ADVERTISING
and Integrated Brand Promotion

Fifth Edition

Thomas C. O'Guinn
Professor of Marketing
Executive Director,
 Center for Brand and Product Management
University of Wisconsin–Madison

Chris T. Allen
Arthur Beerman Professor of Marketing
University of Cincinnati

Richard J. Semenik
Professor of Marketing and Dean
College of Business
Montana State University

SOUTH-WESTERN
CENGAGE Learning

Australia • Brazil • Japan • Korea • Mexico • Singapore • Spain • United Kingdom • United States

SOUTH-WESTERN
CENGAGE Learning™

Advertising and Integrated Brand Promotion, Fifth Edition
Thomas C. O'Guinn, Chris T. Allen, Richard J. Semenik

Vice President of Editorial, Business: Jack W. Calhoun

Editor-in-Chief: Melissa S. Acuña

Acquisitions Editor: Mike Roche

Managing Developmental Editor: John Abner

Marketing Manager: Mike Aliscad

Managing Media Editor: Pam Wallace

Media Editor: John Rich

Marketing Communication Manager: Sarah Greber

Sr. Marketing Coordinator: Sarah Rose

Sr. Manufacturing Coordinator: Diane Gibbons

Production Service: Lachina

Art Director: Stacy Shirley

Internal Designer: Craig Ramsdell

Cover Designer: Grannan Graphic Design

Cover Image: © Lou Beach

Photography Manager: Don Schlotman

Photo Researcher: Susan van Etten

For product information and technology assistance, contact us at
Cengage Learning Academic Resource Center, 1-800-423-0563

For permission to use material from this text or product,
submit all requests online at **cengage.com/permissions**
Further permissions questions can be emailed to
permissionrequest@cengage.com

Exam*View*® is a registered trademark of eInstruction Corp. Windows is a registered trademark of the Microsoft Corporation used herein under license. Macintosh and Power Macintosh are registered trademarks of Apple Computer, Inc. used herein under license.

© 2009 Cengage Learning. All Rights Reserved.

Cengage Learning WebTutor™ is a trademark of Cengage Learning.

Library of Congress Control Number: 2008922770

Student Edition ISBN 13: 978-0-324-56862-2

Student Edition ISBN 10: 0-324-56862-2

Instructor's Edition ISBN 13: 978-0-324-56940-7

Instructor's Edition ISBN 10: 0-324-56940-8

South-Western Cengage Learning
5191 Natorp Boulevard
Mason, OH 45040
USA

Cengage Learning is a leading provider of customized learning solutions with office locations around the globe, including Singapore, the United Kingdom, Australia, Mexico, Brazil, and Japan. Locate your local office at: **international.cengage.com/region**

Cengage Learning products are represented in Canada by Nelson Education, Ltd.

For your course and learning solutions, visit **academic.cengage.com**

Purchase any of our products at your local college store or at our preferred online store **www.ichapters.com**

Printed in the United States of America
1 2 3 4 5 6 7 11 10 09 08

To

the Faithful, torn and frayed, but always true:

Ron Faber, Rich and Chris, Dries, John Abner (our editor on 5e), Albert Muniz, Jr., John Pracejus, Jim Rockford, Lyndon Baines Johnson, John Wayne, Melanie Wallendorf, William Holden, Patrick Gavin Quinlan, Some Girls, Exile on Main Street, Steve Steward, Bob Dylan, Billy McBroom, Joe Phillippe, John Ford, Annie Leibovitz (http://www.youtube.com/watch?v=u34EcDiHVgY), John Sherry, Jr., Rob Arrol, Galen Gondolfi, Bruce Miller, the artists at Lachina, Lou Beach, Russ Belk, The Heuristics, Aaron Clayton O'Guinn, Mildred Lucille Chambers, John Lynch, Jim and Joan Bettman, Eric Arnould, Mick, Keith, and Charlie, Robert Johnson, Fender, Connie Mae Johnson, Mr. and Mrs. Burt Chambers, May Jo and Hartford, Molly, Sheila, Charles, Jo Ann, Kevin Lane Keller, Don and Caroline Kelley, Bob King, Keith Hunt, Kim and Nancy Rotzoll, Dean James Carey, Blue Velvet, Pulp Fiction, Skip and 1st National Guitar Store—Champaign, Good and Loud Music—Madison, Richard Castle, Fritz and all the truly great folks of Champaign Cycle, Champaign, Illinois, Jesse and Griff, Trek, Madison-West, Molly the Dog, Whitley the Dog, Susan H., the other Susan H., old friends all over, new friends in Madison, Robert (Bob) Norman Arrol, and the beautiful Marilyn A. Boland. And anyone I overlooked; I didn't forget you. Thanks.
    T. C. O.

To Linda, Gillian, and Maddy, my three reasons for being.
  Chris Allen

To the students of marketing, advertising, and communications who define the focus and purpose of this book.
  Rich Semenik

In Memoriam

Bill Arens.

Bill was a true professional and an astute student of advertising and its issues. We had the privilege of knowing Bill as a colleague and author. He will be missed by all the academics, practitioners, and students who were touched by his work. Thanks, Bill.

—t.c.o.
—c.t.a.
—r.j.s.

PREFACE

In 2003, when we launched the *third* edition of this book with a new title: *Advertising and Integrated Brand Promotion*, some people questioned that title: "Isn't it supposed be Advertising and Integrated *Marketing Communication?*" We were convinced back then and we are even more committed now to the proposition that advertisers and agencies alike are focused on the *brand* and *integrated brand promotion* (IBP) and that integrated marketing communication (IMC) was really a thing of the past and was probably the wrong term in the first place. We believe that our perspective has proved to be correct. Advertising and promotion is *all* about the brand, and practitioners are pursing brand awareness and competitive advantage with an ever-expanding array of advertising and promotion brand-building techniques—all of which we are proud and excited to present to you here in *Advertising and Integrated Brand Promotion*, 5e.

One point we want to make emphatically. *Advertising and Integrated Brand Promotion*, 5e remains the most current and forward thinking book on the market. Since the launch of the first edition in 1998, we have alerted students to leading edge issues and challenges facing the advertising and promotion industries. We were the first to devote an entire chapter to the Internet as an advertising medium (1998); the first to alert students to the "dot-com" agency incursion on traditional advertising structure (2000); the first to raise the issue of consumers seeking and seizing control of their personal communications environment (2003); and the first to highlight blogs and DVRs and the role they play in disseminating (or blocking) information about brands (2006).

An Effective Student Resource.

There is a deep and lasting commitment among the authors to seek out both the best traditional and the newest contemporary thinking about advertising from a wide array of both academic and trade publications. You will see this commitment manifest in the breadth, depth, and currency of the references in each chapter. Within this context, let's consider the "personality" features of this new edition. We are confident you will find the content and perspective of this new edition a worthy addition to students' classroom experience

First, we have retained all of the content and chapter features that students and instructors liked in our previous editions. Now more of a good thing: advertising as an integrated brand-building process receives even greater emphasis in the fifth edition. The real ad world is about brands, and we cover the complete set of advertising and promotion tools—including the vast array of new opportunities facing advertisers in the peer-to-peer communications environment. Once again, we lead the market in informative, entertaining ads, illustrations, photos, and graphics (over 500!)—printed on the highest quality paper available—to highlight the features of each visual. Ads come first here.

We were very selective in choosing the content that received the heaviest revision, and we targeted those topics that reflect the important changes in the industry. Every chapter has some new content and a lot of new visuals—they need to as the world of advertising continues to evolve in a dynamic way. But even in these cases, there is still a lot of familiar, foundation material. We think you will find some examples of the changes to the fifth edition exciting and compelling.

Chapter 1: The World of Advertising and Integrated Brand Promotion. The first chapter received a *significant* revision to reflect the latest realities of industry practices, technological change, and the new challenges in using promotional techniques. From the very outset, this chapter alerts students to the fact that companies are trying to keep up with how and where consumers want to receive information about brands. Mass media are not dead, but they are being supplemented and supported by all sorts of new ways to reach consumers.

Chapter 2: The Structure of the Advertising Industry: Advertisers, Agencies, Media Companies, and Support Organizations. A key change in Chapter 2 is the addition of more explicit coverage of media companies as reflected in the change in the chapter title. Users of prior editions wanted more complete and explicit coverage of media options earlier in the book—so we delivered. Chapter 2 provides the essential perspective that consumers, who have been the target of advertising and promotion for decades, are discovering technologies and media options that give them more control over the communications they see and hear. From **MySpace** to **YouTube** to **Wikipedia** to millions of individual **blogs**, consumers are seeking out information environments where *they* control their exposure to information, rather than an advertiser or media company being in control. In addition, we raise the prospects of how **Web 2.0** technologies will affect advertising and IBP.

Chapter 3: The Evolution of Promoting and Advertising Brands. The book continues to distinguish itself with the most comprehensive coverage of the historical antecedents and economic forces that shaped today's modern advertising and promotional practices. Here we offer extended coverage of the recent changes in advertising and IBP set in historical context. This allows students to see what is truly new, and what is recycled from the past.

Chapter 4: Social, Ethical, and Regulatory Aspects of Advertising and Promotion. Chapter 4 includes a title change (the addition of the word "Promotion") and discussions of new restrictions on the advertising and promotion process, such as the Children's Food and Beverage Advertising Initiative (i.e., advertising makes kids fat) and the movement to regulate Internet promotions (Global Business Dialog on Electronic

Commerce [GBDe]). In addition, there is updated coverage on the status of the **"do not call"** list and **anti-spam** legislative movements, as well as extensive discussion of privacy issues relating to both direct mail and Internet communications.

Chapter 5: Advertising, Integrated Brand Promotion, and Consumer Behavior. This chapter dedicates greater attention to the social (peer-to-peer brand communities) and cultural perspectives of advertising and consumer behavior. These perspectives are shown in contrast to the psychological perspective offered in the first half of the chapter. No other book offers these dual and complementary perspectives. In addition, the chapter addresses the willingness of firms to allow brand communities to participate in the development of brand communications and, indeed, brand features.

Chapter 7: Advertising and Promotion Research. Chapter 7 has undergone extensive revision to reflect the newest methods used in copy research. In addition, the chapter is now structured around three stages of the research effort in advertising and IBP: development research, copy research, and results. The results section adds a discussion of the methods used for estimating sales derived from advertising

Chapter 9: Advertising Planning: An International Perspective. This material was revised to reflect the ever-changing cultural environment for advertising and promotion. This has never been more important than it is now.

Chapter 10: Managing Creativity in Advertising and IBP. This chapter has always been a distinguishing feature of the book. We are willing to take on the creative process directly and discuss the complexities and vagaries of this all-powerful aspect of advertising and IBP. This edition marks a significant revision of the chapter—starting with the title. The revised material highlights why creativity is so important to the advertising and IBP process. In addition, the chapter goes well beyond the simple perspective of account management versus the creative effort and provides extensive discussion of creativity across domains; conflict and tension in the creative/management interface; and the all-important team effort in coordination, collaboration, and creativity. This is the most comprehensive coverage of the creative effort you will find—anywhere.

Chapter 14: Media Strategy and Planning for Advertising and IBP. Chapter 14 has been, once again, extensively revised—we mean *extensively*. Advertising is in an era when the media environment is driving change, and we want to insure that students have the most up-to-date and accurate perspective.

Chapter 16: Media Planning: Advertising and IBP on the Internet. For each new edition of the book, we feel that much of the discussion of the role and application of the Internet to advertising and IBP basically must be rewritten from scratch. We still provide students with the basics of the Web and statistics on Internet use and surfing behavior. But this edition, following through on the issues raised in Chapters 1 and 2, highlights the impact of peer-to-peer communication through **blogs** and **personal web sites**. **Paid search** gets a complete update, as do the current status of technological advances like **WiFi**, **WiMax**, and **MobileFi**. The opportunity of community sites like **Facebook** and technology like **widgets** is also covered. Finally, consideration of the communications potential of virtual environments like **Second Life** also receive extensive treatment.

Chapter 17: Sales Promotion, Point-of-Purchase Advertising, and Support Media. This chapter carries a new name, and material is repositioned from earlier editions. Support media (signage, directory advertising, etc.) are now combined with sales promotion and point-of-purchase advertising. We felt these topics fit better together and offered the opportunity for expanded coverage of branded entertainment and product placement in Chapter 18 (see below).

Chapter 18: Event Sponsorship, Product Placements, and Branded Entertainment. As contemporary as we have tried to keep the entire book, this chapter is the most contemporary of all. As firms have moved budgets from traditional mass media to other IBP options, the investment in **event sponsorship**, **product placement**, and **branded entertainment** has soared. This chapter offers the best contemporary examples and applications of these three powerful IBP tools.

Chapter 19: Integrating Direct Marketing and Personal Selling. Long-time users of the text will recognize the significant change here. We have added **personal selling** to our coverage of IBP. While firms rely on traditional and old media to accomplish much of what used to be in the personal selling task, there are product categories and circumstances in which direct contact still is the best promotional choice. We wanted students to gain exposure to the personal selling effort.

Chapter 20: Public Relations, Influencer Marketing, and Corporate Advertising. We are excited to present students with new content related to "**influencer marketing**," now highlighted in this chapter. **Professional influencers, peer-to-peer communications, buzz, and viral marketing** are given extensive coverage.

These examples really do just scratch the surface of what is new with respect to topical coverage and the discussions of contemporary issues that reflect the leading-edge coverage that *Advertising and Integrated Brand Promotion*, 5e provides students. As with past editions, we continue the practice of extensive use of written and visual examples to demonstrate points throughout each chapter. Notice the large number of references throughout the book to literature from 2006 and 2007. Plus, over 40 percent of the ads, illustrations, and photos are new in this edition. We work very hard to make the text current and relevant . . . and we think it shows.

Why We Write This Book.

When we introduced the first edition of *Advertising*, we summed up our attitude and passion about advertising in this way:

Advertising is a lot of things. It's democratic pop culture, capitalist tool, oppressor, liberator, art, and theater, all rolled into one. It's free speech, it's creative flow, it's information, and it helps businesses get things sold. Above all, it's fun.

Advertising is fun, and this book reflects it. Advertising is also a business, and this edition carries forward a perspective that clearly conveys that message as well. Like other aspects of business, advertising and integrated brand promotion are the result of hard work and careful planning. Creating good advertising is an enormous challenge . . . and we understand that and give homage to the creative process. We understand advertising and promotion in its business, marketing, and creative context.

This book was written by three people with lots of experience in both academic and professional settings. We have collectively been consultants for many firms and their agencies. Thus, this book is grounded in real-world experience. It is not, however, a book that seeks to sell you a "show-and-tell coffee-table book" version of the advertising industry. Rather, we highlight the challenges facing advertisers and offer complete treatment of the tools they use to meet those challenges.

Much has happened since we released the first edition that has strengthened our resolve to write and deliver the best advertising and promotions book on the market. First, we learned from our adopters (over 500 of you) and from our students that the book's (sometimes brutally) honest discussion of advertising practice was welcomed and applauded. We are not here to be cheerleaders for advertising, or to tell you we know what and where the magic bullets are. We truly love advertising, but we also know that it is not always wonderful. It can be frustrating to work with, particularly when you first learn there is *no* magic bullet. Advertising can also have a dark side. We understand that, and try to put it in a realistic context. We treat students like adults. When the best answer is "no one knows," we tell you that.

As much as we respected our academic and practitioner colleagues the first four times around, we respect them even more now. Research for the fifth edition turned up phenomenal industry talent, and we share our findings and surprises with you. This book is completely real-world, but the real world is also explained in terms of some really smart scholarship. This book copies no one, yet pays homage to many. More than anything, this book seeks to be honest, thoughtful, and imaginative. It acknowledges the complexity of human communication and consumer behavior while retaining a point of view.

We have tried our best to make life easier for the overworked instructor by offering a wide variety of ancillary materials that will assist in teaching from the book and in fully engaging students on this fascinating topic.

Students like this book—they tell us so over and over. You liked the last four editions, and you'll like this one even more. We've spent considerable time reviewing student and instructor likes and dislikes of other advertising textbooks, in addition to examining their reactions to our own book. With this feedback, we've devoted pages and pictures, ideas and intelligence, to creating a place for student and teacher to meet and discuss one of the most important and intrinsically interesting phenomena of contemporary times: advertising and promotion in the service of brands.

From Chapter 1 to Chapter 20.
As we said at the outset, *Advertising and Integrated Brand Promotion*, 5e is different in that it explicitly acknowledges that advertising and promotion are all about brands. Brands can be goods or services, things or people (for example, political candidates, performers), and advertising and promotion are about marketers projecting brands into the consciousness of consumers.

This fifth edition is also about taking a wider view of advertising and promotion. The truth these days is that any boundary between advertising and other forms of promotion is a pretty porous border. We acknowledge that point without making a big deal of it *and* without ignoring the fundamentals of the advertising and promotional processes. In fact, we have made it very easy for instructors to cover what they want. We think that advertising and promotion should be discussed between the covers of the same book, just as their coordinated integration should occur in practice.

Relevant, Intelligent Organization.
We offer an organization we adamantly believe is superior. The organizational structure of this book is unique and highly valued by users. Rather than have a section with 1 or 2 chapters followed by a section with 9 or 10 chapters, we offer a patterned and well-paced five part organization. Instructors and students alike find this approach relevant, intelligent, and easy to follow. The organization of the text is so popular because it lays out the advertising and IBP process the same way it unfolds in practice and application:

Part One: The Process: Advertising and Integrated Brand Promotion in Business and Society. Part One recognizes that students really need to understand just what advertising and IBP are all about, and have a good perspective on how the process works. This section contains the core fundamentals (more about this in a minute). It describes the entire landscape of advertising and promotion, and provides a look at the structure of the industry and a historical perspective on the evolution of the process. Part One concludes with the key social, ethical, and regulatory issues facing practitioners and consumers.

Part Two: Planning: Analyzing Advertising and Integrated Brand Promotion Environments. Part Two provides all the essential perspectives to understand how to carry out effective advertising and IBP. Key strategic concepts of the process, including consumer behavior analysis, market segmentation, brand differentiation, and brand positioning, are considered. Then, this section proceeds to a discussion of the types of research advertising and promotion planners rely on to develop effective advertising and IBP. Additionally, there is special emphasis on "consuming in the real world" and how advertising and IBP need to adapt to consumer lifestyles. The final two chapters in this section provide the key components of developing both a domestic and international advertising and IBP plan.

Whether you are teaching/studying advertising and promotion in a business school curriculum or an advertising/journalism curriculum, the first two parts of the book provide the background and perspective that show how advertising and IBP have become the powerful business and society forces they are in the 21st century.

Part Three: Preparing the Message. Part Three is all about creativity: creativity in general, as a managerial issue, and as a part of art direction, copy writing, and message strategy. Most adopters in advertising and communication programs use this section and put particular focus on Chapter 10, in which the tensions between the creative and management processes are highlighted. Some business-school adopters (particularly those on 6- and 10-week modules or classes) skip some of the creative chapters in Part Three. However, almost everyone uses Chapter 11, which focuses on message development and strategy.

Part Four: Placing the Message in Conventional and "New" Media. Part Four focuses on the use and application of all media—including digital media—to reach target audiences. These chapters are key to understanding many of the execution aspects of good advertising and integrated brand promotion strategies. It is in this section that you will learn not just about the traditional mass media, but also about the array of new media options and consumers' new-found power in managing their information environments through these options.

Part Five: Integrated Brand Promotion. Part Five covers the many tools of integrated brand promotion. We bundled these four chapters together, since our business-school adopters often use them. We think they are good for everyone. Here you will find the best coverage of product placement, direct marketing, branded entertainment, and influencer marketing.

Compelling Fundamentals.

We fully expect our book to continue to set the standard for coverage of new topics and issues. It is loaded with features, insights, and common sense advertising perspectives about the ever-changing nature of the advertising and promotion industry. Now we have incorporated coverage of new issues in *every* chapter.

That said, a truly distinguishing strength of this book is that we do not abandon complete and high-level treatment of the fundamentals of advertising and promotion. You simply *cannot* appreciate the role of the new media or new technologies without a solid understanding of the fundamentals. If you doubt our commitment to the fundamentals, take a good look at Chapters 2 through 9. This is where we, once again, part company with other books on the market. *Advertising and Integrated Brand Promotion*, 5e, is the only book on the market that insures the deep economic roots of advertising and promotion are fully understood. And, we take the time to be sure that not just the business but also the social context of advertising are clear. Check out just how completely the foundational aspects are covered—you'll be surprised and impressed.

Also, notice that we don't wait until the end of the book to bring legal, ethical, social (Chapter 4), and international considerations (Chapter 9) into mainstream thinking about advertising and IBP. While most books put international issues as one of the last chapters—as if they are an afterthought—global topics are covered early and then integrated throughout the text in special box treatments because today's decision makers must possess a global view.

Extensive New Media Coverage. In-depth consideration of new media vehicles is provided in Part Four of the book, "Placing the Message in Conventional and New Media." Chapter 16 is all about advertising and marketing on the Internet, and it reviews many technical considerations for working with this—now not-so-new, but still challenging and evolving—method for reaching and affecting consumers. Chapter 17 highlights all the new ways advertising and promotion can provide an "experiential" encounter with the brand. But, these sections are not the only place new media coverage is prominent. Chapters 1 and 2 highlight how consumers use new media options as a way to control their information flow. And Chapter 5 considers the effects of new media on consumer decision making.

Complete Integrated Brand Promotion Coverage. As we have said, advertising and IBP are all about the brand. The marketing and advertising worlds have always known this, but in the last few years they have placed an even more intense focus on branding. So we make things explicit: This book is about advertising and promotion in the service of brands. Further, it must be an integrated effort. Integrated efforts have come to be the norm. Part 5 of the text offers complete treatment of the full range of promotional tools available to advertisers. We purposely set out to write extensively about sales promotion, point of purchase advertising, direct marketing, personal selling, event sponsorship, branded entertainment, public relations, and corporate advertising. Nearly twenty percent of the book's pages are devoted to promotional tools beyond advertising.

Student Engagement and Learning. You will find that this book provides a clear and sophisticated examination of advertising fundamentals in lively, concise language. We don't beat around the bush; we don't avoid controversies; and we're not shy about challenging conventions. In addition, the book features a stylish internal design (worthy of an advertising book!) and hundreds of illustrations. Reading this book is an engaging experience.

The markers of our commitment to student learning are easily identified throughout the book. Every chapter begins with a statement of the *learning objectives* for that chapter. (For a quick appreciation of the coverage provided by this book, take a pass through it and read the learning objectives on the first page of each chapter.) Chapters are organized to deliver content that responds to each learning objective, and the *chapter summaries* are written to reflect what the chapter has offered with respect to each learning objective.

We also believe that students must be challenged to go beyond their reading to think about the issues raised in the book. Thus, you will note that the *Questions* at the end of each chapter demand thoughtful analysis rather than mere regurgitation, and the *Experiential Exercises* will help students put their learning to use in ways that will help them take more away from the course than just textbook learning. Complete use of this text and its ancillary materials will yield a dramatic and engaging learning experience for students of all ages who are studying advertising for the first time.

A Closer Look at Some Fifth Edition Features.

How the Text Is Organized. As we discussed earlier, *Advertising and Integrated Brand Promotion,* 5e is divided into five major parts reflecting the process of advertising and IBP as it unfolds in practice and application:

- Part One: The Process: Advertising and Integrated Brand Promotion in Business and Society

- Part Two: Planning: Analyzing Advertising and Integrated Brand Promotion Environments
- Part Three: Preparing the Message
- Part Four: Placing the Message in Conventional and New Media
- Part Five: Integrated Brand Promotion

New to this edition we have also included a unique appendix of one-on-one interviews conducted by Tom O'Guinn with three truly compelling individuals with very different perspectives on the world of advertising and IBP:

- **Fred Krupp**, President, Environmental Defense
- **Jim Neupert**, Vice President, Marketing, Abbott Vascular (acquired Guidant Corporation)
- **Dick Antoine**, Senior Vice President, Global Human Resources Officer, Procter & Gamble

Now, let's call your attention to some important chapter highlights.

PART ONE

Part One: The Process: Advertising and Integrated Brand Promotion in Business and Society.

Chapter 1: The World of Advertising and Integrated Brand Promotion. Chapter 1 quickly sets the stage for what's to come. It begins with recognition of the changing consumer information environment. Then, departing from decades-old communication models, the chapter presents a different model of advertising, which highlights the advertiser's sensitivity to target audiences' expectations and motivations. With this opening perspective, we recognize renewed industry emphasis on the integration of the account planning process and creative processes. Students learn that advertising is both a communications process and a business process, and they're shown why this is so. The book's seamless IBP coverage begins right here, with the students being introduced to the terminology and concept of coordinating and integrating promotional efforts to achieve advertising synergy and to speaking to consumers *in a single voice*. It's a great beginning.

This chapter has extensive discussions of the concepts of the brand, brand extensions, and brand equity. The concept of advertising and brand management is introduced here as the premise for the integrated brand promotion dimension of the text. IBP is the logical next step as a departure from integrated marketing communication (IMC).

Chapter 2: The Structure of the Advertising Industry: Advertisers, Agencies, Media Companies, and Support Organizations. In Chapter 2, you'll read about trends that are transforming the advertising industry today and the seismic changes the industry experienced at the end of the millennium. Students will see who the participants are in the ad industry today and the role each plays in the formulation and execution of advertising and IBP campaigns.

The main point is that advertisers are rethinking the way they try to communicate with consumers. Fundamentally, there is a greater focus on integrating more tools with the overall advertising effort into brand promotion programs. More than ever, advertisers are looking to the full complement of promotional opportunities, including sales promotions, event sponsorships, new media options, and public relations, as means to support and enhance the primary advertising effort for brands. There is much more emphasis on the role of the trade in the communications effort. New to this treatment is the recognition that consumers are taking more control of their information environment with the use of new technologies through all aspects of the phenomenon known as Web 2.0.

Chapter 3: The Evolution of Promoting and Advertising Brands. Chapter 3 puts advertising in a historical context. But before the history lesson begins, students are given the straight scoop about advertising as a product of fundamental economic and social conditions—capitalism, the Industrial Revolution, manufacturers' pursuit of power, and modern mass communication—without which there would be no advertising process. Students then study the history of advertising through ten interesting and entertaining eras, seeing how advertising has changed and evolved, and how it is forged out of its social setting. This chapter is rich with some interesting ads representing advertising as a faithful documentation of social life in America. Definitely an entertaining and provocative chapter, it also gives students a necessary and important perspective on advertising before launching into advertising planning concepts and issues. Most strategies were created decades ago, and if you can learn how advertisers took advantage of various social conditions and trends yesterday, you can learn a lot about how to do it today—and tomorrow.

Chapter 4: Social, Ethical, and Regulatory Aspects of Advertising and Promotion. Advertising is dynamic and controversial. In Chapter 4, students will examine a variety of issues concerning advertising's effects on societal well being. Is advertising intrusive, manipulative, and deceptive? Does it waste resources, promote materialism, and perpetuate stereotypes? Or does it inform, give exposure to important issues, and raise the standard of living? After debating the social merits of advertising, students will explore the ethical considerations that underlie the development of campaigns and learn about the regulatory agencies that set guidelines for advertisers. Lastly, students are introduced to the concept of self-regulation and why advertisers must practice it.

There are a couple of important and extensive changes in the fifth edition. First, the issue of privacy is discussed extensively as both a social and ethical issue, given new technologies that can track and profile consumers through the communication process and the risks (such as easy access through WiFi) new technologies present. New material was also added on regulatory issues in direct marketing ("do not call" lists), in e-commerce (anti-spam legislation), in sales promotion, and in public relations.

Part Two: Planning: Analyzing Advertising and Integrated Brand Promotion Environments.

Chapter 5: Advertising, Integrated Brand Promotion, and Consumer Behavior. Chapter 5, which describes consumer behavior from two different perspectives, begins Part Two of the text. The first perspective portrays consumers as systematic decision makers who seek to maximize the benefits they derive from their purchases. The second portrays consumers as active interpreters of advertising, whose membership in various cultures, subcultures, societies, and communities significantly affects their interpretations of and responses to advertising. Students, shown the validity of both perspectives, learn that, like all human behavior, the behavior of consumers is complex, multifaceted, and often symbolic. Understanding buyer behavior is a tremendous challenge to advertisers, who should not settle for easy answers if they want good relationships with their customers. The chapter also includes information about brands and the consumer behavior that makes or breaks them.

Chapter 6: Market Segmentation, Positioning, and the Value Proposition. Chapter 6 opens with a look at how the Folgers brand team used segmentation, position, and targeting in a creative way to reach just-graduated 20-somethings. Students are introduced to the sequence of activities often referred to as STP marketing—segmenting, targeting, and positioning—and how advertising both affects and is affected by these basic marketing strategies. The remainder of the chapter is devoted to detailed analysis of how organizations develop market segmentation, positioning, and product differentiation strategies. The critical role of ad campaigns in successfully executing these strategies is emphasized over and over. Numerous examples of real-world campaigns that contrast different segmentation and positioning strategies keep the narrative fresh and fast moving. The chapter concludes by demonstrating that effective STP marketing strategies result in creating a perception of value in the marketplace.

PART TWO

Chapter 7: Advertising and Promotion Research. Chapter 7, which contains a lot of new content, covers the methods used in developmental research, the procedures used for pre-testing messages prior to the launch of a campaign, the methods used to track the effectiveness of ads during and after a launch, and the many sources of secondary data that can aid the ad-planning effort. This chapter also provides coverage of the agency's new emphasis on account planning as a distinct part of the planning process.

Chapter 8: Planning Advertising and Integrated Brand Promotion. Chapter 8 begins by recounting the sequence of events and strategies behind the exciting launch of Apple's iPhone. Through this opening vignette, students see the importance of constructing a sound ad plan before launching any campaign. In addition, this introductory campaign for the iPhone is an extraordinary example of IBP at work. After reading this chapter, students will be familiar with the basic components of an ad plan. There is emphasis on two fundamental approaches for setting advertising objectives—the budgeting process and the role of the ad agency in formulating an advertising and IBP plan.

Chapter 9: Advertising Planning: An International Perspective. This chapter begins with the fascinating story of how Safeguard soap benefited from the creation a superhero—for the Pakistani market! While many books bury their international chapter at the end of the book, we chose to place this chapter in the heart of the book where it belongs—as part of the overall advertising planning effort. You'll find the chapter engaging in the way the fast-moving discussion unfolds: from a discussion of cultural barriers and overcoming them, to an examination of the creative, media, and regulatory challenges that international advertising presents. Of course, students will also love the ad samples from Japan, Germany, Chile, the Czech Republic, and a host of other countries.

Part Three: Preparing the Message.

Chapter 10: Managing Creativity in Advertising and IBP. Chapter 10 takes on the seemingly awkward task of "talking" about creativity. All you creatives out there know that this is a nearly impossible task. But what we have tried to do for students in this chapter is completely different from what is done in all other texts. Rather than just describing the creative execution *process* (we do that in Chapters 11 and 12), we have tried to discuss the essence of what creativity is. The chapter starts by recounting how the Crispin Porter + Bogusky agency turned creative risk taking into huge advertising and IBP successes. Next, we highlight the commentary and achievements of creative geniuses—both within the advertising industry and completely removed from it. We've also revised and refocused the material on the organizational and managerial tensions of the creative/suit interface. The result is a thought-provoking and enriching treatment like no other that students will find.

Chapter 11: Message Strategy. Building on Chapter 10, Chapter 11 explores the role of creativity in message strategy from a refreshingly honest perspective: No one knows exactly how advertising creativity works. Nine message strategy objectives are presented, along with the creative methods used to accomplish the objectives, including humor, slice-of-life, anxiety, sexual-appeal, slogan, and repetition ads. This chapter makes excellent use of visuals to dramatize the concepts presented. Quite a bit of revision went into this signature chapter, and the many ads offer concrete examples.

Chapter 12: Copywriting. Chapter 12 flows logically from the chapter on message development. In this chapter, students learn about the copywriting process and the importance of good, hard-hitting copy in the development of print, radio, and television advertising. Guidelines for writing headlines, subheads, and body copy for print ads are given, as well as guidelines for writing radio and television ad copy. The chapter closes with a discussion of the most common mistakes copywriters make and a discussion of the copy approval process. And, of course, this chapter also considers the issues surrounding the copywriting process in the highly constrained creative environment of the Internet.

PART THREE

Chapter 13: Art Direction and Production. Feedback from our many adopters told us that they wanted a combined discussion of the art direction and production for both print and broadcast media—so we complied. Here students learn about the strategic and creative impact of illustration, design, and layout, and the production steps required to get to the final ad. Numerous engaging full-color ads are included that illustrate important design, illustration, and layout concepts.

We also introduce students to what is often thought of as the most glamorous side of advertising: television advertising. Students learn about the role of the creative team and the many agency and production company participants involved in the direction and production processes. Students are given six creative guidelines for television ads, with examples of each. Radio is not treated as a second-class citizen in this chapter but is given full treatment, including six guidelines for the production of creative and effective radio ads. This chapter is comprehensive and informative without getting bogged down in production details.

Part Four: Placing the Message in Conventional and "New" Media.

Chapter 14: Media Strategy and Planning for Advertising and IBP. In Chapter 14, which begins Part Four, students see that a well-planned and creatively prepared campaign needs to be placed in media (and not just any media!) to reach a target audience and to stimulate demand. This chapter drives home the point that advertising placed in media that does not reach the target audience—whether new digital media or traditional media—will be much like the proverbial tree that falls in the forest with no one around: Does it make a sound? Students will read about the major media options available to advertisers today, the media-planning process, computer modeling in media planning, and the challenges that complicate the media-planning process. The chapter uses the "real-deal" headings to explain not how things should be done, but how they are done, and why.

Chapter 15: Media Planning: Newspapers, Magazines, Television, and Radio. The opening vignette for Chapter 15 highlights the challenges traditional mass media face from the rising prominence and importance of digital media. The chapter then focuses on evaluating the unique capabilities of different media as an important means for advertisers to reach audiences. The chapter details the advantages and disadvantages of newspapers, magazines, radio, and television as media classes and describes the buying and audience measurement techniques for each. New topics covered in this chapter highlight controversy caused by digital video recorders (DVRs) on television advertising audience measurement, the impact of community portals on newspaper classified advertising, and the changes in listening behavior caused by satellite and Internet radio on the radio medium.

Chapter 16: Media Planning: Advertising and IBP on the Internet. The first edition of *Advertising* was the first introductory advertising book to devote an entire chapter to advertising on the Internet, and this edition continues to set the standard for Internet coverage. Today's employers expect college advertising and promotion students to know about the Internet (inside and out) and the creative and selling opportunities it presents to advertisers as part of their IBP strategy. Chapter 16 presents a complete coverage of advertising on the Internet. The chapter describes who is using the Internet today and the ways they are using it, identifies the advertising and marketing opportunities presented by the Internet, and discusses fundamental requirements for establishing sites on the World Wide Web. The chapter also addresses the challenges inherent in measuring the cost effectiveness of the Internet versus other advertising media.

What has been added to this chapter is an in depth discussion of how firms—large and small—are integrating Web-based, digital media communications into the advertising and promotion plan. In addition, the merging of Web site communication with sales promotion and sales transaction and fulfillment makes this a very powerful communications environment indeed. Finally, possible new communications venues like virtual worlds (e.g. Second Life) are considered for their potential as communications environments.

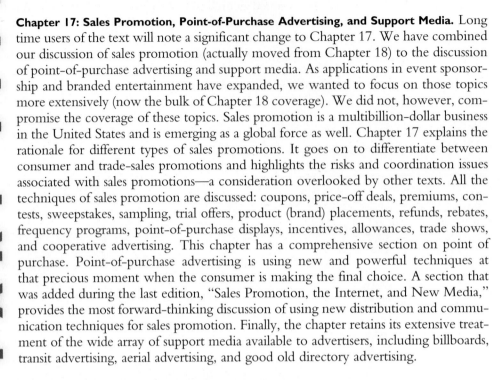

Part Five: Integrated Brand Promotion.

Chapter 17: Sales Promotion, Point-of-Purchase Advertising, and Support Media. Long time users of the text will note a significant change to Chapter 17. We have combined our discussion of sales promotion (actually moved from Chapter 18) to the discussion of point-of-purchase advertising and support media. As applications in event sponsorship and branded entertainment have expanded, we wanted to focus on those topics more extensively (now the bulk of Chapter 18 coverage). We did not, however, compromise the coverage of these topics. Sales promotion is a multibillion-dollar business in the United States and is emerging as a global force as well. Chapter 17 explains the rationale for different types of sales promotions. It goes on to differentiate between consumer and trade-sales promotions and highlights the risks and coordination issues associated with sales promotions—a consideration overlooked by other texts. All the techniques of sales promotion are discussed: coupons, price-off deals, premiums, contests, sweepstakes, sampling, trial offers, product (brand) placements, refunds, rebates, frequency programs, point-of-purchase displays, incentives, allowances, trade shows, and cooperative advertising. This chapter has a comprehensive section on point of purchase. Point-of-purchase advertising is using new and powerful techniques at that precious moment when the consumer is making the final choice. A section that was added during the last edition, "Sales Promotion, the Internet, and New Media," provides the most forward-thinking discussion of using new distribution and communication techniques for sales promotion. Finally, the chapter retains its extensive treatment of the wide array of support media available to advertisers, including billboards, transit advertising, aerial advertising, and good old directory advertising.

Chapter 18: Event Sponsorship, Product Placements, and Branded Entertainment. This chapter begins with the fascinating application of event sponsorship and product placement used by Procter & Gamble in New York City as a way to feature the Charmin brand. From there, the chapter offers a thought provoking discussion of the convergence of Madison & Vine—that is the phenomenon of advertising, branding, and entertainment converging to provide consumers a wider array of "touch points" with brands. The chapter continues from here to review the growing allure of event sponsorships and then takes a deep dive into the provocative subject of branded entertainment. We've come a long way from E.T. eating Reese's Pieces! If students didn't already appreciate the power of integrated brand promotion when they hit this chapter, they certainly will afterward. . .

Chapter 19: Integrating Direct Marketing and Personal Selling. Chapter 19 has undergone a major revision with the addition of coverage of personal selling. In the excitement and, indeed, drama of digital media options, we sometimes forget the powerful role personal selling has across many integrated brand promotion strategies. This chapter opens with a fable about direct marketing guru Les Wunderman and the magic of his little gold box, and then moves quickly on to a historical perspective on direct marketing featuring the well-known L.L. Bean mail-order catalog. Students quickly learn about Bean's emphasis on building an extensive mailing list, which serves as a great segue to database marketing. Students will learn why direct marketing continues to grow in popularity, what media are used by direct marketers to deliver their messages, and how direct marketing creates special challenges for achieving integrated brand promotion.

Chapter 20: Public Relations, Influencer Marketing, and Corporate Advertising. Chapter 20 is another chapter that has new and exciting material with addition of full coverage of "influencer" marketing. This chapter begins with a key discussion of the role of public relations in the overall integrated branding effort. While some firms have turned to PR as a new tool in their overall program, the argument that PR is rising to such prominence that the "death of advertising" is imminent (as some authors have suggested) literally made us laugh out loud. This chapter differentiates between proactive and reactive public relations and the strategies associated with each. You will learn that public relations are an important option in IBP, but they will never take the lead role. The new coverage of influencer marketing is the best and most contemporary you will find anywhere. Professional influencer programs, peer-to-peer programs, buzz, viral marketing, and cultivating "connectors"—it's all here and fully covered. This chapter concludes with a wide-ranging and complete discussion of corporate advertising. Various forms of corporate advertising are identified, and the way each can be used as a means for building the reputation of an organization in the eyes of key constituents is discussed.

Inside Every Chapter.

Inside every chapter of *Advertising and Integrated Brand Promotion*, 5e you will find features that make this new book eminently teachable and academically solid, while at the same time fun to read. As we said earlier, this text was written and the examples were chosen to facilitate an effective meeting place for student and instructor. Who said learning has to be drudgery? It doesn't have to be and it shouldn't.

Dynamic Graphics and over 500 Ads and Exhibits. Ask any student and almost any instructor what an advertising book absolutely *must* have, and the top response will be—lots of ads! As you will see by quickly paging through *Advertising and Integrated Brand Promotion,* 5e, this book sets the standard for ads and other instructional visuals. Over 500 ads, exhibits, illustrations and photos are used to highlight important points made in the chapters. Each exhibit is referenced in the text narrative, tying the visual to the concept being discussed.

As you can see, the book's clean, classic, graphic layout invites you to read it; it dares you to put it down without reading just one more caption or peeking at the next chapter. And, our commitment (and the publisher's) to the power of illustration is clear in the use of the highest quality (read really expensive) paper to make sure the ads "pop" off the pages.

Opening Vignettes. Every chapter includes a classic or current real-world advertising or promotion story to draw students into the chapter and to stimulate classroom discussions. Each vignette illustrates important concepts that will be discussed in the chapter. The chapters throughout the book continue with these types of lively introductions, ensuring that students get off to a good start with every chapter.

In-Chapter Features. Every chapter contains two to three boxed features that highlight interesting, unusual, or just plain entertaining information as it relates to the chapter. The boxes are not diversions unrelated to the text nor are they rambling, page consuming, burdensome tomes. Rather, they provide concise, highly relevant examples that can be fully integrated into classroom lectures. The boxes are for teaching, learning, and reinforcing chapter content. Three different types of boxes are included in the text: Ethics, Globalization, and "Doing It Right." Let's take a look at each.

Ethics: It is important that business decisions be guided by ethical practices. Advertising and integrated brand promotion practices are particularly prone to questions by lay people relating to ethics. Because of the importance of ethics, proper business practice, and its appeal to students' interests, special Ethics boxes appear throughout this edition. Students will gain insights into ethical business practices that will be useful not only in their advertising course, but in future business courses and their careers.

Globalization: The Globalization boxes provide an insightful, real-world look at the numerous challenges advertisers face internationally. Many issues are discussed in these timely boxes, including the development of more standardized advertising across cultures with satellite-based television programming, how U.S.-based media companies such as MTV and Disney/ABC are pursuing the vast potential in global media, obstacles to advertising in emerging markets, and cross-cultural global research.

Doing It Right: Since creativity is often challenging both to teach and to learn, we have fortified the text with some compelling examples that will help students form a better understanding of this nebulous topic within boxes called Doing It Right. These boxes highlight particularly effective or entertaining applications of various IBP techniques.

Also in each chapter:

 Learning Objectives and a Built-In Integrated Learning System. The text and test bank are organized around the learning objectives that appear at the beginning of each chapter, to provide you and your students with an easy-to-use, integrated learning system. A numbered icon like the one shown here identifies each chapter objective and appears next to its related material throughout the chapter. This integrated learning system can provide you with a structure for creating lesson plans as well as tests. A correlation table at the beginning of every chapter in the test bank enables you to create tests that fully cover every learning objective, or ones that emphasize just the objectives you feel are most important.

The integrated system also gives structure to students as they prepare for tests. The icons identify all the material in the text that fulfill each objective. Students can easily check their grasp of each objective by reading the text sections and reviewing the corresponding summary sections. They can also return to appropriate text sections for further review if they have difficulty with end-of-chapter questions.

Concise Chapter Summaries. Each chapter ends with a summary that distills the main points of the chapter. Chapter summaries are organized around the learning objectives so that students can use them as a quick check on their achievement of learning goals.

Key Terms. Each chapter ends with a listing of the key terms found in the chapter. Key terms also appear in boldface in the text. Students can prepare for exams by scanning these lists to be sure they can define or explain each term.

Critical Thinking Questions. End-of-chapter questions are designed to challenge students' thinking and to go beyond the "read, memorize, and regurgitate" learning process. The *Questions for Review* and *Critical Thinking* sections require students to think analytically and to interpret data and information provided for them in the text. Detailed responses to these questions are provided in the Instructor's Manual.

Below is a sampling of the types of critical thinking questions found in *Advertising*:

- If a firm developed a new line of athletic shoes, priced them competitively, and distributed them in appropriate retail shops, would there be any need for advertising? Is advertising really needed for a good product that is priced right?
- The 1950s were marked by great suspicion about advertisers and their potential persuasive powers. Do you see any lingering effects of this era of paranoia in attitudes about advertising today?
- Some contend that self-regulation is the best way to ensure fair and truthful advertising practices. Why would it be in the best interest of the advertising community to aggressively pursue self-regulation?
- Identify several factors or forces that make consumers around the world similar to one another. Conversely, what factors or forces create diversity among consumers in different countries?
- Visit some of the corporate home pages described in this chapter, or think about corporate home pages you visited previously. Of those you have encountered, which would you single out as being most effective in giving the visitor a reason to come back? What conclusions would you draw regarding the best ways to motivate repeat visits to a Web site?

- There's a paradox here, right? On the one hand, it is common to talk about building relationships and loyalty with the tools of direct marketing. On the other hand, direct-marketing tools such as junk e-mail and telephone interruptions at home during dinner are constant irritants. How does one build relationships by using irritants? In your opinion, when is it realistic to think that the tools of direct marketing could be used to build long-term relationships with customers?
- Imagine yourself as a connector. In that role, what kind of inside information would you find interesting enough to tell your friends about a new movie or TV show? What would it take for you to start that conversation?

Experiential Exercises. Many chapters now have at least four of these illuminating exercises—double the number included in the fourth edition. Written by Gail Gibson, these exercises require students to apply the material they have just read by researching well-known brands and issues, writing short papers, preparing brief presentations, or interacting with professionals from the advertising industry. Some exercises require students to get out of the classroom to seek information not provided in the text, while others are especially designed for teamwork both in and outside class.

A Full Array of Teaching/Learning Supplementary Materials.

Supplements:

Instructor's Manual. The instructor's manual was prepared by one of the main text authors, Rich Semenik. We feel that key in-class resources like lecture outlines and PowerPoint® slides simply cannot be properly prepared by a non-author. The manual has been thoroughly revised to update all previous content, including comprehensive lecture outlines that provide suggestions for using other ancillary products associated with the text and suggested answers for all exercises found within the text. The Instructor's Manual is available on the Instructor's Resource CD-ROM.

PowerPoint®. This edition's PowerPoint® presentation is of the highest quality possible and was prepared by one of the main text authors, Rich Semenik. There are many improvements, including additional ads with accompanying discussion questions (answers provided in instructor's manual). All ads are accompanied with commentary on how they illustrate theories and concepts presented in the text and include at least one inductive question to generate classroom discussion. The Power Point® presentation is available on the Instructor's Resource CD-ROM.

Test Bank. Prepared by Christine Wright-Isak at Florida Gulf Coast University, this comprehensive test bank is organized around the main text's learning objectives. Each question is labeled according to the learning objective that is covered, the page number on which the answer can be found, and the type of question (definitional, conceptual, or application). Grouping the questions according to type allows for maximum flexibility in creating tests that are customized to individual classroom needs and preferences. The test bank includes true/false, multiple-choice, scenario application, and essay questions. There are a total of 2,000 questions. All questions have been carefully reviewed for clarity and accuracy. The test bank is available on the Instructor's Resource CD-ROM.

ExamView Testing Software. ExamView Computerized Testing Software, located on the Instructor's Resource CD-ROM, contains all of the questions in the test bank. This program is an easy-to-use test creation software compatible with Microsoft Windows. Instructors can add or edit questions, instructions, and answers and select questions by previewing them on the screen, selecting them randomly, or selecting them by number. Instructors can also create and administer quizzes online, whether over the Internet, a local area network (LAN), or a wide area network (WAN). Contact your sales representative for ordering information.

Instructor's Resource CD-ROM (0-324-56943-2). This CD-ROM includes all the key instructor support materials—instructor's manual, test bank, ExamView, and PowerPoint® slides—providing instructors with a comprehensive capability for customizing their classroom experience.

Product Support Site (http://academic.cengage.com/marketing/o'guinn). The product support site features "Instructor Resources" that include the instructor's manual, test bank, PowerPoint®, and an integrative video guide to accompany the Best of 2007: CLIO GOLD PLUS Collection. For students, we include the following for each chapter: learning objectives, crossword puzzles using key terms, Internet Applications, and interactive quizzes. Students will also find a section on Careers in Marketing Communications, IBP, and Advertising, in which we profile five young professions in the industry.

Video Content:

Best of 2007: CLIO GOLD PLUS Collection (0-324-56941-6). Available to adopting instructors either on DVD or online, this collection offers the best of the Clio gold and silver winners for the year 2007. Entries include Sony Bravia's "Paint," Combos' "Fever," Dove Self-Esteem Fund's "Evolution," Instituto de Apoio à Criança's "Alzheimer's," AIDS Awareness PSA "Sugar Baby Love," Coca-Cola's "Happiness Factory," Toyota Yaris' "Chase," Sprite's "Sublymonal," Vaseline's "Sea of Skin," Microsoft Xbox 360's "Cops and Robbers," JCPenney's "Crazy Beautiful," Sure Deodorant's "Go Wild," Sears' "Arboretum," Travelers Insurance's "Snowball," Nike's "Swing," Adidas' "Equipo," Toyota's "Humanity," and Skittles' "Beard." Contact your sales representative for more information regarding this dynamic supplement.

Acknowledgments

The most pleasant task in writing a textbook is the expression of gratitude to people and institutions that have helped the authors. We appreciate the support and encouragement we received from many individuals, including the following:

- We want to offer our deepest, sincerest, and everlasting thanks to **Susan Van Etten Lawson**, our photo and ad researcher. Remember, this book has approximately 500 ads and illustrations—and every one of them needs documented permission to be used. Some of the ads have needed 2, 3, or even 4 different permissions! Susan patiently and carefully dealt with our requests (and our tardiness) with utmost professionalism. Thank you Susan—we owe you a huge debt.
- Thank you also to acquisitions editor, **Mike Roche**, content project manager, **Tamborah Moore**, and managing developmental editor, **John Abner**, at South-Western for their efforts on this project.
- For great cover art: **Lou Beach** has created art for *The New York Times*, *Time*, David Bowie, Brian Eno, *The Big Lebowski,* and on and on. Lou is the hottest designer around. Thanks for the cover.
- We are very grateful to the following individuals and have featured their work in 5e: **Patricia Dimichele** and **Ed Bello** for their unique point-of-entry program on Folgers, starring those creepy Yellow People, **Aziz Jindani** for the inspiring saga of Commander Safeguard in Pakistan, **Adam Lisook** for Charmin Restrooms on Times Square—a fantastic example of a novel branded experience, **Kerry Cavanaugh** for the great insights about Branded Entertainment grounded in his work with CoverGirl and America's Next Top Model, **Karen Klei** and **Mauricio Troncoso** for teaching us about Bunco and showing how a simple game became a great way to connect with consumers of Prilosec OTC, and **Andrea Zahumensky** for her perfect example of 360 degree/holistic marketing in the launch of Crest Whitening Plus Scope Extreme.
- **David Moore**, Vice President/Executive Producer at Leo Burnett, who gave us invaluable insights on the broadcast production process and helped us secure key materials for the text.
- **Xiaoyan Deng**, The Wharton School, University of Pennsylvania, for all her empirical efforts.

- **Christine Wright-Isak**, Florida Gulf Coast University, for revising the test bank, assuring its accuracy and usefulness.
- **Gail Gibson,** for her professional writing assistance with the experiential exercises and other important elements of the fifth edition.
- **Matt Smith** of Arnold, Finnegan & Martin, for providing us with the Watermark ad and sketches in Chapter 13.
- **Peter Sheldon,** University of Illinois: Chief Exhibitionist (yes, he made us say this). Peter has contributed greatly to all four editions. He makes the book work creatively. He selected many of the ads for this book and provided substantive editorial material and comments. Everybody says this, but in Peter's case it is really true: Without him, we couldn't have done it. He's a pro all the way. His vision, talent, and wonderful humor were our daily blessings. This guy is the real thing. Thanks, Peter.
- **Professors Gray Swicegood** and **Gillian Stevens**, University of Illinois, for their help with consumer demography.
- **Cinda Robbins-Cornstubble**, **Janette Bradley Wright**, and **Robin Price**, University of Illinois at Urbana-Champaign, for their wonderful support and incredible competence.
- **Connie M. Johnson**, for years and years of great and loving observations about the human condition. Connie is connected to the Universe in some very special way.
- **Patrick Gavin Quinlan**, for years of great advice and best friendship.
- **Marilyn A. Boland**, for her love, creativity, smart suggestions, great questions, support, and wonderful images.
- **David Bryan Teets**, University of Illinois, for help with the TV-commercial-director-becomes-movie-director lists and references. Dave knows film.
- **Mildred O'Guinn** (Tom's mom), who actually read every single word of the first edition and found the only misspelled word, one missed by countless computers, editors, authors, proofers, and so on: "Restrictions," in Exhibit 9.16 on page 252. Very good job. Thanks.
- **Professor John Murphy II**, Joe C. Thompson Centennial Professor in Advertising at the University at Austin, who has given us great feedback and continued support. John went well beyond the call with effort and creativity with the author interview film. John also keeps our feet on the ground. Thanks, John.
- **Steve Hall**, who supports, critiques, and gives his all to his students at The University of Illinois. Steve is a creative and gifted teacher, whose continued feedback helps us write better books for real students. Like John Murphy, Steve goes well beyond the call and helped the team produce some really cool video projects for the fourth edition. Steve, thanks.
- **Nancy Roberts** for her office assistance, patience, and friendship.

We are also grateful to the following individuals from the business community:

Dick Antoine
Procter & Gamble

Edward Bello
Procter & Gamble

Patty Bloomfield
Northlich

John Bloomstrom
Northlich

Jack Cassidy
Cincinnati Bell

Kerry Cavanaugh
Procter & Gamble

Lauren Dickson
Saatchi & Saatchi

Patricia Dimichele
Procter & Gamble

Denise Garcia
Conill Advertising Inc.

Emily Neidhardt
Grey

Lisa Hillenbrand
Procter & Gamble

Jim Neupert
Abbott Vascular

Aziz Jindani
Procter & Gamble

Mason Page
imc²

Bharat Kakar
Cincinnati Bell

Jackie Reau
Game Day Communications

Karen Klei
Procter & Gamble

Mark Serrianne
Northlich

Fred Krupp
Environmental Defense

Jim Stengel
Procter & Gamble

Greg Lechner
Luxottica Retail

Meghan Sturges
Saatchi & Saatchi

Liv Lewis
devries-pr

Candace Thomas
Jack Morton Worldwide

Marsha Lindsay
Lindsay, Stone & Briggs

Mauricio Troncoso
Procter & Gamble

Adam Lisook
Procter & Gamble

Ted Woehrle
Newell-Rubbermaid

Vicky Mayer
Procter & Gamble

Andrea Zahumensky
Procter & Gamble

We are particularly indebted to our reviewers—past and present—and the following individuals whose thoughtful comments, suggestions, and specific feedback shaped the content of *Advertising and Integrated Brand Promotion*. Our thanks go to:

Robert B. Affe
Indiana University

Cynthia Frisby
University of Missouri–Columbia

Ron Bernthal
Sullivan County Community College

Gary E. Golden
Muskingum College

Jeff W. Bruns
Bacone College

Corliss L. Green
Georgia State University

Claudia M. Bridges
California State University, Sacramento

Thomas Groth
University of West Florida

Trini Callava
Miami Dade College

Scott Hamula
Keuka College

Joshua Coplen
Santa Monica College

Joseph Helgert
Grand Valley State University

Anne Cunningham
University of Tennessee

Wayne Hilinski
Penn State University

John Davies
University of North Florida

E. Lincoln James
Washington State University

Raj Devasagayam
Siena College

Karen James
Louisiana State University–Shreveport

Robert Dwyer
University of Cincinnati

Michelle Jasso
New Mexico State University

Jon Freiden
Florida State University

Donald Jugenheimer
Southern Illinois University

James Kellaris
University of Cincinnati

Patricia Kennedy
University of Nebraska–Lincoln

Robert Kent
University of Delaware

Priscilla LaBarbera
New York University

Barbara Lafferty
University of South Florida

William LaFief
Frostburg State University

Debbie Laverie
Texas Tech

Gail Love
California State University, Fullerton

Tina M. Lowrey
University of Texas at San Antonio

Nancy Mitchell
University of Nebraska–Lincoln

Elizabeth Moore
University of Notre Dame

Cynthia R. Morton
University of Florida

Darrel Muehling
Washington State University

Andrew T. Norman
Iowa State

John H. Murphy, II
University of Texas–Austin

Marcella M. Norwood
University of Houston

James Pokrywczynski
Marquette University

John Purcell
Castleton State College

Ann H. Rodriguez
Texas Tech University

Jim Rose
Bauder College

Dana K. Saewitz
Temple University

Debra Scammon
University of Utah

Allen D. Schaefer
Missouri State University

Carol Schibi
State Fair Community College

Trina Sego
Boise State University

Kim Sheehan
University of Oregon

Daniel A. Sheinin
University of Rhode Island

Alan Shields
Suffolk County Community College

Sloane Signal
University of Nebraska, Lincoln

Jan Slater
Syracuse University

Lewis Small
York College of Pennsylvania

Barry Solomon
Florida State University

Marla Royne Stafford
University of Memphis

Patricia Stout
University of Texas–Austin

Lynn Walters
Texas A&M

Brian Wansink
University of Illinois

Jon P. Wardrip
University of South Carolina

Robert O. Watson
Quinnipiac University

Marc Weinberger
University of Massachusetts–Amherst

Professor Joan R. Weiss
Bucks County Community College

Gary B. Wilcox
University of Texas–Austin

Kurt Wildermuth
University of Missouri–Columbia

Janice K. Williams
University of Central Oklahoma

Christine Wright-Isak
Young & Rubicam

Molly Ziske
Michigan State University

Lara Zwarun
UT Arlington

Thomas C. O'Guinn
Chris T. Allen
Richard J. Semenik

BRIEF CONTENTS

CONTENTS

PART II

Planning: Analyzing Advertising and Integrated Brand Promotion Environments   148

Chapter 12: Copywriting   374

PART V

Integrated Brand Promotion   558

ADVERTISING
and Integrated Brand Promotion

Fifth Edition

The Process: Advertising and Integrated Brand Promotion in Business and Society

This first part of the book, "The Process: Advertising and Integrated Brand Promotion in Business and Society," sets the tone for our study of advertising. The chapters in this part emphasize that advertising is much more than the old-style mass media messages of the past. Mass media are still, no doubt, a huge part of the advertising effort. But advertising is now much more diverse and dynamic and is part of a process you will learn about called integrated brand promotion (IBP). IBP is the process of using all sorts of different promotional techniques and tools—from television ads to iPod broadcasts—that send messages about brands to consumers. And advertising and IBP communications are not just marketing messages. They are also part of a social communication process that has evolved over time with changes in culture, technology, and business strategies. This is where the "brand" plays a leading role in communications. We all know brands because we hear about them and use them every day—Microsoft, Nike, Pantene, Starbucks, and literally dozens of others. We know (and learn) about brands because companies use advertising and integrated brand promotion to tell us about them. But we also learn about brands by using them and by seeing them being used in society. This first part of the book lays out the broad landscape of the advertising and IBP processes that expose us to brands and what they have to offer.

The World of Advertising and Integrated Brand Promotion introduces and defines advertising and integrated brand promotion and the roles they play within a firm's overall marketing program. We introduce the concept of IBP, which shows that firms communicate to consumers using a broad range of communications that often go far beyond advertising and traditional mass media. Sales promotion, event sponsorship, direct marketing, brand placements in movies and television programs, point-of-purchase displays, the Internet, podcasting, personal selling, and public relations—the tools of IBP—are available to help a firm compete effectively, develop customer loyalty, and generate greater profits. Both advertising and IBP are described as communications processes.

1

The Structure of the Advertising Industry: Advertisers, Agencies, Media Companies, and Support Organizations shows that effective advertising requires the participation of a variety of organizations and specially skilled people, not just the companies who make and sell brands. Advertising agencies, research firms, production facilitators, designers, media companies, Web developers, public relations firms, and Internet portals all play a role. This chapter also highlights that the structure of the industry is in flux. New media options, like streaming video and blogs, and new organizations, like talent agencies and product placement firms, are forcing change. This chapter looks at the basic structure of the industry and how it is evolving with the market and consumer preferences. Special attention is given to the rising prominence of promotion agencies as counterparts to advertising agencies.

2

The Evolution of Promoting and Advertising Brands puts the processes of advertising and integrated brand promotion into both a historical and a contemporary context. Advertising and IBP have evolved and proliferated because of fundamental influences related to free enterprise, economic development, and tradition. Change has also occurred as a reflection of social values and changes in technology and business management practices.

3

Social, Ethical, and Regulatory Aspects of Advertising and Promotion examines the broad societal aspects of advertising and IBP. From a social standpoint, we must understand that advertising and promotion can have positive effects on the standard of living, address lifestyle needs, support communications media, and are contemporary art forms. Critics argue that advertising and other promotions waste resources, promote materialism, are offensive and intrusive, and perpetuate stereotypes, or can make people do things they don't want to do. Ethical issues focus on truthful communication, invasion of privacy, advertising and promoting to children, and advertising and promoting controversial products. Regulatory aspects highlight that while government organizations play a key role, consumer groups and societal values also put pressure on advertising and IBP to change and evolve with cultural values.

4

CHAPTER 1

After reading and thinking about this chapter, you will be able to do the following:

Know what advertising and integrated brand promotion (IBP) are and what they can do.

Discuss a basic model of advertising communication.

Describe the different ways of classifying audiences for advertising and IBP.

Explain the key role of advertising as a business process.

Understand the concept of integrated brand promotion (IBP) and the role advertising plays in the process.

USE ONLY IN SELF-DEFENSE

THE CURIOUSLY STRONG MINTS®

Introductory Scenario: Does This Sound Familiar?

It's a Friday night and you just battled your way through an online quiz in Anthro that had to be submitted by 11 PM and you beat the deadline by a couple of hours. Feeling pretty good about the quiz (and actually leaving a couple hours of a Friday night free), you check a friend's blog on MySpace.com to see where the parties and concerts are for the night. You notice that some friends you haven't seen for awhile are having a party so you IM two of your buddies to ask if they want to hit the party. Then you hurry up and get on the Ticketmaster Web site (http://www.ticketmaster.com) because the Red Hot Chili Peppers are coming to the big arena on campus (you signed up for the Ticketmaster "performer alert" service and got an e-mail this afternoon) and you want to snag a couple tickets as soon as possible. Your buddies IM back and say they are up for the party and will be at your place in half an hour. Before they get there, you have just enough time to buy the new Deftones CD from Amazon (http://www.amazon.com) and set your Slingbox (http://www.slingmedia.com) so you can check the NBA scores on SportsCenter from the Internet on your cell phone while you're at the party.

Does this sound familiar? If you're into being wired and keeping track of things that are important to you, then this scenario probably does sound pretty familiar (except maybe the Slingbox, which is still pretty expensive. If you haven't seen a Slingbox, it's a device that lets you access your television or TiVo from your computer or your cell phone. See Exhibit 1.1.). And you and your friends represent a huge challenge for companies that want to reach you with their advertising and promotion messages. For the last 50 years, firms have primarily been using television, radio, newspapers, magazines, and other traditional media to send messages to consumers about the companies' brands. Well, in this scenario about your (maybe typical) Friday night, you encountered little if *any* mass media advertising, even though you bought concert tickets and a CD and accessed television programming on the Internet! Instead, you had a whole series of individually controlled information sources that let you access all the information *you* wanted to see rather than information some company wanted you to see or hear.[1]

So, what are companies going to do to reach you with their advertising and brand messages? They are still going to try to reach you and every other consumer around the globe that, just like you, is turning to new ways of acquiring information. And these companies are going to use a different blend of mass media and other forms of communication to try to get their brand messages across. But, rather than the old style of mass media reliance, companies are turning to a wide range of new advertising and promotional techniques that complement their mass media advertising.[2]

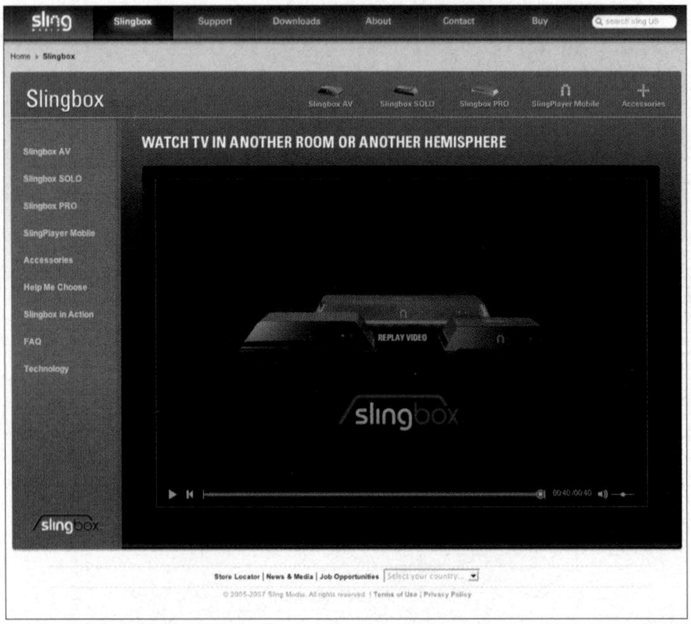

EXHIBIT 1.1

Along with blogs, e-mail, and instant messaging, devices like the Slingbox allow consumers to control their information environment in a way that creates huge challenges for companies trying to get their brand messages to consumers.

1.   Jessi Hempel, "The MySpace Generation," *BusinessWeek*, December 15, 2005, 86–94.
2.   Robert Levine, "Reaching the Unreachables," *Business 2.0*, October 2005, 109–116.

You'll still see advertising during your favorite television show or in your favorite magazine—lots of advertising, in fact. But if you haven't encountered some of the new "smart ads" from companies, you will before too long. If you're a video-game player, your favorite games are already full of ads in the cyberscenery—about $1 billion worth of advertising, actually.[3] The next time you go to the grocery store, you just might find an electronic video tablet attached to the shopping cart that asks you to swipe your store loyalty card before you start touring the aisles. That way the store's computers can prepare a shopping list of items you've purchased before for your convenience. And when you pass a product in the store that a marketer wants to feature, the screen will flash a coupon you can redeem electronically at checkout. When you've finished your shopping and are heading home, your cell phone might alert you to a special on oil changes just as you're approaching a lube shop.[4] Welcome to the new world of advertising and integrated brand promotion.

The New World of Advertising and Integrated Brand Promotion.

As the introductory scenario highlights, the world of advertising and integrated brand promotion is going through enormous change. What you will learn in this book and in your class is that companies are trying to keep up with how and where consumers want to receive information about brands. Mass media are not dead, but they are being supplemented and supported by all sorts of new ways to reach consumers. Consumer preferences and new technology are reshaping the communication environment. You'll also learn that the lines between information, entertainment, and commercial messages are blurring. As one analyst put it, "The line of demarcation was obliterated years ago, when they started naming ballparks after brands."[5] Companies are turning to branded entertainment, the Internet, influencer marketing, and other communication techniques to reach consumers and get their brand messages across. You'll also read about how the world of advertising is being referred to as "Madison & Vine," as Madison Avenue advertising agencies attempt to use Hollywood entertainment-industry techniques to communicate about their brands to consumers.[6] You can go to http://www.adage.com/madisonandvine and read about how new agencies like Madison Road Entertainment are producing brand-filled reality shows like **Treasure Hunters** that expose consumers to dozens of brands, but not in the old "stop the program, show a 30-second ad" kind of way. As the vice president of marketing for Audi America described this new process of integrating brands into consumers' lifestyles, he believes in "acupuncture marketing" where you go "narrow and deep" with your messages.[7]

But we need to remain clear about one thing. No matter how much technology changes or how many new media are available for delivering messages—it's still all about the brand. As consumers, we know what we like and want, and advertising—regardless of the method—helps expose us to brands that can meet our needs. And remember that a brand that does *not* meet our needs will not succeed—no matter how much is spent on advertising or integrated brand promotion. Consider the case of Cadillac. In the early 1950s, Cadillac held a stunning 75 percent share of the luxury car market and was a leading advertiser in the market year after year. But by 2007, that market share had fallen to about 9 percent—an unprecedented loss in the history of the automobile industry. What happened to the Cadillac brand? A series of

3.   Jessica Ramirez, "The New Ad Game," *Newsweek*, July 31, 2006.
4.   David H. Freedman, "The Future of Advertising," *Inc. Magazine*, August 2005, 70–77.
5.   Question of the Week, Ad Infinitum, *BusinessWeek*, November 20, 2006, 18.
6.   To see current "Madison and Vine" campaign strategies, go to *http://www.adage.com/madisonandvine*.
7.   Jean Halliday, "Audi Taps Ad Whiz to Direct Branding," *Advertising Age*, May 8, 2006, 4, 88.

EXHIBIT 1.2

GM is trying to reinvent the Cadillac brand with designs and new "brand story" advertising featuring music by artists like the Teddybears, Explosions in the Sky, and Melikka.

product missteps confused the market's perception of the brand: The 1986 Cimarron, for example, used a Chevy chassis and looked cheap, and the 1987 Allante sports car was slow and leaked like a sieve. And formidable competitors like Lexus and Infiniti entered the market with powerful and stylish alternatives that were effectively advertised. Now GM is reinvesting in Cadillac and has committed $4.3 billion to redesign, advertise, and promote the brand to change consumers' perceptions (see Exhibit 1.2). Advertising (featuring bands like the Teddybears, Explosions in the Sky, and Melikka) and product redesign (dramatic changes in styling and performance) are the key tools being used in revitalizing the brand.[8]

So, as you work your way through the class and the chapters in the book, you'll learn how advertising works and how it is changing. You'll also learn about all the new methods of communicating to consumers through the process of integrated brand promotion.

What Are Advertising and Integrated Brand Promotion?

Now that we've set the new and dynamic context for communication, let's consider the tools companies are going to be using: advertising and integrated brand promotion. We'll start with advertising. You have your own ideas about advertising because you see some advertising every day—even if you try to avoid most of it, like the situation in the introductory scenario. You need to know that advertising means different things to different people, though. It's a business, an art form, an institution, and a cultural phenomenon. To the CEO of a multinational corporation, like Pepsi, advertising is an essential marketing tool that helps create brand awareness and brand loyalty. To the owner of a small retail shop, advertising is a way to bring people into the store. To the art director in an advertising agency, advertising is the creative expression of a concept. To a media planner, advertising is the way a firm uses the mass media to communicate to current and potential customers. To a Web site manager, it's a way to drive traffic to the URL. To scholars and museum curators, advertising is an important cultural artifact, text, and historical record. Advertising means something different to all these people. In fact, sometimes determining just what is and what is not advertising is a difficult task!

While companies believe in and rely heavily on advertising, it is not a process that the average person clearly understands or values. Most people have some significant misperceptions about advertising and what it's supposed to do, what it can do, and what it can't do. Many people think advertising deceives others, but rarely themselves. Most think it's a semi-glamorous profession, but one in which people are either morally bankrupt con artists or pathological liars. At worst, advertising is seen as hype, unfair capitalistic manipulation, banal commercial noise, mind

8.   David Welch and Gerry Khermouch, "Can GM Save An Icon?" *BusinessWeek*, April 8, 2002, 60–67; David Welch, "The Second Coming of Cadillac," *BusinessWeek*, November 24, 2003, 79–80.

It's what makes computers more powerful.

Advertising. The way great brands get to be great brands."

EXHIBIT 1.3

The American Advertising Federation (AAF) ran this ad touting the power of advertising's effect on brand building. The AAF used the Intel logo and brand "look" for this message because Intel is regarded as one of the most successful firms in using advertising to build brand name awareness and recognition. http://www .aaf.org

control, postmodern voodoo, or outright deception. At best, the average person sees advertising as amusing, informative, helpful, and occasionally hip.

The truth about advertising lies somewhere between the extremes. Sometimes advertising is hard-hitting and powerful; at other times, it's boring and ineffective. Advertising can be enormously creative and entertaining, and it can be simply annoying. One thing is for sure: Advertising is anything but unimportant. Advertising plays a pivotal role in world commerce and in the way we experience and live our lives. It is part of our language and our culture. It reflects the way we think about things and the way we see ourselves. It is both a complex communication process and a dynamic business process.

And, as a business process, advertising is relied on by companies big and small to build their brands—this is the central theme of this book. Advertising and integrated brand promotions are key to organizations' strategies to build awareness and preference for brands (see Exhibit 1.3).

Advertising Defined. Keeping in mind that different people in different contexts see advertising so differently and that advertising suffers from some pretty complex controversies, we offer this straightforward definition:

Advertising *is a paid, mass-mediated attempt to persuade.*

As direct and simple as this definition seems, it is loaded with distinctions. First, advertising is *paid* communication by a company or organization that wants its information disseminated. In advertising language, the company or organization that pays for advertising is called the **client** or **sponsor**. If a communication is *not paid for*, it's not advertising. For example, a form of promotion called *publicity* is not advertising because it is not paid for. Let's say Will Smith appears on the *Late Show with David Letterman* to promote his newest movie. Is this advertising? No, because the producer or film studio did not pay the *Late Show with David Letterman* for airtime. In this example, the show gets an interesting and popular guest, the guest star gets exposure, and the film gets plugged. Everyone is happy, but no advertising took place—it might be public relations, but it is not advertising. But when the film studio produces and runs ads on television and in newspapers across the country for the newest Will Smith movie, this communication is paid for by the studio, it is placed in media to reach consumers, and therefore it most definitely is advertising.

For the same reason, public service announcements (PSAs) are not advertising either. True, they look like ads and sound like ads, but they are not ads. They are not commercial in the way an ad is because they are not paid for like an ad. They are offered as information in the public (noncommercial) interest. When you hear a message on the radio that implores you to "Just Say No" to drugs, this sounds very much like an ad, but it is a PSA. Simply put, PSAs are excluded from the definition of advertising because they are unpaid communication.

EXHIBITS 1.4 AND 1.5

The messages in Exhibits 1.4 and 1.5 communicate nearly identical information to the audience, but one is an advertisement and one is not. The message in Exhibit 1.4, sponsored by Trojan, is an advertisement because it is paid-for communication. The message in Exhibit 1.5, sponsored by the U.K.'s Health Education Authority, has a persuasive intent similar to the Trojan ad, but it is not advertising—Exhibit 1.5 is a PSA. Why isn't the Health Education Authority PSA message an ad? http://www.trojancondoms.com

Consider the two messages in Exhibits 1.4 and 1.5. These two messages have similar copy and offer similar advice. Exhibit 1.4 has persuasive intent, is paid-for communication, and appears in the mass media. It is an advertisement. Exhibit 1.5 also has persuasive intent and appears in mass media outlets, but it is not advertising because it is not paid-for communication. PSAs are important and often strongly imitate their commercial cousins.

Second, advertising is *mass mediated*. This means it is delivered through a communication medium designed to reach more than one person, typically a large number—or mass—of people. Advertising is widely disseminated through familiar means—television, radio, newspapers, and magazines—and other media such as direct mail, billboards, the Internet, and iPods. The mass-mediated nature of advertising creates a communication environment where the message is not delivered in a face-to-face manner. This distinguishes advertising from personal selling as a form of communication.

Third, all advertising includes an *attempt to persuade*. To put it bluntly, ads are communications designed to get someone to do something. Even an advertisement with a stated objective of being purely informational still has persuasion at its core. The ad informs the consumer for some purpose, and that purpose is to get the consumer to like the brand and because of that liking to eventually buy the brand. Consider the Pur water filter ad in Exhibit 1.6. It doesn't carry a lot of product information. But it's interesting, and most of us would say, "Yeah, I like that ad." With that reaction, this ad is persuasive. In the absence of a persuasive intent, a communication might be news, but it would not be advertising.

At this point, we can say that for a communication to be classified as advertising, three essential criteria must be met:

1. The communication must be *paid for*.
2. The communication must be delivered to an audience via *mass media*.
3. The communication must be *attempting persuasion*.

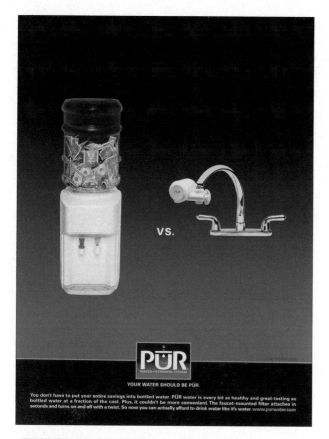

EXHIBIT 1.6

In order for a communication to be advertising, it has to have a persuasive intent. Even though this Pur water filter ad is not overtly persuasive, the fact that it is interesting creates a positive reaction in the audience, which can persuade people to try the brand. http://www .purwater.com

It is important to note here that advertising can be persuasive communication not only about a product or service but also about an idea, a person, or an entire organization. When Colgate and Honda use advertising, this is product advertising and meets all three criteria. When E-Trade, Delta Air Lines, Terminix, or your dentist runs advertisements, it is service advertising and meets all three criteria.

Integrated Brand Promotion Defined.

Now that we have defined advertising, let's consider the other important context for the book—the process of integrated brand promotion, or IBP. To fully understand integrated brand promotion, we need to first define IBP and describe all the tools used for IBP. Then we can talk about how it is related to and yet distinct from advertising. First the definition:

Integrated Brand Promotion (IBP) *is the process of using a wide range of promotional tools working together to create widespread brand exposure.*

Just as the definition of advertising was loaded with meaning, so too is the definition of integrated brand promotion. First, IBP is a process. It has to be. It is complicated and needs to be managed in an integrated fashion. Second, IBP uses a wide range of promotional tools that have to be evaluated and scheduled. Here is a list of the most prominent:

- Advertising in mass media (television, radio, newspapers, magazines, billboards)
- Sales promotions (coupons, premiums, discounts, gift cards, contests, samples, trial offers, rebates, frequent user programs, trade shows)
- Point of purchase (in-store) advertising
- Direct marketing (catalogs, telemarketing, e-mail offers, infomercials)
- Personal selling
- Internet advertising (banners, pop-ups/pop-unders, Web sites)
- Blogs
- Podcasting
- Event sponsorships
- Branded entertainment (product placement in television programming, Webcasts, and films), also referred to as "advertainment"
- Outdoor signage
- Billboard, transit, and aerial advertising
- Public relations
- Influencer marketing (peer-to-peer persuasion)
- Corporate advertising

Notice that this long list of IBP tools includes various types of advertising. From mass media to influencer marketing, the tools of IBP are varied and wide ranging. All of these tools allow a marketer to reach target customers in different ways with different kinds of messages to achieve broad exposure for a brand.

Third, the definition of IBP highlights that all of these tools need to work together. That is, they need to be integrated to create a consistent and compelling impression of the brand. Having mass media advertising send one message and create one image and then have Webcasts or personal selling deliver another message will confuse consumers about the meaning and relevance of the brand—this is a very bad thing!

Finally, the definition of IBP specifies that all of the advertising and promotional effort undertaken by a firm is designed to create widespread exposure for a brand. Unless consumers are reached by these various forms of messages, they will have a difficult time understanding the brand and deciding whether to use it regularly.

Advertisements, Advertising Campaigns, and Integrated Brand Promotion.

Now that we have working definitions of advertising and IBP, we can turn our attention to some other important distinctions and definitions. Let's start with the basics. An **advertisement** refers to a specific message that someone or some organization has placed to persuade an audience. An **advertising campaign** is a series of coordinated advertisements that communicate a reasonably cohesive and integrated theme. The theme may be made up of several claims or points but should advance an essentially singular theme. Successful advertising campaigns can be developed around a single advertisement placed in multiple media, or they can be made up of several different advertisements with a similar look, feel, and message. You are probably familiar with the "Got Milk" campaign as an example. Another example is represented by the Altoids ads in Exhibits 1.7 through 1.10. Notice the excellent use of similar look and feel in this advertising campaign. Advertising campaigns can run for a few weeks or for many years. The advertising campaign is, in many ways, the most challenging aspect of advertising execution. It requires a keen sense of the complex environments within which a company must communicate to different audiences.

And think about this important aspect of advertising campaigns. Most individual ads would make little sense without the knowledge that audience members have accumulated from previous ads for a particular brand. Ads are interpreted by consumers through their experiences with a brand and previous ads for the brand. When you see a new Nike ad, you make sense of the ad through your history with Nike and its previous advertising. Even ads for a new brand or a new product are situated within audiences' broader knowledge of products, brands, and advertising. After years of viewing ads and buying brands, audiences bring a rich history and knowledge base to every communications encounter.

How does IBP fit in with advertisements and advertising campaigns? As we discussed earlier, IBP is the use of many promotional tools, including advertising, in a coordinated manner to build and then maintain brand awareness, identity, and preference. When marketers combine contests, a Web site, event sponsorship, and point-of-purchase displays with advertisements and advertising campaigns, they create an integrated brand promotion. BMW did just that when the firm (re)introduced the Mini Cooper auto to the U.S. market. The IBP campaign used billboards, print ads, an interactive Web site, and "guerrilla" marketing (a Mini was mounted on top of a Chevy Suburban and driven around New York City). Each part of the campaign was coordinated with all the others.[9] Note that the word *coordinated* is central to the IBP effort. Without coordination among these various promotional efforts, there is not an integrated brand promotion. Rather, the consumer will merely encounter a series of unrelated (and often confusing) communications about a brand.

9.   John Gaffney, "Most Innovative Campaign," *Business 2.0*, May 2002, 98–99.

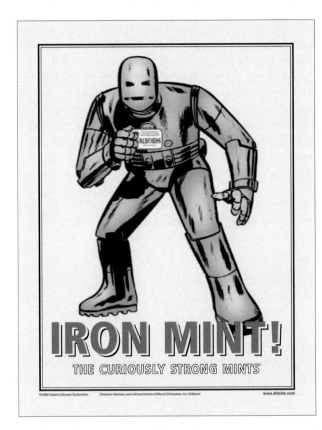

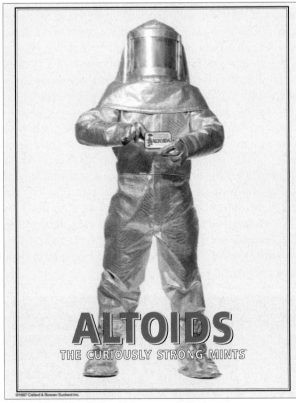

EXHIBITS 1.7 THROUGH 1.10

A well-conceived and well-executed advertising campaign offers consumers a series of messages with a similar look and feel. This series of ads for Altoids is an excellent example of a campaign that communicates with similar images to create a unified look and feel. http://www.altoids.com

A Focus on Advertising. Integrated brand promotion will be a key concept throughout our discussion of advertising. The fact that this phrase is included in the title of the book signals its importance to the contemporary marketing effort. As consumers encounter a daily blitz of commercial messages and appeals, brands and brand identity offers them a way to cope with the overload of information. Brands and the images they project allow consumers to quickly identify and evaluate the relevance of a brand to their lives and value systems. The marketer who does not use advertising and IBP as a way to build brand exposure and meaning for consumers will, frankly, be ignored.

We will develop the concept and describe the execution of IBP throughout the text and demonstrate how advertising is central to the process. The encounters between consumers and advertising, advertisements, and advertising campaigns, specifically, are the focus of our next discussion. The focus on specific features of other IBP tools from the list above will be covered extensively in Part Five of the text.

2 Advertising as a Communication Process. Communication is a
fundamental aspect of human existence, and advertising is one of those communications. To understand advertising at all, you must understand something about communication in general and about mass communication in particular. At the outset, it's important to understand the basics of how advertising works as a means of communication. To help with gaining this understanding, let's consider a contemporary model of mass communication. We'll apply this basic model of communication as a first step toward understanding advertising.

A Model of Mass-Mediated Communication. As we said earlier, advertising is mass-
mediated communication; it occurs not face-to-face, but through a medium (such as radio, magazines, television, on the side of a building, or on your computer). While there are many valuable models of mass communication, a contemporary model of mass-mediated communication is presented in Exhibit 1.11. This model shows mass communication as a process where people, institutions, and messages interact. It has two major components, each representing quasi-independent processes: production and reception. Between production and reception are the mediating (interpretation) processes of accommodation and negotiation. It's not as complex as it sounds. Let's investigate each part of the model.

Moving from left to right in the model, we first see the process of communication production, where the content of any mass communication is produced. An advertisement, like other forms of mass communication, is the product of institutions (such as networks, corporations, advertising agencies, and governments) interacting to produce content (what physically appears on a page as a print ad, or as a television ad, or on a computer screen at a company's Web site). The creation of the advertise-

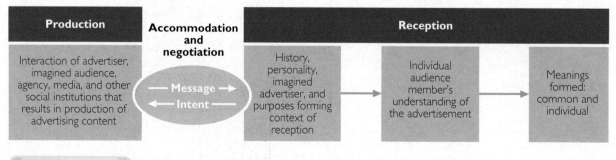

EXHIBIT 1.11

A model of mass-mediated communication.

ment is a complex interaction of the company's message; the company's expectations about the target audience's desire for information; the company's assumptions about how the audience will interpret the words and images in an ad; and the rules and regulations of the medium that transmits the message. Advertising is rarely (if ever) the product of any one individual. Rather, as this model shows, it is a collaborative (social) product between people receiving a message and the institutions (companies and media companies) that send them that message.

Continuing on to the right, we see that the mediating processes of accommodation and negotiation lie between the production and reception phases. Accommodation and negotiation are the ways in which consumers interpret ads. Audience members have some ideas about how the company wants them to interpret the ad (we all know the rules of advertising—somebody is trying to persuade us to buy something). And consumers also have their own needs, agendas, and preferred interpretations. They also know about the way other consumers think about this product and this message, because brands have personalities and send social signals. Given all this, consumers who see an ad arrive at an interpretation of the ad that makes sense to them, serves their needs, and fits their personal history with a product category and a brand.

What's interesting about the whole progression of consumer receipt and interpretation of a communication is that it is usually wholly *incompatible* with the way the company wants consumers to see an ad! In other words, the receivers of the communication must *accommodate* these competing forces, meanings, and agendas and then *negotiate* a meaning, or an interpretation, of the ad. That's why we say that communication is inherently a *social* process: What a message means to any given consumer is a function not of an isolated solitary thinker, but of an inherently social being responding to what he or she knows about the producers of the message (the companies), other receivers of it (peer groups, for example), and the social world in which the brand and the message about it resides. Now, admittedly, all this interpretation happens very fast and without much contemplation. Still, it happens. The level of conscious interpretation might be minimal (mere recognition) or it might be extensive (thoughtful, elaborate processing of an ad), but there is *always* interpretation.

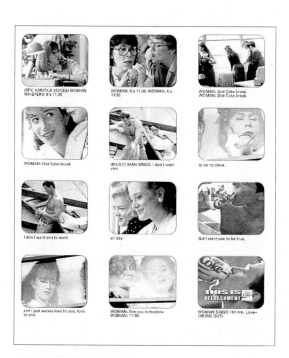

EXHIBIT 1.12

This ad is a good example of how the meaning of an ad can vary for different people. How would you interpret the meaning of this ad? Think of someone very different from you. What meaning might that person give this ad?
http://www.cocacola.com

It has to be emphasized that the processes of production and reception are partially independent. Although the producers of a message can control the placement of a message in a medium, they cannot control or even closely monitor the circumstances that surround reception and interpretation of the ad. Audience members are exposed to advertising outside the direct observation of the company and are capable of interpreting advertising any way they want. (Of course, most audience interpretations are not completely off the wall, either.) Likewise, audience members have little control over or input into the actual production of the message—the company developed a message that audience members are *supposed* to like. Because of these aspects of communication, the model shows that both producers and receivers are thus "imagined," in the sense that the two don't have significant direct contact with each another but have a general sense of what the other is like.

The communication model in Exhibit 1.11 underscores a critical point: No ad contains a single meaning for all audience members. An ad for a pair of women's shoes means something different for women than it does for men. An ad that achieved widespread popularity (and controversy) is the ad for Diet Coke shown in Exhibit 1.12, which may be interpreted differently by men and women. For example, does the ad suggest that men drink Diet Coke so they can be the object of intense daily admiration by a group of female office workers? Or does the ad suggest that Diet

Coke is a part of a modern woman's lifestyle, granting her "permission" to freely admire attractive men in the same way women have been eyed by male construction workers (or executives) for years? The audience decides. Keep in mind that although individual audience members' interpretations will differ to some extent, they may be close enough to the company's intent to make the ad effective. When members of an audience are similar in their background, social standing, and goals, they generally yield similar enough meaning from an ad for it to accomplish its goals.

3 The Audiences for Advertising.

We've been referring to audiences, so now it's time to define them. In the language of advertising, an **audience** is a group of individuals who receive and interpret messages sent from companies. The audience could be made up of household consumers, college students, or business people. Any large group of people can be an audience. A **target audience** is a particular group of consumers singled out by an organization for an advertising or promotion campaign. These target audiences are singled out because the firm has discovered that audience members like or might like the product category. Target audiences are always *potential* audiences because a company can never be sure that the message will actually get through to them as intended. By the way, there is nothing sinister about the targeting process. Targeting audiences simply means that a company wants to reach you with a message. Do you feel like something bad happens to you when the Gap targets you with an ad and you see it on TV? Of course not! Somewhere along the line the word *targeting* and the phrase *target audience* have picked up some negative connotations—ignore them.

While companies can identify dozens of different target audiences, five broad audience categories are commonly described: household consumers, members of business organizations, members of a trade channel, professionals, and government officials and employees.

Audience Categories.

Household consumers are the most conspicuous audience in that most mass media advertising is directed at them. McDonald's, Nissan, Miller Brewing, the Gap, and AIG Insurance have products and services designed for the consumer market, and so their advertising targets household consumers. The most recent information indicates that there are about 111 million households in the United States and approximately 300 million household consumers.[10] Total yearly retail spending by these households is about $5.0 trillion in the United States.[11] This huge audience is typically where the action is in advertising. Under the very broad heading of "consumer advertising," very fine audience distinctions can be made by companies. A target audience definition such as men, 25 to 45, living in metropolitan areas, with incomes greater than $50,000 per year would be the kind of target audience description a company might develop.

Members of business organizations are the focus of advertising for firms that produce business and industrial goods and services, such as office equipment, production machinery, supplies, and software. While products and services targeted to this audience often require personal selling, advertising is used to create an awareness and a favorable attitude among potential buyers. Not-for-profit businesses such as universities, some research laboratories, philanthropic groups, and cultural organizations represent an important and separate business audience for advertising. Exhibit 1.13 is an example of an ad directed at members of business organizations.

10.   "2005 Survey of Buying Power," *Sales and Marketing Management* (2005), 8, 13.
11.   Ibid., 17.

WHEN SERVING YOUR CUSTOMERS, WHATEVER CHOICE YOU MAKE, YOU'RE TOAST.

You know that the only way to succeed is by serving your customers better. But what organization can afford to throw endless dollars at improving the customer experience? With RightNow, you don't have to make a deal with the devil.

RightNow provides a breakthrough solution that lets you enhance your customer experience while reducing costs. By delivering knowledge at every customer touchpoint, RightNow helps you grow your business, one customer

experience at a time. We've enabled more than a billion successful customer interactions for our clients in every major industry. Chances are, we can help you, too.

Find out why RightNow leads in client satisfaction. Download your free executive summary of CRMGuru's Solutions Guide at www.rightnow.com/toast or call us toll-free at 1.877.363.5678.

RIGHT NOW TECHNOLOGIES

EXHIBIT 1.13

RightNow Technologies sells systems used by companies to cut sales costs and improve customer relationship management. When members of business organizations use advertising to communicate, the ads often emphasize creating awareness of the company's brand name. RightNow Technologies is combining high visual appeal with detailed ad copy to accomplish brand name recognition. http://www .rightnow.com

Members of a trade channel include retailers (like Circuit City for consumer electronics), wholesalers (like Castle Wholesalers for construction tools), and distributors (like Sysco Food Services for restaurant supplies). They are a target audience for producers of both household and business goods and services. So, for example, if Microsoft cannot gain adequate retail and wholesale distribution through trade channels for the Xbox, the brand will not reach target customers. That being the case, it's important to direct advertising at the trade level of the market. Various forms of advertising can be used to develop demand among members of a trade channel. The promotional tool used most often to communicate with this group is personal selling. This is because this target audience represents a relatively small, easily identifiable group that can be reached with personal selling. When advertising is also directed at this target audience, it can serve an extremely useful purpose, as we will see later in the section on advertising as a business process.

Professionals form a special target audience and are defined as doctors, lawyers, accountants, teachers, or any other professional group that has special training or certification. This audience warrants a separate classification because its members have specialized needs and interests. Advertising directed to professionals typically highlights products and services uniquely designed to serve their more narrowly defined needs. The language and images used in advertising to this target audience often rely on esoteric terminology and unique circumstances that members of professions readily recognize. Advertising to professionals is predominantly carried out through trade publications. **Trade journals** are magazines published specifically for members of a trade and carry highly technical articles.

Government officials and employees constitute an audience in themselves due to the large dollar volume of buying that federal, state, and local governments do. Government organizations from universities to road maintenance operations buy huge amounts of various types of products. Producers of items such as office furniture, construction materials, vehicles, fertilizers, computers, and business services all target government organizations with advertising. Advertising to this target audience is dominated by direct mail, catalogs, and Web advertising.

GLOBALIZATION

Try This One on for Size

Here's a challenge of global proportions. Imagine that it is your job to develop the advertising for a retail store that sells women's lingerie. This shouldn't be too hard. After all, Victoria's Secret has done a great job with bold television advertising featuring Tyra Banks and Gisele Bündchen, not to mention those direct mail catalogs. It's a product category that's showing strong growth and the media are loosening up on restrictions for visuals.

Well, there is one other little detail that might make this a bit more difficult. The retail lingerie store's name is Al Mashat and it is located in Saudi Arabia. So, you ask? Lingerie is lingerie and women are women. That may be true, but Saudi Arabia is also Saudi Arabia and in Saudi Arabia the detail that is most problematic was well articulated by Margo Chase, founder and executive director of Chase Design Group consulting firm: "The really huge problem is how to market lingerie in a country where you can't show photographs of women." Not being able to show women in lingerie is a somewhat important detail that would make this just a bit more difficult.

So, what *would* you do in a situation like this? One thing is for sure, there is no way that the religious culture of Saudi Arabia and the media restrictions it creates are going to change just because some retail store wants to more effectively advertise. But here are some details that might help you out: Saudi Arabia has an extremely young population, with 42.4 percent being under the age of 15. Additionally, shopping is one of the few recreations available to Saudi women.

Have you figured out an advertising strategy yet? Well, let's take a look at what the U.S. consulting firm Chase Design Group came up with for advertising for Al Mashat. First, the design firm decided that if they could not use the images of women, then the advertising campaign would be carried by "language that was rich, textured, layered, and sensual." An example of the language was a poem featured both in advertising and store banners: "Wrap this beautiful robe of words around you and dream." Second, to carry through on the force of the language, a special font and characters were developed. Finally, advertising was launched using print ads, radio ads, and a direct mail piece featuring bags imprinted with the store logo and filled with potpourri and an invitation card printed on iridescent pearl-colored paper. As a follow-up, another direct mail campaign mailed out gift vouchers worth 50 riyals (about $13) to prospective customers.

How did it all work out? In the first year of the store's operations more than $3.2 million in revenue was generated. The owner expects revenue to grow to $5 million in the store's second full year.

The lesson here is that in global markets, any number of unique circumstances can restrict the way we might use advertising. But the other lesson is that even though there may be what seem to be huge barriers (like not showing women in ads for a product designed exclusively for women), the breadth and creativity of advertising can be used to overcome such barriers.

Source: Arundhati Parmar, "Out from Under," **Marketing News**, July 21, 2003.

Audience Geography. Audiences can also be broken down by geographic location. Because of cultural differences that often accompany geographic location, very few ads can be effective for all consumers worldwide. If an ad is used worldwide with only minor changes it is called **global advertising**. Very few ads can use global advertising. These are typically brands that are considered citizens of the world and whose manner of use does not vary tremendously by culture. Using a Sony television or taking a trip on Singapore Airlines doesn't change much from culture to culture and geographic location to geographic location. Exhibits 1.14 and 1.15 show extremely similar appeals in two different ads for Rolex watches—another product category where product use across cultures is the same. Firms that market brands with global appeal, like Singapore Airlines, IBM, Sony, and Pirelli Tires, try to develop and place advertisements with a common theme and presentation in all markets around the world where the firm's brands are sold. Global placement is possible only when a brand and the messages about that brand have a common appeal across diverse cultures. The Globalization box highlights a situation where a product category widely advertised in the U.S. market, lingerie, is somewhat more complicated to advertise in a different culture—Saudi Arabia.

International advertising occurs when firms prepare and place different advertising in different national markets outside their home market. Each international market often requires unique or original advertising due to product adaptations or message appeals tailored specifically for that market. Unilever prepares different versions of ads for its laundry products for nearly every international market because consumers in different cultures approach the laundry task differently. Consumers in the United States use large and powerful washers and dryers and lots of hot water. Households in Brazil use very little hot water and hang clothes out to dry. Very few

Global advertising can be used for brands where there is little difference in use across cultures or geographic location. The only real difference in these two ads is language (German versus Italian), while other aspects—Rolex's appeal to an affluent elite who likely follow tennis and the Rolex brand imagery—remain the same. An interesting twist with Rolex is that it uses a Web site to describe, but not sell, its products (http://www.rolex .com). Instead, the Web site directs surfers to the retailers who carry the brand. Is the Web likely to be Rolex's best advertising channel, anyway?

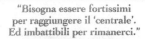

Daffy's (http://www .daffys.com) is a clothing retailer with several shops in the New York/New Jersey metropolitan area. It services a local geographic market. Retailers that serve a small geographic area use local advertising to reach their customers and typically rely on newspaper and radio ads to reach their local target market.

firms enjoy the luxury of having a brand with truly cross-cultural appeal and global recognition, as is necessary for global advertising. International advertising differs from global advertising in that different ads are tailored for each market.

National advertising reaches all geographic areas of one nation. National advertising is the term typically used to describe the kind of advertising we see most often in the mass media in the domestic U.S. market. Does international advertising use many different national advertising efforts? Yes, that is exactly the relationship between international advertising and national advertising.

Regional advertising is carried out by producers, wholesalers, distributors, and retailers that concentrate their efforts in a relatively large, but not national, geographic region. Albertson's, a regional grocery chain, has stores in 31 western, northwestern, midwestern, and southern states. Because of the nature of the firm's markets, it places advertising only in regions where it has stores.

Local advertising is much the same as regional advertising. **Local advertising** is directed at an audience in a single trading area, either a city or state. Exhibit 1.16 shows an example of this type of advertising. Daffy's is a discount clothing retailer with stores in the New York/New Jersey metropolitan area. Retailers with local

EXHIBIT 1.17

National companies will often share advertising expenses with local retail merchants if the retailer features the company's brand in local advertising. This sharing of expenses is called co-op advertising. Here a local retailer, Shapiro Luggage, is featuring TUMI brand luggage in this co-op ad. http://www.tumi.com

markets like Daffy's use all types of local media to reach customers. Under special circumstances, national companies will share advertising expenses in a market with local dealers to achieve specific advertising objectives. This sharing of advertising expenses between national companies and local merchants is called **cooperative advertising** (or **co-op advertising**). Exhibit 1.17 illustrates a co-op advertisement run by TUMI luggage and one of its retailers, Shapiro. In a key strategy move several years ago, General Motors redesigned its co-op advertising program with dealers in an attempt to create a more fully coordinated integrated brand promotion.[12]

4 Advertising as a Business Process.

So far we have talked about advertising as a communication process and as a way companies reach diverse audiences with persuasive brand information. But we need to appreciate another dimension: Advertising is very much a business process as well as a communication process. For multinational organizations like Microsoft, as well as for small local retailers, advertising is a basic business tool that is essential to retaining current customers and attracting new customers. We need to understand that advertising functions as a business process in three ways. First, we'll consider the role advertising plays in the overall marketing and brand development programs in firms. Second, we will look at the types of advertising used by firms. Finally, we will take a broader look at advertising by identifying the economic effects of the process.

The Role of Advertising in Marketing. To truly appreciate advertising as a business process, we have to understand the role advertising plays in a firm's marketing effort. To begin with, realize that every organization *must* make marketing decisions. There simply is no escaping the need to develop brands, price them, distribute them, and advertise and promote them to a target audience. The role of advertising and brand promotion relates to four important aspects of the marketing process: (1) determining the marketing mix; (2) developing and managing the brand; (3) achieving effective market segmentation, differentiation, and positioning; and (4) contributing to revenue and profit generation.

The Role of Advertising in the Marketing Mix. A formal definition of marketing reveals that advertising (as a part of overall promotion) is one of the primary marketing tools available to any organization:

Marketing *is the process of planning and executing the conception, pricing, promotion, and distribution of ideas, goods, and services to create exchanges that satisfy individual and organizational objectives.*[13]

Marketing people assume a wide range of responsibilities in an organization related to conceiving, pricing, promoting, and distributing goods, services, and even ideas. Many of you know that these four areas of responsibility and decision making in marketing are referred to as the **marketing mix**. The word *mix* is used to describe the blend of strategic emphasis on the product versus its price versus its promotion (including advertising) versus its distribution when a brand is marketed to consumers. This blend, or mix, results in the overall marketing program for a brand.

12.   Joe Miller, "Dealers Regain Ad Input as GM Revives Program," *Advertising Age*, October 16, 2000, 80.
13.   This definition of marketing was approved in 1995 by the American Marketing Association (*http://www.marketingpower.com*) and remains the official definition offered by the organization.

Advertising is important, but it is only one of the major areas of marketing responsibility *and* it is only one of many different IBP tools relied on in the marketing mix.

Generally speaking, the role of advertising in the marketing mix is to focus on the ability of advertising to communicate to a target audience the value a brand has to offer. Value consists of more than simply the tangible aspects of the brand itself. Indeed, consumers look for value in the brand, but they also demand such things as convenient location, credit terms, warranties and guarantees, and delivery. In addition, a wide range of emotional values such as security, belonging, affiliation, excitement, and prestige can also be pursued in the brand choice process. If you have any doubts that emotion plays a role, think about the fact that a $14,000 Ford Focus can get you from one place to another in pretty much the same way as a $120,000 BMW M5. Well, maybe without the same thrill and style—but that's the point. People look for more than function in a brand; they often buy the emotional kick that a brand and its features provide.

Because consumers search for such diverse values, marketers must determine which marketing mix ingredients to emphasize and how to blend the mix elements in just the right way to attract customers. These marketing mix decisions play a significant role in determining the message content and media placement of advertising.

Exhibit 1.18 lists factors typically considered in each area of the marketing mix. You can see that decisions under each of the marketing mix areas can directly affect the advertising message. The important point is that a firm's advertising effort must be consistent with and complement the overall marketing mix strategy being used by a firm.

Product	Promotion
Functional features	Amount and type of advertising
Aesthetic design	Number and qualifications of salespeople
Accompanying services	Extent and type of personal selling program
Instructions for use	Sales promotion—coupons, contests, sweepstakes
Warranty	Trade shows
Product differentiation	Public relations activities
Product positioning	Direct mail or telemarketing
	Event sponsorships
	Internet communications
Price	**Distribution**
Level:	Number of retail outlets
Top of the line	Location of retail outlets
Competitive, average prices	Types of retail outlets
Low-price policy	Catalog sales
Terms offered:	Other nonstore retail methods—Internet
Cash only	Number and type of wholesalers
Credit:	Inventories—extent and location
Extended	Services provided by distribution:
Restricted	Credit
Interest charges	Delivery
Lease/rental	Installation
	Training

EXHIBIT 1.18

These are the factors that an organization needs to consider in creating a marketing mix. Advertising messages, media placement, and IBP techniques must be consistent with and complement strategies in all the other areas of the marketing mix.

2007 Brand Rank	2006 Brand Rank	Change in Rank	Brand	Brand Value 2007 (U.S. millions)	Brand Value 2006 (U.S. millions)	% Change in Value from Previous Year	Parent Company	County
1	1	0	Coca-Cola	$65.32	$67.00	−3%	Coca-Cola	U.S.
2	2	0	Microsoft	58.71	56.93	3	Microsoft	U.S.
3	3	0	IBM	57.09	56.20	2	IBM	U.S.
4	4	0	GE	51.57	48.91	5	GE	U.S.
5	6	1	Nokia	33.69	30.13	12	Nokia	Finland
6	7	1	Toyota	32.07	27.94	15	Toyota	Japan
7	5	−2	Intel	30.95	32.32	−4	Intel	U.S.
8	9	1	McDonald's	29.39	27.50	7	McDonald's	U.S.
9	8	−1	Disney	29.21	27.85	5	Walt Disney	U.S.
10	10	0	Mercedes	23.57	21.79	8	Daimler AG	Germany
11	11	0	Citi	23.44	21.46	9	Citigroup	U.S.
12	13	1	Hewlett-Packard	22.19	20.46	9	Hewlett-Packard	U.S.
13	15	2	BMW	21.61	19.62	10	BMW	Germany
14	12	−2	Marlboro	21.28	21.35	0	Altria	U.S.
15	14	−1	American Express	20.83	19.64	6	American Express	U.S.
16	16	0	Gillette	20.42	19.58	4	Procter & Gamble	U.S.
17	17	0	Louis Vuitton	20.32	17.61	15	Louis Vuitton Moët Hennessy	France
18	18	0	Cisco	19.09	17.53	9	Cisco	U.S.
19	19	0	Honda	17.99	17.05	6	Honda Motor	Japan
20	24	4	Google	17.84	12.38	44	Google	U.S.

Source: *BusinessWeek*, August 6, 2007, 59–64.

EXHIBIT 1.19

The World's 20 Most Valuable Brands in 2007.

The Role of Advertising in Brand Management. One of the key issues to understand about the role of advertising is that it plays a critical role in brand development and management. We have been referring to the brand and integrated brand promotion throughout our discussion of the process of advertising so far. All of us have our own understanding of what a brand is. After all, we buy brands every day. A formal definition of a **brand** is a name, term, sign, symbol, or any other feature that identifies one seller's good or service as distinct from those of other sellers.[14] Advertising plays a significant role in brand development and management. A brand is in many ways the most precious business asset owned by a firm. It allows a firm to communicate consistently and efficiently with the market.

BusinessWeek magazine in conjunction with Interbrand, a marketing analysis and consulting firm, has attached a dollar value to brand names based on a combination of sales, earnings, future sales potential and intangibles other than the brand that drive sales. The 20 most valuable brands in the world in 2007 are shown in Exhibit 1.19. Often, the brand name is worth much more than the annual sales of the brand. Coca-Cola, the most valuable brand in the world, is estimated to be worth about $65 billion even though sales of branded Coca-Cola products are only about $20 billion a year.

14.   Peter D. Bennett, *Dictionary of Marketing Terms*, 2nd ed. (Chicago: American Marketing Association, 1995), 4.

A brand can be put at a serious competitive disadvantage without effective communication provided by advertising. Staples, the office supply retailer, was struggling with an outdated advertising campaign featuring the tagline "Yeah, we've got that." Customers were complaining that items were out of stock and sales staff didn't care. So the company's vice president of marketing, Shira Goodman, determined that shoppers wanted an "easier" shopping experience with well-stocked shelves and helpful staff. Once those operational changes were made, Staples introduced the "Staples: That Was Easy" campaign, featuring big red "Easy" buttons that were also available for sale at the stores. Now, with clear, straightforward ads and customers spreading the word (called "viral" marketing) by wearing their "Easy" buttons in offices all over the country, Staples is the runaway leader in office retail.[15]

For every organization, advertising affects brand development and management in five important ways.

Information and Persuasion. Target audiences learn about a brand's features and benefits through the message content of advertising and, to a lesser extent, other promotional tools (most other promotional tools, except the Web, are not heavy on content) that are used in the IBP effort. But advertising has the best capability to inform or persuade target audiences about the values a brand has to offer. No other variable in the marketing mix is designed to accomplish this communication. Analysts agree that branding is crucially important in the multibillion-dollar cell phone market as Verizon, Sprint Nextel, T-Mobile, and AT&T compete for 250 million wireless subscribers.[16] In many ways, marketing and advertising a cellular service brand is much like marketing and advertising brands of bottled water. One cell phone works just like another and there are plenty of alternatives just like one brand of bottled water is pretty much the same as the next brand.

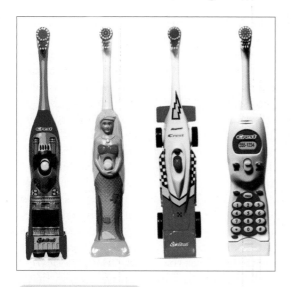

EXHIBIT 1.20

Advertising helps companies with brand extension strategies. Here, the famous Crest name is being used as the company extends the brand name into toothbrushes. What value does the widely recognized nature of a good brand name lend to the brand extension process?

Introduction of New Brand or Brand Extensions. Advertising is absolutely critical when organizations introduce a new brand or extensions of existing brands to the market. A **brand extension** is an adaptation of an existing brand to a new product area. For example, the Snickers Ice Cream Bar is a brand extension of the original Snickers candy bar, and Ivory Shampoo is a brand extension of Ivory Dishwashing Liquid. When brand extensions are brought to market, advertising and IBP play a key role in attracting attention to the brand—so much so that researchers now suggest that "managers should favor the brand extension with a greater allocation of the ad budget.[17] This is often accomplished with advertising working in conjunction with other promotional activities such as sales promotions and point-of-purchase displays. Mars (famous for candy) invested heavily in advertising when it extended the Uncle Ben's Rice brand into ready-to-eat microwave Rice Bowls of all varieties, including Italian, Mexican, and Chinese.[18] Exhibit 1.20 shows another example of advertising being used to extend a famous brand name into a totally different product category.

---

15.   Michael Myser, "Marketing Made Easy, " *Business 2.0,* June 2006, 43–45.

16.   Alice Z. Cuneo, "Cell Giants Plot $1.5B Ad Bonanza," *Advertising Age,* October 6, 2003, 1, 44.

17.   Douglas W. Vorhies, "Brand Extension Helps Parent Gain Influence," *Marketing News,* January 20, 2003, 25. This concept was verified in academic research as well. See Franziska Volckner and Henrik Sattler, "Drivers of Brand Extension Success," *Journal of Marketing,* vol. 70 (April 2006), 18–34.

18.   Stephanie Thompson, "The Bowl Is Where It's At for New Frozen Meal Lines," *Advertising Age,* August 14, 2000, 4.

Building and Maintaining Brand Loyalty among Consumers. Loyalty to a brand is one of the most important assets a firm can have. **Brand loyalty** occurs when a consumer repeatedly purchases the same brand to the exclusion of competitors' brands. This loyalty can result because of habit, because brand names are prominent in the consumer's memory, because of barely conscious associations with brand images, or because consumers have attached some fairly deep meanings to the brands they buy.

While brand features are the most important influence on building and maintaining brand loyalty, advertising plays a key role in the process as well. Advertising reminds consumers of the values—tangible and intangible—of the brand. Advertising and integrated brand promotions often provide an extra incentive to consumers to remain brand loyal. Direct marketing can tailor communications to existing customers. Other promotional tools can offer similarly valuable communications that will help build and strengthen lasting and positive associations with a brand—such as a frequent-flyer or frequent-buyer program. When a firm creates and maintains positive associations with the brand in the mind of consumers, the firm has developed **brand equity**.[19] While brand equity occurs over long periods of time, short-term advertising activities are key to long-term success.[20] This advertising fact of life became clear to strategists at food giant Kraft as it devised a strategy to defend its Kraft Miracle Whip brand against a new campaign by competitor Unilever for Imperial Whip. In order to protect Miracle Whip's $229 million in sales and brand equity with consumers, Kraft invested heavily in television advertising just before Unilever lowered prices on the Imperial Whip brand.[21]

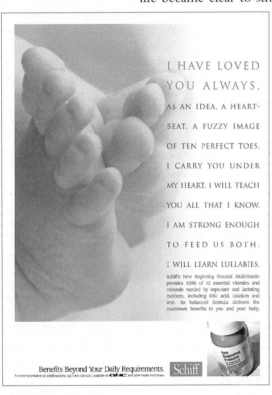

EXHIBIT 1.21

The message in this Schiff ad creates meaning for vitamins that goes beyond the daily nutrition role vitamins can play. What are the many meanings in this message offered to consumers? http://www.schiffvitamins.com

Creating an Image and Meaning for a Brand. As we discussed in the marketing mix section, advertising can communicate how a brand addresses certain needs and desires and therefore plays an important role in attracting customers to brands that appear to be useful and satisfying. But advertising can go further. It can help link a brand's image and meaning to a consumer's social environment and to the larger culture, and in this way actually delivers a sense of personal connection for the consumer.

The Schiff ad for prenatal vitamins in Exhibit 1.21 is a clear example of how advertising can create an image and deeper meaning. The message in this ad is not just about the health advantages of using a nutritional supplement during pregnancy. The message mines associations related to love and caring for an unborn or recently born child. Even the slogan for the brand, "Benefits Beyond Your Daily Requirements," plays on the notion that a vitamin is more than a vehicle for dosing up on folic acid. Other promotional tools in the IBP process, such as personal selling, sales promotions, event sponsorship, or the Internet, simply cannot achieve such creative power or communicate all the potential meanings a brand can have to a consumer as we will see later in the text.

19.   Kevin L. Keller, *Strategic Brand Management: Building, Measuring, and Managing Brand Equity* (Upper Saddle River, NJ: Prentice Hall, 1998), 2.

20.   Kevin L. Keller, "Conceptualizing, Measuring, and Managing Customer-Based Brand Equity," *Journal of Marketing*, vol. 57 (January 1993), 4.

21.   Stephanie Thompson, "Kraft Counters Unilever Launch," *Advertising Age*, August 25, 2003, 4.

Building and Maintaining Brand Loyalty within the Trade. It might not seem as if wholesalers, retailers, distributors, and brokers would be brand loyal, but they will favor one brand over others given the proper support from a manufacturer. Advertising and particularly advertising integrated with other brand promotions is an area where support can be given. Marketers can provide the trade with sales training programs, collateral advertising materials, point-of-purchase advertising displays, premiums (giveaways like key chains or caps), and traffic-building special events. Exide, the battery company, spends several million dollars a year to be the official battery of NASCAR racing. Mike Dever, Exide's vice president of marketing and product management, explains: "Both our distributors and our distributors' customers, for the most part, are race fans so it's the place we want to be."[22]

Also, remember that trade buyers (retailers, wholesalers, distributors, brokers) can be key to the success of new brands or brand extensions, as we pointed out earlier in the discussion of the trade market as a target audience. Marketers have little hope of successfully introducing a brand if there is no cooperation in the trade channel among wholesalers and retailers. This is where IBP as a factor in advertising becomes prominent. This is because the trade is less responsive to advertising messages than they are to other forms of promotion. Direct support to the trade in terms of displays, contests, and personal selling combined with advertising in an IBP program helps ensure the success of a brand. Research also shows that retailer acceptance of a brand extension is key to the success of the new product.[23]

The Role of Advertising in Market Segmentation, Differentiation, and Positioning. The third role for advertising in marketing is helping the firm implement market segmentation, differentiation, and positioning.

Market segmentation is the process of breaking down a large, widely varied *(heterogeneous)* market into submarkets, or segments, that are more similar *(homogeneous)* than dissimilar in terms of what the consumer is looking for. Underlying the strategy of market segmentation are the facts that consumers differ in their wants and that the wants of one person can differ under various circumstances. The market for automobiles can be divided into submarkets for different types of automobiles based on the needs and desires of various groups of buyers. Identifying those groups, or segments, of the population who want and will buy large or small, luxury or economy, or sport or sedan or minivan models is an important part of basic marketing strategy. In addition to needs, markets are often segmented on characteristics of consumers (referred to as demographics) such as age, marital status, gender, and income. These data are widely available and tend to be related to product preference and use. Advertising's role in the market segmentation process is to develop messages that appeal to the wants and desires of different segments and then to transmit those messages via appropriate media. For example, Bayer has four different versions of its basic aspirin brand. There is regular Bayer for headache relief; Bayer Enteric Safety Coated 81 mg aspirin for people with cholesterol and heart concerns; Women's Bayer, which includes a calcium supplement; and Children's Bayer, which is lower dose and chewable. Each of these versions of the Bayer brand of aspirin addresses both needs and characteristics of consumers in the market (see Exhibit 1.22).

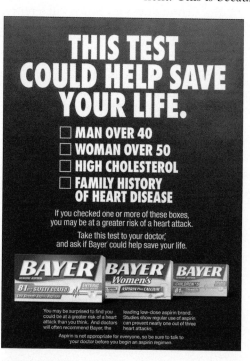

EXHIBIT 1.22

Advertising plays an important role in helping a firm segment the market based on needs and characteristics of consumers. Along with Bayer's regular aspirin for headache relief, Bayer offers these three additional versions of the brand that address both consumer needs (calcium-fortified aspirin for women) and consumer characteristics (a children's lower-dose aspirin). http://www.bayeraspirin.com

22.   Beth Snyder Bulik, "The Company You Keep," *Sales & Marketing Management*, November 2003, 14.

23.   Franziska Volckner and Henrik Sattler, "Drivers of Brand Extension Success," *Journal of Marketing*, vol. 70 (April 2006), 18–34.

DOING IT RIGHT

Old School Bank Discovers New Media

As you have been reading about in this chapter, the world of advertising and integrated brand promotion is going through serious change. Advertising is still a huge force in this world, but other ways of sending messages are gaining favor as more promotional options have been developed.

Consider the case of Wachovia bank—a venerable, old-line institution. The bank has traditionally used network advertising to reach its somewhat conservative and long-loyal customers. But Jim Garrity, the chief marketing officer, has rigorously tested the firm's promotional spending and his findings have led the company to blend old and new approaches to reaching both existing and new customers. He has come to appreciate Web advertising for its clearly identifiable results and feels that event sponsorship like professional golf tournaments allows the firm to reach narrowly defined target markets in a highly efficient way.

Garrity has not abandoned broadcast television advertising completely. The bank still spends over $50 million a year on this traditional medium. But that $50 million is only 30 percent of the ad budget—down from about 37 percent of the total budget just a couple of years earlier. Wachovia does not plan a highly radical reallocation of the budget: The future promises less broadcast advertising with that spending being highly focused; more cable television that is better at targeting niche audiences; and "much more" spending in "new media" like online advertising. The spending will be designed to continue to nurture the relationship the firm has with its current 15 million household and business customers, but, as Garrity puts it, "the company will have to try to win new customers one at a time," which is accomplished better with new media than traditional mass media.

So, when we start to see traditional advertisers with traditional customer groups spreading the promotional budget out among many more IBP options, it is a sign of the times that advertising and IBP are becoming more diverse and more complex.

Source: Jon Fine, "Reworking the Ad Mix," **BusinessWeek**, October 23, 2006, 28.

Differentiation is the process of creating a perceived difference, in the mind of the consumer, between an organization's brand and the competition's. Notice that this definition emphasizes that brand differentiation is based on *consumer perception*. The perceived differences can be tangible differences, or they may be based on image or style factors. Consider the Fendi watch ad in Exhibit 1.23. A $20 Timex and a $12,000 Fendi keep time in exactly the same way. But the two brands are differentiated on perceptions of style and the deeper meaning brands can have, as discussed earlier. The critical issue in differentiation is that consumers *perceive* a difference between brands. If consumers do not perceive a difference, then whether real differences exist or not does not matter. Differentiation is one of the most critical of all marketing strategies. If a firm's brand is not perceived as distinctive and attractive by consumers, then consumers will have no reason to choose that brand over one from the competition or to pay higher prices for the "better" or "more meaningful" brand. Think about bottled water (Evian), bananas (Chiquita), or meat (Niman Ranch) where marketers have been able to differentiate their brands with excellent advertising and branding strategies.[24]

In order for advertising to help create a difference in the mind of the consumer between an organization's brand and its competitors' brands, the ad may emphasize performance features, or it may create a distinctive image for the brand. The essential task for advertising is to develop a message that is different and unmistakably linked to the organization's brand. The ad in Exhibit 1.24 is distinctive and pursues product differentiation.

Positioning is the process of designing a brand so that it can occupy a distinct and valued place in the target consumer's mind relative to other brands and then this distinctiveness is communicated through advertising. Positioning, like differentiation, depends on a perceived image of tangible or intangible features. The importance of positioning can be understood by recognizing that consumers create a *perceptual space* in their minds for all the brands they might consider purchasing. A perceptual space is how one brand is seen on any number of dimensions—such as quality, taste, price, or social display value—in relation to those same dimensions in other brands. Firms are turning to a wider variety of advertising and IBP combinations to achieve effective position, as the Doing It Right box discusses.

24. Paul Kaihla, "Sexing Up a Piece of Meat," *Business 2.0*, April 2006, 72–76.

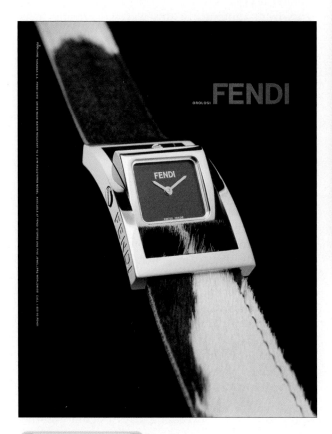

EXHIBIT 1.23

Advertising is key to the marketing strategy of differentiation—creating a perceived difference between the company's brand and competitors' brands. This very expensive Fendi watch keeps time just like a $20 Timex. But you won't see an ad like this for a Timex. What is it about this ad that helps differentiate the Fendi brand from the Timex brand? http://www.fendi.it

Ever Tried To Vacuum A Cat?

Breathe Easy. Hunter Air Purifiers Fight Odors, Allergens, Dust And Dander.

Deal with pet dander, odors, dust, pollen, smoke and mold spores the easy way. Hunter air purifiers provide 99.97% effective air cleaning.* And they reduce common household odors 30% better than other leading brands!** Plus, quiet Hunter air purifiers include handy features like easy-to-use, digital programmable controls. Give the cat a break. Visit www.hunterfan.com to learn more about Hunter air purifiers.

From the Hunter Fan people...quietly improving your indoor air since 1886™

*99.97% effective at removing particles as small as 0.3 microns that pass through the filter.
**Based on tests conducted by human test panels in accordance with ASTM E1593 and ASTM E1958 using competitive pre-filters available in 2002.
© 2004 Hunter Fan Company

EXHIBIT 1.24

An important role for advertising is to help a firm differentiate its brand from the competition with a distinctive message and presentation. This Hunter Fan ad focuses on the function features of its air purifier line as the basis for differentiation. http://www.hunterfan.com

There are really two positioning decisions. A firm must decide on the **external position** for a brand—that is, the niche the brand will pursue relative to all the competitive brands on the market. Additionally, an **internal position** must be achieved with regard to the other similar brands a firm markets. With the external-positioning decision, a firm tries to create a distinctive *competitive* position based on design features, pricing, distribution, or promotion or advertising strategy. Some brands are positioned at the very top of their competitive product category, such as BMW's 550i, priced around $100,000. Other brands seek a position at the low end of all market offerings, such as the Chevrolet Cobalt, with a base price of about $15,000.

Effective internal positioning is accomplished by either developing vastly different products *within* the firm's own product line (Ben & Jerry's ice cream, for example, offers plenty of distinctive flavors, as shown in Exhibit 1.25 on the next page) or creating advertising messages that appeal to different consumer needs and desires. Procter & Gamble successfully positions its many laundry detergent brands both internally and externally using a combination of product design and effective advertising. While some of these brands assume different positions within P&G's line due to substantive differences (a liquid soap versus a powder soap, for example), others with minor differences achieve distinctive positioning through advertising. One P&G brand is advertised as being effective on kids' dirty clothes, while another

EXHIBIT 1.25

Firms with multiple brands in a single product category have to internally position these brands to differentiate them from each other in the minds of consumers. Ben & Jerry's achieves its product positioning by emphasizing the distinctly different flavors of each of its ice creams.
http://www.benjerry.com

brand is portrayed as effective for preventing colors from running. In this way, advertising helps create a distinctive position, both internally and externally.

The methods and strategic options available to an organization with respect to market segmentation, product differentiation, and positioning will be fully discussed in Chapter 6. For now, realize that advertising plays an important role in helping an organization put these most basic marketing strategies into operation.

The Role of Advertising in Revenue and Profit Generation. There are many who believe that the fundamental purpose of marketing (and the advertising that is used in marketing) can be stated quite simply: to generate revenue. Marketing is the only part of an organization that has revenue generation as its primary purpose. In the words of highly regarded management consultant and scholar Peter Drucker, "Marketing and innovation produce results: all the rest are 'costs.'"[25] The "results" Drucker refers to are revenues. The marketing process is designed to generate sales and therefore revenues for the firm.

Creating sales as part of the revenue-generating process is where advertising plays a significant role. As we have seen, advertising communicates persuasive information to audiences based on the values created in the marketing mix related to the product, its price, or its distribution. This advertising communication then highlights brand features—price, emotion, or availability—and then attracts a target market. In this way, advertising makes a direct contribution to the marketing goal of revenue generation. Notice that advertising *contributes* to the process of creating sales and revenue. It cannot be solely responsible for creating sales and revenue—it's not that powerful. Some organizations mistakenly see advertising as a panacea—the salvation for an ambiguous or ineffective overall marketing mix strategy. Advertising alone cannot be held responsible for sales. Sales occur when a brand has a well-conceived and complete marketing mix—including good advertising.

The effect of advertising on profits is a bit more involved and complicated. Its effect on profits comes about when advertising gives an organization greater flexibility in the price it charges for a product or service. Advertising can help create pricing flexibility by (1) contributing to economies of scale and (2) helping create inelasticity of demand. When an organization creates large-scale demand for its brand, the quantity of product produced is increased, and **economies of scale** lead to lower unit production costs. Cost of production decreases because fixed costs (such as rent and equipment costs) are spread over a greater number of units produced.

How does advertising play a role in helping create economies of scale? When Colgate manufactures hundreds of thousands of tubes of its Colgate Total toothpaste and ships them in large quantities to warehouses, the fixed costs of production and shipping per unit are greatly reduced. With lower fixed costs per unit, Colgate can

25.   Peter F. Drucker, *People and Performance: The Best of Peter Drucker* (New York: HarperCollins, 1997), 90.

realize greater profits on each tube of toothpaste sold. Advertising contributes to demand stimulation by communicating to the market about the features and availability of a brand. By contributing to demand stimulation, advertising then contributes to the process of creating these economies of scale, which ultimately translates into higher profits per unit for the organization.

Remember the concept of brand loyalty we discussed earlier? Well, brand loyalty and advertising work together to create another important economic effect related to pricing flexibility and profits. When consumers are brand loyal, they are generally less sensitive to price increases for the brand. In economic terms, this is known as **inelasticity of demand**. When consumers are less price sensitive, firms have the flexibility to raise prices and increase profit margins. Advertising contributes directly to brand loyalty, and thus to inelasticity of demand, by persuading and reminding consumers of the satisfactions and values related to a brand. This argument related to the positive business effects of advertising was recently supported by a large research study. The study found that companies who build strong brands and raise prices are more profitable than companies who cut costs as a way to increase profits—by nearly twice the profit percentage. This research is supported by such real-world examples as Louis Vuitton. The maker of luxury handbags ($1,000 per bag or more) and other luxury items enjoys an operating margin of 45 percent.[26]

EXHIBIT 1.26

When new, innovative products are first introduced to the market, a type of advertising called primary demand stimulation is often used. Primary demand stimulation attempts to stimulate demand for the entire product category by educating consumers about the values of the product itself, rather than the values of a brand within the product category. This ad from the early days of the VHS video cassette recorder is a classic example of primary demand stimulation in a new, innovative product category.

Types of Advertising. So far, we've discussed advertising in a lot of different ways, from its most basic definition through how it can help an organization stimulate demand and generate profits. But to truly understand advertising, we need to go back to some very basic typologies that categorize advertising according to fundamental approaches to communication. Until you understand these aspects of advertising, you really don't understand advertising at all.

Primary versus Selective Demand Stimulation. In **primary demand stimulation**, a company is trying to create demand for an entire product *category*. Primary demand stimulation is challenging and costly, and research evidence suggests that it is likely to have an impact only for totally new products on the market—not brand extensions or product categories that have been around a long time (known as mature products). An example of effective primary demand stimulation was the introduction of the VCR to the consumer market in the 1970s. With a product that is totally new to the market, consumers need to be convinced that the product category itself is valuable and that it is, indeed, available for sale. When the VCR was first introduced in the United States, RCA, Panasonic, and Quasar (see Exhibit 1.26) ran primary demand stimulation advertising to explain to household consumers the value and convenience of taping television programs with this new product called a VHS video recorder—something no one had ever done before at home.

For organizations that have tried to stimulate primary demand in mature product categories, typically trade associations, the results have been dismal. Both the National Fluid Milk Processor Promotion Board and the Florida Department of Citrus have tried to use advertising to stimulate primary demand for the entire product categories of milk and orange juice. Examples of these campaigns are shown in

26.   The research study is reported in Robert G. Docters, Michael R. Reopel, Jeanne-Mey Sun, and Stephen M. Tanney, *Winning the Profit Game: Smarter Pricing, Smarter Branding* (New York: McGraw-Hill, 2004); the information on Louis Vuitton was taken from Carol Matlack et al., "The Vuitton Machine," *BusinessWeek*, March 22, 2004, 98–102.

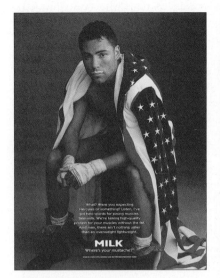

EXHIBIT 1.27

Advertising that attempts to stimulate primary demand is often tried by industry associations and advocacy groups, such as the National Fluid Milk Processor Promotion Board, rather than by specific manufacturers. Trouble is, it doesn't work. Primary demand stimulation has been shown to be ineffective in mature product categories, such as milk, but rather is appropriate for products totally new to the market like PDAs or MP3 players. http:// www.gotmilk.com and http://www.elsie .com

EXHIBIT 1.28

This ad promoting orange juice also attempts to stimulate primary demand, or demand for a product category rather than demand for a particular brand. Decades of literature demonstrate no relationship between aggregate levels of advertising in an industry and overall demand in an industry. It appears that advertising is indeed suited only to selective (brand) demand stimulation. http://www .floridajuice.com

EXHIBIT 1.29

Selective demand stimulation advertising highlights a brand's superiority in providing satisfaction. In this ad, Tropicana touts its superiority as a brand of orange juice with very specific brand features. Compare this ad to the primary demand ad in Exhibit 1.28. http://www.tropicana.com

Exhibits 1.27 and 1.28. While the "mustache" campaign is popular and wins awards, milk consumption has *declined* every year during the time of this campaign.[27] This is despite the fact that many billions of dollars in advertising have been invested in the campaign. Even if the attempts at primary demand have reduced the overall decline in milk consumption (which can't be determined), this is still not a very impressive result. This should come as no surprise, though. Research over decades has clearly indicated that attempts at primary demand stimulation in mature product categories (orange juice, beef, pork, and almonds have also been tried) have never been successful.[28]

While some corporations have tried primary demand stimulation, the true power of advertising is shown when it functions to stimulate demand for a particular company's brand. This is known as selective demand stimulation. The purpose of **selective demand stimulation** advertising is to point out a brand's unique benefits compared to the competition. For example, compare the Tropicana ad in Exhibit 1.29 touting the brand's superiority with the primary demand stimulation ad in Exhibit 1.28.

27.   U.S. Bureau of the Census, *Statistical Abstract of the United States: 1995*, 115th ed. (Washington, D.C.: U.S. Government Printing Office, 1995); "Got Results?" *Marketing News*, March 2, 1998, 1.
28.   For an excellent summary of decades of research on the topic, see Mark S. Abion and Paul W. Farris, *The Advertising Controversy: Evidence of the Economic Effects of Advertising* (Boston: Auburn House, 1981); and J. C. Luik and M. S. Waterson, *Advertising and Markets* (Oxfordshire, England: NTC Publications, 1996).

EXHIBIT 1.30

Direct response advertising asks consumers to take some immediate action. Notice in this ad for Bowflex that advertising copy implores consumers to call the toll free number or visit the Web site for a free DVD or to place an order—calling for a direct response by consumers.

EXHIBIT 1.31

Delayed response advertising attempts to reinforce the benefits of using a brand and create a general liking for the brand. This ad for All detergent is an example of delayed response advertising. It builds an image for the brand rather than asking consumers to take action like the Bowflex ad in Exhibit 1.30.

Direct versus Delayed Response Advertising. Another important type of advertising involves how quickly we want consumers to respond. **Direct response advertising** asks consumers to act immediately. An ad that suggests that you "call this toll-free number" or "mail your $19.95 before midnight tonight" is an example of direct response advertising. In many cases, direct response advertising is used for products that consumers are familiar with, that do not require inspection at the point of purchase, and that are relatively low-cost. However, the proliferation of toll-free numbers, Web sites that provide detailed information, and the widespread use of credit cards have been a boon to direct response for higher priced products, as Exhibit 1.30 demonstrates.

Delayed response advertising relies on imagery and message themes that emphasize the benefits and satisfying characteristics of a brand. Rather than trying to stimulate an immediate action from an audience, delayed response advertising attempts to develop awareness and preference for a brand over time. In general, delayed response advertising attempts to create brand awareness, reinforce the benefits of using a brand, develop a general liking for the brand, and create an image for a brand. When a consumer enters the purchase process, the information from delayed response advertising comes into play. Most advertisements we see on television and in magazines are of the delayed response type. Exhibit 1.31, an ad for hypoallergenic detergent, provides an example of this common form of advertising. In this ad, the message has as much to do with being a good parent (an image and delayed response-type message) as with the actual performance features of the brand.

Corporate versus Brand Advertising. **Corporate advertising** is not designed to promote a specific brand, but is meant to create a favorable attitude toward a company as a whole. Prominent users of corporate advertising include Microsoft, Phillips Petroleum, General Electric, and IBM. As an example, Philips, the Dutch electronics and medical device conglomerate, turned to corporate advertising to unify the image of its brand name across a wide range of superior technologies.[29] **Brand advertising**, as we have seen throughout this chapter, communicates the specific features, values, and benefits of a particular brand offered for sale by a particular organization. By contrast, the firms that have long-established corporate campaigns have designed them to generate favorable public opinion toward the corporation as a whole. This type of advertising can also have an effect on the shareholders of a firm. When shareholders see good corporate advertising, it instills confidence and, ultimately, long-term commitment to the firm and its stock. We'll consider this type of advertising in great detail in Chapter 20.

Another form of corporate advertising is carried out by members of a trade channel, mostly retailers. When corporate advertising takes place in a trade channel it is referred to as *institutional advertising*. Retailers such as Nordstrom, The Home Depot, and Wal-Mart advertise to persuade consumers to shop at their stores. While these retailers may occasionally feature a particular manufacturer's brand in the advertising (Nordstrom features Clinique cosmetics) the main purpose of the advertising is to get the audience to shop at their store. Federated Department Stores, for example, invested $387 million to promote its national brand stores, Macy's and Bloomingdale's. The thrust of Federated's brand strategy comes from marketing research findings that show their target audience "considers shopping an enjoyable activity."[30]

The Economic Effects of Advertising.
Our discussion of advertising as a business process so far has focused strictly on the use of advertising by individual business organizations. But you cannot *truly* understand advertising unless you know something about how advertising has effects across the entire economic system of a country. (This isn't the most fun you'll have reading this book, but it is one of the most important topics.)

Advertising's Effect on Gross Domestic Product.
Gross domestic product (GDP) is the measure of the total value of goods and services produced within an economic system. Earlier, we discussed advertising's role in the marketing mix. Recall that as advertising contributes to marketing mix strategy, it can contribute to sales along with the right product, the right price, and the right distribution. Because of this role, advertising is related to GDP in that it can contribute to levels of overall consumer demand when it plays a key role in introducing new products, such as DVDs, microcomputers, the Internet, or alternative energy sources. As demand for these new products grows, the resultant consumer spending fuels retail sales, housing starts, and corporate investment in finished goods and capital equipment. Consequently, GDP is affected by sales of products in new, innovative product categories.[31]

Advertising's Effect on Business Cycles.
Advertising can have a stabilizing effect on downturns in business activity. There is evidence that many firms increase advertising during times of recession in an effort to spend their way out of a business downturn.

Advertising's Effect on Competition.
Advertising is alleged to stimulate competition and therefore motivate firms to strive for better products, better production methods, and other competitive advantages that ultimately benefit the economy as

29. Kerry Capell, "How Philips Got Brand Buzz," BusinessWeek.com, July 31, 2006, accessed at *http://yahoo.businessweek.com* on August 1, 2006.

30.   Mercedes M. Cardona, "Federated Focuses Campaign on Macy's," *Advertising Age*, December 8, 2003, 6.

31.   There are several historical treatments of how advertising is related to demand. See, for example, Neil H. Borden, *The Economic Effects of Advertising* (Chicago: Richard D. Irwin, 1942), 187–189; and John Kenneth Galbraith, *The New Industrial State* (Boston: Houghton Mifflin, 1967), 203–207.

EXHIBIT 1.32

Advertising affects the competitive environment in an economy. This ad by a plastics manufacturers' council is fostering competition with manufacturers of other packaging materials. http://www.americanchemistry.com/plastics

a whole. Additionally, when advertising serves as a way to enter new markets, competition across the economic system is fostered. For example, Exhibit 1.32 shows an ad in which plastics manufacturers present themselves as competitors to manufacturers of other packaging materials.

Advertising is not universally hailed as a stimulant to competition. Critics point out that the amount of advertising dollars needed to compete effectively in many industries is often prohibitive. As such, advertising can act as a barrier to entry into an industry; that is, a firm may have the capability to compete in an industry in every way except that the advertising dollars needed to compete are so great that the firm cannot afford to get into the business. In this way, advertising can actually serve to decrease the overall amount of competition in an economy.[32]

Advertising's Effect on Prices. One of the widely debated effects of advertising has to do with its effect on the prices consumers pay for products and services. Since we have seen that firms spend millions or even billions of dollars on advertising, then products and services would cost much less if firms did no advertising. Right? Wrong!

First, across all industries, advertising costs incurred by firms range from about 2 percent of sales in the automobile and retail industries up to 30 percent of sales in the personal care and luxury products businesses. Exhibit 1.33 shows the ratio of advertising to sales for various firms in selected industries. Notice that there is no consistent and predictable relationship between advertising spending and sales. Honda spent $1.3 billion in advertising to generate about $51 billion in sales; L'Oréal spent more than Honda on advertising ($1.4 billion) but generated only $4.9 billion in sales; and Wal-Mart spent $1.07 billion on advertising to generate a whopping $271 billion in sales! Different products and different market conditions demand that firms spend different amounts of money on advertising. These same conditions make it difficult to identify a predictable relationship between advertising and sales.

It is true that the cost of advertising is built into product costs, which are ultimately passed on to consumers. But this effect on price must be judged against a couple of cost savings that lower the price. First, there is the reduced time and effort a consumer has to spend in searching for a product or service. Second, economies of scale, discussed earlier, have a direct impact on cost and then on prices. Recall that economies of scale serve to lower the cost of production by spreading fixed costs over a large number of units produced. This lower cost can be passed on to consumers in terms of lower prices, as firms search for competitive advantage with lower prices. Nowhere is this effect more dramatic than the price and performance of personal computers. In the early 1980s, an Apple IIe computer that ran at about 1 MHz and had 64K of total memory cost over $3,000. Today, you can get a computer that is several hundred times faster with vastly increased memory and storage for less than $600. And it is a certainty that companies like HP and Dell are spending more on advertising (even on an inflation-adjusted basis) today than Apple did back in the 1980s.

32.   This fundamental argument about the effect of advertising on competition was identified and well articulated many years ago by Colston E. Warn, "Advertising: A Critic's View," *Journal of Marketing*, vol. 26, no. 4 (October 1962), 12.

Industry	Advertiser	2006 U.S. Ad Spending (millions)	2006 U.S. Sales (millions)	Advertising Spending as % of Sales
Automobiles				
	General Motors	$3,296	$129,041	2.6
	Ford	2,577	81,155	3.2
	Volkswagen	419	18,262	2.3
	Honda	1,351	51,648	2.6
Computers				
	IBM	517	39,511	1.3
	Dell	883	36,100	2.4
	Microsoft	912	29,730	3.1
	Hewlett-Packard	829	32,244	2.6
Drugs				
	Bristol-Myers Squibb	691	9,729	7.1
	Abbott Labs	374	11,995	3.1
	Merck	1,024	13,808	7.4
Food				
	Kraft Foods	1,423	20,931	6.8
	Nestlé	1,315	24,889	5.3
	Kellogg	765	7,349	10.4
	Campbell Soup	564	5,120	11.0
Personal Care				
	Procter & Gamble	4,898	29,462	16.6
	Unilever	2,098	17,222	12.2
	Estée Lauder	1,031	3,446	29.9
	L'Oréal	1,456	4,942	29.5
Retail				
	Wal-Mart	1,073	271,534	0.4
	Target	1,157	59,490	1.9
	Gap	489	12,807	3.8

Source: "100 Leading National Advertisers," *Advertising Age*, June 25, 2007, 5-14. Reprinted with permission. © Crain Communications, Inc., 2007.

EXHIBIT 1.33

Advertising spending as a percentage of sales in selected industries, 2006 (U.S. dollars in millions).

Advertising's Effect on Value. *Value* is the password for successful marketing. **Value**, in modern marketing and advertising, refers to a perception by consumers that a brand provides satisfaction beyond the cost incurred to obtain that brand. The value perspective of the modern consumer is based on wanting every purchase to be a "good deal." Value can be added to the consumption experience by advertising. Consider the effect of branding on bottled water. Advertising helps create enough value in the minds of consumers that they (we) will *pay* for water that comes free out of the tap.

Advertising also affects a consumer's perception of value by contributing to the symbolic value and the social meaning of a brand. **Symbolic value** refers to what

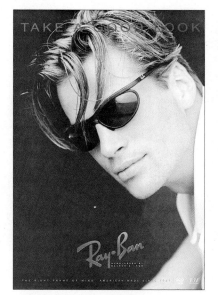

EXHIBIT 1.34

EXHIBIT 1.35

Advertising contributes to the symbolic value that brands have for consumers. What is it about this ad for Ray-Ban sunglasses that contributes to the symbolic value of this brand? http://www.ray-ban.com

Ads communicate social meaning to consumers, as a product or service carries meaning in a societal context beyond its use or purpose. This ad for United Airlines puts the company's service into such a context. http://www.ual.com

a product or service means to consumers in a nonliteral way. For example, branded clothing such as Guess? jeans or Doc Martens shoes can symbolize self-concept for some consumers. Exhibit 1.34 shows an ad that seeks to create symbolic value for Ray-Ban sunglasses. In reality, all branded products rely to some extent on symbolic value; otherwise they would not be brands, but just unmarked commodities (like potatoes).

Social meaning refers to what a product or service means in a societal context. For example, social class is marked by any number of products, such as cars, beverages, and clothes, that are used and displayed to signify class membership. Exhibit 1.35 shows an ad for a service with clear social-class connections. Often, the product's connection to a social class addresses a need within consumers to move up in class.

Researchers from various disciplines have long argued that objects (brands included) are never just objects. They take on meaning from culture, society, and consumers.[33] It is important to remember that these meanings often become just as much a part of the brand as the physical features. Since advertising is an essential way in which the image of a brand is developed, it contributes directly to consumers' perception of the value of the brand. The more value consumers see in a brand, the more they are willing to pay to acquire the brand. If the image of a Gucci watch, a Nissan coupe, or a Four Seasons hotel is valued by consumers, then consumers will pay a premium to acquire that value. Waterford crystal and Gucci watches, shown in Exhibits 1.36 and 1.37 on the next page, are examples of brands that consumers pay a premium to own.

---

33.   For an historical perspective on culture, consumers, and the meaning of goods, see Ernest Ditcher, *Handbook of Consumer Motivations* (New York: McGraw-Hill, 1964), 6. For a contemporary view, see David Glen Mick and Claus Buhl, "A Meaning-Based Model of Advertising Experiences," *Journal of Consumer Research*, vol. 19 (December 1992), 312–338.

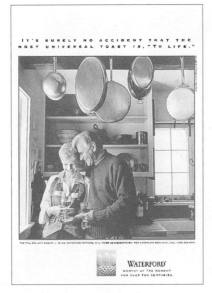 

EXHIBITS 1.36 AND 1.37

Waterford crystal and Gucci watches are two advertised products that consumers will pay premium prices to own. Both products have value in that they epitomize the highest levels of quality craftsmanship. Such craftsmanship, in itself, may not be enough to command premium prices in the marketplace. Advertising that creates an image of exclusivity may also be needed. In what way does the Gucci site (http://www.gucci.com) contribute directly to consumers' perceptions of a brand's value? Compare this site with Waterford's site (http://www.waterford.com) and determine which communicates its brand's social meaning more effectively.

⑤ From Advertising to Integrated Marketing Communications to Integrated Brand Promotion. As we discussed at the beginning of your introduction to the world of advertising and IBP, it is important to recognize that advertising is only one of many promotional tools available to impress and persuade consumers. Another distinction is important for you to recognize as you embark on learning about advertising and IBP.

Beginning in about 1990, the concept of mixing various promotional tools was referred to as **integrated marketing communications (IMC)**. But as the discussions throughout this chapter have highlighted, the reality of promotional strategies in the 21st century demands that the emphasis on *communication* give way to an emphasis on the *brand*.

Recall from the definition earlier in the chapter that integrated brand promotion (IBP) is the use of various communication tools, including advertising, in a coordinated manner to build and maintain brand awareness, identity, and preference. The distinction between IBP and IMC is pretty obvious. IMC emphasizes the communication effort, per se, and the need for coordinated and synergistic messages. IBP retains the emphasis on coordination and synergy of communication, but goes beyond the parameters of IMC. In IBP, the emphasis is on the brand and not just the communication. With a focus on building brand awareness, identity, and ultimately preference, the IBP perspective recognizes that coordinated promotional messages need to have brand-building effects in addition to the communication effects. Recent research and publications on IMC are now quickly recognizing the central role of the brand in communications.[34]

---

34.   A special issue of the *Journal of Advertising* (vol. 34, no. 4, Winter 2005) featuring research and perspectives on IMC contains several articles that focus on the integrated brand promotion aspects of IMC.

SUMMARY

 Know what advertising and integrated brand promotion are and what they can do.

Since advertising has become so pervasive, it would be reasonable to expect that you might have your own working definition for this critical term. But an informed perspective on advertising goes beyond what is obvious and can be seen on a daily basis. Advertising is distinctive and recognizable as a form of communication by its three essential elements: its paid sponsorship, its use of mass media, and its intent to persuade. An advertisement is a specific message that a company has placed to persuade an audience. An advertising campaign is a series of ads and other promotional efforts with a common theme also placed to persuade an audience over a specified period of time. Integrated brand promotion (IBP) is the use of many promotional tools, including advertising, in a coordinated manner to build and maintain brand awareness, identity, and preference.

 Discuss a basic model of advertising communication.

Advertising cannot be effective unless some form of communication takes place between the company and the audience. But advertising is about mass communication. There are many models that might be used to help explain how advertising works or does not work as a communication platform. The model introduced in this chapter features basic considerations such as the message-production process versus the message-reception process, and this model says that consumers create their own meanings when they interpret advertisements.

 Describe the different ways of classifying audiences for advertising and IBP.

While it is possible to provide a simple and clear definition of what advertising is, it is also true that advertising takes many forms and serves different purposes from one application to another. One way to appreciate the complexity and diversity of advertising is to classify it by audience category or by geographic focus. For example, advertising might be directed at households or government officials. Using another perspective, it can be global or local in its focus.

 Explain the key roles of advertising as a business process.

Many different types of organizations use advertising to achieve their business purposes. For major multinational corporations, such as Procter & Gamble, and for smaller, more localized businesses, such as the San Diego Zoo, advertising is one part of a critical business process known as marketing. Advertising is one element of the marketing mix; the other key elements are the firm's products, their prices, and the distribution network. Advertising must work in conjunction with these other marketing mix elements if the organization's marketing objectives are to be achieved. It is important to recognize that of all the roles played by advertising in the marketing process, none is more important than contributing to building brand awareness and brand equity. Similarly, firms have turned to more diverse methods of communication beyond advertising that we have referred to as integrated brand promotion. That is, firms are using communication tools such as public relations, sponsorship, direct marketing, and sales promotion along with advertising to achieve communication goals.

 Understand the concept of integrated brand promotion (IBP) and the role advertising plays in the process.

Integrated brand promotion (IBP) is the use of various promotional tools like event sponsorship, the Internet, public relations, and personal selling, along with advertising, in a coordinated manner to build and maintain brand awareness, identity, and preference. When marketers use advertising in conjunction with other promotional tools, they create an integrated brand promotion that highlights brand features and value. Note that the word *coordinated* is central to this definition. Over the past 30 years, the advertising industry has evolved to recognize that integration and coordination of promotional elements is key to effective communication and lasting brand identity.

KEY TERMS

advertising
client, or sponsor
integrated brand promotion (IBP)
advertisement
advertising campaign
audience
target audience
household consumers
members of business organizations
members of a trade channel
professionals
trade journals
government officials and employees
global advertising
international advertising

national advertising
regional advertising
local advertising
cooperative advertising, or co-op
 advertising
marketing
marketing mix
brand
brand extension
brand loyalty
brand equity
market segmentation
differentiation
positioning
external position

internal position
economies of scale
inelasticity of demand
primary demand stimulation
selective demand stimulation
direct response advertising
delayed response advertising
corporate advertising
brand advertising
gross domestic product (GDP)
value
symbolic value
social meaning
integrated marketing
 communications (IMC)

QUESTIONS

1. As consumers exercise ever greater individual control over when and how they receive information, how are advertisers adapting their messages? What is the role, if any, for traditional media outlets in this new environment?

2. What does it mean when we say that advertising is intended to persuade? How do different ads persuade in different ways?

3. Explain the differences between regional advertising, local advertising, and cooperative advertising. What would you look for in an ad to identify it as a cooperative ad?

4. How do the goals of direct response and delayed response advertising differ? How would you explain marketers' growing interest in direct response advertising?

5. Differentiate between global advertising and international advertising. Do you think consumers in foreign markets will react favorably to GM's new pop band–fueled Cadillac commercials, as do American consumers? Why or why not?

6. How does advertising affect brand management and development? If building brand loyalty is one goal, can

you identify several examples of businesses that have successfully used advertising campaigns to create strong brand equity?

7. If a firm developed a new line of athletic shoes, priced them competitively, and distributed them in appropriate retail shops, would there be any need for advertising? Is advertising really needed for a good product that is priced right?

8. Many companies now spend millions of dollars to sponsor and associate their names with events such as NASCAR races or rock concerts. Do these event sponsorships fit the definition for advertising and IBP given in this chapter?

9. How does the process of market segmentation lead an organization to spend its advertising dollars more efficiently and more effectively?

10. What is the concept of integrated brand promotion (IBP)? How are IBP and advertising related? And how is IBP distinct from the advertising industry's prior emphasis on integrated marketing communications, or IMC?

EXPERIENTIAL EXERCISES

1.   In this chapter, audiences for advertising were divided into five broad audience categories. For each, find one ad that appears to be targeted to members of that audience. Analyze the message and style of each ad and determine whether the message seems effective, given the intended audience category. Why was the ad effective or ineffective? Did you have difficulty locating ads for any specific audience category? If so, explain why you think that might have occurred and what it reveals about the nature and methods of advertising to that audience category.

2.   Very few advertisements or brands have the same appeal to all consumers worldwide. Companies must therefore strategically place ads based on geographic regions. List four of your favorite brands that you use in your everyday life. For each, decide whether it is appropriate to advertise the product at the global, international, national, regional, local, or cooperative level. Explain your answer.

3.   Cellular telephones and wireless computing products are nearly ubiquitous now in American life. In some ways, any one phone or service provider is seen not so much as a brand but as an unmarked commodity. But there are important exceptions. Consider the intense media attention and consumer interest that surrounded the release of Apple's iPhone and AT&T's exclusive contract to provide cellular service to the new phone. Providing examples from current ad campaigns, describe how advertising has affected *value* related to cellular services or products. Contrast that with the iPhone release. How did advertising and integrated brand promotion influence *symbolic value* and *social meaning* related to the new product?

4.   Working in small groups, imagine that you have been hired to create an advertising strategy for the release of a new line of basketball shoes produced by the athletic apparel maker Under Armour. The Maryland-based business has seen rapid growth in recent years, but it is not a globally recognized brand like Nike or Adidas. Beyond the central advertising campaign for the new shoe line, what tools would your team recommend employing to achieve integrated brand promotion? Explain how you would coordinate those efforts to ensure maximum effectiveness.

CHAPTER 2

After reading and thinking about this chapter, you will be able to do the following:

1 Discuss important trends transforming the advertising and promotion industry.

2 Describe the advertising and promotion industry's size, structure, and participants.

3 Discuss the role played by advertising and promotion agencies, the services provided by these agencies, and how the agencies are compensated.

4 Identify key external facilitators who assist in planning and executing advertising and integrated brand promotion campaigns.

5 Discuss the role played by media organizations in executing effective advertising and integrated brand promotion campaigns.

Introductory Scenario: Power Struggle to Beat All Power

Struggles. There have always been power struggles in the advertising and promotion industry: brand versus brand; one agency against another agency; agency versus media company; big advertiser with lots of money versus big retailer with lots of money. But those old-style power struggles were child's play compared with the 21st-century power struggle going on now. Estimates put the number of ads the average consumer encounters in a single day at somewhere between 1,000 and 5,000![1] Guess what: Consumers are tired of the barrage of ads and are looking for ways to avoid most of them. So, the big power struggle now is about how the advertising industry can successfully adapt to the new technologies that consumers are willing and, in fact, eager to use to gain more control over their information environment. Stated more directly, how can the ad industry overcome the fact that none of us is eager to have a 30-second television ad interrupt a television program we are really enjoying?

So consumers, who have been the target of advertising and promotion for decades, are discovering technologies and media options that give them more control over the communications they see and hear. From MySpace to YouTube to Wikipedia to millions of individual blogs, consumers are seeking out information environments where *they* control their exposure to information rather than an advertiser or media company being in control. In fact, consumers are becoming so successful at communicating with each other, *Advertising Age* (the main advertising-industry trade publication) named "the consumer" as its "Best Advertising Agency for 2006" as a way to signify this change in consumer control.[2] The "mass collaboration" of consumers, as it is called, is such a dramatic change from traditional information flow techniques that advertisers, advertising and promotion agencies, and media companies are struggling to reinvent themselves.[3]

We are all living the new technology reality—but how did it used to work? The old system worked like this: An advertiser, like Nike or American Express, would work with an advertising agency, like Leo Burnett or J. Walter Thompson, and think of really creative television, radio, newspaper, magazine, or billboard ads. Then, the advertiser and its agency would work with a media company, like NBC television or Hearst newspapers, and buy time or space to place the ad so that you, as the consumer, would see it when you watched television or read your morning newspaper. Don't get us wrong, this still happens—a lot. Major media like television, radio, and magazines rake in about $600 billion worldwide in a year, and individual media companies like Hearst Corp. generate several billion dollars annually in revenue.[4] But much has changed about the way advertisers, agencies, and media companies are trying to reach control-seeking consumers. And some very smart people think that we are truly heading into a totally new age with the industry on the cusp of even more dramatic changes.[5] Let's explore what's going on in the structure of the industry in some greater detail. First, from the consumer side. With the large number of media options available for news, information, and entertainment, "media fragmentation" is a boon to consumers and a huge headache for advertising agencies. The new "control seeking" generation of consumers is behaving very differently from the cable-TV generation that preceded it. Today's consumers are insisting on the convenience and appeal (and control) of their PC, iPod, and TiVo, or Slingbox (as we saw in Chapter 1). There is some large degree of irony in the control that consumers are starting to exert, however. While the traditional structure of the

1. Matthew Creamer, "Caught in the Clutter Crossfire: Your Brand," *Advertising Age,* April 2, 2007, 1, 35.
2. Teressa Iezzi, "You Got All the Recognition, but Agencies Did Great Work in 2006," *Advertising Age,* January 15, 2007, 15.
3. Robert D. Hof, "The Power of Us," *BusinessWeek,* June 20, 2005, 74–82.
4. Tom Lowry, "A Whole New View at Hearst," *BusinessWeek,* June 6, 2006, 87–88.
5. Bob Garfield, "The Chaos Scenario 2.0: The Post Advertising Age," *Advertising Age,* March 26, 2007, 1, 12–14.

EXHIBIT 2.1

Big advertisers like Coca-Cola (which used to spend about $200 million a year on television advertising) realize that a large portion of the consumer market is gaining more and more control over its exposure advertising. TiVo and consumer-controlled-content options like MySpace are allowing consumers to choose how and when they view information. In response, big advertisers are looking at more and varied ways to reach consumers and have their brands become more a part of consumers' lifestyles through promotional techniques like placing products within television shows and event sponsorships. http://www.cocacola.com

advertising and media industry may be changed forever, the *goal* of that old traditional structure has not changed—the brand needs to be highlighted. In fact, the change in consumer orientation will make product branding even *more* important as consumers choose what persuasive messages they want to be exposed to and where they want to be see them.

To that point, the importance of the brand in advertising and promotion was a key theme in Chapter 1. And advertising and promotion agencies and their media partners are struggling with just how to insert themselves and their clients' brands into this new environment controlled by the consumer. Some think "going with the flow" is the answer by having agencies and media companies allow consumers to contribute to content (à la the Super Bowl ad competitions).[6] Others, like Coca-Cola, understand that consumers will no longer tolerate passive television or magazine ads. Rather, brands are going to have to become part of consumers' daily lives in more subtle and seemingly natural ways. Part of Coke's approach: pay $20 million to have Coke cups on the desks of the judges during Fox Network's *American Idol* program.[7] (See Exhibit 2.1.) Another example is to provide free online video games to players who agree to watch ads (there are over 100 million players in the United States alone).[8]

While big advertisers like Coca-Cola recognize change and are trying to deal with it, so are big media companies. NBC Universal is often referenced as the "classic" big media company with the deepest roots in the old media structure. But now NBC is wooing advertisers by offering to help prepare advertising with the network's vast digital studio resources.[9] Other media companies like Viacom are trying similar experiments within their media-owned programming venues like Nick at Nite. Similarly, MTV Networks is offering new media distribution like broadband channel MotherLoad, which is associated with Comedy Central programming.[10]

This discussion would not be complete, of course, without a discussion of the Internet per se. "Advertising" on the Internet (not all the peer-to-peer information exchanging we have been talking about so far) now exceeds $20 billion through pop-ups, opt-in e-mail, banner ads, paid search, and all the other Internet options.[11] While that sounds like a lot of money (and it is), the total is still less than 10 percent of worldwide expenditures in traditional advertising media. But some analysts believe that the Internet will ultimately become the *primary* form of message delivery

6.   Erick Schonfeld, "Tuning Up Big Media," *Business 2.0,* April 6, 2006, 61–63.

7.   Dean Foust and Brian Grow, "Coke: Wooing the TiVo Generation," *BusinessWeek,* March 1, 2004, 77–78.

8.   Beth Snyder Bulik, "Ad Dollars Flow into Online Games," *Advertising Age,* March 26, 2007, 10.

9.   Jon Fine, "Now, an Ad from Our Network," *BusinessWeek,* November 27, 2006, 26.

10.   Tom Lowry, "The Dilemma Vexing Big Media," *BusinessWeek,* July 3, 2006, 94–98.

11.   Catherine Holahan, "Advertising Goes Off Radio," BusinessWeek.com, December 7, 2006. Accessed at *http://www.businessweek.com* on December 7, 2006.

and that traditional advertising "will become more of a way to simply send people to your Web site."[12] That might be a bit overstated—but maybe not. Google is moving into radio advertising and everyone is working to figure out how to effectively send messages to cell phones and iPods using the Internet without alienating consumers.[13]

Change in the advertising industry is nothing new, as the following section highlights. But the pace of change and the complexity of the change is more challenging than any the industry has ever faced. We'll spend our time in this chapter considering the structure in the industry and all the "players" that are creating and being affected by change.

The Advertising Industry in Constant Transition. The introductory scenario gives some examples of the deep and complex changes that are affecting the advertising industry. To say that the advertising industry is in *constant* transition might seem like an exaggeration, but it's not. If you consider changes in technology, economic conditions, culture, lifestyles, and business philosophies, one or more of these broad business and societal forces is always affecting the advertising and promotion effort.

This chapter highlights how the industry is changing now and has changed over time. While we consider the change and its effects, we need to keep in mind that the fundamental *process* of advertising and the role it plays in organizations remains steadfastly the same: persuasive communications directed at target audiences—no matter what is happening with technology, economic conditions, society, or business philosophies. The underlying role and purpose of advertising and promotion has not changed and will not change.

To appreciate the way the advertising industry is in a state of constant transition and the level of complexity that this transition has reached, it is necessary to understand that advertising is an industry with great breadth and intricacy. The section that follows highlights trends affecting change. Then, we will turn our attention to understanding how advertising and other promotional tools are managed in the communications industry and how that effort is also in a state of constant transition. Along the way, we'll consider all the different participants in the process, particularly the advertisers and their advertising and promotion agencies.

Trends Affecting the Advertising and Promotion Industry.
Often advertisers struggle with whether to use traditional mass media, like television and radio, that have wide reach or whether they should use newer, highly targeted media like personalized e-mail, Web films, podcasting, or other forms of promotion. But in the end what is important is not the Web and new opportunities to communicate that technology has to offer, but rather the critical need to focus on the brand, its image, and a persuasive, integrated presentation of that brand to the target market. It might be the Web, it might not be. It might be television, it might not be. The point is that the right medium needs to be used to achieve the right persuasive impact.

To understand the change that is affecting the advertising and promotion industry and the use of promotional tools, let's consider five broad trends in the marketplace.

12.   Peter Henderson, "Internet Ad Growth Pressures TV to Change," Reuters, December 2, 2005. Accessed at *http://www.news .yahoo.com* on December 2, 2005.

13.   Frant Barnako, "Google Radio Ads Ready to Roll," *Internet Daily,* November 28, 2006. Accessed at *http://www.marketwatch .com* on November 29, 2006.

The "Undoing" of Agency Consolidation and Globalization—or Not?

The advertising industry went through a period of extreme consolidation from 1999 through 2002. Full-service agencies acquired and merged with other full-service agencies and interactive shops. One such merger sequence began when Leo Burnett (the long-standing Chicago-based full-service agency) merged with the MacManus Group to create the $1.7 billion-a-year Bcom3 Group, with 500 operating units in 90 countries and 16,000 employees. Adding globalization to that merger, the Japanese agency Dentsu took a partnership position in the agreement as well. Then, two years later, the Paris-based global agency Publicis bought up the whole Bcom3 setup and by 2007 was a $5.1 billion global conglomerate of agencies.[14] Another global agency, Interpublic Group, acquired more than 300 agencies from 1998 through 2002 at a cost of over $5 billion. Now, Leo Burnett has reemerged as an independent agency and most of the mergers from the 1998 to 2002 period of consolidation have been undone.

But while all this consolidation and globalization provided an enormous array of services to clients, it has created problems as well. First, not all clients were impressed with the giant agencies. In a survey of nearly 300 major companies, only 43 percent said that it was "very important" to have a single agency offer fully integrated services. They felt they would be missing out on the creativity that small shops can offer through the specialization of services.[15] And when agencies get very large, there are inevitably conflicts of interest when trying to go after new business because the potential new client is in the same business as an existing client. Too, bigger has not always meant better or more profitable. Interpublic's buying binge has not increased its net income appreciably, yet it has created crushing debt and made the agency unwieldy. Analysts are now saying that these big agencies need to consolidate, get rid of money-losing operations, and turn what's left "loose to pursue their own clients."

It is unlikely that the giant agencies will dismantle all they have created. Some advertising clients are pleased to be able to consolidate all their integrated brand promotion (IBP) needs with one shop. But there is enough burden on the agencies from debt, conflict of interest, and migration of ad dollars to nontraditional media that some "unconsolidation" is possible—or not. Recent speculation has even more consolidation taking place with Interpublic and Publicis rumored to be considering a merger creating a multi-billion dollar behemoth agency.[16] The main point here is that advertising agencies are trying to do whatever it takes to keep pace with advertisers' needs in effectively reaching and communicating with target audiences.

Media Proliferation, Consolidation, and "Multiplatform" Media Organizations.

At another level of the industry, the media level, proliferation and consolidation have been taking place simultaneously. The proliferation of cable television channels, direct marketing technology, Web options, and alternative new media (podcasting, for example) have caused a visible proliferation of media options. Control of media and the advertising dollars they attract has always been a driving force behind many media companies. Historically, there has been a legal barrier to just how much control any one media company could seize. Well, in 2003, the Federal Communications Commission (FCC) relaxed a decades-old rule that had restricted media ownership. Now a single company can own television stations that reach up to 45 percent of U.S. households—up from the 35 percent specified in the old rule. In addition, the FCC also voted to lift all "cross-ownership" restrictions, ending a ban on one company owning both a newspaper and broadcast station in a city.[17]

14.   Matthew Creamer, "Stars Align for Big Bang, the Sequel," *Advertising Age,* December 4, 2006, 1, 37.
15.   Hillary Chura, "Marketers: One-Stop Shops Could Compromise Creative," *Advertising Age,* June 16, 2003, 6.
16.   Creamer, "Stars Align for Big Bang, the Sequel," 1.
17   David Ho, "FCC Votes to Ease Media Ownership Rules," *Washington Post,* available at *http://news.yahoo.com,* accessed on June 2, 2003.

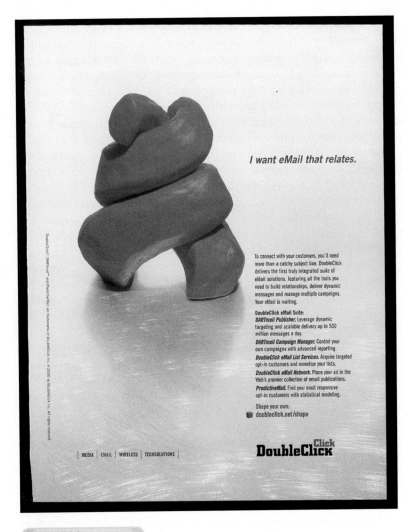

I want eMail that relates.

To connect with your customers, you'll need more than a catchy subject line. DoubleClick delivers the first truly integrated suite of eMail solutions, featuring all the tools you need to build relationships, deliver dynamic messages and manage multiple campaigns. Your eMail is waiting.

DoubleClick eMail Suite:
DARTmail Publisher. Leverage dynamic targeting and scalable delivery up to 500 million messages a day.

DARTmail Campaign Manager. Control your own campaigns with advanced reporting.

DoubleClick eMail List Services. Acquire targeted opt-in customers and monetize your lists.

DoubleClick eMail Network. Place your ad in the Web's premier collection of email publications.

PredictiveMail. Find your most responsive opt-in customers with statistical modeling.

Shape your own:
doubleclick.net/shape

| MEDIA | EMAIL | WIRELESS | TECHSOLUTIONS |

DoubleClick

EXHIBIT 2.2

The proliferation of media alternatives has caused media fragmentation in the advertising and promotion industry. One effect of this change is that new specialized media organizations have emerged to sell and manage new media options. DoubleClick, one of these new media companies, manages targeted e-mail messages. http://www.doubleclick.net

The consolidation is in no way restricted to television. Media companies of all types tend to pursue more and more "properties" if they are allowed to, thus creating what are now referred to as "multiplatform" media organizations.[18] Consider the evolution of media giant News Corp. and its holdings, which include television networks (Fox), newspapers (more than 20 worldwide), magazines (Gemstar-TV Guide International), satellite (DirecTV), and cable systems (Fox News). News Corp.'s worldwide media holdings generate over $40 billion in revenue and reach every corner of the Earth. Now the firm is the proud new owner of MySpace in the peer-to-peer media world. As big as News Corp. is, the ultimate multiplatform may be Disney, which owns the ABC broadcasting network and the ESPN cable network group, plus 10 other cable stations, 15 radio stations, a couple of dozen Web sites, eight podcasting operations, video on demand, books and magazines—you name it, Disney uses it to reach audiences.

Not to be outdone, the Web has its own media conglomerates. InterActiveCorp (IAC) has amassed a media empire of Internet sites that are as diverse as they are successful. The holdings include Ask .com, Match.com, Ticketmaster, and Lending Tree. Together, these sites generate about $7 billion in revenue, which makes IAC nearly as big as better-known Internet merchants like Google, but much more diversified. In turn, the evolution of media options has spawned new specialized agencies to sell, manage, and consult for these new media options (see Exhibit 2.2).

Media Clutter and Fragmentation.
While the media and agency levels of the industry may be consolidating into fewer and fewer large firms, that does not mean that there are fewer media options. Quite the contrary is true. There are more ways to *try* to reach consumers than ever before. In 1994 the consumer had access to about 27 television channels. Today, the average U.S. household has access to well over 100 channels. In 1995, it took three well-placed TV spots to reach 80 percent of women television viewers. By 2003, it took 97 spots to reach them![19] From televi-

---

18. Nat Ives, "Special Report: More Than Magazines," *Advertising Age,* March 12, 2007, s1–s6.
19. Matthew Boyle, "Brand Killers," *Fortune,* April 11, 2003, 89–100.

sion ads to virtual billboards to banner ads on the Internet to podcasts of advertising messages, new and increased media options have resulted in so much clutter that the probability of any one advertisement breaking through and making a real difference continues to diminish. Advertisers are developing a lack of faith in advertising alone, so promotion options such as online communication, brand placement in film and television, point-of-purchase displays, and sponsorships are more attractive to advertisers. For example, advertisers on the Super Bowl, notorious for its clutter and outrageous ad prices (about $2.5 million to $3 million for a 30-second spot), have turned instead to promotional tie-ins to enhance the effect of the advertising. To combat the clutter and expense at one Super Bowl, Miller Brewing distributed thousands of inflatable Miller Lite chairs by game day. The chairs were a tie-in with a national advertising campaign that began during the regular season before the Super Bowl.[20]

Given the backlash against advertising that clutter can cause, advertisers and their agencies are rethinking the way they try to communicate with consumers. Fundamentally, there is a greater focus on integrating more tools within the overall promotional effort in an attempt to reach more consumers in more different ways. This approach by advertisers is wreaking havoc on traditional media expenditures. Consider the decisions by just two advertisers—Johnson & Johnson and General Motors. In 2007, Johnson & Johnson announced that it had shifted $250 million in spending from traditional media—television, magazines, newspapers—to "digital media" including the Internet and blogs. Even more dramatically, General Motors reduced total ad spending by $600 million in that same year with all categories of traditional media being reduced, but Internet spending being increased.[21]

Advertisers are shifting spending out of traditional media because they are looking to the full complement of promotional opportunities in sales promotions (like the Miller chairs), event sponsorships, new media options, and public relations as means to support and enhance the primary advertising effort for brands. In fact, some advertisers are enlisting the help of Hollywood talent agencies in an effort to get their brands featured in television programs and films. The payoff for strategic placement in a film or television show can be huge. Getting Coca-Cola placed on *American Idol*, as we talked about earlier, is estimated to be worth up to $20 million in traditional media advertising.[22] This topic is covered in Chapter 18 when we consider branded entertainment in detail.

Consumer Control: From Blogs to TiVo.
Historically, advertisers controlled information and the flow of information as a one-way communication through mass media. But, as the introductory scenario highlights, consumers are now in greater control of the information they receive about product categories and the brands within those categories. The simplest and most obvious example is when consumers log on to the Internet and visit sites *they* choose to visit for either information or shopping. But it gets a lot more complicated from there. **Blogs**, Web sites frequented by individuals with common interests where they can post facts, opinions, and personal experiences, are emerging as new and sophisticated sources of product and brand information. Once criticized as the "ephemeral scribble" of 13-year-old girls and the babble of techno-geeks, blogs are gaining greater sophistication and organization. Web-based service firms like Blogdrive, Feedster, and Blogger are making blogs easier to use and accessible to the masses. The research firm Gartner forecasts that blogging will peak

20. Betsy Spethmann, "Pre-Game Warmups," *Promo Magazine,* December 2000, 33–34; Bruce Horovitz, "Gee-Whiz Effects Make Super Bowl Ads Super Special," *USA Today,* January 30, 2004, B1–B2.
21. Jack Neff, "J&J Jolts 'Old Media' with $250M Spend Shift," *Advertising Age,* March 19, 2007, 1, 29; Jean Halliday, "GM Cuts $600M off Ad Spend—Yes, Really," *Advertising Age,* February 21, 2007, 1, 25.
22. Betsy Streisand, "Why Great American Brands Are Doing Lunch," *Business 2.0,* September 2003, 146–150.

DOING IT RIGHT

Do Not Call. Do Not Mail. Do Not Text. Do Not Communicate?

Consumers are most certainly exerting their right to control their personal communications environment. The chapter talks about peer-to-peer communication through e-mail and blogs and ways of avoiding ads through devices like TiVo (DVRs) and Slingbox controllers. But consumers' efforts to control the communication environment do not end there. Since 2004, approximately 139 million consumers in the United States have placed their phone numbers on state and federal "do not call" lists to block telemarketer advertising and promotion. (Remember that the U.S. population is about 320 million and about half the population is under 18 years old.) Similarly, consumers can use pop-up blockers and "junk mail" spam blockers (which have varying degrees of effectiveness) to rid their computers of other forms of advertiser communications.

Now more than a dozen states are considering implementing "do not mail" lists similar to the "do not call" list. This would allow consumers to "block" direct mail from their traditional mailboxes and impose a penalty on advertisers who violate the consumer request. In many ways, this block to communication would be more effective than the "do not call" list because the advertiser in violation would be much easier to identify and verify. And if "do not call" and "do not mail" are in place, can "do not text" be far behind? Consumers consider their mobile phones very personal, and as contextual advertising to mobile phones and iPods become more aggressive, a "do not text" movement would not be surprising.

Analyst Pete Blackshaw of Nielsen BuzzMetrics believes that "we've reached this perfect storm of consumer power and ad intrusion" and that the way out of this dilemma is for marketers to figure out a way to "open their doors and lure consumers in." As Liz Vanzura, Cadillac's new marketing chief, puts it, "TiVo and the remote control are killing us. We have to give consumers more reasons to listen to what we have to say." Frito-Lay is one of those advertisers getting creative in order to keep its brands in front of consumers. The snack marketer signed on to embed its Lay's brand in the syndicated reality show *Home Team,* meaning you will see various Lay's products throughout the telecast in a "natural" setting.

The main lesson here for advertisers is that just because technology makes communication possible, it doesn't mean that using that technology is a good idea. As much communication power as advertisers have acquired with new technology, consumers have just as much new technology to block the communications—or at least ignore them effectively. In the end, it will come down to having a compelling message, "done right," delivered in a compelling manner that consumers want to watch or hear.

Sources: David Kiley, "A New Spark Plug for Cadillac," *BusinessWeek,* March 20, 2006, 80–82; Ira Teinowitz and Ken Wheaton, "Do Not Market," *Advertising Age,* March 12, 2007, 1, 44.

in 2007, leveling off when the number of people who maintain a personal Web site reaches 100 million(!), but only about 20,000 blog sites are visited by other than friends and family of the blogger. Gartner analysts expect that the novelty value of the medium will then wear off as most people who are interested in the phenomenon have checked it out.[23] But that is not keeping big firms like Boeing and Procter & Gamble from investing in the process for customers, employees, and the general public.[24]

As discussed earlier, another new and dramatic example of consumer control is the growth in use of digital video recorders (DVRs) like TiVo and controllers like Slingbox. Analysts expect that the use of DVRs will reduce ad viewership by as much as 30 percent. That translates into taking approximately $20 billion out of U.S. advertising industry revenue. And advertisers and their agencies can expect that by 2010, approximately 39 percent of all U.S. television households will have "ad-skipping" capability.[25]

Advertisers and their agencies will need to adapt to the concept that consumers are gaining greater control over the information they choose to receive. How will they adapt? Creativity is one answer. The more entertaining and informative an ad is, the more likely consumers will want to actually watch the ad. Another technique, less creative but certainly effective, is to run advertising messages along the bottom of the programming. Finally, TiVo itself is rolling out a service that sounds crazy: ads on demand.[26] But consumers about to buy expensive items like cars, appliances, or resort vacations may want to watch information about alternative brands. On the other hand, consumers are getting more aggressive about protecting their communication "rights," as the Doing It Right box highlights.

23.   Kim Hart, "Portrait of a Blogger: Under 30 and Sociable," *Washington Post,* July 20, 2006, D5.
24.   Stanley Holmes, "Into the Wild Blog Yonder," *BusinessWeek,* May 22, 2006, 84.
25.   David Kiley, "Learning to Love the Dreaded TiVo," *BusinessWeek,* April 17, 2006, 88.
26.   Ibid.

Web 2.0. We couldn't talk about trends in the advertising industry without talking about Web 2.0. OK, so just what is "Web 2.0" anyway? Web 2.0 is a phrase coined by O'Reilly Media in 2004 and refers to a second generation of Web-based use and services—such as social networking sites and wikis—that emphasize online collaboration and sharing among users. O'Reilly Media used the phrase as a title for a series of conferences, and it has since become widely adopted.

We have discussed the impact of the behaviors associated with Web 2.0, but not everyone believes that the phenomenon is really a phenomenon at all. Since networking (e.g., MySpace) activity and informational services (e.g., Wikipedia) are capabilities that have been part of Web technology from the beginning of the World Wide Web, some analysts challenge whether Web 2.0 is really new or different at all.

Those who champion the concept of Web 2.0 argue that the change in how people are using that technology is so significant that it needs to be recognized as a distinct element of the Web world. When you consider that 70,000 videos are uploaded to YouTube every day by people all over the world, it is hard to argue that this sort of application of Web technology does not deserve its own designation.[27] Consider further that Google believes enough in this particular application of Web technology to have spent $1.65 billion to buy YouTube and that IBM, the icon of old corporate America, believes that Web 2.0 is and can be much more than a "bunch of teenagers posting comments on each other's Facebook pages."[28] IBM is also exploring corporate applications for blogs, wikis, podcasts, social networking, and RSS (Really Simple Syndication). While there are doubters of Web 2.0, you need to be aware that it represents another element of the communication landscape to consider in the application of advertising and promotion tools. An example is Second Life, a network of virtual environments that feature extensive billboard advertising and conspicuous brand use by avatars.

For years to come, these trends and the changes they bring about will force advertisers to think differently about advertising and IBP. Similarly, advertising agencies will need to think about the way they serve their clients and the way communications are delivered to audiences. As you have read, big spenders such as Procter & Gamble, IBM, Miller Brewing, and General Motors are already demanding new and innovative programs to enhance the impact of their advertising and promotional dollars. The goal of creating persuasive communication remains intact—attract attention and develop preference for a brand—and so the dynamics of the communications environment and the changes in the structure of the advertising industry are the central topics of this chapter.

② The Scope and Structure of the Advertising Industry.

To fully appreciate the structure of the advertising industry, let's first consider the size of the advertising industry. Remember from Chapter 1 that the advertising industry is huge: more than $300 billion spent in the United States alone on various categories of advertising, with nearly $600 billion spent worldwide. Spending on all forms of promotion including advertising exceeds a trillion dollars.[29]

Another indicator of the scope of advertising is the amount spent on advertising by individual firms. Exhibit 2.3 shows spending for 2006 and 2005 among the top 20 U.S. advertisers. Hundreds of millions of dollars a year and, in the case of the largest spenders, billions of dollars a year is truly a huge amount of money to spend on advertising. But we have to realize that the $3.2 billion spent by General Motors on advertising was only about 2.6 percent of GM's sales. Similarly,

27.   Lev Grossman, "Invention of the Year," *Time,* November 13, 2006, 61–65.
28.   Tom Lowry and Robert D. Hof, "Smart Move or Silly Money 2.0?" *BusinessWeek,* October 23, 2006, 34–37; Maggie Rauch, "Virtual Reality," *Sales & Marketing Management,* January/February 2007, 18–23.
29.   "100 Leading National Advertisers," *Advertising Age,* June 25, 2007, S-4.

The 20 largest advertisers in the United States in 2006 (U.S. dollars in millions).

Company	2006 Ad Dollars (millions)	2005 Ad Dollars (millions)	% Change
Procter & Gamble	$4,898.0	$4,587.9	6.8%
AT&T	3,344.7	2,653.6	26.0
General Motors	3,296.1	4,110.1	−19.8
Time Warner	3,088.8	3,518.3	−12.2
Verizon Communications	2,821.8	2,481.3	13.7
Ford Motor Co.	2,576.8	2,611.8	−1.3
GlaxoSmithKline	2,444.2	2,249.8	8.6
Walt Disney Co.	2,320.0	2,291.7	1.2
Johnson & Johnson	2,290.5	2,669.4	−14.2
Unilever	2,098.3	1,943.5	8.0
Toyota	1,995.3	1,783.2	11.9
Sony	1,994.0	1,801.8	10.7
DaimlerChrysler	1,952.2	2,181.2	−10.5
General Electric	1,860.2	1,979.9	−6.0
Sprint Nextel	1,775.2	1,715.2	3.5
McDonald's	1,748.3	1,656.8	5.5
Sears Roebuck & Co.	1,652.8	1,715.3	−3.6
L'Oréal	1,456.3	1,464.2	−0.5
Kraft Foods	1,423.2	1,428.9	−0.4
Macy's	1,361.2	1,346.7	1.1

Source: "100 Leading National Advertisers," *Advertising Age*, June 25, 2007, S-4. Reprinted with permission. © Crain Communications, Inc., 2007.

Procter & Gamble spent about $4.8 billion, but this amount represented only about 6 percent of its sales. So while the absolute dollars seem huge, the relative spending is often much more modest. Also note that among the top 20 spenders in Exhibit 2.3, nine showed a *decrease* in ad spending—we will discuss this specifically in Chapter 15.

Overall, the 100 leading advertisers in the United States spent just over $105 billion on advertising in 2006, which was a healthy 3.1 percent increase over 2005.[30] Still, there is no doubt that this rapidly increasing spending is related to increased clutter. Advertising may be quickly becoming its own worst enemy. Exhibit 2.4 shows the increase in advertising across the 20th century and into the 21st century.

Beyond the scope of spending, the structure of the industry is really the key issue. When we understand the structure of the advertising industry, we know *who* does *what, in what order,* during the advertising process. The advertising industry is actually a collection of a wide range of talented people, all of whom have special expertise

30.   Bradley Johnson, "Top 100 Spending Up 3.1% to $105 Billion," *Advertising Age,* June 25, 2007, S-2.

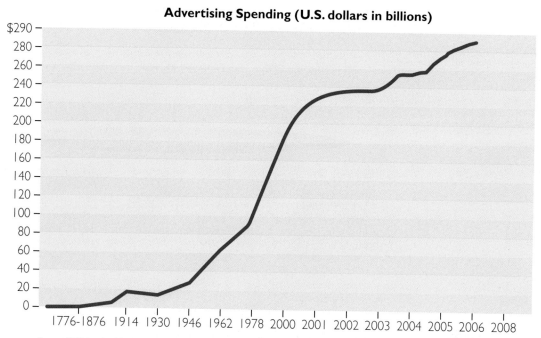

Advertising Spending (U.S. dollars in billions)

Source: "100 Leading National Advertisers," *Advertising Age*, annual estimates. Reprinted with permission. © Crain Communications, Inc., 2007

EXHIBIT 2.4

Advertising spending from the founding of the United States into the 21st century.

and perform a wide variety of tasks in planning, preparing, and placing of advertising. Exhibit 2.5 on page 52 shows the structure of the advertising industry by showing who the different participants are in the process.

Exhibit 2.5 on the next page demonstrates that *advertisers* (such as Kellogg) can employ the services of *advertising agencies* (such as Grey Global Group) that may (or may not) contract for specialized services with various *external facilitators* (such as Simmons Market Research Bureau), which results in advertising being transmitted with the help of various *media organizations* (such as the TBS cable network) to one or more *target audiences* (like you!).

Note the dashed line on the left side of Exhibit 2.5 on the next page. This line indicates that advertisers do not always need to employ the services of advertising agencies. Nor do advertisers or agencies always seek the services of external facilitators. Some advertisers deal directly with media organizations for placement of their advertisements or implementation of their promotions. This happens either when an advertiser has an internal advertising/promotions department that prepares all the materials for the process, or when media organizations (especially radio, television, and newspapers) provide technical assistance in the preparation of materials. The new interactive media formats also provide advertisers the opportunity to work directly with entertainment programming firms, such as Walt Disney, Sony, and SFX Entertainment, to provide integrated programming that features brand placements in films and television programs or at entertainment events. And, as you will see, many of the new media agencies provide the creative and technical assistance advertisers need to implement campaigns through new media.

Each level in the structure of the industry is complex. So let's take a look at each level, with particular emphasis on the nature and activities of agencies. When you need to devise advertising or a fully integrated brand promotion, no source will be more valuable than the advertising or promotion agency you work with. Advertising and promotion agencies provide the essential creative firepower to the process and represent a critical link in the structure.

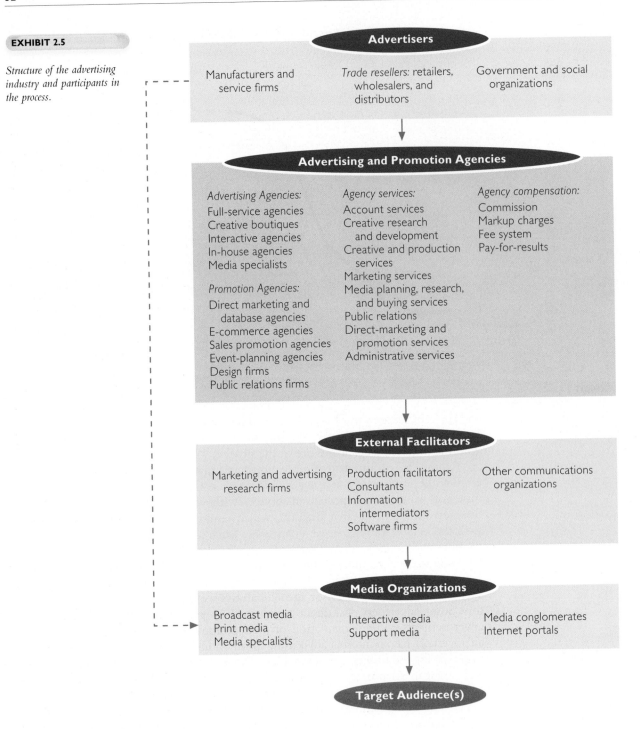

EXHIBIT 2.5

Structure of the advertising industry and participants in the process.

Advertisers

Manufacturers and service firms

Trade resellers: retailers, wholesalers, and distributors

Government and social organizations

Advertising and Promotion Agencies

Advertising Agencies:
Full-service agencies
Creative boutiques
Interactive agencies
In-house agencies
Media specialists

Promotion Agencies:
Direct marketing and database agencies
E-commerce agencies
Sales promotion agencies
Event-planning agencies
Design firms
Public relations firms

Agency services:
Account services
Creative research and development
Creative and production services
Marketing services
Media planning, research, and buying services
Public relations
Direct-marketing and promotion services
Administrative services

Agency compensation:
Commission
Markup charges
Fee system
Pay-for-results

External Facilitators

Marketing and advertising research firms

Production facilitators
Consultants
Information intermediators
Software firms

Other communications organizations

Media Organizations

Broadcast media
Print media
Media specialists

Interactive media
Support media

Media conglomerates
Internet portals

Target Audience(s)

Advertisers. First in the structure of advertising is the advertisers themselves. From your local pet store to multinational corporations, organizations of all types and sizes seek to benefit from the effects of advertising. **Advertisers** are business, not-for-profit, and government organizations that use advertising and other promotional techniques to communicate with target markets and to stimulate awareness and demand for their brands. Advertisers are also referred to as **clients** by their advertising and promotion agency partners. Different types of advertisers use advertising somewhat differently, depending on the type of product or service they market. The following categories describe the different types of advertisers and the role advertising plays for them.

Manufacturers and Service Firms. Large national manufacturers of consumer products and services are the most prominent users of promotion, often spending hundreds of millions of dollars annually. Procter & Gamble, General Foods, Verizon, and Merrill Lynch all have national or global markets for their products and services. The use of advertising, particularly mass media advertising, by these firms is essential to creating awareness and preference for their brands. But advertising is useful not to just national or multinational firms; regional and local producers of household goods and services also rely heavily on advertising. For example, regional dairy companies sell milk, cheese, and other dairy products in regions usually comprising a few states. These firms often use ads placed in newspapers and regional editions of magazines.

Further, couponing and sampling are ways to communicate with target markets with IBPs that are well suited to regional application. Some breweries and wineries also serve only regional markets. Local producers of products are relatively rare, but local service organizations are common. Medical facilities, hair salons, restaurants, auto dealers, and arts organizations are examples of local service providers that use advertising to create awareness and stimulate demand. What car dealer in America has not advertised a holiday event or used a remote local radio broadcast to attract attention!

Firms that produce business goods and services also use advertising on a global, national, regional, and local basis. IBM (computer and business services) and Deloitte (accounting and consulting services) are examples of global companies that produce business goods and services. At the national and regional level, firms that supply agricultural and mining equipment and repair services are common users of promotion, as are consulting and research firms. At the local level, firms that supply janitorial, linen, and bookkeeping services use advertising.

Trade Resellers. The term **trade reseller** is simply a general description for all organizations in the marketing channel of distribution that buy products to resell to customers. As Exhibit 2.5 shows, resellers can be retailers, wholesalers, or distributors. These resellers deal with both household consumers and business buyers at all geographic market levels.

Retailers that sell in national or global markets are the most visible reseller advertisers. Wal-Mart, Gap, and McDonald's are examples of national and global retail companies that use various forms of promotion to communicate with customers. Regional retail chains, typically grocery chains such as Albertson's or department stores such as Dillard's, serve multistate markets and use advertising suited to their regional customers. At the local level, small retail shops of all sorts rely on newspaper, radio, television, and billboard advertising and special promotional events to reach a relatively small geographic area. (See Exhibit 2.6.)

EXHIBIT 2.6

Advertising is not reserved for just big companies with national markets like Microsoft or Nike. Organizations that serve regional and local markets, like Rocky Mountain Choppers, can make effective use of advertising as well. (http://www.rmchoppers.com)

American Red Cross

Together, we can save a life

Make a plan.

How your family reacts in an emergency can make all the difference. Develop a family disaster plan with help from your local Red Cross and learn what everyone in your family can do in the event of a fire or other disaster. When we come together, we become part of something bigger than us all. To learn what you can do, contact your local American Red Cross chapter or visit www.redcross.org

TOGETHERWE   Make a plan | Build a kit | Get trained | Volunteer | Give blood

EXHIBIT 2.7

Government, social, and not-for-profit organizations can use advertising as effectively as corporations. Here the American Red Cross is using advertising to communicate to families the importance of having a "family disaster plan" in case of a fire or other catastrophe. Note how the American Red Cross is highlighting its logo in this ad as a way of developing "brand" recognition—just like corporations do! (http://www.redcross.org)

Wholesalers and distributors, such as Ideal Supply, Inc. (a company that supplies contractors with blasting and surveying equipment), are a completely different breed of reseller. Technically, these types of companies deal only with business customers, since their position in the distribution channel dictates that they sell products either to producers (who buy goods to produce other goods) or to retailers (who resell goods to household consumers). Occasionally, an organization will call itself a wholesaler and sell to the public. Such an organization is actually operating as a retail outlet.

Wholesalers and distributors have little need for mass media advertising over media such as television and radio. Rather, they use trade publications, directory advertising such as the Yellow Pages and trade directories, direct mail, and their Internet Web sites as their main advertising media.

Federal, State, and Local Governments. At first, you might think it is odd to include governments as advertising users, but government bodies invest millions of dollars in advertising annually. The U.S. government often ranks as one of the 50 largest spenders on advertising in the United States, with expenditures typically exceeding $1.0 billion annually.[31] And that's just on advertising. If you add in other IBP expenses like brochures, recruiting fairs, and the personal selling expense of recruiting offices, the U.S. government easily spends well over $2 billion annually. The federal government's spending on advertising and promotion is concentrated in two areas: armed forces recruiting and social issues. As an example, the U.S. government regularly uses broad-based advertising campaigns for military recruiting.[32] The U.S. Army's "Army Strong" campaign uses television, magazine, newspapers, and interactive games ("America's Army") hosted at the Army recruiting Web site (http://www.goarmy.com).

Social and Not-for-Profit Organizations. Advertising by social organizations at the national, state, and local level is common. The Nature Conservancy, United Way, American Red Cross, and art organizations use advertising to raise awareness of their organizations, seek donations, and attempt to shape behavior (deter drug use or encourage breast self-examinations, for example). Organizations such as these use both the mass media and direct mail to promote their causes and services (see Exhibit 2.7). Every state has its own unique statewide organizations, such as Citizens against Hunger, a state arts council, a tourism office, an economic development office, or a historical society. Social organizations in local communities represent a variety of special interests, from computer clubs to fraternal organizations to neighborhood child care organizations. The advertising used by social organizations has the same fundamental purpose as the advertising carried out by major multinational corporations: to stimulate demand and disseminate information. While big multi-

31.   The 2006 ranking for the U.S. Government was 29th at $1.13 billion annual spending on advertising, "100 Leading National Advertisers," *Advertising Age,* June 25, 2007, S-4.

32.   Bob Garfield, "Army Ad Strong—If You Totally Forget We're at War, "*Advertising Age,* November 13, 2006, 57.

nationals might use national or even global advertising, local organizations rely on advertising through local media to reach local audiences.

Do all these advertisers sound familiar? They should. Remember from Chapter 1 that we discussed these types of advertisers as distinct "audiences" as well. Firms are targets for advertising as well as advertisers themselves.

The Role of the Advertiser in IBP.
Very few of the advertisers just discussed have the employees or the financial resources to strategically plan and then totally prepare effective advertising and IBP programs. This is where advertising and promotion agencies play such an important role in the structure of the advertising industry. But there is an important role played by the advertiser *before* the services of an agency are enlisted. Advertisers of all sizes and types, as just discussed, have to be prepared for their interaction with an agency in order for the agency to do *its* job effectively. That is, it is the advertiser's role to

- Fully understand and describe the value that the firm's brand provides to users
- Fully understand and describe the brand's position in the market relative to competitive brands
- Describe the firm's objectives for the brand in the near term and long term (e.g., brand extensions, international market launches)
- Identify the target market(s) that are most likely to respond favorably to the brand
- Identify and manage the supply chain/distribution system that will most effectively reach the target markets
- Be committed to using advertising and other promotional tools as part of the organization's overall marketing strategy to grow the brand

Once an advertiser has done its job with respect to the six factors above, then and *only* then is it time to enlist the services of an agency to help effectively and creatively develop the market for the brand. This is not to say that an agency will not work with an advertiser to help better define and refine these factors. Rather, it is a mistake for an advertiser to enter a relationship with an agency (of any type) without first doing its homework and being prepared for a productive partnership.

Advertising and Promotion Agencies.
Advertisers are fortunate to have a full complement of agencies that specialize in literally every detail of advertising and promotion. Let's take a closer look at the types of agencies advertisers can rely on to help create their advertising and IBP campaigns.

Advertising Agencies.
Most advertisers choose to enlist the services of an advertising agency. An **advertising agency** is an organization of professionals who provide creative and business services to clients in planning, preparing, and placing advertisements. The reason so many firms rely on advertising agencies is that agencies house a collection of professionals with very specialized talent, experience, and expertise that simply cannot be matched by in-house talent.

Most big cities and small towns in the United States have advertising agencies. Advertising agencies often are global businesses as well. As discussed in the section on trends affecting the advertising industry, megamergers between agencies have been occurring for several years. Exhibit 2.8 shows the world's 10 largest advertising organizations and their worldwide gross income. Worldwide revenue for ad agencies reached $28.2 billion in 2006.[33]

---

33. "63rd Annual Agency Report," *Advertising Age,* April 30, 2007, S-4.

Rank 2006	Rank 2005	Company	Headquarters	Worldwide Gross Revenue, 2006 (millions)	% Change
1	1	Dentsu	Tokyo	$2,213	2.2
2	3	BBDO Worldwide	New York	1,539	8.0
3	2	McCann-Erickson Worldwide	New York	1,479	1.2
4	4	JWT	New York	1,286	3.3
5	5	DDB Worldwide	New York	1,263	6.2
6	6	Publicis Groupe	Paris	1,177	2.0
7	7	TBWA Worldwide	New York	1,135	19.4
8	8	Leo Burnett	Chicago	908	2.2
9	10	Y & R	New York	820	4.1
10	9	Hakuhodo	Tokyo	780	−1.0

Source: "63rd Annual Agency Report," *Advertising Age*, April 25, 2007, S-4. Reprinted with permission. © Crain Communications, Inc., 2007.

EXHIBIT 2.8

The world's top 10 advertising organizations (ranked by worldwide gross revenue, U.S. dollars in millions).

The types of agency professionals who help advertisers in the planning, preparation, and placement of advertising and other promotional activities include the following:

Account planners
Marketing specialists
Account executives
Media buyers
Art directors
Lead account planners
Chief executive officers (CEOs)
Chief financial officers (CFOs)
Chief technology officers (CTOs)
Public relations specialists
Creative directors

Sales promotion and event planners
Copywriters
Direct marketing specialists
Radio and television producers
Web developers
Researchers
Interactive media planners
Artists
Technical staff—printers, film editors, and so forth

As this list suggests, some advertising agencies can provide advertisers with a host of services, from campaign planning through creative concepts to e-strategies to measuring effectiveness. Also note from this list that an agency is indeed a business. Agencies have CEOs, CFOs, and CTOs just like any other business. Salaries in the positions listed above range from about several million a year for a big agency chief executive officer (Barry Diller made $295 million in salary and stock options at InterActiveCorp in 2005!) to about $50,000 a year for a media planner.[34] Of course, those salaries change depending on whether you're in a big urban market or a small regional market.

Several different types of agencies are available to the advertiser. Be aware that there are all sorts of agencies with varying degrees of expertise and services. It is up to the advertiser to dig deep into an agency's background and determine which agency or set of multiple agencies will fulfill the advertiser's needs. A short description of the major different types of agencies follows:

Full-Service Agencies. A **full-service agency** typically includes an array of advertising professionals to meet all the promotional needs of clients. Often, such an agency will

34.   Bradley Johnson, "Diller Leads Top Execs in 2005 Pay," *Advertising Age*, December 4, 2006, S-2.

also offer a client global contacts. (See Globalization Box on page 58). Omnicom Group and Dentsu are examples. Full-service agencies are not necessarily large organizations employing hundreds or even thousands of people. Smaller shops can be full service with just a few dozen employees and serve big clients. Crispin Porter + Bogusky is a highly creative shop in Miami—not New York or L.A.—and has produced full service, highly creative campaigns for VW, Burger King, and Mini USA.[35] Similarly, not every full-service agency is built on giant accounts worth hundreds of millions of dollars. Cramer-Krasselt, a midsize agency, has built a stable of international clients one small/medium account at a time. The agency rarely has accounts billing over $20 million. But by serving small accounts from clients such as AirTran, Allen-Edmonds shoes, Rexall, and Bombardier ATVs, the agency now has several million dollars in annual billings.[36]

Creative Boutiques. A **creative boutique** typically emphasizes creative concept development, copywriting, and artistic services to clients. An advertiser can employ this alternative for the strict purpose of infusing greater creativity into the message theme or individual advertisement. As one advertising expert put it, "If all clients want are ideas, lots of them, from which they can pick and mix to their hearts' delight, they won't want conventional, full-service agencies. They all want fast, flashy, fee-based idea factories."[37] Creative boutiques are these idea factories. Some large global agencies such as McCann-Erickson Worldwide and Leo Burnett have set up creative-only project shops that mimic the services provided by creative boutiques, with mixed results. The truth is that as the advertising industry continues to evolve, the creative boutiques may become a casualty of expansion-contraction-expansion by the big global multiservice agencies. Be assured, there are still some great creative boutiques around, like Fusion Idea Lab (http://www.fusionidealab.com).

The creative boutique's greatest advantage, niche expertise, may be its greatest liability as well. As firms search for IBP programs and make a commitment to IBP campaigns, the creative boutique may be an extra expense and step that advertisers simply don't feel they can afford. But, as you will learn in Chapter 10 on creativity and advertising, the creative effort is so essential to effective brand building that creativity will rise to prominence in the process, and creative boutiques are well positioned to deliver that value.

Interactive Agencies. These agencies help advertisers prepare communications for new media such as the Internet, podcasting, interactive kiosks, CD-ROMs, and interactive television. **Interactive agencies** focus on ways to use Web-based solutions for direct marketing and target market communications (see Exhibit 2.9). Interactive agencies do work for BMW, Oracle, Nintendo, and the U.S. Army. But interactive agencies were not spared when the big shake-out occurred among dot-coms

EXHIBIT 2.9

The era of new media has spawned new interactive advertising agencies that specialize in developing banner ads and corporate Web sites. Bluestreak is an agency with the stated purpose of providing the infrastructure for marketers and agencies to create results-driven campaigns that generate dramatically higher click-through, conversion, and transaction rates. Check out its philosophy and purpose at http://www.bluestreak.com.

35.   David Kiley, "The Craziest Ad Guys in America," *BusinessWeek,* May 22, 2006, 72–80.
36.   Hillary Chura and Kate MacArthur, "Cramer-Krasselt Thinks Small," *Advertising Age,* September 11, 2000, 32.
37.   Martin Sorell, "Agencies Face New Battle Grounds," *Advertising Age,* April 13, 1998, 22.

GLOBALIZATION

Hispanic, Chinese, Dutch Agencies—It's All Good and All Growing

The globalization of markets has produced huge growth in specialized agencies both within and outside the United States. One phenomenon is the growth of Hispanic agencies within the United States to develop advertising and promotion for the fast-growing Spanish-speaking consumer market. These agencies have been experiencing double-digit growth for several years with some agencies in Miami and L.A. growing at 30 and 40 percent annually. And now that Hispanic online spending has grown to over $150 million annually, more Latino agencies are starting interactive units.

China, known for its huge growth in GDP and bulging trade surpluses, is struggling to keep up with the need for advertising and promotional materials fueled by that economic growth. In fact, some agencies describe their situation as a "crisis" from the standpoint of trying to find enough talented people to handle dozens of vacancies in creative, research, media—you name it. But they call this a "good" crisis because the need for talent means the market is growing and business is good. Business is especially good when it comes to the opportunities for digital communication. China has 120 million Internet users (and growing fast) and 791 million mobile phones (no, that is not a typo!). The Internet is the third-strongest medium for communication in China, behind television and newspapers, and about 10 percent of all ad dollars go to the Internet.

Finally, Amsterdam has emerged as a very hot agency market. When Sony recently hired a new agency for all its U.S. creative work, it went to Amsterdam and hired a small independent agency called 180. But Sony was not early in the discovery of the highly creative shops in the Netherlands. Adidas, Ikea, and Coca-Cola had been using shops in the metro area of Amsterdam for many years. Why, the city itself is artistic, easily attracts creative talent, and features broad diversity. As one agency exec put it, "Amsterdam allows us to be in touch with the world without being swallowed up by any particular culture."

Sources: Laurel Wentz, "Look at Them Grow: U.S. Hispanic Agencies Thrive," *Advertising Age*, December 4, 2006, 31; Laurel Wentz and Normandy Madden, "China's Ad World: A New Crisis Every Day," *Advertising Age*, December 11, 2006, 6; Jack Ewing, "Amsterdam's Red-Hot Ad Shops," *BusinessWeek*, December 18, 2006, 52.

in 1999. Many simply folded up shop; others were acquired by large agencies. Today, even a midsize full-service agency will offer interactive services to clients. This being the case, many firms have consolidated all their IBP needs, including interactive media, with their main full-service agency.

Here's a heads-up on the next evolution in interactive agencies—the virtual agency. A virtual agency is a Web site (see http://www.pick-n-click.com as an example) where users who pay a flat fee can make their own TV, print, radio, and interactive ads. The idea is being brought "mainstream" by Zimmerman agency (part of the Omnicom Group) as a way for multiunit businesses, like franchises and car dealers, to respond quickly and specifically to varying geographic or competitive needs.[38]

In-House Agencies. An **in-house agency** is often referred to as the advertising department in a firm and takes responsibility for the planning and preparation of advertising materials. This option has the advantage of greater coordination and control in all phases of the advertising and promotion process. Some prominent advertisers who do most of their work in-house are Gap, Calvin Klein, and Revlon. The advertiser's own personnel have control over and knowledge of marketing activities, such as product development and distribution tactics. Another advantage is that the firm can essentially keep all the profits from commissions that an external agency would have earned. While the advantages of doing advertising work in-house are attractive, there are two severe limitations. First, there may be a lack of objectivity, thereby constraining the execution of all phases of the advertising process. Second, it is highly unlikely that an in-house agency could ever match the breadth and depth of talent available in an external agency.

Media Specialists. While not technically agencies, **media specialists** are in organizations that specialize in buying media time and space and offer media strategy consulting to advertising agencies and advertisers. The task of strategic coordination of media and promotional efforts has become more complex because of the prolif-

---

38. Jonah Bloom, "Zimmerman's Virtual Agency Marks the Rise of Machines," *Advertising Age*, January 15, 2007, 15.

eration of media options and extensive use of promotional tools beyond advertising. An example of one of these specialists is Starcom MediaVest Group (http://www .starcommedia.com), a subsidiary of Paris-based Publicis Groupe. Starcom encompasses an integrated network of nearly 3,800 contact architects specializing in media management, Internet and digital communications, response media, entertainment marketing, sports sponsorships, event marketing, and multicultural media. Starcom's network of 110 offices in 104 countries focuses on brand building for many of the world's leading companies.

One additional advantage of using media specialists is that since they buy media in large quantities, they often acquire media time at a much lower cost than an agency or advertiser could. Also, media specialists often have time and space in inventory and can offer last-minute placement to advertisers. Media-buying services have been a part of the advertising industry structure for many years. In recent years, however, media planning has been added to the task of simply buying media space. At one point, Unilever, the Dutch consumer products conglomerate, decided to turn over its $575 million media-buying and planning tasks to a specialized agency, MindShare Worldwide. Firms are finding that the firm that buys space can provide keen insights into the media strategy as well.[39]

Promotion Agencies. While advertisers often rely on an advertising agency as a steering organization for their promotional efforts, many specialized agencies often enter the process and are referred to as **promotion agencies**. This is because advertising agencies, even full-service agencies, will concentrate more on the advertising and often provide only a few key ancillary services for other promotional efforts. This is particularly true in the current era, in which new media are offering so many different ways to communicate to target markets. Promotion agencies can handle everything from sampling to event promotions to in-school promotional tie-ins. Descriptions of the types of agencies and their services follow.

Direct Marketing and Database Agencies. These agencies (sometimes also called **direct response agencies**) provide a variety of direct marketing services. **Direct marketing agencies** and **database agencies** maintain and manage large databases of mailing lists as one of their services. These firms can design direct marketing campaigns that use either mail or telemarketing, or direct response campaigns using all forms of media. These agencies help advertisers construct databases of target customers, merge databases, develop promotional materials, and then execute the campaign. In many cases, these agencies maintain **fulfillment centers**, which ensure that customers receive the product ordered through direct mail. Direct Media, Inc. (http://www .directmedia.com) is the world's largest list management and list brokerage firm, providing clients with services in both the consumer and the business-to-business markets across the country and around the world.

Many of these agencies are set up to provide creative and production services to clients. These firms will design and help execute direct response advertising campaigns using traditional media such as radio, television, magazines, and newspapers. Also, some firms can prepare **infomercials** for clients: a five- to 60-minute information program that promotes a brand and offers direct purchase to viewers. AdProducers.com is an online community that lists infomercial producers around the world. It is part of the Ad Producer.com/Entertainment Producer.com network of advertising providers.

E-Commerce Agencies. There are so many new and different kinds of e-commerce agencies that it is hard to categorize all of them. **E-commerce agencies** handle a

---

39. Richard Linnett, "Unilever Win Affirms MindShare Strategy," *Advertising Age,* December 4, 2000, 4.

variety of planning and execution activities related to promotions using electronic commerce. Note that these agencies are different from the interactive agencies discussed earlier. They do not create Web sites or banner ads, but rather help firms conduct all forms of promotion through electronic media, particularly the Internet. They can run sweepstakes, issue coupons, help in sampling, and do direct response campaigns (see Exhibit 2.10). A firm like 24/7 Real Media (http://www.247media .com) offers advertisers the option of providing consumers with online coupons, contests, and loyalty programs. Old Navy, American Airlines, the World Wildlife Fund, Cisco, and 3M are a few of the firms that have signed on with e-commerce agencies to add another dimension to their IBP campaigns. Another of these new media e-commerce organizations is DoubleClick (featured in Exhibit 2.2 earlier in the chapter), which provides services related to Internet advertising, targeting technology, complete advertising management software solutions, direct response Internet advertising, and Internet advertising developed for regional and local businesses. The best way to view these new e-commerce agencies is to understand that they can provide all forms of promotion using new media technology and usually specializing in Internet solutions.

Sales Promotion Agencies. These specialists design and then operate contests, sweepstakes, special displays, or coupon campaigns for advertisers. It is important to recognize that these agencies can specialize in **consumer sales promotions** and will focus on price-off deals, coupons, sampling, rebates, and premiums. Other firms specialize in **trade-market sales promotions** designed to help advertisers use promotions aimed at wholesalers, retailers, vendors, and trade resellers. These agencies are experts in designing incentive programs, trade shows, sales force contests, in-store merchandising, and point-of-purchase materials.

Event-Planning Agencies. Event sponsorship can also be targeted to household consumers or the trade market. **Event-planning agencies** and organizers are experts in finding locations, securing dates, and putting together a team of people to pull off a promotional event: audio/visual people, caterers, security experts, entertainers, celebrity participants, or whoever is necessary to make the event come about. The event-planning organization will also often take over the task of advertising the event and making sure the press provides coverage (publicity) of the event. When an advertiser sponsors an entire event, such as a PGA golf tournament, managers will work closely with the event-planning agencies. If an advertiser is just one of several sponsors of an event, such as a NASCAR race, then it has less control over planning.

Design Firms. Designers and graphics specialists do not get nearly enough credit in the advertising and promotion process. If you take a job in advertising or promotion, your designer will be one of your first and most important partners. While designers are rarely involved in strategy planning, they are intimately involved in the execution of the advertising or IBP effort. In the most basic sense, **designers** help a firm create a **logo**—the graphic mark that identifies a company—and other visual representations that promote an identity for a firm. This mark will appear on everything from advertising to packaging to the company stationery, business cards, and signage. But beyond the logo, graphic designers will also design most of the materials used in supportive communications such as the package design, coupons, in-store displays, brochures, outdoor banners for events, newsletters, and direct mail pieces. One of the largest consumer package goods firms in the world recently made a larger commitment to design across all aspects of its marketing and promotion, claiming that design was critical to "winning customers in the store with packaging and displays [being] major factors in the outcome."[40]

Public Relations Firms. These firms manage an organization's relationships with the media, the local community, competitors, industry associations, and government organizations. The tools of public relations include press releases, feature stories, lobbying, spokespersons, and company newsletters. Most advertisers do not like to handle their own public relations tasks for two reasons. First, public relations requires highly specialized skills and talent not normally found in an advertising firm. Second, managers are too close to public relations problems and may not be capable of handling a situation, particularly a negative situation, with measured public responses. For these reasons, advertisers, and even advertising agencies, turn to outside **public relations firms**. In keeping with the movement to incorporate the Internet across all forms of promotion, there are even organizations that will handle putting all of a firm's news releases online. One such firm is PR Newswire (http://www.prnews wire.com).

In a search for more and distinctive visibility for their brands, advertisers have been turning to public relations firms to achieve a wide range of film and television placements.[41] William Morris, originally a talent agency and now a public relations firm, has 16 consultants working with top consumer brands like Anheuser-Busch. William Morris succeeded in getting Budweiser to be the first beer advertiser on the Academy Awards.

Agency Services. Advertising and promotion agencies offer a wide range of services. The advertiser may need a large, global, full-service advertising agency to plan, prepare, and execute its advertising and IBP campaigns. On the other hand, a creative boutique may offer the right combination of services. Similarly, a large promotion firm might be needed to manage events and promotions while a design firm is enlisted for design work,

---

40. Jack Neff, "P&G Boosts Design's Role in Marketing," *Advertising Age,* February 9, 2004, 1, 52.
41. Betsy Streisand, "Why Great American Brands Are Doing Lunch," *Business 2.0,* September 2003, 146–150.

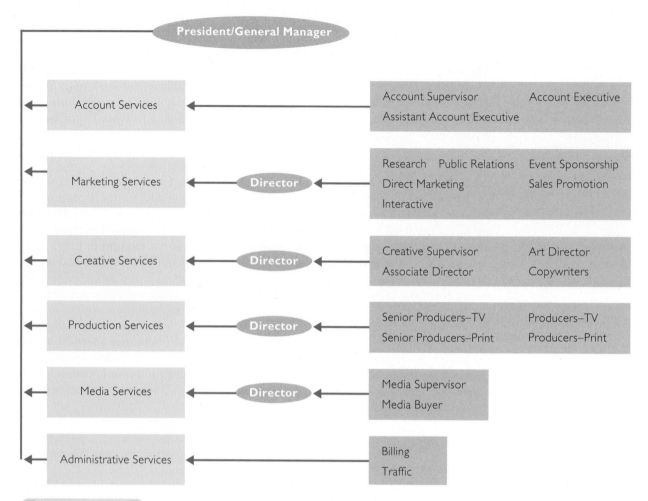

EXHIBIT 2.11

The typical structure of a full-service advertising agency. Note that this structure includes significant integrated brand promotion (IBP) services as well as advertising services.

but nothing else. The most important issue, however, is for the advertiser and the agency to negotiate and reach an agreement on the services being provided before any agency is hired. Exhibit 2.11 shows the typical organizational structure of a full-service advertising agency that also provides a significant number of IBP services. The types of services commonly offered by advertising and promotion agencies are discussed in the following sections.

Account Services. These services are offered by managers who have titles such as account executive, account supervisor, or account manager, and who work with clients to determine how the brand can benefit most from promotion. **Account services** entail identifying the benefits a brand offers, its target audiences, and the best competitive positioning, and then developing a complete promotion plan. In some cases, account services in an agency can provide basic marketing and consumer behavior research, but in general the client should bring this information to the table. Knowing the target segment, the brand's values, and the positioning strategy are really the responsibility of the advertiser (more on this in Chapters 5 and 6).

Account services managers also work with the client in translating cultural and consumer values into advertising and promotional messages through the creative services in the agency. Finally, they work with media services to develop an effective media strategy for determining the best vehicles for reaching the targeted audiences. One of the primary tasks in account services is to keep the various agency teams' creative, production, and media on schedule and within budget (more about this in Chapter 8 when we look at the advertising plan).

FJC[ ]N
AIM HIGHER.

EXHIBIT 2.12

Advertising agencies, from large global agencies to smaller regional shops, provide a wide range of services for clients. Their greatest contribution to the process is, perhaps, their creative prowess. Here, FJCandN, a regional agency, once implored advertisers to "aim higher." A nice bit of creativity to tout the agency's creative talents.

Marketing Research Services. Research conducted by an agency for a client usually consists of the agency locating studies (conducted by commercial research organizations) that have bearing on a client's market or advertising and promotion objectives. The research group will help the client interpret the research and communicate these interpretations to the creative and media people. If existing studies are not sufficient, research may be conducted by the agency itself. As mentioned in the account services discussion, some agencies can assemble consumers from the target audience to evaluate different versions of proposed advertising and determine whether messages are being communicated effectively.

Many agencies have established the position of account planner to coordinate the research effort. An **account planner**'s stature in the organization is on par with an account executive. The account planner is assigned to clients to ensure that research input is included at each stage of development of campaign materials. Some agency leaders, like Jay Chiat of Chiat/Day, think that account planning has been the best new business tool ever invented.[42] Others are a bit more measured in their assessment. Jon Steel, director of account planning at Goody, Silverstein and Partners, described account planning this way: "[Account] planning, when used properly, is the best *old* business tool ever invented."[43] Either way, agencies are understanding that research, signaled by the appointment of an account planner, is key to successful promotional campaigns. The advertising research issue is considered in detail in Chapter 7.

Creative and Production Services. The **creative services** group in an agency comes up with the concepts that express the value of a company's brand in interesting and memorable ways. In simple terms, the creative services group develops the message that will be delivered though advertising, sales promotion, direct marketing, event sponsorship, or public relations. Howard Davis, retired CEO of the full-service advertising agency Tracy-Locke, refers to this process in the industry as the "art of commerce."[44]

Clients will push their agencies hard to come up with interesting and expressive ways to represent the brand. Geoffrey Frost, vice president of consumer communications for Motorola's Personal Communications Sector, expressed his company's approach to demanding creative excellence by saying, "What we've challenged the agencies to do was to help us to figure out how to position Motorola as the company that has really figured out the future."[45] That statement beautifully captures the kind of creative services advertisers seek from their agencies. The creative group in an agency will typically include a creative director, art director, illustrators or designers, and copywriters. In specialized promotion agencies, event planners, contest experts, and interactive media specialists will join the core group. Exhibit 2.12 shows how a small advertising agency, FJCandN, promoted its own creative services.

42.   Jon Steel, *Truth, Lies & Advertising: The Art of Account Planning* (New York: John Wiley & Sons, 1998), 42.
43.   Ibid, 43.
44.   Howard Davis expressed his views in this regard during a keynote speech at the Montana State University College of Business delivered on December 13, 2000.
45.   Tobi Elkin, "Motorola Tenders Brand Challenge," *Advertising Age,* August 14, 2000, 14.

Production services include producers (and sometimes directors) who take creative ideas and turn them into advertisements, direct mail pieces, or events materials. Producers generally manage and oversee the endless details of production of the finished advertisement or other promotion material. Advertising agencies maintain the largest and most sophisticated creative and production staffs.

Media Planning and Buying Services. This service was discussed earlier as a specialized agency through which advertisers can contract for media buying and planning. Advertising agencies themselves provide **media planning and buying services** similar to those of the specialized agencies. The central challenge is to determine how a client's message can most effectively and efficiently reach the target audience. Media planners and buyers examine an enormous number of options to put together an effective media plan within the client's budget. But media planning and buying is much more than simply buying ad space, timing a coupon distribution, or scheduling an event. A wide range of media strategies can be implemented to enhance the impact of the message. Agencies are helping clients sort through the blizzard of new media options such as CD-ROMs, videocassettes, interactive media, and the Internet. Most large agencies, such as Omnicom, Chiat/Day, and Fallon McElligott, set up their own interactive media groups years ago in response to client demands that the Internet media option be included in nearly every IBP plan. The three positions typically found in the media area are media planner, media buyer, and media researcher. This is where most of the client's money is spent; it's very important.

Administrative Services. Like other businesses, agencies have to manage their business affairs. Agencies have personnel departments, accounting and billing departments, and sales staffs that go out and sell the agency to clients. Most important to clients is the traffic department, which has the responsibility of monitoring projects to be sure that deadlines are met. Traffic managers make sure the creative group and media services are coordinated so that deadlines for getting promotional materials to printers and media organizations are met. The job requires tremendous organizational skills and is critical to delivering the other services to clients.

Agency Compensation. The way agencies get paid is somewhat different from the way other professional organizations are compensated. While accountants, doctors, lawyers, and consultants often work on a fee basis, advertising agencies often base compensation on a commission or markup system. Promotion agencies occasionally work on a commission basis, but more often work on a fee or contract basis. We will examine the four most prevalent agency compensation methods: commissions, markup charges, fee systems, and newer pay-for-results plans.

Commissions. The traditional method of agency compensation is the **commission system**, which is based on the amount of money the advertiser spends on media. Under this method, 15 percent of the total amount billed by a media organization is retained by the advertising or promotion agency as compensation for all costs in creating advertising/promotion for the advertiser. The only variation is that the rate typically changes to 16⅔ percent for outdoor media. Exhibit 2.13 shows a simple example of how the commission system works.

EXHIBIT 2.13

Calculation of agency compensation using a traditional commission-based compensation system.

Agency bills client   **$1,000,000**   for television airtime

–

Agency pays television media   **$ 850,000**   for television airtime

=

Agency earns   **$ 150,000**   **15% commission**

Over the past 15 years, and particularly in the past three years with the change in consumer media use, the wisdom of the commission system has been questioned by both advertisers and agencies themselves. As the chairman of a large full-service agency put it long ago, "It's incenting us to do the wrong thing, to recommend network TV and national magazines and radio when other forms of communication like direct marketing or public relations might do the job better."[46] About half of all advertisers compensate their agencies using a commission system based on media cost. But only about 14 percent of advertisers responding to a recent survey still use the traditional 15 percent commission. More advertisers are using other percentage levels of commission, often negotiated levels, as the basis for agency compensation. But even the use of media-based commissions is under fire. Jim Stengel, global marketing officer for Procter & Gamble, laid the foundation for change several years ago when he told American Association of Advertising Agencies members at a media conference that the media-based model dependent on the 30-second spot is "broken" and that the industry needs to understand the complexity of media use by contemporary consumers.[47] This message indirectly calls into question the whole issue of basing compensation on media billings at all.

Markup Charges. Another method of agency compensation is to add a percentage **markup charge** to a variety of services the agency purchases from outside suppliers. In many cases, an agency will turn to outside contractors for art, illustration, photography, printing, research, and production. The agency then, in agreement with the client, adds a markup charge to these services. The reason markup charges became prevalent in the industry is that many promotion agencies were providing services that did not use traditional media. Since the traditional commission method was based on media charges, there was no way for these agencies to receive payment for their work. This being the case, the markup system was developed. A typical markup on outside services is 17.65 to 20 percent.

Fee Systems. A **fee system** is much like that used by consultants or attorneys, whereby the advertiser and the agency agree on an hourly rate for different services provided. The hourly rate can be based on average salaries within departments or on some agreed-on hourly rate across all services. This is the most common basis for promotion agency compensation.

Another version of the fee system is a fixed fee, or contract, set for a project between the client and the agency. It is imperative that the agency and the advertiser agree on precisely what services will be provided, by what departments in the agency, over what specified period of time. In addition, the parties must agree on which supplies, materials, travel costs, and other expenses will be reimbursed beyond the fixed fee. Fixed-fee systems have the potential for causing serious rifts in the client-agency relationship because out-of-scope work can easily spiral out of control when so many variables are at play. When such controversies arise, the client-agency relationship is damaged and trust suffers, as discussed in the Ethics box on the next page.

Agencies are generally vigorously opposed to the fee system approach. They argue that creative impact cannot be measured in "work hours" but rather must be measured in "the value of the materials the agency is creating for the client."[48]

Pay-for-Results. Recently, many advertisers and agencies alike have been working on compensation programs called **pay-for-results** that base the agency's fee on the achievement of agreed-on results. Historically, agencies have not agreed to be

46.   Patricia Sellers, "Do You Need Your Ad Agency?" *Fortune,* November 15, 1993, 148
47.   Jeff Neff and Lisa Sanders, "It's Broken," *Advertising Age,* February 16, 2004, 1, 30.
48.   Lisa Sanders and Alice Z. Cuneo, "Fed-Up Agencies Quit Punching the Clock," *Advertising Age,* January 27, 2007.

ETHICS

Of Course I Trust You—Meet My Auditor

It used to be that advertisers and their agencies had long histories together, and a handshake was the primary way deals got sealed. Well, times have changed. As you saw earlier in the chapter, agencies with 20- or even 30-year histories with a client are being dumped—usually with little ceremony. The days when the agency-advertiser relationship was built purely on trust seem to be gone forever. When advertisers like General Motors refer to their agencies as "flabby organizations," you can be pretty sure that the atmosphere in the industry is changed for good. It doesn't help that recently a federal grand jury indicted two agency executives on charges of defrauding the U.S. government with excess labor charges on a campaign developed for the Office of National Drug Control.

So what has replaced the handshake and the toast at dinner as the basis for the client/agency relationship? Guess who's coming to dinner—the auditor. Today, clients are using outside firms to scrutinize all aspects of agency work, from creative services to billing practices. One such scrutinizer is called Firm Decisions. It is an international ad-agency auditing firm that acts as an intermediary between advertisers and agencies. An example of the work done by Firm Decisions: On one agency project invoice, it found that an agency staffer had billed an average of 17 hours a day including weekends for an entire month. On one day, she even logged 26 hours. David Brocklehurst, founder of Firm Decisions, commented on this particular audit with the deadpan observation, "Even if it was true, how productive could she be?"

So the friendly partnership days are over, and the auditor seems to be showing up more and more often. This is not to say that agencies are not productive and clients aren't happy with the agencies' work. But it really isn't as much fun as it used to be.

Sources: Claire Atkinson, "GM Ad Boss Takes Agencies to Task," ***Advertising Age,*** June 30, 2003, 1, 26; Erin White, "Making Sure the Work Fits the Bill," ***Wall Street Journal,*** February 5, 2004, B8.

evaluated on results because results have often been narrowly defined as sales. The key effects on sales are related to factors outside the agency's control such as product features, pricing strategy, and distribution programs (that is, the overall marketing mix, not just advertising or IBP). An agency may agree to be compensated based on achievement of sales levels, but more often (and more appropriately) communications objectives such as awareness, brand identification, or brand feature knowledge among target audiences will serve as the main results criteria.

One of the most difficult tasks in the compensation system is coordinating all the agencies and coordinating how they get paid. As you have seen, more advertisers are using more different forms of promotion and enlisting the help of multiple agencies. A key to IBP here is integrated agency communication. When all of an advertiser's agencies are working together and coordinating their efforts, not only is integrated brand promotion achieved, but better relations between agencies are achieved.[49]

As if this long list of agencies and intricate compensation schemes weren't complicated enough, let's complicate things a bit more and consider a fairly long list of external facilitators and what their agencies rely on to create and execute promotional campaigns.

 External Facilitators. While agencies offer clients many services and are adding more, advertisers often need to rely on specialized external facilitators in planning, preparing, and executing promotional campaigns. **External facilitators** are organizations or individuals that provide specialized services to advertisers and agencies. The most important of these external facilitators are discussed in the following sections.

Marketing and Advertising Research Firms. Many firms rely on outside assistance during the planning phase of advertising. Research firms such as Burke and Simmons can perform original research for advertisers using focus groups, surveys, or experiments to assist in understanding the potential market or consumer perceptions of a product or services. Other research firms, such as SRI International, routinely

49.   Allen Winneker, "Avoiding Bonus Envy," *Promo Magazine,* November 1999, 35–37.

collect data (from grocery store scanners, for example) and have these data available for a fee.

Advertisers and their agencies also seek measures of promotional program effectiveness after a campaign has run. After an advertisement or promotion has been running for some reasonable amount of time, firms such as Starch INRA Hooper will run recognition tests on print advertisements. Other firms such as Burke offer day-after recall tests of broadcast advertisements. Some firms specialize in message testing to determine whether consumers find advertising messages appealing and understandable.

Consultants. A variety of **consultants** specialize in areas related to the promotional process. Advertisers can seek out marketing consultants for assistance in the planning stage. Creative and communications consultants provide insight on issues related to message strategy and message themes. Consultants in event planning and sponsorships offer their expertise to both advertisers and agencies. Public relations consultants often work with top management. Media experts can help an advertiser determine the proper media mix and efficient media placement.

Three new types of consultants have emerged in recent years. One is a database consultant, who works with both advertisers and agencies. Organizations such as Shepard Associates help firms identify and then manage databases that allow for the development of integrated marketing communications programs. Diverse databases from research sources discussed earlier can be merged or cross-referenced in developing effective communications programs. Another new type of consultant specializes in Web site development and management. These consultants typically have the creative skills to develop Web sites and corporate home pages and the technical skills to advise advertisers on managing the technical aspects of the user interface. The third type of consultant works with a firm to integrate information across a wide variety of customer contacts and to organize all this information to achieve customer relationship management (CRM). Business Objects is one software firm that helps consultants create effective programs (http://www.businessobjects .com). (See Exhibit 2.14.)

In recent years, traditional management consultants—such as IBM, Accenture, and McKinsey—have started to work with agencies on structure and business strategy.[50] These sorts of consultants can also advise on image strategy, market research procedure, and process and account planning. But the combination of traditional consulting and advertising has not always produced compelling results, and the typical role of consultants—focusing on marketing, creative, or technical issues—is the more likely role for consultants in the future.

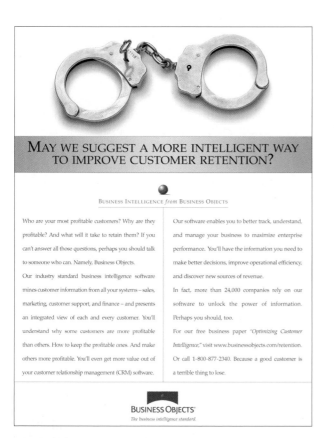

EXHIBIT 2.14

Business Objects is the world's leading business intelligence software company. Business intelligence enables organizations to track, understand, and manage enterprise performance. The company's solutions leverage the information that is stored in an array of corporate databases, enterprise resource planning, and customer relationship management (CRM) systems. http://www.businessobjects.com

50.   Matthew Creamer, "March of the Management Consultants," *Advertising Age,* June 5, 2006, 1, 53.

is it:

what happens when
cousins marry

a centerfold in
Orthodontia Illustrated

Eugene R. Wilton III
Gross Pointe, MI
Platinum Customer #432-A3

Are your online customers
actually who they appear to
be? Now you can know for
sure. With Hyperion® Web
Site Analysis Suite, part
of the eCRM Analysis
family, you can quickly
gather and analyze key
online customer data—so
you can positively identify
who's really visiting your
site—and why. It's insight
that turns hits into sales...
and one-time lookers into
long-term buyers. Which is
sure to make everyone smile.

Hyperion®
what's going on

For a Free White Paper "Customer Analysis: A Survival Guide"
go to www.hyperion.com/free-crm-whitepaper or call 1-888-957-8841.

EXHIBIT 2.15

Software firms like Hyperion are providing advertisers with key assistance in the areas of audience analysis or broadband communications. Hyperion specializes in gathering and analyzing online customer data from Web site visits. http://www.hyperion.com

Production Facilitators. External **production facilitators** offer essential services both during and after the production process. Production is the area where advertisers and their agencies rely most heavily on external facilitators. All forms of media advertising require special expertise that even the largest full-service agency, much less an advertiser, typically does not retain on staff. In broadcast production, directors, production managers, songwriters, camera operators, audio and lighting technicians, and performers are all essential to preparing a professional, high-quality radio or television ad. Production houses can provide the physical facilities, including sets, stages, equipment, and crews, needed for broadcast production. Similarly, in preparing print advertising, brochures, and direct mail pieces, graphic artists, photographers, models, directors, and producers may be hired from outside the advertising agency or firm to provide the specialized skills and facilities needed in preparing advertisements. In-store promotions is another area where designing and producing materials requires the skills of a specialty organization.

The specific activities performed by external facilitators and the techniques employed by the personnel in these firms will be covered in greater detail in Part Three of the text. For now, it is sufficient to recognize the role these firms play in the advertising and promotions industry.

Software Firms. An interesting and complex new category of facilitator in advertising and promotion is that of software firms. The technology in the industry, particularly new media technology, has expanded so rapidly that a variety of software firms facilitate the process. Some of these firms are well established and well known, such as Microsoft, Novell, and Oracle. But others, such as Hyperion (see Exhibit 2.15), are new to the scene. These firms provide software ranging from the gathering and analysis of Web surfer behavior to broadband streaming audio and video to managing relationships with trade partners. These firms provide the kind of expertise that is so esoteric that even the most advanced full-service or e-commerce agency would have to seek their assistance.

5 Media Organizations. The next level in the industry structure, shown in Exhibit 2.16, comprises media available to advertisers. The media available for placing advertising, such as broadcast and print media, are well known to most of us simply because we're exposed to them daily. In addition, the Internet has created media organizations through which advertisers can direct and distribute their advertising and promotional messages.

Advertisers and their agencies turn to media organizations that own and manage the media access to consumers. In traditional media, major television networks such as NBC and Fox, as well as national magazines such as *U.S. News & World Report* and *People,* provide advertisers with time and space for their messages at considerable cost.

EXHIBIT 2.16

Advertisers have an array of media organizations available to them. Notice that the choices range from traditional print and broadcast media to broadband and media conglomerates.

Broadcast

Television
Major network
Independent station
Cable
Broadband

Radio
Network
Local

Print

Magazines
By geographic coverage
By content

Direct Mail
Brochures
Catalogs
Videos

Newspapers
National
Statewide
Local

Specialty
Handbills
Programs

Interactive Media

Online Computer Services

Home-Shopping Broadcasts

**Interactive Broadcast
Entertainment Programming**

Kiosks

CD-ROMs

Internet

iPods

Cell Phones

Support Media

Outdoor
Billboards
Transit
Posters

Directories
Yellow Pages
Electronic directories

Premiums
Keychains
Calendars
Logo clothing
Pens

Point-of-Purchase Displays

**Film and Program Brand
Placement**

Event Sponsorship

Media Conglomerates

Multiple Media Combinations
Time Warner
Viacom
Turner Broadcasting
Comcast
Disney
Clear Channel

STILL WAITING FOR HIGH-SPEED INTERNET ACCESS? ↑ **JUST LOOK UP.**

Tired of waiting for broadband? StarBand® is here now. StarBand is the first company to deliver two-way, high-speed Internet access via satellite to consumers. It's always on and it's available virtually everywhere. If you can see the southern sky, you can get StarBand. Just look up: StarBand is available now at selected DISH Network™ retailers and through MSN® HighSpeed - Satellite at your local RadioShack® store. For more info go to www.StarBand.com or call toll-free 1-800-421-3464.

STARBAND
www.StarBand.com

EXHIBIT 2.17

Broadband offers advertisers the ability to send audio and video through the Internet in a way that lets Web users customize their viewing and listening experiences. To learn more about various streaming services and media-rich content being developed for broadband, visit Akamai (http://www.akamai .com). http://www.starband.com

Other media options are more useful for reaching narrowly defined target audiences. Specialty programming on cable television, tightly focused direct mail pieces, and a well-designed Internet campaign may be better ways to reach a specific audience. One of the new media options, broadband, offers advertisers the chance to target very specific audiences. Broadband allows Internet users to basically customize their programming by calling on only specific broadcasts from various providers. For example, The FeedRoom (http://www.feedroom.com) is an interactive broadband television news network that allows Web users to customize what news broadcasts they receive. Advertisers can target different types of audiences using broadband for interactive broadcasts. The latest step in broadband communications is wireless broadband; firms are already developing technology and access for consumers (see Exhibit 2.17).

Note the inclusion of media conglomerates in the list shown in Exhibit 2.16. This category is included because organizations such as Viacom and Comcast own and operate companies in broadcast, print, and interactive media. Viacom brings you cable networks such as Nickelodeon, VH1, and TV Land. The 2000 merger of AOL and Time Warner (the company, briefly known as AOL Time Warner, is now referred to again as simply Time Warner) created the world's largest media conglomerate, one that provides broadcasting, cable, music, film, print publishing, and a dominant Internet presence.[51]

The support media organizations listed in Exhibit 2.16 include all those places that advertisers want to put their messages other than mainstream traditional or interactive media. Often referred to as out-of-home media, these support media organizations include transit companies (bus and taxi boards), billboard organizations, specialized directory companies, and sports and performance arenas for sponsorships, display materials, and premium items.

Target Audiences. The structure of the advertising and promotion industry (check Exhibit 2.5 again) and the flow of communication would obviously be incomplete without an audience: no audience, no communication. One interesting thing about the audiences for promotional communications is that, with the exception of household consumers, they are also the advertisers who use advertising and IBP communications. We are all familiar with the type of advertising directed at us in our role as consumers: toothpaste, window cleaner, sport-utility vehicles, soft drinks, insurance, and on and on. The text is full of advertising by firms targeting household consumers.

But business and government audiences are key to the success of a large number of firms that sell only to business and government buyers. While many of these firms rely heavily on personal selling in their promotional mix, many also use a variety of advertising and IBP tools. KPMG Consulting uses high-profile television and magazine advertising and sponsors events. Many business and trade sellers regularly need public relations, and most use direct mail to communicate with potential customers as a prelude to a personal selling call.

51.   Clair Atkinson, "AOL Sees Future in Ad Networks," *Advertising Age,* December 11, 2006, 4.

SUMMARY

 Discuss important trends transforming the advertising and promotion industry.

Recent years have proven to be a period of dramatic change for the advertising and promotion industry. The late-1990s trend towards agency consolidation has seen a reversal as numerous industry acquisitions and mergers failed to impress clients or produce greater profitability. Next, the proliferation of media from cable television to the Internet has created new advertising options, and giant media conglomerates are expected to control a majority of these television, radio, and Internet properties. Media proliferation has in turn led to increasing media clutter and fragmentation, reducing the effectiveness of advertisements; as a result, advertisers are utilizing sales promotions, event sponsorships, and public relations to supplement and enhance the primary advertising effort. Finally, today's consumers have greater control over the information they receive about brands. New technology applications from blogs to TiVo empower consumers and diminish the role of advertising in the consumption process. These developments are forcing advertisers to think differently about advertising and IBP.

 Describe the advertising and promotion industry's size, structure, and participants.

Many different types of organizations make up the industry. To truly appreciate what advertising is all about, one must understand who does what and in what order in the creation and delivery of an advertising or IBP campaign. The process begins with an organization that has a message it wishes to communicate to a target audience. This is the advertiser. Next, advertising and promotion agencies are typically hired to launch and manage a campaign, but other external facilitators are often brought in to perform specialized functions, such as assisting in the production of promotional materials or managing databases for efficient direct marketing campaigns. These external facilitators also include consultants with whom advertisers and their agencies may confer regarding advertising and IBP strategy decisions. All advertising and promotional campaigns must use some type of media to reach target markets. Advertisers and their agencies must therefore also work with companies that have media time or space.

 Discuss the role played by advertising and promotion agencies, the services provided by these agencies, and how the agencies are compensated.

Advertising and promotion agencies come in many varieties and offer diverse services to clients with respect to planning, preparing, and executing advertising and IBP campaigns. These services include market research and marketing planning, the actual creation and production of ad materials, the buying of media time or space for placement of the ads, and traffic management to keep production on schedule. Some advertising agencies appeal to clients by offering a full array of services under one roof; others such as creative boutiques develop a particular expertise and win clients with their specialized skills. Promotion agencies specialize in one or more of the other forms of promotion beyond advertising. New media agencies are proliferating to serve the Internet and other new media needs of advertisers. The four most prevalent ways to compensate an agency for services rendered are commissions, markups, fee systems, and the new pay-for-results programs.

 Identify key external facilitators who assist in planning and executing advertising and integrated brand promotion campaigns.

Marketing and advertising research firms assist advertisers and their agencies in understanding the market environment. Consultants of all sorts from marketing strategy through event planning and retail display are another form of external facilitators. Perhaps the most widely used facilitators are in the area of production of promotional materials. In advertising, a wide range of outside facilitators is used in the production of both broadcast and print advertising. In promotions, designers and planners are called on to assist in creation and execution of promotional mix tools. Software firms fill a new role in the structure of the industry. These firms provide expertise in tracking and analyzing consumer usage of new media technology.

 Discuss the role played by media organizations in executing effective advertising and integrated brand promotion campaigns.

Media organizations are the essential link in delivering advertising and IBP communications to target audiences. There are traditional media organizations such as television, radio, newspaper, and magazines. Interactive media options include not just the Internet but CD-ROMs, electronic kiosks, and less widely known communications companies. Media conglomerates such as AT&T, Time Warner, and News Corp. control several different aspects of the communications system, from cable broadcast to Internet connections and emerging broadband communications technologies.

KEY TERMS

blog
advertiser
client
trade reseller
advertising agency
full-service agency
creative boutique
interactive agency
in-house agency
media specialist
promotion agency
direct marketing agency

database agency
direct response agency
fulfillment center
infomercial
e-commerce agency
consumer sales promotion
trade-market sales promotion
event-planning agency
designer
logo
public relations firm
account services

account planner
creative services
production services
media planning and buying services
commission system
markup charge
fee system
pay-for-results
external facilitator
consultant
production facilitator

QUESTIONS

1.   Briefly describe the power struggle now taking place in the advertising industry. Who, beyond the agencies, is exerting power in the industry, and in what ways?

2.   Do you think the increasing independence and control consumers gain through new technologies like TiVo, the Internet, digital music players, and cell phones will make advertising and product branding less important? Explain.

3.   What are the primary characteristics of second-generation Internet use and services, the so-called Web 2.0? In what ways is this advent of Internet technology different—or not—from the Internet's early evolution?

4.   The U.S. government spends millions of dollars each year trying to recruit young men and women into the armed services. What forms of advertising and IBP communication would be best suited to this recruiting effort?

5.   Huge advertisers such as Procter & Gamble spend billions of dollars on advertising every year, yet they still rely on advertising agencies to prepare most of their advertising. Why doesn't a big company like this just do all its own advertising in-house?

6.   What is the advertiser's role in IBP?

7.   As advertisers become more enamored with the idea of IBP, why would it make sense for an advertising agency to develop a reputation as a full-service provider?

8.   Explain the viewpoint that a commission-based compensation system may actually give ad agencies an incentive to do the wrong things for their clients.

9.   What makes production of promotional materials the area where advertisers and their agencies are most likely to call on external facilitators for expertise and assistance?

10. Give an example of how the skills of a public relations firm might be employed to reinforce the message that a sponsor is trying to communicate through other forms of promotion.

EXPERIENTIAL EXERCISES

1. Break up into groups and simulate a small business planning to advertise a new or innovative product. Once you have chosen a general industry and a product to advertise, perform the following tasks and present your answers to the class.

a. Pick the main trend in the advertising industry that you think would have the greatest effect for advertising your product.

b. Determine what advertiser category your business is classified under, and explain the role advertising plays for organizations in that category. How does this apply to your campaign?

c. Select one type of advertising or promotion agency that would be the most effective in providing appropriate services to achieve your advertising or promotion goals. Explain your choice.

d. Select one external facilitator that would provide specialization services to help ensure the success of your campaign and explain your reasoning.

e. Choose an existing media organization that would be best suited for advertising and promoting your brand's identity. What makes it the best choice?

2. This chapter highlights some of the challenges facing advertisers and agencies as consumers have gained greater control of information sources—blocking telemarketing calls, for instance, and carefully guarding the privacy of cell phone numbers and other contact information.

Working in the same groups, brainstorm ways that advertisers still could reach out to consumers and invite them to learn more about your brand or product. As your team develops ideas, also explain how you would address these questions:

a. What ethical issues might arise in your approach to consumers? How would you navigate privacy concerns?

b. Are there any legal risks or potential challenges to your approach?

c. Cadillac's marketing chief talks in this chapter about finding ways to "open their doors and lure customers in." How do your ideas accomplish that?

3. Choose a popular brand from a local or national advertiser and try to determine what media organizations the advertiser is using to target its audience. Does the brand have a special site on the Internet? Can you find television or billboard ads for your product? Are there media organizations you couldn't find that you believe would be suitable or innovative for advertising this brand? Explain.

4. Identify the four primary compensation methods discussed in this chapter and discuss which would best hold both clients and agencies to ethical and responsible business practices. What risks exist in each method? Apart from the threat of regulatory inquiries or criminal investigations, discuss why it is important for agency billing systems to be fully transparent and accountable.

CHAPTER 3

After reading and thinking about this chapter, you will be able to do the following:

1

Tell the story of advertising's birth.

2

Describe the past and current relationship between advertisers, retailers, and consumers.

3

Discuss several significant eras in the evolution of advertising in the United States, and relate important changes in advertising practice to fundamental changes in society and culture. How did successful advertising leverage the social and cultural forces of their day?

4

Tell the story of consumer empowerment and branded entertainment, and understand how it works.

5

Identify forces that will continue to affect the evolution of advertising and integrated brand promotion.

EXHIBIT 3.1

While this ad for Lux laundry powder may seem curious to us today, it reflected the anxiety of the 1930s, during the Great Depression. Just as today's advertising reflects the values of contemporary society, this ad emphasized some very real concerns of the time—the economic well-being and status of women.

The 1935 Lux advertisement shown in Exhibit 3.1 is undoubtedly curious to contemporary audiences. It is, however, typical of its time and probably made perfect sense to its original audience. In the 1930s, in the middle of the Great Depression, anxiety about losing one's husband—and thus one's economic well-being—to divorce was not unfounded. These ads were targeted to a new generation of stay-at-home housewives potentially insecure about their exclusion from the modern world of their husbands, geographically separated from their usually agrarian parents, and living in a rapid and unsure urban environment. These ads went out to women at a time when losing one's source of income (husband) could mean poverty and shame. They were read by women in a society where daily bathing was still relatively new but where self-doubt about personal hygiene was on the rise. Such an ad pushed (maybe even created) just the right buttons. If Lux can "remove perspiration odor from underthings," it might save more than colors and fabrics. It might save affection; it might save marriages. If Bob's romantic indifference continues, Sally may soon be back home with Mom or even on the street. But with Lux on the scene, Bob goes home for dinner.

While some ads today use the very same general strategy to sell deodorants, soaps, and feminine-hygiene products, this ad is not read today as it was in 1935. Ads are part of their times. To really understand advertising and do well in the advertising business, you must understand that successful advertisements convey a particularly perceptive understanding of the contemporary social scene. If you are in the advertising business, you are in the culture and society business. The makers of this 1930s ad really understood, helped create, and used the pressures bearing down on the young married women of that time. Society was changing, and these changes affected Sally and lots of young women like her. Probably many young women of that day felt anxious and uncertain about these changes. This social change and the associated feelings, including uncertainty and anxiety, gave advertisers a chance to offer new products and services to address these very fears, and to leverage this upheaval to their branded benefit. There is a valuable lesson here from history: When the sands of culture and society shift beneath consumers' feet, marketing and advertising opportunities usually present themselves. Today, Sally would likely have a job and be far less economically vulnerable and socially isolated—not to mention that Sally and Bob would both be bathing more often. So we see the 1930s in this ad in the same way that students of the future will view ads of our time: as interesting, revealing, but still somewhat distorted reflections of daily life in the early 21st century. Even in the 1930s, consumers knew that ads were ads; they knew that ads were a little exaggerated; they knew that ads tried to sell things; and they knew that ads didn't exactly mirror everyday life. But ads look enough like life to work, sometimes, but probably not as often as you would think. To get people to do what you want them to do (buy things) is hard work. Consumers are smart; they are not easily convinced. Remember that. Good advertising is in touch with its time and it constantly looks for social and cultural changes that open up marketing and advertising opportunities. Sometimes, these changes and the anxiety and social needs they create can help.

This chapter is about the evolution of advertising. Over the decades, advertisers have tried many different strategies and approaches, and you can learn a lot from their successes and failures. Just about every strategy used today came about decades ago—only the specifics have changed. Studying them will allow you to know when a given advertising technique is really something new, and when and why it worked. You can see how it leveraged the social forces of its time. Besides being interesting, history is very practical. Hint: When you are interviewing for a job in an advertising or marketing position, explain how that advertiser's best ad campaigns worked. That usually impresses them. Sometimes, they ask you that very question. Be ready.

The Rise of Advertising.
In many discussions of the evolution of advertising, the process is often portrayed as having its origins in ancient times, with even primitive peoples practicing some form of advertising. This is substantively incorrect. Whatever those ancients were doing, they weren't advertising. Although the Romans and others communicated with one another with persuasive intent in buying and selling, they were not using advertising. Advertising is a product of modern times and modern media.

Before we get into a brief social history of advertising in the Western world, let's first consider some of the major factors that gave rise to advertising in the first place. Advertising came into being as a result of at least four major factors:

1. The rise of capitalism
2. The Industrial Revolution
3. Manufacturers' pursuit of power in the channel of distribution
4. The rise of modern mass media

The Rise of Capitalism.
The tenets of capitalism warrant that organizations compete for resources, called *capital,* in a free-market environment. Part of the competition for resources involves stimulating demand for the organization's goods or services. When an individual organization successfully stimulates demand, it attracts capital to the organization in the form of money (or other goods) as payment. One of the tools used to stimulate demand is advertising. So, as the Western world turned to capitalism as the foundation of economic systems, the foundation was laid for advertising to become a prominent part of the business environment.

The Industrial Revolution.
The **Industrial Revolution** was an economic force that yielded the need for advertising. Beginning about 1750 in England, the revolution spread to North America and progressed slowly until the early 1800s, when the War of 1812 in the United States boosted domestic production. The emergence of the principle of interchangeable parts and the perfection of the sewing machine, both in 1850, coupled with the American Civil War a decade later, set the scene for widespread industrialization. The Industrial Revolution took Western societies away from household self-sufficiency as a method of fulfilling material needs to dependency on a marketplace as a way of life. The Industrial Revolution was a basic force behind the rapid increase in mass-production goods that required stimulation of demand, something that advertising can be very good at. By providing a need for advertising, the Industrial Revolution was a basic influence in its emergence and growth in Western economies.

Other equally revolutionary developments were part of the broad Industrial Revolution. First, there was a revolution in transportation, most dramatically symbolized by the east-west connection of the United States in 1869 by the railroad. This connection represented the beginnings of the distribution network needed to move the mass quantities of goods for which advertising would help stimulate demand. In the 1840s, the **principle of limited liability**, which restricts an investor's risk in a business venture to only his or her shares in a corporation rather than all personal assets, gained acceptance and resulted in the accumulation of large amounts of capital to finance the Industrial Revolution. Finally, rapid population growth and urbanization began taking place in the 1800s. From 1830 to 1860, the population of the United States nearly tripled, from 12.8 million to 31.4 million. During the same period, the number of cities with more than 20,000 inhabitants grew to 43. Historically, there is a strong relationship between per capita outlays for advertising and an increase in the size of cities.[1] Modernity gave rise to both urbanism and advertising. Overall, the growth and concentration of population provided the marketplaces that were essential to the widespread use of advertising. As the potential grew for goods to be produced, delivered, and introduced to large numbers of people residing in concentrated areas, the stage was set for advertising to emerge and flourish.

②Advertisers, Retailers, and Consumers. Another fundamental influence on the emergence and growth of advertising relates to manufacturers' pursuit of power in the channel of distribution. If a manufacturer can stimulate sizable demand for a brand, then that manufacturer can develop power in the distribution channel and essentially *force* wholesalers and retailers to sell that particular brand. Demand stimulation among consumers causes them to insist on the brand at the retail or wholesale level; retailers and wholesalers then have virtually no choice but to comply with consumers' desires and carry the desired item. Thus, the manufacturer has power in the channel of distribution and not only can force other participants in the channel to stock the brand, but also is in a position to command a higher price for the item. Just recently, this power relationship has swung back in the other direction again due to the increasing power of retail giants like Wal-Mart, Costco, and Tesco. They are so large they can dictate terms to even the P&G's of the world as to what will be carried in their stores and at what price.

A factor that turned out to be critical to manufacturers' pursuit of power was the strategy of **branding** products. Manufacturers had to develop brand names so that consumers could focus their attention on a clearly identified item. Manufacturers began branding previously unmarked commodities, such as work clothes and package goods. In the late 1800s, Ivory (1882), Coca-Cola (1886), Budweiser (1891), and Maxwell House (1892) were among the first branded goods to show up on shopkeepers' shelves. Once a product had a brand mark and name that consumers could identify, marketers gained power. Of course, an essential tool in stimulating demand for a brand was advertising. When Procter & Gamble and Kraft spend many billions of dollars each year to stimulate demand for such popular brands as Crest, Charmin, and Velveeta, wholesalers and retailers carry these brands because advertising has stimulated demand and brought consumers into the retail store looking for and asking for those brands. It is just this sort of pursuit of power by manufacturers that is argued to have caused the widespread use of advertising.[2]

---

1.   Julian Simon, *Issues in the Economics of Advertising* (Urbana: University of Illinois Press, 1970), 41–51.
2.   Vincent P. Norris, "Advertising History—According to the Textbooks," *Journal of Advertising,* vol. 9, no. 3 (1980), 3–12.

The Rise of Modern Mass Media. Advertising is also inextricably tied to the rise of mass communication. With the invention of the telegraph in 1844, a communication revolution was set in motion. The telegraph not only allowed nations to benefit from the inherent efficiencies of rapid communication, but also did a great deal to engender a sense of national identity. People began to know and care about people and things going on thousands of miles away. This changed not only commerce, but society as well.[3] Also, during this period, many new magazines designed for larger and less socially privileged audiences made magazines both a viable mass advertising medium and a democratizing influence on society.[4] Through advertising in these mass-circulation magazines, national brands could be projected into national consciousness. National magazines made national advertising possible; national advertising made national brands possible. Without the rise of mass media, there would be no national brands, and no advertising.

It is critical to realize that for the most part, mass media are supported by advertising. Television networks, radio stations, newspapers, magazines, and Web sites produce shows, articles, films, programs, and Web content not for the ultimate goal of entertaining or informing, but to make a healthy profit from selling brands through advertising and branded entertainment. Media vehicles sell audiences to make money.

3 The Evolution of Advertising.
So far, our discussion of the evolution of advertising has identified the fundamental social and economic influences that fostered its rise. Now we'll turn our focus to the evolution of advertising in practice. Several periods in this evolution can be identified to give us various perspectives on the process of advertising, and how specific brands were able to leverage current events, trends, and social changes to sell things through advertising and other marketing communication.

The Preindustrialization Era (pre-1800).
In the 17th century, printed advertisements appeared in newsbooks (the precursor to the newspaper).[5] The messages were informational in nature and appeared on the last pages of the tabloid. In America, the first newspaper advertisement is said to have appeared in 1704 in the *Boston News Letter*. Two notices were printed under the heading "Advertising" and offered rewards for the return of merchandise stolen from an apparel shop and a wharf.[6]

Advertising grew in popularity during the 18th century in both Britain and the American colonies. The *Pennsylvania Gazette* printed advertisements and was the first newspaper to separate ads with blank lines, which made the ads both easier to read and more prominent.[7] As far as we know; it was also the first newspaper to use illustrations in advertisements. But advertising changed little over the next 70 years. While the early 1800s saw the advent of the penny newspaper, which resulted in widespread distribution of the news media, advertisements in penny newspapers were dominated by simple announcements by skilled laborers. As one historian notes, "Advertising was closer to the classified notices in newspapers than to product promotions in our media today."[8] Advertising was about to change dramatically, however.

3.   James W. Carey, *Communication as Culture: Essays on Media and Society* (Winchester, MA: Unwin Hyman, 1989).

4.   Christopher P. Wilson, "The Rhetoric of Consumption: Mass-Market Magazines and the Demise of the Gentle Reader, 1880–1920," in *The Culture of Consumption: Critical Essays in American History, 1880–1980*, ed. Richard Weightman Fox and T. J. Jackson Lears (New York: Pantheon, 1983), 39–65.

5.   Frank Presbrey, *The History and Development of Advertising* (Garden City, NY: Doubleday, Doran & Co., 1929), 7.

6.   Ibid., 11.

7.   Ibid., 40.

8.   James P. Wood, *The Story of Advertising* (New York: Ronald, 1958), 45–46.

EXHIBIT 3.2

The expansion of newspaper circulation fostered more widespread use of advertising. Unfortunately, some of this new advertising did not contribute positively to the image of the practice. Ads like this one for a patent medicine carried bold claims, such as claiming to cure all liver ailments, including cancer.

The Era of Industrialization (1800 to 1875).
In practice, users of advertising in the mid to late 1800s were trying to cultivate markets for growing production in the context of an increasing urban population. A middle class, spawned by the economic windfall of regular wages from factory jobs, was beginning to emerge. This newly developing populace with economic means was concentrated geographically in cities more than ever before.

By 1850, circulation of the **dailies**, as newspapers were then called, was estimated at 1 million copies per day. The first advertising agent—thought to be Volney Palmer, who opened shop in Philadelphia—basically worked for the newspapers by soliciting orders for advertising and collecting payment from advertisers.[9] This new opportunity to reach consumers was embraced readily by merchants, and at least one newspaper doubled its advertising volume from 1849 to 1850.[10]

With the expansion of newspaper circulation fostered by the railroads, a new era of opportunity emerged for the advertising process. Advertising was not universally hailed as an honorable practice, however. Without any formal regulation of advertising, the process was considered an embarrassment by many segments of society, including some parts of the business community. At one point, firms even risked their credit ratings if they used advertising—banks considered the practice a sign of financial weakness. This image wasn't helped much by advertising for patent medicines, which were the first products heavily advertised on a national scale. These advertisements promised a cure for everything from rheumatism and arthritis to cancer. Exhibit 3.2 shows a typical ad of this period.

The "P. T. Barnum Era" (1875 to 1918).

The only one who could ever reach me was the son of a preacher man.

> —John Hurley and Ronnie Wilkins, "Son of a Preacher Man";
> most notably performed by Dusty Springfield[11]

Shortly after the Civil War in the United States, modern advertising began. This is advertising that we would recognize as advertising. While advertising existed during the era of industrialization, it wasn't until America was well on its way to being an urban, industrialized nation that advertising became a vital and integral part of the social landscape. From about 1875 to 1918, advertising ushered in what has come to be known as **consumer culture**, or a way of life centered on consumption. True, consumer culture was advancing prior to this period, but during this age it really took hold, and the rise of modern advertising had a lot to do with it. Advertising became a full-fledged industry in this period. It was the time of advertising legends:

9.   Daniel Pope, *The Making of Modern Advertising and Its Creators* (New York: William Morrow, 1984), 14.
10.   Cited in Stephen Fox, *The Mirror Makers: A History of American Advertising and Its Creators* (New York: William Morrow, 1984), 14.
11.   John Hurley and Ronnie Wilkins, "Son of a Preacher Man," Atlantic Recording Group, 1968.

Albert Lasker, head of Lord and Thomas in Chicago, possibly the most influential agency of its day; Francis W. Ayer, founder of N. W. Ayer; John E. Powers, the most important copywriter of the period; Earnest Elmo Calkins, champion of advertising design; Claude Hopkins, influential in promoting ads as "dramatic salesmanship"; and John E. Kennedy, creator of "reason why" advertising.[12] These were the founders, the visionaries, and the artists who played principal roles in the establishment of the advertising business. One interesting side note is that several of the founders of this industry had fathers who shared the very same occupation: minister. This very modern and controversial industry was founded in no small part by the sons of preachers. While that seems against the demographic odds, remember that these young men would have been exposed to public speaking and the passionate selling of ideas as well as to the new "religion" of modernity: city life, science, progress, unapologetic fun, and public consumption.

By 1900, total sales of patent medicines in the United States had reached $75 million—an early demonstration of the power of advertising.[13] The stage was set for advertising's modern form. During this period, the first advertising agencies were founded and the practice of branding products became the norm. Advertising was motivated by the need to sell the vastly increased supply of goods brought on by mass production and by the demands of an increasingly urban population seeking social identity through (among other things) branded products. In earlier times, when shoppers went to the general store and bought soap sliced from a large, locally produced cake, advertising had no place. But with advertising's ability to create meaningful differences between near-identical soaps, advertising suddenly held a very prominent place in early consumer culture. Advertising made unmarked commodities into social symbols and identity markers, and it allowed marketers to charge far more money for them. Consumers are quite willing to pay more money for brands (for example, Ivory) than for unmarked commodities (generic soap wrapped in plain paper), even if they are otherwise identical. This is the power of brands.

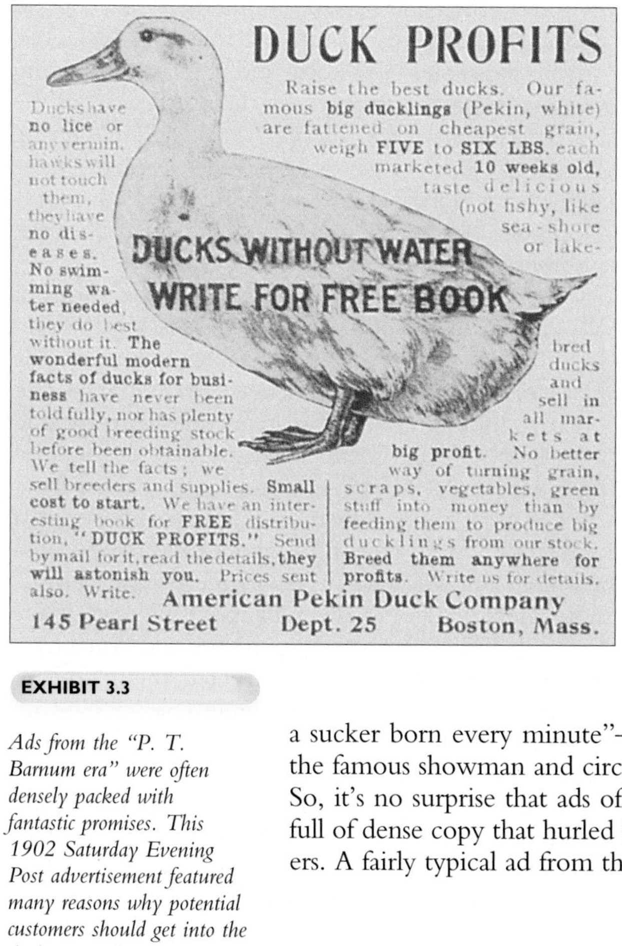

Advertising was completely unregulated in the United States until 1906. In that year, Congress passed the **Pure Food and Drug Act**, which required manufacturers to list the active ingredients of their products on their labels. You could still put some pretty amazing things in products; you just had to now tell the consumer. Still, the direct effect of this federal act on advertising was minimal; advertisers could continue to say just about anything—and usually did. It probably started to slow some of the more outrageous offenders of truth and ethics. Many advertisements still took on the style of a sales pitch for "snake oil." The tone and spirit of advertising owed more to P. T. Barnum—"There's a sucker born every minute"—than to any other influence. Of course, Barnum was the famous showman and circus entrepreneur (Barnum and Bailey Circus) of his day. So, it's no surprise that ads of this period were bold, carnivalesque, garish, and often full of dense copy that hurled fairly incredible claims at prototype "modern" consumers. A fairly typical ad from this era is shown in Exhibit 3.3.

EXHIBIT 3.3

Ads from the "P. T. Barnum era" were often densely packed with fantastic promises. This 1902 Saturday Evening Post advertisement featured many reasons why potential customers should get into the duck-raising business—even without water.

12. Fox, *The Mirror Makers,* 14.
13. Presbrey, *The History and Development of Advertising,* 16.

Several things are notable about these ads: lots of copy (words); the prominence of the product itself and the relative lack of real-world context (visuals) in which the advertised product was to be consumed; ads were small; and they had little color, few photographs, and plenty of hyperbole. Over this period there was variation and steady evolution, but this is what ads were generally like up until World War I.

Consider the world in which these ads existed. It was a period of rapid urbanization, massive immigration, labor unrest, and significant concerns about the abuses of capitalism. Some of capitalism's excesses and abuses, in the form of deceptive and misleading advertising, were the targets of early reformers. It was also the age of suffrage, the progressive movement, motion pictures, and mass culture. The world changed rapidly in this period, and it was no doubt disruptive and unsettling to many—but advertising was there to offer solutions to the stresses of modern life, no matter how real, imagined, or suggested. Advertisers had something to fix just about any problem. Remember: social and cultural change often opens up opportunities for advertisers. Further, had the first World War not occurred, and attention justifiably diverted, it is very possible that there would have been more severe and earlier regulation of advertising.

The 1920s (1918 to 1929). In many ways, the Roaring Twenties really began a couple of years early. After World War I, advertising found respectability, fame, and glamour. It was the most modern of all professions; it was, short of being a movie star, the most fashionable. According to popular perception, it was where the young, smart, and sophisticated worked and played. During the 1920s, it was also a place where institutional freedom rang. The prewar movement to reform and regulate advertising was pretty much dissipated by the distractions of the war and advertising's role in the war effort. During World War I, the advertising industry learned a valuable lesson: Donating time and personnel to the common good is not only good civics but smart business. Exhibit 3.4 is a World War I–era example.

The 1920s were prosperous times. Most (but not all) enjoyed a previously unequaled standard of living. It was an age of considerable hedonism; the pleasure principle was practiced and appreciated, openly and often. The Victorian Age was over, and a great social experiment in the joys of consumption was underway. Victorian repression and modesty gave way to a more open sexuality and a love affair with modernity. Advertising was made for this burgeoning sensuality; advertising gave people permission to enjoy. The 1920s and advertising were made for each other. Ads of the era exhorted consumers to have a good time and instructed them how to do it. Consumption was not only respectable, but expected. Being a consumer became synonymous with being a citizen—a *good* citizen.

During these good economic times, advertising instructed consumers how to be thoroughly modern and how to avoid the pitfalls of this new age. Consumers learned of halitosis from Listerine advertising and about body odor from Lifebuoy advertising (see

EXHIBIT 3.4

A good example of advertisers joining the war effort.

EXHIBIT 3.5

Many ads from the 1920s promised to relieve just about any social anxiety. Here, Lifebuoy offered a solution for people concerned that body odor could be standing in the way of career advancement.

EXHIBIT 3.6

This 1920s-era Gulf advertisement focuses on technological progress and the male prerogative in promoting its advancement. The work world is male space in this period's ads.

EXHIBIT 3.7

Ads from the 1920s often emphasized modernity themes, like the division between public and private workspace. This Fels-Naptha ad shows the private, "feminine" space of the home—where "her work" occurred.

Exhibit 3.5, a Lifebuoy ad from 1926). Not too surprisingly, there just happened to be a product with a cure for just about any social anxiety and personal failing one could imagine, many of which had supposedly been brought on as side effects of modernity. This was perfect for the growth and entrenchment of advertising as an institution: Modern times bring on many wonderful new things, but the new way of life has side effects that, in turn, have to be fixed by even more modern goods and services. For example, modern canned food replaced fresh fruit and vegetables, thus "weakening the gums," causing dental problems—which could be cured by a modern toothbrush. Thus, a seemingly endless consumption chain was created: Needs lead to products, new needs are created by new products, newer products solve newer needs, and on and on. This chain of needs is essential to a capitalist economy, which must continue to expand in order to survive. It also makes a necessity of advertising.

Other ads from the 1920s emphasized other modernity themes, such as the division between public workspace, the male domain of the office (see Exhibit 3.6), and the private, "feminine" space of the home (see Exhibit 3.7). Thus, two separate consumption domains were created, with women placed in charge of the latter, more economically important one. Advertisers soon figured out that women were responsible for as much as 80 percent of household purchases. While 1920s men were out in the "jungle" of the work world, women made most purchase decisions. So, from this time forward, women became advertising's primary target.

Another very important aspect of advertising in the 1920s, and beyond, was the role that science and technology began to play. Science and technology were in many ways the new religions of the modern era. The modern way was the scientific way. So one saw ads appealing to the popularity of science in virtually all product categories of

The cultural theme of modernity in the 1920s emphasized science and technology. These ads for Sonatron Radio Tubes (Exhibit 3.8) and Pet Milk (Exhibit 3.9) tout the science these brands brought to your home.

advertising during this period. Ads even stressed the latest scientific offerings, whether in radio tubes or in "domestic science," as Exhibits 3.8 and 3.9 demonstrate.

The style of 1920s ads was more visual than in the past. Twenties ads showed slices of life, or carefully constructed "snapshots" of social life with the product. In these ads, the relative position, background, and dress of the people using or needing the advertised product were carefully crafted, as they are today. These visual lessons were generally about how to fit in with the "smart" crowd, how to be urbane and modern by using the newest conveniences, and how not to fall victim to the perils and pressure of the new fast-paced modern world. The social context of product use became critical, as one can see in Exhibits 3.10 through 3.13.

Advertising during the 1920s chronicled the state of technology and styles for clothing, furniture, and social functions. Advertising specified social relationships between people and products by depicting the social settings and circumstances into which people and products fit. Consider Exhibits 3.11 and 3.12. Note the attention to the social setting into which plumbing fixtures were to fit. Is the ad really about plumbing? Yes, in a very important way, because it demonstrates plumbing in a social context that works for both advertiser and consumer. Modern consumers, consumers who really care about the best for their family, use modern plumbing. Advertising was becoming sophisticated and had discovered social context in a major way. In terms of pure art direction, the ads in Exhibits 3.14 through 3.16 are examples of the beauty of the period's look.

The J. Walter Thompson advertising agency was the dominant agency of the period. Stanley Resor, Helen Resor, and James Webb Young brought this agency to a leadership position through intelligent management, vision, and great advertising. Helen Resor was the first prominent female advertising executive and was instrumental in J. Walter Thompson's success. Still, the most famous ad person of the era was a very interesting man named Bruce Barton. He was not only the leader of BBDO but also a best-selling author, most notably of a 1924 book called *The Man Nobody Knows*.[14] The book was about Jesus and portrayed him as the archetypal ad man. This blending of Christian and capitalist principles was enormously

14.   Bruce Barton, *The Man Nobody Knows* (New York: Bobbs-Merrill, 1924).

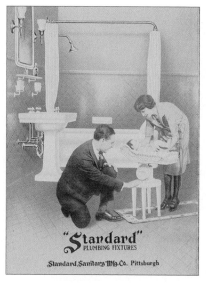

EXHIBITS 3.10 THROUGH 3.13

As the Kodak (Exhibit 3.10), Standard Sanitary (Exhibits 3.11 and 3.12), and Camay (Exhibit 3.13) ads illustrate, ads from the 1920s often showed carefully constructed "snapshots" of social life with the products. The social setting and the product blur together within one image. Setting becomes brand; brand becomes setting. Take a minute and study what's going on in these ads.

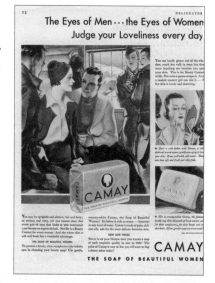

EXHIBITS 3.14 THROUGH 3.16

These three ads are more examples of the beautiful and stylish art direction of the 1920s. (Actually, the Gold Medal ad was produced in the early 1930s, but it is of the 1920s style.) Many believe this era was advertising's finest artistic moment. In an effort to make their advertising depict the technology and style of the era, advertisers in the 1920s enlisted the services of some of the best illustrators and artists of the time.

EXHIBIT 3.17

The very tough times of the Great Depression, depicted in this 1936 photo by Walker Evans, gave Americans reason to distrust big business and its tool, advertising.

attractive to a people struggling to reconcile traditional religious thought, which preached against excess, and the new religion of consumption, which preached just the opposite. Remember: This was a best selling book, clearly indicating the popularity of reconciling public consumption with popular religion and morality.

The Depression (1929 to 1941).

By 1932 a quarter of American workers were unemployed. But matters were worse than this suggests, for three quarters of those who had jobs were working part-time—either working short hours, or faced with chronic and repeated layoffs. . . . Perhaps half the working population at one time or another knew what it was like to lose a job. Millions actually went hungry, not once, but again and again. Millions knew what it was like to eat bread and water for supper, sometimes for days at a stretch. A million people were drifting around the country begging, among them thousands of children, including numbers of girls disguised as boys. People lived in shanty towns on the fields at edges of cities, their foods sometimes weeds plucked from the roadside.[15]

If you weren't there, you have no idea how bad it was. We don't, but your grandparents or great-grandparents did. The Depression was brutal, crushing, and mean. It killed people; it broke lives. Those who lived through it and kept their dignity are to be deeply admired. (See Exhibit 3.17.) Many of this greatest generation then went on to fight in World War II. The **Great Depression** forever changed the way people thought about a great many things: their government, business, money, spending, saving, credit, and, not coincidentally, advertising.

Just as sure as advertising was glamorous in the 1920s, it was villainous in the 1930s. It was part of big business, and big business, big greed, and big lust had gotten America into the great economic depression beginning in 1929—or so the story goes. The public now saw advertising as something bad, something that had tempted and seduced them into the excesses for which they were being punished.

Advertisers responded to this feeling by adopting a tough, no-nonsense advertising style. The stylish and highly aesthetic ads of the 1920s gave way to harsher and more cluttered ads. As one historian said, "The new hard-boiled advertising mystique brought a proliferation of 'ugly,' attention-grabbing, picture-dominated copy in the style of the tabloid newspaper."[16] Clients wanted their money's worth, and agencies responded by cramming every bit of copy and image they could into their ads, or using obviously inappropriate sex appeals. This type of advertising persisted, quite likely making the relationship between the public and the institution of advertising even worse. Regrettably, it is still an industry impulse in bad economic times today. The themes in advertisements traded on the anxieties of the day; losing one's job meant being a bad provider, spouse, or parent, unable to give the family what it needed (as seen in Exhibits 3.18 and 3.19), or when nothing else came to mind: sex.

15. James Lincoln Collier, *The Rise of Selfishness in America* (New York: Oxford University Press, 1991), 162.
16. Ibid., 303–304.

EXHIBITS 3.18 AND 3.19

The themes in advertising during the 1930s traded on the anxieties of the day, as these ads for Paris Garters (Exhibit 3.18) and the Association of American Soap and Glycerine Producers, Inc. (Exhibit 3.19) illustrate.

Another notable event during these years was the emergence of radio as a significant advertising medium. During the 1930s, the number of radio stations rose from a handful to 814 by the end of the decade, and the number of radio sets in use more than quadrupled to 51 million, just over one radio set per household. Radio was in its heyday as a news and entertainment medium, and it would remain so until the 1950s when television emerged. An important aspect of radio was its ability to create a sense of community in which people thousands of miles apart listened to and became involved with their favorite radio soap opera, so named in reference to the soap sponsors of these shows.

Advertising, like the rest of the country, suffered dark days during this period. Agencies cut salaries and forced staff to work four-day weeks without being paid for the mandatory extra day off. Clients demanded frequent review of work, and agencies were compelled to provide more and more free services to keep accounts. Advertising would emerge from this depression, just as the economy itself did, during World War II. However, the advertising industry would never again reach its pre-Depression status. It became the subject of a well-organized and angry consumerism movement. The U.S. Congress passed real reform in this period. In 1938 the Wheeler-Lea Amendments to the Federal Trade Commission Act declared "deceptive acts of commerce" to be against the law; this was interpreted to include advertising. Between 1938 and 1940, the FTC issued 18 injunctions against advertisers, including "forcing Fleischmann's Yeast to stop claiming that it cured crooked teeth, bad skin, constipation and halitosis."[17] Government agencies soon used these new powers against a few large national advertisers, including Lifebuoy and Lux soaps.

World War II and the '50s (1941 to 1960).

Almost one-half of all women married while they were still teenagers. Two out of three white women in college dropped out before they graduated. In 1955, 41 percent of women "thought the ideal number of children was four."[18]

17. Fox, *The Mirror Makers,* 168.
18. Wini Breines, *Young, White and Miserable: Growing Up Female in the Fifties* (Boston: Beacon, 1992).

EXHIBIT 3.20

Advertisers often used America's involvement in World War II as a way to link their products with patriotism. This link provides advertising with a much-needed image boost after the dark period of the late 1930s. http://www.cocacola.com

EXHIBIT 3.21

During the war, advertisers encouraged women to join the workforce, as this ad for Penn Railroad illustrates.

Many people mark the end of the Depression with the start of America's involvement in World War II in December 1941. During the war, advertising often made direct reference to the war effort, as the ad in Exhibit 3.20 shows, linking the product with patriotism and helping to rehabilitate the tarnished image of advertising. During the war advertisers sold war bonds and encouraged conservation. Of all companies, Coca-Cola probably both contributed and benefited the most from their amazingly successful efforts to get Coca-Cola to the front lines. When the war was over Coke had bottling plants all over the globe, and returning American G.I.s were super-loyal to Coke over competitors such as Pepsi by 4:1.[19] In addition, the war got women to join the workforce in what were nontraditional roles, as seen in the so-called Rosie the Riveter ads. The ad in Exhibit 3.21 for the Penn Railroad is a good example. During the war years, many women joined the workforce; of course, many left it (both voluntarily and involuntarily) after the war ended in 1945.

Following World War II, the economy continued (with a few starts and stops) to improve, and the consumption spree was on again. The first shopping malls were built. This time, however, public sentiment toward advertising was fundamentally different from what it had been in the 1920s, following WWI. After WWII, there was widespread belief that America's successful propaganda experts at the War Department simply moved over to Madison Avenue and started manipulating consumer minds. At the same time, there was great concern about the rise of communism and its use of "mind

19.   Pendergrast, Mark, *For God, Country & Coca-Cola: The Definitive History of the Great American Soft Drink and the Company That Makes It* (New York: Basic Books, 2003).

EXHIBIT 3.22

During the 1950s, with fears of communist mind control and a very real nuclear arms race, frightened people built bomb shelters in their backyards and became convinced of advertising's hidden powers.

control." Perhaps it was only natural to believe that advertising was involved in the same type of pursuit, but to get you to buy things rather than become a communist. The United States was filled with suspicion related to McCarthyism, the bomb, repressed sexual thoughts (a resurgence of Freudian thought), and even aliens from outer space. Otherwise-normal people were building bomb shelters in their backyards (see Exhibit 3.22), wondering whether their neighbors were communists and whether listening to "jungle music" (a.k.a. rock 'n' roll) would make their daughters less virtuous.

In this environment of mass fear, stories began circulating in the 1950s that advertising agencies were doing motivation research and using the "psychological sell," which served only to fuel an underlying suspicion of advertising. It was also during this period that Americans began to fear they were being seduced by **subliminal advertising** (subconscious advertising) to buy all sorts of things they didn't really want or need. There had to be a reason that homes and garages were filling up with so much stuff; it must be all that powerful advertising—and so a great excuse for lack of self-control was born. In fact, a best-selling 1957 book, *The Hidden Persuaders,* offered the answer: Slick advertising worked on the subconscious.[20] Suspicions about slick advertising still persist, and is still a big business for the "aren't consumers dumb/aren't advertisers evil" propagandists. Selling fears about advertising has always been good business.

The most incredible story of the period involved a man named James Vicary. According to historian Stuart Rogers, in 1957 Vicary convinced the advertising world, and most of the U.S. population, that he had successfully demonstrated a technique to get consumers to do exactly what advertisers wanted. He claimed to have placed subliminal messages in a motion picture, brought in audiences, and recorded the results. He claimed that the embedded messages of "Eat Popcorn" and "Drink Coca-Cola" had increased sales of popcorn by 57.5 percent and Coca-Cola by 18.1 percent. He held press conferences and took retainer fees from advertising agencies. According to later research, he then skipped town, just ahead of reporters who had figured out that none of his claims had ever happened. He completely disappeared, leaving no bank accounts and no forwarding address. He left town with about $4.5 million (around $28 million in today's dollars) in advertising agency and client money.[21]

Wherever you are, Jim, it appears that you probably pulled off the greatest scam in advertising history. The big problem is that a lot of people, including regulators and members of Congress, still believe in the hype you were selling and that advertisers can actually do such things. That's the real crime.

The 1950s were also about sex, youth culture, rock 'n' roll, and television. In terms of sex, volumes could be written about the very odd and paradoxical '50s. On one hand, this was the time of neo-Freudian pop psychology and *Beach Blanket Bingo,* with sexual innuendo everywhere; at the same time, very conservative pronouncements about sexual mores were giving young people, particularly women, very contradictory messages. What's more, they would be advertised to with a singular focus and force never seen before, becoming, as a result, the first "kid" and then "teen" markets. Because of their sheer numbers, they would ultimately constitute an unstoppable youth culture, one that everyone else had to deal with and try to

20. Vance Packard, *The Hidden Persuaders* (New York: D. McKay, 1957). With respect to the effects of "subliminal advertising," researchers have shown that while subliminal *communication* is possible, subliminal *persuasion,* in the typical real-world environment, remains all but impossible. As it was discussed, as mind control, in the 1950s, it remains a joke. See Timothy E. Moore, "Subliminal Advertising: What You See Is What You Get," *Journal of Marketing,* vol. 46 (Spring 1982), 38–47.

21. Stuart Rogers, "How a Publicity Blitz Created the Myth of Subliminal Advertising," *Public Relations Quarterly* (Winter 1992–1993), 12–17.

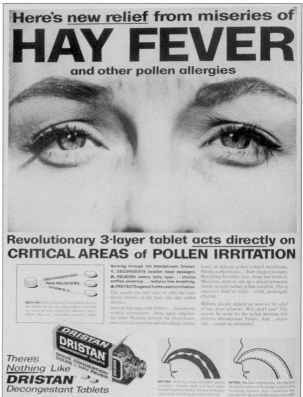

EXHIBIT 3.23

At first, advertisers didn't know what to do with television, the pre–World War II science experiment that reached 90 percent of U.S. households by 1960.

EXHIBIT 3.24

This is an ad from the famous Rosser Reeves at the Ted Bates agency. His style dominated the 1950s: harsh, abrasive, repetitive, and diagrammatic. He believed that selling the brand had virtually nothing to do with art or winning creative awards. His style of advertising is what the creative revolution revolted against.

please—the baby boomers. They would, over their parents' objections, buy rock 'n' roll records in numbers large enough to revolutionize the music industry. Now they buy SUVs, mutual funds, and $8,000 bicycles.

And then there was TV (Exhibit 3.23). Nothing like it had happened before. Its rise from pre–World War II science experiment to 90 percent penetration in U.S. households occurred during this period. At first, advertisers didn't know what to do with it and did two- and three-minute commercials, typically demonstrations. Of course, they soon began to learn TV's look and language.

This era also saw growth in the U.S. economy and in household incomes. The suburbs emerged, and along with them there was an explosion of consumption. Technological change was relentless and was a national obsession. The television, the telephone, and the automatic washer and dryer became common to the American lifestyle. Advertisements of this era were characterized by scenes of modern life, social promises, and reliance on science and technology.

Into all of this, 1950s advertising projected a confused, often harsh, at other times sappy presence. It is rarely remembered as advertising's golden age. Two of the most significant advertising personalities of the period were Rosser Reeves of the Ted Bates agency, who is best remembered for his ultra-hard-sell style (see Exhibit 3.24), and consultant Ernest Dichter, best remembered for his motivational research, which focused on the subconscious and symbolic elements of consumer desire. Exhibits 3.25 through 3.29 are representative of the advertising from this contradictory and jumbled period in American advertising

These ads show mythic nuclear families, well-behaved children, our "buddy" the atom, the last days of unquestioned faith in science, and rigid (but about to break loose) gender roles, while the rumblings of the sexual revolution of the 1960s were just audible. In a few short years, the atom would no longer be our friend; we would question science; youth would rebel and become a hugely important market; women and African Americans would demand inclusion and fairness; bullet bras would be replaced with no bras. A period of great social change would occur, which is usually a very good time for advertisers: new needs, new liberties, new anxieties, new goods and services, and new brands.

EXHIBITS 3.25 THROUGH 3.29

These five ads show the 1950s as they were: contradictory (family values-dominated but titillating) and science obsessed. Exhibit 3.29 shows evidence of the 1950s' paradoxical view on sex: titillating, but still "just an underwear ad."

Peace, Love, and the Creative Revolution (1960 to 1972).

You say you want a revolution, well, you know, we all want to change the world.

—John Lennon and Paul McCartney, "Revolution"[22]

As you well know, there was a cultural revolution in the 1960s. It affected just about everything—including advertising. Ads started to take on the themes, the language, and the look of the 1960s. But as an institution, advertising in the United States during the 1960s was actually slow to respond to the massive social revolution going on all around it. While the nation was struggling with civil rights, the Vietnam War, and the sexual revolution, advertising was often still portraying women and other minorities in subservient roles. Advertising agencies remained one of the whitest industries in America, despite what the ads looked like. And in ads, much of the sexual revolution just made women into boy toys. Gays and lesbians, as far as advertising was concerned, didn't exist.

The only thing truly revolutionary about 1960s advertising was the **creative revolution**. This revolution was characterized by the "creatives" (art directors and copywriters) having a bigger say in the management of their agencies, and the look

22. John Lennon and Paul McCartney, "Revolution," Northern Songs, 1968.

and voice of the ads. The emphasis in advertising turned "from ancillary services to the creative product; from science and research to art, inspiration, and intuition."[23] At first the look of this revolutionary advertising was clean and minimalist, with simple copy and a sense of self-effacing humor. Later (around 1968 or so), it became more. It became very self-aware and unabashedly latched itself onto social revolution—including, ironies of all ironies, to the antimaterialist movement. Advertising admitted being advertising (and even poked fun at itself). More than anything, the creative revolution was about self-awareness, that is, saying, "OK, here's an ad, you know it's an ad—and so do we." The 1960s was also a time when advertising began to understand that it was all about hip, cool, youth, and rebellion. Whatever became cool, ads had to incorporate into their message. The '60s Cultural Revolution soon became ad copy. Everything became rebellion; even an unhip brand like Dodge traded successfully on the "Dodge Rebellion."[24] Once advertising learned that it could successfully attach itself to youth, hipness, and revolution, it never went back. Even hip antiadvertising sentiment could be used to help sell stuff through advertising.

The creative revolution, and the look it produced, is most often associated with four famous advertising agencies: Leo Burnett in Chicago; Ogilvy & Mather in New York (a little less so); Doyle Dane Bernbach in New York (the most); and Wells Rich and Green in New York (deserving of more credit than they get). They were led in this revolution by agency heads Leo Burnett, David Ogilvy, Bill Bernbach, and Mary Wells. The Kellogg's Special K cereal, Rolls-Royce, Volkswagen, and Braniff ads pictured in Exhibits 3.30 through 3.33 are 1960s ads prepared by these four famous agencies, respectively.

Of course, it would be wrong to characterize the entire period as a creative revolution. Many ads in the 1960s still reflected traditional values and relied on relatively uncreative executions. Typical of many of the more traditional ads during the era is the Goodyear ad in Exhibit 3.34. Pepsi (Exhibit 3.35), traded on youth and the idea of youth.

A final point that needs to be made about the era from 1960 to 1972 is that this was a period when advertising became generally aware of its own role in consumer

The new era of advertising in the 1960s was characterized by the creative revolution, during which the creative side of the advertising process rose to new prominence. Note the clean look and minimal copy in the Kellogg's ad in Exhibit 3.30, prepared by Leo Burnett in Chicago. The Rolls-Royce ad in Exhibit 3.31, from David Ogilvy of Ogilvy and Mather, was considered "revolutionary" for its copy (not its look), which took the consumer more seriously than the ads of the 1950s did. http://www.kelloggs.com and http://www.rolls-royce.com

23. Fox, *The Mirror Makers,* 218.
24. Thomas Frank, *The Conquest of Cool: Business Culture, Counterculture, and the Rise of Hip Consumerism* (Chicago: University of Chicago Press, 1997).

EXHIBIT 3.32

Through innovative advertising, Volkswagen has, over the years, been able to refuel its original message that its cars aren't expensive luxuries but as much a household staple as broccoli and ground round (and, at $1.02 a pound, cheaper than either!). These ads from Doyle Dane Bernbach also acknowledged a sophisticated consumer. http://www.vw.com

$1.02 a pound.

EXHIBIT 3.33

This is one of Mary Wells's famously futuristic (and fashionable) ads for Braniff Airlines.

culture—that is, advertising was an icon of a culture fascinated with consumption. While advertising played a role in encouraging consumption, it had become a symbol of consumption itself. The creative revolution did not last long, but advertising was forever changed. After the 1960s it would never again be quite as naïve about its own place in society; it has since become much more self-conscious. It also learned that people (particularly youth) play out their revolutionary phase *through* consumption—even when it's an anticonsumption revolution, you've got to have the right look, the right clothes, the right revolutionary garb. In a very significant

EXHIBIT 3.34

Not all the advertising in the 1960s was characterized by the spirit of the creative revolution. This Goodyear ad relies more on traditional styles and values. http://www.goodyear.com

EXHIBIT 3.35

Pepsi "created" a generation and traded on the discovery of the vast youth market. Pepsi claimed youth as its own. http://www.pepsiworld.com

ETHICS

Discovering Diversity, Courting Gay Consumers

With a simple ad about a couple shopping for a dining room table, Swedish home-furniture manufacturer Ikea in 1994 broke down a long-standing cultural barrier in advertising. What was so special about the no-frills television spot? The couple it featured debating furniture styles and finishing each other's sentences like an old married couple were two gay men.

The ad was one of the first gay-friendly commercials aired by a major corporation, and it generated controversy. But in the decade that followed, the ad became a touchstone for advertisers rethinking how to market to gay and lesbian consumers.

A steady stream of advertising aimed at the gay market followed. The car manufacturer Subaru reached out to lesbian women with tennis great Martina Navratilova, an openly gay athlete. More than 60 major marketers, including Anheuser-Busch, Dell, Sears, and Sony, have advertised on Logo, the fledgling gay cable channel from media giant Viacom. And Ikea in late 2006 prominently featured a gay couple in another mainstream ad, this time with a young child and a golden retriever, in an advertisement for living room furniture that closes with the line: "Why shouldn't sofas come in flavors, just like families?"

Much has changed since Ikea's breakthrough dining room ad in 1994, but minefields still exist. Some gay and lesbian advocates have bristled at the marketing assumption that all homosexual consumers are affluent and urbane, as portrayed in popular television programs such as *Will & Grace* or the Bravo Channel's makeover series *Queer Eye for the Straight Guy*. In late 2005, Ford Motor Co. dropped advertising for its Land Rover and Jaguar brands in gay-oriented publications after the threat of a boycott by the conservative American Family Association.

But the automaker reversed course swiftly. Less than two weeks after saying it would eliminate advertising in gay publications, the company said it actually would expand such advertising to include its core brands such as Ford, Mercury, Mazda, and Lincoln.

Sources: Aparna Kumar, "Commercials: Out of the Closet," http://www.wired.com, May 8, 2001; Stuart Elliott, "Hey, Gay Spender, Marketers Spending Time With You," **New York Times**, June 26, 2006, C8; Jeremy W. Peters, "Ford, Reversing Decision, Will Run Ads in Gay Press," **New York Times**, December 15, 2005, C4.

way, advertising learned how to forever dodge the criticism of capitalism: Hide in plain sight.

Every few years, it seems, the cycles of the sixties repeat themselves on a smaller scale, with new rebel youth cultures bubbling their way to a happy replenishing of the various culture industries' depleted arsenal of cool. New generations obsolete the old, new celebrities render old ones ridiculous, and on and on in an ever-ascending spiral of hip upon hip. As adman Merle Steir wrote back in 1967, "Youth has won. Youth must always win. The new naturally replaces the old." And we will have new generations of youth rebellion as certainly as we will have generations of mufflers or toothpaste or footwear.[25]

The 1970s (1973 to 1980).

Mr. Blutarski, fat, drunk, and stupid is no way to go through life.

—Dean Vernon Wormer (John Vernon) in National Lampoon's *Animal House*, 1978

Dean Wormer's admonition to John Belushi's character in *Animal House* captured essential aspects of the 1970s, a time of excess and self-induced numbness. This was the age of polyester, disco, blow, and driving 55. The reelection of Richard Nixon in 1972 marked the real start of the 1970s. America had just suffered through its first lost war, the memory of four student protesters shot and killed by the National Guard at Kent State University in the spring of 1970 was still vivid, Mideast nations appeared to be dictating the energy policy of the United States, and we were, as President Jimmy Carter suggested late in this period, in a national malaise. In this environment, advertising again retreated into the tried-and-true but hackneyed styles of decades before. The creative revolution of the 1960s gave way to a slowing economy and a return to the hard sell. This period also marked the beginning of the second wave of the American feminist movement. In the 1970s, advertisers actually started to present women in "new" roles and to include people of color, as the ad in Exhibit 3.36 shows. Twenty years later they would admit gays and lesbians exist.

The '70s was the end of "the '60s" and the end of whatever revolution one wished to speak of. This period became known as the era of self-help and selfishness. "Me" became the biggest word in the 1970s. What a great environment for advertising. All of society was telling people that it was not only OK to be selfish, but it was the

25. Frank, *The Conquest of Cool*, 235.

EXHIBIT 3.36

While a bad economy and a national malaise caused a retreat to the tried-and-true styles of decades before, a bright spot of 1970s advertising was the portrayal of people of color. Thomas Burrell created ads that portrayed African Americans with "positive realism."

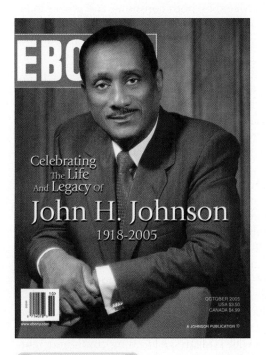

EXHIBIT 3.37

John H. Johnson made so much possible for black Americans in business.

right thing to do. Selfishness was said to be natural and good. A refrain similar to "Hey babe, I can't be good to you if I'm not good to me," became a '70s mantra. Being selfish was now a good thing. Of course, being good to oneself often meant buying stuff—always good for advertising. It's funny how that worked out.

Somewhat surprisingly, the '70s also resulted in added regulation and the protection of special audiences. Advertising encountered a new round of challenges on several fronts. First, there was growing concern over what effect $200 million a year in advertising had on children. A group of women in Boston formed **Action for Children's Television**, which lobbied the government to limit the amount and content of advertising directed at children. Established regulatory bodies, in particular the **Federal Trade Commission (FTC)** and the industry's **National Advertising Review Board**, demanded higher standards of honesty and disclosure from the advertising industry. Several firms were subjected to legislative mandates and fines because their advertising was judged to be misleading. Most notable among these firms were Warner-Lambert (for advertising that Listerine mouthwash could cure and prevent colds), Campbell's (for putting marbles in the bottom of a soup bowl to bolster its look), and Anacin (for advertising that its aspirin could help relieve tension).

While advertising during this period featured more African Americans and women, the effort to adequately represent and serve these consumers was fairly minimal; advertising agency hiring and promotion practices with respect to minorities were formally challenged in the courts. Despite this, two important agencies owned and managed by African Americans emerged and thrived: Thomas J. Burrell founded Burrell Advertising, and Byron Lewis founded Uniworld. Burrell is perhaps best known for ads that rely on the principle of "positive realism." Positive realism is "people working productively; people engaging in family life . . . people being well-rounded . . . and thoughtful; people caring about other people; good neighbors, good parents . . . people with dreams and aspirations; people with ambition." Burrell once said "in 30 seconds you can build a brand and break a stereotype." He also believed that "whites are easier to reach through Black advertising than vise versa."[26] "The idea was that we don't have to be the same as white people to be equal to white people; that we should celebrate our differences while not shying away from demanding our rights."[27]

One of Burrell's ads is shown in Exhibit 3.36. (Go to http://www.littleafrica.com/resources/advertising.htm for a current list of major African-American advertising agencies and resources.) Another very important person was John H. Johnson, founder of *Ebony* magazine, and in many ways the man who made the black American experience in publishing, marketing, and advertising possible (Exhibit 3.37). He opened up enormous opportunities for black entrepreneurs, advertisers, and artists. His funeral was attended by a former

26. http://www.ciadvertising.org/studies/student/99_fall/theory/cal/aainadvertising/folder/burrell.html
27. http://blackmbamagazine.net/articles/docs/2005-2_an%20advertising%20legend%20leads%20with%20passion%20purpose%20and%20power.pdf

One of the significant differences between advertising prepared in the 1960s and in the 1970s is that ads began focusing on the product itself rather than on creative techniques. The Jensen ad in Exhibit 3.38 and the Listerine ad in Exhibit 3.39 represent this product-focused feature of 1970s advertising, which reflects the fact that advertising agency management took control back from creatives during this era. What do current advertising trends tell us about the role of management in today's agencies?

U.S. president, U.S. Senators, celebrities, and a lot of people who simply adored him. He was very important in advertising and beyond.

The 1970s also signaled a period of growth in communications technology. Consumers began to surround themselves with devices related to communication. The VCR, cable television, and the laserdisc player were all developed during the 1970s. Cable TV claimed 20 million subscribers by the end of the decade. Similarly, cable programming grew in quality, with viewing options such as ESPN, CNN, TBS, and Nickelodeon. As cable subscribers and their viewing options increased, advertisers learned how to reach more specific audiences through the diversity of programming on cable systems.

The process of advertising was being restricted by both consumer and governmental regulatory challenges, yet technological advances posed unprecedented opportunities. It was the beginning of the merger mania that swept the industry throughout the end of the decade and into the next, a movement that saw most of the major agencies merge with one another and with non-U.S. agencies as well. It was also the birth of what were essentially program-length commercials, particularly in children's television. Product/show blends for toys like Strawberry Shortcake made regulation more difficult: If it's a show about a product, then it's not really an ad (and can't be regulated as an ad)—or is it? This drove regulators crazy, but program-length commercials were incredibly smart marketing.[28] They were generally treated by regulators as shows and opened the door for countless numbers of imitators. The "new" branded entertainment had its real start here, not 30 years later.

This period in the evolution of advertising presented enormous challenges. In all of this, the look of advertising was about as interesting as it was in the 1950s. Often, advertisements focused on the product itself, rather than on creative technique, as illustrated in the product-focused ads in Exhibits 3.38 and 3.39. During this period, management took control and dominated agency activities. In agencies used to creative control, the idea of "bottom-liners" struck deep at the soul. Of course, all the money they would make in the 1980s would make them feel much better about the whole thing.

But the cultural revolution of the 1960–1970s (and the creative revolution) was over. By the end of the 1970s it was really a very different scene, culturally, and therefore in the ad business as well. There was, as always, a looming youth undercurrent of revolution (with a small "r") and rebellion. This one was more cynical, and ambivalent about consumption and advertising. These youth were the first generation to grow up on TV advertising.

28. Tom Engelhardt, "The Shortcake Strategy," in Todd Gitlin, ed., *Watching Television* (New York: Pantheon, 1986), 68–110.

Do you remember lying in bed
With your covers pulled up over your head?
Radio playin' so no one can see
We need change, we need it fast
Before rock's just part of the past
'Cause lately it all sounds the same to me
Oh oh oh oh, oh oh

Will you remember Jerry Lee,
John Lennon, T. Rex and OI Moulty?
It's the end, the end of the '70s
It's the end, the end of the century

—The Ramones, "Do You Remember Rock 'n' Roll Radio?"[29]

An ad that embodied the tone and style of 1980s advertising was Ronald Reagan's 1984 reelection campaign ad "Morning in America." The ad is soft in texture but firm in its affirmation of the conservative values of family and country.

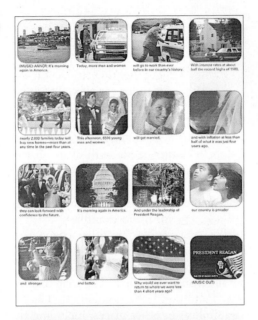

This MasterCard ad demonstrates the social-class and designer consciousness of the 1980s.

The Designer Era (1980 to 1992).

Greed, for a lack of a better word, is good.

—Gordon Gekko (Michael Douglas)
in *Wall Street,* 1987

"In 1980, the average American had twice as much real income as his parents had had at the end of WWII."[30] Consumers had a lot of real income to spend. The political, social, business, and advertising landscape changed in 1980 with the election of Ronald Reagan. The country made a right, and conservative politics were the order of the day. There was, of course, some backlash and many countercurrents, but the conservatives were in the mainstream. Greed was good, stuff was good, and advertising was good.

Many ads from the Republican era are particularly social-class conscious and values conscious. They openly promote consumption, but in a conservative way, all wrapped up in "traditional American values." The quintessential 1980s ad may be the 1984 television ad for President Ronald Reagan's reelection campaign, "Morning in America." The storyboard for this ad is shown in Exhibit 3.40. This ad is soft in texture, but it is a firm reaffirmation of family and country—and capitalism. Other advertisers quickly followed with ads that looked similar to "Morning in America." The 1980s were also about designer labels, social-class consciousness, and having stuff, as the ad in Exhibit 3.41 demonstrates.

29.   Written by Joey Ramone, Sire Records. May 16, 1980. Watch: *http://www.youtube.com/watch?v=kJizV-d3sEQ*
30.   Collier, *The Rise of Selfishness in America,* 230.

I want my MTV.

At the same time, several new communication technology trends were emerging, which led to more-creative, bold, and provocative advertising. Television advertising of this period was influenced by the rapid-cut editing style of MTV. George Lois, himself of the 1960s creative revolution, was hired by MTV to save the fledgling network after a dismal first year. After calling a lot of people who were unwilling to take the chance, he got Mick Jagger to proclaim, "I want my MTV" (see Exhibit 3.42). The network turned around and music television surged into popular consciousness. Most importantly for us, television ads in the 1980s started looking like MTV videos: rapid cuts with a very self-conscious character.

This was also the age of the **infomercial**, a long advertisement that looks like a talk show or a half-hour product demonstration. If you watch late-night cable television, you've probably seen some guy lighting his car on fire as part of a demonstration for car wax. These very long ads initially aired in late-night television time slots, when audiences were small in number and airtime was relatively inexpensive. Infomercials have since spread to other off-peak time slots, including those with somewhat larger audiences, and they have gained respect along the way. The Psychic Friends Network, Bowflex, and a wide assortment of automotive, weight loss, and hair care products are all examples of products and services recently promoted on infomercials. You might check out http://www.as-on-tv-ads.com for more examples.

The advertising of the 1980s had a few other changes. One was the growth and creative impact of British agencies, particularly Saatchi and Saatchi (see Exhibit 3.43). One of the things Saatchi and Saatchi realized earlier than most was that politics, culture, and products all resonate together. The Saatchi and Saatchi ads of this period were often sophisticated and politically nonneutral. They worked, and began to be copied (at least the sensibility) in other places, including the United States.

The late 1970s and into the 1980s was the "golden" age of punk and alternative. The idealism of the 1960s was fading, and cynicism was on the rise. Youth's power

Saatchi and Saatchi, more than anyone, brought a political sensibility to modern advertising.

as a market and as style arbiters continued to grow. If an overall attitude toward commerce can be characterized, it was one of deep ambivalence: People didn't trust commerce—it had somehow helped kill whatever was "authentic"—but they also knew it wasn't going to go away. So, just as author Thomas Frank (author of *Conquest of Cool*) would have predicted, punk, alternative, and anti-1960s cynicism started showing up as the basis for hip ads of this era.

The E-Revolution Begins (1993 to 2000).

Modern advertising had entered its second century, and it was more self-conscious than ever before. In the '90s, self-parody was the inside joke of the day, except everyone was "inside." Winks and nods to the media-savvy audience were becoming pretty common. Advertising was fast, and it was everywhere. Some said it was "dead," killed by the World Wide Web and other new media, but that turned out to be an exaggeration. By the end of the decade, ads were still ads, and they were very much alive. But this was Stage I of the Web revolution in advertising. It ended with mixed results.

There were scary moments. In May 1994, Edwin L. Artzt, then chairman and CEO of Procter & Gamble, the then $40 billion-a-year marketer of consumer packaged goods, dropped a bomb on the advertising industry. During an address to participants at the American Association of Advertising Agencies (4As) annual conference, he warned that agencies must confront a "new media" future that won't be driven by traditional advertising. While at that time P&G was spending about $1 billion a year on television advertising, Artzt told the 4As audience, "From where we stand today, we can't be sure that ad-supported TV programming will have a future in the world being created—a world of video-on-demand, pay-per-view, and subscription TV. These are designed to carry no advertising at all."[31] An icy chill filled the room. Then, just when the industry had almost recovered from Artzt's dire proclamation, William T. Esrey, chairman and CEO of Sprint, gave it another jolt a year later at the same annual conference. Esrey's point was somewhat different but equally challenging to the industry. He said that clients are "going to hold ad agencies more closely accountable for results than ever before. That's not just because we're going to be more demanding in getting value for our advertising dollars. It's also because we know the technology is there to measure advertising impact more precisely than you have done in the past."[32] Esrey's point: **Interactive media** will allow direct measurement of ad exposure and impact, quickly revealing those that perform well and those that do not. Secondly, the agency will be held accountable for results. Well, the former (precise measurement) didn't really work out, but the latter (accountability) became the order of the day. That did change. Ad agencies are now said to be operating with fewer staff and smaller margins than before. Clients are more tight-fisted these days and at least try to demand accountability. Also, there was more competition for the money: the new media wanted it, but so did the old. If you watched the 2000 Super Bowl, you might have noticed that few of those dot-coms that bought all the very expensive advertising are still around, but "new" media are.

The saga continues. Still unsure of what could be delivered and what could be counted, in August 1998 Procter & Gamble hosted an Internet "summit," due to "what is widely perceived as the poky pace of efforts to eliminate the difficulties confronted by marketers using online media to pitch products."[33] Some of these problems were technological: incompatible technical standards, limited bandwidth,

31. This quote and information from this section can be found in Steve Yahn, "Advertising's Grave New World," *Advertising Age,* May 16, 1994, 53.

32. Kevin Goodman, "Sprint Chief Lectures Agencies on Future," *Wall Street Journal,* April 28, 1995, B6.

33. Stuart Elliot, "Procter and Gamble Calls Internet Marketing Executives to Cincinnati for a Summit Meeting," *New York Times,* August 19, 1998, D3; available at http://www.nytimes.com, accessed February 20, 1999.

EXHIBITS 3.44 AND 3.45

1990s ads were generally more visual and self-aware. They didn't try to be realistic; they said "this is an ad."

and disappointing measurement of both audience and return on investment. Others were the result of naïveté. Advertisers such as P&G want to know what they are getting and what it costs when they place an Internet ad. Does anyone notice these ads, or do people click right past them? What would "exposure" in this environment really mean? Is "exposure" really even a meaningful term in the new media ad world? How do you use these new media to build brand relationships? At the end of this summit, P&G reaffirmed its commitment to the Internet.

But history again showed that measurement of bang for buck (return on investment, ROI) in advertising (Internet or not) is very elusive. While better than TV, the Internet was fundamentally unable to yield precise measurements of return on investment in advertisement. Too many variables, too much noise in the system, too many lagged (delayed) effects, and too many uncertainties about who is really online abound.

Not a big surprise for those who pay attention to history: Advertising's impact is always tough to measure. Even with all this technology, it still is. Which bump in sales comes from where is still elusive (more about this in Chapter 15).

Another change has come in the form of a significant challenge on New York's claim as the center of the advertising universe. In the United States, the center has moved west, with the ascendancy of agencies in California, Minnesota, Oregon, and Washington, not to mention international hot spots such as London and Singapore. In the 1990s these agencies tended to be more creatively oriented and less interested in numbers-oriented research than those in New York. Other hot or nearly hot ad-shop markets include Minneapolis, Austin, Atlanta, Houston, and Dallas. Outside the United States, London emerged as the key player, with Singapore and Seoul as close seconds. Nineties ads were generally more visually oriented and much more self-aware. They said "this is an ad" in their look and feel. They had a young and ironic flavor. Some call them "postmodern." Exhibits 3.44 and 3.45 are good examples of this '90s style.

4 Consumer Empowerment and Branded Entertainment (2000–present). As you may be aware, the dot-com bubble burst in 2000. Companies that burned cash like kindling and produced no good estimate of when, if ever, they would turn a profit died off. Part of the problem was the lack of a good Web advertising revenue model. Pop-ups and easy-to-avoid Internet ads had just not generated enough advertising revenue. Online buying continued to grow, but online advertising couldn't catch up until companies became more sophisticated at using alternative media, such as the Internet, to generate calculable and attributable real sales. Since 2001 or so, this has really begun to happen. Phase II of the e-ad-revolution (Web 2.0) has been much more successful. Agencies like StarCom were truly revolutionary and brilliant in their ability to figure how to make real money in this new environment.

With the rise of the Internet something very important has happened: Consumers are more in charge than ever. We believe they always had more power than they were assumed to have, but it's pretty undeniable now. It is widely admitted in industry circles that the day of the heavy hand of the powerful marketer is pretty much over. Consumers can now communicate with each other, actually talk back to the marketer with one voice or millions, and even make their own ads and distribute them on media such as YouTube. The advertising industry has pretty much accepted the fact that consumers can now do many of the very same things that only big studios, agencies, and distributors could do a decade ago. Consumers now really cocreate brands. Consumers' reactions (particularly young peoples') are fused with agency "professional" creative to make ads that are one step from homemade, or in some cases completely homemade. This is typically called **consumer-generated content (CGC)**. This has turned the industry upside down. The industry bible, *Advertising Age,* has declared this era the "post-advertising age." That's probably a bit much, but things really have changed in the last 10 years.

But remember, ad people do get carried away; they have revolutions pretty often, and without much effort. So, it is a bit much to say, even with all these truly amazing and fundamental changes, that advertising is dead, or that advertisers have absolutely no power. Not true. As for the creative trends in ads, ads of this period are diverse, as they are in any period. However, they continue to be self-aware—to proclaim "This is an ad"—and they portray a newfound consumer awareness, that is, an awareness of a very savvy, very connected, and easily turned-off consumer. Many ads are very aware (and proud) of being ads. Everyone is in on it (see Exhibits 3.46 through 3.48). They

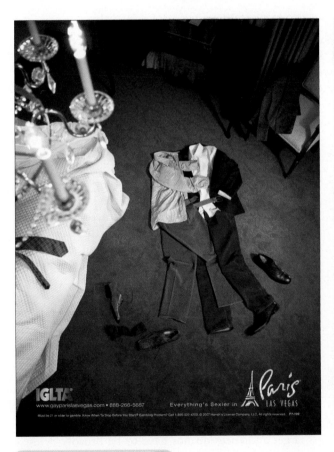

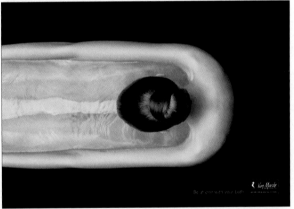

EXHIBITS 3.46 THROUGH 3.48

Exhibits 3.46 through 3.48 are good examples of recent advertising. They are visual, usually self-aware, young, and stylish. They are ads that are comfortable being ads.

EXHIBIT 3.49

Nice ad, though the company was a casualty of the dot-com bust.

EXHIBIT 3.50

Despite the surge in creativity, there are still lots of traditional ads like this one.

are comfortable being ads. They are also visual, young, and stylish (Exhibit 3.49). But people should not kid themselves: Straightforward traditional ads are still a big part of the mix (see Exhibit 3.50).

And don't forget about business-to-business promotion on the Web, known as e-business. **E-business** is another form of e-advertising and promotion in which companies selling to business customers (rather than to household consumers) rely on the Internet to send messages and close sales (we'll cover this in detail in Chapter 16).

Web advertising growth will be fostered by three aspects of technology: interactive, wireless, and broadband. Because of advances in technology, firms like Procter & Gamble continue to invest heavily in these means of sending messages and reaching target customers. P&G has developed and maintains dozens of Web sites for the company's approximately 300 brands to serve and interact with customers.[34] P&G also has gone beyond just product-oriented sites and has launched "relationship building" sites like Beinggirl, a teen community site (Exhibit 3.51). With such a site, the firm can gather data, test new product ideas, and experiment with interactivity. For example, if a Web site visitor wants to

EXHIBIT 3.51

P&G's communal Beinggirl Web site is a good example of online brand community building with global reach.

http://www.beinggirl.com

know what nail polish will match the lipstick she just saw in a commercial, she can get an immediate answer. Thus, target audiences do not have to be broadly defined by age or geographic groups—individual households can be targeted through direct interaction with the audience member. Also note that P&G can reach a global audi-

34.   Beth Snyder Bulik, "Procter & Gamble's Great Web Experiment," *Business 2.0,* November 28, 2000, 48–54.

EXHIBIT 3.52

And, of course, there is YouTube, the first and big mover in social networking and brand communication.

DOING IT RIGHT

Consumers at the Creative Controls

In late 2004, a 36-year-old high school teacher from Southern California created a 60-second video that paid homage to Apple's iPod mini with animated pulsing hearts and swirling 1970s-style graphics, all set to the beat of the song "Tiny Machine" by the 1980s pop band the Darling Buds. With his single short video, George Masters also launched a new advertising era—one that literally put the consumer at the controls.

Masters's ad was considered to be the first strictly consumer-produced advertisement, and it turned out to be a huge hit. Within days of its first posting on the Internet, the ad was viewed tens of thousands of times on blogs and through e-mail. The spot didn't just attract the notice of other devoted Apple fans, either. Marketers and firms quickly realized that one powerful way to capture consumers' attention in the era of increasing audience fragmentation was to put the audience in charge of the message.

The subsequent rise of consumer-generated advertising was swift. In February 2007, four consumer-created ads aired on the Super Bowl, one of advertising's premier events. The makers of Firefox, an open-source Web browser distributed by the Mozilla Corporation, received some 280 entries when it requested user submissions for an advertising campaign. The winning entry featured a teenage girl who says "I love things fast," talks about surfing, and then declares: "My other browser is a surfboard."

For brands, amateur ads can be double-edged swords. When General Motors asked consumers to help shape its ad campaign for the Chevy Tahoe online, the automaker was deluged with sharp anti-SUV environmental messages. But for marketers, letting the public play at the advertising game often means that a small investment can bring big buzz.

Sources: David Kiley, "Advertising Of, By, And For the People," ***BusinessWeek,*** July 25, 2005, p.63; Frank Ahrens, "$2 Million Airtime, $13 Ad," ***Washington Post,*** Jan. 31, 2007, D1.

ence through beinggirl.com without the cost and time-consuming effort of placing traditional media ads in dozens of markets. Furthermore, the consumer comes willingly to the advertiser, not the other way around as in the case of the more intrusive traditional media that seek consumers out, like it or not. Social networking sites such as Facebook or YouTube (see Exhibit 3.52) have made brand communities and personal identity projects the stuff of e-commerce.

Branded Entertainment.

There is no aspect of the evolution of advertising more significant than the emergence of "branded entertainment." **Branded entertainment** is the blending of advertising and integrated brand promotion with entertainment, primarily film, music, and television programming. A subset of branded entertainment is *product placement,* the significant placement of brands within films or television programs. When Tom Cruise wore Ray-Bans in the film *Top Gun,* when James Bond switched to the BMW Z8 from his beloved Aston Martin (by the way, he has switched back), and when the cast of *Friends* drank Pepsi, audiences

EXHIBIT 3.53

The ultimate in branded entertainment, the BMW Web films entertain viewers by featuring BMW cars in short Web-accessed films. The films have attracted millions of viewers who stay at the BMW site for an average of 16 to 20 minutes—far longer viewership than any traditional advertising could ever hope for.

took notice. Well, branded entertainment takes product placement a quantum leap forward. With branded entertainment, a brand is not just a bit player; it is the star of the program. An early participant in branded entertainment and still a leader in using the technique is BMW. BMW launched the BMW Web film series in 2001 and has featured the work of well-known directors, including Wong Kar-Wai, Ang Lee, John Frankenheimer, Guy Ritchie, and Alejandro González Iñárritu (Exhibit 3.53). Other sites featuring entertainment by featuring the brand include Lipton Tea (http://www.lipton.com), Oldsmobile with Tiger Woods in "Tiger Trap" (http://www.oldsmobile .com), and the U.S. Army at its Web-based computer game (http://www.goarmy.com). There are many advantages to branded entertainment— among them, not running into the consumer's well-trained resistance mechanisms to ads and not having to go through all the ad regulations. In an ad BMW has to use a disclaimer ("closed track, professional driver") when it shows its cars tearing around, but in movies, like *The Italian Job,* no such disclaimer is required. Also, movies have been seen by the courts as artistic speech, not as the less protected "commercial speech." Branded entertainment, therefore, gets more First Amendment protection than ordinary advertising does. This is an important distinction, since regulation and legal fights surrounding ads represent a large cost of doing business. This merger of advertising with music, film, television, and other telecom arenas (such as cell phones) is often referred to as Madison & Vine, a nod to New York's Madison Avenue, the traditional home of the advertising industry, and the famous Hollywood intersection of Hollywood and Vine. We will talk more about this later. Suffice it to say for now, branded entertainment has opened up enormous real possibilities for what has become a much cluttered and a bit beat-up traditional advertising industry.

But the Web is only one part of the branded entertainment process. Recently, firms are seeing the beauty of partnering with film studios. For example, the highly successful 2003 film *Pirates of the Caribbean* can easily be argued as a 90-minute advertisement for Disneyland. Going the other way, Universal Studios now has an Indiana Jones ride at its Universal Studios Park in Orlando. In this case, the film came first and the amusement ride was developed based on the success of the film.

As you can imagine, advertisers love the exposure that branded entertainment can provide. And entertainment venues are more fully protected (as artistic expression) by the First Amendment provisions for free speech in the United States and therefore skirt much of the regulation imposed on traditional advertising. But not all consumers are wildly enthusiastic about the blurring line between advertising and entertainment. One survey showed that 52 percent of respondents were worried about advertisers influencing entertainment content.

But in just exactly what real world is it that there are no real brands visible and being used? Personally, we don't think today's consumers find it particularly distracting at all, particularly if it's done well.

Many consumers have turned to solutions like TiVo to avoid traditional advertising. With technology like TiVo, consumers can skip commercials, and 63 percent of TiVo users report that they do just that.[35] This is another reason for branded entertainment.

5 The Value of an Evolutionary Perspective.

As intriguing as new technology like Wi-Fi is and as exciting as new communications options like Web films may be, we shouldn't jump to the conclusion that everything about advertising will change. So far, it hasn't. Advertising will still be a paid attempt to persuade. As a business process, advertising will still be one of the primary marketing mix tools that contribute to revenues and profits by stimulating demand and nurturing brand loyalty. Even though the executives at P&G believe there is a whole new world of communication and have developed dozens of Web sites to take advantage of this new world, the firm still spends about $3.5 billion a year on traditional advertising through traditional media.[36] It is also safe to argue that consumers will still be highly involved in some product decisions and not so involved in others, so that some messages will be particularly relevant and others will be completely irrelevant to forming and maintaining beliefs and feelings about brands. To this date, technology (particularly e-commerce) has changed the way people shop, gather information, and purchase. And while the advance in online advertising continues, net TV revenues are still attractive. Where else are you going to get such an enormous audience with sight and sound?

In this chapter, we have tried to offer an evolutionary perspective on advertising, and a very practical one. Get this; history is very, very relevant and practiced. You don't have to make the same mistakes over and over. Avoid Groundhog Day reality. Learn what works and doesn't work from the past. It's a smart thing to do.

---

35. Claire Atkinson, "Ad Distraction Up, Say Consumers," *Advertising Age*, January 6, 2003, 19.
36. "100 Leading National Advertisers," *Advertising Age,* June 28, 2004, S4.

SUMMARY

 Tell the story of advertising's birth.

Although some might contend that the practice of advertising began thousands of years ago, it is more meaningful to connect advertising as we know it today with the emergence of capitalistic economic systems. In such systems, business organizations must compete for survival in a free market setting. In this setting, it is natural that a firm would embrace a tool that assists it in persuading potential customers to choose its products over those offered by others. The explosion in production capacity that marked the Industrial Revolution gave demand-stimulation tools added importance. Mass moves of consumers to cities and modern times helped create, along with advertising, consumer culture.

 Describe the past and current relationship between advertisers, retailers, and consumers.

Advertising and branding play a key role in the ongoing power struggle between manufacturers and their retailers. U.S. manufacturers began branding their products in the late 1800s. Advertising could thus be used to build awareness of and desire for the various offerings of a particular manufacturer. Retailers have power in the marketplace deriving from the fact that they are closer to the customer. When manufacturers can use advertising to build customer loyalty to their brands, they take part of that power back. Lately, big retailers have been reclaiming that power. Of course, in a capitalistic system, power and profitability are usually related.

 Discuss several significant eras in the evolution of advertising in the United States, and relate important changes in advertising practice to more fundamental changes in society and culture. How did successful advertising leverage the social and cultural forces of their day?

Social and economic trends, along with technological developments, are major determinants of the way advertising is practiced in any society. Before the Industrial Revolution, advertising's presence in the United States was barely noticeable. With an explosion in economic growth around the turn of the century, modern advertising was born: The "P. T. Barnum era" and the 1920s established advertising as a major force in the U.S. economic system. With the Great Depression and World War II, cynicism and paranoia regarding advertising began to grow. This concern led to refinements in practice and more careful regulation of advertising in the 1960s and 1970s. Consumption was once again in vogue during the designer era of the 1980s. The new communication technologies that emerged in the 1990s era seem certain to effect significant changes in future practice. Finally, the interactive, wireless, and broadband technologies that are leading advertising into the 21st century hold great promise but a hard-to-predict future.

 Tell the story of consumer empowerment and branded entertainment, and understand how it works.

Integrated, interactive, and *wireless* have become the advertising buzzwords of the early 21st century. These words represent notable developments that are reshaping advertising practice. This is so because the technologies present advertisers with new options like Web films or feature films that highlight brands—a process known as advertainment. In addition, consumers can use Wi-Fi systems, limited-area wireless access systems, to provide more mobility in their use of computers. Integrated brand promotion may continue to grow in importance as advertisers work with more-varied media options to reach markets that are becoming even more fragmented. A variety of advertisers are using interactive media to reach consumers in the digital realm, while the use of services like TiVo demonstrates a consumer backlash against the ubiquity of advertising. Consumers are taking over many of the functions of traditional marketers and advertisers.

 Identify forces that will continue to affect the evolution of advertising and integrated brand promotion.

History is practical. Consumers will always be affected by social and cultural change and thus represent advertising and IBP opportunity.

KEY TERMS

Industrial Revolution
principle of limited liability
branding
dailies
consumer culture
Pure Food and Drug Act

Great Depression
subliminal advertising
creative revolution
Action for Children's Television
Federal Trade Commission (FTC)
National Advertising Review Board

infomercial
interactive media
consumer-generated content (CGC)
e-business
branded entertainment
TiVo

QUESTIONS

1. As formerly communist countries make the conversion to free market economies, advertising typically becomes more visible and important. Why would this be the case?

2. Explain why there is a strong relationship between increasing urbanization and per capita spending.

3. How do manufacturers gain or lose power in the channel of distribution? What other parties are involved in this power struggle?

4. Describe the various factors that produced an explosion of advertising activity in the "P. T. Barnum era."

5. The 1950s were marked by great suspicion about advertisers and their potential persuasive powers. Do you see any lingering effects of this era in attitudes about advertising today?

6. The "creative revolution" that handed more authority to agency art directors and copywriters in the 1960s led to key shifts in the appearance and message of mainstream advertising. Describe these changes and how they continue to influence advertising today.

7. There were many important developments in the 1970s that set the stage for advertising in the Reagan era. Which of these developments are likely to have the most enduring effects on advertising practice in the future?

8. Ed Artzt, then chairman and CEO of Procter & Gamble, made a speech in May 1994 that rattled the cages of many advertising professionals. What did Artzt have to say that got people in the ad business so excited?

9. Review the technological developments that have had the greatest impact on the advertising business. What new technologies are emerging that promise more profound changes for advertisers in the next decade?

10. What creative trends in ads have emerged in the period from 2001 to the present?

EXPERIENTIAL EXERCISES

1. The practice of advertising has steadily evolved over the past century, adapting to the culture's social and economic changes. Following the directions below, analyze distinctions between some of the key eras in advertising inside the United States using the online database http://www.adflip.com, which features advertisements from the 1940s to the present.

a. Browse Adflip's extensive database and select two ads from different decades of advertising history. Briefly describe the ads and explain how they fit the general characteristics of other advertising during that era as defined in the chapter.

b. Select an ad from the site that does not seem to reflect its era's general characteristics. How does it differ from ads typical of this period? If it would it fit better in a different era, what might have been the intentions of the advertiser?

2. Many current well-known advertising campaigns are marked by irony and quirky, self-referential attempts at humor with a wink. Select three prominent ads from television, radio, or new media, and analyze the content and themes used in the ads to communicate the brands. For each, answer the following questions. Does the theme rely on high fashion, comedy, patriotism, or pop-culture trends? How well does the ad communicate the value of the brand? In what way is the ad a product of the times in which we live?

3. During the period from 1980 to 1992, half-hour television product demonstrations known as infomercials emerged to help sell a variety of products, from diets and cosmetic to housewares and body-training equipment. While some viewers question the integrity of these advertisements, they have earned respect for their success in eliciting spontaneous purchases from broad target audiences.

Working in small teams, identify three common products or brands that are promoted through infomercials and evaluate why this type of advertising proves successful for the product. In your analysis, identify what the product or service is, what the likely target audience is, and whether other forms of advertising could be equally effective.

4. As early as the 1920s, advertisers recognized that women had authority over as much as 80 percent of household purchases. From that point forward, women have been primary targets for the ad world—even in product categories that might traditionally be viewed as male oriented.

To evaluate how that remains true today, locate a prominent advertisement for a product or service in each of these three categories: home improvement, automotive, and financial. For each ad, identify how the brand is appealing to women and why. Do you believe the campaign is likely to be successful in attracting female consumers? Why or why not?

CHAPTER 4

After reading and thinking about this chapter, you will be able to do the following:

1 Identify the benefits and problems of advertising and promotion in a capitalistic society and debate a variety of issues concerning their effects on society's well-being.

2 Explain how ethical considerations affect the development of advertising and IBP campaigns.

3 Discuss the role of government agencies and consumers in the regulation of advertising and promotion.

4 Explain the meaning and importance of self-regulation for firms that develop and use advertising and promotion.

5 Discuss the regulation of the full range of techniques used in the IBP process.

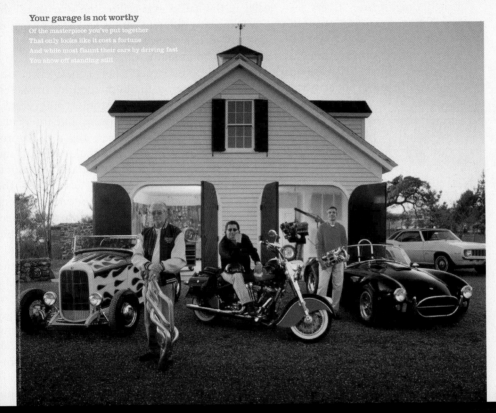

Your garage is not worthy

Of the masterpiece you've put together
That only looks like it cost a fortune
And while most flaunt their cars by driving fast
You show off standing still

Here's why thousands of you turn to eBay Motors to find everything you need.

Buy It Now Don't want to bid on an item? If the thing you want has the "Buy it Now" icon next to it, you can buy it right away without waiting.

It's easy to find what you're looking for. Save three of your favorite searches and be notified when items you want become available.

Every eBay user has a feedback rating. This rating is based on past transactions. It helps ensure we all know who we're dealing with.

 PayPal is the fast, easy and secure way to pay on eBay. Use your credit card or bank account to pay instantly and get your items faster.

Do it
ebaY *Motors*

Introductory Scenario: I Didn't Sign Up for This!

Has this ever happened to you? You see an ad in a magazine or the newspaper that announces a "Big Sweepstakes" where you can win a fabulous vacation to Hawaii, a killer speedboat, or $1 million in a drawing. You fill in the entry form, mail it, and wait. After a few months, it dawns on you that you haven't won the sweepstakes, but what you have won is a mailbox (or e-mail box) full of stuff from advertisers who got your name from the outfit that ran the sweepstakes!

This is exactly what happened to Anne Marie when she saw the Eddie Bauer edition of a Ford Explorer as a sweepstakes giveaway. It was her dream car and she entered the sweepstakes. But in the end, she decided that entering the sweepstakes created a nightmare. "Every Jeep dealer in the galaxy was calling me after that," she says. "There was a span of about two weeks that a different car dealer called or mailed something [every day] about me coming in to test drive a car. I was furious." [1]

What happened to Anne Marie happens to millions of Americans every day. Advertisers call it "database marketing." Contests, sweepstakes, supermarket discount cards, and product warranty cards are common methods used by marketers to gather information about customers and create a database to be used for advertising and integrated brand promotion (IBP) strategies. Big data "warehouse" companies such as Metromail, Acxiom, and R. L. Polk specialize in collecting massive amounts of consumer information. They then sell the data—including names, addresses, phone numbers, and e-mail addresses—to companies that use direct marketing, such as catalog publishers, Internet companies, charities, credit card issuers, book clubs, and music clubs—you know, the ones who send you all the stuff in the (e-)mail. (See Exhibit 4.1.) Some database management companies, however, do not infringe on customer privacy because they do not collect individual data. One such company is Watchfire (http://www.watchfire.com), which provides aggregate data only on visitors to a company's Web site with respect to where the visitors came from and what behavior they exhibited while at the site.

While marketers call this process database marketing, some consumer advocates are calling it an invasion of privacy. The leader of Junkbusters, a consumer advocacy group that opposes invasions of consumer privacy, calls the practice of database development "Orwellian," a reference to George Orwell's futuristic novel *1984,* in which each home had a television-like device that watched the occupants. And there is ample and growing evidence that consumers are getting more and more aggravated with these database marketing efforts. A recent survey by Planetfeedback.com showed that 80 percent of respondents were "very annoyed" by pop-up ads and spam e-mail; in comparison, only about 10–15 percent of these respondents reported being "very annoyed" by print or TV ads. [2]

But advertisers defend themselves by saying that good marketing research (including database development) leads to greater efficiency and more value for customers.

Some Things Are Still A Mystery.

Your Online Visitors Shouldn't Be One Of Them.

EXHIBIT 4.1

Many firms are in the business of providing information for advertisers to effectively and efficiently deliver advertising and integrated brand promotion messages to target audiences. Firms like Buystream (now owned by Watchfire) sell consumers' names and addresses that they have gathered and organized into easy-to-use databases.

1.   Teena Massingill, "Buyer Beware: Retailers Sharing Data," Knight Ridder News Service, September 17, 1999.
2.   Jack Neff, "Spam Research Reveals Disgust with Pop-Up Ads," *Advertising Age,* August 23, 2003, 1, 21.

The argument goes that the more effective direct marketers get, the more they know about you, the better they can serve you.[3] For example, grocers argue that with the databases they can target coupons and other specially advertised offers to the people most likely to use them, instead of wasting money on coupons and mailings that are never used.

Consumer advocates argue that any good that might come from the "data mining" process is far outweighed by the annoyance created by the avalanche of offers plaguing consumers. These advocates are arguing for so-called "permission marketing," in which marketers can direct advertising and promotions *only* to people who give them express permission to do so by indicating clearly that they "opt-in" to receiving offers through the mail or e-mail.[4]

The repercussions of database marketing and not heeding consumers' frustration are already being felt in the form of new regulations. The year 2004 saw the implementation of restrictive legislation. The most important was the "do not call list" devised by the Federal Trade Commission; the list now exceeds 60 million American phone numbers registered in an attempt to restrict telemarketing calls.[5]

We have to realize that nothing about database development or sending advertising messages and promotional offers to consumers is unethical or illegal—yet. We will need to wait and see whether any restrictions are placed on the database process by either government mandate or consumer pressure. Or we could all do what some people do. They don't enter sweepstakes, they never shop on the Internet, they throw junk mail and surveys directly into the trash, and they have unlisted phone numbers.

The story of Anne Marie (and perhaps even your own experience) highlights that the social, ethical, and regulatory aspects of advertising are as dynamic and controversial as any of the strategic or creative elements of the process. What is socially responsible or irresponsible, ethically debatable, politically correct, or legal? The answers are constantly changing. As a society changes, so, too, do its perspectives. Like anything else with social roots and implications, advertising will be affected by these changes.

The history of advertising and promotion includes all sorts of social, ethical, and legal issues and controversies—no doubt about it. But advertising and promotion also have their triumphs, moral as well as financial. One important thing you will learn in this chapter is that many criticisms of advertising and promotion can be uninformed, naïve, and simplistic, often failing to consider the complex social and legal environment in which contemporary advertising and promotion operate. Don't get us wrong; sometimes the criticisms are right on because of overzealous advertising and promotion efforts. Other times, the criticism comes from intuition and emotion not supported by facts or reality.

In this chapter, we will consider a wide range of social, ethical, and legal issues related to advertising and the many tools of integrated brand promotion, and we will do so in an analytical and straightforward fashion. We will start with advertising—the promotional tool that tends to get the most scrutiny because of its global presence—and then we will move on to the other promotional tools in IBP.

The Social Aspects of Advertising.
The social aspects of advertising are often volatile. For those who feel that advertising is intrusive and manipulative, the social aspects usually provide the most fuel for heated debate.

We can consider the social aspects of advertising in several broad areas that highlight both the positive and negative social aspects of advertising. On the positive

---

3.   Erika Rasmusson, "What Price Knowledge?" *Sales and Marketing Management,* December 1998, 56.
4.   Stephen Baker, "Where Danger Lurks," *Business Week,* August 25, 2003, 114–118.
5.   Ira Teinowitz, "FCC Extends Do-Not-Call-List," *Advertising Age,* June 30, 2003, 1, 29.

side, we'll consider advertising's effect on consumers' knowledge, standard of living, and feelings of happiness and well-being, and its potential positive effects on the mass media. On the negative side, we'll examine a variety of social criticisms of advertising, ranging from the charge that advertising wastes resources and promotes materialism to the argument that advertising perpetuates stereotypes.

Our approach is to offer the pros and cons on several issues that critics and advertisers commonly argue about. Be forewarned—these are matters of opinion, with no clear right and wrong answers. You will have to draw your own conclusions. But above all, be analytical and thoughtful. These are important issues and without understanding and contemplating these issues, you really haven't studied advertising and promotion at all.

Advertising Educates Consumers.
Does advertising provide valuable information to consumers, or does it seek only to confuse or entice them? Here's what the experts on both sides have to say.

Pro: Advertising Informs.
Supporters of advertising argue that advertising educates consumers, equipping them with the information they need to make informed purchase decisions. By regularly assessing information and advertising claims, consumers become more educated regarding the features, benefits, functions, and value of products. Further, consumers can become more aware of their own tendencies toward being persuaded and relying on certain types of product information.

Historically, the view has been that advertising is "clearly an immensely powerful instrument for the elimination of ignorance."[6] Now, that might be a *little* bit overstated, but according to this argument, better-educated consumers enhance their lifestyles and economic power through astute marketplace decision making—can't argue with that.

A related argument is that advertising *reduces product search time*—that is, the amount of time an individual must spend to search for desired products and services is reduced because of advertising and access to the Web. The large amount of information readily available through advertising and Web sites allows consumers to easily assess information about the potential value of brands without spending time and effort traveling from retail store to retail store trying to evaluate each one. The information contained in an advertisement "reduces drastically the cost of search."[7]

EXHIBIT 4.2

Advertising can be used to inform the public about important social issues. Miller Brewing spends millions of dollars a year promoting responsible drinking behavior. http://www.millerbrewing.com

Another aspect of informing the public has to do with the role advertising can play in communicating about important social issues. Miller Brewing devotes millions of dollars a year to promoting responsible drinking with both print and television advertisements like the one shown in Exhibit 4.2. As described in the Doing It Right box, another brewer, Anheuser-Busch, hosts a unique Web site at http://www.beeresponsible.com as part of an IBP campaign designed to combat

6.   George J. Stigler, "The Economics of Information," *Journal of Political Economy* (June 1961), 213–220.
7.   Ibid., 220.

DOING IT RIGHT

Tackling Alcohol Abuse through Integrated Brand Promotion

Since 1982, when Anheuser-Busch launched its "Know When to Say When" ad campaign, the firm has spent over $500 million on advertising and other programs to promote responsible drinking among adults who choose to drink. In November 1997, Anheuser-Busch celebrated the campaign's 15-year anniversary by launching the Web site http://www.beeresponsible.com to continue the fight against alcohol abuse "one person at a time."

Anheuser-Busch's approach to fighting alcohol abuse is no different from its philosophy about selling beer: It wants to be the best and it wants to get results. The firm has been at the forefront of alcohol awareness and education initiatives since the early 1900s, when it ran a series of print ads reminding Americans to drink responsibly, with the slogan "Budweiser Means Moderation." In 1982, with the launch of the now famous "Know When to Say When" campaign, Anheuser-Busch began a new era in its efforts to fight alcohol abuse and underage drinking by promoting personal responsibility.

Successful promotions to prevent drunk driving through the use of designated drivers and cab rides home began in 1984. The following year, Anheuser-Busch was the first in the alcohol beverage industry to bring responsible-drinking messages to television. The company's efforts have helped to make *designated driver* a household term and changed public attitudes about drinking and driving.

Anheuser-Busch's strong opposition to underage drinking then led to the development in 1990 of the "Let's Stop Underage Drinking Before It Starts" campaign. Ads in this campaign were focused on helping parents (who children say are the leading influence in their decision whether to drink) address this important issue with their children and are also designed to be used with students in schools.

In the fall of 1999, a new chapter in its awareness and education efforts began with the launch of its "We All Make a Difference" advertising campaign. "We All Make a Difference" reinforces the good practices of drinkers who exercise personal responsibility, designate a driver, or call a cab; salutes those parents who talk to their children about illegal underage drinking; and builds on the momentum of the positive downward trend in drunk driving fatalities and the decline in teen drinking. Starting in 2003, the firm launched a new national advertising campaign ("Responsibility Matters") and has created more than two dozen community-based programs that fight drunk driving and underage drinking and that promote responsible drinking among adults who choose to drink.

Anheuser-Busch is a good example of a firm that has made a commitment to social responsibility and has used advertising and promotion in a consistent manner over many years to achieve a positive effect. This is IBP applied to a social issue rather than to promote the company's brands.

Source: http://www.beeresponsible.com, accessed May 26, 2007.

drunk driving, underage drinking, and binge drinking.

Con: Advertising Is Superficial and Intrusive. Critics argue that advertising does not provide good product information at all and that it is so pervasive and intrusive to daily life that it is impossible to escape. The basic criticism of advertising with respect to it being superficial focuses on the claim that many ads carry little, if any, actual product information (see Exhibit 4.3 on the next page). What it does carry is said to be hollow ad-speak. Ads are rhetorical; there is no pure "information." All information in an ad is biased, limited, and inherently deceptive.

Continuing on, critics of advertising believe that ads should contain information on brands that relates strictly to functional features and performance results—things that can be measured and tested brand by brand. Advertisers argue in response that, in many instances, consumers are interested in more than a physical, tangible material good with performance features and purely functional value. The functional features of a brand may be secondary in importance to consumers in both the information search and the choice process. Emotional factors play an important role in consumer's choices (see Exhibit 4.4 on the next page).

The advertisers' counterpoint is that critics often dismiss as unimportant or ignore the totality of brand benefits that consumers seek, including emotional, hedonic (pleasure-seeking), or aesthetic aspects. The relevant information being used by a buyer may focus on criteria that are nonutilitarian or nonfunctional in nature.

With respect to the intrusive aspect of advertising, the argument is that advertising has become so widespread (in some critics' view, ubiquitous) that consumers are starting to revolt. In a Planetfeedback.com survey where respondents expressed their annoyance with pop-up ads, the study found that over 95 percent of consumers considered themselves "angry" or "furious" over spam and pop-up ads.[8] Similarly, consumers are getting increasingly concerned and frustrated with brands working

---

8.   Jack Neff, "Spam Research Reveals Disgust with Pop-Up Ads," *Advertising Age,* August 23, 2003, 1, 21.

EXHIBITS 4.3 AND 4.4

Critics of advertising complain that ads often carry little, if any, product information and would prefer that all advertising be rich in "information" like the Toyota ad in Exhibit 4.3. Is the Honda ad in Exhibit 4.4 devoid of "information"?

their way into entertainment programming. The so-called commerce-content crossover—product placement and integration highlighted at the beginning of the chapter—was rated as allowing advertising to become too pervasive by 72 percent of consumers surveyed.[9] Despite widespread consumer aggravation, it would seem that advertisers really aren't paying much attention. On the one hand, consumers seem to be saying loud and clear that advertising is getting just too widespread and intruding on their lives and lifestyles. On the other hand, big advertisers like American Express are pushing to become more "relevant" to consumers than a mere 30-second advertising spot and to make their brands part of consumer lifestyles. So much so that the chief marketing officer at American Express said in a keynote speech to a large advertising audience, "We need to adapt to the new landscape by thinking not in day-parts [referring to television advertising schedules] but to mindparts."[10] We'll let you decide what you think of that one.

But the advertising industry should really be paying attention to consumers' aggravation with the clutter and intrusiveness of advertising for one very important reason—clutter and intrusiveness reduce the effectiveness of advertising. According to one expert, "The ability of the average consumer to even remember advertising 24 hours later is at the lowest level in the history of our business."[11] Is the industry

9.   Clair Atkinson, "Ad Intrusion Up, Say Consumers," *Advertising Age,* January 6, 2003, 1, 19.
10.   Hank Kim, "Just Risk It," *Advertising Age,* February 9, 2004, 1, 51.
11.   Matthew Creamer, "Caught in the Clutter Crossfire: Your Brand," *Advertising Age,* April 2, 2007, 1, 35.

likely to work to reduce clutter? Probably not. Another industry expert suggests that "New media have more potential to deliver even more saturation, clutter, and intrusiveness than traditional media, in which case the new media will only worsen marketing resistance."[12]

Advertising Improves the Standard of Living.
Whether advertising raises or lowers the general standard of living is hotly debated. Opinions vary widely on this issue and go right to the heart of whether advertising is a good use or a waste of energy and resources.

Pro: Advertising Lowers the Cost of Products.
Four aspects of the nature of advertising, supporters argue, help lower the cost of products:

- Due to the economies of scale (it costs less to produce products in large quantities) partly created by advertising's contribution to stimulating demand, products cost less than if there were no advertising at all. As broad-based demand stimulation results in lower production and administrative costs per unit produced, lower prices are passed on to consumers.
- Consumers have a greater variety of choice in products and services because advertising increases the probability of success that new products will succeed.
- The pressures of competition and the desire to have fresh, marketable brands motivates firms to produce improved products and brands and introduce lower-priced brands.
- The speed and reach of the advertising process aids in the diffusion of innovations. This means that new discoveries can be communicated to a large percentage of the marketplace very quickly. Innovations succeed when advertising communicates their benefits to the customer.

All four of these factors can contribute positively to the standard of living and quality of life in a society. Advertising may be instrumental in bringing about these effects because it serves an important role in demand stimulation and keeping customers informed.

Con: Advertising Wastes Resources and Raises the Standard of Living Only for Some.
One of the traditional criticisms of advertising is that it represents an inefficient, wasteful process that channels monetary and human resources in a society to the "shuffling of existing total demand," rather than to the expansion of total demand.[13] Critics say that a society is no better off with advertising because it does not stimulate demand—it only shifts demand from one brand to another. Advertising thus brings about economic stagnation and a *lower* standard of living, not a higher standard of living. Similarly, critics argue that brand differences are trivial and that the proliferation of brands does not offer a greater variety of choice but rather a meaningless waste of resources, with confusion and frustration for the consumer. Finally, they argue that advertising is a tool of capitalism that just helps widen the gap between rich and poor, creating strife between social classes.

Advertising Affects Happiness and General Well-Being.
Critics and supporters of advertising differ significantly in their views about how advertising affects consumers' happiness and general well-being. As you will see, this is a complex issue with multiple pros and cons.

12. Ibid., 35.
13. Richard Caves, *American Industry: Structure, Conduct, Performance* (Englewood Cliffs, N.J.: Prentice-Hall, 1964), 102.

Con: Advertising Creates Needs. A common cry among critics is that advertising creates needs and makes people buy things they don't really need or even want. The argument is that consumers are relatively easy to seduce into wanting the next shiny bauble offered by marketers. Critics would say, for example, that a quick examination of any issue of *Seventeen* magazine reveals a magazine intent on teaching the young women of the world to covet slim bodies and a glamorous complexion. Cosmetics giants like Estée Lauder and Revlon typically spend from 15 to 30 cents from every dollar of sales to promote their brands as the ultimate solution for those in search of the ideal complexion.

Pro: Advertising Addresses a Wide Variety of Basic Human Needs. A good place to start in discussing whether advertising can create needs or not is to consider the basic nature of human needs. Abraham Maslow, a pioneer in the study of human motivation (and someone you probably read about in your psych class), conceived that human behavior progresses through the following hierarchy of need states:[14]

- *Physiological needs:* Biological needs that require the satisfaction of hunger, thirst, and basic bodily functions.
- *Safety needs:* The need to provide shelter and protection for the body and to maintain a comfortable existence.
- *Love and belonging needs:* The need for affiliation and affection. A person will strive for both the giving and receiving of love.
- *Esteem needs:* The need for recognition, status, and prestige. In addition to the respect of others, there is a need and desire for self-respect.

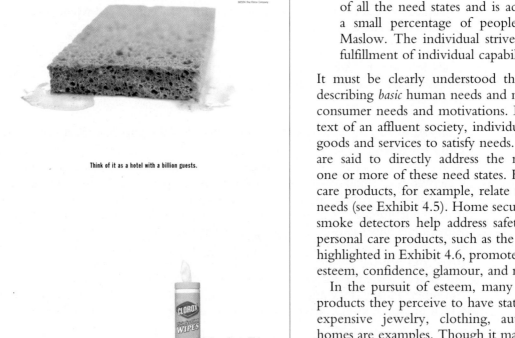

Think of it as a hotel with a billion guests.

Don't spread germs. Kill them.

EXHIBIT 4.5

An ad like this appeals to our physiological needs (protecting our health) in Maslow's Hierarchy of Needs.

- *Self-actualization needs:* This is the highest of all the need states and is achieved by only a small percentage of people, according to Maslow. The individual strives for maximum fulfillment of individual capabilities.

It must be clearly understood that Maslow was describing *basic* human needs and motivations, not consumer needs and motivations. But in the context of an affluent society, individuals will turn to goods and services to satisfy needs. Many products are said to directly address the requirements of one or more of these need states. Food and health care products, for example, relate to physiological needs (see Exhibit 4.5). Home security systems and smoke detectors help address safety needs. Many personal care products, such as the skin care brand highlighted in Exhibit 4.6, promote feelings of self-esteem, confidence, glamour, and romance.

In the pursuit of esteem, many consumers buy products they perceive to have status and prestige: expensive jewelry, clothing, automobiles, and homes are examples. Though it may be difficult to buy self-actualization (the highest level of Maslow's hierarchy), educational pursuits and high-intensity leisure activities (e.g., extreme sports) can certainly foster feelings of pride and accomplishment that contribute to self-actualization. Supporters maintain that advertising may be directed at many different forms of need fulfillment, but it is in no way powerful enough to *create* basic human needs.

14.   A. H. Maslow, *Motivation and Personality* (New York: Harper & Row, 1970).

EXHIBIT 4.6

*"All you need is Guinot."
In what sense might a person
need Guinot? Does the
Guinot site (*http://www
.guinotusa.com*) tie in to
consumers' happiness and
general well-being? Click
around the site and identify
message and design elements
that target consumers' various
need states.*

Con: Advertising Promotes Materialism. It is also claimed that individuals' wants and aspirations may be distorted by advertising. The long-standing argument is that in societies characterized by heavy advertising, there is a tendency for conformity and status-seeking behavior, both of which are considered materialistic and superficial.[15] Material goods are placed ahead of spiritual and intellectual pursuits. Advertising, which portrays brands as symbols of status, success, and happiness, contributes to the materialism and superficiality in a society. It creates wants and aspirations that are artificial and self-centered. This, in turn, results in an overemphasis on the production of private goods, to the detriment of public goods (such as highways, parks, schools, and infrastructure).[16]

Pro: Advertising Only Reflects Society's Priorities. Although advertising is undeniably in the business of promoting the good life, defenders of advertising argue that it did not create the American emphasis on materialism. For example, in the United States, major holidays such as Christmas (gifts), Thanksgiving (food), and Easter (candy and clothing) have become festivals of consumption. This is the American way. Historian and social observer Stephen Fox concludes his treatise on the history of American advertising as follows:

One may build a compelling case that American culture is—beyond redemption—money-mad, hedonistic, superficial, rushing heedlessly down a railroad track called Progress. Tocqueville and other observers of the young republic described America in these terms in the early 1800s, decades before the development of national advertising. To blame advertising now for these most basic tendencies in American history is to miss the point. . . . The people who have created modern advertising are not hidden persuaders pushing our buttons in the service of some malevolent purpose. They are just producing an especially visible manifestation, good and bad, of the American way of life.[17]

While we clearly live in the age of consumption, goods and possessions have been used by all cultures throughout history to mark special events, to play significant roles in rituals, and to serve as vessels of special meaning long before there was modern advertising. Still, have we taken it too far? Is excess what we do best in consumer cultures?

Advertising: Demeaning and Deceitful, or Liberating and Artful?
Without a doubt, advertisers are always on the lookout for creative and novel ways to grab and hold the attention of their audience. Additionally, an advertiser has a very specific profile of the target customer in mind (more about this in Chapter 6) when an ad is being created. Both of these fundamental propositions about how ads get developed can spark controversy.

15.   Vance Packard, *The Status Seekers* (New York: David McKay, 1959).

16.   This argument was first offered by authors George Katona, *The Mass Consumption Society* (New York: McGraw-Hill, 1964), 54–61, and John Kenneth Galbraith, *The Affluent Society* (Boston: Houghton Mifflin, 1958).

17.   Fox, *The Mirror Makers: A History of American Advertising and Its Creators* (New York: William Morrow, 1984), 330.

Con: Advertising Perpetuates Stereotypes. Advertisers often portray people in advertisements that look like members of their target audience with the hope that people who see the ad will be more prone to relate to the ad and attend to its message. Critics charge that this practice yields a very negative effect—it perpetuates stereotypes. The portrayal of women, the elderly, and ethnic minorities is of particular concern. It is argued that women are still predominantly cast as homemakers or objects of desire (see Exhibit 4.7), despite the fact that women now hold top management positions and deftly head households. The elderly are often shown as helpless or ill, even though many active seniors enjoy a rich lifestyle. Critics contend that advertisers' propensity to feature African-American or Latin athletes in ads is simply a more contemporary form of stereotyping.

Pro: Advertisers Are Showing Much More Sensitivity. Much of this sort of stereotyping is becoming part of the past. Advertisements from prior generations do show a vivid stereotyping problem. But in today's setting, the Dove ad in Exhibit 4.8 shows that women can be featured as strong and feminine in contemporary advertising. Dove launched its "Campaign for Real Beauty" in September 2004 with an ad campaign featuring real women whose appearances do not conform to the stereotypical and relatively narrow norms of beauty. The ads asked viewers to judge the women's looks (*Oversized? Outstanding?* or *Wrinkled? Wonderful?*) and invited them to cast their votes and join in a discussion of beauty issues at http://www.campaignforrealbeauty.com. More than one million votes have been tabulated globally. Advertisers are realizing that a diverse world requires diversity in the social reality that ads represent and help construct. However, many remain dissatisfied with the pace of change; the Body Shop ad in Exhibit 4.9, promoting something other than the body of a supermodel as a valid point of reference for women, is still the exception, not the rule.

EXHIBIT 4.7

What is the advertiser claiming in this ad? How about—a Versace gown is the ultimate in chic. http://www.versace.com

EXHIBIT 4.8

Advertisers today realize the diverse reality of consumers' lives. This Dove ad is a beautiful example of advertisers' efforts to represent diversity. http://www.campaignforrealbeauty.com

EXHIBIT 4.9

The Body Shop (http://www.bodyshop.com) is bucking trends by protesting the "supermodel" imagery often used in product advertising. While men's magazine sites, such as Playboy (http://www.playboy.com), triumphantly display airbrushed perfection and countless companies adorn everything from automobiles to breakfast cereal with the svelte and athletic, the Web is (currently) a rather low-fidelity medium for transmitting glossy photographs. Sex may sell, but simple, bold, and clever graphics may be as useful for "eye candy" as anything ever exhibited by Versace Couture.

EXHIBIT 4.10

Oddly, frank talk about real-life issues is not all that common in advertising. Do you know anyone who would be put off by such frankness?
http://www.tampax.com

Con: Advertising Is Often Offensive. A long-standing criticism of advertising is that it is often offensive and the appeals are in poor taste. Moreover, some would say that the trend in American advertising is to be rude, crude, and sometimes lewd, as advertisers struggle to grab the attention of consumers who have learned to tune out the avalanche of advertising messages they are confronted with each day. Of course, taste is just that, a personal and inherently subjective evaluation. What is offensive to one person is merely satiric to another. What should we call an ad prepared for the Australian market that shows the owner of an older Honda Accord admiring a newer model? The owner's admiration of the new car spurs the old version to lock its doors, rev its motor, and drive off a cliff—with the owner still inside. Critics decry the ad as trivializing suicide—an acute problem among young people, who are also the target market for this ad.[18]

But not all advertising deemed offensive has to be as extreme as these examples. Many times, advertisers get caught in a firestorm of controversy because certain, and sometimes relatively small, segments of the population are offended. The history of advertising is loaded with examples. An AIDS prevention campaign run by the Centers for Disease Control and Prevention (CDC), a highly respected government agency, has been criticized for being too explicit. A spokesperson for the Family Research Council said about the ads, "They're very offensive—I thought I was watching *NYPD* Blue."[19] A highly popular ad seen as controversial by some was the "People Taking Diet Coke Break" ad (this ad was featured in Exhibit 1.12 in Chapter 1). In this television spot, a group of female office workers is shown eyeing a construction worker as he takes off his T-shirt and enjoys a Diet Coke. Coca-Cola was criticized for using reverse sexism in this ad. While Coca-Cola and the CDC may have ventured into delicate areas, consider these advertisers, who were caught completely by surprise when their ads were deemed offensive:

- In a public service spot developed by Aetna Life & Casualty insurance for a measles vaccine, a wicked witch with green skin and a wart was cause for a challenge to the firm's ad from a witches' rights group.
- A Nynex spot was criticized by animal-rights activists because it showed a rabbit colored with blue dye.
- A commercial for Black Flag bug spray had to be altered after a war veterans' group objected to the playing of "Taps" over dead bugs.

Advertisers have long felt that they need to carefully consider the tastefulness of their ads. Expect the unexpected. An unpretentious ad like that in Exhibit 4.10, featuring frank copy about mundane aspects of menstruation, could be expected to breach some consumers' sensibilities. However, the marketer in this case is willing to take the risk in the hopes that the frank approach will get attention and ring true with the target customer.

18. Normandy Madden, "Honda Pulls Suicide Car Ad from Australian TV Market," *Advertising Age,* September 22, 2003, 3.
19. Kevin Goldman, "From Witches to Anorexics, Critical Eyes Scrutinize Ads for Political Correctness," *Wall Street Journal,* May 19, 1994, B1, B10.

On the other hand, maybe hypersensitivity to consumer reaction is not all that necessary. GoDaddy.com is making a nice living running risqué ads on the Super Bowl every year. In 2006, the Web firm had its first 13 ad submissions to Super Bowl broadcaster ABC rejected as "tasteless." The still-racy ad that finally ran created a 15-fold spike in traffic to the firm's Web site.[20]

In the end, we have to consider whether advertising is offensive or whether society is merely pushing the limits of what is appropriate for freedom of speech and expression. The now infamous "costume malfunction" that plagued Janet Jackson during a Super Bowl halftime show and incidents like shock radio DJs' profanity are drawing attention not just from fed-up consumers but from the U.S. Senate as well, which has approved a tenfold increase in fines for television and radio stations that violate rules on airing profanity and sexually explicit materials.[21] And while government may move to provide a legal remedy to deter offensive broadcasts—advertising messages or programming—the fact is that what is acceptable and what is offensive changes over time in a culture.

Pro: Advertising Is a Source of Fulfillment and Liberation. On the other end of the spectrum, some argue that the consumption that advertising glorifies is actually quite good for society. Most people sincerely appreciate modern conveniences that liberate us from the more foul facets of everyday life, such as body odor, close contact with dirty diapers, and washing clothes by hand. Some observers remind us that when the Berlin Wall came down, those in East Germany did not immediately run to libraries and churches—they ran to department stores and shops. Before the modern consumer age, the consumption of many goods was restricted by social class. Modern advertising has helped bring us a "democratization" of goods. Observers argue that there is a liberating quality to advertising and consumption that should be appreciated and encouraged.

Con: Advertisers Deceive via Subliminal Stimulation. There is much controversy, and almost a complete lack of understanding that persists about the issue of subliminal (below the threshold of consciousness) communication and advertising.[22] Since there is much confusion surrounding the issue of subliminal advertising, let us clarify: No one ever sold anything by putting images of breasts in ice cubes or the word *sex* in the background of an ad. Furthermore, no one at an advertising agency, except the very bored or the very eager to retire, has time to sit around dreaming up such things (see the Ethics box on page 122). We realize it makes for a great story, but hiding pictures in other pictures doesn't work to get anyone to buy anything. Although there is some evidence for some types of unconscious ad processing, these effects are very short-lived and found only in laboratories. The Svengali-type hocus-pocus that has become advertising mythology simply does not exist.[23] If the rumors are true that some advertisers are actually trying to use subliminal messages in their ads, the best research on the topic would conclude that they're wasting their money.[24]

Pro: Advertising Is Democratic Art. Some argue that one of the best aspects of advertising is its artistic nature. The pop art movement of the late 1950s and

20.   Georgia Flight, "Hits and Misses," *Business 2.0,* April 2006, 140.
21.   Jeremy Pelofsky, "U.S. Senate Backs Ten Fold Hike in Indecency Fines," Reuters News Service, May 18, 2006, accessed at *www.yahoo.reuters.com* on May 19, 2006.
22.   Don E. Schultz, "Subliminal Ad Notions Still Resonate Today," *Marketing News,* March 15, 2007, 5, 9.
23.   Murphy, Monahan, and Zajonc, "Additivity of Nonconscious Affect: Combined Effects of Priming and Exposure," *Journal of Personality and Social Psychology,* vol. 69 (1995), 589–602.
24.   Timothy E. Moore, "Subliminal Advertising: What You See Is What You Get," *Journal of Marketing,* vol. 46 (Spring 1982), 38–47; Timothy E. Moore, "The Case Against Subliminal Manipulation," *Psychology and Marketing,* vol. 5, no. 4 (Winter 1988), 297–317.

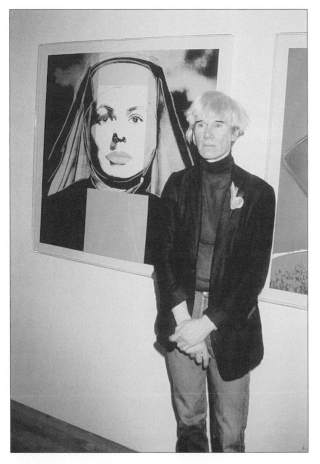

EXHIBIT 4.11

Artist Andy Warhol demonstrated that the most accessible art was advertising. Intel (Blue Man Group) and Microsoft (butterflies) have both used contemporary and fine art in their advertising.

1960s, particularly in London and New York, was characterized by a fascination with commercial culture. Some of this art critiqued consumer culture and simultaneously celebrated it. Above all, Andy Warhol (see Exhibit 4.11), himself a commercial illustrator, demonstrated that art was for the people and that the most accessible art was advertising. Art was not restricted to museum walls; it was on Campbell's soup cans, LifeSavers candy rolls, and Brillo pads. Advertising is anti-elitist, pro-democratic art. As Warhol said about America, democracy, and Coke,

What's great about this country is that America started the tradition where the richest consumers buy essentially the same things as the poorest. You can be watching TV and see Coca-Cola, and you can know that the President drinks Coke, Liz Taylor drinks Coke, and just think, you can drink Coke, too. A Coke is a Coke and no amount of money can get you a better Coke than the one the bum on the corner is drinking. All the Cokes are the same and all the Cokes are good. Liz Taylor knows it, the President knows it, the bum knows it, and you know it.[25]

Advertising Has a Powerful Effect on the Mass Media. One final issue that advertisers and their critics debate is the matter of advertising's influence on the mass media. Here again, we find a very wide range of viewpoints.

Pro: Advertising Fosters a Diverse and Affordable Mass Media. Advertising fans argue that advertising is the best thing that can happened to an informed democracy. Magazines, newspapers, television and radio stations, and Web sites are supported by advertising expenditures. In 2006, mass media advertising expenditures in the United States exceeded $300 billion.[26] Much of this spending went to support television, radio, magazines, and newspapers. If you include online advertising's support of Web sites, the number approaches $400 billion. With this sort of monetary support of the media, citizens have access to a variety of information and entertainment sources at low cost. Network television and radio broadcasts would not be free commodities, and newspapers and magazines would likely cost two to four times more in the absence of advertising support.

Another argument in support of advertising is that it provides invaluable exposure to issues. When noncommercial organizations (like social service organizations) use advertising, members of society receive information on important social and political issues. A dramatic example of the noncommercial use of advertising was a multimedia campaign launched by the U.S. government, working in conjunction with the Partnership for a Drug-Free America, to remind the American public of the ruinous power of drugs such as heroin.[27] At the campaign's launch, the pledge was made to outspend major advertisers, and indeed, over five years the campaign spending is estimated to have approached $1 billion. A stockpile of nearly 400 ads was available for use in this

25.   Andy Warhol, *The Philosophy of Andy Warhol: From A to B and Back Again* (New York: Harcourt Brace Jovanovich, 1975), 101.
26.   "100 Leading National Advertisers," *Advertising Age*, June 25, 2007, S1.
27.   B. G. Gregg, "Tax Funds Bankroll New Anti-Drug Ads," Cincinnati Enquirer, July 10, 1998, A1, A17.

ETHICS

Subliminal Advertising: A Really Bad Idea

Every few years, a story will surface claiming that an advertiser tried to sell a brand by putting subliminal (below the conscious threshold of awareness) messages or images in an ad. To set the record straight, subliminal advertising doesn't work—and you'll get in a lot of trouble if you try it.

This is how subliminal *communication* does work. Research has shown that people can, indeed, process information that is transmitted to them below the level of conscious awareness, that is, subliminally. What is not proven is that you can send a *persuasive* message subliminally. Ever since a crackpot allegedly inserted the phrases "Eat Popcorn" and "Drink Coca-Cola" in a movie back in the 1950s, the world has been terrified that unscrupulous marketers will use the technique to sell products. Well, you can rest easy. Subliminal advertising doesn't work, but it does make for some really interesting stories:

- French TV network M6 and its production house Expand got in hot water in 2001 with French regulators over the alleged insertion of 33 subliminal images of a Kodak disposable camera during the airing of an episode of a hit reality TV show called *Popstars.*

- Russian TV network ATN was pulled off the air in 2000 when Russian officials discovered that the broadcaster had been inserting the message "Sit and Watch Only ATN" into every 25th frame of its broadcasting during the summer of 2000. The station was off the air for nearly two years.

- During the 2000 presidential election campaigns in the United States, Democrats accused Republicans of using subliminal advertising in the so-called Rats ad, which attacked Democratic candidate Al Gore's prescription drug plan. The allegation charged that during the ads the word "bureaucrats" was reduced to the word "rats," visible for a split second.

In none of these recent transgressions into subliminal messaging is there any evidence that the intended effects were achieved. Recently, the issue has resurfaced as a research topic among neural scientists, but what they seem to be "rediscovering" is that yes, you can communicate commercial messages to people below the conscious threshold of awareness. But the next effect has never been discovered—you cannot get people to *act* on the information they may have received.

Whether subliminal advertising works or not, it does provide some great entertainment. And as long as people are suspicious of advertising, claims will surface that subliminal advertising is being used on unsuspecting consumers.

Sources: Lawrence J. Speer, "Off in a Flash," **Ad Age Global**, February 2002, 6; Bob Garfield, "Subliminal Seduction and Other Urban Myths," **Advertising Age**, September 18, 2000, 41; Don E. Schultz, "Subliminal Ad Notions Still Resonate Today," **Marketing News**, March 15, 2007, 5, 9.

comprehensive campaign. Some, like the one shown in Exhibit 4.12 on the next page, involved powerful messages about the ultimate consequence of drug abuse.

Con: Advertising Affects Programming. Critics argue that advertisers who place ads in media have an unhealthy effect on shaping the content of information contained in the media. This issue was highlighted in the introduction to the chapter as both GM and Morgan Stanley appeared to be trying to influence the editorial content of the publications in which the firms placed ads. And there are more blatant examples. The CEO of a firm headed for prosecution was accused of hiring a public relations firm to turn out a series of newspaper articles sympathetic to the CEO's firm.[28] Similarly, there have been several instances of "stealth sponsorship" of newspaper opinion editorials where the journalists were being paid by corporations who were receiving favorable treatment in the editorials.[29]

Another charge leveled at advertisers is that they purchase air time only on programs that draw large audiences. Critics argue that these mass market programs lower the quality of television because cultural and educational programs, which draw smaller and more selective markets, are dropped in favor of mass market programs. Watch a few episodes of *Survivor* or *Lost* and it's hard to argue against the proposition that shallow content is indeed winning out over culture and education.

Additionally, television programmers have a difficult time attracting advertisers to shows that may be valuable, yet controversial. Programs that deal with abortion, sexual abuse, or AIDS may have trouble drawing advertisers who fear the consequences of any association with controversial issues given the predictable public reaction that would come from the religious right.

28.   Jay Reeves, "Scrushy Said to Pay for Positive Stories," Associated Press, January 19, 2006, accessed at *www.news.yahoo.com* on January 20, 2006.
29.   Eamon Javers, "This Opinion Brought to You By. . . ." *BusinessWeek,* January 30, 2006, 35.

Jim Morrison 1943-1971   Janis Joplin 1943-1970

In advertising, they say one of the surest ways to get your message across is to put celebrities in your ad.

John Belushi 1949-1982   River Phoenix 1970-1993

Partnership for a Drug-Free America®

EXHIBIT 4.12

This ad both appeals to our fascination with celebrity and shocks the viewer with the realization that drug use can be fatal. At http://www .drugfreeamerica.org, *the Partnership for a Drug-Free America hones its message that drug use is anything but glamorous.*

The Ethical Aspects of Advertising.
Many of the ethical aspects of advertising border on and interact with both the social and legal considerations of the advertising process. **Ethics** are moral standards and principles against which behavior is judged. Honesty, integrity, fairness, and sensitivity are all included in a broad definition of ethical behavior. Much of what is judged as ethical or unethical comes down to personal judgment. We will discuss the ethical aspects of advertising in three areas: truth in advertising, advertising to children, and advertising controversial products.

Truth in Advertising. While truth in advertising is a key legal issue, it has ethical dimensions as well. The most fundamental ethical issue has to do with **deception**—making false or misleading statements in an advertisement. The difficulty regarding this issue, of course, is in determining just what is deceptive. A manufacturer who claims a laundry product can remove grass stains is exposed to legal sanctions if the product cannot perform the task. Another manufacturer who claims to have "The Best Laundry Detergent in the World," however, is perfectly within its rights to employ superlatives. Just what constitutes "The Best" is a purely subjective determination; it cannot be proved or disproved. The use of absolute superlatives such as "Number One" or "Best in the World" is called **puffery** and is considered completely legal. The courts have long held that superlatives are understood by consumers as simply the exaggerated language of advertising and are interpreted by consumers as such.

We also need to be aware that various promotional tools are often challenged as being deceptive. The "small print" that accompanies many contests or sweepstakes are often challenged by consumers. Similarly, the appeal of a "free" gift for listening to a pitch on a resort time share often draws a harsh reaction from consumers. Now, a consumer watchdog group is challenging brand placements in television shows as deceptive. The group Commercial Alert argues that television networks are deceiving consumers by not disclosing that they are taking money for highlighting brands within shows and films.[30]

Another area of debate regarding truth in advertising relates to emotional appeals. It is likely impossible to legislate against emotional appeals such as those made about the beauty- or prestige-enhancing qualities of a brand, because these claims are unquantifiable (take another look at Exhibits 4.6 and 4.7). Since these types of appeals are legal, the ethics of such appeals fall into a gray area. Beauty and prestige, it is argued, are in the eye of the beholder, and such appeals are neither illegal nor unethical.

As you can see, there is nothing clear cut about the issue of ethics in advertising. Showing beautiful, slim, successful people in an ad is completely legal and puts a

30.   Claire Atkinson, "Watchdog Group Hits TV Product Placement," *Advertising Age,* October 6, 2003, 12.

brand in a favorable setting—do you think that is unethical? If a newspaper or magazine features a brand in an editorial—do you think that is unethical? The challenge is to develop your own ethical standards and values against which you will judge yourself and the actions of any organization for which you may work.

Advertising to Children.

The desire to restrict advertising aimed at children is based on a wide range of concerns, particularly since it is estimated that children between two and 11 years old see 25,600 advertisements in a year. One concern is that advertising promotes superficiality and values founded in material goods and consumption, as we discussed earlier in the broader context of society as a whole. Another is that children are inexperienced consumers and easy prey for the sophisticated persuasions of advertisers, and as such, advertising influences children's demands for everything from toys to snack foods. These demands, in turn, create an environment of child-parent conflict. Parents find themselves having to say no over and over again to children whose desires are piqued by effective advertising. Child psychologists contend that advertising advocates violence, is responsible for child obesity, creates a breakdown in early learning skills, and results in a destruction of parental authority.[31]

There is also concern that many programs aimed at children constitute program-length commercials. Many critics argue that programs featuring commercial products, especially products aimed at children, are simply long advertisements. This movement began in 1990 when critics argued that 70 programs airing at the time were based on commercial products such as He-Man, the Smurfs, and the Muppets.[32] There have been several attempts by special-interest groups to strictly regulate this type of programming aimed at children, but, to date, the Federal Communications Commission permits such programming to continue.

One of the earliest restrictions on advertising to children came about due to the efforts of the special-interest group Action for Children's Television. The group disbanded in 1992, but before it did, it helped get the Children's Television Act passed in 1990. This regulation restricts advertising on children's programming to 10.5 minutes per hour on weekends and 12 minutes per hour on weekdays.[33] Most recently, in an attempt to head off government regulation, big food and beverage marketers—like McDonald's, Kraft, Pepsi, and General Mills—signed the Children's Food and Beverage Advertising Initiative. The initiative is a voluntary commitment by firms to address the issue of obesity among children. A key element of the agreement is that food and beverage marketers will devote half of their advertising dollars on ads directed to children to promote more healthy eating alternatives.[34]

Advertising Controversial Products.

Some people question the wisdom of allowing the advertising of controversial goods and services, such as tobacco, alcoholic beverages, gambling and lotteries, and firearms.

Critics charge that tobacco and alcoholic beverage firms are targeting adolescents with advertising and with making dangerous and addictive products appealing.[35] This is, indeed, a complex issue. Many medical journals have published survey research that claims that advertising "caused" cigarette and alcohol consumption—particularly among teenagers.[36]

31.   Richard Linnett, "Psychologists Protest Kids' Ads," *Advertising Age,* September 11, 2000, 4.

32.   Patrick J. Sheridan, "FCC Sets Children's Ad Limits," *1990 Information Access Company,* vol. 119, no. 20 (1990), 33.

33.   Laura Bird, "NBC Special Is One Long Prime-Time Ad," *Wall Street Journal,* January 21, 1994, B1, B4.

34.   Stephanie Thompson and Ira Teinowitz, "Big Food's Big Deal Not Such a Big Concession," *Advertising Age,* November 20, 2006, 1, 29.

35.   Kathleen Deveny, "Joe Camel Ads Reach Children, Research Finds," *Wall Street Journal,* December 11, 1991, B1, B6.

36.   See, for example, Joseph R. DiFranza et al., "RJR Nabisco's Cartoon Camel Promotes Camel Cigarettes to Children," *Journal of the American Medical Association,* vol. 266, no. 22 (1991), 3168–3153.

It is interesting to note, however, that these recent studies contradict research conducted since the 1950s carried out by marketing, communications, psychology, and economics researchers—including assessments of all the available research by the Federal Trade Commission.[37] These early studies (as well as several Gallup polls during the 1990s) found that family, friends, and peers—not advertising—are the primary influence on the use of tobacco and alcohol products. Studies published in the late 1990s and early in this decade have reaffirmed the findings of this earlier research.[38] While children at a very early age can, indeed, recognize tobacco advertising characters like "Joe Camel," they also recognize as easily the Energizer Bunny (batteries), the Jolly Green Giant (canned vegetables), and Snoopy (life insurance)—all characters associated with adult products. Kids are also aware that cigarettes cause disease and know that they are intended as an adult product. Research in Europe offers the same conclusion: "Every study on the subject [of advertising effects on the use of tobacco and alcohol] finds that children are more influenced by parents and playmates than by the mass media."[39]

Why doesn't advertising cause people to smoke and drink? The simple answer is that advertising just isn't that powerful. Eight out of 10 new products fail and if advertising were so powerful, no new products would fail. The more detailed answer is that advertising cannot create primary demand in mature product categories. **Primary demand** is demand for an entire product category (recall the discussion from Chapter 1). With mature products—like milk, automobiles, toothpaste, cigarettes, and alcohol—advertising isn't powerful enough to have that effect. Research across several decades has demonstrated repeatedly that advertising does not create primary demand for tobacco or alcohol.[40]

No one has ever said that smoking or drinking is good for you. (Except for maybe that glass of wine with dinner.) That's not what we're saying here, either. The point is that these behaviors emerge in a complex social context, and the vast weight of research evidence over 40 years suggests that advertising is not a significant causal influence on initiation behavior (e.g., smoking, drinking). Rather, advertising plays its most important role in consumers' choice of brands (e.g., Camel, Coors) after they have decided to use a product category (e.g., cigarettes, beer).

Gambling and state-run lotteries represent another controversial product area with respect to advertising. What is the purpose of this advertising? Is it meant to inform gamblers and lottery players of the choices available? This would be selective demand stimulation. Or is such advertising designed to stimulate demand for engaging in wagering behavior? This would be primary demand stimulation. What about compulsive gamblers? What is the state's obligation to protect "vulnerable" citizens by restricting the placement or content of lottery advertising?

---

37.   For a summary of more than 60 articles that address the issue of alcohol and cigarette advertising and the lack of a relationship between advertising and cigarette and alcohol industry demand, see Mark Frankena et al., "Alcohol, Consumption, and Abuse," Bureau of Economics, Federal Trade Commission, March 5, 1985. For a similar listing of research articles where the same conclusions were drawn during congressional hearings on the topic, see "Advertising of Tobacco Products," Hearings before the Subcommittee on Health and the Environment, Committee on Energy and Commerce, House of Representatives, 99th Congress, July 18 and August 1, 1986, No. 99–167.

38.   For examples of the more recent studies that reaffirm peers and family rather than advertising as the basis for smoking initiation see Charles R. Taylor and P. Greg Bonner, "Comment on 'American Media and the Smoking-Related Behaviors of Asian Adolescents,'" *Journal of Advertising Research* (December 2003), 419–430; Bruce Simons Morton, "Peer and Parent Influences on Smoking and Drinking Among Early Adolescents," *Journal of Health Education and Behavior* (February 2000); and Karen H. Smith and Mary Ann Stutz, "Factors that Influence Adolescents to Smoke," *Journal of Consumer Affairs*, vol. 33, no. 2 (Winter 1999), 321–357.

39.   With regard to cartoon characters see, for example, Lucy L. Henke, "Young Children's Perceptions of Cigarette Brand Advertising: Awareness, Affect and Target Market Identification," *Journal of Advertising*, vol. 24, no. 4 (Winter 1995), 13–27, and Richard Mizerski, "The Relationship between Cartoon Trade Character Recognition and Attitude toward the Product Category," *Journal of Marketing*, vol. 59 (October 1995), 58–70. The evidence in Europe is provided by Jeffrey Goldstein, "Children and Advertising—the Research," *Commercial Communications*, July 1998, 4–8.

40.   For research on this topic across several decades, see Richard Schmalensee, *The Economics of Advertising* (Amsterdam and London: North-Holland, 1972); Mark S. Albion and Paul W. Farris, *The Advertising Controversy* (Boston: Auburn House, 1981); and Michael J. Waterson, "Advertising and Tobacco Consumption: An Analysis of the Two Major Aspects of the Debate," *International Journal of Advertising*, 9 (1990), 59–72.

When these vulnerable audiences are discussed, questions as to the basis for this vulnerability can become complex and emotionally charged. Those on one side of the issue argue that gamblers as an audiences are among the "information poor." That is, they are not prone to seeking out information from a wide range of sources. Those on the other side find such claims of "information poverty" demeaning, patronizing, and paternalistic. And a new era of gambling emerged in the late 1990s as online gambling became widespread and proved to be a fast and easy way for people to lose their life savings. Stories of out-of-control online gambling were widespread.[41] Then as online gaming revenues approached $1 billion dollars, the U.S. government took the bold move of banning all online gambling in the United States in October of 2006.[42]

The issue of advertising controversial products is complex. In 2003 we wrote in this textbook:

But consider this as you contemplate the role advertising plays in people's decisions regarding these types of products. Currently, one in three children in the United States is diagnosed as clinically obese. Will parents of these kids begin to sue McDonald's, Coca-Cola, Kellogg's, and General Mills because they advertise food products to children? Think this is unbelievable? Think again.

Now that's a little spooky! As you are now aware, this is *exactly* what happened. McDonald's and other food companies had to prepare themselves for lawsuits from people who are claiming food providers "made them fat." The food industry has countered with the proposition that kids are fat because of unconcerned parents, underfunded school systems that have dropped physical activity programs, and sedentary entertainment like home video games.[43]

This issue is troublesome enough that the U.S. government had to pass legislation barring people from suing food companies for their obesity. In March 2004, the U.S. House of Representatives overwhelmingly approved legislation nicknamed the "cheeseburger bill" that would block lawsuits blaming the food industry for making people fat. During the debate on the bill, one of the bill's sponsors said it was about "common sense and personal responsibility."[44] Many marketers are worried about the intense focus on this global health problem. The chief creative officer of Coca-Cola Co. put it this way: "Our Achilles heel is the discussion about obesity. It dilutes our marketing and works against us. It's a huge, huge issue."[45] And, as you read earlier, advertisers have entered into a voluntary agreement to devote 50 percent of their ad dollars to promoting healthy food alternatives.

While we can group these ethical issues of advertising into some reasonable categories—truth in advertising, advertising to children, and advertising controversial products—it is not as easy to make definitive statements about the status of ethics in advertising. Ethics will always be a matter of personal values and personal interpretation. And as long as there are unethical people in the world, there will be ethics problems in advertising just like in every other phase of business and life.

The Regulatory Aspects of Advertising. The term *regulation* immediately brings to mind government scrutiny and control of the advertising process. Indeed, various government bodies do regulate advertising. But consumers themselves and several different industry organizations exert as much regulatory power

41. Ira Singer, et al., "The Underground Web," *BusinessWeek,* September 2, 2002, 67–74.
42. Bloomberg News, "Frank Eyes Restoring Web Gaming," March 17, 2007, accessed at *www.boston.com/news* on May 30, 2007.
43. Mercedes M. Cardona, "Marketers Bite Back as Fat Fight Flares Up," *Advertising Age,* March 1, 2004, 3, 35.
44. Rep. Ric Keller (R-Florida), quoted in Joanne Kenen, "U.S. House Backs Ban on Obesity Lawsuits," Reuters, published on the Internet at *http://biz.yahoo.com/rc/040310/congress_obesity_3.html* on March 10, 2004; accessed March 14, 2004.
45. Stephanie Thompson and Kate MacArthur, "Obesity Fear Frenzy Grips Food Industry," *Advertising Age,* April 23, 2007, 1, 46.

over advertising as government agencies. Three primary groups—consumers, industry organizations, and government bodies—regulate advertising in the truest sense: Together they shape and restrict the process. The government relies on legal restrictions, while consumers and industry groups use less-formal controls. Like the other topics in this chapter, regulation of advertising can be controversial, and opinions about what does and doesn't need to be regulated can be highly variable. Moreover, the topic of regulation could easily be an entire course of study in its own right, so here we present just an overview of major issues and major players.

First we'll consider the areas of regulation pursued most ardently, whether it be by the government, consumers, or industry groups. Then we'll examine the nature of the regulation and the amount of influence exerted by these groups.

Areas of Advertising Regulation.
There are three basic areas of advertising regulation: deception and unfairness in advertising, competitive issues, and advertising to children. Each area is a focal point for regulation.

Deception and Unfairness.
Agreement is widespread that deception in advertising is unacceptable. The problem, of course, is that it is as difficult to determine what is deceptive from a regulatory standpoint as it is from an ethical standpoint. The Federal Trade Commission's (FTC's) policy statement on deception is the authoritative source when it comes to defining deceptive advertising. It specifies the following three elements as essential in declaring an ad deceptive:[46]

1. There must be a representation, omission, or practice that is likely to mislead the consumer.
2. This representation, omission, or practice must be judged from the perspective of a consumer acting reasonably in the circumstance.
3. The representation, omission, or practice must be a "material" one. The basic question is whether the act or the practice is likely to affect the consumer's conduct or decision with regard to the product or service. If so, the practice is material, and consumer injury is likely because consumers are likely to have chosen differently if not for the deception.

If this definition of deception sounds like carefully worded legal jargon, that's because it is. It is also a definition that can lead to diverse interpretations when it is actually applied to advertisements in real life. Fortunately, the FTC now provides highly practical advice for anticipating what can make an ad deceptive (go to http://www.ftc.gov/bcp/guides/guides.htm and under the Advertising section click on "Frequently Asked Advertising Questions"). One critical point about the FTC's approach to deception is that both implied claims and *missing* information can be bases for deeming an ad deceptive. Obviously, the FTC expects any explicit claim made in an ad to be truthful, but it also is on the lookout for ads that deceive through allusion and innuendo or ads that deceive by not telling the whole story.

Many instances of deceptive advertising and packaging have resulted in formal government programs designed to regulate such practices. But as we discussed earlier, there can be complications in regulating puffery. Conventional wisdom has argued that consumers don't actually believe extreme claims and realize that advertisers are just trying to attract attention. There are those, however, who disagree with this view of puffery and feel that it actually represents "soft-core" deception, because some consumers may believe these exaggerated claims.[47]

46.   One of the best discussions of the FTC's definition of deception was offered many years ago by Gary T. Ford and John E. Calfee, "Recent Developments in FTC Policy on Deception," *Journal of Marketing,* vol. 50 (July 1986), 82–103.
47.   Ivan Preston, *The Great American Blow Up* (Madison: University of Wisconsin Press, 1975), 4.

While the FTC and the courts have been reasonably specific about what constitutes deception, the definition of unfairness in advertising has been left relatively vague. In 1994, Congress ended a long-running dispute in the courts and in the advertising industry by approving legislation that defines **unfair advertising** as "acts or practices that cause or are likely to cause substantial injury to consumers, which is not reasonably avoidable by consumers themselves, and not outweighed by the countervailing benefits to consumers or competition."[48] This definition obligates the FTC to assess both the benefits and costs of advertising, and rules out reckless acts on the part of consumers, before a judgment can be rendered that an advertiser has been unfair.

Competitive Issues. Because the large dollar amounts spent on advertising may foster inequities that literally can destroy competition, several advertising practices relating to maintaining fair competition are regulated. Among these practices are cooperative advertising, comparison advertising, and the use of monopoly power.

Vertical cooperative advertising is an advertising technique whereby a manufacturer and dealer (either a wholesaler or retailer) share the expense of advertising. This technique is commonly used in regional or local markets where a manufacturer wants a brand to benefit from a special promotion run by local dealers (recall the co-op advertising example in Chapter 1). There is nothing illegal, per se, about this practice and it is used regularly.

The competitive threat inherent in the process, however, is that dealers (especially since the advent of first department store chains and now mega retailers like Wal-Mart, Target, and Home Depot) can be given bogus cooperative advertising allowances. These allowances require little or no effort or expenditure on the part of the dealer/retailer and thus represent hidden price concessions. As such, they are a form of unfair competition and are deemed illegal. If an advertising allowance is granted to a dealer, that dealer must demonstrate that the funds are applied specifically to advertising.

The potential exists for firms to engage in unfair competition if they use comparison ads inappropriately. **Comparison advertisements** are those in which an advertiser makes a comparison between the firm's brand and competitors' brands. The comparison may or may not explicitly identify the competition. Again, comparison ads are completely legal and are used frequently by all sorts of organizations. The ad in Exhibit 4.13 is an example of straightforward and completely legal comparison advertising.

If an advertisement is carried out in such a way that the comparison is not fair, then there is an unfair competitive effect. The American Association of Advertising Agencies (4As) has issued a set of guidelines, shown in Exhibit 4.14, regarding the use of comparison ads. Further, the FTC may require a firm using comparison to substantiate claims made in an advertisement and prove that the claims do not tend to deceive. A slightly different remedy is the use of a disclaimer to help consumers understand comparative product claims. That's what Duracell had to do when it claimed its "Coppertop" battery lasted longer than

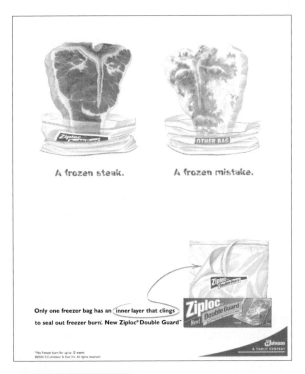

EXHIBIT 4.13

The advertising industry provides guidelines to advertisers to ensure that comparison ads, like this one, offer fair comparisons between brands. http://www.ziploc.com

48. Christy Fisher, "How Congress Broke Unfair Ad Impasse," *Advertising Age*, August 22, 1994, 34. For additional discussion of the FTC's definition of unfairness, see Ivan Preston, "Unfairness Developments in FTC Advertising Cases," *Journal of Public Policy and Marketing*, vol. 14, no. 2 (1995), 318–321.

EXHIBIT 4.14

American Association of Advertising Agencies guidelines for comparison advertising. http://www .aaaa.org

The Board of Directors of the American Association of Advertising Agencies recognizes that when used truthfully and fairly, comparative advertising provides the consumer with needed and useful information. However, extreme caution should be exercised. The use of comparative advertising, by its very nature, can distort facts and, by implication, convey to the consumer information that misrepresents the truth. Therefore, the Board believes that comparative advertising should follow certain guidelines:

1. The intent and connotation of the ad should be to inform and never to discredit or unfairly attack competitors.
2. When a competitive product is named, it should be one that exists in the marketplace as significant competition.
3. The competition should be fairly and properly identified, but never in a manner or tone of voice that degrades the competitive product or service.
4. The advertising should compare related or similar properties or ingredients of the product, dimension to dimension, feature to feature.
5. The identification should be for honest comparison purposes and not simply to upgrade by association.
6. If a competitive test is conducted, it should be done by an objective testing source, preferably an independent one, so that there will be no doubt as to the veracity of the test.
7. In all cases, the test should be supportive of all claims made in the advertising based on the test.
8. The advertising should never use partial results or stress insignificant differences to cause the consumer to draw an improper conclusion.
9. The property being compared should be significant in terms of value or usefulness of the product to the consumer.
10. Comparatives delivered through the use of testimonials should not imply that the testimonial is more than one individual's thought unless that individual represents a sample of the majority viewpoint.

Source: American Association of Advertising Agencies.

Energizer's heavy duty battery. While the claim was technically true, the Coppertop is an alkaline battery and was not being compared to Energizer's alkaline battery. Gillette, makers of Duracell, agreed to include a disclaimer in subsequent ads and then finally pulled the campaign altogether.[49]

Finally, some firms are so powerful in their use of advertising that **monopoly power** by virtue of their advertising spending can become a problem. This issue normally arises in the context of mergers and acquisitions. As an example, the U.S. Supreme Court blocked the acquisition of Clorox by Procter & Gamble because the advertising power of the two firms combined would (in the opinion of the Court) make it nearly impossible for another firm to compete.

Advertising to Children. As we discussed in the area of ethics, critics argue that continually bombarding children with persuasive stimuli can alter their motivation and behavior. While government organizations such as the FTC have been active in trying to regulate advertising directed at children, industry and consumer groups have been more successful in securing restrictions. Recall that the consumer group known as Action for Children's Television (disbanded in 1992) was actively involved in getting Congress to approve the Children's Television Act (1990). This act limits

49.   Daniel Golden and Suzanne Vranica, "Duracell's Duck Will Carry Disclaimer," *Wall Street Journal,* February 7, 2002, B2.

the amount of commercial airtime during children's programs to 10.5 minutes on weekends and 12 minutes on weekdays.

The Council of Better Business Bureaus established a Children's Advertising Review Unit and has issued a set of guidelines for advertising directed at children. These guidelines emphasize that advertisers should be sensitive to the level of knowledge and sophistication of children as decision makers. The guidelines also urge advertisers to make a constructive contribution to the social development of children by emphasizing positive social standards in advertising, such as friendship, kindness, honesty, and generosity. Similarly, the major television networks have set their own guidelines for advertising aimed at children. The guidelines restrict the use of celebrities, prohibit exhortative language (such as "Go ask Dad"), and restrict the use of animation to one-third of the total time of the commercial.

The regulation of children's advertising seems to be having some direct effect. The astounding statistics are that children ages two to 11 see 25,600 television ads a year constituting 10,700 minutes of promotional communications. Over 50 percent of these ads are viewed between 4 PM and midnight and (interestingly) only 5 percent of the ads are viewed during Saturday morning programming. The good news—kids are actually seeing *fewer* ads than they were 20 years ago.[50]

Regulatory Agents. Earlier in this section, we noted that consumer and industry groups as well as government agencies all participate in the regulation of advertising. We will now discuss examples of each of these agents along with the kinds of influence they exert. Given the multiple participants, this turns out to be a highly complex activity that we can only overview in this discussion. Additionally, our discussion focuses on regulatory activities in the United States, but advertising regulation can vary dramatically from country to country. Chapter 9, "Advertising Planning: An International Perspective," provides additional insights on advertising regulation around the world, but we must caution that becoming an expert on the complex and dynamic topic of global ad regulation would require a lifetime of study.

Government Regulation.
Governments have a powerful tool available for regulating advertising: the threat of legal action. In the United States, several different government agencies have been given the power and responsibility to regulate the advertising process. Exhibit 4.15 identifies the six agencies that have legal mandates concerning advertising and their areas of regulatory responsibility.

Several other agencies have minor powers in the regulation of advertising, such as the Civil Aeronautics Board (advertising by air carriers), the Patent Office (trademark infringement), and the Library of Congress (copyright protection). The agencies listed in Exhibit 4.15 are the most directly involved in advertising regulation. Most active among these agencies is the Federal Trade Commission, which has the most power and is most directly involved in controlling the advertising process. The FTC has been granted legal power through legislative mandates and also has developed programs for regulating advertising.

The FTC Legislative Mandates.
The Federal Trade Commission was created by the Federal Trade Commission Act in 1914. The original purpose of the agency was to prohibit unfair methods of competition. In 1916, the FTC concluded that false advertising was one way in which a firm could take unfair advantage of another, and advertising was established as a primary concern of the agency.

---

50.   "Children Not Seeing More Food Ads on Television," Federal Trade Commission Report, June 1, 2007, accessed at http://www.ftc.gov on June 4, 2007.

Government Agency	Areas of Advertising Regulation
Federal Trade Commission (FTC)	Most widely empowered agency in government. Controls unfair methods of competition, regulates deceptive advertising, and has various programs for controlling the advertising process.
Federal Communications Commission (FCC)	Prohibits obscenity, fraud, and lotteries on radio and television. Ultimate power lies in the ability to deny or revoke broadcast licenses.
Food and Drug Administration (FDA)	Regulates the advertising of food, drug, cosmetic, and medical products. Can require special labeling for hazardous products such as household cleaners. Prohibits false labeling and packaging.
Securities and Exchange Commission (SEC)	Regulates the advertising of securities and the disclosure of information in annual reports.
U.S. Postal Service (USPS)	Responsible for regulating direct mail advertising and prohibiting lotteries, fraud, and misrepresentation. It can also regulate and impose fines for materials deemed to be obscene.
Bureau of Alcohol, Tobacco, Firearms, and Explosives (ATF)	Most direct influence has been on regulation of advertising for alcoholic beverages. This agency was responsible for putting warning labels on alcoholic beverage advertising and banning active athletes as celebrities in beer ads. It has the power to determine what constitutes misleading advertising in these product areas.

It was not until 1938 that the effects of deceptive advertising on consumers became a key issue for the FTC. Until the passage of the Wheeler-Lea Amendment (1938), the commission was primarily concerned with the direct effect of advertising on competition. The amendment broadened the FTC's powers to include regulation of advertising that was misleading to the public (regardless of the effect on competition). Through this amendment, the agency could order a firm to stop its deceptive practices. The amendment also granted the agency specific jurisdiction over drug, medical device, cosmetic, and food advertising.

Several other acts provide the FTC with legal powers over advertising. The Robinson-Patman Act (1936) prohibits firms from providing phantom cooperative-advertising allowances as a way to court important dealers. The Wool Products Labeling Act (1939), the Fur Products Labeling Act (1951), and the Textile Fiber Products Identification Act (1958) provided the commission with regulatory power over labeling and advertising for specific products. Consumer protection legislation, which seeks to increase the ability of consumers to make more-informed product comparisons, includes the Fair Packaging and Labeling Act (1966), the Truth in Lending Act (1969), and the Fair Credit Reporting Act (1970). The FTC Improvement Act (1975) expanded the authority of the commission by giving it the power to issue trade regulation rules.

Recent legislation has expanded the FTC's role in monitoring and regulating product labeling and advertising. For example, the 1990 Nutrition Labeling and Education Act (NLEA) requires uniformity in the nutrition labeling of food products and establishes strict rules for claims about the nutritional attributes of food products. The standard "Nutrition Facts" label required by the NLEA now appears on everything from breakfast cereals to barbecue sauce. The NLEA is a notable piece of legislation from the standpoint that two government agencies—the FTC and the FDA—play key roles in its enforcement.

Of course, the Internet has spawned all sorts of scrutiny by the FTC. One area of particular scrutiny regarding children is privacy, which led to the Children's Online Privacy Act of 1998 in which the FTC states explicitly that

It is unlawful for an operator of a website or online service directed to children, or any operator that has actual knowledge that it is collecting personal information from a child, to collect personal information from a child in a manner that violates the regulations prescribed under subsection (b). [51]

Subsection (b) mandates that full disclosure of the Web site's information gathering (if any) must plainly appear on the Web site.

The FTC's Regulatory Programs and Remedies. The application of legislation has evolved as the FTC exercises its powers and expands its role as a regulatory agency. This evolution of the FTC has spawned several regulatory programs and remedies to help enforce legislative mandates in specific situations.

The **advertising substantiation program** of the FTC was initiated in 1971 with the intention of ensuring that advertisers make supporting evidence for their claims available to consumers. The program was strengthened in 1972 when the commission forwarded the notion of "reasonable basis" for the substantiation of advertising. This extension suggests not only that advertisers should substantiate their claims, but also that the substantiation should provide a reasonable basis for believing the claims are true.[52] Simply put, before a company runs an ad, it must have documented evidence that supports the claim it wants to make in that ad. The kind of evidence required depends on the kind of claim being made. For example, health and safety claims will require competent and reliable scientific evidence that has been examined and validated by experts in the field (go to http://www.ftc.gov for additional guidance).

The consent order and the cease-and-desist order are the most basic remedies used by the FTC in dealing with deceptive or unfair advertising. In a **consent order**, an advertiser accused of running deceptive or unfair advertising agrees to stop running the advertisements in question, without admitting guilt. For advertisers who do not comply voluntarily, the FTC can issue a **cease-and-desist order**, which generally requires that the advertising in question be stopped within 30 days so that a hearing can be held to determine whether the advertising is deceptive or unfair. For products that have a direct effect on consumers' health or safety (for example, foods), the FTC can issue an immediate cease-and-desist order.

Affirmative disclosure is another remedy available to the FTC. An advertisement that fails to disclose important material facts about a product can be deemed deceptive, and the FTC may require **affirmative disclosure**, whereby the important material absent from prior ads must be included in subsequent advertisements. The absence of important material information may cause consumers to make false assumptions about products in comparison to the competition.

---

51.   The full text and specifications of the Children's Online Privacy Act can be found at *http://www.ftc.gov/ogc/coppa1.htm*.

52.   For a discussion of the origins and intent of the FTC's advertising substantiation program and its extension to require reasonable basis, see Debra L. Scammon and Richard J. Semenik, "The FTC's 'Reasonable Basis' for Substantiation of Advertising: Expanded Standards and Implications," *Journal of Advertising*, vol. 12, no. 1 (1983), 4–11.

The most extensive remedy for advertising determined to be misleading is **corrective advertising**.[53] In cases where evidence suggests that consumers have developed incorrect beliefs about a brand based on deceptive or unfair advertising, the firm may be required to run corrective ads in an attempt to dispel those faulty beliefs. The commission has specified not only the message content for corrective ads, but also the budgetary allocation, the duration of transmission, and the placement of the advertising. The goal of corrective advertising is to rectify erroneous beliefs created by deceptive advertising, but it hasn't always worked as intended. Over its long history, the corrective advertising remedy has been required of ads ranging from Warner Lambert's Listerine mouthwash claims that it could "cure and prevent colds" (which it couldn't) to more recent ad campaigns that tout new flavors and other brand features that were, in fact, not new.

Another area of FTC regulation and remedy involves **celebrity endorsements**. The FTC has specific rules for advertisements that use an expert or celebrity as a spokesperson for a product. In the case of experts (those whose experience or training allows a superior judgment of products), the endorser's actual qualifications must justify his or her status as an expert. In the case of celebrities (such as Tiger Woods as a spokesperson for Buick or Nike), FTC guidelines state that the celebrity must be an actual user of the product, or the ad is considered deceptive.

These regulatory programs and remedies provide the FTC a great deal of control over the advertising process. Numerous ads have been interpreted as questionable under the guidelines of these programs, and advertisements have been altered. It is also likely that advertisers and their agencies, who are keenly aware of the ramifications of violating FTC precepts, have developed ads with these constraints in mind.

State Regulation. State governments do not have extensive policing powers over the promotional activities of firms. Since the vast majority of companies are involved in interstate marketing of goods and services, any violation of fair practice or existing regulation is a federal government issue.

There is typically one state government organization, the attorney general's office, that is responsible for investigating questionable promotional practices. The state attorney general's office in Texas, for example, claimed a demonstration used by Volvo was misleading. In the ad, a monster truck with oversized tires was shown rolling over the roofs of a row of cars, crushing all of them except a Volvo. The problem was, the Volvo in the test had its roof reinforced while the other cars' roof supports had been weakened.[54]

Since the 1980s, the National Association of Attorneys General, whose members include the attorneys general from all 50 states, has been active as a group in monitoring advertising and sharing its findings. Overall, however, states will rely on the vigilance of the federal agencies discussed earlier to monitor promotional practices and then act against firms with questionable activities.

Finally, in 1995, thirteen states passed prize notification laws regarding sweepstakes and contests. The new laws require marketers to make full disclosure of rules, odds, and retail value of prizes. The states were responding to what they felt was widespread fraud and deception. Some states aggressively prosecuted the sweepstakes companies in court.

 Industry Self-Regulation. The promotion industry has come far in terms of self-control and restraint. Some of this improvement is due to tougher government regulation, and some to industry self-regulation. **Self-regulation** is the promotion industry's attempt to police itself. Supporters say it is a shining example of how unnecessary government intervention is, while critics point to it as a joke, an elaborate shell game. According to the critics, meaningful self-regulation occurs only

53.   The history and intent of the corrective-advertising concept and several of its applications are provided by Debra L. Scammon and Richard J. Semenik, "Corrective Advertising: Evolution of the Legal Theory and Application of the Remedy," *Journal of Advertising,* vol. 11, no. 1 (1982), 10–20.

54.   Steven W. Colford and Raymond Serafin, "Scali Pays for Volvo Ad: FTC," *Advertising Age,* August 26, 1991, 4.

Organization	Code Established
Advertising Associations	
American Advertising Federation	1965
American Association of Advertising Agencies	1924
Association of National Advertisers	1972
Business/Professional Advertising Association	1975
Special Industry Groups	
Council of Better Business Bureaus	1912
Household furniture	1978
Automobiles and trucks	1978
Carpet and rugs	1978
Home improvement	1975
Charitable solicitations	1974
Children's Advertising Review Unit	1974
National Advertising Division/National Advertising Review Board	1971
Media Associations	
American Business Press	1910
Direct Mail Marketing Association	1960
Direct Selling Association	1970
National Association of Broadcasters	
Radio	1937
Television	1952
Outdoor Advertising Association of America	1950
Selected Trade Associations	
American Wine Association	1949
Wine Institute	1949
Distilled Spirits Association	1934
United States Brewers Association	1955
Pharmaceutical Manufacturers Association	1958
Proprietary Association	1934
Bank Marketing Association	1976
Motion Picture Association of America	1930
National Swimming Pool Institute	1970
Toy Manufacturers Association	1962

when the threat of government action is imminent. How you see this controversy is largely dependent on your own personal experience and level of cynicism.

Several industry and trade associations and public service organizations have voluntarily established guidelines for promotion within their industries. The reasoning is that self-regulation is good for the promotion community as a whole and creates credibility for, and therefore enhances the effectiveness of, promotion itself. Exhibit 4.16 lists some organizations that have taken on the task of regulating and monitoring promotional activities, and the year when each established a code of standards.

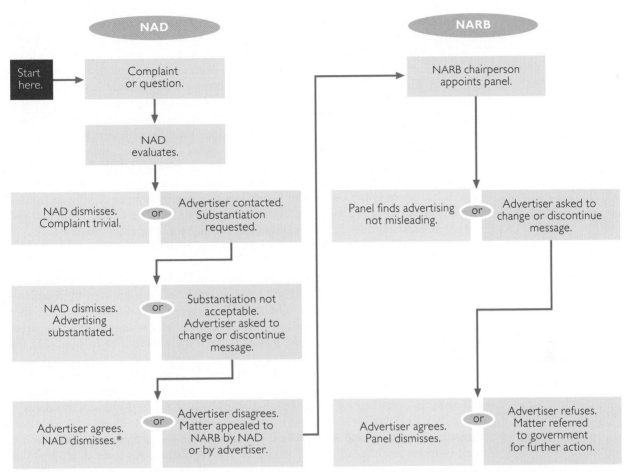

*If the complaint originated outside the system, the outside complainant can appeal at this point to the NARB chairperson for a panel adjudication. Granting of such an appeal is at the chairperson's discretion.

EXHIBIT 4.17

The NAD and NARB regulatory process.

The purpose of self-regulation by these organizations is to evaluate the content and quality of promotion specific to their industries. The effectiveness of such organizations depends on the cooperation of members and the policing mechanisms used. Each organization exerts an influence on the nature of promotion in its industry. Some are particularly noteworthy in their activities and warrant further discussion.

The National Advertising Review Board. One important self-regulation organization is the National Advertising Review Board (NARB). The NARB is the operations arm of the National Advertising Division (NAD) of the Council of Better Business Bureaus. Complaints received from consumers, competitors, or local branches of the Better Business Bureau (BBB) are forwarded to the NAD. Most such complaints come from competitors. After a full review of the complaint, the issue may be forwarded to the NARB and evaluated by a panel. The complete procedure for dealing with complaints is detailed in Exhibit 4.17. Some examples of the types of complaints received and processed include:

- Hardee's sued rival Jack in the Box to stop TV ads that it says suggest that Hardee's uses cow anus to make Angus beef burgers.
- The Sugar Association sued Johnson & Johnson over a marketing campaign related to J&J's artificial sweetener Splenda accusing the company of misleading buyers into believing that Splenda is a natural product.
- Procter & Gamble sued McLane Company, Salado Sales, and Consumer Value Products charging that the companies are selling products in packages that copy P&G's packaging for Bounty, Charmin, and Vicks NyQuil and DayQuil.[55]

55. Gary Gentile, "Jack in the Box Ads Called Misleading," Associated Press, May 25, 2007, accessed at *http://biz.yahoo.com* on May 26, 2007; Sophie Walker, "J&J Sued Over Splenda Ad Campaign" Reuters News Service, January 31, 2005, accessed at *http://story.news.yahoo.com* on February 1, 2005; Bizjournals.com, "P&G Sues Companies over Product Packaging," December 22, 2005, accessed at *http://biz.yahoo.com/bizj* on December 22, 2005.

The NAD maintains a permanent professional staff that works to resolve complaints with the advertiser and its agency before the issue gets to the NARB. If no resolution is achieved, the complaint is appealed to the NARB, which appoints a panel made up of three advertiser representatives, one agency representative, and one public representative. This panel then holds hearings regarding the advertising in question. The advertiser is allowed to present its case. If no agreement can be reached by the panel either to dismiss the case or to persuade the advertiser to change the advertising, then the NARB initiates two actions. First, the NARB publicly identifies the advertiser, the complaint against the advertiser, and the panel's findings. Second, the case is forwarded to an appropriate government regulatory agency (usually the FTC).

The NAD and the NARB are not empowered to impose penalties on advertisers, but the threat of going before the board acts as a deterrent to deceptive and questionable advertising practices. Further, the regulatory process of the NAD and the NARB is probably less costly and time-consuming for all parties involved than if every complaint were handled by a government agency.

State and Local Better Business Bureaus. Aside from the national BBB, there are more than 140 separate local bureaus. Each local organization is supported by membership dues paid by area businesses. The three divisions of a local BBB—merchandise, financial, and solicitations—investigate the advertising and selling practices of firms in their areas. A local BBB has the power to forward a complaint to the NAD for evaluation.

Beyond its regulatory activities, the BBB tries to avert problems associated with advertising by counseling new businesses and providing information to advertisers and agencies regarding legislation, potential problem areas, and industry standards.

Advertising Agencies and Associations. It makes sense that advertising agencies and their industry associations would engage in self-regulation. An individual agency is legally responsible for the advertising it produces and is subject to reprisal for deceptive claims. The agency is in a difficult position in that it must monitor not only the activities of its own people, but also the information that clients provide to the agency. Should a client direct an agency to use a product appeal that turns out to be untruthful, the agency is still responsible.

The American Association of Advertising Agencies (4As) has no legal or binding power over its agency members, but it can apply pressure when its board feels that industry standards are not being upheld. The 4As also publishes guidelines for its members regarding various aspects of advertising messages. One of the most widely recognized industry standards is the 4As' Creative Code. The code outlines the responsibilities and social impact advertising can have and promotes high ethical standards of honesty and decency. You can view the 4As standards of practice, including the creative code, at http://www.aaaa.org.

Media Organizations. Individual media organizations evaluate the advertising they receive for broadcast and publication. The National Association of Broadcasters (NAB) has a policing arm known as the Code Authority, which implements and interprets separate radio and television codes. These codes deal with truth, fairness, and good taste in broadcast advertising. Newspapers have historically been rigorous in their screening of advertising. Many newspapers have internal departments to screen and censor ads believed to be in violation of the newspaper's advertising standards. While the magazine industry does not have a formal code, many individual publications have very high standards.

Direct mail may have a poor image among many consumers, but its industry association, the Direct Marketing Association (DMA), is active in promoting ethical behavior and standards among its members. It has published guidelines for ethical business practices. In 1971, the association established the Direct Mail Preference

Service, which allows consumers to have their names removed from most direct mail lists.

A review of all aspects of industry self-regulation suggests not only that a variety of programs and organizations are designed to monitor advertising, but also that many of these programs are effective. Those whose livelihoods depend on advertising are just as interested as consumers and legislators in maintaining high standards. If advertising deteriorates into an unethical and untrustworthy business activity, the economic vitality of many organizations will be compromised. Self-regulation can help prevent such a circumstance and is in the best interest of all the organizations discussed here.

Internet Self-Regulation. Because there are few federal guidelines established for advertising and promotion on the Internet (with the exception of anti-spam legislation), the industry itself has been the governing body. So far, no industry-wide trade association has emerged to offer guidelines or standards. You will see later in this chapter that several special interest groups are questioning the ethics of some Internet promotional practices. And there are those who are skeptical that the industry can regulate itself.

A new group, the Global Business Dialog on Electronic Commerce (GBDe), is trying to establish itself as a trade association for the online industry. But while it counts some big companies among its 200 members—Time Warner, Daimler AG, Toshiba—not one of the Internet heavyweights, like Amazon.com or Yahoo!, have joined the ranks. The GBDe has drawn up a proposal for dealing with harmful content (pornography), protecting personal information, enforcing copyrights, and handling disputes in e-commerce. But the organization's efforts have not created great enthusiasm. Lester Thurow, the prominent public policy professor from the Massachusetts Institute of Technology, said, "Self-regulation can play a role if you have real regulation that will come piling in if you don't do it."[56]

Consumers as Regulatory Agents. Consumers themselves are motivated to act as regulatory agents based on a variety of interests, including product safety, reasonable choice, and the right to information. Advertising tends to be a focus of consumer regulatory activities because of its conspicuousness. Consumerism and consumer organizations have provided the primary vehicles for consumer regulatory efforts.

Consumerism, the actions of individual consumers or groups of consumers designed to exert power in the marketplace, is by no means a recent phenomenon. The earliest consumerism efforts can be traced to 17th-century England. In the United States, there have been recurring consumer movements throughout the 20th century. *Adbusters* magazine and Web site is a recent example.

In general, these movements have focused on the same issue: Consumers want a greater voice in the whole process of product development, distribution, and information dissemination. Consumers commonly try to create pressures on firms by withholding patronage through boycotts. Some boycotts have been effective. Firms as powerful as Procter & Gamble, Kimberly-Clark, and General Mills all have historically responded to threats of boycotts by pulling advertising from programs consumers found offensive. Sparked by the Janet Jackson Super Bowl incident, advertisers themselves are threatening to withhold their advertising dollars unless they can be assured of decency in programming by producers and networks.[57]

56.   Neal Boudette, "Internet Self-Regulation Seen Lacking Punch," *Reuters News Services*, September 14, 1999, accessed at *http://biz.yahoo.com* on September 14, 1999.
57.   An Advertising Age Roundup, "Upstaged Advertisers Riled by Bowl Stunt," *Advertising Age*, February 9, 2004, 1.

Consumer Organizations. The other major consumer effort to bring about regulation is through established consumer organizations. The following are the most prominent consumer organizations and their prime activities:

- *Consumer Federation of America (CFA).* This organization, founded in 1968, now includes more than 200 national, state, and local consumer groups and labor unions as affiliate members. The goals of the CFA are to encourage the creation of consumer organizations, provide services to consumer groups, and act as a clearinghouse for information exchange between consumer groups (http://www.consumerfed.org).
- *Consumers Union.* This nonprofit consumer organization is best known for its publication of *Consumer Reports.* Established in 1936, Consumers Union has as its stated purpose "to provide consumers with information and advice on goods, services, health, and personal finance; and to initiate and cooperate with individual and group efforts to maintain and enhance the quality of life for consumers."[58] This organization supports itself through the sale of publications and accepts no funding, including advertising revenues, from any commercial organization (http://www.consumersunion.org).
- *Consumer Alert.* Founded in 1977, Consumer Alert champions consumer causes through testimony and comments to legislative and regulatory bodies, legal action, issues management, and media outreach. In addition, the organization promotes the need for sound science and sound economic data in public policy decisions (http://www.consumeralert.org).
- *Commercial Alert.* Commercial Alert is headed by Ralph Nader, a historic figure in consumer rights and protection. The organization's stated mission is to keep the commercial culture within its proper sphere and to prevent it from exploiting children and subverting the higher values of family, community, environmental integrity, and democracy (http://www.commercialalert.org).

These four consumer organizations are the most active and potent of the consumer groups, but there are hundreds of such groups organized by geographic location or product category. Consumers have proven that when faced with an organized effort, corporations can and will change their practices. In one of the most publicized events in recent times, consumers applied pressure to Coca-Cola and, in part, were responsible for forcing the firm to re-market the original formula of Coca-Cola (as Coca-Cola Classic). If consumers are able to exert such a powerful and nearly immediate influence on a firm such as Coca-Cola, one wonders what other changes they could effect in the market.

5 **The Regulation of Other Promotional Tools.** As firms broaden the scope of the promotional effort beyond advertising, the regulatory constraints placed on other IBP tools become relevant. We will consider the current and emerging regulatory environment for direct marketing, e-commerce, sales promotion, and public relations.

Regulatory Issues in Direct Marketing and E-Commerce.

The most pressing regulatory issue facing direct marketing and e-commerce is database development and the privacy debate that accompanies the practice. The crux of the privacy issue has to do with the developing ability of firms to merge offline databases with the online Web search and shopping behavior of consumers.

Privacy. E-commerce privacy issues focus on a wide range, from database development to **cookies**, those online tracking markers that advertisers place on a Web

---

58.   This statement of purpose can be found inside the cover of any issue of *Consumer Reports.*

surfer's hard drive to track that person's online behavior. The current environment is annoying and feels like a huge invasion of privacy. But it is nothing compared to the emerging possibilities. Currently, cookies do not reveal a person's name or address. But what is looming as a real possibility is the widespread use of offline databases that *do* include a consumer's name, address, phone number, credit card numbers, medical records, credit records, and Social Security number that are merged with online tracking data from Web browsing behavior.[59] With this combination of data, the following could easily happen: You are browsing a Web page on mutual funds and seconds later, you get a phone call from a telemarketer trying to sell you financial services!

This scenario may not be too far in the future, and the data/browsing merge has already occurred. The merger of DoubleClick with Abacus Direct created a database that contains transactional data from 1,700 cataloguers, retailers, and publishers—data that chronicles more than 3.6 *billion* transactions by 90 million U.S. households. (By the way, there are only about 102 million households in the United States.) Double-Click, now a part of Google, offers a digital marketplace that connects ad agencies, marketers and Web site publishers. It has more than 1,500 corporate clients. As an example of its database activities, DoubleClick has signed up more than 275 online retailers that contribute detailed transaction, geographic, and demographic information to a database.[60] If you're in that database, it can sure feel like an invasion of privacy. Firms are searching for ways to guarantee to consumers that their privacy will be preserved (see Exhibit 4.18).

In the meantime, the concern is great enough that Congress and the FTC are carefully scrutinizing mergers of firms that would create such comprehensive online and offline databases and privacy advocates are trying to alert people to the invasion.[61]

EXHIBIT 4.18

Web sites like eBay are very conscientious about protecting the privacy of their customers and have detailed privacy statements that explain their efforts. http://pages.ebay .com/help/privacycentral2 .html

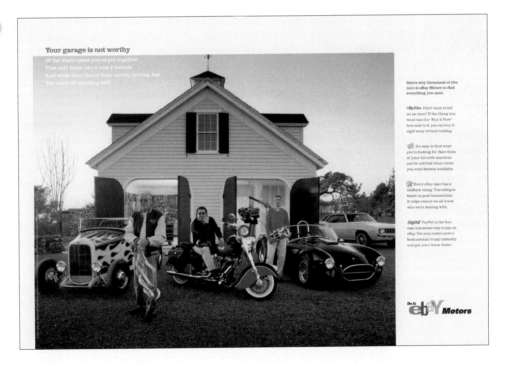

59. Marcia Stepanek, "Protecting E-Privacy: Washington Must Step In," *Business Week E.Biz,* July 26, 1999, EB30; Michael Krauss, "Get a Handle on the Privacy Wild Card," *Marketing News,* February 28, 2000, 12.

60. G. Beato, "Big Data's Big Business," *Business 2.0,* February 2001, 62

61. Peter Kaplan, "FTC Wants More Data on Google-DoubleClick Deal" Reuters News Service, May 29, 2007, accessed at *http://www.reuters.com,* on June 7, 2007.

We have to realize, though, that while this tracking of behavior seems pretty scary, many people don't really seem to care. A recent survey of Web surfers asked if they read a site's privacy policy before making a purchase—only 6 percent responded that they always do, and 77 percent said they rarely or never do. The story in the Ethics box certainly supports those results.

ETHICS

All News and Entertainment—All the Time. Maybe.

We all enjoy many different things in life—kayaking, world politics, photography, power lifting, travel, biking, fashion—whatever helps us relax and enjoy life a little more. And there are all sorts of ways to receive information about these avocations—magazine and newspaper articles, enthusiast Web sites, blogs. We pretty much figure that when we read about our favorite pastime that we're getting somebody's honest views about the topic—sometimes a professional writer, sometimes a news report, sometimes another average person who is sharing his or her experiences. Well, that might not always be true. There are, let's say, "forces" at work that, on occasion, can shape the content in media so that the article you just read or the blog you've been relying on may not be totally objective.

In fact, some people are getting fairly cynical about media content and argue that "You can't believe anything you see or read." This may seem a little extreme, but that quote is from the founder of an interactive ad agency that *pays* bloggers to write nice things about corporate sponsors—without worrying much about whether the bloggers disclose the pay arrangement. To make things even more complicated, there are Web sites being launched to hook up advertisers with bloggers. These sites offer advertisers the opportunity to post details about how they want bloggers to write about their brands—and will provide photos and product stats. The bloggers are then paid for featuring the advertiser's brand—in a positive way, of course. How does that spin your ethical compass?

Defenders of these blogs point out that while the bloggers are paid for their comments, that doesn't mean that they are not giving an honest opinion. Besides, there may be dozens of blogs and hundreds of posts commenting on a brand's features or a company's practices so the totality of the information can still be representative. These defenders also point to a number of questionable practices in "old media." One such practice is when a brand shows up not just in an advertisement but also in the editorial content of a magazine or newspaper article in the same issue. Marketers call this product placement (like the Coke cups on *American Idol* we talked about in Chapter 2); journalistic types call it "product integration" and are finding it to be a new source of revenue in an era of declining readership (and therefore declining ad dollars).

The situation gets more complicated when you consider some even more overt attempts by advertisers to try to ensure a positive information environment for their brands. Consider these situations. In April of 2005, General Motors began an advertising boycott of the *Los Angeles Times*. The big auto company felt that the newspaper's editorial coverage of the company's cars contained "factual errors and misrepresentations." GM and the newspaper resolved their differences after a few months with GM issuing a press release indicating that the two organizations "had productive discussions regarding our complaints." Similarly, other firms have issued guidelines to publications specifying that the firm will pull its advertising from publications whenever a negative story about the bank is about to be published. Such clauses, called "pull-ad clauses," are common across many industries. But the pull-ad clauses are typically used by firms to avoid advertising when news of major catastrophes would conflict with advertising—such as airline advertising after the 9/11 terrorist attacks.

We started this discussion with the premise that when we go to information sources—like magazines, newspapers, or blogs—we figure everything we read is true and objective. Well, we are not saying that people "lie" in articles or in their blog postings—not at all. What *may* happen, though, is that advertisers can be involved in the process—when it is not totally obvious that any were involved. Or, the blog you like so much might have bloggers who are paid by advertisers to write about the advertisers' brands. But you will have to decide if you think the bloggers are being unethical (none of these practices are illegal). Things just aren't as simple as they seem—or as we might like them to be. That is the nature of social, ethical, and legal issues in advertising and promotion.

Sources: Jon Fine, "An Onslaught of Hidden Ads," **BusinessWeek**, June 27, 2005, 24; Associated Press, "GM Ends Boycott of LA Times," August 2, 2005, accessed at http://news.yahoo.com, on August 3, 2005; Liz Moyer, "Managing Ads, Not News," **Forbes.com**, May 23, 2005, accessed at http://www.forbes.com on May 23, 2005.

Spam. Few of us would argue with the allegation that **spam**, unsolicited commercial messages sent through the e-mail system, is the scourge of the Internet. To put the problem into perspective, it is estimated that about 30 million spam e-mails are sent every *minute* worldwide—that comes out to about 50 billion messages a day.[62] Spam can be so bad it has actually shut down a company's entire operations. To cope with the onslaught, individuals and companies are turning to spam filtering software to stem flow and take back control of their e-mail systems. The rise in spam has prompted Internet services providers to form a coalition against spammers. In the spring of 2003, Yahoo!, AOL, and MSN announced a joint anti-spam offensive relying on technological and legal remedies. About that same time, the FTC convened a brainstorming session to determine what, if anything, could be done legally. Then in October of 2003, the U.S. Senate voted unanimously 97–0 to implement the CAN SPAM Act. The Senate followed in November of 2003 with its support, voting 392–5 in favor of the legislation. The act does not outlaw all unsolicited e-mail, but rather targets fraudulent, deceptive, and pornographic messages, which is estimated to make up about two-thirds of all commercial unsolicited e-mail.[63] The most severe prosecution to date has been notorious spammer Alan Soloway, operator of Newport Internet Marketing, which offered "broadcast e-mail" software. Soloway is accused of facilitating the distribution of hundreds of millions of spam e-mails via hijacked networks.[64]

Spammers are not taking the legislation lying down, as you might expect. They are challenging the legislation on legal grounds, claiming that it violates First Amendment free speech rights. And they are doing what they do best—slamming their opponents with a barrage of e-mails. The concern of course is that legitimate marketers and advertisers who could use e-mail in a reasonable way will be caught in this legislation.

Contests, Sweepstakes, Coupons. While privacy and spam are huge direct marketing and e-commerce issues, they are not the only ones. The next biggest legal issue has to do with sweepstakes, contests, and coupons. Because of the success and widespread use of sweepstakes in direct marketing (such as the Publishers Clearing House sweepstakes), Congress has imposed limits on such promotions. The existing limits on direct mail sweepstakes include the requirement that the phrases "No purchase is necessary to win" and "A purchase will not improve an individual's chance of winning" must be repeated three times in letters to consumers and again on the entry form. In addition, penalties can be imposed on marketers who do not promptly remove consumers' names from mailing lists at the consumer's request.[65]

The online version of sweepstakes and contests also has the attention of the U.S. Congress. Sweepstakes, like the ones promoted at LuckySurf.com (shown in Exhibit 4.19), play a lot like traditional sweepstakes, lotteries, games, or contests. At the LuckySurf site, you merely need to register (providing name, home address, e-mail address, and password), pick seven numbers, then click on one of four banner ads to activate your entry in a $1-million-a-day drawing. So far, these online games have avoided both lawsuits and regulation, but they have attracted the attention of policymakers.[66]

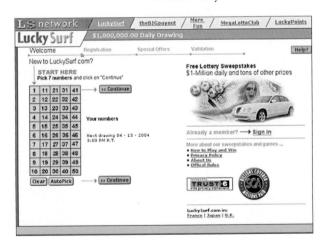

EXHIBIT 4.19

Online contests and sweepstakes are being monitored by government regulatory agents. http://www.luckysurf.com

62.   "Image Spam: The E-Mail Epidemic of 2006," Security Trends Overview, Special Report, IronPort Systems, Inc., September 2006.
63.   "Senate Approves Antispam Bill," Reuters News, reported on the Internet on October 22, 2003, at *http://news.reuters.com*.
64.   Elaine Porterfield, ""First Arrest Under Spam Law Could Dent E-Mail Flood," Reuters News Service, May 31, 2007.
65.   Ira Teinowitz, "Congress Nears Accord on Sweepstakes Limits," *Advertising Age*, August 9, 1999, 33.
66.   James Heckman, "Online, but Not on Trial, though Privacy Looms Large," *Marketing News*, December 6, 1999, 8.

Coupons distributed through direct mail, newspapers, magazines, or the Internet require legal protection for the *marketer* more than anything else. Fraud abounds in the area of couponing, aggravated by the fact that approximately 76 percent of the U.S. population still uses coupons and redeems 2.6 billion coupons every year.[67] Phony coupons can easily be reproduced and redeemed well after the firm's planned promotional campaign. Starbucks ended up with a promotional nightmare by not enacting safeguards for a "Free Iced Beverage" coupon that it intended for a small e-mail distribution. Instead, the coupons were forwarded in huge numbers, and consumers all over the United States tried to redeem them. Because of the unexpected nationwide demand, Starbucks had to cancel the offer before the coupons' expiration date, frustrating many customers.[68] Safeguards like stating strict limitations on redemption, geographic limitations, or encrypted bar codes that can be scanned to detect fraud are all ways to reduce problems with contests, sweepstakes, and coupons.[69]

Telemarketing. Another legal issue in direct marketing that has hit the headlines in recent years has to do with telemarketing practices. The first restriction on telemarketing was the Telephone Consumer Fraud and Abuse Prevention Act of 1994 (later strengthened by the FTC in 1995), which requires telemarketers to state their name, the purpose of the call, and the company they work for. The act prohibits telemarketers from calling before 8 AM and after 9 PM, and they cannot call the same customer more than once every three months. In addition, they cannot use automatic dialing machines that contain recorded messages, and they must keep a list of consumers who do not want to be called.

That original telemarketing law was benign compared to recent legislation aimed at telemarketers. At the center of new regulation restricting telemarketing is the Do Not Call Law, which allows consumers to sign up for a Do Not Call Registry (see Exhibit 4.20) (http://www.donotcall.gov). The Federal Trade Commission, the

EXHIBIT 4.20

The Federal Trade Commission, the Federal Communications Commission, and states started to enforce the Do Not Call Registry on October 1, 2003. Registering your phone number(s) with the registry blocks a wide variety of telemarketers from calling you with a sales pitch. http://www.donotcall.gov

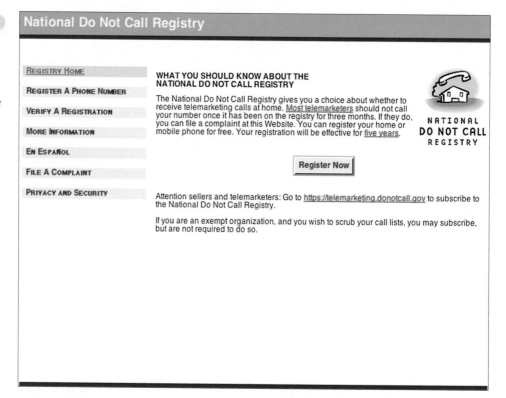

67.   Jack Neff, "Package-Goods Players Just Can't Quit Coupons," *Advertising Age,* May 14, 2007, 8.
68.   Melissa Allison, "Starbucks Coupon Gets out of Hand," *Seattle Times,* August 31, 2006, available at http://archives.seattletimes .nwsource.com/web.
69.   Ibid.

Federal Communications Commission, and states started to enforce the registry on October 1, 2003. The program exempts political and charitable fund-raisers as well as pollsters. When the program was launched, about 60 million phone numbers were registered by consumers as "do not call" numbers.

There are organizations with rights to continue telemarketing efforts, so even if you have registered with the Do Not Call Registry, you can still get calls from[70]

- Charities, politicians, pollsters, and market researchers
- Companies you do business with
- Companies that have sold you something or delivered something to you within the previous 18 months
- Businesses *you've* contacted in the past three months
- Companies that obtain your permission to call you

Regulatory Issues in Sales Promotion. Regulatory issues in sales promotion focus on three areas: premium offers, trade allowances, and contests and sweepstakes.

Premium Offers. With respect to **premiums** (an item offered for "free" or at a greatly reduced price with the purchase of another item), the main area of regulation has do with requiring marketers to state the fair retail value of the item offered as a premium.

Trade Allowances. In the area of trade allowances, marketers need to be familiar with the guidelines set forth in the original Robinson–Patman Act of 1936. Even though this is an old piece of legislation, it still applies to contemporary trade promotion practices. The Robinson–Patman Act requires marketers to offer similar customers similar prices on similar merchandise. This means that a marketer cannot use special allowances as a way to discount the price to highly attractive customers. This issue was raised earlier in the context of vertical cooperative advertising.

Contests and Sweepstakes. In the area of sweepstakes and contests, the issues discussed in the previous section under direct marketing and e-commerce also apply, but there are other issues as well. The FTC has specified four violations of regulations that marketers must avoid in carrying out sweepstakes and contests:

- Misrepresentations about the value (for example, stating an inflated retail price) of the prizes being offered
- Failure to provide complete disclosure about the conditions necessary to win (are there behaviors required on the part of the contestant?)
- Failure to disclose the conditions necessary to obtain a prize (are there behaviors required of the contestant after the contestant is designated a "winner"?)
- Failure to ensure that a contest or sweepstakes is not classified as a lottery, which is considered gambling—a contest or sweepstakes is a lottery if a prize is offered based on chance and the contestant has to give up something of value in order to play

Product/Brand Placement. The area of sales promotion receiving attention most recently in the regulatory arena is brand/product placement in television programs and films. As discussed earlier, consumer groups feel that unless television networks and film producers reveal that brands are placed into a program or film for a fee, consumers could be deceived into believing that the product use is natural and real. The industry counterclaim is, "There is a paranoia about our business that shouldn't be there. We don't control the storyline, or the brands that are included. The writers

---

70. Lorraine Woellert, "The Do-Not-Call Law Won't Stop the Calls," *BusinessWeek,* September 29, 2003, 89.

and producers do."[71] Philip Morris has gone so far as to run print ads in *Variety* and the *Hollywood Reporter* urging film makers not to put its products in films.[72]

Regulatory Issues in Public Relations. Public relations is not bound by the same sorts of laws as other elements of the promotional mix. Because public relations activities deal with public press and public figures, much of the regulation relates to these issues. The public relations activities of a firm may place it on either side of legal issues with respect to privacy, copyright infringement, or defamation through slander and libel.

Privacy. The privacy problems facing a public relations firm center on the issue of appropriation. **Appropriation** is the use of pictures or images owned by someone else without permission. If a firm uses a model's photo or a photographer's work in an advertisement or company brochure without permission, then the work has been appropriated without the owner's permission. The same is true of public relations materials prepared for release to the press or as part of a company's public relations kit.

Copyright Infringement. Copyright infringement can occur when a public relations effort uses written, recorded, or photographic material in public relations materials. Much as with appropriation, written permission must be obtained to use such works.

Defamation. When a communication occurs that damages the reputation of an individual because the information in the communication was untrue, this is called **defamation** (you many have heard it referred to as "defamation of character"). Defamation can occur either through slander or libel. **Slander** is oral defamation and in the context of promotion would occur during television or radio broadcast of an event involving a company and its employees. **Libel** is defamation that occurs in print and would relate to magazine, newspaper, direct mail, or Internet reports.

The public relations practitioner's job is to protect clients from slanderous or libelous reports about a company's activities. Inflammatory TV "investigative" news programs are often sued for slander and are challenged to prove the allegations they make about a company and personnel working for a company. The issues revolve around whether negative comments can be fully substantiated. Erroneous reports in major magazines and newspapers about a firm can result in a defamation lawsuit as well. Less frequently, public relations experts need to defend a client accused of making defamatory remarks.

71.   Claire Atkinson, "Watchdog Group Hits TV Product Placement," *Advertising Age,* October 6, 2003, 12.
72.   Rich Thomaselli, "Philip Morris: No Smoking in Movies," *Advertising Age,* November 20, 2006, 3, 27.

SUMMARY

 Identify the benefits and problems of advertising and promotion in a capitalistic society and debate a variety of issues concerning their effects on society's well-being.

Advertisers have always been followed by proponents and critics. Proponents of advertising argue that it offers benefits for individual consumers and society at large. At the societal level, proponents claim, advertising helps promote a higher standard of living by allowing marketers to reap the rewards of product improvements and innovation. Advertising also "pays for" mass media in many countries and provides consumers with a constant flow of information not only about products and services, but also about political and social issues.

Over the years critics have leveled many charges at advertising and advertising practitioners. Advertising expenditures in the multibillions are condemned as wasteful, offensive, and a source of frustration for many in society who see the lavish lifestyle portrayed in advertising, knowing they will never be able to afford such a lifestyle. Critics also contend that advertisements rarely furnish useful information but instead perpetuate superficial stereotypes of many cultural subgroups. For many years, some critics have been concerned that advertisers are controlling us against our will with subliminal advertising messages.

 Explain how ethical considerations affect the development of advertising and IBP campaigns.

Ethical considerations are a concern when creating advertising, especially when that advertising will be targeted to children or will involve controversial products such as firearms, gambling, alcohol, or cigarettes. While ethical standards are a matter for personal reflection, it certainly is the case that unethical people can create unethical advertising. But there are also many safeguards against such behavior, including the corporate and personal integrity of advertisers.

 Discuss the role of government agencies in the regulation of advertising and promotion.

Governments typically are involved in the regulation of advertising. It is important to recognize that advertising regulations can vary dramatically from one country to the next. In the United States, the Federal Trade Commission (FTC) has been especially active in trying to deter deception and unfairness in advertising. The FTC was established in 1914, and since then a variety of legislation has been passed to clarify its powers. The FTC has also developed regulatory remedies that have expanded its involvement in advertising regulation, such as the advertising substantiation program.

 Explain the meaning and importance of self-regulation for firms that develop and use advertising and promotion.

Some of the most important controls on advertising are voluntary; that is, they are a matter of self-regulation by advertising and marketing professionals. For example, the American Association of Advertising Agencies has issued guidelines for promoting fairness and accuracy when using comparative advertisements. Many other organizations, such as the Better Business Bureau, the National Association of Broadcasters, and the Direct Marketing Association, participate in the process to help ensure fairness and assess consumer complaints about advertising and promotion.

 Discuss the regulation of the full range of techniques used in the IBP process.

The regulation of other tools in the IBP process focuses on direct marketing, e-commerce, sales promotions, and public relations. In direct marketing and e-commerce, the primary concern has to do with consumer privacy. New legislation, like the Do Not Call Registry and the CAN SPAM Act, is restricting ways in which companies can contact consumers with a sales offer. The legislation is a reaction to new technologies that have enabled firms to match consumers' online behavior with offline personal information. Another aspect of e-commerce has to do with contests and sweepstakes and the potential for such games to actually be gambling opportunities. In sales promotions, premium offers, trade allowances, and offline contests and sweepstakes are subject to regulation. Firms are required to state the fair value of "free" premiums, trade allowances must follow the guidelines of fair competition, and contests and sweepstakes must follow strict rules specified by the FTC. The regulation of public relations efforts has to do with privacy, copyright infringement, and defamation. Firms must be aware of the strict legal parameters of these factors.

KEY TERMS

ethics
deception
puffery
primary demand
unfair advertising
vertical cooperative advertising
comparison advertisements
monopoly power

advertising substantiation program
consent order
cease-and-desist order
affirmative disclosure
corrective advertising
celebrity endorsements
self-regulation
consumerism

cookies
spam
premiums
appropriation
defamation
slander
libel

QUESTIONS

1. Advertising has been a focal point of criticism for many decades. In your opinion, what are some of the key factors that make advertising controversial?

2. As blogs have proliferated across the media landscape, so have efforts by businesses and manufacturers to gain positive mentions, reviews, and commentary on these seemingly grassroots sites. What ethical issues are raised if a blogger is paid to comment on a product? Does it matter if the blogger discloses any such financial agreements?

3. You have probably been exposed to hundreds of thousands of advertisements in your lifetime. In what ways does exposure to advertising make you a better or worse consumer?

4. Use Maslow's Hierarchy of Needs to address critics' concerns that too much advertising is directed at creating demand for products that are irrelevant to people's true needs.

5. One type of advertising that attracts the attention of regulators, critics, and consumer advocates is advertising directed at children. Why is it the focus of so much attention?

6. What are the pros and cons of database marketing, and what can consumers do to protect themselves and their privacy from unwanted or intrusive advertising and promotion campaigns?

7. What is comparison advertising, and why does this form of advertising need a special set of guidelines to prevent unfair competition?

8. Explain why a marketer might be tempted to misuse cooperative-advertising allowances to favor some kinds of retailers over others. What piece of legislation empowered the FTC to stop these bogus allowances?

9. Various methods of industry self-regulation are discussed in the chapter. Do you think self regulation can be effective or is government regulation the only really effective way to control advertising and promotional efforts?

10. Spam is considered the scourge of not just the Internet but IBP as well. In this chapter, you have read about attempts to limit spam. What would you suggest as ways spam can be limited—or eliminated?

EXPERIENTIAL EXERCISES

1.   The Federal Trade Commission's National Do Not Call Registry is one of the most popular and successful consumer initiatives undertaken by the federal government, attracting millions of registrants and permitting consumers to block most telemarketers from calling their personal telephone numbers. Violators face steep fines. While the registry's popularity is without question, its constitutionality is not. Commerce groups have taken the FTC to court, claiming that the registry violates free speech rights—in this case, commercial speech. The case could eventually make it all the way to the Supreme Court. Write a report on the current progress of the National Do Not Call Registry (http://www.donotcall .gov), and be sure to discuss the latest court judgments concerning its constitutionality. Provide your opinion on whether the registry violates the constitutional right to free speech, and defend your position. Finally, discuss the effect the registry is having on the direct marketing industry.

2.   Cut out an ad from a magazine. Choose three pros or cons in the social aspects of advertising. Explain how the ad you chose educates consumers, affects the standard of living, affects happiness, influences mass media, and is demeaning or artful.

3.   List two product categories—other than cigarettes—that you think require some kind of advertising regulation and explain why. Do you think they require government regulation, industry self-regulation, or consumer regulation? Explain. Based on your answer, list regulatory agents that might get involved in controlling the advertising process for these products. Finally, go to the Internet and do a search for one or more agency or watchdog sites that are relevant to the regulatory process. How does the site encourage consumers to get involved, and what resources does the site offer to empower their participation in the process?

4.   As discussed in this chapter, one recurring criticism of advertising is that it often is offensive or in poor taste.

In 2007, the makers of Trojan condoms faced backlash over an advertising campaign that portrayed pigs sitting next to attractive women in bars with the tagline, "Evolve. Use a Condom Every Time." Television stations in some cities refused to air the commercials, and both the CBS and Fox networks rejected the ads for national programming. After viewing the television and print ads from the campaign at http://www.trojanevolve .com, consider the following questions:

a.   Do you agree or disagree with the decision by the two networks and some local television stations not to air the commercials? Why or why not?

b.   In what ways is the ad campaign effective? In what ways is it offensive?

c.   Imagine that you are part of the creative team working for Trojan on the campaign. Would you revise the ad to make it more acceptable to the networks and individual affiliates? How? What arguments could you make that the ad should *not* be changed to appease critics? How could the controversy surrounding the campaign help or hurt the brand?

5.   Working in small teams, imagine that you have been hired by a large pizza chain to develop an IBP campaign for a new product, the KidZa Meal, which will consist of a four-inch-diameter pizza, a small drink, and a doll that looks like a traditional Italian pizza chef. The chain is hoping sales of KidZa Meals will drive more families to its dine-in restaurants and increase takeout orders. But the chain is concerned about perceptions that it is targeting children in its advertising or contributing to concerns about childhood obesity rates. What type of campaign would you suggest for this client? As you evaluate the components of the marketing mix, what recommendations would you make regarding the product?

PART TWO

Planning: Analyzing Advertising and Integrated Brand Promotion Environments

Successful advertising and integrated brand promotion rely on a clear understanding of how and why consumers make their purchase decisions. Successful brand communication is rooted in sound marketing strategies and careful research about a brand's market environment. This understanding of the consumer and the market, sound strategy, and research are brought together in a formal advertising plan. Part Two, "Planning: Analyzing Advertising and Integrated Brand Promotion Environments," discusses the many important bases for the development of an advertising plan. Consumer behavior must be understood, segments must be analyzed, positioning the brand needs to be determined, and research must be carried out in a systematic and analytical manner. This section concludes with two chapters that lay out the process of planning advertising and integrated brand promotion and the unique challenges of planning for international markets.

Advertising, Integrated Brand Promotion, and Consumer Behavior Chapter 5, "Advertising, Integrated Brand Promotion, and Consumer Behavior," begins with an assessment of the way consumers make product and brand choices. These decisions depend on consumers' involvement and prior experiences with brands in a product category. This chapter also addresses consumer behavior and advertising from both psychological and socio-cultural points of view, considering individual and social/cultural influences on brand choice. This includes a discussion of ads as social text and how they transmit socio-cultural meaning.

5

Market Segmentation, Positioning, and the Value Proposition Chapter 6, "Market Segmentation, Positioning, and the Value Proposition," details how these three fundamental marketing planning efforts are developed by an organization. With a combination of audience and competitive information, including psychographics and lifestyle research, product and service brands are developed to provide benefits that are both valued by target customers and different from those of the competition. The process for segmenting business markets is also addressed. Finally, the way advertising contributes to communicating value to consumers is explained and modeled.

6

Advertising and Promotion Research Chapter 7, "Advertising and Promotion Research," is organized into three main parts that discuss the key types of research conducted by advertisers and their part in planning an advertising and IBP effort. These three parts are developmental advertising and IBP research, copy research, and results research. The methods used to track the effectiveness of ads during and after a launch are highlighted. Finally, account planning's role is also covered in this chapter.

7

Planning Advertising and Integrated Brand Promotion Chapter 8, "Planning Advertising and Integrated Brand Promotion," explains how formal advertising plans are developed. The chapter begins by putting the advertising and IBP planning process into the context of the overall marketing planning process. The inputs to the advertising and IBP plan are laid out in detail, and the process of setting advertising objectives—both communications and sales objectives—is described. The methods for setting budgets are presented, including the widely adopted and preferred objective-and-task approach.

8

Advertising Planning: An International Perspective Chapter 9, "Advertising Planning: An International Perspective," introduces issues related to planning advertising targeted to international audiences with emphasis on overcoming cultural barriers to communication. Global forces are creating more accessible markets. In the midst of this trend toward international trade, marketers are redefining the nature and scope of the markets for their goods and services while adjusting to the creative, media, and regulatory challenges of competing across national boundaries.

9

CHAPTER 5

After reading and thinking about this chapter,
you will be able to do the following:

Describe the four basic stages of consumer decision making.

Explain how consumers adapt their decision-making processes as a function of involvement and experience.

Discuss how advertising may influence consumer behavior through its effects on various psychological states.

Discuss the interaction of culture and advertising.

Discuss the role of sociological factors in consumer behavior and advertising response.

6

Discuss how advertising transmits sociocultural meaning in order to sell things.

Introductory Scenario: Ay Caramba!

In the summer of 2007, 7–Eleven and *The Simpsons* teamed up for a very contemporary piece of branded entertainment, cross-promotion, and buzz advertising.[1] Literally overnight, twelve U.S. and Canadian 7–Elevens were remodeled into Kwik-E-Marts from *The Simpsons* show. (The new look lasted one month, and then the stores reverted to 7–Elevens.) The idea was to promote the release of *The Simpsons Movie* and, for 7–Eleven, to attract a crop of new customers: die-hard Simpson fans. The change was total: Professional set designers installed over a thousand items including KrustyO's and Buzz Cola (see Exhibit 5.1). Duff Beer was not included due to concerns of the rating of the movie (PG) and the age of some consumers . . . d'oh! Gracie Films, the production company for *The Simpsons*, fought hard but failed to get month-old stale hot dogs into the deal. The Squishee made it in. Some have called this "reverse product placement." Tim Stock, of Scenario DNA, said, "It's pop culture commenting on pop culture commenting on itself." So, what do you think? Good idea? Who wins? Both? None? Welcome to 21st-century consumer culture and advertising. The agency was FreshWorks, an Omnicom Group virtual-agency network headed up by Tracy Locke of Dallas.

Consumer behavior is defined as the broad spectrum of things that consumers do or experience. In other words, if it has anything to do with consuming things; it's part of consumer behavior. Like all human behavior, the behavior of consumers is complicated, rich, and varied. However, advertisers must make it their job to understand consumers if they want to experience sustained success. Sometimes this

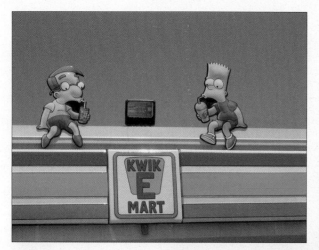

EXHIBIT 5.1

Buzz Cola wasn't the only buzz created by this partnership between the makers of The Simpsons Movie and 7-Eleven.

---

1.   Kate MacArthur, "Marriage of Convenience: 7-Eleven, 'Simpsons'," *Advertising Age*, July 16, 2007.

understanding comes from comprehensive research efforts. Other times it comes from years of experience and implicit theories; truly brilliant, creative, and expert management; or blind, dumb luck (rarely attributed as such). However this understanding comes about, it is a key factor for advertising success.

This chapter summarizes the concepts and frameworks we believe are most helpful in trying to understand consumer behavior. We will describe consumer behavior and attempt to explain it, in its incredible diversity, from two different but major perspectives. The first portrays consumers as reasonably systematic decision makers who seek to maximize the benefits they derive from their purchases. The second views consumers as active interpreters (meaning-makers) of advertising, whose membership in various cultures, societies, and communities significantly affects their interpretation and response to advertising. It sees ads as cultural texts that are "read" by culturally informed consumers, individuals that have been part of a consumer culture since birth and speak and understand the advertising and consumer language. These two perspectives are different ways of looking at the exact same people and many of the exact same behaviors. Though different in some assumptions, both of these perspectives offer something very valuable to the task of actually getting the work of advertising done.

The point is that no one perspective can adequately explain consumer behavior. Consumers are psychological, social, cultural, historical, and economic beings all at the same time. For example, suppose a sociologist and a psychologist both saw someone buying a car. The psychologist might explain this behavior in terms of attitudes, decision criteria, and the like, while the sociologist would probably explain it in terms of the buyer's social environment and circumstances (that is, income, housing conditions, social class, the "badge" value or "cultural capital" of the brand, and so on). Both explanations may be perfectly valid, but each is to some degree incomplete. The bottom line is that all consumer behavior is complex. Why you or any other consumer buys a movie ticket rather than a lottery ticket, or Pepsi rather than Coke, or KFC rather than Wendy's is a function of psychological, economic, sociological, anthropological, historical, textual, and other forces. No single explanation is entirely sufficient. With this in mind, we offer two basic perspectives on consumer behavior.

Perspective One: The Consumer as Decision Maker. One

way to view consumer behavior is as a fairly predictable sequential process culminating with the individual's reaping a set of benefits from a product or service that satisfies that person's perceived needs. In this basic view, we can think of individuals as fairly purposeful decision makers who either weigh and balance alternatives or resort, typically in times of complexity and too much information, to simple decision rules of thumb (heuristics) to make things easier. Often (but not always) this process occurs in a very straightforward sequence and is a good way to think about consumer decision making generally. Many consumption episodes might then be conceived as a sequence of four basic stages:

1. Need recognition
2. Information search and alternative evaluation
3. Purchase
4. Postpurchase use and evaluation

The Consumer Decision-Making Process. A brief discussion of what typically happens at each

stage will give us a foundation for understanding consumers, and it can also illuminate opportunities for developing more powerful advertising.

EXHIBIT 5.2

Every season has its holidays, and with those holidays come a particular array of consumption needs. Even jelly beans.

Need Recognition. The consumption process begins when people perceive a need. A **need state** arises when one's desired state of affairs differs from one's actual state of affairs. Need states are accompanied by a mental discomfort or anxiety that motivates action; the severity of this discomfort can be widely variable depending on the genesis of the need. For example, the need state that arises when one runs out of toothpaste would involve very mild discomfort for most people, whereas the need state that accompanies the breakdown of one's automobile on a dark and deserted highway in North Dakota or Sweden in mid-February can approach true desperation.

One way advertising works is to point to and thereby activate needs that will motivate consumers to buy a product or service. For instance, in the fall, advertisers from product categories as diverse as autos, snowblowers, and footwear roll out predictions for another severe winter and encourage consumers to prepare themselves before it's too late. Every change of season brings new needs, large and small, and advertisers are always at the ready. The coming of spring is typically a cause for celebration, which for some will include Starburst jelly beans (per Exhibit 5.2), along with a delicious Honeybaked Ham for Easter dinner. Isn't life juicy? You can probably think of plenty of examples of an ad saying, "Hey, you need this because. . . ."

Many factors can influence the need states of consumers. For instance, Maslow's hierarchy of needs suggests that a consumer's level of affluence can have a dramatic effect on what types of needs he or she perceives as relevant. The less fortunate are concerned with fundamental needs, such as food and shelter; more-affluent consumers may fret over which new piece of Williams-Sonoma kitchen gadgetry or other accoutrement to place in their uptown condo. The former's needs are predominantly for physiological survival and basic comfort, while the latter's may have more to do with seeking to validate personal accomplishments and derive status and recognition through consumption and social display. While income clearly matters in this regard, it would be a mistake to believe that the poor have no aesthetic concerns, or that the rich are always oblivious to the need for basic essentials. The central point is that a variety of needs can be fulfilled through consumption, and it is reasonable to suggest that consumers' needs are often sufficiently recognized and motivating to many consumers. Products and services should provide benefits that fulfill consumers' needs; hence, one of the advertiser's primary jobs is to make the connection between the two for the consumer. Benefits come in many forms. Some are more "functional"—that is, they derive from the more objective performance characteristics of a product or service. Convenience, reliability, nutritious, durability, and energy efficiency are descriptors that refer to **functional benefits**. Consumers may also choose products that provide **emotional benefits**; these are not typically found in some tangible feature or objective characteristic of a product. Emotional benefits are more subjective and may be perceived differently from one consumer to the next. Products and services help consumers feel pride, avoid guilt, relieve fear, and experience pleasure. These are powerful consumption motives that advertisers often try to activate. Can you find the emotional benefits promised in Exhibit 5.3? (You should know that some scholars believe that *all* benefits are functional, even

EXHIBIT 5.3

All parents want to be good to their child. This ad promises both functional benefits and emotional rewards for diligent parents.
http://www.jnj.com

emotional ones; in other words, they believe all benefits serve a purpose. But for the time being we will continue to make the distinction, as a lot of advertisers do.)

Advertisers must develop a keen appreciation for the kinds of benefits that consumers derive from their brands. Even within the same product category, the benefits promised may vary widely. For instance, as shown in Exhibit 5.4, the makers of Ernst Benz timepieces present a simple, important promise. You buy an Ernst Benz watch and you will always know the precise time. Conversely, the ad for Duby & Schaldenbrand watches, shown in Exhibit 5.5, is more about feelings than performance. Here, the implied benefit is the pride one feels from being recognized as the owner of a prestigious timepiece. These dramatically disparate ads illustrate that consumers will look for different kinds of benefits, even in a seemingly straightforward product category like watches. To create advertising that resonates with your consumers, you better have a good handle on the benefits they are looking for, or might look for, if only you suggested it.

Information Search and Alternative Evaluation.
Given that a consumer has recognized a need, it is often not obvious what would be the best way to satisfy that need. For example, if you have a fear of being trapped in a blizzard in North Dakota, a condo on Miami Beach may be a much better solution than a Jeep or new snow tires. Need recognition simply sets in motion a process that may involve

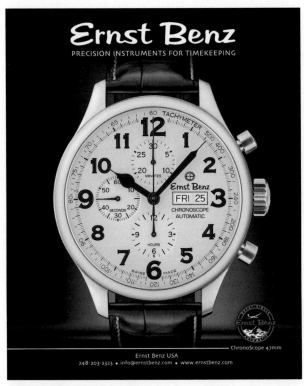

EXHIBIT 5.4

Functional benefits rule in this ad. It's all about precision and accuracy in time keeping.

EXHIBIT 5.5

This ad for a Duby & Schaldenbrand watch is as much about feeling as it is about performance.

an extensive information search and careful evaluation of alternatives prior to purchase. Of course, during this search and evaluation, there are numerous opportunities for the advertiser to influence the final decision.

Once a need has been recognized, information for the decision is acquired through an internal or external search. The consumer's first option for information is to draw on personal experience and prior knowledge. This **internal search** for information may be all that is required. When a consumer has considerable prior experience with the products in question, attitudes about the alternatives may be well established and determine choice, as the Campbell's soup ad shown in Exhibit 5.6 suggests.

An internal search can also tap into information that has accumulated in one's memory as a result of repeated advertising exposures, such as "Tide's In, Dirt's Out," or stored judgments, for example, "Apple computers are best; that's what I've decided." Advertisers want the result of internal search to result in their brand being in the "evoked set," that is the set of brands (usually two to five) that come to mind when a category is mentioned. I say "laundry detergent, and you say "Tide, All, Wisk." Here, the evoked set consists of three brands, all stored internally, found through internal search, and probably the product of advertising, use, and habit. The evoked set is usually highly related to the **consideration set**, the set of the brands the consumer will consider for purchase. If your brand is the first mentioned, you have achieved something even better: "top of mind." Many people believe that top-of-mind awareness best predicts purchase of fairly inexpensive and low-risk consumer packaged goods. Affecting people's beliefs about a brand before their actual use of it, or merely establishing the existence of the brand in the consumer's consciousness, is a critical function of advertising and other integrated brand promotion. As noted in Chapter 1, the purpose of delayed response advertising is to generate recognition of and a favorable predisposition toward a brand so that when consumers enter into search mode, that brand will be one they immediately consider as a possible solution to their needs. If the consumer has not used a brand previously and has no recollection that it even exists, then that brand probably will not be the brand of choice. Good retailing (such as point-of-purchase displays) can help, but prior awareness is a very good thing, and something advertising can do.

It is certainly plausible that an internal search will not turn up enough information to yield a decision. The consumer then proceeds with an **external search**.

EXHIBIT 5.6

For a cultural icon such as Campbell's soup, an advertiser can assume that consumers have some prior knowledge. Here the advertiser seeks to enhance that knowledge to lead people to use more canned soup. http://www.campbellsoups.com

An external search involves visiting retail stores to examine the alternatives, seeking input from friends and relatives about their experiences with the products in question, or perusing professional product evaluations furnished in various publications such as *Consumer Reports* or *Car and Driver*. In addition, when consumers are in an active information-gathering mode, they may be receptive to detailed, informative advertisements delivered through any of the print media, or they may deploy a shopping agent or a search engine to scour the Internet for the best deal or for opinions of other users.

During an internal or external search, consumers are not merely gathering information for its own sake. They have some need that is propelling the process, and their goal is to make a decision that yields benefits for them. The consumer searches for and is simultaneously forming attitudes about possible alternatives. This is the alternative-evaluation component of the decision process, and it is another key phase for the advertiser to target.

Alternative evaluation will be structured by the consumer's consideration set and evaluative criteria. The consideration set is the subset of brands from a particular product category that becomes the focal point of the consumer's evaluation. Most product categories contain too many brands for all to be considered, so the consumer finds some way to focus the search and evaluation. For example, for autos, consumers may consider only cars priced less than $20,000, or only cars that have antilock brakes, or only foreign-made cars, or only cars sold at dealerships within a five-mile radius of their work or home. A critical function of advertising is to make consumers aware of the brand and keep them aware so that the brand has a chance to be part of the consideration set. A great many ads try to do just this.

As the search-and-evaluation process proceeds, consumers form evaluations based on the characteristics or attributes those brands in their consideration set have in common. These product attributes or performance characteristics are referred to as **evaluative criteria**. Evaluative criteria differ from one product category to the next and can include many factors, such as price, texture, warranty terms, service support, color, scent, or carb content. As Exhibit 5.7 suggests, one traditional evaluative criterion for judging airlines has been on-time arrivals.

It is critical for advertisers to have as complete an understanding as possible of the evaluative criteria that consumers use to make their buying decisions. They must also know how consumers rate their brand in comparison with others from the consideration set. Understanding consumers' evaluative criteria furnishes a powerful starting point for any advertising campaign and will be examined in more depth later in the chapter.

Purchase. At this third stage, purchase occurs. The consumer has made a decision, and a sale is made. Great, right? Well, to a point. As nice as it is to make a sale, things are far from over at the point of sale. In fact, it would be a big mistake to view purchase as the culmination of the decision-making process. No matter what the product or service category, the consumer is likely to buy from it again in the future. So, what

RECENTLY, SCIENTISTS IN BRAUNSCHWEIG, GERMANY, SET THE ATOMIC CLOCK BACK ONE FULL SECOND. OUR FLIGHT SCHEDULES HAVE BEEN ADJUSTED ACCORDINGLY.

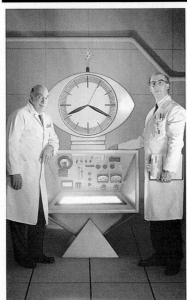

EXHIBIT 5.7

Advertisers must know the relevant evaluative criteria for their products. For an airline, on-time arrival is certainly an important matter. http://www.nwa.com

happens after the sale is very important to advertisers. Advertisers want trial; they then want conversion (repeat purchase). They want brand loyalty. Some want to create brand ambassadors, users who will become apostles for the brand, spreading its gospel. At the same time, competitors will be working to convince consumers to give their brand a try.

Postpurchase Use and Evaluation. The goal for marketers and advertisers must not be simply to generate a sale; it must be to create satisfied and, ultimately, loyal customers. The data to support this position are quite astounding. Research shows that about 65 percent of the average company's business comes from its present, satisfied customers, and that 91 percent of dissatisfied customers will never buy again from the company that disappointed them.[2] Thus, consumers' evaluations of products in use become a major determinant of which brands will be in the consideration set the next time around.

   Customer satisfaction derives from a favorable postpurchase experience. It may develop after a single use, but more likely it will require sustained use. Advertising can play an important role in inducing customer satisfaction by creating appropriate expectations for a brand's performance, or by helping the consumer who has already bought the advertised brand to feel good about doing so.

   Advertising plays an important role in alleviating the **cognitive dissonance** that can occur after a purchase. Cognitive dissonance is the anxiety or regret that lingers after a difficult decision, sometimes called "buyer's remorse." Often, rejected alternatives have attractive features that lead people to second-guess their own decisions. If the goal is to generate satisfied customers, this dissonance must be resolved in a way that leads consumers to conclude that they did make the right decision after all. Purchasing high-cost items or choosing from categories that include many desirable and comparable brands can yield high levels of cognitive dissonance.

   When dissonance is expected, it makes good sense for the advertiser to reassure buyers with detailed information about its brands. Postpurchase reinforcement programs might involve direct mail, e-mail, or other types of personalized contacts with the customer. This postpurchase period represents a great opportunity for the advertiser to have the undivided attention of the consumer and to provide information and advice about product use that will increase customer satisfaction. That's the name of the game: customer satisfaction. Without satisfied customers, we can't have a successful business. Nowadays, consumers often go to the Internet to find other purchasers of the product to tell them they did the right thing. Want to reduce your anxiety that you bought the right car? Go to a chat group or brand community for that brand, and the members will almost always tell you that you were really smart buying what you did. Some advertisers even provide this type of information to make you a satisfied customer. Here, an actual buyer of a Saturn, looks to a use.net group to help her with her buyer's remorse. What better group of people to go to online than a group of Saturn brand-community members?

Subject: Re: Why are Saturns so expensive?

> *The only cars that we found comfortable were the Ford Escort and the Saturn*

Good buy on the Saturn, the resale value on the Ford Escorts drops fast . . . you might have been able to "haggle" for a low price on the Escort, but your long-term ownership costs will be much lower on the Saturn.

                              —A posting at the newsgroup rec.autos.makers.Saturn

---

2.   Terry G. Vavra, *Aftermarketing: How to Keep Customers for Life through Relationship Marketing* (Homewood, IL: Business One Irwin, 1992), 13.

Four Modes of Consumer Decision Making. As you may be thinking about now, consumers aren't always deliberate and systematic; sometimes they are hasty, impulsive, or even irrational. The search time that people put into their purchases can vary dramatically for different types of products. Would you give the purchase of a tube of toothpaste the same amount of effort as the purchase of a new backpack? Probably not, unless you've been chastised by your dentist recently: Buy a tartar control toothpaste! Why is that T-shirt you bought at a Dave Matthews concert more important to you than the brand of orange juice you had for breakfast this morning? Does buying a Valentine's gift from Victoria's Secret create different feelings than buying a newspaper for your father? When you view a TV ad for car batteries, do you carefully memorize the information being presented so you can draw on it the next time you're evaluating the brands in your consideration set, or will you wait to seek out that information when you really need it—like when your car won't start and the guy in the wrecker says your battery is dead?

Let's face it, some purchase decisions are just more engaging than others. In the following sections we will elaborate on the view of consumer as decision maker by explaining four decision-making modes that help advertisers appreciate the richness and complexity of consumer behavior. These four modes are determined by a consumer's involvement and prior experiences with the product or service in question.

Sources of Involvement. To accommodate the complexity of consumption decisions, those who study consumer behavior typically talk about the involvement level of any particular decision. **Involvement** is the degree of perceived relevance and personal importance accompanying the choice of a certain product or service within a particular context. Many factors have been identified as potential contributors to an individual's level of involvement with a consumption decision.[3] People can develop interests and avocations in many different areas, such as cooking, photography, pet ownership, and exercise and fitness. Such ongoing personal interests can enhance involvement levels in a variety of product categories. Also, any time a great deal of risk is associated with a purchase—perhaps as a result of the high price of the item, or because the consumer will have to live with the decision for a long period of time—one should also expect elevated involvement.

Consumers can also derive important symbolic meaning from products and brands. Ownership or use of some products can help people reinforce some aspect of their self-image or make a statement to other people who are important to them. If a purchase carries great symbolic and real consequences—such as choosing the right gift for a special someone on Valentine's Day—it will be highly involving.

Some purchases can also tap into deep emotional concerns or motives. For example, many marketers, from Wal-Mart to Marathon Oil, have solicited consumers with an appeal to their patriotism. With Tide Bleach Alternative, as suggested in Exhibit 5.8, you don't have to be concerned with

EXHIBIT 5.8

Sometimes feelings of patriotism can be aroused in a subtle, understated manner.

3.   Michael R. Solomon, *Consumer Behavior* (Upper Saddle River, NJ: Pearson/Prentice Hall, 2004), ch. 4.

EXHIBIT 5.9

The emotional appeal in this Casio ad is just one of the many involvement devices. The play on water resistance also increases involvement as the reader perceives the double meaning. Describe how these involvement devices work. How does Casio use involvement devices at its Web site, http://www.casio-usa.com, to encourage visitors to further explore its products on the site? Describe the involvement devices used by competitor Timex at its home page, http://www.timex.com.

the red, white, and blue fading away. The ad for Casio watches (a Japanese product) in Exhibit 5.9 demonstrates that a product doesn't even have to be American to wrap itself in the Stars and Stripes. As Lou Dobbs of CNN (Exhibit 5.10) will tell you just about any day, Wal-Mart, which touts itself as a very patriotic company, sells a lot of stuff from China, and Dobbs doesn't think it's good for the United States. The passions of patriotism can significantly affect many things, including a person's level of involvement with a consumption decision.

Involvement levels vary not only among product categories for any given individual, but also among individuals for any given product category. For example, some pet owners will feed their pets only the expensive canned products that look and smell like people food. IAMS, whose ad is featured in Exhibit 5.11, understands this and made a special premium dog food for consumers who think of their pets as close-to-humans. Many other pet owners, however, are perfectly happy with feeding Rover from a 50-pound, economy-size bag of dry dog food.

Now we will use the ideas of involvement and prior experience to help conceive four different types of consumer decision making. These four modes are shown in Exhibit 5.12. Any specific consumption decision is based on a high or low level of prior experience with the product or service in question, and a high or low level of involvement. This yields the four modes of decision making: (1) extended problem solving; (2) limited problem solving; (3) habit or variety seeking; and (4) brand loyalty. Each is described in the following sections.

EXHIBIT 5.10

Does it matter to you where a product is made? Lou Dobbs certainly has issues with Chinese-made goods and U.S. policy makers who seem to him not to care about the negative impact on middle class Americans and national security.

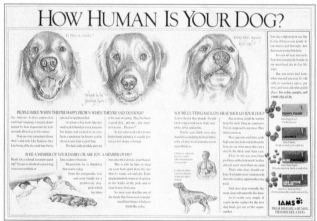

EXHIBIT 5.11

People who think of their pets as human take their selection of pet food very seriously. IAMS offers serious pet food for the serious dog owner. http://www.iams.com

EXHIBIT 5.12

Four modes of consumer decision making.

	High Involvement	Low Involvement
Low Experience	Extended problem solving	Limited problem solving
High Experience	Brand loyalty	Habit or variety seeking

Extended Problem Solving. When consumers are inexperienced in a particular consumption setting yet find the setting highly involving, they are likely to engage in **extended problem solving**. In this mode, consumers go through a deliberate decision-making process that begins with explicit need recognition, proceeds with careful internal and external search, continues through alternative evaluation and purchase, and ends with a lengthy postpurchase evaluation.

Examples of extended problem solving come with decisions such as choosing a home or a diamond ring, as suggested by Exhibit 5.13. These products are expensive, are publicly evaluated, and can carry a considerable amount of risk in terms of making an uneducated decision. Buying one's first new automobile and choosing a college are two other consumption settings that may require extended problem solving. Extended problem solving is the exception, not the rule.

Limited Problem Solving. In this decision-making mode, experience and involvement are both low. **Limited problem solving** is a more common mode of decision making. In this mode, a consumer is less systematic in his or her decision making. The consumer has a new problem to solve, but it is not a problem that is interesting or engaging, so the information search is limited to simply trying the first brand encountered. For example, let's say a young couple has just brought home a new baby, and suddenly they perceive a very real need for disposable diapers. At the hospital they received complimentary trial packs of several products, including Pampers disposables. They try the Pampers, find them an acceptable solution to their messy new problem, and take the discount coupon that came with the sample to their local grocery, where they buy several packages. In the limited problem-solving mode, we often see consumers simply seeking adequate solutions to mundane problems. It is also a mode in which just trying a brand or two may be the most efficient way of collecting information about one's options. Of course, smart marketers realize that trial offers can be a preferred means of collecting information, and they facilitate trial of their brands through free samples, inexpensive "trial sizes," or discount coupons.

A MAN'S GUIDE *to buying* DIAMONDS

She's expecting DIAMONDS.
Don't PANIC. We can help.

EXHIBIT 5.13

High involvement and low experience typically yield extended problem solving. Buying an engagement ring is a perfect example of this scenario. This ad offers lots of advice for the extended problem solver. De Beers is more than happy to be helpful here. http://www.adiamondisforever.com

Habit or Variety Seeking. Habit and variety seeking occur in settings where a decision isn't involving and a consumer repurchases from the category over and over again. In terms of sheer numbers, habitual purchases are probably the most common decision-making mode. Consumers find a brand of laundry detergent that suits their needs, they run out of the product, and they buy it again. The cycle repeats itself many times per year in an almost mind-less fashion. Getting in the habit of buying just one brand can be a way to simplify life and minimize the time invested in "nuisance" purchases. When a consumer perceives little difference among the various competitive brands, it is easier to buy the same brand repeatedly. A lot of consumption decisions are boring but necessary. Habits help us minimize the inconvenience.

In some product categories where a buying habit would be expected, an interest-ing phenomenon called variety seeking may be observed instead. Remember, **habit** refers to buying a single brand repeatedly as a solution to a simple consumption problem. This can be very tedious, and some consumers fight the boredom through variety seeking; this of course happens in many life domains. **Variety seeking** refers to the tendency of consumers to switch their selection among various brands in a given category in a seemingly random pattern. This is not to say that a consumer will buy just any brand; he or she probably has two to five brands that all provide similar levels of satisfaction to a particular consumption problem. However, from one purchase occasion to the next, the individual will switch brands from within this set, just for the sake of variety.

Variety seeking is most likely to occur in frequently purchased categories where sensory experience, such as taste or smell, accompanies product use. In such catego-ries, no amount of ad spending can overcome the consumer's basic desire for fresh sensory experience.[4] Satiation occurs after repeated use and leaves the consumer looking for a change of pace. Product categories such as soft drinks and alcoholic beverages, snack foods, breakfast cereals, and fast food are prone to variety seeking, so marketers in these categories must constantly be introducing new possibilities to consumers to feed their craving for variety. One day you open your lunch and your old, faithful bologna and cheese on white bread just doesn't cut it anymore—especially if a marketer has presented you with a fresh, new choice (see Exhibit 5.14).

Brand Loyalty. The final decision-making mode is typified by high involvement and rich prior experience. In this mode, **brand loyalty** becomes a major consideration in the purchase decision. Consumers demonstrate brand loyalty when they repeatedly purchase a single brand as their choice to fulfill a specific need. (Perhaps it is getting grease off dishes, as demonstrated in the Globalization box.) In one sense, brand-loyal purchasers may look as if they have developed a simple buying habit; however, it is important to distinguish brand loyalty from simple habit. Brand loyalty is based on highly favorable attitudes toward the brand and a conscious commitment to find this brand each time the consumer purchases from this category. Conversely, habits are merely consumption sim-plifiers that are not based on deeply held convic-tions. Habits can be disrupted through a skillful combination of advertising and sales promotions.

EXHIBIT 5.14

Bored with bread? Thomas offers you a chance for a little variety.

4.   Shirley Leung, "Fast-Food Firms Big Budgets Don't Buy Consumer Loyalty," *Wall Street Journal*, July 24, 2003, B4.

GLOBALIZATION

Selling Joy in Japan

The Japanese marketplace is among the most affluent and educated in the world. It also is one of the toughest competitive arenas for marketers to crack, even for global giants like Procter & Gamble. Until 1995, P&G did not sell any of its dishwashing products—such well-known brands as Dawn, Joy, Ivory, and Cascade—inside Japan.

Determined to change that, P&G began paying close attention to the basic tenets of consumer behavior. Managers in the field watched and videotaped Japanese homemakers as they washed dishes, then talked to them about the process. What did they learn? As Japanese diets had adopted more meat and fried foods, it had become more difficult to scrub grease stains out of plastic dishes and storage containers. So when it came time to wash dishes, Japanese homemakers again and again used far more dish soap than was necessary.

P&G responded with a highly concentrated Joy dish soap, specially formulated for the Japanese market, and then launched the product with a straightforward television ad demonstrating how one squirt of Joy could make a grease slick in a sink full of dirty dishes disappear. The results were impressive. Joy rapidly gained market share throughout Japan, and research conducted by P&G's leading Japanese competitor showed that more than 70 percent of Joy users in the country began using it because of the television advertisements.

For advertisers, it was a salient reminder that before they launch any campaign or devise any new product, they must first understand what matters to the consumer. Many things must go right for a new brand to enter a crowded marketplace and succeed. But when that happens, it usually is because the brand managers understand their consumers, create products that meet their needs, and create ad campaigns that convince those consumers that only one product has exactly what they want.

Source: Norihiko Shirouzu, "P&G's Joy Makes an Unlikely Splash in Japan," **Wall Street Journal**, December 10, 1997, B1.

Spending advertising dollars to persuade truly brand-loyal consumers to try an alternative can be a great waste of resources.

Brands such as Starbucks, eBay, Apple, Gerber, Oakley, Coke, Heineken, Ikea, Calvin Klein, Tide, and Harley-Davidson have inspired very loyal consumers. Brand loyalty is something that any marketer aspires to have, but in a world filled with more-savvy consumers and endless product (and advertising) proliferation, it is becoming harder and harder to attain. Brand loyalty may emerge because the consumer perceives that one brand simply outperforms all others in providing some critical functional benefit. For example, the harried business executive may have grown loyal to FedEx's overnight delivery service as a result of repeated satisfactory experiences with FedEx—and as a result of FedEx's advertising that has repeatedly posed the question, "Why fool around with anyone else?"

Perhaps even more important, brand loyalty can be due to the emotional benefits that accompany certain brands. One of the strongest indicators for brand loyalty has to be the tendency on the part of some loyal consumers to tattoo their bodies with the insignia of their favorite brand. While statistics are pretty new on this sort of thing, it is claimed that the worldwide leader in brand-name tattoos is Harley-Davidson. So, you are going to put something on your body for a lifetime, a brand name. What accounts for Harley's fervent following? Is Harley's brand loyalty simply a function of performing better than its many competitors? Or does a Harley rider derive some deep emotional benefit from taking that big bike out on the open road and leaving civilization far behind? To understand loyalty for a brand such as Harley, one must turn to the emotional benefits, such as feelings of pride, kinship, community with other Harley riders. Owning a Harley—and perhaps the tattoo—makes a person feel different and special. Harley ads are designed to reaffirm the deep emotional appeal of this product.

Strong emotional benefits might be expected from consumption decisions that we classify as highly involving, and they are major determinants of brand loyalty. Indeed, with so many brands in the marketplace, it is becoming harder and harder to create loyalty for one's brand through functional benefits alone. In fact, brand loyalty is usually much more about meaning and feelings than some often fictional "functional" benefit in the first place. There are a lot of product categories out there that could easily slip into being nothing more than interchangeable commodities (e.g., Wintel computers). To break free of this brand-parity problem and provide consumers with enduring reasons to become or stay loyal, advertisers are investing more and more effort in communicating the emotional benefits that might be derived from brands in categories as diverse as greeting cards (Hallmark—"When you care enough to send the very best") and vacation hot spots (Las Vegas—"What happens in Vegas, stays in Vegas"). You might go to YouTube and check out one of those Vegas spots, or some of the consumer-generated parodies. Many, probably most, companies are exploring ways to use the Internet to create dialogue and manage relations and even community with their customers. To do this, one must look for means to connect with customers at an emotional level.

③ Key Psychological Processes.

To complete our consideration of the consumer as a fairly thoughtful decision maker, one key issue remains. We need to examine the explicit psychological consequences of advertising. What does advertising leave in the minds of consumers that ultimately may influence their behavior? For those of you who have taken psychology courses, many of the topics in this section will sound familiar.

As we noted earlier in the chapter, a good deal of advertising is designed to ensure recognition and create favorable predispositions toward a brand so that as consumers search for solutions to their problems, they will think of the brand immediately. The goal of any delayed-response ad is to affect some psychological state that will subsequently influence a purchase.

Two ideas borrowed from social psychology are usually the center of attention when discussing the psychological aspects of advertising. First is attitude. **Attitude** is defined as an overall evaluation of any object, person, or issue that varies along a continuum, such as favorable to unfavorable or positive to negative. Attitudes are learned, and if they are based on substantial experience with the object or issue in question, they can be held with great conviction. Attitudes make our lives easier because they simplify decision making; that is, when faced with a choice among several alternatives, we do not need to process new information or analyze the merits of the alternatives. We merely select the alternative we think is the most favorable. We all possess attitudes on thousands of topics, ranging from political candidates to underage drinking. Marketers and advertisers, however, are most interested in one particular class of attitudes—brand attitudes.

Brand attitudes are summary evaluations that reflect preferences for various products and services. The next time you are waiting in a checkout line at the grocery, take a good look at the items in your cart. Those items are a direct reflection of your brand attitudes, or so the theory goes.

But what is the basis for these summary evaluations? Where do brand attitudes come from? Here we need a second idea from social psychology. To understand why people hold certain attitudes, we need to assess their specific beliefs. **Beliefs** represent the knowledge and feelings a person has accumulated about an object or issue. They can be logical and factual in nature, or biased and self-serving. A person might believe that the Mini Cooper is cute, that garlic consumption promotes weight loss, and that pet owners are lonely people. For that person, all these beliefs are valid and can serve as a basis for attitudes toward Minis, garlic, and pets.

If we know a person's beliefs, it is usually possible to infer attitude. Consider the two consumers' beliefs about Cadillac summarized in Exhibit 5.15. From their beliefs, we might suspect that one of these consumers is a prospective Cadillac owner, while the other will need a dramatic change in beliefs to ever make Cadillac part of his or her consideration set. It follows that the brand attitudes of the two individuals are at opposite ends of the favorableness continuum.

You may be aware that in recent years General Motors has spent billions of dollars on its Cadillac brand in a determined effort to take on Japanese and German models like the exquisite BMW 5 Series, which is exalted on the Toronto billboard in Exhibit 5.16. Simply put, the folks at General Motors will need to change a lot of consumers' beliefs about Cadillac if they are to have success in regaining market

EXHIBIT 5.15

An example of two consumers' beliefs about Caddies.

Consumer 1	Consumer 2
Cadillacs are clumsy to drive.	Cadillacs are luxurious.
Cadillacs are expensive.	Cadillacs have great resale value.
Cadillacs are gas guzzlers.	Cadillacs have OnStar.
Cadillacs are large.	Cadillac's TV ads rock!
Cadillacs are for senior citizens.	Cadillacs aren't what they used to be.

share from the likes of Lexus and BMW. Among other things, our beliefs help determine the cars we drive (subject of course to the limitations of our pocketbooks).

People have many beliefs about various features and attributes of products and brands. Some beliefs are more important than others in determining a person's final evaluation of a brand. Typically, a small number of beliefs—on the order of five to nine—underlie brand attitudes.[5] These beliefs are the critical determinants of an attitude and are referred to as **salient beliefs**.

Clearly, we would expect the number of salient beliefs to vary between product categories. The loyal Harley owner who proudly displays a tattoo will have many more salient beliefs about his bike than he has about his brand of shaving cream. Also, salient beliefs can be modified, replaced, or extinguished. For example, many people may have the belief that Nicorette Stop Smoking Gum doesn't taste very good. The ad for Nicorette Fruit Chill Gum in Exhibit 5.17 seeks to challenge that belief.

Since belief shaping and reinforcement can be one of the principal goals of advertising, it should come as no surprise that advertisers make belief assessment a focal point in their attempts to understand consumer behavior.

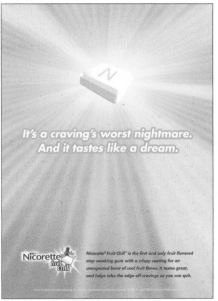

EXHIBIT 5.16

Changing consumers' beliefs is never an easy task. And the challenge is always made more complex by the fact that your best competition will only keep getting better. So for Cadillac the question becomes, even with a series of dramatic improvements, can they ever catch the Ultimate Driving Machine? It's the job of everyone who works for BMW to make sure that they don't. . . .

EXHIBIT 5.17

Belief change is a common goal in advertising. Does this ad make you think differently about Nicorette?

5.   Icek Ajzen and Martin Fishbein, *Understanding Attitudes and Predicting Social Behavior* (Englewood Cliffs, NJ: Prentice Hall, 1980), 63.

Multi-Attribute Attitude Models (MAAMS). **Multi-attribute attitude models (MAAMS)** provide a framework and a set of research procedures for collecting information from consumers to assess their salient beliefs and attitudes about competitive brands. Here we will highlight the basic components of a MAAMs analysis and illustrate how such an analysis can benefit the advertiser.

Any MAAMs analysis will feature four fundamental components:

- *Evaluative criteria* are the attributes or performance characteristics that consumers use in comparing competitive brands. In pursuing a MAAMs analysis, an advertiser must identify all evaluative criteria relevant to its product category.
- *Importance weights* reflect the priority that a particular evaluative criterion receives in the consumer's decision-making process. Importance weights can vary dramatically from one consumer to the next; for instance, some people will merely want good taste from their bowl of cereal, while others will be more concerned about fat and fiber content.
- The *consideration set* is that group of brands that represents the real focal point for the consumer's decision. For example, the potential buyer of a luxury sedan might be focusing on Acura, BMW, and Lexus. These and comparable brands would be featured in a MAAMs analysis. Cadillac could have a model, such as its reasonably new STS sedan, that aspired to be part of this consideration set, leading General Motors to conduct a MAAMs analysis featuring the STS and its foreign rivals. Conversely, it would be silly for GM to include the Chevy Malibu in a MAAMs analysis with this set of luxury/performance imports.
- *Beliefs* represent the knowledge and feelings that a consumer has about various brands. In a MAAMs analysis, beliefs about each brand's performance on all relevant evaluative criteria are assessed. Beliefs can be matters of fact—a 12-ounce Pepsi has 150 calories; a 12-ounce Coke Classic has 140—or highly subjective—the Cadillac XLR roadster is the sleekest, sexiest car on the street. It is common for beliefs to vary widely among consumers.

In conducting a MAAMs analysis, we must specify the relevant evaluative criteria for our category, as well as our direct competitors. We then go to consumers and let them tell us what's important and how our brand fares against the competition on the various evaluative criteria. The information generated from this survey research will give us a better appreciation for the salient beliefs that underlie brand attitudes, and it may suggest important opportunities for changing our marketing or advertising to yield more favorable brand attitudes.

Three basic attitude-change strategies can be developed from the MAAMs framework. First, a MAAMs analysis may reveal that consumers do not have an accurate perception of the relative performance of our brand on an important evaluative criterion. For example, consumers may perceive that Crest is far and away the best brand of toothpaste for fighting cavities, when in fact all brands with a fluoride additive perform equally well on cavity prevention. Correcting this misperception could become our focal point if we compete with Crest.

Second, a MAAMs analysis could uncover that our brand is perceived as the best performer on an evaluative criterion that most consumers do not view as very important. The task for advertising in this instance would be to persuade consumers that what our brand offers (say, lower carb content than any other light beer) is more important than they had thought previously.

Third, the MAAMs framework may lead to the conclusion that the only way to improve attitudes toward our brand would be through the introduction of a new attribute to be featured in our advertising. In some instances we could just add that attribute or feature (e.g., 10X, through the lens, optical zoom) to an existing product (e.g., our Olympus digital camera), and make that the centerpiece in our next ad campaign. Alternatively, if the attribute in question has emerged to be highly valued by 30 million Americans, we may want to reinvent an entire product line to feature this critical attribute. That's exactly what Unilever Bestfoods (makers of Ragu, Lipton, Skippy and Wish-Bone) decided to do for carb-shy consumers when it introduced a line of

INTRODUCING
DELICIOUS NEW OPTIONS
YOU CAN COUNT ON.

CARB OPTIONS™ STEAK SAUCE
1 G CARBS 5 CAL PER SERVING
SEE ALL PRODUCTS >

EXHIBIT 5.18

When fads emerge as major marketplace trends, marketers must respond or risk dramatic erosion in their customer base. Such has been the case in the food business, where carb-consciousness has affected the marketing of everything from peanut butter to steak sauce. Learn more at http://www.carboptions.com.

products like the one in Exhibit 5.18.

When marketers use the MAAMs approach, good things can result in terms of more-favorable brand attitudes and improved market share. When marketers carefully isolate key evaluative criteria, bring products to the marketplace that perform well on the focal criteria, and develop ads that effectively shape salient beliefs about the brand, the results can be dramatic—as we saw in the case of Joy in Japan.

Information Processing and Perceptual Defense. At this point you may have the impression that creating effective advertising is really a straightforward exercise. We carefully analyze consumers' beliefs and attitudes, construct ads to address any problems that might be identified, and choose various media to get the word out to our target customers. Yes, it would be very easy if consumers would just pay close attention and believe everything we tell them, and if our competition would kindly stop all of its advertising so that ours would be the only message that consumers had to worry about. Of course, these things aren't going to happen.

Why would we expect to encounter resistance from consumers as we attempt to influence their beliefs and attitudes about our brand? One way to think about this problem is to portray the consumer as an information processor who must advance through a series of stages before our message can have its intended effect. If we are skillful in selecting appropriate media to reach our target, then the consumer must (1) pay attention to the message, (2) comprehend it correctly, (3) accept the message exactly as we intended, and (4) retain the message until it is needed for a purchase decision. Unfortunately, problems can and do occur at any or all of these four stages, completely negating the effect of our advertising campaign.

There are two major obstacles that we must overcome if our message is to have its intended effect. The first—the **cognitive consistency** impetus—stems from the individual consumer. Remember, a person develops and holds beliefs and attitudes for a reason: They help him or her make efficient decisions that yield pleasing outcomes. When a consumer is satisfied with these outcomes, there is really no reason to alter the belief system that generated them (e.g., why bother with a Cadillac if you love your BMW!). New information that challenges existing beliefs can be ignored or disparaged to prevent modification of the present cognitive system. The consumer's desire to maintain cognitive consistency can be a major roadblock for an advertiser that wants to change beliefs and attitudes.

The second obstacle—**advertising clutter**—derives from the context in which ads are processed. Even if a person wanted to, it would be impossible to process and integrate every advertising message that he or she is exposed to each day. Pick up today's newspaper and start reviewing every ad you come across. Will you have time today to read them all? The clutter problem is further magnified by competitive brands making very similar performance claims.[6] Was it Advil,

---

6.   Clutter creates a variety of problems that compromise the effectiveness of advertising. For instance, research has shown that clutter interferes with basic memory functions, inhibiting a person's ability to keep straight which brands are making what claims. For more details see Anand Kumar and Shanker Krishnan, "Memory Interference in Advertising: A Replication and Extension," *Journal of Consumer Research*, vol. 30 (March 2004), 602–612.

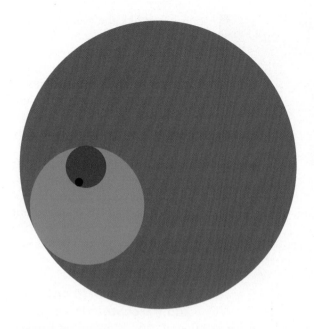

EXHIBIT 5.19

An ad in a sea of ads. So just how much can advertising really do anymore?

Anacin, Aveda, Aleve, Avia, Aflexa, Aveya, Acto-nel, Motrin, Nuprin, or Tylenol Gelcaps that promised you 12 hours of relief from your headache? (Can you select the brands from this list that aren't headache remedies?) The simple fact is that each of us is exposed to hundreds, maybe thousands, of ads each day, and no one has the time or inclination to sort through them all (see Exhibit 5.19). Some industry experts and researchers believe that the simple mass of advertising, the enormous number of ads, is now working very hard against the institution of advertising itself.

Exhibit 5.19 is an excellent illustration of clutter: the outer green circle is the total amount of measured U.S. advertising in a recent year. The smaller and light green circle represents all automotive advertising (the largest category in the U.S.) that same year. The smaller blue circle represents estimated spending of a large automobile company, and the tiny black dot is the amount spent on one of its leading brands. When you do the math, only about one out of every 2000 ads was for this typically advertised brand. So, what chance do you think that ad had to actually affect behavior in a sea of other ads? This is a very big question facing the industry right now.

Consumers thus employ perceptual defenses to simplify and control their own ad processing. It is important here to see that the consumer is in control, and the advertiser must find some way to engage the consumer if an ad is to have any impact. Of course, the best way to engage consumers is to offer them information about a product or service that will address an active need state. Simply stated, it is difficult to get people to process a message about your headache remedy when they don't have a headache. **Selective attention** is certainly the advertiser's greatest challenge and produces tremendous waste of advertising dollars. Most ads are simply ignored by consumers, again providing much of the reason for the growth of other forms of promotion such as branded entertainment. They turn the page, change the station, mute the sound, head for the refrigerator, TiVo past the ad, or just daydream or doze off—rather than process the traditional ad.

Advertisers employ a variety of tactics to break through the clutter. Popular music, celebrity spokespersons, sexy models, rapid scene changes, and anything that is novel are devices for combating selective attention. Remember, as we discussed in Chapter 4, advertisers constantly walk that fine line between novel and obnoxious in their never-ending battle for the attention of the consumer. They really don't want to insult you or anyone else; they just want to be noticed. Of course, they often step over the annoyance line.

The battle for consumers' attention poses another dilemma for advertisers. Without attention, there is no chance that an advertiser's message will have its desired impact; however, the provocative, attention-attracting devices used to engage consumers often become the focal point of consumers' ad processing. They remember seeing an ad featuring 27 Elvis Presley impersonators, but they can't recall what brand was being advertised or what claims were being made about the brand. If advertisers must entertain consumers to win their attention, they must also be careful that the brand and message don't get lost in the shuffle.

Let's assume that an ad gets attention and the consumer comprehends its claims correctly. Will acceptance follow and create the enduring change in brand attitude that is desired, or will there be further resistance? If the message is asking the consumer to alter beliefs about the brand, expect more resistance. When the consumer is involved and attentive and comprehends a claim that challenges current beliefs, the cognitive consistency impetus kicks in, and cognitive responses can be expected. **Cognitive responses** are the thoughts that occur to individuals at that exact moment in time when their beliefs and attitudes are being challenged by some form of persuasive communication. Remember, most ads will not provoke enough mental engagement to yield any form of cognitive response, but when they occur, the valence of these responses is critical to the acceptance of one's message. It is also true that more contemporary models of human memory provide strong evidence that memory is a much more fluid and interpretive system than we have thought in the past.[7, 8]

Human memory is not a mental VCR; it's more likely to combine, delete, add, and rewrite things, etc., because memory is more fluid and intrepretive than previously thought. So, the long-standing idea of just counting up brand name mentions and correctly remembered copy points is still used, and is sometimes appropriate, but is increasingly being disputed by the science of memory research. But it does stand to reason that if a consumer can really remember most of your ad, that's a good thing. As we shall see in the next section, cognitive responses are one of the main components of an influential framework for understanding the impact of advertising labeled the **elaboration likelihood model (ELM)**.

The Elaboration Likelihood Model (ELM). The ELM is another of those ideas that has been borrowed from social psychology and applied to advertising settings.[9] Like all models, it certainly has its limitations, but it is pretty easy to apply to many advertising situations. It has a certain intuitive appeal as well. It is a model that has particular relevance in this chapter because it incorporates ideas such as involvement, information processing, cognitive responses, and attitude formation in a single, integrated framework. The basic premise of the ELM is that to understand how a persuasive communication may affect a person's attitudes, we must consider his or her motivation and ability to elaborate on the message during processing. For most advertising contexts, motivation and ability will be a function of how involved the person is with the consumption decision in question. Involving decisions will result in active, mental elaboration during ad processing, whereas uninvolving decisions will implicate passive ad processing.

As indicated in Exhibit 5.20, the ELM uses the involvement dichotomy in spelling out two unique routes to attitude change. These are typically referred to as the central and peripheral routes to persuasion.

EXHIBIT 5.20

Two routes to attitude change.

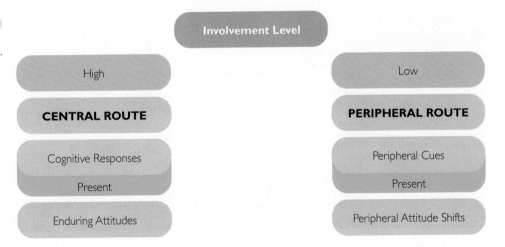

7.   http://depts.washington.edu/uweek/archives/2001.07.JUL_05/_article5.html
8.   Kathryn A. Braun-LaTour, Michael S. LaTour, Jacqueline E. Pickrell, and Elizabeth F. Loftus, "How and When Advertising Can Influence Memory for Consumer Experience," *Journal of Advertising,* vol. 33 (Winter 2004), 7–25.
9.   For an expanded discussion of these issues, see Richard E. Petty, John T. Cacioppo, Alan J. Strathman, and Joseph R. Priester, "To Think or Not to Think: Exploring Two Routes to Persuasion," in *Persuasion: Psychological Insights and Perspectives,* ed. Sharon Shavitt and Timothy C. Brock (Boston: Allyn & Bacon, 1994), 113–147.

When involvement is high, we should expect the consumer to draw on prior knowledge and experience and scrutinize or elaborate on the message arguments that are central to the advertiser's case. The nature of the individual's effortful thinking about the issues at hand could be judged from the cognitive responses that the ad provokes. These cognitive responses may be positive or negative in tone, and can be reactions to specific claims or any executional element of the ad.

Messages designed to reinforce existing beliefs, or shape beliefs for a new brand that the consumer was unaware of previously, are more likely to win uncritical acceptance. Compare the ads in Exhibits 5.21 and 5.22. In this example, think of the cities of New Orleans and Singapore as two brands competing for a tourist's attention (and ultimately, dollars). Each of these ads tries to affect beliefs and attitudes about its focal city. The cognitive consistency impetus that manifests in cognitive responses (thoughts consumers have while viewing an ad) will work against the city that is better known, especially when the ad challenges existing beliefs. Which ad do you find more challenging to your beliefs?

If the cognitive responses provoked by an ad are primarily negative in tone, the ad has backfired: The consumer is maintaining cognitive consistency by disparaging your ad, and that person's negative thoughts are likely to foster negative evaluation of your brand. However, when positive attitudes can be affected through the central route, they have very appealing properties. Because they are based on careful thought, central-route attitudes will (1) come to mind quickly for use in product selection, (2) resist the change efforts of other advertisers, (3) persist in memory

EXHIBIT 5.21

Cities can also engage in persuasive communications. Does this ad present an image of a post-Hurricane Katrina New Orleans that is compatible with your prior beliefs?

EXHIBIT 5.22

Singapore's Tourism Board uses this ad to educate readers about its broad cultural diversity, and to tickle their curiosity (http://www .newasia-singapore.com). Is Singapore an Asian city? Yes, but with influences from many cultures. The ad invites the reader to break out of a conceptual box, just as the Florida orange growers did with their "Orange Juice: It's Not Just for Breakfast Anymore" campaign.

without repeated ad exposures, and (4) be excellent predictors of behavior. These properties cannot be expected of attitudes that are formed in the peripheral route.

For low-involvement products, such as batteries or tortilla chips, cognitive responses to advertising claims are not expected. In such situations, attitude formation will often follow a more peripheral route, and peripheral cues become the focal point for judging the ad's impact. **Peripheral cues** refer to features of the ad other than the actual arguments about the brand's performance. They include an attractive or comical spokesperson, novel imagery, humorous incidents, or a catchy jingle. Any feature of the ad that prompts a pleasant emotional response could be thought of as a peripheral cue. Actually, critics of the ELM find this the weakest part of the model: We can all think of ads where the music and pictures are anything but peripheral, but the ELM fans note how well it does with traditional (i.e., older style) copy-heavy ads. But, remember, those are something of a dying species. In the peripheral route the consumer can still learn from an advertisement, but the learning is passive and typically must be achieved by frequent association of the peripheral cue (for example, the Eveready Energizer Bunny) with the brand in question. It has even been suggested that classical conditioning principles might be employed by advertisers to facilitate and accelerate this associative learning process.[10] As consumers learn to associate pleasant feelings and attractive images with a brand, their attitude toward the brand should become more positive.

What do LeAnn Rimes, James Carville, Queen Latifah, Jerry Seinfeld, Mr. Peanut, Jay-Z, Shakira, Junji Takada, Michelin Man, LeBron (a.k.a. King) James, Paige Davis, the Geico Gecko, Missy Elliott, and the song "Instant Karma" by John Lennon have in common? They and hundreds of others like them have been used as peripheral cues in advertising campaigns. When all brands in a category offer similar benefits, the most fruitful avenue for advertising strategy is likely to be the peripheral route, where the advertiser merely tries to maintain positive or pleasant associations with the brand by constantly presenting it with appealing peripheral cues. Of course, peripheral cues can be more than merely cute, with the right ones adding an undeniable level of "hipness" to aging brands.[11] Selecting peripheral cues can be especially important for mature brands in low-involvement categories where the challenge is to keep the customer from getting bored;[12] however, this is an expensive tactic because any gains made along the peripheral route are short-lived. TV air time, lots of repetition, sponsorship fees, and a never-ending search for the freshest, most popular peripheral cues demand huge budgets. When you think of the peripheral route, think of the advertising campaigns for high-profile, mature brands such as Coke, Pepsi, Budweiser, Gap, McDonald's, Nike, and Doritos. They entertain in an effort to keep you interested. But again, remember that determining just exactly what is "peripheral" is not as easy as it may sound. This is the weakest part of this model in actual practice with real ads in the real world. Of course no model is perfect, and this one works in certain situations with certain kinds of ads, and has been very popular largely for its intuitive appeal and the fact that it's pretty easy to explain.

Perspective Two: The Consumer as Social Being. The view of the consumer as decision maker and information processor has been a popular one. It is not, however, without its limitations or its critics. In fact, its critics are getting louder, particularly in the actual practice of advertising and integrated brand promotion. So we want to give you the other side of the story, a second perspective.

10.   For additional discussion of this issue, see Frances K. McSweeney and Calvin Bierley, "Recent Developments in Classical Conditioning," *Journal of Consumer Research*, vol. 11 (September 1984), 619–631.

11.   Associations like Jay-Z with Heineken, Missy Elliott with Gap, and Queen Latifah with Cover Girl illustrate the influence of Russell Simmons in bringing hip-hop into the advertising mainstream. (See "The CEO of Hip Hop," *BusinessWeek*, October 27, 2003, 91–98.) It is fair to say that Simmons found great success by lining up hip-hop icons as peripheral cues for all sorts of big-name advertisers.

12   The rationale for cultivating brand interest for mature brands is discussed more fully in Karen A. Machleit, Chris T. Allen, and Thomas J. Madden, "The Mature Brand and Brand Interest: An Alternative Consequence of Ad-Evoked Affect," *Journal of Marketing*, vol. 57 (October 1993), 72–82.

First, don't throw the baby out with the bathwater. While we are going to point out the limitations and shortcomings of the decision-maker perspective, we are *not* telling you that what you just learned is wrong or useless. Far from it—there is undeniable value in the perspective presented above. What goes on in consumers' minds is obviously important. But just as certainly it tells only part of the story of consumer behavior and advertising. Advertising and consumer behavior are so many things, and operate on so many levels, that a single-perspective approach is simply inadequate. So we offer more, a second perspective.

What the first perspective is best at is advancing understanding about how consumers make decisions. It is reasonably good at that. For example, it tells us that in general, consumers tend to use less as opposed to more information. That might seem odd, but it's true. Consumers *say* that more information is best, but tend to *actually use* less rather than more. If you think about it, this makes perfect sense. Consumers store and retrieve previously made judgments (e.g., "Honda is the best value") in order to not have to decide all over again every time they make a purchase. If this were not true, a quick trip to the convenience store would take hours: "Let's see, Trident versus Bubble Yum . . . hmmm . . . let me think about the attribute scores and weights of these two choices." In order to make their lives easier, consumers employ all sorts of mental short-cuts and effort-saving strategies. So, with this situation, and for many other reasons, the perspective described above has helped advertisers understand consumer decision making.

But what of understanding advertising and how it works with consumers? In their effort to isolate psychological mechanisms, information-processing academic researchers typically take consumer behavior (and consumers) out of its (their) natural environment in favor of a laboratory. This makes a great deal of sense if your desire is experimental control, the elimination of other possible explanations for a certain effect, or evidence of a mental process. But, as you may have already guessed, few consumers actually watch ads and buy things in laboratories. In fact, under such obviously unrealistic conditions, some argue that these researchers are no longer studying ads at all, but only "stimulus material." Those who criticize this experimental approach believe that ads really exist *only* in the real social world and natural environment. When removed from that environment they are no longer ads in any meaningful sense. Think about it for yourself: When you watch advertising on television, you usually see ten ads in a commercial break. You may or may not be paying attention. You might be talking to friends or family, reading, or just about anything else. Chances are you are not watching an ad on a computer monitor for class credit. In the real world, where you might see 800 to 2,000 ads per day, many ads just become wallpaper, nothing you really focus on. But in a lab the degree of focus is typically far greater. Subjects pay more attention; they watch the "ads" differently. To seriously believe these are the same thing is to believe in some pretty odd notions of reality. More importantly, what the ad means is often completely lost in the quest for "information" being "processed." But the allure of science and its symbols (e.g., labs, the perceived certainty and infallibility of science) is one of the modern period's most well-known seductions and comfortable mythologies. The trappings and appearance of science give people (including clients) feelings of certainty and truth, whether it is deserved or appropriate. And to be fair, the aims of academic experimental research (to advance basic knowledge and theory) are often quite different from the aims of the advertising industry (to make ads that sell things).

Industry critics and more and more academic researchers alike believe that much of the psychological "information processing" research (most popular in the industry in the 1950s) has significantly less to do with the advertising and consumption of real goods and services in the real world than with advancing psychological theory—a completely worthy goal for some college professors, but not necessarily important to the actual practice of advertising. In the real world of advertising, it is real consumers who matter, and how they respond to real ads in real environments.

The move away from purely psychological approaches has been going on in the advertising industry for quite some time, at least 40 years. It gathered enormous momentum in the 1980s. At that time U.S. West Coast agencies began adopting what they called "British Research," which was really just qualitative research as has been practiced by anthropologists, sociologists, and others for well over a century. The only thing really "British" about it at all is that some very hot London agencies had been doing research this way all along. (Actually, many had been, but these agencies used it as a point of differentiation.) At JWT-London, Judie Lannon's emphasis on meaning is a good example. She sums it up beautifully here:

And if Advertising contributes to the meaning of inanimate goods, then the study of these values and meanings are of prime importance . . . the perspective of research must be what people use advertising for.[13]

—Judie Lannon, then creative research director, J. Walter Thompson, London

This industry trend toward qualitative research and naturalistic methods also resonated with a similar move in academic research toward more qualitative field work, interpretive, and textual approaches to the study of human behavior, including consumer behavior. People began to see consumers as more than "information processors" and ads as more than socially isolated attempts at attitude manipulation. The truth is most major companies do very little attitude research apart from tracking studies (this is explained further in Chapter 7). They do almost no experimentation. But they almost all do lots of qualitative research, often under the heading "consumer insights." In this approach, **meaning** becomes more important than attitudes. Consumers do "process" information, but they also do a whole lot more (see Exhibit 5.23). Furthermore, "information" itself is a rich and complex textual product, bound by history, society, and culture, and interpreted in very sophisticated ways by human beings. Advertising practice is not engineering or chemistry; ads are not atoms or molecules. This meaning approach centers on knowing how to connect with human beings around their consumption practices with advertising. That's why advertising agencies

EXHIBIT 5.23

Real consumers do not consume in a social vacuum. Consumers are inherently social beings, connected to other consumers through social identities, families, rituals, cultures, symbols, and shared histories. To have any hope of understanding how real consumers will respond to real ads, you must first consider them and their consumption practices, and not in isolation.

like and hire people who know about material culture (anthropology), demography and social process (sociology), the history of brands and consumption practices (history), memory (psychology), communication, text (literature), and art (what a lot of ads are). Understanding people and ads will not be the same as counting kilos of sulfur, concentrations of acids, or stars in a galaxy. Humans and their creations (like ads and branded goods) are not just processors of information; they are that and much more.

In this section we present a second perspective on consumer behavior, a perspective concerned with social and cultural processes. It should be considered another

13.   Martin Davidson, "Objects of Desire: How Advertising Works," in Martin Davidson, *The Consumerist Manifesto: Advertising in Postmodern Times* (London: Routledge, 1992), 23–60.

part of the larger story of how advertising works. Remember, this is just another perspective. We are still talking about the same consumers discussed in the preceding section; we are just viewing their behavior from a different vantage point. When it comes to the complexities of consumer behavior and advertising, one perspective, one approach, is not enough.

Consuming in the Real World. Let's consider some major components of real consumers' lives:

 Culture. If you are in the ad business, you are in the culture business. Culture infuses, works on, is part of, and generally lands on all consumption. You need to understand what culture is, and what culture does.

Culture is what a people do, or "the total life ways of a people, the social legacy the individual acquires from his (her) group."[14] It is the way we eat, groom ourselves, celebrate, and mark our space and assert our position. It is the way things are done. Cultures are often thought of as large and national, but in reality cultures are usually smaller, and not necessarily geographic, such as *urban hipster culture*, *teen tech-nerd culture*, *goth culture*, *Junior League culture*, and so on. It's usually easier to see and note culture when it's more distant and unfamiliar. For most people, this is when they travel to another place. For example, if you've traveled beyond your own country, you have no doubt noticed that people in other cultures do things differently. If you were to point this out to one of the locals—for example, to a Parisian—and say something like, "Dude, you guys sure do things funny over here in France," you would no doubt be struck (perhaps literally) with the locals' belief that it is not they, but you, who behave oddly. This is a manifestation of culture and points out that members of a culture find the ways they do things to be perfectly natural. Culture is thus said to be invisible to those who are immersed in it. Everyone around us behaves in a similar fashion, so we do not easily think about the existence of some large and powerful force acting on us all. But it's there; this constant background force is the force of culture. To really see the culture that is all around you, to really see what you take as ordinary, to see it like you were a visitor to a strange land, is what the sociocultural perspective offers.

Make no mistake, culture is real, and it affects every aspect of human behavior, including consumer behavior and advertising. Culture surrounds the creation, transmission, reception, and interpretation of ads and brands, just as it touches every aspect of consumption. It is about as "real world" as it gets. For example, if you are Ocean Spray, you want to understand how the U.S. Thanksgiving holiday works so that you can sell more cranberries, and make more profit. Why cranberries? Why cranberries on Thanksgiving, but not on St. Patrick's Day? What is the deal with cranberries? How can we better understand and then leverage that particular pairing to sell more cranberries? Why do we have the particular rituals we perform on certain days? Are there market opportunities in those rituals? Or who makes up the rules of gift giving? If you are Tiffany, Barnes & Noble, Hallmark, or De Beers, you have a very good reason to understand why people do things a certain way (for example, buy things for one holiday, but not for another).

When advertisers spend time and money studying just why consumers consume certain goods or services, or why they consume them in a certain way, they are considering culture. Culture informs consumers' views about food, the body, gifts, possessions, a sense of self versus others, mating, courtship, death, religion, family, jobs, art, holidays, leisure, satisfaction, work—just about everything.

Values are the defining expressions of culture. Values express in words and deeds what is important to a culture. For example, most cultures value individual freedom, while some value duty to the society at large more than others. Some value propriety

---

14.   Gordon Marshall, ed., *The Concise Oxford Dictionary of Sociology* (New York: Oxford University Press, 1994), 104–105.

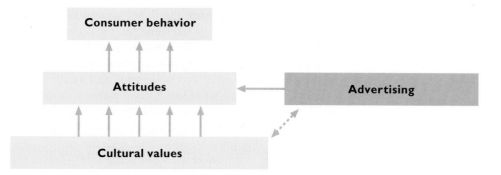

EXHIBIT 5.24

Cultural values, attitudes, and consumer behavior. Some believe that advertising can directly affect consumer behavior and, over time, cultural values as well.

and restrained behavior, while others value open expression. Values are cultural bedrock. Values are enduring. They cannot be changed quickly or easily. They are thus different from attitudes, which can be changed through a single advertising campaign or even a single ad. Think of cultural values as the very strong and rigid foundation on which much more mutable attitudes rest. Exhibit 5.24 illustrates this relationship. Values are the foundation of this structure. Attitudes are, in turn, influenced by values, as well as by many other sources. Advertising has to be consistent with, but cannot easily or quickly change, values. It is thus senseless for an advertiser to speak of using advertising to change values in any substantive way. Advertising influences values in the same way a persistent drip of water wears down a granite slab—very slowly and through cumulative impact, over years and years. It is also the case that cultural values change advertising.

Dear Ketel One Drinker Do you enjoy pushing the envelope, thinking outside the box, zagging when the world zigs, coming from left field, being ahead of the curve, breaking the mold, swimming against the tide, marching to the beat of a different drum, drinking Ketel One Citroen?

EXHIBIT 5.25

Ketel One recognizes that many consumers prefer to think of themselves as outside the mainstream mass market and celebrates their spirit.

Typically, advertisers try to either associate their product with a cultural value or criticize a competitor for being out of step with one. For example, in America, to say that a product "merely hides or masks odors" would be damning criticism, because it suggests that anyone who would use such a product doesn't really value cleanliness and thus isn't like the rest of us.

Advertisements must be consistent with the values of a people. If they are not, they will likely be rejected. Many argue that the best (most effective) ads are those that best express and affirm core cultural values. For example, one core American value is said to be individualism, or the predisposition to value the individual over the group. This value has been part of American culture for a very long time. Thus, advertisements that celebrate or affirm this value are more likely to succeed than ones that denigrate or ignore it. Exhibit 5.25 shows an ad that leans heavily on this value. And we might expect it not to play as well in so-called "collectivist" cultures. This may have been true once, but current thinking on globalization makes this individualism-collectivism dichotomy much less helpful in the real world of global advertising and consuming. Globalization makes the world more homogeneous in media and consumption. The local is swamped by the global. Global brands and a global culture of marketing, branding, advertising, and consuming is the reality, like it or not. Globalization values are commercial values. But, history still matters. Global consumer culture is flavored by history.

For example, do you think that being a poor British colony and losing millions to death in the Great Famine has something to do with Irish culture? You can probably think of other examples where knowing the local history helps in understanding the local culture. How about India's history? China, or Texas, or Mumbai? The trick for transnational companies is to understand this locally flavored globalism.

In the real world, individual agency partners in different countries may tweak or suggest minor changes in most ads, usually over a translation issue or a violation of some local regulation; the local partner either adapts the ad or creates an entirely new version (that must be consistent with the overall creative platform: what is the brand offering and how is the story being told). Travel just about anywhere on this planet and you will be met by the *global brandscape* (see Exhibit 5.26). Sure, advertising from around the globe still reveals cultural differences, but as many have argued those differences are in general disappearing into global consumer culture.

Rituals are "often-repeated formalized behaviors involving symbols."[15] Cultures participate in rituals; consumers participate in rituals. Rituals are core elements of culture. Cultures affirm, express, and maintain their values through rituals. They are a way in which individuals are made part of the culture, and a method by which the culture constantly renews and perpetuates itself. For example, ritual-laden holidays such as Thanksgiving, Christmas, Hanukah, and the Fourth of July help perpetuate aspects of American culture through their repeated reenactment (tradition). In Europe, there are a myriad of very important cultural rituals, all involving consumption (e.g., feasts and gift giving). In fact, this is true all over the world, and rituals help intertwine culture and consumption practices in a very real way. For example, Jell-O may have attained the prominence of an "official" American holiday food because of its regular usage as part of the Thanksgiving dinner ritual.[16] In the American South, it is common to eat black-eyed peas on New Year's Day to ensure good luck. In one sense it is "just done," but in another it is just done because it is a ritual embedded in a culture. If you are a consumer packaged goods manufacturer, understanding these types of ritual is not a trivial concern at all. (See Exhibits 5.27 and 5.28.)

EXHIBIT 5.26

Global brandscape. From Tucson to Tucumcari, Madrid to Cork (photo at right), the global brandscape is there.

---

15.   Ibid., 452.

16.   Melanie Wallendorf and Eric J. Arnould, "We Gather Together: Consumption Rituals of Thanksgiving Day," *Journal of Consumer Research*, vol. 18, no. 1 (June 1991), 13–31.

EXHIBIT 5.27

EXHIBIT 5.28

This ad promotes Kraft products as an integral part of family rituals and traditions. http://www.kraftfoods.com

In this ad, Splenda is made part of holiday ritual.

Rituals also occur every day in millions of other contexts. For example, when someone buys a new car or a new home, they do all sorts of "unnecessary" things to make it theirs. They clean the carpets even if they were just cleaned, they trim trees that don't need trimming, they hang things from the mirror of the used car they just bought, they change oil that was just changed—all to make the new possession theirs and remove any trace of the former owner. These behaviors are not only important to anthropologists, they are also important to those making and trying to sell products such as paint, rug shampoos, household disinfectants, lawn and garden equipment, auto accessories, and on and on.

Rituals don't have to be the biggest events of the year. There are everyday rituals, such as the way we eat, clean ourselves, and groom. Think about all the habitual things you do from the time you get up in the morning until you crawl into bed at night. These things are done in a certain way; they are not random.[17] Members of a common culture tend to do them one way, and members of other cultures do them other ways. Again, if you've ever visited another country, you have no doubt noticed significant differences. An American dining in Paris might be surprised to have sorbet to begin the meal and a salad to end it.

---

17.   For a great review, see Cele C. Otnes and Tina M. Lowrey, eds., *Contemporary Consumption Rituals: A Research Anthology* (Mahwah, NJ: Lawrence Erlbraun, 2004).

EXHIBIT 5.29

EXHIBITS 5.30 AND 5.31

This ad helps Olay become part of an already existing ritual.

Two advertisers incorporate Easter rituals.

Daily rituals seem inconsequential because they are habitual and routine, and thus "invisible." If, however, someone tried to get you to significantly alter the way you do these things, he or she would quickly learn just how important and resistant to change these rituals are. If a product or service cannot be incorporated into an already-existing ritual, it is very difficult and expensive for advertisers to effect a change. If, on the other hand, an advertiser can successfully incorporate the consumption of its good or service into an existing ritual, then success is much more likely. Imagine how important rituals are to the global beauty industry (Exhibit 5.29). Cleaning and beauty practices are highly ritualized.

Clearly, there are incredible opportunities for marketers who can successfully link their products to consumption rituals. In Exhibits 5.30 and 5.31 we see two advertisers incorporating their brands into Easter rituals.

Stratification (social class) refers to a person's relative standing in a social system as produced by systematic inequalities in things such as wealth, income, education, power, and status. For example, some members of society exist within a richer group (stratum), others within a less affluent stratum. Race and gender are also unequally distributed across these strata: For example, men generally have higher incomes than women. Thus a cross-section, or slice, of American society would reveal many different levels (or strata) of the population along these different dimensions. Sociologists used to prefer the term "social class," but many have gotten away from it lately. It seems that contemporary societies have less stable or easy-to-define classes than was once thought. Also, it is argued that the emergence of the *New Class*, a class of technologically skilled and highly educated individuals with great access to information and information technology, has changed the way we define social class: "Knowledge of, and access to, information may begin to challenge property as a determinant of social class."[18]

"Social class" was typically thought most strongly determined by income: Higher-income Americans were generally seen as being in a higher social class, and lower-

18.   Alvin W. Gouldner, "The Future of Intellectuals and the Rise of the New Class," in *Social Stratification in Sociological Perspective: Class, Race and Gender*, ed. David B. Grusky (San Francisco: Westview Press, 1994), 711–729.

income Americans were considered to be in a lower class. But that was an imperfect relationship. For example, successful plumbers often had higher incomes than unsuccessful lawyers, but their occupation was (perhaps) less prestigious, and thus their social class designation was lower. So, the prestige of one's occupation also entered into what we called "social class." Education also has something to do with social class, but a person with a little college experience and a lot of inherited wealth would probably rank higher than an insurance agent with an MBA. Bill Gates left Harvard without a degree, and he has pretty high social standing, not to mention wealth. Thus income, education, and occupation are three important variables for indicating social class, but are still individually, or even collectively, inadequate at capturing its full meaning. Then there are rock stars, professional athletes, and successful actors, who have high incomes but are generally thought to be somewhat outside the social class system. This is another reason the term "social class" has been falling away.

Important to marketers is the belief that members of the same social strata tend to live in similar ways, have similar views and philosophies, and, most critically, tend to consume in somewhat similar ways. You could supposedly tell "social class" from what people consume and how they consume; at least, that's what lots of marketers and advertisers believed. Markers of social class would include what one wears, where one lives, and how one speaks. In a consumer society, consumption marks or indicates stratification in a myriad of ways. Stratification-related consumption preferences reflect value differences and different ways of seeing the world and the role of things in it; they reflect taste.

Lately, the idea that the traditional social class-consumption taste hierarchy has collapsed has gained a lot of momentum. Now that more cheaply produced robotics make better items than "hand made" ones, the money-taste relationship is significantly threatened. Writer John Seabrook notes that now we know social class mostly by "the services you use, where you live, and the control they have over other people's labor."[19] In other words, other than housing, social stratification is marked through consumption only by a consumer's ability to afford all sorts of services, particularly those such as housekeepers, au pairs, personal shoppers, personal trainers, etc.

What do you think? Put it to the test: Go to a mall, walk around, and check people out. Do you think you could guess their income, education, occupation, and whether they live downtown or in the 'burbs from the way they look, what they are wearing, and which stores they shop in? Most advertisers think you can, and that's why stratification matters.

This brings us to taste. **Taste** refers to a generalized set or orientation to consumer preferences. Social class affects consumption through tastes, including media habits, and thus exposure to various advertising media vehicles—for example, *RV Life* versus *Wine Spectator*. We think of tennis more than bowling as belonging to the upper classes, chess more than checkers, and brie more than Velveeta. Ordering wine instead of beer has social significance, as does wearing Tommy Hilfiger rather than Lee jeans, or driving a Volvo rather than a Chevy. Social stratification and taste are intertwined, but perhaps not as closely as we once thought.

Contemporary consumer societies have a much more fluid sense of class, and strata themselves are more in flux and have more permeable boundaries than we once believed. We come down on this in the following way: Yes, in contemporary society there is a more fluid character to social stratification (class) and its consumption markers, but it is still there and still matters. Fashion and taste cycle faster than they once did, and consumers may be more playful in their use of class markers than they once

19. Seabrook, John, "Sunday in Soho," in Nobrow: The Culture of Marketing—The Marketing of Culture, (New York: Knopf, 2000). 161–175. This is available at http://www.booknoise.net/johnseabrook/stories/culture/nobrow/index.html. See also: Steinhauer, Jennifer, "When the Joneses Wear Jeans: Signs of Status are Harder to Spot, but Look Again," in Correspondents of the New York Times, Class Matters, (New York: Times Books, 2005), 134–145.

Over the years, Target has made the logo for its store mean more than the labels on many of its products. It is, in our view, the best branding communication of the past few years.

were, and they are less rigid boundaries than in the past. We refer to this as the Targetization of style in the United States. Since stores led by Target have brought designers to the masses, there has been what some believe to be a democratization of style and taste. So, we believe there is something to this idea of a collapsing taste structure relative to traditional stratification, but not a complete one. Target (see Exhibit 5.32) has been one of the most amazing brands, with amazing ads to match over the last few years. Their ads are almost devoid of words (copy) and are very stylish, hip, and self-aware (remember this was shown in Chapter 3).

A related concept is *cultural capital*, the value that cultures place on certain consumption practices and objects. For example, a certain consumption practice, say snowboarding, has a certain capital or value (like money) for some segment of the population. If you own a snowboard (a certain amount of cultural capital) and can actually use it (more cultural capital), and look good while using it (even more capital), then this activity is like cultural currency or cultural money in the bank. You can "spend" it. It gets you things you want. Cultural capital is a lot like "cool," or "hip," but is more, a broader category. A Porsche has a certain cultural capital among some groups, as does wearing khakis, drinking Bud, ordering the right pinot noir, knowing how to hail a cab, flying first class (maybe not hip or cool, but still high in cultural capital), or knowing about the latest band or cool thing on YouTube. This capital may exist within a hipster culture, or a 40-something wine-snob culture, or a redneck culture—it's still cultural capital. These are all cultures, and certain consumer practices are favored or valued (worth) more in each. Advertisers try to figure out which ones are valued more, and why, and how to make their product sought after because it has higher cultural capital, and can be sold at a higher price. Does an iPhone have more cultural capital than a BlackBerry, or a really thin Motorola? To whom? To what cultural group? To what market segment? Maybe the coolest people don't have any of those things; they are free of their electronic leash. Having good "taste" helps you know which things have high cultural capital. These ads try to emphasize the cultural capital, style, and taste to be found in the product (see Exhibits 5.33 and 5.34), and then on to the consumer.

These two ads point to the high cultural capital of the products.

Stratification and cultural capital becomes apparent when a person moves from one stratum into another. Consider the following example: Bob and Jill move into a more expensive neighborhood. Both grew up in lower-middle-class surroundings and moved into high-paying jobs after graduate school. They have now moved into a fairly upscale neighborhood, composed mostly of "older money." On one of the first warm Sundays, Bob goes out to his driveway and begins to do something he has done all his life: change the oil in his car. One of Bob's neighbors comes over and chats, and ever so subtly suggests to Bob that people in this neighborhood have "someone else" do "that sort of thing." Bob gets the message: It's not cool to change your oil in your own driveway. This is not how the new neighbors behave. It doesn't matter whether you like to do it or not; it is simply not done. To Bob, paying someone else to do this simple job seems wasteful and uppity. He's a bit offended, and a little embarrassed. But, over time, he decides that it's better to go along with the other people in the neighborhood. Over time, Bob begins to see the error of his ways and changes his attitudes and his behavior.

This is an example of the effect of stratification and (negative) cultural capital on consumer behavior. Bob will no longer be a good target for Fram, Purolator, AutoZone, or any other product or service used to change oil at home. On the other hand, Bob is now a perfect candidate for quick-oil-change businesses such as Jiffy Lube.

Family. The consumer behavior of families is also of great interest to advertisers. Advertisers want not only to discern the needs of different kinds of families, but also to discover how decisions are made within families. The first is possible; the latter is much more difficult. For a while, consumer researchers tried to determine who in the traditional nuclear family (that is, Mom, Dad, and the kids) made various purchasing decisions. This was largely an exercise in futility. Due to errors in reporting and conflicting perceptions between partners, it became clear that the family purchasing process is anything but clear. While some types of purchases are handled by one family member, many decisions are actually diffuse nondecisions, arrived at through what consumer researcher C. W. Park aptly calls a "muddling-through" process.[20] These "decisions" just get made, and no one is really sure who made them, or even when. For an advertiser to influence such a diffuse and vague process is indeed a challenge. The consumer behavior of the family is a complex and often subtle type of social negotiation. One person handles this, one takes care of that. Sometimes specific purchases fall along gender lines, but sometimes they don't. While they may not be the buyer in many instances, children can play important roles as initiators, influencers, and users in many categories, such as cereals, clothing, vacation destinations, fast-food restaurants, and technology (like computers). Still, some advertisers capitalize on the flexibility of this social system by suggesting in their ads who *should* take charge of a given consumption task, and then arming that person with the appearance of expertise so that whoever wants the job can take it and defend his or her purchases.

We also know that families have a lasting influence on the consumer preferences of family members. One of the best predictors of the brands adults use is the ones their parents used. This is true for cars, toothpaste, household cleansers, and many more products. Say you go off to college. You eventually have to do laundry, so you go to the store, and you buy Tide. Why Tide? Well, you're not sure, but you saw it around your house when you lived with your parents, and things seemed to

20.   C. Whan Park, "Joint Decisions in Home Purchasing: A Muddling-Through Process," *Journal of Consumer Research*, vol. 9 (September 1982), 151–162.

Who are the Cleavers? Demographically, they (working husband, stay at home mother, two children, upper-middle-class status) have become a pretty small minority, but maybe they still carry an important mythology about stability and the nuclear family. Remember ads and reality are not always the same thing. Do you think more people wish, down deep, that they had a family like this?

have worked out okay for them, so you buy it for yourself. The habit sticks, and you keep buying it. This is called an **intergenerational effect**.

Advertisers often focus on the major or gross differences in types of families, because different families have different needs, buy different things, and are reached by different media. Family roles often change when both parents (or a single parent) are employed outside the home. For instance, a teenage son or daughter may be given the role of initiator and buyer, while the parent or parents serve merely as influences. Furthermore, we should remember that Ward, June, Wally, and the Beaver (Exhibit 5.35) are not the norm. There are a lot of single parents and quite a few second and even third marriages. We know a few that have even surpassed three. *Family* is a very open concept these days. In addition to the "traditional" nuclear family and the single-parent household, there is the extended family (nuclear family plus grandparents, cousins, and others) including single parents and gay and lesbian households with and without children.

Beyond the basic configuration, advertisers are often interested in knowing things such as the age of the youngest child, the size of the family, and the family income. The age of the youngest child living at home tells an advertiser where the family is in terms of its needs and obligations (that is, toys, investment instruments for college savings, clothing, and vacations). When the youngest child leaves home, the consumption patterns of a family radically change. Advertisers like to track the age of the youngest child living at home and use it as a planning criterion. This is called a **life-stage** variable, and is used frequently in advertising and promotion planning.

Celebrity is a unique sociological concept, and it matters a great deal to advertisers. Twenty-first-century society is all about celebrity. Current thinking is that in a celebrity-based culture, celebrities help contemporary consumers with identity. Identity in a consumer culture becomes a "fashion accessory" prop for a day—head banger, corporate slave at work in a screwbed (a term for being assigned to a cubicle rather than the preferred office), and so forth. The idea is that contemporary consumers are very good at putting on and taking off, trying on, switching, and trading various identities, in the same way that they have clicked through the channels since they could reach the remote. E-generation children have become who they are, in some part, through celebrity-inspired identities—the way they do their hair, the way they think about their bodies, their relationships, their aspirations, and certainly their styles. Of course, style is often purchased and accessorized. This means that celebrities and images of them are used moment to moment to help in a personal parade of identity. For this reason, the understanding of the celebrity is much more complex and vital than merely thinking in terms of similar attitudes and behaviors. It affects who we are to some degree, minute to minute, ad to ad, mall to mall, purchase to purchase (Exhibits 5.36 through 5.38). Further, with YouTube, MySpace, and Facebook the line between mass media and daily contemporary life blurs more all the time. Advertisers generally think this is a good thing because rapid identity shifts are just another way of saying marketing opportunity.

Race and Ethnicity. Race and ethnicity provide other ways to think about important social groups. Answering the question of how race figures into consumer behavior is very difficult. Our discomfort stems from having, on the one hand, the

EXHIBITS 5.36 THROUGH 5.38

These ads use celebrity in simple and sophisticated ways. Who do you want to be today?

desire to say, "Race doesn't matter, we're all the same," and on the other hand not wanting (or not being able) to deny the significance of race in terms of reaching ethnic cultures and influencing a wide variety of behaviors, including consumer behavior. The truth is we are less and less sure what *race* is, what it means. Obviously, a person's pigmentation, in and of itself, has almost nothing to do with preferences for one type of product over another. But because race has mattered in culture, it does still matter in consumer behavior. But it is true that the United States, Europe, and much of the world is becoming an increasingly ethnically diverse culture, while at the same time becoming more homogeneous (important exceptions exist) in terms of consumer culture. (Exhibit 5.39 shows the trend of current and projected racial diversity in the United States.) By the middle of the 21st century, whites will probably be very close to only 50 percent of the U.S. population. This demographic reality is very important to advertisers and marketers.

There probably isn't an area in consumer behavior where research is more inadequate. This is probably because everyone is terrified to discuss it, and because most of the findings we do have are suspect. What is attributed to race is often due to another factor that is itself associated with race. For example, consumer behavior textbooks commonly say something to the effect that African Americans

Year	White	Black	Hispanic	Asian	American Indian
1996	194.4 (73.3%)	32.0 (12.1%)	27.8 (10.5%)	9.1 (3.4%)	2.0 (0.7%)
2000	197.1 (71.8%)	33.6 (12.2%)	31.4 (11.4%)	10.6 (3.9%)	2.1 (0.7%)
2010	202.4 (68.0%)	37.5 (12.6%)	41.1 (13.8%)	14.4 (4.8%)	2.3 (0.8%)
2020	207.4 (64.3%)	41.5 (12.9%)	52.7 (16.3%)	18.6 (5.7%)	2.6 (0.8%)
2030	210.0 (60.5%)	45.4 (13.1%)	65.6 (18.9%)	23.0 (6.6%)	2.9 (0.8%)
2040	209.6 (56.7%)	49.4 (13.3%)	80.2 (21.7%)	27.6 (7.5%)	3.2 (0.9%)
2050	207.9 (52.8%)	53.6 (13.6%)	96.5 (24.5%)	32.4 (8.2%)	3.5 (0.9%)

Source: U.S. Census Bureau.

EXHIBIT 5.39

Ethnic diversity in America: projected U.S. population by race in millions (and percentage of total population by race).

EXHIBITS 5.40 THROUGH 5.42

These ads are directed at Hispanics, Asian, and African-American consumers.

and Hispanics are more brand loyal than their Anglo counterparts. Data on the frequency of brand switching is offered, and lo and behold, it does appear that white people switch brands more often. But why? Some ethnic minorities live in areas where there are fewer retail choices. When we statistically remove the effect of income disparities between white people and people of color, we see that the brand-switching effect often disappears. This suggests that brand loyalty is not a function of race, but of disposable income and shopping options.

But race does inform one's social identity to varying degrees. One is not blind to one's own ethnicity. African Americans, Hispanics, and other ethnic groups have culturally related consumption preferences. Certain brands become associated with racial or ethnic groups. It is not enough, however, for advertisers to say one group is different from another group, or that they prefer one brand over another simply because they are members of a racial or ethnic category. If advertisers really want a good, long-term relationship with their customers, they must acquire, through good consumer research, a deeper understanding of who their customers are and how this identity is affected by culture, felt ethnicity, and race. In short, advertisers must ask why groups of consumers are different, or prefer different brands, and not settle for an easy answer. It wasn't until the mid to late 1980s that most American corporations made a concerted effort to court African-American consumers, or even to recognize their existence.[21] Efforts to serve the Hispanic consumer have been intermittent and inconsistent. Sample ads directed at diverse audiences are shown in Exhibits 5.40 through 5.42.

Geo-Politics. Just as there is increasing globalization and general homogeneity at the level of accepting the basic ethos and trappings of consumer culture, there are some important countercurrents: brands for "us." There are many places in the world where religious–ethnic–political strife is abundant, and this gets played out in consumption domains. Exhibit 5.43 shows Mecca Cola, a pretty classic contemporary example. There are also "green" brands (see Exhibit 5.44) and brands that are preferred because of their labor practices and politics (see Exhibit 5.45).

Gender. **Gender** is the social expression of sexual biology, sexual choice, or both. Obviously, gender matters in consumption. But are men and women really that dif-

21.   Jannette L. Dates, "Advertising," in *Split Image: African Americans in the Mass Media,* ed. Jannette L. Dates and William Barlow (Washington, DC: Howard University Press, 1990), 421–454.

EXHIBIT 5.43

This is a brand with pretty clear politics.

EXHIBIT 5.44

This ad for the hybrid Lexus LS 600h L ends with the promise "Gives more to the driver. Takes less from the world." Have you noticed an increase in the number of companies taking a "green" approach to their advertising message?

EXHIBIT 5.45

Having a social conscience isn't necessarily incompatible with smart marketing.

ferent in any meaningful way in their consumption behavior, beyond the obvious? Again, to the extent that gender informs a "culture of gender," the answer is yes. As long as men and women are the products of differential socialization, then they will continue to be different in some significant ways. There is, however, no definitive list of gender differences in consumption, because the expression of gender, just like anything else social, depends on the situation and the social circumstances. In the 1920s, advertisers openly referred to women as less logical, more emotional, the cultural stewards of beauty.[22] (Some say that the same soft, irrational, emotional feminine persona is still invoked in advertising.) Advertising helps construct a social reality, with gender a predominant feature. Not only is it a matter of conscience and social responsibility to be aware of this, but it is good business as well. Advertisers must keep in mind, though, that it's hard to keep the business of people you patronize, insult, or ignore.

22.   Roland Marchand, *Advertising: The American Dream* (Berkeley: University of California Press, 1984), 25.

Obviously, gender's impact on consumer behavior is not limited to heterosexual men and women. Gay men and lesbians are large and significant markets. Of late, these markets have been targeted by corporate titans such as IBM, United Airlines, and Citibank.[23] Again, these are markets that desire to be acknowledged and served, but not stereotyped and patronized. Exhibits 5.46 and 5.47 are ads directed at lesbian and gay audiences.

In the late 1970s, advertisers discovered working women. In the 1980s, marketers discovered African-American consumers, about the same time they discovered Hispanic consumers. Later they discovered Asian Americans, and just lately they discovered gays and lesbians. Of course, these people weren't missing. They were there all along. These "discoveries" of forgotten and marginalized social groups create some interesting problems for advertisers. Members of these groups, quite reasonably, want to be served just like any other consumers. To serve these markets, consider what Wally Snyder of the American Advertising Federation said:

Advertising that addresses the realities of America's multicultural population must be created by qualified professionals who understand the nuances of the disparate cultures. Otherwise, agencies and marketers run the risk of losing or, worse, alienating millions of consumers eager to buy their products or services. Building a business that "looks like" the nation's increasingly multicultural population is no longer simply a moral choice, it is a business imperative.[24]

EXHIBIT 5.46

Quite a few advertisers are beginning to recognize the advantages of marketing to gay and lesbian consumers. Here, American Express recognizes the special financial challenges faced by lesbian couples. http://www. americanexpress.com

EXHIBIT 5.47

Here, Volvo attempts to appeal to gay consumers.

23.   Laura Koss-Feder, "Out and About: Firms Introduce Gay-Specific Ads for Mainstream Products, Services," *Marketing News*, May 25, 1998, 1, 20.
24.   Wally Snyder, "Advertising's Ethical and Economic Imperative," *American Advertising* (Fall 1992), 28.

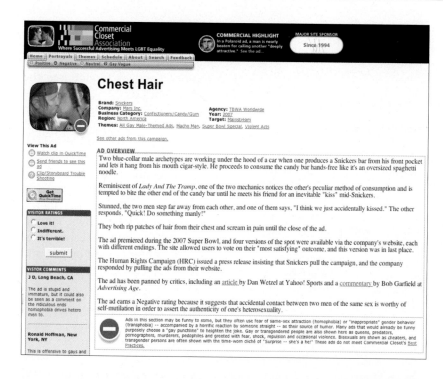

EXHIBIT 5.48

Commercial Closet reviews two ads here. What do you think?

Attention and representation without stereotyping from a medium and a genre that is known for stereotyping might be a lot to expect, but it's not that much. Web sites such as Commercial Closet (Exhibit 5.48) offer reviews and opinions on LGBT representation in ads.

Community. Community is a powerful and traditional sociological concept. Its meaning extends well beyond the idea of a specific geographic place. Communities can be imagined or even virtual. Community members believe that they belong to a group of people who are similar to them in some important way, and different from those not in the community. Members of communities often share rituals and traditions, and feel some sort of responsibility to one another and the community.

Advertisers are becoming increasingly aware of the power of community. Products have social meanings, and community is the quintessential social domain, so consumption is inseparable from the notion of where we live (actually or virtually), and with whom we feel a kinship or a sense of belonging. Communities often exert a great deal of power. A community may be your neighborhood, or it may be people like you with whom you feel a kinship, such as members of social clubs, other consumers who collect the same things you do, or people who have, use, or admire the same brands you do.

DOING IT RIGHT

A Brand Community That Makes the Brand

Plenty of companies try to build communities around their brands. In Chicago, two young entrepreneurs took a more radical approach. When they launched the online T-shirt business Threadless in 2000, owners Jake Nickell and Jacob DeHart decided that all of the designs would come not from big-name stylists, but from the company's own customers.

Their business model is a simple one. The company accepts design ideas from anybody who wants to submit one, with about 125 new submissions coming in each day. The entries then are posted online, where visitors rate each design on a zero-to-five scale. Each week, the company picks six of the most popular designs to be printed on T-shirts. The winning designers each get $2,000, and Threadless.com gets a product pre-approved by its customers. The business has sold out of nearly every T-shirt it has offered; in 2006, the company sold $16 million worth of T-shirts.

Threadless.com also relies on its powerful online community to be the company's primary marketing tool. New visitors are encouraged to upload photos, leave comments, post blog entries, and refer friends. This powerful consumer audience even creates its own design stars. One 16-time winner, Ross Zietz, went to work for Threadless after graduating from Louisiana State University and has picked up freelance work designing shirts for musicians such as the Dave Matthews Band.

Threadless has gone well beyond merely cultivating a loyal customer community. In effect, its customers have become the company. "The bigger and more active the community, the more sales go up," said creative director Jeffrey Kalmikoff. "It's hard to argue with that formula."

Sources: Mark Weingarten, "Designed to Grow," **Business 2.0**, June 2007, p. 35; Rob Walker, "Consumed: Mass Appeal," **New York Times Magazine**, July 8, 2007, p. 16.

Brand communities are groups of consumers who feel a commonality and a shared purpose attached to a consumer good or service (see the Doing It Right box).[25]

When owners of Doc Martens, Saabs, Mountain Dews, or Saturns experience a sense of connectedness by virtue of their common ownership or usage, a brand community exists. When two perfect strangers stand in a parking lot and act like old friends simply because they both own Saturns, a type of community is revealed. Most of these communities exist online, and some reveal a certain level of brand fanaticism:

Coke is the best drink ever created. . . . And with popularity, the imitators came. These imitators make money, are not as good as the Real Thing, they gained popularity and must be stopped. This is why we must rally around our beverage in its time of need. We cannot see the horrible things pepsico does anymore. It is times these crimes stop.

Join the Coke Army.

—From the Web site of a 16-year-old male in Belgium

Other times, these communities reveal an important and more "mainstream" connection between owners, users or admirers of brands, that with the rise of the Internet, has made these communities and this type of community conversation anything but trivial:

Truth be told, I just "found" this group and I'm a happy little person now that I've found there are other people out there like me that love their Miatas!

—From a Miata user-group post

This quote reveals the writer's joy at realizing that there are others out there who get it—who see what this "happy little person" sees in this material object, this car, and this brand: Miata. The promise of community—not to be alone, to share appreciation and admiration of something or someone, no matter how odd or inappropriate others feel it to be—is fulfilled in online communities. The language looks much like that of people pleased that they discovered others with the same sexual orientation, the same health problems, or the same religion, in this case a brand and model of car. It is a rewarding and embracing social collective centered on a brand.

25.   Albert Muniz, Jr., and Thomas O'Guinn, "Brand Community," *Journal of Consumer Research*, vol. 27 (2001), 412–432.

EXPERIENTIAL EXERCISES

1.   Create a list of three products or services to which you are brand-loyal. For each, explain why you have highly favorable attitudes toward the brand and consciously seek to buy it whenever you make a purchase from that product category. Describe what factors could cause you to change your loyalty and switch to a competing brand.

2.   Find ads that address the following four modes of decision making: extended problem solving, limited problem solving, habit or variety seeking, and brand loyalty. Explain why each ad fits with that particular decision-making mode and state whether you think the ad is effective in persuading consumers. Be sure to include the concepts of involvement and prior experience in your answer.

3.   A key issue in postpurchase evaluation is cognitive dissonance—the anxiety or "buyer's remorse" that can linger after high-involvement purchasing decisions. Research has shown that some consumers are more likely to read ads for a product they already have purchased than ads for competing brands.

With this in mind, imagine that you have been hired by the luxury watchmaker Breitling to design an ad campaign specifically intended to ease potential cognitive dissonance. What steps could the company make to reach out to consumers after the purchase? What advertising messages and imagery could be most effective in reinforcing the consumer's decision to purchase the watch?

4.   Working in small teams, brainstorm ideas for an advertising campaign that has as its primary target audience the community of consumers who are intensely loyal to Vans, the surf and skateboard brand best known for its quirky, slip-on canvas shoes. What steps would you take to tap into this brand community? As you develop ideas, explain how those approaches would connect to the rituals and values of that community. Also consider what sociocultural meaning the campaign would convey about the brand and its users.

CHAPTER 6

After reading and thinking about this chapter, you will be able to do the following:

1

Explain the process known as STP marketing.

2

Describe different bases that marketers use to identify target segments.

3

Discuss the criteria used for choosing a target segment.

4

Identify the essential elements of an effective positioning strategy.

5

Review the necessary ingredients for creating a brand's value proposition.

Introductory Scenario: How Well Do You "Tolerate Mornings"?

You know by now that advertising in its many forms is always sponsored for a reason. Generally that reason has something to do with winning new customers or reinforcing the habits of existing customers.[1] However, advertising has no chance of producing a desired result if we are unclear about whom we want to reach. We need a target audience.

One special problem that most companies face is reaching potential customers just as they are experimenting in a product category for the first time. This is a pivotal time when one wants the consumer to have a great experience with your brand. So, for example, if we are Gillette and seek to market anything and everything associated with shaving, we will want one of our shavers in the hands of the consumer the first time he or she shaves. First-time users are not heavy users, but they represent the future. If we don't keep winning these beginners, eventually, we are out of business. Developing advertising campaigns to win with first time users is often referred to as point-of-entry marketing. More on that later . . .

Folgers does a huge business in the coffee category but can take nothing for granted when it comes to new users. Thus, the marketers of Folgers must launch campaigns to appeal specifically to the next generation of coffee drinkers. These of course would be young people just learning the coffee habit. Attracted by coffee titans like Starbucks and Dunkin' Donuts, many people get to know coffee in their teens. But when it's time to start brewing coffee at home, Folgers sees its big chance to get in your cupboard.

Recently, the Folgers brand team launched a new advertising initiative aimed to attract just-graduated 20-somethings. When young adults move into the "real world" and take that first job with a new apartment in a strange city they are primed to develop the coffee habit. Folgers aspires to be the brand of choice for this target as they potentially commit to a morning brew-it-yourself coffee ritual. We all know that mornings are tough, so Folgers just wants to make them tolerable. But how does Folgers, your grandparents' brand, make a connection with a new generation of coffee drinkers? Tried and true slogans ("The best part of waking up is Folgers in your cup") and 30-second TV spots just won't do.

Working with its ad agency Saatchi & Saatchi, the Folgers brand team found another way. It started with the premise that mornings are hard, filled with e-mails and bosses making demands and those darn "morning people" (who for some bizarre reason seem to love sunrises). Folgers exists to help a person tolerate mornings, and especially to tolerate those morning people. A short film, titled something like "Happy Mornings: The Revenge of the Yellow People," was produced to show Folgers as your first line of defense when the fanatical Yellow People try to invade your space first thing in the morning (that's them coming out of the sunrise and across the lake in Exhibit 6.1). The

EXHIBIT 6.1

The Yellow People glow like a sunrise and they want you!

1.   Christie L. Nordhielm, *Marketing Management: The Big Picture* (Hoboken, NJ: John Wiley & Sons, Inc. 2006).

EXHIBIT 6.2

Your best defense when the Yellow People show up unannounced.

film was also designed to generate traffic to toleratemornings.com (per Exhibit 6.2), where other tools (boss-tracker, auto e-mails, wake-up calls, screensaver) for making mornings go better were available. The campaign also included print ads code-named "Dreamscapes," reflecting that frightful moment just before dawn when the creepy Yellow People are planning their attack.

The provocative aspect of the Yellow People film is that zero dollars were spent on media. That's right, zero dollars. Rather, the spot was submitted to three Web sites (Adcritic, BestadsonTV.com, and Boards) where 20-somethings had their way with it. Chatter quickly spread across the blogosphere, Web site hits increased, and the film was soon posted on YouTube (receiving 4 out of 5 stars and over 300,000 viewings). This little sample of YouTube comments suggests that the Folgers team is on the right track in their effort to engage new users:

"I now watch this every morning to wake up, cause it's just so damn funny and awesome that it wakes me right up. If I ever get rich I'm going to hire a bunch of people to dress like happy yellow people and come wake me up with that song every morning."

"I am without speech at the sheer brilliance. If commercials were like this . . . I wouldn't skip them on the DVR."

"I took one look at that video and went straight into the kitchen and made a cup of coffee at 9:30 pm, because after all, I can sleep when I am dead!"

Many companies large and small share the problem we see embedded in the Folgers example. Simply stated, we must be clear on who we are trying to reach and then on what we can say that will resonate with them. Companies address this challenge through a process referred to as STP marketing. It is a critical process from our standpoint because it leads to decisions about *who* we need to advertise to, *what* value proposition we want to present to them, and *how* we plan to reach them with our message.

STP Marketing and the Evolution of Marketing Strategies.

The Folgers example illustrates the process that marketers use to decide who to advertise to and what to say. The Folgers brand team started with the diverse market of all possible coffee drinkers, and broke the market down by age segments. They then selected *just-graduated 20-somethings* as their target segment. The **target segment** is the subgroup (of the larger market) chosen as the focal point for the marketing program and advertising campaign.

Markets are segmented; products are positioned. To pursue the target segment, a firm organizes its marketing and advertising efforts around a coherent positioning

EXHIBIT 6.3

Laying the foundation for effective advertising campaigns through STP marketing.

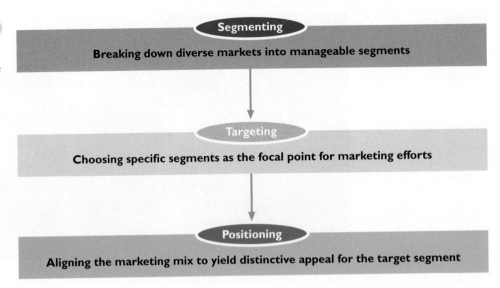

strategy. **Positioning** is the process of designing and representing one's product or service so that it will occupy a distinct and valued place in the target consumer's mind. **Positioning strategy** involves the selection of key themes or concepts that the organization will feature when communicating this distinctiveness to the target segment. In Folgers's case the positioning concept may not seem all that inspiring: it's all about "Tolerate Mornings." But the idea is to position Folgers in such a way that just-graduated 20-somethings can relate. Folks on the Folgers team assumed that they would not convert this segment with an old-fashioned slogan like "The best part of waking up is Folgers in your cup." And of course we see in this example a skillful, low-cost approach to getting the message in front of the target: Let YouTube do it!

Notice the specific sequence illustrated in Exhibit 6.3 that was played out in the Folgers example: The marketing strategy evolved as a result of *segmenting, targeting,* and *positioning.* This sequence of activities is often referred to as **STP marketing**, and it represents a sound basis for generating effective advertising.[2] While no formulas or models guarantee success, the STP approach is strongly recommended for markets characterized by diversity in consumers' needs and preferences. In markets with any significant degree of diversity, it is impossible to design one product that would appeal to everyone, or one advertising campaign that would communicate with everyone. Organizations that lose sight of this simple premise run into trouble.

Indeed, in most product categories one finds that different consumers are looking for different things, and the only way for a company to take advantage of the sales potential represented by different customer segments is to develop and market a different brand for each segment. No company has done this better than cosmetics juggernaut Estée Lauder.[3] Lauder has more than a dozen cosmetic brands, each developed for a different target segment. For example, there is the original Estée Lauder brand, for women with conservative values and upscale tastes. Then there is Clinique, a no-nonsense brand that represents functional grooming for Middle America. Bobbi Brown is for the working mom who skillfully manages a career and her family and manages to look good in the process. M.A.C. is a brand for those who want to make a bolder statement: Its spokespersons have been RuPaul, a 6-foot-7-inch drag queen; Boy George; Missy Elliot; Linda Evangelista; and a host of others.[4] Prescriptives is marketed to a hip, urban, multiethnic target segment, and Origins, with its earthy packaging and natural ingredients, celebrates the connection

---

2.   For more on STP marketing, see Philip Kotler, *Marketing Management* (Upper Saddle River, NJ: Prentice Hall, 2003), ch. 10, 11.

3.   Nina Munk, "Why Women Find Lauder Mesmerizing," *Fortune,* May 25, 1998, 96–106.

4.   Stephanie Thompson, "Gager Mixes Art, Commerce to Boost M.A.C. Sales, Image," *Advertising Age,* April 12, 2004, 60.

The U.S. Armed Forces, including the Marines, are very aggressive and sophisticated advertisers. Note how they position themselves with their advertising slogan: The Few, The Proud, The Marines (http://www.marines.com).

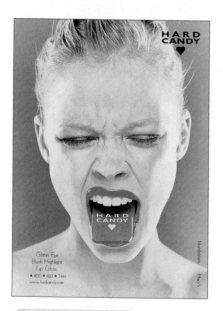

Hard Candy comes by its hip style perhaps in large part because of its uninhibitedly energetic founding by Gen-Xer Dineh Mohajer, who was unhappy with the choices traditional cosmetics firms offered her and her market demographic (http://www.hardcandy.com). There must be something in that California air. Internet technology company Cisco co-founder Sandy Lerner created Urban Decay (http://www.urbandecay.com)—another alternative for the fashion-mad—out of a similar dissatisfaction with the offerings of companies like Lancôme (http://www.lancome.com).

between Mother Nature and human nature. These are just some of the cosmetics brands that Estée Lauder has marketed to appeal to diverse target segments. Check out the company's current brand lineup at http://www.elcompanies.com.

We offer the Estée Lauder example to make two key points before moving on. First, the Folgers case may have made things seem too simple: STP marketing is a lot more complicated than just deciding to target a particular age group. Age alone is rarely specific enough to serve as a complete identifier of a target segment. Second, the cosmetics' example shows that many factors beyond demographics can come into play when trying to identify valid target segments. For these diverse cosmetics' brands we see that considerations such as attitudes, lifestyles, and basic values all may play a role in identifying and describing customer segments.

To illustrate these points, examine the two ads in Exhibits 6.4 and 6.5. Both ran in *Seventeen* magazine, so it is safe to say that in each case the advertiser was trying to reach adolescent females. But as you compare these exhibits, it should be pretty obvious that the advertisers were really trying to reach out to very different segments of adolescent females. To put it bluntly, it is hard to imagine a marine captain wearing Hard Candy lip gloss. These ads were designed to appeal to different target segments, even though the people in these segments would seem the same if we considered only their age and gender.

Beyond STP Marketing. If an organization uses STP marketing as its framework for strategy development, at some point it will find the right strategy, develop the right advertising, make a lot of money, and live happily ever after. Right? As you might expect, it's not quite that simple. Even when STP marketing yields profitable outcomes, one must presume that success will not last indefinitely. Indeed, an important feature of marketing and advertising—a feature that can make these professions both terribly interesting and terribly frustrating—is their dynamic nature. To paraphrase a popular saying, shifts happen—consumer preferences shift. Competitors improve their marketing strategies, or technology changes and makes a popular product obsolete. Successful marketing strategies need to be modified or may even need to be reinvented as shifts occur in the organization's competitive environment.

To maintain the vitality and profitability of its products or services, an organization has two options. The first entails reassessment of the segmentation strategy. This may come through a more detailed examination of the current target segment to develop new and better ways of meeting its needs, or it may be necessary to adopt new targets and position new brands for them, as illustrated by the Estée Lauder example.

The second option is to pursue a product differentiation strategy. As defined in Chapter 1, product differentiation focuses the firm's efforts on emphasizing or even creating differences for its brands to distinguish them from competitors' offerings. Advertising plays a critical role as part of the product differentiation strategy because often the consumer will have to be convinced that the intended difference is meaningful. For example, Schick's response to Gillette's Mach3 Turbo was the Schick Quattro with four blades instead of three. But does that fourth blade really deliver a better shave? How could it be better than The Best a Man Can Get? Following a product differentiation strategy, the role for Schick's advertising is to convince men that that fourth blade is essential for a close shave. But next up is Gillette's Fusion, with five blades to shave you closer than close. And so it goes.

The message is that marketing strategies and the advertising that supports them are never really final. Successes realized through proper application of STP marketing can be short-lived in highly competitive markets where any successful innovation is almost sure to be copied or "one-upped" by competitors. Thus, the value creation process for marketers and advertisers is continuous; STP marketing must be pursued over and over again and may be supplemented with product differentiation strategies.

Virtually every organization must compete for the attention and business of some customer groups while de-emphasizing or ignoring others. In this chapter we will examine in detail the way organizations decide who to target and who to ignore in laying the foundation for their marketing programs and advertising campaigns. The critical role of advertising campaigns in executing these strategies is also highlighted.

② Identifying Target Segments.

The first step in STP marketing involves breaking down large, heterogeneous markets into more manageable submarkets or customer segments. This activity is known as **market segmentation**. It can be accomplished in many ways, but keep in mind that advertisers need to identify a segment with common characteristics that will lead the members of that segment to respond distinctively to a marketing program. For a segment to be really useful, advertisers also must be able to reach that segment with information about the product. Typically this means that advertisers must be able to identify the media the segment uses that will allow them to get a message to the segment. For example, teenage males can be reached through product placements in video games and movies; selected rap, contemporary rock, or country radio stations; and all things Internet. The favorite syndicated TV show among highly affluent households (i.e., annual household income over $100,000) is *Seinfeld*, making it a popular choice for advertisers looking to reach big spenders.

In this section we will review several ways that consumer markets are commonly segmented. Markets can be segmented on the basis of usage patterns and commitment levels, demographic and geographic information, psychographics and lifestyles, or benefits sought. Many times, segmentation schemes evolve in such a way that multiple variables are used to identify and describe the target segment. Such an outcome is desirable because more knowledge about the target will usually translate into better marketing and advertising programs.

Usage Patterns and Commitment Levels.

One of the most common ways to segment markets is by consumers' usage patterns or commitment levels. With respect to usage patterns, it is important to recognize that for most products and services, some users will purchase much more frequently than others. It is common to find that **heavy users** in a category account for the majority of a product's sales and thus become the preferred or primary target segment. [5]

To illustrate, Coffee-mate executives launched a program to get to know their customers better by returning calls to those who had left a complaint or suggestion using the toll-free number printed on the product packaging. [6] As a result they met Paula Baumgartner, a 44-year-old who consumes four jars of Coffee-mate's mocha-flavored creamer every week. (Yes, that's over 200 jars a year!) Now that's a heavy user. Conventional marketing thought holds that it is in Coffee-mate's best interest

5.   Steve Hughes, "Small Segments, Big Payoff," *Advertising Age*, January 15, 2007, 17.
6.   Deborah Ball, "Toll-Free Tips: Nestle Hotlines Yield Big Ideas," *Wall Street Journal*, September 3, 2004, A7.

to get to know heavy users like Paula in great depth and make them a focal point of the company's marketing strategy. On a side note that the Folgers brand team would love, Baumgartner explained that she got her start as a regular coffee drinker at age 21 in her first full-time job (i.e., she was a *just-graduated 20-something*.) Don't know if she now brews Folgers . . .

While being the standard wisdom, the heavy-user focus has some potential downsides. For one, devoted users may need no encouragement at all to keep consuming. In addition, a heavy-user focus takes attention and resources away from those who do need encouragement to purchase the marketer's brand. Perhaps most important, heavy users may differ significantly from average or infrequent users in terms of their motivations to consume, their approach to the brand, or their image of the brand.

Another segmentation option combines prior usage patterns with commitment levels to identify four fundamental segment types—brand-loyal customers, switchers (or variety seekers), nonusers, and emergent consumers.[7] Each segment represents a unique opportunity for the advertiser. **Nonusers** offer the lowest level of opportunity relative to the other three groups. **Brand-loyal users** are a tremendous asset if they are the advertiser's customers, but they are difficult to convert if they are loyal to a competitor.

Switchers or **variety seekers** often buy what is on sale or choose brands that offer discount-coupons or other price incentives. Whether they are pursued through price incentives, high-profile advertising campaigns, or both, switchers turn out to be a costly target segment. Much can be spent in getting their business merely to have it disappear just as quickly as it was won.

EXHIBIT 6.6

Emergent consumers represent an important source of long-term opportunity for many organizations. Have you ever thought of yourself as an emergent consumer? http://www.wellsfargo.com

Emergent consumers offer the organization an important business opportunity. In most product categories there is a gradual but constant influx of first-time buyers. The reasons for this influx vary by product category and include purchase triggers such as puberty, college graduation, marriage, a new baby, divorce, a new job, a big raise, or retirement. Immigration can also be a source of numerous new customers in many product categories. Generation X attracted the attention of marketers and advertisers because it was a large group of emergent adult consumers. But inevitably, Generation X lost its emergent status and was replaced by a new age cohort—Generation Y—who took their turn as advertisers' darlings.[8]

Emergent consumers are motivated by many different factors, but they share one notable characteristic: Their brand preferences are still under development. Targeting emergents with messages that fit their age or social circumstances may produce modest effects in the short run, but it eventually may yield a brand loyalty that pays handsome rewards for the discerning organization. Developing advertising campaigns to win with first time users is often referred to as **point-of-entry marketing**. Sound familiar? This was exactly Folgers' rationale in targeting *just-graduated 20-somethings*. As another case in point, banks actively recruit college students who have limited financial resources in the short term, but excellent potential as long-term customers. Exhibit 6.6 shows an ad from Wells Fargo Bank with an appeal to emergent consumers at the University of Arizona.

7.   This four-way scheme is detailed in David W. Stewart, "Advertising in Slow-Growth Economies," *American Demographics* (September 1994), 40–46.

8.   Bonnie Tsui, "Generation Next," *Advertising Age,* January 15, 2001, 14, 16.

Demographic Segmentation. **Demographic segmentation** is widely used in selecting target segments and includes basic descriptors such as age, gender, race, marital status, income, education, and occupation (see the array of possibilities at http://www.factfinder.census.gov). Demographic information has special value in market segmentation because if an advertiser knows the demographic characteristics of the target segment, choosing media to efficiently reach that segment is easier.

Demographic information has two specific applications. First, demographics are commonly used to describe or profile segments that have been identified with some other variable. If an organization had first segmented its market in terms of product usage rates, the next step would be to describe or profile its heavy users in terms of demographic characteristics such as age or income. In fact, one of the most common approaches for identifying target segments is to combine information about usage patterns with demographics.

Mobil Oil Corporation used such an approach in segmenting the market for gasoline buyers and identified five basic segments: Road Warriors, True Blues, Generation F3, Homebodies, and Price Shoppers.[9] Extensive research on more than 2,000 motorists revealed considerable insight about these five segments. At one extreme, Road Warriors spend at least $1,200 per year at gas stations; they buy premium gasoline and snacks and beverages and sometimes opt for a car wash. Road Warriors are generally more affluent, middle-aged males who drive 25,000 to 50,000 miles per year. (Note how Mobil combined information about usage patterns with demographics to provide a detailed picture of the segment.) In contrast, Price Shoppers spend no more than $700 annually at gas stations, are generally less affluent, rarely buy premium, and show no loyalty to particular brands or stations. In terms of relative segment sizes, there are about 25 percent more Price Shoppers on the highways than Road Warriors. If you were the marketing vice president at Mobil, which of these two segments would you target? Think about it for a few pages—we'll get back to you.

Second, demographic categories are used frequently as the starting point in market segmentation. This was true in the Folgers example, where young people who had recently graduated from college turned out to be the segment of interest. Since families commonly plan vacations together, demographics will also be a major consideration for targeting by the tourism industry, where families with young children are often the marketer's primary focus. For instance, the Bahamian government launched a program to attract families to their island paradise. But instead of reaching out to mom and dad, Bahamian officials made their appeal to kids by targeting the 2-to-11-year-old viewing audience of Nickelodeon's cable television channel.[10] Marketing to and through children is always complex, and as we saw in Chapter 4, is often controversial as well. The Doing It Right box offers some guidelines for approaching young consumers in a professional manner.

Another demographic group that is receiving renewed attention from advertisers is the "woopies," or well-off older people. In the United States, consumers over 50 years old control two-thirds of the country's wealth, around $28 trillion. The median net worth of households headed by persons 55 to 64 is 15 times larger than the net worth for households headed by a person under age 35. Put in simple terms, for most people age 20, $100 is a lot of money. For woopies, $100 is change back from the purchase of a $10,000 home theatre system. Marketers such as Ford, Sony, Target, Anheuser-Busch, Walt Disney, and Virgin Entertainment Group have all reconsidered their product offerings with woopies in mind.[11] By 2025, the number of people over 50 will grow by 80 percent to become a third of the U.S. population. Growth in the woopie segment will also be dramatic in other countries, such as Japan

9.   Allanna Sullivan, "Mobil Bets Drivers Pick Cappuccino over Low Prices," *Wall Street Journal*, January 30, 1995, B1.
10. Sally Beatty, "Nickelodeon Sets $30 Million Ad Deal with the Bahamas," *Wall Street Journal*, March 14, 2001, B6.
11. Kelly Greene, "Marketing Surprise: Older Consumers Buy Stuff, Too," *Wall Street Journal*, April 6, 2004, A1, A12.

DOING IT RIGHT

Take Special Care with Promotions to Kids

Kids' discretionary income grows as societies become more affluent. Kids also exert significant influence in purchasing decisions made by moms, dads, grandmas, grandpas, aunts, uncles, and so on. When you add it all up, kids either control or influence the expenditure of hundreds of billions of dollars every year. So it is logical that in many instances, tykes, tweens, and/or teens are identified as primary target markets for planning special promotions. When targeting kids for special promotions, here are three good principles to live by.

- *Play by their tools.* When targeting a generation that takes computers, high-tech video games, and the Internet for granted, marketers must learn how to play by their tools. This will usually mean incorporating the Internet as part of the promotion. For example, even a low-tech baseball card giveaway can be moved to the Internet. Skippy peanut butter developed such a promotion featuring its baseball star spokesperson—Derek Jeter of the New York Yankees. Skippy jar tops directed kids to peanutbutter.com, where they entered "the secret code" to receive downloadable cards known as Digibles. These digital baseball cards provided both sound and video featuring the Yankee superstar.
- *Treat them like family.* When moving your promotions to the Internet, privacy should always be a concern, and this goes double for promotions to kids. We encourage you to respect young consumers' privacy because it is the right thing to do, and because there are numerous laws that require it. The Children's Online Privacy Protection Act (COPPA), which is enforced by the FTC, restricts kid-focused Web sites in the areas of data collection, spamming, sweepstakes, and contests. According to Susan Bennett, director of promotions for Fox Kids, "If you're in the kids marketplace, you better know what COPPA is." See the details at http://www.coppa.org/comply.htm.
- *Look for the high road.* Something really cool is happening among young people. Kids are less likely to be ridiculed by their peers for being interested in learning about math, science, reading, and especially the environment and all living things. In other words, it's hip to be smart. Thus, educationally themed promotions are increasingly common among kids' brands, and there are abundant opportunities to build on the premise of engaging kids through participative learning. For instance, in the case of the Bahamas' campaign directed at kids and their families, a featured element was learning about a coral reef in the Bahamas and identifying actions that children can take to help protect endangered waterways. Giveaways are nice, but don't forget to look for the high road.

Sources: John Palmer, "Connecting to Kids," **Promo Magazine**, March 2001, 21–33; and Nancy Keates, "Catering to Kids," **Wall Street Journal**, May 3, 2002, W1, W6.

and the nations of Western Europe. Still, like any other age segment, older consumers are a diverse group, and the temptation to stereotype must be resisted. Some marketers advocate partitioning older consumers into groups aged 50–64, 65–74, 75–84, and 85 or older, as a means of reflecting important differences in needs. That's a good start, but again, age alone will not tell the whole story.

Geographic Segmentation.

Geographic segmentation needs little explanation other than to emphasize how useful geography is in segmenting markets. Geographic segmentation may be conducted within a country by region (for example, the Pacific Northwest versus New England in the United States), by state or province, by city, or even by neighborhood. Climate and topographical features yield dramatic differences in consumption by region for products such as snow tires and surfboards, but geography can also correlate with other differences that are not so obvious. Eating and food preparation habits, entertainment preferences, recreational activities, and other aspects of lifestyle have been shown to vary along geographic lines. As shown in Exhibit 6.7 on the next page, even a brand like Hostess Twinkies has its red and blue states.

In recent years skillful marketers have merged information on where people live with the U.S. Census Bureau's demographic data to produce a form of market segmentation known as geodemographic segmentation.[12] **Geodemographic segmentation** identifies neighborhoods (by zip codes) around the country that share common demographic characteristics. One such system, known as PRIZM (potential rating index by zip marketing), identifies 62 market segments that encompass all the zip codes in the United States. Each of these segments has similar lifestyle characteristics and can be found throughout the country.

12. Amy Merrick, "Counting on the Census," *Wall Street Journal*, February 14, 2001, B1.

For example, the American Dreams segment is found in many metropolitan neighborhoods and comprises upwardly mobile ethnic minorities, many of whom were foreign-born. This segment's brand preferences are different from those of people belonging to the Rural Industrial segment, who are young families with one or both parents working at low-wage jobs in small-town America. Systems such as PRIZM are very popular because of the depth of segment description they provide, along with their ability to precisely identify where the segment can be found (for more details, search for PRIZM at http://www.claritas.com).

EXHIBIT 6.7

People who eat Hostess Twinkies (red marks the highest consumption).

Psychographics and Lifestyle Segmentation. Psychographics is

a term that advertisers created in the mid-1960s to refer to a form of research that emphasizes the understanding of consumers' activities, interests, and opinions (AIOs).[13] Many advertising agencies were using demographic variables for segmentation purposes, but they wanted insights into consumers' motivations, which demographic variables did not provide. Psychographics were created as a tool to supplement the use of demographic data. Because a focus on consumers' activities, interests, and opinions often produces insights into differences in the lifestyles of various segments, this approach usually results in a **lifestyle segmentation**. Knowing details about the lifestyle of a target segment can be valuable for creating advertising messages that ring true to the consumer.

Lifestyle or psychographic segmentation can be customized with a focus on the issues germane to a single product category, or it may be pursued so that the resulting segments have general applicability to many different product or service categories. An illustration of the former is research conducted for Pillsbury to segment the eating habits of American households.[14] This "What's Cookin'" study involved consumer interviews with more than 3,000 people and identified five segments of the population, based on their shared eating styles:

- **Chase & Grabbits**, at 26 percent of the population, are heavy users of all forms of fast food. These are people who can make a meal out of microwave popcorn; as long as the popcorn keeps hunger at bay and is convenient, this segment is happy with its meal.
- **Functional Feeders**, at 18 percent of the population, are a bit older than the Chase & Grabbits but no less convenience-oriented. Since they are more likely to have families, their preferences for convenient foods involve frozen products that are quickly prepared at home. They constantly seek faster ways to prepare the traditional foods they grew up with.
- **Down-Home Stokers**, at 21 percent of the population, involve blue-collar households with modest incomes. They are very loyal to their regional diets, such as meat and potatoes in the Midwest and clam chowder in New England. Fried chicken, biscuits and gravy, and bacon and eggs make this segment the champion of cholesterol.
- **Careful Cooks**, at 20 percent of the population, are more prevalent on the West Coast. They have replaced most of the red meat in their diet with pastas, fish,

13.   Michael R. Solomon, *Consumer Behavior* (Upper Saddle River, NJ: Pearson Prentice Hall, 2007), 215–219.

14.   Rebecca Piirto, *Beyond Mind Games: The Marketing Power of Psychographics* (Ithaca, NY: American Demographics Books, 1991), 222–23.

EXHIBIT 6.8

Which lifestyle segment is Pillsbury targeting with this ad? It looks like a toss-up between Chase & Grabbits and Functional Feeders. Does Pillsbury's site (http://www.pillsbury.com) target the same lifestyle segment as the ads? What features at the site are designed to build customer loyalty? Based on the site's message and design, what lifestyle choices does Pillsbury seem to assume that its target segment has made?

EXHIBIT 6.9

The convenience-oriented Functional Feeders seem the natural target for this novel ad. That Pillsbury Doughboy sure gets around! http://www.pillsbury.com

skinless chicken, and mounds of fresh fruit and vegetables. They believe they are knowledgeable about nutritional issues and are willing to experiment with foods that offer healthful options.

- **Happy Cookers** are the remaining 15 percent of the population but are a shrinking segment. These cooks are family-oriented and take substantial satisfaction from preparing a complete homemade meal for the family. Young mothers in this segment are aware of nutritional issues but will bend the rules with homemade meat dishes, casseroles, pies, cakes, and cookies.

Even these abbreviated descriptions of Pillsbury's five psychographic segments should make it clear that very different marketing and advertising programs are called for to appeal to each group. Exhibits 6.8 and 6.9 show ads from Pillsbury. Which segments are these ads targeting?

As noted, lifestyle segmentation studies can also be pursued with no particular product category as a focus, and the resulting segments could prove useful for many different marketers. A notable example of this approach is the VALS (for "values and lifestyles") system developed by SRI International and marketed by SRI Consulting Business Intelligence of Menlo Park, California.[15] The VALS framework was first introduced in 1978 with nine potential segments, but in recent years it has been revised to feature eight segments.

15.   Ibid.; see chs. 3, 5, and 8 for an extensive discussion of the VALS system.

The eight VALS segments.
http://www.sric-bi.com

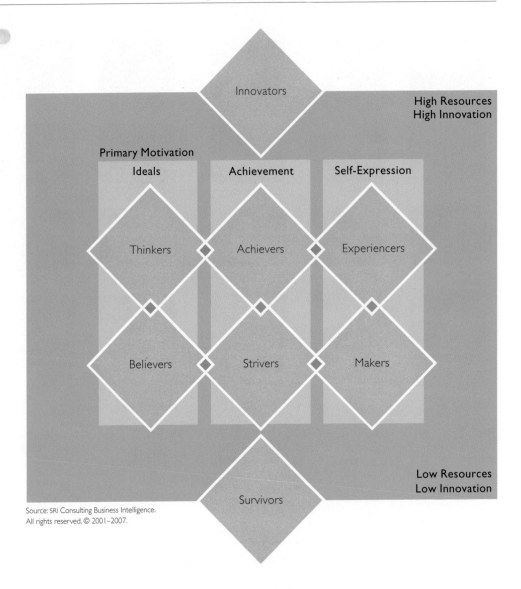

As shown in Exhibit 6.10, the segments are organized in terms of resources (which include age, income, and education) and primary motivation. For instance, the Experiencer is relatively affluent and expressive. This enthusiastic and risk-taking group has yet to establish predictable behavioral patterns. Its members look to sports, recreation, exercise, and social activities as outlets for their abundant energies. SRI Consulting Business Intelligence sells detailed information and marketing recommendations about the eight segments to a variety of marketing organizations.

Benefit Segmentation. Another segmentation approach developed by advertising researchers and used extensively over the past 30 years is **benefit segmentation**. In benefit segmentation, target segments are delineated by the various benefit packages that different consumers want from competing products and brands. For instance, different people want different benefits from their automobiles. Some consumers want efficient and reliable transportation; others want speed, excitement, and glamour; and still others want luxury, comfort, and prestige. One product could not possibly serve such diverse benefit segments. Exhibits 6.11 and 6.12 feature two hair care products that promise different kinds of benefits to comparable consumers.

EXHIBIT 6.11

Benefit segmentation really comes to life in this ad for Bed Head. If that Superstar look is the benefit you desire, Think Thick!

EXHIBIT 6.12

Catwalk promises 3-D benefits: Defrizz— Define—Detangle. And the end result is unDeniable—Curls Rock!

EXHIBIT 6.13

Xerox: The Document Company has taken its brand name and products like the printer/ copier/fax machine around the world with great success. "Multifuncionales" is a feature that business people appreciate in North and South America. http://www.xerox.cl

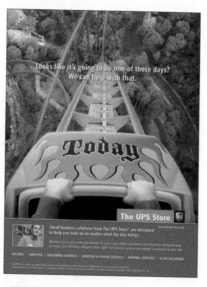

EXHIBIT 6.14

Small business owners are a market segment with a unique set of challenges and thus are a focal point in many advertising campaigns.

Segmenting Business-to-Business Markets.

Thus far, our discussion of segmentation options has focused on ways to segment **consumer markets**. Consumer markets are the markets for products and services purchased by individuals or households to satisfy their specific needs. Consumer marketing is often compared and contrasted with business-to-business marketing. **Business markets** are the institutional buyers who purchase items to be used in other products and services or to be resold to other businesses or households. Although advertising is more prevalent in consumer markets, products and services such as wireless phones, Web hosting, consulting services, and a wide array of business machines and computer-support services (see Exhibits 6.13 and 6.14) are commonly promoted to business customers around the world. Hence, segmentation strategies are also valuable for business-to-business marketers.

Business markets can be segmented using several of the options already discussed.[16] For example, business customers differ in their usage rates and geographic locations, so these variables may be productive bases for segmenting business markets. Additionally, one of the most common approaches uses the Standard Industrial Classification (SIC) codes prepared by the U.S. Census Bureau. SIC information is helpful for identifying categories of businesses and then pinpointing the precise locations of these organizations.

Some of the more sophisticated segmentation methods used by firms that market to individual consumers do not translate well to business markets.[17] For instance, rarely would there be a place for psychographic or lifestyle segmentation in the business-to-business setting. In business markets, advertisers fall back on simpler strategies that

16.   Kotler, *Marketing Management*, 296–298.
17.   Thomas S. Robertson and Howard Barich, "A Successful Approach to Segmenting Industrial Markets," *Planning Forum* (Nov/ Dec 1992), 5–11.

are easier to work with from the perspective of the sales force. Segmentation by a potential customer's stage in the purchase process is one such strategy. It turns out that first-time prospects, novices, and sophisticates want very different packages of benefits from their vendors, and thus they should be targeted separately in advertising and sales programs.

3 Prioritizing Target Segments.

Whether it is done through usage patterns, demographic characteristics, geographic location, benefit packages, or any combination of options, segmenting markets typically yields a mix of segments that vary in their attractiveness to the advertiser. In pursuing STP marketing, the advertiser must get beyond this potentially confusing mixture of segments to a selected subset that will become the target for its marketing and advertising programs. Recall the example of Mobil Oil Corporation and the segments of gasoline buyers it identified via usage patterns and demographic descriptors. What criteria should Mobil use to help decide between Road Warriors and Price Shoppers as possible targets?

Perhaps the most fundamental criterion in segment selection revolves around what the members of the segment want versus the organization's ability to provide it. Every organization has distinctive strengths and weaknesses that must be acknowledged when choosing its target segment. The organization may be particularly strong in some aspect of manufacturing, like Gillette, which has particular expertise in mass production of intricate plastic and metal products. Or perhaps its strength lies in well-trained and loyal service personnel, like those at FedEx, who can effectively implement new service programs initiated for customers, such as next-day delivery "absolutely, positively by 10:30 AM." To serve a target segment, an organization may have to commit substantial resources to acquire or develop the capabilities to provide what that segment wants. If the price tag for these new capabilities is too high, the organization must find another segment.

Another major consideration in segment selection entails the size and growth potential of the segment. Segment size is a function of the number of people, households, or institutions in the segment, plus their willingness to spend in the product category. When assessing size, advertisers must keep in mind that the number of people in a segment of heavy users may be relatively small, but the extraordinary usage rates of these consumers can more than make up for their small numbers. In addition, it is not enough to simply assess a segment's size as of today. Segments are dynamic, and it is common to find marketers most interested in devoting resources to segments projected for dramatic growth. As we have already seen, the purchasing power and growth projections for people age 50 and older have made this a segment that many companies are targeting.

So does bigger always mean better when choosing target segments? The answer is a function of the third major criterion for segment selection. In choosing a target segment, an advertiser must also look at the **competitive field**—companies that compete for the segment's business—and then decide whether it has a particular expertise, or perhaps just a bigger budget, that would allow it to serve the segment more effectively.

Upon considering the competitive field, it often turns out that smaller is better when selecting target segments. Almost by definition, large segments are usually established segments that many companies have identified and targeted previously. Trying to enter the competitive field in a mature segment isn't easy because established competitors (with their many brands) can be expected to respond aggressively with advertising campaigns or price promotions in an effort to repel any newcomer.

Alternatively, large segments may simply be poorly defined segments; that is, a large segment may need to be broken down into smaller categories before a company

EXHIBIT 6.15

Niche marketers are usually able to charge a premium price for their distinctive products. If you decide to go with Svetlana the next time you are buying amplifier tubes, expect to pay a little extra.

can understand consumers' needs well enough to serve them effectively. Again, the segment of older consumers—age 50 and older—is huge, but in most instances it would simply be too big to be valuable as a target. Too much diversity exists in the needs and preferences of this age group, such that further segmentation based on other demographic or perhaps via psychographics variables is called for before an appropriate target can be located.

The smaller-is-better principle has become so popular in choosing target segments that it is now referred to as niche marketing. A market niche is a relatively small group of consumers who have a unique set of needs and who typically are willing to pay a premium price to the firm that specializes in meeting those needs.[18] The small size of a **market niche** often means it would not be profitable for more than one organization to serve it. Thus, when a firm identifies and develops products for market niches, the threat of competitors developing imitative products to attack the niche is reduced. Exhibit 6.15 is an example of an ad directed toward a very small niche, those who prefer imported Russian tubes for their high-end tube stereo amplifiers.

Niche marketing will continue to grow in popularity as the mass media splinter into a more and more complex and narrowly defined array of specialized vehicles. Specialized cable programming—such as the Health & Fitness Channel, the History Channel, or the 24-hour Golf Channel—attracts small and very distinctive groups of consumers, providing advertisers with an efficient way to communicate with market niches.[19] In addition, perhaps the ideal application of the Internet as a marketing tool is in identifying and accessing market niches.

But now let's return to the question faced by Mobil Oil Corporation. Who should it target—Road Warriors or Price Shoppers? Hopefully you will see this as a straightforward decision. Road Warriors are a more attractive segment in terms of both segment size and growth potential. Although there are more Price Shoppers in terms of sheer numbers, Road Warriors spend more at the gas station, making them the larger segment from the standpoint of revenue generation. Road Warriors are also more prone to buy those little extras, such as a sandwich and a coffee, which could be extremely profitable sources of new business. It's just hard (impossible?) to win in gasoline retailing by competing on price.

Mobil selected Road Warriors as its target segment and developed a positioning strategy it referred to as "Friendly Serve." Gas prices went up at Mobil stations, but Mobil also committed new resources to improving all aspects of the gas-purchasing experience. Cleaner restrooms and better lighting alone yielded sales gains between 2 and 5 percent. Next, more attendants were hired to run between the pump and the snack bar to get Road Warriors in and out quickly—complete with their sandwich and beverage. Early results indicated that helpful attendants boosted station sales by another 15 to 20 percent. How can we really say that Mobil made the right choice

18.   Kotler, *Marketing Management,* 280–281.
19.   Timothy Aeppel, "For Parker Hannifin, Cable Is Best," *Wall Street Journal,* August 7, 2003, B3.

EXHIBIT 6.16

EXHIBIT 6.16

When a major competitor like BP imitates our strategy, it's a pretty good sign that we got it right. Unfortunately, this may also mean that it's time for us to look for a new strategy to gain another advantage vis-à-vis our competitive field. This is that part of marketing and advertising that makes these fields both terribly interesting and terribly frustrating. Just when we get it right, it can be time to start over . . .

in targeting Road Warriors? Just look at their competition (e.g., Exhibit 6.16). As suggested by BP's *Wild Bean Café,* coffee is king with the Road Warrior.

4 Formulating the Positioning Strategy.

Now that we have discussed the ways markets are segmented and the criteria used for selecting targets, we turn our attention to positioning strategy. If a firm has been careful in segmenting the market and selecting its targets, then a positioning strategy—such as Mobil's "Friendly Serve" or Gillette's "The Best a Man Can Get"—should occur naturally. In addition, as an aspect of positioning strategy, we entertain ideas about how a firm can best communicate to the target segment what it has to offer. This is where advertising plays its vital role. A positioning strategy will include particular ideas or themes that must be communicated effectively if the marketing program is to be successful.

Essentials for Effective Positioning Strategies.

Any sound positioning strategy includes several essential elements. Effective positioning strategies are based on meaningful commitments of organizational resources to produce substantive value for the target segment. They also are consistent internally and over time, and they feature simple and distinctive themes. Each of these essential elements is described below.

Deliver on the Promise. For a positioning strategy to be effective and remain effective over time, the organization must be committed to creating substantive value for the customer. Take the example of Mobil Oil Corporation and its target segment, the Road Warriors. Road Warriors are willing to pay a little more for gas if it comes with extras such as prompt service or fresh coffee. So Mobil must create an ad campaign that depicts its employees as the brightest, friendliest, most helpful people you'd ever want to meet. The company asks its ad agency to come up with a catchy jingle that will remind people about the great services they can expect at a Mobil station. It spends millions of dollars running these ads over and over and wins the enduring loyalty of the Road Warriors. Right? Well, maybe, and maybe not. Certainly, a new ad campaign will have to be created to make Road Warriors aware of the new Mobil, but it all falls apart if they drive in with great expectations and the company's people do not live up to them.

EXHIBIT 6.17

Consistency is a definite virtue in choosing and executing a positioning strategy. State Farm's "Good Neighbor" theme has been a hallmark of its advertising for many years. Does State Farm's site (http://www .statefarm.com) produce substantive value for its target segment? How? What simple and distinctive themes can you find? Why are these elements essential to State Farm's positioning strategy?

Effective positioning begins with substance. In the case of Mobil's "Friendly Serve" strategy, this means keeping restrooms attractive and clean, adding better lighting to all areas of the station, and upgrading the quality of the snacks and beverages available in each station's convenience store. It also means hiring more attendants and training and motivating them to anticipate and fulfill the needs of the harried Road Warrior. Effecting meaningful change in service levels at thousands of stations nationwide is an expensive and time-consuming process, but without some substantive change, there can be no hope of retaining the Road Warrior's lucrative business.

There's Magic in Consistency. A positioning strategy also must be consistent internally and consistent over time. Regarding internal consistency, everything must work in combination to reinforce a distinct perception in the consumer's eyes about what a brand stands for. If we have chosen to position our airline as the one that will be known for on-time reliability, then we certainly would invest in things like extensive preventive maintenance and state-of-the-art baggage-handling facilities. There would be no need for exclusive airport lounges as part of this strategy, nor would any special emphasis need to be placed on in-flight food and beverage services. If our target segment wants reliable transportation, then this should be our obsession. This particular obsession has made Southwest Airlines a very formidable competitor, even against much larger airlines, as it has expanded its routes to different regions of the United States.[20]

A strategy also needs consistency over time. Consumers have perceptual defenses that allow them to screen or ignore most of the ad messages they are exposed to. Breaking through the clutter and establishing what a brand stands for is a tremendous challenge, but it is a challenge made easier by consistent positioning. If year in and year out an advertiser communicates the same basic themes, then the message may get through and shape the way consumers perceive the brand. An example of a consistent approach is the long-running "Good Neighbor" ads of State Farm Insurance. While the specific copy changes, the thematic core of the campaign does not change. Exhibit 6.17 shows an exemplar from this long-running campaign, including the "We Live Where You Live" extension to their "Good Neighbor" premise.

Make It Different Simply. Simplicity and distinctiveness are essential to the advertising task. No matter how much substance has been built into a product, it will fail in the marketplace if the consumer doesn't perceive what the product can do. In a world of harried consumers who can be expected to ignore, distort, or forget most of the ads they are exposed to, complicated, imitative messages simply have no chance of getting through. The basic premise of a positioning strategy must be simple and distinctive if it is to be communicated effectively to the target segment.

The value of simplicity and distinctiveness in positioning strategy is nicely illustrated by the approach of GM's Pontiac division, starting in the mid-1980s. This was

20.   Scott McCartney, "Profit for Southwest Air Is Industry Rarity," *Wall Street Journal,* October 18, 2002, B4.

EXHIBIT 6.18

"We Build Excitement" is a good example of a single-benefit positioning theme. More recently Pontiac has updated that theme as "Designed for Action," and a great relationship with NCAA basketball creates a unique identity for Pontiac. But to compete in today's automotive marketplace, models like the GTO must deliver legendary performance. http://www.gto.com

the time when Japanese automakers started taking market share from their U.S. counterparts, and no American car company was being hit harder than General Motors. Pontiac, however, grew its market share in this period with a positioning strategy that involved a return to Pontiac's heritage from the 1960s as a performance car. Pontiac's positioning strategy involved a number of different variations of an "excitement" promise, including, "We Build Excitement," "We Are Driving Excitement," and "Excitement Well Built."

It was that last phrase ("Well Built") that ultimately led to erosion in the effectiveness of Pontiac's strategy. While simple, distinctive, and consistent, their strategy began to suffer when their product didn't live up to the promise. Plastic fenders, under-powered engines borrowed from GM's Chevy and Buick divisions, and premium pricing turned off consumers looking for excitement.[21] But to the credit of the Pontiac division, they didn't back down on the basic premise. Models like the legendary GTO (Gran Turismo Omologato, Italian for a race car that has been made street legal) were rebuilt and re-launched to deliver substance. Other new products like the Solstice two-seater and the sporty G6 added excitement. Distinctive affiliations like the Official Performance Machines of the NCAA supported Pontiac's updated positioning message: "Designed for Action." Embedding the Pontiac brand as a regular fixture and supporter of "March Madness" (see Exhibit 6.18) was a real coup for Pontiac marketers, and their invitation to "Google Pontiac" showed increasing brand interest.[22] Pontiac continues to impress with the simplicity, consistency, and distinctiveness of their positioning strategy. It can work for them again, but they must deliver on "Well Built."

Fundamental Positioning Themes. Positioning themes that are simple and distinctive help an organization make internal decisions that yield substantive value for customers, and they assist in the development of focused ad campaigns to break through the clutter of competitors' advertising. Thus, choosing a viable positioning theme is one of the most important decisions faced by advertisers. In many ways, the raison d'être for STP marketing is to generate viable positioning themes.

Positioning themes take many forms, and like any other aspect of marketing and advertising, they can benefit from creative breakthroughs. Yet while novelty and creativity are valued in developing positioning themes, some basic principles should be considered when selecting a theme. Whenever possible, it is helpful if the organization can settle on a single premise—such as "Good Neighbor" or "We Build Excitement" or "Tolerate Mornings" or "Relax, It's FedEx"—to reflect its positioning strategy.[23] In addition, three fundamental options should always be considered in selecting a positioning theme: benefit positioning, user positioning, and competitive positioning.[24]

"We Build Excitement" and "Friendly Serve" are examples of **benefit positioning**. Notice in these premises that a distinctive customer benefit is featured. This single-benefit focus is the first option that should be considered when formulating a positioning strategy. Consumers purchase products to derive functional, emotional,

21.   David Welch, "An 'American BMW'? Don't Hold Your Breath," *BusinessWeek,* March 17, 2003, 98.

22.   Dale Buss, "Change Agents," *Point,* May 2006, 10, 11.

23.   A more elaborate case for the importance of a single, consistent positioning premise is provided in Ries and Trout's classic, *Positioning: The Battle for Your Mind* (New York: Warner Books, 1982).

24.   Other positioning options are discussed in Philip Kotler and Kevin Lane Keller, *A Framework for Marketing Management* (Upper Saddle River, N J: Pearson Prentice Hall, 2007), ch. 9.

or self-expressive benefits, so an emphasis on the primary benefit they can expect to receive from a brand is fundamental. While it might seem that more compelling positioning themes would result from promising consumers a wide array of benefits, keep in mind that multiple-benefit strategies are hard to implement. Not only will they send mixed signals within an organization about what a brand stands for, but they will also place a great burden on advertising to deliver and validate multiple messages.

Functional benefits are the place to start in selecting a positioning theme, but in many mature product categories, the functional benefits provided by the various brands in the competitive field are essentially the same. In these instances the organization may turn to emotion in an effort to distinguish its brand. Emotional benefit positioning may involve a promise of exhilaration, like "Exciting Armpits" (see Exhibit 6.19), or may feature a way to avoid negative feelings—such as the embarrassment felt in social settings due to bad breath, dandruff, or coffee-stained teeth.

Another way to add an emotional benefit in one's positioning is by linking a brand with important causes that provoke intense feelings. Avon Products' former CEO, James E. Preston, insisted that tie-ins with high-profile social issues can cut through the clutter of rivals' marketing messages.[25] Not surprising then that Avon has been a regular sponsor of important causes, such as the Avon Walk for Breast Cancer. Likewise, Sears helped raise money for the homeless, Star-Kist has promoted dolphin-safe fishing practices, Coors Brewing has funded public literacy programs, and Visa in Germany supported the Friendship Card, featured in Exhibit 6.20. There's

EXHIBIT 6.19

When the functional benefits of 24-hour protection and no white residue become old hat, then the advertiser may have no choice but to try to engage consumers through a promise of emotional benefits, as we see in this ad for Lady Speed Stick. http://www.mennen.com

EXHIBIT 6.20

Bonus points for children is the motto of Germany's first charitable credit card. Card users earn "payback" points on every transaction, which are then automatically credited to UNICEF. UNICEF, the United Nations Children's Fund, supports programs for children in 158 countries around the world, in an effort to bring more smiles.

25. Geoffrey Smith and Ron Stodghill, "Are Good Causes Good Marketing?" *BusinessWeek,* March 21, 1994, 64–65.

a meaningful trend here: In a survey of executives from 211 companies, 69 percent said that their companies planned to increase participation in cause-related marketing, as a way to build emotional bonds with their consumers.[26]

Self-expressive benefits can also be the bases for effective positioning strategies. With this approach, the purpose of an advertising campaign is to create distinctive images or personalities for brands, and then invite consumers into brand communities.[27] These brand images or personalities can be of value to individuals as they use the brands to make statements about themselves to other people. For example, feelings of status, pride, and prestige might be derived from the imagery associated with brands such as BMW, Rolex, and Gucci. Brand imagery can also be valued in gift-giving contexts. The woman who gives Calvin Klein's Euphoria for men is expressing something very different than the woman who gives Old Spice. Advertisers help brands acquire meaning and self-expressive benefits to distinguish them beyond their functional forms.

Besides benefit positioning, another fundamental option is **user positioning**. Instead of featuring a benefit or attribute of the brand, this option takes a specific profile of the target user as the focal point of the positioning strategy. Ads like those shown in Exhibits 6.21 and 6.22 make unequivocal statements about who should consider the possibilities offered by Bigen Xpressive and Axe Recovery Shower Gel. Notice how these ads attempt to speak to clearly identifiable user segments.

The third option for a positioning theme is **competitive positioning**. This option is sometimes useful in well-established product categories with a crowded competitive field. Here, the goal is to use an explicit reference to an existing competitor to help define precisely what your brand can do. Many times this approach is used by smaller brands to carve out a position relative to the market share leader in their category. For instance, in the analgesics category, many competitors have used market leader Tylenol as an explicit point of reference in their positioning strategies.

EXHIBIT 6.21

EXHIBIT 6.22

While this ad is busy with competing images and diverse product claims, it still communicates an unmistakable message about who should use this new line of coloring products from Bigen Xpressive.

A shower with Axe Recovery Shower Gel and a cup of Folgers are this fellow's best bet for fending off an attack of those creepy Yellow People.

26.   Stephanie Thompson, "Good Humor's Good Deeds," *Advertising Age,* January 8, 2001, 6.

27.   Albert M. Muniz, Jr., and Thomas C. O'Guinn, "Brand Community," *Journal of Consumer Research,* vol. 27 (2001), 412–432.

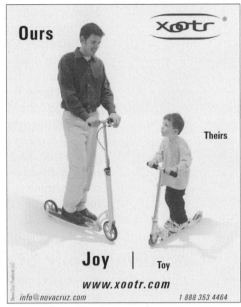

EXHIBIT 6.23

In mature, saturated markets where the performance features of brands don't change much over time, it is common to see competitors making claims back and forth in an effort to steal market share from one another. Powerhouse brands such as Tylenol usually don't initiate these exchanges, because they have the most to lose. This ad is a reply from the makers of Tylenol, responding to a campaign of a smaller competitor. http://www.tylenol.com

EXHIBIT 6.24

The beauty of this ad for Xootr is its simple, unequivocal message. Ours versus Theirs equates to Joy versus Toy. http://www.xootr.com

Excedrin, for one, has attempted to position itself as the best option to treat a simple headache, granting that Tylenol might be the better choice to treat the various symptoms of a cold or the flu. As shown in Exhibit 6.23, Excedrin's strategy must have been effective, because Tylenol came back with a very pointed reply.

Now that you've seen the three fundamental options for creating a positioning strategy, we need to make matters a bit messier. There is nothing that would prevent an advertiser from combining these various options to create a hybrid involving two or more of them working together. The combination of benefit and user is common in creating positioning strategies, and the Xootr ad in Exhibit 6.24 is a superb example of user and competitive positioning combined. Do keep in mind that we're looking for a strategy that reflects substance, consistency, simplicity, and distinctiveness. But the last thing we'd want to do is give you guidelines that would shackle your creativity. So don't be shy about looking for creative combinations.

Repositioning. STP marketing is far from a precise science, so marketers do not always get it right the first time. Furthermore, markets are dynamic. Things change. Even when marketers do get it right, competitors can react, or consumers' preferences may shift for any number of reasons, and what once was a viable positioning strategy must be altered if the brand is to survive. One of the best ways to revive an ailing brand or to fix the lackluster performance of a new market entry is to redeploy the STP process to arrive at a revised positioning strategy. This type of effort is commonly referred to as **repositioning**.

While repositioning efforts are a fact of life for marketers and advertisers, they present a tremendous challenge. When brands that have been around for some time are forced to reposition, perceptions of the brand that have evolved over the years must be changed through advertising. This problem is common for brands that become popular with one generation but fade from the scene as that generation ages and emergent consumers come to view the brand as passé. So, for several years, the makers of Oldsmobile tried to breathe new life into their brand with catchy ad slogans such as "This is not your father's Oldsmobile," "Demand better," and "Defy convention." Ultimately, none of these efforts were able to save a brand that had become passé.[28]

On the other hand, there are numerous examples of brands that have been able to get consumers to take a fresh look at them. Mazda found itself in a funk in the '90s when it tried to go head-to-head with Toyota and Honda around dependability and good value. So Mazda's new CEO decided to return the brand to its roots as a stylish and fun-to-drive vehicle, targeting the 25 percent of the car-buying market that consider themselves auto enthusiasts. The "Zoom Zoom" theme was the outcome of this application of STP marketing, and with it the Mazda brand got its groove back.[29]

⑤ Capturing Your Strategy in a Value Proposition.

In this chapter we have presented several important concepts for understanding how marketers develop strategies for their brands that then have major implications for the integrated advertising campaigns that are executed to build and maintain those brands. One needs to assess customer segments and target markets along with the competitive field to make decisions about various kinds of positioning themes that might be appropriate in guiding the creation of a campaign.

Yes, it can get complicated. Furthermore, as time passes, new people from both the client and agency side will be brought in to work on the brand team. It can be easy for them to lose sight of what the brand used to stand for in the eyes of the target segment. Of course, if the people who create the advertising for a brand get confused about the brand's desired identity, then the consumer is bound to get confused as well. This is a recipe for disaster. Thus, we need a way to capture and keep a record of what our brand is supposed to stand for in the eyes of the target segment. While there are many ways to capture one's strategy on paper, we recommend doing just that by articulating the brand's value proposition. If we are crystal clear on what value we believe our brand offers to consumers, and everyone on the brand team shares that clarity, the foundation is in place for creating effective advertising and integrated brand promotion.

At this point you should find the following definition of a **value proposition** a natural extension of concepts that are already familiar; it simply consolidates the emphasis on customer benefits that has been featured in this chapter:

A brand's value proposition is a statement of the functional, emotional, and self-expressive benefits delivered by the brand that provide value to customers in the target segment. A balanced value proposition is the basis for brand choice and customer loyalty, and is critical to the ongoing success of a firm.[30]

Here are the value propositions for two global brands that are likely familiar to you.[31]

McDonald's
- *Functional benefits:* Good-tasting hamburgers, fries, and drinks served fast; extras such as playgrounds, prizes, premiums, and games.
- *Emotional benefits:* Kids—fun via excitement at birthday parties; relationship with Ronald McDonald and other characters; a feeling of special family times. Adults—warmth via time spent enjoying a meal with the kids; admiration of McDonald's social involvement such as McDonald's Charities and Ronald McDonald Houses.

28. Vanessa O'Connell and Joe White, "After Decades of Brand Bodywork, GM Parks Oldsmobile—For Good," *Wall Street Journal,* December 13, 2000, B1, B4.
29. Jean Halliday, "Mazda Repositioning Begins to Show Results," *Advertising Age,* January 6, 2003, 4.
30. This definition is adapted from David Aaker, *Building Strong Brands* (New York: Free Press, 1996), ch. 3.
31. These examples are adapted from Aaker, *Building Strong Brands,* ch. 3.

ETHICS

Mickey Mouse Tries the High Road

We've heard it over and over again. Many respected groups (including the American Psychological Association, the American Academy of Pediatrics, and the Rudd Policy Center at Yale University) are calling for restrictions on advertising targeted to children. One key concern is that advertising for junk food has played a role in America's obesity crisis. Internet games and Web sites promote products such as Lucky Charms, Cheetos, and Hershey's Syrup. Kids who visit branded sites like these are tantalized by sophisticated entertainment tactics that in the end are selling tactics devised by adults but targeted at kids. One tactic that has drawn special attention from food industry critics is the use of licensed characters, like Scooby-Doo, the Rugrats, or Sponge-Bob SquarePants, to do the selling. Based on its research into the link between marketing practices and childhood obesity, the U.S. Institute of Medicine recommended that food companies stop using licensed, animated characters to sell low-nutrient, high-calorie products.

There is an ethical dilemma here that is becoming impossible to ignore or rationalize away. Maybe, just maybe, we are beginning to see companies step up in an effort to do the right thing. Disney appears to be trying, given its announcement of a companywide initiative to phase out advertising of unhealthy foods to kids and eliminate the same from its theme-park menus and co-promotions with big corporate partners. But fear not. Mickey Mouse is not retiring. We will see Mickey and numerous other Disney characters (e.g., Buzz Lightyear and Woody, Winnie the Pooh and Tigger) on a new line of products branded *Disney Magic Selections*. Disney's goal with this new line of juices, pastas, soups, and snacks is to give parents healthy eating solutions for kids.

Yet who gets to say what is and isn't healthy? Can we trust Disney to set the right standard for itself and its partners? Only time will tell. But the new Disney guidelines do seem to have some teeth. For example, McDonald's Chicken McNuggets don't meet the Disney standard because they contain trans fats. And since there are numerous McDonald's restaurants within Disney theme parks, it will get interesting when Disney executives try to apply their standards to McDonald's. Similar issues loom for Disney and its long time partner Kellogg. Co-promotions involving Disney films and Kellogg's sugary snacks have been common in the past. However, many Kellogg's products linked to recent Disney films don't meet the new Disney guidelines. As these corporate titans wrestle with the question of how to define a healthy snack, one can only hope that they don't set the bar too low or the scales too high.

Sources: Joseph Pereira and Audrey Warren, "Coming Up Next . . .," **Wall Street Journal**, March 15, 2004, B1, B3; Nanci Hellmich, "Food Websites Tempt Kids," **USA Today**, July 20, 2006, 6D; Merissa Marr and Janet Adamy, "Disney Pulls Characters from Junk Food," **Wall Street Journal**, October 17, 2006, D1, D6.

Nike

- *Functional benefits:* High-technology shoe that will improve performance and provide comfort.
- *Emotional benefits:* The exhilaration of athletic performance excellence, feeling engaged, active, and healthy; exhilaration from admiring professional and college athletes as they perform wearing "your brand"—when they win, you win too.
- *Self-expressive benefits:* Using the brand endorsed by high-profile athletes lets your peers know your desire to compete and excel.

Notice from these two statements that over time many different aspects can be built into the value proposition for a brand. Brands like Nike may offer benefits in all three benefit categories; McDonald's from two of the three. Benefit complexity of this type is extremely valuable when the various benefits reinforce one another. In these examples, this cross-benefit reinforcement is especially strong for Nike, with all levels working together to deliver the desired state of performance excellence. The job of advertising is to carry the message to the target segment about the value that is offered by the brand. However, for brands with complex value propositions such as McDonald's and Nike, no single ad could be expected to reflect all aspects of the brand's value. However, if any given ad is not communicating some selected aspects of the brand's purported value, then we have to ask, why run that ad?

So from now on, every time you see an ad, ask yourself, what kind of value or benefit is that ad promising the target customer? What is the value proposition underlying this ad? We expect you to carry forward an ability to assess target segments and isolate value propositions.

One gains tremendous leverage from the process of STP marketing because it is all about anticipating and servicing customers' wants and needs.

But targeting groups for focused advertising and promotion has a controversial side, as do many things. The Ethics box again features the ethical dilemma inherent in choosing children as your target.

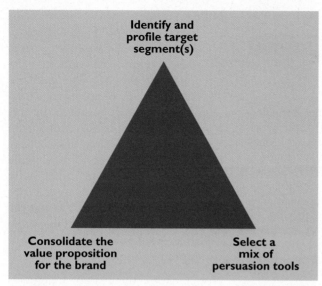

Identify and
profile target
segment(s)

Consolidate the
value proposition
for the brand

Select a
mix of
persuasion tools

Adapted from Esther Thorson and Jeri Moore, *Integrated Communication: Synergy of Persuasive Voices*
(Mahwah, N.J.: Erlbaum, 1996).

EXHIBIT 6.25

*Thorson and Moore's
strategic planning triangle.*

Putting It All Together.

Before moving on it may be helpful to pull together the concepts presented in this chapter using a practical model. The strategic planning triangle proposed by advertising researchers Esther Thorson and Jeri Moore is perfect for this purpose.[32] As reflected in Exhibit 6.25, the apexes of the planning triangle entail the segment(s) selected as targets for the campaign, the brand's value proposition, and the array of persuasion tools that will be deployed to achieve campaign goals.

As we have seen in this chapter, the starting point of STP marketing is identifying who the customers or prospects are and what they want. Hence, Thorson and Moore place identification and specification of the target segment as the paramount apex in their model. Building a consensus between the client and the agency about which segments will be targeted is essential to the campaign's effectiveness. Compelling advertising begins with insights about one's target segment that are both personal and precise.

The second important apex in the planning triangle entails specification of the brand's value proposition. A brand's value proposition is a statement of the functional, emotional, and/or self-expressive benefits delivered by the brand. In formulating the value proposition one should consider both what a brand has stood for or communicated to consumers in the past, and what new types of value or additional benefits one wants to claim for the brand going forward. For mature, successful brands, reaffirming the existing value proposition may be the primary objective for any campaign. When launching a new brand, there is an opportunity to start from scratch in establishing the value proposition.

The final apex of the planning triangle considers the various persuasion tools that may be deployed as part of the campaign. A description of these tools is yet to come. Chapters 14 and 15 emphasize traditional mass media tools; Chapter 16 looks at the Internet advertising option; Chapter 17 considers support media and sales promotions; Chapter 18 examines the exciting new arena of branded entertainment; Chapter 19 provides a comprehensive look at direct marketing; and Chapter 20 fills out the tool box by discussing the public relations function. The mix of tools used will depend on campaign goals. The point here is simply to reinforce our mantra that advertising and integrated brand promotion always entails finding the right mix to do the job: Knowing the target segment and the value proposition are essential to doing the job right.

32.   Esther Thorson and Jeri Moore, *Integrated Communication: Synergy of Persuasive Voices* (Mahwah, N.J.: Erlbaum, 1996).

SUMMARY

 Explain the process known as STP marketing.

The term STP marketing refers to the process of segmenting, targeting, and positioning. Marketers pursue this set of activities in formulating marketing strategies for their brands. STP marketing also provides a strong foundation for the development of advertising campaigns. While no single approach can guarantee success in marketing and advertising, STP marketing should always be considered when consumers in a category have heterogeneous wants and needs.

 Describe different bases that marketers use to identify target segments.

In market segmentation, the goal is to break down a heterogeneous market into more manageable subgroups or segments. Many different bases can be used for this purpose. Markets can be segmented on the basis of usage patterns and commitment levels, demographics, geography, psychographics, lifestyles, benefits sought, SIC codes, or stages in the purchase process. Different bases are typically applied for segmenting consumer versus business-to-business markets.

 Discuss the criteria used for choosing a target segment.

In pursuing STP marketing, an organization must get beyond the stage of segment identification and settle on one or more segments as a target for its marketing and advertising efforts. Several criteria are useful in establishing the organization's target segment. First, the organization must decide whether it has the proper skills to serve the segment in question. The size of the segment and its growth potential must also be taken into consideration. Another key criterion involves the intensity of the competition the firm is likely to face in the segment. Often, small segments known as market niches can be quite attractive because they will not be hotly contested by numerous competitors.

 Identify the essential elements of an effective positioning strategy.

The P in STP marketing refers to the positioning strategy that must be developed as a guide for all marketing and advertising activities that will be undertaken in pursuit of the target segment. As exemplified by Pontiac's "We Build Excitement" and "Designed for Action" campaigns, effective positioning strategies should be linked to the substantive benefits offered by the brand. They are also consistent internally and over time, and they feature simple and distinctive themes. Benefit positioning, user positioning, and competitive positioning are options that should be considered when formulating a positioning strategy.

 Review the necessary ingredients for creating a brand's value proposition.

Many complex considerations underlie marketing and advertising strategies, so some device is called for to summarize the essence of one's strategy. We advance the idea of the value proposition as a useful device for this purpose. A value proposition is a statement of the various benefits (functional, emotional, and self-expressive) offered by a brand which create value for the customer. These benefits as a set justify the price of the product or service. Clarity in expression of the value proposition is critical for development of advertising that sells.

KEY TERMS

target segment	emergent consumers	competitive field
positioning	point-of-entry marketing	market niche
positioning strategy	demographic segmentation	benefit positioning
STP marketing	geodemographic segmentation	user positioning
market segmentation	psychographics	competitive positioning
heavy users	lifestyle segmentation	repositioning
nonusers	benefit segmentation	value proposition
brand-loyal users	consumer markets	
switchers, or variety seekers	business markets	

QUESTIONS

1. While STP marketing often produces successful outcomes, there is no guarantee that these successes will last. What factors can erode the successes produced by STP marketing, forcing a firm to reformulate its marketing strategy?

2. Why does the persuasion required with a product differentiation strategy present more of a challenge than the persuasion required with a market segmentation strategy?

3. Explain the appeal of emergent consumers as a target segment. Identify a current ad campaign (not Folgers!) targeting an emergent-consumer segment.

4. It is often said that psychographics were invented to overcome the weaknesses of demographic information for describing target segments. What unique information can psychographics provide that would be of special value to advertisers?

5. What criteria did Mobil Oil Corporation weigh most heavily in its selection of Road Warriors as a target segment? What do you think will be the biggest source of frustration for Mobil in trying to make this strategy work?

6. Explain why smaller can be better when selecting segments to target in marketing strategies.

7. What essential elements of a positioning strategy can help overcome the consumer's natural tendency to ignore, distort, or forget most of the advertisements he or she is exposed to?

8. On which aspect of its positioning strategy did Pontiac fail to deliver, thus eroding its effectiveness and turning off consumers? How did Pontiac try to recover?

9. Which of the market segmenting strategies discussed in this chapter are likely to be most effective for business-to-business marketing? Why would some techniques that are highly successful in targeting consumer markets, such as lifestyle segmentation, be less effective?

10. Carefully examine the two ads displayed in Exhibits 6.4 and 6.5. What positioning theme (benefit, user, or competitive) is the basis for these ads? If you say benefit positioning, what form of benefit promise (functional, emotional, or self-expressive) is being made in these ads? Write a statement of the value proposition that you believe is reflected by these two ads.

EXPERIENTIAL EXERCISES

1.   Move over, Barbie—here come the Bratz. The race to win the hearts of little girls everywhere has heated up recently as MGA Entertainment's ultra-fashionable Bratz dolls aim to reduce Mattel's Barbie to little more than "the doll mom used to play with." Complete with bare midriffs, bee-stung lips, trendy duds, and funky names, the Bratz are the epitome of the 21st-century girl—sassy and self-aware. Using concepts from the STP marketing approach, analyze the Bratz phenomenon in light of the threat it poses to Barbie's position in the toy-doll market. To find research for your analysis, visit the dolls' respective Web sites, look up news articles on the Internet, and contact a toy-store manager to find out which doll brand is most popular.

2.   Discount pioneer Kmart is repositioning to stay competitive in a challenging retail sector where stores like Wal-Mart and Target are ahead of the pack. Kmart suffered in the past from poor customer service and a lack of consumer enthusiasm toward its brands, but the company is currently making a turnaround. Analysts claim that Kmart, having been outmatched by everyday-low-price giant Wal-Mart, has abandoned the superstore concept, and is instead concentrating on its core competency of merchandising—including promoting exclusive brands. Visit Kmart's e-tail site (http://www.kmart.com) and describe how the company seeks to reconnect with customers through its exclusive brands and services. How does the site compare to those by Target (http://www.target.com) and Wal-Mart (http://www.walmart.com)? Finally, interview someone who is older and ask that person to describe his or her perception of Kmart over the last few decades. How do those perceptions compare to the ones you are gathering through your analysis?

3.   Compose value proposition statements for Starbucks Coffee and Levi Strauss jeans. Each value proposition should crystallize what the brand offers to consumers and serve as a clear mission statement for all subsequent STP marketing efforts.

4.   The Folgers campaign featured in this chapter's introductory scenario was distinctive, in part, because the company spent no money on media, instead allowing the new ads to circulate for free through user sites such as YouTube. That strategic decision reflected an understanding that its young target market was more likely to be online than watching the evening news. What might be the most effective media to reach each of the following target segments?

a.   Upper-income men, ages 45 to 60, for a financial services product.
b.   Young homeowners, ages 30 to 40, for a new interior paint product.
c.   Teenage boys who live in rural areas for a new basketball shoe.
d.   Senior citizens for a new denture-paste product.

5.   Break into teams and imagine you are creating a new online dating service aimed at recent college graduates called SmartDate. Complete each of the following steps in the process of STP marketing and present your campaign to the class in a 10- to 15-slide presentation:

a.   Formulate the value proposition for the new company.
b.   Identify and relevant target segments for the focus of the marketing program. Explain which criteria you used to select the target market and why.
c.   Select a positioning theme for the marketing campaign, choosing among the benefit, user, and competitive positioning options, and explain your decision.

CHAPTER 7

After reading and thinking about this chapter, you will be able to do the following:

1

Explain the purposes served by and methods used in developmental advertising research.

2

Identify sources of secondary data that can aid the IBP planning effort.

3

Discuss the purposes served by and methods used in copy research.

4

Discuss the basic research methods used after ads are in the marketplace.

GOOD MORNING

Introductory Scenario: It's the Brand, Not the Product.

Coca-Cola discovered that consumers generally preferred Pepsi—in blind taste tests. Coke had apparently conducted thousands of taste tests, and knew it was true: When consumers didn't know which cola they were drinking, most preferred Pepsi. To make the point more painful, Coke had been losing market share to Pepsi. What to do?

The Coca-Cola company's answer was a new formula. After conducting 190,000 or so blind taste tests, Coca-Cola discovered that consumers preferred New Coke over both Pepsi and Coke. So they announced the switch: New Coke replaced Coke. As you know, it was a disaster. Consumers were outraged and demanded their friend Coca-Cola back. They stayed away from New Coke in droves.

I do not drink alcoholic beverages, I don't smoke, and I don't chase other women, my only vice has been Coke. Now you have taken that pleasure from me.

Would it be right to rewrite the Constitution? The Bible? To me, changing the Coke formula is of such a serious nature.

—From letters sent to the Coca-Cola Company in 1985 following the introduction of New Coke, which announced the end of "old" Coke.[1]

Why? Didn't the scientific research lead to the right decision? No, it did not. Didn't the psychologists provide all the rights answers? No, they didn't. Maybe that's why Coca-Cola and many other great companies have turned to more socio-cultural approaches.

Why? It's because the right question was never asked, and no one considered the cultural side of the equation. No one bothered to find out if consumers would mind Coke being taken away. And Coca-Cola and its advertising experts broke a cardinal rule of advertising and marketing. They confused the objective taste tests with cultural reality. They confused meaning with physical reality. They confused a mere product with a brand. Coke possessed cultural meaning way beyond simple taste.

As others have noted, never, ever, ever confuse a brand and a product. The blind taste tests were about products; the market reaction of real consumers was about a brand—a brand that had enormous cultural meaning. Brands are about meaning.

Never forget: Meaning makes brands out of products.

Tons of research, and the Coca-Cola company still made a huge mistake. So, never think that just throwing research, no matter how "scientific" it is, at a problem does anything good.[2] Ad luminaries such as Bill Bernbach (responsible for, among many other things, the amazing creative for brands like Volkswagen in the 1960s; see Exhibit 7.1) thought research was worse than a waste. Lately, with shrinking agency margins, research has been regarded as more and more expendable by the bean counters. Advertising agencies have been cutting back on research lately; it's considered a luxury. There are

EXHIBIT 7.1

Bill Bernbach created some of the best advertising of all time and he did it without research. In fact, he thought research got in the way of good advertising.

1.   See Mark Pendergrast, "The Marketing Blunder of the Century," in *For God, Country and Coca-Cola: The Definitive History of the Great American Soft-Drink and the Company That Makes It* (New York: Basic Books, 2000), 356.
2.   Thomas Frank, *The Conquest of Cool: Business Culture, Counterculture, and the Rise of Hip Consumerism* (Chicago: University of Chicago Press, 1997).

Advertising research came to us from the 1950s, a period in which science was popularized to ridiculous heights and was commonly misapplied. Unfortunately, that legacy influenced the advertising industry for decades to come.

a lot of reasons for this, but it actually goes well beyond current trends and economic traditions. It goes back a long way, and involves a basic confusion about what advertising and brand promotion research is, if it does any good, and whether it should even be practiced at all. We won't end the research controversy, but we hope to make things a little clearer and provide some perspective. Real-world bottom line: Research in general is threatened at ad agencies, more and more is being farmed out to external suppliers, and it is being seen as irrelevant. Further, the trend is clearly toward qualitative methods, particularly on-scene, in-home, at usage site, types of fieldwork. In fact, it's more than a trend; it's how most real world advertising and integrated brand promotion research is done. We know because we actually visit and work with real companies.

First, to clarify our terms: Advertising and brand promotion research is any research that helps in the development, execution, or evaluation of advertising and promotion. Good advertising and promotion research can move one closer to producing effective advertising and promotion. It can do that, it just doesn't get the chance very often. The wrong questions are often asked, the wrong methods are often applied, and people generalize way too far on limited data.

Although some advertising agencies have had research specialists or even departments for over 100 years, their real growth occurred in the mid-20th century, with the 1950s being their real heyday. During this period, agencies adopted research departments for three basic reasons: (1) The popularity of, naiveté toward, and overconfidence in "science" during this time legitimized anything called science or research, particularly psychological methods. (2) Other agencies had research departments. (3) There was a real need to better understand how ads worked.

During the 1950s, advertising research established and legitimized itself in the industry. The popular adoration of science was at its height; the books, the plays, the movies, and the ads (see Exhibit 7.2) of this period are full of popular science. There was an economic boom in consumption; agencies could afford research departments: and indulge in the hope (maybe myth) of "scientific advertising." Of course, there was always ambivalence about science after World War II, about its use and misuse. It was a period of great faith in the power of science and technology, and great concern about its misuse for evil, for destructive and manipulative ends like getting people to buy things they really don't need or even really want, particularly by doing this through their subconscious, or subliminally. Go watch some 1950s movies such as anything by Hitchcock or any of the great sci-fi B-movies. They are all about this central cultural theme of great ambivalence toward science. This ambivalence has waxed and waned over the years, but has always remained. It exists today.

Due in large part to popular belief in the success of propaganda and psychological warfare in World War II, there was a ready-made acceptance of the "science of persuasion." There was a widely held belief that sophisticated mind-control techniques used in the war effort were now being turned into Madison Avenue mind control

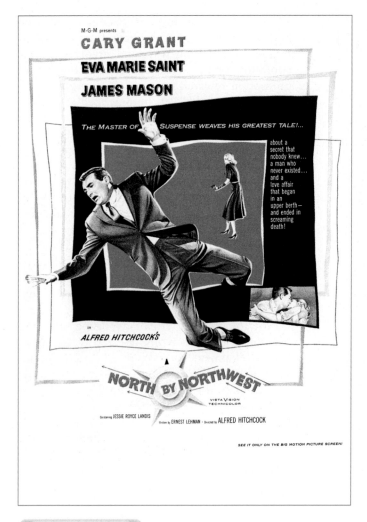

EXHIBIT 7.3

Advertising research had its biggest growth in the "mind control" fears and pop psychology of the 1950s. Unfortunately, this legacy lasted a long time.

through sophisticated advertising. A belief in hidden mass persuasion was a cornerstone of Cold War ideology. Amazingly overconfident social psychologists of the 1950s and 1960s actually thought they were going to eliminate racism, win the Cold War, and take on the relatively easy task of getting people to buy things they neither wanted or needed. Of course, it didn't work out that way.

Into this already strange social context, add a popular renaissance in everything Freud, particularly his obsession with the repressed subconscious (typically sexual in nature). It was a period of fear about mind control, seduction, moral and mental subversion, and repressed desires (see Exhibit 7.3). In university environments, psychologists embraced science and experimentation as the only path to understanding persuasion, rather than the more popularized Freudian approach. This stream of work also had an impact on the industry and its mass importation of college-trained persuasion "experts." It was, not coincidently, the same time that many American universities decided they should spend resources on training advertising professionals; most of the advertising departments and courses were formed during this period. The reasons this class and book exists, part of the reason you are taking the class, has to do with this period. All of these things are related.

So into this social environment were born the advertising research departments. In the 1950s, advertising agencies and their clients clamored for more research, more science, and some for more hidden messages. Agency research departments were justified by the sacred name of "science" and the reality of scared consumers, scared by the Cold War, by the very real possibility of instant annihilation from a nuclear war, by a rapidly changing social system, and by the very idea that someone could control your mind (see *The Manchurian Candidate*). We tell you all this because this history still absolutely influences what we call advertising and promotion research. This legacy is still with us; it's still in common beliefs about advertising, and even in the law. There are a few in the industry who still insist on using 1950s-era methods, appropriate or not, meaningful or not, useful or not.

But, there is change, significant change. In the early 1980s advertising agencies began to openly voice their distrust for the sacred research methods established in 1950s America. These voices of dissent began in London, moved to the U.S. West Coast, and lately are heard just about everywhere. As we said before, in the past decade several advertising agencies have come to believe that stand-alone research departments are a luxury that they can no longer afford given increased demands for accountability, profit, and relevance. At least two things are being seen as replacements, when there are replacements: (1) the account planning system, in which research is a more integral part of planning advertising and promotion strategy and execution, and (2) much greater research outsourcing, that is,

EXHIBIT 7.4

Words to judge research by.

- **Reliability** means that the method generates generally consistent findings over time.

- **Validity** means that the information generated is relevant to the research questions being investigated. In other words, the research investigates what it seeks to investigate.

- **Trustworthiness** is a term usually applied to qualitative data, and it means exactly what it implies: Can one, knowing how the data were collected, trust them, and to what extent?

- **Meaningfulness** is the most difficult of all these terms. Just what does a piece of research really mean (if anything)? Meaningfulness is determined by asking what the methods and measures really have to do with determining a good ad. This simple question is not asked enough.

Good advertising and promotions research can actually help make better advertising and promotions.

going outside the agency for specific advertising research when and only when the need arises. Now, don't get us wrong: Science is essential in many contexts, somewhat valuable in some, and can be in advertising, but not in the immodest and all-encompassing way previously thought (or at least practiced). Actual industry practice quickly showed 1950s-era research to be limited, and over the next half century advertising research morphed many times.

There are a lot of ways to judge research. Exhibit 7.4 gives you some terms and concepts that are very useful when talking about research.

Advertising and IBP Research.
A lot of things are called "advertising and promotion research." Not all of it, or even most of it, is done on the actual ads or promotions themselves. Most of this research is really done in preparation for making the ads and promotions. A lot is done on "the client" or brand side, at companies like P&G or Sony or Nokia. But the best way to divide the research world into three parts: (1) developmental advertising and promotion research (before ads are made); (2) copy research (as the ads are being finished or are finished); and (3) results-oriented research (after the ads are actually out there, running).

Stage One: Developmental Advertising and IBP Research.
Developmental advertising and promotion research is used to generate opportunities and messages. It helps the creatives (the people who dream up and actually make the ads) and the account team figure out the target audience's identity, what they perceive themselves as needing and wanting in a given good or service, and their usage expectations, history, and context, among others. It can provide critical information used by creatives in actually producing ads and promotions. It is conducted early in the process so there is still an opportunity to influence the way the ads, branded entertainment, or other integrated brand promotions turn out. Because of this, many consider it the most valuable kind of research. It occurs when you can still do something about it, before you have spent a ton of money and made some really bad mistakes. It is sometimes called *consumer insight*.

Method: Concept Testing. A **concept test** seeks feedback designed to screen the quality of a new idea, using consumers as the judge and jury. Concept testing may be used to screen new ideas for specific advertisements or to assess new product concepts.

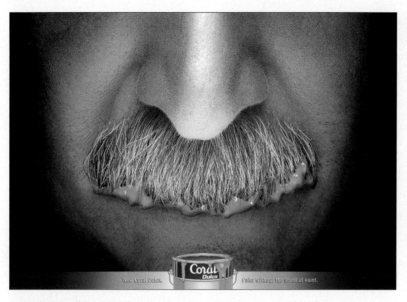

EXHIBIT 7.5

EXHIBIT 7.6

Will consumers embrace the idea of a house paint that doesn't have that new paint smell? The innovators behind this Brazilian product certainly hope so.

Hungry for more on the history of M&Ms? Check out http://www.mms.com.

Before a new product like the one in Exhibit 7.5 is launched, the advertiser must have a deep understanding of how the product fits current needs and how much consumers are willing to pay for the new product. Concept tests of many kinds are commonly included as part of the agenda of focus groups to get quick feedback on new product or advertising ideas. Sometimes an ad agency is called on to invent new ways of presenting an advertised good or service to a target audience. Pretty much everyone knows where M&Ms melt and where they don't. But in Exhibit 7.6, the story of M&Ms is expanded to include its rich history.

Further, just where does an advertiser get ideas for new and meaningful ways to portray a brand? Direct contact with the customer can be an excellent place to start. Qualitative research involving observation of customers and extended interviewing of customers can be great devices for fostering fresh thinking about a brand. Direct contact with and aggressive listening to the customer can fuel the creative process at the heart of a great advertising campaign. It can also be a great way to anticipate and shape marketplace trends, as seen in the Globalization box.

Method: Audience Profiling. Perhaps the most important service provided by developmental advertising research is the profiling of target audiences for the creatives. Creatives need to know as much as they can about the people to whom their ads will speak. This research is done in many ways. One way is through lifestyle research. Lifestyle research, also known as AIO (activities, interests, and opinions) research, uses survey data from consumers who have answered questions about themselves. From the answers to a wide variety of such questions, advertisers can get a pretty good profile of the consumers they are most interested in talking to. Since the data also contain other product usage questions, advertisers can account for a consumption lifestyle as well. For example, it may turn out that the target for a brand of roach killer consists of male consumers, age 35 to 45, living in larger cities, who are more afraid of "unseen dirt" than most people and who think of themselves as extremely organized and bothered by messes. Maybe they also tend to enjoy hunting more than average, and tend to be gun owners. They read *Guns & Ammo* and watch *Cops*. Profiles like this present the creative staff with a finer-grained picture of the target audience and their needs, wants, and motivations. Of course, the answers to these questions are only as valuable as the questions are valid. In-depth interviews

GLOBALIZATION

Girl Power: Tokyo's Teens Influence Global Marketers

Marketers in Japan long ago figured out that some of the best developmental research begins and ends with their country's trendy teenage girls. When Coca-Cola needed help fine-tuning the marketing program for a fermented-milk drink known as Lactia, focus groups of Japanese adolescent girls suggested a light and smooth consistency for the product and a short, squat bottle with a pink label for the packaging. Coke followed their advice, handed out 30,000 bottles of the new drink to high school girls to generate favorable word-of-mouth endorsements, and saw Lactia become one of Japan's most popular beverages.

Now firms inside the United States are paying close attention to this bellwether crowd as well. Over the past decade, trends as varied as Pokemon, Hello Kitty, photo sticker machines, and Zen-inspired décor all traced back to Tokyo teen girls who first sported streaked hair, wore cell phones dangling like charms on chains, and shortened their school uniforms into trend-setting minis.

What accounts for their special influence? In Japan, marketers say, teenage girls are more open and honest than their tradition-bound elders. They also tend to have substantial influence over purchases their parents make for the entire family. When Meji Milk Products of Japan introduced a breath-cleansing Chinese tea under the brand name Oolong Socha, it did so with the advice of teenage girls. The tea fast became a family favorite.

Inside the United States, marketers are paying close attention to this group's influential decisions on the next "kawaii"—incredibly cute—thing that will show up in the world's trendiest cities, whether it's anime and manga (animation and comics) or Japan's early embrace of reality television. For American entrepreneurs who are paying close attention, those hits can mean big business.

Sources: Norihiko Shirouzu, "Japan's High-School Girls Excel in Art of Setting Trends," **Wall Street Journal**, April 24, 1998, B1; Laura Tiffany, "Big in Japan: Forget Hondo, Fujitsu and Sony–Take Your Next Big Cue From Tokyo's Teenage Girls," **Entrepreneur**, December 2001, p.20.

with individual consumers provide an excellent source of information to supplement the findings from AIO research, and vice versa.

Method: Real Usage (What the Consumer Really Wants). One of things research (particularly qualitative field work) can do is to show how consumers really use a product in their real lives, and why. Believe it or not, the makers of some products and services really don't understand how their consumers use their products or feel about them, or what they really want or need. They do not know how to *design* their brand for the consumer. Anti-static laundry dryer sheets, for example, were developed for one thing: for women to rub over their heads to reduce static electricity in their hair. Consumers quickly told marketers that they had a better use for them: Put them in the clothes dryer to remove static cling from clothes. There are literally thousands of these examples. There are many times when marketers invented one thing only to learn that consumers wanted something entirely different, or used the product in an entirely different manner than the marketing and advertising told them to.

Method: Focus Groups. A focus group is a discussion session with (typically) six to 12 target customers who have been brought together to come up with new insights about the good or service. With a professional moderator guiding the discussion, the consumers are first asked some general questions; then, as the session progresses, the questioning becomes more focused and moves to detailed issues about the brand in question. Advertisers tend to like focus groups because they can understand them and observe the data being collected. While focus groups provide an opportunity for in-depth discussion with consumers, they are not without limitations. Even multiple focus groups represent a very small sample of the target audience and are prone to all sorts of errors caused by group dynamics and pleasing the researcher. But remember that generalization is not the goal. The real goal is to get or test a new idea and gain depth of understanding. Deeper understanding of consumers is a good thing. More than once in a while, what ends up being actual ad copy comes from the mouths of focus group members.

It takes great skill to lead a focus group effectively. If the group does not have a well-trained and experienced moderator, some individuals will completely dominate the others. Focus group members also feel empowered and privileged; they have been made experts by their selection, and they will sometimes give the moderator all sorts of strange answers that may be more a function of trying to impress other group members than anything having to do with the product in question. Like most things, focus groups are good at what they do, but people feel compelled to push them in ways they were never designed to be pushed. Again, focus groups are for understanding and insight, not scientific generalizations. They are very low in reliability, sometimes valid, but often produce trustworthy and meaningful insight.

Method: Projective Techniques. Projective techniques are designed to allow consumers to "project" their thoughts, but mostly feelings (conscious or unconscious), onto a "blank" or neutral "surface," like an inkblot or benign painting or scene. It's like seeing zoo animals in clouds, or faces in ice cubes. Projective techniques share a history with Freudian psychology and depend on notions of unconscious or even repressed thoughts. Projective techniques often consist of offering consumers fragments of pictures or words and asking them to complete the fragment. The most common projective techniques are association tests, dialogue balloons, story construction, and sentence or picture completion.

Dialogue balloons offer consumers the chance to fill in the dialogue of cartoon-like stories, much like those in the comics in the Sunday paper. The story usually has to do with a product use situation. The idea is that the consumers will "project" appropriate thoughts into the balloons. Supposedly, their true feelings will emerge.

Story construction is another projective technique. It asks consumers to tell a story about people depicted in a scene or picture. Respondents might be asked to tell a story about the personalities of the people in the scene, what they are doing, what they were doing just before this scene, what type of car they drive, and what type of house they live in. Again, the idea is to use a less direct method to less obtrusively bring to the surface some often unconscious mapping of the brand and its associations.

Another method of projection is **sentence and picture completion**. Here a researcher presents consumers with part of a picture or a sentence with words deleted and then asks that the stimulus be completed. The picture or sentence relates to one or several brands of products in the category of interest. For example, a sentence completion task might be *Most American-made cars are _____*. The basic idea is to elicit honest and un-edited thoughts and feelings. Researchers can get some pretty good information from this method; other times they learn more about a particular individual than a meaningful group of consumers.

Another method that has enjoyed growing popularity in advertising and promotional developmental is the **Zaltman Metaphor Elicitation Technique (ZMET)**.[3] It is also projective in nature. This technique claims to draw out people's buried thoughts and feelings about products and brands by encouraging participants to think in terms of metaphors. A metaphor simply involves defining one thing in terms of another. ZMET draws metaphors from consumers by asking them to spend time thinking about how they would visually represent their experiences with a particular product or service. Participants are asked to make a collection of photographs and pictures from magazines that reflect their experience. For example, in research conducted for DuPont, which supplies raw material for many pantyhose marketers, one person's picture of spilled ice cream reflected her deep disappointment when she spots a run in her hose. In-depth interviews with several dozen of these metaphor-collecting consumers can often reveal new insights about consumers' consumption motives, which then may be useful in the creation of products and ad campaigns to appeal to those motives. Metaphors are believed by many to be one of the most powerful and useful organizing and expressive structures of the human mind, and if they can be tapped successfully can provide advertisers with very useful information. The

3.   For three different viewpoints on ZMET, compare Kevin Lane Keller, *Strategic Brand Management* (Upper Saddle River, NJ: Prentice-Hall, 1988), 317–320; Ronald B. Liever, "Storytelling: A New Way to Get Close to Your Customer," *Fortune*, February 3, 1997, 102–108; and Gerald Zaltman, "Rethinking Market Research: Putting People Back In," *Journal of Marketing Research*, vol. 34 (November 1997), 424–437.

Cookies aren't the only things
that can be dipped with milk.

Nothing keeps me going during a night out,
like the refreshing sensation of milk.
It tastes great and keeps my body limber
and my bones strong – necessities for
the twists and twirls of the tango!

got milk?

EXHIBIT 7.7

This campaign was largely inspired by qualitative research: Researchers actually went out into the "field" and found that there was nothing worse than having a cookie/brownie/etc., but no milk.

ZMET is now widely used by marketers and advertisers.

Method: Field Work. Field work is conducted outside the agency (i.e., in the "field"), usually in the home or site of consumption. Its purpose is to learn from the experiences of the consumer and from direct observation. Consumers live real lives, and their behavior as consumers is intertwined throughout these real lives. Their consumption practices are **embedded**; that is, they are tightly connected to their social context. More and more, researchers are attempting to capture more of the real embedded experiences of consumers. This research philosophy and related methods are very popular today. It is difficult to find actual companies that do not now use this technique. Campaigns such as the award-winning and successful "Got Milk?" campaign (see Exhibit 7.7) used field work to get at the real consumption opportunity for milk—a mouth full of cookies and an empty milk carton. This helped form, and then drive, the strategy and creative execution.

Consumers began to remember to be sure to have milk at home, to ask themselves when at the grocery store, "Got milk?" Other advertisers and their agencies make videorecordings, or have consumers themselves shoot home movies on digital video, to get at the real usage opportunities and consumption practices of real consumers in real settings. Advertising researchers can make better messages if they understand the lives of their target audience, and understand it in its actual usage context. Field research uses observation and in-depth study of individuals or small groups of consumers in their own social environment. The advertising industry has long appreciated the value of qualitative data and is currently moving to even more strongly embrace extended types of fieldwork.

A special type of field work is the **coolhunt**. Coolhunters actually go to the site or sites where they believe cool resides, stalk it, and bring it back to be used in the product and its advertising. Exhibit 7.8 on the next page gives an example of coolhunting. For some product categories like shoes, electronics, clothing, and beverages, the idea is that this thing called cool can be located and then leveraged to sell more cool stuff. There are not a lot of actual coolhunts done, but they still exist here and there and it sounds like a pretty nice gig. There is, however, still a lot of interest in the idea of cool, and determining where and when it will show up next. More and more cool is chased in cyberspace through things like *brand communities*.[4]

4.   Craig J. Thompson, William B. Locander, and Howard Pollio, "Putting Consumer Experience Back into Consumer Research: The Philosophy and Method of Existential Phenomenology," *Journal of Consumer Research*, vol. 16 (June 1989), 133–147.

COOLHUNT

Baysie Wightman met DeeDee Gordon, appropriately enough, on a coolhunt. It was 1992. Baysie was a big shot for Converse, and DeeDee, who was barely twenty-one, was running a very cool boutique called Placid Planet, on Newbury Street in Boston. Baysie came in with a camera crew—one she often used when she was coolhunting—and said, "I've been watching your store, I've seen you, I've heard you know what's up," because it was Baysie's job at Converse to find people who knew what was up and she thought DeeDee was one of those people. DeeDee says that she responded with reserve—that "I was like, 'Whatever' "—but Baysie said that if DeeDee ever wanted to come and work at Converse she should just call, and nine months later DeeDee called. This was about the time the cool kids had decided they didn't want the hundred-and-twenty-five-dollar basketball sneaker with seventeen different kinds of high-technology materials and colors and air-cushioned heels anymore. They wanted simplicity and authenticity, and Baysie picked up on that. She brought back the Converse One Star, which was a vulcanized, suede, low-top classic old-school sneaker from the nineteen-seventies, and, sure enough, the One Star quickly became the signature shoe of the retro era. Remember what Kurt Cobain was wearing in the famous picture of him lying dead on the ground after committing suicide? Black Converse One Stars. DeeDee's big score was calling the sandal craze. She had been out in Los Angeles and had kept seeing the white teenage girls dressing up like cholos, Mexican gangsters, in tight white tank tops known as "wife beaters," with a bra strap hanging out, and long shorts and tube socks and shower sandals. DeeDee recalls, "I'm like, 'I'm telling you, Baysie, this is going to hit. There are just too many people wearing it. We have to make a shower sandal.' " So Baysie, DeeDee, and a designer came up with the idea of making a retro sneaker-sandal, cutting the back off the One Star and putting a thick outsole on it. It was huge, and amazingly, it's still huge.

Today, Baysie works for Reebok as general-merchandise manager—part of the team trying to return Reebok to the position it enjoyed in the mid-nineteen-eighties as the country's hottest sneaker company. DeeDee works for an advertising agency in Del Mar called Lambesis, where she puts out a quarterly tip sheet called the L Report on what the cool kids in major American cities are thinking and doing and buying. Baysie and DeeDee are best friends. They talk on the phone all the time. They get together whenever Baysie is in L.A. (DeeDee: "It's, like, how many times can you drive past O.J. Simpson's house?"), and between them they can talk for hours about the art of the coolhunt. They're the Lewis and Clark of cool.

What they have is what everybody seems to want these days, which is a window on the world of the street. Once, when fashion trends were set by the big couture houses—when cool was trickle-down—that wasn't important. But sometime in the past few decades things got turned over, and fashion became trickle-up. It's now about chase and flight—designers and retailers and the mass consumer giving chase to the elusive prey of street cool—and the rise of coolhunting as a profession shows how serious the chase has become. The sneakers of Nike and Reebok used to come out yearly. Now a new style comes out every season. Apparel designers used to have an eighteen-month lead time between concept and sale. Now they're reducing that to a year, or even six months, in order to react faster to new ideas from the street. The paradox, or course, is that the better coolhunters become at bringing the mainstream close to the cutting edge, the more elusive the cutting edge becomes. This is the first rule of the cool: The quicker the chase, the quicker the flight. The act of discovering what's cool is what causes cool to move on, which explains the triumphant circularity of coolhunting: because we have coolhunters like DeeDee and Baysie, cool changes more quickly, and because cool changes more quickly, we need coolhunters like DeeDee and Baysie.

One day last month, Baysie took me on a coolhunt to the Bronx and Harlem, lugging a big black canvas bag with twenty-four different shoes that Reebok is about to bring out, and as we drove down Fordham Road, she had her head out the window like a little kid, checking out what everyone on the street was wearing. We went to Dr. Jay's, which is the cool place to buy sneakers in the Bronx, and Baysie crouched down on the floor and started pulling the shoes out of her bag one by one, soliciting opinions from customers who gathered around and asking one question after another, in rapid sequence. One guy she listened closely to was maybe eighteen or nineteen, with a diamond stud in his ear and a thin beard. He was wearing a Polo baseball cap, a brown leather jacket, and the big, oversized leather boots that are everywhere uptown right now. Baysie would hand him a shoe and he would hold it, look at the top, and move it up and down and flip it over. The first one he didn't like: "Oh-kay." The second one he hated: he made a growling sound in his throat even before Baysie could give it to him, as if to say, "Put it back in the bag—now!" But when she handed him a new DMX RXT—a low-cut run/walk shoe in white and blue and mesh with a translucent "ice" sole, which retails for a hundred and ten dollars—he looked at it long and hard and shook his head in pure admiration and just said two words, dragging each of them out: "No doubt."

Baysie was interested in what he was saying, because the DMX RXT she had was a girls' shoe that actually hadn't been doing all that well. Later, she explained to me that the fact that the boys loved the shoe was critical news, because it suggested that Reebok had a potential hit if it just switched the shoe to the men's section. How she managed to distill this piece of information from the crowd of teenagers around her, how she made any sense of the two dozen shoes in her bag, most of which (to my eyes, anyway) looked pretty much the same, and how she knew which of the teens to really focus on was a mystery. Baysie is a Wasp from New England, and she crouched on the floor in Dr. Jay's for almost an hour, talking and joking with the homeboys without a trace of condescension or self-consciousness.

Near the end of her visit, a young boy walked up and sat down on the bench next to her. He was wearing a black woolen cap with white stripes pulled low, a blue North Face pleated down jacket, a pair of baggy Guess jeans, and on his feet, Nike Air Jordans. He couldn't have been more than thirteen. But when he started talking you could see Baysie's eyes light up, because somehow she knew the kid was the real thing.

"How many pairs of shoes do you buy a month?" Baysie asked.

"Two," the kid answered. "And if at the end I find one more I like I get to buy that, too."

Baysie was on to him. "Does your mother spoil you?"

The kid blushed, but a friend next to him was laughing. "Whatever he wants, he gets."

Baysie laughed, too. She had the DMX RXT in his size. He tried them on. He rocked back and forth, testing them. He looked back at Baysie. He was dead serious now: "Make sure these come out."

Baysie handed him the new "Rush" Emmitt Smith shoe due out in the fall. One of the boys had already pronounced it "phat," and another had looked through the marbleized-foam cradle in the heel and cried out in delight, "This is bug!" But this kid was the acid test, because this kid knew cool. He paused. He looked at it hard. "Reebok," he said, soberly and carefully, "is trying to get butter."

When Baysie comes back from a coolhunt, she sits down with marketing experts and sales representatives and designers, and reconnects them to the street, making sure they have the right shoes going to the right places at the right price. When she got back from the Bronx, for example, the first thing she did was tell all these people they had to get a new DMX RXT out, fast, because the kids on the street loved the women's version. "It's hotter than we realized," she told them. The coolhunter's job in this instance is very specific. What DeeDee does, on the other hand, is a little more ambitious. With the L Report, she tries to construct a kind of grand matrix of cool, comprising not just shoes but everything kids like, and not just kids of certain East Coast urban markets but kids all over. DeeDee and her staff put it out four times a year, in six different versions—for New York, Los Angeles, San Francisco, Austin-Dallas, Seattle, and Chicago—and then sell it to manufacturers, retailers, and ad agencies (among others) for twenty thousand dollars a year. They go to each city and find the coolest bars and clubs, and ask the coolest kids to fill out questionnaires. The information is then divided into six categories—You Saw It Here First, Entertainment and Leisure, Clothing and Accessories, Personal and Individual, Aspirations, and Food and Beverages—which are, in turn, broken up into dozens of subcategories, so that Personal and Individual, for example, include Cool Date, Cool Evening, Free Time, Favorite Possession, and on and on. The information in those subcategories is subdivided again by sex and by age bracket (14–18, 19–24, 25–30), and then, as a control, the L Report gives you the corresponding set of preferences for "mainstream kids."

What DeeDee argues, though, is that cool is too subtle and too variegated to be captured with these kind of broad strokes. Cool is a set of dialects, not a language. The L Report can tell you, for example, that nineteen-to-twenty-four-year-old male trendsetters in Seattle would most like to meet, among others, King Solomon and Dr. Seuss, and that nineteen-to-twenty-four-year-old female trendsetters in San Francisco have turned their backs on Calvin Klein, Nintendo Game Boy, and sex. What's cool right now? Among male New York trendsetters: North Face jackets, rubber and latex, khakis, and the rock band Kiss. Among female trendsetters: ska music, old-lady clothing, and cyber tech. In Chicago, snowboarding is huge among trendsetters of both sexes and all ages. Women over nineteen are into short hair, while those in their teens have embraced mod culture, rock climbing, tag watches, and bootleg pants. In Austin-Dallas, meanwhile, twenty-five-to-thirty-year-old women trendsetters are into hats, heroin, computers, cigars, Adidas, and velvet, while men in their twenties are into video games and hemp. In all, the typical L Report runs over one hundred pages. But with the flood of data comes an obsolescence disclaimer: "The fluctuating nature of the trendsetting market makes keeping up with trends a difficult task." By the spring, in other words, everything may have changed.

The key to coolhunting, then, is to look for cool people first and cool things later, and not the other way around. Since cool things are always changing, you can't look for them, because the very fact they are cool means you have no idea what to look for. What you would be doing is thinking back on what was cool before and extrapolating, which is about as useful as presuming that because the Dow rose ten points yesterday it will rise another ten points today. Cool people, on the other hand, are a constant.

Source: From Malcolm Gladwell, "The Coolhunt," in *The Consumer Society Reader*, Juliet B. Schor and Douglas B. Holt, eds. (New York: New Press, 2000), 360–374.

EXHIBIT 7.8

This is a description of coolhunting.

Internal Company Sources. Some of the most valuable data are available within a firm itself and are, therefore, referred to as "internal company sources." Commonly available information within a company includes strategic marketing plans, research reports, customer service records, warranty registration cards, letters from customers, customer complaints, and various sales data (broken down by region, by customer type, by product line). All of these provide a wealth of information relating to the proficiency of the company's advertising programs and, more generally, changing consumer tastes and preferences. Sometimes really great data are right there under the client's or agency's nose. More and more of these data are gathered online.

② Government Sources. Various government organizations generate data on factors of interest to advertising planners; information on population and housing trends, transportation, consumer spending, and recreational activities in the United States is available through government documents.[5] Go to http://www.lib.umich.edu/govdocs/federal.html for a couple hundred or so pages of great links to data from federal, state, and international government sources. The Census of Population and Housing is conducted every 10 years in years ending in 0. The data (actually tables, not the data itself, unfortunately) are released at various times over the following handful of years after the census. The Census Bureau has a great Web site with access to numerous tables and papers (http://www.census.gov/).

A great source of data in the United States is the American Community Survey, which the Census Bureau actually hopes will replace many aspects of the census in 2010. It came online in 2003. The ACS is a new approach for collecting accurate, timely information. It is designed as an ongoing survey that will replace the so-called long form in the 2010 census. The ACS provides estimates of demographic, housing, social, and economic characteristics every year for states, cities, counties, metropolitan areas, and population groups of 65,000 people or more (http://www.factfinder.census.gov/home/en/acsdata.html). (See Exhibit 7.9, from the ACS.) Demographic changes are key to so many advertising and branding opportunities. Think of how many ads you see for retirement services and planning; do you think the enormous number of aging baby boomers has something to do with that? It's no accident that *Advertising Age*'s parent company, Crain Communications, bought the magazine *American Demographics*, and offers it bundled with the bible of the advertising industry. Demographics are important.

There is also the commonly used Current Population Survey, which is a national survey that has been conducted monthly since 1940 by the Bureau of the Census for the Bureau of Labor Statistics. It provides information on unemployment, occupation, income, and sources of income, as well as a rotating set of topics such as health, work schedules, school enrollment, fertility, households, immigration, and language (http://www.census.gov/cps). Who could really believe, given all the immigration occurring in North America and Europe, and many other parts of the world, that rapidly changing populations don't affect consumer taste, needs, and preferences? Who could think that? For European surveys, check out Eurobarometer, http://ec.europa.eu/public_opinion (Exhibit 7.10)

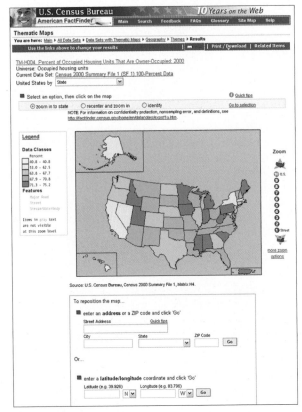

EXHIBIT 7.9

The American Community Survey is a great resource for defining target audiences.

5.   We would like to thank Professor Gillian Stevens of the University of Illinois for her assistance with government data sources.

You might also check out the International Social Survey Programme at http://www.issp.org. Here you could get valuable data on the feelings of consumers from 30 or so nations on, for example, environmental issues, quite a find for companies trying to market "green products." (Exhibit 7.11) Another great site is the National Archives and Records Administration, http://www.nara.gov. This site has an incredible array of information about Americans and American culture—all available, for no charge, from any computer. The array of consumer data available from government sources is a wonderful resource in advertising and planning for businesses of all sizes. These publications/sites are reasonably current. Print versions are available at public libraries. This means that even a small-business owner can access large amounts of information for advertising planning purposes at little or no cost. Again, the Internet has changed the world and the practice of advertising and promotion. Small marketers and their agencies can now obtain data that would have simply either been unavailable or cost too much just a few years ago.

Method: Commercial Sources. First, let us be truthful: This is not a complete list. There are lots and lots of commercial research suppliers, particularly in the developmental stage. We list a few, but more important are the ideas that underlie most of them. Since information has become such a critical resource in marketing and advertising decision making, commercial data services have emerged to provide data of various types and to package existing data. So, while traditional advertising agencies are more and more getting out or downsizing the research business, innovative companies (some of them start-ups) see an opportunity opening up here, particularly for those who can collect, package, or repackage online data. Some firms specialize in data-gathering efforts at the household or neighborhood level. Prizm is a good example. Prizm's owner, Claritas, collects data at the zip-code level on consumption. This way, a marketer can see

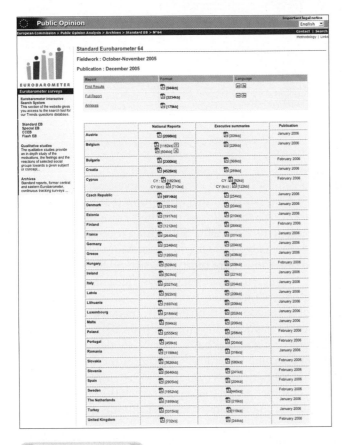

EXHIBIT 7.10

Eurobarometer is a great resource for opinions of EU consumers.

EXHIBIT 7.11

Recognition of the need for cleaner-burning fuels continues to grow across a long list of nations.

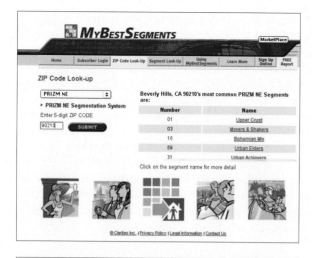

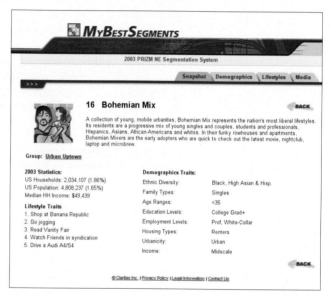

EXHIBIT 7.12

*Here is zip-code consumer data from Prizm. Nice zip code: 90210.
Here are the menu and three of the "best" segments for Beverly Hills,
California.*

a pretty interesting profile of who is most likely to consume a given good or service,
and also *where* (see Exhibit 7.12). This is based on the assumption that most consumers within a given zip code are more alike than different in their consumption habits.
However, this assumption is not accepted universally. Sometimes there are significant
variations in consumer practices within a given geographic area. More often than not,
people living in close proximity to one another are more like each other (in consumption practices) than people living in different geographic areas. That simple reality is
what makes geographic clustering research methods work at all.

Information from commercial data vendors is reasonably comprehensive and is normally gathered using reasonably sound methods. Information from these sources costs
more than information from government sources, but is specifically designed to be of
benefit to advertisers and marketers. Exhibit 7.13 details several of the major companies and their offerings. Many offer consumer surveys (one-shot attempts: one person
answers the survey one time) and consumer panels (surveys in which the same members
stay on the panel and are asked questions numerous times over months or years.)

Method: Professional Publications. Another secondary data source is professional publications. Professional publications are periodicals in which marketing and advertising
professionals report significant information related to industry trends or new research
findings. Examples include be *Progressive Grocer* and *Beverage*.

Commercial Information Source	Type of Information
Dun & Bradstreet Market Identifiers	DMI is a listing of 4.3 million businesses that is updated monthly. Information includes number of employees, relevant SIC codes that relate to the businesses' activities, location, and chief executive. Marketing and advertising managers can use the information to identify markets, build mailing lists, and specify media to reach an organization. http://www.dnb.com
Nielsen Retail Index	Nielsen auditors collect product inventory turnover data from 1,600 grocery stores, 750 drugstores, and 150 mass merchandise outlets. Information is also gathered on retail prices, in-store displays, and local advertising. Data from the index are available by store type and geographic location. http://www.nielsenmedia.com
National Purchase Diary Panel	With more than 13,000 families participating, NPD is the largest diary panel in the United States. Families record on preprinted sheets their monthly purchases in 50 product categories. Information recorded includes brand, amount purchased, price paid, use of coupons, store, specific version of the product (flavor, scent, etc.), and intended use.
Consumer Mail Panel	This panel is operated by a firm called Market Facts. There are 45,000 active participants at any point in time. Samples are drawn in lots of 1,000. The overall panel is said to be representative of different geographic regions in the United States and Canada, then broken down by household income, urbanization, and age of the respondent. Data are provided on demographic and socioeconomic characteristics as well as type of dwelling and durable goods ownership. http://www.marketfacts.com

EXHIBIT 7.13

Examples of the commercial data sources available to advertisers.

EXHIBIT 7.14

At MySpace you will find thousands and thousands of discussion groups, many of them consumer- and brand-based. Here, advertisers can gain incredibly rich, unobtrusive, and sophisticated data from real consumers at virtually no cost. Sophisticated newsreader programs can quickly search and organize these data.

Method: The Internet. It probably goes without saying for today's Web-savvy college student that the Internet can be an advertiser's best friend when looking for secondary data of almost any kind. The Internet has revolutionized developmental research, particularly for smaller agencies and advertisers. Common search engines allow the search of enormous amounts of data previously available only to the wealthiest agencies. Human search costs have been slashed. Beyond commonly available engines, some companies buy customized engines to search the Web for their own particular needs. Of particular value are Web-based interest groups, or online communities. Google Groups, Facebook and MySpace (see Exhibit 7.14) are great resources. Without ever leaving your office, you can do "coolhunting" and see the spread of market ideas through on-line social network data. As search engines get more and more sophisticated anyone can find just about anything. But then there are also all the advances in spyware and tracking software: software designed to let companies know where you go on their site, what you do when you are there, where else you go, with whom you share this information, and presumably with what result (although that's still a bit optimistic in terms of return on investment. If you can figure that out, please let us know).

③ Stage Two: Copy Research. The second major type of advertising and promotion research is known as copy research, or *evaluative research*. It is the kind that people usually think of when one says "advertising research." It is research on the actual ads or promotional texts themselves, finished or unfinished. It is used to judge or *evaluate* ads and promotions. Even though most contemporary ads are more pictures than words, the name "copy" still reflects the time when it was the effect of advertising copy (words) that was supposed to be most important. These usually occur right before or after the ad is finalized.

In the best case, reliable, valid, trustworthy, and meaningful tests are appropriately applied. In the worst case, tests in which few still believe continue to survive because they represent "the way we have always done things." The pressure of history and the felt need for normative or historically comparative data significantly obscure questions of appropriateness and meaningfulness. This makes for an environment in which the best test is not always done, the wrong tests are more than occasionally done, and the right questions are not always asked. But such is life in the real world.

This brings us to motives and expectations of the agency and the client: Why are certain tests done? Aren't these smart people, trying to make money; why would they do these things? Well we all do things because of history and habit that we know don't make sense, some due to tradition. It may also be that we don't have anything much better with which to replace them. Maybe advertising is so complex that it defies simple measures, and even complex and involved (expensive) ones. Just what is it that advertising professionals want out of their copy research? The answer, of course, depends on who you ask. Generally speaking, the account team (AKA "suits") wants some assurance that the ad does essentially what it's supposed to do, or at least is defensible in terms of copy test scores. Many times, the team simply wants whatever the client wants. The client typically wants to see some numbers, generally meaning **normative test scores**—scores relative to the average for a category of ads. In other words, the client wants to see how well a particular ad scored against average commercials of its type that were tested previously. From a purely practical standpoint, having a good normative copy test score (above the average for the category) lowers the probability of getting fired later. You can point to the score and say it "tested well," and then assert that you (and/or your agency) should not be fired. There is a lot of cover in these scores, perhaps in reality their greatest value.

How about the people who actually make the ads, the creatives? What do they want in all of this? Well, generally they hate copy testing and wish it would go away. They are generally uninterested in normative tests. The creatives who actually produced the ad typically believe there is no such thing as the average commercial, and they are quite sure that if there are average commercials, theirs are not among them. Besides benefiting the sales of the advertised product or service, the creatives wouldn't mind another striking ad on their reel or in their book, another Addy or Clio on their wall. But copy research scores are unlikely to predict awards, which are the official currency of creatives. So creatives don't tend to be fans of copy tests. Creatives want awards. Copy tests often stand in the way and seem meaningless.

Copy tests generate a type of report card, and some people, particularly on the creative side of advertising, resent getting report cards from people in suits. Cre-

Bob, a creative at a large agency, has learned from experience how to deal with lower-than-average day-after recall (DAR) scores. As he explains it, there are two basic strategies: (1) Do things that you know will pump up the DAR. For example, if you want high DARs, never simply super (superimpose) the brand name or tag at the end of the ad. Always voice it over as well, whether it fits or not. You can also work in a couple of additional mentions in dialogue; they may stand out like a sore thumb and make consumers think, "Man, is that a stupid commercial," because people don't talk that way. But it will raise your DARs. (2) Tell them (the account executive or brand manager and other suits) that this is not the kind of product situation that demands high DARs. In fact, high DARs would actually hurt them in the long run due to quick wearout and annoyance. Tell them, "You're too sophisticated for that ham-handed kind of treatment. It would never work with our customers." You can use the second strategy only occasionally, but it usually works. It's amazing.

atives also argue that these numbers are often misleading and misapplied. More often than not, they're right. Further, they argue that ads are artistic endeavors, not kitchen appliances to be rated by *Consumer Reports*. Advertising, they say, is art, not science. Again, they have a point. Because of these problems, and the often conflicting career agenda of creatives (awards, career as a filmmaker or writer) and account managers (keep your job, sell more stuff, maybe get to move to the brand side), copy research is often the center of agency tensions. Other than corner offices, copy tests have probably been at the center of more agency fights than just about anything.

Whenever people begin looking at the numbers, there is a danger that trivial differences can be made monumental. Other times, the mandatory measure is simply inappropriate. Still other times, creatives wishing to keep their jobs simply give the client what he or she wants, as suggested in Exhibit 7.15. If simple recall is what the client wants, then increasing the frequency of brand mentions might be the answer. It may not make for a better commercial, but it may make for a better score and, presumably, a happy client in the short run. A lot of games are played with copy tests.

Despite the politics involved, copy testing research is *probably* a good idea, at least some of the time. Properly conceived, correctly conducted and appropriately applied, copy research can yield important data that management can then use to determine the suitability of an ad. Knowing when it is appropriate and when it is not, and sticking to your guns is, quite simply, very hard in the advertising and integrated brand promotion world—too many careers and too much money are on the line. Simple memory measures have lately found their way into product placement and branded entertainment. The following section will help you understand which test to use, and when to test at all.

Evaluative Criteria and Methods. There are a few common ways ads are judged. Again, these "tests" are usually done right as the ad is being finished, or is finished. They are, more than anything else, traditional. Some make a great deal of sense and are very useful for brand advertising and integrated promotion; others are horribly overused and misapplied. Below we go through and discuss the major evaluative criteria and the major methods of assessing ads and promotions on these criteria. Of the three types of research, this is probably the least useful in actual industry practice. It is, however, alive (if not well) because of tradition.

EXHIBITS 7.16 AND 7.17

Do you get it? Does the main message come across? Is the right image projected?

Getting It. Sometimes advertisers just want to know if audience members "get" the ad. Do they generally understand it, get the joke, see the connection, or get the main point? The reasoning behind this assessment is so obvious it hurts. It makes sense; it can be easily defended—even to copy-research-hating creatives. Brand managers understand this criterion; so do account executives. Do you get the ads in Exhibits 7.16 and 7.17?

Method: Communication Tests. A **communication test** simply seeks to discover whether a message is communicating something close to what the advertiser desired. They are most often used with television. Communication tests are usually done in a group setting, with data coming from a combination of pencil-and-paper questionnaires and group discussion. Members of the target audience are shown the ad, or some preliminary or rough version of it. They typically see it several times. Then a discussion is held. One reason communication tests are performed is to prevent a major disaster, to prevent communicating something completely wrong, something the creators of the ad are too close to see but that is entirely obvious to consumers. This could be an unintended double entendre, an inadvertent sexual allusion, or anything else "off the wall." With more transnational or global advertising, it could be an unexpected interpretation of the imagery that emerges as that ad is moved from country to country around the world. Remember, if the consumer sees things, it doesn't matter whether they're intended or not—to the consumer, they're there. However, advertisers should balance this against the fact that communication test members feel privileged and special, and thus they may try too hard to see things, and see things that no one else sees. This is another instance where well-trained and experienced researchers must be counted on to draw a proper conclusion from the testing. These tests are conducted both in-house (at advertising agency itself) or outsourced to a commercial testing service

What Do They Remember? It is assumed that if the consumer was exposed to the ad, something of that ad remains in the consumer's mind: cognitive residue, pieces of the ads mixed with the consumer's own thoughts and reactions. It might be a memory of the headline, the brand name, the joke in a TV spot, a stray piece of copy, a vague memory trace of an executional element in the ad, or just about anything. So for decades advertisers have tried to score this cognitive residue, or the things left in consumer's minds from the ads. If "remembering stuff" from the ad matters, this makes sense at some basic level, yet we have known for at least 30 to 40 years that most memory measures of ads (not brands) don't tend to predict actual sales very well at all. Why is this? Well, for one thing, consumers may remember all sorts of things in ads, and not care for the advertised brand at all. Or they remember things that are completely irrelevant to the advertiser's intended message, or some of their thoughts actually interfere with associating the advertiser's brand name with the ad itself. Humorous ads are great example of this. The consumer remembers what is funny, but not the brand name—or worse yet, remembers the competitor's brand name. Now some companies, some very smart ones, are insisting on recall measures for branded entertainment.

It is also the case that these tests are premised on an increasingly out-of-fashion view of human memory. Not so very long ago, psychologists thought that whatever a human experienced made its way into memory pretty much like streaming video or an unedited movie of one's life. It is becoming clear that motivation is much more important in what is remembered than previously recognized. So the focus of lots of advertising research was on the accurate and faithful retrieval of an ad, or at least important pieces of the ad, as if it existed unaltered in memory. Lately, though, a new way of thinking about human memory has emerged. Inspired from research into false memories in child abuse cases, psychologists now know that human memory is much messier than previously assumed. Psychologists now believe memory to be fluid and highly subject to motivation: remembering things as we care to remember them, even things that never happened. Memory appears to be much more of an interpretive act than previously thought. Advertising researcher Kathryn Braun-LaTour has shown that one can actually be fairly easily made to remember brands that don't exist and consumption experiences that never happened.[6] This work tells us that to rely so strongly on memory as a measure of advertising effectiveness is a very bad idea. There are certainly times when such measures are appropriate, but nowhere near as much as they are used. There will be more on this in Chapter 11.

Common Methods for Assessing Cognitive Residue.

Method: Thought Listings. It is commonly assumed that advertising and promotions generate some thoughts during and following exposure. Wow, what an insght. Copy research that tries to identify specific thoughts that were generated by an ad is referred to as **thought listing**, or **cognitive response analysis**. These are tests of knowledge, cognitive residue, and to a lesser degree feelings and emotions. Thought-listing tests are either conducted in-house or obtained from a commercial testing service. They are most often used with television ads, although they can be applied to all ads. Here the researcher is interested in the thoughts that an ad or promotion generates in the mind of the audience. Typically, cognitive responses are collected by having individuals watch the commercial in groups and, as soon as it is over, asking them to write down all the thoughts that were in their minds while watching the commercial. They are then asked about these thoughts and asked to explain or amplify them. The hope is that this will capture what the potential audience members made of the ad and how they responded, or "talked back to it in their head."

These verbatim responses can then be analyzed in a number of ways. Usually, simple percentages or box scores of word counts are used. The ratio of favorable to unfavorable thoughts may be the primary interest of the researcher. Alternatively,

---

6.   Kathryn A. Braun, "Postexperience Advertising Effects on Consumer Memory," *Journal of Consumer Research*, vol. 25 (March 1999), 319–334.

the number of times the person made a self-relevant connection—that is, "That would be good for me" or "That looks like something I'd like"—could be tallied and compared for different ad executions. The idea itself is appealing: capturing people's stream of thoughts about an ad at time of exposure. But in its actual practice problems arise. These thoughts are in reality more retrospective than online; in other words, people are usually asked to write these down seconds to minutes after their thoughts actually occurred. They are also highly self-edited—some of your thoughts are not very likely to be shared. These thoughts are obtained in artificial environments and mental states typically unlike those in which real people are actually exposed to ads in real environments, such as sitting in their living room, talking, half-listening to the TV, and so on. But the researchers asked; you have to tell them something. Still, even with all these problems, there is something of value in these thoughts. The trick, of course, is to know what is valuable and what is just "noise." A lot has to do with how well matched the ad and the procedure are. Some ads, for example, are designed in such a way that the last thing the advertiser really wants is a lot of deep thought (more on this in Chapter 11). For other ads (those where certain conclusions and judgments are the desired goal), it can be a good test. Interestingly, research has shown that the single most common cognitive response to an ad is a counter-argument. The ad makes some claim, and the consumer says, "no it isn't; that's not true."[7] Do you think that's because it's being done in an artificial setting and the test consumer wants to look smart, or is that really most people's first and foremost reaction to ads? What do you think?

Method: Recall Tests. These are one of the most commonly employed tests in advertising, and the most controversial. They are used to get at the cognitive residue of ads. The basic idea is that if the ad is to work, it has to be remembered. Following on this premise is the further assumption that the ads best remembered are the ones most likely to work. Thus the objective of these tests is to see just how much, if anything, the viewer of an ad remembers of the message. Recall is used most in testing television advertising. In television **recall tests** the big companies are Ipsos-ASI and Burke. In print, the major recall testing services are Gallup & Robinson and Mapes and Ross. In print, however, **recognition** is generally the industry standard. Recognition simply means that the audience members indicate that they have seen an ad before (i.e., recognize it), whereas recall requires more actual memory (recalling from memory) of an ad. Recall is more common for television, recognition for print.

In television, the basic recall procedure is to recruit a group of individuals from the target market who will be watching a certain channel during a certain time on a test date. They are asked to participate ahead of time, and simply told to watch the show. A day after exposure, the testing company calls the individuals on the phone and determines, of those who actually saw the ad, how much they can recall. The day-after-recall (DAR) procedure generally starts with questions such as, "Do you remember seeing a commercial for any laundry detergents? If not, do you remember seeing a commercial for Tide?" If the respondent remembers, he or she is asked what the commercial said about the product: What did the commercial show? What did the commercial look like? The interview is recorded and transcribed. The verbatim interview is coded into various categories representing levels of recall, typically reported as a percentage. *Unaided recall* is when the respondent demonstrates that he or she saw the commercial and remembered the brand name without having the brand name mentioned. If the person had to be asked about a Tide commercial, it would be scored as *aided recall*. Industry leader Burke reports two specific measures: *claim-recall* (percent who claim seeing the ad), and *related-recall* (percent who accurately recall specific elements of the ad).[8] Ipsos-ASI uses a similar

7.   Thomas J. Robertson, Joan Zielinski, and Scott Ward, *Consumer Behavior*, (Glenview: Scott, Foresman and Company, 1984).

8.   Terence A. Shimp, *Advertising, Promotion and Supplemental Aspects of Integrated Marketing Communications* (Cincinnati: South-Western, 2002).

procedure, but with one major difference. Like Burke, Ipsos-ASI recruits a sample, but tells the participants that they are evaluating potential new television shows. What they are really evaluating are the ads. The shows are mailed to the sample audience members' home and they are given instructions. One day after viewing, the company contacts the viewers and asks them questions about the shows and the ads. From their responses, various measures are gathered, including recall. The advantage is the deception. If audience members think they are evaluating the shows, the researchers may get a more realistic assessment of the ads. It is not the same as a truly natural exposure environment, but it's probably an improvement over asking directly about the ad only.

Recall is done a bit differently in print. Remember, recognition, not recall, is considered the standard test in print. But when recall is assessed for print, it is done in the following way. In a typical print recall test, a consumer is recruited from the target market, generally at a shopping mall. He or she is given a magazine to take home. Many times the magazine is an advance issue of a real publication; other times it is a fictitious magazine created only for testing purposes. The ads are "tipped in," or inserted, into the vehicle. Some companies alter the mix of remaining ads; others do not. Some rotate the ads (put them in different spots in the magazine) for each recruited consumer so as not to get effects due to either editorial context or order.

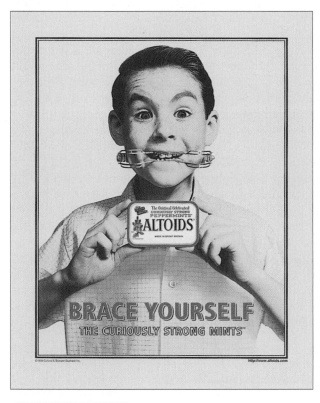

EXHIBIT 7.18

Recognition testing uses the ad itself to test whether consumers remember it and can associate it with its brand and message. This unusual, comically fanciful image would likely make this ad easy to recognize. But imagine this ad with the Altoids brand name blacked out. If consumers recognize the ad, will they also remember the Altoids brand name? Novel imagery sometimes actually distracts readers, enticing them to overlook brand names. Visit the Altoids site (http://www.altoids.com) and evaluate how it reinforces or dilutes recognition in the minds of consumers. Are the interactive features useful or distracting? Does the site achieve "cool," or is it too over-the-top to reinforce brand recognition?

The participants are told that they should look at the magazine and that they will be telephoned the following day and asked some questions. During the telephone interview, aided recall is assessed. This involves a product category cue, such as, "Do you remember seeing any ads for personal computers?" The percentage who respond affirmatively and provide some evidence of actually remembering the ad are scored as exhibiting aided recall. Other tests go into more detail by actually bringing the ad back to the respondent and asking about various components of the ad, such as the headline and body copy. Sometimes a deck of cards with brand names is given to consumers, and they are asked to stop if they can remember any ads from the brands on the cards. If they can, then they are asked to describe everything they can remember about the ad. These are scored in a manner similar to television DAR tests.

Method: Recognition Tests. Recognition tests are the standard memory test for print ads and promotions. Rather than asking you if you recall something, they ask if you *recognize* an ad, or something in an ad. This type of testing attempts to get at little more than evidence of exposure residue. Recognition tests ask magazine readers and (sometimes television viewers) whether they remember having seen particular advertisements and whether they can name the company sponsoring the ad. For print advertising, the actual advertisement is shown to respondents, and for television advertising, a script with accompanying photos is shown. For instance, a recognition test might ask, "Do you remember seeing [the ad in Exhibit 7.18]?" This is a much easier task than recall in that respondents are cued by the very

EXHIBIT 7.19

Though the correlation between seduction and candy is not new, consumers might mistake this imagery for a valentine, not an advertisement. What is the advantage to the placement of the product in this ad?

STARCH™ AD-AS-A-WHOLE		
Noted %	Associated %	Read Most %
W 55	50	23-

EXHIBIT 7.20

55% of Starch respondents said they noticed an ad, 50% said they associated it with the advertised brand, and 23% said they read more than half the body copy.

stimulus they are supposed to remember, and they aren't asked to do anything more than say yes or no. Do you think any complications might arise in establishing recognition of the ad displayed in Exhibit 7.19?

Companies such as **Starch Readership Services** that do this kind of research follow some general procedures. Subscribers to a relevant magazine are contacted and asked if an interview can be set up in their home. The readers must have at least glanced at the issue to qualify. Then each target ad is shown, and the readers are asked if they remember seeing the ad (if they *noted* it), if they read or saw enough of the ad to notice the brand name (if they *associated* it), if they *read any* part of the ad copy, or if they claim to have read at least 50 percent of the copy *(read most)*. This testing is usually conducted just a few days after the current issue becomes available. The *noted, associated,* and *read most* scores are calculated (see Exhibit 7.20). With print ads, Starch is the major supplier of recognition (they also term them "readership") tests.

Bruzzone Research Company provides recognition scores for TV ads. Essentially, a sample of television viewers is selected. A photoboard (a board with still frames from the actual ad) of the TV commercial is sent out to a sample of viewers, but the brand name is obscured (both in picture and copy). Then recognition questions such as "Do you remember seeing this commercial on TV?" are asked. The respondent is asked to identify the brand and answer some attitude items. A recognition score is then presented to the client, along with attitude data. This method has advantages in that it is fairly inexpensive (and may be becoming less so through use of the Internet), and, due to its manner of blocking brand names, may provide a more valid measure of recognition (see Exhibit 7.21).

EXHIBIT 7.21

Try the test: http://www .brcsurvey.com/brc demosurvey4.htm.

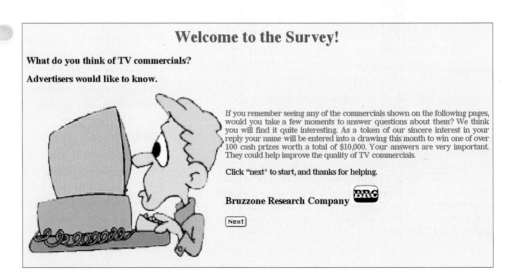

Welcome to the Survey!

What do you think of TV commercials?

Advertisers would like to know.

If you remember seeing any of the commercials shown on the following pages, would you take a few moments to answer questions about them? We think you will find it quite interesting. As a token of our sincere interest in your reply your name will be entered into a drawing this month to win one of over 100 cash prizes worth a total of $10,000. Your answers are very important. They could help improve the quality of TV commercials.

Click "next" to start, and thanks for helping.

Bruzzone Research Company BRC

Next

EXHIBITS 7.22 THROUGH 7.24

All of these ads, so strikingly similar, do little to (1) differentiate the product, (2) make it memorable for the consumer, or (3) promote the brand, though presumably GM and Ford had intended to do all three with these ads. Compare and contrast the new Cadillac models (http://www .cadillac.com) with the Ford luxury models (http://www.lincolnvehicles.com). Has either company broken any new ground in its approach to advertising these vehicles? Do you think in a few days you could distinguish between these models or remember the message of these Web sites?

Recognition scores have been collected for a long time, which allows advertisers to compare their current ads with similar ones done last week, last month, or 50 years ago. This is a big attraction of recognition scores. The biggest problem with this test is that of a yea-saying bias. In other words, many people say they recognize an ad that in fact they haven't seen. After a few days, do you really think you could correctly remember which of the three ads in Exhibits 7.22 through 7.24 you really saw, if you saw the ads under natural viewing conditions? Still, on a relative basis, these tests may tell which ads are way better or way worse than others.

Now here's the rub: Considerable research indicates there is little relation between recall or recognition scores and actual sales.[9] But doesn't it make sense that the best ads are the ads best remembered? Well, the evidence for that is simply not there. This seeming contradiction has perplexed scholars and practitioners for a long time. And as ads become more and more visual, recall of words and claims is more and more irrelevant except, usually, simple brand names. The fact is that, as measured, the level of recall for an ad seems to have relatively little (if anything) to do with sales. This may be due to highly inflated and artificial recall scores. It may also be that ads that were never designed to elicit recall are being tested as if they were. By doing this, by applying this test so widely and so indiscriminately, it makes the test itself look bad. We believe that when, but only when, recall or recognition is the desired result, are these tests appropriate and worthwhile.

9.   Rajeev Batra, John G. Meyers, and David A. Aaker, *Advertising Management*, 5th ed. (Upper Saddle River, NJ: Prentice Hall, 1996), 469.

A recall measurement does make sense when simple memory goals are the aim of the commercial. For example, saying "Kibbles and Bits" 80 times or so in 30 seconds indicates an ad aimed at one simple goal: Remember "Kibbles and Bits." That's all. For an ad like that, recall is the perfect measure. But as advertising moves to fewer words and more pictures, recognition tests, good recognition tests, may become much more valuable than recall. And for most ads or branded entertainment that operate at a far more sophisticated and advanced level than either recall or recognition, these measures are insufficient.

Method: Implicit Memory Measures. What we have been discussing up to this point are explicit memory measures, measures and procedures that require the research subject to recall the actual exposure. As a contrast, **implicit memory measures** do not refer back to the ad or exposure, but try to get at memory by using tasks like word fragments: say, part of a brand name, like S R N T for Sprint. Subjects are asked to complete the brand name (that is scored), along with other recollections. The idea is that this is a much more sensitive, less demanding (artificial), and perhaps a more meaningful measure of advertising. It is being used occasionally in actual practice, but its intensive procedure and instrumentation make it more of an academic pursuit than an applied one.

Knowledge. Knowledge is a big step up from cognitive residue. To have knowledge about a brand that could have come only from an ad is a much more meaningful measure of advertising effectiveness. This knowledge may take several forms. It could be a brand claim, or a belief about the brand. For example, the advertisers may believe that Brand X cleans twice as well as Brand Y. If Brand X's advertising and promotion has been stressing this very fact, then we may generally assume that the consumer has learned something from the promotion and advertising, and that brand knowledge has been created. But with the explosion in available information for consumers, it's really getting hard to figure out just where some piece of knowledge came from.

Method: Communication Tests. See the description of communication tests in the "Getting It" section on page 242.

Method: Surveys. In **surveys**, consumers are asked to answer questions about the advertised brand after the commercial. Sometimes this is immediately after, other times it is hours, days, or even weeks later. This is often done on-site, by phone, or on the Internet.

Attitude Change. Attitudes suggest where a brand stands in the consumer's mind. Attitudes can be influenced both by what people know and by what people feel about a brand. In this sense, attitude or preference is a summary evaluation that ties together the influences of many different factors. Advertisers thus may view attitude change as an important dimension for assessing advertising.

Common sense tells us that sometimes attitudes would be worthwhile in assessing ads. Did the ads change the consumer's attitudes in the right direction? Even though the attitude concept itself has come under fire, attitude studies are still used, though more often at the results stage. One of the big problems is getting advertisers to run true scientific experiments with tight controls. They just don't seem to see the value in it, or the relevance of it. There just isn't much of this done other than on college campuses by professors generally pretending that stimulus material are the same as real ads. They are not. Industry rarely uses experiments. One cannot assume that a favorable attitude toward the ad will always lead to a favorable and meaningful attitude toward the brand. We can all think of ads we love for brands we don't. Still, in the right circumstance, when the correct attitude dimensions are defined, assessing summary evaluations makes perfect sense. There will more on this when we discuss specific methods and message strategies in Chapter 11.

Method: Attitude Studies. The typical industry **attitude study** measures consumer attitudes after exposure to an ad. Television ads are typically seen in a group setting; print ads are often shown one-on-one. The studies may also be administered by survey, including Internet surveys. Essentially, people from the target market are recruited, and their attitudes toward the advertised brand as well as toward competitors' brands are noted. Ideally, there would be pre- and postexposure attitude measurement, so that one could see the change related to seeing the ad in question. Unfortunately, industry practice and thinner agency profit margins have created a situation in which only postexposure measures are now typically taken. True pre-post tests are becoming rare, but are seeing some renewed interest via the Internet.

To the extent that attitudes reflect something meaningful, and something important, these tests may be very useful. Their validity is typically premised on a single ad exposure (sometimes two) in an unnatural viewing environment (such as a theater). Many advertisers believe that commercials don't register their impact until after three or four exposures in a real environment; others believe the number is much higher. Still, a significant swing in attitude scores with a single exposure suggests that something is going on, and that some of this effect might be expected when the ad reaches real consumers in the comfort of their homes. John Philip Jones of Syracuse University has conducted analyses on these data and his conclusions are actually very supportive of attitude studies.[10] He contends that even if this form of message pretesting yields some incorrect predictions about ads' potential effectiveness (as it surely will), an advertiser's success rate is bound to improve with this tool. On the other hand, it is difficult to really know whether the respondent is expressing feelings toward the ad itself or the advertised product, and these can be very different things. The hard cold bottom line is that attitude studies have not been very predictive of actual behavior. For this reason, the attitude paradigm itself is falling from grace. In our view, this is not exactly something to bank much money on.

To test attitude change in print ads, test ads can be dropped off at the participants' homes in the form of magazines. The test ads have been tipped in. Subjects are told that the researcher will return the next day for an interview. They are also told that as part of their compensation for participating, they are being entered in a drawing. At that point, they are asked to indicate their preferences on a wide range of potential prizes. The next day when the interviewer returns, he or she asks for these preferences a second time. This is the postexposure attitude measure.

As you may remember from above, Bruzzone's recognition tests also collect attitude measures. This is a postexposure measure, but because it is linked to recognition scores, it may prove quite useful. Similarly, ASI Next-TV collects postexposure attitude scores. To our knowledge the only prominent testing service to offer true pre-post attitude testing is the **ARS Persuasion Method**. This is a theater-type test in which commercials are embedded in television shows. Audience members indicate brand attitude as preference for brands should they win a basket of free items. Because they are asked this same question before and after exposure, attitude change scores can be determined. While this is a significant improvement over post-only attitude measurement, there is still the pesky problem of the very artificial setting and manner in which these TV ads are viewed. First, they are not on TV, and most of us rarely watch TV with a few hundred other people, knowing that we are supposed to pay attention.

10.   John Philip Jones, "Advertising Pre-Testing: Will Europe Follow America's Lead?" *Commercial Communications*, June 1997, 21–26.

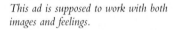

EXHIBIT 7.25

EXHIBIT 7.26

This ad is supposed to work with both images and feelings.

Words and arguments are not what makes this ad work.

Feelings and Emotions. Advertisers have always had a special interest in feelings and emotions. Ever since the "atmospheric" ads of the 1920s, there has been the belief that feelings may be more important than thoughts as a reaction to ads. Recent research by business professor Michel Pham and others[11] have shown that feelings have three distinct properties that makes them very powerful in reactions to advertisements and the advertised goods and services: (1) Consumers monitor and access feelings very quickly—consumers often know how they feel before they know what they think; (2) there is much more agreement in how consumers feel about ads and brands than in what they think about them; and (3) feelings are very good predictors of thoughts. This research adds a great deal of support to the argument that, in many ways, feelings are more important than thoughts when it comes to advertising. It also appears that ads that use feelings produce stronger and more lasting effects than those that try to persuade by thought alone. For example, the way a consumer feels about the imagery in the ads in Exhibits 7.25 and 7.26 may be far more important than what they say they think about them.

Method: Resonance Tests. In a **resonance test** the goal is to determine to what extent the message resonates or rings true with target-audience members.[12] The question becomes: Does this ad match consumers' own experiences? Does it produce an affinity reaction? Do consumers who view it say, "Yeah, that's right; I feel just like that" (Exhibit 7.27)? Do consumers read the ad and make it their own?[13] The method is pretty much the same as a communication test. Consumers see an ad in a group several times, and then discuss it. It can be conducted in-house by agency planners and researchers or "sent out" to a research supplier. How do you feel about this ad? How does it make you feel?

11.   Michel Tuan Pham, Joel B. Cohen, John W. Pracejus, and G. David Hughes, "Affect Monitoring and the Primacy of Feelings in Judgment," *Journal of Consumer Research*, vol. 28 (September 2001), 167–188.

12.   David Glen Mick and Claus Buhl, "A Meaning-Based Model of Advertising Experiences," *Journal of Consumer Research*, vol. 19 (December 1992), 317–338.

13.   Stuart J. Agres, Julie A. Edell, and Tony M. Dubitsky, eds., *Emotion in Advertising* (Westport, Conn.: Quorum Books, 1990). See especially Chapters 7 and 8.

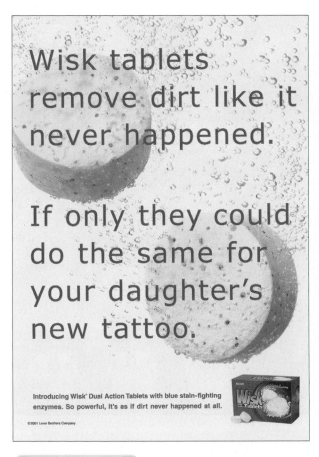

Some ads are judged by their resonance, or how true they ring. http://www.wisk.com

Method: Frame-by-Frame Tests. Frame-by-frame tests are usually employed for ads where the emotional component is seen as key, although they may also be used to obtain thought listing as well. These tests typically work by getting consumers to turn dials (like/dislike) while viewing television commercials in a theater setting. The data from these dials are then collected, averaged, and later superimposed over the commercial for the researchers in the form of a line graph. The height of the line reflects the level of interest in the ad. The high points in the line represent periods of higher interest in the ad, and the dips show where the audience had less interest in that particular point of the ad. While some research companies do ask consumers what they were thinking or feeling at certain points along the trace, and sometimes these responses are diagnostic, others do not. In those cases (such as the one shown in Exhibit 7.28), what the trace line really does then is measure the levels of interest at each specific moment in the execution—it does not explain whether or why consumers' reactions were positive or negative. The downside of frame-by-frame tests is that they involve somewhat higher costs than other methods, and there are some validity concerns in that you are asking consumers to do something they do not normally do while watching television. On the other hand, the method has some fans. It is sexy; it impresses clients.

There is a lot of current interest in developing better measures of the feelings and emotions generated by advertising.[14] This has included better paper-and-pencil measures as well as dial-turning devices. Assessment of feelings evoked by ads is becoming much more important goal of the advertising industry.

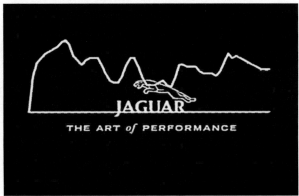

Here consumers' interest levels are measured while they watch an ad in real time.

14.   Ibid.

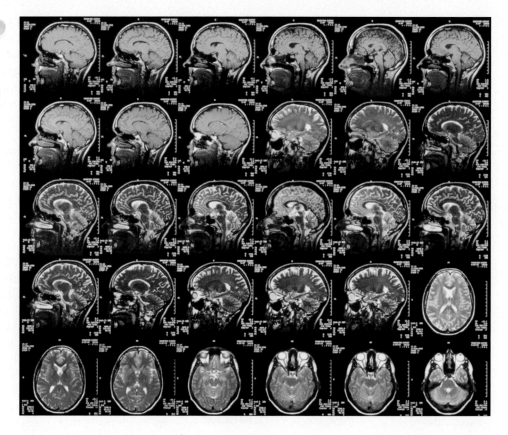

Physiological Changes. Every few years there is renewed interest in the technology of **physiological assessment** of advertising. Then, just as surely, the excitement falls way. Most recently, advances in brain imaging have again raised hopes of understanding how the human mind actually processes advertisements. At this point most of the work involves PT scans, a procedure where subjects breathe or otherwise ingest radioactive isotopes and then are scanned by a sensing device in real time to see how those isotopes are used by the brain, or Magnetic Resonance Imaging (MRI). The idea is to see which parts "light up" during exposure to various stimuli, or during certain tasks, and to understand what is happening when they light up. (Exhibit 7.29 shows MRI testing.) But at least at this point understanding of actual process—beyond isolating the activity in certain parts of the brain known to be involved in certain types of processing—has been promising, but still generally elusive. Practical applications to advertising appear at the level of a better basic understanding of the human mind, which is valuable in and of itself. Actual common use in copy research seems distant and unlikely.

The reasons for the recurring infatuation have to do with our general cultural fascination with science and technology, and the fairly reasonable belief that ads that really affect consumers must affect them at the physiological level. So, technologies come and go that seek to capture changes in the bodies of people exposed to ads. Before all the excitement about PT scans and MRIs, this was typically assessed by eye movement tracking. Dimensions measured by lie-detector-like devices such as skin conductivity, respiration, and pulse have also been employed, but proven disappointing. Other older brain electrical-activity tests proved impractical even at the basic level in that it was very hard to separate "noise" from "signal." Bottom line: None of these technologies has, as of yet, proven to be of much practical value. But again, any increase in basic knowledge of how the mind uses information and deals with more complex texts could be of great value whether or not it is ever used in actual advertising and integrated brand communication research.

Method: Eye Tracking. Eye-tracking systems have been developed to monitor eye movements across print ads. With one such system, respondents wear a goggle-like device that records (on a computer system) pupil dilations, eye movements, and length of time each sector of an advertisement is viewed.

Method: Voice-Response Analysis. The idea with **voice-response analysis**, another medium-tech research procedure, is that inflections in the voice when discussing an ad indicate excitement and other physiological states. In a typical application, a subject is asked to respond to a series of ads. These responses are tape-recorded and then computer-analyzed. Deviations from a flat response are claimed to be meaningful.

All physiological measures suffer from the same drawbacks. While we may be able to detect a physiological response to an advertisement, there is no way to determine whether the response is to the ad or the product, or which part of the advertisement was responsible for the response. In some sense, even the positive-negative dimension is obscured. Without being able to correlate specific effects with other dimensions of an ad, physiological measures are of minimal benefit.

Since the earliest days of advertising, there has been a fascination with physiological measurement. Advertising's fascination with science is obvious, with early attempts at physiological measurement being far more successful as a sales tool than as a way to actually gauge ad effectiveness. There is something provocative about scientists (sometimes even in white lab coats) wiring people up; it seems so precise and legitimate. Unfortunately—or fortunately, depending on your perspective—these measures tell us little beyond the simple degree of arousal attributable to an ad. For most advertisers, this minimal benefit doesn't justify the expense and intrusion involved with physiological measurement.

Behavioral Intent. This is essentially what consumers say they intend to do. If, after exposure to Brand X's advertising, consumers' stated intent to purchase Brand X goes up, there is some reason to believe that the tested advertising had something to do with it. Of course, we all know the problem with intended behavior: It's a poor substitute for actual behavior. Think about it: You really intended to call your mom, put the check in the mail, "I'll call you," and all those other things we say and maybe mean at the time. But it just didn't work out that way. The same thing is true when these are the criteria for testing consumer response to advertising. On a relative basis (say, percentage who intend to buy Pepsi versus percentage who intend to buy Coke, or at least who tell some researcher that), these measures can be meaningful and helpful, particularly if the changes are really large. Beyond that, don't take them to the bank.

Method: Pilot Testing. Before committing to the expense of a major campaign, advertisers sometimes test their messages in the marketplace via **pilot testing**. Pilots are television episodes for new shows the networks are considering putting on the air. They have the advantage of having never been seen by the research audience and thus provide both a good cover story and the lack of spillover feelings from a familiar show to the ads. There are three major types of pilot testing. **Split-transmission** (often on cable television systems) is where different signals (or ads) can be sent to different neighborhoods or households. This allows testing of two different versions of an advertisement through direct transmission to two separate samples of similar households. This method provides exposure in a natural setting for heightened realism. Factors such as frequency of transmission and timing of transmission can be carefully controlled. The advertisements are then compared on all sorts of measures, but predominantly behavioral intent.

Method: Internet Experiments. As described earlier, in **Internet experiments** subjects come or are recruited to a Web site, where they are assigned to different experimental conditions. There have been many things studied in this emerging method, but a lot of industry focus so far has been on intent to buy or actual purchase.

4 Stage Three: Results. At this stage, the ads are already out in the world, and the advertisers are trying to assess whether or not they are working.

Method: Tracking Studies. Tracking studies are one of the most commonly used advertising and promotion research methods. Basically, they "track" the apparent effect of advertising and branded entertainment over time. They typically assess attitude change, knowledge, behavioral intent, and self-reported behavior. They assess the performance of advertisements before, during, or after the launch of an advertising campaign or branded entertainment. This type of advertising research is almost always conducted as a survey. Members of the target market are surveyed on a fairly regular basis to detect any changes. Any change in awareness, belief, or attitude is usually attributed (rightly or wrongly) to the advertising effort. Even though the participants are susceptible to other influences (e.g., news stories about the brand or category), these are fairly valuable tests because they do occur over time and provide ongoing assessment, rather than the one-time, one-shot approach of so many other methods. The method has been extended to even things like advertising within gaming, which presents new ethical issues given that most gamers are young (see Ethics Box). Their weakness resides largely in the meaningfulness of the specific measures. Sometimes attitudes shift a bit, but translate into no noticeable increase in sales and no return on investment (ROI).

Method: Direct Response. Direct response advertisements in print, the Internet, and broadcast media offer the audience the opportunity to place an inquiry or respond directly through a Web site, reply card, or toll-free phone number. These ads produce **inquiry/ direct response measures**. An example is displayed in Exhibit 7.30. These measures are quite straightforward in the sense that advertisements that generate a high number of inquiries or direct responses, compared to historical benchmarks, are deemed effective. Additional analyses may compare the

---

ETHICS

A New Frontier, An Old Controversy

When Madison Avenue came under fire for food advertising that could contribute to childhood obesity, it fired back with a 2004 study showing that kids were watching less broadcast television than they did a decade earlier.

The argument was simple. If kids were watching fewer hours of television, then they also were seeing fewer of the fast-food and packaged-food ads that had come under scrutiny amid rising childhood obesity rates.

"Kids today are playing more video games, watching more videos," said the author of one study that showed that the percentage of eighth, 10th, and 12th graders who watched four or more hours of television a day had been steadily dropping since 1991. "They have more screen time, but they see less ads."

That argument, though, could come back to haunt advertisers as they scramble now to chase the fast-growing in-game advertising market. By some estimates, the video game advertising business is expected to grow to as much as $1 billion by 2010, reaching an audience of at least 132 million gamers 13 years or older inside the United States.

With new ad-serving technology, new gaming consoles, and new metrics to measure when gamers notice a flickering soda billboard or stop at an in-game fast food restaurant, the market is considered prime to reach some of advertising's most prized consumers, men between the ages of 18 and 34.

For advertisers and health advocates, it also could reignite the debate about screen time, obesity rates, and who takes the blame. The television might be turned off, but the ratings firm Nielsen has reported that young men now spend an average of 12.5 hours each week engrossed in video games.

Sources: Ira Teinowitz, "Don't Blame Ads: Kids View Fewer Food Commercials," **Advertising Age**, June 14, 2004, p.10; Jessica Ramirez, "The New Ad Game; Advanced Technology Is Finally Allowing Advertisers to Get Inside Videogames Like Never Before," **Newsweek**, July 31, 2006, p. 42.

COST ACCOUNTING

Traditions & Innovations, 5e

To request your complimentary exam copy of *Cost Accounting: Traditions and Innovations*, 5e by Barfield, Raiborn, and Kinney (ISBN 0-324-18090-X), please fill out all information and...

❶ **Mail** this pre-addressed card, or

❷ **Fax** your request to **513-229-1027** or

❸ Go to the **Internet** at http://snapshot.swcollege.com

☐ Have a South-Western Publishing representative contact me.

Name _____
School _____
Address _____
City _____ State _____ Zip _____
Office Phone _____
Fax _____
E-mail Address _____
Would you like updates on our products by e-mail? ☐ Yes ☐ No
Office Hours _____
Text Currently in Use _____
Estimated Annual Enrollment _____
Adoption Decision Date _____
Probability of Text Change:
☐ Strong ☐ Moderate ☐ Unlikely
Type of Decision: ☐ Individual ☐ Committee

Adopters: You may be eligible for additional supporting resources. Available materials will vary by products/adoptions. Contact your South-Western representative for more information.

EXHIBIT 7.30

An ad like this allows for a very simple kind of advertising response management. When consumers call, click, or write, the advertiser knows.

number of inquiries or responses to the number of sales generated. For example, some print ads will use different 800 numbers for different versions of the ad so that the agency can compute which ad is generating more inquiries. These measures are not relevant for all types of advertising, however. Ads designed to have long-term image building or brand identity effects should not be judged using such short-term response measures.

Internet response measures will be discussed in more detail in Chapter 16. With the Internet, various measures of drill-down, click-through, and actual purchase are employed. Again, there will be more on this in Chapter 15.

Method: Estimating Sales Derived from Advertising. Other advertisers really want to see evidence that the new ads will actually get people to do something: generally, to buy their product. It is, to some, the gold standard. But for reasons explained earlier, there are so many things that can affect sales that the use of actual sales as a measure of advertising effectiveness is considered inherently flawed, but not flawed enough not to be used. Here is a place where advertising and promotion are really different. In the case of the more easily and precisely tracked effects of promotions, some integrated brand promotions, and some sales data collected via the Internet, sales are the gold standard. That's because you can actually isolate the effect of the promotion, or come pretty close to isolating it. In the case of media advertising, statistical models are employed to try to isolate the effect of advertising on sales. Work by Dominique Hanssens, a marketing professor at the University of California at Los Angeles, has demonstrated that in some industries, such as automotive, very sophisticated and fairly time-intensive modeling can isolate advertising effects over time, but these powerful models are underemployed by industry and require more time, data, and expertise than many companies have at their disposal. Results generally indicate that advertising has its greatest impact on sales early in the product life cycle, or when a new version or model or other innovation is made. After that, advertising loses steam. Sometimes a host of other variables that might also affect sales, from the weather (say you represent a theme park) to competing advertising, are factored into these mathematical models.

Another downside is that these models are constructed long after the fact, long after the ad campaign to be assessed has been in place, and sales data have come in. But if the model is strong (robust) enough, it will be applicable to many situations. Behavioral data are sometimes derived from test markets, situations where the advertising is tested in a few select geographic areas before its wider application. While expensive, these tests can be very telling. Ideally, measures of actual behavior would come from tightly controlled field experiments. It's just that meaningfully controlled field experiments are incredibly difficult and expensive, and thus very rare in real advertising and IBP practice. The area of greatest hope for those who believe real behavior is the best test of advertising effectiveness is the use of the Internet for experiments, although that is still in its early stages; there have been some very promising and successful results (particularly in consumer electronics and software), but the jury is still out on a more widespread application.

Method: All-in-One Single-Source Data. With the advent of universal product codes (UPCs) on product packages and the proliferation of cable television, research firms are now able to engage in *single-source research* to document the behavior of individuals—or, more typically, households—in a respondent pool by tracking their behavior from the television set to the checkout counter. **Single–source data** provide information from individual households about brand purchases, coupon use, and television advertising exposure by combining grocery store scanner data with TV-viewing data from monitoring devices attached to the households' televisions. With these different types of data combined, a better assessment can be made of the real impact of advertising and promotion on consumers' actual purchases. This is not an inexpensive method of assessment, and it still remains difficult (if not impossible) to know exactly what specific aspects of advertising had what effects on consumers. The best-known supplier of this type of testing is **IRI BehaviorScan**.

Account Planning versus Advertising Research.

Jon Steel, director of account planning and vice chairman of Goodby, Silverstein and Partners—its clients include Anheuser-Busch, the California Milk Processors Board ("Got Milk?"), Nike, Porsche, and Hewlett-Packard—has called account planning "the biggest thing to hit American advertising since Doyle Dane Bernbach's Volkswagen campaign."[15] That is stretching it a bit, but account planning is a big story in the industry. What is it? Well, good question. (See Exhibit 7.31.)

You will hear a lot about **account planning**. It's quite the term, and has been for a decade or so. It is defined in contrast to traditional advertising research. We've mentioned this before, but it probably deserves repeating. It differs mostly in three ways. First, in terms of organization, agencies that use this system typically assign an "account planner" to work cooperatively with the account executive on a given client's business. Rather than depending on a separate research department's occasional involvement, the agency assigns the planner to a single client (just like an advertising executive) to stay with the projects on a continuous basis—even though, in this organizational scheme, there is typically an account planning department. In the more traditional system, the research department would get involved from time to time as needed, and members of the research department would work on several different clients' advertising. (There are several variations on this theme.)

Another difference is that this organizational structure puts research in a different, more prominent role. In this system, researchers (or "planners") seem to be more actively involved throughout the entire advertising process and

EXHIBIT 7.31

Much ado is made about the account planner versus traditional advertising research.

15.   Jon Steel, *Truth, Lies & Advertising: The Art of Account Planning* (New York: John Wiley & Sons, 1998), jacket.

seem to have a bigger impact on it as well. (Of course, some of the difference is more agency self-promotion than reality.) Agencies that practice "account planning" tend to do more developmental and less evaluative research. Third, "planning agencies" tend to do more qualitative and naturalistic research than their more traditional counterparts. But these differences, too, seem fairly exaggerated—even though Jay Chiat called planning "the best new business tool ever invented."[16] There is another, more cynical side to this story: Many advertising agencies have decided that they simply cannot afford the cost of a full-time research staff. It's cheaper and maybe even better to outsource the work. But a quieter and more devious way of downsizing (or eliminating these expensive departments) is to go to the "account planning" system, in which a researcher will always be a part of the team.

One Last Thought on Message Testing.

None of these methods are perfect. There are challenges to reliability, validity, trustworthiness, and meaningfulness with all of them. Advertisers sometimes think that consumers watch new television commercials the way they watch new, eagerly awaited feature films, or that they listen to radio spots like they listen to a symphony, or read magazine ads like a Steinbeck novel. We watch TV while we work, talk, eat, and study; we use it as a night light, background noise, and babysitter. Likewise, we typically thumb through magazines very, very quickly. While these traditional methods of message testing have their strengths, more naturalistic methods are clearly recommended. Still, it would be a mistake to throw the baby out with the bathwater; good and appropriate behavioral science can produce better advertising.

What We Need.

Advertising and integrated brand promotion research could do with some change. The way we think about ads and advertising is certainly changing. The move to a visual advertising style has also put into question the appropriateness of a set of tests that focus on the acceptance of message claims, as well as verbatim remembrance of words (copy). Also, the Internet has significantly challenged and changed the whole concept of audience, response and associated measures. It's a brave new world.

The account planning way of thinking merges the research and the brand management business. Good research can play an important role in this; it can be very helpful or an enormous hindrance, as advertisers are realizing more and more. Top-down delivered marketing is not considered realistic by many in the industry. With this new realization comes new terms. One is the idea of account planning as a substitute for the traditional research efforts of an agency. There has been a very recent but very significant turn in thinking about research and its role in advertising, promotion, and brand management.

As you can see, advertising and promotion research is used to judge advertising, but who judges advertising research, and how? First of all, not enough people, in our opinion, question and judge advertising research. Research is not magic or truth and it should never be confused with such. Issues of reliability, validity, trustworthiness, and meaningfulness should be seriously considered when research is used to make important decisions. Otherwise, you're just using research as a ritual that you know has limited meaning. Research can be a wonderful tool when applied correctly, but is routinely poorly matched to the real-world situation.

16.   Ibid., p. 42.

SUMMARY

 1 Explain the purposes served by and methods used in developmental advertising research.

Advertising and promotion research can serve many purposes in the development of a campaign. There is no better way to generate fresh ideas for a campaign than to listen carefully to the customer. Qualitative research involving customers is essential for fostering fresh thinking about a brand. Audience definition and profiling are fundamental to effective campaign planning and rely on advertising research. In the developmental phase, advertisers use diverse methods for gathering information. Focus groups, projective techniques, the ZMET, and field work are trusted research methods that directly involve consumers and aid in idea generation and concept testing.

 2 Identify sources of secondary data that can aid the IBP planning effort.

Because information is such a critical resource in the decision-making process, several sources of data are widely used. Internal company sources such as strategic marketing plans, research reports, customer service records, and sales data provide a wealth of information on consumer tastes and preferences. Government sources generate a wide range of census and labor statistics, providing key data on trends in population, consumer spending, employment, and immigration. Commercial data sources provide advertisers with a wealth of information on household consumers. Professional publications share insider information on industry trends and new research. Finally, the Internet is a revolutionary research tool that delivers rich data at virtually no cost. In particular, advertisers can obtain sophisticated research data at thousands of consumer- and brand-based online community sites.

 3 Discuss the purposes served by and methods used in copy research.

Copy research (evaluative research) aims to judge the effectiveness of actual ads. Advertisers and clients try to

determine if audiences "get" the joke of an ad or retain key knowledge concerning the brand. Tracking changes in audience attitudes, feelings and emotions, behavior, and physiological response is important in gauging the overall success of an ad, and various methods are employed before and after the launch of a campaign to assess the impact on audiences. Communication tests, recall testing, pilot testing, and the thought-listing technique are a few of the methods that try to measure the persuasiveness of a message. Some agencies, attempting to bypass the high cost and inconclusive results of research, substitute account planning for traditional advertising and promotion research. Advocates of this trend believe an account planning system merges the best in research and brand management.

 4 Discuss the basic research methods used after ads are in the marketplace.

Once an ad campaign has reached the marketplace, agencies and firms turn to results-oriented research to try to determine whether the ad has succeeded—whether, quite simply, the ad prompted consumers to buy the product or service. One of the most commonly employed methods of results-oriented research is the use of tracking studies to measure the apparent affect of advertising over time. Another long-standing method is the use of reply cards or toll-free numbers, which can track the direct responses of consumers to a particular campaign. Technology also is producing new results-oriented techniques. The development of universal product codes, combined with television monitoring devices, allows advertisers in some instances to track household consumption patterns from the television to the checkout lane. Researchers also are evaluating sophisticated models to more accurately track estimated sales from advertising, what has been a painstaking and expensive endeavor.

KEY TERMS

concept test
focus group
projective techniques
dialogue balloons
story construction
sentence and picture completion
Zaltman Metaphor Elicitation Technique (ZMET)
field work
embedded
coolhunt
normative test scores
communication test

thought listing, or cognitive response analysis
recall tests
recognition
recognition tests
Starch Readership Services
implicit memory measures
surveys
attitude study
ARS Persuasion Method
resonance test
frame-by-frame test
physiological assessment

eye-tracking systems
voice-response analysis
pilot testing
split-transmission
split-run distribution
split-list experiment
Internet experiment
tracking studies
direct response
inquiry/direct response measures
single-source data
IRI BehaviorScan
account planning

QUESTIONS

1.   Read the chapter opening and list two important lessons that can be learned from Coca-Cola's advertising and promotion research blunder with New Coke.

2.   What historic factors led to the development and prominence of advertising and promotion research departments during the mid-1900s?

3.   Focus groups are one of the advertising researcher's most versatile tools. Describe the basic features of focus group research that could lead to inappropriate generalizations about the preferences of the target audience.

4.   ZMET is a technique that advertisers may use in place of focus groups. What aspects of ZMET and focus groups are similar? What particular features of ZMET could foster richer understanding of consumers' motives than is typically achieved with focus groups?

5.   List the sources and uses of secondary data. What are the benefits of secondary data? What are the limitations?

6.   Identify issues that could become sources of conflict between account managers and advertising creatives in the message-testing process. What could go wrong if people in an ad agency take the position that what the client wants, the client gets?

7.   Criteria for judging ad effectiveness include "getting it," cognitive residue, knowledge, attitude change, feelings and emotions, physiological changes, and behavior. Identify specific evaluative advertising research methods that could be used to test an ad's impact on any of these dimensions.

8.   How would you explain the finding that ads that achieve high recall scores don't always turn out to be ads that do a good job in generating sales? Are there some features of ads that make them memorable but could also turn off consumers and dissuade them from buying the brand? Give an example from your experience.

9.   What is single-source research, and what is its connection to the universal product codes (UPCs) one finds on nearly every product in the grocery store?

10. Explain the industry trend of substituting account planning for traditional advertising and promotion research. Why do some agency directors claim that this trend is the biggest thing in advertising since the famous Bernbach Volkswagen campaign? Do you tend to believe the hype surrounding this trend, or are you cynical that forces of downsizing are driving it? Explain your reasoning.

EXPERIENTIAL EXERCISES

1.   Working in the same small teams, create a focus group study for the hypothetical method campaign, then conduct the study using members of another class team as the focus group. Prepare a report outlining the key findings of the focus group, including how your findings were similar to or different from the lifestyle research conducted in the first exercise. Also report on what difficulties or challenges, if any, your team encountered in conducting a focus group study—and how that might have influenced the outcome.

2.   Advertisers increasingly are using metaphor associations in promotional development, tapping into the powerful organizing and expressive function that metaphor serves in the human brain. Test this method on yourself using each of these well-known brands or products discussed in the chapter: Coca-Cola, M&Ms, and milk. For each example, consider how you would visually represent your experiences with that brand or product, and then find photographs or graphics from magazines that best convey that experience.

3.   The chapter identified several online sources that provide a variety of demographic information compiled by the government. This kind of widely available, no-cost information can be a boon to advertisers—particularly small businesses that might otherwise be unable to afford information compiled by commercial data vendors. Develop a demographic portrait of the city or metro area where your school is located using online government resources. What are your primary findings? How accurate do you think this demographic snapshot is? What brands or products do you think would find this community to be attractive? Why?

CHAPTER 8

After reading and thinking about this chapter, you will be able to do the following:

1

Describe the basic components of an advertising plan.

2

Compare and contrast two fundamental approaches for setting advertising objectives.

3

Explain various methods for setting advertising budgets.

4

Discuss the role of the agency in formulating an advertising plan.

Introductory Scenario: Polishing the Apple (Again and Again).

Advertising does not exist in a vacuum. Advertising and IBP are most often conceived to serve a business purpose, and the stakes are always high. Whether you are a small business investing $50,000 in a local ad campaign or a global marketer investing hundreds of millions of dollars around the world, you want your advertising to serve its purpose. All parties involved in the effort must be aware of things like goals, strategies and timetables. There will need to be a plan.

When it comes to high-stakes advertising campaigns, no one does it better than Apple. Let's consider Apple's launch of the iPhone in 2007. After a series of game-changing market successes like candy-colored iMacs (per Exhibit 8.1), launched in 1998, and later the ubiquitous iPods + iTunes, it was time for another act in the remarkable evolution of the company. The next big thing from Apple would be iPhone, which promised to revolutionize the cell phone business, just as iPods + iTunes had revolutionized the music business.[1] But the scale of the potential opportunity for iPhone made Apple's success with iPod seem small by comparison. While Apple sold 100 million iPods from 2001 to 2007, every year the cell phone market represents one billion units sold. Analysts projected that iPhone could quickly become a $10 billion business for Apple.[2] Now that's high stakes.

The iPhone was scheduled to be available for purchase on June 29, 2007. But the launch campaign began months before and followed a plan much like previous Apple launches. It all started at Macworld in January of 2007 when Steve Jobs pulled an iPhone from the pocket of his blue jeans, and the adoring audience gave him a standing ovation. Then a teaser ad, created by long-time Apple partner TBWA/Chiat/Day, ran during the Academy Awards broadcast. At the end of this ad the iPhone appeared ever so briefly, followed by the word "Hello" and the line "Coming in June." This commercial explained nothing about the product and no additional ads appeared for several months. If the buzz was to build, it would have to build on its own. And sure enough, it did.

Apple's less-is-more advertising approach fueled discussions and speculation about its new product in all media venues. As one cell phone analyst from the Yankee Group exclaimed, "This is all a big part of the branding exercise for these guys. We're pawns in the Apple brand game."[3] One should conclude that a little

EXHIBIT 8.1

Apple's launch of the iMac in 1998 used billboards like this one to show off its chic new Internet appliances.

1.   Nick Wingfield, "Great Expectations Juice Up Apple's Trade Show," *Wall Street Journal,* January 9, 2007, B1, B8; Peter Burrows and Roger Crockett, "Turning Cell Phones on Their Ear," *BusinessWeek,* January 22, 2007, 40, 41.
2.   Peter Burrows, "How Big Will iPhone Be?" *BusinessWeek,* June 18, 2007, 43.
3.   Paul Thomasch, "Apple Builds Hype for iPhone with Less," *ScientificAmerican.com,* June 20, 2007.

bit of mystery and ambiguity can be a very good thing in the early stages of an ad campaign. And of course a little bit of mystery is a perfect way to foster person-to-person buzz, both around the water cooler and over the Internet. Bloggers went crazy speculating about the virtues of iPhone, and by March of 2007 more than a million e-mail requests for information had been sent to AT&T, the exclusive U.S. carrier for iPhone.[4] When June finally rolled around, most cell phone users were aware of iPhone, traffic at the Web site continued to build, and surveys showed that on the order of 19 million consumers were very interested in purchasing an iPhone, even with its projected $500-plus pricing.[5] The advertising plan was definitely working . . .

As June 29 approached, Steve Jobs and his team had done their job in stimulating demand for iPhone. Their next big test would be around delivering the goods, literally. It would be a big test, dwarfing anything attempted previously by Apple. The plan was to have 3 million units ready for sale on June 29. But in terms of functionality, the iPhone is a far more complex device than an iPod, with plenty of possibilities for glitches, recalls, and disappointed consumers. Would Apple prove as skillful in their manufacturing and logistics as they were in their advertising and brand-building? Time will tell.

As a CEO with rock-star status, Steve Jobs is constantly in the media limelight and is commonly praised for his marketing savvy. Comments like "Better now than he's ever been—and he's always been good," and "What Jobs does is he focuses like a laser on what makes the thing cool," are routine.[6] But Steve Jobs knows that he's not in the thing alone, and he has always assigned credit elsewhere, especially when it comes to his advertising agency—TBWA/Chiat/Day of Venice, California. Said Jobs: "Creating great advertising, like creating great products, is a team effort. I am lucky to work with the best talent in the industry."[7] Indeed, it would be impossible to launch campaigns like those we have seen for iMac, iPod and iPhone (compare also Exhibits 8.2 and 8.3) without great teamwork between agency and client.

We have merely scratched the surface in describing all that is involved in a campaign for a significant product introduction like iPhone; however, we hope this

EXHIBIT 8.2

The elegant iPhone extended Apple's track record of high-profile product launches.

EXHIBIT 8.3

Very early on, the folks at Apple learned that the interactivity of the Web makes it the perfect means for anticipating and answering questions about the technical features of its products.

4.   Ibid.
5.   Amol Sharma and Nick Wingfield, "Is iPhone AT&T's Magic Bullet?" *Wall Street Journal,* June 15, 2007, B4.
6.   Thomasch, "Apple Builds Hype for iPhone with Less."
7.   Bradley Johnson, "Jobs Orchestrates Ad Blitz for Apple's New iMac PC," *Advertising Age,* August 10, 1998, 6.

example gives you a taste for the complexity that can be involved in executing a comprehensive advertising and IBP effort. You don't go out and spend millions of dollars promoting a new product that is vital to the success of a firm without giving the entire endeavor considerable forethought. Such an endeavor will call for a plan. As you will see in this chapter, Jobs, Apple, and TWBA Chiat/Day followed the process of building an advertising effort based on several key features of the advertising plan. An advertising plan is the culmination of the planning effort needed to deliver effective advertising and IBP.

The Advertising Plan and Its Marketing Context. An ad plan

should be a direct extension of a firm's marketing plan. As suggested in the closing section of Chapter 6, one device that can be used to explicitly connect the marketing plan with the advertising plan is the statement of a brand's value proposition. A statement of what the brand is supposed to stand for in the eyes of the target segment derives from the firm's marketing strategy, and will guide all ad-planning activities. The advertising plan, including all integrated brand promotion, is a subset of the larger marketing plan. The IBP component must be built into the plan in a seamless and synergistic way. Everything has to work together, whether the plan is for Apple or for a business with far fewer resources. And as Steve Jobs has said, there is no substitute for good teamwork between agency and client in the development of compelling marketing and advertising plans.

An **advertising plan** specifies the thinking, tasks, and timetable needed to conceive and implement an effective advertising effort. We particularly like Apple examples because they always illustrate the wide array of options that can be deployed in creating interest and communicating the value proposition for brands like iPod or iPhone. Jobs and his agency choreograph public relations activities, promotions and events, cooperative advertising, broadcast advertising, billboard advertising, Web site development, and more as part of their launches. Advertising planners should review all the options before selecting an integrated set to communicate with the target audience.

For a variety of reasons that will become increasingly clear to you, it is critical to think beyond traditional broadcast media when considering the best way to break through the clutter of the modern marketplace and get a message out to your customer. Miami's Crispin Porter + Bogusky is another agency that has built its reputation on finding novel ways to register clients' messages with consumers. As you will learn in Chapter 10, one of CP+B's principles for success in campaign planning is to consider literally everything as media. When you adopt the philosophy that *everything* is media, it's much easier to surround the consumer with a message and make a deep connection on behalf of the brand.

Exhibit 8.4 shows the components of an advertising plan. It should be noted that there is a great deal of variation in advertising plans from advertiser to advertiser. Our discussion of the advertising plan will focus on the seven major components shown in Exhibit 8.4: the introduction, situation analysis, objectives, budgeting, strategy, execution, and evaluation. Each component is discussed in the following sections.

Introduction. The introduction of an advertising plan consists of an executive summary and an overview. An executive summary, typically two paragraphs to a page in length, is offered to state the most important aspects of the plan. This is the take-away; that is, it is what the reader should remember from the plan. It is the essence of the plan.

As with many documents, an overview is also customary. An overview ranges in length from a paragraph to a few pages. It sets out what is to be covered, and it structures the context. All plans are different, and some require more setup than others. Don't underestimate the benefit of a good introduction. It's where you can make or lose a lot of points with your boss or client.

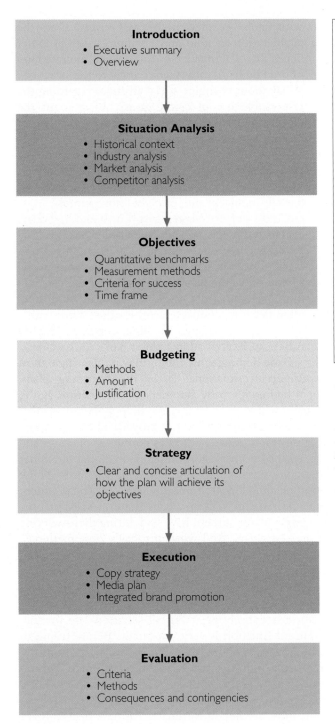

Introduction
- Executive summary
- Overview

Situation Analysis
- Historical context
- Industry analysis
- Market analysis
- Competitor analysis

Objectives
- Quantitative benchmarks
- Measurement methods
- Criteria for success
- Time frame

Budgeting
- Methods
- Amount
- Justification

Strategy
- Clear and concise articulation of how the plan will achieve its objectives

Execution
- Copy strategy
- Media plan
- Integrated brand promotion

Evaluation
- Criteria
- Methods
- Consequences and contingencies

EXHIBIT 8.4

The advertising plan.

EXHIBIT 8.5

What is the image this ad establishes for the American Express card? How is this image a response to the company's situation analysis? Link your answer to a discussion of market segmentation and product positioning. Who is reached by this ad and how does reaching this segment fit into the overall strategy for American Express?

Situation Analysis. When someone asks you to explain a decision you've made, you may say something like, "Well, here's the situation. . . ." In what follows, you try to distill the situation down to the most important points and how they are connected in order to explain why you made the decision. An ad plan **situation analysis** is no different. It is where the client and agency lay out the most important factors that define the situation, and then explain the importance of each factor.

A lengthy list of potential factors (e.g., demographic, technology, social and cultural, economic, and political/regulatory) can define a situation analysis. Some books offer long but incomplete lists. We prefer to play it straight with you: There is no complete or perfect list of situational factors. The idea is not to be exhaustive or encyclopedic when writing a plan, but to be smart in choosing the few important factors that really describe the situation, and then explain how the factors relate to the advertising task at hand. Market segmentation and consumer behavior research provide the organization with insights that can be used for a situation analysis, but ultimately you have to decide which of the many factors are really the most critical to address in your advertising. This is the essence of smart management.

Let's say you represent American Express. How would you define the firm's current advertising situation? What are the most critical factors? What image has prior advertising, like that in Exhibit 8.5, established for the card? Would you consider the changing view of prestige cards to be critical? What about the problem of hanging onto an exclusive image while trying to increase your customer base by having

Want to save 10-20% on FedEx Express?

Let's say, 3 packages a day.

Times 5 days a week.

That's $1,500 a year just by using one of these.

Only the Corporate Cards for Small Business get you savings at FedEx Express, Mobil? Hertz, Hilton and Quest? What can we do for your business?

Call 1-800-SUCCESS
americanexpress.com/smallbusiness

EXHIBIT 8.6

Here we see American Express offering a specific package of benefits to a well-defined target segment. Obviously, the folks at AMEX understand STP marketing (explained in Chapter 6).

your cards accepted at discount stores? Does the proliferation of gold and platinum cards by other banks rate as critical? Do the diverse interest rates offered by bank cards seem critical to the situation? What about changing social attitudes regarding the responsible use of credit cards? What about the current high level of consumer debt?

Think about how credit card marketing is influenced by the economic conditions of the day and the cultural beliefs about the proper way to display status. In the 1980s, it was acceptable for advertisers to tout the self-indulgent side of plastic (for example, MasterCard's slogan "MasterCard, I'm bored"). Today, charge and credit card ads often point out just how prudent it is to use your card for the right reasons. Now, instead of just suggesting you use your plastic to hop off to the islands when you feel the first stirrings of a bout with boredom, credit card companies often detail functional benefits for their cards with a specific market segment in mind, as reflected by the American Express ad in Exhibit 8.6.

Basic demographic trends may be the single most important situational factor in advertising plans. Whether it's baby boomers or Generation X, Y, or Z, where the people are is usually where the sales are. As the population age distribution varies with time, new markets are created and destroyed. The baby boom generation of post–World War II disproportionately dictates consumer offerings and demand simply because of its size. As the boomers age, companies that offer the things needed by tens of millions of aging boomers will have to devise new appeals. Think of the consumers of this generation needing long-term health care, geriatric products, and things to amuse themselves in retirement. Will they have the disposable income necessary to have the bountiful lifestyle many of them have had during their working years? After all, they aren't the greatest savers. And what of today's 20-somethings? When do you tend to model your parents? When do you look to put space between yourself and your parents? Knowing which generation(s) you are targeting is critical in your situation analysis.

Historical Context. No situation is entirely new, but all situations are unique. Just how a firm arrived at the current situation is very important. Before trying to design Apple's iPhone campaign, an agency should certainly know a lot about the history of all the principal players, the industry, the brand, the corporate culture, critical moments in the company's past, its big mistakes and big successes. Long relationships between client and agency, as between Apple and TBWA Chiat/Day, will obviously help with this, but most are not so fortunate. All new decisions are situated in a firm's history, and an agency should be diligent in studying that history. For example, would an agency pitch new business to Green Giant without knowing something of the brand's history and the rationale behind the Green Giant character? The history of the Green Giant dates back decades, as suggested in Exhibit 8.7. The fact is that no matter what advertising decisions are made in the present, the past has a significant impact.

Apart from history's intrinsic value, sometimes the real business goal is to convince the client that the agency knows the client's business, its major concerns, and its corporate culture. A brief history of the company and brand are included in ad plans to demonstrate the thoroughness of the agency's research, the depth of its knowledge, and the scope of its concern.

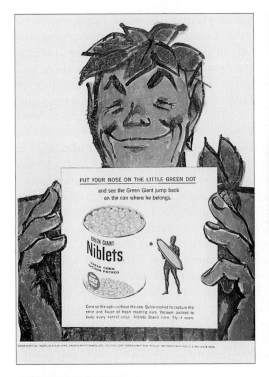

EXHIBIT 8.7

EXHIBIT 8.8

Knowing a brand's history can guide the development of future campaigns. Visit the Green Giant corporate site and read all about the history of the Green Giant character. He first appeared in advertising in 1928. How might this history determine future Green Giant ads? Is it time to ditch the Green Giant? Can you think of brands that made drastic changes in their popular icons? What might motivate a company to modernize or change an icon?

Pizzeria Uno built its business around the classic Chicago-style deep-dish pizza. But in a world gone mad with carb counting, the deep-dish pizza was bound to lose some appeal. Enter Uno Chicago Grill and Lemon Basil Salmon with just 7 net carbs. Can carb counters and deep-dish pizza lovers find a way to peacefully coexist? For Uno's sake, let's hope so.

Industry Analysis. An **industry analysis** is just that; it focuses on developments and trends within an entire industry and on any other factors that may make a difference in how an advertiser proceeds with an advertising plan. An industry analysis should enumerate and discuss the most important aspects of a given industry, including the supply side of the supply-demand equation. When great advertising overstimulates demand that can't be matched by supply, one can end up with lots of unhappy customers. This, of course, was a big concern for Steve Jobs in the days and weeks leading up to June 29, 2007.

No industry faces more dramatic trends and swings in consumers' tastes than the food business. In recent years the low-carb craze has challenged industry giants from Nestlé to Hershey Foods to H.J. Heinz Co. to McDonald's to come up with new products and reposition old ones to satisfy consumers' growing concerns about sugar and white flour. When your industry research tells you that 30 million Americans describe themselves as being on a low-carb diet, and another 100 million are expected to join them in a matter of months, it's time to reposition and reformulate.[8] It is hard to imagine the marketing and advertising plans of any food maker not giving some consideration to the carb issue as part of an analysis of their industry. As suggested by Exhibit 8.8, no one is immune.

8.   Stephanie Thompson, "Low-Carb Craze Blitzes Food Biz," *Advertising Age,* January 5, 2004, 1, 22.

Cable bills bite.

Total Home Bundle
DIRECTV® service, Home Phone and ZoomTown

$89 a month
for the first year*

• Over 140 digital TV channels
• Unlimited local & long distance calling
• Internet access to over 900 WiFi HotSpots

ASK US about a FREE upgrade
to a DVR or HD receiver

Time Warner's cable rates have risen
a painful 93% in the last ten years.*

Cincinnati Bell's Total Home Bundle
is the antidote to rising cable costs.

Call, click or come see us. 513-565-CBTV (2288)

Cincinnati Bell.com

EXHIBIT 8.9

Cincinnati Bell takes direct aim at the market share of a key competitor with a compelling visual element that works perfectly with its headline—Cable bills bite. The value proposition is based on packaging a bundle of services for one low monthly fee . . . perhaps the perfect antidote for cable bills that keep going up, up, and up.

Market Analysis. A **market analysis** complements the industry analysis, emphasizing the demand side of the equation. In a market analysis, an advertiser examines the factors that drive and determine the market for the firm's product or service. First, the advertiser needs to decide just exactly what the market is for the product. Most often, the market for a given good or service is simply defined as current users. The idea here is that consumers figure out for themselves whether they want the product or not and thus define the market for themselves, and for the advertiser. This approach has some wisdom to it. It's simple, easy to defend, and very conservative. Few executives get fired for choosing this market definition. However, it completely ignores those consumers who might otherwise be persuaded to use the product.

A market analysis commonly begins by stating just who the current users are, and (hopefully) why they are current users. Consumers' motivations for using one product or service but not another may very well provide the advertiser with the means toward a significant expansion of the entire market. If the entire pie grows, the firm's slice usually does as well. The advertiser's job in a market analysis is to find out the most important market factors and why they are so important. It is at this stage in the situation analysis that account planning can play an important role.

Competitor Analysis. Once the industry and market are studied and analyzed, attention turns to **competitor analysis**. Here an advertiser determines just exactly who the competitors are, discussing their strengths, weaknesses, tendencies, and any threats they pose. Think about that launch of iPhone back in 2007 and consider the long list of competitors who were watching Apple's every move. Cell phone providers like T-Mobile USA, Verizon Wireless, and Sprint were watching closely and preparing advertising plans of their own as responses to the iPhone threat. For example, executives at Verizon were confident that network quality was its strongest feature and planned to continue to emphasize this point after the iPhone debut.[9] Additionally, handset makers like Nokia, LG, Samsung, and Motorola all had to be drawing up plans for how they would counter this next smooth move by Steve Jobs.[10]

When competing companies go head-to-head trying to win customers' loyalty, one frequently sees advertisements using what we labeled in Chapter 6 as a competitive positioning strategy. An excellent illustration of this approach is featured in Exhibit 8.9. Here we see a regional telecom provider (Cincinnati Bell) taking on an arch rival, Time Warner. In conjunction with its partner, DirecTV, Cincinnati Bell is seeking to win over Time Warner's core customer, the cable subscriber. After all, it's pretty hard to argue with the premise that "Cable bills bite."

Objectives. Advertising objectives lay the framework for the subsequent tasks in an advertising plan and take many different forms. Objectives identify the goals of the advertiser in concrete terms. The advertiser, more often than not, has more than one objective for an ad campaign. An advertiser's objective may be (1) to increase consumer awareness of

9.   Sharma and Wingfield, "Is iPhone AT&T's Magic Bullet?"
10.   Alice Cuneo, "Telecoms Shore Up Defenses for iPhone Invasion," *Advertising Age,* June 4, 2007, 14.

EXHIBIT 8.10

The makers of Bose audio equipment have the philosophy that sound reproduction is a matter of science, so it follows that the best way to impress a consumer is to simply lay out the facts. Learn more about Dr. Amar Bose and the philosophy behind his company at http://www.bose.com.

EXHIBIT 8.11

The approach taken by Sony plugs into any air traveler's nightmare scenario: a screaming baby on a flight to Paris!

and curiosity about its brand, (2) to change consumers' beliefs or attitudes about its product, (3) to influence the purchase intent of its customers, (4) to stimulate trial use of its product or service, (5) to convert one-time product users into repeat purchasers, (6) to switch consumers from a competing brand to its brand, or (7) to increase sales. (Each of these objectives is discussed briefly in the following paragraphs.) The advertiser may have more than one objective at the same time. For example, a swimwear company may state its advertising objectives as follows: to maintain the company's brand image as the market leader in adult female swimwear and to increase revenue in this product line by 15 percent.

Creating or maintaining brand awareness is a fundamental advertising objective. Brand awareness is an indicator of consumer knowledge about the existence of the brand and how easily that knowledge can be retrieved from memory. For example, a market researcher might ask a consumer to name five insurance companies. **Top-of-the-mind awareness** is represented by the brand listed first. Ease of retrieval from memory is important because for many goods or services, ease of retrieval is predictive of market share.

This proved to be the case for Aflac (American Family Life Assurance Co.), an insurance company that used a determined duck quacking *aaa-flack* in its ad campaign as a means to building brand awareness. If you've seen these ads, we suspect that you'll never forget that duck. If you haven't seen them, you might be thinking that a duck as your primary spokesperson sounds pretty dopey. Maybe yes, maybe no, but that duck helped Aflac become a major player in the U.S. insurance market. Similarly, the Geico Gecko was so effective in winning attention for Geico Corp. that the chief marketing officer of rival Allstate Insurance has said, "I'd like to squash it."[11]

Creating, changing, or reinforcing attitudes is another important function of advertising, and thus makes for a common advertising objective. As we saw in Chapter 5, one way to go about changing people's attitudes is to give them information designed to alter their beliefs. There are many ways to approach this task. One way is exemplified by the Bose ad in Exhibit 8.10. Here we see an information-dense approach where a number of logical arguments are developed to shape beliefs regarding the QuietComfort 2 Noise-Cancelling Headphones. For the consumer willing to digest this complex, text-based ad, the arguments are likely to prove quite compelling. Conversely, one can let a picture tell the entire story, as in Exhibit 8.11. Here the approach depends on the visual imagery and the consumer's willingness to interpret the loudspeaker heads. Not a problem for anyone who has traveled coach class. The obvious serenity of the handsome young man wearing the Sony Noise-Canceling Headphones speaks for itself. One thus infers something

11.   Suzanne Vranica, "How a Gecko Shook Up Insurance Ads," *Wall Street Journal,* January 2, 2007, B1.

about Sony without any text. Whether through direct, logical arguments, or thought-provoking visual imagery, advertisements are frequently designed to deliver their objective of belief formation and attitude change.

Purchase intent is another popular criterion in setting objectives. Purchase intent is determined by asking consumers whether they intend to buy a product or service in the near future. The appeal of influencing purchase intent is that intent is closer to actual behavior, and thus closer to the desired sale, than attitudes are. While this makes sense, it does presuppose that consumers can express their intentions with a reasonably high degree of reliability. Sometimes they can, sometimes they cannot. Purchase intent, however, is fairly reliable as an indicator of relative intention to buy, and it is, therefore, a worthwhile advertising objective.

Trial usage reflects actual behavior and is commonly used as an advertising objective. Many times, the best that we can ask of advertising is to encourage the consumer to try our brand. At that point, the product or service must live up to the expectations created by our advertising. In the case of new products, stimulating trial usage is critically important. In the marketing realm, the angels sing when the initial purchase rate of a new product or service is high.

The **repeat purchase**, or conversion, objective is aimed at the percentage of consumers who try a new product and then purchase it a second time. A second purchase is reason for great rejoicing. The odds of long-term product success go way up when this percentage is high.

Brand switching is the last of the advertising objectives mentioned here. In some brand categories, switching is commonplace, even the norm. In others it is rare. When setting a brand-switching objective, the advertiser must neither expect too much, nor rejoice too much, over a temporary gain. Persuading consumers to switch brands can be a long and expensive task.

❷ Communications versus Sales Objectives. Some analysts argue that

as a single variable in a firm's overall marketing mix, it is not reasonable to set sales expectations for advertising when other variables in the mix might undermine the advertising effort or be responsible for sales in the first place. In fact, some advertising analysts argue that communications objectives are the *only* legitimate objectives for advertising. This perspective has its underpinnings in the proposition that advertising is but one variable in the marketing mix and cannot be held solely responsible for sales. Rather, advertising should be held responsible for creating awareness of a brand, communicating information about product features or availability, or developing a favorable attitude that can lead to consumer preference for a brand. All of these outcomes are long term and based on communications impact.

There are some major benefits to maintaining a strict communications perspective in setting advertising objectives. First, by viewing advertising as primarily a communications effort, marketers can consider a broader range of advertising strategies. Second, they can gain a greater appreciation for the complexity of the overall communications process. Designing an integrated communications program with sales as the sole objective neglects aspects of message design, media choice, public relations, or sales force deployment that should be effectively integrated across all phases of a firm's communication efforts. Using advertising messages to support the efforts of the sales force and/or drive people to your Web site is an example of integrating diverse communication tools to build synergy that then may ultimately produce a sale.

Yet there is always a voice reminding us that there is only one rule: *Advertising must sell.*[12] Nowhere is the tension between communication and sales objectives bet-

---

12.   Sergio Zyman, *The End of Advertising As We Know It* (Hoboken, NJ: Wiley, 2002).

ter exemplified than in the annual debate about what advertisers really get for the tremendous sums of money they spend on Super Bowl ads. Every year great fanfare accompanies the ads that appear during the Super Bowl, and numerous polls are taken after the game to assess the year's most memorable ads. One such study showed that among the five most memorable ads (for Budweiser, Pepsi, VW, E-Trade, and Doritos) that ran during a Super Bowl, only the Doritos ad moved people to say that they were much more likely to purchase the product as a result of seeing the ad.[13] If a Super Bowl ad introducing Sheryl Crow as the new spokesperson for a Revlon hair coloring product doesn't affect women's purchase intentions, can it be worth the millions of dollars it takes to produce and air it? And for that matter, who really believes that Sheryl Crow colors her hair herself out of a box?

While there is a natural tension between those who advocate sales objectives and those who push communications objectives, nothing precludes a marketer from using both types when developing an advertising plan. Indeed, combining sales objectives such as market share and household penetration with communication objectives such as awareness and attitude change can be an excellent means of motivating and evaluating an advertising campaign.[14]

Objectives that enable a firm to make intelligent decisions about resource allocation must be stated in an advertising plan in terms specific to the organization. Articulating such well-stated objectives is easier when advertising planners do the following:

1. ***Establish a quantitative benchmark.*** Objectives for advertising are measurable only in the context of quantifiable variables. Advertising planners should begin with quantified measures of the current status of market share, awareness, attitude, or other factors that advertising is expected to influence. The measurement of effectiveness in quantitative terms requires a knowledge of the level of variables of interest before an advertising effort, and then afterward. For example, a statement of objectives in quantified terms might be, "Increase the market share of heavy users of the product category using our brand from 22 to 25 percent." In this case, a quantifiable and measurable market share objective is specified.

2. ***Specify measurement methods and criteria for success.*** It is important that the factors being measured be directly related to the objectives being pursued. It is of little use to try to increase the awareness of a brand with advertising and then judge the effects based on changes in sales. If changes in sales are expected, then measure sales. If increased awareness is the goal, then change in consumer awareness is the legitimate measure of success. This may seem obvious, but in a classic study of advertising objectives, it was found that claims of success for advertising were unrelated to the original statements of objective in 69 percent of the cases.[15] In this research, firms cited increases in sales as proof of success of advertising when the original objectives were related to factors such as awareness, conviction to a brand, or product-use information. But maybe that just says when sales do go up, we forget about everything else.

3. ***Specify a time frame.*** Objectives for advertising should include a statement of the period of time allowed for the desired results to occur. In some cases, as with direct response advertising, the time frame may be related to a seasonal selling opportunity like the Christmas holiday period. For communications-based objectives, the measurement of results may not be undertaken until the end of an entire multiweek campaign. The point is that the time period for accomplishment of an objective and the related measurement period must be stated in advance in the ad plan.

13.   Bonnie Tsui, "Bowl Poll: Ads Don't Mean Sales," *Advertising Age*, February 5, 2001, 33.
14.   John Philip Jones, "Advertising's Crisis of Confidence," *Marketing Management*, vol. 2, no. 1 (1993), 15–24.
15.   Stewart Henderson Britt, "Are So-Called Successful Advertising Campaigns Really Successful?" *Journal of Advertising Research*, vol. 9 (1969), 5–15.

These criteria for setting objectives help ensure that the planning process is organized and well directed. By relying on quantitative benchmarks, an advertiser has guidelines for making future decisions. Linking measurement criteria to objectives provides a basis for the equitable evaluation of the success or failure of advertising. Finally, the specification of a time frame for judging results keeps the planning process moving forward. As in all things, however, moderation is a good thing. A single-minded obsession with watching the numbers can be dangerous in that it minimizes or entirely misses the importance of qualitative and intuitive factors.

③ Budgeting. One of the most agonizing tasks is budgeting the funds for an advertising effort. Normally, the responsibility for the advertising budget lies with the firm itself. Within a firm, budget recommendations come up through the ranks; e.g., from a brand manager to a category manager and ultimately to the executive in charge of marketing. The sequence then reverses itself for the allocation and spending of funds. In a small firm, such as an independent retailer, the sequence just described may include only one individual who plays all the roles.

In many cases, a firm will rely on its advertising agency to make recommendations regarding the size of the advertising budget. When this is done, it is typically the account executive in charge of the brand who will analyze the firm's objectives and its creative and media needs and then make a recommendation to the company. The account supervisor's budget planning will likely include working closely with brand and product-group managers to determine an appropriate spending level.

To be as judicious and accountable as possible in spending money on advertising and IBP, marketers rely on various methods for setting an advertising budget. To appreciate the benefits (and failings) of these methods, we will consider each of them in turn.

Percentage of Sales. A **percentage-of-sales approach** to advertising budgeting calculates the advertising budget based on a percentage of the prior year's sales or the projected year's sales. This technique is easy to understand and implement. The budget decision makers merely specify that a particular percentage of either last year's sales or the current year's estimated sales will be allocated to the advertising process. It is common to spend between 2 and 12 percent of sales on advertising.

While simplicity is certainly an advantage in decision making, the percentage-of-sales approach is fraught with problems. First, when a firm's sales are decreasing, the advertising budget will automatically decline. Periods of decreasing sales may be precisely the time when a firm needs to increase spending on advertising; if a percentage-of-sales budgeting method is being used, this won't happen. Second, this budgeting method can easily result in overspending on advertising. Once funds have been earmarked, the tendency is to find ways to spend the budgeted amount. Third, and the most serious drawback from a strategic standpoint, is that the percentage-of-sales approach does not relate advertising dollars to advertising objectives. Basing spending on past or future sales is devoid of analytical evaluation and implicitly presumes a direct cause-and-effect relationship between advertising and sales. But here, we have sales "causing" advertising. That's backward!

A variation on the percentage-of-sales approach that firms may use is the **unit-of-sales approach** to budgeting, which simply allocates a specified dollar amount of advertising for each unit of a brand sold (or expected to be sold). This is merely a translation of the percentage-of-sales method into dollars per units sold. The unit-of-sales approach has the same advantages and disadvantages as the percentage-of-sales approach.

Share of Market/Share of Voice. With this method, a firm monitors the amount spent by various significant competitors on advertising and allocates an amount equal to the amount of money spent by competitors or an amount proportional to (or

EXHIBIT 8.12

Share of market versus share of voice, major car manufacturers in 2002 (U.S. dollars in millions).

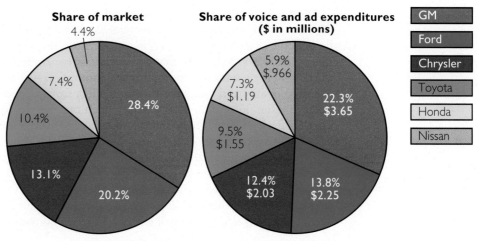

Source: Market share information taken from *Market Share Report, 2004* (Los Angeles Times, January 4, 2003, p. C1). Share of voice/ad expenditures calculated from *100 Leading National Advertisers*, AdAge, Special Report, 6.23.03 and *Domestic Advertising Spending by Category*, AdAge, 2002.

GLOBALIZATION

Trying to Be King Is Not the Danish Way

While the United States is at the top of the list of beer-drinking countries in the world, there are plenty of beer drinkers outside of North America. China, Germany, Brazil, and Russia are also huge markets. Thus, Nils Andersen, chief executive of Carlsberg, the world's fifth-largest brewer, summarizes his company's strategy this way: "I don't mean to offend Americans, but we can be a successful global brewer without the U.S."

Some industry analysts criticize Carlsberg for this strategy; however, it is also wise to consider that the four largest beer marketers in the world spend heavily to support their brands (e.g., Budweiser, Miller Lite, Heineken, Labatt Blue) in the United States, on the order of $1 billion in beer advertising among them. (Those are some deep pockets.) One of the essential decisions that global marketers are always faced with is how much of the globe can we really cover with the advertising funds that our company has available. Andersen's priorities for supporting his brand are clear. For example, he recently commissioned a new analysis of the fast-growing beer market in Serbia. He has no plans for spending any money on further investigation of the United States any time soon.

But in marketing and advertising, the analysis of one's situation is an ongoing process, so executives at Carlsberg won't rule out the possibility of someday making a big advertising push in North America. If they do, it is likely to be a unique campaign, because the Danes seem to think different when it comes to positioning their brands. As expressed by one Carlsberg executive, "We don't like to brag about ourselves. We would never be so bold and say that our beer is king." Probably a good idea to stay away from that line anyway, because last time we checked, "King of Beers" was already taken.

Source: Dan Bilefsky, "Not on Tap: Carlsberg Skips U.S. Beer Market for . . . Serbia?" ***Wall Street Journal***, October 7, 2003, B1.

slightly greater than) the firm's market share relative to the competition.[16] This will provide the advertiser with a **share of voice**, or an advertising presence in the market, that is equal to or greater than the competitors' share of advertising voice. Exhibit 8.12 shows the share of market and share of voice for automakers in the United States.

This method is often used for advertising-budget allocations when a new product is introduced. Conventional wisdom suggests that some multiple of the desired first-year market share, often 2.5 to 4 times, should be spent in terms of share-of-voice advertising expenditures. For example, if an advertiser wants a 2 percent first-year share, it would need to spend up to 8 percent of the total dollar amount spent in the industry (for an 8 percent share of voice). The logic is that a new product will need a significant share of voice to gain notice among a group of existing, well-established brands.[17] So, if you brew beer in Denmark and wanted to promote your Carlsberg brand in North America, how much money will you have to spend to steal market share from the likes of Anheuser-Busch and Miller? As explained in the Globalization box, executives at Carlsberg decided the right answer for them was $0.

16.   The classic treatment of this method was first offered by James O. Peckham, "Can We Relate Advertising Dollars to Market-Share Objectives?" in Malcolm A. McGiven, ed., *How Much to Spend for Advertising* (New York: Association of National Advertisers, 1969), 24.

17.   James C. Shroer, "Ad Spending: Growing Market Share," *Harvard Business Review* (January–February 1990), 44—50.

Although the share-of-voice approach is sound in its emphasis on competitors' activities, there are important challenges to consider with this approach. First, it may be difficult to gain access to precise information on competitors' spending. Second, there is no reason to believe that competitors are spending their money wisely. Third, the flaw in logic with this method is the assumption that every advertising effort is of the same quality and will have the same effect from a creative-execution standpoint. Such an assumption is especially shaky when one tries to compare expenditure levels across today's diverse advertising forms. Take Dove's experience with Super Bowl advertising versus its short film placed on YouTube. The film, "Dove Evolution," generated the biggest traffic spike ever at CampaignForRealBeauty.com, three times more than Dove's Super Bowl ad.[18] The YouTube video aired for $0, versus $2 million or so for the Super Bowl ad. No doubt that "Dove Evolution" was a huge contributor to Dove's share-of-voice at the time, but predicting the effects of innovative executions such as this one will always challenge conventional models.

Response Models. Using response models to aid the budgeting process is a fairly widespread practice among larger firms.[19] The belief is that greater objectivity can be maintained with such models. While this may or may not be the case, response models do provide useful information on what a given company's advertising response function looks like. An **advertising response function** is a mathematical relationship that associates dollars spent on advertising and sales generated. To the extent that past advertising predicts future sales, this method is valuable. Using marginal analysis, an advertiser would continue spending on advertising as long as its marginal spending was exceeded by marginal sales. Margin analysis answers the advertiser's question, "How much more will sales increase if we spend an additional dollar on advertising?" As the rate of return on advertising expenditures declines, the wisdom of additional spending is challenged.

Theoretically, this method leads to a point where an optimal advertising expenditure results in an optimal sales level and, in turn, an optimal profit. The relationship between sales, profit, and advertising spending is shown in the marginal analysis graph in Exhibit 8.13. Data on sales, prior advertising expenditures, and consumer awareness are typical of the numerical input to such quantitative models.

Unfortunately, the advertising-to-sales relationship assumes simple causality, and we know that that assumption isn't true. Many other factors, in addition to advertising, affect sales directly. Still, some feel that the use of response models is a better budgeting method than guessing or applying the percentage-of-sales or other budgeting methods discussed thus far.

Objective and Task. The methods for establishing an advertising budget just discussed all suffer from the same fundamental deficiency: a lack of

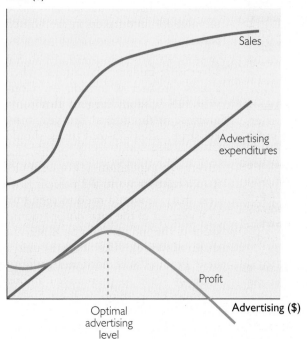

Sales ($)

Advertising ($)

Source: David A. Aaker, Rajeev Batra, and John G. Meyers, *Advertising Management*, 4th ed. (Englewood Cliffs, N.J.: Prentice-Hall, 1992), 469. Reprinted by permission of the authors.

EXHIBIT 8.13

Sales, profit, and advertising curves used in marginal analysis.

18.   Jack Neff, "A Real Beauty: Dove's Viral Makes a Big Splash for No Cash," *Advertising Age,* October 10, 2006, 1, 45.

19.   James E. Lynch and Graham J. Hooley, "Increasing Sophistication in Advertising Budget Setting," *Journal of Advertising Research* (February–March 1990), 72.

specification of how expenditures are related to advertising goals. The only method of budget setting that focuses on the relationship between spending and advertising objectives is the **objective-and-task approach**. This method begins with the stated objectives for an advertising effort. Goals related to production costs, target audience reach, message effects, behavioral effects, media placement, duration of the effort, and the like are specified. The budget is formulated by identifying the specific tasks necessary to achieve different aspects of the objectives.

There is a lot to recommend this procedure for budgeting. A firm identifies any and all tasks it believes are related to achieving its objectives. Should the total dollar figure for the necessary tasks be beyond the firm's financial capability, reconciliation must be found. But even if reconciliation and a subsequent reduction of the budget results, the firm has at least identified what *should* have been budgeted to pursue its advertising objectives.

The objective-and-task approach is the most logical and defensible method for calculating and then allocating an advertising budget. It is the only budgeting method that specifically relates advertising spending to the advertising objectives being pursued. It is widely used among major advertisers. For these reasons, we will consider the specific procedures for implementing the objective-and-task budgeting method.

Implementing the Objective-and-Task Budgeting Method. Proper implementation of the objective-and-task approach requires a data-based, systematic procedure. Since the approach ties spending levels to specific advertising goals, the process depends on proper execution of the objective-setting process described earlier. Once a firm and its agency are satisfied with the specificity and direction of stated objectives, a series of well-defined steps can be taken to implement the objective-and-task method. These steps are shown in Exhibit 8.14 and summarized in the following sections.

Determine Costs Based on Build-up Analysis. Having identified specific objectives, an advertiser can now begin determining what tasks are necessary for the accomplishment of those objectives. In using a **build-up analysis**—building up the expenditure levels for tasks—the following factors must be considered in terms of costs:

- **Reach.** The advertiser must identify the geographic and demographic exposure the advertising is to achieve.
- **Frequency.** The advertiser must determine the number of exposures required to accomplish desired objectives.
- **Time frame.** The advertiser must estimate when communications will occur and over what period of time.
- **Production costs.** The decision maker can rely on creative personnel and producers to estimate the costs associated with the planned execution of advertisements.
- **Media expenditures.** Given the preceding factors, the advertiser can now define the appropriate media, media mix, and frequency of insertions that will directly address objectives. Further, differences in geographic allocation, with special attention to regional or local media strategies, are considered at this point.

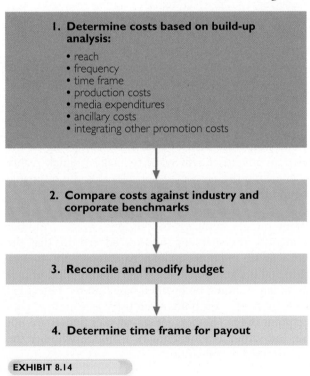

EXHIBIT 8.14

Steps in implementing the objective-and-task approach.

What could be better on a warm summer day than a stroll down Chicago's Navy Pier? Smart marketers like Best Buy want to be part of your day, and thus they bring their high tech playground right to where the action is. The idea here is to build deeper relationships with potential customers by contributing to their good times in a special venue. Concerts, sporting events, fairs, and carnivals are all great places to show off your brand.

- *Ancillary costs.* There will be a variety of related costs not directly accounted for in the preceding factors. Prominent among these are costs associated with advertising to the trade and specialized research unique to the campaign.
- *Integrating other promotional costs.* In this era of advertising and integrated brand promotion, sometimes it is the novel promotion that delivers the best bang for the buck. New and improved forms of brand promotion, like the one illustrated in Exhibit 8.15, must also be considered as part of the planning and budgeting process.

Compare Costs against Industry and Corporate Benchmarks. After compiling all the costs through a build-up analysis, an advertiser will want to make a quick reality check. This is accomplished by checking the percentage of sales that the estimated set of costs represents relative to industry standards for percentage of sales allocated to advertising. If most competitors are spending 4 to 6 percent of gross sales on advertising, how does the current budget compare to this percentage? Another recommended technique is to identify the share of industry advertising that the firm's budget represents. Another relevant reference point is to compare the current budget with prior budgets. If the total dollar amount is extraordinarily high or low compared to previous years, this variance should be justified based on the objectives being pursued. The use of percentage of sales on both an industry and internal corporate basis provides a reference point only. The percentage-of-sales figures are not used for decision making per se, but rather as a benchmark to judge whether the budgeted amount is so unusual as to need reevaluation.

Reconcile and Modify the Budget. It is always a fear that the proposed budget will not meet with approval. It may not be viewed as consistent with corporate policy related to advertising expense, or it may be considered beyond the financial capabilities of the organization. Modifications to a proposed budget are common, but having to make radical cuts in proposed spending is disruptive and potentially devastating. The objective-and-task approach is designed to identify what a firm will need to spend in order to achieve a desired advertising impact. To have the budget level compromised after such planning can result in an impotent advertising effort because necessary tasks cannot be funded.

Every precaution should be taken against having to radically modify a budget. Planners should be totally aware of corporate policy and financial circumstance *during* the objective-setting and subsequent task-planning phases. This will help reduce the extent of budget modification, should any be required.

Determine a Time Frame for Payout. It is important that budget decision makers recognize when the budget will be available for funding the tasks associated with the proposed effort. Travel expenses, production expenses, and media time and space are tied to specific calendar dates. For example, media time and space are often acquired and paid for far in advance of the completion of finished advertisements. Knowing when and how much money is needed improves the odds of the plan being carried out smoothly.

If these procedures are followed for the objective-and-task approach, an advertiser will have a defendable budget with which to pursue key objectives. One point to be made, however, is that the budget should not be viewed as the final word in funding an advertising effort. The dynamic nature of the market and rapid developments in media require flexibility in budget execution. This can mean changes in expenditure levels, but it can also mean changes in payout allocation.

Like any other business activity, a marketer must take on an advertising effort with clearly specified intentions for what is to be accomplished. Intentions and expectations for advertising are embodied in the process of setting objectives. Armed with information from market planning and an assessment of the type of advertising needed to support marketing plans, advertising objectives can be set. These objectives should be in place before steps are taken to determine a budget for the advertising effort, and before the creative work begins. Again, this is not always the order of things, even though it should be. These objectives will also affect the plans for media placement.

Strategy. Returning now to the other major components of the advertising plan (revisiting Exhibit 8.4 is a good idea at this point), next up is strategy. Strategy represents the mechanism by which something is to be done. It is an expression of the means to an end. All of the other factors are supposed to result in a strategy. Strategy is what you do, given the situation and objectives. There are numerous possibilities for advertising strategies. For example, if you are trying to get more top-of-the-mind awareness for your brand of chewing gum, a simple strategy would be to employ a high-frequency, name-repetition campaign (Double your pleasure with Doublemint, Doublemint, Doublemint gum). Exhibit 8.16 on the next page presents an ad from Danskin's campaign designed to address a more ambitious objective; that is, broadening the appeal of the brand beyond dance accessories to the much larger fitness-wear market. Danskin's advertising strategy thus features unique "fitness" celebrities as implicit endorsers of the brand.

More sophisticated goals call for more sophisticated strategies. You are limited only by your resources: financial, organizational, and creative. Ultimately, strategy formulation is a creative endeavor. It is best learned through the study of what others have done in similar situations and through a thorough analysis of the focal consumer. To assist in strategy formulation, a growing number of ad agencies have created a position called the account planner. This person's job is to synthesize

EXHIBIT 8.16

This ad provides an excellent example of repositioning. The slogan says it all: "Danskin—Not Just for Dancing."

all relevant consumer research and draw inferences from it that will help define a coherent advertising strategy. You will learn a great deal more about the connection between ad objectives and strategy options when you get to Chapter 11.

Execution. The actual "doing" is the execution of the plan. It is the making and placing of ads across all media. To quote a famous bit of advertising copy from a tire manufacturer, this is where "the rubber meets the road." There are two elements to the execution of an advertising plan: determining the copy strategy and devising a media plan.

Copy Strategy. A copy strategy consists of copy objectives and methods, or tactics. The objectives state what the advertiser intends to accomplish, while the methods describe how the objectives will be achieved. Part Three of this text will deal extensively with these executional issues.

Media Plan. The media plan specifies exactly where ads will be placed and what strategy is behind their placement. In an integrated communications environment, this is much more complicated than it might first appear. Back when there were just three broadcast television networks, there were already more than a million different combinations of placements that could be made. With the explosion of media and promotion options today, the permutations are almost infinite.

It is at this point—devising a media plan—where all the money is spent, and so much could be saved. This is where the profitability of many agencies is really determined. Media placement strategy can make a huge difference in profits or losses and is considered in great depth in Part Four of this text.

Integrated Brand Promotion. Many different forms of brand promotion may accompany the advertising effort in launching or maintaining a brand; these should be spelled out as part of the overall plan. There should be a complete integration of all communication tools in working up the plan. For example, in the launch of its Venus shaving system for women, Gillette had the usual multimillion-dollar budget allocation for traditional mass media. But along with its aggressive advertising effort, several other promotional tools were deployed.[20] At the Gillette Venus Web site, per Exhibit 8.17, women could sign up for an online sweepstakes to win vacations in Hawaii, New York City, and Tuscany, and provide friends' e-mail addresses to increase their own chances of winning. Gillette also put a pair of 18-wheelers on the road (see Exhibit 8.18) to spread the word about Venus at beaches, concerts, college campuses, and store openings. So the launch of Venus integrated tools that ran the gamut from TV ads to the World Wide Web to Interstate 95. You'll learn much more about a variety of IBP tools in Part Five.

EXHIBIT 8.17

The Venus Web site has offered many possibilities, including the prospect of winning a great vacation, a beauty IQ test, and a way to "Reveal the goddess in you." http://www.gillettevenus .com

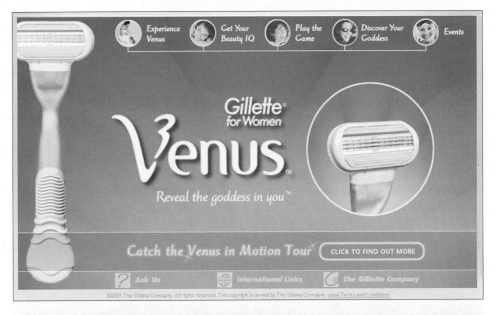

EXHIBIT 8.18

Hard to imagine goddesses going on the road in an 18-wheeler, but in today's world of integrated brand promotion, just about anything goes.

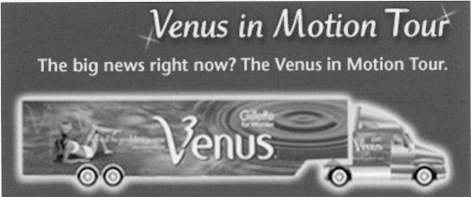

20.   Betsy Spethmann, "Venus Rising," *Promo Magazine,* April 2001, 52–61.

DOING IT RIGHT

Who Wants What?

Great advertising is much more likely when client and agency have a strong relationship where each knows its role and also knows how to support the other. Relationships are critical to success in advertising and they need to be proactively managed from both sides. Of course, it is much easier to do this when one is clear on the things your partner wants from you. But it's really no mystery what agencies and clients want from each other.

Marketers consistently want several things from their agencies. To begin with, at least in principle, everyone buys into the notion that collaboration and mutual respect are essential to doing advertising right. But in today's complex and dynamic ad environment, clients know they need help in two key areas. The first involves integration. Clients have trouble keeping up with the dynamic media environment and they expect their agency to be an expert on a wide array of options for getting the message out to the target consumer. So they need the various divisions and departments in an agency to be working as a team, coming up with communication solutions that build synergy between and among multiple channels. Simply stated, they want *integrated* brand promotion. Second, clients know they need new ideas and fresh approaches to break through the ever-increasing clutter in today's marketplace. Here again, the agency will be expected to ride to the rescue. While creativity can be an illusive aim, nonetheless, clients expect it.

Additionally, an agency should never be shocked to learn that clients expect results from their investment in advertising. The relationship will unravel quickly if an agency is not sensitive to this issue. The best way for agencies to stay on top of this key issue is to spend lots of time and attention on the client's business during the ad planning process so that everyone is clear on the goals for a campaign and the metrics that will be used in judging the success or failure of a campaign. Most clients are normal, reasonable people. They don't expect magic. They can live with an occasional failure. But if a campaign didn't work, the client will want to understand why, and will certainly expect better results the next time around.

Agencies too have a set of things that they want from every client. Here again the list starts with the need for collaboration and mutual respect. The agency wants to be treated as a partner, not a vendor. The agency also needs the time and resources so it can do its best work. But of course, there is never enough time and the budget is never large enough. There are two things clients must do to help everyone cope with resource issues. First, get the agency involved early in the planning process so the agency is well informed about dates and deadlines. Second, the agency needs honest, upfront assessments regarding budget. Everyone is used to a world where one must do more with less. But it kills a relationship to find out at the last minute, "Oh no, we never had the funding for something like that."

Finally, since agencies know that clients are going to be results oriented, they are looking for clients that will set them up for success. Agencies love clients who can articulate clearly the outcomes they seek. Agencies love clients that provide constructive and timely feedback. Agencies love clients who respect and value their expertise and are ready to step aside and let the agency do its thing when the time is right. When you have that kind of trust in your expertise, you also have a partner.

Sources: Tim Williams and Ronald Baker, "New Value-Based Comp Model Needed," *Advertising Age*, June 11, 2007, 20, 21; Deborah Vence, "Proving Ground," *Marketing News*, May 15, 2007, 12–15.

Evaluation. Last but not least in an ad plan is the evaluation component. This is where an advertiser determines how the agency will be graded: what criteria will be applied and how long the agency will have to achieve the agreed-on objectives. It's critically important for the advertiser and agency to align around evaluation criteria up front. John Wanamaker's classic line still captures the challenge associated with evaluation; he said, "I know half my advertising is wasted, I just don't know which half." In a world where the pressures on companies to deliver short-term profitability continue to intensify, advertising agencies find themselves under increasing pressure to show quantifiable outcomes from all advertising and IBP activities.[21]

4 The Role of the Agency in Planning Advertising and IBP.

Now that we have covered key aspects of the advertising planning process, one other issue should be considered. Because many marketers rely heavily on the expertise of an advertising agency, understanding the role an agency plays in the advertising planning process is important. Various agencies will approach their craft with different points of emphasis. But while not everyone does it the same way, it is still important to ask: What contribution to the planning effort can and should an advertiser expect from its agency?

The discussion of advertising planning to this point has emphasized that the marketer is responsible for the marketing-planning inputs as a type of self-assessment that identifies the firm's basis for offer-

21. Laura Q. Hughes, "Measuring Up," *Advertising Age*, February 5, 2001, 1, 34; Deborah Vence, "Proving Ground," *Marketing News,* May 15, 2007, 12–15.

ing value to customers. This assessment should also clearly identify, in the external environment, the opportunities and threats that can be addressed with advertising. A firm should bring to the planning effort a well-articulated statement of a brand's value proposition and the marketing mix elements designed to gain and sustain competitive advantage. However, when client and agency are working in harmony, the agency may take an active role in helping the client formulate the marketing plan. Indeed, when things are going right, it can be hard to say exactly where the client's work ended and the agency's work began. This is the essence of teamwork, and as Steve Jobs noted about working with Apple's long-time partner, TBWA/Chiat/Day: "Creating great advertising, like creating great products, is a team effort."

The agency's crucial role is to translate the current market and marketing status of a firm and its advertising objectives into advertising strategy and, ultimately, finished advertisements and IBP materials. An agency can serve its clients best by taking charge of the preparation and placement stages. Here, message strategies and tactics for the advertising effort and for the efficient and effective placement of ads in media need to be hammered out. At this point, the firm (as a good client) should turn to its agency for the expertise and talent needed for planning and executing at the stage where design and creative execution bring marketing strategies to life. There are two basic models for the relationship between agencies and their clients: adversarial or partnering. The former is too common; the latter is certainly preferred. The Doing It Right box on the facing page makes the case that partnerships are more likely to develop when each side has a clear understanding of what the other values.

SUMMARY

 Describe the basic components of an advertising plan.

An advertising plan is motivated by the marketing planning process and provides the direction that ensures proper implementation of an advertising campaign. An advertising plan incorporates decisions about the segments to be targeted, communications and/or sales objectives with respect to these segments, and salient message appeals. The plan should also specify the dollars budgeted for the campaign, the various communication tools that will be employed to deliver the messages, and the measures that will be relied on to assess the campaign's effectiveness.

 Compare and contrast two fundamental approaches for setting advertising objectives.

Setting appropriate objectives is a crucial step in developing any advertising plan. These objectives are typically stated in terms of either communications or sales goals. Both types of goals have their proponents, and the appropriate types of objectives to emphasize will vary with the situation. Communication objectives feature goals such as building brand awareness or reinforcing consumers' beliefs about a brand's key benefits. Sales objectives are just that: They hold advertising directly responsible for increasing sales of a brand.

 Explain various methods for setting advertising budgets.

Perhaps the most challenging aspect of any advertising campaign is arriving at a proper budget allocation. Companies and their advertising agencies work with several different methods to arrive at an advertising budget. A percentage-of-sales approach is a simple but naive way to deal with this issue. In the share-of-voice approach, the activities of key competitors are factored into the budget-setting process. A variety of quantitative models may also be used for budget determination. The objective-and-task approach is difficult to implement, but with practice it is likely to yield the best value for a client's advertising dollars.

 Discuss the role of the agency in formulating an advertising plan.

An advertising plan will be a powerful tool when firms partner with their advertising agencies in its development. The firm can lead this process by doing its homework with respect to marketing strategy development and objective setting. The agency can then play a key role in managing the preparation and placement phases of campaign execution.

KEY TERMS

advertising plan
situation analysis
industry analysis
market analysis
competitor analysis
top-of-the-mind awareness

purchase intent
trial usage
repeat purchase
brand switching
percentage-of-sales approach
unit-of-sales approach

share of voice
advertising response function
objective-and-task approach
build-up analysis

QUESTIONS

1. Review the materials presented in this chapter (and anything else you may be able to find) about Apple's launch of the iPhone. Based on the advertising utilized, what do you surmise must have been the value proposition for iPhone at the time of its launch?

2. Now that some time has passed since the official launch of iPhone, has this product lived up to its early hype? Has it become the next "big thing" for Steve Jobs and Apple?

3. Explain the connection between marketing strategies and advertising plans. What is the role of target segments in making this connection?

4. Describe five key elements in a situation analysis and provide an example of how each of these elements may ultimately influence the final form of an advertising campaign.

5. How would it ever be possible to justify anything other than sales growth as a proper objective for an advertising campaign? Is it possible that advertising could be effective yet not yield growth in sales?

6. What types of objectives would you expect to find in an ad plan that featured direct response advertising?

7. Write an example of a workable advertising objective that would be appropriate for a service like the Geek Squad.

8. In what situations would share of voice be an important consideration in setting an advertising budget? What are the drawbacks of trying to incorporate share of voice in budgeting decisions?

9. What is it about the objective-and-task method that makes it the preferred approach for the sophisticated advertiser? Describe how build-up analysis is used in implementing the objective-and-task method.

10. Briefly discuss the appropriate role to be played by advertising agencies and their clients in the formulation of marketing and advertising plans.

EXPERIENTIAL EXERCISES

1. Five of the most common objectives for advertising are listed in this chapter: top-of-the-mind awareness, purchase intent, trial usage, repeat purchase, and brand switching. For each, find a magazine or newspaper ad that you think aims primarily to accomplish this objective and give an analysis as to whether or not the ad is successful.

2. Select three full-page magazine advertisements that you consider to be effective. For each ad, describe what you think was the likely strategy developed as part of the advertising plan for the campaign and identify ways that advertisers could evaluate whether those strategy goals were met.

3. Working in small teams, prepare a situation analysis that could be included in an advertising plan for the online employment site Monster. The analysis should identify key factors that you consider most relevant to such a campaign and a brief assessment of each. Present your findings to the class in a 10- to 15-slide presentation.

4. Working in the same teams, identify potential placement and promotional opportunities that could be part of the media plan for a Monster campaign.

CHAPTER 9

After reading and thinking about this chapter, you will be able to do the following:

1

Explain the types of audience research that are useful for understanding cultural barriers that can interfere with effective communication.

2

Identify three distinctive challenges that complicate the execution of advertising and IBP in international settings.

3

Describe the three basic types of agencies that can assist in the placement of advertising around the world.

4

Discuss the advantages and disadvantages of globalized versus localized advertising campaigns.

Introductory Scenario: Commander Safeguard to the Rescue!

In 2003 the Safeguard soap brand was floundering in Pakistan. There was plenty of competition from traditional favorites like Unilever's Lifebuoy, and the antibacterial claim that had become the essence of Safeguard's positioning in other markets was taking it nowhere. The anti-bac message was just not resonating with consumers in Pakistan; as evidenced by the fact that in 2003, all anti-bac brands combined held just a skimpy 7 percent share of the bar soap market.

But Pakistan had serious public health challenges that are common in less-developed economies. For example, 250,000 children were dying every year because of diarrhea. Many of these deaths were preventable through basic hygiene, like hand washing. But no one was getting this message out. A country struggling with poverty, terrorism threats, and a longstanding border war didn't have the resources to devote to public service announcements about hygiene. And even if it did, how effective are mundane public service announcements in changing people's everyday habits? Typically . . . not very. Yet dire situations like this one often hold great opportunity; and the marketers of Safeguard found a way to unlock it.

So how do you reach families with a message that many infectious diseases are preventable through basic hygiene? How do you elevate this message to make it fun and engaging, especially for children, rather than glum and forgettable? And one more thing: How does one accomplish all this on a shoestring budget so that it also leads to more sales for Safeguard?

Sounds like a job that only a superhero could handle. Someone on the order of a Voltron, Captain Planet, or even Spiderman: all popular cartoon characters in Pakistan at the time of the Safeguard turnaround. Inspired by these characters, the marketers of Safeguard launched one of their own in 2003. "Commander Safeguard" was conceived as someone who could capture the imagination of kids, but also partner with mothers in their efforts to keep their children in good health. And of course, for every superhero, there has to be a villain. Commander Safeguard's first foe would be "Dirtoo," the germ king, who had it as his mission to stalk children at every turn to spoil their health. Indeed, prior to the arrival of Commander Safeguard, Dirtoo was having his way with the kids of Pakistan.

Initially Commander Safeguard was introduced to children via a 15-minute cartoon program code-named "Clean Sweep." This programming was delivered as part of a school edutainment program for kids. The aim from the beginning was to fuse entertainment with education to make the program high-impact. Commander Safeguard storybooks were also provided for the kids to take home and share with their mothers. This engaged both kids and moms around something both fun and lifesaving. Not a bad combination!

Kids sparked to this new superhero and soon there was a series of new Commander Safeguard adventures made for national TV and radio. As with any superhero fantasy, new villains were invented (to represent different types of infectious diseases), but Commander Safeguard would defeat them all. The series deepened its connection to the local culture by using Pakistani celebrities to do the voiceovers in each episode and creating plots around themes that engaged kids (e.g., Dirtoo plans to spoil kids' enjoyment of a cricket match by making them all sick!). This gave Commander Safeguard a unique status in Pakistan. He wasn't a borrowed superhero from some other country or culture; he was Pakistan's own superhero. Now that's a pretty big deal.

Ultimately, an art gallery hosted at http://www.commandersafeguard.com let children post drawings and poems created in school-sponsored Health Day contests to celebrate both good hygiene and Pakistan's first superhero. Exhibit 9.1 provides an overview of the look and feel of Health Day with Commander Safeguard as the star of the show. This popular program benefits from the ongoing support of the Safeguard brand as well as the Pakistan Medical Association and the Infectious Diseases Society of Pakistan.

So what did all this do for Safeguard soap in Pakistan? In combination with other TV communication targeted to mothers, this program helped Safeguard double its sales over the next two years and made Pakistan the fastest-growing Safeguard market in the world. The campaign made germ protection emerge as the most important attribute influencing choice of a bar soap. Safeguard became the brand recommended by doctors and the brand associated with a movement to improve the health and hygiene of Pakistan. By 2007,

EXHIBIT 9.1

Commander Safeguard's message about good hygiene has been embraced by the children of Pakistan (and their teachers, too!).

anti-bac brands held a combined 50 percent share of the bar soap market and Unilever was repositioning its Lifebuoy brand as a germ buster that would "Bash, Trash, and Smash" disease-spreading germs. But there was one and only one Commander Safeguard. And soon this success model would be exported to other countries around the world, like China and the Philippines, where good hygiene and superheroes were also in short supply.

The remarkable story about the success of Safeguard in Pakistan (and the pictures that tell the story in Exhibit 9.1) has many intriguing elements. Some of these elements are likely familiar for you in your culture (like a superhero), and some are likely less familiar (like a superhero saving the day by besting Dirtoo at a cricket match). As suggested in the Globalization box on the next page, savvy marketers don't always get it right, and it is the unanticipated or underappreciated elements that will get you in trouble every time. Toyota's mishap in launching its Land Cruiser in China illustrates the difficulties that even the savviest companies must overcome as they take their products and brands to new, international markets.

International advertising is advertising that reaches across national and cultural boundaries. As with all the advertising you've learned about thus far, it can take many forms, from Internet ads to superhero spokespersons to signage on the sides of buses. In the past, a great deal of international advertising was nothing more than translations of domestic advertising. Often these simple translations were ineffective, and sometimes they were even offensive. The day has passed—if there ever was such a day—when advertisers based in industrialized nations can simply "do a foreign translation" of their ads. Today, international advertisers have learned they must pay greater attention to local cultures. For example, the Safeguard campaign was a success in Pakistan because the managers who created it were there on the ground and were totally immersed in the local culture.

GLOBALIZATION

Stumbling Into China

With a population of well over a billion people, a robustly growing economy, new global status associated with hosting the 2008 Olympic games, and greater acceptance of capitalistic ways and means, it follows that many companies large and small have turned to China as a new source of business opportunity. It also follows that advertising spending in China is growing at unprecedented rates. Many experts are already predicting that in this decade China will overtake Japan as the second largest advertising market in the world. Yet China presents many incredible challenges for advertisers from around the world. Some of these derive from the gargantuan nature of this country. China has 31 provinces, 656 cities, and 48,000 districts. There is no one Chinese language; rather, there are seven major tongues with 80 spoken dialects. The north of China is a frozen plateau and the south of China is tropical. There are huge income and lifestyle differences between city-dwellers and farmers, and between the prosperous east and the impoverished west. When you come right down to it, there really is no such thing as a single "China." And that's just the obvious stuff.

Matters get even more complex when one factors in the unique aspects of the Chinese culture, where the norms of a Confucian society often are in conflict with the drive toward economic reform and Western lifestyles. The Chinese are also keenly aware and proud of their rich history, which spans thousands of years. (Recall that Marco Polo set out to explore the mysteries of China in the 13th century.) For any outsider, China presents many mysteries that will need to be solved in the development of appropriate and effective advertising.

Toyota's launch of the Prado Land Cruiser in China provides a nice example of the challenges one must overcome in developing advertising to reach across national (and cultural) boundaries. Now keep in mind, this is Toyota, from just across the East China Sea in Toyota City, Japan, not some newcomer to the Asian continent. To launch its big SUV in China, Toyota's ad agency Saatchi & Saatchi created a print campaign showing a Prado driving past two large stone lions, which were saluting and bowing to the Prado. This seems to make sense because the stone lion is a traditional sign of power in the Chinese culture. As one Saatchi executive put it, "These ads were intended to reflect Prado's imposing presence when driving in the city: You cannot but respect the Prado."

Chinese consumers saw it differently. For starters, Chinese words often have multiple meanings, and Prado can be translated into Chinese as **badao**, which means "rule by force" or "overbearing." In addition, the use of the stone lions prompted scathing commentary on the Internet about a contentious time in China's relationship with Japan. Some thought the stone lions in the Prado ad resembled those that flank the Marco Polo Bridge in China, a site near Beijing that marked the opening battle of Japan's invasion of China in 1937. These of course are not the kind of reactions that an advertiser is looking for when launching a new product. The automaker quickly pulled 30 magazine and newspaper ads and issued a formal apology, illustrating that no one is immune to the subtle but powerful influences of culture.

Sources: Geoffrey Fowler, "China's Cultural Fabric Is a Challenge to Marketers," **Wall Street Journal**, January 21, 2004, B7; Sameena Ahmad, "A Billion Three, But Not for Me," **The Economist**, March 20, 2004, 5, 6; Norihiko Shirouzu, "In Chinese Market, Toyota's Strategy Is Made in USA," **Wall Street Journal**, May 26, 2006, A1, A8; Laurel Wentz, "China's Ad World: A New Crisis Every Day," **Advertising Age**, December 11, 2006, 6; Dexter Roberts, "Cautious Consumers," **BusinessWeek**, April 30, 2007, 32–34.

As we said in Chapter 5, culture is a set of values, rituals, and behaviors that define a way of life. Culture is typically invisible to those who are immersed within it. Communicating *across* cultures is not easy. It is, in fact, one of the most difficult of all communication tasks, largely because there is no such thing as culture-free communication. Advertising is a cultural product; it means nothing outside of culture. Culture surrounds advertising, informs it, gives it meaning. To transport an ad across cultural borders, one must respect, and hopefully understand, the influence of culture.

Ads depend on effective communication, and effective communication depends on shared meaning. The degree of shared meaning is significantly affected by cultural membership. When an advertiser in culture A wants to communicate with consumers in culture B, it is culture B that will surround the created message, form its cultural context, and significantly affect how it will be interpreted.

Some products and brands may belong to a global consumer culture more than to any one national culture. Such brands travel well, as do their ads, because there is already common cultural ground on which to build effective advertising. The Jack Daniel's and LG ads in Exhibits 9.2 and 9.3 provide examples of products and brands with wide, if not "global," appeal. Jack Daniels began distilling whiskey in 1866. With ads like the one in Exhibit 9.2, the legend of Jack Daniel's spread around the world, and Tennessee became associated with smooth sippin' whiskey. One common bond among Jack Daniel's drinkers worldwide is the nostalgic premise that their whiskey is distilled the old-fashioned way. Tennessee pride guarantees it!

LG Electronics, headquartered in Seoul, South Korea, markets its products in dozens of countries around the world. If you're in the market for a plasma TV with a 7-foot screen and high definition DVR, they've got the perfect product for you, just as they do for consumers in Asia, Europe, Latin America, and the rest of the world. But brands like Jack Daniel's and LG

EXHIBIT 9.3

You don't need to be able to read Japanese to get the point here, in part because this ad follows the same style as other Jack Daniel's ads around the world. If you want a smooth sippin' whiskey, it can't be rushed. And in the back hills of Tennessee, no one is rushing anything. . . .

EXHIBIT 9.2

Electronics is a product category that lends itself to global brands (e.g., LG, Sony, Panasonic, Nintendo, Philips, Nokia, Apple) because, for consumers who have the disposable income to afford them, performance is performance, whether you watch, play, or listen in Montreal, Madrid, or Mexico City. To get a good appreciation of the scale and reach of a company like LG Electronics, check out their global network at http://www.lge.com/general/globalsite.jsp Oh, yeah—Life's Good.

are more the exceptions rather than the rule, and as "global" as they may be, they are still affected by local culture as to their use and, ultimately, their meaning.

This chapter augments and extends the advertising planning framework offered in Chapter 8. We add some necessary international planning tools along with additional insights about the special challenges found in advertising around the world. There is likely to be a Brazil or China or India in your future, so now's the time to begin thinking about the challenges of communicating with different cultures.

Overcoming Cultural Barriers.
It's not hard to identify the companies that are making a major commitment to international advertising. Just follow the money! Exhibit 9.4 offers perspective on those that are most committed and successful in marketing and advertising around the world. Canada, China, Germany, and South Korea are large and diverse markets. In Exhibit 9.4 on the next page you will see many familiar names that span the globe in their quest for consumers. These are corporate titans such as Procter & Gamble, Unilever, Volkswagen, LG, General Motors, and L'Oréal. It is also interesting to note that in China the predominant advertisers are often Chinese, suggesting that many global marketers (e.g., Toyota) are still trying to solve the mysteries of China. But the key point is that most companies today consider their markets to extend beyond national boundaries and across cultures. Hence, advertisers must come to terms with how they are going to effectively overcome cultural barriers in trying to communicate with consumers around the world.

Canada Advertiser	2005	2004	% chg
Procter & Gamble Co.	$172	$170	1.3
Rogers Communications	106	100	6.9
General Motors Corp.	99	84	17.5
Telus Corp.	71	44	59.7
BCE	67	56	19.0
Wendy's International	61	56	9.1
L'Oreal	59	58	2.3
Sony Corp.	57	50	13.9
Toyota Motor Corp.	56	57	−1.0
Hyundai Motor Co.	54	47	14.9

China Advertiser	2005	2004	% chg
Procter & Gamble Co.	$891	$707	25.9
Hayao Group	382	318	20.4
Unilever	213	124	71.3
Stone Group Holdings	154	125	23.6
Colgate-Palmolive Co.	115	62	86.1
China Mobile Communications Corp.	115	89	28.2
Yum Brands	76	55	38.4
L'Oreal	75	53	43.1
Lafang Group	70	54	31.4
Arche Group	67	94	−28.5

Germany Advertiser	2005	2004	% chg
Metro Group	$332	$304	9.2
Lidl & Schwarz Stiftung & Co.	268	262	2.4
Deutsche Telekom	254	224	13.3
Procter & Gamble Co.	248	286	−13.2
Unilever	226	182	24.4
Volkswagen	223	202	10.6
Axel Springer Verlag	213	220	−3.3
Aldi Group	205	192	6.6
L'Oreal	196	187	4.9
Bertelsmann	181	194	−6.7

South Korea Advertiser	2005	2004	% chg
Samsung Group	$268	$253	5.6
LG Group	204	203	0.3
SK Group	148	161	−8.3
Lotte Group	134	138	−3.0
KT Corp.	132	173	−23.3
Hyundai Motor Co.	65	57	14.7
American International Group	56	30	85.4
Amore Pacific Corp.	50	57	−12.1
Kia Motors Corp.	46	51	−8.4
GS Holdings Corp.	45	17	167.0

Source: *Advertising Age*, November 20, 2006, 56. Reprinted with permission. © Crain Communications, Inc., 2006.

EXHIBIT 9.4

Advertising leaders in four major global markets (U.S. dollars in millions).

Barriers to Successful International Advertising. Adopting an international perspective is often difficult for marketers. The reason is that experience gained over a career and a lifetime creates a cultural "comfort zone"—that is, one's own cultural values, experiences, and knowledge serve as a subconscious guide for decision making and behavior. International advertisers are particularly beset with this problem.

Managers must overcome two related biases to be successful in international markets. **Ethnocentrism** is the tendency to view and value things from the perspective of one's own culture. A **self-reference criterion (SRC)** is the unconscious reference to one's own cultural values, experiences, and knowledge as a basis for decisions. These two closely related biases are primary obstacles to success when conducting marketing and advertising planning that demand a cross-cultural perspective.

A decision maker's SRC and ethnocentrism can inhibit his or her ability to sense important cultural distinctions between markets. This in turn can blind advertisers to their own culture's "fingerprints" on the ads they've created. Sometimes these are offensive or, at a minimum, markers of "outsider" influence. Outsiders are sometimes welcome; other times, they just appear ignorant.

Let's take an issue that all of us could readily overlook in developing ads for diverse cultures. Sense of humor is a very culturally bounded thing. U.S. media companies such as Time Warner and Walt Disney Co. commonly run into problems transferring comedic programming that was successful in America to other countries. For instance, while HBO's relationships-based *Sex in the City* was very popular in

Germany, the ironic humor of *Seinfeld* was lost on Germans.[1] Of course we also know that humor is one of advertisers' favorite tactics for engaging their audiences, so differences in sense of humor can become a huge issue when trying to roll out ad campaigns across cultures.

Apple ran into "humor problems" with its quirky campaign "Mac vs. PC." You may have seen it: A nerdy PC keeps getting embarrassed by a hip Mac. Created in America, with droll *Daily Show* commentator John Hodgman personifying the bumbling PC and comic actor Justin Long as the Mac, the campaign had just the right amount of dry humor to tickle American funny bones. But in Japan the ads had to be completely revamped, because in the Japanese culture, direct-comparison ads are viewed as rude and showing a lack of class. For the United Kingdom, Apple tried to recreate the exchanges between Mac and PC using British comedians and a new script, but the humor seemed to get lost along the way, and a local polling firm found that Apple's reputation suffered after the ads started showing in cinemas and on the Web.[2] Here again we can see that even the most proficient of advertisers are challenged when they try to go across cultures with an idea formulated at home.

The only way to counteract the confounding influence that ethnocentrism and SRC have on international advertising decision making is to be constantly sensitive to their existence and to the virtual certainty of important differences among cultures that will constrain your best thinking. Even with thorough cross-cultural research, it is still likely that problems will present themselves. However, without research, problems are a virtual certainty.

Cross-Cultural Audience Research.

Analyzing audiences in international markets can be a humbling task. If firms have worldwide product distribution networks—like Nestlé, Unilever, and Procter & Gamble—then international audience research will require dozens of separate analyses. There really is no way to avoid the task of specific audience analysis. This typically involves research in each different country, generally from a local research supplier. There are, however, good secondary resources that provide broad-based information to advertisers about international markets. The U.S. Department of Commerce has an International Trade Administration (ITA) division, which helps companies based in the United States develop foreign market opportunities for their products and services. The ITA publishes specialized reports that cover most of the major markets in the world and provide economic and regulatory information (see http://www.ita.doc.gov). The United Nations' *Statistical Yearbook* is another source of general economic and population data (http://unstats .un.org/unsd). The yearbook, updated annually, provides information for more than 200 countries. These sources provide helpful information for the international advertiser. Unfortunately, it's rarely enough.

An international audience analysis will also involve evaluation of economic conditions, demographic characteristics, values, custom and ritual, and product use and preferences.

Economic Conditions.

One way to think about the economic conditions of a potential international audience is to break the world's markets into three broad classes of economic development: less-developed countries, newly industrialized countries, and highly industrialized countries. These categories provide a basic understanding of the economic capability of the average consumer in a market and

---

1.   Matthew Karnitschnig, "Comedy Central Export Aims for Local Laughs," *Wall Street Journal*, March 2, 2007, B1.
2.   Gregory Fowler, "Mac and PC's Overseas Adventures," *Wall Street Journal*, March 1, 2007, B1.

EXHIBIT 9.5

Gross domestic product (GDP) per capita in dollars (2006), adjusted to parity in purchasing power.

Luxembourg	$68,800	Malaysia	12,700
Norway	47,800	Mexico	10,600
Ireland	43,600	**World Average**	**10,000**
United States	43,500	Thailand	9,100
Denmark	37,000	Turkey	8,900
Canada	35,200	Brazil	8,600
Japan	33,100	China	7,600
Germany	31,400	Philippines	5,000
France	30,100	Egypt	4,200
Israel	26,200	India	3,700
New Zealand	26,000	Pakistan	2,600
Portugal	19,100	Nigeria	1,400
South Africa	13,000	Afghanistan	800

Source: World Fact Book, http://www.cia.gov/cia/publications, accessed April 8, 2007.

thus help place consumption in the context of economic realities. Exhibit 9.5 lists gross domestic product (GDP) per capita for 25 countries to give you additional appreciation for the vast differences in resources available to consumers around the world.

Less-developed countries represent nearly 75 percent of the world's population. Some of these countries are plagued by drought and civil war, and their economies lack almost all the resources necessary for development: capital, infrastructure, political stability, and trained workers. Many of the products sold in these less-developed economies are typically not consumer products, but rather business products used for building infrastructure (such as heavy construction equipment) or agricultural equipment.

Newly industrialized countries have economies defined by change; they are places where traditional ways of life that have endured for centuries are changing and modern consumer cultures are emerging. This creates a very particular set of problems for the outside advertiser trying to hit a moving target, or a culture in rapid flux. But many marketers now see low-income consumers as an opportunity deserving more attention, in part because in counties like Brazil, India and China, we are talking about billions of consumers. So, for example, Nestlé Brazil saw sales of its Bono cookies jump 40 percent after it shrank its package from 200 to 140 grams and lowered its price;[3] a prudent move when marketing to low-income consumers.

But communicating with low-income consumers is an ongoing challenge for the big, multinational firms, in part because their employees and those of their ad agencies are well educated and highly affluent. It is always hard to understand the wants and needs of a person living with fundamentally different economic circumstances. Johnny Wei, director of Nestlé Brazil's regional marketing programs, puts it more bluntly: a trip to the slums of a city like Sao Paulo is frequently a "mind-blowing" experience for advertising executives.[4] Of course, from such experiences meaningful insights emerge that can foster improved advertising.

The **highly industrialized countries** of the world are those with mature economies and high levels of affluence as indicated by data such as GDP per capita (several such countries are apparent in Exhibit 9.5). These countries have also invested heav-

3.   Antonio Regalado, "Marketers Pursue the Shallow-Pocketed," *Wall Street Journal*, January 26, 2007, B3.
4.   Ibid.

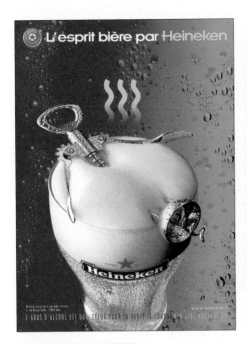

EXHIBIT 9.6

EXHIBIT 9.7

Heineken's distinctive red star is a logo known around the world. Here Heineken challenges partygoers in France to choose the bottle opener over the corkscrew for their next celebration.
http://www.heineken.com

Big Mac Tuesdays play well in many places. In this instance it's Toronto, so that's $1.69, Canadian.

ily over many years in infrastructure—roads, hospitals, airports, power-generating plants, educational institutions, and the Internet. Within this broad grouping, an audience assessment will focus on more-detailed analyses of the market, including the nature and extent of competition, marketing trade channels, lifestyle trends, and market potential. Firms pursuing opportunities in highly industrialized countries proceed with market analysis in much the same way that they would in the United States. While the advertising in these countries will often vary based on unique cultural and lifestyle factors, consumers in these markets are accustomed to seeing a full range of creative appeals for goods and services. The Heineken and McDonald's ads in Exhibits 9.6 and 9.7 provide familiar examples.

Demographic Characteristics. Information on the demographic characteristics of nations is generally available. Both the U.S. Department of Commerce and the United Nations publish annual studies of population for hundreds of countries. Advertisers must be sensitive to the demographic similarities and differences in international markets, along with key trends. Demographics, including size of population, age distribution, income distribution, education levels, occupations, literacy rates, and household size, can dramatically affect the type of advertising prepared for a market. And it is always true that advertising dollars flow to where the purchasing power resides. Big advertisers generally place a higher priority on wealthy nations with their high levels of purchasing power per household, but as noted above, the sheer number of households in countries like India and China is changing the dynamics of advertising spending.

The world's wealthy nations are, for the most part, getting older[5] and this also creates the potential for wealth redistribution around the world.[6] It could work

5.   Clay Chandler, "Changing Places," *Fortune*, September 18, 2006, 61–64.
6.   Gautam Naik, "Leveraging the Age Gap," *Wall Street Journal*, February 27, 2003, B1, B4.

this way: While the United States, Japan, and Western Europe will struggle in the future with pension plan shortfalls and rising health care costs, countries like Brazil and Mexico have an opportunity to surge ahead economically because of something referred to as the **demographic dividend**. In these developing nations, falling labor costs, a younger and healthier population, and the entry of millions of women into the work force produce a favorable climate for economic expansion. The experts say that these developing nations have about a 30-year window to capitalize on their demographic dividend. Better education for more of their populations will be an essential element in realizing this dividend.

Here again the point is simply that understanding fundamental demographic trends around the world is essential for marketing and advertising planning. Increases and decreases in the proportion of the population in specific age groups are closely related to the demand for particular products and services. As populations continue to increase in developing countries, new market opportunities emerge for products and services for teens and young families. Similarly, as advanced-age groups continue to increase in countries with stable population rates, the demand for consumer services such as health care, travel, and retirement planning will increase. It is fair to conclude that knowing the age segment you want to target is especially critical for developing effective international advertising.

Values. Cultural values are enduring beliefs about what is important to the members of a culture. They are the defining bedrock of a culture. They are an outgrowth of the culture's history and its collective experience. (Even though there are many cultures within any given nation, many believe that there are still enough shared values to constitute a meaningful "national culture," such as "American culture.") For example, the value of individualism enjoys a long and prominent place in American history and is considered by many to be a core American value. Other cultures seem to value the group or collective more. Even though a "collectivist" country like Japan may be becoming more individualistic, there is still a Japanese tradition that favors the needs of the group over those of the individual. In Japan, organizational loyalty and social interdependence are values that promote a group mentality. Japanese consumers are thus thought to be more sensitive to appeals that feature stability, longevity, and reliability, and they find appeals using competitive comparisons to be rude and inappropriate[7] (recall the "Mac vs. PC" example). Some researchers believe this continuum from individualism to collectivism to be a stable and dependably observed difference among the people of the world, or at least stable enough for crafting different ads for different cultures.[8]

Custom and Ritual. Among other things, rituals perpetuate a culture's connections to its core values. They seem perfectly natural to members of a culture, and they can often be performed without much thought (in some cases, none at all) regarding their deeper meaning. Many consumer behaviors involve rituals, such as grooming, gift giving, or food preparation. As reflected in Exhibit 9.8, something as simple as preparing breakfast cereal can entail different rituals from one culture to another (and, of course, in many cultures breakfast cereal is a totally alien concept). To do a good job in cross-cultural advertising, the rituals of other cultures must be not only appreciated, but also understood. This requires in-depth and extended research efforts, explaining the growing popularity of ethnographic studies.[9] Quick marketing surveys rarely do anything in this context except invite disaster.

7.   Johny Johansson, "The Sense of Nonsense: Japanese TV Advertising," *Journal of Advertising* (March 1994), 17–26.
8.   S. Han and S. Shavitt, "Persuasion and Culture: Advertising Appeals in Individualistic and Collectivistic Societies," *Journal of Experimental Social Psychology*, vol. 30 (1994), 326–350.
9.   Spencer Ante, "The Science of Desire," *BusinessWeek*, June 5, 2006, 98–106.

MÖVENPICK
OF SWITZERLAND

NEU

Am Ende glauben Sie noch,
Sie hätten es selbst gemacht.

MÖVENPICK
Birchermüesli

Das Müesli.

EXHIBIT 9.8

In many European countries it is common to create a "homemade" batch of breakfast cereal each morning with natural grains and fresh fruit. In this ad from Switzerland's Mövenpick, we see the advertiser attempting to align the convenient packaging of its new product with the homemade tradition. The headline reads, "At the end, you'll even think that you made it yourself." Or, more simply, tastes like homemade! When was the last time you looked for a breakfast cereal that "tastes like homemade"?

One of the most devastating mistakes an advertiser can make is to presume that consumers in one culture have the same rituals as those in another. Religion is an obvious expression of values in a culture. In countries adhering to the precepts of the Islamic religion, which includes most Arab nations, traditional religious beliefs restrict several products from being advertised at all, such as alcohol and pork. Other restrictions related to religious and cultural values include not allowing women to appear in advertising and restricting the manner in which children can be portrayed in advertisements. Each market must be evaluated for the extent to which prevalent customs or values translate into product choice and other consumer behaviors.

Understanding values and rituals can represent a special challenge (or opportunity) when economic development in a country or region creates tensions between the old and the new. The classic example is the dilemma advertisers face as more wives leave the home for outside employment, creating tensions in the home about who should do the housework. This tension over traditional gender assignments in household chores has been particularly acute in Asia, and advertisers there have tried to respond by featuring husbands as homemakers. For example, an ad for vacuum cleaners made by LG Electronics showed a woman lying on the floor exercising and giving herself a facial with slices of cucumbers, while her husband cleaned around her. The ad received mixed reviews from women in Hong Kong and South Korea, with younger women approving, but their mothers disapproving.[10] (Sound familiar?) The advertiser's dilemma in situations like these is how to make ads that reflect real changes in a culture without alienating important segments of consumers by appearing to push the changes. Not an easy task!

Product Use and Preferences. Information about product use and preferences is available for many markets. The major markets of North America, Europe, and the Pacific Rim typically are relatively heavily researched. In recent years, A. C. Nielsen has developed an international database on consumer product use in 26 countries. Also, Roper Starch Worldwide has conducted "global" studies on product preferences, brand loyalty, and price sensitivity in 40 countries.

Studies by firms such as Nielsen and Roper document how consumers around the world display different product use characteristics and preferences. One area of great variation is personal-care products. There is no market in the world like the United States, where consumers are preoccupied with the use of personal-care products such as toothpaste, shampoo, deodorant, and mouthwash. Procter & Gamble, maker of brands such as Crest, Head & Shoulders, Secret, and Scope, among others, learned the hard way in Russia with its Wash & Go shampoo. Wash & Go was a shampoo and conditioner designed for the consumer who prefers the ease, convenience, and speed of one-step washing and conditioning. Russian consumers, accustomed to washing their hair with bar soap, didn't understand the concept of a hair conditioner and didn't perceive a need to make shampooing any more convenient.

---

10. Louise Lee, "Depicting Men Doing Housework Can Be Risky for Marketers in Asia," *Wall Street Journal*, August 14, 1998, B6.

Van Cleef & Arpels

Thumb through a French fashion magazine and you'll appreciate both the passion for art and the passion for perfume that are hallmarks of French culture.

Other examples of unique and culture-specific product uses and preferences come from Brazil and France. In Brazil, many women still wash clothes by hand in metal tubs, using cold water. Because of this behavior, Unilever must specially formulate its Umo laundry powder and tout its effectiveness under these washing conditions. In France, men commonly use cosmetics like those used by women in the United States. Advertising must, therefore, be specifically prepared for men and placed in media to reach them with specific male-oriented appeals. Perfume is another product category that inspires distinctive approaches around the world. As exemplified by Exhibit 9.9, the French have a passion for perfume that transforms their advertisements in this category to near works of art.

2   The Challenges in Executing Advertising Worldwide.

Cross-cultural audience research on basic economic, social, and cultural conditions is an essential starting point for planning international advertising. But even with excellent audience analysis, three formidable and unique challenges face the advertiser: the creative challenge, the media challenge, and the regulatory challenge.

The Creative Challenge. Written or spoken language is a basic barrier to cross-cultural communication. Ads written in Japanese are typically difficult for those who speak only Spanish—this much is obvious. But language issues will always be a formidable challenge. We've all heard stories of how some literal translation of an ad said something very different than what was intended. International blunders are a rich part of advertising lore, and the anecdotes are plentiful:[11]

- The name *Coca-Cola* in China was first rendered as "Ke-kou-ke-la." Unfortunately, Coke did not discover until after thousands of signs had been printed that the phrase means "bite the wax tadpole" or "female horse stuffed with wax," depending on the dialect. Coke then researched 40,000 Chinese characters and found a close phonetic equivalent, "ko-kou-ko-le," which can be loosely translated as "happiness in the mouth."
- In Taiwan, the translation of the Pepsi slogan "Come alive with the Pepsi generation" came out as "Pepsi will bring your ancestors back from the dead."
- Scandinavian vacuum manufacturer Electrolux used the following in an American ad campaign: "Nothing sucks like an Electrolux."
- When Parker Pen marketed a ballpoint pen in Mexico, its ads were supposed to say, "It won't leak in your pocket and embarrass you." Instead the ads said that "It won't leak in your pocket and make you pregnant."

11.   Robert Kirby, "Kirby: Advertising Translates Into Laughs," *Salt Lake Tribune*, *http://www.sltrib.com*, accessed February 24, 1998.

True or not, such tales remind us that communicating with consumers around the world is a special challenge, just in terms of the obvious issue of language.

What is less obvious, however, is the role of **picturing** in cross-cultural communication. There is a widely held belief that pictures are less culturally bound than words are, and that pictures can speak to many cultures at once. International advertisers are increasingly using ads that feature few words and rely on visuals to communicate. This is, as you might expect, a bit more complicated than it sounds.

First, picturing is culturally bound. Different cultures use different conventions or rules to create representations (or pictures) of things. Pictures, just like words, must be "read" or interpreted, and the "rules of reading" pictures vary from culture to culture. People living in Western cultures often assume that everyone knows what a certain picture means. This is not true and is another example of ethnocentrism. Photographic two-dimensional representations are not even recognizable as pictures to those who have not learned to interpret such representations. Symbolic representations that seem so absolute, common, and harmless in one culture can have varied, unusual, and even threatening meaning in another. A picture may be worth a thousand words, but those words may not mean something appropriate—or they may be entirely unintelligible or tasteless—to those in another culture.

Think about the ads in Exhibits 9.10 through 9.12. Which of these ads seem culture-bound? Which would seem to easily cross cultural borders? Why? All of these ads depend on knowing the way to correctly interpret the ad, but some require more cultural knowledge than others. For U.S. consumers, the message of the Visa ad in Exhibit 9.10 is perfectly clear: Visa will help you acquire more stuff. But in less materialistic cultures, the premise of collecting material possessions as an expression of self may be completely incomprehensible. Exhibit 9.11 is a stylized ad created to present a romantic vision of a vacation in Thailand, with German consumers as the target segment. Do you suppose that this ad has any meaning to the average person in Thailand? And the ad in Exhibit 9.12 promises that Sears has everything you need to be the shining star at your high school prom. But while this ad ran in Spanish-speaking countries throughout South America, the high school prom is a more common ritual in North America. Can a teen in Santiago spark to the offer of a formal prom dress when she has no cultural context for interpreting the meaning of "prom"? Not likely.

EXHIBITS 9.10 THROUGH 9.12

Which of these ads seem most bound to specific cultures, based on the pictures in the ads? Are any of them not *culturally bound?*

A few human expressions, such as a smile, are widely accepted to mean a positive feeling. Such expressions and their representations, even though culturally connected, have widespread commonality. But cultureless picture meanings are rare. Larger contributors to cross-cultural commonalities are those representations that are a part of a far-flung culture of commerce and have thus taken on similar meanings in many (but certainly not all) nations. With sports playing an ever-larger role in international commerce, the sports hero is often used to symbolize common meaning across the world. What do you think? Is Tiger Woods Tiger Woods, no matter what he is selling or where he is selling it? Can the Williams sisters revive the Avon cosmetics brand around the world? Avon signed the tennis champs to an endorsement deal to do just that.[12] Similarly, other types of celebrities add their star power in many advertising campaigns around the world. But again, not even Heidi Klum or David Beckham will have common, desirable meaning across all cultures.

The Media Challenge. Of all the challenges faced by advertisers in international markets, the media challenge may be the greatest. Your assumptions about media availability are likely to be faulty in other cultures.

Media Availability and Coverage. Some international markets simply have too few media options. In addition, even if diverse media are available in a particular international market, there may be severe restrictions on the type of advertising that can be done or the way in which advertising is organized in a certain medium.

Many countries have dozens of subcultures and language dialects within their borders, each with its own newspapers and radio stations. This complicates the problem of deciding which combination of newspapers or radio stations will achieve the desired coverage of the market. The presence of a particular medium in a country does not necessarily make it useful for advertisers if there are restrictions on accepting advertising. A prominent example is the BBC networks in the United Kingdom, where advertising is still not accepted. While the United Kingdom does have commercial networks in both radio and television, the BBC stations are still widely popular. Or consider the situation with regard to television advertising in the Netherlands. There, television advertising cannot constitute more than 5 percent of total programming time, and most time slots must be purchased nearly a year in advance. Similar circumstances exist in many markets around the world.

Newspapers are actually the most localized medium worldwide, and they require the greatest amount of local market knowledge to be used correctly as an advertising option. Turkey, for example, has hundreds of daily newspapers; the Netherlands has only a handful. Further, many newspapers (particularly regional papers) are positioned in the market based on a particular political philosophy. Advertisers must be aware of this, making certain that their brand's position with the target audience does not conflict with the politics of the medium.

The best news for advertisers from the standpoint of media availability and coverage is the emergence of several global television networks made possible by cable and satellite technology. Viacom bills its combined MTV Networks (MTVN) as the largest TV network in the world, with a capability to reach over 300 million households worldwide. MTVN also offers expertise in developing special promotions to Generations X, Y, and Z around the world. MTVN has facilitated international campaigns for global brands such as Pepsi, Swatch, Sega, and BMX Bikes. Additionally, MTV has proven expertise in producing programs for specific country markets, like *Mochilao*, a backpack travel show hosted by a popular Brazilian model, as well as programming designed to appeal to its key demographic across cultures.[13] If there is such a thing as a "global consumer," MTVN offers an efficient means for reaching them.

12.   Mercedes Cardona, "Venus and Serena Become Avon's New Leading Ladies," *Advertising Age*, January 22, 2001, 8.
13.   Charles Goldsmith, "MTV Seeks Global Appeal," *Wall Street Journal*, July 21, 2003, B1, B3.

見たい番組ばっかり、見ていたい、そんなわ
がままは、1チャンネル1ジャンルのCSにま
かせなさい。6つのTV放送と5つの通信放
送が見られるCSスカイポートなら、好きな
ジャンルを次から次へと楽しめます。CSチ
ューナー内蔵テレビや、CSチューナー内蔵
ビデオがあれば、あとはCSアンテナを設置
するだけ。そろいもそろった11チャンネルが、
あなたの好奇心を欲求不満にさせません。

EXHIBIT 9.13

Direct broadcast by satellite allows households to receive television transmission via a small, low-cost receiving dish. This is an ad for Skyport TV, one of the early DBS services to serve Japan.

Another development affecting Europe and Asia is direct broadcast by satellite (DBS), via systems like SkyPort (see Exhibit 9.13). DBS transmissions are received through the small, low-cost receiving dishes that have become a familiar sight on rooftops around the world. STAR, which stands for Satellite Televisions Asian Region, sends BBC, U.S., Bollywood, and local programming to 300 million households in 53 countries across Asia.[14] With literally billions of people in its viewing area, STAR has the potential to become one of the world's most influential broadcasting systems.

Media Costs and Pricing. Confounding the media challenge is the issue of media costs and pricing. As discussed earlier, some markets have literally hundreds of media options (recall the Turkish newspapers). Whenever a different medium is chosen, separate payment and placement must be made. Additionally, in many markets, media prices are subject to negotiation—no matter what the official rate cards say. The time needed to negotiate these rates is a tremendous cost in and of itself.

Global coverage is an expensive proposition and both ad rates and the demand for ad space are on the increase. In some markets, advertising time and space are in such short supply that, regardless of the published rate, a bidding system is used to escalate the prices. As you will see in Chapter 14, media costs represent the majority of costs in an advertising budget. With the seemingly chaotic buying practices in some international markets, media costs are indeed a great challenge in executing cost-effective advertising campaigns.

The Regulatory Challenge. The regulatory restrictions on international advertising are many and varied, reflecting diverse cultural values, market by market. The range and specificity of regulation can be aggravatingly complex. Tobacco and liquor advertising are restricted (typically banned from television) in many countries, including India, where the beer market has been slow to develop in part because there is no beer advertising.[15] With respect to advertising to children, Austria, Canada, Germany, and the United States have specific regulations. Other products and topics monitored or restricted throughout the world are drugs (Austria, Switzerland, Germany, Greece, and the Netherlands), gambling (United Kingdom, Italy, and Portugal), and religion (Germany, United Kingdom, and the Netherlands).

This regulatory complexity, if anything, continues to grow. For instance, the European Union, the world's largest trading bloc, has strict regulations protecting citizens' privacy, thus limiting marketers' access to data that are readily available in North America. To cope with these regulations many global companies have dozens of employees in Europe whose job is to keep their companies in compliance with various regulations.[16] Generally, advertisers must be sensitive to the fact that advertising regulations can, depending on the international market, impose limitations on the following:

14.   From the STAR Web site, *http://www.startv.com*, accessed April 6, 2007.

15.   Nandini Lakshman, "The Great Indian Beer Rush," *BusinessWeek*, April 23, 2007, 50.

16.   David Scheer, "Europe's New High-Tech Role: Playing Privacy Cop to the World," *Wall Street Journal*, October 10, 2003, A1, A16.

ETHICS

Who's to Blame for Child Obesity?

Much like the United States, debate is raging across Europe about who is to blame for increases in childhood obesity; and perhaps more importantly, what actions to take to reverse the trend. In Sweden and Norway a ban on TV advertising to children under 12 years old hasn't been effective in reversing the trend. France is considering regulations that force advertisers to add a pro-health message to any ad for processed foods, or pay a tax equal to 1.5 percent of their annual ad budgets to fund public service campaigns promoting better eating habits. And in the United Kingdom, regulators have moved even more aggressively to control advertising for foods high in fat, salt, and sugar (referred to as HFSS products).

Advertisers of course are never fans of ad bans, and in Europe many advertisers tried to change their ways to head off legal dictates. For example, in the United Kingdom, Burger King and KFC stopped all promotions around toy giveaways; Coca-Cola, Cadbury, Kraft, and McDonald's all promised to stop ad campaigns directed at youth under age 12. A trade group of British advertisers also drafted a set of guidelines to discourage member companies from using cartoon or licensed characters, or celebrities, in any ads directed at preteens. Turns out, none of this was enough to satisfy regulators in Britain.

In 2007 U.K. regulator Ofcam announced a sweeping ban on all TV junk-food ads targeted to children under age 16. Britain's health minister at the time, Caroline Flint, also made it clear that she expected the industry to apply the ban to any and all print, poster, online, and cinema ads. As always, the challenge with this regulation was defining what exactly is and is not a "junk food." Ofcam came up with a nutrient-profiling system to decide which foods get designated as HFSS. Among other things, ads for low-fat cheese, butter, dark chocolate, and a 100 year-old sandwich spread known as Marmite got banned. (As Brits have been saying for 100 years, you either love Marmite or hate it because of its odd taste.) Media owners in Britain were upset, to say the least, calling Ofcam's regulations stringent and even "draconian." No surprise there.

At the time of this writing, European Union regulators were discussing whether to apply more restrictions to advertisers in all their member countries. Will any of this stem the tide in the obesity epidemic? We can only hope that someone, somewhere in the world, will find an answer.

Sources: Emma Hall, "Brit Ban on Junk-Food Ads to Cost TV Titans $75 mil," ***Advertising Age***, November 27, 2006, 18; Emma Hall, "In Europe, the Clash over Junk-Food Ads Heats Up," ***Advertising Age***, March 5, 2007, 32.

- The types of products that can be advertised
- The kinds of data that can be collected from consumers
- The types of message appeals that can be used
- The times during which ads for certain products can appear on television
- Advertising to children
- The use of foreign languages (and talent) in advertisements
- The use of national symbols, such as flags and government seals, in advertisements
- The taxes levied against advertising expenditures

In short, just about every aspect of advertising can be regulated, and every country has some peculiarities with respect to ad regulation. A specific case in point is discussed in the Ethics box, where we find regulators in the United Kingdom clearly at odds with the junk-food industry.

③ Advertising Agencies around the World.

An experienced and astute agency can help an advertiser deal with the creative, media, and regulatory challenges just discussed. In Brazil, using a local agency is essential to getting the creative style and tone just right. In Australia, Australian nationals must be involved in certain parts of the production process. And in China, trying to work through the government and media bureaucracy is nearly impossible without the assistance of a local agency. There are nearly 80,000 to choose from in China.[17]

Advertisers have three basic alternatives in selecting an agency to help them prepare and place advertising in other countries: They can use a global agency, an international affiliate, or a local agency.

17. Normandy Madden, "Culture Clash Thwarts Shops from Enjoying China's Boom," *Advertising Age*, May 3, 2004, 20.

EXHIBIT 9.14

Primary holdings of the world's top two global agencies by 2005 revenues.

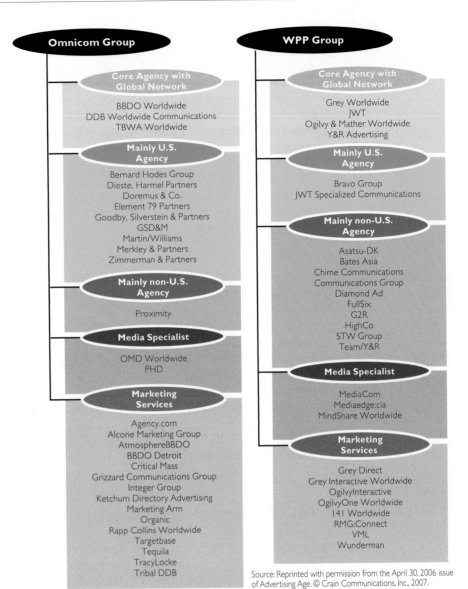

Source: Reprinted with permission from the April 30, 2006 issue of Advertising Age. © Crain Communications, Inc., 2007.

The Global Agency. The consolidation and mergers taking place in the advertising industry are creating more and more **global agencies**, or worldwide advertising groups. Among the giants are Omnicom Group, WPP Group, Interpublic Group of Companies, Publicis Groupe, and Dentsu. The lineup of companies affiliated with Omnicom and WPP Group is detailed in Exhibit 9.14. Note how these multibillion-dollar businesses have assembled a network of diverse service providers to deliver advertising and integrated brand promotion for clients who demand global reach.

The great advantage of a global organization is that it will know the advertiser's products and current advertising programs (presuming it handles the domestic advertising duties). With this knowledge, the agency can either adapt domestic campaigns for international markets or launch entirely new campaigns. Another advantage is the geographic proximity of the advertiser to the agency headquarters, which can often facilitate planning and preparation of ads. The size of a global agency can be a benefit in terms of economies of scale and political leverage.

Global agencies' greatest disadvantage stems from their distance from the local culture. Exporting meaning is never easy. This is no small disadvantage to agencies that actually believe they can do this. Most, however, are not that naive, and they have procedures for acquiring local knowledge.

The International Affiliate. Many agencies do not own and operate worldwide offices, but rather have established foreign-market **international affiliates** to handle clients' international advertising needs. Many times these agencies join a network of foreign agencies or take minority ownership positions in several foreign agencies. The benefit of this arrangement is that the advertiser typically has access to a large number of international agencies that can provide local market expertise. These international agencies are usually well established and managed by foreign nationals, giving the advertiser a local presence in the international market while avoiding any resistance to foreign ownership.

The risk of these arrangements is that while an international affiliate will know the local market, it may be less knowledgeable about the advertiser's brands and competitive strategy. The threat is that the real value and relevance of the brand will not be incorporated into the foreign campaign.

The Local Agency. The final option is for an advertiser to choose a **local agency** in every foreign market where advertising will be carried out. Local agencies have the same advantages as the affiliate agencies just discussed: They will be knowledgeable about the culture and local market conditions. Such agencies tend to have well-established contacts for market information, production, and media buys. But the advertiser that chooses this option is open to administrative problems. There is less opportunity for standardization of the creative effort; each agency in each market will feel compelled to provide a unique creative execution. This lack of standardization can be expensive and potentially disastrous for brand imagery when the local agency seeks to make its own creative statement without a good working knowledge of a brand's heritage. Finally, working with local agencies can create internal communication problems, which increases the risk of delays and errors in execution.

4 Globalized versus Localized Campaigns.

One additional issue needs to be considered in advertising planning for international markets. It involves the extent to which a campaign will be standardized across markets versus localized by market. In discussions of this issue, the question is often posed as: How much can the advertiser globalize the approach? **Globalized campaigns** use the same message and creative execution across all (or most) international markets. Exhibit 9.15 shows an ad from a globalized campaign that you'll find familiar, even though this version appeared in a magazine targeting the Spanish-speaking countries of South America. By contrast, **localized campaigns** involve preparing specific messages and/or creative executions for a particular market. Compare Exhibits 9.15 and 9.16. It should be evident that the dairy producers of Deutschland wanted an ad campaign focused on their local market, not something for a global stage.

The issue is more complex than simply a question of globalized versus localized advertising. Both the brand and its overall marketing strategy must be examined. The marketer must first consider the extent to which the brand can be standardized across markets, and then the extent to which the advertising can be globalized across markets. The degree to which advertising in international markets can use a common appeal, versus whether the ads prepared for each market must be customized, has been a widely debated issue.[18]

18.   For contrasting points of view compare Douglas B. Holt, John A. Quelch and Earl L. Taylor, "How Global Brands Compete," *Harvard Business Review*, September 2004, 68–75; with Darrell K. Rigby and Vijay Vishwanath, "Localization: The Revolution in Consumer Markets," *Harvard Business Review*, April 2006, 82–92.

EXHIBIT 9.15

EXHIBIT 9.16

Globalized advertising campaigns maintain a similar look and feel across international markets. This "got milk" ad could easily work in San Antonio or San Diego, even though it ran in Santiago, Chile.

Here the key message is that German dairy products are best for Germans. And perhaps, "got butter"?

Those who favor the globalized campaign assume that similarities as well as differences between markets can be taken into account. They argue that standardization of messages should occur whenever possible, adapting the message only when absolutely necessary. For example, Mars's U.S. advertisements for Pedigree dog food have used golden retrievers, while poodles were deemed more effective for the brand's positioning and image in Asia. Otherwise, the advertising campaigns were identical in terms of basic message appeal.

Those who argue for the localized approach see each country or region as a unique communication context, and claim that the only way to achieve advertising success is to develop separate campaigns for each market.

The two most fundamental arguments for globalized campaigns are based on potential cost savings and creative advantages. Just as organizations seek to gain economies of scale in production, they also look for opportunities to streamline the communication process. Having one standard theme to communicate allows an advertiser to focus on a uniform brand or corporate image worldwide, develop plans more quickly, and make maximum use of good ideas. Thus, while Gillette sells hundreds of different products in more than 200 countries around the world, its corporate philosophy of globalization is expressed in its "Gillette—The Best a Man Can Get" tagline, which has been repeated again and again all over the world.

Several trends in the global marketplace are working in combination to create conditions that are supportive of globalized campaigns, in that they facilitate the creation of a global consumer. Some of the conditions that support the use of globalized ad campaigns are as follows.

- *Global communications*. Worldwide cable and satellite networks have resulted in television becoming a truly global communications medium. Almost all of MTVN's 200 European advertisers run English-language-only campaigns in the station's 28-nation broadcast area. These standardized messages will themselves serve to homogenize the viewers within these market areas. Similarly, common experience and exposure on the Internet serves to create shared values around the world, especially among young people.
- *Global youth*. As suggested by the Nokia ad from the Czech Republic in Exhibit 9.17, young people around the world have a lot in common. Global communications, global travel, and the demise of communism are argued to have created common norms and values among teenagers around the world.[19] And it's not just teenagers. Toymakers like Mattel, Hasbro, and Lego once worked under the assumption that children around the world would value different toys that carried some local flavor. No more. The large toymakers now create and launch standardized products for children worldwide.[20]
- *Common demographic and lifestyle trends*. Demographic and related lifestyle trends that emerged in the 1980s in the United States are now manifesting themselves in other countries. More working women, more single-person households, increasing divorce rates, and fewer children per household are now widespread demographic phenomena that are effecting common lifestyles worldwide, with advertisers sure to follow. For instance, the rising number of working women in Japan caused Ford Motor Company to prepare ads specifically targeted to this audience.
- *The Americanization of consumption values*. Another advantage for U.S. advertisers has been the Americanization of consumption values around the world. American icons have gained popularity worldwide, especially due to the exportation of pop culture fueled by the U.S. entertainment industry. Adulation of Hollywood, high fashion, and celebrities transcends the United States. On the other hand, high-profile events in recent years like rejecting of the Kyoto treaty on greenhouse gas emissions and the Afghan and Iraq wars are altering America's image around the world. This has yielded a backlash against American brands in some countries.

Arguments against globalization tend to center on issues relating to local market requirements and cultural constraints within markets. The target audiences in different countries must understand and place the same level of importance on brand features or attributes for a globalized campaign to be effective. In many cases, different features are valued at different levels of intensity, making a common message inappropriate. Also, if a globalized campaign defies local customs, values, and regulations, or if it ignores the efforts of local competition, then it has little chance of being successful.

EXHIBIT 9.17

You don't need to speak Czech to appreciate the intent of this ad. As with any Nokia product, it's all about "connecting people" (especially young people).

19.   Arundhati Parmar, "Global Youth United," *Marketing News*, October 28, 2002, 1, 49.
20.   Lisa Bannon, "One-Toy-Fits-All: How Industry Learned to Love the Global Kid," *Wall Street Journal*, April 29, 2003, A1, A12.

It is also the case that local managers do not always appreciate the value of global-ized campaigns. Since they did not help create the campaign, they may drag their feet in implementing it. Without the support of local managers, no globalized cam-paign can ever achieve its potential.

Developing global brands through standardized campaigns can be successful only when advertisers can find similar needs, feelings, or emotions as a basis for communi-cation across cultures. Take McDonald's as a case in point. They have something like 30,000 restaurants in over 100 countries. They work to accommodate local interests by using Olympic champions as spokespersons in China and excluding beef prod-ucts from their menu in India. But wherever they go, McDonald's always stands for family friendly. That's a premise that resonates from Moscow to Memphis, making McDonald's a legitimate global brand.[21]

Finally, global marketers need to distinguish between strategy and execution when using a global approach to advertising. The basic need identified may well be universal, but communication about the product or service that offers satisfaction of the need may be strongly influenced by cultural values in different markets, and thus may work against globalization. For example, have a look at Exhibit 9.18. What do you think of this Italian ad for Yokohama tires? Would it play in Peoria? Everyone wants a tire that performs well, but for Peoria, there are better ways to execute a performance claim for your tire.

EXHIBIT 9.18

This Yokohama ad may fit Italian tastes, but will it play in the United States? American tire ads often stress safety (for example, the Michelin ad showing a baby securely nestled in a solid, sensible tire) and performance in adverse weather, but not usually a torrid romance with the road.

21.   Michael Fielding, "Walk the Line," *Marketing News*, September 1, 2006, 8–10.

Explain the types of audience research that are useful for understanding cultural barriers that can interfere with effective communication.

All of us wear cultural blinders, and as a result we must overcome substantial barriers in trying to communicate with people from other countries. This is a major problem for international advertisers as they seek to promote their brands around the world. To overcome this problem and avoid errors in advertising planning, cross-cultural audience analysis is needed. Such analyses involve evaluation of economic conditions, demographic characteristics, customs, values, rituals, and product use and preferences in the target countries.

 Identify three distinctive challenges that complicate the execution of advertising and IBP in international settings.

Worldwide advertisers face three distinctive challenges in executing their campaigns. The first of these is a creative challenge that derives from differences in experience and meaning among cultures. Even the pictures featured in an ad may be translated differently from one country to the next. Media availability, media coverage, and media costs vary dramatically around the world, adding a second complication to international advertising. Finally, the amount and nature of advertising regulations vary dramatically from country to country and may force a complete reformulation of an ad campaign.

 Describe the three basic types of advertising agencies that can assist in the placement of advertising around the world.

Advertising agencies provide marketers with the expertise needed to develop and execute advertising campaigns in international markets. Marketers can choose to work with global agencies, local agencies in the targeted market, or an international affiliate of the agency they use in their home country. Each of these agency types brings different advantages and disadvantages on evaluative dimensions such as geographic proximity, economies of scale, political leverage, awareness of the client's strategy, and knowledge of the local culture.

 Discuss the advantages and disadvantages of globalized versus localized advertising campaigns.

A final concern for international advertising entails the degree of customization an advertiser should attempt in campaigns designed to cross national boundaries. Globalized campaigns involve little customization among countries, whereas localized campaigns feature heavy customization for each market. Standardized messages bring cost savings and create a common brand image worldwide, but they may miss the mark with consumers in different nations. As consumers around the world become more similar, globalized campaigns may become more prevalent. Teenagers in many countries share similar values and lifestyles and thus make a natural target for globalized campaigns.

KEY TERMS

international advertising
ethnocentrism
self-reference criterion (SRC)
less-developed countries
newly industrialized countries

highly industrialized countries
demographic dividend
picturing
global agencies
international affiliates

local agency
globalized campaigns
localized campaigns

QUESTIONS

1. What was a key factor that contributed to the success of the "Commander Safeguard" ad campaign in Pakistan? Would the company have likely seen the same results from the campaign if it had borrowed an existing American superhero instead of creating one specifically for the Pakistani market?

2. What perils did Japanese automaker Toyota face during its campaign to launch the Prado Land Cruiser in China? How did Toyota ad agency Saatchi & Saatchi respond to the controversy?

3. From the various facts and figures presented throughout this chapter, which did you find most compelling in making the case for the global nature of the advertising business?

4. In this chapter we discuss the challenges advertisers face in Asia when it comes to representing husbands and wives in ads for products such as laundry detergents and vacuum cleaners. Why is this issue challenging in Asia? Would you expect that advertisers face this same challenge in other parts of the world? Where?

5. If you were creating a media strategy for a global advertising campaign, what emphasis would you put on newspapers in executing your strategy? What factors complicate their value for achieving broad market coverage?

6. Explain the appeal of new media options such as direct broadcast by satellite and the Internet for marketers who have created globalized advertising campaigns.

7. Compare and contrast the advantages of global versus local ad agencies for implementing international advertising.

8. Identify several factors or forces that make consumers around the world more similar to one another. Conversely, what factors or forces create diversity among consumers in different countries?

9. Teens and retired people are two market segments found worldwide. If these two segments of European consumers were each being targeted for new advertising campaigns, which one would be most responsive to a globalized ad campaign? Why?

10. The chapter discusses how Apple's quirky "Mac vs. PC" campaign—while popular among American consumers—flopped in both Japan and the United Kingdom. What happened, and how could the advertising team have avoided those problems?

EXPERIENTIAL EXERCISES

1. Select a particular brand or product category that you think would succeed internationally with the right IBP campaign. To accompany the product's global launch, you are asked to identify the best spokesperson for the product, one with broad appeal to international audiences. Who would you choose and why? Explain how a celebrity endorsement, in particular, is the best fit for your product's international launch.

2. Conduct an informal study on the concept of *picturing* in cross-cultural communication. Using library resources, examine a collection of international magazines or newspapers that include ads with photographic representations. What contrasts or similarities can you identify when you compare the ads to American promotions for similar products? What can you infer about the values of a culture based on the types of photographic images that are used?

3. Working in small teams, imagine that you have been hired by cosmetic giant Maybelline to promote its various product lines in China's expanding markets. Identify some of the cultural barriers the company could face—addressing specifically questions about economic conditions, values, customs, and current product use patterns—and then recommend whether the company should adopt a globalized or localized campaign to extend its reach in China.

4. While this chapter discusses the Americanization of consumption values—a phenomenon that has benefited many U.S. firms—American brands also have faced backlash in recent years, as some U.S. companies suffer from perceptions of arrogance, cultural insensitivity, and an overemphasis on consumerism. Working in small groups, brainstorm ways that American business and advertising executives could counteract negative perceptions about the role of the United States in the global economy. Present your ideas to the class.

Preparing the Message

Part Three, "Preparing the Message," marks an important transition in our study of advertising and IBP. The topics to this point have raised the essential process and planning issues that make advertising and integrated brand promotion essential business communication tools. Now we need to take the plunge into the actual preparation of advertising and IBP materials.

Creativity is the soul of advertising and IBP. Without the creative function, there is no advertising or promotion. It's the one thing that communication cannot get by without. Yet most advertising and promotion books treat it as either a bunch of creative "rules" or dry lectures about the value of various fonts. We take a different approach. We first consider the idea of creativity itself: what is it, what distinguishes it, what is its beauty, when is it a beast? What makes creative people creative? We then quickly present the organizational and managerial/creative interface. We discuss honestly what many textbooks don't mention at all: the problem of the competing reward systems of brand managers, account executives, and the creatives. We then offer a chapter like no other—message strategy—in which we detail nine time-honored message strategies and their strategic pluses and minuses. We then offer the best basic chapters on copywriting and art direction available. These chapters have been developed and refined with constant input from industry professionals. If you read them carefully, you will know a lot about art direction and copywriting.

Managing Creativity in Advertising and IBP A famous
dancer once said, "If I could describe dancing, I wouldn't have to do it." Well, we
feel the same way about creativity in advertising—it really is impossible to describe
fully. But in Chapter 10, "Managing Creativity in Advertising and IBP," we do our
best to give you insights into the creative process by giving examples of how the
creative process is worked out in an advertising context—how the "creatives" work
with the "strategists." But we also try to provide insight into this wonderfully slippery
thing called creativity. We do it by drawing on many sources and the examples of
some of the most creative minds of the past century, from physics to painting. While
creativity is creativity, we move from the general to discussing the particular context
of advertising creativity and its unique opportunities and problems. Creativity is the
soul of advertising, and this chapter tries to reveal the magic of advertising.

10

Message Strategy Chapter 11, "Message Strategy," is a chapter like no
other anywhere. We take nine key and primary message objectives and the multiple
matching strategies of each and explore them in detail. We give you lots of specific
real-world examples and walk you through each one. We discuss their advantages
and disadvantages and tell you when they should be used and when they should
not.

11

Copywriting Chapter 12, "Copywriting," explores the development of copy
from the creative plan through dealing with the constraints and opportunities of the
medium that will carry the message. This chapter also highlights guidelines for writing
effective copy and common mistakes in copywriting. A full discussion of radio and
television advertising formats, which provide the context for copy development, is
provided. Writing for the Web is covered. At the end of this chapter is a discussion
of a typical copy approval process used by advertisers and agencies. This chapter
received enormous input from real live advertising professionals with years of
copywriting experience in real advertising agencies. It's a very experience-driven
chapter.

12

Art Direction and Production In Chapter 13, "Art Direction
and Production," you will first learn about creating effective print advertisements
destined for magazines, newspapers, and direct-marketing promotions. The nature
of the illustration, design, and layout components of print advertising are considered.
Then the exciting and complex process of creating broadcast advertising is
discussed. The emphasis in this chapter is on the creative team and how creative
concepts are brought to life. The chapter follows a preproduction, production, and
postproduction sequence. Also highlighted in this chapter are the large numbers of
people outside the agency who facilitate the production effort. Again, this chapter
was overseen by advertising and promotion professionals who have worked in art
direction for years. This is experience talking.

13

CHAPTER 10

After reading and thinking about this chapter, you will be able to do the following:

Describe the core characteristics of great creative minds.

2

Contrast the role of an agency's creative department with that of business managers/account executives and explain the tensions between them.

3

Assess the role of teams in managing tensions and promoting creativity in advertising and IBP applications.

Examine yourself and your own passion for creativity.

Introductory Scenario: Creativity Begets a Creepy King.

In 2004 Crispin Porter + Bogusky (CP+B) was the hot little underdog agency working on low-budget but high-buzz campaigns for clients like Mini, Ikea, and Molson. The business press had fallen in love with CP+B as the so-called prototype of ad agency fused with PR firm.[1] The agency's chief creative force, Alex Bogusky, was anointed as the ad industry guru who had figured out how to thrive in a world where 30-second TV ads appeared on everybody's death watch.[2] CP+B was thriving in its role as the underdog, but then along came the King—Burger King, that is—and nothing would ever be the same.

In 2004 Burger King was in pretty rough shape. Customer traffic was steadily declining and the product line was in need of some serious excitement. Poor results hadn't been good for Burger King's ad agencies either; four of them had been hired and fired in the previous four years. Given this track record, many agencies might have shied away from signing on with the King, but not feisty little CP+B. Skeptics, however, predicted doom and gloom. The sentiment was that CP+B had yet to prove itself with a major mass-market client. Doomsayers expected that CP+B's culture of creativity would be stifled by a company that expected to communicate with customers through 30-second TV spots.[3] Could the underdog survive?

It didn't take long for CP+B to give the King a new look. Right from the start CP+B showed its dexterity with creative that befuddled the skeptics and maxed out the buzz factor. And confirming the basic theses of Chapter 6, newfound success started with an unequivocal focus on the one target segment that everyone agreed Burger King had to win: 18- to 35-year-old males, who are among the heaviest users of fast foods of all kinds. With the target segment well defined, CP+B unleashed a series of offbeat characters to engage the segment. "Subservient Chicken" started it all with a viral, online campaign hyping the new TenderCrisp chicken sandwich. Next up was "Blingo," an

over-the-top rapper who mocked diet-crazed consumers and pushed the Angus steak burger as the antidote to politically correct fast food. And of course, CP+B would resurrect The King, with a new and very strange persona. The King's first job would be to revive the breakfast menu, but ultimately he introduced us to a whole new dimension for evaluating corporate icons: No one does *creepy* better than The King.

It's not just the offbeat and out-of-the-box characters that make this story worth telling. Unlike its predecessors, CP+B did not get fired after one year. More importantly, it really did help turn around the fast food business for Burger King. Three years into the relationship Burger King was celebrating 12 consecutive quarters of revenue growth.[4] Burger King was relevant again and a part of the everyday conversations of men 18 to 35. No doubt CP+B's creative executions helped make this happen.

That Creepy King is clearly on a roll. His holiday promo with Xbox for adver-games like Pocketbike Racer and Big Bumpin (see Exhibit 10.1) set sales records.[5] Here again we see the genius of CP+B at work. Not only did over two million people pay $3.99 for a videogame, they also took home with them a stealth advertisement for Burger King. Every time they play the game, it's one more subtle plug for Burger King. And it just so happens

---

EXHIBIT 10.1

The King offered his loyal subjects a great deal with value meals; few could resist his creepy charm.

1.   Warren Berger, "Dare-Devils," *Business 2.0,* April 2004, 111–116.
2.   Matthew Creamer, "Crispin Ups Ante," *Advertising Age,* January 10, 2005, S-1, S-2.
3.   Ibid.
4.   Eloy Trevino and Scott Davis, "There's Nothing New in Desperate Marketing," *Advertising Age,* April 23, 2007, 22.
5.   Kate MacArthur, "BK Sets High Score with its Adver-games," *Advertising Age,* January 8, 2007, 3, 31.

ETHICS

CP+B's Not-So-Secret Recipe for "Hoopla"

Many have tried to decode the CP+B model to understand the agency's process for achieving creative breakthroughs. Now it turns out that the principals at CP+B have written a book (with Warren Berger) to give us the treasure map. If we can take them at their word (and keep in mind that these are folks who love a good practical joke) then the creatives at CP+B try to follow a few soft and loose principles to help them "rock the boat." They say it's just a matter of emulating P. T. Barnum and focusing on the Hoopla. In their own words, the seven key elements for manufacturing Hoopla are mutation, invention, candor, mischief, connection, pragmatism, and momentum. See if you believe . . .

Mutation: Make a decision that you will always do things differently. Give yourself an attitude adjustment. Start by looking for the established rules and then find a way to violate them. The folks at CP+B claim that "just about every major success we had came as a result of a conscious decision to reject a basic premise or fundamental principle of our industry or of our client's category."

Invention: Consumers constantly crave things that are new and different. As a result, invention is at the heart of Hoopla. CP+B likes to portray itself as an idea factory: constantly in the business of inventing new ideas. One business publication, *Fast Company,* even described CP+B as an agency where "ideas are an almost unhealthy obsession." What's the best way to get started in finding new ideas? Per Bogusky: "Do the opposite of what everybody else does."

Candor: Don't overlook your flaws and limitations. Don't be afraid to talk about them. "If you have a big wart on your face, you'd better make that your thing. Make people love the wart. Convince everyone that it's a beauty mark. Don't waste a second trying to hide it." CP+B claims that it is possible to generate a barrage of Hoopla around a product's "wart-like" limitations, and it is often the case that these limitations are the things that make the product unique and special.

Mischief: No surprise here. CP+B has always tended to "celebrate the troublemaker and pay attention to the rebel." Tricks, pranks, and playfully naughty behavior keep people interested and potentially more engaged with the ultimate message. But of course if you push it too far; mischief can backfire and alienate the audience. Make a lot of people nervous. Make a lot of columnists write stories about you giving free exposure. While communicating "on the edge" takes a delicate balance, at CP+B the default setting appears to be—make more mischief.

Connection: When you adopt the philosophy that *everything* is media, it's much easier to surround the consumer with your message and make a deep connection on behalf of the brand. This also makes it possible to build momentum at the grassroots level without spending huge sums of money. To really connect, stop shouting and get into a conversation. Remember, the good conversationalist "listens, answers questions, and engages the other party in a discussion." Interactive media make the conversation easy to do.

Pragmatism: People like stuff they can use. And fun stuff. Stuff they can pass around. There's no reason that advertising has to be useless stuff that people just ignore or dispose of as fast as possible. Alex Bogusky maintains that the most pragmatic way to promote a product is to just make the product experience better in some way, say by wrapping the product in better or reusable packaging, or by adding little gifts or perks for a repeat customer. Critical to Hoopla: Zero in on the product; find lots of little ways to make it more useful.

Momentum: Choose the right goal. Brand awareness is a simple goal. Momentum is what you really want. Brands have momentum when people are talking about them. News stories are being done about them. Bloggers are arguing about them. Celebrities are seen with them. Product enthusiasts are putting up YouTube videos showing their latest goofy antics. And so on. It's thus very easy to know whether or not your brand has momentum. This is what you're after. Momentum is about constant reinvention and doing tons of work. But it makes clients very happy.

Sources: Warren Berger, "Dare-Devils," *Business 2.0*, April 2004, 111–116; David Kiley, "The Craziest Ad Guys in America," *BusinessWeek*, May 22, 2006, 73–80; Crispin Porter + Bogusky with Warren Berger, *Hoopla*, Brooklyn, NY: powerHouse Books, 2006.

that purchasers were those young-adult males who don't watch much TV but instead spend some 20 hours per week playing video games. Gone are the concerns about CP+B's ability to survive a relationship with a hard-to-please, mass-market client.

So in a matter of just a few years, CP+B went from Underdog to Big Dog. More high-profile (and struggling) clients like Volkswagen and Miller Lite presented big challenges, and it's noteworthy that Crispin remains an agency that the professional critics love to hate.[6] Hence, the agency's seven elements for creating "Hoopla," described in the Ethics box, will likely rile its disbelievers. But in a chapter on

---

6.   Jonah Bloom, "Savaging Crispin May Be Fun, but the Agency Is Not the Enemy," *Advertising Age,* January 29, 2007, 11.

advertising creativity, this is exactly what we should expect. Creative people and creative organizations have to be risk takers. They shake things up. They step on some people's toes. They are commonly boastful, which of course irks their critics even more. They do things differently. So in a discussion of creativity, we should expect stories about great successes, and stories about great failures. But there can be absolutely no doubt that creativity is the secret ingredient in great advertising. In this chapter we will attempt both to convince you of that and to help you understand how to get more of the secret ingredient into your recipe.

Why Does Advertising Need Creativity?

So what is it about creativity that makes it such a big deal in the advertising business? Why do big successful marketing firms like Procter & Gamble send their employees on expensive junkets to the Cannes Lions International Advertising Festival to make connections with the best creative minds in the ad business? Why is creativity the secret sauce that determines the winners and losers? What gives?

There are numerous ways that creativity contributes, but let's start with the pervasive problem of advertiser clutter. Everyone hates ad clutter. So to try to overcome it advertisers generate more ads, which typically just increase the clutter. Yes, clutter begets more clutter in a process that no one seems to be able to shut off.[7] If you want your message heard, you'll need a way to stand out from the crowd, and that will require good creative. Research shows that a primary benefit of award-winning, creative ads is that they break through the clutter and get remembered.[8] But as suggested by the cartoon in Exhibit 10.2, part of the challenge is always to make sure that the brand gets remembered as part of the process.

So for starters we need to get the consumer's attention and be memorable. But that's hardly enough. Going back to Burger King's issues in 2004, the problem wasn't that consumers were unaware of Burger King or didn't know they served Whoppers. It was that Burger King was boring. Largely irrelevant. No momentum. A syndrome one could expect with many mature brands.[9] Burger King needed to become relevant again with its core customers. It needed to get back in their everyday conversations. That's what Subservient Chicken and the creepy King did for Burger King. All of a sudden, it's relevant, in play. This clearly called for a huge dose of creativity. Another brand that stays relevant with its core customers through hip design and creative advertising is featured in Exhibit 10.3.

EXHIBIT 10.2

FoxTrot reminds us of an all too common occurrence with "creative advertising."

7.   Matthew Creamer, "Caught in the Clutter Crossfire: Your Brand," *Advertising Age,* April 2, 2007, 1, 35

8.   Brian Till and Daniel Baack, "Recall and Persuasion: Does Creative Advertising Matter?" *Journal of Advertising,* Fall 2005, 47–57.

9.   Karen Machleit, Chris Allen, and Thomas Madden, "The Mature Brand and Brand Interest," *Journal of Marketing,* October 1993, 72–82.

EXHIBIT 10.3

Creative advertising keeps the brand relevant and interesting for its core customer.

target.com

Another way of saying it is that great brands make emotional connections with consumers. Brands make emotional connections when they engage consumers through complex sensory experiences and deep emotional episodes.[10] Advertising and IBP in its many forms helps create these experiences, but great creative execution brings it all to life. For instance, Apple's iPod wasn't the first MP3 player. Creative Technology Ltd. had a good one on the market almost two years before Apple.[11] But iPod was the first MP3 player to be brought to the market with great advertising; advertising that made iPod synonymous with hip and cool; advertising that made the brand relevant in a social context. And it all worked because of the simple creative genius of the iPod silhouettes. They were everywhere and we couldn't stop watching them. They showed us what we needed to do if we too wanted to become cool. Get that thing. So is creativity important to advertising? In today's world, there would be no advertising without it.

Creativity across Domains.

The creative mind plays with the objects it loves.

—C. G. Jung[12]

Before examining how the creative function plays out in the world of advertising and IBP, let's consider creativity as it manifests in other domains. Creativity, in its essence, is the same no matter what the domain. People who create, create, whether they write novels, take photographs, ponder the particle physics that drives the universe, craft poetry, write songs, play a musical instrument, dance, make films, design buildings, paint, or make ads. Great ads can be truly great creative accomplishments.

Creativity is the ability to consider and hold together seemingly inconsistent elements and forces, making a new connection. This ability to step outside of everyday logic, to free oneself of thinking in terms of "the way things are" or "the way things have to be," apparently allows creative people to put things together in a way that, once we see it, makes sense, is interesting, is creative. To see love and hate as the same entity, to see "round squares," or to imagine time bending like molten steel is

10.   Marc Gobe, *Emotional Branding: The New Paradigm for Connecting Brands to People* (New York: Allworth, 2001).
11.   Cris Prystay, "When Being First Doesn't Make You No. 1," *Wall Street Journal,* August 12, 2004, B1, B2.
12.   Carl G. Jung, cited in Astrid Fitzgerald, *An Artist's Book of Inspiration: A Collection of Thoughts on Art, Artists, and Creativity* (New York: Lindisfarne, 1996), 58.

EXHIBIT 10.4

Pablo Picasso, seen here in a self-portrait, was one of the greatest creative minds of the 20th century. Read about the life of Pablo Picasso at Artcyclopedia (http://www.artcyclopedia.com), or visit the official Pablo Picasso Web site (http://www.picasso.fr).

to have this ability. Ideas born of creativity reveal their own logic, and then we all say, "Oh, I see."

Creativity is sometimes seen as a gift; a special way of seeing the world. Throughout the ages, creative people have been seen as special, revered and reviled, loved and hated. They have served as powerful political instruments (for good and evil), and they have been ostracized, imprisoned, and killed for their art. For example, creativity has been associated with various forms of madness:

Madness, provided it comes as the gift of heaven, is the channel by which we receive the greatest blessings. . . . [T]he men of old who gave their names saw no disgrace or reproach in madness; otherwise they would not have connected it with the name of the noblest of all arts, the art of discerning the future, and called by our ancestors, madness is a nobler thing than sober sense. . . . [M]adness comes from God, whereas sober sense is merely human.

—Socrates[13]

Creativity reflects early childhood experiences, social circumstances, and cognitive styles. In one of the best books ever written on creativity, *Creating Minds,* Howard Gardner examines the lives and works of seven of the greatest creative minds of the 20th century: Sigmund Freud, Albert Einstein, Pablo Picasso (see Exhibit 10.4), Igor Stravinsky, T. S. Eliot, Martha Graham, and Mahatma Gandhi.[14] His work reveals fascinating similarities among great creators. All seven of these individuals, from physicist to modern dancer, were

self confident, alert, unconventional, hardworking, and committed obsessively to their work. Social life or hobbies are almost immaterial, representing at most a fringe on the creator's work time.[15]

Apparently, total commitment to one's craft is the rule. While this commitment sounds positive, there is also a darker reflection:

[T]he self confidence merges with egotism, egocentrism, and narcissism: highly absorbed, not only wholly involved in his or her own projects, but likely to pursue them at costs of other individuals.[16]

Let's be clear: One should not stand between a great creator and his or her work. It's not safe; you'll have tracks down your back. Or maybe the creator will just ignore you. Not coincidentally, these great creative minds had troubled personal lives and simply did not have time for ordinary people (such as their families). According to Gardner, they were generally not very good to those around them. This was true even of Gandhi.

All seven of these great creative geniuses were also great self-promoters. Well-recognized creative people are not typically shy about seeking exposure for their work. Apparently, fame in the creative realm rarely comes to the self-effacing and timid. (A lesson we also see illustrated nicely by CP+B's self-promotional book *Hoopla.*)

13.   Socrates, quoted in Plato, *Phaedrus and the Seventh and Eighth Letters,* Walter Hamilton, trans. (Middlesex, England: Penguin, 1970), 46–47, cited in Kay Redfield Jamison, *Touched with Fire: Manic-Depressive Illness and the Artistic Temperament* (New York: Free Press, 1993), 51.

14.   Howard Gardner, *Creating Minds: An Anatomy of Creativity Seen through the Lives of Freud, Einstein, Picasso, Stravinsky, Eliot, Graham, and Gandhi* (New York: Basic Books, 1993).

15.   Gardner, *Creating Minds,* 364.

16.   Ibid.

All seven of these great creators were, very significantly, childlike in a critical way. All of them had the ability to see things as a child does. Einstein spent much of his career revolutionizing physics by pursuing in no small way an idea he produced as a child: What would it be like to move along with a strand of pure light? Picasso commented that it ultimately was his ability to paint like a child (along with amazingly superior technical skills) that explained much of his greatness. Freud's obsession with and interpretation of his childhood dreams had a significant role in what is one of his most significant works, *The Interpretation of Dreams*.[17] T. S. Eliot's poetry demonstrated imaginative abilities that typically disappear past childhood. The same is true of Martha Graham's modern dance. Even Gandhi's particular form of social action was formulated with a very simple and childlike logic at its base. These artists and creative thinkers never lost the ability to see the ordinary as extraordinary, to not have their particular form of imagination beaten out of them by the process of "growing up."

Of course, the problem with this childlike thinking is that these individuals also behaved as children throughout most of their lives. Their social behavior was egocentric and selfish. They expected those around them to be willing to sacrifice at the altar of their gift. Gardner put it this way: "[T]he carnage around a great creator is not a pretty sight, and this destructiveness occurs whether the individual is engaged in solitary pursuit or ostensibly working for the betterment of humankind."[18] They can, however, be extraordinarily charming when it suits their ambitions. They could be monsters at home, and darlings when performing.

Apparently, the creative mind also desires marginality;[19] they love being outsiders. They revel in it. This marginality seems to have been absolutely necessary to these people, and provided them with some requisite energy.

Emotional stability did not mark these creative lives either. All but Gandhi had a major mental breakdown at some point in their lives, and Gandhi suffered from at least two periods of severe depression. Extreme creativity, just as the popular myth suggests, seems to come at some psychological price.

¡Yo Quiero Taco Bell!

EXHIBIT 10.5

Chihuahuas want Taco Bell.

Creative Genius in the Advertising Business. While perhaps not as influential as the Gandhis or the Freuds, it is common to see individuals from the ad business praised for remarkable careers that have clearly revealed sparks of creative genius. One example is Lee Clow, who at the time of this writing was 63 years old and still the main creative force with TBWA/Chiat/Day. You know his work. The Energizer Bunny, billboards for Nike, "Dogs Rule" for Pedigree, the "1984" spot that launched Apple's Mac, and those iPod silhouettes are all from his portfolio. Another example is provided in Exhibit 10.5.

17. Gardner, *Creating Minds*, 145; Sigmund Freud, *The Interpretation of Dreams*, in A. A. Brill, ed., *The Basic Writings of Sigmund Freud* (New York: Modern Library, 1900/1938).
18. Gardner, *Creating Minds*, 369.
19. Ibid.

Lee Clow is one of the great creative maestros of the modern advertising business. *Ad Age* referred to him simply as "The Dude Who Thought Different."[20] But those who have worked at his side say his real gift is as the synthesizer. Sorting through a wall full of creative ideas in the form of rough sketches, Lee is the guy who knows how to pick a winner. The one simplest marketing idea that is most likely to resonate with consumers, as in "Impossible is Nothing" for Adidas or "Shift" for Nissan. Some say he is fervent about great creativity; others say he is prone to fits of temper and can be mean to those who don't see things his way.[21] Now doesn't that sound a lot like the other great creators discussed above?

Creativity in the Business World. The difficulty of determining who is creative and who is not or what is creative and what is not in the artistic world is paralleled in the business world. Certainly, no matter how this trait is defined, creativity is viewed in the business world as a positive quality for employees. It's been said that creative individuals assume almost mythical status in the corporate world. Everybody needs them, but no one is sure who or what they are. Furthermore, business types often expect that working with creative people will not be easy. Often, they are right.

Can One Become Creative? This is an important question. The popular answer in a democratic society would be to say, "Yes, sure; you too can be a Picasso." But in the end the genius of a Picasso or an Einstein is a pretty high standard, one that most of us will not be able to achieve. And given some of the costs associated with intense creativity, maybe we don't want to be that anyway. But this question really depends on what one means by *creativity*. Is a person creative because he or she can produce a creative result? Or is a person creative because of the way he or she thinks? Further, who gets to determine what is creative and what is not? When an elephant paints holding a brush with its trunk, and the paintings sell for thousands of dollars, does it mean that the elephant is creative?

While there are numerous elusive elements on the path to being creative, we need to keep coming back to the point that in the advertising business, we can't do without it. So we will take the point of view that while few of us are destined to become the next Pablo Picasso or even Lee Clow, that doesn't mean that we can't learn how to improve our own level of creativity. We all start from a different baseline, but we all can learn to be more creative and contribute to the creativity process in an advertising application. We'll revisit this later in the chapter.

Against Stereotype. In concluding our discussion about the traits of extraordinarily creative people, a couple of notes of caution are in order. First, it should be understood that just because you are in a "creative" job, it doesn't follow that you are actually creative. Second, just because you are on the account or business side (a.k.a. "a suit") doesn't mean you are uninspired (as in Exhibit 10.6). As the folks at CP+B will tell you, good ideas can come from anyone, anywhere.[22] Sometimes even the client (gasp!) can have a good idea. Tension and conflict (a.k.a., suits versus the creatives) are regular occurrences in producing great advertising. It's normal. One needs to anticipate and manage this conflict in positive ways to get good outcomes. We take up the issues involved in this challenge in the section to follow.

---

20.   Alice Cuneo, "The Dude Who Thought Different," *Advertising Age,* July 31, 2006, 1, 25.
21.   Ibid.
22.   Warren Berger, "Dare-Devils," *Business 2.0,* April 2004, 111–116.

Artist David Ross's Swimming Suits, a view of corporate individuality and creativity that is often shared by art directors and copywriters.

Agencies, Clients, and the Creative Process.

As an employee in an agency creative department, you will spend most of your time with your feet up on a desk working on an ad. Across the desk, also with his feet up, will be your partner—in my case, an art director. And he will want to talk about movies.

In fact, if the truth be known, you will spend fully one-fourth of your career with your feet up talking about movies.

The ad is due in two days. The media space has been bought and paid for. The pressure's building. And your muse is sleeping off a drunk behind a dumpster somewhere. Your pen lies useless. So you talk movies.

That's when the traffic person comes by. Traffic people stay on top of a job as it moves through the agency; which means they also stay on top of you. They'll come by to remind you of the horrid things that happen to snail-assed creative people who don't come through with the goods on time . . .

So you try to get your pen moving. And you begin to work; and working in this business means staring at your partner's shoes.

That's what I've been doing from 9 to 5 for almost 20 years. Staring at the bottom of the disgusting tennis shoes on the feet of my partner, parked on the desk across from my disgusting tennis shoes. This is the sum and substance of life at an agency.

—Luke Sullivan, copywriter and author[23]

Exhibit 10.7 is illustrative of many creative pursuits: lots of time trying to get an idea, or the right idea. You turn things over and over in your head, trying to see the light. You try to find that one way of seeing it that makes it all fall into place. Or it just comes to you, real easy, just

Companies like ibid (http://www.ibidphoto.com) cater to the creative: The ibid catalog offers images to jumpstart the imagination.

23. Luke Sullivan, "Staring at Your Partner's Shoes," in *Hey Whipple, Squeeze This: A Guide to Creating Great Ads* (New York: Wiley, 1998), 20–22.

like that. Magic. Every creative pursuit involves this sort of thing. However, advertising and IBP, like all creative pursuits, are unique in some respects. Ad people come into an office and try to solve a problem, always under time pressure, given to them by some businessperson. Often the problem is poorly defined, and there are competing agendas. They work for people who seem not to be creative at all, and who seem to be doing their best not to let them be creative. They are housed in the "creative department," which makes it seem as if it's some sort of warehouse where the executives keep all the creativity so they can find it when they need it, and so it won't get away. This implies that one can pick some up, like getting extra batteries at Target.

Oil and Water: Conflicts and Tensions in the Creative/Management Interface.

Here are some thoughts on management and creativity by two advertising greats:

The majority of businessmen are incapable of original thinking, because they are unable to escape from the tyranny of reason. Their imaginations are blocked.

—William Bernbach[24]

If you're not a bad boy, if you're not a big pain in the ass, then you are in some mush in this business.

—George Lois[25]

As you can see, this topic rarely yields tepid, diplomatic comments. Advertising is produced through a social process. As a social process, however, it's marked by the struggles for control and power that occur within departments, between departments, and between the agency and its clients on a daily basis.

Most research concerning the contentious environment in advertising agencies places the creative department in a central position within these conflicts. We know of no research that has explored conflict within or between departments in an advertising agency that doesn't place the creative department as a focus of the conflict. One explanation hinges on reactions to the uncertain nature of the product of the creative department. What do they do? From the outside it sometimes appears that they are having a lot of fun and just screwing around while everyone else has to wear a suit to the office and try to sell more stuff for their client. This creates tension between the creative department and the account services department.

Additionally, the two departments do not always share the same ultimate goals for advertisements. Individuals in the creative department see an ad as a vehicle to communicate a personal creative ideology that will further their careers. (See Exhibit 10.8.) The account manager, serving as liaison between client and agency, sees the goal of the communication as achieving some predetermined objective in the marketplace.[26]

Another source of conflict is attributed to differing perspectives due to differing background knowledge of members of creative groups versus account services teams. Account managers must be generalists with broad knowledge, whereas creatives are specialists who must possess great expertise in a single area.[27]

Regardless of its role as a participant in conflict, the creative department is recognized as an essential part of any agency's success. It is a primary consideration of potential clients when they select advertising agencies.[28] Creativity has been found

24.   William Bernbach, quoted in Thomas Frank, *The Conquest of Cool: Business Culture, Consumer Culture, and the Rise of Hip Consumerism* (Chicago: University of Chicago Press, 1997).
25.   George Lois, quoted in Randall Rothenberg, *Where the Suckers Moon* (New York: Knopf, 1994), 135–172.
26.   Elizabeth Hirschman, "The Effect of Verbal and Pictorial Advertising Stimuli on Aesthetic, Utilitarian and Familiarity Perceptions," *Journal of Advertising,* 1985, 27–34.
27.   B. G. Vanden Berg, S. J. Smith, and J. W. Wickes, "Internal Agency Relationships: Account Service and Creative Personnel," *Journal of Advertising,* vol. 15, no. 2 (1986), 55–60.
28.   D. West, "Restricted Creativity: Advertising Agency Work Practices in the U.S., Canada and the U.K.," *Journal of Creative Behavior,* vol. 27, no. 3 (1993), 200–213; D. C. West, "Cross-National Creative Personalities, Processes, and Agency Philosophies," *Journal of Advertising Research,* vol. 33, no. 5 (1993), 53–62.

EXHIBIT 10.8

Team One Advertising (http://www.teamoneadv.com) *has an interesting spin on what motivates agency creatives; here, it parodies Maslow's hierarchy to make its point.*

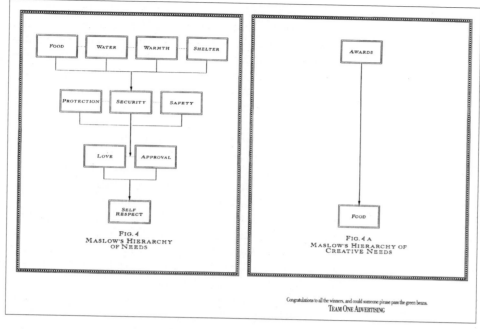

to be crucial to a positive client/advertiser relationship. Interestingly, clients see creativity as an overall agency trait, whereas agency people place the responsibility for it firmly on the shoulders of the creative department.[29]

However, many clients don't recognize their role in killing the very same breakthrough ideas that they claim to be looking for (see Exhibit 10.9). Anyone who has worked in the creative department of an advertising agency for any length of time has a full quiver of client stories—like the one about the client who wanted to produce a single 30-second spot for his ice cream novelty company. The creative team went to work and brought in a single spot that everyone agreed delivered the strategy perfectly, set up further possible spots in the same campaign, and, in the words of the copywriter, was just damn funny. It was the kind of commercial that you actually look forward to seeing on television. During the storyboard presentation, the client laughed in all the right places, and admitted the spot was on strategy.

EXHIBIT 10.9

What clients like and what clients approve are often two very different things.

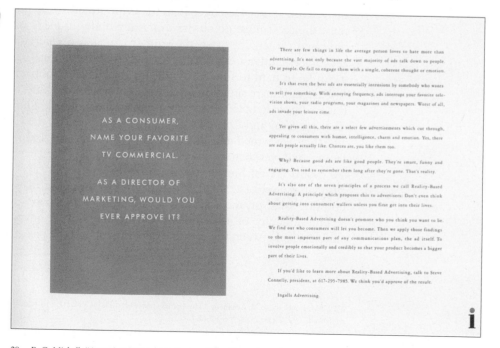

29.   P. C. Michell, "Accord and Discord in Agency-Client Perceptions of Creativity," *Journal of Advertising Research,* vol. 24, no. 5 (1984), 9–24.

The client said the agency was trying to force him into a corner where he had to approve the spot, since they didn't show him any alternatives. The agency went back to work. Thirty-seven alternatives were presented over the next six months. Thirty-seven alternatives were killed. Finally, the client approved a spot, the first spot from half a year earlier. There was much rejoicing. One week later, he canceled the production, saying he wanted to put the money behind a national coupon drop instead. Then he took the account executive out to lunch and asked why none of the creatives liked him.

It's easy and sometimes fun to blame clients for all of the anxieties and frustrations of the creatives; especially if you've worked in a creative department. You can criticize the clients all you want and, since they aren't in the office next to you, they can't hear you. But, despite the obvious stake that creative departments have in generating superior advertising, it should be mentioned that no creative ever put $10 million of his or her own money behind a campaign.

Indeed, you can't always blame the client. Sometimes the conflicts and problems that preclude wonderful creative work occur within the walls of the advertising agency itself. To say there can be conflict between the creative department and other departments within an agency is a bit like saying there will be conflict when Jerry Springer walks into a studio. In advertising, the conflict often centers on the creative department versus account services. So why doesn't everybody pull together and love each other within an agency?

When a client is unhappy, it fires the agency. Billings and revenue drop. Budgets are cut. And pink slips fly. It's no wonder that conflict occurs. When someone is looking out for his or her job, it's tough not to get involved in struggles over control of the creative product. **Account executives** (AEs) are the liaison between the agency and the client. Every day when they walk in the door, their prime responsibility is to see that the client is happy. Since clients hold the final power of approval over creative output, the members of the account team see an advertisement as a product they must control before the client sees it.[30] Members of the account team perceive the creatives as experts in the written word or in visual expression. However, they believe that creatives don't understand advertising strategy or business dealings. Members of the creative department resent all that.

For AEs to rise in their career, they must excel in the care and feeding of clients. It's a job of negotiation, gentle prodding, and ambassadorship. For creatives to rise, their work must challenge. It must arrest attention. It must provoke. At times, it must shock. It must do all the things a wonderful piece of art must do. Yet, as we indicated earlier, this is all the stuff that makes for nervous clients. And that is an account executive's nightmare. As suggested in Exhibit 10.10, it is little wonder that it can be so hard to find AEs with just the right disposition.

This nightmare situation for the AEs produces the kind of ads that win awards for the creatives. People who win awards are recognized: Their work gets published in *The One Show* and *Communication Arts* and appears on the Clios. They are in demand and they are wined and dined by rival agencies (see Exhibit 10.11). They become famous and, yes, rich by advertising standards. Are they happier, better people? Some are. Some aren't. So the trick is, how do you get creatives to want to pursue cool ads that also sell? Let them win awards even though it may have nothing to do with boosting sales, or, more simply, let them keep their job?

The difficulty of assessing the effectiveness of an advertisement can also create antagonism between the creative department and the research department.[31] Vaughn

30.   A. J. Kover and S. M. Goldberg, "The Games Copywriters Play: Conflict, Quasi-Control, a New Proposal," *Journal of Advertising Research,* vol. 25, no. 4 (1995), 52–62.
31.   Ibid.

EXHIBIT 10.10

How to identify a good AE.

For some 25 years I was an advertising agency "AE," eventually rising through the crabgrass to become a founder, president, chairman and now chairman emeritus of Borders, Perrin and Norrander, Inc.

During all those years, I pondered the eternal question: Why do some advertising agencies consistently turn out a superior creative product while others merely perpetuate mediocrity? Is the answer simply to hire great writers and art directors? Well, certainly that has a lot to do with it, but I would suggest that there is another vital component in the equation for creative success.

Outstanding creative work in an ad agency requires a ferocious commitment from all staffers, but especially from the account service person. The job title is irrelevant—account executive, account manager, account supervisor—but the job function is critical, particularly when it comes to client approvals. Yes, I am speaking of the oft-maligned AE, the "suit" who so frequently is the bane of the Creative Department.

So how in the wide world does one identify this rare species, this unusual human being who is sensitive to the creative process and defends the agency recommendations with conviction and vigor? As you might expect, it is not easy. But there are some signals, some semihypothetical tests that can be used as diagnostic tools:

To begin with, look for unflappability, a splendid trait to possess in the heat of battle. In Australia last year I heard a chap tell about arriving home to "find a bit of a problem" under his bed. An eight-foot python had slithered in and coiled around the man's small dog. Hearing its cries, he yanked the snake out from under the mattress, pried it loose from the mutt, tossed it out the door and "dispatched it with a garden hoe." Was he particularly frightened or distressed? Not at all. "I've seen bigger snakes," he said, helping himself to another Foster's Lager. Now, that's the kind of disposition which wears well in account service land.

Source: Wes Perrin, "How to Identify a Good AE," *Communication Arts Advertising Annual* 1988 (Palo Alto, Calif: Coyne and Blanchard, Inc., 1988), 210.

EXHIBIT 10.11

Foote, Cone & Belding used a bit of sassy, tongue-in-cheekiness to signal that résumés were wanted.

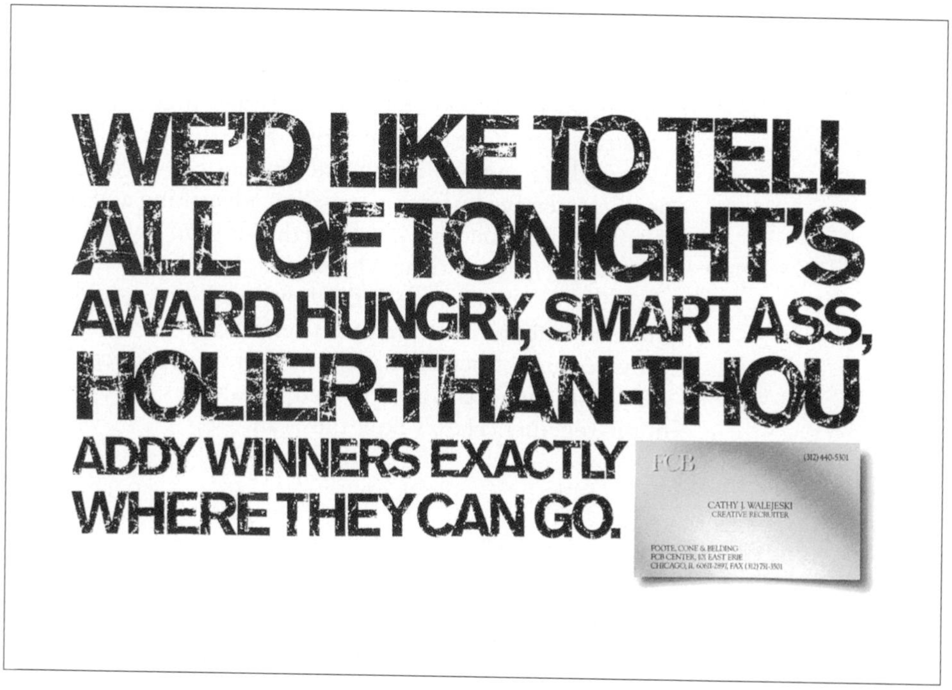

If you don't like this ad, we'll find out why.

For accurate and objective advertising research, call Kevin Menk at (612) 331-9222.

Project Research, Inc.

1313 Fifth Street SE, Minneapolis, MN 55414

We could fill this page with interesting information about our research company, but research indicates you wouldn't read it.

Project Research, Inc.

1313 Fifth Street SE, Minneapolis, MN 55414
(612) 331-9222

EXHIBITS 10.12 AND 10.13

Research on an ad's effectiveness is important and difficult but not always a popular task.

states that the tumultuous social environment between creative departments and ad testers represents the "historical conflict between art and science . . . these polarities have been argued philosophically as the conflict between Idealism and Materialism or Rationalism and Empiricism."[32] In the world of advertising, people in research departments are put in the unenviable position of judging the creatives (see Exhibits 10.12 and 10.13). So, again, "science" judges art. Creatives don't like this, particularly when it's bad science or not science at all. Of course, researchers are sometimes creative themselves, and they don't typically enjoy being an additional constraint on those in the creative department.

So is there any way around all the tension and conflict that is inherent in the very people-intensive business of creating advertising and integrated brand promotion? As detailed in Exhibit 10.14, the insights of John Sweeney—a true expert on advertising creativity—make it clear what *not* to do if creativity is the goal. Professor Sweeney also gives us the hint we need about what we should do. He notes that bad work is more a matter of structure than talent. So given a pool of talented people, we have to provide some structure that allows them to produce their best work. Creative types, AEs, marketing managers, and ad researchers have to find a way to make beautiful music together. Here's how they can.

32.   R. L. Vaughn, "Point of View. Creatives versus Researchers—Must They Be Adversaries?" *Journal of Advertising Research,* vol. 22, no. 6 (1983), 45–48.

One of the advantages of being a practitioner-turned-educator is the opportunity to interact with a large number of agencies. Much like Switzerland, an academic is viewed as a neutral in current affairs and not subject to the suspicions of a potential competitor.

The result of my neutral status has been the opportunity to watch different agencies produce both great and poor work. And, as a former associate creative director, I'd like to share the trends I've seen in the development of bad creative. The revelation: Bad work is more a matter of structure than talent. Here are 12 pieces of advice if you want to institutionalize bad creative work in your agency:

1. Treat your target audience like a statistic.

Substituting numbers for getting a feel for living, breathing people is a great way to make bad work inevitable. It allows you to use your gut instinct about "women 55 to 64" rather than the instinct that evolves from really understanding a group of folks. The beauty with staying on the statistical level is that you get to claim you did your homework when the creative turns out dreadful. After all, there were 47 pages of stats on the target.

2. Make your strategy a hodgepodge.

Good ads have one dominant message, just one. Most strategies that result in lousy work have lots more than one. They are political junkyards that defy a creative wunderkind to produce anything but mediocrity. So make everybody happy with the strategy and then tell your creatives to find a way to make it all work. You'll get bad work, for sure.

3. Have no philosophy.

William Bernbach believed in a certain kind of work. His people emulated his philosophy and produced a consistent kind of advertising that built a great agency. Now, to be controversial, I'll say the exact same thing about Rosser Reeves. Both men knew what they wanted, got it, and prospered.

The agency leaders who do hard sell one day, then new wave the next, create only confusion. More important, the work does not flow from a consistent vision of advertising and a code of behavior to achieve that advertising. Instead, there is the wild embrace of the latest fashion or the currently faddish bromide making the rounds at conventions. So beware of those who have a philosophy and really are true to it. They are historically at odds with lousy work.

4. Analyze your creative as you do a research report.

The cold, analytical mind does a wonderful job destroying uncomfortable, unexpected work. Demand that every detail be present in every piece of creative and say it is a matter of thoroughness. The creative work that survives your ice storm will be timid and compromised and will make no one proud.

5. Make the creative process professional.

"Creative types collect a paycheck every two weeks. They'd better produce and do it now. This is, after all, a business." The corporate performance approach is a highly recommended way of developing drab print and TV. Treating the unashamedly artistic process of making ads as if it were an offshoot of the local oil filter assembly plant promises to destroy risk-taking and morale. Your work will become every bit as distinctive as a gray suit. More important, it will be on schedule. And both are fine qualities in business and we are a business, aren't we?

6. Say one thing and do another.

Every bad agency says all the right things about risk-taking, loving great creative, and admiring strong creative people. It is mandatory to talk a good game and then do all the things that destroy great work. This will help keep spirits low and turnover high in the creatives who are actually talented. And then you'll feel better when they leave after a few months because you really do like strong creative people—if they just weren't so damn defensive.

7. Give your client a candy store.

To prove how hard you work, insist on showing numerous half-thought-out ideas to your client. The approved campaign will have lots of problems nobody thought about and that will make the final work a mess.

Campaigns with strong ideas are rare birds, and they need a great deal of thinking to make sure they're right. So insist on numerous campaigns and guarantee yourself a series of sparrows rather than a pair of eagles.

Continued

EXHIBIT 10.14

Assuring poor creative.

8. Mix and match your campaigns.

Bring three campaigns to your client, and then mix them up. Take a little bit of one and stick it on another. Even better, do it internally. It's like mixing blue, red, and green. All are fine colors, but red lacks the coolness of blue. Can't we add a little? The result of the mix will be a thick muddy clump. Just like so many commercials currently on the air.

9. Fix it in production.

Now that your procedure has created a half-baked campaign that is being mixed up with another, tell the creative to make it work by excellent production values. Then you can fire the incompetent hack when the jingle with 11 sales points is dull.

10. Blame the creative for bad creative.

After all, you told them what they should do. ("Make it totally unexpected, but use the company president and the old jingle.") The fault lies in the fact that you just can't find good talent anymore. Never mind that some creative departments have low turnover and pay smaller salaries than you do.

11. Let your people imitate.

"Chiat/Day won awards and sales for the Apple *1984* commercial, so let's do something like that for our stereo store account." This approach works wonders because your imitation appears lacking the original surprise that came from a totally expected piece of work. You can even avoid the controversy that surrounded Chiat/Day when half the industry said the ad was rotten. Your imitation can blend right in with all the other imitations and, even better, will have no strategic rationale for your bizarre execution.

12. Believe posttesting when you get a good score.

That way you can be slaughtered by your client when your sensitive, different commercial gets a score 20 points below norm. The nice things you said about posttesting when you got an excellent score with your "singing mop" commercial cannot be taken back. If you want to do good work, clients must somehow be made to use research as a tool. If you want to do bad creative, go ahead, and believe that posttesting rewards excellent work.

Naturally, a lot of bad creative results from egomania, laziness, incompetence, and client intractability—but a lot less than most believe. I have found that bad work usually comes from structures that make talented people ineffective and that demand hard work, human dedication, and tremendous financial investment to produce work that can be topped by your average high school senior.

John Sweeney, a former associate creative director at Foote, Cone & Belding, Chicago, teaches advertising at the University of North Carolina–Chapel Hill.

3 Making Beautiful Music Together: Coordination, Collaboration, and Creativity.

Metaphors help us understand, so let's use a metaphor to appreciate the challenge of executing sophisticated advertising and IBP campaigns. Executing an IBP campaign is very much like the performance of a symphony orchestra. To produce glorious music, many individuals must make their unique contributions to the performance, but it sounds right only if the maestro brings it all together at the critical moment. Make it a point to attend a symphony and get there early so that you can hear each individual musician warming up his or her instrument. Reflect on the many years of dedicated practice that this individual put in to master that instrument. Reflect on the many hours of practice that this individual put in to learn his or her specific part for tonight's performance. As you sit there listening to the warm-up, notice how the random collection of sounds becomes increasingly painful to the ears. With each musician doing his or her own thing, the sound is a collection of hoots and clangs that grows louder as the performance approaches. Mercifully, the maestro finally steps to the podium to quell the cacophony. All is quiet for a moment. The musicians focus on their sheet music for reassurance, even though by now they could play their individual parts in their sleep. Finally, the maestro calls the orchestra into action. As a group, as a collective, as a team, with each person executing a specific assignment as defined by the composer, under the direction of the maestro, they make beautiful music together.

So it goes in the world of advertising. Preparing and executing breakthrough IBP campaigns is a people-intensive business. Many different kinds of expertise will be needed to pull it off, and this means many different people must be enlisted to play a variety of roles. But some order must be imposed on the collection of players.

Frequently, a maestro will need to step in to give the various players a common theme or direction for their work. Lee Clow of TBWA Worldwide quite naturally received a conductor's baton as a gift. About the role of maestro he has said: "I was a pretty good soloist when I joined the orchestra, but I think I'm a much better conductor than I was a soloist. If we can make beautiful music together, that makes me happy. . . . And different people end up getting to do the solos and get the standing ovations."[33] Lee Clow definitely gets it and now you do too.

Coordination and collaboration will be required for executing any kind of advertising, which means simply that advertising is a team sport. Moreover, the creative essence of the campaign can be aided and elevated by skillful use of teams. Teams can generate a synergy that allows them to rise above the talents of their individual members on many kinds of tasks. (Yes, the whole can be greater than the sum of the individual parts.) So even without an Igor Stravinsky, Pablo Picasso, or Martha Graham in our midst, a group of diverse and motivated people can be expected to not only generate big ideas, but also put them into action.

Great advertising and great teamwork go hand in hand, which of course means that we don't just want to hope for a good team, we need to make it happen. Great teamwork can't be left to chance. It must be planned for and facilitated if it is to occur with regularity. So next we will introduce several concepts and insights about teams to make you better at teamwork. In addition, you will come to appreciate how important teams can be in producing that one elusive thing that everyone wants: *creativity*.

What We Know about Teams.
No doubt you have taken a class where part of your grade was determined by teamwork. Get used to it. More and more instructors in all sorts of classes are incorporating teamwork as part of their courses because they know that interpersonal skills are highly valued in the real world of work. In fact, an impressive body of research indicates that teams have become essential to the effectiveness of modern organizations. In their book *The Wisdom of Teams*, consultants Jon Katzenbach and Douglas Smith review many valuable insights about the importance of teams. Here we summarize several of their key conclusions.[34]

Teams Rule! There can be little doubt that in a variety of organizations, teams have become the primary means for getting things done. The growing number of performance challenges faced by most businesses—as a result of factors such as more demanding customers, technological changes, government regulation, and intensifying competition—demand speed and quality in work products that are simply beyond the scope of what an individual can offer. In most instances, teams are the only valid option for getting things done. This is certainly the case for advertising.

It's All about Performance. Research shows that teams are effective in organizations where the leadership makes it perfectly clear that teams will be held accountable for performance. Teams are expected to produce results that satisfy the client and yield financial gains for the organization.

Synergy through Teams. Modern organizations require many kinds of expertise to get the work done. The only reliable way to mix people with different expertise to generate solutions where the whole is greater than the sum of the parts is through team discipline. Research shows that blending expertise from diverse disciplines often produces the most innovative solutions to many different types of business problems.[35] The "blending" must be done through teams.

33.   Alice Cuneo, "The Dude Who Thought Different," *Advertising Age,* July 31, 2006, 25.

34.   Jon R. Katzenbach and Douglas K. Smith, *The Wisdom of Teams: Creating the High-Performance Organization* (Boston: Harvard Business School Press, 1993).

35.   Dorothy Leonard and Susaan Straus, "Putting Your Company's Whole Brain to Work," *Harvard Business Review,* July–August 1997, 111–121.

The Demise of Individualism? Rugged individualism is the American Way. Always look out for number one! Are we suggesting that a growing reliance on teams in the workplace must mean a devaluation of the individual and a greater emphasis on conforming to what the group thinks? Not at all. Left unchecked, of course, an "always look out for number one" mentality can destroy teams. But teams are not incompatible with individual excellence. Effective teams find ways to let each individual bring his or her unique contributions to the forefront. When an individual does not have his or her own contribution to make, then one can question that person's value to the team. As the old saying goes, "If you and I think alike, then one of us is unnecessary."

Teams Promote Personal Growth. An added benefit of teamwork is that it promotes learning for each individual team member. In a team, people learn about their own work styles and observe the work styles of others. This learning makes them more effective team players in their next assignment. Once team principles take hold in an organization, momentum builds.

Leadership in Teams. A critical element in the equation for successful teams is leadership. Leaders do many things for their teams to help them succeed.[36] Teams ultimately must reach a goal to justify their standing, and here is where the leader's job starts. The leader's first job is to help the team build consensus about the goals they hope to achieve and the approach they will take to reach those goals. Without a clear sense of purpose, the team is doomed. Once goals and purpose are agreed upon, then the leader plays a role in ensuring that the work of the team is consistent with the strategy or plan. This is a particularly important role in the context of creating IBP campaigns.

Finally, team leaders must help do the real work of the team. Here the team leader must be careful to contribute ideas without dominating the team. There are also two key things that team leaders should never do: *They should not blame or allow specific individuals to fail, and they should never excuse away shortfalls in team performance.*[37] Mutual accountability must be emphasized over individual performance.

Direct Applications to the Account Team. Think of an agency's **account team** as a bicycle wheel, with the team leader as the hub of a wheel. Spokes of the wheel then reach out to the diverse disciplinary expertise needed in today's world of advertising and IBP. The spokes will represent team members from direct marketing, public relations, broadcast media, graphic design, interactive, creative, accounting, and so on. The hub connects the spokes and ensures that all of them work in tandem to make the wheel roll smoothly. To illustrate the multilayered nature of the team approach to IBP, each account team member can also be thought of as a hub in his or her very own wheel. For example, the direct marketing member on the account team is team leader for her own set of specialists charged with preparing direct marketing materials. Through this type of multilevel "hub-and-spokes" design, the coordination and collaboration essential for effective IBP campaigns can be achieved.

Fostering Collaboration through the Creative Brief. The **creative brief** is a little document with a huge role in promoting good teamwork and fostering the creative process. It sets up the goal for any advertising effort in a way that gets everyone moving in the same direction, but should never force or mandate a particular solution. It provides basic guidelines with plenty of room for the creatives to be creative. Preparation of the creative brief is a joint activity involving the client lead and the AE. When the creative brief is done right, a whole bunch of potential conflicts are prevented. An efficient template for the creative brief is featured in Exhibit 10.15.

---

36.   Katzenbach and Smith, *The Wisdom of Teams,* ch. 7.
37.   Katzenbach and Smith, *The Wisdom of Teams,* 144.

CLIENT: **DATE:**   **JOB NO.:**
Prepared by:

WHAT IS THE PRODUCT OR SERVICE?
Simple description or name of product or service.

WHO/WHAT IS THE COMPETITION?
Provide a snapshot of the brand situation including current position in the category, brand challenges, competitive threats, and future goals.

WHO ARE WE TALKING TO?
Clear definition of who the target is both demographically and psychographically. Be as specific as possible in defining the target so the creative can connect target and brand in the most compelling way.

WHAT CONSUMER NEED OR PROBLEM DO WE ADDRESS?
Describe the unmet consumer need that this product or service fills or how this product addresses a need in a way that's unique.

WHAT DOES THE CONSUMER CURRENTLY THINK ABOUT US?
Uncover target insights to get at attitudes and behaviors related to broader context as well as specific category and brand. Determine whether insights currently exist or whether new research needs to be conducted.

WHAT ONE THING DO WE WANT THEM TO BELIEVE?
Be as single-minded as possible. Write in benefit (functional, emotional, or self-expressive) language. Should differentiate us . . . no other brand in the category can or is currently saying it.

WHAT CAN WE TELL THEM THAT WILL MAKE THEM BELIEVE THIS?
Not a laundry list of available support but the few things that clearly support the "one thing we want them to believe."

WHAT IS THE TONALITY OF THE ADVERTISING?
A few adjectives or phrase that captures the tonality and personality of the advertising.

Of particular note:
Write it in the consumer's language; not business-speak.

Make every word count; be simple and concise.

Make as evocative as possible. Think of the brief as the first "ad." The brief should make creatives jump up and down in their excitement to start executing it!

Courtesy of Northlich (http://www.northlich.com).

EXHIBIT 10.15

Template for a creative brief.

DOING IT RIGHT

Setting the Stage for Creativity

Researchers in many fields have tackled the issue of how to foster creativity in the workplace and have generated pretty good lists of do's and don'ts if the objective is to get more creative. Teresa Amabile, a researcher at Harvard, has identified what she refers to as the six keys to creativity in any organization: challenge, freedom, resources, work-group features, supervisory encouragement, and organizational support.

According to Amabile, the foundation for creativity is setting people up with just the right amount of challenge and then giving them the freedom to choose a path for resolving it. In other words, give your teams a challenging goal, and then get out of their way as they look for ways to accomplish it. In the advertising world, it is often the creative brief that lays out the challenge for a team in a simple framework that should not restrict or dictate solutions in any way. Next comes resources, both time and money. Here again it is a matter of finding just the right balance. For example, setting deadlines is extremely important and it's fine to make people stretch themselves, but fabricated deadlines or impossibly short time frames will just kill the team's motivation and stifle creativity.

Next is a theme you'll see over and over again in any literature about creativity: Pay careful attention to the design of your teams. Homogeneous teams get things done quickly and without a lot of conflict or problems, but they produce ordinary solutions. If you want creative solutions you need to assemble teams characterized by diversity of thought and expertise. Such teams will make more waves, but will produce more creative solutions. As well, the team leader must communicate that new ideas are valued and must prevent the critics from destroying momentum around new ideas. Finally, no one person or no one team will produce creative solutions if the overall organization they are part of doesn't brand itself as creative and then continually reinforce that message to its employees. As you should recall, Crispin, Porter + Bogusky is an agency that prides itself on creative. It is not shy about making this claim or promoting it to the world (as in its book *Hoopla*). Leaders at all levels of an organization must reinforce the creativity mantra if individual employees in those organizations are to take it seriously.

That's what the research says about creativity, and it's pretty good research. But there is some fun stuff too. The business of advertising is a unique business and ad agencies clearly do special things to let their employees know that creativity is job one. A nonscientific survey of ad agencies found that lots of perks are the norm in the workplace today: on-site yoga and game rooms; espresso bars and celebrity chefs; Halloween parties and movie nights; tai chi classes and concierge services. All things designed to attract and retain interesting people and keep them happy about their jobs. As one agency leader put it: "We sell ideas, and if your employees are unhappy, you are not going to get a lot of good ideas." Maybe it's as simple as that.

Sources: Teresa Amabile, "How to Kill Creativity," **Harvard Business Review**, Fall 1998, 77–87; Brooke Capps, "Playtime, Events, Perks Go Long Way in Team Building," **Advertising Age**, January 15, 2007, 30; Jaafar El-Murad and Douglas C. West, "The Definition and Measurement of Creativity: What Do We Know?" **Journal of Advertising Research**, June 2004, 188–201.

Teams Liberate Decision Making. With the right combination of expertise assembled on the account team, a carefully crafted creative brief, and a leader that has the team working well as a unit, what appears to be casual or spur-of-the-moment decision making can turn out to be breakthrough decision making. This is one of the huge benefits of good teamwork. As they say at CP+B, a good idea can come from anywhere. Teams composed of members that trust one another are liberated to be more creative because no one is worried about having their best ideas stolen. No one is worried about trying to look good for the boss. It's the team that counts. This type of "safe" team environment allows everyone to contribute and lets the whole be greater than the sum of the parts. The Doing It Right box goes deeper in explaining how to create the "right conditions" to foster breakthrough performance by teams.

When Sparks Fly: Igniting Creativity through Teams.

Whether account teams, sub-specialist teams, creative teams, or hybrid teams involving persons from both the client and agency side; all will play critical roles in preparing and executing integrated advertising campaigns. Moreover, impressive evidence shows that when managed in a proactive way, teams come up with better ideas; that is, ideas that are both creative and useful in the process of building brands.[38] One can get pretty serious about the subject of managing creativity, and as reflected in Exhibit 10.16, good teamwork may be serious stuff. But it doesn't have to be complicated and it certainly will get rowdy at times. The key elements are building teams with the right expertise and diversity of thought, pushing individuals in those teams to challenge and build on each others' ideas, and creating just the right amount of tension to get the sparks flying.

---

38.   Jacob Goldenberg, David Mazursky, and Sorin Solomon, "The Fundamental Templates of Quality Ads," *Marketing Science,* vol. 18, no. 3 (1999), 333–351.

EXHIBIT 10.16

Teamwork really is both those things.

Cognitive Styles. According to the stereotype, business types favor left-brain thinking and advertising types favor right-brain thinking. Business types like to talk about testing and data and return on investment, while advertising types like to talk about movies and the Cannes Film Festival.[39] While such stereotypes misrepresent individual differences, the old left brain/right brain metaphor serves to remind us that people approach problem solving with different styles. That is, people prefer to think about things in their own style.

The unique preferences of each person for thinking about and solving a problem is a reflection of **cognitive style**. For instance, some people prefer logical and analytical thinking; others prefer intuitive and nonlinear thinking. Numerous categorization schemes have been developed for classifying people based on their cognitive styles. Psychologist Carl Jung was an early pioneer among cognitive stylists. He proposed essential differences among individuals along three dimensions of cognitive style: Sensing versus Intuiting; Thinking versus Feeling; and Extraverted versus Introverted. The important point for teams and creativity is that the more homogeneous a team is in terms of cognitive styles, the more limited will be the range of their solutions to a problem. Simply stated, diversity of thought nourishes creativity.

Creative Abrasion. Teamwork is not a picnic in the park. That's why it's called team*work*. Moreover, when teams bring together people with diverse cognitive styles, and they truly get engaged in the task, there will be friction. Friction can be both good and bad.[40] On the one hand we can have **creative abrasion**, which is the clash of ideas, and from which new ideas and breakthrough solutions can evolve. That's obviously the good thing. On the other hand, we can have **interpersonal abrasion**, which is the clash of people, from which communication shuts down and new ideas get slaughtered. That's obviously the bad thing. So as we pointed out earlier, teams must have leadership that creates a safe environment allowing creative abrasion to flourish, while always looking to defuse interpersonal abrasion. It's a fine line, but getting it right means the difference between creativity and chaos.

---

39.   Dale Buss, "Bridging the Great Divide in Marketing Thinking," *Advertising Age,* March 26, 2007, 18, 19.
40.   Dorothy Leonard and Walter Swap, *When Sparks Fly: Igniting Creativity in Groups* (Boston: Harvard Business School Press, 1999).

Using Brainstorming and Alien Visitors. Many of us have sat in a conference room and shot the breeze for an hour and when it was all over decided we just wasted another hour. Groups can waste a lot of time if not proactively managed, and one of the key means for getting groups or teams to generate novel solutions is through the use of a process called brainstorming. **Brainstorming** is an organized approach to idea generation in groups. As suggested by Exhibit 10.17, there is a right way and a wrong way to brainstorm. Follow the rules laid out in Exhibit 10.17, and you can call it brainstorming. Otherwise, you're just shooting the breeze, and most likely wasting time.

Adding more diversity to the group is always a way to foster creative abrasion; moreover, well-established teams can get stale and stuck in a rut. To ramp up the creative abrasion may require a visit from an alien. If you can get one from Pluto or Mars that's fine, but more likely this alien will just be a person or persons from outside the normal network. They can be from elsewhere in your organization, or from outside the organization entirely. Perhaps the team will need to take a field trip together to visit some aliens. Teams that insulate themselves from outside influences run the risk over time of loosing their spark.[41] Tranquility and sameness can be enemies of creativity.

Final Thoughts on Teams and Creativity. Creativity in the preparation of an IBP campaign can be fostered by the trust and open communication that are hallmarks of effective teams. But it is also true that the creativity required for breakthrough campaigns will evolve as personal work products generated by individuals laboring on their own. Both personal and team creativity are critical in the preparation of IBP campaigns. The daunting task of facilitating both usually falls in the lap of an agency's creative director.

The position of creative director in any ad agency is very special because, much like the maestro of the symphony orchestra, the creative director must encourage

EXHIBIT 10.17

Don't waste time; do it right!

Eight Rules for Brilliant Brainstorming

#1—Build off each other. One proven path to creativity entails building on existing ideas; don't just generate ideas, build on each others'.

#2—Fear drives out creativity. If people believe they will be teased, demoted, or otherwise humiliated in the group, no need to even consider brainstorming. It won't work.

#3—Prime individuals before and after. Encourage individuals to learn about the problem before and after the group session; teams always benefit when individuals apply their unique expertise.

#4—Make it happen. Great organizations develop a brainstorming culture where everyone knows the rules and honors them; to achieve such a culture, it is essential that ideas developed in brainstorm sessions lead to actions. We can't just talk big ideas; we must also put them to work.

#5—It's a skill. Leading a productive brainstorming session is not a job for amateurs; facilitating a brainstorming session is a skill that takes months or years to master. Don't pretend to brainstorm without a skilled facilitator.

#6—Embrace creative abrasion. If your team has been formed appropriately, it will contain people with conflicting cognitive styles. Celebrate that diversity, welcome everybody into the group, and then let the sparks fly!

#7—Listen and learn. Good brainstorming sessions foster learning among people who have diverse expertise and divergent cognitive styles. Trust builds and suspicion fades.

#8—Follow the rules, or you're not brainstorming (and pretending just wastes everybody's time).

Source: Robert I. Sutton, "The Truth about Brainstorming," *Inside Business Week*, September 25, 2006, 17–21.

41. Ibid.

personal excellence but at the same time demand team accountability. We interviewed veteran creative directors to get more insights about the challenge of channeling the creative energies of their teams. All acknowledge that creativity has an intensely personal element, often motivated by the desire to satisfy one's own ego or sense of self. But despite this interpersonal element, team unity has to be a priority. In orchestrating creative teams, these are some good principles to follow:

- Take great care in assigning individuals to a team in the first place. Be sensitive to their existing workloads and the proper mix of expertise required to do the job for the client.
- Get to know the cognitive style of each individual. Listen carefully. Since creativity can be an intensely personal matter, one has to know when it is best to leave people alone, versus when one needs to support them in working through the inevitable rejection.
- Make teams responsible to the client. Individuals and teams are empowered when they have sole responsibility for performance outcomes.
- Beware of adversarial and competitive relationships between individuals and between teams. They can quickly lead to mistrust that destroys camaraderie and synergy.
- In situations where the same set of individuals will work on multiple teams over time, rotate team assignments to foster fresh thinking, or bring in some aliens!

Here we see once again that the fundamentals of effective teams—communication, trust, complementary expertise, and leadership—produce the desired performance outcome. There's simply no alternative. Advertising is a team sport.

4 Have *You* Decided to Become More Creative?

Most of us are not going to model our lives after creative geniuses like Pablo Picasso or Martha Graham. While it's great to have role models to inspire us, we don't think it's realistic to aspire to be the next Gandhi or Einstein. But we all can take stock of our own special skills and abilities and should candidly assess our own strengths and weaknesses.

For example, referring to some of the terminology used earlier in this chapter, we all can complete assessments that reveal our own cognitive styles and then compare ourselves to others. And if you want to calibrate your level of creativity, just search the Internet for "creativity tests" or "creativity assessments" and a host of options will present themselves. It is a good thing to get to know your self and start thinking about skills and abilities. In addition, if you have any interest in a career in advertising, it would be a good thing to decide right now that you are going to make yourself more creative. Although we all may start in different places, it is a worthy goal to aspire to become more creative. Yale psychologist Robert Sternberg, who has devoted his professional career to the study of intelligence and creativity, advises his students as follows.

To make yourself more creative, decide now to:
Redefine problems to see them differently from other people;
Be the first to analyze and critique your own ideas, since we all have good ones and bad ones;
Be prepared for opposition whenever you have a really creative idea;
Recognize that it is impossible to be creative without adequate knowledge;
Recognize that too much knowledge can stifle creativity;
Find the standard, safe solution and then decide when you want to take a risk by defying it;
Keep growing and experiencing, and challenging your own comfort zone;
Believe in yourself, especially when surrounded by doubters;
Learn to cherish ambiguity, because from it comes the new ideas;
Remember that research has shown that people are most likely to be creative when doing something they love.[42]

It's good advice.

42. Robert J. Sternberg, "Creativity as a Decision," *American Psychologist,* May 2002, 376; and Robert J. Sternberg, "Identifying and Developing Creative Giftedness," *Roeper Review,* vol. 23, no. 2 (2000), 60–65.

SUMMARY

Describe the core characteristics of great creative minds.

A look at the shared sensibilities of great creative minds provides a constructive starting point for assessing the role of creativity in the production of great advertising. What Picasso had in common with Gandhi, Freud, Eliot, Stravinsky, Graham, and Einstein—including a strikingly exuberant self-confidence, (childlike) alertness, unconventionality, and an obsessive commitment to the work—both charms and alarms us. Self-confidence, at some point, becomes crass self-promotion; an unconstrained childlike ability to see the world as forever new devolves, somewhere along the line, into childish self-indulgence. Without creativity, there can be no advertising. How we recognize and define creativity in advertising rests on our understanding of the achievements of acknowledged creative geniuses from the worlds of art, literature, music, science, and politics.

Contrast the role of an agency's creative department with that of business managers/account executives and explain the tensions between them.

What it takes to get the right idea (a lot of hard work), and the ease with which a client may dismiss that idea, underlies the contentiousness between an agency's creative staff and its AEs and clients. Creatives provoke. Managers restrain. Ads that win awards for creative excellence don't necessarily fulfill a client's business goals. All organizations deal with the competing agendas of one department versus another, but in advertising agencies, this competition plays out at an amplified level. The difficulty of assessing the effectiveness of any form of advertisement only adds to the problem. Advertising researchers are put in the unenviable position of judging the creatives, pitting "science" against art. None of these tensions changes the fact that creativity is essential to the vitality of brands. Creativity makes a brand, and it is creativity that reinvents established brands in new and desired ways.

Assess the role of teams in managing tensions and promoting creativity in advertising and IBP applications.

There are many sources of conflict and tension in the business of creating great advertising. It's the nature of the beast. One way that many organizations attempt to address this challenging issue is through systematic utilization of teams. Teams, when effectively managed, will produce outputs that are greater than the sum of their individual parts. Teams need to be managed proactively to promote creative abrasion but limit interpersonal abrasion if they are to produce "beautiful music together." Guidance from a maestro (like a Lee Clow or Alex Bogusky) will be required. Another important tool to get teams headed in the right direction and to pre-empt many forms of conflict in the advertising arena is the creative brief. It's a little document with a very big function.

Examine yourself and your own passion for creativity.

Self assessment is an important part of learning and growing and now is the perfect time to be thinking about yourself and your passion for creativity. If advertising is a profession that interests you, then improving your own creative abilities should be a lifelong quest. Now is the time to decide to become more creative.

KEY TERMS

creativity
account executive
account team

creative brief
cognitive style
creative abrasion

interpersonal abrasion
brainstorming

QUESTIONS

1.   Over the years, creativity has been associated with various forms of madness and mental instability. In your opinion, what is it about creative people that prompt this kind of characterization?

2.   Think about a favorite artist, musician, or writer. What is unique about the way he or she represents the world? What fascinates you about the vision he or she creates?

3.   Much credence is given in this chapter to the idea that tension (of various sorts) is part of creative pursuits. Explain the connection between creativity and tension.

4.   Which side of this debate do you have more affinity for: Are people creative because they can produce creative results, or are they creative because of the way they think? Explain.

5.   What forces inside an advertising agency can potentially compromise its creative work? Is compromise always to be avoided? Imagine that you are an agency creative. Define "compromise." Now imagine that you are an account executive. How does your definition of compromise change?

6.   Describe the conflict between the creative department and the research department. Do you think creatives are jus-

tified in their hesitancy to subject their work to advertising researchers? Is science capable of judging art any more than art is capable of judging science? Explain.

7.   Examine Exhibit 10.14. Using this exhibit as your guide, generate a list of ten principles to foster creativity in an ad agency.

8.   The creative director in any agency has the daunting task of channeling the creative energies of dozens of individuals, while demanding team accountability. If the expression of creativity is personal and highly individualized, how can teamwork possibly foster creativity? What might a creative director do to "allow creativity to happen" in a team environment? Explain how the saying "The whole is greater than the sum of its parts" fits into a discussion of creativity and teamwork.

9.   Advertising always has been a team sport, but the advent of advertising and IBP has made effective teamwork more important than ever. It also has made it more difficult to achieve. Explain how the growing emphasis on IBP makes effective teamwork more challenging.

10. Choose any ad from this book that represents exemplary creativity to you. Explain your choice.

EXPERIENTIAL EXERCISES

1.   Creativity with brands is often directly related to the names marketers choose for their products and services. Identify and research two brands that you think have especially creative names. For each, describe tangible ways that the brand's name influences the creativity expressed in its advertising and promotion themes and campaigns.

2.   Write a one-page analysis of a creative song, video, or other work created by an artist, writer, or musician. In your own words, describe what makes the work uniquely creative (be sure to use chapter concepts concerning creativity and creative personalities). Finally, given the contentious conflicts between creativity and management in the advertising industry, do you think this artist or musician could succeed in a career in advertising? Explain.

3.   This chapter emphasizes the importance of coordination and collaboration in the creative process for IBP campaigns. Break into small groups to conduct the following creative brainstorming exercises. When you are done, present your ideas to the class and explain how the "Eight Rules for Brilliant Brainstorming" listed in Exhibit 10.17 helped your team's collaborative effort. How did your ideas, in number and in substance, compare to others in the class?

Spend 10 minutes brainstorming each of these topics:

- How many uses can you identify for baking soda?
- Put a ballpoint pen, a baseball cap, and a belt on a desk. How many alternative uses can you identify for those objects?
- What words do you associate with the following well-known brands? Taco Bell, Pampers, and John Deere.

4.   Working in the same small teams, develop a creative brief for one of the three brands listed above. The brief should establish the goal of any future advertising efforts and offer some basic guidance to the creative division. Your team should use the template at Exhibit 10.15 to develop the creative brief, but you may make adjustments as necessary to that model.

5.   This chapter identifies several steps individuals can take to make themselves become more creative thinkers. Consider the following situation and then identify how you might use Robert Sternberg's creative thinking suggestions, listed at the end of the chapter, to formulate an action plan:

   You have decided to launch a tutoring service for graduate school entrance exams. While wishing you well, investors and your friends have voiced the same concern: It will be tough sledding for a small tutoring start-up in a field already crowded with sophisticated test-coaching services. How do you proceed?

CHAPTER 11

After reading and thinking about this chapter,
you will be able to do the following:

Identify nine objectives of message strategy.

Identify methods for executing each message strategy objective.

3

Discuss the strategic implications of various methods used to execute each message strategy objective.

AND NOW
FOR OUR
NEXT ACT.
**HEADLIGHTS
THAT SEE
AROUND
CORNERS.**

No, it's not the latest in espionage equipment. Just our way of helping you see whatever may lie around the next bend. These ingenious headlights respond to curves by pivoting up to 15 degrees as you turn, acting in much the same way as your peripheral vision does. Allowing you more of a chance to respond. At Lexus, we stay ahead of the curve, so you can, too. To learn more about our pursuit of perfection, please visit lexus.com.

Introductory Scenario: Power to the People.
Most say it was brilliant and inspired. Others argue it was an arrogant and expensive exercise in grandstanding. In January 1984, during the third quarter of the Super Bowl, Apple Computer introduced the Macintosh with a 60-second spot. The ad, known as "1984," climaxed with a young athletic woman hurling a mallet through a huge projection screen in a monochromatic vision of a hypercorporate and ugly future.[1] On the big screen was an Orwellian Big Brother instructing the masses. As the ad closed, with the near-soulless masses obediently chanting the corporate-state mantra in the background, the following simple statement appeared on the television screens of millions of viewers: "On January 24th, Apple Computer will introduce Macintosh. And you'll see why 1984 won't be like 1984."

What made this advertisement particularly newsworthy is that it cost $400,000 to produce (very expensive for its day) and another $500,000 to broadcast, yet it was broadcast only *once*. It was a creative super event. The three major networks covered the event on the evening news, and the ad went on to become *Advertising Age*'s Commercial of the Decade for the 1980s. But why? It wasn't just its high cost and single play. It wasn't just its very stylish but disturbing look (directed by Ridley Scott [*Blade Runner, Alien, Gladiator, G.I. Jane, Black Hawk Down*]). It wasn't just another ad that told us who or what we could be. The ad captured and expressed something important lying just below the surface of early 1980s American culture. It was about us versus them, threatened individuals versus faceless corporations. It was about the defiant rejection of sterile corporate life and the celebration of individuality through, of all things, a computer. Archrival IBM was implicitly cast as the oppressive Big Blue (that is, Big Brother) and Apple as the good and liberating anticorporate corporation. The ad captured the moment and, most critically, served up a consumer product as popular ideology. Apple became the hip, the young, the cool, the democratic, and the antiestablishment computer. It was the computer of the nonsellout, or at least of those who wished to think of themselves that way.

The really great ads of all time have captured the cultural moment, have wrapped their brands in the words and images of that cultural moment, and then have served that package up for sale to that very same culture. If you can also serve a large and underserved market segment (for example, cyber-insecure consumers who are generally anti-button-down corporate), even better. Steve Hayden, the "1984" copywriter, described the ad this way: "We thought of it as an ideology, a value set. It was a way of letting the whole world access the power of computing and letting them talk to one another. The democratization of technology—the computer for the rest of us."[2]

With "1984," Apple and advertising agency Chiat/Day wanted to focus attention on a new product and completely distinguish Apple and the Macintosh from Big Blue, IBM. Macintosh was going to offer computing power to the people. This declaration of computing independence was made on the most-watched broadcast of the year. Forty-six percent of all U.S. households tuned into the 1984 Super Bowl. With the Macintosh, Apple offered an alternative and very hip cyber-ethos for those who felt alienated or intimidated by the IBM world. The "1984" ad offered a clear choice, a clear instruction: *Buy a Mac, keep your soul*. And it worked. Macintosh and Apple grew and prospered. For quite a while, "the rest of us" was a pretty big group.

Of course, there is another lesson here: Nothing lasts forever, not even a great creative idea. Things change. Advertising has to evolve along with the situation, or the brand may suffer. As great as this ad was (and it was) and as much success as the Mac

---

1.   The term *ugly future* was first used in this context (and beautifully so) by Connie Johnson, University of Illinois, in the late 1970s. We thank her.
2.   This quote appears in Bradley Johnson, "10 Years after 1984: The Commercial and the Product That Changed Advertising," *Advertising Age*, January 10, 1994, 12.

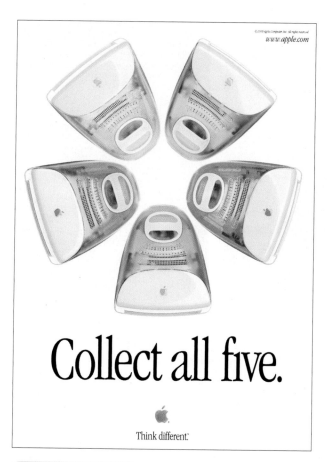

©2000 apple computer, inc. all rights reserved.
www.apple.com

Collect all five.

Think different.

EXHIBIT 11.1

The launch of the iMac.
http://www.apple.com

and Apple had (and they did), things didn't stay so good. Some believe that the seeds of Apple's own near demise were sown with the "rest of us" idea. Apple effectively cultivated an us–versus–them ethic, which worked well to help establish a brand position and even a sense of brand community, but Apple failed to keep the Apple tent inclusive and big. The rest-of-us ethos became something of a problem.

By 2000, Apple's market share had dropped to around 3 percent. Many believed that Apple was forever damaged by a failure to recognize and adapt to changes in the marketplace. Because Apple refused to license its operating system until 1995 (and then changed its mind again), Macs became a relatively expensive alternative to PCs. Coupled to a premium price, they came to be regarded by some as evidence of Apple's snooty and elitist nature. The "rest of us" seemed to think they were better (more hip, cooler, more arty, and so on) than us—not necessarily a desirable product attribute if a company hopes to sell a lot of computers. Once the skid hit software availability, Apple came perilously close to extinction.

Then came the iMac. With the return of cofounder Steve Jobs to the company, Apple once again teamed up with TBWA/Chiat/Day to launch the iMac (see Exhibit 11.1), and things turned around. The company made a profit of around $309 million after a loss of $1 billion in the previous Jobs-less year. And over 278,000 people took iMacs home with them in the first six weeks on the market.[3] The stylish iMac started a trend in the computer industry similar to what General Motors did in the 1920s—when all cars were black and were in some danger of eventually becoming undifferentiated commodities, GM began to produce them in color and introduced elements of style. This created brand distinctiveness, added value, and period obsolescence (style change).

In the 1990s, computers were quickly becoming low-margin commodities—so, taking a page from GM and others 70 years previously, Apple introduced style, design, and color. This was very smart marketing and required smart advertising. But within a few months, most everyone else was offering style and design as product benefits as well. Still, Apple was there first, and still "owns" the computer "style segment."

What about the present? Is Apple again tapping into the soul of American culture? Well, sort of; Apple and its advertising are highly regarded, but still only 6 percent or so of the U.S. market actually buys an Apple computer. Of course, this represents a doubling of their market share in just a few years. So, while doing pretty well, Apple computers have not conquered the American consciousness (or market) the way they did in 1984. Back then, Apple's advertising was unquestionably amazing. No one can ever take that away. It was truly creative, and it advanced Apple's strategy. Apple and Chiat/Day deserve a great deal of credit. But now the world is different, and the computer market is different. In 1984 it was still an open question as to who would win the operating system platform race; that race had appeared to be over for a long time now. Expecting people to switch platforms at this point is an entirely different marketing and advertising problem. But wait.

---

3.   David Kirkpatrick, "The Second Coming of Apple," *Fortune*, November 9, 1998, 86–92.

EXHIBITS 11.2 AND 11.3

Twenty-some years after 1984, Apple has become much more than a company that just makes computers.

Now Apple is more than computers. Perhaps more importantly, small share, or "microbrands," have turned out to be both popular and profitable. Companies are questioning the wisdom of the mass market model. Sometimes, less is more. Apple is still reinventing itself. Apple is many things, including the wildly successful iPod and iTunes, and is still trading on its brand equity of cyber-cool (see Exhibits 11.2 and 11.3). Now we have the iPhone: How will it do after all the buzz dies down? What will be the results of a scaled-down and less-pricey model? Does owning an iPod or an iPhone raise the odds of a consumer buying an Apple computer? It appears that it does. Initial launch numbers for the iPhone were far below analysts' estimates (146,000 actual sales in the first two days versus a predicted 1 million). Then came the awful launch of Microsoft's VISTA operating system. In the computer industry, when a program is very buggy, there are two choices: push back the launch date and fix the bugs or do what is called "launch and learn. . ." meaning inviting a few hundred million beta testers (a.k.a., consumers) to test your product and de-bug it for you. Launch and learn seems to have been Microsoft's decision. Folks at Apple say it is the number one reason people in large numbers are now buying their first Mac. After 25 years of unwavering loyalty to Windows, I bought a Mac. VISTA drove me to Mac. Consumer purchases may be affected not only by a brand's own marketing decisions, but also by the marketing decisions of its competition.

Stay tuned for more of the Apple saga.

Message Strategy.
So, now we come to talking about message: how to create a message with advertising and integrated brand promotion that advances the marketers' strategy. One major component of the larger advertising and promotion strategy is the **message strategy**. The message strategy consists of objectives and methods. The message strategy defines the goals of the advertiser (objectives) and how those goals will be achieved. This chapter offers nine message strategies, and then discusses and illustrates the methods most often used to satisfy them. This is not an exhaustive list, but it covers the most common and important message strategies. Exhibit 11.4 summarizes the nine message strategies presented here.

We will discuss these objectives in order from simple to complex. This is an important distinction. The first ads we describe work at a very simple level; the last at a very complex one. Also, you must understand that you will certainly see ads that

Message strategy objectives and methods.

Objective: What the Advertiser Hopes to Achieve	Method: How the Advertiser Plans to Achieve the Objective
Promote brand recall: To get consumers to recall its brand name(s) first; that is, before any of the competitors' brand names	Repetition Slogans and jingles
Link a key attribute to the brand name: To get consumers to associate a key attribute with a brand name and vice versa	Unique selling proposition (USP)
Persuade the consumer: To convince consumers to buy a product or service through high-engagement arguments	Reason-why ads Hard-sell ads Comparison ads Testimonials Demonstration Advertorials Infomercials
Instill brand preference: To get consumers to like or prefer its brand above all others	Feel-good ads Humor ads Sexual-appeal ads
Scare the consumer into action: To get consumers to buy a product or service by instilling fear	Fear-appeal ads
Change behavior by inducing anxiety: To get consumers to make a purchase decision by playing to their anxieties; often, the anxieties are social in nature	Anxiety ads Social anxiety ads
Transform consumption experiences: To create a feeling, image, or mood about a brand that is activated when the consumer uses the product or service	Transformational ads
Situate the brand socially: To give the brand meaning by placing it in a desirable social context	Slice-of-life ads Product placement/ short Internet films Light-fantasy ads
Define the brand image: To create an image for a brand by relying predominantly on visuals rather than words and argument	Image ads

are not pure cases, and ads that are combinations of strategies. We offer these nine pure types as examples. When you see an ad you should ask: What is this ad trying to do, and how is it trying to accomplish that? What is its *main* message method?

Essential Message Objectives and Strategies. Again, these are presented from simplest to most complex. For each one we will tell you about the logic behind the strategy, the basic mechanisms involved, how it works, how success or failure is typically determined, and a strategic summary of those methods.

Objective #1: Promote Brand Recall. This is the simplest type of advertising there is. Since modern advertising's very beginning, getting consumers to remember the advertised brand's name has been a goal. The obvious idea behind this objective is that if consumers remember the brand name, and can easily recall it, they are more likely to buy it. It's a pretty simple and straightforward idea.

Although human memory is a very complex topic, the relationship between repetition and recall has been pretty well understood for a very long time. We know that repetition generally increases the odds of recall. So, by repeating a brand name over and over, the odds of recalling that brand name go up—pretty simple.

But advertisers typically don't just want consumers to remember their name; they want their name to be the *first* brand consumers remember, or what advertisers call *top of mind*. At a minimum, they want them to be in the *evoked set*, a small list of brand names (typically five or less) that come to mind when a product or service category (for example, airlines [United, American, Delta], soft drinks [Coke, Pepsi], or toothpaste [Crest, Colgate]) is mentioned. So, if someone says "soft drink," the folks in Atlanta (Coca-Cola headquarters) want you to say "Coke."

Again, the odds of being either top of mind or in the evoked set increase with recall. In the case of parity products (those with few major objective differences between brands—for example, laundry soaps) and other "low-involvement" goods and services, the first brand remembered is often the most likely to be purchased. First-remembered brands are often the most popular brands. In fact, consumers may actually infer popularity, desirability, and even superiority from the ease with which they recall brands. The most easily recalled brand may be seen as the leading brand (most popular, highest market share), even when it isn't. Of course, in time if people think a brand is the leading brand, it can actually become the leading brand. For things purchased routinely, you can't expect consumers to deliberate and engage in extensive consideration of product attributes. Instead, in the real world of advertising and brand promotion, you rely on recall of the brand name, recall of a previously made judgment (e.g., *I like Tide*) to get the advertised brand in the shopping cart. Sometimes, the simplest strategy is the best strategy.

So, how do advertisers promote easy recall? There are two popular methods: repetition, and memory encoding (storing in memory) and retrieval (remembering) aids: slogans and jingles.

Method A: Repetition. Repetition is a tried-and-true way of gaining easier retrieval of brand names from consumer's memory. Advertisers do this by buying lots of ads and/or by frequently repeating the brand name within the ad itself. This is typically a strategy for television and radio, but can be accomplished visually in print, with promotional placement in television shows and movies, and on the Web. The idea is that things said (or shown) more often will be remembered more easily than things said (or shown) less frequently. So the advertiser repeats the brand name over and over and over again. Then, when the consumer stands in front of, say, the cosmetics aisle, the advertised brand name is recalled from memory. In the contemporary IBP world, marketers often use point-of-purchase displays (see Exhibit 11.5) that help trigger, or cue, the brand name from memory.

In other cases, the aisle itself (its look, smells, etc.) or the packaging may cue the category. That is, on the shopper's highly repeated and routinized path down this aisle, the aisle or the packaging may prompt recollections about the category (say, detergent) and may make the heavily advertised brand (say, Tide) come right to mind. The more accessible (easier to remember) brand names are retrieved first and fastest from memory, making them (all else being equal) more likely to end up in the shopping cart. Getting into the consumer's evoked set gets you close to actual purchase, and achieving top of mind gets you even closer.

Repetition strategies are being used use on the Internet as well: Familiar names are placed so that consumers will see them again and again. In fact, many IBP efforts work in this way. Think sports arenas: Seeing a name over and over (and having it in a TV shot) is certainly one of the ideas behind named arenas such as Qualcomm Stadium, AT&T Park, and Minute Maid Park.

EXHIBIT 11.5

Point-of-purchase (POP) displays are great for promoting recall.

EXHIBIT 11.6

This ad may hold the all-time record for most brand mentions in a single 30-second ad. Kibbles and Bits, Kibbles and Bits. . . .

Does repetition always work? No, of course it doesn't. There are plenty of times when consumers remember one brand, and then buy another. Still, this type of advertising plays a probability game—being easily recalled tilts the odds of being purchased in favor of the advertisers willing to pay for the recall that repetition buys.

We think the all-time record for most brand mentions in a single ad might be a tie: either "Kibbles and Bits, Kibbles and Bits, I gotta get me some Kibbles and Bits" over and over and over (see Exhibit 11.6), or the endless "Meow, Meow, Meow, Meow" for Meow Mix. Can you think of one with more?

Method B: Slogans and Jingles. Slogans are one small step up from raw repetition in degree of complexity. Here, slogans and jingles are used to enhance the odds of recalling the brand name. The basic mechanism at work here is still memory, and the goal is still brand-name recall. Slogans are linguistic devices that link a brand name to something memorable by means of the slogan's simplicity, meter, rhyme, or some other factor. Jingles do the same thing, just set to a melody. Examples are numerous: "You Deserve a Break Today"; "You're in Good Hands with Allstate"; "Like a Good Neighbor, State Farm Is There"; "Two, Two, Two Mints in One"; "Get Met, It Pays"; and "It Keeps on Going and Going and Going." No doubt you've heard a few of these before. Slogans and jingles provide rehearsal, that is, encourage repetition because they are catchy, or prone to repeating, and the inherent properties of the slogan or jingle provide a retrieval cue for the brand name.

Also consider a practical application of the human need to complete or "close" a verse: For example, when you say, "Like a good neighbor," you pretty much are compelled to complete the phrase with "State Farm is there." As you know, slogans and jingles are hard to get out of your head. That's the idea.

Evaluation of repetition, slogans, and jingles is typically done through day-after-recall (DAR) tests and tracking studies emphasizing recall (e.g., "name three detergents"). In other words, these ads are evaluated with the most traditional ad copy research there is: simple recall measures. This is one time when the method of evaluation actually makes perfect sense: You are trying to get recall, you test for recall.

3 **Strategic Implications of Repetition, Slogans, and Jingles.**

- *Extremely resistant to forgetting.* These methods make it virtually impossible to forget the brand. Once established, the residual amount of impact from the campaign is huge. If some advertisers stopped advertising today, you would remember their slogans, jingles, and names for a long, long time.
- *Efficient for consumer.* For routinely purchased items, consumers rely on a simple and easy decision "rule": Buy what you remember. So, this kind of advertising works well in repeat-purchase and low-involvement items.
- *Long-term commitment/expense.* To achieve this carryover, or sales in the absence of advertising once advertising has stopped, advertisers have to sign on for a lot of advertising, at least initially. It's not easy in a cluttered media environment to build this type of enduring recall. It takes lots and lots of repetition, particularly early on, or a very memorable slogan or jingle. Once advertisers have achieved a high recall level, they can fine-tune their spending so that they are spending just enough to stay where they want. But they have to get there first, and it can be a very expensive trip.
- *Competitive interference.* This is less a problem with repetition, but consumers may learn a slogan or jingle only to associate it with the wrong brand. This has happened more times than you might imagine. For example, "It keeps on going, and going, and going. . . ." It's Duracell, right? Wait, maybe it's Eveready? Not absolutely sure? Not good. This is why it is absolutely vital to firmly link brand name to slogan. You don't want to pay for your competitor's success.
- *Creative resistance.* Creatives generally hate this type of advertising. Can you imagine why? These ads are rarely called creative and don't usually win a lot of creative awards. So creatives are less likely to enjoy working on them. Thus, the client paying the bills is less likely to get the "hot" or even senior creative teams. A lot of rookies get these assignments.

Objective #2: Link Key Attribute(s) to the Brand Name. Sometimes advertisers want

consumers to remember the brand and associate it with one or two attributes. This type of advertising is most closely identified with the **unique selling proposition (USP)** style, a type of ad that strongly emphasizes a supposedly unique quality (or qualities) of the advertised brand. It is more complicated than simple brand recall, and a bit more challenging. It is one step up from objective #1 in complexity. It requires more of the consumer, a little more thought, a little more learning. So, it requires more from those planning and making the ads. The ads provide a reason to buy, but don't require the consumer to think too much about that reason, just associate it with the brand name. In fact, many experts believe these ads work best if consumers don't think too much about the claim, just associate the two: the name and the claim. The primary mechanisms are memory and learning. The appeal may be through words (copy), or visuals (art direction). Contemporary advertising relies more and more on

visuals to communicate key brand attributes, but there is still a lot of copywriting involved in these ads.

Method: USP. The idea of emphasizing one and only one brand attribute is a very good idea—sometimes two are used if they are complementary, such as "strong but gentle." Ads that try to link several attributes to a brand while working to establish recall generally fail—they are too confusing and give too much information. Too much is attempted. Consider the Lexus ad in Exhibit 11.7. Clearly, the USP is that the car is built with headlights that turn in concert with the car. The headline delivers the single-minded message. The body copy explains it further. It's the headlights that make this car different. It's the headlights that make this car safer. That's all you have to know. Sometimes this type of advertising relies on a soft logic. The ad makes sense, but don't think too much about it: Listerine is strong, Ivory is pure. Evaluation of the USP method is typically done through recall tests, communication tests, and tracking studies. Did the consumer remember the USP?

Strategic Implications of the USP Method.

- 👍 Big carryover. USP advertising is very efficient. Once this link has been firmly established, it can last a very long time. An investment in this kind of advertising can carry you through some lean times.
- 👍 **Very resistant.** This type of advertising can be incredibly resistant to competitive challenge. Generations of consumers have been born, lived, and died remembering that Ivory is pure. Being the first to claim an attribute can be a huge advantage. Professionals will often say "Brand X owns that space" (meaning that attribute). For example, "Ivory owns the purity space," "Cheer owns the all temperature space."
- 👎 **Long-term commitment and expense.** If advertisers are going to use the USP method, they have to be in it for the long haul. You can't keep switching strategies and expect good results. Pick an attribute and stay with it.
- 👎 **Some creative resistance.** Creatives tend not to hate this quite as much as simple repetition, but it does seem to get old with them pretty fast. Don't expect the best or most experienced creative teams.

Objective #3: Persuade the Consumer.

This style of advertising is about arguments. In this type of advertising we move up from linking one (possibly two) attributes to a brand name using soft logic and simple learning to actually posing one or more (usually more) logical arguments to an engaged consumer. This is high-engagement advertising. That is, it assumes an actively engaged consumer, paying attention and considering the presented arguments. Its goal is to convince the consumer through arguments that the advertised brand is superior, the right choice. The advertiser says, in effect, you should buy my brand because of *x*, *y*, and *z* reasons. These arguments have typically been verbal (copy), but have in the past few decades employed more visual arguments (visual rhetoric) as well. As detailed below, there are several forms of this genre of advertising.

For this general type of advertising to work as planned, the consumer has to think about what the advertiser is saying. The receiver must "get" the ad, understand the argument, and agree with it. In a persuasion ad there is an assumed dialogue between the ad and the receiver, and some of the dialogue is the consumer disagreeing and counterarguing with the message. This is not good, but completely expected. As mentioned in Chapter 7, some research has found counterarguments to be the single most common consumer response to these types of ads. This, its inherent wordiness, and its antiquated style are the reasons such advertising is becoming less popular. However, these ads are still found in the earliest phases of a technological innovation, where a new good or service has to be explained to consumers or in categories where the very nature of the product or service is complex. But generally, ads that resemble high school debates are going away.

EXHIBIT 11.8

Kia uses reason-why.

EXHIBIT 11.9

Metamucil. Makes sense, right?

Method A: Reason-Why Ads. In a reason-why ad, the advertiser reasons with the potential consumer. The ad points out to the receiver that there are good reasons why this brand will be satisfying and beneficial. Advertisers are usually relentless in their attempt to reason with consumers when using this method. They begin with some claim, like "Seven great reasons to buy Brand X," and then proceed to list all seven, finishing with the conclusion (implicit or explicit) that only a moron would, after such compelling evidence, do anything other than purchase Brand X (see Exhibit 11.8). Other times, the reason or reasons to use a product can be presented deftly. The biggest trick to this method is making sure that the reason makes sense and that consumers care. Very often, consumers couldn't care less. The reason-why approach is used in direct mail and other forms of IBP and on the Web (see Exhibit 11.9).

Strategic Implications of Reason-Why Ads.

👍 *Permission to buy.* Gives consumers a great reason or reasons for purchasing the advertised brand.

👍 *Socially acceptable defense.* We all know that we sometimes have to defend our purchase decisions to friends and family. These types of ads are chock full o' reasons why it was a smart idea.

👎 *High level of involvement.* Consumers have to be paying attention for these ads to work. How much of the time do you think that happens? It's most likely right before or after a major purchase.

👎 *Potential for counterarguments.* This type of advertising might actually convince consumers why *not* to buy the advertised brand.

👎 *Legal/regulatory challenges/exposure.* The makers of these ads tend to get dragged into court or summoned by a regulatory body of some sort quite a bit. You'd better make sure that all your reasons why can stand up in court. Some haven't.

👎 *Some creative resistance.* This type of advertising rarely advances a creative career. Don't expect the best creative talent.

Method B: Hard-Sell Ads. Hard-sell ads are a subcategory of reason-why ads. They are characteristically high pressure and urgent, thus "hard." Phrases such as "act now," "limited time offer," "your last chance to save," and "one-time-only sale" are representative of this method. The idea is to create a sense of urgency so consumers will act quickly (see Exhibit 11.10). Sometimes these are done as IBP, and include "call or click *now*." Of course, many consumers have learned to ignore or otherwise discount these messages. We've all seen "Going Out of Business Sale" signs that remained up and the store open for months and even years. As one of our editors noted, this happens all the time. She lived in NYC; on the stretch of Fifth Avenue from 42nd to 48th she once (in four years of living and working in Midtown) saw one electronics store that *didn't* have a "Going Out of Business" sign.

When I moved to L.A. my roommate told me to look for the waterbed/futon shop with the "Going Out of Business Sign" for some good deals on furnishings. When I left two years later, it was still going out of business. Hey, nobody said when, right?

Strategic Implications of Hard-Sell Approaches.

👍 *"Permission to buy now."* The sale was about to end.

👍 *Socially acceptable defense.* "I had to act"; "It was on sale that day only"; "It was such a good deal."

👎 *Legal/regulatory challenges/exposure.* The makers of these ads tend to face the same legal and regulatory problems as the reason-why ads.

👎 *Some creative resistance.* Again, these are not the kind of ads creatives beg for.

Method C: Comparison Ads. Comparison advertisements are another form of advertising designed to persuade the consumer. Comparison ads try to demonstrate a brand's ability to satisfy consumers by comparing its features to those of competitive brands. Comparisons can be an effective and efficient means of communicating a large amount of information in a clear, interesting, and convincing way, or they can be extremely confusing and create a situation of information overload in which the market leader usually wins. Comparison advertising as a technique has traditionally been used by marketers of convenience

EXHIBIT 11.10

Hurry! You better act fast to get the benefits of JCPenney. http://www.jcpenney.com

A straight comparison ad. http://www.castrolusa.com

Considering buying a Rolls Royce or a Bentley? Perhaps you might rethink your decision after you compare them to the Lexus LS 430.

goods, such as pain relievers, laundry detergents, and household cleaners. Advertisers in a wide range of product categories have tried comparison advertising from time to time. For several years, AT&T and MCI had a long-running feud over whose rates were lower for household consumers. The ads seemed to have thoroughly confused everyone. Luxury car makers BMW and Lexus have targeted each other with comparative claims.[4] In one ad, BMW attacks the sluggish performance of Lexus with the message, "According to recent test results, Lexus' greatest achievement in acceleration is its price." Not to be left out, the Acura dealers of Southern California entered the luxury car advertising skirmish by stating, "We could use a lesser leather in our automobiles, but then we'd be no better than Rolls-Royce." Evaluation of comparison ads is typically done through tracking studies that measure attitudes, beliefs, and preferences over time.

Using comparison in an advertisement can be direct and name competitors' brands, or it can be indirect and refer only to the "leading brand" or "Brand X." Here are a few rules gleaned from consumer research.

• Direct comparison by a low-share brand (say Apple) to a high-share brand (say Windows) increases receivers' attention and increases their intent to purchase the low-share brand (Apple).
• Direct comparison by a high-share brand to a low-share brand does not attract additional attention to the high share brand, but actually helps the low-share brand. This is not good. Direct comparison is more effective if members of the target audience have not demonstrated clear brand preference in their product choices.[5]

For these reasons, established market leaders almost never use comparison ads. These ads are almost always used by the underdog brand, the brand that wishes to be seen in the company of the market leader. What do you think of the ads in Exhibits 11.11 and 11.12?

Strategic Implications of Comparison Ads.

- Can help a low-share brand, largely through awareness.
- Provides social justification for purchase.
- Gives permission to buy. Lets the consumer work through and then come to his or her own conclusion that it really is the best brand. (Consumer-generated conclusions are more powerful than those made on behalf of the advertiser).
- Significant legal/regulatory exposure.
- Not done much outside the United States; in much of the world, comparison advertising is either outlawed, not done by mutual agreement, or simply considered in such poor taste as to never be done.
- Not for established market leaders.
- These ads are sometimes evaluated as more offensive and less interesting than noncomparative ads. They have a tendency to turn some readers off.

4. Jim Henry, "Comparative Ads Speed Ahead for Luxury Imports," *Advertising Age*, September 12, 1994, 10.
5. Conclusions in this list are drawn from William R. Swinyard, "The Interaction between Comparative Advertising and Copy Claim Variation," *Journal of Marketing Research* 18 (May 1981), 175–186; Cornelia Pechmann and David Stewart, "The Effects of Comparative Advertising on Attention, Memory, and Purchase Intentions," *Journal of Consumer Research* (September 1990), 180–191; and Sanjay Petruvu and Kenneth R. Lord, "Comparative and Noncomparative Advertising: Attitudinal Effects under Cognitive and Affective Involvement Conditions," *Journal of Advertising* (June 1994), 77–90.

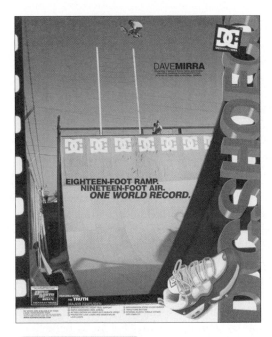

Dave Mirra is known as the Miracle Boy of freestyle BMX riding. What type of audience might find his testimonials persuasive?

This testimonial is done with facial expression, body attitude, and "look." These days even testimonials don't have to have words. There is no doubt they are testifying.
http://www.skechers.com

Method D: Testimonials. Testimonials are another type of persuade-the-consumer ad. A frequently used message tactic is to have a spokesperson who champions the brand in an advertisement, rather than simply providing information. When an advocacy position is taken by a spokesperson in an advertisement, it is known as a **testimonial**. The value of the testimonial lies in the authoritative presentation of a brand's attributes and benefits by the spokesperson. There are three basic versions of the testimonial message tactic.

The most conspicuous version is the *celebrity testimonial.* Sports stars such as Michael Jordan and Tiger Woods are favorites. Supermodels are also widely used. The belief is that a celebrity testimonial will increase an ad's ability to attract attention and produce a desire in receivers to emulate or imitate the celebrities they admire (see Exhibit 11.13).

Whether this is really true or not, the fact remains that a list of top commercials is dominated by ads that feature celebrities.[6] Of course, there is the ever-present risk that a celebrity will fall from grace, as several have in recent years, and potentially damage the reputation of the brand for which he or she was once the champion.

Expert spokespeople for a brand are viewed by the target audience as having expert product knowledge. The GM Parts Service Division created an expert in Mr. Goodwrench, who was presented as a knowledgeable source of information. A spokesperson portrayed as a doctor, lawyer, scientist, gardener, or any other expert relevant to a brand is intended to increase the credibility of the message being transmitted. There are also real experts. Advertising for the Club, a steering-wheel locking device that deters auto theft, uses police officers from several cities to demonstrate the effectiveness of the product. Some experts can also be celebrities. This is the case when Michael Jordan gives a testimonial for Nike basketball shoes.

There is also the *average-user testimonial.* Here, the spokesperson is not a celebrity or portrayed as an expert but rather as an average user speaking for the brand. The philosophy is that the target market can relate to this person. Solid theoretical support for this testimonial approach comes from reference-group theory. An interpretation of reference-group theory in this context suggests that consumers may rely on opinions or testimonials from people they consider similar to themselves, rather than on objective product information. Simply put, the consumer's logic in this situation is, "That person is similar to me and likes that brand; therefore, I will also like that brand." In theory, this sort of logic frees the receiver from having to scrutinize detailed product information by simply substituting the reference-group information (see Exhibit 11.14). Of course, in practice, the execution of this strategy is rarely that easy. Consumers are very sophisticated at detecting this attempt at persuasion. Evaluation is usually through tracking studies and communications tests.

6.   Kevin Goldman, "Year's Top Commercials Propelled by Star Power," *Wall Street Journal*, March 16, 1994, B1.

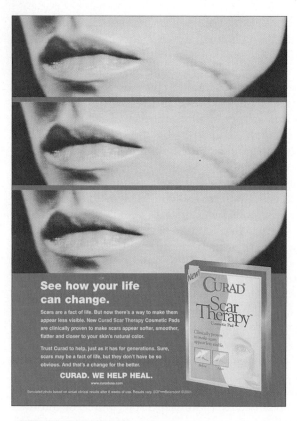

See how your life can change.

Scars are a fact of life. But now there's a way to make them appear less visible. New Curad Scar Therapy Cosmetic Pads are clinically proven to make scars appear softer, smoother, flatter and closer to your skin's natural color.

Trust Curad to help, just as it has for generations. Sure, scars may be a fact of life, but they don't have to be so obvious. And that's a change for the better.

CURAD. WE HELP HEAL.
www.curadusa.com

Simulated photo based on actual clinical results after 8 weeks of use. Results vary. BDF—Beiersdorf ©2001

EXHIBIT 11.15

Straight demonstration of a product benefit by Curad.
www.curadusa.com

Strategic Implications of Testimonial Advertising.

- 👍 Very popular people can generate popularity for the brand.
- 👍 People perceived to be very similar to the consumer, or an expert, can be powerful advocates for the brand.
- 👎 Consumers often forget who likes what, particularly when stars promote multiple goods and services.
- 👎 Can generate more popularity for the star than for the brand. This happens way too often.

Celebrities, being human, are not as easy to manage as packages or cartoon characters: think Tony the Tiger versus Martha Stewart.

Method E: Demonstration. How close an electric razor shaves, how green a fertilizer makes a lawn, or how easy an exercise machine is to use are all product features that can be demonstrated by using a method known simply as demonstration. "Seeing is believing" is the motto of this school of advertising. When it's done well, the results are striking (see Exhibit 11.15). Evaluation of demonstration ads is typically done through tracking studies that measure attitudes, beliefs, and brand preferences over time.

Strategic Implications of Demonstration Ads.

- 👍 Inherent credibility of "seeing is believing."
- 👍 Can be used as social justification; helps the consumer defend his or her decision to buy.
- 👍 Provides clear permission to buy. ("I saw a test; it was best.")
- 👎 Fairly heavy regulatory/legal exposure.

Method F: Infomercials. With the **infomercial**, an advertiser typically buys from five to 60 minutes of television time and runs an information/entertainment program that is really an extended advertisement. Real estate investment programs, weight-loss and fitness products, motivational programs, and cookware have dominated the infomercial format. The program usually has a host who provides information about a product and typically brings on guests to give testimonials about how successful they have been using the featured product. Most infomercials run on cable or satellite stations, although networks have sold early-morning and late-night time as well.

Not all advertisers have had success with infomercials. After spending nearly half a million dollars to produce and air a 30-minute infomercial promoting a Broadway show, the producers pulled the ad after three weeks. The toll-free number to order tickets drew an average of only 14 calls each time the ad ran.[7] However, infomercials can have tremendous sales impact. Many leading infomercials rely on celebrity spokespeople as part of the program. Infomercials are often used in an integrated

---

7.   Kevin Goldman, "Broadway Hopeful Flops with Debut of Infomercial," *Wall Street Journal*, April 1992, 1.

communications effort with promotional efforts. The infomercial can suck you in; mail and telephone promotions follow up; and then some type of sales promotion effort, such as a "free" trip to hear more about this amazing offer, concludes the approach.

Strategic Implications of Infomercials.

- Long format gives advertisers plenty of time to make their case.
- As network ratings fall, day-parts (e.g., Sunday mornings 9–11) that were previously unaffordable have now opened up, making infomercials better deals for advertisers.
- Has the advantage of looking like an entertainment show, when it's really an ad.
- The genre of ads has a somewhat negative public image, which doesn't help build credibility or trust in the advertised brand.

Others. There are other persuade-the-consumer formats, including ads posing as newspaper articles (advertorials), but all have the same basic mechanism at their core: Here's why you should buy this—providing supportive arguments for purchase.

Objective #4: Affective Association: Get the Consumer to Feel Good about the

Brand. Advertisers want consumers to like their brand. They believe that liking leads to preference. But rather than provide the consumer with hard reasons to like the brand, these ads work more through feelings—although let's be clear about this, completely separating thoughts and feelings in real-world human responses to advertising is largely undemonstrated. Instead, what we are talking about here are ads that are *more* geared toward eliciting feelings relative to those *more* designed to elicit thought. Again, this is another pretty big step up in complexity.

There are several well-known approaches to getting the consumer to like one's brand. Let's look at some of the general approaches; most specific examples are merely finer distinctions within these more general categories.

Method A: Feel-Good Ads. These ads are supposed to work through affective (feeling) association. They are supposed to link the good feeling elicited by the ad with the brand: You like the ad, you like the brand. While the actual theory and mechanics of this seemingly simple association are far more complex than you can imagine, the basic idea is that by creating ads with positive feelings, advertisers will lead consumers to associate those positive feelings with the advertised brand, leading to a higher probability of purchase. As Steve Sweitzer of the Hal Riney and Partners advertising agency said:

[C]onsumers want to do business with companies they like. If they like us, they just may give us a try at the store. What a concept. Sometimes just being liked is a strategy.[8]

Of course, getting from liking the ad to liking the brand is one gigantic leap. The evidence on how well this method works is mixed. It may be that positive feelings are transferred to the brand, or it could be that they actually interfere with remembering the message or the brand name. Liking the ad doesn't necessarily mean liking the brand. But message strategy development is a game of probability, and liking the ad may lead to a higher probability of purchase. There are certainly practitioners who believe in the method's intuitive appeal. This may be the result of fairly simple

---

8.   The One Club e-mail discussion, July 27, 1997, as published in *One: A Magazine for Members of the One Club for Art and Copy*, vol. 1, no. 2 (Fall 1997), 18.

DOING IT RIGHT

Feeling Good Again About the NFL

A string of player arrests and a drumbeat of bad news stories about off-field antics had left the National Football League as bruised and battered as a quarterback on Monday morning. The league wanted to repair its image and protect its powerful brand, but it was wary of any direct discussion about the problems faced by individual players.

So in 2007, NFL executives rolled out a new ad campaign focusing on the positive aspects of the lives of its players. One spot featured Matt Hasselbeck of the Seattle Seahawks reading to his young children. In another ad, the Cleveland Browns' Brady Quinn talked about working hard as a student at Notre Dame because he dreamed of going to law school.

"If you keep the focus on the good the players do, people will realize there's this whole other side to their behavior," said Abe Novick, a business development director with the Baltimore office of Euro RSCG Worldwide. "This humanizes them, and that's a good thing."

Source: Stuart Elliott, "Mending a Bruised Image: NFL Campaign Spotlights Players and Their Good Deed," **New York Times**, August 30, 2007, C1.

associations or by more complex and elaborate thoughts. The interpretive processes of humans are very sophisticated. Humans can make sense of and otherwise "get" complex advertising texts loaded with symbols, innuendo, jokes, cultural references and so on, in a second. We don't completely understand why some feel-good ads work and others do not. Some positive attitudes toward the ad don't seem to result in positive attitudes toward the brand because they are not "read" for that purpose, or it could be that consumers easily separate their feelings for the ad and their feelings for the brand. Consumers are pretty sophisticated at keeping these straight. If the theory was as simple (and consumers as simple-minded) as some believe, seeing *The Producers* would make you like Nazis more. Clearly not the intent; hopefully it's not the case. You may love ads for Miller Lite but be a Budweiser drinker. You may think, "Nice ads—wish they made a better beer."

Some feel-good advertising campaigns do work. For example, the long-running Chevrolet truck television campaign "Like a Rock," shown in Exhibit 11.16, featured the music of Bob Seger and scenes of hardworking, patriotic Americans and their families. The good feeling it produces may be the result of widely shared patriotic associations and the celebration of working-class Americans evoked by the advertising. It may map easily onto the brand because sophisticated consumers know that the brand and the advertising are symbolically consistent in theory and practice—and consumer experience. It must have worked for a lot of consumers. Because when the "Like a Rock" campaign finally ended, the familiar themes and images continued. At press time it's John Mellencamp singing "Our Country" against iconic images of American history for Chevy.

Sometimes, feel good ads try to get the consumer *not* to think about certain things. United Airlines could show how often its planes depart and arrive on schedule. Of course, why would they want to? Instead, it has shown successful business meetings and the happy reunion of family members, which create a much richer message, a wider field of shared meanings. And you don't have to think about being stuck at O'Hare or a rude ticket agent. The emotions become the product attribute linked to the brand. But remember, if the actual usage experience is widely discrepant with the ad, the chance of a backfire is significant. Other times, it works beautifully. Consider Kodak's highly successful print and television campaign that highlighted the "Memories of Our Lives" with powerful scenes: a son coming home from the military just in time for Christmas dinner, a father's reception dance with his newly married daughter. Here, Kodak makes it clear that it is in the memory business, and Kodak memories are good memories. Kodak has done this type of advertising, with occasional breaks, for about 100 years. It has worked. In Exhibit 11.17, Martex attempts to evoke warm feelings associated with the relationship between a father and son.

Chevy's feel-good "Like a Rock" truck ads created positive association for working-class Americans. http://www.chevrolet.com

A touching ad for Martex Bath and Bedding. http://www.martex .com

Evaluation of feel-good ads is typically done by measuring attitude change via pre- and postexposure tests, tracking studies, theater dial-turning tests, and communication tests.

Recently, there has been progress in understanding the mechanisms involved in feel-good advertising.[9] It is becoming clearer that thought and feelings are, at some basic level, separate systems. Feelings are believed to be a more "primitive" system. That is, they emanate from a part of the brain that responds quickly to stimuli in the environment. The classic example is that a loud noise frightens (feeling) us, before we know what we are frightened of (thought). So emotions are faster than thought, and sometimes even stronger. There is also evidence that as the media environment gets more cluttered, the affective (or feeling) ads may actually do better than thought-based ads that require a great deal of processing. The feelings may even outlast the thought, although highly emotional ads tend to "wear out" sooner; that is, consumers get tired of them and the ads quickly lose their emotional punch. The secret is finding just the right level of feeling. Feeling ads may have a leg up in the contemporary media environment.

9.   See Michel Tuan Pham, Joel B. Cohen, John W. Pracejus and G. David Hughes, "Affect Monitoring and the Primacy of Feelings in Judgment," *Journal of Consumer Research*, vol. 28 (September 2001), 167–188.

Strategic Implications of Feel-Good Advertising.

- 👍 Eager creatives. Creatives win awards and advance their careers with this style of advertising.
- 👍 May perform better in cluttered media environment.
- 👎 Can have wear-out problems if the emotional appeal is too strong.

Method B: Humor Ads. The goal of a humor ad is pretty much the same as that of other feel-good ads, but humor is a different animal. Generally, the goal of humor in advertising is to create in the receiver a pleasant and memorable association with the brand. Recent advertising campaigns as diverse as those for ESPN ("This Is SportsCenter"), California Milk Processor Board ("Got Milk?") and Las Vegas ("What Happens in Vegas, Stays in Vegas") have all successfully used humor as the primary message theme. But research suggests that the positive impact of humor is not as strong as the intuitive appeal of the approach. Quite simply, humorous versions of advertisements often do not prove to be more persuasive than nonhumorous versions of the same ad. Funny ads are usually great entertainment, but may often be pretty bad business investments.

How many times have you been talking to friends about your favorite ads, and you say something like, "Remember the one where the guy knocks over the drink, and then says. . . ." Everybody laughs, and then maybe someone says something like, "I can't remember who it's for, but what a great ad." Wrong; this is not a great ad. You remember the gag, but not the brand. Not good. You and your friends didn't pay for the ad. How come with some funny ads you can recall the brand? The difference may be that in the ads you recall the payoff for the humor is an integral part of the message strategy. Thus, it better ensures the memory link between humor and brand. If the ad is merely funny and doesn't link the joke (or the punch line) to the brand name, then the advertiser may have bought some very expensive laughs. Clients rarely consider this funny.

A great example of an explicitly linked payoff is the Bud Light "Give Me a Light" campaign of the early 1980s. "Miller Lite" was quickly becoming the generic term for light beer. To do something about this, Bud Light came up with the series of "Give Me a Light" ads to remind light beer drinkers that they had to be a little more specific in what they were ordering. The ads showed customers ordering "a light" and instead getting spotlights, landing lights, searchlights, lights in Wrigley Field, and all sorts of other types of lights. The customer in the ad would then say, "No, a Bud Light." The ads not only were funny, but also made the point perfectly: Say "Bud Light," not just "a light," when ordering a beer. In addition, the message allowed thousands of customers and would-be comedians in bars and restaurants to repeat the line in person, which amounted to a lot of free advertising. The campaign, by Needham, Harper and Steers-Chicago (now DDB Chicago), was a huge success. Why? Because the punch line was firmly linked to the brand name, and the ad actually got consumers to repeat the tag line in actual consumer practice.

Miller Brewing has both reaped the benefits of humor in its recent ad campaigns and suffered from its risks. The original "Less Filling—Tastes Great" campaigns that pitted famous retired athletes against one another rose to great prominence in the late 1970s and through nearly the entire decade of the 1980s. Sports fans could hardly wait for the next installment of the campaign. But the campaign, while highly successful overall, ultimately ran into the problem of wear-out. The brand began to lose market share and is still struggling to regain past glories. In fact, Miller advertising has been all over the place for the last decade or so. Any ideas for Miller?

Pretty funny, eh? Is it good advertising?

Not Sure What Page You're On?

Just check the top corner of this page to find out.

Page numbers. Only in The Onion.

Evaluation of humorous ads is typically done through pre- and postexposure tests; dial-turning attitude tests; tracking studies that measure attitudes, beliefs, and preferences over time.

Strategic Implications of Humor Advertising.

👍 If the joke is integral to the copy platform, humor can be very effective. If it is not, it is just free entertainment.

👍 Very eager creatives. Creatives love to do funny ads. Funny ads tend to win awards and advance careers.

👎 Humorous messages may adversely affect comprehension. Humor can actually interfere with memory processes: The consumer doesn't remember what brand the ad was for.

👎 Very funny messages can wear out very quickly, leaving no one laughing, especially the advertiser.[10] It's like hearing the same joke over and over. Advertisers who use this technique have to keep changing the gag. Think "So Simple Even a Caveman Can Do It." They keep adding new gags to keep it interesting.

Because you have to keep the gag fresh, these can be very expensive ad campaigns.

Method C: Sex-Appeal Ads. Sex ads are a type of feelings-based advertising. Because they are directed toward humans, ads tend to focus on sex from time to time. Not a big surprise: Humans tend to think about sex from time to time. Sex ads are thought not to require much thought, just arousal and affect (feelings). But does sex sell? In a literal sense, the answer is no, because nothing, not even sex, *makes* someone buy something. However, sexual appeals are attention-getting and occasionally arousing, which may affect how consumers feel about a product. The advertiser is trying to get attention and link some degree of sexual arousal to the brand. Some believe in a type of classical conditioning involving sex in ads. Evidence for the effect is mixed.

Like all other interpretation of ads by humans, context is extremely important in sexual-appeal messages. Knowing just what constitutes sex appeal is not easy. Is it showing skin? How much skin? What's the difference between the celebration of a beautiful body and its objectification? Motive? Politics? Who says? What was the deal with the Nipple-Gate scandal of the 2004 Super Bowl?

Can you use sex to help create a brand image? Sure you can. Calvin Klein and many other advertisers have used sexual imagery successfully to mold brand image. But these are for products such as clothes and perfumes, which emphasize how one

10. This claim is made by Video Storyboards Tests, based on its extensive research of humor ads, and cited in Kevin Goldman, "Ever Hear the One about the Funny Ad?" *Wall Street Journal*, November 2, 1993, B11.

intelligence: ergonomic design

intelligence **(M)** everywhere

The Motorola V.Series 120

MOTOROLA

EXHIBIT 11.19

Historically, muted sex ads have scored well in recall tests. Is recall all you really want here? What about feeling toward the brand? http:// www.motorola.com/phonefeel

looks, feels, and smells. Does the same appeal work as well for cars, telephones, computer peripherals, and file cabinets? How about breakfast cereals? In general, no. But because humans are complex and messy creatures, we cannot say that sex-appeal ads never work in such categories. Sometimes they do (See Exhibit 11.19). As recently noted by Professor Tom Reichert at the University of Georgia,[11] traditional wisdom in the ad business was that the use of sex is "amateurish and sophomoric, and a desperate—not to mention ineffective—attempt to rescue plummeting sales." But, in the very next breath, advertising professionals will recount several examples where it has worked wonderfully. So, which is it? This may be one of those classic examples of what is said (by ad industry spokespeople) being very different from what is actually done and what actually works. This should not be too surprising in that humans in general, and Americans in particular, are chronically vexed by the topic of sex, and their own ambivalence on the topic shows.

The most important aspect for effectiveness seems to be the match (or appropriateness) of the category and the appeal. The ads shown in Exhibit 11.20 use a sex-appeal message to one degree or another. How effective do you think these ads are in fulfilling the objective of instilling brand preference? Are they gratuitous? Are they on target strategically? In which of these is the sex appeal relevant, appropriate, distracting, sexist, demeaning, fun, innocent, playful, or good advertising? What do you think? Sex appeals are certainly used in all sorts of promotional efforts. But what is sexy or constitutes sex appeal seems to vary widely according to audience members' gender, appropriateness for the product or service category, and so on. There is more discussion of sex in advertising than just about any other topic. So look at these ads and think about what is good, bad, effective, ineffective, OK, not OK, and why. Talk about which of these ads are good advertising, gratuitous advertising, demeaning, appropriate, and so on. You will be engaging in the same debate that advertising professionals do all the time. It's good training.

One of the biggest problems that all agencies have is the headache of censorship. There is simply no reason to it. Censorship, any kind of censorship, is pure whim and fancy. It's one guy's idea of what is right for him. It's based on everything arbitrary. . . . There's a classic Lenny Bruce bit. He's doing a father talking to his son while they're both watching a pornographic film. Bruce says, "Son, I can't let you watch this. This is terrible and disgusting. Son, I'm going to have to cover your eyes now. That man is going to kiss that woman and they're going to make love and there's going to be pleasure and everything else and this is terrible, it's not for you until you are at least twenty-one. Instead son, I am going to take you to a nice war movie."

—Famous adman Jerry Della Femina[12]

11.   Tom Reichert, , *The Erotic History of Advertising* (Amherst, NY: Prometheus, 2004).
12.   Jerry Della Femina, "Censorship," in *From Those Wonderful Folks Who Gave You Pearl Harbor: Front-Line Dispatches from the Advertising War*, Charles Sopkin, ed. (New York: Simon and Schuster, 1970), 179, 190.

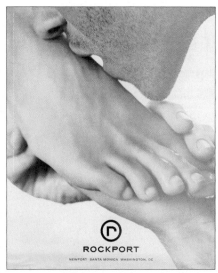

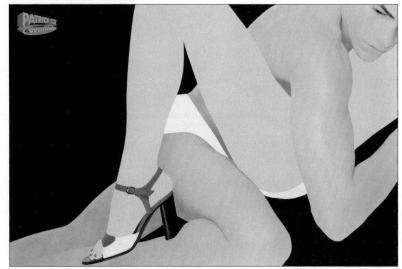

EXHIBIT 11.20

Sex-appeal ads are among the most common and the most controversial in advertising. But often the issues of "what is appropriate" and "why" get completely mixed up and confused. Here, we provide a selection of current ads for your inspection and discussion. As future advertising professionals, which do you think are good, sound, on-strategy advertising? Which do you think use sex inappropriately? Which are in poor taste? Which may do the brand more harm than good? What might women think and feel about these ads and the companies that sponsor them? How about men? Should there be more regulations, or not? What do you think?

EXHIBIT 11.21

What do you think? Puritanism, good taste, bad taste, desperate for ratings?

No kidding. If you use sex in an ad, you will probably have "issues" with clients, or regulators, or advocacy groups, or lawmakers, or municipalities, on and on. You will hear of all the harms that can occur if you use sex. Some on the political right will tell you to avoid promoting promiscuity (and lost sales), and some on the political left will tell you to protect women from degrading images (and lost sales). Whatever your politics, the fear of losing sales is an entirely reasonable concern, but rarely a very realistic problem in practice. Just as consumers do not typically buy something (like a lawn mower) because of a poor-fitting sex appeal, they will rarely refrain from buying it either. After Nipple-Gate the advertising industry wondered publicly whether we were entering a new age of puritanical thought (see Exhibit 11.21). We think the last few years have pretty much answered the question: no.

Evaluation of sex-appeal ads is typically done through communication tests, focus groups, pre- and postexposure tests, and tracking studies that measure attitudes, beliefs, and preferences over time. When using sex appeal, clients are sometimes a little nervous and order more focus groups, communication tests, and qualitative work because they want to make sure that they are not going to go over some fairly invisible line and be punished for it.

Strategic Implications of Sexual-Appeal Advertising.

- 👍 Higher attention levels.
- 👍 Higher arousal and affective (feeling).
- 👎 Possible poor memorability of brand due to interference at the time of exposure. In other words, the viewer is thinking about something else.
- 👎 Product-theme continuity excludes many goods and services.
- 👎 Legal, political, and regulatory exposure.

Objective #5: Scare the Consumer into Action.
Sometimes the strategy is to scare the consumer into acting. Fear appeals are typically designed to illicit a specific feeling (fear) as well as thought. Fear is an extraordinarily powerful emotion and may be used to get consumers to take some very important action. But this fear must be coupled with some degree of thought in order for it to work. That's why we place this strategy a bit higher up the ladder in terms of its degree of complexity. It is generally considered hard to use effectively, and is fairly limited in application. Still, you should know how they work.

Method: Fear-Appeal Ads.
A fear appeal highlights the risk of harm or other negative consequences of not using the advertised brand or not taking some recommended action. The appeal is usually a combination of reason-why and affect attachment. Often it's a little bit of fear designed to induce a little bit of thought, and then action. Getting the balance right can be very tricky. The intuitive belief about fear as a message tactic is that fear will motivate the receiver to buy a product that will reduce or eliminate the portrayed threat. For example, Radio Shack spent $6 million to run a series of ads showing a dimly lit unprotected house, including a peacefully

EXHIBIT 11.22

Fairly scary. Get the point?

sleeping child, as a way to raise concerns about the safety of the receiver's valuables as well as his or her family. The campaign used the theme "If Security Is the Question, We've Got the Answer." The ad closed with the Radio Shack logo and the National Crime Prevention Council slogan, "United against Crime."[13] Similarly, the ad in Exhibit 11.22 for Body Alarm cuts right to the chase: It capitalizes on fears of not being able to cry for help during a bodily attack.

The contemporary social environment has provided advertisers with an ideal context for using fear appeals. In an era of drive-by shootings, carjackings, gang violence, and terrorism, Americans fear for their personal safety. Manufacturers of security products such as alarm and lighting security systems play on this fearful environment.[14] Other advertisers have recently tried fear as an appeal. One such advertiser, the Asthma Zero Mortality Coalition, urges people who have asthma to seek professional help and uses a fear appeal in its ad copy: "When those painful, strained breaths start coming, keep in mind that any one of them could easily be your last."[15] In Exhibit 11.23, Electrolux shows us the things that live in all our carpets, and how to get rid of them.

Research indicates that until a consumer gets to very high fear levels, more is better. So, moderate levels of fear appear to work better than low levels. However, the effect of truly intense levels of fear is either unknown or thought to be counterproductive.

EXHIBIT 11.23

Just to look at a dust mite close up is a little scary.

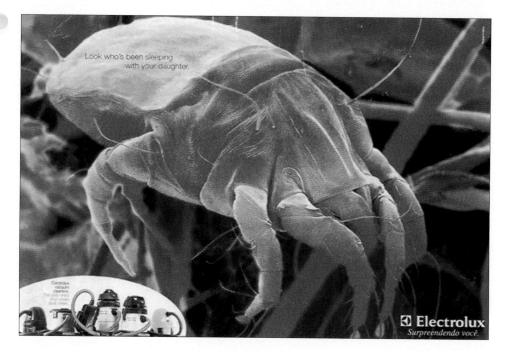

13. Jeffrey D. Zbar, "Fear!," *Advertising Age*, November 14, 1994, 18.
14. Ibid.
15. Emily DeNitto, "Healthcare Ads Employ Scare Tactics," *Advertising Age*, November 7, 1994, 12.

ETHICS

Automakers Shift Gears in Ad Campaign

When Washington lawmakers were considering new fuel economy standards in 2007, the nation's top three automakers and Toyota Motor Corp. came out swinging with an aggressive advertising campaign intended to strike fear in American consumers.

One ad raised the prospect that soccer moms might be prevented from buying big sport utility vehicles to haul their children safely around town. Another spot featured men discussing whether they would be able to purchase a new pickup truck.

"You might want to do that fast," one of the men said in the script, suggesting that new fuel standards are "going to really jack up the price."

But the scare tactics backfired. The ads, which targeted key senators in 11 states, served only to spur environmental groups and rile some lawmakers. One senator, North Dakota Democrat Byron Dorgan, angrily told auto executives that new fuel standards "will not take your pickup truck away." The Senate then passed a bill that would require an increase in the average fuel economy of cars and trucks by 2010.

When they went back to the ad drawing board, the automakers returned with a kinder, gentler tone. A $1 million print and radio campaign from the Alliance of Automobile Manufacturers that followed the Senate vote in the summer of 2007 dropped the fear appeal, and the automakers stood down. "We are the first to voice a mea culpa," one of the group's leaders said. "We played a role in a public debate that sounded like a *Crossfire* show."

The new campaign echoed that sentiment. "We don't have all the answers to questions about reasonable fuel economy standards. No one does," one ad intoned. "Together, we can find the answers America deserves."

Sources: Micheline Maynard, "Politics Forcing Detroit to Back New Fuel Rules," **New York Times**, June 20, 2007, A1; David Shepardson, "Carmakers Ditch Scare Tactics in New Fuel Ads," **Detroit News**, July 14, 2007.

Because they are so rarely used, either in a research setting or in the real world, no one is entirely sure. Traditional wisdom holds that intense fear appeals actually short-circuit persuasion and result in a negative attitude toward the advertised brand.[16] Other researchers argue that the tactic is beneficial to the advertiser.[17] So no one really knows for sure, it may very much depend on varying definitions of fear, its close association with anxiety, individual differences in consumers, and the extent a "way out" of harm's way is offered. Advances in brain research employing technologies such as PT scans and MRIs may finally give us a more definitive answer. What is fairly clear, though, is that two factors seem to produce better results when moderate fear appeals are used: that the message is plausible, and that the ad presents a very clear action to be taken to avoid harm. The ideal fear-appeal ad would thus be a moderate level of fear that is entirely believable[18] (one that people can't easily say doesn't apply to them or seems unlikely to be a real threat), and offers a very clear (completely obvious) and very easy way to avoid the bad thing threatened by the ad. Evaluation of fear-appeal ads is typically done through tracking studies that measure attitudes, beliefs, and preferences over time; pre- and postexposure tests, and communication tests.

Strategic Implications of Fear-Appeal Advertising.

- 👍 Moderate levels of fear appear to works the best.
- 👍 You must have a plausible threat to motivate consumers.
- 👍 You must have a completely clear and easy-to-discern link between the threat and the use of the advertised brand.
- 👎 Too little or too much fear may do nothing.
- 👎 Legal, regulatory, and ethical problems.
- 👎 Some fear ads are simply ridiculous and have low impact.

16. Irving L. Janis and Seymour Feshbach, "Effects of Fear Arousing Communication," *Journal of Abnormal Social Psychology* 48 (1953), 78–92.

17. Michael Ray and William Wilkie, "Fear: The Potential of an Appeal Neglected by Marketing," *Journal of Marketing*, vol. 34, no. 1 (January 1970), 54–62.

18. E. H. H. J. Das, J. B. F. de Wit, and W. Strobe, "Fear Appeals Motivate Acceptance of Action Recommendations: Evidence for a Positive Bias in the Processing of Persuasive Messages," *Personality and Social Psychology Bulletin*, vol. 29 (2003), 650–664.

Objective #6: Change Behavior by Inducing Anxiety.

Anxiety is fear's cousin. Anxiety is not quite outright fear, but it is uncomfortable and can last longer. While it's hard to keep people in a state of outright fear, people can feel anxious for a good long time. People try to avoid feeling anxious. They try to minimize, moderate, and alleviate anxiety. They use all sorts of mechanisms to avoid anxiety from thought to behavior. Often people will buy or consume things to help them in their continuing struggle with anxiety. They might watch television, smoke, exercise, eat, or take medication. They might also buy mouthwash, deodorant, condoms, a safer car, life insurance, or a retirement account, and advertisers know this. Advertisers pursue a change-behavior-by-inducing-anxiety objective by playing on consumer anxieties. The ads work through both thought and feelings. Regrettably, this is one of the most effective types of advertising around.

Method A: Anxiety Ads. There are many things to be anxious about. Advertisers realize this and use many settings to demonstrate why you should be anxious and what you can do to alleviate the anxiety. Social, medical, and personal-care products frequently use anxiety ads. The message conveyed in anxiety ads is that (1) there is a clear and present problem, and (2) the way to avoid this problem is to buy the advertised brand. Anxiety ads tout the likelihood of being stricken by gingivitis, athlete's foot, calcium deficiency, body odor, heart disease and on and on. The idea is that these anxiety-producing conditions are out there, and they may affect you unless you take the appropriate action. What anxieties might the ad in Exhibit 11.24 arouse?

EXHIBIT 11.24

This ad is designed to produce anxiety. What is the target market supposed to worry about? http://www.lvidocs.com

Method B: Social Anxiety Ads. This is a subcategory of anxiety ads where the danger is negative social judgment, as opposed to a physical threat. Procter & Gamble has long relied on such presentations for its household and personal-care brands. In fact, Procter & Gamble has used this approach so consistently over the years that in some circles the anxiety tactic is referred to as the P&G approach. When Head & Shoulders dandruff shampoo is advertised with the theme "You Never Get a Second Chance to Make a First Impression," the audience realizes that Head & Shoulders could spare them the embarrassment of having dandruff. One of the more memorable P&G social anxiety ads is the scene where husband and wife are busily cleaning the spots off the water glasses before dinner guests arrive because they didn't use P&G's Cascade dishwashing product, which, of course, would have prevented the glasses from spotting. Most personal-care products have used this type of appeal. In Exhibit 11.25 on the next page, Eclipse suggests that you might be sharing unwanted leftovers from lunch. Feel a touch of anxiety? How's your breath? Evaluation of anxiety ads is typically done by measuring attitudes and beliefs through tracking studies and communication tests.

EXHIBIT 11.25

Here is another example of a social anxiety ad. Also, antiperspirant brands are a natural fit for advertising messages that play upon social anxiety. Do products sites for Old Spice (http://www.oldspice .com) or Secret (http://www.secretstrength.com) capitalize on faux pas anxieties?

Strategic Implications of Anxiety Advertising.

- Can generate perception of widespread (and thus personal) threat and motivate action (buying and using the advertised product). These ads have a pretty good track record of working.
- The brand can become the solution to the ever-present problem, and this results in long-term commitment to the brand. Once a solution (brand) is found, the consumer doesn't have to think about it again.
- Efficient: A little anxiety goes a long way.
- Too much anxiety, like fear, may overwhelm the consumer, and the ad and the brand may be avoided because it produces too much discomfort.
- If the anxiety-producing threat is not linked tightly enough to your brand, you may increase category demand and provide business for your competitors, particularly the market leader. If total category share goes up, market leaders get most of it. Still, if the creative is good and the link to the specific brand is strong, it is a good method for any size player.
- Ethical issues: Some believe there is more than enough to feel anxious about without advertisers adding more.
- These ads have historically been disproportionately targeted at women. Critics note the inherent unfairness and sexism.

Objective #7: Transform Consumption Experiences. Let's get even more sophisticated:
transformational advertising and IBP. You know how sometimes it's hard to explain to someone else just exactly why a certain experience was so special, why it felt so good? It wasn't just this thing, or that thing; the entire experience was somehow better than the sum of the individual parts. Sometimes that feeling is at least partly due to your expectations of what something will be like, your positive memories of previous experiences, or both. Sometimes advertisers try to provide that anticipation and/or familiarity bundled up in a positive memory of an advertisement or other brand promotion, to be activated during the consumption experience itself, and recalled positively after the experience. The advertising or other forms of integrated brand promotion are thus said to have transformed the actual consumption experience, both at the time of consumption and in the consumer's memory.

Method: Transformational Ads. The idea behind transformational advertising
is that it can actually make the consumption experience better. For example, after years of transformational advertising by McDonald's, the experience of actually eating at McDonald's may be transformed or made better by virtue of what you know and feel about McDonald's each time you walk in. Transformational advertising attempts to create a brand feeling, expectation, and mood that are activated when the consumer uses the product or service. Actual usage is thus transformed, made better. Transformational ads that are effective are said to connect the experience of the advertisement so closely with the brand experience that consumers cannot help but

EXHIBIT 11.26

Does this ad actually transform the consumption experience? That's the idea.

think of material from the ads (or in a more general sense, the memory of many things from many ads) when they think of the brand. Exhibit 11.26 is as much about the fun feelings connected with having a Miller Lite with friends as it is about the taste of beer. If, as researchers have shown, it is possible to create false memories of brands that don't even exist, isn't it possible that over time commercial content and actual experience begin to merge in memory, and the consumer remembers things as they and the advertisers want them to? What if Disney mailed you a videotape of a perfect trip to the Magic Kingdom before you went, and one after you returned? Maybe in a year or two those memories would merge in a fashion that benefits Disney. Product placements in movies and television shows, and other forms of branded entertainment, can accomplish the same thing. Evaluation of transformational ads and other forms of IBP are typically done through field studies, tracking studies, ethnographic (on-site, qualitative) methods, and communication tests. On rare occasions, small-scale experiments are conducted.

Strategic Implications of Transformational Advertising.

- 👍 Can be extremely powerful due to a merging of ad and brand experience.
- 👍 Fosters long-term commitment.
- 👎 Can ring absolutely false.
- 👎 Ethical issues: Some believe that this manipulation of experience is unethical.

Objective #8: Situate the Brand Socially. Maybe you haven't given it much thought, but if you're ever going to understand advertising, you have to get this: Objects have social meanings. While it applies to all cultures, this simple truth is at the very center of consumer cultures. In consumer cultures, billions of dollars are spent in efforts to achieve specific social meanings for advertised brands. As an advertiser you have to try to make material objects, which already carry some meaning, have the meaning you want them to have. How do you do it?

Advertisers have long known that when they place their product in the right social setting either in an ad, a branded promotion in a real environment, or a product placement in a television, show, movie, or video game, their brand takes on some of the characteristics of its surroundings. The social setting and the brand rub off on each other. These social brandscapes are often created within ads. In advertising, a product is placed into a custom-created social setting hopefully perfect for the brand, a setting in which the brand hopefully excels. If all goes right, this becomes the way in which the consumer remembers the brand, as fitting into this manufactured and desirable social reality. Let us say it again: Objects have social meaning; they are not just things. Good social reality advertising can let us shape that meaning. Amazingly, many forget this. If done well, these can be effective ads. This is really where the action is these days.

EXHIBIT 11.27

By carefully constructing a social world within the frame of the ad into which the product is carefully placed, meaning is transferred to the product. "Background" and product meanings merge. This is the sophistication behind "slice-of-life" advertising. http://www.louisboston.com

Method A: Slice-of-Life Ads. A brand placed in a social context gains social meaning by association. Slice-of-life advertisements depict an ideal usage situation for the brand. The social context surrounding the brand rubs off and gives the brand social meaning (see Exhibit 11.27). Consumers may, of course, reject or significantly alter that meaning, but often they accept it. Think about it. You put the brand into a social setting and transfer meaning from that social setting to the brand. Look at Exhibit 11.28. Think about it, about how it works. Evaluation of slice-of-life ads is typically done through tracking studies that measure attitudes, beliefs, and preferences over time; pre- and postexposure tests; communication tests; and qualitative interviews.

EXHIBIT 11.28

This is an excellent slice-of-life ad. It shows the brand in an idealized social context. Great ad. http://www.verizon.com

Strategic Implications of Slice-of-Life Ads.

- 👍 Generally, fewer counterarguments made by consumers.
- 👍 Legal/regulatory advantages. Advertisers' attorneys like pictures more than words because determining the truth or falsity of a picture is much tougher than words. Have you ever noticed how heavily regulated industries tend to use lots of pictures and little copy (other than mandated warning labels?)
- 👍 Iconic potential. To make their brands another Coca-Cola is many advertisers' dream. Socially embedding your brand in everyday life gives you this chance.
- 👍 Creation of ad-social-realities. You may be able to create the perfect social world for the brand, and its space in it.
- 👎 Fairly common. Unless the creative is outstanding (particularly visually) and you are generally willing to spend a reasonable amount for repetition, these ads can get lost in the clutter. In certain categories, such as fashion, almost all ads are of this type.
- 👎 If not done very well, the picture presented by the advertiser rings false and is rejected.
- 👎 These ads don't tend to copy-test well. This is because so much of copy-testing is still designed

around remembering words and verbal claims. Copy-testing has simply not caught up with the new reality of the prominence of visual forms of persuasion (visual rhetoric).

☞ Managerial (brand side) resistance. You will sometimes get pushback on these ads from a brand manager or bean-counter type who says something like "Why are we paying so much and saying nothing? Where are the words?" What can you say to a statement like that: that it's simply an uninformed opinion from someone not in the profession of persuading? If "trust me" doesn't work, you might ask the nay-sayer to walk through a museum or study the great propaganda campaigns of all time (many heavily visual), or look at the greatest ads of all time (VW in the 1960s, etc.) and note the prominence of the visual in the persuasion attempt. Tell them to leave advertising to the professionals.

👍 Creatives tend to love these ads (at least, art directors do); you will get some top-flight creative folks on the job.

Method B: Branded Entertainment: Product Placement/Short Internet Films/Other Madison & Vine Techniques. In the age of new media, we have gone well beyond a few product placements in movies and TV shows to a more and more broad-spectrum and integrated set of methods to bring brand messages to consumers. These methods are often gathered under one umbrella called Madison & Vine. It began as a conference to bring together Hollywood (the famous intersection of "Hollywood and Vine") and the advertising industry (traditionally based along New York's Madison Avenue, although agencies are now all over the place): thus "Madison & Vine." Madison & Vine then became a book, an *Ad Age* column, and now encompasses a wide array of nontraditional integrated brand promotions (IBP). Recording, gaming, and cell phone industries are involved as well now. The most important development is how many major advertisers are now involved in producing movies that are really brand promotions, TV shows that are really brand promotions, cell phone content that is really brand promotion, TV spots for new musical recordings that are also ads for products (a Sting video promoted Jaguar while a Jaguar TV spot promoted Sting; *The Bourne Ultimatum* promoted Volkswagen (Exhibit 11.29) as Volkswagen promoted *The Bourne Ultimatum* . . . on and on and on.) We will dig deeper into this topic in Chapter 18, but for now focus on a common form and one that is in this strategic set: product placement and integration.

EXHIBIT 11.29

Many products were integrated into The Bourne Ultimatum. If you saw the movie, did you notice them?

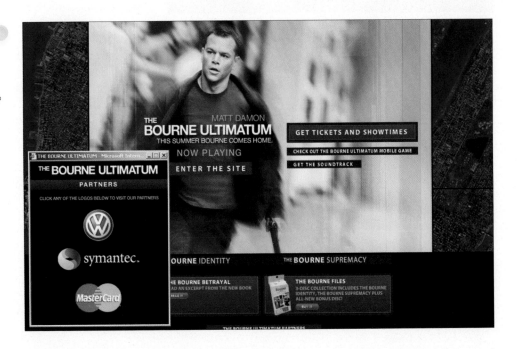

One way to integrate the product into a desired setting is to place the product in a television show or film. An actor picks up a can of Coke, rather than just any soda, and hopefully the correct image association is made. Even more explicit are short films (usually less than 10 minutes) made for the Internet. A few years ago, BMW released six such films showing its cars in dramatic contexts. The most famous was a film starring Madonna and directed by her husband, British film director Guy Ritchie (*Lock, Stock, and Two Smoking Barrels; Snatch*). The films were all made by hot directors and had amazing story content, yet they were also a way of demonstrating the product by placing it in a deliberately and carefully created social world. BMW sales responded very nicely and executives believed it was a much better media buy than network television, where getting lost in the crowd is so easy. Ford alone spends nearly $2 billion a year on national advertising. What would BMW have to spend just to get noticed in that environment? BMW eventually pulled these films from their Web site, either because the models in the films were getting outdated as new models were out, or for some other reason we simply don't know. However, since that time, the idea or similar ones has really caught on. It's worth running a quick YouTube or Google "BMW film" search to see what started the trend.

You can follow this evolving saga of this on http://adage.com/madisonandvine, so we will mention just a few other examples. Ford Motor Co. has decided to be partners in the new motion picture studio Our Stories Films, a joint venture of Ford, entrepreneur and BET founder Robert L. Johnson, and movie moguls Bob and Harvey Weinstein to produce what Ford has called "the black Walt Disney." Their initial goal is to produce three to five "African-American family films." According to *Advertising Age*, Ford will have "script integration, sponsorships, and promotions." According to theory, everyone wins: Ford gets its cars into movies, the cost of producing the films is partially underwritten by the car company, and Robert L. Johnson serves an African-American audience.

The producers of *24* made a deal through their prequel *CTU Rookie* (Exhibit 11.30) and the animated *DayZero* with Unilever to promote Degree deodorant. In no time at all, Unilever had over 1.5 million hits to its related Web site. Sales went up at least 20 percent in a category that is growing.[19] At the same time, Degree was running more traditional TV spots.

There are thousands of these examples. To give you an idea of just how much branded content there is out there, check out Exhibit 11.31. In one week *CSI: NY* had 36 product placement occurrences in a 60-minute show (about 42 minutes of actual airtime).

Exhibit 11.32 lists the most recalled in-product placements for a similar period. There is, however, debate about whether recall is even really desirable. Perhaps what advertisers really want is for their brand to become integral parts of a desired social reality, a media-created world where the brand is absolutely normal and expected, almost invisible. Some contemporary theories of memory suggest

EXHIBIT 11.30

Product placement deals are becoming the norm.

19. Jack Neff, "Case Study: Why Unilever Execs Are Loving '24.' Webisode Partnership with Fox Show Helps Degree Men Sales Climb 20%" http://adage.com, published June 21, 2007.

EXHIBIT 11.31

Nielsen Product Placement Report

Program	Network	Total Occurrences
Happy Birthday Elton	MNT	216
King of Queens	CBS	211
So You Think You Can Dance	Fox	180
TV's Funniest Moments	Fox	107
On the Lot	Fox	78
CSI: NY	CBS	36
Gilmore Girls	CW	36
30 Rock	NBC	32
Studio 60 on the Sunset Strip	NBC	30
Extreme Makeover: Home Edition	ABC	27

Source: "Happy Birthday Elton Tops Week of May 28 to June 3. Reprinted with permission from the June 7, 2007 issue of AdAge.com. © Crain Communications, Inc., 2007.

EXHIBIT 11.32

IAG Product Placement Recall Report

Rank	Brand	In-Program Placement Description	Program Airing Info	Recall Index
1	Jeep	Lorelai and Rory drive to the inn to meet a famous journalist	*Gilmore Girls* (CW, May 15)	238
2	Cisco	Acting Pres. Daniels talks to Russian Pres. Suvarov via TelePresence service	24 (Fox, May 14)	213
3	Modern Bride	Alan catches Charlie reading magazine in the living room	*Two and a Half Men* (CBS, May 14)	209
4	Toyota	Oncsreen graphic identifies Yaris as sponsor of the "Smallville Legends" segment	*Smallville* (CW, May 10)	191
5	Marvel Silver Surfer	Micah holds up a copy of the original comic book	*Heroes* (NBC, May 14)	188
6	MySpace	Angela shows Brennan and Booth the deceased's Web page in her office	*Bones* (Fox, May 9)	187
7	Cisco	Announcer directs viewers to visit sponsored Web site and send in plot theories	*Heroes* (NBC, May 7)	184
8	Hershey's Kisses	Jordan says that there are only two chocolates when the team is stranded	*Crossing Jordan* (NBC, May 16)	179
9	Xanax	Kate throws a container of perscription medication into a pile of food	*Crossing Jordan* (NBC, May 16)	173
10	Dell	Karen Hayes watches video on monitor; Chloe uses laptop at CTU office	24 (Fox, May 21)	172

The IAG Top 10 Most Recalled In-Program Placements focuses on brand/product placements occuring in Sitcom and Drama programs on the broadcast networks during the May 7 to June 3 period. The Recall Score is the percentage of television viewers who can recall within 24 hours the brand/product of an in-program placement they were exposed to during the normal course of viewing network sitcoms and dramas. These scores are then indexed against the mean score for all placements occurring in this genre during the time period (Recall Index). 100 equals average. Note: For this analysis, in-program placements were considered only if the occurrence had visual elements (i.e., was seen onscreen) or both visual and auditory element (i.e., was both seen and mentioned). Only first-run episodes were considered. Both planned and incidental exposures are tracked through IAG's In-Program Performance measurement system.

Source: "IAG Top 10 Most-Recalled In-Program Product Placements: Network Sitcoms and Dramas, May 7 to June 3, 2007. Reprinted with permission from June 14, 2007 issue of AdAge.com. © Crain Communications, Inc., 2007.

that this would indeed be best over time, as the source of the brand image becomes disassociated from the brand memory. In other words, consumers believe Degree is a very popular brand among the desired target market, part of their world.

Strategic Implications of Branded Entertainment.

- 👍 Low counterargument, if not too obvious.
- 👍 Outside normal ad context; may reduce all sorts of defensive measures by consumers, such as source discounting.
- 👍 May actually increase consumer's estimates about how many other people use the brand, thus making it appear more prevalent and popular than it actually is.
- 👍 A perceived cost advantage over the very expensive network TV.
- 👎 Can be horribly ineffective when it's really, really obvious.
- 👎 Nonstandardized rate structure; hard to price these; deals done in private.

Objective #9: Define the Brand Image.
Madonna has an image; Michael Jordan has an image; so do Prada and Pepsi. Even fictional characters such as the wildly popular Harry Potter have images. Brands have images. Images are the most apparent and most prominently associated characteristics of a brand. Advertisers are in the business of creating, adjusting, and maintaining brand images—in other words, they often engage in the define-the-brand-image objective.

Method: Image Ads.
Image advertising means different things to different people. To some, it means the absence of hard product information (see Exhibit 11.33). To others, it refers to advertising that is almost exclusively visual (see Exhibit 11.34).

Image advertising attempts to project (usually through visuals) a sense—a set of feelings and generally unelaborated thoughts—about a brand to the consumer. This method can still link defined attributes to the brand. Sometimes these linkages are quite explicit, such as using a tiger to indicate the strength of a brand. Other times, the linkages are implicit and subtle, such as the colors and tones associated with a brand. Check out the ads in Exhibit 11.35.

EXHIBIT 11.33

EXHIBIT 11.34

Image.

Stylish visual ads for stylish Prada.

EXHIBIT 11.35

These are all image ads. Even though some people think of these ads as light and fluffy, they are anything but that. They are carefully constructed to yield the right set of connections and the right images. Think about these. Do you get them?

Evaluation of image ads can be tricky. Qualitative methods are often employed; sometimes associative tests are used, along with attribute-related tracking studies done over time. As we've said before, the evaluation of visual communication is still not where it should be. Further, these ads are often figurative rather than literal, and require evaluation methods like the Zaltman (ZMET) metaphor-based techniques (discussed in Chapter 7). They are also heavily dependent upon the maker of the ad being completely in touch with the contemporary culture so that the audience "gets" the ad. It is the skillful use of this social and cultural knowledge that turns brands into very successful brands, or even brand icons.[20]

What is often really needed is a very cultural connected creative, and management wise enough to either help them or leave them alone.

Strategic Implications of Image Advertising.

- 👍 Generally, less counterarguments generated by consumers.
- 👍 Relatively little or no legal/regulatory exposure.
- 👍 Iconic potential: Think Marlboro Man.
- 👎 Very common in some product categories; can get lost in clutter.
- 👎 Can be quickly rejected if advertised image rings untrue or poorly matches what the consumer currently thinks of the brand, particularly through direct experience.
- 👎 Don't tend to copy-test well. Why? Well, once again, existing copy-test procedures are designed predominately for words, not images.
- 👎 Managerial resistance: Client often argues for more words.
- 👍 Creatives tend to love them; you can get great people on your communication team.

In the End. In the end, message development is where the advertising and branding battle is usually won or lost. It's where real creativity exists. It's where the agency has to be smart and figure out just how to turn the wishes of the client into effective advertising. It is where the creatives have to get into the minds of consumers, realizing that the advertisement will be received by different people in different ways. It is where advertisers merge culture, mind, and brand. Great messages are developed by people who can put themselves into the minds (and culture) of their audience members and anticipate their response, leading to the best outcome: selling the advertised brand.

---

20.   Douglas B. Holt, "What Becomes an Icon Most?" *Harvard Business Review* (March 2003).

SUMMARY

 Identify nine objectives of message strategy.

Advertisers can choose from a wide array of message strategy objectives as well as methods for implementing these objectives. Three fundamental message objectives are promoting brand recall, linking key attributes to the brand name, and persuading the customer. The advertiser may also wish to create an affective association in consumers' minds by linking good feelings, humor, and sex appeal with the brand itself. Such positive feelings associated with the advertised brand can lead consumers to a higher probability of purchase. The advertiser may try to scare the consumer into action or change behavior by inducing anxiety, using negative emotional states as the means to motivate purchases. Transformational advertising aims to transform the nature of the consumption experience so that a consumer's experience of a brand becomes connected to the glorified experiences portrayed in ads. A message may also situate the brand in an important social context to heighten the brand's appeal. Finally, advertisers seek to define a brand's image by linking certain attributes to the brand, mostly using visual cues.

 Identify methods for executing each message strategy objective.

Advertisers employ any number of methods to achieve their objectives. To get consumers to recall a brand name, advertisers use repetition, slogans, and jingles. When the advertiser's objective is to link a key attribute to a brand, USP ads emphasizing unique brand qualities are employed. If the goal is to persuade a consumer to make a purchase, reason-why ads, hard-sell ads, comparison ads, testimonials, demonstrations, and infomercials all do the trick. Feel-good ads, humorous ads, and sexual-appeal ads can raise a consumer's preferences for one brand over another through affective association. Fear-appeal ads, judiciously used, can motivate purchases, as can ads that play on other anxieties. Transformational ads attempt to enrich the consumption experience. With slice-of-life ads, product placement, and short Internet films, the goal is to situate a brand in a desirable social context. Finally, ads that primarily use visuals work to define brand image.

 Discuss the strategic implications of various methods used to execute each message strategy objective.

Each method used to execute a message strategy objective has pros and cons. Methods that promote brand recall or link key attributes to a brand name can be extremely successful in training consumers to remember a brand name or its specific, beneficial attributes. However, these methods require long-term commitment and repetition to work properly, and advertisers can pay high expense while generating disdain from creatives. Methods used to persuade consumers generally aim to provide rhetorical arguments and demonstrations for why consumers should prefer a brand, resulting in strong, cognitive loyalty to products. However, these methods assume a high level of involvement and are vulnerable to counterarguments that neutralize their effectiveness—more-sophisticated audiences tune them out altogether, rejecting them as misleading, insipid, or dishonest. Methods used in creating affective association have short-term results and please creatives; however, the effect on audiences wears out quickly and high expense dissuades some advertisers from taking the risk. Methods designed to play on fear or anxiety are compelling, but legal and ethical issues arise, and most advertisers wish to avoid instigating consumer panic. Finally, methods that transform consumption experiences, situate the brand socially, or define brand image have powerful enduring qualities, but often get lost in the clutter and can ring false to audiences.

KEY TERMS

message strategy   comparison advertisements   infomercial
unique selling proposition (USP)   testimonial

QUESTIONS

1.   Review the chapter opener about the success of Apple's "1984" commercial. What was the idea at the heart of this ad that helped make the Macintosh a success? A decade later, Apple's big idea had failed to pan out. What went wrong?

2.   Once again, reflect on the "1984" commercial. As this chapter suggested, consumers are active interpreters of ads, and one of the virtues of the "1984" ad was that it invited the audience to become involved and make an interpretation. What sorts of interpretations could a viewer of the "1984" ad make that would benefit the brand? Conversely, what sorts of interpretations might a person make, after a single exposure to this ad, that would be detrimental to Macintosh?

3.   How has Apple reinvented itself and tapped back into the soul of American culture since the near-demise of the Macintosh back in the mid-1990s?

4.   Explain the difference between brand recall and affective association as message objectives. Which of these objectives do you think would be harder to achieve, and why?

5.   Discuss the merits of unique selling proposition (USP) ads. Is it possible to have a USP that is not the "big idea" for an ad campaign?

6.   Review the do's and don'ts of comparison advertising and then think about each of the brand pairs listed here. Comment on whether you think comparison ads would be a good choice for the product category in question, and if so, which brand in the pair would be in the more appropriate position to use comparisons: Ford versus Chevy trucks; Coors Light versus Bud Light beer; Nuprin versus Tylenol pain reliever; Brut versus Obsession cologne; Wendy's versus McDonald's hamburgers.

7.   Procter & Gamble has had considerable success with the message strategy involving anxiety arousal. How does P&G's success with this strategy refute the general premise that the best way to appeal to American consumers is to appeal to their pursuit of personal freedom and individuality?

8.   What are some of the ways advertisers can use the Internet to execute message strategy objectives?

9.   Do you think product placement and short Internet films are effective in executing the message strategy of situating the brand socially? Have you ever consciously made a correlation between the products actors used during a film and your own brand preferences?

10. Think of a major purchase you have made recently. Which of the nine message strategy objectives do you think were the most effective in influencing your purchase decision? Explain.

EXPERIENTIAL EXERCISES

1.   For each of the nine message strategies identified in the chapter, find one example of an advertisement, commercial, or specific product placement that demonstrates the strategy in action. For each example, also identify what method the advertising agency employed to achieve the objective and state briefly whether you think it was an appropriate and effective message strategy.

2.   Choose a popular radio or television slogan or jingle and evaluate its effectiveness based on what you learned in the chapter. Does the slogan or jingle immediately make you think of the brand? Does the slogan or jingle evoke a positive response? If not, does this matter? Do you think you will remember this slogan or jingle years from now? Why might creatives in the industry be averse to repetition, slogans, and jingles?

3.   Advertisers are increasingly employing product placement in television, film, and online to help give brands cultural meaning and significance by situating them in desirable social settings. Watch a 60-minute television series or drama, and identify how many times you can spot a specific product placement. List the brands that you were able to identify, describe the setting in which they appeared, and provide a brief analysis of how the particular show, character, or plotline could be effective to help situate the brand socially.

4.   Humor can be effective as a method to help consumers feel good about a particular brand. But humorous ad messages can be difficult to pull off and are not always successful in building brand awareness. Identify three current ad campaigns where you think the creator has attempted to use humor to boost the brand's likeability factor, and then answer these questions: Does the joke work? Is the joke quickly and easily linked to the brand's name or identity? Could the same joke work over a long period of time?

CHAPTER 12

After reading and thinking about this chapter, you will be able to do the following:

Explain the need for a creative plan in the copywriting process.

Detail the components of print copy, along with important guidelines for writing effective print copy.

Describe various formatting alternatives for radio ads and articulate guidelines for writing effective radio copy.

4

Describe various formatting alternatives for television ads and articulate guidelines for writing effective television copy.

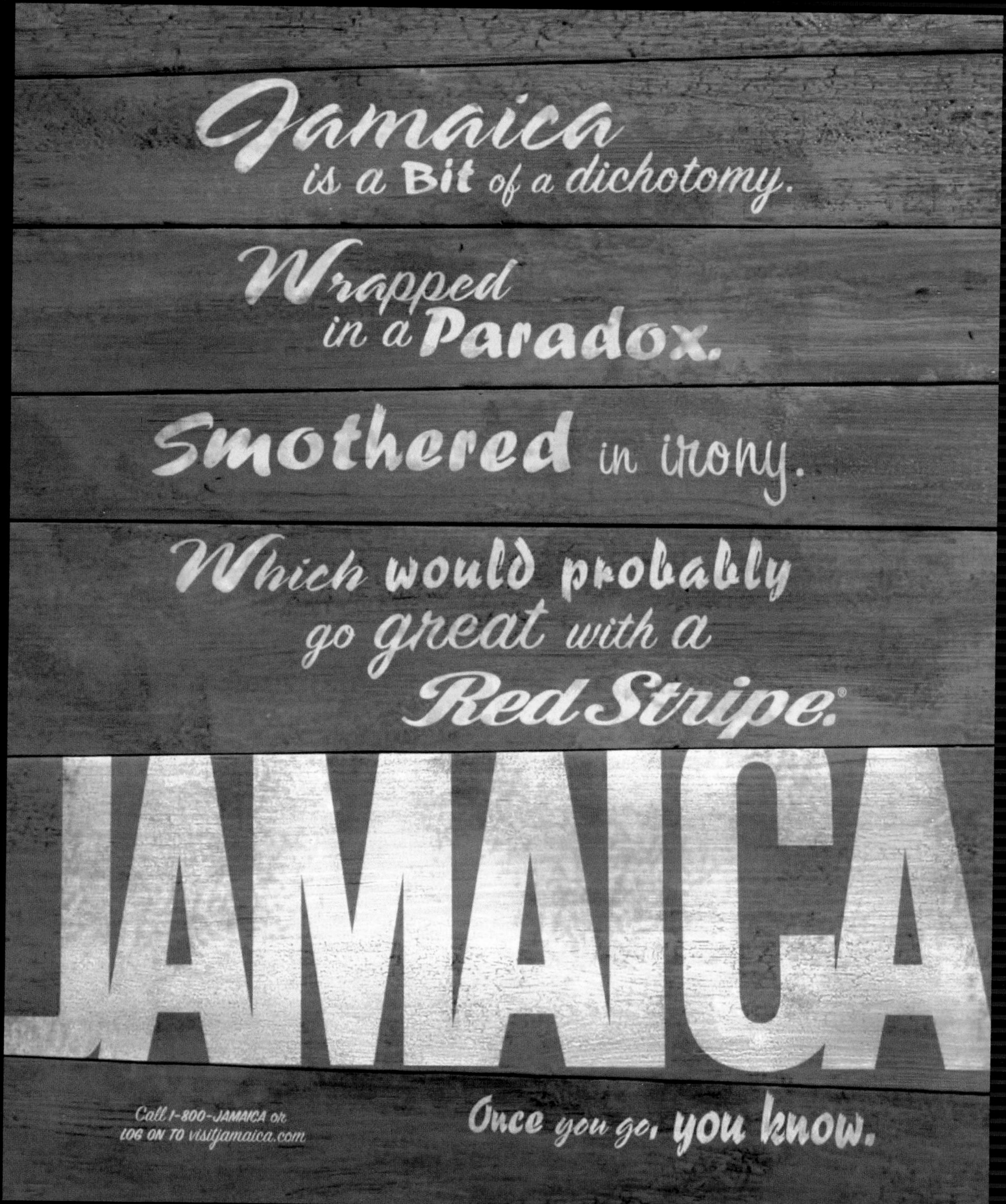
Jamaica
is a Bit of a dichotomy.
Wrapped
in a Paradox.
Smothered in irony.
Which would probably
go great with a
Red Stripe.®
JAMAICA
Call 1-800-JAMAICA or
LOG ON TO visitjamaica.com
Once you go, you know.

WARNING: The Difference Between Copywriters And Art Directors May Not Be As Great As You Think.

We live in an age when just about everything carries a warning label of some sort. Objects in rearview mirrors may be closer than they appear. Hair dryers should not be used in the shower. Using a lawn mower to trim the hedge may result in injury.

In this spirit, the authors of this book urge you to read the warning label in Exhibit 12.1. Yet, unlike the examples given earlier, the truth expressed here may not be quite so obvious, the danger not so clear. You know how some people just have to divide up the world into neat little parcels and categories. These are the same people who neatly place copywriters in one box on the organizational chart, and art directors in another. But in practice, it's not that simple. It's far too simplistic to state that copywriters are responsible for the verbal elements in an ad and art directors are responsible for the visual elements. In fact, copywriters and art directors function as partners and are referred to as the **creative team** in agencies. The creative team is responsible for coming up with the **creative concept** and for guiding its execution. The creative concept, which can be thought of as the unique creative thought behind a campaign, is then turned into individual advertisements. During this process, copywriters often suggest the idea for magnificent, arresting visuals. Likewise, art directors often come up with killer headlines.

As you can see in Exhibits 12.2 and 12.3, some ads have no headlines at all; some have no pictures. Still, in most cases, both a copywriter and an art director

GLOBALIZATION

You Know That Kissing Thing— It Works for Global Ads, Too

Years ago, some management guru said, "Keep It Simple, Stupid," giving birth to the KISS rule in American management philosophy. Well, it turns out that KISS has a place in global advertising as well.

Over the past decade, advertisers have been getting better and better at creating advertising campaigns that succeed on a global level. The International Advertising Festival at Cannes demonstrates that fact annually. More and more of the winning campaigns are global campaigns, not just domestic market campaigns. They work as well in Boston as they do in Brussels. What is also a demonstrated fact annually is that these winning campaigns are actually quite simple in terms of message theme and visual structure. Certainly, particular product categories lend themselves more readily to a global stage than do others. Lifestyle products such as soft drinks, jeans, sneakers, and candy translate well across cultures. Nike, Pepsi, and Levi's speak to the world and each has been the subject of memorable, award-winning campaigns. But what makes these brands so well suited to a global audience—even beyond the natural fit of lifestyle product categories?

The campaigns that work best on a global scale are those where the brand and its imagery are inextricably one and the same. In addition, advertising that succeeds in the global arena draws on four constants: Simplicity, Clarity, Humor, and Clever demonstration. SCHC doesn't exactly spell KISS, but the reason that global ads that highlight these qualities can bridge the complexities and distinctiveness of one culture to another is simple. Granted, what is funny to a Brit may be lost on a Brazilian, but the key is to find not the culturally bound humor in a demonstration, but the culturally shared humor. When it comes to copy, simplicity and clarity rule. Aside from their inherent value, their ability to communicate across cultures is, well, clear. In short, actually trying to bridge cultures may be just the thing that complicates the situation. Reducing a brand and its message to the simplest and most common human values has a great chance of succeeding.

Source: Jay Schulberg, "Successful Global Ads Need Simplicity, Clarity," **Advertising Age**, June 30, 1997, 17.

are equally involved in creating an ad. This doesn't mean that copywriting and art directing are one and the same. This chapter and the next will show that the talent and knowledge needed to excel in one area differ in many ways from those needed to excel in the other. Still, one must recognize that not all copywriting is done by copywriters and not all art directing is done by art directors.

Understanding copywriting is as much about the people who write copy as it is about the product studies, audience research, and other information that copywriters draw upon to create effective copy. Copywriting is, in fact, mostly about the fairly magical relationship between creator and creation, between writer and text, writer and brand. It is more about art than science. Copywriting is writing, and writing is a form of crafted magic. Magic cannot be taught. If (and it's a big if) you have a gift to begin with, then you can learn technique. But technique alone is not enough. Gifts are gifts—they come from somewhere else. Writing long paragraphs won't make you William Faulkner any more than writing self-effacing copy will make you Bill Bernbach. Likewise, trying to treat a discussion of copywriting like a step-by-step discussion of how to change the oil in your car is sadly silly and thoroughly useless. Still, there are things—some of them principles, some of them hints and tips—that can be learned from the creators of some of the greatest advertising of all time. Furthermore, even if you don't plan to be a copywriter, knowing something about the craft is essential to any working understanding of advertising. Knowing something about the craft is also essential to selling good ideas in global markets, as shown in the Globalization box.

Let's begin with some fairly general thoughts on copywriting from some of the most influential people in the history of advertising:

If you think you have a better mousetrap, or shirt, or whatever, you've got to tell people, and I don't think that has to be done with trickery, or insults, or by talking down to people. . . . The smartest advertising is the advertising that communicates the best and respects consumers' intelligence. It's advertising that lets them bring something to the communication process, as opposed to some of the more validly criticized work in our profession which tries to grind the benefits of a soap or a cake mix into a poor housewife's head by repeating it 37 times in 30 seconds.

—Lee Clow, creator of the Apple Macintosh "1984" advertisement[1]

---

1.   Jennifer Pendleton, "Bringing New Clow-T to Ads, Chiat's Unlikely Creative," *Advertising Age*, February 7, 1985, 1.

As I have observed it, great advertising writing either in print or television is disarmingly simple. It has the common touch without being or sounding patronizing. If you are writing about baloney, don't try to make it sound like Cornish hen, because that is the worst kind of baloney. Just make it darned good baloney.

—Leo Burnett, founder of the Leo Burnett agency, Chicago[2]

Why should anyone look at your ad? The reader doesn't buy his magazine or tune his radio and TV to see and hear what you have to say. . . . What is the use of saying all the right things in the world if nobody is going to read them? And, believe me, nobody is going to read them if they are not said with freshness, originality and imagination.

—William Bernbach, cofounder of one of the most influential agencies during the 1960s, Doyle Dane Bernbach[3]

Never write an advertisement which you wouldn't want your family to read. Good products can be sold by honest advertising. If you don't think the product is good, you have no business to be advertising it. If you tell lies, or weasel, you do your client a disservice, you increase your load of guilt, and you fan the flames of public resentment against the whole business of advertising.

—David Ogilvy's ninth of eleven commandments of advertising[4]

Finally, the following observation on the power of a good advertisement, brilliant in its simplicity, is offered by one of the modern-day geniuses of advertising:

Imagination is one of the last remaining legal means to gain an unfair advantage over your competition.

—Tom McElligott, cofounder of a highly creative and successful Minneapolis advertising agency[5]

Good copywriters must always bring spirit and imagination to advertising. Lee Clow, Leo Burnett, William Bernbach, and David Ogilvy have created some of the most memorable advertising in history: the "We're Number 2, We Try Harder" Avis campaign (William Bernbach); the Hathaway Shirt Man ads (David Ogilvy); the Jolly Green Giant ads (Leo Burnett); and the "1984" Apple Macintosh ad (Lee Clow). See Exhibits 12.4 and 12.5 for samples of their work. When these advertising legends speak of creating good ads that respect the consumer's intelligence and rely on imagination, they assume good copywriting.

1 Copywriting and the Creative Plan.

Writing well, rule #1: Write well.

—Luke Sullivan, copywriter and author

Copywriting is the process of expressing the value and benefits a brand has to offer, via written or verbal descriptions. Copywriting requires far more than the ability to string product descriptions together in coherent sentences. One apt description of copywriting is that it is a never-ending search for ideas combined with a never-ending search for new and different ways to express those ideas.

---

2.   Leo Burnett, "Keep Listening to That Wee, Small Voice," in *Communications of an Advertising Man* (Chicago: Leo Burnett, 1961), 160.
3.   Cited in Martin Mayer, *Madison Avenue, U.S.A.* (New York: Pocket Books, 1954), 66.
4.   David Ogilvy, *Confessions of an Advertising Man* (New York: Atheneum, 1964), 102.
5.   Tom McElligott is credited with making this statement in several public speeches during the 1980s.

When you're only No.2, you try harder. Or else.

Avis can't afford to relax.

Little fish have to keep moving all of the time. The big ones never stop picking on them.

Avis knows all about the problems of little fish.

We're only No.2 in rent a cars. We'd be swallowed up if we didn't try harder.

There's no rest for us.

We're always emptying ashtrays. Making sure gas tanks are full before we rent our cars. Seeing that the batteries are full of life. Checking our windshield wipers.

And the cars we rent out can't be anything less than spanking new Plymouths.

And since we're not the big fish, you won't feel like a sardine when you come to our counter.

We're not jammed with customers.

© AVIS RENT A CAR SYSTEM, INC.

EXHIBIT 12.4

One of the great names in advertising is William Bernbach, and the memorable and highly effective "We Try Harder" campaign for Avis Rent a Car was produced by his agency, Doyle Dane Bernbach.

Hathaway and the Duke's stud groom

EXHIBIT 12.5

David Ogilvy, to many a guru in advertising, created the Hathaway Shirt Man (complete with an eye patch) as a way to attract attention and create an image for the Hathaway brand.

Imagine you're a copywriter on the MasterCard account. You've sat through meeting after meeting in which your client, account executives, and researchers have presented a myriad of benefits one gets from using a MasterCard for online purchases. You've talked to customers about their experiences. You've even gone online to try the card out for yourself. All along, your boss has been reminding you that the work you come up with must be as inspiring as the work that focuses on building interest for the brand (see Exhibit 12.6 on the next page). Now your job is simple. Take all the charts, numbers, and strategies and turn them into a simple, emotionally involving, intellectually challenging campaign such as the one in Exhibits 12.7 and 12.8 on the next page.

Effective copywriters are well-informed, astute advertising decision makers with creative talent. Copywriters are able to comprehend and then incorporate the complexities of marketing strategies, consumer behavior, and advertising strategies into a brief yet powerful communication. They must do so in such a way that the copy does not interfere with but rather enhances the visual aspects of the message.

An astute advertiser will go to great lengths to provide copywriters with as much information as possible about the objectives for a particular advertising effort. The responsibility for keeping copywriters informed lies with the client's marketing managers in conjunction with account executives and creative directors in the ad agency. They must communicate the foundations and intricacies of the firm's marketing strategies to the copywriters. Without this information, copywriters are left without guidance and direction, and they must rely on intuition about what sorts of

Your boss has been reminding you that the work you come up with must be as good as the work that focuses on building interest for the brand. http://www.mastercard.com

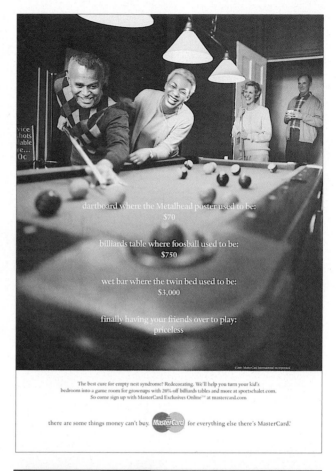

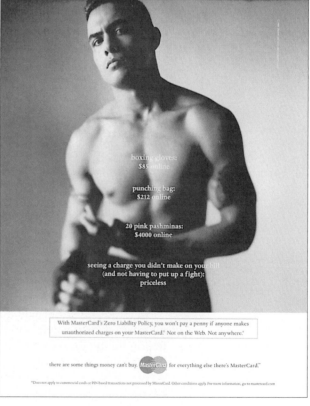

Take all the charts, numbers, and strategies and turn them into a simple, emotionally involving, intellectually challenging campaign.

Expected product feature, unexpected creative delivery.

information are relevant and meaningful to a target audience. Sometimes that works; most of the time, it does not.

A **creative plan** is a guideline used during the copywriting process to specify the message elements that must be coordinated during the preparation of copy. These elements include main product claims, creative devices, media that will be used, and special creative needs a product or service might have. One of the main challenges faced by a copywriter is to make creative sense out of the maze of information that comes from the message development process. Part of the challenge is creating excitement around what can otherwise be dull product features. For example, just about any lint roller can be expected to remove pet hair. But the creative team responsible for the ad in Exhibit 12.9 made the claim in an unexpected way. In the ad in Exhibit 12.10, the expected feature of insect-killing ability in an insecticide was presented in an unexpected fashion.

Another aspect of the challenge is bringing together various creative tools (such as illustration, color, sound, and action) and the copy. Copy must also be coordinated with the media that will be used. All of these factors are coordinated through the use of a creative plan. Some of the elements considered in devising a creative plan are the following:

- The single most important thought you want a member of the target market to take away from the advertisement
- The product features to be emphasized
- The benefits a user receives from these features
- The media chosen for transmitting the information and the length of time the advertisement will run
- The suggested mood or tone for the ad
- The ways in which mood and atmosphere will be achieved in the ad
- The production budget for the ad[6]

These considerations can be modified or disregarded entirely during the process of creating an ad. For example, sometimes a brilliant creative execution demands that television, rather than print, be the media vehicle of choice. Occasionally, a particular creative thought may suggest a completely different mood or tone than the one listed in the creative plan. A creative plan is best thought of as a starting point, not an endpoint, for the creative team. Like anything else in advertising, the plan should evolve and grow as new insights are gained. Once the creative plan is devised, the creative team can get on with the task of creating the actual advertisement.

6.   The last two points in this list were adapted from A. Jerome Jewler, *Creative Strategy in Advertising,* 3rd ed. (Belmont, CA: Wadsworth, 1989), 196.

② Copywriting for Print Advertising.

In preparing copy for a print ad, the first step in the copy development process is deciding how to use (or not use) the three separate components of print copy: the headline, the subhead, and the body copy. Be aware that the full range of components applies most directly to print ads that appear in magazines, newspapers, or direct mail pieces. These guidelines also apply to other "print" media such as billboards, transit advertising, and specialty advertising, but all media are in effect different animals. More detail on these "support" media is presented in Chapter 17.

The Headline.

The **headline** in an advertisement is the leading sentence or sentences, usually at the top or bottom of the ad, that attracts attention, communicates a key selling point, or achieves brand identification. Many headlines fail to attract attention, and the ad itself then becomes another bit of clutter in consumers' lives. Lifeless headlines do not compel the reader to examine other parts of the ad. Simply stated, a headline can either motivate a reader to move on to the rest of an ad or lose the reader for good.

Purposes of a Headline.

In preparing a headline, a copywriter begins by considering the variety of purposes a headline can have in terms of gaining attention or actually convincing the consumer. In general, a headline can be written to pursue the following purposes:

- **Give news about the brand.** A headline can proclaim a newsworthy event focused on the brand. "Champion Wins Mt. Everest Run" and "25 of 40 Major Titles Won with Titleist" are examples of headlines that communicate newsworthy events about Champion spark plugs and Titleist golf balls. The Mount Sinai hospital ad in Exhibit 12.11 uses this approach in a gripping, emotional manner.

- **Emphasize a brand claim.** A primary and perhaps differentiating feature of the brand is a likely candidate for the headline theme. "30% More Mileage on Firestone Tires" highlights durability. Exhibit 12.12 reminds people of how durable a Hummer is.

- **Give advice to the reader.** A headline can give the reader a recommendation that (usually) is supported by results provided in the body copy. "Increase Your Reading Skills" and "Save up to 90% on Commissions" both implore the reader to take the advice of the ad. The headline in Exhibit 12.13 advises readers to make sure that bad radio stations don't ever ruin a road trip.

- **Select prospects.** Headlines can attract the attention of the intended audience. "Good News for Arthritis Sufferers" and "Attention June Graduates" are examples of headlines designed to achieve prospect selection. The headline in Exhibit 12.14 suggests in no uncertain terms who its audience is.

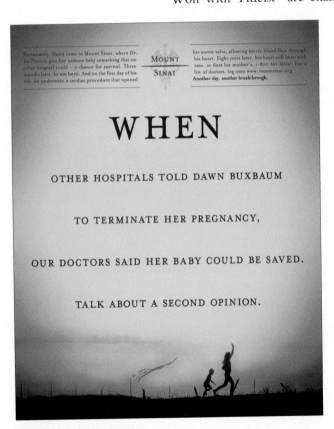

EXHIBIT 12.11

This ad gives important news about the brand.

EXHIBIT 12.12

This headline emphasizes a straight-ahead brand feature. http://www.hummer.com

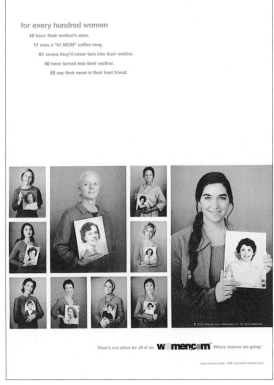

EXHIBIT 12.13

This headline offers advice. http://www.roxio.com

EXHIBIT 12.14

The headline in this ad calls out the intended audience.

- **Stimulate the reader's curiosity.** Posing a riddle with a headline can serve to attract attention and stimulate readership. Curiosity can be stimulated with a clever play on words or a contradiction. Take, for example, the headline "With MCI, Gerber's Baby Talk Never Sounded Better." The body copy goes on to explain that Gerber Products (a maker of baby products) uses the high technology of MCI for its communication needs. Does the headline in the ad shown in Exhibit 12.15 get your attention? It was written for that purpose.

- **Set a tone or establish an emotion.** Language can be used to establish a mood that the advertiser wants associated with its product. Teva sports sandals has an ad with the headline "When you die, they put you in a nice suit and shiny shoes. As if death didn't suck enough already." Even though there is no direct reference to the product being advertised, the reader has learned quite a bit about the company doing the advertising and the types of people expected to buy the product. The headline in the ad shown in Exhibit 12.16 is far more about establishing the mood or tone of a Jamaican visit than it is about talking about its beaches and attractions.

- **Identify the brand.** This is the most straightforward of all headline purposes. The brand name or label is used as the headline, either alone or in conjunction with a word or two. The goal is to simply identify the brand and reinforce brand-name recognition. Advertising for Brut men's fragrance products often uses merely the brand name as the headline.

Guidelines for Writing Headlines. Once a copywriter has firmly established the purpose a headline will serve in an advertisement, several guidelines can be followed in preparing the headline. The following are basic guidelines for writing a good headline for print advertisements:

- Make the headline a major persuasive component of the ad. Five times as many people read the headline as the body copy of an ad. If this is your only opportunity to communicate, what should you say? The headline "New Power. New

EXHIBIT 12.15

A headline that creates curiosity motivates readers to continue reading, perhaps after a slight disconcerting pause.

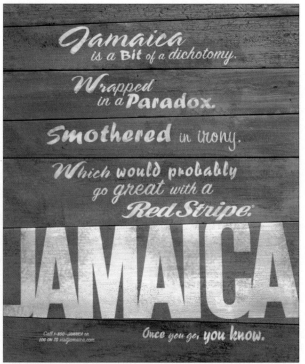

EXHIBIT 12.16

Even though there are no explicit product features being advertised, the reader has learned quite a bit about the island, its natives, and its tourists.

Comfort. New Technology. New Yorker" in a Chrysler ad communicates major improvements in the product quickly and clearly.

- Appeal to the reader's self-interest with a basic promise of benefits coming from the brand. For example, "The Temperature Never Drops Below Zerex" promises engine protection in freezing weather from Zerex antifreeze.

- Inject the maximum information in the headline without making it cumbersome or wordy.
- Limit headlines to about five to eight words.[7] Research indicates that recall drops off significantly for sentences longer than eight words.
- Include the brand name in the headline.
- Entice the reader to read the body copy.
- Entice the reader to examine the visual in the ad. An intriguing headline can lead the reader to carefully examine the visual components of the ad.
- Never change typefaces within a headline. Changing the form and style of the print can increase the complexity of visual impression and negatively affect the readership.
- Never use a headline whose persuasive impact depends on reading the body copy.
- Use simple, common, familiar words. Recognition and comprehension are aided by words that are easy to understand and recognize.

This set of guidelines is meant only as a starting point. A headline may violate one or even all of these basic premises and still be effective. And it is unrealistic to try to fulfill the requirements of each guideline in every headline. This list simply offers general safeguards to be considered. Test the list for yourself using the ads in Exhibits 12.17 through 12.19. Which, if any, of these 10 guidelines do

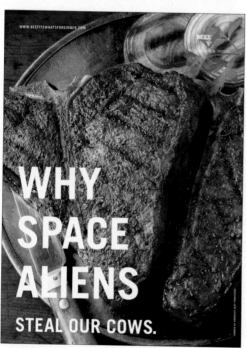

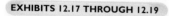

EXHIBITS 12.17 THROUGH 12.19

There are 10 general guidelines for writing headlines. How do you rate the headlines in these ads relative to the guidelines?

7.   Based in part on Jewler, *Creative Strategy in Advertising,* 232–233; Albert C. Book, Norman D. Cary, and Stanley I. Tannenbaum, *The Radio and Television Commercial* (Lincolnwood, IL.: NTC Business Books, 1984), 22–26.

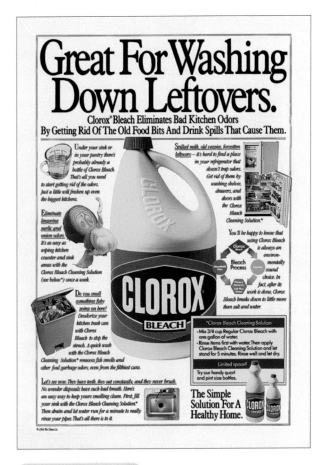

EXHIBIT 12.20

Subheads include important brand information not included in the headline. Where is the subhead in this Clorox ad? What does the subhead accomplish that the headline does not? http://www.clorox.com

these ads comply with? And which ones do they torch? Which of these guidelines would you say are most important for creating effective headlines?

A truly great piece of advice:

Certain headlines are currently checked out. You may use them when they are returned. Lines like "Contrary to popular belief . . ." or "Something is wrong when . . ." These are dead. Elvis is dead. John Lennon is dead. Deal with it. Remember, anything that you even think you've seen, forget about it. The stuff you've never seen? You'll know when you see it, too. It raises the hair on the back of your neck.

—Luke Sullivan[8]

Originality is good.

The Subhead. A **subhead** consists of a few words or a short sentence and usually appears above or below the headline. It includes important brand information not included in the headline. The subhead in the ad for Clorox in Exhibit 12.20 is an excellent example of how a subhead is used to convey important brand information not communicated in the headline. A subhead serves basically the same purpose as a headline—to communicate key selling points or brand information quickly. A subhead is normally in print smaller than the headline, but larger than the body copy. In many cases, the subhead is more lengthy than the headline and can be used to communicate more complex selling points. The subhead should reinforce the headline and, again, entice the reader to proceed to the body copy.

Subheads can serve another important purpose: stimulating a more complete reading of the entire ad. If the headline attracts attention, the subhead can stimulate movement through the physical space of the ad, including the visual. A good rule of thumb is the longer the body copy, the more appropriate the use of subheads. Most creative directors try to keep the use of subheads to the barest minimum, however. They feel that if an ad's visual and headline can't communicate the benefit of a product quickly and clearly, the ad isn't very good.

The Body Copy. More good advice:

I don't think people read body copy. I think we've entered a frenzied era of coffee-guzzling, fax-sending channel surfers who honk the microsecond the light turns green and have the attention span of a flashcube. If the first five words of body copy aren't "May we send you $700.00?," word 6 isn't read. Just my opinion, mind you.

—Luke Sullivan[9]

It's our opinion too.

8.   Luke Sullivan, *Hey Whipple, Squeeze This: A Guide to Creating Great Ads* (New York: Wiley, 1998), 78.
9.   Ibid, 85.

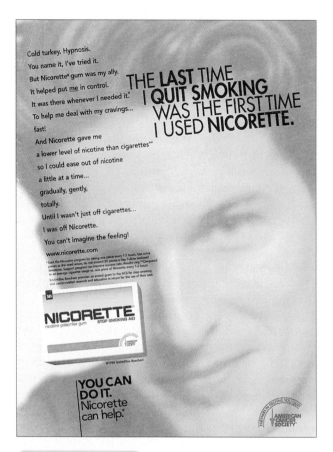

EXHIBIT 12.21

In this testimonial ad from Nicorette, a spokesperson tells his story directly to the reader. Is this same copy technique used at the Nicorette site (http://www.nicorette.com)? What does Nicorette offer to its customers at the Committed Quitters resource site (http://www.committedquitters.com), and is the copy at this site more geared toward eliciting a direct response from consumers?

Body copy is the textual component of an advertisement and tells a more complete story of a brand. Effective body copy is written in a fashion that takes advantage of and reinforces the headline and subhead, is compatible with and gains strength from the visual, and is interesting to the reader. Whether body copy is interesting is a function of how accurately the copywriter and other decision makers have assessed various components of message development, and how good the copywriter is. The most elaborate body copy will probably be ineffective if it is "off strategy." It will not matter if it's very clever, but has little to do in advancing the strategy.

There are several standard techniques for preparing body copy. The **straight-line copy** approach explains in straightforward terms why a reader will benefit from use of a brand. This technique is used many times in conjunction with a benefits message strategy. Body copy that uses **dialogue** delivers the selling points of a message to the audience through a character or characters in the ad. Dialogue can also depict two people in the ad having a conversation, a technique often used in slice-of-life messages. A **testimonial** uses dialogue as if the spokesperson is having a one-sided conversation with the reader through the body copy. The Nicorette ad shown in Exhibit 12.21 is an example of the testimonial technique.

Narrative as a method for preparing body copy simply displays a series of statements about a brand. A person may or may not be portrayed as delivering the copy. It is difficult to make this technique lively for the reader, so the threat of writing a dull ad using this technique is ever present. **Direct response copy** is, in many ways, the least complex of copy techniques. In writing direct response copy, the copywriter is trying to highlight the urgency of acting immediately. Hence, the range of possibilities for direct response copy is more limited. In addition, many direct response advertisements rely on sales promotion devices, such as coupons, contests, and rebates, as a means of stimulating action. Giving deadlines to the reader is also a common approach in direct response advertising.

These techniques for copywriting establish a general set of styles that can be used as the format for body copy. Again, be aware that any message objective can be employed within any particular copy technique. There are a vast number of compatible combinations.

Guidelines for Writing Body Copy.
Regardless of the specific technique used to develop body copy, the probability of writing effective body copy can be increased if certain guidelines are followed. However, guidelines are meant to be just that—guidelines. Copywriters have created excellent ads that violate one or more of these recommendations. Generally, however, body copy for print ads has a better chance of being effective if these guidelines are followed:

- *Use the present tense whenever possible.* Casting brand claims in the past or future reduces their credibility and timeliness. Speaking to the target audience about things that have happened or will happen sounds like hollow promises.
- *Use singular nouns and verbs.* An ad is normally read by only one person at a time, and that person is evaluating only one brand. Using plural nouns and verbs simply reduces the focus on the item or brand attribute being touted and makes the ad less personal.
- *Use active verbs.* The passive form of a verb does little to stimulate excitement or interest. The use of the active verb in Pontiac's "We Build Excitement" slogan suggests that something is happening, and it's happening *now.*
- *Use familiar words and phrases.* Relying on familiar words and phrases to communicate in an interesting and unique way poses a formidable challenge for a copywriter. Familiar words can seem common and ordinary. The challenge is to creatively stylize what is familiar and comfortable to the reader so that interest and excitement result.
- *Vary the length of sentences and paragraphs.* Using sentences and paragraphs of varying lengths not only serves to increase interest but also has a visual impact that can make an ad more inviting and readable.
- *Involve the reader.* Talking at the receiver or creating a condescending mood with copy results in a short-circuited communication. Copy that impresses the reader as having been written specifically for him or her reduces the chances of the ad being perceived as a generalized, mass communication.
- *Provide support for the unbelievable.* A brand may have features or functions that the reader finds hard to believe. Where such claims are critical to the brand's positioning in the market and value to the consumer, it is necessary to document (through test results or testimonials) that the brand actually lives up to the claims made. Without proper support of claims, the brand will lose its credibility and therefore its relevance to the consumer.
- *Avoid clichés and superlatives.* Clichés are rarely effective or attention-getting. The average consumer assumes that a brand touted through the use of clichés is old-fashioned and stale. Even though the foundation for puffery as a message method is the use of superlatives (*best, superior, unbeatable*), it is wise to avoid their use. These terms are worn out and can signal to the consumer that the brand has little new or different to offer.[10]

Copywriting for Cyberspace.

While some take the position that writing is writing, we see enough evidence that the rapidly evolving medium of cyberspace has its own style, its own feel, and its own writing. Part of this is due to its history. Cybercopy evolved from a very techno-speak community, with a twentysomething, Gen-X-meets-techno-nerd kind of voice. Cybercopy's style has been influenced by this history. The medium itself, its structure and its active nature, suggests a type of writing closer to print than to television copy, but not really traditional print copy either. This is a medium where *audience* has a significantly different meaning than it does in traditional one-way (noninteractive) media. Audience members often come to cyberads, that is they seek out the ads or other online IBP material, rather than the other way around. In other cases, cyberads pop up as one moves from Web page to Web page. The medium itself (online computer) is a fundamentally more

---

10.   The last three points in this list were adapted from Kenneth Roman and Jan Maas, *The New How to Advertise* (New York: St. Martin's Press, 1992), 18–19.

user-directed medium than print, television, or radio. This means that consumers approach (and read) cyberads somewhat differently than other ads. Most have more incentive to read cybercopy than traditional print advertising. Further, much cybercopy is direct response, thus dictating copy style. At this point we believe that the basic principles of good print advertising discussed earlier in the chapter generally apply, but the copy should assume a more active and engaged audience. Still, remember that odds are that they are not there for your ads, and they have a mouse in their hands. Consider the cyberads in Exhibits 12.22 through 12.25. What do these different forms suggest to you about cyberwriting?

EXHIBITS 12.22 THROUGH 12.25

Cybercopy represents a new type of ad writing—closer to print than to television copy, but not really traditional print copy either. What do these four cyberads suggest to you about cyberwriting?

Copywriting for Broadcast Advertising. Relative to the print media, radio

and television present totally different challenges for a copywriter. It is obvious that the audio and audiovisual capabilities of radio and television provide different opportunities for a copywriter. The use of sound effects and voices on radio and the ability to combine copy with color and motion on television provide vast and exciting creative possibilities.

Compared to print media, however, broadcast media have inherent limitations for a copywriter. In print media, a copywriter can write longer and more involved copy to better communicate complex brand features. For consumer shopping goods such as automobiles or home satellite systems, a brand's basis for competitive differentiation and positioning may lie with complex, unique functional features. In this case, print media provide a copywriter the time and space to communicate these details, complete with illustrations. In addition, the printed page allows a reader to dwell on the copy and process the information at a personalized, comfortable rate.

These advantages do not exist in the broadcast media. Radio and television offer a fleeting exposure. In addition, introducing sound effects and visual stimuli can distract the listener or viewer from the copy of the advertisement. Despite the additional creative opportunities that radio and television offer, the essential challenge of copywriting remains.

③ Writing Copy for Radio.

Your spot just interrupted your listener's music. It's like interrupting people having sex. If you're going to lean in the bedroom door to say something, make it good: "Hey your car's on fire."

—Luke Sullivan[11]

Some writers consider radio the ultimate forum for copywriting creativity. Because the radio is restricted to an audio-only presentation, a copywriter is free from some of the harsher realities of visual presentations. Yet it has been said that radio *is* visual. The copywriter must (it is almost inevitable) create images in the minds of listeners. The creative potential of radio rests in its ability to stimulate a theater of the mind, which allows a copywriter to create images and moods for an audience that transcend those created in any other medium.

Despite these creative opportunities, the drawbacks of this medium should never be underestimated. Few radio listeners ever actively listen to radio programming (talk radio is an obvious exception), much less the commercial interruptions. Radio may be viewed by some as the theater of the mind, but others have labeled it audio wallpaper—wallpaper in the sense that radio is used as filler or unobtrusive accompaniment to reading, driving, household chores, or homework. If it were absent, the average person would miss it, but the average person would be hard-pressed to recall the radio ads aired during dinner last evening.

The most reasonable view of copywriting for radio is to temper both the enthusiasm of the theater-of-the-mind perspective and the pessimism of the audio-wallpaper view. (Of course, "reasonable" creative solutions often are destined to be mind-numbingly dull.) A radio copywriter should recognize the unique character of radio and exploit the opportunities it offers. First, radio adds the dimension of sound to the copywriting task, and sound (other than voices) can become a primary tool in creating copy. Second, radio can conjure images in the mind of the receiver that extend beyond the starkness of the brand "information" actually being provided. Radio copywriting should, therefore, strive to stimulate each receiver's imagination.

Writing copy for radio should begin the same way that writing copy for print begins. The copywriter must review components of the creative plan so as to take advantage of and follow through on the marketing and advertising strategies speci-

11.   Sullivan, *Hey Whipple, Squeeze This: A Guide to Creating Great Ads,* 131.

fied and integral to the brand's market potential. Beyond that fundamental task, there are particular formats for radio ads and guidelines for copy preparation the writer can rely on for direction.

Radio Advertising Formats. There are four basic formats for radio advertisements, and these formats provide the structure within which copy is prepared: the music format, the dialogue format, the announcement format, and the celebrity announcer format. Each of these formats is discussed here.

Music. Since radio provides audio opportunities, music is often used in radio ads. One use of music is to write a song or jingle in an attempt to communicate in an attention-getting and memorable fashion. Songs and jingles are generally written specifically to accommodate unique brand copy. On occasion, an existing tune can be used, and the copy is fit to its meter and rhythm. This is done when the music is being used to capture the attention of a particular target segment. Tunes popular with certain target segments can be licensed for use by advertisers. Advertisements using popular tunes by Garbage and Barry Manilow would presumably attract two very different audiences. Singing and music can do much to attract the listener's attention and enhance recall. Singing can also create a mood and image with which the product is associated. Modern scores can create a contemporary mood, while sultry music and lyrics create a totally different mood.

But what of jingles? While some love them—and let's face it, they have survived for over a hundred years in advertising—there are some hazards in the use of singing or jingles. Few copywriters are trained lyricists or composers. The threat is ever present that a musical score or a jingle will strike receivers as amateurish and silly. To avoid this, expert songwriters are often used. Further, ensuring that the copy information dominates the musical accompaniment takes great skill. The musical impact can easily overwhelm the persuasion and selling purposes of an ad. Still, just try to get a really good jingle out of your head. You may go to your grave with it on your mind.

Another use of music in radio commercials is to open the ad with a musical score and/or have music playing in the background while the copy is being read. The role of music here is generally to attract attention. This application of music, as well as music used in a song or jingle, is subject to an ongoing debate. If a radio ad is scheduled for airing on music-format stations, should the music in the ad be the same type of music the station is noted for playing, or should it be different? One argument says that if the station format is rock, for example, then the ad should use rock music to appeal to the listener's taste. The opposite argument states that using the same type of music simply buries the ad in the regular programming and reduces its impact. There is no good evidence to suggest that music similar to or different from station programming is superior.

Dialogue. The dialogue technique, described in the section on print copywriting, is commonly used in radio. There are difficulties in making narrative copy work in the short periods of time afforded by the radio medium (typically 15 to 60 seconds). The threat is that dialogue will result in a dull drone of two or more people having a conversation. (You hear enough of that, right?) To reduce the threat of boredom, many dialogues are written with humor, like the one in Exhibit 12.26. Of course, some believe that humor is overused in radio.

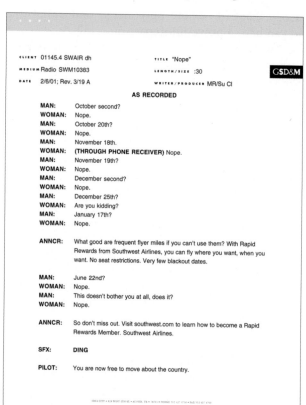

EXHIBIT 12.26

To reduce the threat of boredom, many dialogues are written with humor.

Announcement. Radio copy delivered by an announcer is similar to narrative copy in print advertising. The announcer reads important product information as it has been prepared by the copywriter. Announcement is the prevalent technique for live radio spots delivered by disc jockeys or news commentators. The live setting leaves little opportunity for much else. If the ad is prerecorded, sound effects or music may be added to enhance the transmission.

Celebrity Announcer. Having a famous person deliver the copy is alleged to increase the attention paid to a radio ad. Most radio ads that use celebrities do not fall into the testimonial category. The celebrity is not expressing his or her satisfaction with the product, but merely acting as an announcer. Some celebrities (such as James Earl Jones) have distinctive voice qualities or are expert at the emphatic delivery of copy. It is argued that these qualities, as well as listener recognition of the celebrity, increase attention to the ad.

Guidelines for Writing Radio Copy. The unique opportunities and challenges of the radio medium warrant a set of guidelines for the copywriter to increase the probability of effective communication. The following are a few suggestions for writing effective radio copy:

- *Use common, familiar language.* The use of words and language easily understood and recognized by the receiver is even more important in radio than in print copy preparation.
- *Use short words and sentences.* The probability of communicating verbally increases if short, easily processed words and sentences are used. Long, involved, elaborate verbal descriptions make it difficult for the listener to follow the copy.
- *Stimulate the imagination.* Copy that can conjure up concrete and stimulating images in the receiver's mind can have a powerful impact on recall.
- *Repeat the name of the product.* Since the impression made by a radio ad is fleeting, it may be necessary to repeat the brand name several times before it will register. The same is true for location if the ad is being used to promote a retail organization.
- *Stress the main selling point or points.* The premise of the advertising should revolve around the information that needs to be presented. If selling points are mentioned only in passing, there is little reason to believe they'll be remembered.
- *Use sound and music with care.* By all means, a copywriter should take advantage of all the audio capabilities afforded by the radio medium, including the use of sound effects and music. While these devices can contribute greatly to attracting and holding the listener's attention, care must be taken to ensure that the devices do not overwhelm the copy and therefore the persuasive impact of the commercial.
- *Tailor the copy to the time, place, and specific audience.* Take advantage of any unique aspect of the advertising context. If the ad is specified for a particular geographic region, use colloquialisms unique to that region as a way to tailor the message. The same is true with time-of-day factors or unique aspects of the audience.[12]

The Radio Production Process. Radio commercial production highlights the role of the copywriter. There is no art director involved in the process. Further, the

12.   Book, Cary, and Tannenbaum, *The Radio and Television Commercial.*

writer is relatively free to plan nearly any radio production he or she chooses because of the significantly reduced costs of radio execution compared to television. In radio, there are far fewer expert participants than in television. This more streamlined form of production does not mean, however, that the process is more casual. Successful fulfillment of the objectives of an advertisement still requires the careful planning and execution of the production process.

Once the copy strategy and methods for the commercial are approved, the process begins with soliciting bids from production houses. The producer reviews bids and submits the best bid for advertiser approval. When the best bid (not always the lowest-priced bid) is identified, the agency submits an estimate to the advertiser for approval. The bid estimate includes both the production house bid and the agency's estimates of its own costs associated with production. When the agency and the advertiser agree, then the producer can award the job to a production house.

After awarding the job to a production house, the next step is to cast the ad. A radio ad may have only an announcer, in which case the casting job is relatively simple. If the dialogue technique is used, two or more actors and actresses may be needed. Additionally, musical scores often accompany radio ads, and either the music has to be recorded, which includes a search for musicians and possibly singers, or prerecorded music has to be obtained for use by permission. Securing permission for existing music, especially if it is currently popular, can be costly. Much music is in the public domain—that is, it is no longer rigidly protected by copyright laws and is available for far less cost. Closely following the casting is the planning of special elements for the ad, which can include sound effects or special effects, such as time compression or stretching, to create distinct sounds.

Final preparation and production entails scheduling a sound studio and arranging for the actors and actresses to record their pieces in the ad. If an announcer is used in addition to acting talent, the announcer may or may not record with the full cast; her or his lines can be incorporated into the tape at some later time. Music is generally recorded separately and simply added to the commercial during the sound-mixing stage.

Radio and television production have some similarities. As in television production, the copywriter will have drawn on the copy platform plans approved in the message development stage to write copy for the radio spot. Additionally, the script used in the production of a radio advertisement serves the same purpose that the storyboard does in television production. Exhibit 12.27 on the next page shows a typical radio script.

Note that the copywriter must indicate the use of sound effects (SFX) on a separate line to specify the timing of these devices. Further, each player in the advertisement is listed by role, including the announcer if one is used.

One important element of writing radio copy not yet discussed is the number of words of copy to use given the length of the radio ad. As a general rule, word count relative to airtime is as follows:

10 seconds	20 to 25 words
20 seconds	40 to 45 words
30 seconds	60 to 65 words
60 seconds	120 to 125 words
90 seconds	85 to 190 words[13]

13. Sandra E. Moriarty, *Creative Advertising: Theory and Practice*, 2nd ed. (Englewood Cliffs, N J: Prentice Hall, 1991), 293.

MERIT AWARD: Consumer Radio: Single
WRITER: Adam Chasnow
AGENCY PRODUCER: Andy Lerner
CLIENT: Hollywood Video
AGENCY: Cliff Freeman & Partners/New York
ID 00 0542A

ANNOUNCER:	Hollywood Video presents "Sixty Second Theater," where we try, unsuccessfully, to pack all the action and suspense of a two-hour Hollywood production into 60 seconds. Today's presentation, "The Matrix."
SFX:	TECHNO/ACTION MUSIC; KNOCK KNOCK.
TRINITY:	(CARRIE-ANN MOSS SOUNDALIKE; FROM BEHIND DOOR) Hello, Neo?
NEO:	(KEANU REEVES SOUNDALIKE) Yeah.
TRINITY:	You gotta come with me to meet Morpheus and learn about the Matrix.
NEO:	But I don't know you.
TRINITY:	I'm wearing a skin-tight leather catsuit.
SFX:	DOOR OPENS.
NEO:	Oh, I'll get my coat.
SFX:	TECHNO/ACTION MUSIC TRANSITION.
TRINITY:	Morpheus, this is Neo. He's going to save the world from the machines that control the virtual reality the entire human race believes they live in.
MORPHEUS:	(LAURENCE FISHBURNE SOUNDALIKE) Hi, Neo.
NEO:	(VERY KEANU) Hey, dude.
MORPHEUS:	(TO TRINITY UNDER HIS BREATH) This guy's going to save the world?
TRINITY:	Yeah. Isn't he hot?
MORPHEUS:	We better get started. Plug the computer into his head.
SFX:	PLUG INTO HEAD.
NEO:	Ouch!
SFX:	COMPUTER SOUNDS.
MORPHEUS:	Download everything he needs to know. First, kung fu.
SFX:	COMPUTER SOUNDS.
NEO:	Hi-yah!
MORPHEUS:	Now, judo.
SFX:	KARATE SOUNDS; BODY SLAM.
NEO:	Whoa!
MORPHEUS:	And wine tasting.
SFX:	COMPUTER SOUNDS; WINE POURING FROM BOTTLE.
NEO:	Mmm. Is this a merlot or a cabernet?
MORPHEUS:	Cabernet.
SFX:	WINE GLASSES CLINKING. TECHNO/ACTION MUSIC TRANSITION.
MORPHEUS:	Now you're ready to save the world, which doesn't exist.
NEO:	Wait. This isn't actually happening?
MORPHEUS:	It is, but it isn't.
NEO:	You mean, I don't know kung fu?
MORPHEUS:	No.
NEO:	And that wasn't a cabernet?
MORPHEUS:	Sorry.
NEO:	What about her leather catsuit?
MORPHEUS:	I'm afraid not.
NEO:	Dude!
SFX:	HOLLYWOOD VIDEO THEME MUSIC.
ANNOUNCER:	If this doesn't satisfy your urge to see "The Matrix," and we can't say we blame you, then rent it today at Hollywood Video. The only place to get five-day rentals on new releases like "Prince of Egypt" and "The Mummy," available September 28th. Welcome to Hollywood. Hollywood Video. Celebrity voices impersonated.

EXHIBIT 12.27

A typical radio script. http://www.hollywoodvideo.com

EXHIBIT 12.28

A live script radio ad has an on-air personality read a detailed script over the air. Normally, there are no sound effects or music to accompany the ad—just the announcer's voice.

The inclusion of musical introductions, special effects, or local tag lines (specific information for local markets) reduces the amount of copy in the advertisement. Special sound effects interspersed with copy also shorten copy length. The general rules for number of words relative to ad time change depending on the form and structure of the commercial.

After production, the tape goes through editing to create the best version of the production. Then, after advertiser approval, a sound mix is completed in which all music, special sound effects, and announcer copy are mixed together. The mixing process achieves proper timing between all audio elements in the ad and ensures that all sounds are at the desired levels. After mixing, the tape is duplicated and sent to radio stations for airing.

Expenses for a radio ad should be in the $30,000 to $50,000 range, although big-name talent can push that cost way up.

The most loosely structured production option essentially requires no production at all. It is called a fact sheet. A **fact sheet radio ad** is merely a listing of important selling points that a radio announcer can use to ad-lib a radio spot. This method works best with radio personalities who draw an audience because of their lively, entertaining monologues. The fact sheet provides a loose structure so the announcer can work in the ad during these informal monologues. The risk, of course, is that the ad will get lost in the chatter and the selling points will not be convincingly delivered. On the positive side, radio personalities many times go beyond the scheduled 30 or 60 seconds allotted for the ad.

Another loosely structured technique is the live script. The **live script radio ad** involves having an on-air radio personality, such as a DJ or talk-show host, read the detailed script of an advertisement. Normally there are no sound effects, since such effects would require special production. The live script ensures that all the selling points are included when the commercial is delivered by the announcer. These scripts are not rehearsed, however, and the emphasis, tone, and tempo in the delivery may not be ideal. The advantage of a live script is that it allows an advertiser to submit a relatively structured commercial for airing in a very short period of time. Most stations can work in a live script commercial in a matter of hours after it is received. Exhibit 12.28 shows that a live script is, indeed, read right over the air.

4 Writing Copy for Television.

Great print can make you famous. Great TV can make you rich.

—Anonymous[14]

Rule #1 in producing a great tv commercial. First, you must write one.

—Luke Sullivan[15]

---

14.   Cited in Sullivan, *Hey Whipple, Squeeze This: A Guide to Creating Great Ads,* 103.
15.   Sullivan, *Hey Whipple, Squeeze This: A Guide to Creating Great Ads,* 104.

The ability to create a mood or demonstrate a brand in use gives television wonderful capabilities; it also affords you the ability to really screw up in magnificent fashion for a very large and expensive audience (no pressure here!). Obviously, copy for television must be highly sensitive to the ad's visual aspects. It is a visual medium; you should try to not let the words get in the way.

The opportunities inherent to television as an advertising medium represent challenges for the copywriter as well. Certainly, the inherent capabilities of television can do much to bring a copywriter's words to life. But the action qualities of television can create problems. First, the copywriter must remember that words do not stand alone. Visuals, special effects, and sound techniques may ultimately convey a message far better than the cleverest turn of phrase. Second, television commercials represent a difficult timing challenge for the copywriter. It is necessary for the copy to be precisely coordinated with the video. If the video portion were one continuous illustration, the task would be difficult enough. Contemporary television ads, however, tend to be heavily edited (that is, lots of cuts), and the copywriting task can be a nightmare. The copywriter not only has to fulfill all the responsibilities of proper information inclusion (based on creative platform and strategy decisions), but also has to carefully fit all the information within, between, and around the visual display taking place. To make sure this coordination is precise, the copywriter, producer, and director assigned to a television advertisement work together closely to make sure the copy supports and enhances the video element. The road map for this coordination effort is known as a **storyboard**. A storyboard is an important shot-by-important-shot sketch depicting in sequence the visual scenes and copy that will be used in a television advertisement. The procedures for coordinating audio and visual elements through the use of storyboards will be presented in Chapter 13, when television production is discussed in more detail.

Television Advertising Formats. Because of the broad creative capability of the television medium, there are several alternative formats for a television ad: demonstration, problem and solution, music and song, spokesperson, dialogue, vignette, and narrative. Each is discussed here. Again, this is not an exhaustive list, but rather a sampling of popular forms.

Demonstration. Due to television's abilities to demonstrate a brand in action, demonstration is an obvious format for a television ad. Do it if you can. Brands whose benefits result from some tangible function can effectively use this format. Copy that accompanies this sort of ad embellishes the visual demonstration. The copy in a demonstration is usually straight-line copy, but drama can easily be introduced into this format, such as with the Radio Shack home security system that scares off a burglar or the Fiat braking system that saves a motorist from an accident. Demonstration with sight and sound lets viewers appreciate the full range of features a brand has to offer. The commercial in Exhibit 12.29 was created at an agency in São Paulo, Brazil, but the clarity of the demonstration is convincing in just about any culture.

Problem and Solution. In this format, a brand is introduced as the savior in a difficult situation. This format often takes shape as a slice-of-life message, in which a consumer solves a problem with the advertised brand. Dishwashing liquids, drain openers, and numerous other household products are commonly promoted with this technique. A variation on the basic format is to promote a brand on the basis of problem prevention. A variety of auto maintenance items and even insurance products have used this approach.

Music and Song. Many television commercials use music and singing as a creative technique. The various beverage industries (soft drinks, beer, and wine) frequently use this format to create the desired mood for their brands. Additionally, the growth of image advertising has resulted in many ads that show a product in action accom-

EXHIBIT 12.29

Demonstration with sight and sound lets viewers appreciate the full range of features a brand has to offer. This commercial created by an ad agency in Brazil is a good example. http://www .honda.com

(**SFX:** MOTORCYCLE SOUNDS)
SUPER: Honda C-100 Dream. Up to 700 Km per
                liter or 30 seconds with a single drop.
SUPER: C-100 Dream, Start It, Ride It, And Love It.
SUPER: Honda. The World's Best Emotion.

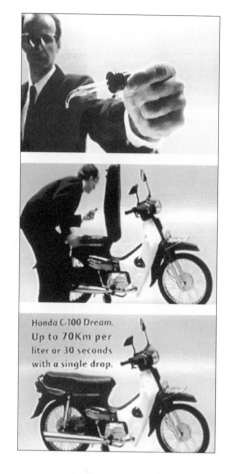

Honda C-100 Dream. Up to 70Km per liter or 30 seconds with a single drop.

panied by music and only visual overlays of the copy. This format for television advertising tends to restrict the amount of copy and presents the same difficulties for copywriting as the use of music and song in radio copywriting. Did you wonder if Burger King would ever run out of pop songs to use to peddle fast food? A logo, a few captions, a product shot, and songs ranging from "Tempted" to "So Hot" to the theme from *Welcome Back, Kotter* have been used to great success for the franchise.

Spokesperson. The delivery of a message by a spokesperson can place a heavy emphasis on the copy. The copy is given precedence over the visual and is supported by the visual, rather than vice versa. Expert, average-person, and celebrity testimonials fall into this formatting alternative. An example of the effective use of an expert spokesperson is Tiger Woods for Titleist.

Dialogue. As in a radio commercial, a television ad may feature a dialogue between two or more people. Dialogue-format ads pressure a copywriter to compose dialogue that is believable and keeps the ad moving forward. Most slice-of-life ads in which a husband and wife or friends are depicted using a brand employ a dialogue format.

Vignette. A vignette format uses a sequence of related advertisements as a device to maintain viewer interest. Vignettes also give the advertising a recognizable look, which can help achieve awareness and recognition. The Taster's Choice couple featured in a series of advertisements in the United States and Great Britain is an example of the vignette format.

Narrative. A narrative is similar to a vignette but is not part of a series of related ads. Narrative is a distinct format in that it tells a story, like a vignette, but the mood of

EXHIBIT 12.30

A narrative ad often focuses on storytelling and indirectly touches on the benefits of the brand. http://www .jhancock.com

SUPER:	Your parents, your children, yourself.
SIGOURNEY WEAVER:	You owe it to your parents, for they brought you into this world.
SUPER:	Who do you love the least?
WEAVER:	You owe it to your children, for you did the same for them. But the day may arrive when both debts come due. When you may have no choice but to borrow from your own retirement to educate a child or care for a parent. Into whose eyes can you look and say you just can't help?
SUPER:	Insurance for the unexpected.
WEAVER:	For in both, you will surely see your own.
SUPER:	Investments for the opportunities.
SUPER:	John Hancock (Olympic rings) worldwide sponsor.

the ad is highly personal, emotional, and involving. A narrative ad often focuses on storytelling and only indirectly touches on the benefits of the brand. Many of the "heart-sell" ads by McDonald's, Kodak, and Hallmark use the narrative technique to great effect. (See Exhibit 12.30.)

Guidelines for Writing Television Copy. Writing copy for television advertising has its own set of unique opportunities and challenges. The following are some general guidelines:

- *Use the video.* Allow the video portion of the commercial to enhance and embellish the audio portion. Given the strength and power of the visual presentation in television advertising, take advantage of its impact with copy.
- *Support the video.* Make sure that the copy doesn't simply hitchhike on the video. If all the copy does is verbally describe what the audience is watching, an opportunity to either communicate additional information or strengthen the video communication has been lost.
- *Coordinate the audio with the video.* In addition to strategically using the video, it is essential that the audio and video do not tell entirely different stories.
- *Sell the product as well as entertain the audience.* Television ads can sometimes be more entertaining than television programming. A temptation for the copywriter and art director is to get caught up in the excitement of a good video presentation and forget that the main purpose is to deliver persuasive communication.
- *Be flexible.* Due to media-scheduling strategies, commercials are produced to run as 15-, 20-, 30-, or 60-second spots. The copywriter may need to ensure that the audio portion of an ad is complete and comprehensive within varying time lengths.
- *Use copy judiciously.* If an ad is too wordy, it can create information overload and interfere with the visual impact. Ensure that every word is a working word and contributes to the impact of the message.

- *Reflect the brand personality and image.* All aspects of an ad, copy and visuals, should be consistent with the personality and image the advertiser wants to build or maintain for the brand.
- *Build campaigns.* When copy for a particular advertisement is being written, evaluate its potential as a sustainable idea. Can the basic appeal in the advertisement be developed into multiple versions that form a campaign?[16]

Slogans. Copywriters are often asked to come up with a good slogan or tagline for a product or service. A **slogan** is a short phrase in part used to help establish an image, identity, or position for a brand or an organization, but mostly used to increase memorability. A slogan is established by repeating the phrase in a firm's advertising and other public communication as well as through salespeople and event promotions. Slogans are often used as a headline or subhead in print advertisements, or as the tagline at the conclusion of radio and television advertisements. Slogans typically appear directly below the brand or company name, as "The Brand That Fits" does in all Lee jeans advertising. Some memorable and enduring ad slogans are listed in Exhibit 12.31.

EXHIBIT 12.31

Slogans used for brands and organizations.

Brand/Company	Slogan
Allstate Insurance	You're in Good Hands with Allstate.
American Express	Don't Leave Home Without It.
AT&T (consumer)	Reach Out and Touch Someone.
AT&T (business)	AT&T. Your True Choice.
Beef Industry Council	Real Food for Real People.
Best Buy	Turn on the Fun.
BMW	The Ultimate Driving Machine.
Budweiser	This Bud's for You.
Chevrolet trucks	Like a Rock.
Cotton Industry	The Fabric of Our Lives.
DeBeers	Diamonds Are Forever.
Ford	Have You Driven a Ford Lately?
Goodyear	The Best Tires in the World Have Goodyear Written All Over Them.
Harley-Davidson	The Legend Rolls On.
Lincoln	What a Luxury Car Should Be.
Maybelline	Maybe She's Born with It. Maybe It's Maybelline.
Microsoft (online)	Where Do You Want to Go Today?
Panasonic	Just Slightly Ahead of Our Time.
Prudential Insurance	Get a Piece of the Rock.
Rogaine	Stronger Than Heredity.
Saturn	A Different Kind of Company. A Different Kind of Car.
Sharp	From Sharp Minds Come Sharp Products.
Toshiba	In Touch with Tomorrow.
VH1	Music First.
Visa	It's Everywhere You Want to Be.
VW	Drivers Wanted.

16. The last three points in this list were adapted from Roman and Maas, *The New How to Advertise*.

A good slogan can serve several positive purposes for a brand or a firm. First, a slogan can be an integral part of a brand's image and personality. BMW's slogan, "The Ultimate Driving Machine," does much to establish and maintain the personality and image of the brand. Second, if a slogan is carefully and consistently developed over time, it can act as a shorthand identification for the brand and provide information on important brand benefits. The long-standing slogan for Allstate Insurance, "You're in Good Hands with Allstate," communicates the benefits of dealing with a well-established insurance firm. A good slogan also provides continuity across different media and between advertising campaigns. Nike's "Just Do It" slogan has given the firm an underlying theme for a wide range of campaigns and other promotions. In this sense, a slogan is a useful tool in helping to bring about thematic integrated marketing communications for a firm. Microsoft's slogan—"Where do you want to go today?"—is all about freedom, but the company approach to integrated communications is more sophisticated than just brandishing its slogan with a vengeance.

Common Mistakes in Copywriting.
The preceding discussions have shown that print, radio, and television advertising present the copywriter with unique challenges and opportunities. Copy in each arena must be compatible with the various types of ads run in each medium and the particular capabilities and liabilities of each medium and format. Beyond the guidelines for effective copy in each area, some common mistakes made in copywriting can and should be avoided:

- *Vagueness.* Avoid generalizations and imprecise words. To say that a car is stylish is not nearly as meaningful as saying it has sleek, aerodynamic lines. And when being precise, always be justified. The Ethics box shows the penalty for a precise but misleading claim.

- *Wordiness.* Being economical with descriptions is paramount. Copy has to fit in a limited time frame (or space), and receivers bore easily. When boredom sets in, effective communication often ceases.

- *Triteness.* Using clichés and worn-out superlatives was mentioned as a threat to print copywriting. The same threat (to a lesser degree, due to audio and audiovisual capabilities) exists in radio and television advertising. Trite copy creates a boring, outdated image for a brand or firm.

- *Creativity for creativity's sake.* Some copywriters get carried away with a clever idea. It's essential that the copy in an ad remain true to its primary responsibility: communicating the selling message. Copy that is extraordinarily funny or poses an intriguing riddle yet fails to register the main selling theme will simply produce another amusing advertising failure.

ETHICS

Plaque Flap: For Listerine, Fallout from a False Claim

Listerine mouthwash has long touted its ability to fight bad breath and kill germs. But when a new ad campaign claimed that Listerine was "as effective as floss" in preventing plaque and gum disease, the mouthwash maker found itself on the losing side of a false-claims lawsuit.

Johnson & Johnson, the leading manufacturer of dental floss, sued Listerine's parent Pfizer for false advertising and unfair competition, and won. A federal judge in New York ruled that the claims were not just misleading, but literally false and could potentially pose a health risk by "undermining the efforts of dental professionals . . . to convince consumers to floss on a daily basis."

For copywriters, the courtroom battle between the two corporate giants was a lesson in the basic principles of creating ads. Advertisers can claim attributes and superiority only if they can substantiate the claims.

The contested mouthwash commercials had claimed, "Listerine's as effective as floss at fighting plaque and gingivitis. Clinical studies prove it." The ads, based on two Pfizer-funded studies, also included the disclaimer "there's no replacement for flossing," in the television version. Print ads contained the words "floss daily" in small print.

But the court said the studies had shown only that the mouthwash was as effective as improperly used floss. For Pfizer, it was a costly mistake. Not only did the company have to pull the ads, it also was forced to dispatch workers to stores to sticker over Listerine bottles bearing the claim "clinically proven as effective as floss."

Source: Anthony Lin, "Listerine's Advertising Claim is Found False," **New York Law Journal**, January 10, 2005.

The Copy Approval Process.

"The client has some issues and concerns about your ads." This is how account executives announce the death of your labors: "issues and concerns." To understand the portent of this phrase, picture the men lying on the floor of that Chicago garage on St. Valentine's Day. Al Capone had issues and concerns with these men.

I've had account executives beat around the bush for 15 minutes before they could tell me the bad news. "Well, we had a good meeting."

"Yes," you say, "but are the ads dead?"

"We learned a lot?"

"But are they dead?"

"Wellll, . . . They're really not dead. They are just in a new and better place."

—Luke Sullivan[17]

The final step in copywriting is getting the copy approved. For many copywriters, this is the most dreaded part of their existence. During the approval process, the proposed copy is likely to pass through the hands of a wide range of client and agency people, many of whom are ill-prepared to judge the quality of the copy. The challenge at this stage is to keep the creative potency of the copy intact. As David Ogilvy suggests in his commandments for advertising, "Committees can criticize advertisements, but they can't write them."[18]

The copy approval process usually begins within the creative department of an advertising agency. A copywriter submits draft copy to either the senior writer or the creative director, or both. From there, the redrafted copy is forwarded to the account management team within the agency. The main concern at this level is to evaluate the copy on legal grounds. After the account management team has made recommendations, a meeting is likely held to present the copy, along with proposed visuals, to the client's product manager, brand manager, and/or marketing staff. Inevitably, the client representatives feel compelled to make recommendations for altering the copy. In some cases, these recommendations realign the copy in accordance with important marketing strategy objectives. In other cases, the recommendations are amateurish and problematic. From the copywriter's point of view, they are rarely welcome, although the copywriter usually has to act as if they are.

Depending on the assignment, the client, and the traditions of the agency, the creative team may also rely on various forms of copy research. Typically, copy research is either developmental or evaluative. **Developmental copy research** can actually help copywriters at the early stages of copy development by providing audience interpretations and reactions to the proposed copy. **Evaluative copy research** is used to judge copy after it's been produced. Here, the audience expresses its approval or disapproval of the copy used in an ad. Copywriters are not fond of these evaluative report cards. In our view, they are completely justified in their suspicion; for many reasons, state-of-the-art evaluative copy research just isn't very good.

Finally, copy should always be submitted for final approval to the advertiser's senior executives. Many times, these executives have little interest in evaluating advertising plans, and they leave this responsibility to middle managers. In some firms, however, top executives get very involved in the approval process.

17. Sullivan, *Hey Whipple, Squeeze This: A Guide to Creating Great Ads*, 182.
18. Ogilvy, *Confessions of an Advertising Man*, 101.

EXHIBIT 12.32

The copy approval process.

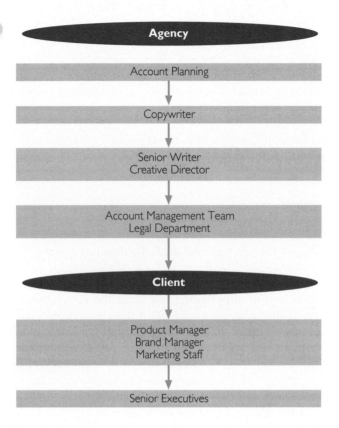

The various levels of approval for copy are summarized in Exhibit 12.32 and paro-died in Exhibit 12.33. For the advertiser, it is best to recognize that copywriters, like other creative talent in an agency, should be allowed to exercise their creative exper-tise with guidance but not overbearing interference. Copywriters seek to provide energy and originality to an often dry marketing strategy. To override their creative effort violates their reason for being.

EXHIBIT 12.33

Advertisers should allow copywriters to exercise their creative expertise, as suggested by this Dilbert cartoon.

Source: DILBERT © UFS. Reprinted by permission.

SUMMARY

 Explain the need for a creative plan in the copywriting process.

Effective ad copy must be based on a variety of individual inputs and information sources. Making sense out of these diverse inputs and building from them creatively is a copywriter's primary challenge. A creative plan is used as a device to assist the copywriter in dealing with this challenge. Key elements in the creative plan include product features and benefits that must be communicated to the audience, the mood or tone appropriate for the audience, and the intended media for the ad.

 Detail the components of print copy, along with important guidelines for writing effective print copy.

The three unique components of print copy are the headline, subhead, and body copy. Headlines need to motivate additional processing of the ad. Good headlines communicate information about the brand or make a promise about the benefits the consumer can expect from the brand. If the brand name is not featured in the headline, then that headline must entice the reader to examine the body copy or visual material. Subheads can also be valuable in helping lead the reader to and through the body copy. In the body copy, the brand's complete story can be told. Effective body copy must be crafted carefully to engage the reader, furnish supportive evidence for claims made about the brand, and avoid clichés and exaggeration that the consumer will dismiss as hype.

 Describe various formatting alternatives for radio ads and articulate guidelines for writing effective radio copy.

Four basic formats can be used to create radio copy. These are the music format, the dialogue format, the announcement format, and the celebrity announcer format. Guidelines for writing effective radio copy start with using simple sentence construction and language familiar to the intended audience. When the copy stimulates the listener's imagination, the advertiser can expect improved results as long as the brand name and the primary selling points don't get lost. When using music or humor to attract and hold the listener's attention, the copywriter must take care not to shortchange key selling points for the sake of simple entertainment.

 Describe various formatting alternatives for television ads and articulate guidelines for writing effective television copy.

Several formats can be considered in preparing television ad copy. These are demonstration, problem and solution, music and song, spokesperson, dialogue, vignette, and narrative. To achieve effective copy in the television medium, it is essential to coordinate the copy with the visual presentation, seeking a synergistic effect between audio and video. Entertaining to attract attention should again not be emphasized to the point that the brand name or selling points of the ad get lost. Developing copy consistent with the heritage and image of the brand is also essential. Finally, copy that can be adapted to various time lengths and modified to sustain audience interest over the life of a campaign is most desirable.

KEY TERMS

creative team
creative concept
copywriting
creative plan
headline
subhead

straight-line copy
dialogue
testimonial
narrative
direct response copy
fact sheet radio ad

live script radio ad
storyboard
slogan
developmental copy research
evaluative copy research

QUESTIONS

1.   Explain the applications for copy research in the copywriting process. What other forms of consumer or market research might be particularly helpful in developing effective ad copy?

2.   What are the primary purposes that headlines serve in print advertising copy? Can a print ad ever be effective without a headline?

3.   How does audience influence the style of writing exhibited in online advertising copy? How do you characterize the writing at Dove.com?

4.   Discuss the advantages and disadvantages of music as a tool for constructing effective radio ads.

5.   Listen with care to the radio ads in 30 minutes of programming on your favorite radio station. Then do the same for 30 minutes of programming on a parent's or grandparent's favorite station. Identify ads that did the best job of using terms and jargon familiar to the target audience of each station. What differences in mood or tone did you detect among ads on the two stations?

6.   Compare and contrast the dialogue and narrative formats for television ads. What common requirement must be met to construct convincing TV ads using these two formats?

7.   Entertainment is both the blessing and the curse of a copywriter. Is it conceivable that ads that merely entertain could actually prove valuable in stimulating sales? If so, how so?

8.   Describe the four common categories of mistakes that copywriters must avoid. From your personal experience with all types of ads, are there other common mistakes that you believe copywriters are prone to make on a regular basis?

9.   Copywriters often are asked to develop slogans for a product or service. What role does an effective slogan play in promoting a brand's image and personality? Exhibit 12.32 provides a list of some commonly recognized slogans. Pick three of the listed brands and try to write a new slogan for each.

10. Everyone has his or her own opinion on what makes advertisements effective or ineffective. How does this fundamental aspect of human nature complicate a copywriter's life when it comes to winning approval for his or her ad copy?

EXPERIENTIAL EXERCISES

1.   Working in small teams, write a script for a 15- to 60-second radio commercial for the campus bookstore that you will then present to the class. As you work on this project, clearly identify which of the radio advertising formats the script will follow. Also pay close attention to the radio copy guidelines and word count relative to airtime as you prepare the script.

2.   Pull 10 print ads from a favorite magazine. Using the classifications outlined in the chapter, identify for each ad the headline, the subhead, and the body copy. For each ad, also offer a brief assessment of what you think was the copywriter's intended purpose and whether it was accomplished.

3.   Review the online advertising copy at the home pages of the following well-known brands: L'eggs (http://www.leggs.com), Sirius satellite radio (http://

www.sirius.com), Mini (http://www.miniusa.com), and Puffs tissues (http://www.puffs.com). Then answer the following questions:

- Do these sites have headlines, much like in print ads? How are the headlines similar to traditional print copy? How are they different?
- How is the body copy at these sites distinct from body copy in traditional print ads and why?
- Does the copy support the overall creative plan of the site?

4.   Identify seven current television commercials that represent each of the television advertising formats discussed in the chapter. For each ad, write a brief summary of the commercial and then analyze how well the ad adheres to the television copywriting guidelines.

CHAPTER 13

After reading and thinking about this chapter, you will be able to do the following:

1

Identify the basic purposes, components, and formats of print ad illustrations.

2

Describe the principles and components that help ensure the effective design of print ads.

3

Detail the stages that art directors follow in developing the layout of a print ad.

4

Discuss the activities and decisions involved in the final production of print ads.

5

Identify the various players who must function as a team to produce television ads.

6

Discuss the specific stages and costs involved in producing television ads.

7

Describe the major formatting options for television ad production.

A hundred years ago advertisers largely relied on words to persuade consumers. They argued with consumers, attempted to reason with them, pleaded with them, and cajoled them. Then sometime in the early 20th century, particularly noticeable after about 1910, advertisers began to move away from words and toward pictures. This trend would extend throughout the 20th century and into the 21st. Advertising has become more and more visual. Marsha Lindsay, founder, owner, and CEO of Lindsay, Stone & Briggs in Madison, a medium-size agency, says her agency doesn't even interview copywriters anymore: "everything is visual." There are several reasons for this. Among them are (1) improved technologies, which facilitate better and more affordable illustration; (2) the inherent advantage of pictures to quickly demonstrate goods and services; (3) the ability to build brand "images" through visuals; (4) the legal advantage of pictures over words in that the truth or falsity of a picture is almost impossible to determine; (5) the widely held belief that pictures, although just as cultural as words, permit a certain type of portability that words do not; and (6) the fact that pictures allow advertisers to place brands in desired social contexts, thus transferring important social meaning to them.

Not coincidentally, the role of the art director has grown more and more important relative to the copywriter. This is a visual age, and like it or not, the primacy of the word has been challenged by pictures in contemporary advertising. Make no mistake, copywriting is still vital. This is a place where we can learn from the experience of real advertising practice.

Illustration, Design, and Layout.
We begin with a discussion of three primary visual elements of a print ad: illustration, design, and layout. We then identify aspects of each that should be specified, or at least considered, as a print ad is being prepared. An advertiser must appreciate the technical aspects of coordinating the visual elements in an ad with the mechanics of the layout and ultimately with the procedures for print production. A discussion of illustration, design, and layout brings to the fore the role of art direction in print advertising.

Initially, the art director and copywriter decide on the content of an illustration. Then the art director, usually in conjunction with a graphic designer, takes this raw idea for the visual and develops it further. Art directors, with their specialized skills and training, coordinate the design and illustration components of a print ad. The creative director oversees the entire process. Most often, the copywriter is still very much in the loop.

Illustration.
Illustration, in the context of print advertising, is the actual drawing, painting, photography, or computer-generated art that forms the picture in an advertisement.

Illustration Purposes. There are several specific, strategic purposes for illustration, which can greatly increase the chances of effective communication. The basic purposes of an illustration are the following:

- To attract the attention of the target audience
- To make the brand heroic
- To communicate product features or benefits
- To create a mood, feeling, or image
- To stimulate reading of the body copy
- To create the desired social context for the brand

Attract the Attention of the Target Audience. One of the primary roles of an illustration is to attract and hold attention. With all the advertising clutter out there today, this is no easy task. In some advertising situations (for example, the very early stages

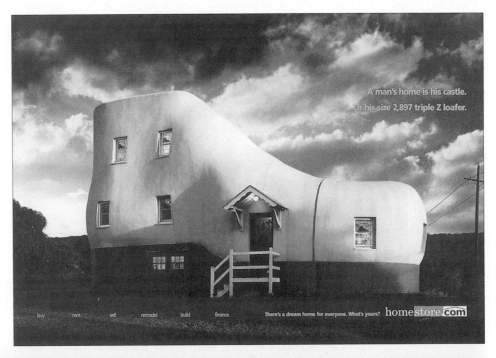

of a new product launch or for very "low-involvement" repeat purchase items), just being noticed by consumers may be enough. In most cases, however, being noticed is a necessary, but not sufficient, goal. An illustration is made to communicate with a particular target audience and, generally, must support other components of the ad to achieve the intended communication impact. So, what do you think of the impact of the ads in Exhibits 13.1 and 13.2? Will they get noticed?

Make the Brand Heroic. One traditional role of art direction is to make the brand heroic. Very often this is done by the manner in which the brand is presented via illustration. Visual techniques such as backlighting, low-angle shots, and dramatic use of color can communicate heroic proportions and qualities. Professionals even call this the "hero" or "beauty shot" (see Exhibit 13.3 on the next page). David Ogilvy suggests that if you don't have a particular story to tell in the ad, then make the package the subject of the illustration.[1] Product and package design have always been important, but have been particularly recognized as so lately. Some MBA programs now require or strongly suggest those planning to be brand managers take a course or two in design.

---

1.   David Ogilvy, *Ogilvy on Advertising* (New York: Vintage Books, 1985), 77.

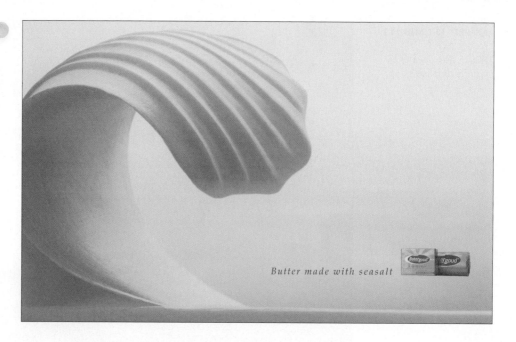

Butter made with seasalt

Communicate Product Features or Benefits. Perhaps the most straightforward illustration is one that simply displays brand features, benefits, or both (see Exhibit 13.4). Even though a print ad is static, the product can be shown in use through an "action" scene or even through a series of illustrations. The benefits of product use can be demonstrated with before-and-after shots or by demonstrating the result of having used the product.

Create a Mood, Feeling, or Image. Brand image is projected through illustration. The myriad of ways this is done is beyond enumeration, but the illustration interacts with the packaging, associated brand imagery (for example, the brand logo), and evoked feelings, which all contribute. The "mood" of an ad can help this along. Whether these goals are achieved with a print ad depends on the technical execution of the illustration. The lighting, color, tone, and texture of the illustration can have a huge impact. In Exhibit 13.5, the photograph used as the illustration in the print ad for a video rental store that specializes in horror movies captures an eerie, disconcerting feeling.

Stimulate Reading of the Body Copy. Just as a headline can stimulate examination of the illustration, the illustration can stimulate reading of the body copy. Since body copy generally carries the essential selling message, any tactic that encourages reading is useful. (See Exhibit 13.6.) Illustrations can create curiosity and interest in readers. To satisfy that curiosity, readers may proceed to the body copy for clarification. (This is not easy; body copy often looks boring and tedious.) Normally, an illustration and headline need to be fully coordinated and play off each other for this level of interest to occur. One caution is to avoid making the illustration too clever a stimulus for motivating copy reading. Putting cleverness ahead of clarity in choosing an illustration can confuse the receiver and cause the body copy to be ignored, which in reality it usually is. As one expert puts it, such ads win awards but can camouflage the benefit offered by the product.[2] To be both fair and realistic, there simply aren't that many print ads that motivate consumers to actually read the body copy. But it has to be there, and it has to be good, in case they do.

---

2.   Tony Antin, *Great Print Advertising* (New York: Wiley, 1993), 38.

EXHIBIT 13.4

Sometimes a photograph of a product in use can present brand features or benefits in a simple, powerful manner.

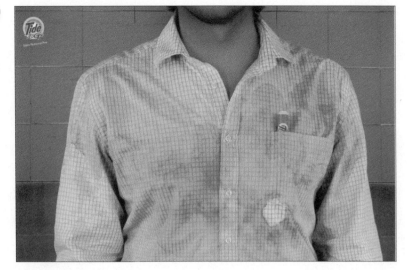

EXHIBIT 13.5

Contrast and eerie lighting work here.

EXHIBIT 13.6

This ad tries to get you to read the body copy. Does it work?

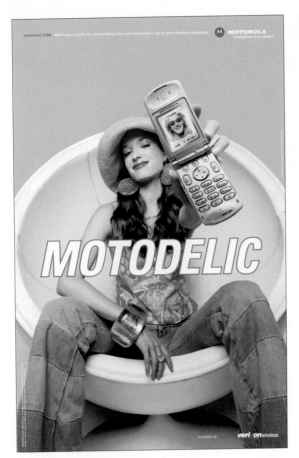

EXHIBITS 13.7 AND 13.8

Context is (almost) everything. When you remove the advertised brand from the advertiser created context, it isn't the same, is it?

Create the Desired Social Context for the Brand. As described earlier, advertisers need to associate or situate their brand within a type of social setting, thereby linking it with certain "types" of people and certain lifestyles. Establishing desired social contexts is probably the most important function of modern art direction. Look at the ad in Exhibit 13.7 and then think about what it would mean if the product were divorced from the social context. (See Exhibit 13.8.) See what we mean? Context can be everything.

Illustration Components. Various factors contribute to the overall visual presentation and impact of an illustration. Size, color, and medium affect viewers. Individual decisions regarding size, color, and medium are a matter of artistic discretion and creative execution. There is some evidence of the differing effects of various decisions made in each of these areas. But remember, the interpretation and meaning of any visual representation cannot be explained completely by a series of rules or prescriptive how-tos. Thankfully, it's not that simple.

Size. There is no question that greater size in an illustration may allow an ad to compete more successfully for the reader's attention, especially in a cluttered media environment. Consumers appear to infer brand importance from the relative size of an ad. Generally speaking, illustrations with a focal point immediately recognizable by the reader are more likely to be noticed and comprehended. Conversely, illustrations that arouse curiosity or incorporate action score high in attracting attention but have been found to score low in inducing the reading of the total ad.[3]

---

3.   Daniel Starch, *Measuring Advertising Readership and Results* (New York: McGraw-Hill, 1966), 83.

Color. While not every execution of print advertising allows for the use of color (because of either expense or the medium being employed), color is a creative tool with important potential. Some products (such as furniture, floor coverings, or expensive clothing) may depend on color to accurately communicate a principal value. Color can also be used to emphasize a product feature or attract the reader's attention to a particular part of an ad. But remember, color has no fixed meaning, so no hard rules can be offered. Color is cultural, situational, and contextual. To say that red always means this or blue always means that is to rely on a popular but unfounded myth. It's simply not true, but you will run into those who are absolutely sure that a certain shade of red is why Marlboro is the leading cigarette, or that a certain shade of green always means this or that. Sorry, these are just myths.

Medium. The choice of **medium** for an illustration is the decision regarding the use of drawing, photography, or computer graphics.[4] Drawing represents a wide range of creative presentations, from cartoons to pen-and-ink drawings to elaborate watercolor or oil paintings. Photos have an element of believability as representations of reality (even though they can be just as manipulated as any other form of representation). Further, photos can often be prepared more quickly and at much less expense than other forms of art. Photographers all over the world specialize in different types of photography: landscape, seascape, portrait, food, or architecture, for example. The American Society of Media Photographers (originally the Society of Magazine Photographers and later the American Society of Magazine Photographers) is a trade association for more than 5,000 photographers whose work is primarily used for publication.[5] This society can help buyers find professional photographers. Buyers can also purchase photographs from various stock agencies, such as Corbis, Getty Images, or PhotoEdit. These photographs can usually be cropped to any size or shape, retouched, color-corrected, and doctored in a number of ways to create the user's desired effect.

With advancing technology, artists have discovered the application of computer graphics to advertising illustrations. Computer graphics specialists can create and manipulate images. With respect to illustrations for print advertising, the key development has been the ability to digitize images. Digitizing is a computer process of breaking an image (illustration) into a grid of small squares. Each square is assigned a computer code for identification. With a digitized image, computer graphics specialists can break down an illustration and reassemble it or import other components into the original image. Age can be added to or taken away from a model's face, or the Eiffel Tower can magically appear on Madison Avenue. The creative possibilities are endless with computer graphics. Exhibit 13.9 is an example of an ad with multiple images imported through computer graphics. Some art directors are very fond of these software solutions.

The size, color, and media decisions regarding an illustration are difficult ones. It is likely that strategic and budgetary considerations will heavily influence choices in these areas. Once again, advertisers should not constrain the creative process more than

EXHIBIT 13.9

Computer graphics make this ad.

4. This section is adapted from Sandra E. Moriarty, *Creative Advertising: Theory and Practice*, 2nd ed. (Englewood Cliffs, NJ: Prentice-Hall, 1991), 139–141.

5. G. Robert Cox and Edward J. McGee, *The Ad Game: Playing to Win* (Englewood Cliffs, NJ: Prentice Hall, 1990), 44.

is absolutely necessary, and even then they should probably back off a bit. Great art directors know the language and syntax of visual persuasion (rhetoric) even if they can't always explain it in a way that brand managers and account executives understand.

Illustration Formats. The just-discussed components represent a series of decisions that must be made in conceiving an illustration. Another important decision is how the product or brand will appear as part of the illustration. **Illustration format** refers to the choices the advertiser has for displaying its product. There are product shots of all sorts: Some emphasize the social context and meaning of the product or service; some are more abstract (see Exhibit 13.10); some are minimal. Obviously, the illustration format must be consistent with the copy strategy set for the ad. The creative department and the marketing planners must communicate with one another so that the illustration format selected helps pursue the specific objectives set for the total ad campaign.

The Strategic and Creative Impact of Illustration. Defining effectiveness is a matter of first considering the basic illustration purposes, components, and formats we've just discussed. Next, these factors need to be evaluated in the context of marketing strategy, consumer behavior, and campaign planning. At this point there is a lot of negotiation, discussion, and explaining. If everything works out, the ad goes forward.

2 **Design.** **Design** is "the structure itself and the plan behind that structure" for the aesthetic and stylistic aspects of a print advertisement.[6] Design represents the effort on the part of creatives to physically arrange all the components of a printed advertisement in such a way that order and beauty are achieved—order in the sense that the illustration, headline, body copy, and special features of the ad are easy to read; beauty in the sense that the ad is visually pleasing to a reader.

Certainly, not every advertiser has an appreciation for the elements that constitute effective design, nor will every advertiser be fortunate enough to have highly skilled designers as part of the team creating a print ad. As you will see in the following discussions, however, there are aspects of design that directly relate to the potential

6.   This discussion is based on Roy Paul Nelson, *The Design of Advertising*, 5th ed. (Dubuque, Iowa: Wm. C. Brown, 1985), 126.

for a print ad to communicate effectively based on its artistic form. As such, design factors are highly relevant to creating effective print advertising.

Principles of Design. Principles of design govern how a print advertisement should be prepared. The word *should* is carefully chosen in this context. It is used because, just as language has rules of grammar and syntax, visual presentation has rules of design. The **principles of design** relate to each element within an advertisement and to the arrangement of and relationship between elements as a whole.[7] Principles of design suggest the following:

- A design should be in balance.
- The proportion within an advertisement should be pleasing to the viewer.
- The components within an advertisement should have an ordered and directional pattern.
- There should be a unifying force within the ad.
- One element of the ad should be emphasized above all others.

We will consider each of these principles of design and how they relate to the development of an effective print advertisement. Of course, as surely as there are rules, there are occasions when the rules need to be broken. An experienced designer knows the rules and follows them, but is also prepared to break the rules to achieve a desired outcome. But first, you learn the rules.

Balance. Balance in an ad is an orderliness and compatibility of presentation. Balance can be either formal or informal. **Formal balance** emphasizes symmetrical presentation—components on one side of an imaginary vertical line through the ad are repeated in approximate size and shape on the other side of the imaginary line. Formal balance creates a mood of seriousness and directness and offers the viewer an orderly, easy-to-follow visual presentation (see Exhibit 13.11).

EXHIBIT 13.11

This ad achieves balance.
http://www.miniusa.com

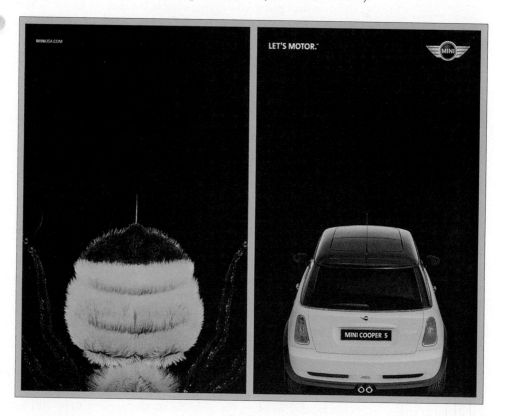

7.   Ibid., 129–136.

Informal balance emphasizes asymmetry—the optical weighing of nonsimilar sizes and shapes. Exhibit 13.12 shows an advertisement using a range of type sizes, visuals, and colors to create a powerful visual effect that achieves informal balance. Informal balance in an ad should not be interpreted as imbalance. Rather, components of different sizes, shapes, and colors are arranged in a more complex relationship providing asymmetrical balance to an ad. Informal balance is more difficult to manage in that the placement of unusual shapes and sizes must be precisely coordinated.

Proportion. Proportion has to do with the size and tonal relationships between different elements in an advertisement. Whenever two elements are placed in proximity, proportion results. In a printed advertisement, proportional considerations include the relationship of the width of an ad to its depth; the width of each element to the depth of each element; the size of one element relative to the size of every other element; the space between two elements and the relationship of that space to a third element; and the amount of light area as opposed to the amount of dark area. Ideally, factors of proportion vary so as to avoid monotony in an ad. Further, the designer should pursue pleasing proportions, which means the viewer will not detect mathematical relationships between elements. In general, unequal dimensions and distances make for the liveliest designs in advertising (see Exhibit 13.13).

Order. Order in an advertisement is also referred to as sequence or, in terms of its effects on the reader, "gaze motion." The designer's goal is to establish a relationship among elements that leads the reader through the ad in some controlled fashion. A designer can create a logical path of visual components to control eye movement. The eye has a "natural" tendency to move from left to right, from up to down, from large elements to small elements, from light to dark, and from color to noncolor. Exhibit 13.14 is an example of an ad that takes advantage of many of these tendencies. The bright lights on top of the Land Rover and the white headlines against a dark background initially attract the gaze. The eye then moves down the shape of the car, and the headlights bring the gaze down to the body copy and logo. The natural tendency for the eye to move from top to bottom leads the eye to a final shot of the Land

Proportion, when expertly controlled, can result in an inspired display of the oversized versus the undersized. http://www .parmalat.com

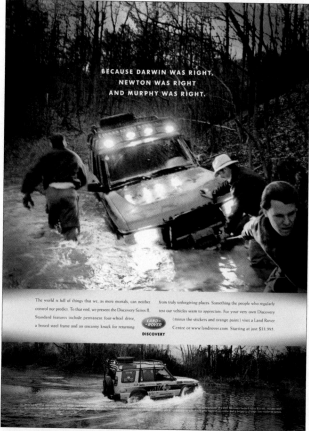

The order of elements in this ad for the Land Rover controls the reader's eye, moving it from the top of the ad through the body copy and logo, then down to the product shot at the bottom. http://www .landrover.com

Rover. Order also includes inducing the reader to jump from one space in the ad to another, creating a sense of action. The essential contribution of this design component is to establish a visual format that results in a focus or several focuses.

Unity. Ensuring that the elements of an advertisement are tied together and appear to be related is the purpose of unity. Considered the most important of the design principles, unity results in harmony among the diverse components of print advertising: headline, subhead, body copy, and illustration. Several design techniques contribute to unity. The **border** surrounding an ad keeps the ad elements from spilling over into other ads or into the printed matter next to the ad. **White space** at the outside edges creates an informal border effect. The indiscriminate use of white space within an ad can separate elements and give an impression of disorder. The proper use of white space can be dramatic and powerful and draw the receiver's attention to the most critical elements of an ad. Exhibit 13.15 on the next page shows a classic example of the effective use of white space. Exhibit 13.16 on the next page shows that it wasn't just the look of the Beetle that made a comeback decades later: The effective use of white space came along for the ride, too. White space (sometimes called "negative space," and not necessarily white, just "empty") is typically used to communicate (and is understood by consumers to convey) qualities such as elegance, leadership, and trustworthiness.

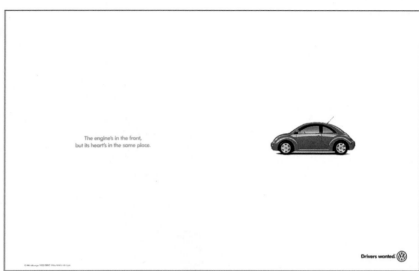

EXHIBITS 13.15 AND 13.16

The effective use of white space—past and present—to highlight the critical aspect of the ad: the product. http://www.vw.com

The final construct of unity is the axis. In every advertisement, an axis will naturally emerge. The **axis** is a line, real or imagined, that runs through an ad and from which the elements in the advertisement flare out. A single ad may have one, two, or even three axes running vertically and horizontally. An axis can be created by blocks of copy, by the placement of illustrations, or by the items within an illustration, such as the position and direction of a model's arm or leg. Elements in an ad may violate the axes, but when two or more elements use a common axis as a starting point, unity is enhanced. Note all the different axes that appear in Exhibit 13.17.

A design can be more forceful in creating unity by using either a three-point layout or a parallel layout. A **three-point layout structure** establishes three elements in the ad as dominant forces. The uneven number of prominent elements is critical for creating a gaze motion in the viewer (see Exhibit 13.18). **Parallel layout structure** employs art on the right-hand side of the page and repeats the art on the left-hand side. This is an obvious and highly structured technique to achieve unity (see Exhibit 13.19).

EXHIBIT 13.17

Look at all the different axes that appear in this ad.

EXHIBIT 13.18

There are three prominent visual elements here.

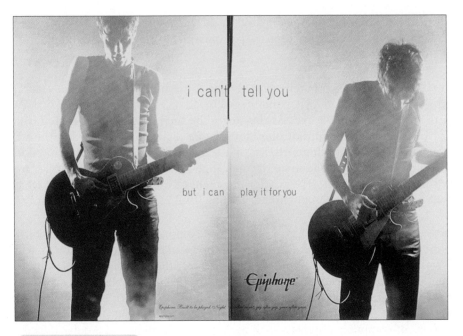

i can't   tell you

but i can   play it for you

Epiphone

EXHIBIT 13.19

Here, the visual layout on the left is repeated on the right. http://www .epiphone.com

Emphasis. At some point in the decision-making process, someone needs to decide which major component—the headline, subhead, body copy, or illustration—will be emphasized. The key to good design relative to emphasis is that one item is the primary but not the only focus in an ad. If one element is emphasized to the total exclusion of the others, then a poor design has been achieved, and ultimately a poor communication will result.

Balance, proportion, order, unity, and emphasis are the basic principles of design. As you can see, the designer's objectives go beyond the strategic and message-development elements associated with an advertisement. Design principles relate to the aesthetic impression an ad produces. Once a designer has been informed of the components that will make up the headline, subhead, body copy, and illustration to be included in the ad, then advertising and marketing decision makers *must* allow the designer to arrange those components according to the principles of creative design.

3 **Layout.** In contrast to design, which emphasizes the structural concept behind a print ad, layout is the mechanical aspect of design—the physical manifestation of design concepts. A **layout** is a drawing or digital rendering of a proposed print advertisement, showing where all the elements in the ad are positioned. An art director uses a layout to work through various alternatives for visual presentation and sequentially develop the print ad to its final stages. It is part and parcel of the design process and inextricably linked to the development of an effective design. While some art directors still work with traditional tools—layout tissue, T-square, triangle, and markers—most work in computerized layout programs, such as QuarkXPress.

An art director typically proceeds through various stages in the construction of a final design for an ad. The following are the different stages of layout development, in order of detail and completeness, that an art director typically uses.

Thumbnails. Thumbnails are the first drafts of an advertising layout. The art director will produce several thumbnail sketches to work out the general presentation of the ad. While the creative team refines the creative concept, thumbnails represent placement of elements—headline, images, body copy, and tagline. Headlines are often represented with zigzag lines and body copy with straight, parallel lines. An example of a thumbnail is shown in Exhibit 13.20 on page 423. Typically, thumbnails are drawn at one-quarter the size of the finished ad.

Rough Layouts. The next step in the layout process is the **rough layout**. Unlike a thumbnail sketch, a rough layout is done in the actual size of the proposed ad and is usually created with a computer layout program, such as QuarkXPress. This allows the art director to experiment with different headline fonts and easily manipulate the placement and size of images to be used in the ad. A rough layout is often used by the advertising agency for preliminary presentation to the client. Exhibit 13.21 features a rough layout.

Comprehensives. The comprehensive layout, or **comp**, is a polished version of an ad. Now for the most part computer-generated, a comp is a representation of what the final ad will look like. At this stage, the final headline font is used, the images to be used—photographs or illustrations—are digitized and placed in the ad, and the actual body copy is often included on the ad. Comps are generally printed in full color, if the final ad is to be in color, on a high-quality printer. Comps that are produced in this way make it very easy for the client to imagine (and approve) what the ad will look like when it is published. Exhibit 13.22 features a comp layout.

Mechanicals. After the client has approved the comprehensive layouts, the production art department creates the final version of an ad, the **mechanical** that will be sent to the printer. Working with the art director, the production artist refines the ad by adjusting the headline spacing (kerning), making any copy changes the client has requested, and placing high-quality digitized (scanned or digitally created) versions of images (illustrations or photographs) to be used. The production artist uses a variety of computer programs such as Adobe Photoshop and Adobe Illustrator to create the ad. A layout program is used to assemble all of the elements of the ad—images and type. Although there are many programs available to perform these tasks, QuarkXPress is the standard for the advertising industry, along with the Macintosh computer platform.

The client will make one last approval of the mechanical before it is sent to the printer. Changes that a client requests, prior to the ad being sent to the printer, are still easily and quickly made. A digital file is then sent either electronically or by mail to the printer. (Prior to the use of computers to generate mechanicals, a small copy change could result in hours of work on the part of the production artists and a large bill to the client.)

The stages of layout development discussed here provide the artistic blueprint for a print advertisement (see Exhibit 13.23). We now turn our attention to the matter of print production.

④ Production in Print Advertising.

The production process in print advertising represents the technical and mechanical activities that transform a creative concept and rough layout into a finished print advertisement. While the process is fundamentally technical, some aspects of print production directly relate to the strategic and design goals of the print ad. Different type styles can contribute to the design quality, readability, and mood in an advertisement. Our purpose in this section, however, is to provide a basic familiarity with production details. Here we will outline the sequence of activities and proper time frame related to print production and the various options available for print preparation.

The Print Production Schedule.

The advertiser is only partly in control of the timing of the print advertisement. While plans can be made to coordinate the appearance of the ad with overall marketing strategies, it must be recognized that the print media have specifications regarding how far in advance and in what form an ad must be received to appear in print. The deadline for receipt of an ad is referred to as the **closing date**. Closing dates for newspapers can be one or two days before publication. For magazines, the closing date may be months ahead of publication.

EXHIBIT 13.20

A thumbnail showing the transition from idea to advertisement.

EXHIBIT 13.21

A rough layout.

EXHIBIT 13.22

A comp layout.

EXHIBIT 13.23

The finished ad.

Advertisers must be aware that advance planning is necessary to accommodate the basic nature of print production. Computers have certainly speeded things up, but there are still pressures (often more financial than anything else) to close earlier than is truly necessary from a production standpoint.

Print Production Processes. Seven major processes can be used in print production.[8] Depending on the medium (newspaper, magazine, direct mail, or specialty advertising), the length of the print run (quantity), the type of paper being used, and the quality desired in reproduction, one of the following processes is used: letterpress, offset lithography, gravure, flexography, electronic, laser, and inkjet printing. Advances in technology have made computer print production an ideal alternative under certain conditions.

Letterpress draws its name from the way it "presses" type onto a page. Typesetters hand-placed, or *set*, each letter for a printed page in a tray, separating lines of text with bars of lead. These trays would then be inked and "pressed" onto the paper to transfer the ink type or image, similar to how we might currently use a rubber stamp. Today, handset type is a thing of the past, and individual metal type has been replaced with metal or rubber plates that are typeset from a computer program. The most common use for the letterpress today is finishing activities, such as embossing and scoring.

Offset lithography is by far the most common printing method. This process prints from a flat, chemically treated surface—a plate—wrapped around a cylinder that attracts ink to the areas to be printed and repels ink from other areas; the basic idea is that oil and water don't mix. The inked image is then transferred to a rubber blanket on a roller and from this roller the impression is carried to paper. Depending on the length of the run (quantity of pieces needed), either a sheetfed or web (not associated with the World Wide Web) press would be used.

The **gravure** method of printing also prints from a plate. However, unlike the offset plate, the gravure plate is engraved. This method of printing is most commonly used for very large runs, such as the Sunday newspaper supplements, to maintain a high quality of printing clarity.

Flexography is similar to offset lithography because it also uses a rubber blanket to transfer images. It differs from offset in that this process uses water-based ink instead of oil-based ink, and printing can be done on any surface. Because of this versatility of printing surface, flexography is most commonly used in packaging.

Electronic, laser, and inkjet printing are also known as plateless printing. The widespread use of computer technology has made printing very small runs, as few as one piece, in full color or black and white, with very sharp image quality on a variety of different papers, very easy. The advertising industry often uses software connected to a color photocopier to generate color comps for clients. The colors may not be exactly as they would have been if a printer had produced the piece, but for comping purposes this method is both timely and inexpensive. Laser and inkjet printing are also plateless printing processes that are directly connected to a computer to transfer information. However, unlike the large color comping machines, laser and inkjet printers are affordable for home use. On a larger scale, both *Time* and *Fortune* use inkjet printers to address magazines to their subscribers.

Computer Print Production. Integrating the print production process with the computer has changed the printing business considerably. First, by having digital files, printers no longer need to photograph pasted-up versions of ads. Film can be

---

8.   This discussion is based in part on Michael H. Bruno, ed., *Pocket Pal: A Graphic Arts Production Handbook*, 19th ed. (New York: Graphic Arts Technical Foundation, 2004).

generated directly from digital files and, in turn, printing plates are made from the film. Second, the proofing process—double-checking that the colors to be printed are correct—can be performed well before the print job is on the press. Iris prints, polar proofs, and watermark prints are all extremely high-quality proofing methods. Though these proofing methods are expensive, their cost is only a small fraction of the cost to reprint a piece. Last, with the increasing use of electronic file transfer, files can be sent quickly to printers.

As stated earlier, choice of the proper printing process depends on the requirements of the advertisement with regard to the medium being used, the quantity being printed, the type of paper being printed on, and the level of quality needed. With respect to magazines, the production process is mandated by the publisher of a particular vehicle within the medium. Print production processes are independent publishing decisions.

Typography in Print Production.

The issues associated with typography have to do with the typeface chosen for headlines, subheads, and body copy, as well as the various size components of the type (height, width, and running length). Designers agonize over the type to use in a print ad because decisions about type affect both the readability and the mood of the overall visual impression. For our purposes, some knowledge of the basic considerations of typography is useful for an appreciation of the choices that must be made.

Categories of Type.

Typefaces have distinct personalities, and each can communicate a different mood and image. A **type font** is a basic set of typeface letters. For those of us who do word processing on computers, the choice of type font is a common decision. In choosing type for an advertisement, however, the art director has thousands of choices based on typeface alone.

There are six basic typeface groups: blackletter, roman, script, serif, sans serif, and miscellaneous. The families are divided by characteristics that reflect the personality and tone of the font. **Blackletter**, also called *gothic*, is characterized by the ornate design of the letters. This style is patterned after hand-drawn letters in monasteries where illuminated manuscripts were created. You can see blackletter fonts used today in very formal documents, such as college diplomas. **Roman** is the most common group of fonts used for body copy because of its legibility. This family is characterized by the use of thick and thin strokes in the creation of the letterforms. **Script** is easy to distinguish by the linkage of the letters in the way that cursive handwriting is connected. Script is often found on wedding invitations and documents that are intended to look elegant or of high quality. **Serif** refers to the strokes or "feet" at the ends of the letterforms. Notice the serifs that are present in these letters as you read. Their presence helps move your eye across the page, allowing you to read for a long time without losing your place or tiring your eyes. **Sans serif** fonts, as the name suggests, do not have serifs, hence the use of the French word *sans*, meaning "without." Sans serif fonts are typically used for headlines and not for body copy. **Miscellaneous** includes typefaces that do not fit easily into the other categories. Novelty display, garage, and deconstructed fonts all fall into this group. These fonts were designed specifically to draw attention to themselves and not necessarily for their legibility. The following example displays serif and sans serif type:

This line is set in serif type.
This line is set in sans serif type.

Type Measurement.

There are two elements of type size. **Point** refers to the size of type in height. In the printing industry, type sizes run from 6 to 120 points. Now,

This is 8 point type

This is 12 point type

This is 18 point type

This is 36 point type

This is 60 point type

A range of type point sizes.

with computer layout programs such as QuarkXPress, the range is much larger, between 2 and 720 points. Exhibit 13.24 shows a range of type sizes for comparison purposes. **Picas** measure the width of lines. A pica is 12 points wide, and each pica measures about one-sixth of an inch. Layout programs make it very easy for the art director to fit copy into a designated space on an ad by reducing or enlarging a font with a few strokes on the keyboard.

Readability. It is critical in choosing type to consider readability. Type should facilitate the communication process. The following are some traditional recommendations when deciding what type to use (however, remember that these are only guidelines and should not necessarily be followed in every instance):

- Use capitals and lowercase, NOT ALL CAPITALS.
- Arrange letters from left to right, not up and down.
- Run lines of type horizontally, not vertically.
- Use even spacing between letters and words.

Different typefaces and styles also affect the mood conveyed by an ad. Depending on the choices made, typefaces can connote grace, power, beauty, modernity, simplicity, or any number of other qualities.

Art Direction and Production in Cyberspace.

Cyberspace is its own space. It is its own medium, too. It's not television or radio, but, at this point, it's closer to print than to anything else. By the next edition of this book, it will probably be closer to television; that seems to be the way we are going. But for now, cyberads are still pretty print oriented. Like print, the Internet is an active medium rather than a passive one (people generally come to it rather than the other way around). Television is considered a more passive medium. While the basic principles of art direction (design and concept) apply, the cyber medium is fundamentally different in the way its audience comes to it, navigates it, and responds to it. This difference presents one of the real challenges of electronic advertising.

In most respects, cyber-production does not differ significantly from print, radio, or television production, but it does differ from these traditional media in how aspects of production are combined with programming language, such as HTML, and with each other. Advances in streaming audio and digital video keep art direction and production in cyberspace a fast moving target. Still, most cyberads are either produced in traditional ways and then digitized and combined with text or created entirely with computer design packages. Exhibits 13.25 through 13.28 are pretty representative of what's out there.

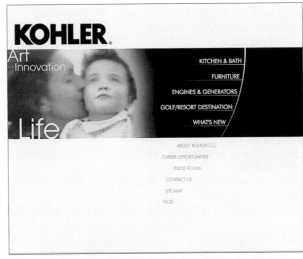

EXHIBITS 13.25 THROUGH 13.28

These ads are pretty typical of contemporary cyberads. Visit the promotion site for pop group They Might Be Giants (http://www.tmbg.com) and its companion site (http://www.dialasong.com). Do these sites suggest that the future of art direction and production in cyberspace will be more like television than print, or do the interactive features make the medium unique? Do you think highly interactive Web sites add clutter, or do they make browsing a more efficient experience?

DOING IT RIGHT

In Web Production, the Next Next Thing

After paying a whopping $1.65 billion for YouTube, technology giant Google had to find some way to generate revenue from the online video site. Linking ads to YouTube's previously sponsor-free content, though, risked alienating viewers. And early testing showed a particularly high user-abandonment rate associated with widely used "pre-roll ads," which play for 15 to 60 seconds before a requested video begins.

In the continuously evolving world of Internet ad production, Google turned instead to a relatively new form of online selling, called "overlay advertising." Translucent overlay ads appear roughly 15 seconds after the start of a requested video, showing up along the bottom of the screen much like scroll messages on traditional television. Viewers are invited to click on the overlay, which opens a new screen and launches the extended advertisement—all while the regular video content is paused.

In contrast to pre-roll ads, Google said that less than 10 percent of overlay ads were closed by viewers. Advertisers, meanwhile, are able to reach viewers who indicate at least some receptiveness to the message. They also can tailor ads according to programming, demographics, locations, and even time of day.

The launch of overlay advertising on YouTube in summer 2007 appeared promising, said Greg Sterling, an analyst at Sterling Market Intelligence. If the new model is accepted, Sterling said, "it has the potential to alter the landscape."

Sources: Jefferson Graham, "Google Plans Ad Overlays For Some YouTube Videos," **USA Today**, August 22, 2007, B1; Catherine Holahan, "Now Playing on YouTube: Ads," **BusinessWeek Online**, August 22, 2007; Staff, "Google Puts Ads in YouTube Videos," **InformationWeek**, August 22, 2007.

All media have to find their own way, their own voice. This is not just an aesthetic matter. It's figuring out what works, which has something to do with design. How the information is laid out matters. If you go back and look at the first few years of television advertising, you have to say that they really didn't fully understand the medium or the ways audiences would use this new technology. The ads went on forever and seemed to be written for radio. In fact, many of the early TV writers were radio writers. They tried to make television radio.

This same phenomenon seems to be happening with Web sites. At first, they looked more like print ads than something truly cyber. Yet, unlike print ads, Web sites have the ability to change almost immediately. If a client wants to change a copy point, for example, it can happen many times in one afternoon. And Web consumers demand change. Though frequent changes may seem time-consuming and expensive, they ensure return visits from audiences.

Web pages are often very busy, with lots of information crammed into small spaces. Advertisers, while not yet knowing what this medium can do, are convinced that they must be in it. But they really haven't yet found its best face. In short, the Web is not print *or* television: It is electronic and fluid, and must be thought of in this way. In terms of design, this means trying to understand why people come to various sites, what they are looking for, what they expect to encounter, what they expect in return for their very valuable click. As suggested in the Doing It Right box, this is a truly dynamic undertaking.

One of the most valuable lessons out there right now is the case of consumer generated content (CGC). As you know, people are making their own ads for their favorite brands. One Apple cyberad that was incredibly popular on the Web was not made by Apple's high-priced ad agency—a college kid did it. YouTube and other venues have allowed consumers to say, "Hey, it's my brand too . . . I get it more than you do . . . here's my ad." And sometimes, the big companies are more than happy to invite you to lunch, per Exhibit 13.29.

Art Direction and Production in Television Advertising. There

have been few (if any) things that have changed the face of advertising (or contemporary culture) more than television. Like other media, television first struggled to find its best form, but soon did. In many ways, television was simply made for advertising. It is everywhere, serving as background to much of daily life. If you are in a room and a television is on, you will find yourself watching it. Want to kill a good

Several advertisers, including Doritos, ran consumer-generated ads during Super Bowl XLI.

party? Turn on a television. Did you ever try to talk to someone sitting across from you when your back is to the television? You just about have to offer money to get their attention. In the Oscar-winning film *Network*, a television anchorman believes that God has chosen him as a modern-day prophet. When he asks God, "Why me?" God replies, "Because you're on television, dummy." Everybody watches TV, no matter what they tell you.

Television is about moving visuals. Sometimes, it's just about leaving impressions, or setting moods, or getting you to notice; sometimes it tells stories. Many believe that the very best television ads work just as well with the sound turned off, that the best television tells its story visually. Of course, this is what film critics have said about master film directors, such as John Ford (Exhibit 13.30) and Alfred Hitchcock (Exhibit 13.31), both of whom learned their craft in silent films.

Still, it must be said that an awful lot of TV spots are very reliant on copy. In fact, entire genres of television ads rely heavily on repetitive brand mentions, or dialogue-dependent narratives. Of late, rapid cuts and sparse dialogue seem to be the way of the TV creatives, but this phase will probably change before the next full moon. Advertising is, in so many respects, fashion.

Two of the very best filmmakers—and storytellers—ever: John Ford and Alfred Hitchcock.

Art Direction in Television Advertising. The primary creative directive for TV is the same as for other media: effective communication. Television presents some unique challenges, however. Due to its complexity, television production involves a lot of people. These people have different but often overlapping expertise, responsibility, and authority. This makes for a myriad of complications and calls for tremendous organizational skills. At some point, individuals who actually shoot the film or the tape are brought in to execute the copywriter's and art director's concepts. At this point, the creative process becomes intensely collaborative: The film director applies his or her craft and is responsible for the actual production. The creative team (that is, the art director and copywriter) rarely relinquishes control of the project, even though the film director may prefer exactly that. But who really has creative authorship is typically unclear. Getting the various players to perform their particular specialty at just the right time, while avoiding conflict with other team members, is an ongoing challenge in TV ad production.

GLOBALIZATION

An Ad Plan for Brand USA Falls Short

Charlotte Beers was considered one of the most powerful women in advertising when she was tapped shortly after the Sept. 11, 2001, terrorist attacks to help the federal government boost the global image of the United States. The appointment seemed like a sure winner. Beers was the only woman to have chaired two top-10 worldwide advertising agencies, and she had helped shape such powerful brands as Uncle Ben's Rice and Head & Shoulders.

But the plan to promote "Brand America" to deeply skeptical Arab and Muslim nations proved to be too tough a sell, even for the woman known as the Queen of Madison Avenue. After serving two years as undersecretary of state for public diplomacy, Beers resigned, citing health reasons.

Her short tenure was a rocky one. Videos that her office produced featuring American Muslims speaking favorably about the United States were rebuffed by several Arab countries. Some diplomats inside the State Department who had been based in Islamic countries criticized the promotional scripts as being simplistic and patronizing.

To reshape the image of the United States in the Muslim world, Beers had worked with international media-reaction teams and public affairs officers in embassies around the world. "The principles of persuasive communication hold true whether you find yourself in the world of marketing or of foreign affairs," she said in a speech at The Citadel as she prepared to launch the effort.

But when the controversial $15 million campaign led by Beers faltered, the U.S. government shifted its approach. Most visibly, U.S. officials turned to a long-time political strategist, Margaret Tutwiler, to replace Beers instead of searching for another ad whiz—a move even top advertising executives called a good thing.

"It's not an advertising job we are facing right now," said Dick O'Brien, a top official with the Washington office of the American Association of Advertising Agencies, "because the nature of the anger toward America is so deep that it requires a solution that is more complex than advertising alone."

Sources: Wendy Melillo, "No Brand USA Expected from New Diplomacy Chief," *Adweek*, October 20, 2003, p. 9; Jane Perlez, "Muslim-as-Apple-Pie Videos are Greeted with Skepticism," *New York Times*, October 30, 2002, A1.

⑤ The Creative Team in Television Advertising. The vast and ever-increasing capability of the broadcast media introduces new challenges and complexities to the production process. One aspect of these complexities is that aside from the creative directors, copywriters, and art directors who assume the burden of responsibility in the production of print advertising, we now encounter a host of new and irreplaceable creative and technical participants. The proper and effective production of broadcast advertising depends on a team of highly capable creative people: agency personnel, production experts, editorial specialists, and music companies. An advertiser and its agency must consider and evaluate the role of each of these participants. Descriptions of the roles played by the participants in television advertising are provided in Exhibit 13.32. The Globalization box describes how Charlotte Beers, an advertising superstar, faced the challenge of assembling a creative team to enhance the global image of the United States.

Creative Guidelines for Television Advertising. Just as

for print advertising, there are general creative principles for television advertising.[9] These principles are not foolproof or definitive, but they certainly

---

9.   These guidelines were adapted from A. Jerome Jewler, *Creative Strategy in Advertising*, 3rd ed. (Belmont, CA.: Wadsworth, 1989), 210–211; Nelson, *The Design of Advertising*, 296.

Agency Participants

Creative director (CD): The creative director manages the creative process in an agency for several different clients. Creative directors typically come from the art or copywriting side of the business. The main role of the CD is to oversee the creative product of an agency across all clients.

Art director (AD): The art director and the copywriter work together to develop the concept for a commercial. The AD either oversees the production of the television storyboard or actually constructs the storyboards. In addition, the AD works with the director of the commercial to develop the overall look of the spot.

Copywriter: The copywriter is responsible for the words and phrases used in an ad. In television and radio advertising, these words and phrases appear as a script from which the director, creative director, and art director work during the production process. Together with the AD, the copywriter also makes recommendations on choice of director, casting, and editing facility.

Account executive (AE): The account executive acts as a liaison between the creative team and the client. The AE has the responsibility for coordinating scheduling, budgeting, and the various approvals needed during the production process. The AE can be quite valuable in helping the advertiser understand the various aspects of the production process. Account executives rarely have direct input into either the creative or technical execution of an ad.

Executive producer: The executive producer in an agency is in charge of many line producers, who manage the production at the production site. Executive producers help manage the production bid process. They also assign the appropriate producers to particular production jobs.

Producer: The producer supervises and coordinates all the activities related to a broadcast production. Producers screen director reels, send out production bid forms, review bids, and recommend the production house to be used. The producer also participates in choosing locations, sets, and talent. Normally, the producer will be on the set throughout the production and in the editing room during postproduction, representing agency and client interests.

Production Company Participants

Director: The director is in charge of the filming or taping of a broadcast advertising production. From a creative standpoint, the director is the visionary who brings the copy strategy to life on film or tape. The director also manages the actors, actresses, musicians, and announcers used in an ad to ensure that their performances contribute to the creative strategy being pursued. Finally, the director manages and coordinates the activities of technical staff. Camera operators, sound and lighting technicians, and special effects experts get their assignments from the director.

Producer: The production company also has a producer present, who manages the production at the site. This producer is in charge of the production crew and sets up each shoot. The position of cameras and readiness of production personnel are the responsibility of this producer.

Production manager: The production manager is on the set of a shoot, providing all the ancillary services needed to ensure a successful production. These range from making sure that food service is available on the set to providing dressing rooms and fax, phone, and photocopy services. The production manager typically has a production assistant (PA) to help take care of details.

Camera department: Another critical part of the production team is the camera department. This group includes the director of photography, camera operator, and assistant camera operator. This group ensures that the lighting, angles, and movement are carried out according to the plan and the director's specification.

Art department: The art department that accompanies the production company includes the art director and other personnel responsible for creating the set. This group designs the set, builds background or stunt structures, and provides props.

Editors: Editors enter the production process at the postproduction stage. It is their job, with direction from the art director, creative director, producer, or director, to create the finished advertisement. Editors typically work for independent postproduction houses and use highly specialized equipment to cut and join frames of film or audiotape together to create the finished version of a television or radio advertisement. Editors also synchronize the audio track with visual images in television advertisements and perform the transfer and duplication processes to prepare a commercial for shipping to the media.

EXHIBIT 13.32

The creative team for television advertising production.

represent good advice. Again, truly great creative work has no doubt violated some or all of these conventions.

- *Use an attention-getting and relevant opening.* The first few seconds of a television commercial are crucial. A receiver can make a split-second assessment of the relevance and interest a message holds. An ad can either turn a receiver off or grab his or her attention for the balance of the commercial with the opening. Remember, remote controls and DVRs are ubiquitous. It is getting so incredibly easy to avoid commercials that you, as an advertiser, must have a good hook to suck viewers in. Ads just don't get much time to develop. Of course, there is the belief that "slower" ads (ads that take time to develop) don't wear out as quickly as the quick hit-and-run ads. So, if you have a huge (almost inexhaustible) supply of money, an ad that

"Grace" :30
(A very manly-looking mother, Man Mom, sits at a table with her two grown-up sons. There's a bag of Cheddar Cheese Pretzel Combos on the table. One of the sons reaches for the Combos)
Man Mom: Ahem.
(The son quickly retracts his arm)
Son: Sorry, mom.
(All three join hands to say grace)
Man Mom: We thank you for this bounty of pretzels filled with creamy-tasting cheddar cheese that we're about to receive. And please, please let Dallas cover the spread this weekend.
(The son opens the bag of Combos, takes some and then passes the bag to Man Mom. Cut to Combos end treatment)
Anncr. (VO): Combos. What your mom would feed you if your mom were a man.

"Trade" :45
(Open on a guy holding a bag of Skittles. His friend is holding a rabbit that is singing in an operatic voice)
Rabbit: Yaaaaaa yaaaaaa yaaaaaaaaaaaaa....
(The friend trades the rabbit for the guy's Skittles. Cut to the guy at home. The rabbit is singing loudly)
Rabbit: Yaaaaaa yaaaaaa yaaaaaaaaaaaaa....
(Realizing he made a bad trade, the guy runs through the rain with the singing rabbit to his friend's house only to watch him through the window enjoying the Skittles)
Rabbit: Yaaaaaa yaaaaaa yaaaaaaaaaaaaa....
(The rabbit bites the guy's hand, and runs away)
Rabbit: Yaaaaaa yaaaaaa yaaaaaaaaaaaaa....
Card/AVO: Treasure the rainbow. Taste the rainbow.

EXHIBIT 13.33

If the first seconds of this ad draw you in, there's a pretty good chance you'll stick around for the slogan at the end. "Combos. What your mom would feed you if your mom were a man."

EXHIBIT 13.34

Even the opera-singing rabbit doesn't need words in this spot for Skittles.

"builds" might be best. If you don't, go for the quick hook. In Exhibit 13.33, the TV spot opens with a shot of "ManMom" sitting at a table with two young men and a bag of Combos. It's hard to not wonder what's going to come next.

- *Emphasize the visual.* The video capability of television should be highlighted in every production effort. To some degree, this emphasis is dependent on the creative concept, but the visual should carry the selling message even if the audio portion is ignored by the receiver. In Exhibit 13.34, Skittles tells its story with a minimum of words. Exhibit 13.35 shows one of the most famous political ads of all time, an ad that helped cement Lyndon Johnson's win over Barry Goldwater in 1964 by painting Goldwater as a near madman who might get us into a nuclear war.

- *Coordinate the audio with the visual.* The images and copy of a television commercial must reinforce each other. Divergence between the audio and visual portions

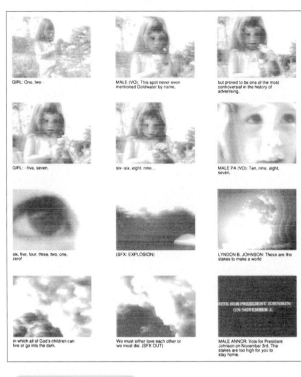

GIRL: One, two—

MALE (VO): This spot never even mentioned Goldwater by name,

but proved to be one of the most controversial in the history of advertising.

GIRL: —five, seven,

six—six, eight, nine...

MALE PA (VO): Ten, nine, eight, seven,

six, five, four, three, two, one, zero!

(SFX: EXPLOSION)

LYNDON B. JOHNSON: These are the stakes to make a world

in which all of God's children can live or go into the dark.

We must either love each other or we must die. (SFX OUT)

MALE ANNCR: Vote for President Johnson on November 3rd. The stakes are too high for you to stay home.

EXHIBIT 13.35

The most famous political ad of all time (Doyle Dane Bernbach).

(single and part of series)

"Donut" :30

(OPEN ON A CLOSE-UP OF BEER, DONUTS AND A MAN'S DIRTY HANDS ON TABLE. HE PICKS UP A DONUT)

ANNCR. (VO):   Sometimes a man gets too hungry to clean his hands properly.

(CUT TO CLOSE-UP OF DONUTS)

ANNCR. (VO):   The powdered sugar on this donut puts a semi-protective barrier between your fingerprint and your nutrition.

(CUT TO A MAN HOLDING BEER AND EATING DONUTS)

ANNCR. (VO):   But even if some grease does get on that donut, that's just flavor to a High Life man.

TITLE CARD: (FADE UP) Miller Time logo.

ART DIRECTOR: Jeff Williams
WRITER: Jeff Kling
CREATIVE DIRECTOR: Susan Hoffman
PRODUCER: Jeff Selis
DIRECTOR: Errol Morris
PRODUCTION COMPANY: @radical.media
AD AGENCY: Wieden & Kennedy (Portland, OR)
CLIENT: Miller Brewing Company

EXHIBIT 13.36

Here's to the High Life!

(SFX: QUIET TICKING OF CLOCK)
(SFX: WRESTLING ON TV)
GRANDPA: Ohhhhhh!
(SFX: THUD)
BABY: Wahhhhhhhhhh!
GRANDPA: Don't worry, honey. Mom and Dad will be right back.
GRANDPA: Pretty baby!
BABY: Wahhhhhhhhhh!
(SFX: SUDDEN QUIET)
(SFX: CLOCK TICKING)
ANNCR: HP photo-quality printers. Good enough to fool almost anyone.
SUPER: BUILT BY ENGINEERS. USED BY NORMAL PEOPLE.

EXHIBIT 13.37

Humor meets demonstration. http://www.hp.com

---

of an ad only serves to confuse and distract the viewer. In Exhibit 13.36, Miller High Life uses both words and visuals to create the world of a High Life man.

- ***Persuade as well as entertain.*** It is tempting to produce a beautifully creative television advertisement rather than a beautifully effective television advertisement. The vast potential of film lures the creative urge in all the production participants. Creating an entertaining commercial is an inherently praiseworthy goal *except* when the entertainment value of the commercial completely overwhelms its persuasive impact. In Exhibit 13.37, Hewlett-Packard sells its photo-quality printers with a humorous yet persuasive demonstration of their reproductive powers.

- ***Show the product.*** Unless a commercial is using intrigue and mystery surrounding the product, the product should be highlighted in the ad. Close-ups and shots of the brand in action help receivers recall the brand and its appearance.

The Production Process in Television Advertising.

The television production process can best be understood by identifying the activities that take place before, during, and after the actual production of an ad. These stages are referred to as preproduction, production, and postproduction. (Hope we're not getting too technical.) By breaking the process down into this sequence, we can appreciate both the technical and the strategic aspects of each stage.

Preproduction. The **preproduction** stage is that part of the television production process in which the advertiser and the advertising agency carefully work out the precise details of how the creative planning behind an ad can best be brought to life with the opportunities offered by television. Exhibit 13.38 shows the sequence of six events in the preproduction stage.

Storyboard and Script Approval. As Exhibit 13.38 shows, the preproduction stage begins with storyboard and script approval. A **storyboard** is a shot-by-shot sketch depicting, in sequence, the visual scenes and copy that will be used in an advertisement. A **script** is the written version of an ad; it specifies the coordination of the copy elements with the video scenes. The script is used by the producer and director to set the location and content of scenes, by the casting department to choose actors and actresses, and by the producer in budgeting and scheduling the shoot. Exhibit 13.39 is part of a storyboard from the Miller Lite "Can Your Beer Do This?" campaign, and Exhibit 13.40 shows the related script. This particular spot was entitled "Ski Jump" and involved rigging a dummy to a recliner and launching the chair and the dummy from a 60-meter ski jump.

The art director and copywriter are significantly involved at this stage of production. It is important that the producer has discussed the storyboard and script with the creative team and fully understands the creative concept and objectives for the advertisement before production begins. Since it is the producer's responsibility to solicit bids for the project from production houses, the producer must be able to fully explain to bidders the requirements of the job so that cost estimates are as accurate as possible.

Budget Approval. Once there is agreement on the scope and intent of the production as depicted in the storyboard and script, the advertiser must give budget approval. The producer needs to work carefully with the creative team and the advertiser to estimate the approximate cost of the shoot, including production staging, location costs, actors, technical requirements, staffing, and a multitude of other considerations. It is essential that these discussions be as detailed and comprehensive as possible, because it is from this budget discussion that the producer will evaluate candidates for the directing role and solicit bids from production houses to handle the job.

Assessment of Directors, Editorial Houses, Music Suppliers. A producer has dozens (if not hundreds) of directors, postproduction editorial houses, and music suppliers from which to choose. An assessment of those well-suited to the task must take place early in the preproduction process. The combination of the creative talents of ad agencies and production houses can produce creative, eye-catching ads. Directors of television commercials, like directors of feature films, develop specializations and reputations. Some directors are known for their work with action or special effects. Others are more highly

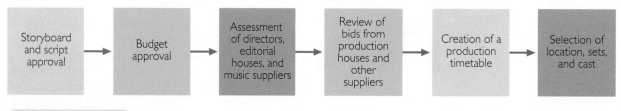

EXHIBIT 13.38

Sequence of events in the preproduction stage of television advertising.

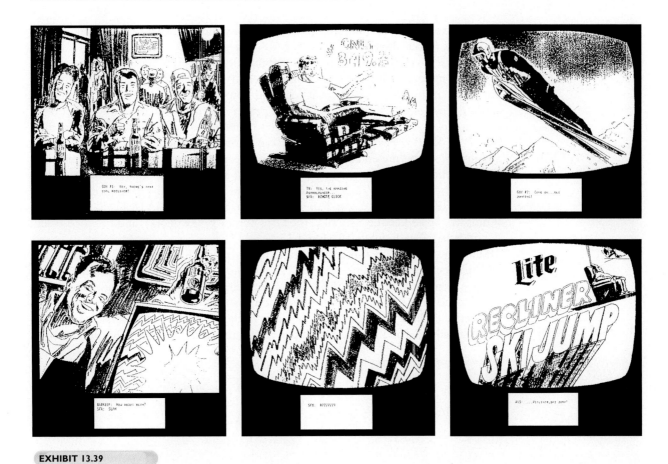

EXHIBIT 13.39

How does this storyboard for a Miller Lite Beer ad save the advertiser time and money during the television production process?

EXHIBIT 13.40

This is the script for the Miller Lite "Can Your Beer Do This?" ad. The producer and director use the script to set locations and the content of scenes and for budgeting and scheduling. The script is also used to choose actors and actresses.

skilled in working with children, animals, outdoor settings, or shots of beverages flowing into a glass ("pour shots").

The director of an advertisement is responsible for interpreting the storyboard and script and managing the talent to bring the creative concept to life. A director specifies the precise nature of a scene, how it is lit, and how it is filmed. In this way, the director acts as the eye of the camera. Choosing the proper director is crucial to the execution of a commercial. Aside from the fact that a good director commands a fee anywhere from $8,000 to $25,000 per day, the director can have a tremendous effect on the quality and impact of the presentation. An excellent creative concept can be undermined by poor direction. The agency creative team should be intimately involved in the choice of directors. Among the now-famous feature film directors who have made television commercials are Ridley Scott (Apple), John Frankenheimer (AT&T), Woody Allen (Campari), Spike Lee (Levi's, Nike, the Gap, Barney's New York), and Federico Fellini (Coop Italia). (See Exhibits 13.41 and 13.42.)

Similarly, editorial houses (and their editors) and music suppliers (and musicians) have particular expertise and reputations. The producer, the director, and the agency creative team actively review the work of the editorial suppliers and music houses that are particularly well suited to the production. In most cases, geographic proximity to the agency facilities is important; as members of the agency team try to maintain a tight schedule, editorial and music services that are nearby facilitate the timely completion of

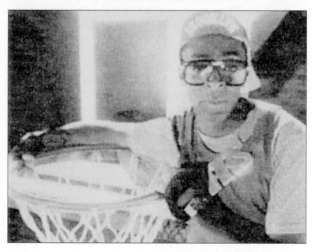

EXHIBITS 13.41 AND 13.42

Examples of famous feature film directors who have made television commercials are Ridley Scott, director of Apple's "1984" campaign and the 1982 movie Blade Runner, and Spike Lee, who directed 1989's Do the Right Thing as well as the "Morris Blackman" Nike ads. http://www.apple.com *and* http://www.nike.com

Personnel	Cost
Director	$8,000–25,000/day
Director of photography	3,000/day
Producer	800/day
Production assistant	200/day
Camera operator	600/day
Unit manager	450/day
Equipment	
Production van (including camera, lighting kit, microphones, monitoring equipment)	$2,500–4,000/day
Camera	750–1,000/day
Grip truck with lighting equipment and driver	400–500/day
Telescript with operator	600–700/day
Online editing with editor and assistant editor	250–400/hour

an ad. Because of this need, editorial and music suppliers have tended to cluster near agencies in Chicago, New York, and Los Angeles.

Review of Bids from Production Houses and Other Suppliers. Production houses and other suppliers, such as lighting specialists, represent a collection of specialized talent and also provide needed equipment for ad preparation. The expertise in production houses relates to the technical aspects of filming a commercial. Producers, production managers, sound and art specialists, camera operators, and others are part of a production house team. The agency sends a bid package to several production houses. The package contains all the details of the commercial to be produced and includes a description of the production requirements and a timetable for the production. An accurate timetable is essential because many production personnel work on an hourly or daily compensation rate.

To give you some idea of the cost of the technical personnel and equipment available from production houses, Exhibit 13.43 lists some key production house personnel who would participate in shooting a commercial, and the typical daily rates (for a 10-hour day) for such personnel and related equipment. Also listed are the rental costs of various pieces of equipment. These costs vary from market to market, but it is obvious why production expenses can run into the hundreds of thousands of dollars. The costs listed in the exhibit represent only the daily rates for production time or postproduction work. In addition to these costs are overtime costs, travel, and lodging (if an overnight stay is necessary).

Most agencies send out a bid package on a form developed by the agency. An example of such a bid form is provided in Exhibit 13.44. By using a standardized form, an agency can make direct comparisons between production house bids. A similar form can be used to solicit bids from other suppliers providing editorial or music services. The producer reviews each of the bids and revises them if necessary. From the production house bids *and* the agency's estimate of its own costs associated with production (travel, expenses, editorial services, music, on-camera talent, and agency markups), a production cost estimate is prepared for advertiser review and approval. Once the advertiser has approved the estimate, one of the production houses is awarded the job. The lowest production bid is not always the one chosen. Aside from cost, there are creative and technical considerations. A hot director costs more than last year's model. The agency's evaluation of the reliability of a production house also enters into the decision.

Creation of a Production Timetable. In conjunction with the stages of preproduction just discussed, the producer will be working on a **production timetable**. This timetable projects a realistic schedule for all the preproduction, production, and postproduction activities. To stay on budget and complete the production in time to ship the final advertisement to television stations for airing, an accurate and realistic timetable is essential. A timetable must allow a reasonable amount of time to complete all production tasks in a quality manner. Exhibit 13.45 is a timetable for a national 30-second spot, using location shooting.

Realize that a reasonable timetable is rarely achieved. Advertisers often request (or demand) that an agency provide a finished spot (or even several spots) in times as short as four or five weeks. Because of competitive pressures or corporate urgency for change, production timetables are compromised. Advertisers have to accept the reality that violating a reasonable timetable can dramatically increase costs and puts undue pressure on the creative process—no matter what the reason for the urgency. In fact, a creative director at one agency often told clients that they could pick any two selections from the following list for their television commercials: good, fast, and reasonably priced.[10]

Selection of Location, Sets, and Cast. Once a bid has been approved and accepted, both the production house and the agency production team begin to search for appropriate, affordable locations if the commercial is to be shot outside a studio setting. Studio production warrants the design and construction of the sets to be used.

A delicate stage in preproduction is casting. While not every ad uses actors and actresses, when an ad calls for individuals to perform roles, casting is crucial. Every individual appearing in an ad is, in a very real sense, a representative of the advertiser. This is another reason why the agency creative team stays involved. Actors and actresses help set the mood and tone for an ad and affect the image of the brand. The successful execution of various message strategies depends on proper casting. For instance, a slice-of-life message requires actors and actresses with whom the target audience can readily identify. Testimonial message tactics require a search for particular types of people, either celebrities or common folks, who will attract attention and be credible to the

EXHIBIT 13.45

Example of a reasonable timetable for shooting a 30-second television advertisement.

Activity	Time
Assess directors/editorial houses/music suppliers	1 week
Solicit bids from production houses/other suppliers	1 week
Review bids, award jobs to suppliers, submit production estimate to advertiser	1 week
Begin preproduction (location, sets, casting)	1 to 2 weeks
Final preparation and shooting	1 to 2 weeks
Edit film	1 week
Agency/advertiser review of rough-cut film	1 week
Postproduction (final editing, voice mix, record music, special effects, etc.) and transfer of film to video; ship to media	2 weeks
Transfer film to videotape; ship to stations	1 week
Total	10 to 12 weeks

10.   Peter Sheldon, former creative director and head of creative sequences, University of Illinois Advertising Department.

DOING IT RIGHT

Casting Call: A Big Name Might Not Be the Right Name

Tiger Woods was the face of Buick for eight years. And for eight years, consciously or not, General Motors found itself having to convince viewers that the young golf phenomenon at the center of its long-running television campaign really wanted to drive a Buick.

The average Buick buyer is 63. Tiger Woods was still just 31 when, in June 2007, General Motors said it would begin using Woods primarily to pitch its OnStar service and let Buick's long tradition as a classic, premium American car speak for itself.

Buick surely gained visibility by casting a sports figure as well known and popular as Woods as its primary spokesperson. But in spite of the millions spent on the campaign—a five-year contract through 2009 was reportedly worth $40 million—the century-old car brand continued to steadily lose market share. For advertisers eyeing celebrity talent, a basic question has to be: Is it worth it?

"There was just no believability that Tiger was dying to drive a Buick," said Laura Ries, president of Ries & Ries, an Atlanta-based marketing strategy firm. "The brand personalities just didn't go together, like oil and water. Buick is an older person's car. Tiger is very young, very cool, and at the top of his game. You can imagine him driving a Bentley or a Mercedes or a Lexus."

For its part, Buick maintained that Woods was an effective spokesperson and a contented GM customer. Even as their costly relationship shifted, Buick officials said Woods had recently taken delivery of a fully loaded Enclave CXL.

Sources: Nick Bunkley, "G.M. To Alter Tiger Woods' Role in Its Ads," **New York Times**, June 22, 2007, C4; Leslie J. Allen, "Buick's Plan: Sell Luxury, Not Tiger," **Automotive News**, June 25, 2007, p. 47.

audience. The point to remember is that successfully casting a television commercial depends on much more than simply picking people with good acting abilities. Individuals must be matched to the personality of the brand, the nature of the audience, and the scene depicted in the ad. As suggested in the Doing It Right box, even Tiger Woods isn't always the perfect choice.

Production. The **production stage** of the process, or the **shoot**, is where the storyboard and script come to life and are filmed. The actual production of the spot may also include some final preparations before the shoot begins. The most common final preparation activities are lighting checks and rehearsals. An entire day may be devoted to *prelight*, which involves setting up lighting or identifying times for the best natural lighting to ensure that the shooting day runs smoothly. Similarly, the director may want to work with the on-camera talent along with the camera operators to practice the positioning and movement planned for the ad. This work, known as *blocking*, can save a lot of time on a shoot day, when many more costly personnel are on the set.

Lighting, blocking, and other special factors are typically specified by the director in the script. Exhibit 13.46 on the next page is a list of common directorial specifications that show up in a script and are used by a director to manage the audio and visual components of a commercial shoot.

Shoot days are the culmination of an enormous amount of effort beginning all the way back at the development of the copy platform. They are the execution of all the well-laid plans by the advertiser and agency personnel. The set on a shoot day is a world all its own. For the uninformed, it can appear to be little more than high-energy chaos, or a lot of nothing going on between camera setups. For the professionals involved, however, a shoot has its own tempo and direction, including a whole lot of nothing going on.

Production activities during a shoot require the highest level of professionalism and expertise. A successful shoot depends on the effective management of a large number of diverse individuals—creative performers, highly trained technicians, and skilled laborers. Logistical and technical problems always arise, not to mention the ever-present threat of a random event (a thunderstorm or intrusive noise) that disrupts filming and tries everyone's patience. There is a degree of tension and spontaneity on the set that is a necessary part of the creative process but must be kept at a manageable level. Much of the tension stems from trying to execute the various tasks of production correctly and at the proper time.

Another dimension to this tension, however, has to do with expense. As pointed out earlier, most directors, technicians, and talent are paid a daily rate plus overtime after 10 hours. Daily shooting expenses, including director's fees, can run $80,000 to $120,000 for just an average production, so the agency and advertiser, understandably, want the shoot to run as smoothly and quickly as possible.

There is the real problem of not rushing creativity, however, and advertisers often have to learn to accept the pace of production. For example, a well-known director made a

Script Specification	Meaning
CU	Close-up.
ECU	Extreme close-up.
MS	Medium shot.
LS	Long shot.
Zoom	Movement in or out on subject with camera fixed.
Dolly	Movement in or out on subject moving the camera (generally slower than a zoom).
Pan	Camera scanning right or left from stationary position.
Truck	Camera *moving* right or left, creating a different visual angle.
Tilt	Camera panning vertically.
Cut	Abrupt movement from one scene to another.
Dissolve	Smoother transition from one scene to another, compared to a cut.
Wipe	Horizontal or vertical removal of one image to replace it with a new image (inserted vertically or horizontally).
Split screen	Two or more independent video sources occupying the screen.
Skip frame	Replacement of one image with another through pulsating (frame insertion of) the second image into the first. Used for dramatic transitions.
Key insert, matte, chromakey	Insertion of one image onto another background. Often used to impose product over the scene taking place in the commercial.
Super title	Lettering superimposed over visual. Often used to emphasize a major selling point or to display disclaimers/product warnings.
SFX	Sound effects.
VO	Introducing a voice over the visual.
ANN	Announcer entering the commercial.
Music under	Music playing in the background.
Music down and out	Music fading out of commercial.
Music up and out	Music volume ascending and abruptly ending.

EXHIBIT 13.46

Instructions commonly appearing in television commercial scripts.

Honda commercial in South Florida, where he shot film for only one hour per day—a half-hour in the morning and a half-hour at twilight. His explanation? "From experience you learn that cars look flat and unattractive in direct light, so you have to catch the shot when the angle [of the sun] is just right."[11] Despite the fact that the cameras were rolling only an hour a day, the $9,000-per-hour cost for the production crew was charged all day for each day of shooting. Advertisers have to accept, on occasion, that the television advertising production process is not like an assembly line production process. Sweating the details to achieve just the right look can provoke controversy—and often does.

The Cost of Television Production. Coordinating and taking advantage of the skills offered by creative talent is a big challenge for advertisers. The average 30-second television commercial prepared by a national advertiser can run up production charges from $100,000 to $500,000 and even more if special effects or celebrities are used in the spot.[12] As with most things, these costs have continued to rise, partly because of the escalating cost of creative talent, such as directors and editors. Other aspects of the cost have to do with more and better equipment being used at all stages

---

11.　Jeffrey A. Trachtenberg, "Where the Money Goes," *Forbes*, September 21, 1987, 180.
12.　Joe Mandese, "Study Shows Cost of TV Spots," *Advertising Age*, August 1, 1994, 32.

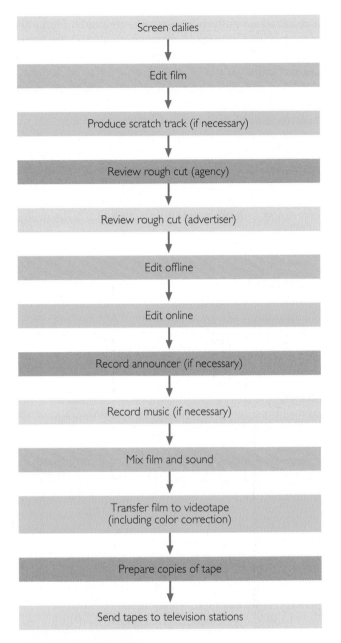

EXHIBIT 13.47

Sequence of events in television commercial postproduction.

of the production process, and longer shooting schedules to ensure advertiser satisfaction.

The average expense for a 30-second spot tends to be higher for commercials in highly competitive consumer markets, such as beer, soft drinks, autos, and banking, where image campaigns (which require high-quality production) are commonly used. Conversely, average production costs tend to be lower for advertisements in which functional features or shots of the product often dominate the spot, as with household cleansers and office equipment.

The high and rising cost of television production has created some tensions between advertisers and their ad agencies. Most agencies and production companies respond by saying that advertisers are demanding to stand out from the clutter, and to do so requires complex concepts and high-priced talent. Conversely, when an advertiser is not so image conscious, ways can be found to stand out without spending huge dollar amounts.

The important issue in the preparation of all television advertising, regardless of cost, is that the production process has direct and significant effects on the communication impact of a finished advertisement. A well-conceived copy strategy can fall flat if the execution at the point of production is poor. One rule of thumb is to ask for 10 percent of the planned media buy for production. They may not give it to you, but it's nice if you can get it, unless they are planning a very small media buy.

Postproduction. Once filming is completed, several postproduction activities are required before the commercial is ready for airing. At this point, a host of additional professional talent enters the process. Film editors, audio technicians, voice-over specialists, and musicians may be contracted. Exhibit 13.47 shows the sequence of events in the postproduction phase.

The first step in postproduction is review of the **dailies**—scenes shot during the previous day's production. Such screening may result in reshooting certain segments of the ad. Once dailies are acceptable to the agency, the editing process begins. **Editing** involves piecing together various scenes or shots of scenes, called *takes*, to bring about the desired visual effect. Most editing involves making decisions about takes shot at different angles, or subtle differences in the performance of the talent. If music is to be included, it will be prepared at this point using a **scratch track**, which is a rough approximation of the musical score using only a piano and vocalists.

A rough cut of the commercial is then prepared by loading the video dailies into an *Avid computer* to digitize and timecode the tape. The **rough cut** is an assembly of the best scenes from the shoot edited together using the quick and precise access afforded by digital technology. Using the offline Avid computer on the digitized rough cut, various technical aspects of the look of a commercial can be refined—color alterations and background images, for example. The final editing of the advertisement—which includes repositioning of elements, correcting final color, and adding fades, titles, blowups, dissolves, final audio, and special effects—is done with online equipment in specially-equipped facilities. **Online editing** involves transferring the finalized rough cut onto one-inch videotape, which is of on-air quality suitable for media transmission.

The personnel and equipment required for postproduction tasks are costly. Film editors charge about $150 to $200 per hour, and an editing assistant is about $50 per hour. An offline computer costs about $100 per hour. When online editing begins, the cost goes up, with online rooms running about $700 per hour. The reason for the dramatic difference in cost between offline editing and online editing is that offline edits are done on a single machine to produce a rough, working version of an ad. The online room typically includes many specialized machines for all the final effects desired in the ad. Additionally, a mixing room for voice and music costs about $400 per day.

In all, it is easy to see why filmed television commercials are so costly. Scores of people with specialized skills and a large number of separate tasks are included in the process. The procedures also reflect the complexity of the process. Aside from the mechanics of production, a constant vigil must be kept over the creative concept of the advertisement. Despite the complexities, the advertising industry continues to turn out high-quality television commercials on a timely basis.

⑦ Production Options in Television Advertising. Several production options are available to an advertiser in preparing a television commercial. Eighty percent of all television commercials prepared by national advertisers use film as the medium for production. The previous discussion of production procedures, in fact, described the production process for a filmed advertisement. **Film** (typically 35mm) is the most versatile medium and produces the highest-quality visual impression. It is, however, the most expensive medium for production and is also the most time consuming.

A less expensive option is **videotape**. Videotape is not as popular among directors or advertisers for a variety of reasons. Tape has far fewer lines of resolution, and some say videotape results in a flatter image than film. Its visual impressions are starker and have less depth and less color intensity. While this can sometimes add to the realism of a commercial, it can also detract from the appearance of the product and the people in the ad. New **digital video (DV)** formats are replacing traditional videotape, and even challenging film in some productions due to DV's much lower cost and high-quality look. It doesn't look like film exactly, but it sure looks better than videotape.

There is always the choice of live television commercial production. **Live production** can result in realism and the capturing of spontaneous reactions and events that couldn't possibly be recreated in a rehearsed scene. It is clear, however, that the loss of control in live settings threatens the carefully worked-out objectives for a commercial. On occasion, local retailers (such as auto dealers) use live commercials to execute direct response message strategies. Such a technique can capture the urgency of an appeal.

Two techniques that do not neatly fit the production process described earlier are animation and stills. **Animation** (and the variation known as Claymation) is the use of drawn figures and scenes (such as cartoons) to produce a commercial. Keebler cookie and California Raisin commercials use characters created by animators and Claymation artists. Animated characters, such as Tony the Tiger, are frequently incorporated into filmed commercials for added emphasis. A newer form of animation uses computer-generated images. Several firms, such as TRW, have developed commercials totally through the use of computers. The graphics capabilities of giant-capacity computers make futuristic, eye-catching animation ads an attractive alternative. And the actors always show up on time.

Still production is a technique whereby a series of photographs or slides is filmed and edited so that the resulting ad appears to have movement and action. Through the use of pans, zooms, and dissolves with the camera, still photographs can be used to produce an interesting yet low-cost finished advertisement.

The production option chosen should always be justified on both a creative and a cost basis. The dominance of filmed commercials is explainable by the level of quality of the finished ad and the versatility afforded by the technique. A local retailer or social service organization may not need or may not be able to afford the quality of film. In cases where quality is less significant or costs are primary, other production techniques are used.

SUMMARY

 Identify the basic purposes, components, and formats of print ad illustrations.

With few exceptions, illustrations are critical to the effectiveness of print ads. Specifically, illustrations can serve to attract attention, make the brand heroic, communicate product features or benefits, create a mood and enhance brand image, stimulate reading of the body copy, or create the desired social context for the brand. The overall impact of an illustration is determined in part by its most basic components: size, use of color, and the medium used to create the illustration. Another critical aspect of the illustration's effectiveness has to do with the format chosen for the product in the illustration. Obviously, a print ad cannot work if the consumer doesn't easily identify the product or service being advertised.

 Describe the principles and components that help ensure the effective design of print ads.

In print ad design, all the verbal and visual components of an ad are arranged for maximum impact and appeal. Several principles can be followed as a basis for a compelling design. These principles feature issues such as balance, proportion, order, unity, and emphasis. The first component of an effective design is focus—drawing the reader's attention to specific areas of the ad. The second component is movement and direction—directing the reader's eye movement through the ad. The third component is clarity and simplicity—avoiding a complex and chaotic look that will deter most consumers.

 Detail the stages that art directors follow in developing the layout of a print ad.

The layout is the physical manifestation of all this design planning. An art director uses various forms of layouts to bring a print ad to life. There are several predictable stages in the evolution of a layout. The art director starts with a hand-drawn thumbnail, proceeds to the digitized rough layout, and continues with a tight comp that represents the look of the final ad. With each stage, the layout becomes more concrete and more like the final form of the advertisement. The last stage, the mechanical, is the form the ad takes as it goes to final production.

 Discuss the activities and decisions involved in the final production of print ads.

Timing is critical to advertising effectiveness: Advertisers must have a keen understanding of production cycles to have an ad in the consumer's hands at just the right time. In addition, there are many possible means for

actually printing an ad. These range from letterpress to screen printing to computer print production. As with many aspects of modern life, the computer has had a dramatic impact on print ad preparation and production. Before a print ad can reach its audience, a host of small but important decisions need to be made about the type styles and sizes that will best serve the campaign's purposes.

 Identify the various players who must function as a team to produce television ads.

The complexity of ad production for television is unrivaled and thus demands the input of a variety of functional specialists. From the ad agency come familiar players such as the art director, copywriter, and account executive. Then there are a host of individuals who have special skills in various aspects of production for this medium. These include directors, producers, production managers, and camera crews. Editors will also be needed to bring all the raw material together into a finished commercial. Organizational and team-management skills are essential to make all these people and pieces work together.

 Discuss the specific stages and costs involved in producing television ads.

The intricate process of TV ad production can be broken into three major stages: preproduction, production, and postproduction. In the preproduction stage, scripts and storyboards are prepared, budgets are set, production houses are engaged, and a timetable is formulated. Production includes all those activities involved in the actual filming of the ad. The shoot is a high-stress activity that usually carries a high price tag. The raw materials from the shoot are mixed and refined in the postproduction stage. Today's editors work almost exclusively with computers to create the final product—a finished television ad. If all this sounds expensive, it is!

 Describe the major formatting options for television ad production.

Film is the preferred option for most TV ads because of the high-quality visual impression it provides. Videotape suffers on the quality issue, and live television is not practical in most cases. Animation is probably the second most popular formatting option. With continuing improvements in computer graphics, computer-generated images may one day become a preferred source of material for TV ad production. Still production can be an economical means to bring a message to television.

KEY TERMS

illustration	mechanical	storyboard
medium	closing date	script (television ad)
illustration format	letterpress	production timetable
design	offset lithography	production stage, or shoot
principles of design	gravure	dailies
balance	flexography	editing
formal balance	electronic, laser, and inkjet printing	scratch track
informal balance	type font	rough cut
border	blackletter	online editing
white space	roman	film
axis	script (typeface)	videotape
three-point layout structure	serif	digital video (DV)
parallel layout structure	sans serif	live production
layout	miscellaneous	animation
thumbnails	point	still production
rough layout	picas	
comp	preproduction	

QUESTIONS

1. Is there anyone out there who would rather watch black-and-white television than color? If not, why would any advertiser choose to run a black-and-white print ad in a medium that supports color? Can you think of a situation where a black-and-white ad might be more effective than a color ad?

2. Identify the strategic roles that illustration plays in increasing the effectiveness of a print advertisement from a communications and marketing perspective.

3. This chapter reviewed five basic principles for print ad design: balance, proportion, order, unity, and emphasis. Give an example of how each of these principles might be employed to enhance the selling message of a print ad.

4. Why is it appropriate to think of print as a static medium? Given print's static nature, explain how movement and direction can be relevant concepts to the layout of a print ad.

5. For an art director who has reached the mechanicals stage of the ad layout process, explain the appeal of computer-aided design versus the old-fashioned paste-up approach.

6. Explain the role of the production company in the evolution of a television commercial. As part of this explanation, be certain you have identified each of the unique skills and specialties that people in the production company bring to the ad development process.

7. Compare and contrast the creative guidelines for TV offered in this chapter with those offered for print ads in the previous chapter. Based on this analysis, what conclusions would you offer about the keys to effective communication in these two media?

8. Identify the six steps involved in the preproduction of a television ad and describe the issues that an art director must attend to at each step if his or her goals for the ad are to be achieved.

9. In television ad production, shoot days are notoriously pressure-packed. What factors contribute to the tension and excitement that surrounds an ad shoot?

10. Review the formatting options that an art director can choose from when conceiving a television ad. Discuss the advantages of each option and describe the situation for which each is best suited.

EXPERIENTIAL EXERCISES

1.   Using six print ads from popular magazines, assess whether the primary illustration accomplishes the strategic goals discussed in the chapter and whether the ad follows the principles of design. If a particular ad fails to accomplish the primary illustration goals or to follow general design principles, do you still find it to be effective? Why?

2.   Many advertisers include their Web address at the end of television commercials, encouraging viewers to visit the site. One highly visible example of this practice is the television campaign for Geico. For this exercise, evaluate one of the insurer's television spots and determine whether the ad follows the general creative principles for television advertising discussed in the chapter. Next, visit the company's home page, http://www .geico.com, and evaluate the site based on the principles of illustration. Does the home page more closely

resemble a print advertisement, or does it share common features with the television campaign? How well does the company integrate its message across different media?

3.   Divide into small teams and imagine that you have been asked to develop a campaign for retail giant Wal-Mart that is intended to increase sales among recent college graduates. Your first assignment is to design a thumbnail and rough layout for a single print advertisement that could be presented to the client for evaluation.

4.   Working in the same teams, extend your Wal-Mart campaign to include a television spot. Create a script and rough storyboard that could be presented to the client. As you work on this second assignment, consider how the mood and social context created for the campaign's print advertisement should be extended to television.

Placing the Message in Conventional and "New" Media

Once again we pass into a new and totally different area of advertising and IBP, "Placing the Message in Conventional and 'New' Media." We are now at the point where reaching the target audience is the key issue.

Beyond the basic and formidable challenge of effectively choosing the right media to reach a target audience, contemporary advertisers and promotion professionals are demanding even more from the media placement decision: synergy and integration. Throughout the first three parts of the text, the issue of integrated brand communications has been raised whenever the opportunity existed to create coordinated communications. But nowhere is IBP more critical than at the media placement. Here, audiences may be exposed to brand messages through a wide range of different media, each with a unique quality and tone to the communication. The challenge is to ensure that if diverse communications media options are chosen for placing the message, there is still a "one-voice" quality to the overall communication program.

PART FOUR

Media Strategy and Planning for Advertising and IBP.

Maintaining integration is indeed a challenge in the contemporary media environment. Chapter 14, "Media Strategy and Planning for Advertising and IBP," begins with a discussion of the major changes that have altered and now define the contemporary media landscape. Next, the fundamentals of media planning are explained, followed by the details. We then tell it like it really is in the real world by discussing the "real deals" of media planning. Next, we discuss how the complex communications environment impacts the entire process, followed by particular attention to IBP's impact. We finish with a reminder of the value of traditional advertising and its continued prominence in the communications landscape.

14

Media Planning: Newspapers, Magazines, Television, and Radio.

Chapter 15, "Media Planning: Print, Television, and Radio," offers an analysis of the major media options available to advertisers. The vast majority of the creative effort—and money—is expended on print and broadcast advertising campaigns. Despite the many intriguing opportunities that new media options offer, print and broadcast media will likely form the foundation of most advertising campaigns for years to come. But we also raise the issue that these traditional media are turning to new, digital media opportunities as well. The chapter follows a sequence in which the advantages and disadvantages of each medium are discussed, followed by considerations of costs, buying procedures, and audience measurement techniques.

15

Media Planning: Advertising and IBP on the Internet.

The newest and perhaps greatest challenge for advertisers has recently presented itself—the Internet. Chapter 16, "Media Planning: Advertising and IBP on the Internet," describes this formidable technology. This chapter is key to understanding the contemporary advertising and IBP environment. Basic terminology and procedures are described, as well as who is using the Internet and for what purposes. Most of the discussion in this chapter focuses on two fundamental issues: the structure of the Internet and the potential of the Internet as an advertising and IBP media option. Through these discussions, we will come to a better understanding of how to use the Internet as part of an effective advertising and integrated brand promotion effort. We will consider a short history of the Internet, an overview of cyberspace, the different types of advertising that can be used, and some of the technical aspects of the process. We also discuss the peer-to-peer communications options that now present themselves, as well as the potential for "virtual worlds" as venues for advertising and IBP.

16

CHAPTER 14

After reading and thinking about this chapter, you will be able to do the following:

1

Describe the important changes that have altered the advertising and IBP media landscape, such as agency compensation, ROI demands, globalization, and multicultural media.

2

Describe the fundamentals of media planning.

3

Know the bottom line of IBP's impact on media planning.

4

Discuss the "real deals" in media planning.

5

Discuss the essentials of the contemporary media planning environment.

6

Discuss the value of traditional advertising.

WE THOUGHT OF CHANGING OUR NAME TO THE MUSEUM OF TELEVISION, RADIO, CABLE, SATELLITE, VIDCAST, PODCAST, BLOGS, VLOGS, CLIPS, AND MOBISODES, BUT THAT WOULDN'T FIT ON OUR BUSINESS CARDS.

Media isn't the only thing that's changing. The Museum of Television &
Radio is now officially **The Paley Center for Media**. Stay tuned to see
how we evolve as media transforms our world.

paleycenter.org

In 1967, Super Bowl I was simultaneously telecast on CBS and NBC. It reached about 41 percent of U.S. households (a 41 rating), or about 43 million people. A 30-second ad on Super Bowl I cost $42,000, or about $208,000 in 2003 dollars. In 2003, Super Bowl XXXVII also reached about 41 percent of U.S. households, now about 88 million people, but 30 seconds of advertising cost $2.1 million dollars—that's right, $2.1 million dollars for a 30-second ad that in 1967 cost (in current dollars) one-tenth that amount. (See Exhibit 14.1.) CBS asked $2.7 million for a 30-second ad on the 2008 Super Bowl. That means that the cost of network television Super Bowl advertising has risen more than tenfold since the late 1960s even though its total audience has gone up only twofold and its rating (41 percent of U.S. households) has not changed at all. It's not just the Super Bowl; television advertising has become very expensive. More than a few people have noticed and have taken their media money elsewhere. Advertisers who feel they need a truly mega-audience may continue to buy media on events like the Olympics. But at some point, one has to wonder how much is enough, figure skating or not. (See Exhibit 14.2.)

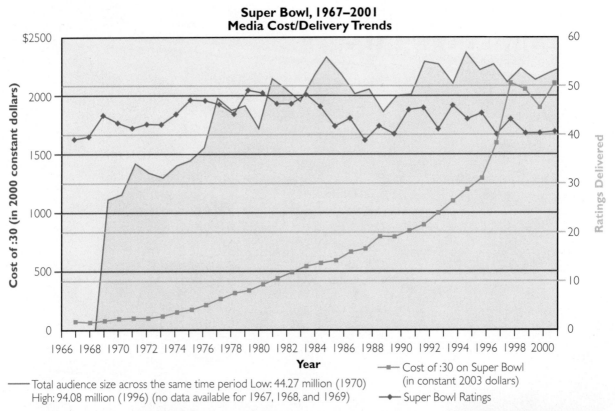

Super Bowl, 1967–2001
Media Cost/Delivery Trends

——— Total audience size across the same time period Low: 44.27 million (1970)
High: 94.08 million (1996) (no data available for 1967, 1968, and 1969)

■ Cost of :30 on Super Bowl (in constant 2003 dollars)

◆ Super Bowl Ratings

EXHIBIT 14.1

In 1967 the Super Bowl reached 41 percent of U.S. households. It still reaches about 41 percent of U.S. households. Now it just costs more than 10 times as much for a 30-second ad. TV advertising has become very expensive.

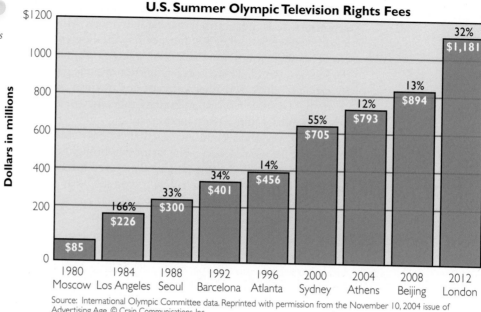

Source: International Olympic Committee data. Reprinted with permission from the November 10, 2004 issue of Advertising Age. © Crain Communications, Inc.

A few years ago a few people were saying, "Advertising is dead; long live new media." Hyperbole; advertising was not dead. Now, things have changed. A better metaphor is that advertising has merged, morphed, and meaningfully mingles with all sorts of other forms of brand communications, both new and not-new. And, by the way, advertising is still alive; evolving, but alive. There are now more ways to promote brands than ever before.

The Very Wide World of Brand Media Vehicles. Enter the world of integrated brand promotion: a world where new media and ways of using them are merging with the more traditional ones. The media arena (new or old) is vitally important, always has been, always will be. This is where the money is spent, invested wisely, or wasted. It is also a place where much has changed. We begin by noting the changes, explaining some underlying reasons, and discussing their real-world implications.

ⓘ Very Important Changes.

Agency Compensation. Thirty years ago it was a pretty simple system: Around 80 percent of all advertising and promotional dollars went to media advertising (television, radio, newspapers, magazines, and outdoor). The advertising was created, produced, and placed by full-service advertising agencies—most everything was done under one roof. The agency purchased the media at a 15 percent discount, and that's how ad agencies made their money. Back in the day, ad agencies (say, J. Walter Thompson) got a 15 percent discount from the media (e.g., NBC), but they charged their clients (e.g., Ford) full price; the agencies kept the change, the 15 percent. Fifteen percent of a few million dollars (per account) was good money. The more ads a client bought through their ad agency, the more money the agencies made. Back then agencies would deny with their last breath that they ever encouraged clients to spend more just so the agency would make more money. Sure. It was very simple math and the more cynical among us suspect that it was a system that produced the massive growth in media advertised and agency profits. But those simple days are long gone.

The 15 percent commission is pretty much history. In its place are individually negotiated deals; not much is standard anymore. Most clients now pay agencies on a fee-for-service basis; they pay for specific jobs. Lots of staff time is billed out to the client. The new system more resembles a law firm's billing system than anything else in the business world. There is still significant revenue generated through media discounts to agencies, but it is neither constant nor uniform. Further, the people who actually create the ads may work at an entirely different agency from the people who actually buy the media. Quite a bit of media planning and buying is outsourced, or split off from the agency with the account management and/or creative function. The demise of the 15 percent flat commission is one factor that brought on the new media age. When the way agencies got paid changed, and it involved less financial reward for buying lots of mass media, there was less incentive to consider only the traditional forms.

More Media. Even more fundamentally challenging to the old system is that "media" now include all sorts of new species: the Internet, cross-promotions, product placements, buzz and viral marketing, movies that are really feature-length commercials, and so on. The line between public relations and advertising has become a busy blur. Companies supply and push "news" stories about their brands or categories to media outlets as part of their overall integrated brand promotion effort. These "news" stories cost the companies nothing other than the salaries of the staff writers and placement specialists, so in a pure sense, no ads are actually purchased. But IBP is clearly being done. Obvious examples occur around holidays when food stories (let's say about cooking turkeys) show up on the local early news as a feature story. These "stories" are often written and produced by a poultry or seasoning marketer and sent out to the news media as news, not advertising. Lazy journalists are usually more than willing to let marketers write and produce their stories for them. Newspapers, most struggling desperately for revenue just to survive, find a way to put aside ethical considerations and run the stories. Money rarely changes hands in a direct way, but having free stories allow newspapers to trim staff. We know of at least one major U.S. consumer package goods advertiser that has very quietly moved a small, but significant percentage of its overall promotional budget into this type of news/media/advertising. A senior executive told us that the growth of ads as "news" is fast, strong, and significant, and suggests the model of the future. Other times, public relation firms are quick to write and disseminate a news story when their product is rated highly, say a car by Consumer Reports. This is sometimes called "earned media" as opposed to "paid media" (advertising). The same is true in entertainment, where movies can work as promotional vehicles for products while still entertaining. (See Exhibit 14.3.) There is now IBP in video and computer games on cell phones, just about everywhere. So, this large expansion of what we call "media" is another factor in bringing about this new media world.

Going Public. Agencies have become leaner operations since moving from being privately held to publicly traded companies. Now there is much more stockholder pressure for short-term profitability. In the ad world, the two quickest routes to greater short-term profit are (1) to fire staff and (2) to make more money on fees and media buys. As the ad world has moved away from flat media commissions, traditional media, and privately held companies, they have become much more like other traditional businesses and are constantly searching for ways to optimize short-term profits. This often pushes them in the direction of higher-return media buys and deals, often in the nonstandardized realm of "new media" where rate books and compensation formula either don't exist or are rarely made public. To understand media, and how it is bought and used to generate profit for the agency, is to understand a great deal about real-

■ **MADISON+VINE**

GOLDEN GIRL: Sales of Uma's Asics have taken off in Asia, Europe and the U.S.

Asics sneaks are 'Kill Bill' sleeper hit

world advertising and marketing practice. So, these changes in agency profitability and stockholder pressure have also helped usher in the age of new media.

Greater Accountability: Return on Investment (ROI). Another big change directly related to media is agency accountability. In the past, the standard reply from advertising agencies to client questions concerning results was, "Well, there is really no way to precisely isolate the effects of advertising from all the other things going on in the consumer's environment—maybe sales went up/down because of weather, a change in packaging, or a competitor's actions. But clearly our advertising is doing great things for your brand. Trust us."

Well, trust is in short supply these days. One big reason for the shift out of traditional media advertising and into other forms of IBP is the at least perceived greater accountability of other promotional forms. For example, proponents of direct mail advertising say that they can pretty much determine the effect of each promotional mailing in real dollar terms. This answer makes brand managers much happier than the traditional "relax, trust us" answer. Also, advances in mathematical modeling and access to better integrated data have increased the ability of sophisticated marketers to estimate (not perfectly) the return on investment (ROI) of many forms of IBP. Now the pressure to produce a documented ROI for all forms of advertising and IBP is significant. Clients want more accountability out of their advertising and integrated brand promotion. So, the desire for accountability is another factor that has led to the creation of this new media world.

Globalization. Then there is globalization. More and more, advertising and IBP media are truly world-wide. Contemporary media are not so contained by national borders, or even particularly concerned with them. Transnational corporations, particularly media, don't really care much about the borders of nation-states. From CNN to Al Jazeera, media exist in transnational space, and must be thought of that way. This is the new media reality. Even vehicles strongly associated with one particular country are more and more trying to soften that association. Have you noticed how CNN is looking less like a U.S. news agency and more like a global one? Watch CNN midday and it's pretty much CNN-Europe. The Web is worldwide; search engines don't really care about nation-state boundaries. Many of these global media organizations have large audiences outside of North America. BBC Worldwide TV, based in London, has several million viewers throughout Asia. As the European Union solidifies (if it does), the big media muscle of united Europe will be felt all over the globe. Then there are the BRIC countries, countries with huge emerging consumer markets: Brazil, Russia, India, and China. Companies must pay special attention to these four and are actively developing media platforms and vehicles just for these emerging mega-markets. For example, in 2008 India has 1.1 billion people, at least 25 percent of them under 16. By 2050, it will have nearly 1.7 billion people. It is currently adding "an Australia" to its population every single year. It also has a growing middle class. That's why P&G, Coke, Pepsi, Microsoft, Motorola, Unilever, General Mills, J. Walter Thompson, and on and on all have operations there. It is also significant that indigenous Indian brands like Kingfisher and Tatta are both huge and hugely successful. You cannot ignore numbers and signs of growth like these. Neither can you ignore the media challenge of reaching them. In India today, television remains the best media buy due largely to the high population density and the concentration of wealth in the even denser urban centers. But globalization is more than a marketplace phenomenon. It's a way of thinking, a mindset, a homogenized world of brand culture. Globalization is yet another factor in the rise of the "new media." There are no more meaningful "individualism-collectivism" nation-state differences; there is only globalization and global consumer culture.

Globalization presents media planners with a few new problems. The most serious one is lack of international standardized audience measurement and pricing. Pricing and buying media around the globe is very complicated. Typically, agencies partner with local agencies or media buyers. One advantage of the "new" media is that it tends to be more or less international in scope and offers fewer of these problems, although a few countries block or filter content, including commercial content containing IBP. We are, however, generally optimistic about this getting better in most places.

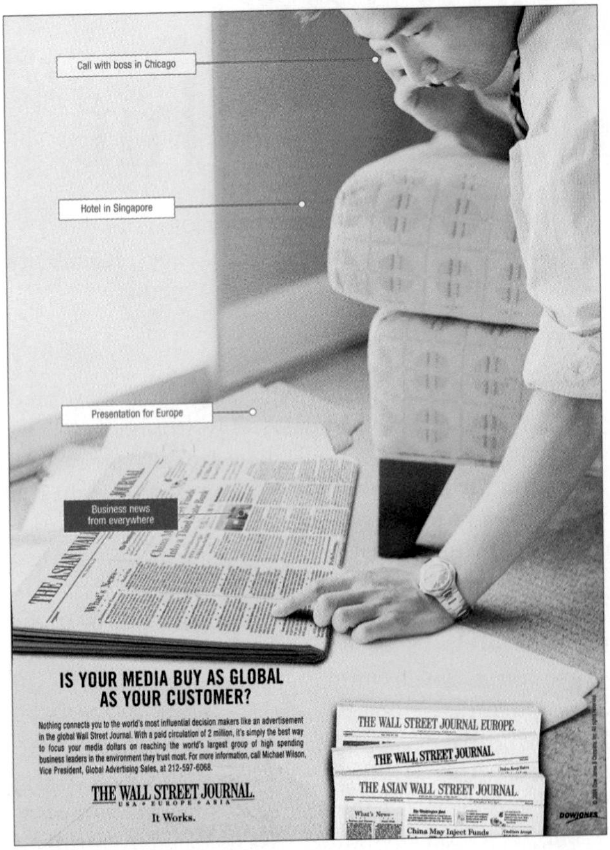

EXHIBIT 14.4

The Wall Street Journal is read all around the globe. Media are going global.

Free Content. Maybe the single biggest change in the media world is the flood of "free" media content. Largely due to the Internet and other telecommunications changes, consumers are getting used to getting cool stuff for free, or next to free. So, why should they buy a magazine at a bookstore for $4.50 that's full of ads? They can go online and get much of the same, maybe better content without paying a dime, and can avoid the ads—if there are any ads at all. This is making traditional ad-supported paid media vehicles an increasingly endangered species. So advertisers are putting more of their total promotional budget into nontraditional media, media environments that contemporary consumers clearly enjoy and use more.

Consumer-Generated Content. Another real surprise is the case of consumer-generated content, including IBP. That's right, consumers are making and distributing brand material and even ads on the Internet for their favorite brands, or mocking ads for disliked brands. These ads cost the marketer nothing, make the agency nothing, and may or may not be on target. Several major advertisers tell the story of getting lots of great feedback for an Internet ad, calling their agency to congratulate them, and finding out that their agency has no idea what they are talking about: the ad turns out to have been made by some 14-year-old kid in Ohio. This has become a worry for some advertisers; they really enjoy being in control.

Consumer in Charge. It is now widely accepted that the days of the marketer as the sole creator of brand image is over. This admission has appeared on the cover of *Advertising Age,* been said by scores of major CEOs, and is now the accepted reality being practiced by most large advertisers. With the rise of the Internet, the rise of connected consumers capable and willing to talk back to marketers, and a changing consumer culture and consumer mind-set, there is a real battle for who owns the brand and who gets to say things about it. This is yet another big difference when describing the new media world. Brands and brand communication are now meaningfully co-created. Advertisers bring something to the table, and so do consumers.

E-commerce has been wildly successful. It has truly revolutionized the way consumers shop and consume. Its impact has been more than technological; it has been cultural and economic. It has given consumers considerably more power in the marketing channel: access to more and better information, access to millions of other consumers and their opinions of goods and services, and much higher expectations of finding good deals (see Exhibit 14.5). In fact, two of the biggest changes the Internet has wrought are the rise of **deal-proneness** in consumers and **price/cost transparency**. It is now so incredibly easy to get a deal, to know what a good deal is, to operate with knowledge of what a good price would be, and even to know what the seller's cost is. A new-car buyer can very easily find out online what the local

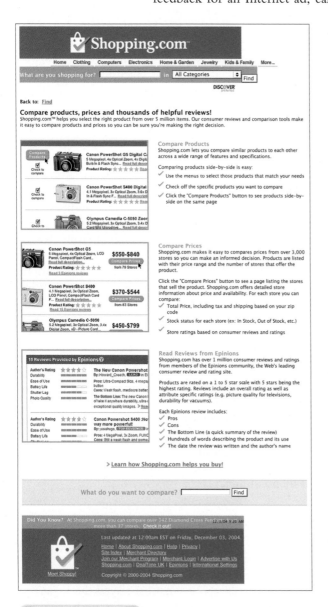

EXHIBIT 14.5

It's become much easier to find the best deal. http://www.shopping.com

TIENES SEGURO DE INQUILINO, ¿CIERTO?

Pues deberías, no importa si tus cosas son caras o no ya que siempre será más costoso reponerlas. Además, el dueño de tu edificio sólo es responsable por el edificio y nada más. Pero no te preocupes, State Farm® te ofrece el SEGURO DE INQUILINO que por unos centavos al día te cubre por incendio, robo y muchas cosas más. Llama a un agente hoy y sal de casa tranquilo.

STATE FARM INSURANCE   UN BUEN VECINO

statefarm.com®

EXHIBIT 14.6

Advertisers reach out to serve increasingly diverse populations.

car dealer's invoice price was (how much it paid for the car) and what the breakeven point is for the dealer. Consumers can do the same for countless goods and services through the World Wide Web. It's now cool to talk about how little you paid for something; in the 1980's consumers bragged about how much they paid. Consumers have now become prone to seek deals more than ever before. E-commerce (shopping and consuming online), much more than e-advertising per se, has changed the ad and promotion world. Learning how to fit in and leverage that new world is now the key to success.

This gives the consumer unprecedented marketplace power. This is power that consumers are not going to easily give up. So this means that going forward consumers are going to want media that gives them this kind of information and power, often for free and without obtrusive and annoying ads. This has changed the media environment in a fundamental way.

Hyperclutter and Ad Avoidance.

While it has always been the case that consumers felt there were lots of ads in their environment, it has now become the stuff of serious industry concern. It is probably most threatening to network television. Before, consumers pretty much had no choice. Now they do. They can watch ad-free premium channels such as HBO or they can "TiVo" past the ads from network television shows. On the Internet, pop-up ad filters are some of the most popular software offerings available. People will pay to avoid ads. Too many ads have made traditional advertising less powerful. Ironically, traditional advertising is a victim of itself.

Multicultural Media.
If you haven't noticed, there is a lot more ethnic media these days. There are many reasons for this; in the United States, one of the most obvious is the growing population of several prominent ethnic groups. In the United States, the most attention is on the Hispanic/Latino(a) market, due mostly to its size and growth rate. Most major advertisers are paying lots of attention to this (see Exhibit 14.6). There are at least 10 major cities in the United States now where English is the minority language, and this trend will continue. This is nothing compared to other parts of the world. In India, for example, there are 16 major dialects of Hindi as well as English, and a mix of world religions and their cultures.

2 The Fundamentals of Media Planning.
OK, so a lot has changed in media land, but not everything. There are still some ideas, names, concepts, and principles that are just as they always were. Traditional concepts still matter. Some basic tools remain the same. So now we are going to talk about what has stayed the same and still matters. There are those things that endure, principles. One of them is the principle of good planning.

Good planning remains good planning regardless of the media employed. We'll give you an example. While I was writing an earlier version of this chapter, I went downstairs to get the mail. One envelope was from "Unique Customized Dog Food." Enclosed was a bright blue bag labeled "Stool Sample Collection Instructions." That's right; these guys wanted me to send them some dog feces for customized analysis, so they could make some dog food that would be "optimized for your dog's DNA (Digestive Nutrient Absorption)." This is a form of promotion. The marketer selected me to receive this offer, betting that I would be more likely than others to scoop up some of Fido's fertilizer and send it in. Of course, there is a problem—I don't have a dog. I used to, but I haven't for a while. Clearly, this company relied on some old data.

No matter how new the media are, how great a marketing plan is, and how insightful or visionary advertising strategists are, poor message placement will undermine even the best-laid plans and the coolest media. Advertising placed in media that do not reach the target audience—whether via new media or traditional media—will be much like the proverbial tree that falls in the forest with no one around: Does it make a sound? From an advertising standpoint, no; it doesn't. Advertising placed in media that do not reach target audiences will not achieve the communications or sales impact an advertiser desires.

Now, let's think about some fundamentals, some hard, cold realities.

The Big Pie. Think of all the money used to promote a brand as a big pie. The big pie (see Exhibit 14.7) includes advertising, direct mail, point of purchase promotion, coupons, promotional e-mails, buzz marketing, product placement, brand integration in computer games, everything spent to promote a good or service. Traditionally, companies would make the distinction between (1) **above-the-line promotion**, which meant traditional **measured media** advertising, and (2) **below-the-line promotion**, which is everything else. For consumer package goods companies, below-the-line promotion might be desirable retail shelving, in-store promotions, coupons, and events; for durable goods (say cars) it might be for dealer incentives and financing incentives. Below-the-line is also referred to as **unmeasured media**. These terms are still used, but it's getting harder to say exactly what is above or below the line, measured or unmeasured. To be fair, it should probably be termed "publicly estimated" vs. "best guess." All the newer forms of media have really complicated this.

As defined by Competitive Media Reporting, the industry leader in the tracking of ad placement and spending, "measured media" include network TV, cable TV, spot TV, syndicated TV, network Spanish TV, the Internet (excluding broadband video and paid search), Net radio, spot radio, local radio (500 stations, top 28 markets), magazines (Sunday, consumer, business-to-business, and 30 local magazines), 250 local newspapers, Spanish newspapers, national newspapers (*Wall Street Journal, USA Today, New York Times*), and outdoor (200-plus markets). Unmeasured media is everything else: paid Internet search, coupons, product placement, events, and the like.

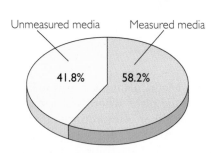

EXHIBIT 14.7

The Total Promotions Pie.

This is a very big pie. Let's call everything companies spend to promote the brand the Total Brand Promotions Pie. The most recent data (late 2007) reveal that measured media account for 58.2 percent and unmeasured account for 41.8 percent of total spending. Estimates for 2008, 2009, and beyond indicate this trend continuing: less traditional advertising, more unmeasured "new" media. The thing to remember is that unmeasured media slice has been growing at the expense of the measured.

Advertising Age reported that Procter & Gamble, the largest U.S. advertiser, increased its unmeasured U.S. spending by 15 percent from 2006 to 2007 while measured media increased only 3.9 percent. P&G Chairman and CEO A. G. Lafley Jr. said, "If you step back and look at our [marketing] mix across most of the major brands, it's clearly shifting, and it's shifting from measured media

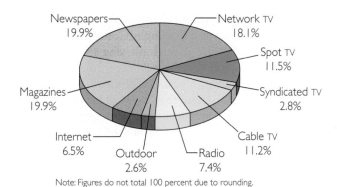

EXHIBIT 14.8

This is how measured brand communication in the United States breaks down by medium.

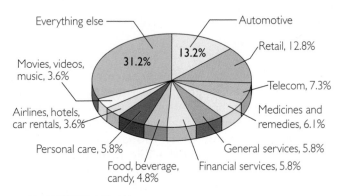

EXHIBIT 14.9

Top 10 measured media advertising categories.

EXHIBIT 14.10

Different categories spend advertising in different media. Think about the difference in these two categories and why they spend the media budgets the way they do.

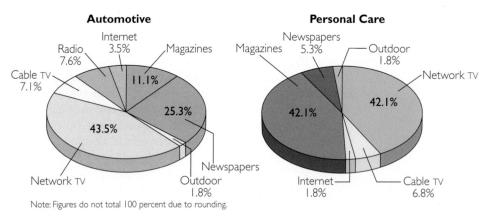

to in-store, to the Internet and to trial activity (i.e., product sampling.)" This not happening at only P&G; for example, Johnson & Johnson recently moved a significant amount of its brand communications money into unmeasured media. Why? Well, the simple answer is that these large companies believe these forms are more efficient than traditional mass media advertising, which is too expensive and offers little accountability where ROI is concerned. Just about everyone is shifting in the direction of "new media," even though new media ROI has proven to be more elusive than first thought.

If you break things down a bit more, you can see the relative standing of the different measured media (see Exhibit 14.8). Television in all its forms is still king by a long way. The Internet, which is growing rapidly, still amounts to only 6.5 percent of measured media spending, but that does not include paid search, and that 6.5 percent is very significant. It is more than double all outdoor advertising, on the heels of radio (which has been around since the 1920s), and climbing. That's big.

It is also interesting to see who spends where (see Exhibit 14.9).

Marketers in some product categories spend more on media and rely more on certain types of media than others. For example, compare how the two industries shown in Exhibit 14.10 spread around their media money.

Media Planning.
The ad world can be a pretty interesting place. Media planning is particularly interesting these days. While everyone knows this is the place where vast fortunes can be saved by better media buying, media jobs are neither glamorous (like being a creative), nor high paying (like account executives). A lot of people enter the ad industry through the media department. It has traditionally been a job of numbers, schedules, and deadlines, and relatively low salaries. But as the world of media has opened up, it has become considerably more interesting, more desirable, and even a

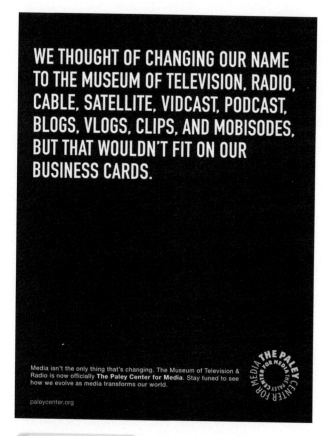

WE THOUGHT OF CHANGING OUR NAME TO THE MUSEUM OF TELEVISION, RADIO, CABLE, SATELLITE, VIDCAST, PODCAST, BLOGS, VLOGS, CLIPS, AND MOBISODES, BUT THAT WOULDN'T FIT ON OUR BUSINESS CARDS.

Media isn't the only thing that's changing. The Museum of Television & Radio is now officially **The Paley Center for Media.** Stay tuned to see how we evolve as media transforms our world.

paleycenter.org

EXHIBIT 14.11

The Paley Center for Television and Radio embraced the world of new media by changing its name to The Paley Center for Media.

little better paying. Now, with the merger of movies, music, gaming, and other entertainment, media planning is getting a lot more interesting and powerful. Think about creating a television show, a TV channel, movies, or music rather than just pulling numbers and making buys. Media planning is a lot more interesting than it was just five years ago. It is now a more realistic path to senior management at big multi-national agencies.

True, the big matrix of media options demands attention to detail in media planning. But, at the same time, you should never lose sight of what it is you are really trying to do. Media planning requires creativity and strategic thinking. Sure, you need to know how to do the basic math, and know the key terms, but you should never let the raw numbers and techno-buzzwords obscure the strategy. What you need to understand is what you are trying to do with media, why you are doing it and the key aspects of the various tools at your disposal. You should also realize with all the "new" media and the way things have opened up, you can do some pretty amazing and cool things (see Exhibit 14.11).

Some important terms:

A **media plan** specifies the media in which advertising messages will be placed to reach the desired target audience. A **media class** is a broad category of media, such as television, radio, or newspapers. A **media vehicle** is a particular option for placement within a media class. For example, *Newsweek* is a media vehicle within the magazine-media class. The media mix is the blend of different media that will be used to effectively reach the target audience.

A media plan includes strategy, objectives, media choices, and a media schedule for placing a message. And remember: Everything must fit together. The advertising plan (Chapter 8) is developed during the planning stage of the advertising effort, and is the driving force behind a media plan. Market and advertising research determines that certain media options hold the highest potential for shaping the consumer behavior (Chapter 5) of the target audience. The message strategy (Chapter 11) has enormous implications for where to place the messages, that is, in which media. Thus, in reality, the media-planning process takes place soon after the overall development of the advertising plan.

Media Strategies, Objectives, and Data.
The true power of a media plan rests in the media strategy. What are you trying to do with your media: buy simple awareness, counter a competitor's claims, reposition your brand, react to good or bad media publicity, or establish an image and good feel surrounding your brand? You have to know this before you start thinking about actual media buys. This strategy is then tactically executed in media terms of message weight, reach, frequency, continuity, audience duplication, and newer terms associated with branded entertainment and e-advertising; such as click-throughs. Don't miss the big picture; you should always know and pay close attention to the fundamental qualities of each medium and specific vehicle in terms of what your brand is trying to do. To be really good you need to be able to see the media buys in the strategic context of brand communication and consumer behavior goals.

Perhaps the most obvious media objective is that the vehicle chosen *reaches the target audience*. Recall that a target audience can be defined by demographics, geography, lifestyle, attitude dimensions, or usage category. But this is actually where a lot of problems happen in the real advertising and IBP world.

Here's what happens too often. The people making the ads, the creatives, along with (maybe) account planners and/or folks from the research department, account executives, and brand managers, have "determined" a target market of something similar to this example: "housewives 18–49 who hate cooking, long for the day when their children are out of the house, and need a better nonstick cooking spray for baking." Now, unfortunately, most media are bought and sold with much, much broader variables: age, income, geography, family size—in other words, very basic demographics associated with the total audience of a particular vehicle, say *Newsweek*. All that other stuff helps the creatives, but doesn't do much for the media buyer. You really can't call a salesperson at *Newsweek* and say, "Give me just those women who meet this very specific profile." Sorry, can't do it; getting closer, but still can't do it. So media planners are often (very often) put in the awkward and unenviable position of trying to deliver very specific audience characteristics based on inadequate data from media organizations. This is an industry-wide problem. Most of the time, there is simply no way to identify which television shows are watched by "women who really like strawberries" *and* "regularly shop at Bed Bath & Beyond." Those data are not routinely collected in a single source and are not available. And no matter how many times you tell account executives and creatives this, they seem to still think these data exist. No, generally speaking, they don't, not yet. Media buyers have to use their creativity to figure out what the next best thing would be. A lot of the creativity involved in media planning is trying to find that next best thing. The Internet actually offers some behavioral targeting that can effectively get at this problem, but this is still in its beginning stages.

Sometimes, however, if advertisers are willing to spend the money, and you are reasonably lucky in terms of what you asked for, the data will be available from a media research organization. These organizations don't cover everything, but they sometimes cover what you are looking for. This information can greatly increase the precision and usefulness of media buys. The two most prominent providers of demographic information correlated with product usage data are Mediamark Research (MRI) (http://www .mediamark.com) and Simmons Market Research Bureau (SMRB) (http://www .smrb.com). An example of the type of information supplied is shown in Exhibit 14.12, where market statistics for four brands of men's aftershave and cologne are compared: Eternity for Men, Jovan Musk, Lagerfeld, and Obsession for Men. The most-revealing data are contained in columns C and D. Column C shows each brand's strength relative to a demographic variable, such as age or income. Column D provides an index indicating that particular segments of the population are heavier users of a particular brand. Specifically, the number expresses each brand's share of volume as a percentage of its share of users. An index number above 100 shows particular strength for a brand. The strength of Eternity for Men as well as Obsession for Men is apparent in both the 18–24 and the 25–34 age cohorts. In magazines (their known specialty) and other print, Standard Rate and Data Service provides the exposure data (http://www .srds.com/portal/main?action=LinkHit&frameset=yes&link=ips).

Even more sophisticated data have become available. Research services such as A. C. Nielsen's Homescan and Information Resources' BehaviorScan are referred to as **single-source tracking services**, which offer information not just on demographics but also on brands, purchase size, purchase frequency, prices paid, and media exposure. BehaviorScan is the most comprehensive, in that exposure to particular television programs, magazines, and newspapers can be measured by the service. With demographic, behavioral, and media-exposure correlates provided by research services like these, advertising and media planners can address issues such as the following:

Aftershave Lotion & Cologne for Men

BASE: MEN	TOTAL U.S. '000	Eternity for Men A '000	B % DOWN	C % ACROSS	D INDEX	Jovan Musk A '000	B % DOWN	C % ACROSS	D INDEX	Lagerfeld A '000	B % DOWN	C % ACROSS	D INDEX	Obsession for Men A '000	B % DOWN	C % ACROSS	D INDEX
All Men	92674	2466	100.0	2.7	100	3194	100.0	3.4	100	1269	100.0	1.4	100	3925	100.0	4.2	100
Men	92674	2466	100.0	2.7	100	3194	100.0	3.4	100	1269	100.0	1.4	100	3925	100.0	4.2	100
Women	—	—	—	—	—	—	—	—	—	—	—	—	—	—	—	—	—
Household Heads	77421	1936	78.5	2.5	94	2567	80.4	3.3	96	1172	92.4	1.5	111	2856	72.7	3.7	87
Homemakers	31541	967	39.2	3.1	115	1158	36.3	3.7	107	451	35.5	1.4	104	1443	36.8	4.6	108
Graduated College	21727	583	23.7	2.7	101	503	15.8	2.3	67	348	27.4	1.6	117	901	23.0	4.1	98
Attended College	23842	814	33.0	3.4	128	933	29.2	3.9	113	*270	21.3	1.1	83	1283	32.7	5.4	127
Graduated High School	29730	688	27.9	2.3	87	1043	32.7	3.5	102	*460	36.3	1.5	113	1266	32.2	4.3	101
Did not Graduate H.S.	17374	*380	15.4	2.2	82	*715	22.4	4.1	119	*191	15.0	1.1	80	*475	12.1	2.7	65
18–24	12276	754	30.6	6.1	231	*391	12.2	3.2	92	*7	0.5	0.1	4	747	19.0	6.1	144
25–34	20924	775	31.4	3.7	139	705	22.1	3.4	98	*234	18.5	1.1	82	1440	36.7	6.9	162
35–44	21237	586	23.8	2.8	104	1031	32.3	4.9	141	*311	24.5	1.5	107	838	21.3	3.9	93
45–54	14964	*202	8.2	1.4	51	*510	16.0	3.4	99	*305	24.0	2.0	149	481	12.3	3.2	76
55–64	10104	*112	4.6	1.1	42	*215	6.7	2.1	62	*214	16.9	2.1	155	*245	6.2	2.4	57
65 or over	13168	*37	1.5	0.3	10	*342	10.7	2.6	75	*198	15.6	1.5	110	*175	4.4	1.3	31
18–34	33200	1529	62.0	4.6	173	1096	34.3	3.3	96	*241	19.0	0.7	53	2187	55.7	6.6	156
18–49	62950	2228	90.4	3.5	133	2460	77.0	3.9	113	683	53.9	1.1	79	3315	84.5	5.3	124
25–54	57125	1563	63.4	2.7	103	2246	70.3	3.9	114	850	67.0	1.5	109	2758	70.3	4.8	114
Employed Full Time	62271	1955	79.3	3.1	118	2141	67.0	3.4	100	977	77.0	1.6	115	2981	76.0	4.8	113
Part-time	5250	*227	9.2	4.3	163	*141	4.4	2.7	78	*10	0.8	0.2	14	*300	7.7	5.7	135
Sole Wage Earner	21027	554	22.5	2.6	99	794	24.9	3.8	110	332	26.2	1.6	115	894	22.8	4.3	100
Not Employed	25153	*284	11.5	1.1	42	912	28.6	3.6	105	*281	22.2	1.1	82	643	16.4	2.6	60
Professional	9010	*232	9.4	2.6	97	*168	5.3	1.9	54	*143	11.3	1.6	116	504	12.8	5.6	132
Executive/Admin./Mgr.	10114	*259	10.5	2.6	96	*305	9.6	3.0	88	*185	14.6	1.8	134	353	9.0	3.5	82
Clerical/Sales/Technical	13212	436	17.7	3.3	124	*420	13.2	3.2	92	*231	18.2	1.7	128	741	18.9	5.6	132
Precision/Crafts/Repair	12162	624	25.3	5.1	193	*317	9.9	2.6	76	*168	13.2	1.4	101	511	13.0	4.2	99
Other Employed	23022	631	25.6	2.7	103	1071	33.5	4.7	135	*261	20.6	1.1	83	1173	29.9	5.1	120
H/D Income																	
$75,000 or More	17969	481	19.5	2.7	101	*320	10.0	1.8	52	413	32.5	2.3	168	912	23.2	5.1	120
$60,000–74,999	10346	*368	14.9	3.6	134	*309	9.7	3.0	87	*142	11.2	1.4	100	495	12.6	4.8	113
$50,000–59,999	9175	*250	10.2	2.7	103	*424	13.3	4.6	134	*153	12.1	1.7	122	*371	9.4	4.0	95
$40,000–49,999	11384	*308	12.5	2.7	102	*387	12.1	3.4	99	*134	10.6	1.2	86	580	14.8	5.1	120
$30,000–39,999	12981	*360	14.6	2.8	104	542	17.0	4.2	121	*126	10.0	1.0	71	*416	10.6	3.2	76
$20,000–29,999	13422	*266	10.8	2.0	75	*528	16.5	3.9	114	*164	12.9	1.2	89	*475	12.1	3.5	84
$10,000–19,999	11867	*401	16.3	3.4	127	*394	12.3	3.3	96	*67	5.3	0.6	41	*481	12.3	4.1	96
Less than $10,000	5528	*31	1.3	0.6	21	*291	9.1	5.3	153	*69	5.4	1.2	91	*194	4.9	3.5	83

Source: Mediamark Research Inc., Mediamark Research Men's, Women's Personal Care Products Report (Mediamark Research Inc., Spring 1997), 16.

EXHIBIT 14.12

Commercial research firms can provide advertisers with an evaluation of a brand's relative strength within demographic segments. This typical data table from Mediamark Research shows how various men's aftershave and cologne brands perform in different demographic segments. http://www.mediamark.com

- How many members of the target audience have tried the advertiser's brand, and how many are repeat purchasers?
- What appears to affect brand sales more—increased amounts of advertising, or changes in advertising copy?
- What other products do buyers of the advertiser's brand purchase regularly?
- What television programs, magazines, and newspapers reach the largest number of the advertiser's audience?

Another critical element in setting advertising objectives is determining the **geographic scope** of media placement. Media planners need to identify media that cover the same geographic area as the advertiser's distribution system. Obviously, spending money on the placement of ads in media that cover geographic areas where the advertiser's brand is not distributed is wasteful.

Some analysts suggest that when certain geographic markets demonstrate unusually high purchasing tendencies by product category or by brand, then geo-targeting

Weekday Prime audience up **99%**

Primetime is up **11** share points

75% of Telemundo's primetime shows are original. No wonder people can't take their eyes off us.

Call Steve Mandala, EVP Sales, 212-664-3599.

Gabriela Spanic, *Prisionera*

FRESH ORIGINAL TELEMUNDO

EXHIBIT 14.13

Reach is an important measure of a media vehicle's effectiveness. Who you reach is very important.

should be the basis for the media placement decision. **Geo-targeting** is the placement of ads in geographic regions where higher purchase tendencies for a brand are evident. For example, in one geographic area the average consumer purchases of Prego spaghetti sauce were 36 percent greater than the average consumer purchases nationwide. With this kind of information, media buys can be geo-targeted to reinforce high-volume users.[1]

Reach refers to the number of people or households in a target audience that will be exposed to a media vehicle or schedule at least one time during a given period of time. It is often expressed as a percentage. If an advertisement placed on the hit network television program *ER* is watched at least once by 10 percent of the advertiser's target audience, then the reach is said to be 10 percent. Media vehicles with broad reach are ideal for consumer convenience goods, such as toothpaste and cold remedies. These are products with fairly simple features, and they are frequently purchased by a broad cross-section of the market. Broadcast television, cable television, and national magazines have the largest and broadest reach of any of the media, due to their national and even global coverage. But their audiences have been shrinking. Now, vehicles like Telemundo (Exhibit 14.13) are claiming respectable reach among selected but prized "demos" (demographics).

Frequency is the average number of times an individual or household within a target audience is exposed to a media vehicle in a given period of time (typically a week or a month). For example, say an advertiser places an ad on a weekly television show with a 20 rating (20 percent of households) four weeks in a row. The show has an (unduplicated) reach of 43 (percent) over the four-week period. So, frequency is then equal to $(20 \times 4)/43$, or 1.9. This means that an audience member had the opportunity to see the ad an average of 1.9 times.

Advertisers often struggle with the dilemma of increasing reach at the expense of frequency, or vice versa. At the core in this struggle are the concepts of effective frequency and effective reach. **Effective frequency** is the number of times a target audience needs to be exposed to a message before the objectives of the advertiser are met—either communications objectives or sales impact. Many factors affect the level of effective frequency. New brands and brands laden with features may demand high frequency. Simple messages for well-known products may require less frequent exposure for consumers to be affected. While most analysts agree that one exposure will typically not be enough, there is debate about how many exposures are enough. A common industry practice is to place effective frequency at three exposures, but analysts argue that as few as two or as many as nine exposures are needed to achieve effective frequency.

Effective reach is the number or percentage of consumers in the target audience that are exposed to an ad some minimum number of times. The minimum-number estimate for effective reach is based on a determination of effective frequency. If effective reach is set at four exposures, then a media schedule must be devised that

---

1.   This section and the example are drawn from Erwin Ephron, "The Organizing Principle of Media," *Inside Media,* November 2, 1992.

achieves at least four exposures over a specified time period within the target audience. With all the advertising clutter (too many ads) that exists today, effective reach is likely a much higher number; some experts have advocated six as a minimum.

Message weight is another media measure; it is the total mass of advertising delivered. Message weight is the gross number of advertising messages or exposure opportunities delivered by the vehicles in a schedule. Media planners are interested in the message weight of a media plan because it provides a simple indication of the size of the advertising effort being placed against a specific market.

Message weight (at least in traditional media) is typically expressed in terms of gross impressions. **Gross impressions** represent the sum of exposures to the entire media placement in a media plan. Planners often distinguish between two types of exposure. *Potential ad impressions* or *opportunities* to be exposed to ads are the most common meanings and refer to exposures by the media vehicle carrying advertisements (for example, a program or publication). *Message impressions*, on the other hand, refers to exposures to the ads themselves. Information on ad exposure probabilities can be obtained from a number of companies, including Nielsen, Simmons, Roper-Starch, Gallup & Robinson, Harvey Research, and Readex. This information can pertain to particular advertisements, campaigns, media vehicles, product categories, ad characteristics, and target groups.

For example, consider a media plan that, in a one-week period, places ads on three television programs and in two national newspapers. The sum of the exposures to the media placement might be as follows:

	Gross Impressions	
	Media Vehicle	**Advertisement**
Television		
Program A audience	16,250,000	5,037,500
Program B audience	4,500,000	1,395,000
Program C audience	7,350,000	2,278,500
Sum of TV exposures	28,100,000	8,711,000
Newspapers		
Newspaper 1	1,900,000	376,200
Newspaper 2	450,000	89,100
Sum of newspaper exposures	2,350,000	465,300
Total gross impressions	**30,450,000**	**9,176,300**

The total gross impressions figure is the media weight.

Of course, this does not mean that 30,450,000 separate people were exposed to the programs and newspapers or that 9,176,300 separate people were exposed to the advertisements. Some people who watched TV program A also saw program B and read newspaper 1, as well as all other possible combinations. This is called **between-vehicle duplication** (remember, "vehicles" are shows, newspapers, magazines—things that carry ads). It is also possible that someone who saw the ad in newspaper 1 on Monday saw it again in newspaper 1 on Tuesday. This is **within-vehicle duplication**. That's why we say that the total *gross* impressions number contains audience duplication. Data available from services such as SMRB report both types of duplication so that they may be removed from the gross impressions to produce the *unduplicated* estimate of audience, or *reach,* as discussed above. (You should know, however, that the math involved in such calculations is fairly complex.)

EXHIBIT 14.14

Gross rating points (GRP) for a media plan.

Media Class/Vehicle	Rating (reach)	Number of Ad Insertions (frequency)	GRP
Television			
ER	25	4	100
Law & Order	20	4	80
Good Morning America	12	4	48
Days of Our Lives	7	2	14
Magazines			
People	22	2	44
Travel & Leisure	11	2	22
U.S. News & World Report	9	6	54
Total			**362**

Another way of expressing media weight is in terms of gross rating points (GRP). GRP is the product of reach times frequency ($GRP = r \times f$). When media planners calculate the GRP for a media plan, they multiply the rating (reach) of each vehicle in a plan times the number of times an ad will be inserted in the media vehicle and sum these figures across all vehicles in the plan. Exhibit 14.14 shows the GRP for a combined magazine and television schedule. The GRP number is used as a relative measure of the intensity of one media plan versus another. Whether a media plan is appropriate is ultimately based on the judgment of the media planner.

The message weight objective provides only a broad perspective for a media planner. What does it mean when we say that a media plan for a week produced more than 30 million gross impressions? It means only that a fairly large number of people were potentially exposed to the advertiser's message. It provides a general point of reference. When Toyota introduced the Avalon in the U.S. market, the $40 million introductory ad campaign featured 30-second television spots, newspaper and magazine print ads (see Exhibit 14.15 for an example), and direct mail pieces. The high-

EXHIBIT 14.15

What is the importance of message weight for the introduction of a new product such as the Avalon? Is it important that the advertiser be able to distinguish between gross impressions and audience reach in this type of campaign? http://www
.toyota.com

EXHIBIT 14.16

An example of a print ad that was flighted during December—a month in which whipped-cream dessert toppings figure prominently.
http://www.reddi-wip.com

light of the campaign was a nine-spot placement on a heavily watched Thursday evening TV show, costing more than $2 million. The message weight of this campaign in a single week was enormous—just the type of objective Toyota's media planners wanted for the brand introduction.[2]

Continuity is the pattern of placement of advertisements in a media schedule. There are three strategic scheduling alternatives: continuous, flighting, and pulsing. **Continuous scheduling** is a pattern of placing ads at a steady rate over a period of time. Running one ad each day for four weeks during the soap opera *General Hospital* would be a continuous pattern. Similarly, an ad that appeared in every issue of *Redbook* magazine for a year would also be continuous. **Flighting** is another media-scheduling strategy. Flighting is achieved by scheduling heavy advertising for a period of time, usually two weeks, then stopping advertising altogether for a period, only to come back with another heavy schedule.

Flighting is often used to support special seasonal merchandising efforts or new product intro-ductions, or as a response to competitors' activities. The financial advantages of flighting are that discounts might be gained by concentrating media buys in larger blocks. Communication effectiveness may be enhanced because a heavy schedule can achieve the repeat exposures necessary to achieve consumer awareness. For example, the ad in Exhibit 14.16 was run heavily in December issues of magazines, to take advantage of seasonal dessert-consumption patterns.

Finally, **pulsing** is a media-scheduling strategy that combines elements from continuous and flighting techniques. Advertisements are scheduled continuously in media over a period of time, but with periods of much heavier scheduling (the flight). Pulsing is most appropriate for products that are sold fairly regularly all year long but have certain seasonal requirements, such as clothing.

Continuity and the Forgetting Function. While many may not know it, industry media continuity practices were actually strongly influenced by academic research in the area of human memory. When people first started trying to understand how and when to place ads, the idea of forgetting soon came into play. It makes sense. Very early in advertising's history, this very useful piece of psychological research was recognized. It turns out that people's forgetting is fairly predictable; that is, all else being equal, we know at about what interval things fade from people's memory. It seems to obey a mathematical function pretty well; thus it is often called the **forgetting function**. The original work for this was done over a century ago by psychologist Hermann Ebbinghaus in the late 19th century and most notably in the advertising world by Hubert Zielske in 1958. In his very famous study, Zielske sent food ads to two randomly selected groups of women. One received the ad every four weeks for 52 weeks (13 total exposures), the other received the ad once

2.   Bradley Johnson, "Toyota's New Avalon Thinks Big, American," *Advertising Age,* November 14, 1994, 46.

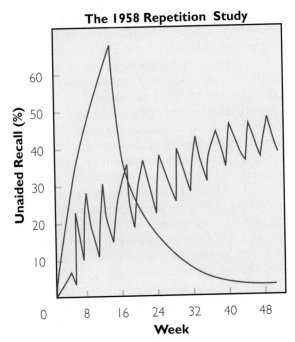

The 1958 Repetition Study

Source: Adapted from Hubert A. Zielske, "The Remembering and Forgetting of Advertising," *Journal of Marketing*, American Marketing Association, January 23, 1959, 239–243. Reprinted in R. Batra, J. Myers, and D. Aaker, *Advertising Management*, 4th ed. (Englewood Cliffs, N.J.: Prentice Hall, 1992).

EXHIBIT 14.17

Work your way through this graph of a very important and influential piece of media research. It links what we know about the manner in which humans forget things with the optimal frequency of advertising.

every week for 13 straight weeks (13 total exposures). Exhibit 14.17 shows what happened. The group that received all 13 ads in the first 13 weeks (called a flighting schedule) scored much higher in terms of peak unaided recall, but the level of recall fell off very fast, and by halfway through the year was very low. The group that got the ads at an evenly spaced schedule (called a continuous schedule) never attained as a high a level of recall as the other group, but finished much higher at the end of the year, and had an overall higher average recall.

This research has been very influential in terms of guiding industry media planners for several decades. The real-world implications are pretty clear. If you need rapid and very high levels of recall—say for the introduction of a new product, a strategic move to block the message of a competitor, or a political ad campaign, where there is only one day of actual shopping (election day)—use a flighting (sometimes called "heavy-up") schedule. A continuous schedule would be more broadly effective, and would be used for established brands with an established message.

We do, however, offer a note of caution here. As you know, the idea of recall and its measurement have received considerable criticism from both industry managers and academic researchers. We agree with this criticism; simple memory measures are inadequate at best in most advertising situations. As discussed earlier, they are most appropriate when a simple outcome like brand name recall is sought. In that case, forgetting (or not forgetting) is an important factor in advertising success or failure.

Length or Size of Advertisements. Beyond whom to reach, how often to reach them, and in what pattern, media planners must make strategic decisions regarding the length of an ad in electronic media or the size of an ad in print media. Certainly, the advertiser, creative director, art director, and copywriter have made determinations in this regard as well. Television advertisements (excluding infomercials) can range from 10 seconds to 60 seconds, and sometimes even two minutes, in length. Is a 60-second television commercial always six times more effective than a 10-second spot? Of course, the answer is no. Is a full-page newspaper ad always more effective than a two-inch, one-column ad? Again, not necessarily. Some research shows an increase in recognition scores of print advertising with increasing image size. Some call this the **square root law**; that is, "the recognition of print ads increases with the square of the illustration."[3] So a full-page ad should be twice as memorable as a quarter-page ad. Such "laws" should not be considered laws, but rather general guidelines; they show a general relationship, but are not completely precise. Still, advertisers use full-page newspaper ads when a product claim, brand image, or market situation warrants it.

The decision about the length or size of an advertisement depends on the creative requirements for the ad, the media budget, and the competitive environment within

3.   John R. Rossiter, "Visual Imagery: Applications to Advertising," *Advances in Consumer Research* (Provo, UT: Association for Consumer Research, 1982), 101–106.

which the ad is running. From a creative standpoint, ads attempting to develop an image for a brand may need to be longer in broadcast media or larger in print media to offer more creative opportunities. On the other hand, a simple, straightforward message announcing a sale may be quite short or small, but it may need heavy repetition. From the standpoint of the media budget, shorter and smaller ads are, with few exceptions, much less expensive. If a media plan includes some level of repetition to accomplish its objectives, the lower-cost option may be mandatory. From a competitive perspective, matching a competitor's presence with messages of similar size or length may be essential to maintain the share of mind in a target audience.

Media Context. This used to be referred to as "editorial climate." It refers to the feel, spirit, look, or image of the media vehicle. There is the belief that you are known by the company you keep, and that an ad is colored, to some extent, by where it appears. These are sometimes called **context effects**. It means that some of the meaning of your ad's surroundings rubs off on it. So advertisers and media professionals have to be very aware of the social meaning of context. Some advertisers will not do direct mail because they feel it is beneath them, that to do so would tarnish their brand's upper-crust image. Others will not use certain magazines, or sponsor a NASCAR driver, or cross-promote certain kinds of movies. Conversely, some purposefully choose exclusive magazines or other media, including sponsorships, precisely because they want to be elevated by their surroundings. While there have been attempts to grade, quantify, and automate editorial climate in media selection models, it has proven to be a task best suited for knowledgeable human interpretation. You should always make media context a consideration in media strategy. Quantifiable or not, it counts. As branded entertainment and other forms of new media spread, context will become more critical. For an example, see the Globalization box concerning context in Toyota's efforts in Japan.

GLOBALIZATION

A Plot Path into the Ad Break

Product placement is widespread in American television and film. But the practice still is rare in Japan, where research has shown that viewers simply don't respond to advertising that is too obvious. So Japanese advertising agencies are trying a new approach: "context-linked" ads that extend the characters and plot of a regular program into the commercial break.

The idea builds on the notion that advertising's impact is influenced, at least in part, by where it appears. The first context-linked commercials in Japan, for instance, were incorporated into a television drama called *37 Degrees*, which tracked the lives of three young, urban couples.

One of the commercials featured a character pondering life as a mother as she watches a young family emerge from a Toyota Sienta minivan. In another, a character complains about her love life to a bartender, who then pours her a glass of Suntory whiskey. The whiskey maker's yellow logo in one corner of the television screen tipped viewers that they had been watching a paid commercial.

"Regular product placement can easily look too obvious to viewers, but we made sure the product was necessary to the story," said Eiichi Hirano, the media account director who helped guide the project.

The extended storylines kept viewers watching through the commercial breaks, time usually spent grabbing a drink or bite to eat. Research showed a 3 percent increase in the number of viewers who stayed tuned to the screen during the ad break. But did those viewers feel duped when they realized they had been watching a paid commercial? A Toyota spokesman said reaction was mixed.

"Some people wondered if it was a drama or a commercial, and when they found out that it was an advert, they said they felt cheated because they thought it had been part of the show," Toyota spokesman Tomomi Imai commented. "Other people said it had been interesting."

Source: Julian Ryall, "In Japan, 'Context' Ads to Story Line," **Hollywood Reporter**, May 1, 2007, p.8.

Competitive Media Assessment.

While media planners normally do not base an overall media plan on how much competitors are spending or where competitors are placing their ads, a competitive media assessment can provide a useful perspective. A competitive media assessment is particularly important for product categories in which all the competitors are focused on a narrowly defined target audience. This condition exists in several product categories in which heavy-user segments dominate consumption—for example, snack foods, soft drinks, beer and wine, and chewing gum. Brands of luxury cars and financial services also compete for common-buyer segments.

When a target audience is narrow and attracts the attention of several major competitors, an advertiser must assess its competitors' spending and the relative share of voice its brand is getting. **Share of voice** is a calculation of any one advertiser's brand expenditures relative to the overall spending in a category:

$$\text{Share of voice} = \frac{\text{one brand's advertising expenditures in a medium}}{\text{total product category advertising expenditures in a medium}}$$

This calculation can be done for all advertising by a brand in relation to all advertising in a product category, or it can be done to determine a brand's share of product category spending on a particular advertising medium, such as network television or magazines. For example, athletic-footwear marketers spend approximately $310 million per year in measured advertising media. Nike and Reebok are the two top brands, with approximately $160 million and $55 million respectively in annual expenditures in measured advertising media. The share-of-voice calculations for both brands follow.

$$\text{Share of voice, Nike} = \frac{\$160 \text{ million} \times 100}{\$310 \text{ million}} = 51.6\%$$

$$\text{Share of voice, Reebok} = \frac{\$55 \text{ million} \times 100}{\$310 \text{ million}} = 17.7\%$$

Together, both brands dominate the product category advertising with a nearly 70 percent combined share of voice. Yet Nike's share of voice is nearly three times that of Reebok.

Research data, such as that provided by Competitive Media Reporting, can provide an assessment of share of voice in up to 10 media categories. A detailed report shows how much a brand was advertised in a particular media category versus the combined media category total for all other brands in the same product category. Knowing what competitors are spending in a medium and how dominant they might be allows an advertiser to strategically schedule within a medium. Some strategists believe that scheduling in and around a competitor's schedule can create a bigger presence for a small advertiser.[4]

Media Efficiency. The advertiser and the agency team determine which media class is appropriate for the current effort, based on criteria similar to those listed in Exhibit 14.18. These criteria give a general orientation to major media and the inherent capabilities of each media class.

Each medium under consideration in a media plan must be scrutinized for the efficiency with which it performs. In other words, which media deliver the largest target audiences at the lowest cost? A common measure of media efficiency is **cost per thousand (CPM)**, which is the dollar cost of reaching 1,000 (the M in CPM comes from the Roman numeral for 1,000) members of an audience using a particular medium. The CPM calculation can be used to compare the relative efficiency

---

4.   Andrea Rothman, "Timing Techniques Can Make Small Ad Budgets Seem Bigger," *Wall Street Journal,* February 3, 1989, B4; see also Robert J. Kent and Chris T. Allen, "Competitive Interference Effects in Consumer Memory for Advertising: The Role of Brand Familiarity," *Journal of Marketing* (July 1994), 97–105.

Characteristics	Broadcast TV	Cable TV	Radio	News-paper	Maga-zines	Direct Mail	Outdoor	Transit	Directory
Reach									
Local	M	M	H	H	L	H	H	H	M
National	H	H	L	L	H	M	L	L	M
Frequency	H	H	H	M	L	L	M	M	L
Selectivity									
Audience	M	H	H	L	H	H	L	L	L
Geographic	L	M	H	H	M	H	H	H	H
Audience reactions									
Involvement	L	M	L	M	H	M	L	L	H
Acceptance	M	M	M	H	M	L	M	M	H
Audience data	M	L	L	M	H	H	L	L	M
Clutter	H	H	H	M	M	M	M	L	H
Creative flexibility	H	H	H	L	M	M	L	L	L
Cost factors									
Per contact	L	L	L	M	M	H	L	L	M
Absolute cost	H	H	M	M	H	H	M	M	M

H = High, M = Moderate, L = Low

EXHIBIT 14.18

Essential qualities of media options.

of two media choices within a media class (magazine versus magazine) or between media classes (magazine versus radio). The basic measure of CPM is fairly straightforward; the dollar cost for placement of an ad in a medium is divided by the total audience and multiplied by 1,000. Let's calculate the CPM for a full-page black-and-white ad in the Friday edition of *USA Today*:

$$\text{CPM} = \frac{\text{cost of media buy} \times 1,000}{\text{total audience}}$$

$$\text{CPM for } USA\ Today = \frac{\$72,000 \times 1,000}{5,206,000} = \$13.83$$

These calculations show that *USA Today* has a CPM of \$13.83 for a full-page black-and-white ad. But this calculation shows the cost of reaching the entire readership of *USA Today*. If the target audience is college graduates in professional occupations, then the cost per thousand–target market (CPM–TM) calculation might be much higher for a general publication such as *USA Today* than for a more specialized publication such as *Fortune* magazine:

$$\text{CPM–TM for } USA\ Today = \frac{\$72,000 \times 1,000}{840,000} = \$85.71$$

$$\text{CPM–TM for } Fortune = \frac{\$54,800 \times 1,000}{940,000} = \$58.30$$

You can see that the relative efficiency of *Fortune* is much greater than that of *USA Today* when the target audience is specified more carefully and a CPM–TM calculation is made. An advertisement for business services appearing in *Fortune* will have a better CPM–TM than the same ad appearing in *USA Today*.

Information about ad cost, gross impressions, and target audience size is usually available from the medium itself. Detailed audience information to make a cost per thousand–target market analysis also is available from media research organizations, such as Simmons Market Research Bureau (for magazines) and A. C. Nielsen (for television). Cost information also can be obtained from Standard Rate and Data Service (SRDS) and Bacon's Media Directories, for example.

Like CPM, a **cost per rating point (CPRP)** calculation provides a relative efficiency comparison between media options. In this calculation, the cost of a media vehicle, such as a spot television program, is divided by the program's rating. (A rating point is equivalent to 1 percent of the target audience—for example, television households in the designated rating area tuned to a specific program.) Like the CPM calculation, the CPRP calculation gives a dollar figure, which can be used for comparing TV program efficiency. The calculation for CPRP is as follows, using television as an example.

$$\text{CPRP} = \frac{\text{dollar cost of ad placement on a program}}{\text{program rating}}$$

For example, an advertiser on WLTV (Univision 23) in the Miami–Ft. Lauderdale market may wish to compare household CPRP figures for 30-second announcements in various dayparts on the station. The calculations for early news and prime-time programs are as follows.

$$\text{CPRP for WLTV early news} = \frac{\$2,205}{9} = \$245$$

$$\text{CPRP for WLTV prime time} = \frac{\$5,100}{10} = \$510$$

Clearly an early news daypart program delivers households more efficiently at $245 CPRP, less than half that of prime time, with 90 percent of the typical prime-time rating.

It is important to remember that these efficiency assessments are based solely on costs and coverage. They say nothing about the quality of the advertising and thus should not be viewed as indicators of advertising effectiveness. When media efficiency measures such as CPM and CPM–TM are combined with an assessment of media objectives and media strategies, they can be quite useful. Taken alone and out of the broader campaign-planning context, such efficiency measures may lead to ineffective media buying.

Internet Media. We cover the topic of Internet media in considerable detail in Chapter 16. We devote an entire chapter to it because Internet media has its own terms, its own unique calculation issues. Many Internet portals post their advertising rates. Other good resources include the Interactive Advertising Bureau (http://www.iab.net) and Iconocast (http://www.iconocast.com). The most important thing to remember is that these media are fundamentally different in one very major way: they are "pull" media. With pull media, the consumer goes looking for the advertiser or advertising and thus "pulls" the advertised brand toward them. This is just the opposite of the traditional "push" media (e.g., a 30-second television ad) in which the brand is "pushed" at the consumer.

In Internet media, advertisers generally buy search terms on search engines, so that when a user searchers for a certain thing, say snowboards, your company comes up near the top. This is the basic revenue model for most search engines. Google AdSence

TOP BIDS FOR SELECT PAID SEARCH TERMS ON YAHOO

Term	TOP BIDS BY POSITION				
	No. 1	No. 2	No. 3	No. 4	No. 5
Hotel	$2.00	$1.30	$1.29	$1.20	$1.13
Car Rental	1.50	1.50	1.50	1.49	1.25
Computer	8.50	2.01	2.00	1.01	1.00
Bicycle	0.39	0.38	0.28	0.20	0.18
Automobile	0.98	0.98	0.97	0.97	0.96
Viagra	1.69	1.68	1.50	0.89	0.88
Sopranos	0.88	0.62	0.17	0.11	0.11
Subaru Forester	1.02	1.02	1.01	1.00	1.00
Real estate San Francisco	2.27	2.16	2.15	2.12	2.11
Starbucks	0.30	0.21	0.20	0.16	0.14

Source: *Advertising Age*, "Search Marketing Fact Pack 2006," p. 32. Reprinted with permission. © Crain Communications, Inc., 2006.

eMarketer using Yahoo Search Marketing (formerly Overture) to identify high bids for the top five positions as of Jan. 23, 2006 at 2:30 p.m. EST.

ENGINE	OVERALL COST PER CLICK		
	2005	2004	%CHG
Google AdWords	$1.61	$1.29	24.8
Yahoo/Overture PPC	1.34	1.03	30.1
Shopping engines	2.56	1.87	36.9
2nd tier search properties	0.58	0.00	NA

Source: *Advertising Age*, "Search Marketing Fact Pack 2006," p. 33. Reprinted with permission. © Crain Communications, Inc., 2006.

Data from MarketingSherpa, March 2006, via eMarketer. Notes: N=3,271 SEM marketers & agencies and 776 affiliate marketers & merchants. Data are for U.S. paid search ads only.

ONLINE AD SPENDING

Term	PROJECTED 2006	AS% TOTAL
Paid search	$6.47	41.5
Rich media	1.79	11.5
Classified	2.73	17.5
Display ads	2.89	18.5
Sponsorships	0.62	4.0
Referrals	0.78	5.0
E-mail	0.16	1.0
Slotting fees	0.16	1.0
Total	15.60	100.0

Source: *Advertising Age*, "Search Marketing Fact Pack 2006," p. 3.
Data from eMarketer, which benchmarks projections against Interactive Advertising Bureau/PricewaterhouseCoopers data, for which the last full year measured was 2005. Dollars in billions. Reprinted with permission. © Crain Communications, Inc., 2006.

matches subscriber site content with ads, and then delivers the ads to the right computer. According to Google's promise, the Web site holder earns money whenever a visitor clicks on one of these ads (https://www.google.com/adsense/login/en_US/?sourceid=aso&subid=ww-en-ha-adsense&medium=sem).

Search engine and browser companies now offer ad-related information well beyond simple clicks. For example, social network data tells advertisers who saw what (e.g., an internet ad), did what with it (e.g., clicked on it, drilled down, or even purchased), and then did what (e.g. went to a related site, told online friends about the purchase, looked for a better deal, etc.). But still, search terms are the big money maker. The process typically involves bidding for those terms by potential buyers. High bid wins. Exhibit 14.19 shows what words cost, according to *Ad Age*. Exhibit 14.20 shows cost-per-click data. Exhibit 14.21 shows how these clicks add up.

Online and interactive media have become popular even among upscale, traditional organizations. http://www .christies.com

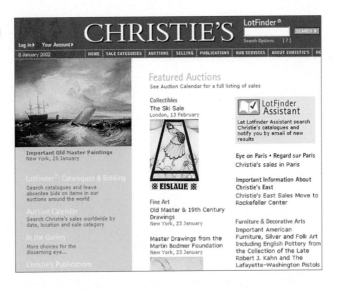

In Internet media, determining message weight is still being worked out, but clicks, hits, and click-throughs are all commonly used for this purpose.

Interactive Media. The media environment has gotten considerably more challenging as interactive media have been refined. First, the term is, in our opinion, overused and imprecise. To be truly interactive, consumers, the media itself, marketers (and other consumers sometimes) have to actually deal with one another in a meaningful way. But for now the term is pretty broad and includes things from kiosks to Internet shopping environments to **RSS (Really Simple Syndication)**. RSS is simply a channel or feed from blogs, podcasts, or other content that the computer user has linked to. Often an aggregator is used to collect, assemble, and deliver the RSS content. Of course, these RSS are often commercial in nature. Also included are interactive telephones, interactive CDs, online services, the Internet, computer gaming, and online versions of magazines. Absolut Vodka has developed a successful interactive Internet campaign. Even such traditional, upscale outlets as Christie's auction house have started using home pages on the World Wide Web to publicize upcoming events (see Exhibit 14.22). The confounding factor for media placement decisions is that if consumers truly do begin to spend time with interactive media, they will have less time to spend with traditional media such as television and newspapers. This will force advertisers to choose whether to participate in (or develop their own) interactive media. (Chapter 16 deals exclusively with the Internet, media buying on the Internet, and audience measurement problems.)

The biggest lessons here are (1) this type of advertising and IBP is growing rapidly, and (2) it works, for the most part, in a fundamentally different way: consumers seek out the advertiser/advertising (pull) and then interact (two-way, or **multiway communication**) with brand communication, rather than the traditional model where ads intrude in programming and seek consumers out. It's more the consumer's choice: The consumer chooses to go there and interact; it is not pushed at them.

③ Media Choice and Integrated Brand Promotions.
A final complicating factor in the media environment is that more firms are adopting an integrated brand promotion perspective, which relies on a broader mix of communication tools. As you know, IBP is the use of various promotional tools, including advertising, in a coordinated manner to build and maintain brand awareness, identity, and preference. Promotional options such as event sponsorship, direct marketing, sales promotion (see Exhibit 14.23), and public relations are drawing many firms away from traditional mass media advertising. But even these new approaches still require coordination with the advertising that remains.

EXHIBIT 14.23

Sunglass Hut and American Pie 2 cross-promote.

Madison & Vine Media.

> *"It's a magnitude and urgency of change that isn't evolutionary—it's transformational. . . . If a new model isn't developed, the old one will simply collapse."*

> Steven J. Heyer, President and COO, Coca-Cola Co.[5]

This is the chief operating officer of Coca-Cola saying in no uncertain terms that something has to change: 30-second spot advertising just isn't doing it anymore.

The credit for coining the enormously popular term *Madison & Vine* goes to Scott Donaton at *Advertising Age* and his very good book by the same title. The term refers to the combination and meaningful merger of entertainment media and advertising. While this is covered elsewhere as well in the book, let us just say a few things about this very exciting turn of events. This concept is also referred to as branded entertainment. It began, actually long ago, with simple product placements in movies, radio, and then television shows. It actually goes back to the 1920s and 1930s, but really began to escalate in the late 1980s. The basis for the idea was that traditional advertising was no longer cost effective and that the cost of making and promoting films and music was also out of control. Hollywood, the record industry, and advertising all had a stake in finding a better, less regulated, less expensive, accountable, and more effective means of marketing communications. So, Madison & Vine was born: a recognized, full-fledged attempt to merge media in the form of branded entertainment on television, in games, in retail settings called brandscapes (think of stores such as NikeTown), on mobile phones, all across the board. We discussed the basic mechanism in Chapter 11, but it also is important to consider branded entertainment from the media side of things.

5.   Stephen J. Heyer (keynote address, Advertising Age Madison & Vine Conference, Beverly Hills, CA, February 5, 2003).

In an interview with Advertising Age, Sony Vice President-Music Licensing Kenny Ochoa, explained how linking music and advertising can benefit both the brand and the artist.

Q: What do you think are some of the new and creative approaches to licensing?

A: I think creating a dialog directly between artists, labels and brands as early as possible in the creative process is imperative for the future. It's important that we can get beyond our relationship of a simple "transaction" for goods or budgetary element and treat music as talent, which it really is, and a brand in itself that the client can tap into for many benefits.

Q: Why do you think consumers are more open to artists pairing themselves with brands now than they were 10 years ago?

A: Consumers have a different perspective now than 10 years ago, when there were several more filters to what they were exposed to, which the Internet has completely removed, thus possibly making them more open-minded and accepting as the artist's individual choice and right.

Q: Any particular triumphs you are proud of?

A: Personally, the exposure of a new or unknown artist in a commercial to an audience they normally would not be in front of, not to mention contributing to the income to an artist in the early stages of their career, is rewarding… We (had) Columbia recording artist Nicole Atkins appearing in and having her music featured in an American Express spot, which during the first week of the campaign she landed at No. 2 on Google Trends, received a mention in the New York Post and got more than 3,000 hits in one day on her MySpace page.

Source: Brooke Capps, "Meet the Matchmaker: Hooking up Song Artists and Marketers," *Advertising Age*, August 23, 2007. Reprinted with permission. © Crain Communications, Inc. 2007.

EXHIBIT 14.24

Music meets brand. Of course, who is the brand: the musical artists, the car, the airline, or the box of cereal? Under this model, they all are.

In Exhibit 14.24, Kenny Ochoa, the vice president for music licensing at Sony, discusses how the use of music in advertising and marketing campaigns can benefit both brands and recording artists. That is just one example of how branded entertainment is helping build the kind of new advertising model that Coca-Cola's Heyer so clearly stated was needed. In other instances, branded entertainment starts with a 30-second television spot that grows into something much larger. That was the case with the Geico cavemen, who were created as quirky pitchmen for the automobile insurance company and then found themselves with their own half-hour television show in fall 2007. Joe Lawson, who was writing the caveman ad scripts as head of Geico's creative team, knew the company wanted to expand into other branded entertainment. So he developed full-length television scripts, tapped some Hollywood connections, then pitched the networks—and succeeded. Of course, by the time you are reading this, the show could be cancelled. Things move fast in branded entertainment land.

For clients seeking branded entertainment opportunities, there typically are three primary approaches. The most straightforward and least expensive is product placement. A character on television might be seen drinking Diet Pepsi, driving a Cadillac, or dropping off a FedEx package. A more sophisticated approach involves storyline integration, such as putting a UPS delivery truck in an EA Sports NASCAR game or sending the Geico cavemen down the red carpet during the Oscars (see Exhibit 14.25). Original content, as when the cavemen graduated to their own primetime show or BMW produced short online film clips featuring their vehicles, is the most expensive, but potentially most compelling, form of branded entertain-

Cavemen and three levels of branded entertainment: A Very Good Example.

ment. Yet, as Lawson notes, measuring the value of these various forms of branded entertainment is difficult. "We're trying to find meaningful ways to measure this sort of stuff," Lawson says. "Ultimately, the clients still want that, and as they spend more money in that area, they will want to feel more comfortable knowing that their message is getting out there in a meaningful way."[6]

In terms of media measurement: IAG gives scores to the most recalled brand placement (see Exhibit 14.26)

IAG provides a list of the most recalled brands.

Rank	Brand	In-Program Placement Description	Program Airing Info	Recall Index
1	Green Valley Ranch	Julia and Jen win trip to resort as reward for winning a challenge	Hell's Kitchen (FOX, Jul 23)	252
2	Green Valley Ranch	Announcer says the winner will be head chef of a restaurant in resort	Hell's Kitchen (FOX, Jul 9)	228
3	Lipton	Kail hides her veto box in package of tea bags during challenge	Big Brother 8 (CBS, Jul 10)	221
4	Green Valley Ranch	Announcer says the winner will be head chef of a restaurant in resort	Hell's Kitchen (FOX, Jul 30)	213
5	Capital One	Sponsor of the "Audience Favorite" award	Last Comic Standing (NBC, Aug 1)	204
6	Capital One	Sponsor of the "Audience Favorite" award	Last Comic Standing (NBC, Jul 18)	191
7	Red Rock	Julia and Jen visit resort to meet Heather, last season's winner	Hell's Kitchen (FOX, Jul 23)	188
8	Capital One	Sponsor of the "Audience Favorite" award	Last Comic Standing (NBC, Jul 11)	186
9	InTouch Magazine	Red Team has a photo shoot as reward for winning a challenge	Hell's Kitchen (FOX, Jul 9)	160
10	Nike	Logo is visible on Jayanna's sneakers during camping trip	Age of Love (NBC, Jul 23)	144

The IAG Top 10 Most Recalled In-Program Placements focuses on brand/product placements occurring in Reality programs on the broadcast networks during the July 9 to August 5 period. The Recall Score is the percentage of television viewers who can recall within 24 hours the brand/product of an In-Program placement they were exposed to during the normal course of viewing Network Reality shows. These scores are then indexed against the mean score for all placements occurring in this genre during the time period (Recall Index). 100 equals average. Note: For this analysis, In-Program placements were only considered if the occurrence had visual elements (i.e., was "seen" on-screen) or both visual and auditory element (i.e., was both "seen" and "mentioned"). Only first-run episodes were considered. Both planned and incidental exposures are tracked by IAG.

6.   Brooke Capps, "The Man Who Brought UPS to NASCAR and Geico Cavemen to Hollywood," *Advertising Age*, May 3, 2007.

TOP 10 SHOWS WITH PRODUCT PLACEMENT
Week of July 23–29, 2007

Program	Network	Total Occurrences
CMA Music Festival	ABC	142
Hell's Kitchen	Fox	142
King of Queens	CBS	114
America's Next Top Model	CW	111
Big Brother 8	CBS	65
Extreme Makeover: Home Edition	ABC	51
So You Think You Can Dance	Fox	45
Just for Laughs	ABC	34
Reba	CW	33
Age of Love	NBC	33

TOP 10 BRANDS WITH TV PRODUCT PLACEMENT
Week of July 23–29, 2007

Brand	Category	Total # Occurrences
Chef Revival	Apparel	91
Tribal Streetwear	Apparel	31
Mack	Trucks	25
Nike	Footware	20
1-800-skydive	Referral Services	19
Ludwig	Drums	17
LRG	Apparel	16
Nike	Apparel	14
Abercrombie & Fitch	Apparel	14
Houston Texans	Football Teams	13

Source: "Nielsen Place Views," *Advertising Age,* August 9, 2007. Reprinted with permission. © Crain Communications, Inc., 2007.

EXHIBIT 14.27

The biggest player in all media measurement, A.C. Nielsen also offers product placement data.

Nielsen is also in the interactive game. The company measures, among other things, the number of placements in shows. Check out Exhibit 14.27.

Social Networking. Facebook, MySpace, and others have revolutionized the way we think about mediated communication. From the earliest work on brand communities, Muniz and O'Guinn noted that this new paradigm is represented by three nodes rather than the traditional two: marketer-consumer-consumer (see Exhibit 14.28). Consumers talk to other consumers and like to talk to other consumers, and like to talk to other consumers about stuff, consumer stuff. Now, through the Internet, they can, for almost no cost, instantaneously, and with the power of huge numbers. That changed everything. Now, it is so easy to leverage this through sites like Facebook and MySpace. They all vary a bit, but in Facebook the advertiser pays fees to promote groups through paid-for stories as "news." As social networking has become hugely important, so has the data acquired through it. In 2007, the media research giant Nielsen launched a social network data gathering service called Hey!Nielsen, intended to reach exactly that audience, as the Doing It Right box explains.

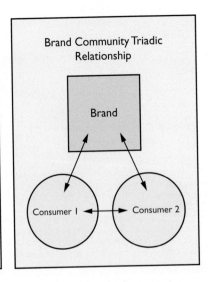

EXHIBIT 14.28

The World Wide Web has made us re-think the brand-consumer relationship.

④ The Real Deal.

The Real Deal: Data Quality.
A problem that gets way too little attention, at least in textbooks, is this: GIGO. This is an old, but still very appropriate, rule

DOING IT RIGHT

With Hey!Nielsen, Research Giant Tracks Pop Culture Buzz the Facebook Way

The British rock band Radiohead touched off a hot debate about consumer behavior and the future of the music industry in October 2007 when it announced that its new album would be independently released as a pay-what-you-will download. The question of the moment for the band's many fans became: What are you willing to pay?

For music executives keenly interested in the answer, the world's largest media research firm offered a new way to tap into that consumer conversation. The Nielsen company in September 2007 launched an online social networking site designed to let pop culture enthusiasts share their views about everything from television and the Internet to movies to music. Modeled after networking sites like Facebook and MySpace, the site lets users sound off about their pop culture interests, while Nielsen tracks demographic information, comments, and topic scores for its clients.

At Hey!Nielsen.com, the discussion about Radiohead's unusual pricing strategy was lively—and insightful. "Very exciting idea," one fan posted. "I hate downloading, legal or illegal. I want to hold a CD in my hand and have a high-fidelity hard copy, no matter what. Pay-as-you-wish is a novel idea, though; I will totally throw down $5 for the download and buy the physical CD when it's at retail."

Developers of Hey!Nielsen said the site was designed to be part opinion engine, part trend tracker, part social glue. Said Nielsen Media Research CEO Susan Whiting, "We hope people will come because they understand that we have clients who will be listening to them and want to listen to them. It really will be their Web site. It's really about the users coming on and telling us what they think."

Regular posters at Hey!Nielsen can earn perks such as sneak previews and passes to invitation-only events. For Nielsen clients, the benefits could be far more substantial. One likely extension of the product will be broad online panels for conducting experimental marketing and other consumer research for the entertainment industry.

Sources: Staff report, "Nielsen Rolls Out Hey!Nielsen: Online Social Network for Popular Culture," **Wireless News**, September 30, 2007; Joe Mandese, "Hey!Nielsen, Why Are You Going Viral? Researcher Develops Social Network to Measure TV, Internet, Music, Celebrities," **Media Post**, August 24, 2007.

in computer data management: garbage in, garbage out. In other words, no matter how much you process data, if it was garbage coming in to the system, it is still garbage going out. In media planning, there is enormous reliance on very sophisticated mathematical models and computer programs to optimize media schedules. But throwing the calculus book at the problem isn't sufficient. We have a big cultural hang-up about numbers. In fact, let us say that again: We have a big cultural hang-up about numbers. When we put a number to something it makes it appear more precise, more scientific, and more certain. But that is often pure illusion. Yes, these optimization programs are good, they are valuable, they save clients billions of dollars—but they also distract attention from a more basic problem: Media exposure data are often just not very good. We are not saying that media data are complete trash, but we are saying that what it means to be exposed to an advertisement is not adequately addressed by most exposure data. This is a sad reality, and one that is well known but rarely acknowledged until fairly recently. With the radically changing media landscape, clients are less willing to pay for, or rely on, an even highly "optimized" media schedule when the data going into those calculations are highly suspect. There are now too many other games in town with better and more meaningful exposure estimates and ROIs to have to pay for poor data. This is now a common industry complaint. It is almost at crisis stage.

Think about it: Is being in the room when a TV is on sufficient to say you were exposed to the ad? Did you see it in any meaningful way? Shouldn't "exposure" be more, mean more than that? Well, sure it should. But the media measurement companies argue that (1) it's the best we have, (2) everyone is playing by the same rules, and if you use the measures simply to judge *relative* strengths, then they are OK, and (3) they are always working on better methods. They are right about the second point: If used only for relative measurement (one schedule against another), exposure data are probably reasonably good. Unfortunately, most exposure data in all mass media are a long way from capturing and delivering what it means to see or hear an ad. You need to keep this in mind when you see all those precise-looking numbers.

No doubt, in response to considerable desire for something better, Nielsen released Project Apollo, as featured in Exhibit 14.29: Lots more data, better measurement.

EXHIBIT 14.29

A.C. Nielsen has unveiled its newest measurement system. This is an attempt to make media data more meaningful and practical.

For marketers, one of the most critical questions is whether the money spent on ad campaigns and promotions really influences consumer choices. That question is made even more difficult as media choices expand at an unprecedented rate, retail channels are blurred, and consumers face seemingly limitless options for even the most basic products.

A new national tracking service, known as Project Apollo, promises to help cut through those issues by collecting and connecting three kinds of single-source consumer information: exposure to multi-media messages, brand recognition and preference, and actual purchase behavior.

Project Apollo launched in early 2006, with about 5,000 households included in its pilot study. The consumer volunteers agreed to have their exposure to electronic media messages monitored and to track all of their product pruchases, providing marketers with rare objective data about what specific messages get relayed to consumers—and how those individual consumers respond.

The accompanying chart, for instance, records how exposure to a television commercial for the Lincoln Navigator might have prompted a subsequent visit to a Lincoln/Mercury dealership or how a lunch stop at McDonald's followed a radio ad spot for the fast food chain.

To collect that kind of detailed information, Project Apollo relies on two key technologies. One, the Portable People Meter, is a pager-like device that continuously records the wearer's exposure to electronic media. The other primary technology, the ACNielsen Homescan scanner, allows the panelist consumers to create an electronic record of all packaged goods they purchase.

The result is a holistic system of measuring media exposure, integrated with demographic and purchasing data that offers marketers a new way to know with greater certainty whether they're getting the most bang for the buck.

Chart 2: Project Apollo–Pulling Together the Elements of a "Day In The Life."

Wife, Age 41

Key Statistics
- Post-graduate degree
- Drives a Mercury Sable
- Health conscious
- Hectic life—willing to pay for convenience
- Active in community
- Married with 2 kids, ages 13 & 1
- Uses Visa and MasterCard
- Eats out 4–6 times a week
- Family owns 3 cell phones

Other Media Usage
- *American Baby*
- *National Geographic*
- *Cosmopolitan*
- *Self*
- *People*

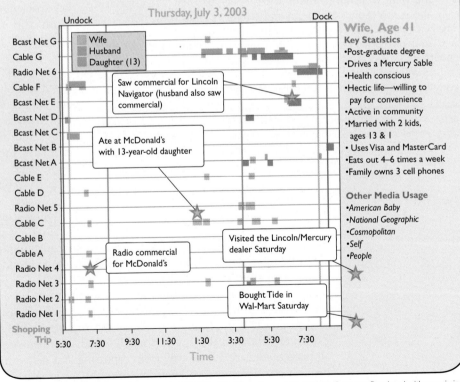

Source: http://us.acneilsen.com/pubs/documents/media_000.pdf, Arbitron, Inc. and the Nielson Company. Reprinted with permission.

The Real Deal: Ads For Advertisers. Another thing that is generally poorly covered in other books is the institutional sales function. How do media vehicles sell themselves to advertisers and advertising agencies? What is the role of this business-to-business (B2B) advertising? Well, it's a big effort, and a big role. Media companies spend lots of money selling their time and space to advertisers thorough their ad agencies. Pick up any issue of *Ad Age* and count the ads. Who is spending the money? Exhibits 14.30 through 14.33 are some pretty creative ads for media vehicles placed in *Ad Age* and *Adweek* to attract advertisers. This is an important part of the real-world of advertising and IBP media.

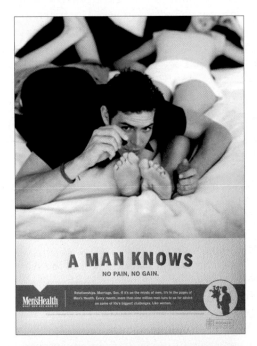

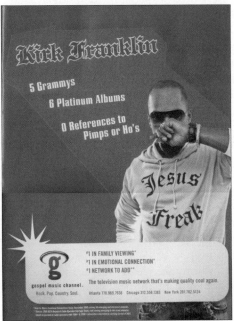

EXHIBITS 14.30 THROUGH 14.33

These are ads for advertising professionals, particularly media buyers. They tell why their particular vehicle is the best at reaching some desired audience.

The Real Deal: The Media Lunch. It's the real world. It's Friday afternoon, and *Big National Magazine* is throwing a party at your agency. Wow, what nice folks: free drinks, great food, nice socializing. One of the sales reps took some of us to a bar afterward. Wow, those reps over at *Big National Magazine* are sure some great guys.

But wait, why the party? Well, let's look at the guest list: The party is being held on the floor of the building where the media buyers work. Look around the room. There are some account people, the occasional hungry creative, but almost everyone there is a media planner or buyer. Hmm. Well, yes, that's because a lot of media buying does not depend on sophisticated math from a computer program, but on good old-fashioned schmoozing and sales pitches. The media planner has options beyond what the canned software recommends—he/she can make deals, can and does play favorites. This is why, despite the relatively low pay, entry-level ad people tend to like the job. It has good perks. It's also why certain ads get in certain vehicles.

⑤ Computer Media-Planning Models. The explosion of available data on markets and consumers has motivated media planners to rely heavily on electronic databases, computers, and software to assist with the various parts of the media-planning effort.

Nearly all of the major syndicated research services offer electronic data to their subscribers, including advertisers, agencies, and media organizations. These databases contain information helpful in identifying target markets and audiences, estimating or projecting media vehicle audiences and costs, and analyzing competitive advertising activity, among many others. Companies that offer data electronically, such as Nielsen, Arbitron, MRI, SMRB, Scarborough, and the Audit Bureau of Circulations, also typically provide software designed to analyze their own data. Such software often produces summary reports, tabulations, ranking, reach-frequency analysis, optimization, simulation, scheduling, buying, flowcharts, and a variety of graphical presentations.

Advertisers that use a mix of media in their advertising campaigns often subscribe to a variety of electronic data services representing the media they use or consider using. However, the various syndicated services do not provide standardized data, reports, and analyses that are necessarily comparable across media categories. Also, individual syndicated service reports and analyses may not offer the content and depth that some users prefer. Nor do they typically analyze media categories that they do not measure. Consequently, media software houses such as Interactive Market Systems (IMS) and Telmar Information Services Corp. (Telmar) offer hundreds of specialized and standardized software products that help advertisers, agencies, and media organizations worldwide develop and evaluate markets, audiences, and multimedia plans. Exhibit 14.34 shows typical screens from one such computer program. The first screen is reach and cost data for spot TV ads, and the second screen is the combined reach and cost data for spot TV and newspaper ads.

Computerization and modeling can never substitute for planning and judgment by media strategists. Computer modeling does, however, allow for the assessment of a wide range of possibilities before making costly media buys. It can, and does, save advertisers a lot of money.

One of the most important aspects of the media-scheduling phase involves creating a visual representation of the media schedule. Exhibit 14.35 shows a media schedule flowchart that includes both print and electronic media placement. With this visual representation of the schedule, the advertiser has tangible documentation of the overall media plan.

Making the Buy. Once an overall media plan and schedule are in place, the focus must turn to **media buying**. Media buying entails securing the electronic media time and print media space specified in the schedule. An important part of the media-buying process is the

Left Table

ADplus(TM) RESULTS: SPOT TV (30S)
Walt Disney World
Off-Season Promotion
Monthly
Target: 973,900
Jacksonville DMA Adults

Message/vehicle = 32.0%

Frequency (f) Distributions

f	VEHICLE % f+	% f+	MESSAGE % f	% f+
0	5.1	–	9.1	–
1	2.0	94.9	7.5	90.9
2	2.2	92.9	8.1	83.4
3	2.3	90.7	8.1	75.2
4	2.4	88.3	7.8	67.1
5	2.4	85.9	7.2	59.3
6	2.5	83.5	6.6	52.1
7	2.5	81.0	6.0	45.5
8	2.5	78.5	5.3	39.5
9	2.5	76.0	4.7	34.2
10+	73.5	73.5	29.5	29.5
20+	49.8	49.8	6.1	6.1

Summary Evaluation

Reach 1+ (%)	94.9%	90.9%
Reach 1+ (000s)	923.9	885.3
Reach 3+ (%)	90.7%	75.2%
Reach 3+ (000s)	882.9	732.8
Gross rating points (GRPs)	2,340.0	748.8
Average frequency (f)	24.7	8.2
Gross impressions (000s)	22,789.3	7,292.6
Cost-per-thousand (CPM)	6.10	19.06
Cost-per-rating point (CPP)	59	186

Vehicle List	RATING	AD COST	CPM-MSG	ADS	TOTAL COST	MIX %
WJKS-ABC-AM	6.00	234	12.51	30	7,020	5.1
WJXT-CBS-AM	6.00	234	12.51	30	7,020	5.1
WTLV-NBC-AM	6.00	234	12.51	30	7,020	5.1
WJKS-ABC-DAY	5.00	230	14.76	60	13,800	9.9
WJXT-CBS-DAY	5.00	230	14.76	60	13,800	9.9
WTLV-NBC-DAY	5.00	230	14.76	60	13,800	9.9
WJKS-ABC-PRIM	10.00	850	27.27	30	25,500	18.4
WJXT-CBS-PRIM	10.00	850	27.27	30	25,500	18.4
WTLV-NBC-PRIM	10.00	850	27.27	30	25,500	18.4
Totals:			19.06	360	138,960	100.0

Right Table

ADplus(TM) RESULTS: DAILY NEWSPAPERS (1/2 PAGE), SPOT TV (30S)
Walt Disney World
Off-Season Promotion
Monthly
Target: 973,900
Jacksonville DMA Adults

Message/vehicle = 28.1%

Frequency (f) Distributions

f	VEHICLE % f+	% f+	MESSAGE % f	% f+
0	1.2	–	4.0	–
1	0.8	98.8	4.9	96.0
2	0.9	98.0	5.9	91.1
3	0.9	97.2	6.5	85.2
4	1.0	96.2	6.7	78.7
5	1.1	95.2	6.8	72.0
6	1.1	94.2	6.6	65.2
7	1.2	93.0	6.3	58.6
8	1.3	91.8	5.9	52.4
9	1.3	90.6	5.5	46.5
10+	89.3	89.3	41.0	41.0
20+	73.3	73.3	9.6	9.6

Summary Evaluation

Reach 1+ (%)	98.8%	96.0%
Reach 1+ (000s)	962.6	934.6
Reach 3+ (%)	97.2%	85.2%
Reach 3+ (000s)	946.5	829.7
Gross rating points (GRPs)	3,372.0	948.0
Average frequency (f)	34.1	9.9
Gross impressions (000s)	32,839.9	9,232.3
Cost-per-thousand (CPM)	10.96	38.99
Cost-per-rating point (CPP)	107	380

Vehicle List	RATING	AD COST	CPM-MSG	ADS	TOTAL COST	MIX %
1 Daily Newspapers		Totals:	114.00	80	221,040	61.4
Times-Union	42.00	8,284	104.93	20	165,680	46.0
Record	4.00	866	115.18	20	17,320	4.8
News	3.20	926	153.95	20	18,520	5.1
Reporter	2.40	976	216.35	20	19,520	5.4
2 Spot TV (30s)		Totals:	19.00	360	138,960	38.6
WJKS-ABC-AM	6.00	234	12.51	30	7,020	2.0
WJXT-CBS-AM	6.00	234	12.51	30	7,020	2.0
WTLV-NBC-AM	6.00	234	12.51	30	7,020	2.0
WJKS-ABC-DAY	5.00	230	14.76	60	13,800	3.8
WJXT-CBS-DAY	5.00	230	14.76	60	13,800	3.8
WTLV-NBC-DAY	5.00	230	14.76	60	13,800	3.8
WJKS-ABC-PRIM	10.00	850	27.27	30	25,500	7.1
WJXT-CBS-PRIM	10.00	850	27.27	30	25,500	7.1
WTLV-NBC-PRIM	10.00	850	27.27	30	25,500	7.1
Totals:			38.99	440	360,000	100.0

EXHIBIT 14.34

The explosion of data about markets and consumers has caused advertisers to rely more on computerized media-planning tools.

EXHIBIT 14.35

A media flowchart gives an advertiser a visual representation of the overall media plan.

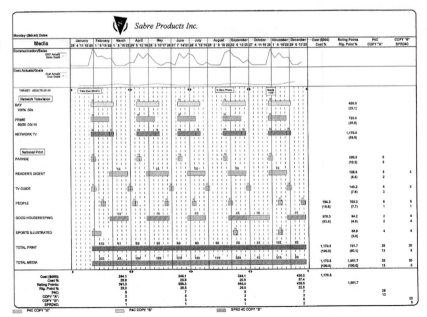

Source: Telmar Information Services Corp., FlowMaster for Windows™, New York, 1999. Reprinted with permission.

Wanna go outside?

NEWSPAPER BUYS—THAT SELL   (800) 638 9798

EXHIBIT 14.36

An example of a media-buying service. Internet-based media-buying services enable media professionals to purchase advertising more efficiently for print, online, and broadcast media. Explore the services and capabilities of Marketron International (http://www.marketron .com). How does this Web-based advertising-exchange service increase the efficiency of media scheduling and buying?

agency of record. The **agency of record** is the advertising agency chosen by the advertiser to purchase time and space. The agency of record coordinates media discounts and negotiates all contracts for time and space. Any other agencies involved in the advertising effort submit insertion orders for time and space within those contracts.

Each spring, television programming and ad execs participate in a ritual called the "**upfronts**." The upfronts is a period where the television networks reveal their fall line-ups and presell advertising on them. About 75 percent of prime time television advertising is bought this way, in advance. Only the remaining 25 percent is really "in play" for the season. There are all sorts of unofficial rules in this ritual. Viewed from the outside, it's much like a typical American trying to understand cricket. Let's just say it's played a bit like poker—you can see some cards for free; others will cost you. Whatever the best game metaphor, it looks like the TV networks are not getting as much premium pricing as they use to. Why? It's the TV clutter, TiVo, branded entertainment, competition from computer-delivered entertainment, and its very high price. Several media soothsayers predict the end of the up-fronts within the next decade. Personally, we think they will probably still be around.

Rather than using an agency of record, some advertisers use a **media-buying service**, which is an independent organization that specializes in buying large blocks of media time and space and reselling it to advertisers (see Exhibit 14.36). Some agencies and companies have developed their own media-buying units (e.g., GM's GMPlanworks) to control both the planning and the buying process. Regardless of the structure used to make the buys, media buyers evaluate the audience reach, CPM, and timing of each buy. The organization responsible for the buy also monitors the ads and estimates the actual audience reach delivered. If the expected audience is not delivered, then media organizations have to *make good* by repeating ad placements or offering a refund or price reduction on future ads. For example, making good to advertisers because of shortfalls in delivering 1998 Winter Olympics prime-time cost CBS an estimated 400 additional 30-second spots.[7]

⑥ In Defense of Traditional Advertising. While it is absolutely undeni-

able that the world of media advertising and promotion has changed a great deal, we would like to throw a bit of cold water (maybe more like a light mist) on the media revolution. Traditional advertising, even the "30 Net-TV" (30-second network television) ad and the magazine ad, are not dead. They still perform a very valuable function. There are just some things you can't accomplish without them, like a Super Bowl or Olympics: delivering the truly mass audience. Sometimes their unique qualities get lost in the optimized promotional numbers. Brand building still needs traditional ads, at least for a while longer. Yet the traditional ad world has learned that it can never rest on its laurels, nor can the traditional media. But throwing around planning buzzwords doesn't work either. As Kevin Roberts, CEO of Saatchi and Saatchi recently said in obvious rebuke of the integrated communication frenzy: "If I hear the words 'touchpoints' or 'holistic' one more time, I'm going to throw up."

7.   "CBS Faces Olympics Make-Goods," *http://www.adage.com*, February 19, 1998.

SUMMARY

 Describe the important changes that have altered the advertising and IBP media landscape, such as agency compensation, ROI demands, globalization, and multicultural media.

The demise of the 15 percent commission means that there is less economic incentive for agencies to buy media advertising. With more media of all sorts of advertising and IBP out there, dollars get spread around a lot more than they used to. The consolidated media buying allows agencies to get better deals and exert more power on the media. Still, agencies now operate with fewer staff to do even bigger jobs, thus making the newer and more lucrative types of media more attractive than traditional media. Globalization of media is exerting considerable pressure on the industry to standardize media measurement across the globe. Consumers who are spoiled by free content are less and less interested in obtrusive advertising, thus favoring alternative pull communications forms going forward. The increasing deal-proneness and cost transparency provided by the Internet has made consumers considerably more powerful in their ability to get consumer information without having to rely on traditional media advertising. Add to this the incredibly ad-cluttered state of traditional media, and you can see why nothing in advertising media is sacred, nothing. Don't forget the growing influence of multicultural media available across the globe. It's a new world of media out there. Last, but far from least, advertisers are now demanding greater accountability and documented return on investment (ROI) from their media buys, traditional or new media.

 Describe the fundamentals of media planning.

Although many important changes are taking place in the advertising industry, the components of the media-planning process remain essentially the same. A media plan specifies the media vehicles that will be used to deliver the advertiser's message. Developing a media plan entails setting objectives such as effective reach and frequency and determining strategies to achieve those objectives. Media planners use several quantitative indicators, such as CPM and CPRP, to help them judge the efficiency of prospective media choices. The media-planning process culminates in the scheduling and purchase of a mix of media vehicles expected to deliver the advertiser's message to specific target audiences at precisely the right time to affect their consumption decisions. While media planning is a methodical process, it cannot be reduced to computer decision-making models and statistical measurements; data quality and human and personal factors prohibit media planning from being an exact science.

 Know the bottom line of IBP's impact on media planning.

There is a very real possibility of a continued decline in advertising's reliance on traditional media. IBP efforts that rely on database efforts are very attractive due to their highly selective targeting and measured response. It's also true that better and better measures of advertising effectiveness will be required with more reliance on IBP. To work in the contemporary ad and IBP environment you will have to know a lot about a much wider array of "media." Further, central control of these far-flung promotional efforts is a must. Things can really get away from you in this new environment.

 Discuss the "real deals" in media planning.

In the real ad and IBP world there is an illusion of precision because of all the numbers used. In reality there is a lot of slop in the media measurement system. Data quality is just not all that great. They are good enough for some purposes, but don't be fooled into thinking numbers equal truth. Not so. Bad measurement is still bad measurement no matter how many computers crunch the data. Also, a lot of real world media planning comes from ads for advertisers. Media planners are the target market of lots of ads for lots of media outlets. And never forget the power of the media lunch: the "free lunch" or cocktail party hosted by your friendly media rep. That's how a lot of media get planned. Truth.

 Discuss the essentials of the contemporary media planning environment.

You should know the particular measurement demands and essential terms of Internet media. You should also know the importance of share-of-voice calculations; they allow you to see, across all kinds of contemporary media, what percent your brand's spending is of the total category, and they provide quick and easy competitive comparisons. You should also understand that standard practice these days involves the uses of computer-media models that optimize media schedules for the most mathematically cost efficient media buy. This should be used as a tool, but not a substitute for media strategy. You should also understand that the growing category of interactive media demands special attention from media planners and will probably make traditional media less important over time. You should also know that more and more media buys are made by a stand-alone media buying company.

 Discuss the value of traditional advertising.

A lot of very smart, creative, and powerful people believe in traditional advertising, and don't see it going away . . . at all, ever.

KEY TERMS

deal-proneness	frequency	share of voice
price/cost transparency	effective frequency	cost per thousand (CPM)
above-the-line promotion	effective reach	cost per thousand–target market
measured media	message weight	(CPM–TM)
below-the-line promotion	gross impressions	cost per rating point (CPRP)
unmeasured media	between-vehicle duplication	RSS (Really Simple Syndication)
media plan	within-vehicle duplication	multiway communication
media class	continuity	media buying
media vehicle	continuous scheduling	agency of record
media mix	flighting	upfronts
single-source tracking services	pulsing	media-buying service
geographic scope	forgetting function	Push marketing
geo-targeting	square-root law	Pull marketing
reach	context effects	

QUESTIONS

1. The opening section of this chapter describes radical changes that have taken place in the world of media planning. Compare and contrast the way things used to be and the way they are now. What factors contributed to this shift? Do you think the job of media planning has become more or less complicated? Explain.

2. Of all the changes taking place in the in the world of media planning, which do you think will continue to have the greatest impact on the future of the advertising industry?

3. The proliferation of media options has created increasing complexities for media planners, but useful distinctions can still be made concerning the relative standing of the different choices available to advertisers. What advertising and brand promotion options dominate the "big pie" of total promotion options? Who is doing the most ad spending?

4. Media plans should of course take a proactive stance with respect to customers. Explain how geo-targeting can be used in making a media plan more proactive with respect to customers.

5. Media strategy models allow planners to compare the impact of different media plans, using criteria such as reach, frequency, and gross impressions. What other kinds of criteria should a planner take into account before deciding on a final plan?

6. Review the mathematics of the CPM and CPRP calculations, and explain how these two indicators can be used to assess the efficiency and effectiveness of a media schedule.

7. Why is data quality becoming an increasingly important issue in real-world media planning?

8. In the real world, do media planners always make strategic decisions based on sophisticated data, or are there other influences that sway their media-buying decisions? Explain.

9. How has the increased emphasis on branded entertainment and the meteoric rise in popularity of social networking sites such as MySpace influenced media planning?

10. Discuss the issues raised in this chapter that represent challenges for those who champion integrated brand promotions. Why would central control be required for achieving IBP? If media planners wish to play the role of central controller, what must they do to qualify for the role?

EXPERIENTIAL EXERCISES

1.   Watch one hour of prime-time television and for each advertisement, record the time length and a brief description of the spot. Using your perceptions about the most and least persuasive ads during this hour of television, develop a hypothesis about the value of long versus short advertising messages. When should an advertiser use long instead of short television ads? When does the opposite hold true?

2.   Assume that you are advising a regional snack-food manufacturer whose brands have a low share of voice. Which pattern of continuity would you recommend for such an advertiser? Would you place your ads in television program that is also sponsored by competing national brands such as Pringles or Doritos? Why or why not?

3.   As discussed in the chapter, context is a critical part of the media planning equation. To better understand context effects, obtain recent copies of *Sports Illustrated, InStyle,* and the *New Yorker.* For each magazine, what are the primary types of brands, products, and services advertised? What similarities do you find between brands and their ad messages within each magazine? What social meaning does the magazine itself lend to the advertisers? Also list five examples of brands, products, or services you would least expect to advertise in each magazine and explain why.

4.   Divide into small teams and outline a media strategy for the makers of Jovan Musk based on the demographic research provided for men's aftershave and cologne in Exhibit 14.12. Your strategy outline should offer guidelines for any subsequent media planning, identifying the best target audience, the appropriate media mix, and what media vehicles would be a logical fit for the campaign. In your answer, also address the limitations of such demographic data in media planning.

CHAPTER 15

After reading and thinking about this chapter, you will be able to do the following:

1

Understand the changes taking place in the traditional media of newspapers, magazines, television, and radio relative to new electronic media options.

2

Detail the pros and cons of newspapers as a media class, identify newspaper categories, and describe buying and audience measurement for newspapers.

3

Detail the pros and cons of magazines as a media class, identify magazine categories, and describe buying and audience measurement for magazines.

4

Detail the pros and cons of television as a media class, identify television categories, and describe buying and audience measurement for television.

5

Detail the pros and cons of radio as a media class, identify radio categories, and describe buying and audience measurement for radio.

Spring 2007 • $3

fedflyfishers.org

FLYFISHER

MAGAZINE OF THE FEDERATION OF FLY FISHERS

Conserving, Restoring & Educating Through Fly Fishing

Tips from the masters on

EARLY SEASON
TROUT
REDFISH
WHITEFISH
BASS

GILA TROUT
making a comeback

A Whole New "Traditional" Media World.

In Chapters 1 and 2 we discussed that the advertising industry as a whole continues to evolve and change in very significant ways. No place is that change more tangible or dramatic than in the traditional media of newspapers, magazines, television, and radio. For 70 years, choosing media to deliver advertising messages was a fairly simple and straightforward process. Advertisers would work with their advertising agency to develop messages for their brands. Then the agencies would negotiate for airtime with television and radio networks or space with newspapers and magazines. Most of these media options were owned by a few big media companies.

Well, it just doesn't work like that anymore. Advertisers are fast adopting the belief that digital media—primarily Internet ads—offer a more cost-effective way to reach target markets. In addition, digital media allow advertisers to make rapid changes in campaigns, changes that might take months to accomplish with traditional media. And let's not forget that an Internet campaign can be a global campaign if the advertiser chooses to make it so—a monumental task in traditional media.

These advantages of digital media are changing not just advertisers' perceptions of how to develop campaigns, but also the way they are spending their money on media. Internet advertising is now a $20 billion industry, or about 6 percent of total U.S. spending on advertising, up from just 4 percent in 2004.[1] The other important change is that media companies are catching on to the fact that the old traditional way of delivering content (and the ads that support that content) are fading. One example is that total advertising dollars spent on newspapers by advertisers has dropped from 23 percent of all ad spending to just 18 percent—taking hundreds of millions of dollars of revenue away from newspaper publishers.[2] Google and Yahoo! can offer precisely targeted local ads (the power of newspapers in the past), craigslist .com has free classified ads, and news information is free *everywhere* on the Web. In response, newspaper companies like E.W. Scripps have made aggressive moves into interactive media to shore up flagging print revenues.[3]

While newspapers have been particularly hard hit by interactive media, television companies are feeling the pinch as well—and responding with their own makeovers. Consider the case of CBS, the 50-plus-year-old traditional media television network (you know, the folks that bring you all the *CSI* programs). In 2006 CBS began to set up partnerships with two dozen online organizations like Bebo and Veoh to syndicate CBS programming online and will receive about 90 percent of the ad revenue sold around the content it provides.[4] In addition, the network has purchased outright online media organizations like music-based social network Last.fm and financial video start-up Wallstrip. The reason for all these modern media maneuvers by an old-style media company: CBS wants ad revenue coming in from as many sources as possible related to the ways people are seeking information in this new media environment.

Big traditional media companies like CBS *have* to get into new media because of the way advertisers are setting their media strategies. Consider the way Delta Air Lines designed its advertising campaign for the firm's emergence from bankruptcy. First, the company enlisted the services of traditional ad agency SS&K and digital marketing company Publicis Modem. The two agencies worked out the message, images, and story line for the Delta campaign. Then SS&K developed a traditional media campaign (primarily print media—see Exhibit 15.1) and Publicis designed different ads for online media including banner ads and e-mails to frequent fliers. The new digital media campaign also included a social networking site and the purchase of paid search terms.[5]

The media environment is by no means settled into any predictable structure, and media companies on all sides of the "digital divide" are scrambling to properly posi-

1.   Emily Steel, "Advertising's Brave New World," *Wall Street Journal*, May 25, 2007, B1, B3.
2.   Brian Deagon, "Digital Era Leaves No Time for Newspapers to Rest In Print," *Investor's Business Daily*, February 17, 2006, accessed at *http://www.biz.yahoo.com* on February 20, 2006
3.   Abbey Klaassen, "How Scripps Turned into a Digital Darling," *Advertising Age*, January 22, 2007, 3, 23.
4.   Jon Fine, "Not Bad, for a TV Network," *BusinessWeek*, June 25, 2007, 24.
5.   Steel, "Advertising's Brave New World."

Delta used both the traditional medium of magazines and online digital media for the airline's advertising/IBP campaign as it emerged from bankruptcy.

tion themselves for the new ways consumers seek out brand information. The discussions that follow will give you an overview of all the traditional media options so you'll be aware of the options available to advertisers as they plan their brand advertising strategies. The next chapter, Chapter 16—Media Planning: Advertising and IBP on the Internet, addresses the digital media options.

Which Media? Strategic Planning Considerations.

Media decisions made by advertisers are critically important for two reasons. First, advertisers need media to reach the audiences that are likely to buy their brands. Not much of a mystery there. Second, when advertisers choose their media, these choices ultimately determine which media companies earn the billions of dollars spent on newspaper, magazine, television/cable, and radio advertising slots.

This chapter focuses on the challenge advertisers face in evaluating these major print and broadcast media options as key ways to reach their audiences. As the discussion of media planning in the previous chapter emphasized, even great advertising can't achieve communications and sales objectives if the media placement misses the target audience.

Our discussion of print, television, and radio media will concentrate on several key aspects of using these major traditional media. With respect to the print media—newspapers and magazines—we'll first consider the advantages and disadvantages of the media themselves. Both newspapers and magazines have inherent capabilities and limitations that advertisers must take into consideration in building a media plan. Next, we'll look at the types of newspapers and magazines from which advertisers can choose. Finally, we will identify buying procedures and audience measurement techniques.

After we look at the print media, we will consider television and radio in the same way. First, the types of television and radio options are described. Next, the advantages and disadvantages of television and radio are considered and the buying procedures and audience measurement techniques are identified. Finally, the future of television and radio in the context of new Internet, satellite, and broadband technology is considered.

Print, television, and radio media represent major traditional alternatives available to advertisers for reaching audiences. As the introductory scenario to this chapter points out, there is significant spending on new media, but about 50 percent of all advertising dollars in the United States still go to traditional print, radio, and television media.[6] In addition, the vast majority of the creative effort—and money—is expended on print and broadcast advertising campaigns. Despite the many intriguing opportunities that new digital media might offer, print and broadcast media will likely form the foundation of most advertising campaigns for years to come. The discussions in this chapter will demonstrate why these media represent such rich—and necessary—communication alternatives for advertisers.

---

6.   Bradley Johnson, "It's Been a Good 5 Years—Unless You're in Media," *Advertising Age,* December 11, 2006, 16.

Print Media.

You might think that the print media—newspapers and magazines—are lifeless lumps and lack impact compared to dynamic broadcast media options like Spike TV. Think again. Consider the problems that faced Absolut vodka. At one point in its illustrious history, Absolut was on the verge of extinction. The Swedish brand was selling only 12,000 cases a year in the United States—not enough to register even a single percentage point of market share. The name Absolut was seen as gimmicky; bartenders thought the bottle was ugly and hard to pour from; and to top things off, consumers gave no credibility at all to a vodka produced in Sweden, which they knew as the land of boxy-looking cars and hot tubs.

TBWA advertising agency in New York set about the task of overcoming these liabilities of the brand and decided to rely on print advertising *alone*—primarily because spirits ads were banned from broadcast at the time. The agency took on the challenge of developing magazine and newspaper ads that would build awareness, communicate quality, achieve credibility, and avoid Swedish clichés etched in the minds of American consumers. The firm came up with one of the most famous and successful print campaigns of all time. The concept was to feature the strange-shaped Absolut bottle as the hero of each ad, in which the only copy was a two-word tag line always beginning with *Absolut* and ending with a "quality" word such as *perfection* or *clarity*. The two-word description evolved from the original quality concept to a variety of clever combinations. "Absolut Centerfold" appeared in *Playboy* and featured an Absolut bottle with all the printing removed, and "Absolut Wonderland" was a Christmas-season ad with the bottle in a snow globe like the ones that feature snowy Christmas scenes.

In the end, the Absolut campaign was not only a creative masterpiece but also a resounding market success—using print media alone, without the flashier television or digital media. Absolut has become one of the leading imported vodkas in the United States. The vodka with no credibility and the ugly bottle has become sophisticated and fashionable with a well-conceived and well-placed print campaign.[7] To this day, the Absolut brand still relies heavily on magazine advertising in the IBP mix with continued success.

② Newspapers.

Despite efforts by Internet media, the newspaper is the still the medium that is most accessible to the widest range of advertisers. Advertisers big and small—even you and I when we want to sell that old bike or snowboard—can use newspaper advertising. In fact, investment in newspaper advertising now stands at about $47 billion—more than any of the other traditional medium and more than double the spending on Internet advertising.[8] Exhibit 15.2 shows the top 10 advertisers in newspapers. Several national newspapers reach primarily business audiences. Newspapers are, of course, ideally suited to reaching a narrow geographic area—precisely the type of audience retailers want to reach.

There are some sad truths, however, about the current status of newspapers as a medium. Since the 1980s, newspapers across the United States have been suffering circulation declines, and the trend has continued into the 21st century. Note that this decline in readership and circulation is reflected in the fact that more than half of the advertisers in Exhibit 15.2 have reduced their newspaper spending—significantly.

What may be worse is that the percentage of adults reading daily newspapers is also declining. About 52 percent of adults in the United States read a daily newspaper, compared with about 78 percent in 1970.[9] Much of the decline in both circulation

---

7. Historical information about the Absolut vodka campaign was adapted from information in Nicholas Ind, "Absolut Vodka in the U.S.," in *Great Advertising Campaigns* (Lincolnwood, Ill.: NTC Business Books, 1993), 15–32.

8. 100 Leading National Advertisers, *Advertising Age*, June 25, 2007, S-15.

9. Data on newspaper readership is available at the Newspaper Association of America Web site, *http://www.nnn-naa.com*. Data cited here were drawn from that site on June 22, 2007.

Top 10 newspaper advertisers (U.S. dollars in millions).

Rank	Advertiser	National Newspaper Ad Spending		
		2006	2005	% Change
1	Macy's	$714.8	$793.3	−9.9
2	Verizon Communications	687.7	635.7	8.2
3	Sprint Nextel Corp.	495.6	551.1	−10.1
4	AT&T	483.5	661.5	−26.9
5	Time Warner	297.6	362.7	−17.96
6	Sears Holding Corp.	234.2	247.8	−5.57
7	General Motors Corp.	219.6	580.6	−62.2
8	Fry's Electronics	215.1	204.2	5.3
9	General Electric Co.	212.8	211.6	0.6
10	Procter & Gamble Co.	206.8	198.0	4.4

Source: *Advertising Age*, January 1, 2007, 20.

and readership comes from the fact that both morning and evening newspapers have been losing patronage to television news programs and Internet news sites. While shows such as *Good Morning America* and *Fox Nightly News* cannot provide the breadth of coverage that newspapers can, they still offer news, and they offer it in a lively multisensory format. On the Internet, news seekers can access news 24/7, not just when a newspaper is delivered. Be aware, however, that newspapers' successful foray into digital media means that many newspaper companies themselves are healthy, even if readership in the "traditional" format is waning.

Advantages of Newspapers. Newspapers may have lost some of their luster over the past two decades, but they still do reach more than 50 percent of U.S. households, representing about 150 million adults. And, as mentioned earlier, the newspaper is still an excellent medium for retailers targeting local geographic markets. But broad reach isn't the only attractive feature of newspapers as a medium. Newspapers offer other advantages to advertisers:

Geographic Selectivity. Daily newspapers in cities and towns across the United States offer advertisers the opportunity to reach a geographically well-defined target audience. Some newspapers are beginning to run zoned editions, which target even more narrow geographic areas within a metropolitan market. Zoned editions are typically used by merchants doing business in the local area; national marketers such as Kellogg and Colgate can use the paper carrier to deliver free samples to these zoned areas.

Timeliness. The newspaper is one of the most timely of the traditional major media. Because of the short time needed for producing a typical newspaper ad and the regularity of daily publication, the newspaper allows advertisers to reach audiences in a timely way. This doesn't mean on just a daily basis. Newspaper ads can take advantage of special events or a unique occurrence in a community.

Creative Opportunities. While the newspaper page does not offer the breadth of creative options available in the broadcast media, there are things advertisers can do in a newspaper that represent important creative opportunities. Since the newspaper page offers a large and relatively inexpensive format, advertisers can provide a lot of information to the target audience at relatively low cost. This is important for

DOING IT RIGHT

Myth: The Web Will Dominate Classified Advertising. Reality: Newspapers Don't Have to Worry—They're Going Digital, Too.

Classified advertising is the lifeblood of local newspapers. It often represents 30 to 40 percent of a newspaper's total revenues. Currently, classifieds bring in about $18 billion a year, according to the Newspaper Association of America.

It is no wonder that when big portals like Yahoo!, Microsoft, and America Online began creating local sites, newspapers were concerned that Web-based classifieds would seriously cut into their revenues. After all, wasn't the Web a better and more accessible venue for classified ads? A consumer-seller's photo of the house or the bike or the dog that was for sale made a much better presentation than the itty-bitty box with the three terse lines of description. And the consumer-buyer could come to the classified advertising environment anytime—no need to trek out onto the lawn to grab the paper that never quite seems to make it to the front porch. Because Web classifieds seemed so much better than newspaper-based, dot-com companies such as Monster (help wanted/employees available) and Autobytel (automobile classifieds) were even able to offer classified ads for free, with costs supported by sales of banner ads. How could newspapers ever compete with a better presentation format *and* free advertising space?

Well, there are a few reality checks in order. First, while classified advertising is down a bit over the past couple of years (and that probably has to more with circulation than with Web competition), the prospect of the Web swallowing up all the classified advertising dollars never turned into a reality. Second, local newspapers have combated the Web attack by providing their own localized version of ads on the Internet. Third, the really big newspaper chains like the McClatchy Company and newspapers like the *Washington Post* are investing in online social networks like Friendster, MeetUp, and Tribe. These online venues reach local audiences but in a networking context rather than with merely a classified ad.

Sources: Dan Mitchell, "Hello Webmaster—Get Me a Rewrite," ***Business 2.0***, March 6, 2001, 42; Tobi Elkin, "Newspaper Giants Buy into Tribe," ***Advertising Age***, December 8, 2003, 36. Brian Deagon, "Digital Era Leaves No Time for Newspapers to Rest in Print," ***Investors Business Daily***, February 17, 2006.

products or services with extensive or complex features that may need lengthy and detailed copy. The Tire America ad in Exhibit 15.3 needs just such a large format to provide detail about tire sizes and prices.

Credibility. Newspapers still benefit from the perception that "if it's in the paper it must be the truth." As an example, this credibility element played a key role in the decision by Glaxo Wellcome and SmithKline Beecham to announce their megamerger (creating the $73 billion GlaxoSmithKline Corporation) using newspapers.[10]

Audience Interest. Regular newspaper readers are truly interested in the information they are reading. While overall readership may be down in the United States, those readers that remain are loyal and interested. Many readers buy the newspaper specifically to see what's on sale at stores in the local area, making this an ideal environment for local merchants. And newspapers are the primary medium for local classified advertising despite an early concern that the Internet would cut deeply into classified revenue, as the Doing It Right box suggests.

Cost. In terms of both production and space, newspapers offer a low-cost alternative to advertisers. The cost per contact may be higher than with television and radio options, but the absolute cost for placing a black-and-white ad is still within reach of even a small advertising budget.

Disadvantages of Newspapers. Newspapers offer advertisers many good opportunities. Like every other media option, however, newspapers have some significant disadvantages.

Limited Segmentation. While newspapers can achieve good geographic selectivity, the ability to target a specific audience ends there. Newspaper circulation simply cuts across too broad an economic, social, and demographic audience to allow the isolation of specific targets. The placement of ads within certain sections can achieve minimal targeting by gender, but even this effort is somewhat fruitless. Some newspapers are developing special sections to enhance their segmentation capabilities (see Exhibit 15.4). Many papers are developing sections on e-business and e-film reviews to target specific audiences.[11] In addition, more and more newspapers are

10.   David Goetzl, "GlaxoSmithKline Launches Print Ads," *Advertising Age*, January 8, 2001, 30.
11.   Jon Fine, "Tribune Seeks National Ads with 3 New Special Sections," *Advertising Age*, October 9, 2000, 42.

The newspaper medium offers a large format for advertisers. This is important when an advertiser needs space to provide the target audience with extensive information, as Tire America has done with this ad featuring tire sizes and prices.

Many newspapers are trying to increase their target selectivity by developing special sections for advertisers, such as a NASCAR section for race fans.

being published to serve specific ethnic groups, which is another form of segmentation. The industry feels it has made great progress in this regard and is approaching advertisers with the argument that newspaper advertising, if purchased strategically, can rival the targeting capability of magazines.[12]

Creative Constraints. The opportunities for creative executions in newspapers are certainly outweighed by the creative constraints. First, newspapers have poor reproduction quality. Led by *USA Today,* most newspapers now print some of their pages in color. But even the color reproduction does not enhance the look of most products in advertisements. For advertisers whose brand images depend on accurate, high-quality reproduction (color or not), newspapers simply have severe limitations compared to other media options. Second, newspapers are a unidimensional medium—no sound, no action. For brands that demand a broad creative execution, this medium is often not the best choice.

Cluttered Environment. The average newspaper is filled with headlines, subheads, photos, and announcements—not to mention the news stories. This presents a terribly cluttered environment for an advertisement. To make things worse, most advertisers in a product category try to use the same sections to target audiences. For example, all the home equity loan and financial services ads are in the business section, and all the women's clothing ads are in the metro, or local, section.

Short Life. In most U.S. households, newspapers are read quickly and then discarded (or, hopefully, stacked in the recycling pile). The only way advertisers can overcome this limitation is to buy several insertions in each daily issue, buy space several times during the week, or both. In this way, even if a reader doesn't spend much time with the newspaper, at least multiple exposures are a possibility.

12.   Jon Fine, "Papers' Ad Group Goes on Offensive," *Advertising Age,* February 9, 2004, 6.

The newspaper has creative limitations, but what the average newspaper does, it does well. If an advertiser wants to reach a local audience with a simple black-and-white ad in a timely manner, then the newspaper is the superior choice.

Categories of Newspapers. All newspapers enjoy the same advantages and suffer from the same limitations to one degree or another. But there are different types of newspapers from which advertisers can choose. Newspapers are categorized by target audience, geographic coverage, and frequency of publication.

Target Audience. Newspapers can be classified by the target audience they reach. The five primary types of newspapers serving different target audiences are general-population newspapers, business newspapers, ethnic newspapers, gay and lesbian newspapers, and the alternative press. **General-population newspapers** serve local communities and report news of interest to the local population. Newspapers such as the *Kansas City Star,* the *Dayton Daily News,* and the *Columbus Dispatch* are examples. **Business newspapers** such as the *Wall Street Journal, Investor's Business Daily* (United States), and the *Financial Times* (United Kingdom) serve a specialized business audience. **Ethnic newspapers** that target specific ethnic groups are growing in popularity. Most of these newspapers are published weekly. The *New York Amsterdam News* and the *Michigan Chronicle* are two of the more than 200 newspapers in the United States that serve African-American communities. The Hispanic community in the United States has more than 300 newspapers. One of the most prominent is *El Diario de las Americas* in Miami. **Gay and lesbian newspapers** exist in most major (and many smaller) markets, such as San Francisco's *Bay Area Reporter* and Boston's *Bay Windows.* Readership typically extends considerably beyond gay and lesbian readers. So-called **alternative press newspapers**, such as *L.A. Weekly,* the *Austin Chronicle,* and New Orleans's *Gambit Weekly,* are very viable vehicles for reaching typically young and entertainment-oriented audiences.

EXHIBIT 15.5

Sunday supplements such as Parade (http://www .parade.com) and USA Weekend (http://www .usaweekend.com) offer advertisers another alternative for placing newspaper ads. How do these differ from alternative press weeklies such as the Village Voice (http:// www.villagevoice.com)? Does USA Weekend's Web site offer any features that attract repeat visits from readers, thus increasing the life of the weekly publication?

Geographic Coverage. As noted earlier, the vast majority of newspapers are distributed in a relatively restricted geographic area—either a large metropolitan area or a state. Newspapers such as the *Tulsa World* and the *Atlanta Journal-Constitution,* with weekly readership of 288,000 and 900,000, respectively, serve a local geographic area. The other type of newspaper in the United States is the national newspaper. *USA Today* and the *Wall Street Journal* were, from their inception, designed to be distributed nationally, and now have a weekly readership of about 6.2 million and 5.0 million respectively. The *New York Times* and the *Los Angeles Times,* each with weekly readership of about 2.0 million, have evolved into national newspapers.[13]

Frequency of Publication. The majority of newspapers in the United States are called *dailies* because they are published each day of the week, including Sunday. There are a smaller number of *weeklies,* and these tend to serve smaller towns or rural communities. Finally, another alternative for advertisers is the Sunday supplement, which is published only on Sunday and is usually delivered along with the Sunday edition of a local newspaper. The most widely distributed Sunday supplements—*Parade* magazine and *USA Weekend*—are illustrated in Exhibit 15.5.

13.   Data from Newspaper Association of America, *http://www.nnn-naa.com,* accessed on June 22. 2007.

Categories of Newspaper Advertising. Just as there are categories of newspapers, there are categories of newspaper advertising: display advertising, inserts, and classified advertising.

Display Advertising. Advertisers of goods and services rely most on display advertising. **Display advertising** in newspapers includes the standard components of a print ad—headline, body copy, and often an illustration—to set it off from the news content of the paper. An important form of display advertising is co-op advertising sponsored by manufacturers. In **co-op advertising**, a manufacturer pays part of the media bill when a local merchant features the manufacturer's brand in advertising. Co-op advertising can be done on a national scale as well. (See Exhibit 15.6.) Intel invests heavily in co-op advertising with computer manufacturers who feature the "Intel Inside" logo in their print ads.

Inserts. There are two types of insert advertisements. Inserts do not appear on the printed newspaper page but rather are folded into the newspaper before distribution. An advertiser can use a **preprinted insert**, which is an advertisement delivered to the newspaper fully printed and ready for insertion into the newspaper

The second type of insert ad is a **free-standing insert (FSI)**, which contains cents-off coupons for a variety of products and is typically delivered with Sunday newspapers. The Pizza Hut ad in Exhibit 15.7 is part of a free-standing insert. Nearly $2 billion per year is spent by advertisers on free-standing inserts.[14]

Retailers who feature a particular brand can receive co-op advertising money for media placement. http://www.ebel.com

This example of a free-standing insert (FSI) from Pizza Hut shows how an ad can be delivered via a newspaper distribution system without having to become part of the paper itself. What are the production and attention-getting advantages that this insert provides? http://www.pizzahut.com

14. "100 Leading National Advertisers," *Advertising Age,* June 25, 2007, S-15.

Classified Advertising. Classified advertising is newspaper advertising that appears as all-copy messages under categories such as sporting goods, employment, and automobiles. Many classified ads are taken out by individuals, but real estate firms, automobile dealers, and construction firms also buy classified advertising.

Costs and Buying Procedures for Newspaper Advertising. When an advertiser wishes to place advertising in a newspaper, the first step is to obtain a rate card from the newspaper. A **rate card** contains information on costs, closing times (when ads have to be submitted), specifications for submitting an ad, and special pages or features available in the newspaper. The rate card also summarizes the circulation for the designated market area and any circulation outside the designated area.

The cost of a newspaper ad depends on how large the advertisement is, whether it is black-and-white or color, how large the total audience is, and whether the newspaper has local or national coverage. Advertising space is sold in newspapers by the **column inch**, which is a unit of space one inch deep by one column wide. Each column is 2¹⁄₁₆ inches wide. Most newspapers have adopted the **standard advertising unit (SAU)** system for selling ad space, which defines unit sizes for advertisements. There are 57 defined SAU sizes for advertisements in the system, so that advertisers can prepare ads to fit one of the sizes. Many newspapers offer a volume discount to advertisers who buy more than one ad in an issue or buy multiple ads over some time period.

When an advertiser buys space on a **run-of-paper (ROP)** basis, which is also referred to as a *run-of-press basis,* the ad may appear anywhere, on any page in the paper. A higher rate is charged for **preferred position**, in which the ad is placed in a specific section of the paper. **Full position** places an ad near the top of a page or in the middle of editorial material.

Measuring Newspaper Audiences. There are several different dimensions to measuring newspaper audiences. The reach of a newspaper is reported as the newspaper's circulation. **Circulation** is the number of newspapers distributed each day (for daily newspapers) or each week (for weekly publications). **Paid circulation** reports the number of copies sold through subscriptions and newsstand distribution. **Controlled circulation** refers to the number of copies of the newspaper that are given away free. The Audit Bureau of Circulations (ABC) is an independent organization that verifies the actual circulation of newspapers.

Rates for newspaper advertising are not based solely on circulation numbers, however. The Newspaper Association of America estimates that about 2.3 people read each copy of a daily newspaper distributed in the United States. **Readership** of a newspaper is a measure of the circulation multiplied by the number of readers of a copy. This number, of course, is much higher than the circulation number and provides a total audience figure on which advertisers base advertising rates. To give you some idea of costs, a full-page four-color ad in *USA Today* costs about $150,000, and a full-page black-and-white ad in the *Wall Street Journal* costs about $200,000. A full-page ad in your local newspaper is, of course, considerably less—probably $10,000 to $25,000 for a good-sized city and much less for small-town newspapers. Remember, though, that few advertisers, national or local, purchase an entire page.

The Future of Newspapers. Earlier in the chapter, we talked about the fact that newspaper circulation has been in a long, sustained downward trend, and that traditional print readership is following the same pattern. To survive as a viable advertising medium, newspapers will have to evolve with the demands of both audiences and advertisers, who provide them with the majority of their revenue. Primarily, newspapers will have to exploit their role as a source for local news—something new media like the Web cannot do effectively. To compete in the future as a viable advertising medium, newspapers will have to do the following:[15]

---

15.   Based in part on Jon Fine, "The Daily Paper of Tomorrow," *BusinessWeek*, January 9, 2006, 20.

- Continue to provide in-depth coverage of issues that focus on the local community.
- Increase coverage of national and international news.
- Borrow from Google's approach to advertisers—be accountable to advertisers and offer local advertisers unlimited pages in both paper and online editions.
- Maintain and expand their role as the best local source for consumers to find specific information on advertised product features, availability, and prices.
- Provide consumer-buyers the option of shopping through an online newspaper computer service.
- Use bloggers to cover events.
- Become more mainstream in integrated brand promotions particularly relating to new media (see Exhibit 15.8).

③ Magazines. While newspapers have struggled in a changing media world, magazines are flourishing, with advertisers spending over $30 billion for advertising space in consumer, business, and Sunday magazines annually.[16] A big part of the reason is that big advertisers like Procter & Gamble are finding that magazines "work hard" for the firm in reaching target customers effectively and efficiently (see Exhibit 15.9). P&G strategists have moved media spending from television to magazines, and magazines now

Nothing attracts online shoppers to your website like newspapers.

Newspapers can help your website achieve the critical mass it needs to drive your business. According to a recent study, daily newspapers reached over 59% of those who had made a purchase on the Internet within the previous 30 days. No other medium delivers this amount of traffic with greater velocity. So if you're looking for shoppers you'll find them browsing through newspapers. For more information call the number below. *Nobody delivers the paper like we do.*

Call Jack Grandcolas, VP of High Tech advertising, at 415-454-9168 or e-mail granj@nnn-naa.com

EXHIBIT 15.8

The future of newspapers will be greatly enhanced if the medium adapts to the demands of a new media environment and particularly if newspapers can become part of the integrated brand promotion process that includes new media. This ad touts just such a role for newspapers in IBP. http://www.nnn-naa.com

EXHIBIT 15.9

*Specialty magazines like FlyFisher (*http://www.fedflyfishers.org*) help advertisers target highly specialized markets with efficiency and effectiveness.*

Top 10 magazines by circulation for 2006.

Rank	Magazine	Paid Circulation	% Change
1	AARP The Magazine	23,067,712	2.3
2	Reader's Digest	10,094,286	−0.3
3	Better Homes & Gardens	7,615,179	−0.2
4	National Geographic	5,073,822	−6.6
5	Good Housekeeping	4,609,206	0.1
6	Ladies' Home Journal	4,103,480	−0.7
7	Time	4,009,582	1.2
8	Family Circle	4,054,870	−5.7
9	Woman's Day	4,002,870	−0.3
10	People	3,823,604	1.2

Source: *Advertising Age*, June 25, 2007, S-16. Reprinted with permission. © Crain Communications, Inc., 2007.

Top 10 magazine advertisers for 2006 (U.S. dollars in millions).

Rank	Advertiser	Magazine Ad Spending 2006	2005	% Change
1	Procter & Gamble	$887.9	$810.0	9.6
2	GlaxoSmithKline	439.3	266.6	64.8
3	Kraft Foods	438.8	508.6	−13.7
4	General Motors Corp.	401.7	493.8	−18.6
5	Johnson & Johnson	355.9	415.4	−14.3
6	Ford Motor Co.	337.0	339.0	−0.6
7	L'Oreal	325.5	344.4	−5.5
8	Time Warner	294.0	355.4	−17.3
9	Pfizer	291.3	222.7	30.8
10	AstraZeneca	282.8	161.4	75.2

Source: *Advertising Age*, June 25, 2007, S-16. Reprinted with permission. © Crain Communications, Inc., 2007.

capture about 25 percent of the consumer goods marketer's nearly $5 billion annual media spending.[17]

No doubt, many of the most popular and successful magazines are ones you read yourself—*People, Sports Illustrated, Elle,* and *Car and Driver* make the annual list of leading magazines. The top 10 magazines in the United States, based on circulation, are listed in Exhibit 15.10. This list suggests the diversity of magazines as a media class. Exhibit 15.11 shows the top 10 advertisers in magazines.

Like newspapers, magazines have advantages and disadvantages, come in different types, offer various ad costs and buying procedures, and measure their audiences in specific ways. We will consider these issues now.

Advantages of Magazines. Magazines have many advantages relative to newspapers. These advantages make them more than just an ideal print medium—many analysts conclude that magazines are, in many ways, superior to even broadcast media alternatives.

17.   Jeff Neff, "P&G Pumps Up Ring Spending, Trims TV," *Advertising Age*, November 6, 2006, 1, 78.

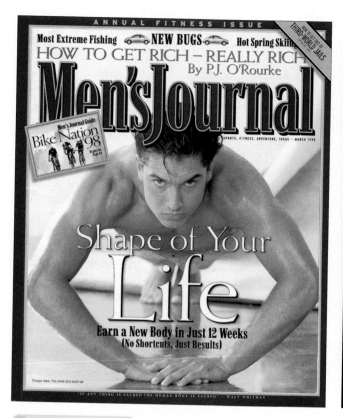

One distinct advantage of magazines over most other media options is the ability to attract and target a highly selective audience. Magazines such as Men's Journal attract an audience based on special interests and activities—in this case, readers interested in health issues.

The advantage of magazines: Specialized content attracts audiences with special interests, and those audiences attract advertisers. This ad by Escort Radar appeared in Car and Driver magazine.

Audience Selectivity. The overwhelming advantage of magazines relative to other media—print or broadcast—is the ability of magazines to attract and target a highly selective audience. This selectivity can be based on demographics (*Woman's Day*), lifestyle (*Muscle & Fitness*), or special interests (*Men's Journal*), as shown in Exhibit 15.12. The audience segment can be narrowly defined, as is the one that reads *Modern Bride,* or it may cut across a variety of interests, like *Newsweek* readers. Magazines also offer geographic selectivity on a regional basis, as does *Southern Living,* or city magazines, such as *Atlanta,* which highlight happenings in major metropolitan areas. Also, large national publications have multiple editions for advertisers to choose from. *Better Homes & Gardens* has 85 different specific market editions, and *Time* offers advertisers a different edition for each of the 50 states.

Audience Interest. Perhaps more than any other medium, magazines attract an audience because of content. While television programming can attract audiences through interest as well, magazines have the additional advantage of voluntary exposure to the advertising. Parents seek out publications that address the joys and challenges of parenting in a wide range of strong-circulation magazines like *American Baby* and *Cookie.*[18] When a magazine attracts a highly interested readership, advertisers, in turn, find a highly receptive audience for their brand messages (see Exhibit 15.13).

18.   Joseph Weber, "The Boomlet in Baby News," *BusinessWeek,* May 15, 2006, 82

Magazines offer unique creative opportunities to advertisers. Perfume marketers such as Clarins include scent strips in the magazine ads for consumers to sample.

Creative Opportunities. Magazines offer a wide range of creative opportunities. Because of the ability to vary the size of an ad, use color, use white space, and play off the special interests of the audience, magazines represent a favorable creative environment. Also, because the paper quality of most magazines is quite high, color reproduction can be outstanding—another creative opportunity.

These factors are precisely why Infiniti invests nearly $60 million annually in magazine advertising. A case in point was when the firm introduced its full-size QX56 SUV. Magazines offered the perfect combination of audience selectivity and high-quality visual presentation to effectively advertise the brand.[19] In an attempt to expand the creative environment even further, some advertisers have tried various other creative techniques: pop-up ads, scratch-and-sniff ads, ads with perfume scent strips, and even ads with small computer chips that flash lights and play music. The Clarins ad in Exhibit 15.14 shows how an advertiser can take advantage of the creative opportunities offered by magazines.

Long Life. Many magazines are saved issue-to-issue by their subscribers. This means that, unlike newspapers, a magazine can be reexamined over a week or a month. Some magazines are saved for long periods for future reference, such as *Architectural Digest, National Geographic,* and *Travel & Leisure.* In addition to multiple subscriber exposure, this long life increases the chance of pass-along readership as people visit the subscriber's home (or professional offices) and look at magazines.

Many magazines are experiencing some difficulty in growing both circulation and revenue. In just one year, 2006, several high-profile magazines were pulled from the market, including *ElleGirl, Teen People,* and *Premiere.*[20] All these magazines failed for the same reason—they did not deliver the circulation to target markets that advertisers wanted. Conversely, specialty magazines with narrow target audiences, such as *Maxim* and *Car and Driver,* have recently shown solid gains in circulation of up to 20 percent.[21] It would appear that the main advantage of magazines—their appeal to a selective audience—is translating into market success.

Disadvantages of Magazines.
The disadvantages of magazines as a media choice have to do with their being too selective in their reach and with the recent proliferation of magazines.

Limited Reach and Frequency. The tremendous advantage of selectivity discussed in the previous section actually creates a limitation for magazines. The more narrowly defined the interest group, the less overall reach a magazine will have.

Since most magazines are published monthly or perhaps every two weeks, there is little chance for an advertiser to achieve frequent exposure using a single magazine.

19.   Jean Halliday, "Auto Industry Pushes Print's Creative Limits," *Advertising Age,* March 8, 2004, 4.
20.   Nat Ives, "'Premiere' Death Stands Out in an Era of Mag Closings," *Advertising Age,* March 12, 2007, 10.
21.   Halliday, "Auto Industry Pushes Print's Creative Limits."

EXHIBIT 15.15

In the consumer magazine category, publishers try to appeal to target audiences' special interests. Boy Crazy! is one of many titles targeted to teenagers.

To overcome this limitation, advertisers often use several magazines targeted at the same audience. For example, many readers of *Better Homes & Gardens* may also be readers of *Architectural Digest*. By placing ads in both publications, an advertiser can increase both reach and frequency within a targeted audience.

Clutter. Magazines are not quite as cluttered as newspapers, but they still represent a fairly difficult context for message delivery. The average magazine is about half editorial and entertainment content and half advertising material, but some highly specialized magazines, like *Bride*, can have as much as 80 percent of their pages devoted to advertising. And given the narrowly defined audiences, this advertising tends to be for brands in direct competition with each other. In addition to this clutter, there is another sort of clutter that has recently begun to plague magazines. As soon as a new market segment is recognized, there is a flood of "me too" magazines. The teen magazine market suffered precisely this problem from 2000 to 2005. Traditional titles like *Seventeen* and *YM* suddenly found themselves amid a glut of teen girl magazines including *Teen, Teen People, Teen Vogue, Cosmo Girl, ElleGirl,* and *Boy Crazy!* (See Exhibit 15.15.) This may be good in terms of coverage, but it may devalue individual ads, and the magazines in which they appear may reach fewer consumers than the advertiser expected (note that two of the newer teen girl magazines have already failed, as discussed above).

Long Lead Times. Advertisers are required to submit their ads as much as 90 days in advance of the date of publication. If the submission date is missed, there can be as much as a full month's delay in placing the next ad. And once an ad is submitted, it cannot be changed during that 90-day period, even if some significant event alters the communications environment.

Cost. While the cost per contact in magazines is not nearly as high as in some media (direct mail in particular), it is more expensive than most newspaper space, and many times the cost per contact in the broadcast media. The absolute cost for a single insertion can be prohibitive. For magazines with large circulations, such as *Modern Maturity* (20 million) and *Good Housekeeping* (5 million), the cost for a one-time, full page, four-color ad runs from $100,000 to about $250,000.

Categories of Magazines. The magazine medium is highly fragmented, with more than 12,000 magazine titles published annually in the United States and literally hundreds of titles introduced every year. A useful classification scheme for magazines is to categorize them by major target audience: consumer, business, and farm publications.

Consumer Publications. Magazines that appeal to consumer interests run the gamut from international news to sports, education, age-group information, and hobbies. These include magazines written specifically for men (like *Men's Journal*), women (*Woman's Day*), and ethnic groups (*Ebony*). Many new consumer magazines appeal

EXHIBIT 15.16

Top five consumer magazine categories, ranked by revenue, 2006 (U.S. dollars in millions).

Magazine Category	Total Revenue	Ad Revenue	Ad Revenue 2005–2006 % Change
Women's	$6,389	$4,942	4.4
Newsweeklies	4,581	3,132	0.3
General editorial	3,963	2,994	−1.1
Home service and home	3,532	2,680	2.1
Business and finance	1,911	1,574	−3.3

Source: *Advertising Age,* "Magazine 300," October 28, 2007, S4. Reprinted with permission. © Crain Communications, Inc., 2007.

EXHIBIT 15.17

Top five business magazine categories, ranked by revenue, 2006 (U.S. dollars in millions).

Magazine Category	Total Revenue	Ad Revenue	Ad Revenue 2005–2006 % Change
Computer/Internet	$1,164.0	$1,041.0	0.0
Business (20)	336.0	211.0	−4.6
Electronic engineering (40)	150.0	62.0	−0.8
Travel, retail (149B)	149.0	149.0	−21.5
Multi-specialty primary care (21)	141.0	141.0	0.0

Source: *Advertising Age,* "Magazine 300," October 28, 2007, S4. Reprinted with permission. © Crain Communications, Inc., 2007.

to the lifestyle changes of the 2000s: *Cooking Light, Men's Health.* Advertisers invested more than $26 billion in advertising in consumer magazines in 2006.[22] The top five consumer magazine categories are listed in Exhibit 15.16.

Business Publications. Business magazines come in many different forms. Each major industry has a trade publication, such as *PC World* in the computer industry, that highlights events and issues in that industry. The digital age has been a huge boon to the magazine industry with dozens of new titles, like *Wired,* serving the needs of Internet and Web service professionals.[23] Professional publications are written for doctors, lawyers, accountants, and other professional groups. *American Family Physician* publishes articles for family practitioners and carries advertising from many pharmaceutical manufacturers. General-interest business magazines such as *Fortune* and *Forbes* cut across all trades, industries, and professions. The leading business magazine categories are listed in Exhibit 15.17.

Farm Publications. The three major farm publications in the United States and their approximate paid circulations are *Farm Journal* (175,000), *Successful Farming* (450,000), and *Progressive Farmer* (250,000). These magazines provide technical information about farming techniques as well as business management articles to improve farmers' profitability. In addition to national publications, regional farm magazines and publications focus on specific aspects of the industry.

22. *Advertising Age,* "Magazine 300," October 28, 2007, S4.
23. Gary Wolf, "The Magazine That Launched a Decade," *Business 2.0,* July 2003, 87–91.

EXHIBIT 15.18

Gatefold ads display extra-wide advertisements, like this one for Lenox dishes. http://www.lenox.com

Costs and Buying Procedures for Magazine Advertising. The cost for magazine space varies dramatically. As with newspapers, the size of an ad, its position in a publication, its creative execution (black and white or color, or any special techniques), and its placement in a regular or special edition of the magazine all affect costs. The main cost, of course, is based on the magazine's circulation. A full-page four-color ad in *Reader's Digest* costs about $226,000 (based on 11 million readers); a full-page four-color ad in *People* costs about $200,000; a full-page ad in *Skiing* costs about $35,000; and a full-page ad in *UpHere*, the magazine about Canada's northern frontier with a circulation of about 30,000, is only $3,000.

Each magazine has a rate card that shows the cost for full-page, half-page, two-column, one-column, and half-column ads. The rate card also shows the cost for black-and-white, two-color, and four-color ads. Rate cards for magazines, as with newspapers, have been the standard pricing method for many years. In recent years, however, more and more publishers have been willing to negotiate rates and give deep discounts for volume purchases—discounts as large as 30 to 40 percent off the published card rate.

In addition to standard rates, there is an extra charge for a **bleed page**. On a bleed page, the background color of an ad runs to the edge of the page, replacing the standard white border. **Gatefold ads**, or ads that fold out of a magazine to display an extra-wide advertisement, also carry an extra charge. Gatefolds are often used by advertisers on the inside cover of upscale magazines. An example of a gatefold is the ad for dishes and flatware in Exhibit 15.18.

Placement. When buying space in a magazine, advertisers must decide among several placement options. A run-of-paper advertisement, as mentioned earlier, can appear anywhere in the magazine, at the discretion of the publisher. The advertiser may pay for a preferred position, however. **First cover page** is the front cover of a magazine; **second cover page** is the inside front cover; **third cover page** is the inside back cover; and **fourth cover page** is the back cover. When advertisers prepare **double-page spreads**—advertisements that bridge two facing pages—it is important that no headlines or body copy run through the *gutter,* which is the fold between the magazine pages.

Buying procedures for magazine advertising demand that an advertiser follow several guidelines and honor several key dates. A **space contract** establishes a rate for all advertising placed in a publication by an advertiser over a specified period. A **space order**, also referred to as an *insertion order,* is a commitment by an advertiser to advertising space in a particular issue. It is accompanied by production specifications for the ad or ads that will appear in the issue. The dates that an advertiser must be aware of are as follows:

- **Closing date:** The date when production-ready advertising materials must be delivered to a publisher for an ad to appear in an issue.
- **On-sale date:** The date on which a magazine is issued to subscribers and for newsstand distribution. Most magazines put issues on sale far in advance of the cover date.
- **Cover date:** The date of publication that appears on a magazine.

Measuring Magazine Audiences. Most magazines base their published advertising rates on **guaranteed circulation**, which is a stated minimum number of copies of a particular issue that will be delivered to readers. This number guarantees for advertisers that they are achieving a certain minimum reach with an ad placement. In addition, publishers estimate **pass-along readership**, which is an additional number of people, other than the original readers, who may see a publication. Advertisers can verify circulation through the Audit Bureau of Circulations, which reports total and state-by-state circulation for magazines, as well as subscriber versus newsstand circulation. When an advertiser wants to go beyond basic circulation numbers, the syndicated magazine research services such as Simmons Market Research Bureau and Mediamark Research can provide additional information. Through personal interviews and respondent-kept diaries, these services provide advertisers with information on reader demographics, media use, and product usage.

A controversy has presented itself with magazine audience measurement. While magazines do report guaranteed circulation, they only guarantee *average* paid circulation, not the paid circulation of specific issues. Advertisers are starting to insist on guaranteed circulation issue by issue, and you can understand why. An issue with hot, controversial news may show considerably more circulation than an issue with relative mundane news or stories. Some big magazine advertising spenders like Kraft, Wal-Mart, and Coca-Cola have threatened to pull advertising dollars until the specific issue-by-issue metric is available.[24]

The Future of Magazines. Magazines have had a roller-coaster history over the past 10 to 15 years. The most recent data show that circulation is generally on an upward trend, but that ad revenues are either up slightly or down slightly, depending on the year. The growing circulation is testimony to the fact that advertisers still find the advantages of magazines well suited to their current needs.

Three factors need to be considered as influences on magazines as an advertising medium in the future. First, magazines will, like other traditional media, have to determine how to adapt to new media options. In the late 1990s, magazines rushed to publish online, with more than 250 magazines offered in online versions. As discussed earlier, these electronic versions were touted as having several advantages to both the publisher and the subscriber, but it appears that neither readers nor advertisers are particularly happy with the "digizine." Consider the fact that the paid circulation for the print version of *Reader's Digest* is 11 million copies, while there are only about 100,000 subscribers online.[25] And, in 2003, Ziff Davis, one of the largest newspaper publishers, dropped *Yahoo! Internet Life* from its publication lineup. To date, these digizines have attracted minimal ad spending, and fewer are being offered. But with the advent of more read-friendly devices such as the Tablet PC—a sleek and portable part laptop, part digital notepad—is encouraging some publishers

24.   Nat Ives, "Marketers to Mags: Give Us Guarantees or We'll Walk," *Advertising Age*, May 7, 2007, 1,46.
25.   Jon Fine, "Magazines Recorded Declines in Late 2003," *Advertising Age*, February 23, 2004, 39.

EXHIBIT 15.19

While the rush to "digizines" (online versions of magazines) was pretty much a bust, magazine publishers are encouraged by the introduction of the Tablet PC as a vehicle for digital delivery of magazine content.

to reconsider digital formats for their magazines. (See Exhibit 15.19.) The *New Yorker,* the *Financial Times,* and *Forbes* have all prepared digital versions for Tablet PC application.[26]

The second factor affecting the future of magazines is a robust environment for mergers and acquisitions. Recent years have seen dozens of merger and acquisition deals each year in the magazine industry. Buyers are looking for two benefits in acquiring publications: economies of scale in traditional print publication, and new media outlets. In the past few years, the pursuit of these advantages has resulted in publishing corporations investing over $2 billion a year in mergers and acquisitions.[27]

Third, magazines are exploring other ways to take advantage of the digital environment. In an effort to generate additional revenue, some magazines are starting to make the products in their editorial titles available for sale online. *Maxim* has opened Shop Maxim Online, which allows readers direct access to products seen in the publication; *Maxim* gets a cut of sales. This is particularly important as the crowding continues in certain magazine publishing spaces. *Maxim* turned to the new digital opportunity as the publication saw ad pages decline 6.2 percent over a three year period.[28]

Television and Radio: Strategic Planning Considerations.

When you say the word *advertising,* the average person thinks of television and radio advertising. It's easy to understand why. Television advertising can be advertising at its very best. With the benefit of sight and sound, color and music, action and special effects, television advertising can be the most powerful advertising of all. It has some other advantages as well. In many parts of the world, particularly in the United States, television is the medium most widely used by consumers for entertainment and information. Radio advertising also has key advantages. The ability to reach consumers in multiple locations and the creative power of radio rank as important communications opportunities. Advertisers readily appreciate the power of television and radio advertising and invest billions of dollars a year in these media.

4 Television. To many, television is the medium that defines what advertising is. With its multisensory stimulation, television offers the chance for advertising to be all that it can be. Television presents two extraordinary opportunities to advertisers. First, the diversity of communication possibilities allows for outstanding creative expression of a brand's value. Dramatic color, sweeping action, and spectacular sound effects can cast a brand in an exciting and unique light—especially in an era of widescreen and HDTV. Second, once this expressive presentation of a brand is prepared, it can be disseminated to millions of consumers, often at a fraction of a penny per contact.

26.   Tobi Elkin, "Publishers Bet on Tablet PC Content," *Advertising Age,* January 6, 2003, 17.
27.   Tom Lowry, "How Many Magazines Did We Buy Today?" *BusinessWeek,* January 22, 2001, 98–99.
28.   Nat Ives, "Magazines Dabble in E-commerce," *Advertising Age,* December 11, 2006, 18.

These opportunities have not been lost on advertisers. In the United States in 2008, advertisers invested about $85 billion in television advertising for media time alone—this does not include the many billions of dollars spent on production costs.[29] To fully appreciate all that television means to advertisers, we need to understand much more about this complex medium.

Television Categories. Without careful evaluation, the natural tendency is to classify television as a single type of broadcast medium. When we turn on the television, we simply decide what program we find interesting and then settle in for some entertainment. The reality is that over the past 15 to 20 years, several distinct versions of television have evolved, from which consumers can choose for entertainment and advertisers can choose for reaching those consumers. There are four categories: network, cable, syndicated, and local television. The delivery system varies as well, with broadcast, cable, satellite, and emerging Internet delivery systems available. Exhibit 15.20 shows the spending in these four television categories for 2005 and 2006. Notice that all of the options with the exception of syndication showed steady growth in advertising receipts. Let's examine the nature of each of the four categories for television advertising and the growing satellite/closed-circuit option as well.

Network Television. Network television broadcasts programming over airwaves to affiliate stations across the United States under a contract agreement. Advertisers can buy time within these programs to reach audiences in hundreds of markets. There are currently six major broadcast television networks in the United States. The original big three networks were American Broadcasting Company (ABC, now owned by Disney), the Columbia Broadcasting System (CBS), and the National Broadcasting Company (NBC). The next large broadcast company to be added was the Fox network (now owned by News Corp.). Estimates are that network television reaches more than 90 percent of U.S. households. Exhibit 15.21 shows the top 10 advertisers on network television.

Despite speculation over the last decade that alternative television options (discussed next) would ultimately undermine network television, the broadcast networks still continue to flourish—mostly due to innovative programming. For example, episodes of *Survivor* on CBS regularly draw audiences in the range of 30 million viewers and the Super Bowl now draws over 90 million viewers, with a 30-second spot costing over $2.6 million.[30] Regular programming costs are somewhat more reasonable. Thirty seconds on *Deal or No Deal* costs about $167,000 and on *Lost* costs $328,000; *Ugly Betty* seems like a bargain at $93,000.[31] No other television option gives advertisers the breadth of reach of network television.

EXHIBIT 15.20

Spending by advertisers in the four major television categories (U.S. dollars in billions).

Category	Total Measured Advertising Spending		
	2006	**2005**	**% Change**
Spot TV	$25.9	$25.0	3.5
Network TV	18.5	16.6	11.1
Cable TV	16.7	16.2	3.4
Syndicated TV	4.2	4.2	0.0

Source: *Advertising Age*, June 25, 2007, S-16. Reprinted with permission. © Crain Communications, Inc., 2007.

29. "Marketing Fact Book," *Marketing News*, July 15, 2006, 32.
30. Bradley Johnson, "CFOs Cringe at Price, but Bowl Delivers the Masses," *Advertising Age*, January 29, 2007, 8.
31. AdAge Annual, *Advertising Age*, January 1, 2007, 22.

EXHIBIT 15.21

Top 10 network TV advertisers (U.S. dollars in millions).

		Network TV Ad Spending		
Rank	**Advertiser**	**2006**	**2005**	**% Change**
1	Procter & Gamble	$1,112.8	$1,002.0	11.1
2	General Motors	875.4	924.6	−5.3
3	AT&T	683.3	430.0	58.9
4	Ford Motor Co.	563.7	496.6	13.5
5	Johnson & Johnson	538.6	717.8	−25.0
6	Verizon	470.7	374.6	25.6
7	Time Warner	467.5	486.9	−4.0
8	GlaxoSmithKline	430.1	441.1	−2.5
9	Pepsi Co.	403.6	504.9	−20.1
10	Toyota Motor	399.9	385.8	3.6

Source: *Advertising Age*, June 25, 2007, S-16. Reprinted with permission. © Crain Communications, Inc., 2007.

Cable Television. From its modest beginnings as community antenna television (CATV) in the 1940s, cable television has grown into a worldwide communications force.

EXHIBIT 15.22

The power and success of cable comes from offering very specific programming through a wide range of cable networks. An example is the Speed Channel, which offers all forms of motor sports programming and commentary.

Cable television transmits a wide range of programming to subscribers through wires rather than over airwaves. In the United States, more than 65 million basic-cable subscribers (nearly 58 percent of all U.S. households) are wired for cable reception and receive on average more than 40 channels of sports, entertainment, news, music video, and home-shopping programming.[32] Cable's power as an advertising option has grown enormously over the past decade as cable's share of the prime-time viewing audience has grown, and advertisers now invest about $20 billion for advertising time on cable.

Aside from more channels and hence more programming, three other aspects distinguish cable from network television. First is the willingness of cable networks to invest in original programming. With the success of programs such as USA network's *JAG*, cable networks are investing record dollar amounts in new programs to continue to attract well-defined audiences (see Exhibit 15.22). Second, because of cable's unique delivery technology, cable firms are now investing in software that can send different ads to different viewers. Time Warner is testing a system that tracks what channel each TV in any household is tuned to and what channels the household surfs. The software then can track the age, gender, and probable interests of the viewer.[33] This offers much more targeting efficiency for the advertiser and allows the cable company to increase ad placement prices. Finally, the cable industry is investigating the feasibility and potential revenue from **video on demand (VOD)**. While providing films and other programming through VOD has revenue potential, cable firms are also interested in ways advertising can be sold along with the VOD.[34]

32.   Data drawn from the National Cable & Telecommunications Association, Industry Statistics, accessed at *http://www.ncta.com* on June 24, 2007.
33.   David Kiley, "Cable's Big Bet on Hyper-Targeting," *BusinessWeek*, July 4, 2005, 58–59.
34.   Andrew Hampp, "Cablers Chase Revenue from VOD, Online Video," *Advertising Age*, May 14, 2007, 14.

Syndicated Television. Television syndication is either original programming or programming that first appeared on network television. It is then rebroadcast on either network or cable stations with pending distribution on the Internet. Syndicated programs provide advertisers with proven programming that typically attracts a well-defined, if not enormous, audience. There are several types of television syndication. **Off-network syndication** refers to programs that were previously run in network prime time. The popular off-network syndicated shows *Home Improvement* and *Seinfeld* command significant ad dollars—$175,000 to $225,000 for a 30-second ad. Less popular shows are more affordable, with prices set between about $25,000 and $60,000.[35] **First-run syndication** refers to programs developed specifically for sale to individual stations. The most famous first-run syndication show is *Star Trek: The Next Generation*. **Barter syndication** takes both off-network and first-run syndication shows and offers them free or at a reduced rate to local television stations, with some national advertising pre-sold within the programs. Local stations can then sell the remainder of the time to generate revenues. This option allows national advertisers to participate in the national syndication market conveniently. Two of the most widely recognized barter syndication shows are *Jeopardy* and *Wheel of Fortune*.

Local Television. Local television is the programming other than the network broadcast that independent stations and network affiliates offer local audiences. Completely independent stations air old movies, sitcoms, or children's programming. Network affiliates get about 90 hours of programming a week from the major networks, but they are free to air other programming beyond that provided by the network. News, movies, syndicated programs, and community-interest programs typically round out the local television fare.

Satellite/Closed-Circuit. New technology offers another version of television available to advertisers. Programming can now be transmitted to highly segmented audiences via **satellite and closed-circuit** transmission. The best known of these systems is the CNN Airport Network, which transmits news and weather programming directly to airport terminals around the world. A growing segment in this area is programming delivered via satellite to college campuses. CTN (College Television Network) reaches 8.2 million college students each week through closed-circuit programming delivered by satellite to thousands of TV monitors on 750 college and university campuses.[36]

As you can see, while all television may look the same to the average consumer, advertisers actually have five distinct options to consider. Regardless of which type of television transmission advertisers choose, television offers distinct advantages to advertisers as a way to communicate with target audiences.

Web/iPod/Cell TV. We would be remiss if we did not address the issue of transmitting television programs over the Web, as iPod downloads, or through cell phone reception. Since this capability is just emerging, it is premature to call this a television "category," but the capability has advertisers excited and we need to consider the potential here. Bear with us if by the time you read this, delivery of video through the Web and cell phones has changed dramatically.

First, let's consider the distribution of video over the Web. Cable industry execs believe there is huge revenue potential and advertiser interest in the convergence of on-air and on-screen programming. For example, during a sports broadcast you could watch a specific athlete on your computer while simultaneously watching the broader game on the television. And there certainly seems to be viewer interest in accessing video via the Web. CNN reports up to 26 million unique visitors monthly who download video from the network's Web site.[37]

35.   Richard Linnett, "Host of TV Superstars Boost Bullish Syndication Market," *Advertising Age*, March 8, 2004, S-4.
36.   Data drawn from TrendCentral accessed at *http://www.trendcentral.com* on June 24, 2007.
37.   Kate Fitzgerald, "Cable Websites Boost Content, Tighten TV Ties," *Advertising Age*, April 9, 2007, S-6.

Second, when Apple unveiled the video iPod, ABC started selling $1.99 downloads. But this option for video delivery needs some major sorting out. Shortly after ABC started its iPod downloads, it announced it would stream shows over the Web with the big advantage to ABC of selling ads around them due to the opportunity of putting ads within the shows.[38] The sorting out that needs to take place is whether iPod users will tolerate ads within the shows received over their iPods.

Finally, cell TV seems to have huge potential. Verizon Wireless's V CAST Mobile TV started with distribution in 25 markets in 2007 and has aggressive plans to expand the distribution. Broadcast shows need to be watched as scheduled—there is no on-demand viewing (yet). With a 2.2-inch display, 20 available channels, and a monthly fee of $15 dollars for the cell phone (in addition to voice and text fees), there seems to be good potential for generating ad revenue. But some analysts are wondering about how big that potential is once the novelty wears off.[39] One estimate suggests that by 2009, more than half of the U.S. population will be using computers, iPods, and cell phones to access video content and $2.9 billion will be spent by advertisers to reach these users with advertising messages.[40]

Advantages of Television. Throughout the book, we have referred to the unique capability of television as an advertising medium. There must be some very good reasons why advertisers such as AT&T, General Motors, and Procter & Gamble invest hundreds of millions of dollars annually in television advertising. The specific advantages of this medium are as follows.

Creative Opportunities. The overriding advantage of television compared to other media is, of course, the ability to send a message using both sight and sound. With recent advances in transmission and reception equipment, households now have brilliantly clear visuals and stereo-enhanced audio to further increase the impact of television advertising. Now, with HDTV capabilities becoming mainstream, all sorts of new creative opportunities present themselves.

Coverage, Reach, and Repetition. Television, in one form or another, reaches more than 98 percent of all households in the United States—an estimated 290 million people. These households represent every demographic segment in the United States, which allows advertisers to achieve broad coverage. We have also seen that the cable television option provides reach to hundreds of millions of households throughout the world. With the new mobile TV options just discussed, coverage and reach capabilities are enhanced even more. Further, no other medium allows an advertiser to repeat a message as frequently as television.

Cost per Contact. For advertisers that sell to broadly defined mass markets, television offers a cost-effective way to reach millions of members of a target audience. The average prime-time television program reaches 11 million households, and top-rated shows can reach more than 30 million households. This brings an advertiser's cost-per-contact figure down to an amount unmatched by any other media option—literally fractions of a penny per contact.

Audience Selectivity. Television programmers are doing a better job of developing shows that attract well-defined target audiences. **Narrowcasting** is the development and delivery of specialized programming to well-defined audiences. Cable television is far and away the most selective television option. Cable provides not only well-defined programming, but also entire networks—such as MTV and ESPN—built around the concept of attracting selective audiences. Also, recall the new software

38. Jon Fine, "Local TV's Clear Shot at the Web," *BusinessWeek*, May 15, 2006, 26.
39. Stephen H. Wildstrom, "A Giant Step for Tiny TV," *BusinessWeek*, May 21. 2007, 24.
40. Erick Schonfeld, "Make Way for Must Stream TV," *Business 2.0*, March 2007, 95–98.

DOING IT RIGHT

Cable and the Web: The Perfect Combination for High Selectivity

The discussion of cable television in the chapter highlights that one of the key advantages of cable is its ability to reach narrowly defined target segments. There are several other advantages of cable related to such "narrowcasting," such as combining cable with Web placement to achieve integrated brand promotion. The key advantages of cable include the following:

The expanded reach of cable. Cable's appeal is growing among key demographic groups such as teens, who spend more time watching cable than watching network television. Overall, cable now reaches nearly 60 percent of all U.S. households. Cable networks like TBS Superstation, ESPN, and AMC reach over 85 million homes. Consumers are highly favorable toward cable as a medium. In a recent survey of consumer perceptions of quality across major media (TV, radio, magazines, and newspapers), cable ranked first in 15 of 25 ratings while network television ranked first in only two categories.

Highly selective markets/minimal waste. Cable is much more efficient at reaching target markets than network television is. Viewers have more choices, and those more precisely defined choices attract a better-defined demographic, psychographic, and geographic audience. One of the fastest-growing categories for television spending is the kids' TV program. Because of increasing demand, the cost of a 30-second spot on cable networks like Nickelodeon and the Cartoon Network has increased 20 percent over the last few years.

Integrated brand promotion. For advertisers who want to add new media options to the media mix, cable offers an interesting combination with the Internet. Cable offers many branded Web sites. In fact, cable-branded Web sites attract more than 60 percent of the audience for media-affiliated Web sites. At the Comedy Central Web site, where viewers can catch up on programs they missed on television, ads are integrated into the video content so that instead of seeing "pre-roll" ads (those that ran during the original programming), they see video ads between video clips.

Sources: John Heilemann, "Cable's Niche Player," *Business 2.0*, May 2006, 36,39; Kate Fitzgerald, "Cable Websites Boost Content, Tighten TV Ties," *Advertising Age*, April 9, 2007, S-6-S-7.

being developed by Time Warner that will allow sending different ads to different households—the ultimate in selectivity. The ability to narrowcast is enhanced even further when cable is combined with other media, as the Doing It Right box highlights.

Disadvantages of Television. Television has great capabilities as an advertising medium, but it is not without limitations. Some of these limitations are serious enough to significantly detract from the power of television advertising.

Fleeting Message. One problem with the sight and sound of a television advertisement is that it is gone in an instant. The fleeting nature of a television message, as opposed to a print ad (which a receiver can contemplate), makes message impact difficult. Some advertisers invest huge amounts of money in the production of television ads to overcome this disadvantage.

High Absolute Cost. While the cost per contact of television advertising is the best of all traditional media, the absolute cost may be the worst. The average cost of air time for a single 30-second television spot during prime time is about $200,000, with the most popular shows, like *American Idol,* bringing in as much as $600,000 for a 30-second spot. Other popular shows command impressive numbers as well, such as *Grey's Anatomy,* $344,000; *CSI,* $340,000, and *Two and a Half Men,* $275,000.[41] Remember this is prime-time pricing. Off-prime-time slots go for a more modest $20,000 to $50,000 for 30 seconds. In addition, the average cost of producing a quality 30-second television spot is around $300,000 to $400,000. These costs make television advertising prohibitively expensive for many advertisers. Of course, large, national consumer products companies—for which television advertising is best suited anyway—find the absolute cost acceptable for the coverage, reach, and repetition advantages discussed earlier.

Poor Geographic Selectivity. While programming can be developed to attract specific audiences, program transmission cannot target geographic areas nearly as well.

41. AdAge Annual, *Advertising Age*, January 1, 2007, 22.

This is especially true for satellite subscribers. For a national advertiser that wants to target a city market, the reach of a television broadcast is too broad. Similarly, for a local retailer that wants to use television for reaching local segments, the television transmission is likely to reach a several-hundred-mile radius—which will increase the advertiser's cost with little likelihood of drawing patrons.

Poor Audience Attitude and Attentiveness. Since the inception of television advertising, consumers have bemoaned the intrusive nature of the commercials. Just when a movie is reaching its thrilling conclusion—on come the ads. The involuntary and frequent intrusion of advertisements on television has made television advertising the most distrusted form of advertising among consumers. In one of the few surveys tracking consumer sentiment, only 17 percent of consumers surveyed felt that television advertising affected them in their purchase of a new car, compared with 48 percent who claimed that direct mail advertising was a factor in their decision.[42] But be aware that it is not fundamentally the job of television advertising to motivate an immediate purchase. Image building and awareness are the key achievements for television ads.

Along with—and perhaps as a result of—this generally bad attitude toward television advertising, consumers have developed ways of avoiding exposure. Making a trip to the refrigerator or conversing with fellow viewers are the preferred low-tech ways to avoid exposure. On the high-tech side, **channel grazing**, or using a remote control to monitor programming on other channels while an advertisement is being broadcast, is the favorite way to avoid commercials.

New technology has created yet another potential method for avoiding advertising—and this development has advertisers greatly concerned. The problems centers on the so-called "V-chip." The **V-chip** is a device that can block television programming based on the program rating system. It was developed as a way for parents to block programming that they do not want their children to see. While that was the original and intended use for the V-chip, the technology can be easily adapted to block advertisements as well. Two manufacturers, RCA and Panasonic, say they want to build television sets with this sort of technology. Advertisers and broadcasters, of course, are challenging the rights of these manufacturers to build such sets. The consequences of sets with V-chips that block ads could be devastating to advertising revenues.

And, of course, the biggest news and highest-tech way to avoid television advertising is with TiVo. **TiVo**, and similar devices, are digital video recorders (DVRs) that use computer hard drives to store up to 140 hours of television programming. Consumers can use the devices to skip commercials and watch only the programming itself. Indeed, the overwhelming reason consumers use DVRs *is* to skip commercials. A survey of DVR users revealed that 81 percent of them invested in a DVR primarily to skip commercials, and they claim to fast-forward through 75 percent of the ads that appear in the programming that they watch. By 2008, about 25 percent of U.S. households had DVRs, and that percentage is expected to rise rapidly when cable companies like Comcast and Time Warner make built-in DVRs an option with set-top boxes.[43] Obviously, widespread use of DVRs has advertisers looking for ways to get exposure for their brands on television. More brand placement within programming and those annoying little "runners" at the bottom of the screen during programs are ways to reach DVR users.

Clutter. All the advantages of television as an advertising medium have created one significant disadvantage: clutter. The major television networks run about 15

---

42.   Jean Halliday, "Study Claims TV Advertising Doesn't Work on Car Buyers," *Advertising Age*, October 13, 2003, 8.

43.   Ronald Grover, "The Sound of Many Hands Zapping," *BusinessWeek*, May 22, 2006, 38.

minutes of advertising during each hour of prime-time programming, and cable channels carry about 14 minutes of advertising per hour.[44] Research has found that 65 percent of a surveyed group of consumers felt that they were "constantly bombarded with too much" advertising.[45]

A communications environment cluttered with advertising can cause viewers to invoke various information overload defenses to avoid information, as we discussed in Chapter 5.

Buying Procedures for Television Advertising. Discussions in Chapter 13 as well as in this chapter have identified the costs associated with television advertising from both a production and a space standpoint. Here we will concentrate on the issue of buying time on television. Advertisers buy time for television advertising through sponsorship, participation, and spot advertising.

Sponsorship. In a **sponsorship** arrangement, an advertiser agrees to pay for the production of a television program and for most (and often all) of the advertising that appears in the program. Sponsorship is not nearly as popular today as it was in the early days of network television. Contemporary sponsorship agreements have attracted big-name companies such as AT&T and IBM, who often sponsor sporting events, and Hallmark, known for its sponsorship of dramatic series.

Participation. The vast majority of advertising time is purchased on a participation basis. **Participation** means that several different advertisers buy commercial time during a specific television program. No single advertiser has a responsibility for the production of the program or a commitment to the program beyond the time contracted for.

Spot Advertising. Spot advertising refers to all television advertising time purchased from and aired through local television stations. Spot advertising provides national advertisers the opportunity to either adjust advertising messages for different markets or intensify their media schedules in particularly competitive markets. Spot advertising is the primary manner in which local advertisers, such as car dealers, furniture stores, and restaurants, reach their target audiences with television.

A final issue with respect to buying television advertising has to do with the time periods and programs during which the advertising will run. Once an advertiser has determined that sponsorship, participation, or spot advertising (or, more likely, some combination of the last two) meets its needs, the time periods and specific programs must be chosen. Exhibit 15.23 shows the way in which television programming times are broken into **dayparts**, which represent segments of time during a television broadcast day.

EXHIBIT 15.23

Television dayparts (in Eastern U.S. time zone segments).

Morning	7:00 A.M.	to	9:00 A.M.,	Monday through Friday
Daytime	9:00 A.M.	to	4:30 P.M.,	Monday through Friday
Early fringe	4:30 P.M.	to	7:30 P.M.,	Monday through Friday
Prime-time access	7:30 P.M.	to	8:00 P.M.,	Sunday through Saturday
Prime time	8:00 P.M.	to	11:00 P.M.,	Monday through Saturday
	7:00 P.M.	to	11:00 P.M.,	Sunday
Late news	11:00 P.M.	to	11:30 P.M.,	Monday through Friday
Late fringe	11:30 P.M.	to	1:00 A.M.,	Monday through Friday

44 . Andrew Green, "Clutter Crisis Countdown," *Advertising Age,* April 21, 2003, 22.

45. 2004 Yankelovich Partners poll, cited in Gary Ruskin, "A 'Deal Spiral of Disrespect,'" *Advertising Age,* April 26, 2004, 18.

Measuring Television Audiences. Television audience measurements identify the size and composition of audiences for different television programming. Advertisers choose where to buy television time based on these factors. These measures also set the cost for television time. The larger the audience or the more attractive the composition, the more costly the time will be.

The following are brief summaries of the information used to measure television audiences.

Television Households. **Television households** is an estimate of the number of households that are in a market and own a television. Since more than 98 percent of all households in the United States own a television, the number of total households and the number of television households are virtually the same, about 101 million. Markets around the world do not have the same level of television penetration.

Households Using Television. **Households using television (HUT)**, also referred to as sets in use, is a measure of the number of households tuned to a television program during a particular time period.

Program Rating. A **program rating** is the percentage of television households that are in a market and are tuned to a specific program during a specific time period. Expressed as a formula, program rating is:

$$\text{program rating} = \frac{\text{TV households tuned to a program}}{\text{total TV households in the market}}$$

A **ratings point** indicates that 1 percent of all the television households in an area were tuned to the program measured. If an episode of *CSI* is watched by 19.5 million households, then the program rating would be calculated as follows:

$$CSI \text{ rating} = \frac{19,500,000}{95,900,000} = 20 \text{ rating}$$

The program rating is the best-known measure of television audience, and it is the basis for the rates television stations charge for advertising on different programs. Recall that it is also the way advertisers develop their media plans from the standpoint of calculating reach and frequency estimates, such as gross rating points.

Share of Audience. **Share of audience** provides a measure of the proportion of households that are using television during a specific time period and are tuned to a particular program. If 65 million households are using their televisions during the *CSI* time slot, and *CSI* attracts 19.5 million viewers, then the share of audience is:

$$CSI \text{ share} = \frac{\text{TV households tuned to a program}}{\text{total TV households using TV}} = \frac{19,500,000}{65,000,000} = 30 \text{ share}$$

Controversy in Television Measurement. There has been some controversy in the area of measuring television audiences in that advertisers have been disputing Nielsen Media ratings (Nielsen is the premier provider of television audience data). The importance of this controversy is that advertisers rely on Nielsen ratings to determine the programs on which they will by time and media companies rely on the same ratings as the basis for how much they will charge advertisers for the time.

There are two key aspects to this controversy surrounding the rating data. First, since Nielsen data report households "tuned" to a program, that measure does not really measure "commercial" viewership in the first place nor does it account for all of us who leave the room during commercial breaks. Second, there is the issue of technological change, like the digital video recorders discussed earlier, and their effect on actual television viewing behavior since DVR users can "skip" the ads all together.[46] Obviously, advertisers do not want to pay for mere "program" viewership but rather want to pay for "commercial" viewership—potentially a lower number at lower cost.[47] The first foray into "commercial" ratings took place in the spring of 2007 with great success as advertisers signed up for commercial airtime on the upcoming network season. One industry analyst said, "It was a truly transformational 'upfront' [buying season]," given the new commercial rating metric.[48]

The Future of Television. The future of television is exciting for several reasons. First, the emerging interactive era will undoubtedly affect television as an advertising medium. Prospects include viewer participation in mystery programs and game shows in which household viewers play right along with studio contestants. Equally as important, though, is that technology is creating the ability to transmit advertising to a wide range of new devices from cell phones to personal digital assistants to pagers. Estimates are that by the year 2010 global mobile advertising will be a $10 billion industry.[49] And recall the discussion from Chapter 2 regarding the growth of broadband access. By the year 2006, about 42 percent of all adult Americans (about 84 million people) had broadband connections,[50] and that figure is growing rapidly, increasing the prospect that television advertising will be transmitted via the Internet to either PCs or handheld devices. Advertisers will have to seriously consider the implications of this mode of communication and how well it will serve as a way to send persuasive communications.

Another major change that will affect the future of television is transmission technology. **Direct broadcast by satellite (DBS)** is a program delivery system whereby television and radio (like XM) programs are sent directly from a satellite to homes equipped with small receiving dishes. This transmission offers the prospect of hundreds of different channels. While advertisers will still be able to insert advertising in programs, the role of networks and cable stations in the advertising process will change dramatically.

Television advertisers and their agencies also have to be prepared for high-definition television broadcasts. **High-definition television (HDTV)** promises to offer consumers picture and audio clarity that is a vast improvement over current technology. While HDTV equipment will certainly have the capability to reproduce images and sound with extraordinary quality, the uncertainties of visual and audio transmission may compromise the ability of the new HDTV sets to do so.

Television advertising, as discussed, is now migrating to a variety of mobile devices. As programming capability becomes more technologically sound and consumers are more willing to view that programming via the Web, an iPod or cell phone, advertisers will have multiple new ways of reaching consumers with their brand messages.

Finally, consolidation in the industry cannot be ignored. In 2004, Comcast made a $51 billion bid for all the media owned by Disney. The offer was finally dropped after pressure from both Comcast and Disney shareholders. But Comcast still has acquired about $20 billion in cable companies.[51] Similarly, Rupert Murdock has

46.   David Bauder, "Network Execs Question Nielsen Accuracy," Yahoo! News, November 16, 2003, accessed at *http://www .news.yahoo.com* on November 17, 2003.

47.   Brian Steinberg and Andrew Hampp, "Commercial Ratings? Nets Talk TiVo Instead," *Advertising Age,* June 4, 2007, 3, 60.

48.   Nat Worden, "Ratings Metric Boosts TV Ad Buys," TheStreet.com, June 26, 2007, accessed via the Web at *http://www .thestreet.com* on June 26, 2007.

49.   Digital Marketing & Media FactPack, "Mobile Device Use and Content Consumption," April 23, 2007, 43.

50.   Peter Svensson, "Middle Class Goes Broadband as Price Falls," Associated Press Yahoo! Finance, May 29, 2006, accessed at http://biz.yahoo.com/ap/.

51.   Tom Lowry, Amy Barrett, and Ronald Grover, "A New Cable Giant," *BusinessWeek,* November 18, 2002, 108–118.

been expanding the DirecTV empire of cable holdings and media holdings that generates $30 billion in revenue from literally every corner of the earth.[52] And let's not forget media giants GE, Time Warner, and Disney, all of which in their own right have great broadcast media power. The issue, of course, is the extent to which these big and powerful media companies can end up controlling programming content. It is not automatically the case that big media companies shape programming in a biased way, but that is the concern of media watchdogs.

While it is hard to predict what the future will hold, one thing seems sure—television will continue to grow as an entertainment and information medium for households. The convenience, low cost, and diversity of programming make television an ideal medium for consumers. Additionally, television's expansion around the world will generate access to huge new markets. Television, despite its limitations, will continue to be an important part of the integrated communications mix of many advertisers.

5 Radio. Radio may seem like the least glamorous and most inconspicuous of the major media. This perception does not jibe with reality. Radio plays an integral role in the media plans of some of the most astute advertisers. Because of the unique features of radio, advertisers invest about $20 billion annually in radio advertising to reach national and local audiences.[53] There are good reasons why advertisers of all sorts use radio to reach target audiences. Let's turn our attention to the different radio options available to advertisers.

Radio Categories. Radio offers an advertiser several options for reaching target audiences. The basic split of national and local radio broadcasts presents an obvious geographic choice. More specifically, though, advertisers can choose among the following categories, each with specific characteristics: networks, syndication, AM versus FM, satellite, and Internet.

Networks. Radio networks operate much like television networks in that they deliver programming via satellite to affiliate stations across the United States. Network radio programming concentrates on news, sports, business reports, and short features. Some of the more successful radio networks that draw large audiences are ABC, CNN, and AP News Network.

Syndication. Radio syndication provides complete programs to stations on a contract basis. Large syndicators offer stations complete 24-hour-a-day programming packages that totally relieve a station of any programming effort. Aside from full-day programming, they also supply individual programs, such as talk shows. Large syndication organizations such as Westwood One and Satellite Music Network place advertising within programming, making syndication a good outlet for advertisers.

AM versus FM. AM radio stations send signals that use amplitude modulation (AM) and operate on the AM radio dial at signal designations 540 to 1600. AM was the foundation of radio until the 1970s. Today, AM radio broadcasts, even the new stereo AM transmissions, cannot match the sound quality of FM. Thus, most AM stations focus on local community broadcasting or news and talk formats that do not require high-quality audio. Talk radio has, in many ways, been the salvation of AM radio. FM radio stations transmit using frequency modulation (FM). FM radio transmission is of a much higher quality. Because of this, FM radio has attracted the wide range of music formats that most listeners prefer. Radio is, of course, now available via the Web.

---

52.   Catherine Young, et .al., "Rupert's World," *BusinessWeek*, January 19, 2004, 53–61.
53.   AdAge Annual, *Advertising Age*, January 1, 2007, 20.

EXHIBIT 15.24

Satellite radio providers like Sirius are betting that consumers are willing to pay for commercial-free radio and get a greater variety of music and higher-quality sound.

Satellite Radio. Of course one of the newest options in radio is satellite radio, which is transmitted from satellites circling the earth. Currently, satellite radio costs a consumer anywhere from $99 to $200 to set up and then about $10 per month for a subscription. The advantages of satellite radio have to do with variety of program, more crisp and clear sound reproduction, and, of course, *no ads on the music channels.* By 2007, the two leading satellite radio providers, XM Satellite Radio and Sirius Satellite Radio, had only 13 million subscribers combined; both were losing money and were in active merger negotiations (see Exhibit 15.24). It remains to be seen whether consumers like the variety and quality offered by satellite radio or whether they will prefer to keep "free" radio and listen to ads. (See the Doing It Right box.)

Internet Radio. It is truly hard to predict what will happen to this radio option. Internet radio was launched basically because the technology allowed music transmission. But Internet radio Webcasters like Yahoo's LAUNCHcast and RealNetworks' Rhapsody are being hit with higher and higher royalty costs for transmitting copyrighted music. A huge hike in 2007 prompted some Internet radio transmitters like Live365 to go "silent" for a day in protest. It is possible that all Internet radio will go silent if royalty rates make the medium unsustainable.[54]

Types of Radio Advertising. Advertisers have three basic choices in radio advertising: local spot radio advertising, network radio advertising, or national spot radio advertising. Local spot radio advertising attracts 80 percent of all radio advertising dollars in a year. In **local spot radio advertising**, an advertiser places advertisements directly with individual stations rather than with a network or syndicate. Local spot radio dominates the three classes of radio advertising because there are more than 9,000 individual radio stations in the United States, giving advertisers a wide range of choices. And local spot radio reaches well-defined geographic audiences, making it the ideal choice for local retailers.

   Network radio advertising is advertising placed within national network programs. Since there are few network radio programs being broadcast, only about $600 million a year is invested by advertisers in this format.

   The last option, **national spot radio advertising**, offers an advertiser the opportunity to place advertising in nationally syndicated radio programming. An advertiser can reach millions of listeners nationwide on over 400 radio stations by contracting with Clear Channel's Premiere Radio Networks.

54.   Rick Aristotle Munarriz, "The Day Internet Radio Died," *Motley Fool*, June 26, 2007, accessed at *http://www.fool.com* on June 27, 2007.

DOING IT RIGHT

The Death of Radio?

In 2001, Sirius Satellite Radio launched its third satellite into space from the Soviet Union's once-secret Baikonur Cosmodrome in Kazakhstan. This is the same site where the first Earth satellite was launched in 1957 and where the first human in orbit blasted off in 1961. Will this site also be known as the place where the slow death of radio began? Right now, Sirius delivers 65 streams of commercial-free music in every radio genre and over 50 streams of news, sports, weather, talk, comedy, public radio, and children's programming. Sirius's programming is not available on conventional radio in any market in the United States. The CD-quality sound broadcasts can be accessed only through subscription (about $10 per month). The company holds one of only two licenses issued by the Federal Communications Commission (FCC) to operate a national satellite radio system. The other is held by XM Satellite Radio.

If the advantages of subscription satellite radio are appealing to radio listeners, it could rattle the very foundation of the $20 billion-a-year broadcast radio industry. And satellite has some very high-profile believers. Corporations like General Motors, DaimlerChrysler, and Clear Channel Communications as well as venture capital investors like Prime 66 Partners, Apollo, and Blackstone have sunk over $3 billion into Sirius and XM. In 2003, one industry analyst believed that satellite radio was the "next big consumer phenomenon" and that by 2007 it will be generating up to $10 billion a year.

While all this sounds very exciting and convincing, the reality is that no satellite company has made a profit—quite the contrary. By the end of 2007, Sirius counted about 6 million subscribers but only $7 million in revenue, and lost over $700 million that year. XM radio had more subscribers, about 8 million, and generated about $1 billion in revenue but also lost about $700 million. So the question remains: Will Sirius and XM grow dramatically and "kill" commercial radio as we have always known it? Or are consumers too accustomed to free radio, and the death of radio is greatly exaggerated? It looks like exaggeration is winning right now and free radio is not ready to die.

Sources: Bethany McLean, "Satellite Killed the Radio Star," **Fortune**, January 22, 2001, 95. Financial data taken from Sirius and XM radio financial statements accessed via the Web at **http://www.finance.yahoo.com** on June 27, 2007.

Advantages of Radio. While radio may not be the most glamorous or sophisticated of the major media options, it has some distinct advantages over newspapers, magazines, and television.

Cost. On both a per-contact and absolute basis, radio is often the most cost-effective medium available to an advertiser. A full minute of network radio time can cost between $5,000 and $10,000—an amazing bargain compared with the other media we've discussed. In addition, production costs for preparing radio ads are quite low; an ad often costs nothing to prepare if the spot is read live during a local broadcast.

Reach and Frequency. Radio has the widest exposure of any medium. It reaches consumers in their homes, cars, offices, and backyards, and even while they exercise. The wireless and portable features of radio provide an opportunity to reach consumers that exceeds all other media. The low cost of radio time gives advertisers the opportunity to frequently repeat messages at low absolute cost and cost per contact.

Target Audience Selectivity. Radio can selectively target audiences on a geographic, demographic, and psychographic basis. The narrow transmission of local radio stations gives advertisers the best opportunity to reach narrowly defined geographic audiences. For a local merchant with one store, this is an ideal opportunity. Radio programming formats and different dayparts also allow target audience selectivity.

CBS Radio made the decision several years ago to convert four of its 13 stations to a rock 'n' roll oldies format to target 35-to-49-year-olds—in other words, the baby boomers. Hard rock, new age, easy listening, country, classical, and talk radio formats all attract different audiences. Radio dayparts, shown in Exhibit 15.25, also attract different audiences. Morning and afternoon/evening drive times attract a male audience. Daytime attracts predominantly woman; nighttime, teens.

EXHIBIT 15.25

Radio dayparts used for advertising scheduling.

Morning drive time	6:00 A.M. to 10:00 A.M.
Daytime	10:00 A.M. to 3:00 P.M.
Afternoon/evening drive time	3:00 P.M. to 7:00 P.M.
Nighttime	7:00 P.M. to 12:00 A.M.
Late night	12:00 A.M. to 6:00 A.M.

Flexibility and Timeliness. Radio is the most flexible medium because of very short closing periods for submitting an ad. This means an advertiser can wait until close to an air date before submitting an ad. With this flexibility, advertisers can take advantage of special events or unique competitive opportunities in a timely fashion.

Creative Opportunities. While radio may be unidimensional in sensory stimulation, it can still have powerful creative impact. Recall that radio has been described as the theater of the mind. Ads such as the folksy tales of Tom Bodett for Motel 6 or the eccentric humor of Stan Freberg are memorable and can have tremendous impact on the attitude toward a brand. In addition, the musical formats that attract audiences to radio stations can also attract attention to radio ads. Research has discovered that audiences who favor certain music may be more prone to listen to an ad that uses songs they recognize and like.

Disadvantages of Radio. As good as radio can be, it also suffers from some severe limitations as an advertising medium. Advertising strategists must recognize these disadvantages when deciding what role radio can play in an integrated marketing communications program.

Poor Audience Attentiveness. Just because radio reaches audiences almost everywhere doesn't mean that anyone is paying attention. Remember that radio has also been described as audio wallpaper. It provides a comfortable background distraction while a consumer does something else—hardly an ideal level of attentiveness for advertising communication. Consumers who are listening and traveling in a car often switch stations when an ad comes on and divide their attention between the radio and the road.

Creative Limitations. While the theater of the mind may be a wonderful creative opportunity, taking advantage of that opportunity can be difficult indeed. The audio-only nature of radio communication is a tremendous creative compromise. An advertiser whose product depends on demonstration or visual impact is at a loss when it comes to radio. And like its television counterpart, a radio message creates a fleeting impression that is often gone in an instant.

Fragmented Audiences. The large number of stations that try to attract the same audience in a market has created tremendous fragmentation. Think about your own local radio market. There are probably four or five different stations that play the kind of music you like. Or consider that in the past few years, more than 1,000 radio stations in the United States have adopted the talk-radio format. This fragmentation means that the percentage of listeners tuned to any one station is likely very small.

Chaotic Buying Procedures. For an advertiser who wants to include radio as part of a national advertising program, the buying process can be sheer chaos. Since national networks and syndicated broadcasts do not reach every geographic market, an advertiser has to buy time in individual markets on a station-by-station basis. This could involve dozens of different negotiations and individual contracts.

Buying Procedures for Radio Advertising. While buying procedures to achieve national coverage may be chaotic, this does not mean they are completely without structure. Although the actual buying may be time-consuming and expensive if many stations are involved, the structure is actually quite straightforward. Advertising time can be purchased from networks, syndications, or local radio stations. Recall that among these options, advertisers invest most heavily in local placement. About 80 percent of annual radio advertising is placed locally. About 15 percent is allocated to national spot placement, and only 5 percent is invested in network broadcasts.

The other factor in buying radio time relates to the time period of purchase. Refer again to Exhibit 15.25. This shows the five basic daypart segments from which an advertiser can choose. The time period decision is based primarily on a demographic description of the advertiser's target audience. Recall that drive-time dayparts attract a mostly male audience, while daytime is primarily female, and nighttime is mostly teen. This information, combined with programming formats, guides an advertiser in a buying decision.

As with magazine buying, radio advertising time is purchased from rate cards issued by individual stations. Run-of-station ads—ads that the station chooses when to run—cost less than ads scheduled during a specific daypart. The price can also increase if an advertiser wants the ad read live on the air by a popular local radio personality hosting a show during a daypart.

The actual process of buying radio time is relatively simple. A media planner identifies the stations and the dayparts that will reach the target audience. Then the rates and daypart availabilities are checked to be sure they match the media-planning objectives. At this point, agreements are made regarding the number of spots to run in specified time frames.

Measuring Radio Audiences. There are two primary sources of information on radio audiences. Arbitron ratings cover 260 local radio markets. The ratings are developed through the use of diaries maintained by listeners who record when they listened to the radio and to what station they were tuned. The *Arbitron Ratings/Radio* book gives audience estimates by time period and selected demographic characteristics. Several specific measures are compiled from the Arbitron diaries:

- **Average quarter-hour persons:** The average number of listeners tuned to a station during a specified 15-minute segment of a daypart.
- **Average quarter-hour share:** The percentage of the total radio audience that was listening to a radio station during a specified quarter-hour daypart.
- **Average quarter-hour rating:** The audience during a quarter-hour daypart expressed as a percentage of the population of the measurement area. This provides an estimate of the popularity of each station in an area.
- **Cume:** The cumulative audience, which is the total number of different people who listen to a station for at least five minutes in a quarter-hour period within a specified daypart. Cume is the best estimate of the reach of a station.
- RADAR (Radio's All Dimension Audience Research) is the other major measure of radio audiences. Sponsored by the major radio networks, RADAR collects audience data twice a year based on interviews with radio listeners. Designated listeners are called daily for a one-week period and asked about their listening behavior. Estimates include measures of the overall audience for different network stations and audience estimates by market area. The results of the studies are reported in an annual publication, *Radio Usage and Network Radio Audiences*. Media planners can refer to published measures such as Arbitron and RADAR to identify which stations will reach target audiences at what times across various markets.

The Future of Radio. Three factors must be considered with respect to the future of radio. First, the prospects for subscription satellite radio, event with the current troubles facing Sirius and XM, should not be underestimated. Satellite radio does away with radio advertising clutter and offers listeners multiple, detailed choices to match their listening preferences. This is a huge advantage along with the increased audio quality. The key issue, of course, is whether radio listeners will be willing to pay for an entertainment medium that has been free from its inception.

Second, radio will be affected by emerging technologies much in the same way that television will be affected. High-definition radio, HD radio, is becoming a reality and big firms like Clear Channel have plans for 100 digital channels in 50 cities.[55]

55.   Tom Lowry, "From Vanilla to Full Metal Racket," *BusinessWeek*, May 1, 2006, 42.

EXHIBIT 15.26

The radio industry is in a state of flux. While Sirius and XM are providing subscription-based satellite radio programming, Clear Channel Communications has continued to expand its ownership of traditional radio stations and now owns and operates about 1,200 stations throughout the United States and is expanding into HD radio with transmission in 50 U.S. cities.

There are no subscription fees, but an HD receiver will cost a radio fan about $200, which may present a barrier to adoption and use. Finally, there has been a large degree of consolidation going on in the traditional radio market. Led by Clear Channel Communications (see Exhibit 15.26), fewer big competitors are owning more and more radio stations. Through an aggressive period of acquisitions in the early 2000s, Clear Channel now owns approximately 1,200 radio stations in all regions of the United States, generates about $8 billion in revenue, and makes a profit of about $1 billion. Consolidation provides both opportunities and liabilities for both consumers and advertisers. Opportunities for consumers relate to the consistency of quality in the radio programming available and advertisers have an easier time buying and placing radio spots.

SUMMARY

 Understand the changes taking place in the traditional media of newspapers, magazines, television, and radio relative to new electronic media options.

The changes in the advertising industry are tangible and dramatic with respect to advertisers' use of the traditional media of newspapers, magazines, television, and radio. For decades, advertisers would work with their advertising agencies to develop messages for their brands and then the agencies would negotiate for airtime with television and radio networks or for space in newspapers, and magazines. Most of these media options were owned by a few big media companies. Now, advertisers are fast adopting the belief that digital media—primarily Internet ads—offer a more cost-effective way to reach target markets. In additional, digital media allow advertisers to rapidly make changes in campaigns that might take months to accomplish with traditional media. In addition, if the advertiser chooses, an Internet campaign can easily be a global campaign—a monumental task in traditional media. Advertisers are shifting literally billions of dollars out of traditional media in preference for digital media.

 Detail the pros and cons of newspapers as a media class, identify newspaper categories, and describe buying and audience measurement for newspapers.

Newspapers can be categorized by target audience, geographic coverage, and frequency of publication. As a media class, newspapers provide an excellent means for reaching local audiences with informative advertising messages. Precise timing of message delivery can be achieved at modest expenditure levels. But for products that demand creative and colorful executions, this medium simply cannot deliver. Newspaper costs are typically transmitted via rate cards and are primarily a function of a paper's readership levels.

 Detail the pros and cons of magazines as a media class, identify magazine categories, and describe buying and audience measurement for magazines.

Three important magazine categories are consumer, business, and farm publications. Because of their specific editorial content, magazines can be effective in attracting distinctive groups of readers with common interests. Thus, magazines can be superb tools for reaching specific market segments. Also, magazines facilitate a wide range of creative executions. Of course, the selectivity advantage turns into a disadvantage for advertisers trying to achieve high reach levels. Costs of magazine ad space can vary dramatically because of the wide range of circulation levels achieved by different types of magazines.

 Detail the pros and cons of television as a media class, identify television categories, and describe buying and audience measurement for television.

The four basic forms of television are network, cable, syndicated, and local television. Television's principal advantage is obvious: Because it allows for almost limitless possibilities in creative execution, it can be an extraordinary tool for affecting consumers' perceptions of a brand. Also, it can be an efficient device for reaching huge audiences; however, the absolute costs for reaching these audiences can be staggering. Lack of audience interest and involvement certainly limit the effectiveness of commercials in this medium, and digital devices like TiVo that allow the viewer to skip commercials make TV advertising nonexistent for many. The three ways that advertisers can buy time are through sponsorship, participation, and spot advertising. As with any medium, advertising rates will vary as a function of the size and composition of the audience that is watching—yet audience measurement for television is not an exact science and its methods are often disputed.

 Detail the pros and cons of radio as a media class, identify radio categories, and describe buying and audience measurement for radio.

Advertisers can choose from three basic types of radio advertising: local spot, network radio, or national spot advertising. Radio can be a cost-effective medium, and because of the wide diversity in radio programming, it can be an excellent tool for reaching well-defined audiences. Poor listener attentiveness is a drawback to radio, and the audio-only format places obvious constraints on creative execution. Satellite radio, which is subscriber-based, does away with advertising entirely on its music stations. Radio ad rates are driven by considerations such as the average number of listeners tuned to a station at specific times throughout the day. Buying and placing ads for radio is becoming easier due to ever-increasing consolidation in the industry.

KEY TERMS

general-population newspapers
business newspapers
ethnic newspapers
gay and lesbian newspapers
alternative press newspapers
display advertising
co-op advertising
preprinted insert
free-standing insert (FSI)
classified advertising
rate card
column inch
standard advertising unit (SAU)
run-of-paper (ROP) or run-of-press
preferred position
full position
circulation
paid circulation
controlled circulation
readership
bleed page
gatefold ads

first cover page
second cover page
third cover page
fourth cover page
double-page spreads
space contract
space order
closing date
on-sale date
cover date
guaranteed circulation
pass-along readership
network television
cable television
video on demand (VOD)
off-network syndication
first-run syndication
barter syndication
local television
satellite and closed-circuit
narrowcasting
channel grazing

V-chip
TiVo
sponsorship
participation
spot advertising
dayparts
television households
households using television (HUT)
program rating
ratings point
share of audience
direct broadcast by satellite (DBS)
high-definition television (HDTV)
radio networks
radio syndication
local spot radio advertising
network radio advertising
national spot radio advertising
average quarter-hour persons
average quarter-hour share
average quarter-hour rating
cume

QUESTIONS

1. With reference to the chapter opener, why are advertisers shifting billions of dollars from the traditional media of newspapers, magazines, television, and radio to digital media? What is your preference for viewing brand messages—traditional media or the Internet?

2. Why are newspapers losing circulation and what effect does that have on their advertising revenue?

3. Magazines certainly proved to be the right media class for selling Absolut vodka. Why are magazines a natural choice for vodka advertisements? What has Absolut done with its advertising to take full advantage of this medium?

4. Peruse several recent editions of your town's newspaper and select three examples of co-op advertising. What objectives do you believe the manufacturers and retailers are attempting to achieve in each of the three ads you've selected?

5. Place your local newspaper and an issue of your favorite magazine side by side and carefully review the content of each. From the standpoint of a prospective advertiser, which of the two publications has a more dramatic problem with clutter? Identify tactics being used by advertisers in each publication to break through the clutter and get their brands noticed.

6. The costs involved in preparing and placing ads in television programming such as the Super Bowl broadcast can be simply incredible. How is it that advertisers such as Pepsi and Nissan can justify the incredible costs that come with this media vehicle?

7. Think about the television viewing behavior you've observed in your household. Of the five ways people avoid TV ad exposure discussed in this chapter, which have you observed in your household? What other avoidance tactics do your friends and family use?

8. The choice between print and broadcast media is often portrayed as a choice between high- and low-involvement media. What makes one medium inherently more involving than another? How will the characteristics of an ad's message affect the decision to employ an involving versus an uninvolving medium?

9. For an advertiser that seeks to achieve nationwide reach, can radio be a good buy? What frustrations are likely to be encountered in using radio for this purpose?

10. What are the potential liabilities and risks to consumers and advertisers of the consolidation of radio station ownership by a few, large media companies?

EXPERIENTIAL EXERCISES

1.   Look up the following four sites on the Internet and evaluate which medium (radio, television, magazines, or newspaper) you think is best suited for advertising each brand. Justify your choices based on an evaluation of these brands, and based on the pros and cons of each medium discussed in the chapter.

K2 Snowboards: http://www.k2snowboards.com

CoverGirl: http://www.covergirl.com

Metro-Goldwyn-Mayer: http://www.mgm.com

Zingerman's: http://www.zingermans.com

2.   This chapter discusses the cost and buying procedures of four different types of media. Select a favorite magazine, newspaper, radio station, or television station and look over its media cost and buying procedures. (You can obtain rate cards at the company's Internet site or by contacting the sales department.) Using this chapter's cost and buying information as your guide, gather specific ad rate information from the publication or station you selected. How do the rates and specifications of your selection compare with what is listed in the text? If the rates or buying procedures for your selected medium seem different from the ones listed in the text, explain why you think they varied. Do you think the advertising costs are justified for the medium you selected? Explain.

3.   Program sponsorship is one way for advertisers to cut through the clutter of television advertising. In 2007, the beauty brand Pond's sponsorship of the USA Network's mini-series *The Starter Wife* drew attention for its fully integrated marketing and promotions campaign, which included product placements and input during the show's creation. Similarly, Hallmark has long sponsored dramatic television specials.

Working in small teams, propose both existing and potential television series or specials that would present powerful sponsorship opportunities for the sports-drink maker Gatorade. Identify any additional marketing opportunities that could accompany such a sponsorship.

4.   Draft a media plan for a new cosmetics line with a target segment of Hispanic women between the ages of 15 and 25. Identify examples within each of the traditional media groups—newspapers, magazines, television, and radio—that could be effective and then recommend which of the four areas is the best choice for the campaign.

CHAPTER 16

After reading and thinking about this chapter,
you will be able to do the following:

1

Understand the role of the Internet in
advertising and IBP.

2

Identify the nature of the Internet as
a medium available for communicating
advertising and promotion messages.

Describe the different advertising options
on the Web.

4

Discuss the issues involved in establishing a
site on the World Wide Web.

Discuss the future of advertising and IBP
on the Web.

Introductory Scenario: Old Media Meets New Media. When

Unilever, one of the world's largest consumer products companies (http://www .unilever.com), wanted a fresh and powerful advertising campaign for its Axe spray deodorant brand for men, the firm turned to London-based advertising agency Bartle Bogle Hegarty Limited (BBH, http://www.bbh.co.uk). What Unilever wanted was a truly global advertising message that would work in all 75 countries where it sold Axe. What BBH created was a new phrase, universally global, that guys would come to know and love as an expression of female attraction for any guy wearing Axe— and the phrase BomChickaWahWah was born.[1] The brand managers at Unilever and creatives at BBH went to work and released a wave of BomChickaWahWahs around the world through videos of an all-female band singing BomChickaWah-Wah (which would show up on YouTube), online games, live performances by the band, and television ads also destined to end up on social networking sites. The goal was to make the phrase stick in the mind of millions of young guys around the globe with (hopefully) the same kind of longevity as Homer Simpson's "D'oh!" The campaign ran through 2007 and attracted widespread attention. To check out the newest offerings for Axe on the Web go to http://www.theaxeeffect.com.

The whole idea behind combining Web content with traditional media is that the Web generation (of which you are a key part) will seek out messages on the Web and attend to those messages more readily than traditional media messages sent through magazines or television (although the Axe campaign does rely on these types of ads too—see Exhibit 16.1). Advertising messages that find their way on to YouTube, MySpace, or Flickr are believed to communicate in a more "social" way. That is, when a message shows up on a social networking site, it seems to be more part of "life" and less like big corporate, commercial-speak. And, as with the Axe strategy, global target markets can be reached nearly instantaneously if the right message catches on and spreads through the networks.

Unilever is not, of course, the first firm to think of using strategies that unleash the power of the Web on a brand. Red Bull does little traditional media advertising in the 100 countries where the energy drink is sold. Instead you'll find Web-based contests where people create sculptures out of Red Bull cans and win a trip to Switzerland. Another example is DirecTV's organization of a championship video-gaming series with tournaments broadcast on satellite television. Firms around the world are discovering that working brand messages into media that will be "voluntarily" viewed is powerful

So how does this story end? Did BomChicka-WahWah work? Did Unilever and BBH score in the world of Web 2.0? Well, it may be too soon to say it was a global smash success, but Axe now holds significant market share in the men's deodorant market around the world: 8.9 percent in Germany, 13.5 percent in the United States, 17.6 percent in Australia, and 28.6 percent in India as examples.[2] But what do you think? Do you encounter brands on the Web and find the

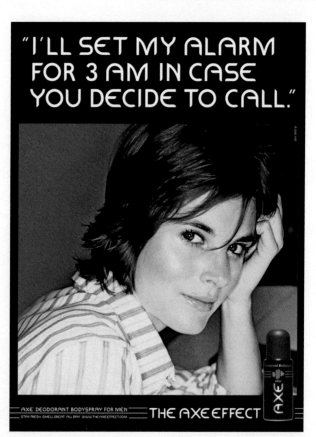

"I'LL SET MY ALARM FOR 3 AM IN CASE YOU DECIDE TO CALL."

AXE DEODORANT BODYSPRAY FOR MEN THE AXE EFFECT

EXHIBIT 16.1

Unilever wanted a Web-based campaign for its men's spray deodorant Axe that would communicate the message that women are attracted to men who use Axe. This print ad for Axe is an example of a traditional media (magazine) ad used by Unilever in the past. Go to http://www .theaxeeffect.com to see the Web version of the Axe campaign.

1.   Steve Hamm, "Children of the Web," *BusinessWeek*, July 2, 2007, 51–58.
2.   Ibid, 56.

message more appealing and interesting than a television or radio ad? What about BomChickaWahWah—did you like it? Did you buy Axe? If you want to express yourself and join the networking around Axe you can go to http://www.rateitall .com and rate the campaign yourself!

No Wires Means New Rules.
The Internet has been a wild ride since 1999. First a boom. Then the dot.bomb. Now we are firmly into another boom—and it is permanent. Despite terrorism, recession, and skepticism resulting from the large list of high-profile Internet sites that went from dot.darlings to dot.nots—including eToys, Garden.com, and Pets.com—the Internet is growing at an astounding rate. Networked business-to-business Internet transactions now exceed $10 *trillion* annually. Consumer e-commerce is just as spectacular, also exceeding $10 trillion annually with over $6 trillion spent by consumers on services (online mortgages, music downloads, information subscription sites, etc.).[3]

The Web has also finally become the advertising option that everyone expected it to be. As we talked about in Chapter 2 and Chapter 15, marketers are discovering that they can incorporate Web advertising messages into their IBP programs and are, indeed, channeling money from traditional media over to the Web. Expenditures on Web advertising now exceed $20 billion annually with "paid search" (more on this later) leading the way at about $10 billion followed by rich media/video at about $3 billion.[4]

But for all that the Internet is fundamentally—an information search, e-mail, entertainment medium—it has become so much more in the last few years. Why? One word—wireless. No doubt, you are all occasionally accessing the Web through WiFi on campus or at your favorite coffeeshop. **WiFi** first became widely popular in 2004 because it allowed Internet-access connections that reach out about 300 feet. So everyone from coffee drinkers at Starbucks to emergency workers at disaster sites could have wireless access to information through their laptops. But WiFi was just the beginning. Now, the new wireless revolution makes WiFi look like child's play for all kinds of applications, including the use of the Internet for advertising and promotion. Over the next few years WiFi will likely yield to three innovative technologies that will push wireless networking into every facet of life from cars to homes to offices to the beach. These technologies are:

- **WiMax** (**W**orldwide **I**nteroperability for **M**icrowave **Acc**ess), which like WiFi creates "hot spots" around a central antenna within which people can wirelessly tap into the Net. But while WiFi creates a hot spot of perhaps 300 feet, WiMax has a potential range of 25–30 miles! The new technology, telecom industry scientists say, could be used in place of cable or DSL to deliver the "last mile" (final leg) of wireless broadband to the customer. WiMax won't replace DSL and cable modems in urban areas but is ideally suited to rural areas, as the Globalization Box describes.
- **Mobile-Fi**, similar to WiMax in that it has multimile access but adds the capability of accessing the Net while the user is moving in a car or a train.
- **Ultrabroadband**, a technology that will allow people to move extremely large files quickly over short distances. On the road, a driver could download a large file from an on-board PC to a handheld computer. Or, at home, you could do a wireless upload of your favorite concert from your PC to your TV.

Scientists at Intel, Alcatel-Lucent, and Motorola are working on these technologies primarily as modes of communication for the high-speed transmission of data. But, in their practical application, these technologies will allow advertisers to communicate with audiences as Net surfers access the Internet through WiMax or

3.   Data on e-commerce is available at *http://www.census.gov/eos/www/2005/2005reportfinal.pdf.*
4.   Digital Marketing & Media Fact Pack, *Advertising Age,* April 23, 2007, 6.

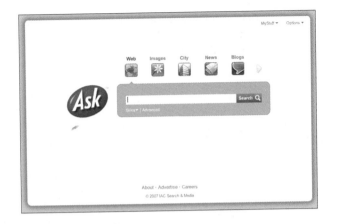

EXHIBIT 16.2

In the next decade, new technologies like WiMax will provide wireless access to the Net that extends up to 30 miles. This will open up more ways for consumers to tap into their favorite information sources, like Ask.com, and more ways for advertisers to reach those surfers.

GLOBALIZATION

To Russia with WiMax

The Russian market is a mystery in many ways when it comes to advertising and promotion. Data on just how much money is spent in what media to send commercial messages is hard to come by. But when it comes to the technology that advertisers want and need to send messages over the Internet, the picture is getting much more clear. Alcatel-Lucent, developers of WiMax technology and hardware, just landed a deal to build a nationwide rural WiMax access network in Russia—the most rural country in the world. There are over 160 cities and towns in Russia with 50,000 to 100,000 people and hundreds more with a population less than 50,000.

Alcatel-Lucent will work with Russian telecom company Synterra, the firm that holds the national license for the 2.5 GHz bands needed for WiMax communications, to build the WiMax infrastructure in towns with populations smaller than 100,000. The project will install "steered beams" that will provide greater range and coverage than any other form of transmission.

The project is enormous, providing Internet access to more than 40 million Russians who do not have DSL or cable modem connection to the Internet. This, in turn, will give advertisers and Internet service providers a vast new market of Russian consumers who, up to this point, had limited or no access to the Web. Which leaves one burning question: Do you think BomChickaWahWah will sell in rural Russia?

Sources: Dan O'Shea, "Study: WiMax, MobileFi No Threat to DSL," *TelephonyOnline*, June 8, 2004, accessed at http://www.telephonyonline.com on July 13, 2007; Kevin Fitchard, "Alcatel-Lucent to Build WiMax in Russia," *TelephonyOnline*, July 6, 2007, accessed at http://www.telephonyonline.com on July 13, 2007.

Mobile-Fi. We are all just now getting accustomed to WiFi and the convenience it provides. These new technologies are going to make it that much easier for consumers using search services like Ask .com to find what they are searching for faster, from wherever they are! (See Exhibit 16.2.)

The Role of the Internet in the Advertising and IBP Process.

As the Internet has developed as a legitimate option for advertisers, many firms like Pepsi (http://www.pepsiworld.com) and BMW (http://www.bmw.com) have been highly successful in folding the Internet into their integrated brand promotion strategies. A trip to these sites shows that these firms funnel a lot of information and promotion through their Web sites. But what about the Internet *overall* as a medium? What can and what will likely be the role of the Internet in a promotional effort? A few "truths" have made themselves evident to this point.

First, the Internet will *not* be replacing all other forms of advertising. Nor is it even likely that the biggest spenders on advertising and promotion (you know those multibillion-dollar types) will use the Internet as the *main* method of communicating with target audiences. But, like Pepsi and BMW, advertisers are discovering ways to use the Internet as a key component of integrated brand promotions. The music company Arista, which represents artists like Pink, Dido, and Sarah McLachlan, uses Internet access like AOL's Music Discovery Network to deliver digital music streams of popular artists. Exposure through the Web has become a primary method of promoting both new artists and new singles.[5]

Second, yes, things are changing dramatically regarding all aspects of the Internet. Auction sites like eBay have provided huge opportunities for small business all over the world. And as we have pointed out throughout the book, Web 2.0 and its social networking emphasis provides a whole new way of delivering promotional messages.

In the current view of the Internet and advertising, we will spend most of our time in this chapter focusing on two fundamental issues: the structure of the Internet

---

5.   Tobi Elkin, "Record Labels Turning to Web to Boost Sales," *Advertising Age,* June 9, 2003, 16.

and the potential of the Internet as an advertising medium. Through these discussions, we will come to a better understanding of how to use the Internet as part of an effective overall advertising and integrated brand promotion effort. First, we will consider a short history of the evolution of the Internet. Then, we'll have an overview of cyberspace and some of the basics of the way the Internet works. Next, we will consider the different types of advertising that can be used and some of the technical aspects of the process. Finally, we will look at the issues involved in establishing a Web site and developing a brand in the "e-community."

The (R)evolution of the Internet.

Technology changes everything—or at least it has the power and potential to change everything. When it's communications technology, such as the Internet, it can change something very fundamental about human existence. The Internet-connected consumer is connected to other consumers in real time, and with connection comes community, empowerment, even liberation.

Is the proliferation of the Internet an evolution in communication or a revolution? While revolutions are more common than they used to be, we have witnessed the Internet go through some growing pains. Still, what can be truly revolutionary about the Internet is its ability to alter the basic nature of communication within a commercial channel. And, despite the recent and ongoing shakeout of Internet sites talked about earlier, if you want an e-evolutionary perspective on the Internet and advertising, consider the short history of communication in this channel.

In 1994, advertisers began working with Prodigy and CompuServe, which were the first Internet service providers (ISPs). These advertisers had the idea that they would send standard television commercials online. Well, the technology was not in place back then for that to work. That technological fact sent the advertisers and the ISPs back to the drawing board. With the emergence of more commercial ISPs such as America Online and EarthLink, the new Web browsers were worth exploring as a way to send commercial messages. The first Web browser was Mosaic, the precursor to Netscape 1.0, and the first ads began appearing in *HotWired* magazine (the online version of *Wired* magazine) in October 1994. The magazine boasted 12 advertisers including MCI, AT&T, Sprint, Volvo, and Club Med, and each one paid $30,000 for a 12-week run of online display/banner ads with no guarantee of the number or profile of the viewers.

Well, things have certainly changed since those early days. Now, the Internet is being accessed worldwide by just over 1 billion users.[6] In historical perspective, advertising spending on the Internet was estimated at about $12 billion in 2005 and is estimated to grow to over $36 billion by 2011.[7] The medium is used by all forms of companies, large, small, bricks and mortar, virtual, e-commerce, not-for-profit, you name it. Further, the medium is home to literally millions of Web sites, and the value of the Internet to individual consumers is growing daily. Let's turn our attention to some of the technical aspects of the Internet and then we'll explore the Internet as a strategic advertising and IBP option for advertisers.

An Overview of Cyberspace.

We refer to the Internet casually because it has become so prominent in the technological landscape. But just what is this thing called the Internet? The **Internet** is a global collection of computer networks linking both public and private computer systems. It was originally designed by the U.S. military to be a decentralized, highly redundant, and thus reliable communications system in the event of a national emergency. Even if some of the military's computers crashed,

---

6.   Global use of the Web statistics obtained from Clickz at *http://www.clickz.com/showPage.html?page=stats/web_worldwide,* accessed on July 13, 2007.

7.   Digital Marketing & Media Fact Pack, *Advertising Age,* April 23, 2007, 6.

the Internet would continue to perform. Today the Internet comprises a combination of computers from government, educational, military, and commercial sources. In the beginning, the number of computers connected to the Internet would roughly double every year, from 2 million in 1994 to 5 million in 1995 to about 10 million in 1996. But beginning in 1998, Internet use accelerated with around 90 million people being connected in the United States and Canada and 155 million people worldwide. Exhibit 16.3 shows that Internet access around the world has continued its accelerated rate of increase with about 1.1 *billion* users estimated worldwide as of 2006—a seven-fold increase in just an 8-year period.[8]

Do not overlook the potential that still remains for Internet communications, however. Note from Exhibit 16.3 that the 1.1 billion Internet users worldwide represent only about 16 percent of the world's population. Further, some large-population countries, such as Russia, China, and India, have only recently begun to provide widespread access to the Internet and represent billions more potential users.

After years of use, much of the vocabulary of the Web is common knowledge or intuitive. But some is still fairly esoteric. The short glossary in Exhibit 16.4 defines some of the terms you may have heard dozens of times, but may not be exactly sure what they really mean.

EXHIBIT 16.3

Estimates of Internet users worldwide as of 2006.

Country	Number Online	Percent of Total Population
Europe		
Austria	4.65 million	58.1%
Belgium	10.39 million	49.0
Czech Republic	4.80 million	46.9
Denmark	3.76 million	68.9
Finland	3.29 million	62.9
Italy	28.87 million	49.6
Lithuania	.96 million	26.9
Netherlands	10.81 million	65.5
Norway	3.41 million	68.1
Spain	17.14 million	42.4
Brazil	190.01 million	13.6
Bulgaria	1.61 million	21.9
Canada	20.90 million	62.5
China	111.00 million	8.4
Iceland	.22 million	75.2
India	50.60 million	4.6
Japan	86.30 million	67.7
Mexico	17.00 million	15.8
Russia	23.70 million	16.5
United Kingdom	37.80 million	62.3
United States	203.44 million	68.2
World Total	**1.1 billion**	**16.6%**

Source: ClickZ Stats, Web Worldwide, data available at http://www.clickz.com, accessed via the Internet on July 13, 2007.

8. Global use of the Web statistics obtained from ClickZ at *http://www.clickz.com/showPage.html?page=stats/web_worldwide,* accessed on July 13, 2007.

Term	Definition
applet	A Java program that can be inserted into an HTML page (see definition for HTML below).
banner ad	An advertisement, typically rectangular, used to catch a consumer's eye on a Web page. Banner ads serve as a gateway to send a consumer to an expanded Web page where more extensive information is provided for a firm or a product. Many include an electronic commerce capability whereby a product or service can be ordered through the banner itself.
bandwidth	The capacity for transmitting information through an Internet connection. Internet connections are available through phone lines, cable, or various wireless options.
baud	A measure of data transmission speed, typically referring to a modem.
button	Small clickable square or circle running down the side of a Web site leading to an ad.
clicks	Number of times users click on a banner ad.
click-through	The process of a Web site visitor clicking on a banner ad and being sent to a marketer's home page for further information. Ad banner click-through rates average about 1 percent.
cookie	A piece of information sent by a Web server to a Web browser that tracks Web page activity. Because they identify users and their browsing habits, cookies are at the center of Web privacy issues.
CPC	*Cost per click*, the price advertisers pay for a banner ad based on the number of clicks the ad registers from Web site visitors.
CPM	*Cost per thousand impressions*, the long-standing measure of advertising rates used in traditional media and now carried over as a standard for the Internet.
domain name	The unique name of a Web site chosen by a marketer. There are twelve designations for domain names after the unique name chosen by the marketer: .com and .net refer to business and commercial sites; .org refers to an institution or nonprofit organization; .gov identifies government Web sites; .edu refers to academic institutions; .aero for the air transport industry; .biz for businesses; .coop for cooperatives; .info, unrestricted by organizational type; .museum for museums; .name for individuals; .pro for accountants, lawyers, and other professionals.
e-mail	Text messages exchanged via computer, Web TV, and various wireless devices such as Palm Pilots and cell phones.
hit	Used to measure the "traffic" at a Web site. Hits are measured by each time a file server sends a file to a browser. Hits may represent multiple requests by the same visitor and do not provide a measure of the number of people who visit a site (see "unique users" below).
HTML	An acronym that stands for *hypertext markup language*, which is used to display and link documents to the Web.
interstitial	Pop-up ads that appear when a Web user clicks on a designated (or not designated) area of a Web page.
intranet	An online network *internal* to a company that can be used by employees. Intranets are even showing up in some households.
link	The clickable connection between two Web sites.
opt-in email	A list of Internet users who sign up for commercial e-mail and give permission to have messages relayed to them via their e-mail addresses.
page views	The number of times a Web site visitor requests a page containing an ad. This measure serves as an indication of the number of times the ad was potentially viewed. Page views is analogous to gross impressions in traditional media.
rich media	Special technology effects used in Internet ads that provide enhanced audio and visual presentation. An example is streaming video.
spam	"Junk" e-mail sent to consumers who haven't requested the information. Not an acronym, the Internet term is said to have derived from a Monty Python skit about a restaurant where everything comes with Spam—the Hormel lunch meat, that is.
sponsorship	Site content paid for by an advertiser.
unique visitors	The number of different individuals who visit a Web site in a specified period of time.
views	Number of times a banner ad is downloaded.

EXHIBIT 16.4

A glossary of basic Internet terminology.

② Internet Media. Internet media for advertising consist of e-mail (including electronic mailing lists), Usenet, and the World Wide Web.

E-Mail. E-mail is frequently used by advertisers to reach potential and existing customers. A variety of companies collect e-mail addresses and profiles that allow advertisers to direct e-mail to a specific group. Widespread, targeted e-mail advertising is facilitated by organizations like Advertising.com (http://www.advertising .com) (See Exhibit 16.5). These organizations target, prepare, and deliver e-mails to highly specific audiences for advertisers.

Advertisers are addressing consumer resistance to e-mail advertising through "opt-in e-mail." **Opt-in e-mail** is commercial e-mail that is sent with the recipient's consent, such as when Web site visitors give their permission to receive commercial e-mail about topics and products that interest them. If you have purchased a product online, it is likely you were asked to check a box acknowledging that you would like to receive future information about the company and its products. Service providers like Opt In Inc. (http://www.optininc.com) help firms like OfficeMax, American Express, and Exxon manage their opt-in e-mail promotions. Other firms like L-Soft (http://www.lsoft.com) offer software for managing electronic mailing lists, providing advertisers with readily available target market access (see Exhibit 16.6).

As we discussed in Chapter 4 as an ethical/social issue, uninvited commercial messages sent to electronic mailing lists, Usenet groups, or some other compilation of e-mail addresses is a notorious practice known as **spam**. Various estimates suggest 120 *billion* spam e-mails are being sent every day worldwide.[9] As we saw in Chap-

EXHIBIT 16.5

Various firms help marketers place highly targeted e-mail messages on the Internet that serve as customized one-on-one advertising. http://www.advertising.com

EXHIBIT 16.6

Similar to e-mail messaging, firms can buy complete lists of e-mail groups from companies like L-Soft to distribute e-mail newsletters opt-in e-mail marketing campaigns.

---

9.   Allison Enright, "Guerrilla-Style Spam Wars," *Marketing News,* November 1, 2006, 13–14.

ter 4, few promotional techniques have drawn as much wrath from consumers and regulators. But before we close the discussion on spam, here is an interesting note: As annoying as spam seems to be to Web users, it appears to be effective. Those mass e-mailings can get a 5 to 7 percent response compared with 1 to 3 percent for offline direct marketing efforts.[10] So before we write off mass e-mails, we had better consider the results, not just the public reaction.

Usenet. **Usenet** is a collection of discussion groups in cyberspace. People can read messages pertaining to a given topic, post new messages, and answer messages. Users read and post e-mail-like messages (called "articles" or "posts") to one or more of a number of categories, called newsgroups. Usenet resembles bulletin board systems (BBS) in most respects. One crucial difference from a BBS is that with Usenet there is no central server or central system owner. Usenet is distributed among a large, constantly changing conglomeration of servers that store and forward messages to one another. These servers are loosely connected in a variable mesh. Individual users usually read from and post messages to a local server operated by their ISP, university, employer, or some other local organization. Then, the servers exchange the messages between one another.

The World Wide Web. Finally, the **World Wide Web (WWW)** is a "web" of information available to most Internet users, and its graphical environment makes navigation simple and exciting. Of all the options available for Internet advertisers, the WWW provides the greatest breadth and depth of opportunity. It allows for detailed and full-color graphics, audio transmission, delivery of customized messages, 24-hour availability, and two-way information exchanges between the marketer and customer. For some people, spending time on the Web is replacing time spent viewing other media, such as print, radio, and television. There is one great difference between the Web and other cyber-advertising vehicles: The consumer actively searches for the marketer's home page. Of course, Web advertisers are attempting to make their pages much easier to find and, in reality, harder to avoid.

To learn how a firm can make highly effective use of all the Internet media, see the Doing It Right box (on the next page) describing how RCA records put together a Web-based strategy to create a buzz around Christina Aguilera's debut album.

Surfing the World Wide Web.
About 70 percent of Americans use the World Wide Web. Of these users, 75 percent use e-mail, 50 percent use the Web to the access the latest news and special interest information sites, 34 percent have made a purchase on line and over 30 percent use the Web to pay bills.[11]

This desire for information, entertainment, and personal services leads to **surfing**—gliding from page to page. Users can seek and find different sites in a variety of ways: through search engines, through direct links with other sites, and by word of mouth.

Surfing is made fast and efficient by various search engine technology. A **search engine** allows an Internet user to surf by typing in a few keywords, and the search engine then finds all sites that contain the keywords. Search engines all have the same basic user interface but differ in how they perform the search and in the amount of the WWW accessed. The big Internet sites like Yahoo! and Google use search

---

10. Tobi Elkin, "Spam: Annoying but Effective," *Advertising Age,* September 22, 2003, 40.
11. Digital Marketing & Media Fact Pack, *Advertising Age,* April 23, 2007, 32.

DOING IT RIGHT

Chatting a Star up the Charts

We all know Christina Aguilera as a superstar. But you may not know that the Web played a huge part in her path to stardom. When executives at RCA records started plotting the advertising strategy for Christina Aguilera's debut album, they knew the Internet would play a crucial role in the introductory campaign. They understood that the teen target audience was skeptical and not receptive to traditional media. Or, in the words of one Internet marketing strategist, "They have their B.S. detectors on 11." With that knowledge, RCA put into motion an Internet-based advertising/word-of-mouth strategy to create an Internet buzz around Aguilera and her new album. The strategy was executed in four stages by Electric Artists, an Internet marketing firm that specializes in music marketing.

Stage 1: To find out what teens already knew about Aguilera and what they were saying, Electric Artists began monitoring popular teen sites such as Alloy (http://www.alloy.com) and gURL (http://www.gurl.com) as well as sites created for other teen stars such as the Backstreet Boys and Britney Spears. The firm compiled some important information about fans' reactions to Aguilera's single "Genie in a Bottle" and also learned that there was a budding rivalry between Aguilera fans and Spears fans.

Stage 2: Electric sent a team of cybersurfers to popular sites to start chatting up Aguilera, her single, her past, and the rumor of her new album. The surfers posted messages on sites or e-mailed individual fans with comments like "Does anyone remember Christina Aguilera—she sang the song from Mulan called 'Reflection'? I heard she has a new song out called 'Genie in a Bottle' and a new album is supposed to be out this summer." Electric strategists point out, "It's kids marketing to each other."

Stage 3: The promotional strategy ascended to a new level as Electric shifted the emphasis of its Internet com-

munication from Aguilera's single to the album itself. One challenge included motivating fans to go from a $1.98 purchase to a $16.00 purchase. Another hurdle was to convince big music retailers such as Amazon.com and CDNow that Aguilera deserved prominent visibility on their Web sites. To complement these strategies, Electric ensured that the album cover and album name were highly memorable to parents who were shopping for their teenagers. This included lots of major magazine and entertainment television media coverage that parents, particularly mothers, would come in contact with.

Stage 4: To retain the momentum gained from the initial Internet effort, Electric continued to strengthen and broaden Aguilera's fan base using a variety of additional Internet strategies. The continually updated Web site offers teen audiences access to concert and TV appearances, chats, fan club information, merchandise, and e-mail. Electric also continues to monitor teen interest in competitors such as Mariah Carey and Whitney Houston to stay connected to the broader teen music scene.

The result of this Internet-based campaign was a number one album for Christina Aguilera and eventually the Best New Artist award at the 2000 Grammy Awards. This story shows that the power of Internet advertising lies in its ability to specifically target and communicate in very specific language to an audience. That is the distinguishing feature of the Internet as an advertising media alternative. The Aguilera story demonstrates that Internet advertising is much more than just display/banner ads. Currently, major record labels still find the Internet, particularly with the ability to use rich media like streaming video, to be a powerful way to promote new artists and new material.

Sources: Erin White, "Chatting a Singer up the Pop Charts," **Wall Street Journal**, December 5, 1999, B1, B4; Christopher John Farley and David E. Thigpen, "Christina Aguilera: Building a 21st Century Star," **Time**, March 6, 2000, 70–71; Tobi Elkin, "Record Labels Turning to Web to Boost Sales," **Advertising Age**, June 9, 2003, 16.

engine technology to optimize the search results that direct surfers to alternative sites of possible interest (see Exhibit 16.7). One feature of surf engines that provide convenience and speed are "bots" that basically do the surfing for a user (see Exhibit 16.8).

Portals and Web Sites. The word "portal" has assumed the position as the most overused, misused, abused, and confused term in Internet vocabulary. A **portal** is a starting point for Web access and search. Portals can be general, like Yahoo!; vertical (serving a specialized market or industries, such as Jobster, http://www.jobster.com, for employment opportunities); horizontal (providing access and links across industries, such as Verticalnet, http://www.verticalnet.com, with access to business trade com-

EXHIBIT 16.7

Big Internet sites like Yahoo! and Google offer Internet users quick and efficient searches thorough search engine technology for their information, entertainment, and service needs. http://www.yahoo.com; http://www.google.com

EXHIBIT 16.8

One way to search the Internet is with "shopbots" or "bots." These automated Internet search engines take directions on what to search for and then deliver it automatically back to the user. http://www.mysimon.com

munities); or community-based (such as Latina Online, http://www.latina.com; see Exhibit 16.9 on the next page). With big portals like Google having 8 billion pages in their search indexes, vertical and horizontal subject-specific search engines are proliferating to make searching a topic a bit easier.[12]

In addition to the portals, the Web is, of course, dominated by individual company or brand Web sites. Formally defined, a **Web site** is a collection of Web pages, images, videos, and other digital content that is hosted on a Web server. Think about your own surfing behavior. You probably start out at a portal and then navigate your way around a series of Web sites. A variation of the standard Web site is the "mash-up." A **mash-up** is the combination of one or more Web sites into a single site. An example is Chicagocrime.org, where local crime statistics are overlaid on GoogleMaps so you can see what crimes have been committed in your neighborhood. Another is Book Burro, which shows the price for a book at several competing online booksellers.[13]

12.   Om Malik, "Growing in the Shadow of Google," *Business 2.0,* December 2006, 40.
13.   Robert D. Hof, "Mix, Match, and Mutate," *BusinessWeek,* July 25, 2005, 72–74

EXHIBIT 16.9

Community portals like Latina Online offer a site that matches surfers' interests for information on a variety of topics from politics to culture to entertainment. What is teen site Alloy (http://www.alloy.com) doing to make sure it wins the community portal war? Are Alloy's search functions and navigational features designed to direct surfers to particular sites?

Personal Web Sites and Blogs. Many people have created their own Web pages that list their favorite sites. This is a fabulous way of finding new and interesting sites—as well as feeding a person's narcissism. For example, the Web site for this book, http://academic.cengage.com/marketing/oguinn, is a resource for information about advertising and IBP including links to a wide range of industry resources.

Although most people find Web pages via Internet resources (over 80 percent of respondents in one survey found Web pages through search engines or other Web pages), sites can also be discovered through traditional word-of-mouth communications. Internet enthusiasts tend to share their experiences on the Web through discussions in coffeehouses, by reading and writing articles, and via other non-Web venues. There are also mega–search engines, like Dogpile (http://www.dogpile.com), which combine several search engines at once.

The newest personal use of the Web is the blog. On a Web site, a **blog**, a short form for Weblog, is a personal journal that is frequently updated and intended for public access. Blogs generally represent the personality of the author or the Web site and its purpose. Topics include brief philosophical musings, favorite hobbies and music, political leanings, commentary on Internet and other social issues, and links to other sites the author favors. The essential characteristics of the blog are its journal form, typically a new entry each day, and its informal style. The author of a blog is often referred to as a **blogger**. People who post new journal entries to their blog may often say they blogged today, they blogged it to their site, or that they still have to blog.

While blogs get a lot of publicity, let's get some perspective. About 57 million people reported using blogs, but only about 12 percent of those blog users visit a blog once a week or more frequently. And 88 percent of all Internet users seldom or never read blogs.[14] But big corporations like Procter & Gamble are finding that some of their brands, like Swiffer (a long plastic stick with a swatch of dust-attracting cloth attached to the end), are featured on customer blogs, and advertisers in general feel this aspect of the Web holds great potential for peer-to-peer communication and the power of persuasion such communication can have on brands.[15]

③ Advertising on the Internet. As we have referenced before, the growth of advertising via the Internet is growing dramatically but sporadically. In 1995, $54.7 million was spent advertising on the Internet, and the year 2000 logged in at just over $8 billion. Then the boom turned to bust and the dot.bomb hit. In 2002, billions went out of the Internet ad market and revenues came in at just over $6 billion (see Exhibit 16.10). By 2003, a recovery was in process and revenues spiked back to $7.25 billion, reached about $16 billion in 2006, and are now estimated to be in the range of $20 billion in 2008.[16]

14.   Digital Marketing & Media Fact Pack, *Advertising Age*, April 23, 2007, 21.

15.   Nancy Einhart, "Clean Sweep of the Market," *Business 2.0*, March 2003, 56.

16.   PricewaterhouseCoopers, "IAB Internet Advertising Report," April 2004, 5; 2003 Marketing Fact Book, *Advertising Age*, July 7, 2003, 21, Digital Marketing & Media Fact Pack, *Advertising Age*, April 23, 2007, 6.

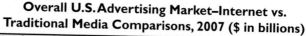

EXHIBIT 16.10

Internet advertising revenues grew dramatically through the year 2000 and then made an abrupt downturn. By 2007, a recovery was firmly taking place with spending reaching $17.1 billion annually. Here is a comparison of advertising spending for the Internet and other major media.

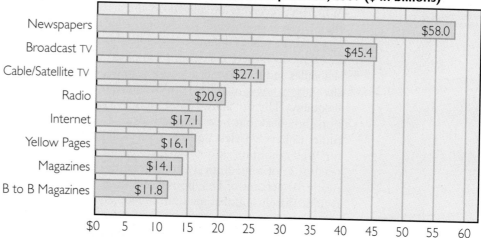

Overall U.S. Advertising Market–Internet vs. Traditional Media Comparisons, 2007 ($ in billions)

Newspapers	$58.0
Broadcast TV	$45.4
Cable/Satellite TV	$27.1
Radio	$20.9
Internet	$17.1
Yellow Pages	$16.1
Magazines	$14.1
B to B Magazines	$11.8

A variety of complex issues are associated with using the Internet for advertising purposes. This section begins by exploring the advantages of Internet advertising. Then we'll look at who is advertising on the Internet, the costs associated with Internet advertising, and the different types of Internet advertising.

The Advantages of Internet Advertising.

Internet advertising has finally emerged as a legitimate advertising option for advertisers—and it is not just because the Web represents a new and different technological option. Several unique characteristics of the Internet offer advantages for advertising over traditional media options.

Target Market Selectivity.

The Web offers advertisers a new and precise way to target market segments. Not only are the segments precisely defined—you can place an ad on the numismatist (coin collecting) society page, for example—but the Internet allows forms of targeting that truly enhance traditional segmentation schemes such as demographics, geographics, and psychographics. Advertisers can focus on specific interest areas, but they can also target based on geographic regions (including global), time of day, computer platform, or browser. As example, Filipacchi Media U.S. shut down its print version of *ElleGirl* and instead created a Web site. The publisher discovered that teen girls were forgoing print media altogether in preference for Web access to information.[17] When American Airlines enlisted the help of TM Advertising to track the Web behavior of the readers of *Wall Street Journal* (http://www.wsj.com) online travel columns and then "follow" those surfers around with American Airlines ads at various other sections, response to the online advertising increased 115 percent.[18]

Tracking.

The Internet allows advertisers to track how users interact with their brands and learn what interests current and potential customers. Display/banner ads and Web sites also provide the opportunity to measure the response to an ad by means of hits, a measure that is unattainable in traditional media. We'll discuss tracking and measurement in more detail a bit later in the chapter.

17.   Jon Fine, "Smells Like Teen Progress," *BusinessWeek,* May 8, 2006, 22.

18.   Kris Oser, "Targeting Web Behavior Pays, America Airlines Study Finds," *Advertising Age,* May 17, 2004, 8.

Deliverability, Flexibility, and Reach. Online advertising and Web site content is delivered 24 hours a day, seven days a week, at the convenience of the receiver. Whenever receivers are logged on and active, advertising is there and ready to greet them. Just as important, a campaign can be tracked on a daily basis and updated, changed, or replaced almost immediately. This is a dramatic difference from traditional media, where changing a campaign might be delayed for weeks, given media schedules and the time needed for production of ads. The Maui Jim sunglasses Web site (http://www.mauijim.com) is a perfect example of this kind of deliverability and flexibility. The site allows consumers to visit the site at any time to dig for information and check out new products. And, as mentioned earlier, as Web delivery continues to have wireless options, there will be even more flexibility and deliverability for Web communications. Finally, behind television and radio, no medium has the reach (use of a medium by audiences) of the Internet. As we saw in Exhibit 16.3, nearly 70 percent of U.S. households have Internet access. In addition, the Internet is immediately a global medium unlike any traditional media option.

Interactivity. A lofty and often unattainable goal for a marketer is to engage a prospective customer with the brand and the firm. This can be done with Internet advertising in a way that just cannot be accomplished in traditional media. A consumer can go to a company Web site or click through from a display/banner ad and take a tour of the brand's features and values. A **click-through** is a measure of the number of page elements (hyperlinks) that have actually been requested (that is, "clicked through" from the display/banner ad to the link). Software is a perfect example of this sort of advantage of the Web. Let's say you are looking for software to do your taxes. You can log on to H&R Block tax consulting (http://www.hrblock.com) and you will find all the software, tax forms, and online information you need to prepare your taxes. Then you can actually file your taxes with both the IRS and your state tax agency! And this sort of interactivity is not reserved for big national companies. Try this as an exercise. Find a signage company in your local area. It is likely that one will have a Web site where you can design your own sign, order it, and ask for it to be delivered. You have complete interaction with the firm and its product without ever leaving your computer.

The click-through is an important component of Web advertising for another very important reason. If advertisers can attract surfers to the company or brand Web site, then there is the opportunity to convert that surfer to a buyer if the site is set up for e-commerce (more on this in Chapter 19, Direct Marketing and Personal Selling). Researchers are discovering that design components of various Internet ad formats can have an important effect on click-through and therefore sales potential.[19]

Integration. Web advertising is the most easily integrated and coordinated with other forms of promotion. In the most basic sense, all traditional media advertising being used by a marketer can carry the Web site URL (uniform resource locator; basically, the Web site's address). Web display/banner ads can highlight themes and images from television or print campaigns. Special events or contests can be featured in display/banner ads and on Web sites. Overall, the integration of Web activities with other components of the marketing mix is one of the easiest integration tasks in the IBP process. This is due to the flexibility and deliverability of Web advertising discussed earlier. A great example of integrating consumer Web behavior with another part of the promotional process, personal selling, is the strategy used by Mazda Corp. It used to be that the salespeople hated the Web because shoppers would come to the showrooms armed with "cost" data on every vehicle, obtained from various Web sites. Rather than battle consumers, Mazda embraced the fact that car shoppers surf the Web and search out pricing information. Now, visitors to Mazda showrooms can access Web data from onsite Internet kiosks. Rather than

19.   Kelli S. Burns and Richard J. Lutz, "The Function of Format," *Journal of Advertising*, vol. 35, no. 1 (Spring 2006), 53–63.

interfering with the personal selling process, one dealership owner claims that the Internet access right at the dealership "helps build trust and close sales faster."[20]

The Cost of Internet Advertising.

It used to be that you could prepare and buy banner ads for a few thousand dollars. But now, with the huge audiences that can now be reached on the Web and new technology that can track the number of people who "visit" a Web site and click on an ad, the cost has skyrocketed. A banner ad on a leading portal like Yahoo! or MSN now costs about $500,000 per day—about the same as a 30-second television spot on *CSI*. Granted, the ad runs all day versus one 30-second insertion, but costs are escalating dramatically.[21]

On a cost-per-thousand (CPM) basis, the cost of Web ads for the most part compares favorably with ads placed in traditional media. Exhibit 16.11 shows the comparison of absolute cost and CPM for ads placed in traditional media and on the Web. The real attraction of the Internet is not found in raw numbers and CPMs, but rather in terms of highly desirable, highly segmentable, and highly motivated audiences (see Exhibit 16.12 on the next page). The Internet is ideally suited for niche marketing—that is, for reaching only those consumers most likely to buy what the marketer is selling. This aspect of the Internet as an advertising option has always been its great attraction: the ability to identify segments and deliver almost-customized (or in the case of e-mail, actually customized) messages directly to them—one by one. With respect to banner ads specifically, most agencies (about 90 percent) price banner ads on a cost per thousand basis (CPM) while a smaller number (about 33 percent) use click-throughs (i.e., the number of times an ad visitor goes to the advertiser's site) as the basis for pricing.[22]

EXHIBIT 16.11

The cost per thousand (CPM) for display/banner ads has been falling steadily over the past several years. However, compared with television or radio broadcasts display/banner ad CPM is still relatively high. Notice, however, that the absolute cost in dollars of placing display/banner ads and other Internet-based communications can be much lower than traditional media.

	Absolute Cost	Cost per Thousand (CPM)
Traditional Media		
Local TV (30-second spot)	$4,000 to $45,000	$12 to $15
National TV (30-second spot)	80,000 to 600,000	10 to 20
Cable TV (30-second spot)	5,000 to 10,000	3 to 8
Radio (30-second spot)	200 to 1,000	1 to 5
Newspaper (top-10 markets)	40,000 to 80,000	80 to 120
Magazines (regional coverage)	40,000 to 100,000	50 to 120
Direct mail (inserts)	10,000 to 20,000	15 to 40
Billboards	5,000 to 25,000	—
Internet Media		
Banner ads	$1,000 to $5,000	$5 to $50
Rich media	1,000 to 10,000	40 to 50
E-mail newsletters	1,000 to 5,000	25 to 200
Sponsorship	Variable based on duration	30 to 75
Pop-up/pop-under	500 to 2,000	2 to 50

Sources: Forrester Research, http://www.forrester.com; Jennifer Rewick, "Choices, Choices," *Wall Street Journal*, April 23, 2001, R12.

20.   Bob Parks, "Let's Remake a Dealership," *Business 2.0*, June 2004, 65–67.
21.   Ibid.
22.   Fuyuan Shen, "Banner Advertisement Pricing, Measurement, and Pretesting Practices: Perspectives from Interactive Agencies," *Journal of Advertising*, vol. 31. no. 3 (Fall 2002), 59–68.

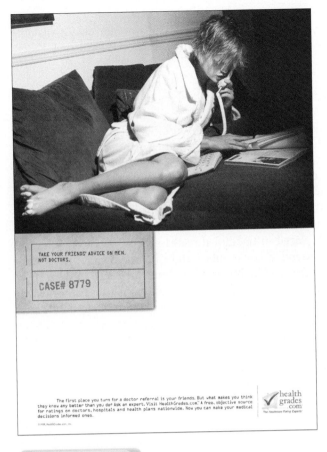

TAKE YOUR FRIENDS' ADVICE ON MEN.
NOT DOCTORS.

CASE# 8779

The first place you turn for a doctor referral is your friends. But what makes you think they know any better than you do? Ask an expert. Visit HealthGrades.com. A free, objective source for ratings on doctors, hospitals and health plans nationwide. Now you can make your medical decisions informed ones.

health grades .com
The Healthcare Rating Experts

EXHIBIT 16.12

One of the key advantages of the Internet is that Web sites can be targeted to the very specific information needs of narrowly defined segments. http://www.healthgrades.com

Types of Internet Advertising. There are several ways for advertisers to place advertising messages on the Web. "Paid search" is now the most prominent, though display/banner ads are more widely known. And many more options exist, including sponsorship, pop-up and pop-under ads, e-mail communication, rich media/video and audio, corporate Web sites, virtual malls, widgets, and virtual worlds and video games. We will consider the features and advantages of each of these types of Internet advertising options.

Paid Search. The biggest news in Internet advertising is "paid search." **Paid search** is the process by which advertisers pay Web sites and portals to place ads in or near relevant search results based on key words. For example, if you Google "running shoes," you will find links to Onlineshoes.com and Zappos.com next to the search results as sources for purchasing running shoes. Paid search has grown astronomically and is expected to reach $6 billion by 2008 and represents about 40 percent of the online ad spending by advertisers.[23] The catalyst for growth in paid search is the success of Google, which pushed the concept from its beginning although all sites can accommodate paid search. Paid-search technology can fine-tune a Web user's search to more relevant and specific Web sites. For example, if an astronomy buff enters the word "saturn" in a search, paid search results would be returned for the planet, not the car company.

Paid search is extremely valued by firms as they try to improve the effectiveness and efficiency of their use of the Internet as a promotional tool. Steve St. Andre, president of Ford Direct, spends 25 percent of his media budget on paid search and says, "Our goal is to drive online transactions. We want keywords to convert into leads and then sales. . . . Search allows you to rethink the entire advertising model and immediately see which keyword buys are successful and which aren't."[24] The top "key words" that lead Internet users to advertiser sites are health and medical, education, food and beverage, and government.[25] Paid search is not particularly cheap—about 58 cents per verified click for second-tier search sites to about $1.61 on Google.[26] But 80 percent of advertisers using paid search report that it increased the traffic to their Web sites.[27]

Another term you should be familiar with related to paid search is **search engine optimization (SEO)**. SEO is a process whereby the volume and quality of traffic to a Web site from search engines is improved based on surfers' profiles. Basically, the higher a site is presented in a surfer's search results, the more likely surfers are to visit that site.

23. Search Marketing Fact Pack 2006, *Advertising Age,* November 6, 2006, 6.
24. Tobi Elkin, "Paid Search's Appeal Escalates," *Advertising Age,* October 13, 2003, 62.
25. Search Marketing Fact Pack 2006, *Advertising Age,* November 6, 2006, 20
26. Ibid., 33.
27. Ibid., 36

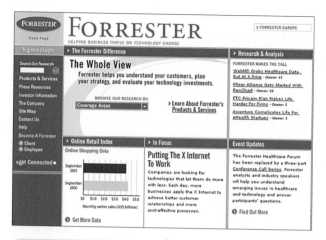

EXHIBIT 16.13

New service and research organizations can track advertising cost and audience delivered for various Web sites. http://www .forrester.com

Display/Banner Ads. **Display/banner ads** are paid placements of advertising on Web sites that contain editorial material. A feature of display/banner ads is that consumers not only see the ad but also can make a quick trip to the marketer's home page by clicking on the ad (this is the "click-through" defined earlier). Thus, the challenge of creating and placing display/banner ads is not only to catch people's attention but also to entice them to visit the marketer's home page and stay for a while. Research indicates that the ability to create curiosity and provide the viewer resolution to that curiosity can have important impact on learning and brand attitude.[28]

A more targeted option is to place these ads on sites that attract specific market niches. For example, a display or banner ad for running shoes would be placed on a site that offers information related to running. This option is emerging as a way for advertisers to focus more closely on their target audiences. Currently, advertisers consider WWW users to be a focused segment of their own. However, as the Web continues to blossom, advertisers will begin to realize that, even across the entire Web, there are sites that draw specific subgroups of Web users. These niche users have particular interests that may represent important opportunities for the right marketer.

A pricing evaluation service for these types of ads is offered by Interactive Traffic. The I-Traffic Index computes a site's advertising value based on traffic, placement and size of ads, ad rates, and evaluations of the site's quality. Firms such as Forrester Research (see Exhibit 16.13) assess the costs of display/banner ads on a variety of sites and provide an estimate to advertisers of the audience delivered.

Sponsorship. **Sponsorship** occurs when a firm pays to maintain a section of a site. In some instances a firm may also provide content for a site along with sponsorship. If you go to Yahoo!'s home page (http://www.yahoo.com) you'll find that the Yahoo! Movies section and Yahoo! Marketplace section are almost always "sponsored by" a major movie studio and a brokerage house respectively. The Weather Channel Web site (http://www.weather.com) is also a site that attracts sponsors. Public service or not-for-profit Web sites often try to recruit local sponsors. In the context of more animated display/banner ads and paid search, it appears that sponsorships are becoming less and less popular. About $500 million is spent annually by advertisers on sponsorship.[29]

Pop-Up/Pop-Under Ads. The only thing surfers hate more than display/banner ads is pop-up Internet ads. The idea is borrowed from TV. A **pop-up ad** is an Internet advertisement that opens in a separate window while a Web page is loading. The more times people click on these ads, the more money can be charged for the privilege of advertising. The future of pop-ups must be considered—a recent study found that nearly 80 percent of surfers said that pop-ups were annoying and about 65 percent felt that display/banner ads were annoying.[30] But, like spam, pop-ups are relatively effective, with 2 percent of Web visitors clicking on the pop-up—that's nearly double the click-through rate for display/banner ads.[31] But many service providers are offering "blockers" that greatly reduce an advertiser's ability to get a pop-up onto a user's screen.

28.   Satya Menon and Dilip Soman, "Managing the Power of Curiosity for Effective Web Advertising Strategies," *Journal of Advertising,* vol. 31. no. 3 (Fall 2002), 1–14.

29.   Ibid., 6

30.   The statistics referenced here were from a Forrester Research survey cited in Digital Marketing & Media Fact Pack, *Advertising Age,* April 23, 2007, 45.

31.   Stephen Baker, "Pop-Up Ads Had Better Start Pleasing," *BusinessWeek,* December 8, 2003, 40.

A subcategory of pop-up ads is the *interstitial,* also called "splash screen." These appear on a site after a page has been requested but before it has loaded, and stay onscreen long enough for the message to be registered. So a surfer who wants to go to a certain site has to wade through an ad page first, just as a television viewer must watch a commercial before seeing a favorite show. It is often not merely a word from a sponsor, but an invitation to link to another related site.

Pop-under ads are ads that are present "under" the Web user's active window and are visible only once the surfer closes that window. It is debatable as to whether pop-ups or pop-unders are the greater nuisance. Regardless, if the click-through rate is not identifiable or if paid search begins to completely dominate online advertising investment (as it appears it may), then the pop-up and pop-under ad may end up being a bit of curious Internet history (please!).

E-Mail Communication. As mentioned earlier, e-mail communication may be the Internet's most advantageous application. Through e-mail, the Internet is the only mass medium capable of customizing a message for thousands or even millions of receivers. The message is delivered in a unique way, one at a time, which no other medium is capable of doing. There are about 170 million e-mail users in the United States alone and advertisers are spending over $1.6 billion annually on newsletters, direct messaging, and e-mail list rental. E-mail from organizations is most effective when Web users have agreed to receive it; this is called opt-in e-mail, as discussed earlier, or **permission marketing**. Some Web firms, such as InetGiant (see Exhibit 16.14), specialize in developing "opt-in" lists of Web users who have agreed to accept commercial e-mails.

The data on permission-based e-mailing versus spamming are compelling. Sixty-six percent of Web users who give their permission to have e-mail sent to them indicate that they are either eager or curious to read the e-mail. This compares with only 15 percent of Web users who receive e-mail through spamming. And e-mail advertisers are turning to some traditional message strategies such as humor to make the e-mail messages more palatable and interesting. BitMagic, an Amsterdam-based Web advertising specialty firm, has Web users download software containing a joke, cartoon, or game along with the e-mail message.[32]

Through e-mail and electronic mailing lists, advertisers can encourage viral marketing. **Viral marketing** is the process of consumers marketing to consumers over the Internet through word of mouth transmitted through e-mails and electronic mailing lists. Hotmail (http://www.hotmail.com) is the king of viral marketing. Every e-mail from every Hotmail subscriber used to conclude with the tagline "Get your private, free e-mail at www.hotmail.com." That viral marketing program helped sign up 12 million subscribers.[33]

EXHIBIT 16.14

E-mail as an advertising alternative can meet with some heavy resistance from Web users. One way to avoid the resistance is to use a permission marketing firm. These firms have lists of consumers who "opt in," or agree to have e-mail sent to them by commercial sources. http://www.inetgiant.com

32.   Kathryn Kranhold, "Internet Advertisers Use Humor in Effort to Entice Web Surfers," *Wall Street Journal,* August 17, 1999, B9.
33.   Steve Jurvetson, "Turning Customers into a Sales Force,: *Business 2.0,* March 2000, 231.

EXHIBIT 16.15

Some corporate Web sites are developed to be purely information sites. The Saturn site provides extensive product information for the full line of Saturn vehicles. http:// www.saturn.com

EXHIBIT 16.16

In contrast to purely information sites, other Web sites are more "lifestyle" sites. The Crayola site (http://www .crayola.com) offers parents, educators, and kids all sorts of interesting, entertaining, and educational options. Compare the Crayola site to the Good Humor–Breyer's Popsicle site (http://www.popsicle.com), and evaluate which one does a better job of focusing on the needs of parents and children.

Rich Media/Video and Audio. Rich media/video and audio is the process in which a Web ad uses advanced technology like streaming video or audio that interacts with the user when the user's mouse passes over the ad. For example, if you go the Yahoo! main page, you may see an ad for a new movie about to be released. As you pass your mouse over the ad, it launches a video clip from the film. Firms such as RealNetworks, NetRadio, and MusicVision insert streaming video into ads for advertisers. The future of such ads will depend on the ability to deliver bandwidth to accommodate the transmission and on consumer access to high-speed Internet connections. The advantage, aside from being more interesting than a display/banner or a pop-up, is that streaming audio and video can realize click-through rates of 3.5 percent—hundreds of times greater than display/banner click-throughs. There is also academic literature that supports the proposition that adding animation to Internet ads increases click-through rates, recall, and favorable attitudes toward Web ads.[34] One firm that experienced great success with streaming video over the Net is Adidas. When Adidas launched an online version of its television ad "Impossible is Nothing," which featured a fantasy bout between Muhammad Ali and his daughter Laila, the two-week Net placement attracted 5 million streams, or viewings. More importantly, the streams drew a large part of its audience from the 12-to-24-year-old consumer that is highly prized by sport-shoe sellers. Similarly, when American Express launched its Superman and Jerry Seinfeld "Webisodes," the firm found much greater receptivity to the four-minute Web video than to its typical 30-second television spot.

Corporate Home Pages. A corporate home page is simply the Web site where a business provides current and potential customers with information about the firm and usually its brands in great detail. The best corporate home pages not only provide corporate and brand information but also offer other content of interest to site visitors. The Saturn site (http://www.saturn.com) in Exhibit 16.15 allows people to find out about the line of Saturn cars, including pricing and specifications. This product-oriented site also allows consumers to build their own car, compare vehicles, communicate their comments and questions to the Saturn Corporation, and find nearby dealers when they are ready to make a purchase. A corporate site that falls toward the lifestyle end of the spectrum is the Crayola site (http://www.crayola.com) in Exhibit 16.16. Rather than focusing on its rather famous product, the company decided to focus on the needs of the parents and children who use Crayola crayons. Visitors can do such things plan parties, look up family travel ideas and, of course, create art with computerized Crayolas.

34. Heather Green and Ben Elgin, "Do E-Ads Have a Future?" *BusinessWeek e.biz,* January 22, 2001, 46–49; S. Shyam Sundar and Sriram Kalyanaraman, "Arousal, Memory, and Impression Formation Effects of Animation Speed in Web Advertising," *Journal of Advertising,* vol. 33, no.1 (Spring 2004), 7–17.

Virtual Malls. A variation on the corporate Web site is a Web site placed inside a virtual mall. A **virtual mall** is a gateway to a group of Internet storefronts that provide access to mall sites by simply clicking on a category of store, as shown on the Mall Internet site (http://www.mall-internet.com). Notice that this site is set up to lead shoppers to product categories. Also notice that when a click is made to a product category, Mall Internet offers "featured store" click-throughs that lead to corporate Web sites and home pages. Having this additional presence gives stores such as the Sharper Image, Shoes.com, and Target more exposure.

Widgets. A very new piece of technology that has potential as an advertising option is a "widget." A **widget** is a module of software that people can drag and drop on to their personal Web page of their social network (e.g., FaceBook) or on to a blog. Widgets look like a Web site window, but carry the power of a full Web site. Advertisers can create widgets that feature their brands or that direct the widget clicker to an e-commerce site. The advertiser will pay a fee each time a user installs the widget. While this is a very new application, Reebok has created a widget where users can create a customized virtual "fighting" sport shoe and place it on their Web page to "fight" other people's sneakers.[35]

Second Life/Virtual Worlds. Another new Internet option available to advertisers is within virtual worlds. The most prominent of the virtual worlds is **Second Life**, an online virtual world where participants log into a space, then use their mouse and keyboard to roam landscapes, chat, create virtual homes, or conduct real business. Participants "exist" in Second Life as avatars—onscreen graphical characters. (See Exhibit 16.17.)

Virtual worlds, like Second Life, offer opportunities for advertisers to insert advertising and IBP messages into virtual world spaces, like this one. It remains to be seen, however, whether virtual world residents will accept commercial messages in their spaces.

35.   Spencer E. Ante, Heather Green, and Catherine Holahan, "The Next Small Thing," *BusinessWeek*, July 23, 2007, 58–62.

While Second Life is primarily a virtual world where Web enthusiasts can create idyllic environments, interact with virtual acquaintances, or play games and accumulate "Linden dollars," the growth of participation in this world has attracted the attention of advertisers for three reasons. First, there are about 2 million active participants in Second Life and that number is growing astronomically.[36] Second, since participants in Second Life can "own" the objects they create, there is real commerce going on within the virtual world. Third, the landscapes and cityscapes created in Second Life offer an ideal environment for advertising and brand visibility in this virtual world. If you visit the Second Life site (http://www.secondlife.com) you will find paid search at the site but also several "merchants" available to outfit your "second life."

Within the virtual world, advertisers can create "billboards" and branded product use (remember the discussion of brand placement), and avatars can wear branded apparel or use branded items. Several automobile firms have already committed to Second Life as a good branding and IBP opportunity. Pontiac, Nissan, and Toyota have all established virtual dealerships and "sell" some of their most popular youth-oriented brands: the Pontiac Solstice GXP, the Toyota Scion, and the Nissan Sentra.[37]

But despite all the intuitive excitement virtual worlds create in advertisers' minds, the ultimate potential of this venue as an advertising/IBP venue is most certainly still in question. One analyst described Second Life as "so popular, no one goes there anymore." And that "Madison Avenue is wasting millions of dollars creating ads for an empty digital world."[38] An evaluation by this analyst of "actual" visitors and then repeat visitors to Second Life numbered only about 100,000 Americans per week available for targeting by U.S. marketers. And on visits to virtual islands owned by American Apparel, Reebok, and Scion, "There was nobody around."[39] So, there is the real prospect that virtual worlds may offer Internet users another social networking venue, but they may not offer advertisers a very good message-communication venue.

Video Games. Video games offer a very attractive option for advertisers because they reach the elusive 18-to-34-year-old-male segment that has abandoned many traditional media for digital media. For example, the hot auto-racing game from Electronic Arts, ***Need for Speed: Carbon***, is full of ads. Advertising spending within video games, primarily through embedded billboards and posters, is expected to reach over $700 million by 2010. A question for advertisers to address, however, is that while the games are full of ads, there is some evidence that players focusing on the game pay almost no attention to the ads embedded in the game.[40]

4 Establishing a Site on the World Wide Web.
While setting up a Web site can be done fairly easily, setting up a commercially viable one is a lot harder and a lot more expensive. The top commercial sites can cost $1 million to develop, about $4.9 million for the initial launch, and about $500,000 to over $1 million a year to maintain.[41] Setting up an attractive site costs so much because of the need for specialized designers to create the site and, most important, to constantly update the site. The basic

36.   Robert D. Hof, "My Virtual Life," *BusinessWeek,* May 1, 2006, 72–80. A visit to Second Life on July 23, 2007, showed 8,310,736 total residents; 1,548,131 logged in within the last 60 days; 33,940 online at the moment; US$1,761,092 spent in the last 24 hours.
37.   Peter Valdes-Dapena, "Real Cars Drive into Second Life," CNNMoney.com, November 18, 2006, accessed at *http://www .cnn.com* on July 22, 2007.
38.   Frank Rose, "Lonely Planet," *Wired,* August 2007, 140–145.
39.   Ibid., 142.
40.   Frank Rose, " Blind Spots," *Wired,* August 2007, 144–145.
41.   Lynn Ward, "Hidden Costs of Building an E-Commerce Site," available at *http://www.ecommercetimes.com,* accessed on April 28, 2003.
42.   Duff McDonald, "A Website as Big (and Cheap) as the Great Outdoors," *Business 2.0,* October 2003, 70–71.

GLOBALIZATION

The Next Net Wave

It's no secret that the instant you establish a Web site, you have become a "global" company. Any computer user from any part of the globe can access your site and navigate through all the features and information opportunities you care to provide. But as much as we know about the Web as a global medium, it is still hard to appreciate the vast potential that is still available for cultivating a global customer base.

When Internet global opportunities are considered, there is no greater opportunity than China. Currently about 100 million Chinese users have piled on to the Net. That makes China second only to the United States as the county with the most Internet subscribers. But it is expected that China will not be number two for very long: Piper Jaffery and Co. estimates that China will soon pass the United States. Since 100 million subscribers represent only 10 percent of the Chinese population, whereas nearly 70 percent of the U.S. population is already online, China has huge opportunity for future growth.

The growth is being fueled by several factors. First, Chinese consumers like the Internet for the same reasons Americans do—there is a lot of information and entertainment available. Second, a strong economy is letting more Chinese households buy PCs for access to the Internet. And third, the Internet offers the opportunity for the average Chinese citizen to skirt the Chinese government's tight censorship rules.

Here's a look at the firms currently serving the Chinese market with specific Internet services:

- Sina is the most popular portal in the country, with 95 million registered visitors. It has links to online gaming and Yahoo! Auctions.
- Soho sends Internet content to its customers' cellular phones in the form of short text messages.
- Netease is a traditional portal earning revenue through online advertising, text messages, and games.
- Shanda is China's first indigenous online gaming company.
- Tom Online is a new portal that is a spin-off of China's largest traditional media group and will focus on cutting-edge wireless services.

Source: Bruce Einhorn, "The Net's Second Superpower," *BusinessWeek*, March 15, 2004, 54–56.

hardware for a site can be a personal computer, and the software to run the site ranges from free to several thousand dollars, depending on the number of extras needed. A site anticipating considerable traffic will need to plan for higher-capacity connections—and hence, a bigger phone bill.

But what if you're not a big Internet firm with several million to spend for the first year of operating of a Web site? Not to fear. There are actually some very inexpensive ways of setting up a site and finding hosts to maintain it if you are a small or medium-size business and want an Internet presence. Companies like 1&1 Internet (http://www.1and1.com) offer a wide range of services to the small business including hosting at extremely low cost. These small-business service firms offer hosting that includes maintenance of domain names, Web site connectivity, e-mail accounts, and some limited e-commerce applications for as little as $9.99 per month. One company that set up an inexpensive site (and still maintains a very simple structure) that is experiencing great success is Backcountry.com (http://www.backcountry.com). The two founders, former ski bums, started with $2,000 in the year 2000 and now run the second-largest online outdoor gear organization, behind REI.[42] So, while there are ways to spend millions to develop and maintain a site, it is not an absolute necessity.

We also need to keep in mind that using the Web as a key component of a brand-building strategy is not reserved just for consumer brands. Business products advertisers—large firms like Caterpillar (http://www.cat.com) or small firms like PrintingForLess.com (http://www.printingforless.com)—are discovering the power of the Web in providing both customer service and brand building (see Exhibit 16.18). Plus, there is no more efficient or speedy way to reach a global market. The Globalization box explains the vast and still emerging potential of the Web for global commerce and brand building.

Getting Surfers to Come Back. Once a site is set up, getting those who spend considerable time on the Internet to spend time at the site and to come back often is a primary concern.

---

43.   Gary L. Geissler, George M. Zinkhan, and Richard T. Watson, "The Influence of Home Page Complexity on Consumer Atten-

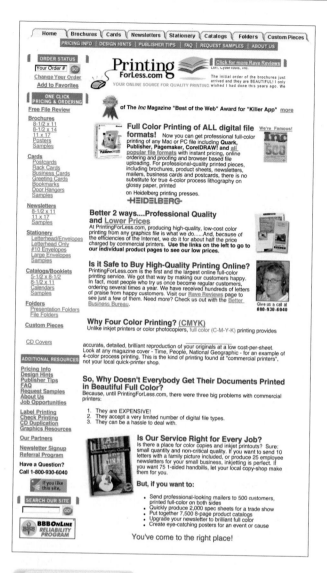

The Web is not just effective in serving household consumers. Business product and service firms of all sorts can use the Web to provide customer service and build brand awareness. From large multinational corporations like Caterpillar (http://www.cat.com) to smaller firms like PrintingForLess.com (http://www.printing forless.com), the Web is highly effective in providing customer contact, customer service, and brand building.

When a site is able to attract visitors over and over again and keep them for a long time, it is said to be a **sticky site** or to have features that are "sticky." A site with pages and pages showing the product and its specifications may have no appeal beyond attracting a single visit. Even a quick tour of various home pages reveals countless, boring corporate Web pages. Often Web sites merely include rich product descriptions that simply mimic printed brochures. Although such Web sites might satisfy the needs of consumers searching for specific product information, they are unlikely to attract and capture the interest of surfers long enough to get them to come back. The whole idea is to satisfy visitors and get them to come back. Research indicates that a home page that is moderately complex with respect to the number of links, graphics, and overall home page length influences consumer attention, attitudes, and purchase intent.[43]

To make a site sticky, a marketer should incorporate engaging, interactive features into the site. For the major hosting sites and portals, recurring information such as the weather, late-breaking news, sports scores, and stock quotes are key to attracting visitors daily or even several times a day. In an effort to break into the world of portals, iWon (http://www.iwon.com) offers all sorts of links to current information—as well as the chance to win $10,000 a day or $1 million each month for using the site—pretty much an all-out assault on trying to get surfers to come back (see Exhibit 16.19 on the next page). For home pages or Web sites, entertaining features such as online games or videos can also get surfers to stay at a site and get them to come back. One site that does a good job of using devices such as these is the U.S. Army. Its Web site, http://www.goarmy .com, has over 1 million people registered to play the Army's Web-based computer games.[44]

There are service firms available to advertisers that provide all the tools and expertise needed to develop a sticky site. One such firm is Ingenux (http://www.ingenux .com), which provides design and features for Web sites to attract visitors and keep them coming back. And as Web design technology has become widely known, many, many firms are available locally to serve firms.

Finally, success in getting repeat visitors depends on substance, ease of use, and entertainment value. Web users are discriminating. While pretty pictures are interesting, sites that have high user loyalty offer something more. This can be brand information and ongoing technical support, or it can be general news about a brand category, original writing, or the latest information about just about anything. That's precisely what King Arthur Flour company did when it made the most mundane of commodi-

tion, Attitudes, and Purchase Intent," *Journal of Advertising*, vol. 35, no. 2 (Summer 2006), 69–80.

44.   Thomas Mucha, "Operation Sign 'Em Up," *Business 2.0*, April 2003, 44.

45.   Vicki Powers, "Flour Power," *Business 2.0*, June 2004, 80–81.

One of the biggest challenges facing Web marketers is making a site "sticky." A sticky site gets consumers to stay a long time and come back often. Notice that at the iWon site, you not only have a chance to win big money on a daily basis and bigger money on a monthly basis, but you also have access to all sorts of options such as checking sports scores, sending greeting cards, or visiting a chat room. http://www.iwon.com

ties, baking flour, the feature of an energized Web site called the Baking Circle (http://www.bakingcircle.com). At this site, members swap recipes, post messages, and upload pictures of baked goods (honest). Is the site popular? Even in our carb-conscious society, the Baking Circle has more than 100,000 online members.[45]

One thing advertisers should know is that the interactivity of a site has important consequences for loyalty to a site and intention to purchase items from a site. Research shows that when consumers engage in more human–message (an interactive message) or human–human interaction (like a chat room), there is a more positive attitude toward the site which, in turn, relates to higher purchase intention.[46]

Developing a Domain Name. A **domain name** is a company's unique identity on the Internet, such as www.yourcompany.com. If you are the Gap (http://www.gap.com) or Sony (http://www.sony.com), your domain name is your corporate name and consumers know how to search for your location. But for thousands of Web startups that provide specialized Web products and services, the domain name issue is a dilemma. You want the name to be descriptive but unique, and intuitive but distinctive. That was the strategy used by Dennis Scheyer, a consultant, when he recommended that GoToTix.com, a ticketing and entertainment site, stick with its original name. The name was intuitive and easy to remember. But the firm insisted on running a consumer contest to rename the company. Scheyer said of the names that made the final cut, "One sounded like a breakfast cereal you wouldn't eat. One sounded like a cough medicine. And one sounded like a prophylactic." In the end, the firm chose Acteva.com (we suspect this is Scheyer's cough medicine entry) because "Act conveys activity. E signifies E-commerce and 'va' has that international flavor." The company has morphed beyond just tickets and now provides online registration and tracking for all sorts of events from fundraisers to corporate meetings (http://www.acteva.com).[47] Companies like VeriSign help companies identify, register, and manage Internet names and keywords in both domestic and global markets (see Exhibit 16.20).

The newest issue in domain names is the issuance of new top-level domains. The **top-level domain (TLD)** is the suffix that follows the Web site name. Until late 2000, there were only five TLDs—.com, .edu, .org, .gov, and .net. The Internet Corporation for Assigned Names and Numbers (ICANN) is a nonprofit formed in 1998 to coordinate technical management of the domain name system. You can visit its Web site at http://www.icann.org and learn about the TLD extensions available and the new country-specific TLDs (e.g., .us and .uk).

The whole idea behind releasing new TLDs, like .tv and .us, is, of course, to relieve the pressure on the original five top-level domains. But there is the prospect of a degree of confusion among consumers as similar or identical prefixes are paired with the new

46.   Hanjun Ko, Chang-Hoan Cho, and Marilyn S. Roberts, "Internet Uses and Gratifications," *Journal of Advertising,* vol. 34, no. 2 (Summer 2005), 57–70.

47.   Laurie Freeman, "Domain-Name Dilemma Worsens," *Advertising Age,* November 8, 1999, 100.

48.   Paul Sloan, "Masters of Their Domain," *Business 2.0,* December 2005, 138–144.

EXHIBIT 16.20

Firms like VeriSign (http://www.verisign.com) are in the business of registering names so surfers have direct access to company Web sites—a process made considerably more complicated by the introduction of TLDs (top-level domains) such as .biz and .name.

suffixes. Domain names are big business as well—so if you have an idea, be sure to register the URL for your company ASAP with a provider like Register.com. The cost can be less than $20 per year, and that price often includes e-mail. The reason to hurry? There are folks out there called "domainers" who register every name they can think of. The URL http://www.cellphones.com was resold for $4.2 million dollars![48] It is estimated that 90,000 domain names are purchased each day and that Internet domain purchasing will be a $10 billion per year industry by 2010.[49]

Promoting Web Sites. Building a Web site is only the first step; the next is promoting it. Throughout the text, you have seen advertising by companies promoting their Web sites. Several agencies, including BBDO, Wieden & Kennedy, and OgilvyOne, specialize in promoting Web sites. The first and most obvious way to promote a Web site is to feature the Web site address in traditional media advertising. Most print ads and may radio and television ads will feature the advertiser's Web address in the message. A quick and low-cost way to promote a Web site is to notify Usenet groups. Another key method is to register the site with search engines such as Yahoo! and Ask.com. With Yahoo!, because it is a hierarchical search engine, it is important to pick keywords that are commonly chosen, yet describe and differentiate that site. Other places to register are with the growing Yellow Pages on the Internet (for example, SuperPages, [http://www.bigyellow.com]) and with appropriate electronic mailing lists. It is also important to send out press releases to Internet news sites. E-mail as a form of direct mail is another method to promote the site.

Security and Privacy Issues. Any Web user can download text, images, and graphics from the World Wide Web. Although advertisers place trademark and copyright disclaimers in their online messages, advertisers on the Web have to be willing to accept the consequence that their trademarks and logos can easily be copied without authorization. Currently, there is no viable policing of this practice by users. So far, advertisers have taken legal action only against users who have taken proprietary materials and blatantly used them in a fashion that is detrimental to the brand or infringes on the exclusivity of the marketer's own site. This may change.

In Chapter 4 we discussed privacy as an ethical and regulatory issue. At this point, we can consider privacy from a strategic-management standpoint. As we saw in Chapter 4, privacy is a very complex and sensitive topic. Discussions at the highest levels focus on the extent to which regulations should be mandated for gathering and disseminating information about Web use. The concern among advertisers is not just the regulatory aspects of the issue. In addition, consumers often express concerns about using the Internet for fear of invasion of privacy—clearly a strategic-management issue.

With respect to consumer privacy, the Coalition for Advertising Supported Information and Entertainment (CASIE) has suggested five goals for advertisers, which we've reproduced in Exhibit 16.21. Striving for these goals will certainly contribute to

49. Adam Goldman, "Domain Names: 21st Century Real Estate," Associated Press, July 22, 2007 accessed at *http://biz.yahoo.com* on July 22, 2007.

50. Ann Harrison, "Privacy? Who Cares," *Business 2.0,* June 12, 2001, 48–49.

EXHIBIT 16.21

CASIE—the Coalition for Advertising Supported Information and Entertainment—has issued a set of privacy goals for advertisers on the Internet.

1. We believe it is important to educate consumers about how they can use interactive technology to save time and customize product and service information to meet their individual needs. By choosing to share pertinent data about themselves, consumers can be provided the product information most relevant to them and can help marketers service them more economically and effectively.

2. We believe any interactive electronic communication from a marketer ought to disclose the marketer's identity.

3. We believe that marketers need to respect privacy in the use of "personal information" about individual consumers collected via interactive technology. "Personal information" is data not otherwise available via public sources. In our view, personal information ought to be used by a marketer to determine how it can effectively respond to a consumer's needs.

4. We believe that if the marketer seeks personal information via interactive electronic communication, it ought to inform the consumer whether the information will be shared with others. We also believe that before a marketer shares such personal information with others, the consumer ought to be offered an option to request that personal information not be shared. Upon receiving such a request, the marketer ought to keep such personal information confidential and not share it.

5. We believe consumers ought to have the ability to obtain a summary of what personal information about them is on record with a marketer that has solicited them via interactive electronic communication. In addition, a consumer ought to be offered the opportunity to correct personal information, request that such information be removed from the marketer's database (unless the marketer needs to retain it for generally accepted and customary accounting and business purposes), or request that the marketer no longer solicit the customer.

Source: Coalition for Advertising Supported Information and Entertainment, http://www.casie.com/guide1/priv.html, accessed June 6, 2004.

the loyalty and confidence that consumers possess for a brand. Privacy is a legitimate concern for Internet users, and will likely continue to be one for civil libertarians and regulators as well. But it is not clear that consumers themselves (as opposed to critics or watchdog groups) really do care much about privacy. A survey of consumers found that only 6 percent of U.S. consumers always read a site's privacy policy and only another 15 percent "sometimes" read the policy.[50] Some very interesting research has discovered that for people from countries with "weak rule of law," privacy/security issues affect the perceived value of a Web site, whereas for people from countries that are high on national identity, privacy/security is less important than the cultural congruity between the site and themselves.[51]

But let's remember that technology is changing rapidly and a whole new level of concern and controversy may be finding its way into the privacy discussions. More and more consumers are accessing the Internet through WiFi and in the near future many will do so through WiMax, methods that are often subject to easy monitoring. In addition, in-home or in-firm wireless systems are easy to hack without the proper security hardware that creates restrictions. It's as easy as sitting in a car with a laptop with an antenna. That's how thieves allegedly snatched credit-card numbers of customers shopping at a Lowe's home improvement store. To protect WiFi systems, firms need to install encryption software known as WiFi Protected Access or develop a "virtual private network" that creates a secure pathway by requiring passwords for access.[52]

51.　Jan-Benedict E.M. Steenkamp and Inge Geyskens, "How Country Characteristics Affect the Perceived Value of Web Sites," *Journal of Marketing,* vol. 70, no. 3 (July 2006), 136–150.

52.　Roger O. Crockett, "For Now, Wi-Fi Is a Hacker's Delight," *BusinessWeek,* January 19, 2004, 79.

53.　Definitions in this section adapted from Brian Getting, "Web Analytics: Understanding Visitor Behavior," *Practical eCommerce,*

Measuring the Effectiveness of Internet Advertising.

The information a Web site typically gets when a user connects with a site is the IP address of the computer that is requesting the page, what page is requested, and the time of the request. This is the minimum amount of information available to a Web site. If a site is an opt-in site and requires registration, then additional information (for example, e-mail address, zip code, gender, age, or household income) is typically requested directly from the user. Attempts at registration (and easy audience assessment) have been largely rejected by consumers because of the privacy concern, but plenty of service providers, such Nielsen//NetRatings (http://www.nielsen-netratings.com), are available to guide marketers through Web measurement options (see Exhibit 16.22).

Several terms are used in Web audience measurement. We will consider the most meaningful of these measurement factors. **Hits** represent the number of elements requested from a given page and consequently provide almost no indication of actual Web traffic. For instance, when a user requests a page with four graphical images, it counts as five hits. Thus by inflating the number of images, a site can quickly pull up its hit count. Consider what might happen at the *Seventeen* magazine site (http://www.seventeen.com). The *Seventeen* site may get three million hits a day, placing it among the top Web sites. However, this total of three million hits translates into perhaps only 80,000 people daily. Thus, hits do not translate into the number of people visiting a site. But another measure of site effectiveness is the extent to which a site will motivate visitors to click through and request information from an ad, as we have discussed before. Most analysts feel that the click-through number (and percentage) is the best measure of the effectiveness of Web advertising. If an ad is good enough to motivate a visitor to click on it and follow the link to more information, then that is verification that the ad was viewed and was motivating (more on this later).

Page views are defined as the pages (actually the number of HTML files) sent to the requesting user's computer. However, if a downloaded page occupies several screens, there is no indication that the user examined the entire page. Also, the page-view count doesn't tell you how many visitors the page actually has: 100,000 page views in a week could be 10 people reading 10,000 pages, or 100,000 people reading one page, or any variation in between.

Visits are the number of occasions in which a user X interacted with site Y after time Z has elapsed. Usually Z is set to some standard time such as 30 minutes. If the user interacts with a site and then interacts again more than 30 minutes later, the second interaction would be counted as a new visit.

Unique visitors are the number of different "people" visiting a site (a new user is determined from the user's registration with the site) during a specified period of time. Besides the address, page, and time, a Web site can find out the referring link address. This allows a Web site to discover what links are directing people to the site. This can be extremely helpful in Internet advertising planning. The problem is that what is really counted are unique IP numbers. Many Internet service providers use a dynamic IP number, which changes every time a given user logs in through the service, so you might show up as 30 different unique visitors to a site you visited daily for a month.

Web analytic software is measurement software that not only provides information on hits, pages, visits, and users, but also lets a site track audience traffic within the site. A site could determine which pages are popular and expand on them. It is also possible

EXHIBIT 16.22

Because of the technology of the Web, tracking the behavior of Web site visitors is relatively easy. Firms like Nielsen//NetRatings help marketers measure the behavior of Web visitors. http://www.nielsen-netratings.com

to track the behavior of people as they go through the site, thus providing inferential information on what people find appealing and unappealing. An example of this software is MaxInfo's WebC, which allows marketers to track what information is viewed, when it is viewed, how often it is viewed, and where users go within a site. An advertiser can then modify the content and structure accordingly. It can also help marketers understand how buyers make purchase decisions in general. But although it is possible to know a lot about users' behavior at sites, it still isn't possible to know what people actually do with Web site information (see the discussion that follows).[53]

Plenty of companies offer measurement services for interactive media. Yet there is really no industry standard for measuring the effectiveness of one interactive ad placement over another. There also is no standard for comparing Internet with traditional media placements. Moreover, demographic information on who is using the WWW is severely limited to consumers who have signed up for opt-in programs and, for example, allow targeted e-mails to be sent to them. Until these limitations are overcome, many marketers will remain hesitant about spending substantial dollars for advertising on the World Wide Web. Here is a list of just come of the companies providing measurement and evaluation services:

- *Arbitron* (http://www.arbitron.com). One of the oldest advertising measurement firms and better know for its traditional media (especially radio and television) measures, Arbitron also specializes in providing data on Internet radio broadcasts.
- *Audit Bureau of Circulations* (http://www.accessabc.com). The Audit Bureau has been for many years the main print circulation auditing organization. Recently, the firm has established ABC Interactive (ABCi), which offers independent measurement of online activity to ensure that Web site traffic and ad delivery metrics are accurately reported.
- *ClickTracks* (http://www.clicktracks.com) is a Web analytics program that makes it easy for marketers to compile Web site navigation patterns by users and ROI stats for Web advertising.
- *eMarketer* (http://www.emarketer.com). One of the newer entrants in the advertising measurement area, eMarketer accumulates data from various research sources and provides summary statistics.
- *Jupiter Research* (http://www.jupiterresearch.com). This firm provides a wide range of data analysis, research, and advice for firms using the Internet for both promotion and e-commerce.
- *Nielsen//NetRatings* (http://www.nielsen-netratings.com). Probably the highest-profile of the data providers, Nielsen has ruled the ratings game for many years. Nielsen relies on its traditional method of finding consumers who are willing to have their media behavior (in this case Internet use) monitored by a device attached to the consumers' computers.
- *Ranking.com* (http://www.ranking.com). Performs market research on a statistically, geographically, and demographically significant number of Internet surfers. By recording these surfers' Web site visits, the company calculates the ranking for the top 1 million (and growing every month) most visited Web sites. This is one of the very few free Web-data-research sites.
- *Simmons Market Research Bureau–SMRB* (http://www.smrb.com). Simmons measures the media and purchase behaviors of consumers and offers data on more than 8,000 brands across over 460 product categories then creates 600 lifestyle profiles linked to every media genre. Included in these analyses is information on Web use and product purchase.

Internet Measurement. No medium is able to provide detail on audiences like the Internet. With Internet tracking services, an advertiser used to just be able to know how many people see an ad and how many respond to it with a click. But new technologies now allow track-

January 2006, 8.
54.   Stephen Baker, "Wiser About the Web," *BusinessWeek*, March 27, 2006, 55.

ETHICS

Click Fraud—A Nasty Business

Martin Fleischmann built his business with online advertising. Most-Choice offers consumers rate quotes and information on insurance and mortgages. Fleischmann paid Yahoo! and Google a total of $2 million in advertising fees based on clicks (or click-throughs) from the sites to his MostChoice Web page.

But after a while, he noticed a growing number of clicks coming from places like Botswana, Mongolia, and Syria. This was odd since his customers primarily were U.S.-based and seeking information on car insurance and mortgage rates in U.S. cities. Fleischmann found some specialized software to track the click patterns and found that his ads were being clicked not on the pages of Google or Yahoo but on curious sites with names like insurance1472.com and insurance060.com. In the end, he calculated that he had paid more than $100,000 for bogus clicks over a three-year period.

MostChoice.com was the victim of "click fraud." Fleischmann paid for clicks on his ads that were made by people or computer programs that imitate legitimate Web users, thereby generating a charge per click without having actual interest in the ad's link. Scammers that perpetrate click fraud can use a "clickbot," a program that can be used to produce automatic clicks on ads. These are sophisticated programs that can hide the origin and timing of clicks to mimic the behavior of real Web surfers. So, Fleichmann had to pay for the clicks generated by the computer program when no "real" prospects were visiting his sites.

Click fraud is a big and growing problem. About half of all Internet advertising spending is tied to deals requiring advertisers to pay by the click. Experts estimate that 10 to 15 percent of all ad clicks are fake, meaning that click fraud costs about $1 billion a year. And it is pervasive. Forty-two percent of Internet advertisers report that they have been a victim of click fraud, although 78 percent of them have received credit for fake clicks from their paid search provider. Not all of the click fraud is promulgated by off-shore, shadowy crooks. Of the advertisers reporting being victimized, over half report that the click fraud was initiated by competitors in an attempt to deplete advertising dollars.

An important question is what is being done about the problem. Yahoo! has named a senior executive to lead the company's effort to combat click fraud in its advertising business. The Internet media company also discards as invalid or inferior quality about 12 to 15 percent of clicks on advertisements; in the case of invalid clicks, it will not charge the advertiser. In a similar move, Google said its computers automatically reject up to 10 percent of potential advertising billings resulting from invalid clicks.

Use of a computer to commit this type of Internet fraud is a felony in many jurisdictions. It is covered by Penal Code 502 in California and the Computer Misuse Act 1990 in the United Kingdom. The Internet industry is doing what it can in a "self regulation" way, but it may take harsh legal action, as in the case of spammers going to jail, to effectively deal with the issue.

Sources: Brian Grow and Ben Elgin, "Click Fraud," **BusinessWeek**, October 2, 2006, 46–57: Search Marketing Fact Pack, Advertising Age, November 6, 2006, 46: "Yahoo Taps Click Fraud Watchdog," Reuters News Service, March 22, 2007 accessed at http://www.cnnmoney.com on March 22, 2007.

ing of mouse movement on Web pages and grouping of shoppers by age, zip code, and reading habits. DoubleClick, which places 200 billion ads a month for customers, can now provide 50 different types of metrics for an Internet campaign. With mouse tracking, advertisers can know which parts of a banner ad appear to be of interest to visitors and how long they spend on different parts of an ad. With new control monitors, referred to as "dashboards," advertising strategists can check the performance of their online ads in real time. There is so much data available that agencies are hiring teams of analytic people, including Ph.D.s in statistics, to make sense of the data. And if you had any doubt that the Web was high tech, one agency, Tacoda Systems, is going to wire a group of Web surfers with brain scanners to see which ads register in their minds.[54] Any volunteers? And academics are deep into the evaluation process, researching such things as the effect of animation speed on attention, memory, and impression formation.[55]

One issue you need to be aware of is **click fraud**—clicking on Internet advertising solely to generate illegitimate revenue for the Web site carrying the ad. Those doing the clicking typically also get paid.[56] Click fraud is a crime and occurs when an advertiser has a pay-per-click agreement with a Web site. Click fraud takes place when a person is paid to visit Web sites, or when a computer program roams the Web and imitates a legitimate Web user by "clicking" on ads. Click fraud thus generates a charge per click without there having been actual interest in the ad's link. There have been arrests related to click fraud with regard to malicious clicking in order to deplete a competitor's advertising budget. And this is no small problem. Forty percent of Web advertisers claim they have been victims of click fraud. Google and Yahoo!, prime targets for click scammers, are working to stop click fraud by monitoring Web traffic for repeated clicks or unusual visit patterns from anonymous servers.[57] See the Ethics box for more on this issue.

55. Sundar and Kalyanaraman, "Arousal, Memory, and Impression Formation Effects of Animation Speed in Web Advertising."
56. Brian Grow and Ben Elgin, "Click Fraud," *BusinessWeek,* October 2, 2006, 46–57.
57. Burt Helm, "How Do You Clock the Clicks?" *BusinessWeek,* March 13, 2006, 44.
58. Digital Marketing & Media Fact Pack, *Advertising Age,* April 23, 2007, 46.

Managing the Brand in an E-Community. A final strategic issue to be considered is the concept of creating a brand community, or e-community, for a brand by using the Internet. The Internet, in addition to providing a new means for advertisers to communicate to consumers, also provides consumers a new and efficient way to communicate with one another. In fact, the social aspect of the Internet is one of the most important reasons for its success. Via Usenet newsgroups, e-mail, blogs, and social networking Web pages, consumers have a way to interact and form communities.

Sometimes communities are formed online among users of a particular brand. These online brand communities behave much like a community in the traditional sense, such as a small town or ethnic neighborhood. They have their own cultures, rituals, and traditions. Members create detailed Web pages devoted to the brand. Members even feel a sense of duty or moral responsibility to other members of the community. For example, among many Volkswagen drivers, it is a common courtesy to pull over to help another VW broken down on the side of the road. Harley-Davidson riders feel a similar sense of affinity and desire to help others who use the same brand when they are in trouble.

We have referenced social networking sites extensively throughout the chapter, but the affinity to these sites cannot be underestimated—or ignored. Sites like MySpace and Facebook attract 20 to 50 million unique visitors per month![58] It seems clear that the credibility of these sites is appealing to consumers who are weary of the blatant promotional intent of both traditional media and commerce-oriented Web sites.

Since the Internet makes it easier for members of these communities to interact, brand communities are likely to continue to proliferate in coming years. Consequently, dealing effectively with these communities will be one of the challenges facing advertisers. Several sites, such as Collabrio Technologies' MyEvents (http://www.myevents .com), have emerged to facilitate the community interaction process by providing shared access to the site that promotes communication between members. (See Exhibit 16.23.) Harley-Davidson is a company whose site tries to accomplish e-community interaction. Notice at the Harley Web site (http://www.harley-davidson.com) that the events around the country are a highlight for riders. Another technique is to create a community around the brand in a portal-like manner—that is, drawing consumers to a brand site with content and features that include lifestyle and entertainment information much like what the big portals provide. One firm that has always tried to develop community within its Web site is teen apparel seller Candie's. Visit http://www.candies.com to see how the Candie's site is as community-oriented as it is sales-oriented.

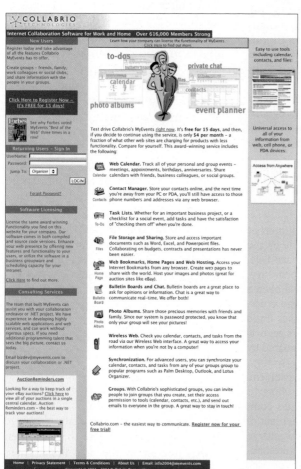

EXHIBIT 16.23

Building an e-community with great loyalty to a site is a tall task. Today's typical computer users have islands of disparate information located everywhere, from on their computer and home bulletin board to in their electronic organizer. Collabrio Technologies provides these users with a free, central place to manage and organize their lives and to share information with any group of people—their friends or family, their investment or book club, or even their co-workers.

59.   Robert D. Hof and Catherine Holahan, *BusinessWeek,* May 21, 2007, 46.

⑤ The Future of Advertising and IBP and the Internet.

When it comes to the Internet, talking about the future is usually futile. The future seems to come with every new issue of *BusinessWeek, Fortune, Wired,* or *Business 2.0.* But the future of the Internet and advertising and IBP seems unavoidably linked to two influences: technology and strategic IBP.

From a technological standpoint, two technologies—wireless communication and Web-launched video—will have the biggest impact. (See Exhibit 16.24.) Early on, the AOL/Time Warner merger in 2001 signaled the future direction for the Web and Web advertising. Time Warner brought to this merger all of its movie studio properties as well as an emerging Internet movie business and digital delivery of Warner Bros. movies on demand. What AOL brought to the merger, of course, was AOL's online services, including Netscape, CompuServe, MovieFone, and Instant Messenger. Then interactive media giant IAC/InterActiveCorp put together a conglomerate of Internet companies that can promote and sell each other's products. The Web sellers now included in InterActiveCorp (http://www.iac.com) are IAC Travel, which includes Expedia, Hotels.com, Hotwire, Interval International, and TV Travel Shop; HSN; Ticketmaster, which oversees ReserveAmerica; Match .com; and LendingTree. Finally, a wave of acquisitions are occurring that are aimed at amassing better online data to help track consumer interests and intentions, thereby letting Web sites target audiences with more relevant ads—which they can charge more for. Google spent $3.1 billion to buy DoubleClick and Yahoo paid $680 million to assume complete ownership of RightMedia Inc.[59]

EXHIBIT 16.24

Whatever direction the dynamic nature of Web advertising and IBP takes, it will no doubt be influenced by wireless technology and high speed (broadband) access. As more consumers access the Web through their laptops or cell phones, advertisers have more and more ways of sending messages and communicating about their brands.

Mergers and partnerships of broadcast and Internet firms are one side of the story. On the other side, advertisers and advertising agencies are preparing for new opportunities with "broadcast Web." Spending on mobile phone advertising alone is approaching $3 billion per year, and podcast ad spending is nearly at $250 million per year.[60] Does this mean that in the near future every television ad is really a Web ad? Well, maybe it won't be that extreme, but the technology is available to provide direct links to Web sites for information and purchasing through television ads—a huge opportunity and potential for advertisers. And as more Web users have access to broadband—as more than 60 percent of users in the United States now do—more complex data can be streamed to them.[61] The possibilities are attracting all the big players—Microsoft, ABC, CBS, and Warner Brothers Online, to name just a few. They all see video streaming as another piece of this Web broadcast puzzle.[62]

Of course, this next step in the evolution of the Internet and its potential as an advertising alternative depends on the consumer's willingness to allow mobile wireless communication to occur. At this stage, consumers are showing resistance. Only 10 percent of mobile phone users surveyed indicated they were very willing to receive advertising and promotional messages over their cell phone, while 51 percent said they were "not willing at all."[63]

60. Digital Marketing & Media Fact Pack, *Advertising Age,* April 23, 2007, 43, 50.

61. Ibid., 30.

62. John Kuczala, "Online Video Ads Get Ready to Grab You," *Business 2.0,* May 2005, 25.

63. Ibid, 42.

64. Parks, "Let's Remake a Dealership."

With respect to the strategic use of the Internet, we are seeing some very clever and effective integrated brand promotions that rely on the Web, but are not dominated by it. For example, when Mazda wanted to reposition its brand and appeal more broadly to a younger market, understanding the Web behavior of 24-to-36-year-old males was critical. But it wasn't just the knowledge that this target segment was Web savvy when it came to buying cars. The dealership itself and the salespeople had to be changed as well. Mazda's strategy—drive traffic to the dealership through the Web, redesign the dealerships' physical appearance (coffeeshops and hip waiting rooms), make sure the salespeople are as Web-savvy as the shopper. The resulting of combining the promotional tools of the Web and salespeople has been impressive—sales at Web-savvy Mazda dealerships are up 32 percent and profits are up 50 percent.[64] Chrysler discovered the same thing when it developed a e-newsletter for customers.[65]

A less elaborate but equally effective IBP that features the Web is using television advertising to drive traffic to the Web site. Mitsubishi had enormous success with its "seewhathappensnext.com" campaign. The firm ran action-packed television ads that ended just before the climax of the scene. As the scene came to a stop, the television screen went black except for the words "seewhathappensnext.com." When TV viewers arrive at the Web site, they can watch the conclusion of the scene in streaming video. Mitsubishi debuted the campaign during the Super Bowl, and the Web site drew 11 million hits in six hours.[66]

Finally, we cannot underestimate the potential of Second Life and "widgets" as new technological venues for Web advertising and IBP campaigns. These new options offer wide-ranging possibilities that advertisers are just now starting to understand and employ.

It seems likely that as advertisers try to "engage" consumers in brand messages that the Internet will play an increasing role in IBP campaigns. Will Internet advertising and promotion become the "lead" tool in most IBP campaigns? Not likely. But expect that as technology advances and consumers become accustomed to accessing information in nontraditional ways, the Internet will be an increasingly valued tool in the IBP kit.

65. Michael Fielding, "Dealer Options," *Marketing News,* July 15, 2006, 11.
66. Jean Halliday, "Bowl Ads Spark Web Upticks," *Advertising Age,* February 9, 2004, 48.

SUMMARY

1 Understand the role of the Internet in advertising and IBP.

First, it is unlikely that the Internet will replace all other forms of advertising and promotion through IBP. It is even unlikely that the biggest spenders on advertising and promotion will use the Internet as the *main* method of communicating with target audiences.

Second, technologies and opportunities are changing dramatically regarding all aspects of the Internet. Auction sites like eBay have provided huge opportunities for small business all over the world. Web 2.0 and its social networking emphasis provide a whole new way of delivering promotional messages. New venues like Second Life offer communication opportunities very different from existing message delivery.

Third, the structure of the Internet and the potential of the Internet as an advertising medium offer ways for advertisers to both create and deliver messages that are significantly different from traditional mass media.

2 Identify the nature of the Internet as a medium available for communicating advertising and promotion messages.

The Web has several advantages as a medium for communicating advertising and IBP messages: target market selectivity, tracking, deliverability, flexibility, reach, and integration.

Target Market Selectivity. The Web offers advertisers a way to target market segments very precisely. This precision allows targeting that is more finely tuned than traditional segmentation schemes such as demographics, geographics, and psychographics. Advertisers can focus on specific interest areas of Internet users and can also target users based on geographic regions (including global), time of day, computer platform, or browser.

Tracking. The Internet allows advertisers to track how users interact with their brands and learn what interests current and potential customers.

Deliverability, Flexibility, and Reach. Online advertising and Web site content is delivered 24 hours a day, seven days a week, at the convenience of the receiver. Whenever receivers are logged on and active, advertising is there and ready to greet them. A campaign can be tracked on a daily basis and updated, changed, or replaced almost immediately. In addition, the Internet is immediately a global medium unlike any traditional media option.

Interactivity. A marketer is able to engage a prospective customer with the brand and the firm with Internet advertising in a way that just cannot be accomplished in traditional media. A consumer can go to a company Web site or click through from a display/banner ad and take a tour of the brand's features and values.

Integration. Web advertising is the most easily integrated and coordinated with other forms of promotion. In the most basic sense, all traditional media advertising being used by a marketer can carry the Web site URL. Web display/banner ads can highlight themes and images from television or print campaigns. Special events or contests can be featured in display/banner ads and on Web sites. Overall, the integration of Web activities with other components of the marketing mix is one of the easiest integration tasks in the IBP process.

3 Describe the different advertising options on the Web.

Paid search is the process by which advertisers pay Web sites and portals to place ads in or near relevant search results based on key words.

Display/banner ads are paid placements of advertising on other sites that contain editorial material. These ads allow advertisers to have their brands associated with popular Web sites.

Sponsorship occurs when a firm pays to maintain a section of a site. In some instances a firm may also provide content for a site along with sponsorship.

A *pop-up/pop-under ad* is an Internet advertisement that appears as a Web site page is loading or after a page has loaded.

Through *e-mail,* the Internet is the only mass medium capable of customizing a message for thousands or even millions of receivers delivered directly to each receiver.

Rich media/video and audio is the process of inserting TV- and radio-like ads into music and video clips that advertisers send to Web users as they visit content networks.

A *corporate home page* is a Web site where a marketer provides current and potential customers with information about the firm in great detail.

A *virtual mall* is a gateway to a group of Internet storefronts that provides access to mall sites by simply clicking on a category of store. Advertisers can take up residence in a virtual mall and provide target markets with access to brand information and purchase.

A *widget* is a module of software that people can drag and drop on to their personal Web page of their social network (e.g., FaceBook) or on to a blog. Advertisers can create widgets that feature their brands or that direct the widget clicker to an e-commerce site.

Second Life is an online virtual world where participants log into a space, then use their mouse and keyboard to roam landscapes, chat, create virtual homes, or conduct real business. Participants "exist" in Second Life as avatars—on screen graphic characters. Advertisers can create "billboards" within the virtual world and avatars can wear branded apparel or use branded items.

SUMMARY (CONTINUED)

 Discuss the issues involved in establishing a site on the World Wide Web.

There are three key issues to successfully establishing and maintaining a site on the World Wide Web: getting surfers to come back by creating a "sticky" site; purchasing keywords and developing a domain name; and promoting the Web site.

 Discuss the future of advertising and IBP on the Web.

The future of advertising and IBP on the Web will be guided by the emergence of more wireless delivery systems, the merger of big powerful media companies—particularly those media companies that own both traditional media and digital media properties—and the availability of new and different advertising and IBP venues like Second Life where brands can exist in a new, less commercial-like context.

KEY TERMS

WiFi
WiMax
Mobile-Fi
Ultrabroadband
Internet
opt-in e-mail
spam
Usenet
World Wide Web (WWW)
surfing
search engine
portal
Web site

mash-up
blog
blogger
click-through
paid search
search engine optimization (SEO)
display/banner ads
sponsorship
pop-up/pop-under ad
permission marketing
viral marketing
rich media/video and audio
corporate home page

virtual mall
widget
Second Life
sticky site
domain name
top-level domain (TLD)
hits
page views
visits
unique visitors
Web analytic software
click fraud

QUESTIONS

1. Despite its ups and downs over the past decade, the Internet is experiencing a strong recovery. Why is there reason to believe that the current Internet boom could be permanent?

2. What may have driven advertisers to embrace the Internet early on in its development despite considerable uncertainty about audience size, audience composition, and cost-effectiveness?

3. How effective do you think mobile advertising and IBP will be through delivery systems like the iPod and cell phone?

4. What unique characteristics of Internet advertising offer advantages over traditional forms?

5. Explain the two basic strategies for developing corporate home pages, exemplified in this chapter by Saturn and Crayola.

6. Niche marketing will certainly be facilitated by the WWW. What is it about the WWW that makes it such a powerful tool for niche marketing?

7. Visit some of the corporate home pages and Web sites described in this chapter, or think about Web sites you have visited previously. Of those you have encountered, which would you single out as being most effective in giving the visitor a reason to come back? What conclusions would you draw regarding the best ways to motivate repeat visits to a Web site?

8. The Internet was obviously not conceived or designed to be an advertising medium. Thus, some of its characteristics have proven perplexing to advertisers. If advertising professionals had the chance to redesign the Internet, what single change would you expect they would want to make to enhance its value from an advertising perspective?

9. What are blogs, and what are some of their personal and commercial uses?

10. Do you feel that Web users will accept or reject the presence of advertising and IBP in virtual worlds?

EXPERIENTIAL EXERCISES

1.   Part of what makes digital media such a powerful tool for marketers is the ability to customize content and messages for individuals or specific groups of consumers. That allows marketers to interact with large online communities, such as devoted Saab owners at http://www .saabnet.com or the Harley Owners Group at the motorcycle company's corporate site, http://www .harley-davidson.com.

   Pick one of your favorite hobbies, pastimes, or areas of interest—music, sports, literature, investing—you decide. Visit three or four prominent Web sites featuring your interest area. What similarities and differences can you detect between sites with respect to the advertising or sponsorship at the site? What site features are designed to keep surfers coming back? Do you think they are effective? Explain.

2.   Visit portal sites like Google, Yahoo!, or Ask.com that use *paid search* for sponsored links and display/banner advertising. Search for items related to popular products or personal interests. What sponsored links or display/banner ads appeared along side of your search results? How do those sponsored links or display/banner ads correlate to your search topic, if at all? Next, click on some of the sponsored links or display/banner ads that were produced along with your search results, and describe what happens. Did you get transferred to a product Web site? Were you taken to an online promotion such as a sweepstakes? What purpose did the company have in prompting your click-throughs, and what incentives were you given to oblige the advertiser with your time

and effort? Finally, describe the different experiences you had clicking through different display/banner ads and rate their effectiveness from a consumer perspective.

3.   Much of traditional advertising now incorporates some form of online promotion or information, even if it is as simple as including a Web site URL on a magazine, newspaper, or television advertisement. Each of the Web addresses below lead to the online component of a traditional media ad campaign. Review each site and then answer these questions: What added value does the online component bring to the campaign? What other ways could the advertiser incorporate digital media in the campaign? Why would a consumer go the Web site, and why would he or she stay?
http://www.simpsonizeme.com
http://www.blackberry.com/ask
http://www.apple.com/switch

4.   Clorox Bleach has launched a new ad campaign touting the advice of The Accidental Housewife, also known as book author Julie Edelman. The campaign includes traditional media, such as radio ads with Edelman espousing the benefits of Clorox Wipes, as well as a "Tips from the Accidental Housewife" page on its corporate site:
http://www.clorox.com.

   Working in small teams, brainstorm ways that Clorox could expand its online campaign, using The Accidental Housewife as a central character. Your proposal should address how each of the primary methods of Internet advertising discussed in the chapter could be used.

Integrated Brand Promotion

PART FIVE

Part Five of the text brings us to the end of our journey in the study of advertising and IBP. This part highlights the full range of communications tools a firm can use in creating an integrated brand promotion campaign. Throughout the text, we have been emphasizing that IBP is a key to effective brand development. You will find that the variety and breadth of communications options discussed here represent a tremendous opportunity for marketers to be creative and break through the clutter in today's marketplace. Each of the tools discussed in Part Five has the unique capability to influence the audience's perception of and desire to own a brand. And, this part of the text has gone through significant revision to bring you the latest emerging techniques in support media, product placement, branded entertainment, and influencer marketing.

Sales Promotion, Point-of-Purchase Advertising, and Support Media.

All the techniques of sales promotion are discussed. Coupons, price-off deals, premiums, contests, sweepstakes, sampling, trial offers, refunds, rebates, frequency programs, point-of-purchase displays, incentives, allowances, trade shows, and cooperative advertising are presented in this chapter, as well as comprehensive coverage of point-of-purchase techniques. A section on "Sales Promotion, the Internet, and New Media," provides the most forward-thinking discussion of using new distribution and communication techniques for sales promotion. The chapter concludes with extensive treatment of the wide array of support media available to advertisers, including billboards, transit advertising, aerial advertising, and good old directory advertising.

17

Event Sponsorship, Product Placements, and Branded Entertainment.

This chapter highlights the thought-provoking issue of the convergence of Madison & Vine—that is the phenomenon of advertising, branding, and entertainment converging to provide consumers a wider array of "touch points" with brands. The chapter continues from here to review the growing allure of event sponsorships and then takes a deep dive into the provocative subject of branded entertainment. If you had any lingering doubts about the power of integrated brand promotion, the topics discussed in this chapter will dispel those.

18

Integrating Direct Marketing and Personal Selling.

Consumers' persistent desire for greater convenience and marketers' never-ending search for competitive advantage continue to create an emphasis on direct marketing in IBP programs. With direct marketing, the opportunity exists to not only communicate to a target audience, but also to seek an immediate response. You will learn why direct marketing continues to grow in popularity, what media are used by direct marketers to deliver their messages, and how direct marketing creates special challenges for achieving integrated brand promotion. In the excitement and, indeed, drama of digital media options, we sometimes forget the powerful role personal selling has across many integrated brand promotion strategies. The chapter provides a perspective on this important IBP process.

19

Public Relations, Influencer Marketing, and Corporate Advertising.

Chapter 20 is another chapter that has new and exciting material with the addition of full coverage of "influencer" marketing. This chapter begins with a discussion of the key role public relations can play in the overall IBP effort and differentiates between proactive and reactive public relations strategies. You will learn that public relations is an important option in IBP, but rarely will it ever take the lead role. The new coverage of influencer marketing is the best and most contemporary you will find anywhere. Professional influencer programs, peer-to-peer programs, buzz and viral marketing, cultivating "connectors"—it's all here. This chapter concludes with a wide-ranging and complete discussion of corporate advertising. Various forms of corporate advertising are identified, and the way each can be used as a means for building the reputation of an organization in the eyes of key constituents is discussed.

20

CHAPTER 17

After reading and thinking about this chapter, you will be able to do the following:

1

Explain the importance and growth of sales promotion.

2

Describe the main sales promotion techniques used in the consumer market.

3

Describe the main sales promotion techniques used in the trade channel and business markets.

4

Identify the risks to the brand of using sales promotion.

5

Understand the role and techniques of point-of-purchase advertising.

6

Describe the role of support media in a comprehensive IBP plan.

Introductory Scenario: If You Give It Away, They Will Come.

Sampling is a powerful tool in many IBP campaigns. But no one would ever have imagined the role sampling is now playing in overall corporate strategy. Big, powerful fast-food operations like McDonald's, Starbucks, and KFC are turning to sampling to jump-start sales and win ever-escalating competitive battles. After years of trying to wean themselves off deep discounting (which included excessive sampling), which was seen as cheapening brand image and conditioning consumers to look for deals, these big retailers are once again doling out free products and boasting about how much they give away. After Sonic's inaugural Free Float Night, the fast-food chain's vice president of marketing said, "We believe we gave away well over our goal of 3 million free floats. We exceeded that handily."[1] Sonic is only one of several chains using sampling:

- McDonald's is crediting coffee giveaways with boosting breakfast revenues and margins.
- Wendy's launched a 25-city, six-month "taste tour" offering free hamburgers. The tour features a mobile burger kitchen on a tractor-trailer rig, music, and picnic tables. The chain distributed more than 1,000 free burgers and $5 gift cards at each stop.
- KFC gave out free Colonel's Crispy Strips supported by a full-page ad in *USA Today*. During the first week of the sampling, the chain saw its highest sales for the strips.

But the goal of boosting sales and combating competition is not the only role perceived for sampling these days. A much bigger and broader role is emerging. While sampling has always been useful in attracting consumer attention and making them feel good about getting "something for free," which is the traditional role for sampling in IBP campaigns (see Exhibit 17.1), sampling is now being considered for a much bigger task—building sales at existing sales units in the absence of opportunities to build new stores. Rivals in the fast-food industry have nearly worn themselves out battling one another with menu changes and all sorts of pricing schemes. And

EXHIBIT 17.1

Advertisers have long used sampling, like this free offer from Glad, as a component in IBP campaigns. Fast-food retailers are now turning to extensive sampling as a way to build traffic—and sales— in existing stores, as building new stores becomes more difficult and more expensive.

1.   Kate MacArthur, "Give It Away: Fast Feeders Favor Freebies," *Advertising Age*, June 18, 2007, 10.

real estate is getting more and more scarce and more and more expensive, making building more sales units less attractive—so new-unit growth has slowed considerably. Now, rather than building new stores, these companies are trying to build traffic—and revenues—at existing stores by enticing both old and new customers with free food and drink. There is some sound reasoning behind the strategy. If a customer stops in for free fries, he or she might also buy a burger and drink—an immediate effect on sales. And a free product also presents the chance to "convert the curious into loyalists."[2] McDonald's, for example, claims that at least half the customers who come in for free coffee wind up buying something.

It remains to be seen if these savvy marketers continue to use sampling as a primary IBP technique. As you will learn in this chapter, sampling—and other "discounting" IBP tools—carry the risk of eroding brand value and turning consumers into price-focused bargain hunters. But for now, sampling seems to be having the positive effect on increased sales that strategists hoped it would have.

Sales Promotion Defined. Sales promotion is often a key component within an integrated brand promotion campaign. Sales promotions like dealer incentives and consumer price and discount appeals can attract attention and give new energy to the overall advertising and the IBP effort. While mass media advertising is designed to build a brand image over time, sales promotion is conspicuous and designed to make things happen in a hurry. Used properly, sales promotion is capable of almost instant demand stimulation, like the kind that contests and sweepstakes can create. The "message" in a sales promotion features price reduction, free samples, a prize, or some other incentive for consumers to try a brand or for a retailer to feature the brand in a store. Sales promotion has proven to be a popular complement to mass media advertising because it accomplishes things advertising cannot.

Formally defined, **sales promotion** is the use of incentive techniques that create a perception of greater brand value among consumers, the trade, and business buyers. The intent is to generate a short-term increase in sales by motivating trial use, encouraging larger purchases, or stimulating repeat purchases. **Consumer-market sales promotion** includes

- coupons
- price-off deals
- premiums
- contests and sweepstakes
- sampling and trial offers
- rebates
- loyalty/frequency programs
- phone and gift cards

All these incentives are ways of inducing household consumers to purchase a firm's brand rather than a competitor's brand. Notice that some incentives reduce price, offer a reward, or encourage a trip to the retailer.

Trade-market sales promotion uses the following ways of motivating distributors, wholesalers, and retailers to stock and feature a firm's brand in their store merchandising programs:

- point-of-purchase displays
- incentives
- allowances
- cooperative advertising
- sales training

2.   Ibid., 10.

Business-market sales promotion is designed to cultivate buyers in large corporations who are making purchase decisions about a wide range of products including computers, office supplies, and consulting services. Techniques used for business buyers are similar to the trade-market techniques and include

- trade shows
- premiums
- incentives
- loyalty/frequency programs

The Importance and Growth of Sales Promotion. Sales promotion is designed to affect demand differently than advertising does. As we have learned throughout the text, most advertising is designed to have awareness-, image-, and preference-building effects for a brand over the long run. The role of sales promotion, on the other hand, is primarily to elicit an immediate purchase from a customer group. Coupons, samples, rebates, contests and sweepstakes, and similar techniques offer household consumers, trade buyers, or business buyers an immediate incentive to choose one brand over another, as exemplified in Exhibit 17.2. Notice that Oreck is offering a free product (referred to as a premium offer) just for trying the Oreck vacuum cleaner.

Other sales promotions, such as frequency programs (for example, airline frequent-flyer programs), provide an affiliation value for a brand, which increases a consumer's ability and desire to identify with a particular brand. Sales promotions featuring price reductions, such as coupons, are effective in the convenience goods category, where frequent purchases, brand switching, and a perceived homogeneity (similarity) among brands characterize consumer behavior.

Sales promotions are used across all consumer goods categories and in the trade and business markets as well. When a firm determines that a more immediate response is called for—whether the target customer is a household, business buyer, distributor, or retailer—sales promotions are designed to provide that incentive. The goals for sales promotion versus those of advertising are compared in Exhibit 17.3. Notice the key differences in the goals for these different forms of promotion. Sales promotion encourages more immediate and short-term responses whereas the purpose of advertising is to cultivate an image, loyalty, and repeat purchases over the long term.

EXHIBIT 17.2

Marketers use a wide range of incentives to attract attention to a brand. Here, David Oreck offers new buyers a free iron for trying the Oreck lightweight vacuum.

EXHIBIT 17.3

Sales promotion and advertising serve very different purposes in the promotional mix. What would you describe as the key difference between the two based on the features listed here?

Purpose of Sales Promotion	Purpose of Advertising
Stimulate short-term demand	Cultivate long-term demand
Encourage brand switching	Encourage brand loyalty
Induce trial use	Encourage repeat purchases
Promote price orientation	Promote image/feature orientation
Obtain immediate, often measurable results	Obtain long-term effects, often difficult to measure

The Importance of Sales Promotion.

The importance of sales promotion in the United States should not be underestimated. Sales promotion may not seem as stylish and sophisticated as mass media advertising, but expenditures on this tool are impressive. In recent years, sales promotion expenditures have grown at an annual rate of about 4 to 8 percent, compared to about a 3 to 5 percent rate for advertising. Spending on sales promotion efforts in the United States alone now exceed $300 billion annually (see Exhibit 17.4). The rapid growth is occurring as big consumer products firms shift dollars out of media advertising and into promotions. The chairman and CEO of Procter & Gamble told analysts that the firm's advertising and IBP spending was shifting "and it's shifting from measured media to in-store, to the Internet, and to trial activity [i.e., product sampling]."[3]

It is important to realize that full-service advertising agencies specializing in advertising planning, creative preparation, and media placement typically do not prepare sales promotion materials for clients. These activities are normally assigned to sales promotion agencies (spending on such agencies is also listed in Exhibit 17.4) that specialize in coupons, premiums, displays, or other forms of sales promotion and point-of-purchase techniques that require specific skills and creative preparation.

The development and management of an effective sales promotion program requires a major commitment by a firm. During any given year, it is typical that as much as 30 percent of brand management time is spent on designing, implementing, and overseeing sales promotions.

Growth in the Use of Sales Promotion.

Many marketers have shifted the emphasis of their promotional spending over the past decade. Much of the shift has been away from mass media advertising. Some has made its way to the Internet, as we saw in the last chapter, and more spending has found its way to consumer, trade, and business sales promotions. Currently, the budget allocation on average stands at about 17.5 percent

EXHIBIT 17.4

Marketers rely on several different sales promotion techniques to complement and support the advertising effort. This list shows spending on those techniques as well as the amount spent on promotion agency services and research.

TACTIC	2005	2004	% Change	% of total
Event Marketing	$171.8	$166.0	3.0%	50.2%
Direct Mail	49.8	35.1	41.8	14.5
Premiums & Incentives	47.6	46.5	2.5	13.9
Retail	19.3	18.5	4.8	5.6
Sponsorship	12.1	11.1	8.7	3.5
Coupons	7.2	7.2	0.0	2.1
Specialy Printing	6.1	6.1	0.0	1.7
Licensing	5.9	5.9	0.0	1.7
Agency Revenues	5.2	4.2	23.5	1.5
Fulfillment	4.7	4.7	0.0	1.4
Product Placement	4.5	–	–	1.3
Interactive/Online	2.4	2.4	0.0	0.7
Loyalty	2.0	2.0	1.0	0.5
Games, Contests, Sweeps	1.8	1.8	0.0	0.5
Sampling	1.8	1.8	0.0	0.5
Total (in billions)	**$342.2**	**$313.2**	**9.3%**	**100.0%**

Source: *PROMO* Industry Trends Report 2006.

3.   Bradley Johnson, "Leading National Advertisers Report: Spending up $3.1% to $105 Billion," *Advertising Age*, June 25, 2007, S-2.

for advertising, 54 percent for trade and business promotions, and 28.5 percent for consumer promotions.[4] There are several reasons why many marketers have been shifting funds from mass media advertising to sales promotions, from the need for greater cost accountability to the problem of media clutter.

Demand for Greater Accountability. In an era of cost cutting and shareholder scrutiny, companies are demanding greater accountability across all functions, including marketing, advertising, and promotions. When activities are evaluated for their contribution to sales and profits, it is often difficult to draw specific conclusions regarding the effects of advertising. But the more immediate effects of sales promotions are typically easier to document. Various studies are now showing that only 18 percent of TV advertising campaigns produced a short-term positive return on investment (ROI) on promotional dollars.[5] Conversely, point-of-purchase in-store displays have been shown to positively affect sales by as much as 35 percent in some product categories.[6]

Short-Term Orientation. Several factors have created a short-term orientation among managers. Pressures from stockholders to increase quarter-by-quarter revenue and profit per share are one factor. A bottom-line mentality is another factor. Many organizations are developing marketing plans—with rewards and punishments for manager performance—that are based on short-term revenue generation. This being the case, companies are seeking tactics that can have short-term effects. McDonald's credits its "Play to Win" game with boosting store sales up to 15 percent during the game's promotion period.[7]

Consumer Response to Promotions. The precision shopper in the contemporary marketplace is demanding greater value across all purchase situations, and that trend is battering overpriced brands.[8] These precision shoppers search for extra value in every product purchase. Coupons, premiums, price-off deals, and other sales promotions increase the value of a brand in these shoppers' minds. The positive response to sales promotion goes beyond value-oriented consumers, though. Historically, consumers report that coupons, price, and good value for their money influence 75 to 85 percent of their brand choices.[9] (Be careful here—coupons, price reduction, and value seeking do not necessarily mean consumers are choosing the *lowest*-priced item. The analysis suggests that these sales promotion techniques act as an incentive to purchase the brand *using* a promotion, even if another brand has a lower basic price.)

Proliferation of Brands. Each year, thousands of new brands are introduced into the consumer market. The drive by marketers to design products for specific market segments to satisfy ever more narrowly defined needs has caused a proliferation of brands that creates a mind-dulling maze for consumers. Consider this case of brand proliferation—in one 12-month period, Coca-Cola's new head of marketing launched *1,000* (not a typo) new drinks or new variations of existing brands worldwide (has anybody tried Coca-Cola Blak?).[10] At any point in time, consumers are typically able to choose from about 60 spaghetti sauces, 100 snack chips, 50 laundry detergents, 90 cold remedies, and 60 disposable-diaper varieties. As you can see in Exhibit 17.5, gaining attention in this blizzard of brands is no easy task. Because of this proliferation and "clutter" of brands, marketers turn to sales promotions—contests, coupons, premiums, loyalty programs, point-of-purchase displays—to gain some attention.

4.   2004 Industry Trends Report, *Promo Magazine*.
5.   Jack Neff, "TV Doesn't Sell Packaged Goods," *Advertising Age*, May 24, 2004, 1, 30.
6.   Cara Beardi, "POP Ups Sales Results," *Advertising Age*, July 23, 2001, 27.
7.   Kate MacArthur, "McD's Sees Growth, but Are Ads a Factor?" *Advertising Age*, November 24, 2003, 3, 24.
8.   Jack Neff, "Black Eye in Store for Big Brands," *Advertising Age*, April 30, 2001, 1, 34
9.   Cox Direct 20th Annual Survey of Promotional Practices, Chart 22, 1998, 37.
10. Dean Foust, "Queen of Pop," *BusinessWeek*, August 7, 2006, 44–450.

As you can see by this shelf of spaghetti sauces, getting the consumer to pay attention to any one brand is quite a challenge. This proliferation of brands in the marketplace has made marketers search for ways to attract attention to their brands, and sales promotion techniques often provide an answer. Notice the point-of-purchase promotion attached to the shelves.

ETHICS

Big Brother Has a New Toy

In the constant battle to provide big retailers with reasons to feature one brand over another, manufacturers work hard to come up with new ways to gain favors for their brands versus competitors. As one manufacturer put it, "One Wal-Mart is worth 101 other companies." A new weapon in this battle is the successor to bar codes called radio frequency identification (RFID) tags. These tags can potentially provide an instant assessment of inventory and stock on the shelf.

RFID tags work by combining tiny information chips with an antenna. When a tag is placed on an item, it starts to radio its location. Receivers can be placed in management offices, storerooms, and even consumer shopping carts. And herein lies the problems. Critics of RFID argue that this is just another instance of "Big Brother" intruding on consumers' privacy by tracking consumers' behavior. This is how it would work. When you get to your favorite grocery store, you will grab a shopping cart just like you always do. But this is not your typical shopping cart. With this cart, you swipe your store loyalty card (another kind of tracking) through an RFID reader attached to the cart. Now that you are officially "checked in" (i.e., being tracked), the store can offer you special deals based on the items you put in your cart on this day or, since your purchase history is tracked through your loyalty card, offer you deals on items you have purchased in the past. Eventually, you'll be able to ring up your purchases as you put them in your specially equipped RFID cart and just walk straight out the door when you are done shopping.

Are there real benefits to RFID? Absolutely. The efficiency gained from inventory control, restocking alerts, and automated checkout would no doubt result in significant cost savings. But is this just another way that corporation can track and monitor our behavior? And if they can track our behavior in the store, what's keeping them from tracking our behavior after we leave the store?

Source: Gerry Khermouch and Heather Green, "Bar Codes Better Watch Their Backs," *Business-Week*, July 14, 2003, 42.

Increased Power of Retailers. Big retailers like Target, Home Depot, Costco and the most powerful of all, Wal-Mart, now dominate retailing in the United States. These powerful retailers have responded quickly and accurately to the new environment for retailing, where consumers are demanding more and better products and services at lower prices. Because of these consumer demands, retailers are, in turn, demanding more deals from manufacturers. Many of the deals are delivered in terms of trade-oriented sales promotions: point-of-purchase displays, slotting fees (payment for shelf space), case allowances, and co-op advertising allowances. In the end, manufacturers use more and more sales promotions to gain and maintain good relations with the powerful retailers—a critical link to the consumer. And retailers use the tools of sales promotion as competitive strategies against each other. Manufacturers are coming up with clever ways to provide value to retailers and thus maintain the balance of power. But some of these tools may be just another intrusion on privacy, as the Ethics box highlights.

Media Clutter. A nagging and traditional problem in the advertising process is clutter. Many advertisers target the same customers because their research has led them to the same conclusion about whom to target. The result is that advertising media are cluttered with ads all seeking the attention of the same people. When consumers encounter a barrage of ads, they tune out (remember the discussion in Chapter 5). And clutter is getting worse, not better, across all media—including the Internet, where pop-ups, pop-unders, and banners "clutter" nearly every Web site.[11] One way to break through the clutter is to feature a sales promotion. In print ads, the featured deal is often a coupon. In television and radio advertising, sweepstakes, premium, and rebate offers can attract viewers' and listeners' attention. The combination of advertising and creative sales promotions has proven to be a good way to break through the clutter.

2 Sales Promotion Directed at Consumers.

It is clear that U.S. consumer-product firms have made a tremendous commitment to sales promotion in their overall marketing plans. During the 1970s, consumer goods marketers allocated only about 30 percent of their budgets to sales promotion, with about 70 percent allocated to mass media advertising. Now we see that for many consumer-goods firms, the percentages are just the opposite, with nearly 75 percent of promotional budgets being spent on various forms of promotion and point-of-purchase materials. With this sort of investment in sales promotion and point of purchase as part of the integrated brand promotion process, let's examine in detail the objectives for sales promotion in the consumer market and the wide range of techniques that can be used.

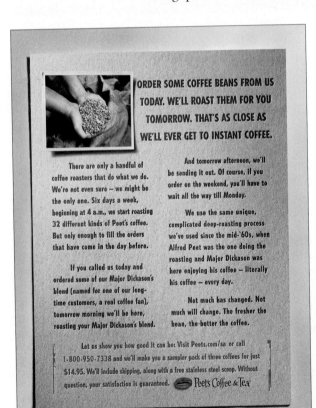

EXHIBIT 17.6

One objective for sales promotion in the consumer market is to stimulate trial use of a brand. Here, Peet's Coffee & Tea is offering consumers a sample pack they can request either online or by calling a toll-free number.

Objectives for Consumer-Market Sales Promotion.

To help ensure the proper application of sales promotion, specific strategic objectives should be set. The following basic objectives can be pursued with sales promotion in the consumer market.

Stimulate Trial Purchase. When a firm wants to attract new users, sales promotion tools can reduce the consumer's risk of trying something new. A reduced price, offer of a rebate, or a free sample may stimulate trial purchase. Exhibit 17.6 illustrates an attempt to stimulate trial use. Note that this promotion is trying to get consumers to try a *brand* for the first time—not the product category. Recall the discussions in Chapters 2 and 4 (primary versus selective demand stimulation) highlighting the fact that advertising and promotion cannot *initiate* product use in mature product categories, like coffee—but can only affect brand choice among people who already use the product category.

Stimulate Repeat Purchases. In-package coupons good for the next purchase, or the accu-

11.   Matthew Creamer, "Caught in the Clutter Crossfire: Your Brand," *Advertising Age*, April 2, 2007, 1,35.

EXHIBIT 17.7

Sales promotions are often used to encourage larger purchases. This coupon for SpaghettiOs offers consumers the opportunity to stock up on three cans.

mulation of points with repeated purchases, can keep consumers loyal to a particular brand. The most prominent frequency programs are found in the airline and hotel industries. Or how about that loyalty "punch card" at your favorite coffee shop—same idea. Firms try to retain their most lucrative customers by enrolling them in frequency programs.

Stimulate Larger Purchases. Price reductions or two-for-one sales can motivate consumers to stock up on a brand, thus allowing firms to reduce inventory or increase cash flow. Shampoo is often double-packaged to offer a value to consumers. Exhibit 17.7 is a sales promotion aimed at stimulating a larger purchase ("Save 30 cents on 3").

Introduce a New Brand. Because sales promotion can attract attention and motivate trial purchase, it is commonly used for new brand introduction. One of the most successful uses of sales promotions to introduce a new brand was when the makers of Curad bandages introduced their new kid-size bandage by distributing 7.5 million sample packs in McDonald's Happy Meal sacks. The promotion was a huge success, with initial sales exceeding estimates by 30 percent.

Combat or Disrupt Competitors' Strategies. Because sales promotions often motivate consumers to buy in larger quantities or try new brands, they can be used to disrupt competitors' marketing strategies. If a firm knows that one of its competitors is launching a new brand or initiating a new advertising campaign, a well-timed sales promotion offering deep discounts or extra quantity can disrupt the competitors' strategy. Add to the original discount an in-package coupon for future purchases, and a marketer can severely compromise competitors' efforts. *TV Guide* magazine used a sweepstakes promotion to combat competition. In an effort to address increasing competition from newspaper TV supplements and cable-guide magazines, *TV Guide* ran a Shopping Spree Sweepstakes in several regional markets. Winners won $200 shopping sprees in grocery stores—precisely the location where 65 percent of *TV Guide* sales are realized.

Contribute to Integrated Brand Promotion. In conjunction with advertising, direct marketing, public relations, and other programs being carried out by a firm, sales promotion can add yet another type of communication to the mix. Sales promotions suggest an additional value, with price reductions, premiums, or the chance to win a prize. This is a different message within the overall communications effort a firm can use in its integrated brand promotion effort.

Consumer-Market Sales Promotion Techniques.
Several techniques are used to stimulate demand and attract attention in the consumer market. Some of these are coupons, price-off deals, premiums, contests and sweepstakes, samples and trial offers, phone and gift cards, rebates, and frequency (continuity) programs.

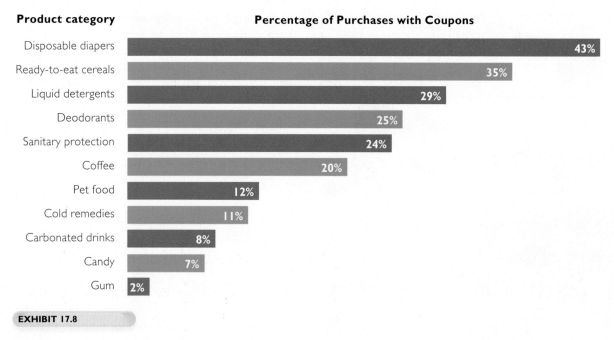

EXHIBIT 17.8

Percentage of purchases made with coupons in various product categories.

Coupons. A **coupon** entitles a buyer to a designated reduction in price for a product or service. Coupons are the oldest and most widely used form of sales promotion. The first use of a coupon is traced to around 1895, when the C. W. Post Company used a penny-off coupon as a way to get people to try its Grape-Nuts cereal. Annually, about 350 billion coupons are distributed to American consumers, with redemption rates ranging from 2 percent for gum purchases to nearly 45 percent for disposable diaper purchases. Exhibit 17.8 shows coupon-redemption rates for several product categories.

There are five advantages to the coupon as a sales promotion tool:

- The use of a coupon makes it possible to give a discount to a price-sensitive consumer while still selling the product at full price to other consumers.
- The coupon-redeeming customer may be a competitive-brand user, so the coupon can induce brand switching.
- A manufacturer can control the timing and distribution of coupons. This way a retailer is not implementing price discounts in a way that can damage brand image.
- A coupon is an excellent method of stimulating repeat purchases. Once a consumer has been attracted to a brand, with or without a coupon, an in-package coupon can induce repeat purchase.
- Coupons can get regular users to trade up within a brand array. For example, users of low-priced disposable diapers may be willing to try the premium version of a brand with a coupon.

The use of coupons is not without its problems. There are administrative burdens and risks with coupon use:

- While coupon price incentives and the timing of distribution can be controlled by a marketer, the timing of redemption cannot. Some consumers redeem coupons immediately; others hold them for months.
- Heavy redemption by regular brand buyers merely reduces a firm's profitability.
- Couponing entails careful administration. Coupon programs include much more than the cost of the face value of the coupon. There are costs for production and distribution and for retailer and manufacturer handling. In fact, the cost for

handling, processing, and distribution of coupons is typically equal to about two-thirds of the face value of the coupon. Marketers need to track these costs against the amount of product sold with and without coupon redemption.

- Fraud is a chronic and serious problem in the couponing process. The problem relates directly to misredemption practices. There are three types of misredemption that cost firms money: redemption of coupons by consumers who do not purchase the couponed brand; redemption of coupons by salesclerks and store managers without consumer purchases; and illegal collection or copying of coupons by individuals who sell them to unethical store merchants, who in turn redeem the coupons without the accompanying consumer purchases.

Price-Off Deals. The price-off deal is another straightforward technique. A **price-off deal** offers a consumer cents or even dollars off merchandise at the point of purchase through specially marked packages. The typical price-off deal is a 10 to 25 percent price reduction. The reduction is taken from the manufacturer's profit margin rather than the retailer's (another point of contention in the power struggle). Manufacturers like the price-off technique because it is controllable. Plus, the price off, judged at the point of purchase, can effect a positive price comparison against competitors. Consumers like a price-off deal because it is straightforward and automatically increases the value of a known brand. Regular users tend to stock up on an item during a price-off deal. Retailers are less enthusiastic about this technique. Price-off promotions can create inventory and pricing problems for retailers. Also, most price-off deals are snapped up by regular customers, so the retailer often doesn't benefit from new business.

Premiums and Advertising Specialties. **Premiums** are items offered free, or at a reduced price, with the purchase of another item. Many firms offer a related product free, such as a free granola bar packed inside a box of granola cereal. Service firms, such as a car wash or dry cleaner, may use a two-for-one offer to persuade consumers to try the service. Premiums represent firms' single largest category of investment in sales promotion, with over $47 billion spent on premiums during 2005.

There are two options available for the use of premiums. A **free premium** provides consumers with an item at no cost; the item is either included in the package of a purchased item or mailed to the consumer after proof of purchase is verified. The most frequently used free premium is an additional package of the original item or a free related item placed in the package (e.g., free conditioner with shampoo purchase).

A **self-liquidating premium** requires a consumer to pay most of the cost of the item received as a premium. For example, Snapple can offer a "Snapple Cooler" with the purchase of six bottles of Snapple for $6.99—the cost of the cooler to Snapple. Self-liquidating premiums are particularly effective with loyal customers. However, these types of premiums must be used cautiously. Unless the premium is related to a value-building strategy for a brand, it can serve to focus consumer attention on the premium rather than on the benefits of the brand. Focusing on the premium rather than the brand erodes brand equity. For example, if consumers buy a brand just to get a really great looking T-shirt at $4.99, then they won't purchase the brand again until there is another great premium available at a low price.

Advertising specialties have three key elements: a message, placed on a useful item, that is given to consumers with no obligation. Popular advertising specialties are baseball caps, T-shirts, coffee mugs, computer mouse pads, pens, and calendars. Sales of promotional products in 2003 increased 4.57 percent over the previous year to $16 billion.[12] Advertising specialties allow a firm to tout its company or brand

---

12.   Data obtained from PPAI: Promotional Products Association International at the association's Web site, *http://www.promotion-clinic.ppa.org*, accessed June 25, 2004.

EXHIBIT 17.9

Advertising specialty items, like these pens and ball caps, allow a firm to regularly remind target customers of the brand name and logo. While a sales promotion item like this will never be the main strategic tool in an IBP campaign, it does serve to create a regular brand presence and conversation piece with consumers.

name with a target customer in an ongoing fashion. Many of us have ball caps or coffee mugs that carry brand names (see Exhibit 17.9).

Contests and Sweepstakes. Contests and sweepstakes can draw attention to a brand like no other sales promotion technique. Technically, there are important differences between contests and sweepstakes. In a **contest**, consumers compete for prizes based on skill or ability. Winners in a contest are determined by a panel of judges or based on which contestant comes closest to a predetermined criterion for winning, such as picking the total points scored in the Super Bowl. Contests tend to be somewhat expensive to administer because each entry must be judged against winning criteria.

A **sweepstakes** is a promotion in which winners are determined purely by chance. Consumers need only to enter their names in the sweepstakes as a criterion for winning. Sweepstakes often use official entry forms as a way for consumers to enter the sweepstakes. Other popular types of sweepstakes use scratch-off cards. Instant-winner scratch-off cards tend to attract customers. Gasoline retailers, grocery stores, and fast-food chains commonly use scratch-off-card sweepstakes as a way of building and maintaining store traffic. Sweepstakes can also be designed so that repeated trips to the retail outlet are necessary to gather a complete set of winning cards. In order for contests and sweepstakes to be effective, advertisers must design them in such a way that consumers perceive value in the prizes and find playing the games intrinsically interesting.

Contests and sweepstakes can span the globe. British Airways ran a contest with the theme "The World's Greatest Offer," in which it gave away thousands of free airline tickets to London and other European destinations. While the contest increased awareness of the airline, there was definitely another benefit. Contests like these create a database of interested customers and potential customers. All the people who didn't win can be mailed information on future programs and other premium offers.

Contests and sweepstakes often create excitement and generate interest for a brand, but the problems of administering these promotions are substantial. Consider these challenges to effectively using contest and sweepstakes in the IBP effort.

- There will always be regulations and restrictions on contests and sweepstakes. Advertisers must be sure that the design and administration of a contest or sweepstakes complies with both federal and state laws. Each state may have slightly different regulations. The legal problems are complex enough that most firms hire agencies that specialize in contests and sweepstakes to administer the programs.
- The game itself may become the consumer's primary focus, while the brand becomes secondary. Like other sales promotion tools, this technique thus fails to build long-term consumer affinity for a brand.
- It is hard to get any meaningful message across in the context of a game. The consumer's interest is focused on the game, rather than on any feature of the brand.
- Administration of a contest or sweepstakes is sufficiently complex that the risk of errors in administration is fairly high and can create negative publicity.[13]

13.   Barry M. Benjamin, "Plan Ahead to Limit Potential Disasters," *Marketing News*, November 10, 2003, 15

- If a firm is trying to develop a quality or prestige image for a brand, contests and sweepstakes may contradict this goal.

Sampling and Trial Offers. As we saw at the opening of the chapter, getting consumers to simply try a brand can have a powerful effect on future decision making. **Sampling** is a sales promotion technique designed to provide a consumer with an opportunity to use a brand on a trial basis with little or no risk. To say that sampling is a popular technique is an understatement. Most consumer-product companies use sampling in some manner, and invest approximately $1.8 billion a year on the technique. Surveys have shown that consumers are very favorable toward sampling, with 43 percent indicating that they would consider switching brands if they liked a free sample that was being offered.[14]

Sampling is particularly useful for new products, but should not be reserved for new products alone. It can be used successfully for established brands with weak market share in specific geographic areas. Ben & Jerry's "Stop & Taste the Ice Cream" tour gave away more than a million scoops of ice cream in high-traffic urban areas in an attempt to reestablish a presence for the brand in weak markets.[15] Six techniques are used in sampling:

- **In-store sampling** is popular for food products and cosmetics. This is a preferred technique for many marketers because the consumer is at the point of purchase and may be swayed by a direct encounter with the brand. Increasingly, in-store demonstrators are handing out coupons as well as samples, as any trip to Costco will verify.
- **Door-to-door sampling** is extremely expensive because of labor costs, but it can be effective if the marketer has information that locates the target segment in a well-defined geographic area. Some firms enlist the services of newspaper delivery people, who package the sample with daily or Sunday newspapers as a way of reducing distribution costs.
- **Mail sampling** allows samples to be delivered through the postal service. Again, the value here is that certain zip-code markets can be targeted. A drawback is that the sample must be small enough to be economically feasible to mail. Specialty sampling firms provide targeted geo-demographic door-to-door distribution as an alternative to the postal service. Cox Target Media has developed a mailer that contains multiple samples related to a specific industry—like car-care products—and that can reach highly targeted market segments.[16]
- **Newspaper sampling** has become very popular in recent years, and 42 percent of consumers report having received samples of health and beauty products in this manner.[17] Much like mail sampling, newspaper samples allow very specific geographic and geodemographic targeting. Big drug companies like Eli Lilly and Bristol-Myers Squibb have used newspaper distribution of coupons to target new users for antidepressant and diabetes drugs.[18]
- **On-package sampling,** a technique in which the sample item is attached to another product package, is useful for brands targeted to current customers. Attaching a small bottle of Ivory conditioner to a regular-sized container of Ivory shampoo is a logical sampling strategy.
- **Mobile sampling** is carried out by logo-emblazoned vehicles that dispense samples, coupons, and premiums to consumers at malls, shopping centers, fairgrounds, and recreational areas.

---

14. Cox Direct 20th Annual Survey of Promotional Practices, 1998, 28
15. Betsy Spethmann, "Branded Moments," *Promo Magazine*, September 2000, 84.
16. Cara Beardi, "Cox's Introz Mailer Bundles Samples in Industry," *Advertising Age*, November 2000, 88
17. Cox Direct 20th Annual Survey of Promotional Practices, 1998, 27.
18. Susan Warner, "Drug Makers Print Coupons to Boost Sales," Knight Ridder Newspapers, June 4, 2001.

Of course, sampling has its critics. Unless the brand has a clear value and benefit over the competition, a trial of the brand is unlikely to persuade a consumer to switch brands. This is especially true for convenience goods because consumers perceive a high degree of similarity among brands, even after trying them. The perception of benefit and superiority may have to be developed through advertising in combination with sampling. In addition, sampling is expensive. This is especially true in cases where a sufficient quantity of a product, such as shampoo or laundry detergent, must be given away for a consumer to truly appreciate a brand's value. Finally, sampling can be a very imprecise process. Despite the emergence of special agencies to handle sampling programs, a firm can never completely ensure that the product is reaching the targeted audience.

Trial offers have the same goal as sampling—to induce consumer trial use of a brand—but they are used for more expensive items. Exercise equipment, appliances, watches, hand tools, and consumer electronics are typical of items offered on a trial basis. Trials offers can be free for low-priced products, as we saw in Exhibit 17.6 with Peet's Coffee. Or trials can be offered for as little as a day to as long as 90 days for more expensive items like vacuum cleaners or computer software. The expense to the firm, of course, can be formidable. Segments chosen for this sales promotion technique must have high sales potential.

Phone and Gift Cards. Phone and gift cards represent a new and increasingly popular form of sales promotion. This technique could be classified as a premium offer, but it has enough unique features to warrant separate classification as a sales promotion technique. The use of phone and gift cards is fairly straightforward. Manufacturers or retailers offer either free or for-purchase debit cards that provide the holder with a preset spending limit or minutes of phone time. The cards are designed to be colorful and memorable. A wide range of marketers, including luxury car manufacturers like Lexus and retailers like the Gap, have made effective use of phone and gift cards. The really good news about gift cards is that gift card holders tend to use them freely to pay the full retail price for items, which means retailers and brand marketers earn higher profit margins from gift card purchases.[19] Exhibit 17.10 shows a Starbucks gift card as a promotional tool.

Rebates. A **rebate** is a money-back offer requiring a buyer to mail in a form requesting the money back from the manufacturer, rather than from the retailer (as in couponing). The rebate technique has been refined over the years and is now used by a wide variety of marketers with over 400 million rebates offered each year for products as diverse as computers (Dell) to mouthwash (Warner-Lambert).[20] Rebates are particularly well suited to increasing the quantity purchased by consumers, so rebates are commonly tied to multiple purchases. For example, if you buy a ten-pack of Kodak film you can mail in a rebate coupon worth $2.

Another reason for the popularity of rebates is that relatively few consumers take advantage of the rebate offer after buying a brand. The best estimate of consumer redemption of rebate offers is that only 60 percent of buyers ever bother to fill out and then mail in the

19.   Louise Lee, "What's Roiling the Selling Season," *BusinessWeek*, January 10, 2005, 38.
20.   Brian Grow, "The Great Rebate Runaround," *BusinessWeek*, December 5, 2005, 34–38.

"WHY IS OUR AWARD PROGRAM SO POPULAR WITH FREQUENT TRAVELERS? WE'RE IN EVERY CITY THEY FREQUENT."

As a business traveler you earn free vacations faster with Marriott's Honored Guest Award program. With over 250 locations worldwide, we're doing business wherever you're doing business. To join the program call 1-800-648-8024. For reservations, call your travel agent or 1-800-228-9290.

Marriott.
HOTELS · RESORTS · SUITES
WE MAKE IT HAPPEN FOR YOU.

EXHIBIT 17.11

Frequency (continuity) programs build customer loyalty and offer opportunities for building a large, targeted database for other promotions.

rebate request—resulting in an extra $2 billion in revenue for manufacturers and retailers who offer rebates.[21]

Frequency (Continuity) Programs. In recent years, one of the most popular sales promotion techniques among consumers has been frequency programs. **Frequency programs**, also referred to as continuity programs, offer consumers discounts or free product rewards for repeat purchase or patronage of the same brand or company. These programs were pioneered by airline companies. Frequent-flyer programs such as Delta Air Lines' Sky-Miles, frequent-stay programs such as Marriott's Honored Guest Award Rewards program, and frequent-renter programs such as Hertz's #1 Club are examples of such loyalty-building activities. But frequency programs are not reserved for big national airline and auto-rental chains. Chart House Enterprises, a chain of 65 upscale restaurants, successfully launched a frequency program for diners, who earned points for every dollar spent. Frequent diners were issued "passports," which were stamped with each visit. Within two years, the program had more than 300,000 members. Exhibit 17.11 features Marriott's frequency program.

③ Sales Promotion Directed at the Trade Channel and Business Markets.

Sales promotions can also be directed at members of the trade—wholesalers, distributors, and retailers—and business markets. For example, Hewlett-Packard designs sales promotion programs for its retailers, like Circuit City, in order to ensure that the HP line gets proper attention and display. But HP will also have sales promotion campaigns aimed at business buyers like Accenture or IHC HealthCare. The purpose of sales promotion as a tool does not change from the consumer market to the trade or business markets. It is still intended to stimulate demand in the short term and help *push* the product through the distribution channel or cause business buyers to act more immediately and positively toward the marketer's brand. Firms spend big money to attract business to their brands with sales promotions. Recent estimates put business-to-business sales promotions at more than $44 billion annually.[22]

Effective trade- and business-market promotions can generate enthusiasm for a product and contribute positively to the loyalty distributors show for a brand. In the business market, sales promotions can mean the difference between landing a very large order and missing out entirely on a revenue opportunity. With the massive proliferation of new brands and brand extensions, manufacturers need to stimulate enthusiasm and loyalty among members of the trade and also need a way to get the attention of business buyers suffering from information overload.

21   Ibid., 34.
22.   2007 Marketing Fact Book, *Marketing News*, July 15, 2007, 32.

Objectives for Promotions in the Trade Channel. As in the consumer market, trade-market sales promotions should be undertaken with specific objectives in mind. Generally speaking, when marketers devise incentives for the trade market they are executing a **push strategy**; that is, sales promotions directed at the trade help push a brand into the distribution channel until it ultimately reaches the consumer. Four primary objectives can be identified for these promotions.

Obtain Initial Distribution. Because of the proliferation of brands in the consumer market, there is fierce competition for shelf space. Sales promotion incentives can help a firm gain initial distribution and shelf placement. Like consumers, members of the trade need a reason to choose one brand over another when it comes to allocating shelf space. A well-conceived promotion incentive may sway them.

Bob's Candies, a small family-owned business in Albany, Georgia, is the largest candy cane manufacturer in the United States. But Bob's old-fashioned candy was having trouble keeping distributors. To reverse the trend, Bob's designed a new name, logo, and packaging for the candy canes. Then, each scheduled attendee at the All-Candy Expo trade show in Chicago was mailed three strategically timed postcards with the teaser question "Wanna Be Striped?" The mailing got a 25 percent response rate, and booth visitations at the trade show were a huge success.[23]

Increase Order Size. One of the struggles in the channel of distribution is over the location of inventory. Manufacturers prefer that members of the trade maintain large inventories so the manufacturer can reduce inventory-carrying costs. Conversely, members of the trade would rather make frequent, small orders and carry little inventory. Sales promotion techniques can encourage wholesalers and retailers to order in larger quantities, thus shifting the inventory burden to the trade channel.

Encourage Cooperation with Consumer-Market Sales Promotions. It does a manufacturer little good to initiate a sales promotion in the consumer market if there is little cooperation in the channel. Wholesalers may need to maintain larger inventories, and retailers may need to provide special displays or handling during consumer-market sales promotions. To achieve synergy, marketers often run trade promotions simultaneously with consumer promotions. When Toys "R" Us ran a "scan and win" promotion, the retailer actually ran out of several very popular toy items during the critical holiday buying season because distributors (and Toys "R" Us) were unprepared for the magnitude of the response to the promotion.

Increase Store Traffic. Retailers can increase store traffic through special promotions or events. Door-prize drawings, parking-lot sales, or live radio broadcasts from the store are common sales promotion traffic builders. Burger King has become a leader in building traffic at its 6,500 outlets with special promotions tied to Disney movie debuts. Beginning in 1991 with a *Beauty and the Beast* tie-in promotion, Burger King has set records for generating store traffic with premium giveaways. The *Pocahontas* campaign distributed 55 million toys and glasses. A promotion tie-in with Disney's enormously successful film *Toy Story* resulted in 50 million toys, based on the film's characters, being given away in $1.99 Kids Meals. Manufacturers can also design sales promotions that increase store traffic for retailers. A promotion that generates a lot of interest within a target audience can drive consumers to retail outlets.

23.   Lee Duffey, "Sweet Talk: Promotions Position Candy Company," *Marketing News,* March 30, 1998, 11.

Trade-Market Sales Promotion Techniques. The sales promotion techniques used with the trade are incentives, allowances, trade shows, sales training programs, and cooperative advertising.

Incentives. Incentives to members of the trade include a variety of tactics not unlike those used in the consumer market. Awards in the form of travel, gifts, or cash bonuses for reaching targeted sales levels can induce retailers and wholesalers to give a firm's brand added attention. Consider this incentive ploy: The Volvo national sales manager put together an incentive program for dealerships, in which the leading dealership in the nation won a trip to the Super Bowl including dinner with Hall of Fame footballer Lynn Swann.[24] But the incentive does not have to be large or expensive to be effective. Weiser Lock offered its dealers a Swiss Army knife with every dozen cases of locks ordered. The program was a huge success. A follow-up promotion featuring a Swiss Army watch was an even bigger hit. And firms are finding that Web-based incentive programs can be highly effective as well. When the sales manager at Netopia, a manufacturer of broadband equipment, wanted to offer an incentive to dealers, he did *not* want to manage the whole process. The solution? Implement innergE, an online incentive-management program that features a Web site where salespeople can track their progress and claim their rewards.[25]

Another form of trade incentive is referred to as push money. **Push money** is carried out through a program in which retail salespeople are offered a monetary reward for featuring a marketer's brand with shoppers. The program is quite simple. If a salesperson sells a particular brand of, say, a refrigerator for a manufacturer as opposed to a competitor's brand, the salesperson will be paid an extra $50 or $75 "bonus" as part of the push money program.

One risk with incentive programs for the trade is that salespeople can be so motivated to win an award or extra push money that they may try to sell the brand to every customer, whether it fits that customer's needs or not. Also, a firm must carefully manage such programs to minimize ethical dilemmas. An incentive technique can look like a bribe unless it is carried out in a highly structured and open fashion.

Allowances. Various forms of allowances are offered to retailers and wholesalers with the purpose of increasing the attention given to a firm's brands. Allowances are typically made available to wholesalers and retailers about every four weeks during a quarter. **Merchandise allowances**, in the form of free products packed with regular shipments, are payments to the trade for setting up and maintaining displays. The payments are typically far less than manufacturers would have to spend to maintain the displays themselves.

In recent years, shelf space has become so highly demanded, especially in supermarkets, that manufacturers are making direct cash payments, known as **slotting fees**, to induce food chains to stock an item. The proliferation of new products has made shelf space such a precious commodity that these fees now run in the hundreds of thousands of dollars per product. Another form of allowance is called a bill-back allowance. **Bill-back allowances** provide retailers a monetary incentive for featuring a marketer's brand in either advertising or in-store displays. If a retailer chooses to participate in either an advertising campaign or a display bill-back program, the marketer requires the retailer to verify the services performed and provide a bill for

---

24.   Ron Donoho, "It's Up! It's Good!" *Sales and Marketing Management*, April 2003, 43–47.
25.   Michelle Gillan, "E-Motivation," *Sales and Marketing Management*, April 2003, 50.

the services. A similar program is the **off-invoice allowance**, in which advertisers allow wholesalers and retailers to deduct a set amount from the invoice they receive for merchandise. This program is really just a price reduction offered to the trade on a particular marketer's brand. The incentive for the trade with this program is that the price reduction increases the margin (and profits) a wholesaler or retailer realizes on the off-invoiced brand.

One risk with allowances is monitoring the extent to which retailers actually use the allowance to either cover extra-effort to feature a brand or reduce prices to consumers. Procter & Gamble alone spends over $2 billion per year on trade promotions and has implemented controls to ensure that displays and other merchandising of the firm's brands are actually occurring.[26]

Sales-Training Programs. An increasingly popular trade promotion is to provide training for retail store personnel. This method is used for consumer durables and specialty goods, such as personal computers, home theater systems, heating and cooling systems, security systems, and exercise equipment. The increased complexity of these products has made it important for manufacturers to ensure that the proper factual information and persuasive themes are reaching consumers at the point of purchase. For personnel at large retail stores, manufacturers can hold special classes that feature product information, demonstrations, and training about sales techniques.

Another popular method for getting sales-training information to retailers is the use of videotapes and brochures. Manufacturers can also send sales trainers into retail stores to work side by side with store personnel. This is a costly method, but it can be very effective because of the one-on-one attention it provides.

Cooperative (Co-op) Advertising. Cooperative advertising as a trade promotion technique is referred to as vertical cooperative advertising and provides dollars directly to retailers for featuring company's brand in local advertising. (Such efforts are also called vendor co-op programs.) Manufacturers try to control the content of this co-op advertising in two ways. They may set strict specifications for the size and content of the ad and then ask for verification that such specifications have been met. Alternatively, manufacturers may send the template for an ad, into which retailers merely insert the names and locations of their stores. Just such an ad is featured in Exhibit 17.12. Notice that the James Bond and Omega watch components are national with the co-op sponsorship of the Hawaiian retailer highlighted in the lower left.

EXHIBIT 17.12

Here is a classic example of co-op advertising between manufacturer and retailer. Omega is being featured by this Hawaiian retailer in a magazine ad. Is there another form of sales promotion going on here as well?

26.   Jack Neff, "P&G Trims Fat off Its $2B Trade-Promotion System," *Advertising Age*, June 5, 2006, 8.

DOING IT RIGHT

Can You Really Do a Trade Show over the Web?

In an odd combination of IBP tools, firms are creating "virtual" booths for the Web much like those used at trade shows to get even more exposure to the business market for their brands. One compelling motivation for the virtual booth is the time and expense of sending people to "real" trade shows. The online version of trade shows are similar to those "Webinars" you hear about that bring together multiple participants, including those outside of the United States. These virtual booths and trade shows feature presentations, product displays, demonstrations, and downloadable brochures—just like the ones that take place live.

There is some question, though, whether the virtual version of the trade show will be sustained. Although the technology is there and the cost-saving incentive is there, analysts wonder whether this technique will flourish at any substantial level. One analyst summed it up this way: "Salespeople will still want to sit down and talk to people one-on-one. This [the virtual booth] may be a good way to generate leads, but you probably won't close any sales this way." But one firm that has had tremendous success is National Instruments, which runs a virtual event year round and generates sales leads from attendees.

Despite some of the drawbacks, experts suggest that if you want to give the virtual show a try, there are ways to increase your "presence" at an online show:

- Design an attractive virtual booth that draws and holds the Web visitor's attention.
- Have someone available at all times to communicate with attendees. This can be done with instant messaging or toll-free telephone access.
- Ensure technical quality and reliability. The Internet connection is the only way to communicate with virtual attendees during the trade show.

One potential boon for the virtual booth is the emergence of virtual worlds and avatars, as discussed in Chapter 16. If attendees "show up" as avatars, a company avatar can greet and communicate with them.

Sources: Ned Shaw, "Building a Virtual Booth," *Sales and Marketing Management*, July 2003, 14; Julia Chang, "Online Trading," *Sales and Marketing Management*, July/August 2007, 12.

Business-Market Sales Promotion Techniques. Often the discussion of sales promotion focuses only on consumer and trade techniques. It is major oversight to leave the business market out of the discussion. The Promotional Product Association estimates that several billion dollars a year in sales promotion is targeted to the business buyer.[27]

Trade Shows. **Trade shows** are events where several related products from many manufacturers are displayed and demonstrated to members of a trade. Literally every industry has trade shows, from ones featuring gourmet products to the granddaddy of them all, Comdex. Comdex is the annual computer and electronics industry trade show held in Las Vegas that attracts over a quarter of a million business buyers. Spending on trade shows continues to grow and now stands at about $11 billion dollars per year.[28] Advertisers are finding that a trade show is an efficient way to reach interested current and potential buyers with the brand right at hand for discussion and actual use. The Promotional Products Association reports that when a trade show visitors receive a promotional item from a firm at a trade show booth, over 70 percent of the visitors remember the name of the company that gave them the item.[29]

At a typical trade show, company representatives staff a booth that displays a company's products or service programs. The representatives are there to explain the products and services and perhaps make an important contact for the sales force. Trade shows can be critically important to a small firm that cannot afford advertising and has a sales staff too small to reach all its potential customers. Through the trade-show route, salespeople can make far more contacts than they could with direct sales calls. And speaking of making more contacts, the trade show has gone high-tech and global, as the Doing It Right box explains.

Trade shows are also an important route for reaching potential wholesalers and distributors for a company's brand. But the proliferation of trade shows has been so extensive in recent years that the technique is really more oriented to business buyers these days.

---

27. Data available at Promotional Products Association International Web site at *http://www.ppa.org*, accessed on August 5, 2007.
28. 2004 Industry Trends Report, *Promo Magazine*, 31.
29. Data available at Promotional Products Association International Web site, *http://www.ppa.org*, accessed on August 5, 2007.

Business Gifts. Estimates are that nearly half of corporate America gives business gifts. These gifts are given as part of building and maintaining a close working relationship with suppliers. Business gifts that are part of a promotional program may include small items like logo golf balls, jackets, or small items of jewelry. Extravagant gifts or expensive trips that might be construed as "buying business" are not included in this category of business-market sales promotion.

Premiums and Advertising Specialties. As mentioned earlier, the key chain, ball cap, T-shirt, mouse pad, or calendar that reminds a buyer of a brand name and slogan can be an inexpensive but useful form of sales promotion. A significant portion of the $14 billion premium and advertising specialty market is directed to business buyers. While business buyers are professionals, they are not immune to the value perceptions that an advertising specialty can create. In other words, getting something for nothing appeals to business buyers as much as it does to household consumers. Will a business buyer choose one consulting firm over another to get a sleeve of golf balls? Probably not. But advertising specialties can create awareness and add to the satisfaction of a transaction nonetheless.

Trial Offers. Trial offers are particularly well suited to the business market. First, since many business products and services are high cost and often result in a significant time commitment to a brand (i.e., many business products and services have long life), trial offers provide a way for buyers to lower the risk of making a commitment to one brand over another. Second, a trial offer is a good way to attract new customers who need a good reason to try something new. The chance to try a new product for 30 days with no financial risk can be a compelling offer.

Frequency Programs. The high degree of travel associated with many business professions makes frequency programs an ideal form of sales promotion for the business market. Airline, hotel, and restaurant frequency programs are dominated by the business market traveler. But frequency programs for the business market are not restricted to travel-related purchases. Retailers of business products like Staples, OfficeMax, and Costco have programs designed to reward the loyalty of the business buyer. Costco has teamed with American Express to offer business buyers an exclusive Costco/American Express credit card. Among the many advantages of the card is a rebate at the end of the year based on the level of buying—the greater the dollar amount of purchases, the greater the percentage rebate.

④ The Risks of Sales Promotion.

Sales promotion can be used to pursue important sales objectives. As we have seen, there are a wide range of sales promotion options for the consumer, trade, and business markets. But there are also significant risks associated with sales promotion, and these risks must be carefully considered.

Creating a Price Orientation.

Since most sales promotions rely on some sort of price incentive or giveaway, a firm runs the risk of having its brand perceived as cheap, with no real value or benefits beyond the low price. Creating this perception in the market contradicts the concept of integrated brand promotion. If advertising messages highlight the value and benefit of a brand only to be contradicted by a price emphasis in sales promotions, then a confusing signal is being sent to the market. Chrysler dealers challenged corporate management on just this point, arguing that escalating price incentives on various vehicles were "wrecking" the brand.[30]

---

30.   Jean Halliday, "Dealers: Chrysler Is Wrecking Brands," *Advertising Age*, June 12, 2006, 1, 39.

Borrowing from Future Sales. Management must admit that sales promotions are typically short-term tactics designed to reduce inventories, increase cash flow, or show periodic boosts in market share. The downside is that a firm may simply be borrowing from future sales. Consumers or trade buyers who would have purchased the brand anyway may be motivated to stock up at the lower price. This results in reduced sales during the next few time periods of measurement. This can play havoc with the measurement and evaluation of the effect of advertising campaigns or other image-building communications. If consumers are responding to sales promotions, it may be impossible to tease out the effects of advertising.

Alienating Customers. When a firm relies heavily on sweepstakes or frequency programs to build loyalty among customers, particularly their best customers, there is the risk of alienating these customers with any change in the program. Airlines suffered just such a fate when they tried to adjust the mileage levels needed for awards in their frequent-flyer programs. Ultimately, many of the airlines had to give concessions to their most frequent flyers as a conciliatory gesture.

Time and Expense. Sales promotions are both costly and time-consuming. The process is time-consuming for the marketer and the retailer in terms of handling promotional materials and protecting against fraud and waste in the process. As we have seen in recent years, funds allocated to sales promotions are taking dollars away from advertising. Advertising is a long-term, franchise-building process that should not be compromised for short-term gains.

Legal Considerations. With the increasing popularity of sales promotions, particularly contests and premiums, there has been an increase in legal scrutiny at both the federal and state levels. Legal experts recommend that before initiating promotions that use coupons, games, sweepstakes, and contests, a firm check into lottery laws, copyright laws, state and federal trademark laws, prize notification laws, right of privacy laws, tax laws, and FTC and FCC regulations. The best advice for staying out of legal trouble with sales promotions is to carefully and clearly state the rules and conditions related to the program so that consumers are fully informed.

⑤ Point-of-Purchase Advertising. From 1981 to 2008, marketers' annual expenditures on point-of-purchase (P-O-P) advertising rose from $5.1 billion to over $17 billion per year.[31] Why this dramatic growth? First, consider that P-O-P is the only medium that places advertising, products, and a consumer together in the same place at the same time. Then, think about these results. Research conducted by the trade association Point-of-Purchase Advertising International (http://www.popai.com) indicates that 70 percent of all product selections involve some final deliberation by consumers at the point of purchase.[32] Additionally, in an early study on the effects of P-O-P sponsored by KMart and Procter & Gamble, the research showed that P-O-P advertising boosted the sales of coffee, paper towels, and toothpaste by 567 percent, 773 percent, and 119 percent, respectively.[33] With results like these, it is plain to see why P-O-P advertising is one of the fastest-growing categories in today's marketplace.

---

31. Data available at Promotional Products Association International Web site at *http://www.ppa.org*, accessed on August 5, 2007.
32. Data on point-of-purchase decision making cited in Kate Fitzgerald, "In-Store Media Ring Cash Register," *Advertising Age*, February 9, 2004, 43–45.
33. Data cited in Lisa Z. Eccles, "P-O-P Scores with Marketers," *Advertising Age*, September 26, 1994.

Point-of-Purchase Advertising Defined.
Point-of-purchase (P-O-P) advertising refers to materials used in the retail setting to attract shoppers' attention to a brand, convey primary brand benefits, or highlight pricing information. P-O-P displays may also feature price-off deals or other consumer sales promotions. A corrugated-cardboard dump bin and an attached header card featuring the brand logo or related brand information can be produced for pennies per unit. When the bin is filled with a brand and placed as a freestanding display at retail, sales gains usually follow. Marketers clearly believe in the power of P-O-P; spending on P-O-P is second only to event and premiums/incentives spending.

As an example of the kind of impact P-O-P advertising can have, a dump bin with tower display was designed for Nabisco's Barnum's Animals crackers. This colorful 76-inch-tall cardboard tower spent 14 weeks in design before being mass-produced and rolled out across the country. The gorilla towers, along with their tiger and elephant predecessors, hold small boxes of animal crackers and are the cornerstone of the advertising strategy for Barnum's. The display had a significant positive impact on sales.[34] Effective deployment of P-O-P advertising requires careful coordination with the marketer's sales force. Gillette found this out when it realized it was wasting money on lots of P-O-P materials and displays that retailers simply ignored.[35] Gillette sales reps visit about 20,000 stores per month, and are in a position to know what retailers will and will not use. Gillette's marketing executives finally woke up to this fact when their sales reps told them, for example, that 50 percent of the shelf signs being shipped to retailers from three separate suppliers were going directly to retailers' garbage bins. Reps helped redesign new display cards that mega-retailers such as Wal-Mart approved for their stores and immediately put into use. Now any time Gillette launches a new P-O-P program, it tracks its success carefully.[36] Having a sales force that can work with retailers to develop and deliver effective P-O-P programs is a critical element for achieving integrated brand promotion.

Objectives for Point-of-Purchase Advertising.
The objectives of point-of-purchase advertising are similar to those for sales promotion. The goal is to create a short-term impact on sales while preserving the long-term image of the brand being developed and maintained by advertising for the brand. Specifically, the objects for sales promotion are as follows:

- Draw consumers' attention to a brand in the retail setting.
- Maintain purchase loyalty among brand-loyal users.
- Stimulate increased or varied usage of the brand.
- Stimulate trial use by users of competitive brands.

These objectives are self-explanatory and follow closely on the objects of sales promotion. Key to the effective use of P-O-P is to maintain the brand image being developed by advertising.

Types of Point-of-Purchase Advertising and Displays.
A myriad of displays and presentations are available to marketers. P-O-P materials generally fall into two categories: **short-term promotional displays**, which are used for six months or less, and **permanent long-term displays**, which are intended to provide point-of-purchase presentation for more than six months. Within these two categories, marketers have a wide range of choices:[37]

---

34.   Yumiko Ono, "'Wobblers' and 'Sidekicks' Clutter Stores, Irk Retailers," *Wall Street Journal*, September 8, 1998, B1.

35.   Nicole Crawford, "Keeping P-O-P Sharp," *Promo Magazine*, January 1998, 52, 53.

36.   Neff, "P&G Trims Fat off Its $2B Trade-Promotion System."

37.   *Retailer Guide to Maximizing In-Store Advertising Effectiveness* (Washington, DC: Point-of-Purchase Advertising International, 1999), 5–7

EXHIBIT 17.13

Displays at a cash register checkout lane are designed to sell impulse items such as candy, or easily forgotten items such as batteries.

EXHIBIT 17.14

End-of-aisle displays provide space to draw attention to a large display of product.

EXHIBIT 17.15

A shopping-cart ad carries an immediate message to shoppers.

- *Window and door signage:* Any sign that identifies and/or advertises a company or brand or gives directions to the consumer.
- *Counter/shelf unit:* A smaller display designed to fit on counters or shelves.
- *Floor stand:* Any P-O-P unit that stands independently on the floor.
- *Shelf talker:* A printed card or sign designed to mount on or under a shelf.
- *Mobile/banner:* An advertising sign suspended from the ceiling of a store or hung across a large wall area.
- *Cash register:* P-O-P signage or small display mounted near a cash register designed to sell impulse items such as gum, lip balm, or candy, as in Exhibit 17.13.
- *Full line merchandiser:* A unit that provides the only selling area for a manufacturer's line. Often located as an end-of-aisle display.
- *End-of-aisle display/gondola:* Usually a large display of products placed at the end of an aisle, as in Exhibit 17.14.
- *Dump bin:* A large bin with graphics or other signage attached.
- *Illuminated sign:* Lighted signage used outside or in-store to promote a brand or the store.
- *Motion display:* Any P-O-P unit that has moving elements to attract attention.
- *Interactive unit:* A computer-based kiosk where shoppers get information such as tips on recipes or how to use the brand. Can also be a unit that flashes and dispenses coupons.
- *Overhead merchandiser:* A display rack that stocks product and is placed above the cash register. The cashier can reach the product for the consumer. The front of an overhead merchandiser usually carries signage.
- *Cart advertising:* Any advertising message adhered to a shopping cart, as in Exhibit 17.15.
- *Aisle directory:* Used to delineate contents of a store aisle; also provides space for an advertising message.
- *Retail digital signage:* The newest P-O-P device available is retail digital signage. These are video displays that have typically been ceiling- or wall-mounted and are now being moved to end-of-aisle caps or given strategic shelf placement to relay special pricing or new product introductions.[38]

This array of in-store options gives marketers the opportunity to attract shoppers' attention, induce purchase, and provide reinforcement for key messages that are being conveyed through other components of the advertising plan. Retailers are increasingly looking to P-O-P displays as ways to differentiate and provide ambience for their individual stores, which means that the kind of displays valued by Wild Oats versus Walgreens versus Albertson's versus Target (to name just a few) will often vary considerably. Once again, it is the marketer's field sales force that will be critical in developing the right P-O-P alternative for each retailer stocking that marketer's products. Without the retailers' cooperation, P-O-P advertising has virtually no chance to work its magic.

38.   Dale Smith, "Coming Down to Eye Level," *Marketing at Retail*, June 2007, 28–31.

P-O-P Advertising and the Trade and Business Markets. While we have focused our discussion of the use of point-of-purchase advertising as a technique to attract consumers, this promotional tool is also strategically valuable to manufacturers as they try to secure the cooperation in the trade and business markets. Product displays and information sheets often encourage retailers to support one distributor or manufacturer's brand over another. P-O-P promotions can help win precious shelf space and exposure in a retail setting. From a retailer's perspective, a P-O-P display can enhance the atmosphere of the store and make the shopping experience easier for customers. Brand manufacturers and distributors obviously share that interest. When the retailer is able to move a particular brand off the shelf, that in turn, positively affects both the manufacturer and distributor's sales. Over $18.8 billion was invested in on P-O-P materials in 2006—a 9.6 percent increase since 2003. This is more than was spent on either magazine or radio advertising.[39]

In an attempt to combat the threat of losing business to online shopping, retailers are trying to enliven the retail environment, and point-of-purchase displays are part of the strategy. Distributors and retailers are trying to create a better and more satisfying shopping experience. The president of a large display company says, "We're trying to bring more of an entertainment factor to our P-O-P programs."[40]

6 Support Media.
This section discusses traditional support media: outdoor signage and billboard advertising, transit and aerial advertising, directory advertising, and packaging. We placed this section in this chapter because these supportive IBP tools are more similar to sales promotion and point-of-purchase devices than they are to the major media covered in Chapters 14–16.

Support media are used to reinforce or supplement a message being delivered via some other media vehicle; hence the name *support media*. Exhibits 17.16 and 17.17

EXHIBIT 17.16

*Brands like Adidas need to be in constant contact with the sports fan. In this case Adidas delivers its "forever sport" mantra through a print ad that appeared in the college football preview issue of **Sports Illustrated**. Hence the first line of copy: "Leaves that let you know it's football season."*

EXHIBIT 17.17

Here we see the Adidas logo providing the backdrop for everyday life in a building-side billboard. Note how this support media vehicle—the billboard—supports the print media message in Exhibit 17.16.

39.   Data available at Promotional Products Association International Web site at *http://www.ppa.org*, accessed on August 5, 2007
40.   2004 Industry Trends Report, *Promo Magazine*.

show a pair of ads for Adidas, with the outdoor signage supporting the print campaign. Support media are especially productive when used to deliver a message near the time or place where consumers are actually contemplating product selections (e.g., imagine that building in Exhibit 17.17 as a Foot Locker store). Since these media can be tailored to local markets, they can have value to any organization that wants to reach consumers in a particular venue, neighborhood, or metropolitan area.

Outdoor Signage and Billboard Advertising. Billboards, posters, and outdoor signs are perhaps the oldest advertising form. Posters first appeared in North America not as promotional pieces, but rather were used during the Revolutionary War to keep the civilian population informed about the war's status. In the 1800s, they became a promotional tool, with circuses and politicians among the first to adopt this new medium. Exhibit 17.18 shows a classic ad execution for "The Greatest Show on Earth."

Today, the creative challenge posed by outdoor advertising is as it has always been—to grab attention and communicate with minimal verbiage and striking imagery, as does the billboard in Exhibit 17.19.

In recent years total spending on outdoor advertising in the United States has been growing steadily since 2003 and now exceeds $7 billion per year.[41] Outdoor advertising offers several distinct advantages.[42] This medium provides an excellent means to achieve wide exposure of a message in specific local markets. Size is, of course, a powerful attraction of this medium, and when combined with special lighting and moving features, billboards can be captivating. Billboards created for a retail store in Minneapolis have even wafted a mint scent throughout the city as part of a candy promotion for Valentine's Day.[43] Billboards also offer around-the-clock exposure for an advertiser's message and are well suited to showing off a brand's distinctive packaging or logo.

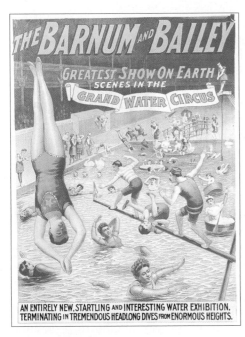

EXHIBIT 17.18

Advertising in the United States began with posters and billboards. Circuses were the early pioneers in this medium. http://www.ringling.com

EXHIBIT 17.19

Minimal verbiage is one key to success with billboard advertising. This example easily satisfies the minimal-verbiage rule. http://www.horst-salons.com

41.   2007 Marketing Fact Book, *Marketing News*, July 15, 2007, 29.

42.   Jack Z. Sissors and Lincoln Bumba, *Advertising Media Planning* (Lincolnwood, IL: NTC Business Books, 1996).

43.   Ronald Grover, "Billboards Aren't Boring Anymore," *BusinessWeek*, September 21, 1998, 88–89

EXHIBIT 17.20

Here is a clever example of how a billboard can deliver the right message at the right time.

Billboards are especially effective when they reach viewers with a message that speaks to a need or desire that is immediately relevant. For instance, they are commonly deployed by fast-food restaurants along major freeways to help hungry travelers know where to exit to enjoy a Whopper or Big Mac. Exhibit 17.20 features a clever example of putting outdoor signage in the right place at the right time to maximize its appeal. The product categories that rely most heavily on outdoor advertising are local services (like gas stations), real estate and insurance companies, hotels, financial institutions and automobile dealers and services.[44]

Billboards have obvious drawbacks. Long and complex messages simply make no sense on billboards; some experts suggest that billboard copy should be limited to no more than six words. Additionally, the impact of billboards can vary dramatically depending on their location, and assessing locations is tedious and time-consuming. To assess locations, companies may have to send individuals to the site to see if the location is desirable. This activity, known in the industry as **riding the boards**, can be a major investment of time and money. Moreover, the Institute of Outdoor Advertising has rated billboards as expensive in comparison to several other media alternatives.[45] Considering that billboards are constrained to short messages, are often in the background, and are certainly not the primary focus of anyone's attention, their costs may be prohibitive for many advertisers.

Despite the cost issue, and frequent criticism by environmentalists that billboards represent a form of visual pollution, there are advocates for this medium who contend that important technological advances will make outdoor advertising an increasingly attractive alternative in the future. The first of these advances offers the prospect of changing what has largely been a static medium to a dynamic medium with heretofore-unimagined possibilities. Digital and wireless technologies have found their way to billboards with remarkable consequences. Both Google and Microsoft are experimenting with digital technology to make billboards a more targeted medium.[46] Digital billboard displays let advertisers rotate their messages on a board at different times during the day. This capability is especially appealing to local marketers—like

---

44.   Data on outdoor advertising categories obtained from Outdoor Advertising Association of America Web site, *http://www.oaaa .org*, accessed on August 4, 2007.
45.   Sissors and Bumba, *Advertising Media Planning*.
46.   Andrew Hampp, "What Are Online Giants Doing in Out-of-Home?" *Advertising Age*, January 29, 2007, 30.

This wonderful old building has a big, flat backside, facing a major interstate freeway. No wonder the Gap wants to keep it in jeans. Does the Gap site (http://www.gap.com) show signs of integrated brand promotion?

Happy Berliners enjoy their Cokes at three degrees Celsius while waiting on the U-bahn (subway).

The story is the same all over the world. Mass transit has become an advertising vehicle too. Can you identify this European city?
http://www.converse.com

television stations and food sellers—whose businesses are very time sensitive. For example, FreshDirect uses this technology to change the messaging for its food-delivery service—morning, noon, and night—on the billboard outside New York City's Queens Midtown Tunnel. Ultimately, billboard time may be sold in day-parts like radio or television, making them more appealing to time-sensitive advertisers.

Another key development that also features amazing technology entails a testing system to profile the people who see a billboard in any given day.[47] For the past 70 years the only information available to assess the impact of billboard advertising came from raw traffic counts. Now, Nielsen Outdoor, part of the company known for rating television viewer-ship, has developed a system using GPS satellites to track minute-by-minute movements in the "impact zone" of a billboard. Drivers in the Nielsen panel are paid a small stipend to have their latitude and longitude recorded by GPS every 20 seconds. Nielsen also knows the demographic characteristics of its panel, so they can advise advertisers about the characteristics of persons who viewed a billboard at any given time. And technology now allows for complete personalization of a billboard thanks to radio frequency identification (RFID) tags—really. Mini USA is experimenting with billboards in four U.S. cities. New Mini owners have volunteered to have RFID tags installed in their key fobs; when they drive by one of the Mini billboards, a personalized message will flash to the driver—like "Have a Great Day John!"[48]

Transit and Aerial Advertising. **Transit advertising** is a close cousin to billboard advertising, and in many instances it is used in tandem with billboards. The phrase **out-of-home media** is commonly used to refer to the combination of transit and billboard advertising; this is a popular advertising form around the world. As illustrated in Exhibits 17.21 and 17.22, out-of-home ads appear in many venues, including on backs of buildings, in subway tunnels, and throughout sports stadiums. Transit ads may also appear as signage on terminal and station platforms, or actually envelop mass transit vehicles, as exemplified in Exhibit 17.23. One of the latest innovations in out-of-home media is taxi-top electronic billboards that deliver customized messages by neighborhood using wireless Internet technology.[49] We've come a long way from the circus poster.

47.   Lisa Sanders, "Nielsen Outdoor Tracks Demo Data," *Advertising Age*, May 31, 2004, 14

48.   Jonathan Mummolo, "Ads Made For You," *BusinessWeek*, March 5, 2007.

49.   Stephen Freitas, "Evolutionary Changes in the Great Outdoors," *Advertising Age*, June 9, 2003, C4

ETHICS

"Street Furniture" Means Big Bucks for Someone

The idea of "street furniture" started in Europe, but is catching on fast in North America. San Francisco, Los Angeles, and Chicago all have street furniture deals. But the biggest prize is New York City. The city has called for proposals to redesign all the city's street furniture to make it a more productive venue for selling ad space. The request for proposals called for the winning bidder to redesign, install, and maintain 3,300 bus-stop shelters, 20 self-cleaning automatic public toilets, 330 newsstands, and a variety of other "public-service structures" like trash cans and information kiosks. New York City is looking for a 20-year deal. Why would anyone want to take on such a task? Well, those in the know estimate that the city's street furniture will generate a *billion* dollars in ad revenue over the life of the contract.

The opportunity has attracted all the big players in outdoor ad media. There is JCDecaux, the French firm that first conceived the premise of street furniture in 1964. Clear Channel Communications is also a player with big plans for customizing the look of each structure to reflect the unique architecture in New York City's many neighborhoods. And Viacom, which previously controlled transit ad space in New York City, definitely knows the value of reaching its legion of commuters. Each hired well-connected lobbyists to help pitch their proposals to City Hall.

For overseeing this street furniture project, one of these media companies stands to gain a major new source of advertising revenue. The City of New York is a winner as well, because around 30 percent of the revenue will be the city's take. But not everyone will profit from the new arrangement. In particular, the Newsstand Operators Association isn't pleased and has threatened to sue the city to thwart the deal. Independent newsstand owners basically will be put out of business if the program isn't amended with them in mind since the proposal calls for city-owned newsstands. As the association's lawyer noted, "We are not too pleased with the scheme. It will transfer ownership of newsstands from private mom-and-pop operations to large corporations with no compensation to us." Until the matter is settled, probably in the courts, New York City's commuters will just have to wait for their bus at a bus stop, perhaps unaware that one day they'll have "street furniture."

What do you think? Should New York City own the newsstands to get the advertising revenue? Would you vote to keep the independent newsstands or is it time for the Big Apple to move on with a more modern approach?

Sources: Lisa Sanders, "Gimme Shelter: NYC Seeks Ad Sites," **Advertising Age**, April 5, 2004, 3; Erin White, "Companies to Bid for Bus-Stop Ads," **Wall Street Journal**, April 7, 2004, B3.

Transit advertising is especially valuable when an advertiser wishes to target adults who live and work in major metropolitan areas. The medium reaches people as they travel to and from work, and because it taps into daily routines repeated week after week, transit advertising offers an excellent means for repetitive message exposure. In large metro areas such as New York City—with its 200 miles of subways and 3 million subway riders—transit ads can reach large numbers of individuals in a cost-efficient manner. The once-utilitarian bus stop has also become big business, with all the usual complications, as outlined in the Ethics box.

When working with this medium, an advertiser may find it most appropriate to buy space on just those train or bus lines that consistently haul people belonging to the demographic segment being targeted. This type of demographic matching of vehicle with target audience derives more value from limited ad budgets. Transit advertising can also be appealing to local merchants because their messages may reach a passenger as he or she is traveling to a store to shop.

Transit advertising works best for building or maintaining brand awareness. But, as with outdoor billboards, lengthy or complex messages simply cannot be worked into this medium. Also, transit ads can easily go unnoticed in the hustle and bustle of daily life. People traveling to and from work via a mass transit system are certainly one of the hardest audiences to engage with an advertising message. They can be bored, exhausted, absorbed by their thoughts about the day, or occupied by some other medium. Given the static nature of a transit poster, breaking through to a harried commuter can be a tremendous challenge.

When advertisers can't break through on the ground or under the ground, they can always look to the sky. **Aerial advertising** can involve airplanes pulling signs or banners, skywriting, or those majestic blimps. For several decades, Goodyear had blimps all to itself; now, the availability of smaller, less-expensive blimps has made this medium more popular to advertisers. For example, Virgin Lightships has created a fleet of small blimps that can be rented for advertising purposes for around $200,000 per month. Aerial billboards, pulled by small planes or jet helicopters equipped with screeching loudspeakers (bring back any spring break memories?), have also proliferated in recent years, as advertisers look for new ways to connect with consumers.[50]

Sanyo, Fuji Photo, MetLife, Outback Steakhouse, and Anheuser-Busch have clearly bought into the appeal of an airborne brand presence by launching blimps. The Family Channel has also been a frequent user of Virgin Lightships' mini-blimps at sporting events such as the Daytona 500 NASCAR race. A recall study done after one such event showed that 70 percent of target consumers remembered the Family Channel as a result of the blimp flyovers.[51] Blimps carrying television cameras at sporting events also provide unique video that can result in the blimp's sponsor getting several on-air mentions. This brand-name exposure comes at a fraction of the cost of similar exposure through television advertising.

When a medium proves itself, more and more marketers will want it in their media mix. Of course, the irony is that as a medium becomes more attractive and hence cluttered, its original appeal begins to be diluted. We already see this occurring with aerial advertising. With more and more blimps showing up at sporting events, networks can be choosy about which one gets the coveted on-air mention, even demanding that blimp sponsors carry an overhead camera for the network's benefit and purchase advertising time during the event in exchange for the mention. Additionally, the sportscasters' casual banter about the beautiful overhead shots from so-and-so's wonderful blimp has now been replaced by scripted commentary that is written out in advance as part of the advertising contract.[52]

Directory Advertising. The last time you reached for a phone directory to appraise the local options for Chinese or Mexican food, you probably didn't think about it as a traditional support medium. However, Yellow Pages advertising plays an important role in the media mix for many types of organizations, as evidenced by the $16 billion spent in this medium annually.[53] A wealth of current facts and figures about this media option are available from the Yellow Pages Association's Web site, http://www.buyyellow.com.

A phone directory can play a unique and important role in consumers' decision-making processes. While most support media keep the brand name or key product information in front of a consumer, Yellow Pages advertising helps people follow through on their decision to buy. By providing the information that consumers need to actually find a particular product or service, the Yellow Pages can serve as the final link in a buying decision. Because of their availability and consumers' familiarity with this advertising tool, Yellow Pages directories provide an excellent means to supplement awareness-building and interest-generating campaigns that an advertiser might be pursuing through other media.

On the downside, the proliferation and fragmentation of phone directories can make this a challenging medium to work in. Many metropolitan areas are covered by multiple directories, some of which are specialty directories designed to serve specific neighborhoods, ethnic groups, or interest groups. Selecting the right set of directories to get full coverage of large sections of the country can be a daunting task. Thus, of the $16 billion spent in this medium annually, less than $2 billion is from

50.   Barry Newman, "Sky-Borne Signs Are on the Rise as Most Ad Budgets Take a Dive," *Wall Street Journal*, August 27, 2002, B3.
51.   Fara Warner, "More Companies Turn to Skies as Medium to Promote Products," *Wall Street Journal*, January 5, 1995, B6.
52.   Bill Richards, "Bright Idea Has Business Looking Up for Ad Blimps," *Wall Street Journal*, October 14, 1997, B1
53.   2007 Marketing Fact Book, *Marketing News* July 15, 2007, 29.

advertisers looking for national coverage.[54] Additionally, working in this medium requires long lead times; and over the course of a year, information in a Yellow Pages ad can easily become dated. There is also limited flexibility for creative execution in the traditional paper format.

Growth of the Internet was once viewed as a major threat to providers of paper directories. Many Web sites such as Switchboard (http://www.switchboard.com) and Superpages (http://www.superpages.com) provide online access to Yellow Pages–style databases that allow individualized searches at one's desktop. Other high-profile players such as Yahoo! and AOL have also developed online directories as components of their service offerings for Web surfers. But as it turns out, consumers still want their old-style Yellow Pages; market research has established that people who spend the most time on the Internet searching for addresses and phone numbers are the same people who make heavy use of paper directories.[55] When people are in an information-gathering mode, they commonly use multiple media. So, thus far the Internet has been more of an opportunity than a threat for Yellow Pages publishers, and "old-fashioned" Yellow Pages directories continue to produce something that has been hard to find on the Web—profitability!

Packaging. Why consider the brand package as an element of support media? It is not a "medium" in the classic sense, but it carries important brand information nonetheless, and that information carries a message. Classic quotes from consultants describe packaging as "the last five seconds of marketing" and "the first moment of truth."[56] While the basic purpose of packaging seems fairly obvious, it can also make a strong positive contribution to the promotional effort. One of the best historical incidents of the power of packaging is when Dean Foods created the "Milk Chug," the first, stylish, single-serving milk package. Dean Foods officials noted that "One thing milk didn't have was the 'cool' factor like Pepsi and Coke."[57] Twelve months after introduction of the new package, sales of white milk increased 25 percent and chocolate and strawberry flavors saw increases as much as 50 percent. Additionally, the Point-of-Purchase Advertising Institute has research to show that more than 70 percent of supermarket purchases now result from in-store decisions.[58] In the simplest terms, **packaging** is the container or wrapping for a product. As Exhibit 17.24 demonstrates, packaging adds another strategic dimension and can serve an important role in IBP.

Promotional Benefits of Packaging to the Advertiser. Packaging provides several strategic benefits to the brand manufacturer. First, there is a general effect on IBP strategy. The package carries the brand name and logo and communicates the name and symbol to a consumer. In the myriad of products displayed at the retail level, a well-designed package can attract a buyer's attention and induce the shopper to more carefully examine the product. Several firms attribute renewed success of their brands to package design changes. Kraft Dairy Group believes that significant package changes helped its Breyer's ice cream brand make inroads in markets west of the Mississippi. A package consulting firm came up with a package with a black background, a radically different look for an ice cream product.

54. Lisa Sanders, "Major Marketers Turn to Yellow Pages," *Advertising Age,* March 8, 2004, 4, 52.

55. Bradley Johnson, "Yellow Pages Deals Red Hot as Telecom Industry Regroups," *Advertising Age,* January 6, 2003, 4, 20.

56. Don Hootstein, "Standing Out in the Aisles," *Marketing at Retail,* June 2007, 22–24.

57. Catherine Arnold, "Way Outside the Box," *Marketing News,* June 23, 2003, 13–14.

58. *An Integrated Look at Integrated Marketing: Uncovering P.O.P.'s Role as the Last Three Feet in the Marketing Mix,* (Washington, DC: Point-of-Purchase Advertising Institute, 2000), 10.

EXHIBIT 17.24

An attractive, attention-grabbing package serves important IBP purposes. Crayons has developed a package for its all-natural fruit juice drink that reflects the quality and excitement of the brand.

Additional value of packaging has to do with creating a perception of value for the product—remember that the "value" message is a key part of IBP communication. The formidable packaging surrounding computer software is made more substantial simply to add tangibility to an intangible product. Similarly, when consumers are buying image, the package must reflect the appropriate image. The color, design, and shape of a package have been found to affect consumer perceptions of a brand's quality, value, and image.[59] Perrier, one of the most expensive bottled waters on the market, has an aesthetically pleasing bottle compared to the rigid plastic packages of it competitors. Perfume manufacturers often have greater packaging costs than product costs to ensure that the product projects the desired image.

When Support Media Are More Than Support Media.

There will be times when the capabilities and economies of support media lead them to be featured in a company's media plan. Obviously, in such instances, it would be a misnomer to label them as merely "supportive." Out-of-home media used creatively and focused in major metropolitan markets are especially effective in this regard. A couple of examples should make this point clear.

Altoids, "the curiously strong mints" made in England since 1780, used out-of-home media to invigorate its brand in 12 major U.S. cities. Altoids' target segment of young, socially active adults living in urban neighborhoods is very hard to reach with traditional broadcast or print advertising. Perhaps they are just too busy being socially active. But using geodemographic segmentation systems like those described in Chapter 6, it is not hard to identify their neighborhoods. So Altoids and its ad agency, Leo Burnett, set out to plaster those neighborhoods with quirky advertising signage on telephone kiosks, bus shelters, and the backs of buses. In each of the 12 targeted metro areas, sales of Altoids increased by more than 50 percent.[60]

59.   Robert L. Underwood and Julie L. Ozanne, "Is Your Package an Effective Communicator? A Normative Framework for Increasing the Communicative Competence of Packaging," *Journal of Marketing Communications,* December 1998, 207–219.
60.   Brad Edmondson, "The Drive/Buy Equation," *Marketing Tools,* May 1998, 28–31

Edgy, often inexpensive promotional initiatives executed in major urban markets have become so popular that they now have their own name—**guerrilla marketing**. And many firms have adopted guerilla marketing as their primary promotional style, tailoring different executions market by market. A great exemplar of guerrilla marketing gone global is provided by Ikea, the Swedish furniture maker.[61] For instance, Ikea China, focusing on low-income customers in Beijing, transformed the elevators of 20 apartment buildings into furnished "rooms" with small cabinets, teapots, and an elevator operator handing out Ikea catalogs. The intent was to illustrate that Ikea offers many things for dressing up small spaces. Ikea Germany went a slightly different route, taking over train stations in Berlin. The walls of the dingy train stations were decorated with brightly colored fabrics and hanging lamps to make the point that any room can be brightened with a little help from Ikea. The Ikea philosophy is to use nontraditional approaches to make a big splash. That's the essence of guerilla marketing and obviously raises out-of-home media from support to a central role in the media mix.

61.   Emma Hall, "Ikea Courts Buyers with Offbeat Ideas," *Advertising Age*, April 12, 2004, 10.

SUMMARY

 Explain the importance and growth of sales promotion.

Sales promotions use diverse incentives to motivate action on the part of consumers, members of the trade channel, and business buyers. They serve different purposes than mass media advertising does, and for some companies, sales promotions receive substantially more funding. The growing reliance on these promotions can be attributed to the heavy pressures placed on marketing managers to account for their spending and meet sales objectives in short time frames. Deal-prone shoppers, brand proliferation, the increasing power of large retailers, and media clutter have also contributed to the rising popularity of sales promotion.

 Describe the main sales promotion techniques used in the consumer market.

Sales promotions directed at consumers can serve various goals. For example, they can be employed as means to stimulate trial, repeat, or large-quantity purchases. They are especially important tools for introducing new brands or for reacting to a competitor's advances. Coupons, price-off deals, phone and gift cards, and premiums provide obvious incentives for purchase. Contests, sweepstakes, and product placements can be excellent devices for stimulating brand interest. A variety of sampling techniques are available to get a product into the hands of the target audience. Rebates and frequency programs provide rewards for repeat purchase.

 Describe the main sales promotion techniques used in the trade channel and business markets.

Sales promotions directed at the trade can also serve multiple objectives. They are a necessity in obtaining initial distribution of a new brand. For established brands, they can be a means to increase distributors' order quantities or obtain retailers' cooperation in implementing a consumer-directed promotion. Incentives and allowances can be offered to distributors to motivate support for a brand. Sales training programs and cooperative advertising programs are additional devices for effecting retailer support.

In the business market, professional buyers are attracted by various sales promotion techniques. Frequency (continuity) programs are very valuable in the travel industry and have spread to business-product advertisers. Trade shows are an efficient way to reach a large number of highly targeted business buyers. Gifts to business buyers are a form of sales promotion that is unique to this market. Finally, premiums, advertising specialties, and trial offers have proven to be successful in the business market.

 Identify the risks to the brand of using sales promotion.

There are important risks associated with heavy reliance on sales promotion. Offering constant deals for a brand can erode brand equity, and sales resulting from a promotion may simply be borrowing from future sales. Constant deals can also create a customer mindset that leads consumers to abandon a brand as soon as a deal is retracted. Sales promotions are expensive to administer and fraught with legal complications. Sales promotions yield their most positive results when carefully integrated with the overall advertising plan.

 Understand the role and techniques of point-of-purchase advertising.

Point-of-purchase (P-O-P) advertising refers to materials used in the retail setting to attract shoppers' attention to a firm's brand, convey primary brand benefits, or highlight pricing information. The effect of P-O-P can be to reinforce a consumer's brand preference or change a consumer's brand choice in the retail setting. P-O-P displays may also feature price-off deals or other consumer and business sales promotions. A myriad of displays and presentations are available to marketers. P-O-P materials generally fall into two categories: short-term promotional displays, which are used for six months or less, and permanent long-term displays, which are intended to provide point-of-purchase presentation for more than six months. In trade and business markets, P-O-P displays encourage retailers to support one manufacturer's brand over another; they can also be used to gain preferred shelf space and exposure in a retail setting.

 Describe the role of support media in a comprehensive IBP plan.

The traditional support media include billboard, transit, aerial, and directory advertising. Billboards and transit advertising are excellent means for carrying simple messages into specific metropolitan markets. Street furniture is becoming increasingly popular as a placard for brand builders around the world. Aerial advertising can also be a great way to break through the clutter and target specific geographic markets in a timely manner. Directory advertising, primarily the Yellow Pages directories, can be a sound investment because it helps a committed customer locate an advertiser's product. Finally, packaging can be considered in the support media category because the brand's package carries important information for consumer choice at the point of purchase including the brand logo and "look and feel" of the brand.

KEY TERMS

sales promotion
consumer-market sales promotion
trade-market sales promotion
business-market sales promotion
coupon
price-off deal
premiums
free premium
self-liquidating premium
advertising specialties
contest
sweepstakes
sampling
in-store sampling

door-to-door sampling
mail sampling
newspaper sampling
on-package sampling
mobile sampling
trial offers
rebate
frequency programs
push strategy
push money
merchandise allowances
slotting fees
bill-back allowances
off-invoice allowances

cooperative advertising
trade shows
point-of-purchase (P-O-P) advertising
short-term promotional displays
permanent long-term displays
support media
riding the boards
transit advertising
out-of-home media
aerial advertising
packaging
guerrilla marketing

QUESTIONS

1. Compare and contrast sales promotion and mass media advertising as promotional tools. In what ways do the strengths of one make up for the limitations of the other? What specific characteristics of sales promotions account for the high levels of expenditures that have been allocated to them in recent years?

2. What is brand proliferation and why is it occurring? Why do consumer sales promotions become more commonplace in the face of rampant brand proliferation? Why do trade sales promotions become more frequent when there is excessive brand proliferation?

3. What role does sales promotion play in the trade channel and in business markets?

4. Why are sales promotions considered "risky" as an IBP tool?

5. Consumers often rationalize their purchase of a new product with a statement such as, "I bought it because I had a 50-cent coupon and our grocery store was doubling all manufacturers' coupons this week." What are the prospects that such a consumer will emerge as a loyal user of the product? What must happen if he or she is to become loyal?

6. In the chapter, it was suggested that large retailers like Wal-Mart are assuming greater power in today's marketplace. What factors contribute to retailers' increasing power? Explain the connection between merchandise allowances and slotting fees and the growth in retailer power.

7. What role does point-of-purchase advertising play as an IBP tool? In what ways can a firm ensure coordination of its P-O-P with other promotional efforts?

8. What advantages do billboards and transit advertising offer an advertiser as part of an IBP program?

9. A consumer can go to various Internet sites to find local businesses and services. Is the Internet a threat to traditional directories like the Yellow Pages?

10. How does packaging function as a support medium? What sort of "message" does a consumer get from a brand package?

EXPERIENTIAL EXERCISES

1.   Working in small teams, imagine that you have been hired by a major American automaker to design a sales promotion campaign to stimulate sales of its newly developed economy car, known as the Zoom. Identify which of the sales promotions techniques described in the chapter could be most effective and why. Your answer also should outline for the manufacturer what potential risks the firm takes in incorporating sales promotions into its broader IBP campaign.

2.   Working in the same teams, imagine that you have been hired by the Gap to develop a support media campaign in Washington, D.C., intended to stimulate sales among young professionals, ages 22 to 30. The clothing manufacturer is particularly interested in developing an edgy, out-of-home media campaign that can capture the attention of the large population of young professionals who work in the city and are frequent users of the Washington subway system. What would you develop, and why do you think it would be effective?

3.   The chapter identifies more than a dozen kinds of point-of-purchase displays, including floor stands, shelf talkers, and dump bins. With the list of examples in mind, visit any major retailer or supermarket and see how many P-O-P displays you can find. Note which advertiser uses which displays, and evaluate each display's likely usefulness as a sales promotion tool.

4.   As brand managers struggle to capture consumer attention through traditional mass media advertising, they are increasingly turning to new packaging innovations to draw consumer interest and stimulate sales. Research the packaging changes and evolution of three common items: Kleenex tissues, Pepsi soda, and Coors beer. Describe the various packaging changes experienced by each brand. What reasons might have prompted the changes? How could the packaging changes stimulate sales?

CHAPTER 18

After reading and thinking about this chapter,
you will be able to do the following:

1

Justify the growing popularity of event
sponsorship as another means of brand
promotion.

2

Summarize the uses and appeal of product
placements in venues like TV, movies, and
video games.

3

Explain the benefits and challenges of connecting with entertainment properties in
building a brand.

4

Discuss the challenges presented by the
ever-increasing variety of communication
and branding tools for achieving integrated
brand promotion.

Introductory Scenario: The Brave New World of IBP.

It's the number one question asked of New York City's finest as they patrol Times Square: "Where's the bathroom?" And in most instances, they don't have a very good answer. But during one recent holiday season in New York City, everyone had an exceptional answer. When is a perfect potty (see Exhibit 18.1) both the answer to the toughest question in Times Square and a robust brand-building tool? When you're Procter & Gamble, maker of Charmin, Puffs, Mr. Clean, Safeguard, Pampers, and Bounty.

From November 20 through December 31, 2006, the makers of Charmin gave New York City and the 15 million visitors to the "Crossroads of the World" an irreplaceable bathroom experience (code named "Charmin Restrooms"). On Broadway between West 45th and West 46th streets, the Charmin team built 20 plush restrooms complete with baby-changing stations, stroller parking, aromatherapy, and Charmin-logo city maps as take-home gifts. More than 10,000 "mega rolls" (four times the size of a regular roll!) of Charmin were stockpiled to get the party started. Flat-screen TVs showed a continuous loop of Charmin commercials, special messages, and something called the Potty Dance, for those waiting patiently for their turn on a perfect potty. Flush-O-Meters were installed to get an accurate count of usage, and for parents with kids in tow, there was a photo opportunity featuring the playful bear that stars in all Charmin ads, like the one in Exhibit 18.2.

That's not all. Street teams roamed the Times Square area on custom-outfitted Charmin Segways looking to foster interest in a restroom break, which is really easy to do when you find people who "gotta go." Additionally, for such a grand undertaking there had to be a celebrity spokesperson to cut the ribbon and execute the official "First Flush." For this high honor, the Charmin folks selected America's favorite mom, Doris Roberts, from the sitcom *Everybody Loves Raymond*. Roberts, a mother and grandmother in real life, called the facility "a modern miracle" for families touring the Big Apple.[1] New York City mayor Michael Bloomberg said of the whole thing: "Whoever thought of this should come work for my team."

EXHIBIT 18.1

Associating brands with unexpected and pleasing experiences is a great way to connect with consumers. Procter & Gamble's CEO, A.G. Lafley, has encouraged such connections for many P&G brands.

1.   Kathryn Holl and Dewayne Guy, "Charmin Restrooms Offer the Plushest Flush in Times Square," P&G press release, November 20, 2006.

EXHIBIT 18.2

No surprise that the Charmin mascot was called in to entertain as part of this unique, family-oriented, branded experience.

It did not take long for P&G, a very results-oriented company, to realize the kind of results it was looking for from this brand-building program. A variety of measures, including the Flush-O-Meter, indicated that the Restrooms program was a runaway success. Using its proprietary system to calculate the numbers, P&G claimed that 191 million media impressions were generated for Charmin in just the first 24 hours. Every major network and newspaper in New York City covered the story of the Restrooms opening, with a *New York Times* editorial calling Time Square's newest attraction "the Disneyland" of restrooms. Families from all 50 states and more than 70 countries visited the Disneyland of restrooms, at a rate of more than 10,000 per day throughout the holiday season, spending on average 21 minutes inside the Charmin-branded experience. Indeed, the Charmin facility racked up more daily visits than popular tourist landmarks like the Statue of Liberty and Rockefeller Center, making this a true brand-building extravaganza for P&G.

The Charmin Restrooms example is the perfect starter for this chapter because it exemplifies the novel means that marketers are now using to create meaningful connections with consumers. Additionally, it reminds us that the unconventional is becoming conventional, and that traditional mass media are no longer enough. As you no doubt have already recognized, perhaps in a restroom near you, advertisers are always on the lookout for new venues to advance their messages, and this can lead them to many different places. Often these efforts are directed at hard-to-reach niche markets, particularly in urban locations, where new market trends often originate. Another example that may be familiar to you involves the beaches of South Florida where students and brand builders gather every March to celebrate in the sun. The youthful crowd that gathers in this setting is of great interest to brands like MTV, Maxim, Coke, Gillette, and Axe. Brand builders are always looking to be where the action is, whether that means Panama City or New York City.[2]

This chapter discusses an array of tools and tactics that marketers are now using to create unique experiences with consumers. The array is so wide that it is not always obvious what these innovations have in common. The dynamic nature of this subject matter also means that the rules for success are hard to pin down. But a new order does appear to be emerging from this dynamic environment, built around the central premise that the fields of advertising, branding, and entertainment are

2.   "Special Report—10 Leading Brand Events," *Advertising Age*, March 19, 2007, S-1.

converging and collapsing on one another. More than ever before, brand builders want to be embedded in the entertainment that their target consumers enjoy.

This chapter assesses event sponsorship, which continues to produce impressive results and thus is receiving increases in funding from many marketers.[3] Related to event sponsorship is the latest rage in advertising circles—branded entertainment. We'll examine this "new" form of brand building and assess what's new about it. When it comes to building brands—as with the Charmin Restrooms—there are very few limits on what one can try, and quirky/edgy/off-the-wall may be just what the doctor ordered. Before we get to the specific applications, let's review briefly the forces that have sparked this brave new world of advertising and integrated brand promotion.

Why the Convergence of Madison & Vine?

As indicated by Charmin's Restrooms in the Big Apple, and the Folgers Yellow People on YouTube (see Chapter 6), and Commander Safeguard in Pakistan (see Chapter 9), and that creepy Burger King starring in his own video game (see Chapter 10), and possibly even a movie,[4] marketers around the world are receptive to many possibilities for brand building and the list continues to grow. Yet think about what all these examples have in common. Whether it's touring New York City, scanning a few videos at YouTube, watching a superhero cartoon after school, or playing "Pocketbike Racer" with the Creepy King, these brands are part of some entertainment activity. Advertising, branding, and entertainment are converging at an accelerating rate, and because of the advertising/entertainment linkage, this convergence is sometimes slotted under the heading of **Madison & Vine**, which of course refers to two renowned avenues representing the advertising and entertainment industries, respectively. Why the accelerating convergence? There are many reasons.

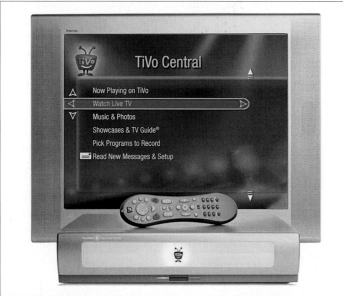

EXHIBIT 18.3

A TiVo DVR automatically finds and records your favorite shows without videotape and allows you to pause live TV, watch in slow motion, and create your own instant replays. You can also fast-forward quickly through any pre-recorded content.

An important issue propelling this search for new ways to reach consumers is the erosion in the effectiveness of traditional broadcast media. By now you have been sensitized to the many forces that are working to undermine "old school" media. One is simply a question of options. People have an ever-expanding set of options to fill their leisure time, from playing video games to surfing the Web to watching DVDs. Does anyone actually watch television any more? And if they do, there is growing concern among advertisers that soon we will all have set-top technology that will make watching TV ads a thing of the past.[5] As noted in Exhibit 18.3, TiVo Central offers an array of features, but in the minds of many, the best one is that it lets you skip commercials. The numbers tell the story. Forrester Research has predicted that DVR penetration will rise to 50

3. Jack Neff, "Specialists Thrive in Fast-Growing Events Segment," *Advertising Age,* March 19, 2007, S-2, S-4.
4. Marc Graser and T.L. Stanley, "Crispin Makes a Movie," *Advertising Age,* July 10, 2006, 1, 37.
5. Jack Neff and Lisa Sanders, "It's Broken," *Advertising Age,* February, 16, 2004, 1, 30; Julia Angwin, "In Embracing Digital Recorders, Cable Companies Take Big Risk," *Wall Street Journal,* April 26, 2004, A1, A11; Ronald Grover, "Can Mad Ave. Make Zap-Proof Ads?" *BusinessWeek,* February 2, 2004, 36–37.

percent of U.S. households by 2010.[6] Marketers claim they will dramatically reduce their TV ad buys well before then.

In the "**Chaos Scenario**" predicted by *Advertising Age*'s Bob Garfield, a mass exodus from the traditional broadcast media is coming. Shifts happen, and this one looks inevitable. According to Garfield, it will work something like this: Advertisers' dollars stop flowing to traditional media because audience fragmentation and ad-avoidance hardware are undermining their value. With reduced funds available, the networks will have less to invest in the quality of their programs, leading to further reductions in the size of their audiences. This then causes even faster advertiser defections, and on and on in what Garfield calls an "inexorable death spiral" for traditional media.[7] He predicts a brave new world where "marketing—and even branding—are conducted without much reliance on the 30-second [television] spot or the glossy [magazine] spread."[8]

As the old model collapses, billions of advertising dollars will be freed up to move to other brand-building tools. As discussed in Chapter 16, online advertising in its many forms will continue to surge because of this new money. But according to a 2007 Trendwatch survey, the brand-building options preferred by marketers as a replacement for old-school advertising comprise the brave new world of events and experiential marketing (think Charmin Restrooms).[9]

Why events and experiential marketing? Well, the reasons are many, and this chapter will explain and celebrate those reasons. But it is important to stress that the collection of tools and tactics featured in this chapter are surging in popularity not just because advertisers *must* find new ways to connect with their consumers. Event sponsorship, product placements, and branded entertainment can work in numerous ways to assist with a brand-building agenda. In theory these things can foster brand awareness and even liking through a process known as mere exposure.[10] In addition, the meaning-transfer process discussed in Chapter 5 can change people's perceptions of the brand. That is, the fun and excitement of a Panama City beach at spring break can become part of your feelings about the brands that were there with you. The brand evokes that pleasant memory. Similarly, consumers' sense of self may be influenced by the events they attend (as in a NASCAR race or a sporting event), and brands associated with such venues may assist in embellishing and communicating that sense of self.[11] But enough with the justifications for now. Let's get to the specific applications.

 Event Sponsorship. One of the time-tested and increasingly popular means for reaching targeted groups of consumers on their terms is event sponsorship. **Event sponsorship** involves a marketer providing financial support to help fund an event, such as a rock concert, tennis tournament, or hot-dog-eating contest. In return, that marketer acquires the rights to display a brand name, logo, or advertising message on-site at the event. If the event is covered on TV, the marketer's brand and logo will most likely receive exposure with the television audience as well. In 2006 marketers spent approximately $32 billion on events for which the sponsoring brand received top billing, or in essence "owned" the event. Another 13 billion was spent for events that existed on their own (e.g., college football or basketball) but marketers paid for

6.   Bob Garfield, "The Post Advertising Age," *Advertising Age*, March 26, 2007, 1, 12–14.
7.   Ibid.
8.   Ibid.
9.   Dan Lippe, "Events Trail Only Ads in Alignment with Brands," *Advertising Age*, March 19, 2007, S-2.
10.   Bettina Cornwell, Clinton Weeks, and Donald Roy, "Sponsor-Linked Marketing: Opening the Black Box," *Journal of Advertising*, Summer 2005, 21–42.
11.   Chris Allen, Susan Fournier, and Felicia Miller, "Brands and Their Meaning Makers," in *Handbook of Consumer Psychology* (Hillsdale, NJ: LEA Publishing, 2007) Chapter 31.

rights to be a branded sponsor. Spending on various types of events has been increasing at a rate of 10 to 15 percent annually.[12]

In fact, in recent years event marketing and sponsorship have been growing at twice the rate of other advertising and branding tools.[13] General Motors, one of the world's foremost old-school ad spenders, typifies the trend to events. GM has experimented with a number of ways to "get closer" to its prospective customers. Most entail sponsoring events that get consumers in direct contact with its vehicles, or events that associate the GM name with causes or activities that are of interest to its target customers. For example, GM has sponsored a traveling slave-ship exhibition, a scholarship program for the Future Farmers of America, the Woodward Dream Cruise hot-rod show, and a week of fashion shows in New York City. GM has also launched a movie theater on wheels that travels to state fairs, fishing contests, and auto races to show its 15-minute "movie" about the Silverado pickup truck. Like many marketers large and small, GM has been shifting more and more of its budget out of the "measured" media and into events and the Web.[14]

EXHIBIT 18.4

While there are no gold medals at the Flying Pig Marathon in Cincinnati (a.k.a. Porkopolis), crossing the "finish swine" at the head of the pack is still cause for a bit of snorting.

Who Else Uses Event Sponsorship? Event sponsorship can take varied forms. The events can be international in scope, as in the 2008 Summer Olympics in Beijing with big-name sponsors like Adidas, McDonald's, Samsung, Lenovo, and Visa. Or they may have a distinctive local flavor, like the Flying Pig Marathon. As shown in Exhibit 18.4, local events provide sponsorship opportunities for organizations like Mercy Health Partners and a regional office of the accounting firm Ernst & Young. Events like the Summer Olympics or the Flying Pig Marathon provide a captive audience, may receive radio and television coverage, and often are reported in the print media. Hence, event sponsorship can both yield face-to-face contact with real consumers and receive simultaneous and follow-up publicity . . . all good things for a brand.

The list of companies participating in various forms of event sponsorships seems to grow every year. Jeep, Best Buy, Reebok, Atlantic Records, Revlon, Heineken, Citibank, and a host of other companies have sponsored tours and special appearances for recording artists such as Faith Hill, Tim McGraw, Jewel, Jay-Z, Sting, Sheryl Crow, Elton John, and 50 Cent. Soon after ESPN launched the X games to attract younger viewers, a host of sponsors signed on, including Taco Bell, Levi Strauss, Kellogg's, Gatorade, and Activision. These brands were looking for benefits through association with something new and hip through a process that anthropologist Grant McCracken has labeled "the movement of meaning."[15]

And of course, the world is absolutely crazy about football—no, not that kind of football. English professional soccer has become one of the darlings of the sports busi-

12.   Neff, "Specialists Thrive in Fast-Growing Events Segment"; "Event & Sponsorship Spending," *AMA* Marketing Fact Book, July 15, 2007, 31.

13.   Neff, "Specialists Thrive in Fast-Growing Events Segment."

14.   Emily Steel, "Measured Media Lose in Spending Cuts," *Wall Street Journal,* March 14, 2007, B3; Mike Spector and Gina Chon, "The Great Texas Truck Fair," *Wall Street Journal,* October 20, 2006, B1, B10.

15.   Grant McCracken, "Culture and Consumption: A Theoretical Account of the Structure and Movement of the Cultural Meaning of Consumer Goods," *Journal of Consumer Research,* June 1986, 71–84.

PUMA is a proud sponsor of the Jamaican Athletics Federation
PUMA
puma.com

EXHIBIT 18.5

It's hard to compete with the Nikes and the Reeboks of the world when it comes to sports sponsorship. The dollars that get thrown around in this regard are simply prohibitive for some companies. But rather than abandoning sport, here we see Puma choose a different path. If all sports fans have a place in their hearts for the underdog, then perhaps it makes perfect sense to be on the sideline with teams from Jamaica.

ness because of the valuable marketing opportunities it supports. For example, Manchester United of the English Premier Soccer League surpasses the New York Yankees in its ability to generate revenues. In this world of big-time sports, global companies like Pepsi, Nike, and Vodafone pay huge amounts to have their names linked to the top players and teams.[16]

Sports sponsorships truly come in all shapes and sizes, including organizations like Professional Bull Riders and the World Hunting Association. Advertisers thus have diverse opportunities to associate their brands with the distinctive images of various participants, sports, and even nations.[17] For yet another example, examine Exhibit 18.5. What benefit might Puma be looking for as a proud sponsor of the Jamaican Athletics Federation?

Finding the Sweet Spot. A major sweet spot in event sponsorship comes when significant overlap is achieved between an event's participants and the marketer's target audience. If the event has big numbers of fans and/or participants, that's even better. Moreover, marketers stand to gain the most in supporting an event as its exclusive sponsor. However, exclusivity can be extremely pricey, if not cost prohibitive, except in those situations where one finds a small, neighborhood event with passionate supporters just waiting to be noticed. Consider, for example, the World Bunco Association (WBA), which was chartered in 1996. Bunco is a dice game, usually played in groups of 8, 12, or 16. It's especially popular with middle-aged women, sort of a ladies' version of "poker night." Bunco is a game of chance, so its leaves players with lots of time for eating, drinking, and intimate conversation about everything from a daughter's new baby to the recipe for yummy Snickers Salad (a concoction of Cool Whip, marshmallow crème, cream cheese, chopped Snickers bars, and just a touch of apple to make it good for you).

"So where is the sponsorship opportunity?" you ask. Consider a few facts: Approximately 14 million women in the United States have played Bunco and 4.6 million play regularly. Six out of 10 women say that recommendations from their Bunco group influence their buying decisions.[18] Additionally, about a third of all regular Bunco players suffer from frequent heartburn and it just so happens that 70 percent of frequent heartburn suffers are women. Can you see where this is going now?

In 2005, the makers of Prilosec OTC®, an over-the-counter heartburn medication, discovered Bunco and went to work learning about the women who play it regularly. They attended Bunco parties, listened to country music, camped in RVs, and watched a lot of NASCAR races. For starters, they entered into a partnership with the World Bunco Association to sponsor the first Bunco World Championship in 2006. With a $50,000 first prize, associated fund raising for the National Breast

16. Charles Goldsmith, "Join the Club: Thai Wants In on U.K. Soccer," *Wall Street Journal,* May 12, 2004, B1, B2.
17. Jim Hanas, "Going Pro: What's with All These Second-Tier Sports?" *Advertising Age,* January 29, 2007, S-3.
18. Ellen Byron, "An Old Dice Game Catches On Again, Pushed by P&G," *Wall Street Journal,* January 30, 2007, A1, A13.

EXHIBIT 18.6

Passionate event participants often become passionate brand advocates through their loyalty to an exclusive sponsor.

EXHIBIT 18.7

The look of a champion.

Cancer Foundation, and lots of favorable word-of-mouth from regional Bunco tournaments, the World Championships caught on fast. It wasn't long before cable TV caught Bunco fever and began covering the championship matches, where the Prilosec OTC purple tablecloths made it a branded experience. Per Exhibit 18.6, the Bunco World Tour now packs plenty of excitement, and as shown in Exhibit 18.7, provides plenty of great photo ops for Prilosec OTC.

The Bunco World Championship is a perfect sponsorship opportunity for a brand like Prilosec OTC and illustrates an ideal scenario. Again, this is a scenario where there is excellent overlap between the lifestyles of event enthusiasts and benefits that your product can deliver. Supporting Bunco allows Prilosec OTC to connect with its core customer in a fun and meaningful way, and the unique connection between Prilosec OTC and Bunco fosters brand loyalty and favorable word-of-mouth. Not surprising then that the marketing director for Prilosec OTC reports that business has responded "phenomenally" on all measures as a result of its Bunco sponsorships.

Assessing the Benefits of Event Sponsorship. In the early days of event sponsorship, it often wasn't clear what an organization was receiving in return for its sponsor's fee. Even today, many critics contend that sponsorships, especially those of the sporting kind, can be ego-driven and thus a waste of money.[19] Company presidents are human, and they like to associate with sports stars and celebrities. This is fine, but when sponsorship of a golf tournament, for example, is motivated mainly by a CEO's desire to play in the same foursome as Annika Sorenstam or Tiger Woods, the company is really just throwing money away.

One of the things fueling the growing interest in event sponsorship is that many companies have found ways to make a case for the effectiveness of their sponsorship dollars. Boston-based financial services company John Hancock has been a pioneer in developing detailed estimates of the advertising equivalencies of its sponsorships. John Hancock began sponsoring a college football bowl game in 1986 and soon after had a means to judge the value of its sponsor's fee. Hancock employees

19.   Amy Hernandez, "Research Studies Gauge Sponsorship ROI," *Marketing News,* May 12, 2003, 16; Ian Mount, "Exploding the Myths of Stadium Naming," *Business 2.0,* April 2004, 82, 83.

scoured magazine and newspaper articles about their bowl game to determine name exposure in print media. Next they'd factor in the exact number of times that the John Hancock name was mentioned in pre-game promos and during the television broadcast. Early on, Hancock executives estimated that they received the equivalent of $5.1 million in advertising exposure for their $1.6 million sponsorship fee. However, as the television audience for the John Hancock bowl dwindled in subsequent years, Hancock's estimates of the bowl's value also plunged. Subsequently, Hancock moved its sports sponsorship dollars into other events, such as the Olympics, the Boston Marathon, and Major League Baseball.

Improving one's ability to gauge the effectiveness of ad dollars spent will generally drive more spending on any IBP tool.[20] Enter a familiar player—Nielsen Media Research—and its Sponsorship Scorecard. Nielsen developed this service to in part give advertisers a read on the impact of their signage in sports stadiums. In one assessment for Fleet Bank in Boston's Fenway Park, Nielsen calculated that Fleet signage received 84 impressions of at least five seconds each during a telecast of the Red Sox/Yankees baseball game. Each impression was time-stamped as to when it appeared during the game. Factoring in the size of the viewing audience, Nielsen determined that the 84 impressions for Fleet resulted in a total of 418 million impressions among adults age 18 and over.[21]

EXHIBIT 18.8

One of the best uses of events is in reaching well-defined audiences that may be hard to reach through other channels. JBL and Trek have teamed up to support events that reach a target segment that interests them both.

As we see illustrated in both the John Hancock and Fleet Bank examples, the practice of judging sponsorship spending through **media impressions** is a popular approach. (Recall also Charmin Restrooms' 191 million media impressions on opening day.) The idea is to create a metric that lets a marketer judge sponsorship spending in a direct comparison to spending in the traditional measured media.

Adding to their appeal, sponsorships can furnish a unique opportunity to foster brand loyalty. When marketers connect their brand with the potent emotional experiences often found at rock concerts, in soccer stadiums, at the Bunco table, or on Fort Lauderdale beaches in March, positive feelings may be attached to the sponsor's brand that linger well beyond the duration of the event. Judging whether your brand is receiving this loyalty dividend is another important aspect of sponsorship assessment. As discussed in the Doing It Right box on the next page, getting a good read on the return from one's sponsorship dollars will require a mix of qualitative and quantitative approaches. This of course is true of most advertising expenditures.

Since various types of events attract well-defined target audiences, marketers should also monitor event participants to ensure they are reaching their desired target. Such is the case for the sponsors featured in Exhibit 18.8. Notice that JBL Electronics has teamed up with Trek Bikes to sponsor nationwide mountain biking events. These so-called "gravity" sports are particularly attractive to

20.   Kate Fitzgerald, "Events No Longer Immune to Marketer Demand for ROI," *Advertising Age,* March 19, 2007, S-3.

21.   Rich Thomaselli, "Nielsen to Measure Sports Sponsorship," *Advertising Age,* May 3, 2004, 14.

DOING IT RIGHT

Find the Right Balance in Assessing Events

The pressure's on. Marketers want proof. They need to be convinced that their spending for events is justified. To make such a case requires a good balance of facts and emotions.

On the factual side, marketers will need at a minimum good data on the number and types of consumers who are making direct contact with their brands at any given event. Technology, as is often the case, provides useful tools like tablet-size wireless computers that allow data collection and input by those scouting the event. Another good approach for generating the facts is the exit survey. As attendees exit, marketers can collect their impressions of the various brands sponsoring the event and ask the all-important question: Is this a brand you will recommend to a friend or family member? But never ever let technology and surveying get in the way of people enjoying the event. That's a sure way to turn your brand into the enemy.

And it's never just about the facts. Sponsorships yield their greatest benefit when they foster a relationship or deep connection between the target consumer and the sponsoring company or brand. This connection is created when the consumer's passion for the event in question (say, World Cup soccer) becomes associated with a sponsoring brand (such as Adidas, Heineken, or MasterCard). There is no guarantee that all brands will realize an emotional connection to the events they sponsor. Indeed, most won't. Although traditional evaluation tools like exit surveys and media impressions are important in assessing the value of sponsorships,

they cannot reveal deep connections. Careful listening is key to uncovering these connections.

When we know the right questions to ask, listening to the consumer can prove very rewarding. Three areas of questioning can provide important insights for evaluating the relationship-building benefits of event sponsorship. This qualitative research process should begin by exploring attendees' subjective experience of an event. Do they have strong feelings about the events they attend? What is it that ignites their passion for an event? Next, it is critical to explore whether fans really understand the role of the sponsor. Most fans know little about the benefits that sponsors provide; research has shown that the more they know, the more the sponsor benefits. Auto-racing fans have the greatest understanding of the role of the sponsor, which helps explain the eagerness of companies to get involved as sponsors of this sport. Finally, one needs to probe the issue of connection: What specific brands do people connect with specific events and how have their opinions of those brands been affected, if at all?

Tapping emotional connections requires sophisticated listening. Listen for fans' descriptions of their emotional experiences, their understanding of the role of the sponsor, and the connections they take away regarding what brands stood out as contributors to what events. Keen listening in these areas will help reveal whether sponsorships are deepening a brand's relevance and meaning in the lives of event goers. Then along with the facts; there will be a case to be made.

Sources: Julie Zdziarski, "Evaluating Sponsorships," *Promo Magazine*, March 2001, 92, 93; Kate Fitzgerald, "Events No Longer Immune to Marketers Demand for ROI," *Advertising Age*, March 19, 2007, S-3.

skeptical teens, who reject traditional broadcast advertising and are even starting to reject other forms of promotion. Their support of these sports at least puts JBL and Trek on the radar screen for this demanding audience.

Leverage, Leverage, Leverage. As noted above, one way to justify event sponsorship is to calculate the number of viewers who will be exposed to a brand either at the event or through media coverage of the event, and then assess whether the sponsorship provides a cost-effective way of reaching the target segment. This approach assesses sponsorship benefits in direct comparison with traditional advertising media. Some experts now maintain, however, that the benefits of sponsorship can be fundamentally different from anything that traditional media might provide. Finding ways to leverage the sponsorship is especially critical. Any collateral communication or activity reinforcing the link between a brand and an event is referred to as **leveraging** or activating a sponsorship.[22]

22. Cornwell, Weeks, and Roy, "Sponsor-Linked Marketing: Opening the Black Box."

Events can be leveraged as ways to entertain important clients, recruit new customers, motivate the firm's salespeople, and generally enhance employee morale. Events provide unique opportunities for face-to-face contact with key customers. Marketers commonly use this point of contact to distribute specialty-advertising items so that attendees will have a branded memento to remind them of the rock concert or their New York City holiday. Marketers may also use this opportunity to sell premiums such as T-shirts and hats, administer consumer surveys as part of their marketing research efforts, or distribute product samples. As you will see in Chapter 20, a firm's event participation may also be the basis for public relations activities that then generate additional media coverage. A checklist of guidelines for selecting the right events and maximizing their benefits for the brand are outlined in Exhibit 18.9.

EXHIBIT 18.9

Guidelines for event sponsorship.

Guidelines for Event Sponsorship

1. **Match the brand to the event.** Be sure that the event matches the brand personality. Stihl stages competitions at Mountain Man events featuring its lumbering equipment. Would the Stihl brand fare as well sponsoring a boat race or a triathalon? Probably not.

2. **Tightly define the target audience.** Closely related to point number one is the fact that the best event in the world won't create impact for a brand if it's the wrong target audience. Too often the only barometer of success is the number of bodies in attendance. Far more important is the fact that the brand is getting exposure to the right audience. This is what JBL and TREK accomplished with the mountain bike tour sponsorship.

3. **Stick to a few key messages.** Most events try to accomplish too much. People are there to experience the event and can accommodate only a limited amount of persuasion. Don't overwhelm them. Stick to a few key messages and repeat them often.

4. **Develop a plot line.** An event is most effective when it is like great theater or a great novel. Try to develop a beginning, a middle, and an exciting ending. Sporting events are naturals in this regard, which explains much of their popularity. In nonsporting events, the plot line needs to be developed and delivered in small increments so the attendees can digest both the event and the brand information.

5. **Deliver exclusivity.** If you are staging a special event, make it by invitation only. Or, if you are a featured sponsor, invite only the most important customers, clients, or suppliers. The target audience wants to know that this event is special. The exclusivity provides a positive aura for the brand.

6. **Deliver relevance.** Events should build reputation, awareness, and relationships. Trying to judge the success of an event in terms of sales is misleading and shortsighted. Don't make the event product-centric; make it a brand-building experience for the attendees.

7. **Use the Internet.** The Internet is a great way to promote the event, maintain continuous communication with the target audience, and follow up with the audience after an event. Plus, it's a good way to reach all the people who can't attend the event in person. For golf fans, pga.com gets viewers involved with each event on the PGA tour and gives sponsors another chance to reach the target audience.

8. **Plan for the before and after.** Moving prospects from brand awareness to trial to brand loyalty doesn't happen overnight. The audience needs to see the event as part of a broad exposure to the brand. This is the synergy that needs to be part of the event-planning process. The event must be integrated with advertising, sales promotions, and advertising specialty items.

Source: Laura Shuler, "Make Sure to Deliver When Staging Events," *Marketing News*, September 13, 1999, 12.

Product Placements. As noted early in this chapter, the fields of advertising, branding, and entertainment are converging and collapsing on one another. Brand builders aspire to be embedded in any form of entertainment that their target consumers enjoy. And while event sponsorship has been around for decades, brand builders are also looking elsewhere to help put on the show. Indeed, in today's world of advertising and integrated brand promotion, no show seems to be off limits. Brands can now be found whenever and wherever consumers are being entertained, whether at a sporting event, in a movie theatre, on the Internet, or in front of a TV set or video game console. If it entertains an audience, some brand will want to be there, on the inside.

Product placement is the practice of placing any branded product into the content and execution of an established entertainment vehicle. These placements are purposeful and paid for by the marketer to expose and/or promote a brand. Product placement has come a long way since E.T. nibbled on Reese's Pieces in the movie *E.T. the Extra-Terrestrial*. But that product (or brand) placement foreshadowed much that has followed. The genie, as they say, is definitely out of the bottle: Estimates suggest that advertisers' spending for product placements around the world will approach $14 billion by the year 2010.[23]

In today's world, product-placement agencies work with marketers to build bridges to the entertainment industry. Working collaboratively, agents, marketers, producers, and writers find ways to incorporate the marketer's brand as part of the show. The show can be of almost any kind. Movies, short films on the Internet, and reality TV are great venues for product placements. Videogames, novels, and magazines (or mag-a-logs) offer great potential. There may be an opportunity for a brand to be involved anywhere and any time people are being entertained.

On Television. Television viewers have become accustomed to product placements. Soap operas and reality shows have helped make product placements seem the norm on TV, and the tactic is spreading like wildfire. On Time Warner's WB network, a shiny orange Volkswagen Beetle convertible played an important role in the teen superhero drama *Smallville*. Ray Romano chased his wife around the grocery store, knocking over a display of Ragu products, in an episode of *Everybody Loves Raymond*. *Queer Eye for the Straight Guy*, on the Bravo network, has provided a bonanza of placement opportunities with brands like Amaretto, Redken, and Diesel. The final episode of NBC's long-running comedy *Frasier* included a special moment where Niles gave his brother a little gift to cheer him up. That gift? Pepperidge Farm Mint Milano cookies. The branded "special moment," like that one on *Frasier*, will only become more commonplace.[24]

There's even a school of thought contending that product placements can be television's savior.[25] Recall Bob Garfield's Chaos Scenario discussed previously in this chapter, with its "inexorable death spiral" for the traditional media like TV. So, if consumers won't watch ads on TV, why not turn the programming itself into an ad vehicle? When Simon has a sip of Coke on *American Idol*, or when contestants get rewarded with a Pringles snack on an episode of *Survivor*, these brands are in effect receiving an implicit endorsement. There were over 100,000 product placements in TV shows in 2005 and that number continues to grow robustly.[26] No telling where this trend is headed; but it is, of course, hard to put the genie back into the bottle. And maybe TV will be saved.

23.   Marc Graser and T.L. Stanley, "Study: Placements to Surge 25% in '06," *Advertising Age,* August 28, 2006, 6.
24.   Brian Steinberg and Suzanne Vranica, "Prime-Time TV's New Guest Stars: Products," *Wall Street Journal,* January 12, 2004, B1, B4; Brian Steinberg, "Frasier Finale: Amid Nostalgia, A Product Plug," *Wall Street Journal,* May 12, 2004, B1, B2; Grover, "Can Mad Ave. Make Zap-Proof Ads?"
25.   Marc Graser, "TV's Savior?" *Advertising Age,* February 6, 2006, S-1, S-2.
26.   Ibid.

EXHIBIT 18.10

The Mini Cooper launch campaign featured many innovative examples of integrated brand promotion, including a starring role in the film The Italian Job. Let's motor!

At the Movies. The "car chase" is a classic component of many action/adventure movies, and in recent years has been seized as a platform for launching new automotive brands.[27] If you'd like to immerse yourself in a superb example of branded entertainment, rent the DVD of *The Italian Job,* a movie released in 2003 starring the lovable Mini Cooper, like the one on display in Exhibit 18.10. The Mini proves to be the perfect getaway car, as it deftly maneuvers in and out of tight spots throughout the movie. BMW has been a pioneer in the product-placement genre, starting with its Z3 placement in the 1995 James Bond thriller *Golden-eye.* Pontiac re-launched its GTO brand in the 2004 made-for-TV movie *The Last Ride,* starring Dennis Hopper and Chris Carmack; Toyota tried to rev up sales of its boxy Scion brand through a featured role in the made-for-the-Internet film *On the D.L.* And Audi touted its futuristic RSQ concept car in the science fiction feature film *I, Robot.* As they say, birds of a feather flock together.

Of course it is not just automakers that have discovered product placements in movies and films. White Castle, American Express, Nokia, and the Weather Channel—to name just a few—have joined the party as well. The 2006 movie *Talladega Nights: The Ballad of Ricky Bobby,* starring Will Ferrell, featured a cornucopia of product placements for everything from Applebee's to Wonder Bread.[28] All this activity is supported by research indicating that persons under 25 years old are most likely to notice product placements in films, and are also willing to try products they see in movies and films.[29] As we have emphasized throughout, young consumers are increasingly difficult to reach via traditional broadcast media. While they are likely to soon get their fill of product placements at the movies, in the near term this looks like a good tactic for reaching an age cohort that can be hard to reach.

In Your Videogame. Speaking of reaching the unreachable, consider these numbers: According to Forrester Research, 100 million U.S. households have at least some gaming capability.[30] Moreover, most analysts conclude that around 40 percent of the hard-core players are in the 18-to-34 age cohort—highly sought after by advertisers because of their discretionary spending but expensive to reach via conventional media. Now factor in that video games are not only an attractive entertainment option but also a form of entertainment where players rarely wander off during a commercial break. With all those focused eyeballs in play, is it any wonder that marketers want to be involved? Indeed, Nielsen forecasts that spending on product placements in video games will grow from $75 million in 2005 to as much as $1 billion in 2010.[31]

27.   Marc Graser, "Automakers: Every Car Needs a Movie," *Advertising Age,* December 11, 2006, 8.

28.   Kate Kelly and Brian Steinberg, "Sony's 'Talladega Nights' Comedy is Product-Plug Rally," *Wall Street Journal,* July 28, 2006, A9, A12.

29.   Emma Hall, "Young Consumers Receptive to Movie Product Placements," *Advertising Age,* March 29, 2004, 8.

30.   David Kiley, "Rated M for Mad Ave," *BusinessWeek,* February 27, 2006, 76, 77.

31.   Ibid.

Billboard ads and virtual products have become standard fare in games like True Crime: Streets of L.A., starring Puma-wearing Nick Kang. In the Ubisoft game Splinter Cell: Chaos Theory, secret agents sneak past Diet Sprite vending machines as they track down terrorists. And Tony Hawk must be a Jeep fan, because Wranglers, Grand Cherokees, and Liberties are always on the scene in his games. Nielsen research has established that the majority of players see brand placements as adding to the quality of play, and because of the repetitive brand exposures in games, they affect purchase intent more than old-style media do. The next big thing for marketers is Web-enabled consoles that allow more dynamic ad placements and precise tracking of where and how often players pause to take a closer look.[32] Whether you call it "game-vertising" or "adver-gaming," you can expect to see more of brands like these in the virtual world: LG Mobile, Coca-Cola, BMW, Sony, Old Spice, Levi Strauss, Nokia, Callaway Golf, Ritz Bits, Target, Radio Shack, the U.S. Army, and oodles more.

What We Know About Product Placement.

The business of product placements has evolved at warp speed over the past decade. An activity that was once rare, haphazard, and opportunistic has become more systematic, and in many cases, even strategic. While product placement will never be as tidy as crafting and running a 30-second TV spot, numerous case histories make several things apparent about using this tool, both in terms of challenges and opportunities.[33]

First, product placements will add the greatest value when they are integrated with other elements of an advertising plan. No big surprise here; it's always about the synergy. As with event sponsorship, the idea is to leverage the placement. One should avoid isolated product placement opportunities and create connections to other elements of the advertising plan. For instance, a placement combined with a well-timed public relations campaign can yield synergy: novel product placements create great media buzz. In addition, a product placement can be just the right thing to complement other advertising initiatives that attend the launch of a new product. We have seen this use on numerous occasions in the launch of new car models and brands.

Also, much like event sponsorship, product placements present marketers with major challenges in terms of measuring the success or return on investment of the activity. Here again the collective wisdom seems to be that calculating media impressions for placements does not tell the whole story regarding their value. Product placements can vary dramatically in the value they offer to the marketer. One key item to look for is the celebrity connection in the placement.[34] When Tom Cruise puts on Wayfarer shades in one of his movies, the implied endorsement drives sales of the product.[35] Astute users of product placements are always looking for plot connections that could be interpreted by the audience as an implied brand endorsement from the star of the show.

Another factor affecting the value of any placement has to do with the illusive concept of authenticity. **Authenticity** refers to the quality of being perceived as genuine and natural. As advertisers and their agents look for more and more chances to write their brands into the script of shows, it is to be expected that some of these placements will come off as phony. For example, when Eva Longoria plugs a new Buick at a shopping mall during an episode of *Desperate Housewives,* the scene looks phony and contrived. No way would Longoria or her character in this TV show ever stoop to such an unflattering activity. Conversely, when Kramer argues with a homeless man in the TV show *Seinfeld* about returning his Tupperware containers,

32. John Gaudiosi, "In-Game Ads Reach the Next Level," *Business 2.0,* July 2007, 36, 37.

33. See also Cristel Russell and Michael Belch, "A Managerial Investigation into the Product Placement Industry," *Journal of Advertising Research,* March 2005, 73—92.

34. James Karrah, Kathy McKee, and Carol Pardun, "Practitioners' Evolving Views on Product Placement Effectiveness," *Journal of Advertising Research,* June 2003, 138—149.

35. Christina Passariello, "Ray-Ban Hopes to Party Like It's 1983 by Re-launching Its Wayfarer Shades," *Wall Street Journal,* October 27, 2006, B1, B4.

the spoof is perfect and adds to the comedic moment. Brands want to be embedded in the entertainment, not detract from it. This is often a difficult goal to achieve.

But like so many other things in the advertising business, success with product placements is fostered through developing deep relationships with the key players in this dynamic business. You need to have the right people looking for the right opportunities that fit with the strategic objectives that have been established for the brand. This too is not a new idea for the business of advertising. As was emphasized in Chapter 8, advertising is a team sport and the best team wins most of its games. You want to be part of a team where the various members understand each other's goals and are working to support one another. Good teams take time to develop. They also move product placement from an opportunistic and haphazard endeavor to one that supports integrated brand promotion. That's always the right thing.

In the next section we will turn our attention to branded entertainment, another topic that is closely related to everything considered in this chapter thus far. To set the stage, one way to see branded entertainment is as a natural extension and outgrowth of product placement. Branded entertainment raises the stakes but also raises the potential payout. With product placement, the question is: "What shows are in development that we might fit our brand into?" With branded entertainment, advertisers create their own shows, so they never have to worry about finding a place for their brand. This of course guarantees that the brand will be one of the stars in the show, as in the Tide car on your TV at the Lowe's Motor Speedway.

③ Branded Entertainment. For a stock-car racing fan, there is nothing quite like being at the Lowe's Motor Speedway on the evening of the Coca-Cola 600. It's NASCAR's longest night. But being there live is a rare treat, and so the NASCAR Nextel Cup Series gets plenty of coverage on television, making it among the most popular televised sporting events in North America.[36] If you've never watched a NASCAR race, you owe it to yourself to do so, because while NASCAR is all about the drivers and the race, every race is also a colossal celebration of brands. There are the cars themselves—as in Exhibit 18.11—carrying the logo large and small

There is something special in the relationship between fans and their brands at a NASCAR event. Each race is truly a celebration, with brands as co-stars of the show. View the galaxy of stars at http://www.nascar .com.

36.   Tom Lowry, "The Prince of NASCAR," *BusinessWeek,* February 23, 2004, 91–98; Rich Thomaselli, "How NASCAR Plans to Get Back on the Fast Track," *Advertising Age,* February 12, 2007, 3, 26.

Automobile racing attracts loyal fans with lots of devotion to their favorite brands. Is it any surprise that advertisers want to be part of this unique venue?

of something like 800 NASCAR sponsors. The announcers keep you informed throughout via the Old Spice Lap Leaders update and the Visa Race Break. We are told that Home Depot is the Official Home Improvement Warehouse of NASCAR and UPS is the Official Delivery Service of NASCAR. At commercial breaks there's the beer ads with Budweiser and Miller shouting at each other, and we rejoin the race to follow the Budweiser or Miller Lite car around the track. None of this comes as any surprise, because NASCAR openly and aggressively bills itself as the best marketing opportunity in sports. Said another way, a NASCAR race is a fantastic example of branded entertainment.

It's not hard to understand why NAPA Auto Parts or Budweiser, the King of Beers, would be willing to shell out millions of dollars to be a featured brand in the NASCAR Nextel Cup Series. But how is it conceivable that a company such as Procter & Gamble could justify sponsorship of the Tide Car, which you see whizzing by in Exhibit 18.12? Well, first of all, lots of women are NASCAR fans and lots of women buy Tide. Additionally, general industry research indicates that NASCAR fans are unusually loyal to the brands that sponsor cars and have absolutely no problem with marketers plastering their logos all over their cars and their drivers. Indeed, many NASCAR fans often wear those logos proudly. Moreover, the data say that race fans are three times more likely to purchase a product promoted by their favorite NASCAR driver, relative to the fans of all other sports.[37] One NASCAR marketing executive put it this way: "Our teams and drivers have done a wonderful job communicating to fans that the more Tide they buy, the faster Ricky Cravens is going to go."[38] Obviously, this entails impressing and connecting with consumers in a most compelling way, making the Tide car or the Bud car or the Viagra car or the Lowe's car all great symbols of branded entertainment.

NASCAR is truly a unique brand building "vehicle" with numerous marketing opportunities for brands large and small.[39] But we use it here as an exemplar of something bigger, something more pervasive, and something that is growing in popularity as a way to support and build brands. Although it has been called many things, we have settled on the label branded entertainment. **Branded entertainment** entails the development and support of any entertainment property (e.g., TV show, theme park, short film, movie, or

37.   Rich Thomaselli, "Nextel Link Takes NASCAR to New Level," *Advertising Age,* October 27, 2003, S-7.
38.   Lisa Napoli, "A New Era in Stock-Car Racing," *New York Times,* available at *http://www.nytimes.com,* July 14, 2003.
39.   Rich Thomaselli, "Hitch a Ride with NASCAR for Under $5M," *Advertising Age,* November 6, 2006, 4, 80.

video game) where a primary objective is to feature one's brand or brands in an effort to impress and connect with consumers in a unique and compelling way.

What distinguishes branded entertainment from product placement is that in branded entertainment, the entertainment would not exist without the marketer's support, and in many instances, it is marketers themselves who create the entertainment property. BMW's efforts in product placement versus branded entertainment provide a perfect example. The appearance of the Z3 in the 1995 James Bond thriller *Goldeneye* is a nice example of product placement. But BMW did not stop there. In 2001 BMW and its ad agency Fallon Minneapolis decided it was time to make their own movies with BMW vehicles as the star of the show. The result was a series of original, Web-distributed short films like *Beat the Devil*, starring Clive Owen, James Brown, Marilyn Manson, and most especially, the BMW Z4. The success of these custom-made BMW films helped launch the new era of branded entertainment.

Many have followed BMW's lead in developing their own forms of entertainment as a means to feature brands.[40] Goen Group has developed a reality show, the *Million Dollar Makeover Challenge,* starring its diet pill Trimspa. Unilever helped produce two specials to promote its Axe body wash that ran on MTV and SpikeTV. *The Fairway Gourmet,* featured on a PBS station near you, promoted images of the good life, courtesy of the Hawaii Visitors & Convention Bureau. By creating shows themselves (often with their ad agencies), marketers seek to attract a specific target audience with a carefully tailored story that shows their brands at their best. This is something quite different from trying to find a special place for one's brand in an existing show. As others have suggested, "clients often enter the (general) realm of entertainment marketing via small product placements that eventually develop into larger promotional programs."[41] On the path of brand building, it is natural to evolve from the simple product placement to the more elaborate enterprise of branded entertainment.

Returning to the NASCAR example, today's NASCAR racing circuit could not exist without big brands like Gillette, Budweiser, Toyota, and Tide sponsoring racing teams and their drivers. Without the brands, there would be no NASCAR. As exemplified by a NASCAR race, in today's world of brand building, it is often impossible to disentangle the brand building from the entertainment. That's a great scenario for brand builders, because, among other things, it makes their efforts TiVo-proof.

Where Are Product Placement and Branded Entertainment Headed?

It is easy to understand the surging popularity of product placements and branded entertainment. Reaching the unreachable through a means that allows your brand to stand out and connect with the consumer can only mean more interest from marketers. But there are always complicating and countervailing forces. No one can really say how rapidly advertising dollars will flow into branded entertainment in the next decade. Several forces could work to undermine that flow.

One of the obvious countervailing forces is instant oversaturation. Like any other faddishly popular promotional tactic, if advertisers pile on too quickly, a jaded consumer and a cluttered environment will be the result. As stated by a former marketing vice president at General Motors, "Any reasonable observer today has to see most of the marketing world is chasing a handful of product-placement deals. This is problematic and limiting. There just aren't enough bona fide hits to go around."[42] Some will argue that creative collaboration can always yield new opportunities for branded entertainment, but you have to acknowledge at some point that yet another motion picture featuring another hot automobile or even that Creepy King will start to feel a little stale. Indeed, we may already be there.

---

40.   Burt Helm, "Bet You Can't TiVo Past This," *BusinessWeek,* April 24, 2006, 38, 40; Louise Story, "Brands Produce Their Own Shows," *New York Times,* available at *http://www.nytimes.com,* November 10, 2006.

41.   Cristel Russell and Michael Belch, "A Managerial Investigation into the Product Placement Industry," *Journal of Advertising Research,* March 2005, 82, 83.

42.   Phil Guarascio, "Decision Time at Mad + Vine," *Advertising Age,* September 1, 2003, 15.

GLOBALIZATION

Europeans Run Hot and Cold on Product Placements

H.J. Heinz will tell you that the world is a very complicated place when it comes to the use of product placements. All you need to know about the United Kingdom is that when reruns of *American Idol* ran there, the U.K.'s Independent Television Commission made producers disguise the Coca-Cola logo on those big red cups. And when Heinz launched a cooking show called *Dinner Doctors* in the U.K., they of course had in mind featuring many of their foods products as part of the show's normal fare. The regulator's response: no way. No products could be mentioned in any part of the programming. When one Heinz executive from the home office in Pittsburgh asked, "How many times is the product shown?" he was told bluntly by Heinz's general manager of corporate affairs in Europe, "It's not shown." Why bother with such programming? Heinz does get sponsorship mentions as part of the credits, and in Britain's sparse product placement environment, apparently that's enough to generate positive feedback from consumers. Perhaps this is just another example of the "law of advertising relativity." In a sparse environment, a little bit of credit can seem like a lot.

The situation for advertisers in Spain couldn't be more different. Turns out that Spain is an advertisers dream come true. But maybe that dream is just an illusion. There is so much advertising clutter on Spanish television that is hard to argue that anyone can break through to engage the consumer. During prime time evening hours, commercial breaks can last up to 15 minutes with as many as 30 ads in a row. By the time the program resumes, many viewers can easily forget what show they were watching. A movie like *The Lord* *of the Rings* runs about three hours in the theatre, but check your program guide in Spain and you'll see it's scheduled for five hours. That's right; two hours of advertisements are embedded in a three-hour movie. Wonder how one says TiVo in Spanish?

How can an advertiser avoid the dreaded TiVo? Build your brand into the show itself. Again, not a problem in Spain. General Motors and McDonald's wanted to be part of Spain's top-rated TV show, *Aqui no hay Quien Viva (No One Can Live Here)*. The show's writers were happy to oblige. During a wedding scene on the show the bride and groom had a special surprise for their guests: They drove to McDonald's in a Hummer and ordered Big Macs, McNuggets, and of course fries, for everyone. But the home-improvement show *Decogarden* sets the standard for product placements on Spanish TV. That would be 105 placements in just four episodes running in four consecutive weeks. As expressed by the head of one ad agency in Spain: "We are a paradise for product placement."

So how about the rest of Europe? Other European countries currently fall somewhere between the two extremes represented by Britain and Spain when it comes to product placement, but the trend is toward the Spanish model. New rules from the European Union are encouraging a more open advertising environment across Europe. But don't expect a quick conversion from the Brits. As one agency executive put it: "We Brits are cynical about clunky brand communications, and as practitioners we also kick against it." It's a good bet that serving McNuggets at a wedding reception would qualify as clunky in a lot of places.

Sources: Erin White, "U.K. TV Can Pose Tricky Hurdles," **Wall Street Journal**, June 27, 2003, B7; Emma Hall, "Product Placement Faces a Wary Welcome in Britain," **Advertising Age**, January 8, 2007, 27; Aaron Patrick and Keith Johnson, "Spanish Television Reigns as King of Product Plugs," **Wall Street Journal**, February 2, 2007, A1, A16.

A related problem involves the processes and systems that currently exist for matching brands with entertainment properties. Traditional media provide a well-established path for reaching consumers. Marketers like that predictability. Branded entertainment is a new and often unpredictable path. As noted by a senior executive at Fallon Minneapolis, a pioneer in branded entertainment with BMW Films, "For every success you have several failures, because you're basically using a machete to cut through the jungle . . . with branded entertainment, every time out, it's new."[43] Lack of predictability causes the process to break down.

A soured relationship between General Motors and Warner Bros. over the promotion of the film *Matrix Reloaded* illustrates that marketers and filmmakers don't always appreciate the needs of the other. In this instance GM's Cadillac division abandoned a big-budget TV campaign associated with the sequel when it couldn't get the talent cooperation or film footage it wanted. Samsung, Heineken, and Coke also com-

43.   Kate MacArthur, "Branded Entertainment, Marketing Tradition Tussle," *Advertising Age,* May 10, 2004, 6.

plained in public about poor treatment from Warner Bros. These kinds of high-profile squabbles make big news and leave the people with the money to spend wondering whether the branded entertainment path is really worth all the aggravation.[44]

Finally, there is a concern about playing it straight with consumers. More specifically, Ralph Nader's Commercial Alert consumer advocacy group has filed a complaint with the Federal Trade Commission and the Federal Communication Commission alleging that TV networks deceive the public by failing to disclose the details of product-placement deals.[45] The group's basic argument seems to be that since most product placements are in fact "paid advertisements," consumers should be advised as such. It is conceivable that a federal agency will call for some form of disclosure when fees have been paid to place brands in U.S. TV shows, although now that the practice has become so prevalent, we expect that consumers already perceive that there is money changing hands behind the scenes. Consumers are generally pretty savvy about this sort of thing. On the global front, this can be one of those issues where you find great differences of opinion from country to country. For example, as described in the Globalization box, the Spanish approach product placements much like we in the United States do, whereas the Brits see things quite a bit differently.

What's Old Is New Again.
Some hate to admit it, but marketers, media moguls, ad agencies, and entertainers have much in common. They do what they do for business reasons. And they have and will continue to do business together. That's reality. It's been reality for decades. Smart advertisers have always recognized this, and then go about their business of trying to reach consumers with a positive message on behalf of their brands.

EXHIBIT 18.13

In the 1920s P&G was an innovator in the new medium of radio, trying to reach consumers on behalf of brands like Crisco, Ivory, and Oxydol.

No firm has managed this collaboration better over the years than Procter & Gamble, and to close this section, we take a then-and-now look at P&G initiatives to acknowledge that, while it is enjoying a huge surge of popularity recently, branded entertainment has been around for decades.

In 1923 P&G was on the cutting edge of branded entertainment in the then new medium of radio. (Try if you dare to imagine a world without television or the Internet—how did people survive?) To promote their shortening product Crisco, they helped create a new radio program called *Crisco Cooking Talks*. This was a fifteen-minute program that featured recipes and advice to encourage cooks, like the one in Exhibit 18.13, to find more uses for Crisco. While it was a good start, P&G's market research soon told them that listeners wanted something more entertaining than just a recipe show. So a new form of entertainment was created just for radio that would come to be known as the soap opera. These dramatic series used a storyline that encouraged listeners to tune in day after day. *Guiding Light,* P&G's most enduring "soap," was started on the radio in 1937. In 1952 *Guiding Light* made a successful transition to television. It thus holds the distinction of being the longest-running show in the history of electronic media.[46] One more thing—P&G has done all right selling soap (and today, many other products as well).

44.   T. L. Stanley, "Sponsors Flee Matrix Sequel," *Advertising Age,* October 13, 2003, 1, 71.
45.   Claire Atkinson, "Watchdog Group Hits TV Product Placements," *Advertising Age,* October 6, 2003, 12.
46.   Davis Dyer, Frederick Dalzell, and Rowena Olegario, *Rising Tide: Lessons from 165 Years of Brand Building at Procter & Gamble* (Boston, MA: Harvard Business School Publishing, 2004).

Following the format of many popular audience participation shows, CoverGirl asks you to help select a winner each week.

Every winner of the Top Model competition goes on to be a CoverGirl model for P&G, delivering an instant endorsement for the brand from this new celebrity.

Fast forward to the new millennium. P&G's consumer has changed. The soap opera has lost much of its traditional appeal and new forms of integrated brand promotion are necessary. Today P&G works with partners like Viacom Plus and Starcom MediaVest Group to ensure that its brands are embedded in the entertainment venues preferred by its targeted consumers. A great example is the integration of P&G's CoverGirl brand in the CW network's *America's Next Top Model,* hosted by former CoverGirl Tyra Banks. At the time of this writing this relationship had already endured through five seasons, and there were plans to do up to five more. In this CoverGirl/*Top Model* relationship, we see exemplified many best practices for branded entertainers.

An enduring relationship is clearly something to strive for. Long-term relationships beget trust, and when partners trust each other, they also look out for each other. So while P&G does not have direct control over the content of *Top Model,* it is able to ask for brand inserts and sometimes influence the show's content because of the relationship. However, P&G has learned to not push too hard to get its brand featured. That can detract from the entertainment value of the programming, which wouldn't help anyone. To maintain the right balance, the CoverGirl brand receives strong integration into the plot in just three episodes per season. But of course, online audience participation, as suggested in Exhibit 18.14, is welcomed every week.

Authenticity of the brand integration is always desirable, and CoverGirl definitely gets that on *Top Model.* For example, each season the three finalists must prepare to be photographed for a magazine ad. This is after all what models get paid to do: appear in ads. So it's perfectly natural that this is part of the show, and it's perfectly natural that the magazine ad will be for CoverGirl, as this is a brand that stands for "enhancing your natural beauty." The content of the show and the essence of the brand become completely intertwined, with an implied endorsement from America's Next Top Model, like Eva in Exhibit 18.15. It doesn't get any better in the brave new world of brand building.

4 The Coordination Challenge.

The choices for delivering messages to a target audience continue to evolve. As you have seen, marketers and advertisers are constantly searching for new, cost-effective ways to break through the clutter and connect with consumers. Today, everything from advertising in restrooms to sponsoring a marathon to adver-gaming to producing short films for the Internet is part of the portfolio.

In concluding this chapter, a critical point about the explosion of advertising and IBP tools needs to be reinforced. Advertisers have a vast and ever-expanding array of options for delivering messages to their potential customers. From cable TV to national newspapers, from high-tech billboards to online contests and giveaways, the variety of options is staggering. The keys to success for any campaign are choosing the right set of options to engage a target segment and then coordinating the placement of messages to ensure coherent and timely communication.

Many factors work against coordination. As advertising and IBP have become more complex, organizations often become reliant on diverse functional specialists. For example, an organization might have separate managers for advertising, event sponsorship, branded entertainment, and Web development. Specialists, by definition, focus on their specialty and can lose sight of what others in the organization are doing.[47] Specialists also want their own budgets and typically argue for more funding for their particular area. This competition for budget dollars often yields rivalries and animosities that work against coordination. Never underestimate the power of competition for the budget. It is exceedingly rare to find anyone who will volunteer to take less of the budget so someone else can have more.

Coordination is further complicated by the fact that there can be an incredible lack of alignment around who is responsible for achieving the integration.[48] Should the client accept this responsibility, or should integration be the responsibility of a "lead" agency? Ad agencies often see themselves in this lead role, but have not played it to anyone's satisfaction.[49] One vision of how things should work has the lead agency playing the role of an architect and general contractor.[50] The campaign architect is charged with drawing up a plan that is media neutral and then hiring subcontractors to deliver those aspects of the project that the agency itself is ill suited to handle. The plan must also be profit-neutral. That is, the budget must go to the subcontractors who can deliver the work called for in the master plan. Here again the question becomes, Will the "architect/general contractor" really spread the wealth, if by so doing it forfeits wealth? Life usually doesn't work that way. But one thing is for sure: When it is not clear who is accountable for delivering an integrated campaign, there is little chance that synergy or integration will be achieved.

Remember finally that the objective underlying the need for coordination is to achieve a synergistic effect. Individual media can work in isolation, but advertisers get more for their dollars if various media and IBP tools build on one another and work together. Even savvy marketers like American Express are challenged by the need for coordination, and especially so as they cut back on their use of the 30-second TV spot and venture into diverse IBP tools. For instance, to launch its Blue card, AmEx employed an innovative mix, starting with Blue-labeled water bottles given away at health clubs and Blue ads printed on millions of popcorn bags. The company sponsored a Sheryl Crow concert in New York's Central Park and transformed L.A.'s House of Blues jazz club into the "House of Blue," with performances by Elvis Costello, Stevie Wonder, and Counting Crows. Print ads and TV have also been used to back the Blue, but AmEx's spending in these traditional media was down by over 50 percent relative to previous campaigns. Making diverse components like these work together and speak to the targeted consumer with a "single voice" is the essence of advertising and integrated brand promotion. AmEx appears to have found a good formula: The Blue card was the most successful new-product launch in the company's history.[51]

The coordination challenge does not end here. Chapters that follow will add more layers of complexity to this challenge: Topics to come include direct marketing, personal selling, public relations, and corporate advertising. These activities entail additional contacts with a target audience that should reinforce the messages being delivered through broadcast, print, and support media. Integrating these efforts to speak with one voice represents a marketer's best and maybe only hope for breaking through the clutter to engage with a target segment in today's crowded marketplace.

47.   Don E. Schultz, Stanley I. Tannenbaum, and Robert F. Lauterborn, *Integrated Marketing Communications* (Lincolnwood, IL: NTC Business Books, 1993); Daniel Klein, "Disintegrated Marketing," *Harvard Business Review,* March 2003, 18–19.
48.   Laura Q. Hughes and Kate MacArthur, "Soft Boiled: Clients Want Integrated Marketing at Their Disposal, but Agencies Are (Still) Struggling to Put the Structure Together," *Advertising Age,* May 28, 2001, 3, 54; Claire Atkinson, "Integration Still a Pipe Dream for Many," *Advertising Age,* March 10, 2003, 1, 47; Burt Helm, "Struggles of a Mad Man: Saatchi & Saatchi CEO Kevin Roberts," *BusinessWeek,* December 3, 2007, 44–50.
49.   Joe Cappo, *The Future of Advertising* (Chicago, IL: McGraw-Hill, 2003), ch. 8.
50.   Ibid, 153, 154.
51.   Suzanne Vranica, "For Big Marketers Like AmEx, TV Ads Lose Starring Role," *Wall Street Journal,* May 17, 2004, B1, B3.

SUMMARY

 Justify the growing popularity of event sponsorship as another means of brand promotion.

The list of companies sponsoring events grows with each passing year, and the events include a wide variety of activities. Of these various activities, sports attract the most sponsorship dollars. Sponsorship can help in building brand familiarity; it can promote brand loyalty by connecting a brand with powerful emotional experiences; and in most instances it allows a marketer to reach a well-defined target audience. Events can also facilitate face-to-face contacts with key customers and present opportunities to distribute product samples, sell premiums, and conduct consumer surveys.

 Summarize the uses and appeal of product placements in venues like TV, movies, and video games.

Product placements have surged in popularity over the past decade and there are many reasons to believe that advertisers will continue to commit more resources to this activity. Like any other advertising tactic, product placements offer the most value when they are connected to other elements of the advertising plan. One common use of the placement is to help create excitement for the launch of a new product. Implicit celebrity endorsements and authenticity are key issue to consider when judging placement opportunities. High-quality placements are most likely to result from great collaboration among marketers, agents, producers, and writers. As always, the best team wins.

 Explain the benefits and challenges of connecting with entertainment properties in building a brand.

Brand builders want to connect with consumers, and to do so they are connecting with the entertainment business. While not everyone can afford a NASCAR sponsorship, in many ways NASCAR sets the standard for celebrating brands in an entertaining setting. Many marketers, such as BMW and Unilever, are now developing their own entertainment properties to feature their brands. However, the rush to participate in branded entertainment ventures raises the risk of oversaturation and consumer backlash, or at least consumer apathy. As with any tool, while it is new and fresh, good things happen. When it gets old and stale, advertisers will turn to the next "big thing."

 Discuss the challenges presented by the ever-increasing variety of communication and branding tools for achieving integrated brand promotion.

The tremendous variety of media options we have seen thus far represents a monumental challenge for an advertiser who wishes to speak to a customer with a single voice. Achieving this single voice is critical for breaking through the clutter of the modern advertising environment. However, the functional specialists required for working in the various media have their own biases and subgoals that can get in the way of integration. We will return to this issue in subsequent chapters as we explore other options available to marketers in their quest to win customers.

KEY TERMS

Madison & Vine
Chaos Scenario
event sponsorship

media impressions
leveraging
product placement

authenticity
branded entertainment

QUESTIONS

1. Read the opening section of this chapter and briefly describe the Charmin Restrooms promotion. In what ways do the Charmin Restrooms exemplify the brave new world of integrated brand promotion?

2. Who is Bob Garfield? Do you agree with his Chaos Scenario?

3. Present statistics to document the claim that the television viewing audience is becoming fragmented. What are the causes of this fragmentation? Develop an argument that links this fragmentation to the growing popularity of event sponsorship and branded entertainment.

4. Event sponsorship can be valuable for building brand loyalty. Search through your closets, drawers, or cupboards and find a premium or memento that you acquired at a sponsored event. Does this memento bring back fond memories? Would you consider yourself loyal to the brand that sponsored this event? If not, why not?

5. What lessons can we learn from Prilosec's sponsorship of the WBA regarding the things one should look for in judging sponsorship opportunities?

6. Why have video games attracted so much interest recently as a venue for product placements? What makes this venue even more appealing for advertisers as games and game players move to the Internet?

7. What is the role for celebrities in the business of product placement and branded entertainment? Describe a scene from a TV show or movie that illustrates the best way to involve a celebrity as part of a product placement.

8. Why is NASCAR a good affiliation for the Tide brand?

9. Using BMW as the example, explain the difference between product placements and branded entertainment.

10. Explain the need for functional specialists in developing IBP campaigns. Who are they and what skills do they offer? What problems do these functional specialists create for the achievement of integrated brand promotion?

EXPERIENTIAL EXERCISES

1. Product placement is the practice of embedding a branded product into the content of an entertainment vehicle, whether a television show, film, or print article. A classic example was the prominent appearance of Reese's Pieces in the movie *E.T. the Extra-Terrestrial*. For this exercise, select a favorite brand and identify placement opportunities for it in popular television series, movies, or video games. List three ways the brand could be placed naturally and explain why you think this product placement would be an appropriate and effective marketing tool for the brand.

2. Event sponsorship is becoming increasingly important to advertisers as the effectiveness of traditional media is eroded due to audience fragmentation. Event sponsorship can take many forms—it's even commonplace on college campuses. Select an example of event sponsorship at your school and describe the relationship between the advertiser and the event. What role does the advertiser perform during the event? Why would a company consider the event an effective method to reach its target audience?

3. Video-game maker Incredible Technologies Inc. has in recent years steadily expanded its corporate partnerships and product placements in its most popular game, the pub-based, Web-connected golfing game Golden Tee Live. Players can purchase Top-Flite branded virtual golfing equipment, and as they work through the course they spot Coca-Cola vending machines, billboards, and even groundhogs that pop up on the screen guzzling from a Coke can.

Working in small groups, brainstorm other possible product placement opportunities for the game and identify how they could be incorporated. Your answers should address specifically how the unique characteristics of a videogame, particularly one with a Web-linked console, support the product placement suggestions.

4. Working in the same teams, create a branded entertainment proposal for the coffee giant Starbucks. As discussed in the chapter, your proposal should identify a specific target audience and describe in detail a proposed storyline for a short film, television series, or other entertainment product that would effectively promote the brand and capture the attention of that market segment.

CHAPTER 19

After reading and thinking about this chapter, you will be able to do the following:

1

Identify the three primary purposes served by direct marketing and explain its growing popularity.

2

Distinguish a mailing list from a marketing database and review the many applications of each.

3

Describe the prominent media used by direct marketers in delivering their messages to the consumer.

4

Explain the key role of direct marketing and personal selling in complementing other advertising activities.

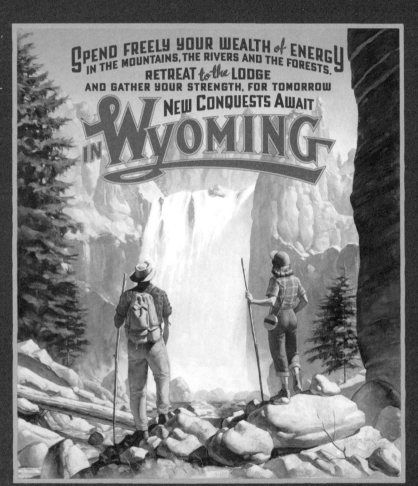

Introductory Scenario: Don't Mess with Les.

In 1958 Lester Wunderman launched a new services firm to help clients with a different style of marketing—a style he would label "direct marketing." It turned out to be a potent style and his firm prospered, changed names, and today is part of WPP Group, the global ad-agency holding company based in London.[1] Over his career Les Wunderman worked with numerous clients to help them grow their businesses. One of his success stories involved Columbia House Music Club, and a brief look back at Wunderman's work with Columbia provides instant insights regarding the unique style of the direct marketer.[2]

Wunderman had worked with Columbia for a number of years when executives at Columbia had a notion to hire another ad agency to help with the job. The other agency was McCann Erickson, renowned for its creativity and sophistication in ad development. To put it mildly, Les was not thrilled about sharing the account with McCann, but Columbia wanted something different. So Les proposed a test. He said, give me 13 cities to work in, give McCann a comparable 13 cities, and the two of us will develop and run new campaigns—winner take all. Everyone agreed a test was in order.

McCann took the classic approach of the traditional ad agency. They developed an awareness-building campaign featuring prime-time TV ads, designed to heighten familiarity with Columbia. Then, as consumers found Columbia House offers in *TV Guide* and *Parade* magazines (you know, Buy One and Get 12 FREE), the more-aware consumer was expected to jump at the offer.

Wunderman used a different approach. Rather than glitzy, prime-time TV ads, he went late night, where airtime is much less expensive (about one-quarter the cost of McCann's programming). However, the key to his plan was the "treasure hunt." In every magazine ad, Wunderman's designers incorporated a little gold box. Then, in his series of TV commercials, a critical theme was the invitation to solve the "Secret of the Gold Box" and win a prize. The gold box gave viewers a reason to look for the companion ads in *TV Guide* and *Parade* magazines. In Wunderman's words, "It made the readers/viewers part of an interactive advertising system. Viewers . . . became participants."[3] The little gold box served to "integrate" the different components of the overall campaign. That's the magic word, so you can already guess who wins this competition.

Both the McCann and Wunderman approaches showed results. Spending four times as much on prime-time media, McCann produced nearly a 20 percent increase in the sign-up rate for Columbia's Music Club. But Wunderman and his, some might say, cheesy idea of the Secret of the Gold Box generated an 80 percent increase in sign-ups. Needless to say, Les preempted the splitting of Columbia's business, and the Gold Box tactic was unveiled as part of Columbia's national campaign.

Several aspects of this story illustrate the mind-set of the direct marketer. First is simply the idea of staging a test. Direct marketers always seek to be in a position to judge results. Clients want results, and the Les Wundermans of the world recommend first going to the marketplace to see what works, and then spending the big dollars after you know the winner. Testing "in-market" is a hallmark of the direct marketer. Second, we see in the Wunderman gold box tactic keen insight about how to initiate a dialogue with the consumer. Use a little bit of mystery and throw in the prospect of winning something and consumers get interested and send you back a response. This proclivity for promoting dialogue is another defining charac-

1.   Catherine Arnold, "Up Close, Personal," *Marketing News*, February 15, 2005, 15, 16.
2.   This account is adapted from Malcolm Gladwell, *The Tipping Point* (Boston: Little, Brown and Company, 2002), 93–95.
3.   Ibid, 95.

teristic of the direct marketer's style. Getting in a dialogue with consumers leads to relationships that can mean multiple purchases over time (as in a CD/DVD club like Columbia's). And that's where the real gold lies—in those multiple purchases.

In this chapter we examine the growing field of direct marketing and explain how it may be used to both complement and supplant other forms of advertising. In addition, we conclude this chapter with a brief introduction to the field of personal selling. Personal selling brings the human element into the marketing process and shares many important features with direct marketing. For instance, as with direct marketing, an organization's sales personnel are looking to develop a dialogue with customers that can result in product sales in the short run, and repeat business over the long run. Trial purchases are a good thing, but a satisfied customer who comes back to purchase again and again (and encourages friends and family to do likewise) is the ultimate goal.

The Evolution of Direct Marketing.
This theme should be familiar to you by now. With the growing concern about fragmenting markets and the diminishing effectiveness of traditional media in reaching those markets, one can expect that more and more advertising dollars will be moved into other options, like direct marketing programs.[4] Before we examine the evolution of direct marketing and look deeper at the reasons for its growing popularity, we need a clear appreciation for what people mean when they use the term *direct marketing*. The "official" definition from the Direct Marketing Association (DMA) provides a starting point:

Direct marketing *is an interactive system of marketing, which uses one or more advertising media to effect a measurable response and/or transaction at any location.*[5]

When examined piece by piece, this definition furnishes an excellent basis for understanding the scope of direct marketing.[6]

Direct marketing is interactive in that the marketer is attempting to develop an ongoing dialogue with the customer. Direct marketing programs are commonly planned with the notion that one contact will lead to another and then another so that the marketer's message can become more focused and refined with each interaction. The DMA's definition also notes that multiple media can be used in direct marketing programs. This is an important point for two reasons. First, we do not want to equate direct mail and direct marketing. Any medium can be used in executing direct marketing programs, not just the mail. Second, as we have noted before, a combination of media is likely to be more effective than any one medium alone.

Another key aspect of direct marketing programs is that they almost always are designed to produce some form of immediate, measurable response. Direct marketing programs are often designed to produce an immediate sale. The customer might be asked to return an order form with check or money order for $189 to get a stylish Klaus Kobec Couture Sports Watch, or to call an 800 number with credit card handy to get 22 timeless hits on a CD called *The Very Best of Tony Bennett*. Because of this emphasis on immediate response, direct marketers are in a position to judge the effectiveness of a particular program. As in the Wunderman example, this ability to gauge the immediate impact of a program has great appeal to clients like Columbia House.

4.   Anthony Bianco, "The Vanishing Mass Market," *BusinessWeek*, July 12, 2004, 61–68.
5.   Bob Stone, *Successful Direct Marketing Methods* (Lincolnwood, IL: NTC Business Books, 1994).
6.   The discussion to follow builds on that of Stone, *Successful Direct Marketing Methods*.

EXHIBIT 19.1

EXHIBIT 19.2

Among other things, pure-play Internet retailers came to realize that when shoppers are dissatisfied with their purchases, many want a physical store where they can return the merchandise for a refund or a trade. In this ad BestBuy.com has some fun with this issue in the context of online CD shopping. At Best Buy, if Folksongs from Rumania is not what you thought it would be, you can always return it to one of their retail stores.

How about a new moose rug or carved loon for your grandparents' cottage Up North? Well, you could visit the Adirondack Country Store in upstate New York, call them at 1–800-LOON-ADK for the catalog, or go online to pick out something nice. Check out the call of the loon at http:// www.adirondackcountrystore.com.

The final phrase of the DMA's definition notes that a direct marketing transaction can take place anywhere. The key idea here is that customers do not have to make a trip to a retail store for a direct marketing program to work. Follow-ups can be made by mail, over the telephone, or on the Internet. At one time the thinking was that Web-based direct marketers such as Amazon.com, pets.com, and eToys.com could ultimately provide so much convenience for shoppers that traditional retail stores might fall by the wayside. Not! It now seems clear that consumers like the option of contacting companies in many ways.[7] So smart retailers both large (see Exhibit 19.1) and small (see Exhibit 19.2) make themselves available in both the physical and virtual worlds.[8] Customers are then free to choose where and how they want to shop.

Direct Marketing—A Look Back. From Johannes Gutenberg and Benjamin Franklin to Richard Sears, Alvah Roebuck, Les Wunderman, and Lillian Vernon, the evolution of direct marketing has involved some of the great pioneers in business. As Exhibit 19.3 shows, the practice of direct marketing today is shaped by the successes of many notable mail-order companies and catalog merchandisers.[9] Among them, none is more exemplary than L. L. Bean. Bean founded his company in 1912 on his integrity and $400. His first product was a unique hunting shoe made from a leather top and rubber bottom sewn together. Other outdoor clothing and equipment soon followed in the Bean catalog.

7.   Louise Lee, "Catalogs, Catalogs, Everywhere," *BusinessWeek*, December 4, 2006, 32–34.
8.   Allanna Sullivan, "From a Call to a Click," *Wall Street Journal*, July 17, 2000, R30.
9.   See Edward Nash, "The Roots of Direct Marketing," *Direct Marketing Magazine*, February 1995, 38–40; Cara Beardi, "Lillian Vernon Sets Sights on Second Half-Century," *Advertising Age*, March 19, 2001, 22.

EXHIBIT 19.3

Direct-marketing milestones.

c. 1450	Johannes Gutenberg invents movable type.
1667	The first gardening catalog is published by William Lucas, an English gardener.
1744	Benjamin Franklin publishes a catalog of books on science and industry and formulates the basic mail-order concept of customer satisfaction guaranteed.
1830s	A few mail-order companies began operating in New England, selling camping and fishing supplies.
1863	The introduction of penny postage facilitates direct mail.
1867	The invention of the typewriter gives a modern appearance to direct-mail materials.
1872	Montgomery Ward publishes his first "catalog," selling 163 items on a single sheet of paper. By 1884 his catalog grows to 240 pages, with thousands of items and a money-back guarantee.
1886	Richard Sears enters the mail-order business by selling gold watches and makes $5,000 in his first six months. He partners with Alvah Roebuck in 1887, and by 1893 they are marketing a wide range of merchandise in a 196-page catalog.
1912	L. L. Bean founds one of today's most admired mail-order companies on the strength of his Maine Hunting Shoe and a guarantee of total satisfaction for the life of the shoe.
1917	The Direct Mail Advertising Association is founded. In 1973 it becomes the Direct Mail/Direct Marketing Association.
1928	Third-class bulk mail becomes a reality, offering economies for the direct-mail industry.
1950	Credit cards first appear, led by the Diners' Club travel and entertainment card. American Express enters in 1958.
1951	Lillian Vernon places an ad for a monogrammed purse and belt and generates $16,000 in immediate business. She reinvests the money in what becomes the Lillian Vernon enterprise. Vernon recognizes early on that catalog shopping has great appeal to time-pressed consumers.
1953	Publishers Clearing House is founded and soon becomes a dominant force in magazine subscriptions.
1955	Columbia Record Club is established, and eventually becomes Columbia House—the music-marketing giant.
1967	The term *telemarketing* first appears in print, and AT&T introduces the first toll-free 800 service.
1983	The Direct Mail/Direct Marketing Association drops Direct Mail from its name to become the DMA, as a reflection of the multiple media being used by direct marketers.
1984	Apple introduces the Macintosh personal computer.
1992	The number of people who shop at home surpasses 100 million in the United States.
1998	The Direct Marketing Association, http://www.the-dma.org, eager to adapt its members' bulk mailing techniques for the Internet, announces it will merge with the Association for Interactive Media, http://www.interactivehq.org.
2003	U.S. consumers register over 10 million phone numbers in the first four days of the national Do Not Call Registry.

Sources: Adapted from the DMA's "Grassroots Advocacy Guide for Direct Marketers" (1993). Reprinted with permission of the Direct Marketing Association, Inc.; Rebecca Quick, "Direct Marketing Association to Merge with Association of Interactive Media," *Wall Street Journal*, October 12, 1998, B6.

A look at the L. L. Bean catalog of 1917 (black and white, just 12 pages) reveals the fundamental strategy underlying Bean's success. It featured the Maine Hunting Shoe and other outdoor clothing with descriptive copy that was informative, factual, and low-key. On the front page was Bean's commitment to quality. It read: "Maine Hunting Shoe—guarantee. We guarantee this pair of shoes to give perfect satisfaction in every way. If the rubber breaks or the tops grow hard, return them together with this guarantee tag and we will replace them, free of charge. Signed, L.L. Bean."[10] Bean realized that long-term relationships with customers must be based on trust, and his guarantee policy was aimed at developing and sustaining that trust.

As an astute direct marketer, Bean also showed a keen appreciation for the importance of building a good mailing list. For many years he used his profits to promote his free catalog via advertisements in hunting and fishing magazines. Those replying to the ads received a rapid response and typically became Bean customers. Bean's obsession with building mailing lists is nicely captured by this quote from his friend, Maine native John Gould: "If you drop in just to shake his hand, you get home to find his catalog in your mailbox."[11]

Today, L. L. Bean is still a family-operated business that emphasizes the basic philosophies of its founder, which are thoughtfully summarized at http://www.llbean .com. Quality products, understated advertising, and sophisticated customer-contact and distribution systems sustain the business. Additionally, L. L.'s 100-percent-satisfaction guarantee can still be found in every Bean catalog. It remains at the heart of the relationship between Bean and its customers.

Direct Marketing Today. Direct marketing today is rooted in the legacy of mail-order giants and catalog merchandisers such as L. L. Bean, Lillian Vernon, Publishers Clearing House, and JCPenney. Today, however, direct marketing has broken free from its mail-order heritage to become a tool used by all types of organizations throughout the world. Although many types of businesses and not-for-profit organizations are using direct marketing, it is common to find that such direct-marketing programs are not carefully integrated with an organization's other advertising efforts. Integration should be the goal for advertising and direct marketing (remember the Gold Box!). Again and again the evidence supports our thesis that integrated programs are more effective than the sum of their parts.[12]

Because the label "direct marketing" now encompasses many different types of activities, it is important to remember the defining characteristics spelled out in the DMA definition given earlier. Direct marketing involves an attempt to interact or create a dialogue with the customer; multiple media are often employed in the process, and direct marketing is characterized by the fact that a measurable response is immediately available for assessing a program's impact. With these defining features in mind, we can see that direct marketing programs are commonly used for three primary purposes.

As you might imagine, the most common use of direct marketing is as a tool to close the sale with a customer. This can be done as a stand-alone program, or it can be coordinated with a firm's other advertising. Telecommunications giants such as AT&T, Sprint, T-Mobile, and Verizon make extensive use of the advertising/direct marketing combination. High-profile mass media campaigns build awareness for their latest offer, followed by systematic direct marketing follow-ups to close the sale.

10.   Allison Cosmedy, *A History of Direct Marketing* (New York: Direct Marketing Association, 1992), 6.
11.   Ibid.
12.   Daniel Klein, "Disintegrated Marketing," *Harvard Business Review*, March 2003, 18, 19; Michael Fielding, "Spread the Word," *Marketing News*, February 15, 2005, 19, 20; Michael Fielding, "Direct Mail Still has its Place," *Marketing News*, November 1, 2006, 31, 33.

EXHIBIT 19.4

Most people are not going to buy a major piece of exercise equipment based on this or any other magazine ad. That's not the intent of this ad. The purchase process could start here, however, with the simple act of ordering that free video.

A second purpose for direct marketing programs is to identify prospects for future contacts and, at the same time, provide in-depth information to selected customers. Any time you respond to an offer for more information or for a free sample, you've identified yourself as a prospect and can expect follow-up sales pitches from a direct marketer. The StairMaster ad in Exhibit 19.4 is a marketer's attempt to initiate a dialogue with prospective customers. Ordering the free catalog and video, whether through the 800 number or at the Web site, begins the process of interactive marketing designed to ultimately produce the sale of another Free-Climber 4600.

Direct marketing programs are also initiated as a means to engage customers, seek their advice, furnish helpful information about using a product, reward customers for using a brand, and in general foster brand loyalty. For instance, the manufacturer of Valvoline motor oil seeks to build loyalty for its brand by encouraging young car owners to join the Valvoline Performance Team.[13] To join the team, young drivers just fill out a questionnaire that enters them into the Valvoline database. Team members receive posters, special offers on racing-team apparel, news about racing events that Valvoline has sponsored, and promotional reminders at regular intervals that reinforce the virtues of Valvoline for the driver's next oil change.

What's Driving the Growing Popularity of Direct Marketing?

The growth in popularity of direct marketing is due to a number of factors. Some of these have to do with changes in consumer lifestyles and technological developments that in effect create a climate more conducive to the practice of direct marketing. In addition, direct marketing programs offer unique advantages vis-à-vis conventional mass media advertising, leading many organizations to shift more of their marketing budgets to direct marketing activities.

From the consumer's standpoint, direct marketing's growing popularity might be summarized in a single word—*convenience*. Dramatic growth in the number of dual-income and single-person households has reduced the time people have to visit retail stores. Direct marketers provide consumers access to a growing range of products and services in their homes, thus saving many households' most precious resource—time.

More liberal attitudes about the use of credit and the accumulation of debt have also contributed to the growth of direct marketing. Credit cards are the primary means of payment in most direct marketing transactions. The widespread availability of credit cards makes it ever more convenient to shop from the comfort of one's home.

Developments in telecommunications have also facilitated the direct marketing transaction. After getting off to a slow start in the late 1960s, toll-free telephone numbers have exploded in popularity to the point where one can hardly find a product or a catalog that does not include an 800 or 888 number for interacting with

---

13. Nash, "The Roots of Direct Marketing."

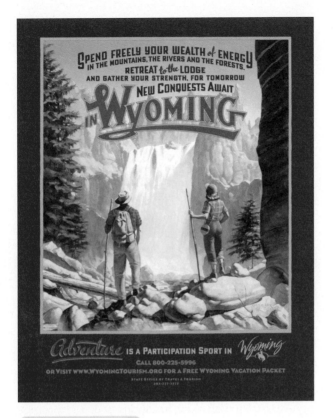

Finding that waterfall in Wyoming will take some planning, and Wyoming's Office of Travel & Tourism is happy to help. The adventure begins with a request for their vacation packet, and if the phone feels a little old fashioned, you know you can start the visit at http://www.wyomingtourism.org.

the seller. Whether one is requesting the StairMaster video, ordering a twill polo shirt from Eddie Bauer, or planning that adventure in Wyoming (see Exhibit 19.5), the preferred mode of access for many consumers has been the 800 number.

Another obvious development having a huge impact on the growth of direct marketing is the computer. The incredible diffusion of computer technology sweeping through all modern societies has been a tremendous boon to direct marketers. The computer now allows firms to track, keep records on, and interact with millions of customers with relative ease. As we will see in an upcoming discussion, the computer power now available for modest dollar amounts is fueling the growth of direct marketing's most potent tool—the marketing database.

And just as the computer has provided marketers with the tool they need to handle massive databases of customer information, it too has provided convenience-oriented consumers with the tool they need to comparison shop with the point and click of a mouse. What could be more convenient than logging on to the Internet and pulling up a shopping agent like PriceScan.com or MySimon to check prices on everything from toaster ovens to snowboards? Why leave the apartment?

Direct marketing programs also offer some unique advantages that make them appealing compared with what might be described as conventional mass marketing. A general manager of marketing communications with AT&T's consumer services unit put it this way: "We want to segment our market more; we want to learn more about individual customers; we want to really serve our customers by giving them very specific products and services. Direct marketing is probably the most effective way in which we can reach customers and establish a relationship with them."[14] As you might expect, AT&T is one of those organizations that has shifted more and more of its marketing dollars into direct-marketing programs.

The appeal of direct marketing is enhanced further by the persistent emphasis on producing measurable effects. For instance, in direct marketing, it is common to find calculations such as **cost per inquiry (CPI)** or **cost per order (CPO)** being featured in program evaluation. These calculations simply divide the number of responses to a program by that program's cost. When calculated for every program an organization conducts over time, CPI and CPO data tell an organization what works and what doesn't work in its competitive arena.

This emphasis on producing and monitoring measurable effects is realized most effectively through an approach called *database marketing*.[15] Working with a database, direct marketers can target specific customers, track their actual purchase behavior over time, and experiment with different programs for affecting the purchasing pat-

14.   Gary Levin, "AT&T Exec: Customer Access Goal of Integration," *Advertising Age*, October 10, 1994, S1.

15.   Like many authors, Winer contends that direct marketing starts with the creation of a database. See Russell Winer, "A Framework for Customer Relationship Management," *California Management Review*, Summer 2001, 89–105.

terns of these customers. Obviously, those programs that produce the best outcomes become the candidates for increased funding in the future. Let's look into database marketing.

② Database Marketing.

If any ambiguity remains about what makes direct marketing different from marketing in general, that ambiguity can be erased by the database. The one characteristic of direct marketing that distinguishes it from marketing more generally is its emphasis on database development. Knowing who the best customers are along with what and how often they buy is a direct marketer's secret weapon.[16] This knowledge accumulates in the form of a marketing database.

Databases used as the centerpieces in direct marketing campaigns take many forms and can contain many different layers of information about customers. At one extreme is the simple mailing list that contains nothing more than the names and addresses of possible customers; at the other extreme is the customized marketing database that augments names and addresses with various additional information about customers' characteristics, past purchases, and product preferences. Understanding this distinction between mailing lists and marketing databases is important in appreciating the scope of database marketing.

Mailing Lists.

A **mailing list** is simply a file of names and addresses that an organization might use for contacting prospective or prior customers. Mailing lists are plentiful, easy to access, and inexpensive. For example, CD-ROM phone directories available for a few hundred dollars provide a cheap and easy way to generate mailing lists. More-targeted mailing lists are available from a variety of suppliers. The range of possibilities is mind-boggling, including groupings like the 238,737 subscribers to *Mickey Mouse Magazine*; 102,961 kindergarten teachers; 4,145,194 physical fitness enthusiasts; 117,758 Lord & Taylor credit card purchasers, and a whopping 269 archaeologists.[17]

Each time you subscribe to a magazine, order from a catalog, register your automobile, fill out a warranty card, redeem a rebate offer, apply for credit, join a professional society, or log in at a Web site, the information you provided about yourself goes on another mailing list. These lists are freely bought and sold through many means, including over the Internet. Sites such as Worldata, HDML, and InfoUSA allow one to buy names and addresses, or e-mail address lists, for as little as 10 cents per record. What's out there is truly remarkable—go have a look.

Two broad categories of lists should be recognized: the internal, or house, list versus the external, or outside, list. **Internal lists** are simply an organization's records of its own customers, subscribers, donors, and inquirers. **External lists** are purchased from a list compiler or rented from a list broker. At the most basic level, internal and external lists facilitate the two fundamental activities of the direct marketer: Internal lists are the starting point for developing better relationships with current customers, whereas external lists help an organization cultivate new business.

List Enhancement.

Name-and-address files, no matter what their source, are merely the starting point for database marketing. The next step in the evolution of a database is mailing-list

---

16. Ibid.
17. *The 2001 Mailing List Catalog* (New York: Hugo Dunhill Mailing Lists, 2001).

enhancement. Typically this involves augmenting an internal list by combining it with other, externally supplied lists or databases. External lists can be appended or merged with a house list.

One of the most straightforward list enhancements entails simply adding or appending more names and addresses to an internal list. Proprietary name-and-address files may be purchased from other companies that operate in noncompetitive businesses. With today's computer capabilities, adding these additional households to an existing mailing list is simple. Many well-known companies such as Sharper Image, American Express, Bloomingdale's, and Hertz sell or rent their customer lists for this purpose.

A second type of list enhancement involves incorporating information from external databases into a house list. Here the number of names and addresses remains the same, but an organization ends up with a more complete description of who its customers are. Typically, this kind of enhancement includes any of four categories of information:

- *Demographic data*—the basic descriptors of individuals and households available from the Census Bureau.
- *Geodemographic data*—information that reveals the characteristics of the neighborhood in which a person resides.
- *Psychographic data*—data that allow for a more qualitative assessment of a customer's general lifestyle, interests, and opinions.
- *Behavioral data*—information about other products and services a customer has purchased; prior purchases can help reveal a customer's preferences.

List enhancements that entail merging existing records with new information rely on software that allows the database manager to match records based on some piece of information the two lists share. For example, matches might be achieved by sorting on zip codes and street addresses. Many suppliers gather and maintain databases that can be used for list enhancement. One of the biggest is InfoUSA of Papillion, Nebraska (see http://www.infousa.com). With over 210 million people in its database, and literally dozens of pieces of information about each person, InfoUSA offers exceptional capabilities for list enhancement. Because of the massive size of the InfoUSA database, it has a high match rate (60 to 80 percent) when it is merged with clients' internal lists. A more common match rate between internal and external lists is around 50 percent.

The Marketing Database. Mailing lists come in all shapes and sizes, and by enhancing internal lists they obviously can become rich sources of information about customers. But for a mailing list to qualify as a marketing database, one important additional type of information is required. Although a marketing database can be viewed as a natural extension of an internal mailing list, a **marketing database** also includes information collected directly from individual customers. Developing a marketing database involves pursuing dialogues with customers and learning about their individual preferences and behavioral patterns. This can be potent information for hatching marketing programs that will hit the mark with consumers.

Aided by the dramatic escalation in processing power that comes from every new generation of computer chip, marketers see the chance to gather and manage more information about every individual who buys, or could buy, from them. Their goal might be portrayed as an attempt to cultivate a kind of cybernetic intimacy with the customer. A marketing database represents an organization's collective memory, which allows the organization to make the kind of personalized offer that once was characteristic of the corner grocer in small-town America. For example, working in conjunction with The Ohio State University Alumni Association, Lands' End created a special autumn promotion to offer OSU football fans all their favorite gear

EXHIBIT 19.6

Cabela's for Women makes it easy to prepare for autumn's chill with style.

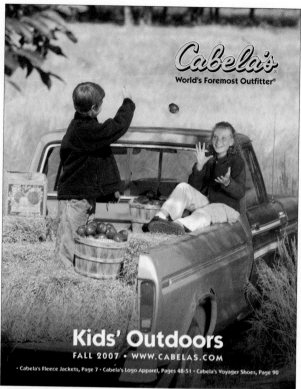

EXHIBIT 19.7

Cabela's for Kids is perfect for the shopper looking for those back-to-school bargains.

just in time for the upcoming session. Prints ads in the September issue of the OSU alumni magazine set the stage for a special catalog of merchandise mailed to Buckeye faithful. Of course, Lands' End had similar arrangements with other major universities to tap into fall football frenzy. Database marketing at its best puts an offer in the hands of the consumer that is both relevant and timely. That's cybernetic intimacy.

Database marketing can also yield important efficiencies that contribute to the marketer's bottom line. As suggested in Exhibits 19.6 and 19.7, like many other multichannel retailers, Cabela's finds it useful to create many targeted versions of its base or master catalogs, with seasonal points of emphasis. Why? The gender or age-specific versions run about 100 pages, versus over 1,000 pages for some of its master catalogs. A customer or household receives the targeted versions based on its profile in Cabela's database and the time of year. These streamlined catalogs are a great way to make timely offerings to targeted households in a cost-effective manner. In a nutshell, that's what database marketing is all about.

It certainly is the case that a marketing database can have many valuable applications. Before we look at more of these applications, let's review the terminology introduced thus far. We now have seen that direct marketers use mailing lists, enhanced mailing lists, and/or marketing databases as the starting points for developing many of their programs. The crucial distinction between a mailing list and a marketing database is that the latter includes direct input from customers. Building a marketing database entails pursuing an ongoing dialogue with customers and

DOING IT RIGHT

Cybernetic Intimacy Meets the NASCAR Fan

When Josh Linkler was young, he bought a lot of Cracker Jacks in hopes of finding decoder rings as his sticky surprise. Always intrigued by the decoder mystique, he used it as the big idea in launching a new marketing service. His company, ePrize, uses decoder contests to drive curious customers to the Web, where they can play games online and in the process provide information about themselves and their interests. Just like that, we have the makings of a marketing database.

In one application Linkler worked with the Michigan International Speedway to build a database to unlock the secrets of NASCAR fans. It all starts with mass distribution of e-decoder game pieces, through ticket-order envelopes, movie theaters, and Pepsi retailers. The game pieces encourage NASCAR fans to go online to win prizes like a $10,000 garage makeover from Gladiator Garage Works (part of Whirlpool Corp. in Benton Harbor, Mich.). First-time players are required to give their name, address, e-mail, age, and gender. With each return visit, more questions must be answered to go deeper into the game. Ultimately, the database gets enriched with answers to something like 150 demographic and lifestyle questions. There are also questions dealing with leisure-time pursuits like camping and fishing, and specific questions like "Do you shop at Cabela's?"

Detailed insights about NASCAR fans help advertisers to connect with them via personalized offers that are timely and relevant. For example, Cabela's, a huge outdoor sports retailer in Dundee, Michigan, can target just the right offers to hunters versus campers versus boaters versus fisherman in the ePrize database. But in this age of privacy concerns, why are these NASCAR fans so willing to divulge their personal information? Well, not all are willing, but Josh Linkler sees it simply as an issue of value. According to Linkler, "If you want consumers to speak to you and provide information, you have to give them something to get them to react." Apparently, the combination of a decoder game and a $10,000 Grand Prize can be pretty hard to resist.

Source: Kris Oser, "Speedway Effort Decodes NASCAR Fans," *Advertising Age*, May 17, 2004, 150.

continuous updating of records with new information, as illustrated in the Doing It Right box. While mailing lists can be rich sources of information for program development, a marketing database has a dynamic quality that sets it apart.

Marketing Database Applications.

Many different types of customer-communication programs are driven by marketing databases. One of the greatest benefits of a database is that it allows an organization to quantify how much business the organization is actually doing with its current best customers. A good way to isolate the best customers is with a recency, frequency, and monetary (RFM) analysis. An **RFM analysis** asks how recently and how often a specific customer is buying from a company, and how much money he or she is spending per order and over time. With this transaction data, it is a simple matter to calculate the value of every customer to the organization and identify customers that have given the organization the most business in the past. Past behavior is an excellent predictor of future behavior, so yesterday's best customers are likely to be any organization's primary source of future business.

A marketing database can be a powerful tool for organizations that seek to create a genuine relationship with their best customers. The makers of Ben & Jerry's ice cream have used their database in two ways: to find out how customers react to potential new flavors and product ideas, and to involve their customers in social causes.[18] In one program, their goal was to find 100,000 people in their marketing database who would volunteer to work with Ben & Jerry's to support the Children's Defense Fund. Jerry Greenfield, cofounder of Ben & Jerry's, justified the program as follows: "We are not some nameless conglomerate that only looks at how much money we make every year. I think the opportunity to use our business and particularly the power of our business as a force for progressive social change is exciting."[19] Of course, when customers feel genuine involvement with a brand like Ben & Jerry's, they also turn out to be very loyal customers.

18.   Murray Raphel, "What's the Scoop on Ben & Jerry?" *Direct Marketing Magazine*, August 1994, 23, 24.
19.   Ibid.

EXHIBIT 19.8

Think of your "best customer" as your most profitable customer. For most businesses, spending more advertising and promotional dollars to win more business from best customers is often money well spent. The real gold lies in not just one purchase, but in a continuous stream of purchases. Can a person ever have too many pairs of cool shades?

Reinforcing and recognizing your best customers is an essential application of the marketing database. This application may be nothing more than a simple follow-up letter that thanks customers for their business or reminds them of the positive features of the brand to reassure them that they made the right choice. Since date of birth is a common piece of information in a marketing database, it naturally follows that another great time to contact customers is on their birthday. Sunglass Hut International uses a birthday card mailing as part of its program to stay in a dialogue with its best customers. Of course, everyone likes a little birthday present too, so along with the card Sunglass Hut includes a Customer Appreciation Check for $20 (shown in Exhibit 19.8) good at any Sunglass Hut store nationwide. Sunglass Hut executives maintain that this birthday card promotion, targeted to current best customers identified from their marketing database, is one of their best investments of advertising dollars.

To recognize and reinforce the behaviors of preferred customers, marketers in many fields are offering frequency-marketing programs that provide concrete rewards to frequent customers. **Frequency-marketing programs** have three basic elements: a *database*, which is the collective memory for the program; a *benefit package*, which is designed to attract and retain customers; and a *communication strategy*, which emphasizes a regular dialogue with the organization's best customers.

The casino industry is renowned for its application of frequency-marketing principles, and Harrah's Entertainment has set the standard for program innovation.[20] Harrah's "Total Rewards" program started out as a way for its 27 million members to accumulate points that could be cashed in for free meals and other casino amenities. This is a good, simple approach, which was quickly copied by the competition. Harrah's subsequently upgraded its program on a number of dimensions. One involved the benefit package: Harrah's upped the ante. Now points can be used for Sony televisions and shopping sprees at Macy's. Harrah's also recognized that it needed separate reward packages for men and women, especially since women make up the majority of its customers. So for the men there are Big Bertha golf clubs and tickets to boxing matches; for the ladies, spa treatments and an evening with Chippendale dancers. That's innovation, Las Vegas style.

20.   Christina Binkley, "Harrah's Is Revamping Rewards Plan," *Wall Street Journal*, June 17, 2003, D4.

Another common application for the marketing database is **cross-selling**. Since most organizations today have many different products or services they hope to sell, one of the best ways to build business is to identify customers who already purchase some of a firm's products and create marketing programs aimed at these customers but featuring other products. If they like our ice cream, perhaps we should also encourage them to try our frozen yogurt. If they have a checking account with us, can we interest them in a credit card? If customers dine in our restaurants on Fridays and Saturdays, with the proper incentives perhaps we can get them to dine with us midweek, when we really need the extra business. A marketing database can provide a myriad of opportunities for cross-selling.

A final application for the marketing database is a natural extension of cross-selling. Once an organization gets to know who its current customers are and what they like about various products, it is in a much stronger position to go out and seek new customers. Knowledge about current customers is especially valuable when an organization is considering purchasing external mailing lists to append to its marketing database. If a firm knows the demographic characteristics of current customers—knows what they like about products, knows where they live, and has insights about their lifestyles and general interests—then the selection of external lists will be much more efficient. The basic premise here is simply to try to find prospects who share many of the same characteristics and interests with current customers. And what's the best vehicle for coming to know the current, best customers? Marketing-database development.

The Privacy Concern. One very large dark cloud looms on the horizon for database marketers: consumers' concerns about invasion of privacy. It is easy for marketers to gather a wide variety of information about consumers, and this is making the general public nervous. Many consumers are uneasy about the way their personal information is being gathered and exchanged by businesses and the government without their knowledge, participation, or consent. Of course, the Internet only amplifies these concerns because the Web makes it easier for all kinds of people and organizations to get access to personal information.

In response to public opinion, state and federal lawmakers have proposed and sometimes passed legislation to limit businesses' access to personal information. Additionally, consumers' desire for privacy was clearly the motivation for the launch of the Federal Trade Commission's Do Not Call Registry. It has proved to be a very popular idea with consumers, but has many opponents in business, including the Direct Marketing Association.[21] The DMA estimated that the list could cost telemarketers on the order of $50 billion in lost sales. How much the "do not call" list will ultimately mean to both sides remains to be seen. If you are one of those people who would like to do more to protect the privacy of your personal information, you can start with a visit to http://www.ftc.gov/privacy/protect.shtm.

As suggested by Exhibit 19.9, many in business are keenly aware of consumers' concerns about the privacy of their personal information. Companies can address customers' concerns about privacy if they remember two fundamental premises of database marketing. First, a primary goal for developing a marketing database is to get to know customers in such a way that an organization can offer them products and services that better meet their needs. The whole point of a marketing database is to keep junk mail to a minimum by targeting only exciting and relevant programs to customers. If customers are offered something of value, they will welcome being in the database.

Second, developing a marketing database is about creating meaningful, long-term relationships with customers. If you want people's trust and loyalty, would you col-

---

21.   Ira Teinowitz and Ken Wheaton, "Do Not Market," *Advertising Age*, March 12, 2007, 1, 44.

EXHIBIT 19.9

This Orwellian ad paints a dark picture of our future if database marketers go unchecked. There is definitely something about the Internet that has heightened people's concerns about who is in control of their personal information. Who controls your personal information? Does it matter to you?

lect personal information from them and then sell it to a third party behind their back? We hope not! When collecting information from customers, an organization must help them understand why it wants the information and how it will use it. If the organization is planning on selling this information to a third party, it must get customers' permission. If the organization pledges that the information will remain confidential, it must honor that pledge. Integrity is fundamental to all meaningful relationships, including those involving direct marketers and their customers. Recall that it was his integrity as much as anything else that enabled L. L. Bean to launch his successful career as a direct marketer. It will work for you too.

Media Applications in Direct Marketing.
While mailing lists and marketing databases are the focal point for originating most direct marketing programs, information and arguments need to be communicated to customers in implementing these programs. As we saw in the definition of direct marketing offered earlier in this chapter, multiple media can be deployed in program implementation, and some form of immediate, measurable response is typically an overriding goal. The immediate response desired may be an actual order for services or merchandise, a request for more information, or the acceptance of a free trial offer. Because advertising conducted in direct marketing campaigns is typified by this emphasis on immediate response, it is commonly referred to as **direct response advertising**.

As you probably suspect, **direct mail** and **telemarketing** are the direct marketer's prime media. However, all conventional media, such as magazines, radio, and television, can be used to deliver direct response advertising; nowadays, a wide array of companies are also deploying e-mail as a most economical means of interacting with customers. In addition, a dramatic transformation of the television commercial—the infomercial—has become especially popular in direct marketing. Let's begin our examination of these media options by considering the advantages and disadvantages of the dominant devices—direct mail and telemarketing.

EXHIBIT 19.10

The U.S. Postal Service is saying, Use our services to drive consumers to your Web site. It's a great point: With millions of Web sites out there in cyberspace, you really must find economical ways to help people notice yours. For help reaching qualified visitors, the Postal Service suggests you visit—where else?—its Web site, http://www.usps .com/directmail/welcome.htm.

Direct Mail. Direct mail has some notable faults as an advertising medium, not the least of which is cost. It can cost 15 to 20 times more to reach a person with a direct mail piece than it would to reach that person with a television commercial or newspaper advertisement.[22] Additionally, in a society where people are constantly on the move, mailing lists are commonly plagued by bad addresses. Each bad address represents advertising dollars wasted. And direct mail delivery dates, especially for bulk, third-class mailings, can be unpredictable. When precise timing of an advertising message is critical to its success, direct mail can be the wrong choice.

But as suggested by the ad from the U.S. Postal Service in Exhibit 19.10, there will be times when direct mail is the right choice. Direct mail's advantages stem from the selectivity of the medium. When an advertiser begins with a database of prospects, direct mail can be the perfect vehicle for reaching those prospects with little waste. Also, direct mail is a flexible medium that allows message adaptations on literally a household-by-household basis. For example, through surveys conducted with its 15 million U.S. subscribers, *Reader's Digest* amassed a huge marketing database detailing the health problems of specific subscribers.[23] In the database were 771,000 people with arthritis, 679,000 people with high blood pressure, 206,000 people with osteoporosis, 460,000 smokers, and so on. Using this information, *Reader's Digest* sent its subscribers disease-specific booklets containing advice on coping with their afflictions, wherein it sold advertising space to drug companies that had tailored messages that they wanted to communicate to those with a particular problem. This kind of precise targeting of tailored messages is the hallmark of direct marketing.

Direct mail as a medium also lends itself to testing and experimentation. With direct mail it is common to test two or more different appeal letters using a modest budget and a small sample of households. The goal is to establish which version yields the largest response. When a winner is decided, that form of the letter is backed by big-budget dollars in launching the organization's primary campaign.

Additionally, the array of formats an organization can send to customers is substantial with direct mail. It can mail large, expensive brochures; videotapes; CDs; or DVDs. It can use pop-ups, foldouts, scratch-and-sniff strips, or a simple, attractive postcard, as in Exhibit 19.11. If a product can be described in a limited space with minimal graphics, there really is no need to get fancy with the direct mail piece. The double postcard (DPC) format has an established track record of outperforming

22.   Stone, *Successful Direct Marketing Methods.*
23.   Sally Beatty, "Drug Companies Are Minding Your Business," *Wall Street Journal,* April 17, 1998, B1, B3.

This postcard for Fleece and Flannel announces the grand opening of its new store in Livingston, Montana. In that part of the world, it's perfectly natural to select a fly-fishing guide and guru to serve as your spokeswoman. Learn more at http://www.MontanaFleeceAndFlannel.com *and* www.visitmt.com.

more expensive and elaborate direct mail packages.[24] Moreover, if an organization follows U.S. Postal Service guidelines carefully in mailing DPCs, the pieces can go out as first-class mail for reasonable rates. Since the Postal Service supplies address corrections on all first-class mail, using DPCs usually turns out to be a winner on either CPI or CPO measures, and DPCs can be an effective tool for cleaning up the bad addresses in a mailing list!

Telemarketing. Telemarketing is probably the direct marketer's most invasive tool. As with direct mail, contacts can be selectively targeted, the impact of programs is easy to track, and experimentation with different scripts and delivery formats is simple and practical. Because telemarketing involves real, live, person-to-person dialogue, no medium produces better response rates. Telemarketing shares many of direct mail's limitations. Telemarketing is very expensive on a cost-per-contact basis: and just as names and addresses go bad as people move, so do phone numbers. Further, telemarketing does not share direct mail's flexibility in terms of delivery options. When you reach people in their home or workplace, you have a limited amount of time to convey information and request some form of response.

If you have a telephone, you already know the biggest concern with telemarketing. It is a powerful yet highly intrusive medium that must be used with discretion. High-pressure telephone calls at inconvenient times can alienate customers. Telemarketing will give best results over the long run if it is used to maintain constructive dialogues with existing customers and qualified prospects.

24.   Michael Edmondson, "Postcards from the Edge," *Marketing Tools*, May 1995, 14.

ETHICS

Meet a Spam Queen

Everybody hates spam. Which raises the question, why is there more all the time? Well, it is probably not accurate to say that everybody hates spam. Laura Betterly prefers to call it commercial or bulk e-mail, and she certainly doesn't hate it. After all, she makes her living by delivering bulk e-mail, direct from her home office to you. The company that Betterly founded with three of her friends, Data Resources Consulting, can send out as many as 60 million e-mail messages a month.

The crown jewel of DRC is its database of 100 million e-mail addresses. Betterly assembled it from a number of sources, including Excite, About.com, and Ms. Cleo's psychic Web site. Like most spammers, she also makes money by selling e-mail addresses to other bulk e-mailers, and she is always looking to add more names to her database when the price is right. While large companies too are in the business of sending unsolicited, bulk e-mail, a large part of this industry is small entrepreneurs like Laura Betterly and DRC. There's nothing hard about it.

Now here's the secret as to why there is more spam all the time—it's a profitable business. According to Betterly, depending on the commission she negotiates, it is possible to make money on a bulk e-mailing when as few as 100 people respond out of a mailing of 10 million. No doubt spammers are able to survive with response rates that could never work for the paper-junk mailer. For "snail mail" the direct marketer is typically looking for a response of 2 percent or better to turn a profit on the program. For bulk e-mail, profits kick in with a response rate of 0.001 percent. Sometimes you wonder how anyone would respond to the kinds of messages we all receive in our e-mail boxes, but the point is, if 1 out of 1,000 responds, Betterly is making money. Those are pretty good odds.

"I'm just trying to make a living like everyone else," is how Laura Betterly sees it. Because of Data Resources Consulting, she can raise her two children comfortably and spend lots of quality time with them. "You can call me a spam queen if you want," she says. "As long as I'm not breaking any laws, you don't have to love me or like what I do for a living."

Sources: Mylene Mangalindan, "Web Vigilantes Give Spammers a Big Dose of Their Medicine," *Wall Street Journal*, May 19, 2003, A1, A13; Mylene Mangalindan, "For Bulk E-Mailer, Pestering Millions Offers a Path to Profit," *Wall Street Journal*, November 13, 2002, A1, A17.

E-Mail. Perhaps the most controversial tool deployed of late by direct marketers has been unsolicited or "bulk" e-mail. Commonly referred to as spam, this junk e-mail can get you in big trouble with consumers. In a worst-case scenario, careless use of the e-mail tool can earn one's company the label of a "spammer," and because of the community-oriented character of the Internet, can then be a continuing source of negative buzz. But is this discouraging companies from deploying this tool? Hardly. In 2006, 70 percent of the 180 billion e-mails sent daily was spam.[25] Better filtering tools are helping control this epidemic, but still it is estimated that by 2010, active e-mail users will receive on average 1,600 spam messages annually.[26] It does make you wonder, with so much spam out there, and with so many who hate it, why does anyone do it? The Ethics box tackles this weighty question.

There definitely is a school of thought that says some consumers are not averse to receiving targeted e-mail advertisements, and that as the Internet continues to evolve as an increasingly commercial medium, those companies that observe proper etiquette on the Net (dare we say "Netiquette"?) will be rewarded through customer loyalty.[27] The key premise of netiquette is to get the consumer's permission to send information about specific products or services, or, to use the current buzzword, they must "opt in." This opt-in premise has spawned a number of e-marketing service providers who claim to have constructed e-mail lists of consumers who have "opted in" for all manner of products and services.

Exhibit 19.12 features an ad from one firm that worked diligently to make e-mail marketing a workable alternative for conscientious advertisers. Others now promise large lists of consumers who have agreed to receive commercial e-mails (e.g., http://www.infousa.com or http://www.yesmail.com). As noted in Exhibit 19.12, the future of direct marketing may be in reaching those people who have already said "Yes."

25. Allison Enright, "Guerrilla-Style SPAM Wars," *Marketing News*, November 1, 2006, 13, 14.
26. Ibid.
27. Cara Beardi, "Opt-In Taken to Great Heights," *Advertising Age*, November 6, 2000, S54; Michael Battisto, "Preparation Yields Spam-Free E-Mail Lists," *Marketing News*, February 17, 2003, 17.

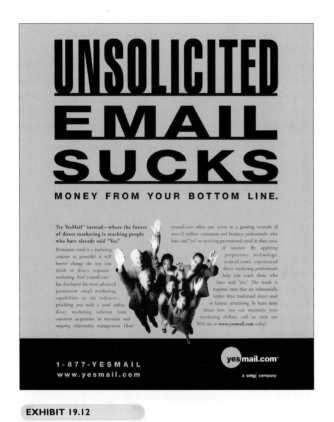

EXHIBIT 19.12

Purveyors of permission e-mail have sprung up like mushrooms in the forest after a rain. It is hard to argue with the premise that unsolicited e-mail sucks. Wouldn't you agree?

Our advice is to stay away from the low-cost temptations of bulk e-mail. The quickest way to get flamed and damage your brand name is to start sending out bulk e-mails to people who do not want to hear from you. Instead, through database development, ask your customers for permission to contact them via e-mail. Honor their requests. Don't abuse the privilege by selling their e-mail addresses to other companies, and when you do contact them, have something important to say. Seth Godin, whose 1999 book *Permission Marketing* really launched the "opt-in" mindset, puts it this way: "The best way to make your [customer] list worthless is to sell it. The future is, this list is mine and it's a secret."[28] Isn't it funny—you can imagine L. L. Bean feeling exactly the same way about his customer list 95 years ago.

Direct Response Advertising in Other Media.

Direct marketers have experimented with many other methods in trying to convey their appeals for a customer response. In magazines, a popular device for executing a direct marketer's agenda is the bind-in insert card. Thumb through a copy of any magazine and you will see how effective these light-cardboard inserts are at stopping the reader and calling attention to themselves. Insert cards not only promote their product, but also provide tempting offers like $25 off your next order at Coldwater Creek, a free sample of Skoal smokeless tobacco, or 12 CDs for the price of one for new members of the BMG Music Club.

When AT&T introduced the first 800 number in 1967, it simply could not have known how important this service would become to direct marketing. Newspaper ads from the *Wall Street Journal* provide toll-free numbers for requesting everything from really cheap online trading services (800–619-SAVE) to leasing a Learjet 40 (800-FLEXJET). If you watch late-night TV, you may know the 800 number to call to order the Grammy-winning CD by Walter Ostanek and his polka band. Finally, magazine ads like the one shown in Exhibit 19.13 on the next page out of *Bon Appetit* are commonly used to provide an 800 number to initiate contact with customers. As these diverse examples indicate, toll-free numbers make it possible to use nearly any medium for direct response purposes.

Infomercials. The infomercial is a novel form of direct response advertising that merits special mention. An **infomercial** is fundamentally just a long television advertisement made possible by the lower cost of ad space on many cable and satellite channels. They range in length from 2 to 60 minutes, but the common length is 30 minutes. Although producing an infomercial is more like producing a television program than it is like producing a 30-second commercial, infomercials are all about selling. There appear to be several keys to successful use of this unique vehicle.[29]

28.   Jodi Mardesich, "Too Much of a Good Thing," *Industry Standard*, March 19, 2001, 85.
29.   Thomas Mucha, "Stronger Sales in Just 28 Minutes," *Business 2.0*, June 2005, 56–60; Elizabeth Holmes, "Golf-Club Designer Hopes to Repeat TV Success," *Wall Street Journal*, January 30, 2007, B4.

A critical factor is testimonials from satisfied users. Celebrity testimonials can help catch a viewer as he or she is channel surfing past the program, but celebrities aren't necessary, and, of course, they add to the production costs. Whether testimonials are from celebrities or from folks just like us, without them your chances of producing a profitable infomercial diminish hugely.

Another key point to remember about infomercials is that viewers are not likely to stay tuned for the full 30 minutes. An infomercial is a 30-minute direct response sales pitch, not a classic episode of *South Park* or *The Simpsons*. The implication here is that the call to action should come not just at the end of the infomercial; most of the audience could be long gone by minute 28 into the show. A good rule of thumb in a 30-minute infomercial is to divide the program into 10-minute increments and close three times. Each closing should feature the 800 number or Web address that allows the viewer to order the product or request more information. And an organization should not offer information to the customer unless it can deliver speedy follow-up; same-day response should be the goal in pursuing leads generated by an infomercial.

Many different types of products and services have been marketed using infomercials, and now via Internet extensions such as http://www.iqvc .com. CD players, self-help videos, home exercise equipment, kitchen appliances, and Annette Funicello Collectible Bears have all had success with the infomercial. While it is easy to associate the infomercial with things such as the Ronco Showtime Rotisserie & BBQ (yours for just four easy payments of $39.95!), many familiar brands have experimented with this medium. Brand marketers such as Quaker State, America Online, Primestar, Lexus, Monster .com, Disney, Hoover, Kal Kan, Pontiac, and yes, Mercedes-Benz, have all used infomercials to help inform consumers about their offerings.[30]

How does one explain the growing appeal of the infomercial for all manner of marketers? New data generated by TiVo's StopWatch service are revealing.[31] They show that bare-bones, direct-response ads for products like Perfect Pushup exercise equipment are among the least likely to be zapped. That kind of result will get lots of scrutiny from all corners of the advertising business.

EXHIBIT 19.13

Nothing fancy here. Just good, sound direct marketing.

30.   Evantheia Schibsted, "Ab Rockers, Ginsu Knives, E320s," *Business 2.0*, May 29, 2001, 46–49; Jean Halliday, "Pontiac Models Get Infomercial Push," *Advertising Age*, April 19, 2004, 12.
31.   Brian Steinberg, "How To Stop Them from Skipping: TiVo Tells All," *Advertising Age*, July 16, 2007, 1, 33.

④ Closing the Sale with Direct Marketing and/or Personal

Selling. As we have pointed out repeatedly, the wide variety of options available to marketers for reaching customers poses a tremendous challenge with respect to coordination and integration. Organizations are looking to achieve the synergy that can come when various options reach the consumer with a common and compelling message. However, to work in various media, functional specialists both inside and outside an organization need to be employed. It then becomes a very real problem to get the advertising manager, special events manager, sales promotion manager, and Web designer to work in harmony.[32] And now we must add to the list of functional specialists the direct marketing or database manager.

The evolution and growing popularity of direct marketing raise the challenge of achieving integrated communication to new heights. In particular, the development of a marketing database commonly leads to interdepartmental rivalries and can create major conflicts between a company and its advertising agency. The marketing database is a powerful source of information about the customer; those who do not have direct access to this information will be envious of those who do. Additionally, the growing use of direct marketing campaigns must mean that someone else's budget is being cut. Typically, direct marketing programs come at the expense of conventional advertising campaigns that might have been run on television, in magazines, or in other mass media. Since direct marketing takes dollars from activities that have been the staples of the traditional ad agency business, it is easy to see why a pure advertising guru like Saatchi's Kevin Roberts views direct marketing with some disdain.[33]

There are no simple solutions for achieving integrated communication, but one classic approach is the establishment of a marketing communications manager, or "marcom" manager for short.[34] A **marcom manager** plans an organization's overall communications program and oversees the various functional specialists inside and outside the organization to ensure that they are working together to deliver the desired message to the customer, which ultimately yields a product sale. Of course the pivotal role for direct marketing programs in this process is to establish dialogue with customers, and then close the sale.

The Critical Role of Personal Selling. This brings us to the field of personal selling, yet another

unique functional specialization in the business world. **Personal selling** is the face-to-face communications and persuasion process. Products that are higher priced, complicated to use, require demonstration, must be tailored to user needs, involve a trade-in, or are judged at the point of purchase are heavily dependent on personal selling. Household consumers and business buyers are frequently confronted with purchase decisions that are facilitated by interaction with a salesperson. In many decision contexts, only a qualified and well-trained salesperson can address the questions and concerns of a potential buyer. Fail to get the dialogue right at this critical stage of the purchase process and all other advertising efforts will end up being wasted.

There are many different types of sales jobs. A salesperson can be engaged in order taking, creative selling, or supportive communication. The discussion that follows demonstrates that the communication task for each type of selling varies dramatically.

---

32.   Laura Q. Hughes and Kate MacArthur, "Soft Boiled," *Advertising Age*, May 28, 2001, 3, 54; Klein, "Disintegrated Marketing," 18,19.

33.   Alessandra Galloni, "Is Saatchi Helping Publicis' Bottom Line?" *Wall Street Journal*, June 22, 2001, B6.

34.   Don E. Schultz, Stanley I. Tannenbaum, and Robert F. Lauterborn, *Integrated Marketing Communications* (Lincolnwood, IL: NTC Business Books, 1993).

The least complex type of personal selling is order taking. Its importance, however, should not be underestimated. **Order taking** involves accepting orders for merchandise or scheduling services. Order takers deal with existing customers who are lucrative to a business due the low cost of generating additional revenues from them. Order takers can also deal with new customers, which means that they need to be trained well enough to answer the basic questions a new customer might have about a product or service. Order takers are responsible for communicating with buyers in such a way that a quality relationship is maintained. This type of selling rarely involves communicating large amounts of information. However, a careless approach to this function can be a real turn-off for the loyal consumer, and can end up damaging the relationship.

Creative selling requires considerable effort and expertise. Situations where creative selling takes place range from retail stores through the selling of services to business and the sale of large industrial installations and component parts. **Creative selling** is the type of selling where customers rely heavily on the salesperson for technical information, advice, and service. In retail settings like those illustrated in Exhibits 19.14 and 19.15, stores selling higher-priced items and specialty goods must have a trained sales staff and emphasize customer and product knowledge. The services of an insurance agent, stockbroker, media representative, or real estate agent represent another type of creative selling. These salespeople provide services customized to the unique needs and circumstances of each buyer.

The most complex and demanding of the creative selling positions is in business-to-business markets. Many times these salespeople have advanced degrees in technical areas like chemical engineering, computer science, or any of the medical professions. Technical salespeople who deal in large-dollar purchases and complex corporate decisions for specialized component parts, medical equipment, or raw materials have tremendous demands placed on them. They are often called on to analyze the customer's product and production needs and carry this information back to the firm so that product design and supply schedules can be tailored for each customer.

Another noteworthy form of creative selling that has emerged in recent years is system selling. **System selling** entails selling a set of interrelated components that fulfill all or a majority of a customer's needs in a particular area. System selling has

EXHIBIT 19.14

Buying gourmet cookware for one's spouse can be risky business. It's the salesperson's job to help the customer find the perfect gift.

Point of purchase is where the salesperson plays a critical role in determining the consumer's ultimate choice. The myriad of options available in today's markets for all sorts of wireless gadgets amplifies the need for knowledgeable and well-trained sales personnel in this category.

emerged because of the desire on the part of customers for "system solutions." Large industrial and government buyers, in particular, have come to seek out one or a small number of suppliers that can provide a full range of products and services needed in an area. Rather than dealing with multiple suppliers, these buyers then "system buy" from a single source. This trend in both buying and selling emphasizes the customer-relationship-management aspects of selling.

Creative selling tasks call for high levels of preparation, expertise, and contact with the customer and are primary to the process of relationship building. This doesn't happen by chance. Companies work hard to train their salespeople to be ready to address the needs of specific target markets. Take, for example, Honda and its recent launch of the Honda Fit.[35] This was an important launch for Honda because Fit represented the company's first true entry-level vehicle since the 1970s. But the buyers of entry-level vehicles have changed dramatically since the '70s, and Honda was keen to bring its 7,500 U.S. sales associates up to speed on the profile of that new buyer. One key issue: This consumer is Internet savvy and likely will come to the showroom with lots of background research on the car. So step one for the salesperson: Find out what the customer already knows about the car. Don't rehash what she already knows. Surprise her and excite her with something new.

Finally, when a sales force is deployed for the purpose of supportive communication, it is not charged directly with closing the sale. Rather, the objective is to provide information to customers, offer services, and generally to foster goodwill. The **missionary salesperson** calls on accounts with the express purpose of monitoring the satisfaction of buyers and updating buyers' needs. They may provide product information after a purchase. Many firms also use direct marketing tools like telephone, fax, and e-mail reminders to complement the efforts of the missionary salesperson in maintaining a dialogue with key customers.

35.   Jacqueline Durett, "Road Warriors," *Sales & Marketing Management*, September 2006, 46–48.

Customer Relationship Management. Salespeople can play a critical role as well in cultivating long-term relationships with customers—which often is referred to as a **customer relationship management (CRM)** program.[36] As an example, Merck spends 12 months training its sales representatives not just in knowledge of pharmaceuticals, but also in trust-building techniques. Reps then are required to take regular refresher courses. Similarly, General Electric went so far as to station its own engineers full time at Praxair, Inc., a user of GE electrical equipment, to help the firm boost productivity. Furthermore, firms are discovering that CRM is a key strategy for gaining competitive advantage in many global markets.

Likewise, salespeople are also instrumental in ensuring customer satisfaction. Salespeople no longer simply approach customers with the intention of making a sale. Rather, they are problem solvers who work in partnership with customers. The salesperson is in the best position to analyze customer needs and propose the right solution on a case-by-case basis. By accepting this role, the sales force helps determine ways in which a firm can provide total customer satisfaction through its entire market offering. The great thing about satisfied consumers is they come back and buy again and again, which ultimately is the mechanism that sustains any business.

A Case in Point. To wrap things up for this chapter, let's consider an example of what happens for a company when it strikes just the right balance among advertising, brand building, direct marketing, and personal selling. Let's start with a quiz. Who's number one in the specialty bedding business? No, it's not Crazy Larry's Mattress Barn or the House of Pillows. Think Sleep Number bed by Select Comfort and their spokesmodel Lindsay Wagner (the original Bionic Woman). Now an actress, mom, and Sleep Number bed owner, Lindsay's number is 35.

The Select Comfort story represents a real metamorphosis from a tiny niche brand to a market leader.[37] For years Select Comfort promoted its air mattresses with late-night infomercials along the lines of the Ronco Showtime Rotisserie & BBQ. Some consumers found value in the product as a good option to pull out of the closet and blow up when friends dropped in for the night. But that's hardly a mainstream market, and Select Comfort was looking for more. Thus, the company invented a new brand, the Sleep Number bed, where the user can adjust the firmness of the mattress with a simple remote control using a numerical range from 1 to 100 (see the really big remote in Exhibit 19.16). But the company had a lot of work to do in building this brand. First, it had to overcome the perception that this is just a *very* expensive air mattress. Second, it had to shed the association with late-night cable TV to be accepted as a high-quality product found in upscale shopping malls across the United States.

Lots of things changed in building the Sleep Number brand. While Select Comfort did not abandon its heritage as a direct marketer, new ad campaigns also included a healthy mix of newspaper advertising and local and prime-time TV spots. Often these ads would feature the first point of difference for the mattress: Couples sharing a bed could each adjust their side to just the right level of firmness (typically less than 50 for gals and over 50 for guys). Patented technology in the remote control made this a sustainable point of difference.

Once basic awareness was established for the brand, Select Comfort next proceeded with the communication objective of associating the bed with deep, restorative sleep. And while all this brand building was taking place, targeted consumers continuously received direct mail pieces like the one in Exhibit 19.17 that were seeking to close the sale. A person typically doesn't buy a $1,000 mattress over an 800 number, but a visit to one of the company's 410 retail stores is another matter. There, well-trained sales personnel (often in their pajamas) patiently helped each customer find his or her sleep number, while reinforcing the importance of deep, restorative sleep. Of course, it is also the job of that salesperson to work to close the sale.

36.   Daniel Tynan, "The 10 Biggest CRM Mistakes," *Sales & Marketing Management*, December 2005, 30–33.
37.   Willow Duttge, "Counting Sleep," *Advertising Age*, June 5, 2006, 4, 50.

Weary travelers in the Minneapolis airport are encouraged to find their Sleep Number in Concourse D.

Hallmarks of the direct mail piece designed to help close the sale are an offer of special pricing, free accessories, encouragement to ACT NOW, and great financing arrangements if you ACT NOW.

The Select Comfort example typifies a theme developed throughout this book. Each marketer must find the right balance of tools and tactics to get its points across to targeted consumers. Different tools and tactics play various roles in the process from building brand awareness, to communicating key brand benefits, and ultimately closing the sale. If the various media and programs an organization employs are sending different messages or mixed signals, the organization is only hurting itself. All the functional specialists who are part of the marketing and sales team must be working as a team. To achieve the synergy that will allow it to overcome the clutter of today's marketplace, and, for example, move to the top spot in the specialty bedding market, an organization has no choice but to pursue advertising and integrated brand promotion.

SUMMARY

  Identify the three primary purposes served by direct marketing and explain its growing popularity.

Many types of organizations are increasing their expenditures on direct marketing. These expenditures serve three primary purposes: direct marketing offers potent tools for closing sales with customers, for identifying prospects for future contacts, and for offering information and incentives that help foster brand loyalty. The growing popularity of direct marketing can be attributed to several factors. Direct marketers make consumption convenient: Credit cards, 800 numbers, and the Internet take the hassle out of shopping. Additionally, today's computing power, which allows marketers to build and mine large customer information files, has enhanced direct marketing's impact. The emphasis on producing and tracking measurable outcomes is also well received by marketers in an era when everyone is trying to do more with less.

  Distinguish a mailing list from a marketing database and review the many applications of each.

A mailing list is a file of names and addresses of current or potential customers, such as lists that might be generated by a credit card company or a catalog retailer. Internal lists are valuable for creating relationships with current customers, and external lists are useful in generating new customers. A marketing database is a natural extension of the internal list, but includes information about individual customers and their specific preferences and purchasing patterns. A marketing database allows organizations to identify and focus their efforts on their best customers. Recognizing and reinforcing preferred customers can be a potent strategy for building loyalty. Cross-selling opportunities also emerge once a database is in place. In addition, as one gains keener information about the motivations of current best customers, insights usually emerge about how to attract new customers.

  Describe the prominent media used by direct marketers in delivering their messages to the customer.

Direct marketing programs emanate from mailing lists and databases, but there is still a need to deliver a message to the customer. Direct mail and telemarketing are the most common means used in executing direct marketing programs. E-mail has recently emerged as a low-cost alternative. Because the advertising done as part of direct marketing programs typically requests an immediate response from the customer, it is known as direct response advertising. Conventional media such as television, newspapers, magazines, and radio can also be used to request a direct response by offering an 800 number or a Web address to facilitate customer contact.

  Explain the key role of direct marketing and personal selling in complementing other advertising activities.

Developing a marketing database, selecting a direct mail format, and producing an infomercial are some of the tasks attributable to direct marketing. These and other related tasks require more functional specialists, who further complicate the challenge of presenting a coordinated face to the customer. Additionally, many products and services must be supported by well-trained sales personnel. Here again, the message consumers hear in advertising for any brand needs to be skillfully reinforced by the sales team. Fail to get the dialogue right at this final, critical stage of the purchase process and all other advertising efforts will end up being wasted. The sales force plays a critical role in the process because theirs is the job of closing the sale, while at the same time ensuring customer satisfaction.

KEY TERMS

direct marketing
cost per inquiry (CPI)
cost per order (CPO)
mailing list
internal lists
external lists
marketing database
RFM analysis

frequency-marketing programs
cross-selling
direct response advertising
direct mail
telemarketing
infomercial
marcom manager
personal selling

order taking
creative selling
system selling
missionary salesperson
customer relationship management (CRM)

QUESTIONS

1.   Who is Lester Wunderman and in what ways does his historic campaign for Columbia House illustrate the mindset of direct marketing?

2.   Direct marketing is defined as an interactive system of marketing. Explain the meaning of the term *interactive system* and give an example of a noninteractive system. How would an interactive system be helpful in the cultivation of brand loyalty?

3.   Review the major forces that have promoted the growth in popularity of direct marketing. Can you come up with any reasons why its popularity might be peaking? What are the threats to its continuing popularity as a marketing approach?

4.   Describe the various categories of information that a credit card company might use to enhance its internal mailing list. For each category, comment on the possible value of the information for improving the company's market segmentation strategy.

5.   What is RFM analysis, and what is it generally used for? How would RFM analysis allow an organization to get more impact from a limited marketing budget? (Keep in mind that every organization views its marketing budget as too small to accomplish all that needs to be done.)

6.   Compare and contrast frequency-marketing programs with the tools described in Chapter 17 as sales promotions directed at consumers. What common motivators do these two types of activities rely on? How are their purposes similar or different? What goal is a frequency-marketing program trying to achieve that would not be a prime concern with a sales promotion?

7.   There's a paradox here, right? On the one hand, it is common to talk about building relationships and loyalty with the tools of direct marketing. On the other hand, direct-marketing tools such as junk e-mail and telephone interruptions at home during dinner are constant irritants. How does one build relationships by using irritants? In your opinion, when is it realistic to think that the tools of direct marketing could be used to build long-term relationships with customers?

8.   What is it about direct marketing that makes its growing popularity a threat to the traditional advertising agency?

9.   Compare and contrast the purposes served by direct marketing versus personal selling.

10. Use the example of the Sleep Number bed to illustrate the importance of a balanced approach in executing advertising and integrated brand promotion.

EXPERIENTIAL EXERCISES

1.   Working in small teams, assess the direct marketing components at the Web site of Moosejaw, the athletic apparel retailer popular on college campuses. (See http://www.moosejaw.com.) For each direct marketing appeal that you can identify on the site, explain how the company would be able to measure the effectiveness of the appeal. As you evaluate the site, also identify any and all opportunities for the company to gather customer information that could enhance its database marketing efforts.

2.   The chapter discusses how database marketing can be used not only as a tool to reach customers and close sales, but also to aid product development. Working again in small teams, identify three distinct offerings that could be developed for well-known brands based on input and knowledge gleaned from customer and sales databases. As you propose the new products or services, identify specific types of database information that could influence the development process.

3.   Imagine that you have been hired by a travel agency to develop a direct appeal letter for a spring break ski trip to Colorado targeting college-age young adults. Write a three- to four-paragraph appeal letter for the vacation package, then explain how the travel agency would measure response to the appeal and what next steps you would recommend in the direct marketing campaign to further engage potential customers and to close the sale.

4.   This chapter discusses serious privacy concerns raised by database marketing. Today's marketers are gathering enormous amounts of information about individuals, and much of the database development occurs without the consent or awareness of consumers. Visit the following sites and explain the contribution of each to the issue of online privacy.

   Better Business Bureau: http://www.bbbonline.org
   TRUSTe: http://www.truste.com

CHAPTER 20

After reading and thinking about this chapter, you will be able to do the following:

1

Explain the role of public relations as part of an organization's overall advertising and IBP strategy.

2

Detail the objectives and tools of public relations.

3

Describe two basic strategies motivating an organization's public relations activities.

4

Illustrate the strategies and tactics used in influencer marketing programs.

5

Discuss the applications and objectives of corporate advertising.

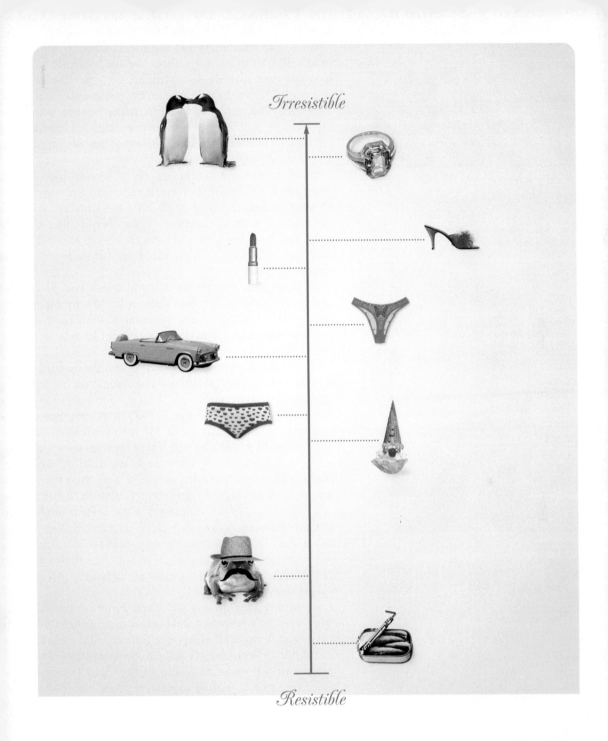

Irresistible

Resistible

Where do you fit in? Take the irresistibility i.q. quiz and enter for a chance to win prizes at **crestiq.com** or text "IQ" to CREST.

Crest Healthy, beautiful smiles for life.

Introductory Scenario: Think Holistic to Build Brand Buzz.

When one has a hip or novel product like Red Bull, Mini Cooper, Apple's iPhone, or Betty Beauty, it's not hard to get consumers and the media buzzing about your

With iPods, Nick Cannon, and free downloads as part of the package, who could resist?

Obviously the folks at P&G understand the importance of social networking among the age group targeted in this product launch.

brand. But in many ways those are the exceptions. Often it is the case that we are working with familiar products and well-known brands where the excitement has faded long ago. The challenge faced by many marketers is creating interest, building buzz, motivating trial (or re-trial), and cultivating relationships for brands that are all too familiar. Take, for example, toothpaste.

Most people use toothpaste on a regular basis. Many don't recall the brand they last bought and believe that it's all pretty much the same stuff. It's a low-interest, hard-to-differentiate product category where brands like Colgate and Crest have been around forever. "Look Ma, No Cavities" was an ad slogan that created great buzz for the Crest brand—50 years ago.

So how does one revive a brand like Crest to get the consumer enthusiastic? And let's make the problem even tougher by targeting young consumers, with their eclectic media habits and built-in skepticism about brands. Where to even begin? You should know by now.

Great advertising and integrated brand promotion always begins with a clear focus on and deep insights into the consumers you are targeting. With its line extension, Crest Whitening Plus Scope Extreme, P&G marketers were clearly focused on women age 18 to 34, with a primary emphasis on women 23 to 24 years old. These women are social, outgoing, and not married. They are heavy users of social networking sites and constantly converse with their friends and family via all forms of wireless communication. A key insight that helped P&G in this campaign: While these women agree that an occasional "bad hair day" is unavoidable, a "bad breath day" is totally unacceptable. Additionally, making a good first impression is a high priority for these women; fresh breath and a big bright smile are definitely perceived as a good thing in that regard.

So the big idea driving the Crest Extreme launch campaign was, let's help her make great first impressions in all social situations, add to her confidence, and enhance her irresistibility. Who doesn't want to be irresistible? The centerpiece of this initiative would be the Crest Extreme Irresistibility IQ Quiz. Before one can become more irresistible, you first have to establish your baseline. Interactive quizzes are common fare for this age group, and of course it would have to be diagnostic with lots of expert and celebrity input, and cool prizes and other incentives for participation.

With the quiz as its centerpiece, P&G launched a holistic, integrated communication campaign to build the buzz. Some of the main components were as follows:

Public Relations. The first people to take the Irresistibility Quiz were MTV personality Nick Cannon and members of the Hispanic boy band Reik. Media junkets and interviews were given by both Cannon and Reik, resulting in local and national media coverage of Crest Extreme, which aided in driving traffic to the English (http://www.Crestiq.com) and Spanish (http://www.AlientoCrest.com) language sites.

EXHIBIT 20.3

Appealing visual elements are a hallmark of great advertising, no matter what the product category.

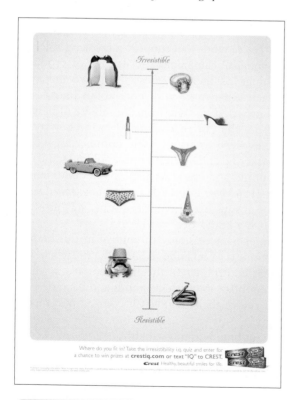

EXHIBIT 20.4

Here low-tech meets high-tech with the perfect buzz builder for any restroom.

Other celebrities, like JoJo, Teddy Geiger, and Lauren Conrad, also took the quiz and had their scores posted.

Online. Banner ads such as the one in Exhibit 20.1 promoted the quiz with all the right stuff. These appeared in the obvious places like Facebook, MySpace, Evite, Batanga, Tickle, and Instant Messenger. In addition, a member profile for a mythical "Miss Irresistibility" was created on MySpace (see Exhibit 20.2), providing lots of opportunity for more dialogue. Members were encouraged to add Miss Irresistibility as a friend with the offer of free Nick Cannon songs and other downloads. Online chats with Nick Cannon and Reik were also hosted on MySpace, with lots of prizes just for the friends of Miss Irresistibility. Samantha Daniels, a renowned dating expert who helped in creating the quiz questions, was also featured on and offline throughout the campaign.

Events and Publicity. Crest Extreme partnered with Vibe.com to host a speed-dating event in Times Square, again featuring Nick Cannon as the cool guy. *Entertainment Tonight* on MTV and *The Insider* broadcast the event live, driving tons of traffic to CrestIQ.com.

Irresistible Visuals, Print Ads and Posters. A print campaign was fielded to drive awareness and encourage people to log on at CrestIQ.com. Embedded in this campaign was a key visual element that promised more irresistible kisses, as shown in Exhibit 20.3. At the local level, consumers saw posters like the one in Exhibit 20.4 in restrooms of their favorite night spots. It was a call to action to take an abbreviated version of the quiz by mobile phone, before leaving the restroom. "You meet a hottie at the club; how do you let him know you're interested?" CrestIQ.com to the rescue!

It's a complex thing bringing a mature brand back to life with a young audience, but if you get all the pieces put together in the right way, the buzz will build again. P&G calls it 360 degree/holistic marketing. Cool name. We call it great execution of advertising and integrated brand promotion, using all the right tools to reach a well-defined target market.

Whatever you call it, it works. At the close of the Extreme campaign Crest had 401,902 quiz completions, 48,760 MySpace Friends, 157 million media impressions, and 1,156,375 visitors to CrestIQ.com. The brand also ended up with a dramatic market share increase versus archrival Colgate, especially among women age 18 to 34.

The launch campaign for Crest Extreme is a great example for us here in Chapter 20 for a number of reasons. For one thing, it reinforces the point that advertising and IBP involves the use of multiple tools, as well as just the right tools for the target segment in question. Moreover, this example features the whole idea of buzz building that is so popular in marketing today, along with the use of public relations activities as a way to get that buzz. Indeed, these two things often go hand in hand, and a focal point of this chapter will be to fold public relations into the tool kit to complete your set.

One can argue that we've entered an exciting new era for public relations. PR and buzz building have never been hotter. Public relations has moved well beyond its traditional role of simply managing goodwill or "relations" with a firm's many "publics," which often takes the form of "damage control" in the face of negative publicity. These traditional functions are still important, but there's much more going on in PR circles today. Another major topic in this chapter—Influencer Marketing—will emphasize public relations activities as a brand-building agenda, reflecting the new emphasis in PR.

Last but not least, corporate advertising is also considered in this final chapter. Corporate advertising typically uses major media to communicate a unique, broad-based message that is distinct from more product-specific brand building. Corporate advertising contributes to the development of an overall image for a firm without touting specific products or services. Corporate advertising has a lot to do with the trustworthiness and reputation of a firm. As consumers are becoming increasingly informed and sophisticated, they are also demanding a higher standard of conduct from the companies they patronize. When a company has established trust and integrity, it is of course much easier to build productive relationships with consumers.

❶ Public Relations.

The classic role of **public relations** is to foster goodwill between a firm and its many constituent groups. These constituent groups include customers, stockholders, suppliers, employees, government entities, citizen action groups, and the general public. The firm's public relations function seeks to highlight positive events like outstanding quarterly sales and profits (to stockholders), or noteworthy community service programs (to government entities and the general public). As well, PR is used strategically for "damage control" when adversity strikes. All organizations at some point face adversity. Additionally, new techniques in public relations have fostered a bolder, more aggressive role for PR in many IBP campaigns.

A New Era for Public Relations?

There are many forces at work that support a growing role for PR activities as part of the advertising and IBP campaigns for all sorts of products and services. Among these are familiar things like increasingly sophisticated and connected consumers who are talking to each other more and more about brands. As noted by Stephen Brown, a prolific and provocative writer on the subject of branding, we are living in a different world from the one that operated in the heyday of mass marketing.[1] As he notes, we have evolved to an intensely commercial world where TV shows feature stories about marketing and consumer psychology, stand-up comics perform skits about shopping routines and brand strategies, and documentaries like *Who Killed the Electric Car?* and *Wal-Mart: The High Cost of Low Price* make great anti-brand entertainment. Industry gossip, executive screw-ups, and product critiques are bloggers' standard fodder. It is a brand-obsessed world.

And as you already know, the consumer is increasingly in control in this brand-obsessed world, using tools like blogs, podcasts, YouTube, RSS feeds, and whatever will be invented next week to exert that control across the Internet.[2] It's a world where marketers must monitor the current buzz about their brands and become part of the dialogue in an effort to rescue or revive their brands. Of course, mass media advertising has never been about dialogue.

Consumers are spreading the word about brands as never before. While marketers have always believed that the most powerful influence in any consumer's decision is the recommendations of friends and family, they have never known exactly what to

1.   Stephen Brown, "Ambi-brand Culture," in *Brand Culture* (New York: Routledge, 2006), 50–66.
2.   Frank Rose, "Let the Seller Beware," *Wall Street Journal,* December 20, 2006, D10.

do about it. Some clues about what to do were provided by Malcolm Gladwell in his bestseller *The Tipping Point,* wherein he makes the case that "mavens" and "connectors" are critically important in fostering social epidemics. The key idea here is that these mavens and connectors can be located, and if you give them useful information or interesting stories about your brand, they may share it with their networks. Of course that sharing is a more robust phenomenon when there exists a medium like the Internet that allows one to spread the word to thousands of one's close, personal friends with the simple click of a mouse.

People talk about brands. The challenge is to give them interesting things to talk about, things that bring one's brand into the conversation in a positive way. Marketers are starting to get it. PR isn't just about managing goodwill; it can be about finding ways to get your brand into the day-to-day conversations of key consumers. We saw this nicely illustrated in the Crest Extreme example with the Irresistibility Quiz. Maytag is another company that is learning how to use PR expertise in a proactive way to build its brand. Its nationwide contest to select the next Maytag Repairman generated 2,000 candidates and lots of buzz in the conventional media and across the Internet. Maytag's vice president of marketing described the effort as a $500,000 campaign that generated $10 million of value, and attributed its success to integrating PR expertise into the planning process for the brand early and often.[3]

In today's dynamic marketplace, where we know there are lots of online and offline conversations taking place about brands, a brand builder needs to take a proactive stance in influencing at least some of those conversations. As always, it takes a strong team effort to ensure integration, and it is becoming increasingly clear that PR expertise needs to be well represented as part of any marketing and advertising team.[4]

Public Relations and Damage Control.
Public relations has always been an important and unique contributor in that PR serves a role that no other promotional tool can. Public relations is the one and only tool that can provide damage control from bad publicity. Such public relations problems can arise from either a firm's own activities or from external forces completely outside a firm's control. Let's consider a classic public relations debacle to illustrate the nature of damage control.

Intel is one of the great success stories of American industry. Intel has risen from relative techno-obscurity as an innovative computer technology company to one of the largest corporations in the world with one of the most visible brands (who doesn't know "Intel Inside"?). Sales have grown from $1.3 billion to more than $40 billion in just 25 years. But all this success did not prepare Intel for the one serious public relations challenge that the firm encountered. In early 1994, Intel introduced its new-generation chip, the now-well-known Pentium, as the successor to the widely used line of X86 chips. But by November 1994, Pentium users were discovering a flaw in the chip. During certain floating-point operations, some Pentium chips were actually producing erroneous calculations—and even though the error showed up in only the fifth or sixth decimal place, power users in scientific laboratories require absolute precision and accuracy in their calculations.

Having a defect in a high-performance technology product such as the Pentium chip was one thing; how Intel handled the problem was another. Intel's initial "official" response was that the flaw in the chip was so insignificant that it would produce an error in calculations only once in 27,000 years. But then IBM, which had shipped thousands of PCs with Pentium chips, challenged the assertion that the flaw was insignificant, claiming that processing errors could occur as often as every 24 days. IBM announced that it would stop shipment of all Pentium-based PCs immediately.[5]

3.   Jeffrey Davidoff, "Want Great PR? Get Your Agencies to Share the Load," *Advertising Age,* August 13, 2007, 12–13.
4.   Claire Stammerjohan, Charles M. Wood, Yuhmiin Chang, and Esther Thorson, "An Empirical Investigation of the Interaction Between Publicity, Advertising, and Previous Brand Attitudes and Knowledge," *Journal of Advertising,* Winter 2005, 55–67; Jonah Bloom, "Marketing, PR Departments Must Bridge the Cultural Gulf," *Advertising Age,* March 12, 2007, 18.
5.   Barbara Grady, "Chastened Intel Steps Carefully with Introduction of New Chip," *Computerlink,* February 14, 1995, 11.

Source: Dilbert reprinted by permission of United Features Syndicate, Inc.

EXHIBIT 20.5

When Intel did not respond quickly and positively to problems with its Pentium chip, the press unloaded a barrage of negative publicity on the firm. Even Dilbert got into the act with this parody of Intel decision making.

From this point on, the Pentium situation became a runaway public relations disaster. Every major newspaper, network newscast, and magazine carried the story of the flawed Pentium chip. Even the cartoon series *Dilbert* got in on the act, running a whole series of cartoon strips that spoofed the Intel controversy (see Exhibit 20.5). One observer characterized it this way: "From a public relations standpoint, the train has left the station and is barreling out of Intel's control."[6] For weeks Intel did nothing but publicly argue that the flaw would not affect the vast majority of users.

Finally Intel decided to provide a free replacement chip to any user who believed he or she was at risk. In announcing the $475 million program to replace customers' chips, Andy Grove, Intel's highly accomplished CEO, admitted publicly that "the Pentium processor divide problem has been a learning experience for Intel."[7]

Firms large and small encounter PR problems; that's not going to change. Indeed, as consumers become more informed and connected, the bad news just travels faster and lingers longer. This "bad news" can take many forms. For Taco Bell it was an Internet video of rats running amok at its Greenwich Village restaurant.[8] You can close the restaurant, but that video is still out there. Johnson & Johnson walked into a PR firestorm by suing the Red Cross for logo infringement.[9] That's a hard case to win in the court of public opinion, but it's definitely a self-inflicted wound for J&J.

And Wal-Mart seems to have developed a penchant for attracting negative news, like the ongoing controversy about how it treats its frontline employees. A group calling itself "Wake Up Wal-Mart" has demonstrated great PR prowess in trashing the Wal-Mart brand.[10] Check out their approach at http://www.WakeUpWalmart .com. The Wal-Mart example also shows what happens when bad publicity is handled poorly. According to a report by McKinsey & Company, a significant number of Wal-Mart customers say they have stopped shopping there because of lingering negative news.[11]

Companies need to learn how to handle the bad news. No company is immune. But while many public relations episodes must be reactive, a firm can be prepared with public relations materials to conduct an orderly and positive relations-building campaign with its constituents. To fully appreciate the potential of public relations, we will next consider the objectives and tools of public relations, and basic public relations strategies.

6.   James G. Kimball, "Can Intel Repair the Pentium PR?" *Advertising Age,* December 19, 1994, 35.

7.   Grady, "Chastened Intel Steps Carefully with Introduction of New Chip."

8.   Kate MacArthur, "Taco Hell: Rodent Video Signals New Era in PR Crises," *Advertising Age,* February 26, 2007, 1, 46.

9.   Jack Neff, "J&J Targets Red Cross, Blunders into PR Firestorm," *Advertising Age,* August 13, 2007, 1, 22.

10. Barney Gimbel, "Attack of the Wal-Martyrs," *Fortune,* December 11, 2006, 125–130.

11. Jon Birger, "The Unending Woes of Lee Scott," *Fortune,* January 22, 2007, 118–122.

2 Objectives for Public Relations. While reacting to a crisis is a necessity, it is always more desirable to take a proactive approach. The key is to have a structured approach to public relations, including a clear understanding of objectives for PR. Within the broad guidelines of image building, damage control, and establishing relationships with constituents, it is possible to identify six primary objectives of public relations:

- *Promoting goodwill.* This is an image-building function of public relations. Industry events or community activities that reflect favorably on a firm are highlighted. When Pepsi launched a program to support school music programs—programs hard-hit by funding decreases—the firm garnered widespread goodwill.
- *Promoting a product or service.* Press releases, events, or brand "news" that increase public awareness of a firm's brands can be pursued through public relations. Large pharmaceutical firms such as Merck and GlaxoSmithKline issue press releases when they discover new drugs or achieve FDA approval. Likewise, BP has been proactive in promoting its "green" initiatives (Beyond Petroleum) in the face of the negative press that follows all the Big Oil companies.
- *Preparing internal communications.* Disseminating information and correcting misinformation within a firm can reduce the impact of rumors and increase employee morale. For events such as reductions in the labor force or mergers of firms, internal communications can do much to dispel rumors circulating among employees and in the local community.
- *Counteracting negative publicity.* This is the damage-control function of public relations, as discussed earlier. The attempt here is not to cover up negative events, but rather to prevent the negative publicity from damaging the image of a firm and its brands. When a lawsuit was filed against NEC alleging that one of its cellular phones had caused cancer, McCaw Cellular Communications used public relations activities to inform the public and especially cellular phone users of scientific knowledge that argued against the claims in the lawsuit. Also, one industry's public relations problems are another industry's golden opportunity, as the ad in Exhibit 20.6 shows.
- *Lobbying.* The public relations function can assist a firm in dealing with government officials and pending legislation. Microsoft reportedly spent $4.6 billion on such lobbying efforts when antitrust violations were leveled at the company. Industry groups also maintain active and aggressive lobbying efforts at both the state and federal levels. As an example, the beer and wine industry has lobbyists monitoring legislation that could restrict beer and wine advertising.
- *Giving advice and counsel.* Assisting management in determining what (if any) position to take on public issues, preparing employees for public appearances, and helping management anticipate public reactions are all part of the advice and counsel function of public relations.

Practice safe cellular.™

Great Gift Item!

Speaker and microphone in one earpiece with comfort-fit EarGels™.

Keep both hands on the wheel, both eyes on the road, and a JABRA® EarSet™ in your ear.

The portable, plug-and-play JABRA EarSet for cellular and PCS mobile phones lets you talk and listen all in your ear. It gives you comfort, great reception and something you can really use on the road: Two free hands.

Find JABRA products at leading retailers, catalogs, websites and wireless carriers worldwide.
1 800 EAR 2230 (USA and Canada) • 1 858 622 9955 • www.jabra.com

JABRA
A GN Netcom Company

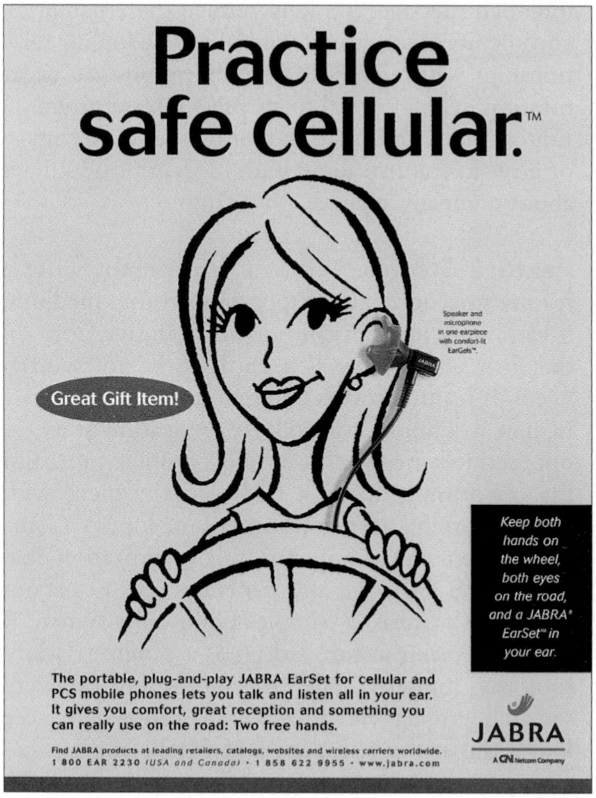

EXHIBIT 20.6

Public relations problems in one industry create opportunities in another. When medical research suggested that extensive cellular phone use could be linked to brain tumors, firms developed cell phone accessories to address the issue. Here, Jabra is alluding to the negative publicity and the medical research as the basis for its brand appeal.

The Tools of Public Relations. There are several means by which a firm can pursue the objectives just cited. The goal is to gain as much control over the process as possible. By using the tools discussed in the following sections, a firm can integrate its public relations efforts with other brand communications.

Press Releases. Having a file of information that makes for good news stories puts the firm in a position to take advantage of free press coverage. Press releases allow a firm to pursue positive publicity from the media. Exhibit 20.7 is a press release announcing Myriad Genetics' discovery of a gene related to high cholesterol. Topics that make for good press releases include

- New products
- New scientific discoveries
- New personnel
- New corporate facilities
- Innovative corporate practices, such as energy-saving programs or employee benefit programs
- Annual shareholder meetings
- Charitable and community service activities

The only drawback to press releases is that a firm often doesn't know if or when the item will appear in the news. Also, journalists are free to edit or interpret a news release, which may alter its intended message. To help reduce these liabilities, consultants recommend carefully developing relationships with editors from publications the organization deems critical to its press release program. Editors prefer information that focuses on technical or how-to features along with in-depth case studies about company successes and failures.

Feature Stories. While a firm cannot write a feature story for a newspaper or any other medium, it can invite journalists to do an exclusive story on the firm when there is a particularly noteworthy event. A feature story is different from a press release in that it is more controllable. A feature story, as opposed to a news release, offers a single journalist the opportunity to do a fairly lengthy piece with exclusive rights to the information. Jupiter Communications, a leading research organization that tracks Internet usage and generates statistics about the Internet, has a simple philosophy when it comes to using feature stories as a public relations tool. Says Jupiter's CEO, "It is our goal to get every research project we do covered somewhere. We know this is the cheapest, and maybe most effective, way to market ourselves."[12]

Company Newsletters. In-house publications such as newsletters can disseminate positive infor-

---

Tuesday, June 5, 6:30 A.M. Eastern Time

Press Release

SOURCE: Myriad Genetics, Inc.

Myriad Genetics Discovers High Cholesterol Gene

CHD2 Enzyme is in Novel Pathway, May Lead to New Class of Cholesterol Lowering Drugs

Salt Lake City, June 5/PRNewswire/—Myriad Genetics, Inc. (NASDAQ: MYGN-news), has discovered a human gene responsible for high total cholesterol and low HDL (also known as "good cholesterol"), in individuals with early age myocardial infarction. The research shows that the gene's protein product is produced in abnormal amounts in these individuals and has enzymatic activity and other characteristics that suggest it will be readily amenable as a drug target. The CHD2 (Coronary Heart Disease 2) protein acts in a novel, previously unknown pathway, distinct from the cholesterol synthesis pathway that is acted upon by the statin class of drugs and other classes of drugs.

The CHD2 gene, and its function, was discovered by a combination of genetic analyses of families whose members had heart attacks at an early age and an analysis of biological pathways. In total, more than 5,000 individuals from 145 families were analyzed to identify the gene. The discovery in this population, made by Myriad in collaboration with scientists from the Cardiovascular Genetics Research Clinic at the University of Utah, means that abnormal levels of the CHD2 protein are critical to the development of disease. Because disorders of the CHD2 gene lead to high LDL cholesterol, low HDL cholesterol, and early-onset heart disease, inhibition of the gene with a small molecule drug is expected to lower cholesterol and reduce the risk of heart disease across the general population of individuals with high cholesterol. Current therapies, including the statins, are inadequate in lowering the total cholesterol to recommended levels in many patients. Heart disease remains the most common cause of death in the United States. Studies estimate that half of all men and one-third of women will develop heart disease during their lives.

"The discovery of this novel drug target for the treatment of heart disease points to the strengths of Myriad's integrated approach to drug development incorporating the best technologies of genomics and proteomics in a high-throughput, industrialized fashion," said Peter Meldrum, President and Chief Executive Officer of Myriad Genetics, Inc. "Myriad now has a full pipeline of earlier stage preclinical compounds to back up our lead prostate cancer drug, which has completed a Phase IIa human clinical trial, and we intend to aggressively advance these compounds toward commercialization."

EXHIBIT 20.7

A press release is good way to communicate positive information about a firm to a wide variety of constituents and stakeholders. Here, Myriad Genetics has issued a press release regarding a new drug designed to lower cholesterol.

---

12. Andy Cohen, "The Jupiter Mission," *Sales and Marketing Management*, April 2000, 56.

mation about a firm through its employees. As members of the community, employees are proud of achievements by their firm. Newsletters can also be distributed to important constituents in the community, such as government officials, the chamber of commerce, or the tourism bureau. Suppliers often enjoy reading about an important customer, so newsletters can be mailed to this group as well. As in other areas, firms have discovered that the Internet is an excellent way to distribute information that traditionally has been the focus of newsletters.

Interviews and Press Conferences. Interviews with key executives or staged press conferences can be highly effective public relations tools. Often they are warranted in a crisis management situation. But firms also call press conferences to announce important scientific breakthroughs or explain the details of a corporate expansion or a new product launch. Of course, no one does this better than Steve Jobs each and every time Apple has big news about a new product. The press conference has an air of credibility because it uses a news format to present salient information.

Sponsored Events. As was discussed in Chapter 18, sponsoring events can also serve as an important public relations tool. Sponsorships run the gamut from supporting community events to mega-events such as the Olympics. At the local level, prominent display of the corporate name and logo offers residents the chance to see that an organization is dedicated to supporting their community.

Another form of sponsorship is the fund-raiser. Fund-raisers for nonprofit organizations of all sorts give positive visibility to corporations. For many years, Chevrolet has sponsored college scholarships through the NCAA by choosing the best offensive and defensive player in televised football games. The scholarships are announced with much fanfare at the conclusion of the game. This sort of publicity for Chevrolet can also make a favorable impression.

Publicity. **Publicity** is essentially "free" media exposure about a firm's activities or brands. The public relations function seeks to monitor and manage publicity, but obviously can never actually control what the media chooses to say or report. This lack of control was demonstrated earlier in the chapter with the examples of Intel, Taco Bell, and Wal-Mart. As suggested by Exhibit 20.8, politics is another walk of life where the tone of one's publicity can be hard to manage. Organizations (or politicians) need to be prepared to take advantage of events that make for good publicity and to counter events that are potentially damaging to their reputation.

The appeal of publicity—when the information is positive—is that it tends to carry heightened credibility. Publicity that appears in news stories on television and radio and in newspapers and magazines assumes an air of believability because of the credibility of the media context. Not-for-profit organizations often use publicity in the form of news stories and public interest stories as ways to gain widespread visibility at little or no cost.

But publicity is not always completely out of the company's control. For instance, during the Academy

"HOW'S THAT PRO-AMERICAN FOREIGN-ADVERTISING P.R. BLITZ THINGY COMING ALONG?"

EXHIBIT 20.8

Managing public perceptions is an ongoing challenge in the world of politics, just as it is in the world of business.

© Jim Borgman, Sept. 6, 2002. Reprinted by special permission, Universal Press Syndicate.

ETHICS

Guerrilla Marketing Run Amok

The ideal scenario for a guerrilla marketing campaign is to use a small marketing budget, typically in a major metro area, and create countercultural buzz, often for offbeat products and brands. If the buzz spills over to the major media, into the blogosphere, and the almost inevitable YouTube videos, so much the better. But for most people, causing a bomb scare and creating a mass panic that brings a city like Boston to a screeching halt crosses the line. Turner Broadcasting felt the sting of negative publicity for a clumsy guerrilla marketing campaign it funded on behalf of its Cartoon Network TV show *Aqua Teen Hunger Force*.

Surely Turner did not intend to cause a bomb scare in Boston. In fact, this campaign ran in nine other large cities and almost no one noticed. But in Boston, things definitely got out of control. Turner's street operatives Sean Stevens and Peter Berdovsky had placed 40 blinking black boxes all around Boston in public places. Both men were charged with violating a Massachusetts law—passed after the anthrax scare of 2001—that makes it a felony to place a hoax device with the intent to cause anxiety. A Turner spokesperson contended that "It was never intended to be a hoax," but the mayor of Boston clearly was not amused. Post-arraignment statements from Stevens and Berdovsky didn't help matters. Both seemed amused at how their little stunt had turned into such a big headache for Boston officials.

A cynic might say that even in this case, the exposure that Turner received for its TV show made the whole incident a very cost-effective marketing investment. Indeed, for a period of about 48 hours, the debacle in Boston even upstaged the Super Bowl for generating media hype. And who knows, maybe guys like Sean Stevens and Peter Berdovsky are inspirational for the prospective viewers of *Aqua Teen Hunger Force*. Or you might say, it was the city of Boston that over-reacted. After all, the blinking lights on each of the 40 boxes were the outline of a cartoon character (albeit a pretty mean one making an obscene gesture). Maybe there really is no such thing as bad publicity.

Call us old-fashioned if you like, but in a post-9/11 world it is just hard to see how any campaign that resurfaces memories of an event like the 2001 anthrax scare could be a good thing. Shortly after the event, Kelly O'Keefe of Virginia Commonwealth University's Adcenter put it this way: "Most people who are involved in guerilla marketing are very responsible advertisers and do very responsible things. This is an irrational act. It is really guerilla marketing gone awry and it is inexcusable." We agree.

Sources: Andrew Hampp, "Lite-Brites, Big City and a Whole Load of Trouble," **Advertising Age,** February 5, 2007, 1, 34; Jennifer Levitz and Emily Steel, "Boston Stunt Draws Legal, Ethical Fire," **Wall Street Journal,** February 2, 2007, B3.

Awards a bracelet worn by actress Julia Roberts caused quite a stir. After Roberts won the award for best actress, she stood smiling (which we all know she does so well) and waving to the cameras, and suddenly the whole world wanted to know about the snowflake-design Van Cleef & Arpels bracelet that adorned her right (waving) wrist. What a lucky break for the designers! Not. The whole episode was carefully planned by Van Cleef's PR agency, Ted, Inc. The agency lobbied hard to convince Roberts that the bracelet and matching earrings were stunning with her dress, knowing that if she won the Oscar, she would be highly photographed waving that pretty bracelet.[13]

Stirring up a controversy is a sure way to get publicity, and many companies and their brands thrive on publicity. (As shown in Exhibit 20.9, Richard Branson was stirring up controversy even at age 15.) In fact, there is an old saying in PR circles that goes something like, "There is no such thing as bad publicity." The point is that in most cases it is a good thing for your brand to be in the news. But controversy can backfire, as in the case of a recent Turner Broadcasting promotion. Read more about how to get bad publicity in the Ethics box.

③ Basic Public Relations Strategies. Given the breadth of possibilities for using public relations as part of a firm's overall advertising and IBP effort, we need to identify basic public relations strategies. Public relations strategies can be categorized as either proactive or reactive. **Proactive public relations strategy** is guided by marketing objectives, seeks to publicize a company and its brands, and takes an offensive rather than defensive posture in the public relations process. **Reactive public relations strategy** is dictated by influences outside the control of a company, focuses on problems to be solved rather than on opportunities, and requires a company to take defensive measures. These two strategies involve different orientations to public relations.[14]

---

13.   Beth Snyder Bulik, "Well-Heeled Heed the Need for PR," *Advertising Age,* June 11, 2001, S2.

14.   These definitions were developed from discussions offered by Jordan Goldman, *Public Relations in the Marketing Mix* (Lincolnwood, IL: NTC Business Books, 1992), xi–xii.

EXHIBIT 20.9

EXHIBIT 20.10

"At age 15, his headmaster said he'd either wind up rich . . . or in prison . . . If his headmaster could only see him now." As the preceding quote from the body copy of this ad and its clever image demonstrate, even as a schoolboy Richard Branson was hard to control. Although he never really outgrew his naughty nature, he did put it to good use promoting all things Virgin.

The biotechnology industry is taking a proactive approach to the controversies surrounding the industry and its processes. See also http://www.whybiotech.com.

Proactive Strategy. In developing a proactive PR strategy, a firm acknowledges opportunities to use public relations efforts to accomplish something positive. Companies often rely heavily on their public relations firms to help them put together a proactive strategy. The biotechnology industry, for example, is subject to much controversy in the press regarding genetically altered food and seed products. The advertisement in Exhibit 20.10 from the biotechnology industry attempts to take a proactive approach to dealing with the controversies by presenting a positive image and information.

In many firms, the positive aspects of employee achievements, corporate contributions to the community, and the organization's social and environmental programs go unnoticed by important constituents. To implement a proactive strategy, a firm needs to develop a comprehensive public relations program. The key components of such a program are as follows:

1. *A public relations audit.* A **public relations audit** identifies the characteristics of a firm or the aspects of the firm's activities that are positive and newsworthy. Information is gathered in much the same way as information related to advertising strategy is gathered. Corporate personnel and customers are questioned to provide information. This information may include descriptions of company products and services, market performance of brands, profitability, goals for products, market trends, new product introductions, important suppliers, important customers, employee programs and facilities, community programs, and charitable activities.

2. *A public relations plan.* Once the firm is armed with information from a public relations audit, the next step is a structured plan. A **public relations plan** identifies the objectives and activities related to the public relations communications issued by a firm. The components of a public relations plan include the following:

   a. *Situation analysis.* This section of the public relations plan summarizes the information obtained from the public relations audit. Information contained here is often broken down by category, such as product performance or community activity.

   b. *Program objectives.* Objectives for a proactive PR program stem from the current situation. Objectives should be set for both short-term and long-term opportunities. Public relations objectives can be as diverse and complex as advertising objectives. The focal point is not sales or profits per se. Rather, factors such as the credibility of product performance (that is, placing products in verified, independent tests) or the stature of the firm's research and development efforts (highlighted in a prestigious trade publication article) are legitimate types of PR objectives.

   c. *Program rationale.* In this section, it is critical to identify the role the public relations program will play relative to all the other communication efforts—particularly advertising—being undertaken by a firm. This is the area where an integrated brand promotion perspective is clearly articulated for the public relations effort.

   d. *Communications vehicles.* This section of the plan specifies precisely what means will be used to implement the public relations plan. The tools discussed earlier in the chapter—press releases, interviews, newsletters—constitute the communications vehicles through which objectives can be implemented. There will likely be discussion of precisely how press releases, interviews, and company newsletters can be used.[15]

   e. *Message content.* Analysts suggest that public relations messages should be researched and developed in much the same way that advertising messages are researched and developed. Focus groups and in-depth interviews are being used to fine-tune PR communications. For example, a pharmaceutical firm learned that calling obesity a "disease" rather than a "condition" increased the overweight population's receptivity to the firm's press release messages regarding a new anti-obesity drug.[16]

A proactive public relations strategy has the potential for making an important supportive contribution to a firm's IBP effort. Carefully placing positive information targeted to potentially influential constituents—such as members of the community or stockholders—supports the overall goal of enhancing the image, reputation, and perception of a firm and its brands.

Reactive Strategy. A reactive PR strategy may seem like a contradiction in terms, but as stated earlier, firms must implement a reactive strategy when events outside the control of the firm create negative publicity. Coca-Cola was able to rein in negative publicity by acting swiftly after an unfortunate incident occurred in Europe. Seven days after a bottling problem caused teens in Belgium and France to become sick after drinking Coke, the firm acted quickly and pulled all Coca-Cola products from the market, with an apology from the CEO.[17] Coca-Cola's quick actions could not prevent negative consequences in terms of product sales. That would call for new marketing programs tailored to meet the needs of consumers on a country-by-country basis. The programs relied heavily on integrated brand promotion

15.   Ibid., 4–14.
16.   Geri Mazur, "Good PR Starts with Good Research," *Marketing News*, September 15, 1997, 16.
17.   Kathleen V. Schmidt, "Coke's Crisis," *Marketing News*, September 27, 1999, 1, 11.

GLOBALIZATION

Public Relations with Global Impact

Few brands generate as much cultural association as Guinness. The 250-year-old brand of stout beer has been attracting tourists to its St. James's Gate brewery in Dublin, Ireland, for more than a century. But executives at Guinness faced a tough challenge: The old reception area was totally inadequate to handle the thousands of tourists who flocked to the brewery each year. The task, however, was much larger than just building a new reception area. The brewery was the very pinnacle of the traditional image of the brand.

The task of building a new reception/visitor area was as much a public relations problem as it was a practical problem. The tradition of the brand image had to be preserved while thousands of tourists had to be accommodated. Guinness strategists conceived the problem this way:

- How to accommodate the ever-growing flock of devotees who come to Dublin to connect with the brand's "spiritual home"
- How to modernize the conference and meeting room facilities for corporate use
- How to maintain its traditional relationships with Guinness loyalists while also appealing to younger consumers, many of whom have watched their fathers quaff many a pint of Guinness

The last point was of particular concern to marketing managers at Guinness. Stout beer has, over the past 10 years, been challenged in Ireland by a wide range of new, contemporary beers and other alcoholic drinks targeted to younger drinkers.

The solution chosen for all the public relations and promotion issues the firm felt it faced was a new seven-story structure called The Guinness Storehouse. The Storehouse preserved and incorporated the five-story Market Street Storehouse, which had served as a Guinness storage facility in the early 1900s. The solution was an expensive one, with a price tag of over $45 million. But the investment seems to be paying off. Within two years of its opening, the visitor center attracted its millionth visitor and the Storehouse is now the number one fee-paying tourist spot in all of Ireland. Most importantly, the Storehouse aims to evoke in visitors an affinity with the brand. With 10 million glasses of Guinness consumed every day around the world, it would appear this PR effort is an appropriate testimony to the brand.

Source: Arundhati Parmar, "Guinness Intoxicates," **Marketing News**, November 10, 2003, 4, 6.

strategies including free samples; dealer incentive programs; and beach parties featuring sound and light shows, DJs, and cocktail bars with free Cokes to win back the critical teen segment.[18] In the end it was a complete and integrated effort that restored consumers' trust and rebuilt the business across Europe.

It is difficult to organize for and provide structure around reactive PR. Since the events that trigger a reactive effort are unpredictable as well as uncontrollable, a firm must simply be prepared to act quickly and thoughtfully. Two steps help firms implement a reactive public relations strategy:

1. *The public relations audit.* The public relations audit that was prepared for the proactive strategy helps a firm also prepare its reactive strategy. The information provided by the audit gives a firm what it needs to issue public statements based on current and accurate data.

2. *The identification of vulnerabilities.* In addition to preparing current information, the other key step in a reactive strategy is to recognize areas where the firm has weaknesses in its operations or products that can negatively affect its relationships with important constituents. From a public relations standpoint, these weaknesses are called *vulnerabilities*. If aspects of a firm's operations are vulnerable to criticism, such as environmental issues related to manufacturing processes, then the public relations function should be prepared to discuss the issues in a broad range of forums with many different constituents. Leaders at Pepsi, Quaker Oats, and Philip Morris were taken somewhat by surprise when shareholders challenged the firms on their practices with respect to genetically modified foods. While the concern was among a minority of shareholders, there were enough concerned constituents to warrant a proxy vote on the issue of genetically modified foods.[19] Of course executives at these firms now understand that pursuing any form of genetically modified foods will always be one of their vulnerabilities.

18.   Amie Smith, "Coke's European Resurgence," *Promo Magazine*, December 1999, 91.
19.   James Cox, "Shareholders Get to Put Bio-Engineered Foods to Vote," *USA Today*, June 6, 2000, 1B.

A Final Word on Public Relations. Public relations is a prime example of how a firm (or an individual) can identify and then manage aspects of communication in an integrated and synergistic manner to diverse audiences. Without recognizing public relations activities as a component of the firm's overall communication effort, misinformation or disinformation could compromise more mainstream communications such as advertising. The coordination of public relations into an integrated program is a matter of recognizing and identifying the process as critical to the overall IBP effort, and, as always, getting the right set of players on your IBP team. As an example of using public relations in a powerful and ideal way, consider how Guinness, the venerable Irish brewer, launched a PR effort that appealed to both long-time Guinness loyalists and a new generation of Guinness drinkers (see the Globalization box on the previous page).

Influencer Marketing.
If public relations is the discipline devoted to monitoring and managing how people view us, then it can also be thought of as a discipline devoted to monitoring and managing what consumers are saying to one another about us. Moreover, as noted earlier in this chapter, consumers have become increasingly predisposed to talk about brands, both online and offline. Since we know they are likely to talk about our brands anyway, it seems prudent to follow the advice of Bonnie Raitt from her album *Luck of the Draw*. As Bonnie says (and sings) in her 1990s blues-rock hit: "Let's give them something to talk about!"

That basic idea, "give 'em something to talk about," underlies the evolution of an important new communication discipline that we will represent under the general label of influencer marketing. As defined by Northlich, a leader in influencer marketing programming, **influencer marketing** refers to a series of personalized marketing techniques directed at individuals or groups who have the credibility and capability to drive positive word of mouth in a broader and salient segment of the population. The idea is to give the influencer something to talk about. Additionally, it is useful to distinguish between professional and peer-to-peer influencer programs. Both can provide one of the most valued assets for any brand builder—an advocacy message from a trusted source.[20]

Professional Influencer Programs. If you're a pet owner, it's likely you've made many visits to the vet. And while visiting the vet, perhaps you asked a few questions about the best products to feed your puppy or kitten. Pet owners always want to do the right thing for their four-legged friends. If you've lived this scenario, you know what comes next. The vet is ready to talk about proper feeding, and not only that, he or she may be ready with product samples or informational brochures describing the benefits of a particular brand of pet food. Coincidence? Not at all. The makers of IAMS, Eukanuba, and Hill's Science Diet know that vets are key influencers in the decision about what to feed one's pet, especially for devoted pet owners who don't mind paying a little extra to get the best. These brands target vets with influencer marketing programs to try to earn their recommendation.

Many professionals are in this position where their advice about products is highly valued by consumers. Your doctor, dentist, neonatal nurse, auto mechanic, and hair stylist all have the credibility to influence product choices in their specific areas of expertise. Sometimes the opportunity is obvious, as with the example of vets and pet food. But more and more we are seeing creative programming that takes influencer programming into new territory. An excellent example is that of Select Comfort, which targets many different types of health care professionals with an influencer program for its Sleep Number bed.

20.   Robert Berner, "I Sold it Through the Grapevine," *BusinessWeek,* May 29, 2006, 32–34.

The information kit that Select Comfort provides to health care professionals includes a DVD and brochures that carefully document the benefits of the Sleep Number bed. The prescription pad allows the therapist to put his or her recommendation in writing.

One particular group of health care professionals targeted by Select Comfort is Occupational Therapists (OTs). Persons in this field provide therapy to individuals with serious physical challenges, and they commonly receive promotional materials for things like the Moen bathtub grab bar, which makes it easier for persons with physical challenges to bathe safely (see other product information offered to OTs at http://www.hartleydata.com/OT). But are OTs experts on sleep? Doesn't matter. Many of their patients are likely to value their opinions, and all health care professionals commonly hear complaints from their patients about having trouble sleeping. So what advice can the OT provide to help a person sleep better?

Obviously, if you're Select Comfort, you'd like the OT to encourage patients to have a look at the Sleep Number bed. The first step is to get that OT to try and use the bed herself. Thus, Select Comfort offers special promotions to encourage OTs to purchase Sleep Number beds for their own bedrooms. Next, the OT needs tools to follow through on their potential advocacy. No problem. Like most professionals, OTs belong to associations and subscribe to journals. Name and address files from such sources allow a company to start building an OT marketing database. Once an OT expresses any kind of interest in the Sleep Number bed, she is sent an advocacy kit. Some key elements of that kit are displayed in Exhibit 20.11. Marketers at Select Comfort cannot control what the OT says to her patient about the Sleep Number bed. But they can put materials in her hands that will make it easy for her to become an advocate, if she believes such advocacy is justified. That's the nature of influencer marketing.

Think of influencer marketing as systematic seeding of conversations involving a consumer, an influencer, and a brand. Professionals in any field of endeavor take their role very seriously, so influencer programs directed to them must be handled with great care. Several points of emphasis should be kept in mind when developing programs for professionals. First, their time is money, so any program that wastes their time will be a waste of money. However, tactics designed to encourage professionals to try the product themselves can be very valuable. Also, messaging with professionals needs to provide intellectual currency and help the professional learn important benefits of the brand. For example, health care professionals' concerns will be better addressed through clinical studies than celebrity endorsements. Additionally, programs directed at professionals require a long-term commitment. For them to be advocates, trust first must develop, and any marketer must show patience and persistence to earn that trust.

Peer-to-Peer Programs.
Peer-to-peer programs typically have a very different tone than programs for professionals. In peer-to-peer programs the idea is to give influencers something fun or provocative to talk about. Think of it as an emphasis on "social currency" for peer-to-peer versus "intellectual currency" for professionals. A great guiding principle for peer-to-peer programs is "Do something remarkable" to get people talking about your brand.[21] To promote Virgin Mobile's "Nothing to Hide" campaign, Richard Branson descended into Time Square on a giant cell phone while performing a striptease act. Pretty remarkable. To launch its G6 model, Pontiac gave away 276 cars to the flabbergasted audience members of Oprah's season-opening show.[22] Pretty remarkable. Just follow that advice from Bonnie Raitt: Give 'em something to talk about is a good starting point.

Buzz and Viral Marketing.
Two hot concepts in this area of peer-to-peer influence are buzz and viral marketing. Essentially, both of these refer to efforts to stimulate word-of-mouth involving key targets that might otherwise be impervious to more traditional advertising and promotional tools. **Buzz marketing** can be defined as creating an event or experience that yields conversations that include the brand. **Viral marketing** is the process of consumers marketing to consumers via the Web (e.g., via blogs or forwarding YouTube links) or through personal contact stimulated by a firm marketing a brand. The idea behind both buzz and viral marketing strategies is to target a handful of carefully chosen trendsetters or connectors as your influencers, and let them spread the word.[23]

So it is often the case that buzz marketing programs are fielded in cities like New York, London, and Los Angeles, because that's where you find these trendsetters. Consider this scene at the cafés on Third Street Promenade in and around Los Angeles. A gang of sleek, impossibly attractive bikers pulls up and, guess what, they seem *genuinely* interested in getting to know you over an iced latte—their treat, no less! Sooner or later the conversation turns to their Vespa scooters glinting in the sun, and they eagerly pull out a pad and jot down an address and phone number—for the nearest Vespa dealer. The scooter-riding, latte-drinking models are on the Vespa payroll, and they're paid to create buzz about the scooters by engaging hip café dwellers in conversation and camaraderie.[24]

Cultivating Connectors.
Publicity stunts can be thought of as buzz builders, and there is nothing new about them. In 1863 P. T. Barnum orchestrated a wedding between two of his circus stars to boost attendance at the circus. The remarkable thing about this circus wedding was that bride and groom were both just 3 feet tall. P. T. Barnum knew how to create a buzz; he just didn't call it that.

But as you might expect, there is a lot that separates old-school publicity stunts from today's practice of influencer marketing. For one thing, there is the level of experience and sophistication of organizations like Northlich and Keller Fay Group when it comes to assisting clients with influencer programming. Keller Fay has developed a tracking system that can estimate the number of word-of-mouth conversations taking place on a daily basis. In 2006 the firm estimated that consumers shared opinions about brands on the order of 3.5 billion times per day. That's 3.5 billion word-of-mouth conversations each day, a majority of which were offline, but with a growing percentage online.[25] Another familiar name and key supplier in this space is Nielsen BuzzMetrics. BuzzMetrics provides services to clients for tracking word-

21.   Michael Krauss, "To Generate Buzz, Do Remarkable Things," *Marketing News,* December 15, 2006, 6.
22.   Matthew Creamer and Jean Halliday, "Dead Giveaways," *Advertising Age,* March 14, 2005, 3.
23.   Gerry Khermouch and Jeff Green, "Buzz-z-z Marketing," *BusinessWeek,* July 30, 2001, 50–56.
24.   Ibid.
25.   Ed Keller and Jon Berry, "Word-of-Mouth: The Real Action is Offline," *Advertising Age,* December 4, 2006, 20.

DOING IT RIGHT

Five Ts Are the Keys

No doubt, any marketer's dream is to have consumers saying positive things to one another about its brands. Now there appears to be a new level of sophistication in obtaining this happy state. And no one has better credentials on the topic than Andy Sernovitz, who founded WOMMA in 2004. In his book *Word of Mouth Marketing: How Smart Companies Get People Talking*, he draws on numerous cases for a wide variety of brands to offer up success principles for those who desire favorable "word of mouth." Turns out it's as simple as the Five Ts.

Talkers. Much like our point about connectors, Andy asserts that you have to find the people who are predisposed to talk about brands in general, and/or your brand in particular. Often you need to be on the Internet to find these people. Find them and get to know them.

Topics. Next, of course, you have to give them something to talk about. This can't be a marketing message or a mission statement. There needs to be a mystery or a cool story or some breaking news that you are sharing to get people talking. Maybe the best at doing this is Steve Jobs at Apple. He definitely has a knack for stirring up interest and conversation with his suspenseful product announcements and his implied promise that our next great thing is just around the corner.

Tools. Make good use of the tools that promote a viral conversation. You can post a story on a Web page and some will find it there, but in the end it just sits there. You put the exact same story on a blog and it's linkable, portable, built to travel across the Internet. Suddenly lots of people are sharing the story.

Taking part. Stop thinking in terms of one-way communication; start thinking in terms of dialogue. If you want favorable word of mouth, you need to be part of the conversation, not ignore it. Dell was slow to take part in a conversation about problems consumers had getting service. Basically, they ignored the conversation. When blogger Jeff Jarvis had big problems with his Dell and couldn't get the company's attention he coined the phrase "Dell Hell," which became a lightning rod for conversation about Dell on the Internet. You've got to be tuned in if you ever want to join the conversation.

Tracking. Word of mouth on the Internet is very measurable. With blogs, people write things down in full view. This is an opportunity for any company to know what people are saying about their brands and why they are saying it. Lots of companies are paying close attention to what consumers are saying about their brands. Even Dell is now among them.

Sources: Andy Sernovitz, **Word of Mouth Marketing: How Smart Companies Get People Talking**, Chicago, IL: Kaplan Publishing, 2006; Michael Krauss, "To Generate Buzz, Do Remarkable Things," **Marketing News**, December 15, 2006.

of-mouth activity across the Internet. The point is, it's no longer just about the publicity stunt (but don't tell that to Richard Branson), and with billions of conversations every day, lots of brand builders, from Beam to Baskin Robbins, want to be involved.

One specific area where we see dramatic advancements in influencer marketing on the peer-to-peer side is in the activity of identifying and cultivating connectors. Meet Donna Wetherell. Donna is an outgoing mom and works at a customer-service call center where she knows about 300 coworkers by name. She likes to talk about shopping and lots of different brands. She always seems to have lots of extra coupons for the brands she likes, so much so that her coworkers call her the coupon lady. Donna is a connector, one of 600,000 that P&G has enrolled for its new influencer program called Vocalpoint.[26]

That's right, your chatty next-door neighbor, who seems to know everyone and loves to talk about her favorite brands, could be one of these highly coveted connectors. For its connector database P&G focuses on women who have large social networks. They search for them over the Internet at sites like iVillage.com, and are always looking for referrals (if you'd like to nominate your chatty neighbor). It seems connectors like the idea of being the first to receive new product samples and to feel that their voice is being heard by a big company.

Once the connector database is developed, it again becomes a matter of giving your connectors something to talk about. That's the part they enjoy. But in the end it's not always a simple thing to get consumers talking about a product like dishwashing detergent, so here again P&G execs assert that "We do tremendous research behind it to give them a reason to care."[27] Just as with professional programs, you can't force someone to be an advocate for your brand. You can identify people who have big social networks, but they're not going

26. Berner, "I Sold it Through the Grapevine."
27. Ibid., 34.

to compromise their relationships with others by sharing dull stories or phony information. You must give them something interesting to talk about.

Developing connector databases, finding the conversation starters, tracking the buzz online and off, that's the new era of influencer marketing. And it doesn't hurt to have a little of the P. T. Barnum flair as part of the process either. An area that once was very mysterious, that is, word-of-mouth marketing, is becoming increasingly demystified and in some ways made more scientific. Another true pioneer in this regard is Andy Sernovitz, who founded the Word of Mouth Marketing Association (WOMMA) in 2004. The WOMMA Web site, http://www .womma.org, is a great resource for learning more about all the topics in this section. Andy's five keys (or five Ts) for success with influencer marketing are featured in the Doing It Right box on the previous page.

5 Corporate Advertising.

Corporate advertising is not designed to promote the benefits of a specific brand, but instead is intended to establish a favorable attitude toward a company as a whole. A variety of highly regarded and successful firms use corporate advertising to enhance the image of the firm and affect consumers' attitudes. This perspective on corporate advertising is gaining favor worldwide. Firms with the stature of General Electric, Toyota, and Hewlett-Packard are investing in corporate ad campaigns. Exhibit 20.12 shows a corporate campaign for Elkay, a high-end manufacturer of sinks and other plumbing fixtures.

Delight in everyday perfection.

ELKAY
elkay.com

specialty collection sinks. Style that endures.

EXHIBIT 20.12

Firms often use corporate advertising as a way to generate name recognition and a positive image for the firm as a whole rather than for any one of its brands. Here Elkay touts the company name rather than any specific features of a brand.

The Scope and Objectives of Corporate Advertising.

Corporate advertising is a significant force in the overall advertising carried out by organizations around the world. Billions of dollars are invested annually in media for corporate campaigns. Interestingly, most corporate campaigns run by consumer-goods manufacturers are undertaken by firms in the shopping-goods category, such as appliance and auto marketers. Studies have also found that larger firms are much more prevalent users of corporate advertising than smaller firms are. Presumably, these larger firms have broader communications programs and more money to invest in advertising, which allows the use of corporate campaigns. Apple is another company that has historically relied on corporate campaigns (see Exhibit 20.13) to support its numerous sub-brands.

In terms of media, both magazines and television are well suited to corporate advertising.[28] Corporate advertising appearing in magazines has the advantage of being able to target particular constituent groups with image- or issue-related messages. Magazines also provide the space for lengthy copy, which is often needed to achieve corporate advertising objectives. Television is a popular choice for corporate campaigns because the creative opportunities provided by television can deliver a powerful, emotional message. Hewlett-Packard chose to use both television and

28.   David W. Schumann, Jan M. Hathcote, and Susan West, "Corporate Advertising in America: A Review of Published Studies on Use, Measurement and Effectiveness," *Journal of Advertising,* September 1991, 40–53.

Corporate image advertising is meant to build a broad image for the company as a whole rather than tout the features of a brand. Does this ad qualify as a corporate image ad?

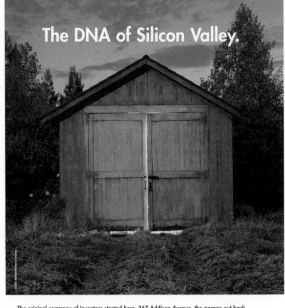

Hewlett-Packard felt the company's image had become fragmented. This is one of the ads in a corporate image campaign designed to unify the image of the firm, harkening back to the roots of the company.

magazine ads (see Exhibit 20.14) in a recent corporate campaign designed to reaffirm its image as an innovator.

The objectives for corporate advertising should be focused. In fact, corporate advertising shares similar purposes with proactive public relations when it comes to what companies hope to accomplish. Here are some of the possibilities for a corporate campaign:

- To build the image of the firm among customers, shareholders, the financial community, and/or the general public
- To boost employee morale or attract new employees
- To communicate an organization's views on social, political, or environmental issues
- To better position the firm's products against competition, particularly foreign competition
- To play a role in the overall advertising and IBP strategy of an organization, providing a platform for more brand-specific campaigns

Notice that corporate advertising is not always targeted at the consumer. A broad range of constituents can be targeted with a corporate advertising effort. For example, when GlaxoWellcome and SmithKline Beecham merged to form a $73 billion pharmaceutical behemoth, the newly created firm, known as GlaxoSmithKline, launched an international print campaign aimed at investors who had doubts about the viability of the new corporate structure. The campaign was all about image and led with the theme: "Disease does not wait. Neither will we."[29]

29.   David Goetzl, "GlaxoSmithKline Launches Print Ads," *Advertising Age,* January 8, 2001, 30.

Types of Corporate Advertising.
Three basic types of corporate advertising dominate the campaigns run by organizations: image advertising, advocacy advertising, and cause-related advertising. Each is discussed in the following sections. We then consider green marketing, which can be considered as a special case of any of these first three.

Corporate Image Advertising.
The majority of corporate advertising efforts focus on enhancing the overall image of a firm among important constituents—typically customers, employees, and the general public. When IBM promotes itself as the firm providing "Solutions for a small planet" or when Toyota uses the slogan "Investing in the things we all care about" to promote its U.S. manufacturing plants, the goal is to enhance the overall image of the firm.

Bolstering a firm's image may not result in immediate effects on sales, but as we saw in Chapter 5, attitude can play an important directive force in consumer decision making. When a firm can enhance its overall image, it may well affect consumer predisposition in brand choice.[30] Exhibit 20.15 is an example of an image-oriented corporate ad. In this ad Bristol-Myers Squibb is touting the life-saving impact of its high-technology line of pharmaceuticals.

Similarly, energy giant BP developed a series of television and print ads that featured real people out on the street candidly answering questions about the environment, pollution, and the use of natural resources and saying things like "I'd rather have a cleaner environment, but I can't imagine me without my car." One critic's assessment is that the spots "don't convey a lot of information" and that the campaign is likely to be successful in "getting the name equated in people's minds with a progressive, forward-thinking company."[31] An appropriate and important goal for corporate image advertising.

While most image advertising intends to communicate a general, favorable image, the effects of such campaigns can be multifaceted. When PPG Industries undertook an image campaign to promote its public identity, the firm found that over a five-year period the number of consumers who claimed to have heard of PPG increased from 39.1 percent to 79.5 percent. Moreover, the perception of the firm's product quality, leadership in new products, and attention to environmental problems were also greatly enhanced over the same period.[32]

Advocacy Advertising.
Advocacy advertising attempts to establish an organization's position on important social or political issues. Advocacy advertising attempts to influence public opinion on issues of concern to a firm. For example, in a corporate advertising program begun in the 1990s, Phillips Petroleum links its commitment to protect and restore bird populations and habitats to its efforts to reduce sulfur in gasoline. Typically, the issue featured in an advocacy campaign is directly relevant to the business operations of the organization.

Cause-Related Advertising.
Cause-related advertising features a firm's affiliation with an important social or societal cause—examples are reducing poverty, increasing literacy, conserving energy, protecting the environment, and curbing drug abuse—and takes place as part of the cause-related marketing efforts undertaken by a firm. The goal of cause-related advertising can be to enhance the image of the firm by associating it with important social issues; this tends to work best when the

---

30.   For an exhaustive assessment of the benefits of corporate advertising, see David M. Bender, Peter H. Farquhar, and Sanford
C. Schulert, "Growing from the Top," *Marketing Management,* (Winter–Spring 1996), 10–19, 24.
31.   "Campaign Close-up—BP," *Sales and Marketing Management,* February 2004, 13.
32.   Schumann, Hathcote, and West, "Corporate Advertising in America," 43, 49.

EXHIBIT 20.15

This corporate image ad for Bristol-Myers Squibb is touting the beneficial, life-enhancing effects of its high-tech pharmaceuticals.

EXHIBIT 20.16

In this cause-related corporate campaign, Anheuser-Busch is promoting the control of teenage drinking. This campaign helps establish the firm as a responsible marketer of alcoholic beverages. See also A-B's programs at http://www.beeresponsible.com.

firm confronts an issue that truly connects to its business. The ad in Exhibit 20.16, in which Anheuser-Busch is promoting the control of teenage drinking, is a good example. This campaign helps establish the firm as a responsible marketer of alcoholic beverages, while also helping society deal with an important problem.

Cause-related advertising often features philanthropic activities that are funded by a company. Each year, *Promo Magazine* provides an extensive list of charitable, philanthropic, and environmental organizations that have formal programs in which corporations may participate. Most of the programs suggest a minimum donation for corporate sponsorship and specify how the organization's resources will be mobilized in conjunction with the sponsor's other resources.

Cause-related marketing is becoming increasingly common. In 2006 IEG forecast that spending on cause-related sponsorships would exceed $1.3 billion, a tenfold increase over spending levels in the 1990s.[33] There are several reasons for this. First, research supports the wisdom of such expenditures. In a 2004 consumer survey conducted by Cone, a Boston-based brand strategy firm, 91 percent of respondents said they have a more favorable impression of companies that support good causes, and

33.   James Tenser, "The New Samaritans," *Advertising Age,* June 12, 2006, S-1, S-6.

also said they believed that the causes a company supports can be a valid reason for switching brands.[34] Other studies indicate that support of good causes can translate into brand preference with the important qualifier that consumers will judge a firm's motives.[35] If the firm's support is perceived as disingenuous, cause-related expenditures are largely wasted.

One would also like to think that the trend toward greater social responsibility by businesses is simply a matter of people wanting to do the right thing. For instance, Whirlpool Corporation is a Habitat Cornerstone Partner and has assisted in the massive rebuilding effort needed in the wake of Hurricane Katrina. Jeff Terry, who manages the program of donations and volunteering on behalf of Whirlpool, says of the experience: "The first time you do this work it will change your life."[36] Sure, Whirlpool's participation in this program brings the company a lot of favorable publicity, but its people's hearts also appear to be in the right place. That makes the program a win/win activity for everyone involved.

The range of firms participating in cause-related marketing programs continues to grow. Eddie Bauer and Crystal Geyser take a pro-environment stance through their support of American Forests' ReLeaf program.[37] Campbell's Soup, Avon, and Yoplait yogurt have ongoing programs that generate funding to support research for a breast cancer cure. Home Depot promotes water conservation in areas of desperate need through its "Use Water Wisely" campaign; Nick at Nite funds an initiative called "National Family Dinner Day."[38] To advance the cause of families spending more time together, Nick at Nite networks shut off for the dinner hour on Family Day to help make their point. These examples illustrate the wide variety of programs that can be launched to support a cause.

Green Marketing. It is heartening to observe that numerous companies have sparked to the idea of supporting any number of causes. One area in particular seems to offer special opportunities in the years ahead. Like so many things, this one has numerous labels, but "green marketing" is probably the most popular. **Green marketing** refers to corporate efforts that embrace a cause or a program in support of the environment. Such efforts include shoe boxes made out of 100 percent recycled materials at Timberland and the "Dawn Saves Wildlife" program sponsored by Procter & Gamble. General Electric and its "Ecomagination" campaign is another high-profile exemplar of this movement. In funding this corporate campaign, GE has taken the stance that it is simply a good business strategy to seek real solutions to problems like air pollution and fossil-fuel dependency.[39] Let's hope they mean it.

The green marketing movement has been on again and off again, especially in the United States. For example, in the early 1990s Jacquelyn Ottman's book *Green Marketing* predicted that going green would be a marketing revolution. It didn't come to pass, at least not in the United States. However, many signs now point to the prospect that this time around, green marketing really will take hold as a major source of opportunity for businesses, maybe just in time to save our planet. Most informed people now accept the inconvenient truth that our addiction to fossil fuels is putting the planet at risk. Surveys show that environmental issues are of major concern to consumers, and a formidable segment is acting on this concern.[40] The green movement looks sustainable this time around.

34. Stephanie Thompson, "Raising Awareness, Doubling Sales," *Advertising Age,* October 2, 2006, 4.
35. Michael J. Barone, Anthony D. Miyazaki, and Kimberly A. Taylor, "The Influence of Cause-Related Marketing on Consumer Choice," *Journal of the Academy of Marketing Science,* Vol. 28, No. 2, 2000, 248–262.
36. Tenser, "The New Samaritans," S-1.
37. Stephanie Thompson, "Good Humor's Good Deeds," *Advertising Age,* January 8, 2001, 6.
38. Tenser, "The New Samaritans."
39. Kathryn Kranhold, "GE's Environment Push Hits Business Realities," *Wall Street Journal,* September 14, 2007, A1, A10.
40. Mya Frazier, "Going Green? Plant Deep Roots," *Advertising Age,* April 30, 2007, 1, 54–55.

In addition, the Internet once again is changing the game. It is no longer possible for companies to pay lip service to environmental causes but hide their true motives. "Green sites" like Green Seal and EnviroLink can assist in determining who is really doing what to protect the environment. Or check out Co-op America, where you can search for any company or brand's track record on the environment. Motivated and well-informed consumers are hard to fool. Hopefully, companies will realize that it doesn't pay to make token gestures on behalf of the planet. Firms really only need to follow the one immutable law of branding to get it right when it comes to green marketing: Underpromise and overdeliver. Here's hoping that you too are getting on board the green bandwagon.

Happy trails.

SUMMARY

 Explain the role of public relations as part of an organization's overall advertising and IBP strategy.

Public relations focuses on communications that can foster goodwill between a firm and constituent groups such as customers, stockholders, employees, government entities, and the general public. Businesses utilize public relations activities to highlight positive events associated with the organization; PR strategies are also employed for "damage control" when adversity strikes. Public relations has entered a new era, as changing corporate demands and new techniques have fostered a bolder, more aggressive role for PR in IBP campaigns.

 Detail the objectives and tools of public relations.

An active public relations effort can serve many objectives, such as building goodwill and counteracting negative publicity. Public relations activities may also be orchestrated to support the launch of new products or communicate with employees on matters of interest to them. The public relations function may also be instrumental to the firm's lobbying efforts and in preparing executives to meet with the press. The primary tools of public relations experts are press releases, feature stories, company newsletters, interviews and press conferences, and participation in the firm's event sponsorship decisions and programs.

 Describe two basic strategies motivating an organization's public relations activities.

When companies perceive public relations as a source of opportunity for shaping public opinion, they are likely to pursue a proactive public relations strategy. With a proactive strategy, a firm strives to build goodwill with key constituents via aggressive programs. The foundation for these proactive programs is a rigorous public relations audit and a comprehensive public relations plan. The plan should include an explicit statement of objectives to guide the overall effort. In many instances, however, public relations activities take the form of damage control. In these instances the firm is obviously in a reactive mode. While a

reactive strategy may seem a contradiction in terms, it certainly is the case that organizations can be prepared to react to bad news. Organizations that understand their inherent vulnerabilities in the eyes of important constituents will be able to react quickly and effectively in the face of hostile publicity.

 Illustrate the strategies and tactics used in influencer marketing programs.

We know that consumers are predisposed to talk about brands, and what they have to say is vital to the health and well-being of those brands. Hence it is no surprise that marketers are pursuing strategies to proactively influence the conversation. Influencer marketing refers to tools and techniques that are directed a driving positive word of mouth about a brand. In professional programs, important gatekeepers like veterinarians or any type of health care professional may be a focal point. In peer-to-peer programs, the new mantra has become finding the connectors. But whether it's professional or peer-to-peer, the marketer is always challenged to give the influencers something meaningful or provocative that they will want to talk about.

 Discuss the applications and objectives of corporate advertising.

Corporate advertising is not undertaken to support an organization's specific brands, but rather to build the general reputation of the organization in the eyes of key constituents. This form of advertising serves goals such as enhancing the firm's image and building fundamental credibility for its line of products. Corporate advertising may also serve diverse objectives, such as improving employee morale, building shareholder confidence, or denouncing competitors. Corporate ad campaigns generally fall into one of three categories: image advertising, advocacy advertising, or cause-related advertising. Corporate advertising may also be orchestrated in such a way to be very newsworthy, and thus it needs to be carefully coordinated with the organization's ongoing public relations programs.

KEY TERMS

public relations
publicity
proactive public relations strategy
reactive public relations strategy
public relations audit

public relations plan
influencer marketing
buzz marketing
viral marketing
corporate advertising

advocacy advertising
cause-related advertising
green marketing

QUESTIONS

1. Review the example of Crest Whitening Plus Scope Extreme and identify the features of their launch campaign that made it resonate with young women, especially those in the 23 to 24 age group.

2. Do you agree with our premise that consumers today are spreading the word about brands like never before? Does that assessment apply to you and the people in your network?

3. Obviously, some events will have more potential for generating favorable publicity than others. What particular criteria should be emphasized in event selection when a firm has the goal of gaining publicity that will build goodwill? How might the benefits of sponsorship be similar or different if that sponsorship involves a sporting event versus a noble cause?

4. Would it be appropriate to conclude that the entire point of public relations activity is to generate favorable publicity and stifle unfavorable publicity? What is it about publicity that makes it such an opportunity and threat?

5. There is an old saying to the effect that "there is no such thing as bad publicity." Can you think of a situation in which bad publicity would actually be good publicity? How is that possible?

6. Most organizations have vulnerabilities they should be aware of to help them anticipate and prepare for unfavorable publicity. What vulnerabilities would you associate with each of the following companies?

*   R. J. Reynolds, makers of Camel cigarettes
*   Procter & Gamble, makers of Pampers disposable diapers
*   Kellogg's, makers of Kellogg's Frosted Flakes
*   ExxonMobil, worldwide fossil-fuel company
*   McDonald's, worldwide restaurateur

7. What key points need to be managed in creating successful influencer programs with medical professionals?

8. Imagine yourself as a connector. In that role, what kind of inside information would you find interesting enough to tell your friends about a new movie or TV show? What would it take for you to start that conversation?

9. Review the different forms of corporate advertising and discuss how useful each would be as a device for boosting a firm's image. Is corporate advertising always an effective image builder?

10. Do you ever select a brand based on the company's environmental track record? Investigate one of your favorite brands at CoopAmerica.org. Did you find anything that changes your feelings about this brand?

EXPERIENTIAL EXERCISES

1. Corporate scandals, environmental disasters, and even general mishaps can quickly snowball into big controversies that can severely damage a company's reputation. Consider the situation Wendy's restaurants faced in 2005 after a woman claimed she found a severed fingertip in a bowl of chili. Although it was later revealed that the woman planted the fingertip, Wendy's still lost an estimated $2.5 million in sales during the controversy, and a corporate plan to woo back diners with a "Free Frosty" campaign got a chilly response from many customers. Review news articles about the Wendy's incident, then answer these questions:

*   Describe the extent of the crisis and who was involved.
*   Identify public relations tools and strategies that Wendy's employed to manage the crisis.
*   How effective was the public relations strategy? Could Wendy's have avoided the controversy altogether or done more to resolve the problem and win back customers? Explain.

2. To better position itself in the competitive college admissions field, your college or university is planning to launch a public relations campaign to encourage more highly qualified high school seniors to apply for admission. Working in small teams, identify what steps you would take to create a proactive public relations strategy for the school's admissions office. Your proposal should clearly identify the plan's objectives and rationale, what steps should be taken prior to the campaign's launch, and what communication methods and content would be most effective.

3. Working in the same teams, propose what steps you would take to launch an effective peer-to-peer marketing campaign as part of the effort to raise awareness of the college and increase applications to the school. In your answer, identify what types of individuals would make the most influential connectors to generate buzz about the school and explain what types of virtual and real-world tools could be developed to help those connectors have a compelling story about the college to share with others.

4. Corporate advertising is broadly intended to boost the reputation of an organization and build credibility for its products and services. Review recent magazines, and identify three examples for each of the primary forms of corporate advertising: image advertising, advocacy advertising, and cause-related advertising. For each ad, prepare a short analysis of how the ad is likely to enhance the firm's general reputation and identify the likely target audience for the advertisement.

APPENDIX: ADVERTISING & IBP IN ACTION

We would like to thank Fred, Jim, Dick, and Marsha for their gracious cooperation. The interview with Marsha Lindsay, President and CEO, Lindsay, Stone & Briggs, is not included here due to technical problems with digital audio file conversion and transcription. Her considerable knowledge and wisdom is, however, employed throughout the book, particularly as it relates to branding, strategy, and creative. Marsha, thank you, and forgive my technical ineptitude and illegible handwriting.

Fred Krupp
President,
Environmental Defense

Dick Antoine
Senior Vice President,
Global Human Resources
Officer,
Procter & Gamble

Jim Neupert
Vice President,
Marketing,
Abbott Vascular
   (acquired Guidant
       Corporation)

Marsha Lindsay
President and CEO,
Lindsay, Stone & Briggs

Fred Krupp

President, Environmental Defense

Conducted by Tom O'Guinn

T.O. First of all, I was very impressed with your talk last spring at the University of Wisconsin Brand Center. It got me thinking about a couple of things. First of all, how you brand an NGO or charitable organization, carve out market niches, and compete in a marketplace for attention and resources. I also was very taken with the pragmatism of your approach.

F.K. I don't think, until recently, we paid enough attention to branding. Thus, there is an opportunity for people who have to have a big impact on us.

Second, we have recently retained Siegel and Gale. They have interviewed dozens of our donors. Over the next few months, we will have a major body of research presented to us, and we're going to have to make some key decisions.

T.O. How many years did you say, 23?

F.K. I've been with Environmental Defense for 23 years.

T.O. What led you to this particular venue; what got you here?

F.K. I became interested in environmental issues and, particularly, in a pragmatic approach to the environmental problems, while in college and at law school at the University of Michigan. After law school, I both worked for a private law firm and helped start a nonprofit environmental group in the state of Connecticut.

After six years of doing both of those things, the public interest entrepreneurial work was much more rewarding. It was also the reason I had gone to law school, to do environmental law.

And, at the time, Environmental Defense was looking for a new head, and some people who had watched me create something from nothing in Connecticut put my name in the hopper. After I was interviewed by 22 different people . . . they selected me and took a chance on a 30-year-old who had no national experience. I had created something from nothing, and that really was the only credential I had.

T.O. Well, that's a pretty big credential. How old is the organization?

F.K. The organization was started in 1967. Our original tagline, informally, was "Sue the bastards." And today, our official tagline is "Finding the Ways That Work." So, there's been quite an evolution over time.

T.O. So now you're the head of this organization, and it's a well known organization, but it certainly has "competitors," groups that are also seeking resources from contributors—passion, time, and commitment. How do you guys do that, compete? Is competition something you talk about, or is it a notion that violates some NGO ideal?"

F.K. Well, it's interesting. We do talk about competitors. But they are also allies in our program work. I suppose we have differentiated ourselves through our work, which we express with the tagline, "Finding The Ways That Work." I think it is a strong brand.

T.O. Yes, it is.

F.K.   And, we were the pioneers among environmental groups in moving from confronting big polluters to co-opting them with solutions. This philosophy really does infuse almost all of our work. It's not that we have created a brand out of five percent of what we do. Our approach infuses over 90% of our work.

We are walking the walk; some others may have simply adopted the rhetoric and improved their positioning. But when you look under the hood, it's not what they run on.

We do put forward our unique selling proposition. But in a way that doesn't demean, denigrate, or impugn other groups. If we do that, we're not making friends and allies who can help us get government to adopt the most effective solutions to these problems.

Our approach is like a martial art. We leverage the weight of potential opponents to our advantage.

At first glance, the idea that my organization, which employs only 300 people, is actually impacting the world in a major way seems preposterous. But ask Tom Friedman or other journalists, and they say it is. So how is it possible that we are able to impact the biggest environmental problems? Partly by hiring top talent.

And partly by partnering with companies to show them that their financial interests can be served by doing right by the environment. And also by advocating for government rules that harness greed to work for the environment. For many problems, you need government rules, incentives that create a playing field that inspires everyone to help solve these problems.

There's a limit to how much bureaucracies can do. We seek to write the rules to create the incentives that enlist people in wanting to solve problems. For fisheries, we have done this with the idea of catch shares. For acid rain, we have the concept of emissions trading. For climate change, we have done this with the imperfect Kyoto Agreement, but it is an agreement that, at its best, set up a market in greenhouse pollution reductions.

In many cases, we seek to set up a playing field that has incentives to enlist the creativity of entrepreneurs and businesses to invent what we need to survive.

We can get not just 300 employees at Environmental Defense, or 15,000 at the EPA, but hundreds of thousands of employees in many corporations, working to solve these problems. Because what we're doing is inculcating a value in everyday decisions to do more than the law requires. And that's the magic of the acid rain example, in which, for the first time, companies, if they reduce more sulfur dioxide pollution than the law required, they made more money.

Greed/capitalism, is a pretty powerful force.

T.O.   Yes, it is.

F.K.   Markets have lifted hundreds of millions of people out of poverty. But we need to align the profit motive with producing the things the world needs to continue to survive.

When people understand that our organization is built around the insight that corporate partnerships and government incentive regulations can enlist millions in creatively solving environmental problems—then they suddenly understand how just 300 people could really have an impact in changing the world. They then become passionate advocates for our way of doing things, for our brand of environmentalism. They become motivated financial supporters, or in the case of corporate or government officials, allies.

Our challenge is to figure out a way to communicate that brand and get it out. And, I think we have to find a good way to get the word out, even though we have doubled our income in the last five years.

When I started, we had revenues of $3 million a year; we are now at $80 million a year. Yet, given the results we've obtained, our brand is woefully under-marketed.

T.O.   I agree that you could be more well known given your accomplishments. But, I know you are interested in more than contributions.

The philosophy you've got and the tagline you've got are unique in the sector. And that sets you apart and makes you attractive to a much broader spectrum of people and contributors than your competitors.

What I like more than anything is your pragmatism. It's very much the Bono approach to getting countries like the U.S., Canada, the U.K., and much of the E.U. to forgive the developing world's debt. There's a general sense in business these days that this is the way the world is going. Corporate responsibility is more salient to consumers than it was ten years ago, and to companies as well. So I think you're in the right place at the right time. And I think you're beautifully positioned as a brand.

F.K.   That, I see, may be our biggest challenge. We're a group who put staff in Bentonville, and our donors are excited about using Wal-Mart's leverage for the environment.

But we need to scale up our brand recognition. When people find out about us they get excited about us. We have yet to figure out ways to market to those people wholesale what we sell so effectively retail, one by one.

T.O.   In terms of marketing the organization there are many audiences that are important. Which are the most important audiences?

F.K.   I'd probably have to start with journalists, just because so many people believe what they read in the newspaper. The media serves to validate which groups are really effective, who's doing important work.

T.O.   Agenda setters?

F.K.   Yes. So I would start with the media. Then our financial supporters. My organization, like others, is dependent on revenue as its lifeblood. It's amazing how people with disposable income, people who have inherited or acquired wealth, want to have impact. Many have an environmental interest. When they hear about our approach, we have a very high batting average in engaging them.

T.O.   Are there geographic regions that tend to be greener?

F.K.   Specifically, Silicon Valley tends to be a little bit libertarian, not so much so that they think environmental problems are going to be solved without government involvement. Rather, they prefer our way of involving government to set standards but not choose technologies, using markets. And similarly, therefore, other areas like Seattle and Austin, same tech wealth, understand the power of our approach.

Beyond that, Wall Streeters, whether working on Wall Street, or in the financial services industry in Boston or Chicago. People who see that capitalism is working really well to bring higher value (iPhones) to market at lower and lower prices but who understand that there's this dark underside . . . that world is in trouble. Something's got to be done. The idea of using capitalism and the power of capitalism to actually harness innovation to make clean energy the most profitable energy: they get that. So, if I had to be restricted to just two demographics, it would be the high tech community and the Wall Street financial services community.

T.O.   You know, there's been in the last ten years a paradigm shift in branding. And essentially, it's gone from being more driven by accountants to now more by those interested in culture. In fact, it's being called "cultural branding," or "social branding." A brand is not some dry summation of attitudes. Brands are about meaning and cultural capital. They are carriers of meaning. It's now cool to be green. How can you leverage that wave with your brand?

F.K.   Unlike Pepsi, we can't buy tens of millions of dollars of advertising. Our basic way of surfing that wave is through the earned media, hence the importance of journalists.

And, awareness of global warming has heightened substantially. All over this country, there are fights over building coal-fired power plants.

We became identified with this fight among the public that follows the news.

The biggest buyout in the history of America occurred when Henry Kravis and KKR were going to buy TXU, the big Texas utility company. But they made that purchase contingent on our approval and they said they wouldn't go ahead unless we approved of their new greenhouse gas management plan. They agreed to cancel 8 of the 11 plants, and they agreed to spend $400 million on wind power, $400 million on energy efficiency.

T.O. Now, having a "green" company is worth a lot of cultural capital.

F.K. So that's one way we benefit from the wave, by being in the news visibly making things happen.

As an NGO with a very limited, tiny paid advertising budget . . . we have to think creatively about . . . what can we make happen next that will positively impact the world and help the issue, but also carry the message about who we are. It is analogous to dreaming up screenplays,

T.O. Have you looked at the Madison & Vine kind of approach, working with Hollywood or television . . . having a hand in developing program content that's essentially branded for your organization and your cause? You accomplish consciousness-raising at the same time you work in some brand recognition, and even very small players can do this through the Web and consumer-generated content.

F.K. We really haven't explored those avenues too much. I don't think we've done anything like a thorough exploration of what kind of money it would take to do that and what the benefits would be.

T.O. The whole changing media environment has benefited the small players.

F.K. You know, I'm very interested in pursuing that idea. I've co-authored a book that will come out next spring.

T.O. Congratulations.

F.K. And it will be about solutions to the global warming problem, kind of an optimistic view of what market-based forces could bring about with the right type of government regulations. But apart from that, the whole notion of guerilla marketing and investigating what a limited budget could buy is fascinating.

T.O. It seems like this is a brand that could have its moment right now.

F.K. I agree with that.

T.O. What are you most proud of in these past 23 years?

F.K. Well, the work we did with President George H.W. Bush on acid rain . . . a system that's reduced sulfur dioxide pollution nationwide by 50 percent.

T.O. Impressive.

F.K. And now that's been tightened; another 70 percent sulfur will come out of the emissions nationwide. That would be high on the list. Many of the projects partnering with companies from McDonald's, where it gets rid of the Styrofoam clamshell, to FedEx to get a truck that has 97 percent less fine particulate pollution, to the antibiotic work with McDonald's where, because of our partnership with them, the major producers of poultry have reduced the use of antibiotics by 90 percent, which is a big deal because 70 percent of all antibiotics used in America are used on farm animals. So a lot of the corporate partnership projects have been high points.

T.O. What is your greatest frustration?

F.K. Probably we've been talking about it.

Yeah, I mean, Sierra Club, Greenpeace, Audubon Society, The Nature Conservancy, we can name a series of environmental groups that are household names, and our brand recognition is dismal.

T.O.   What career paths do you see for young (or not) people wanting to work in this area?

F.K.   Well there's a lot of different roles in the world, there are many ways to have a meaningful job. Many are in the business world, but there are many in the non-profit world too. There are lots of places where one can get compensated, but also do things that are meaningful and fun. I see many folks ending up in work-a-day jobs that they don't like. There's a tendency to settle for a job that doesn't provide meaning. For some they need to settle for that.

But for a lot of people who are going to be reading your textbook, who have good college educations, who will have talents and abilities, my counsel to them would be to spend an extra amount of time so you have more choices for meaningful employment. Put in a little bit extra time into their job search. So many people settle for the first thing, without understanding that they will spend at least a few years, maybe a lifetime in a job. So, it's worth making a few extra phone calls. It's worth pounding the pavement a little more to try to find something that's truly meaningful.

T.O.   That's a great answer, a great way to quit. Thank you so much.

Jim Neupert

Vice President, Marketing, Abbott Vascular (acquired Guidant Corporation)

Conducted by Tom O'Guinn

T.O.   First of all, I'm just curious how you got where you are, the career path. What took you to where you are now? Did you just always have some love of medical devices, or was this just serendipity like most things in life?

J.N.   One of my uncles, in fact, including my dad, my only uncle to go to college . . . was actually a fairly prominent physician in Wisconsin . . . and I was always intrigued by medicine . . . and healthcare. And so coming out of grad school, I got an offer to join a medical technology company, and it looked like the most interesting thing among what I was looking at. And that proved to be right for 29 years so far. And I think the next few will be the same.

T.O.   So you're one of those lucky guys who get up in the morning and are truly happy that you have the job you have.

J.N.   Absolutely.

T.O.   And that's a small percentage of people.

J.N.   I can only think of about four or five days when it wasn't very easy to get up and come in in the morning. But, no, that has been the case for literally 30 years.

T.O.   So in terms of branding do you consider this a B2B, or a B2C business, or both? How do you look at it?

J.N.   Yeah, great question. This is really business to consumer, with the consumer having a slightly different definition. The consumer for our part of the medical world is an incredibly skillful and prominent clinician that does the heavy surgery, does the heavy procedures that we're involved with here. And so they really are the consumer of the product because if they don't believe it, they're not going to touch their patients with our technology.

T.O.   Right. So clearly, branding is important, the Guidant brand name and its reputation?

J.N.   Yes. Because they're going to do something to a person, one at a time, that that individual is going to live with, that their family members are going to be a part of and live with in a way, and that they as a clinician are going to live with for years to come, because you know this is going to change the patient's life.

T.O.   So you're literally talking about lifesaving products.

J.N.   Yes.

T.O.   So I guess Guidant Vascular doesn't get into the DTC kinds of issues as much as big pharma?

J.N.   You know we do a little bit but you have to be at a scale way above what we are. You have to be a pharmaceutical. And you know the scale, Tom . . . if you don't spend $50 million a year for several years . . .

T.O.   No one hears you?

J.N.   You're not going to . . . yeah, nobody hears you. You're not going to move the needle. And you know the companies in this space are spending it on R&D. We don't have that kind of money.

T.O.   So without DTC or some sort of traditional consumer advertising, how do you in that kind of space create and maintain a brand image?

J.N.   Well, through your technology and the training that you provide to clinicians . . . and the clinical studies that you get them involved in . . . your reputation, your brand, your positioning comes through to them. That's how you really build the identity of who you are.

T.O.   Right, but Guidant's a very strong brand achieved with almost no traditional advertising?

J.N.   It is a strong brand.

T.O.   I'm not a clinician, but even without knowing anything about medical devices, I still have an image of Guidant and if I had to click off attributes they'd all be very positive evaluations. They're all strong brand-image kinds of things, and I got that idea somewhere. Guidant must do a really good job of maintaining brand because the name means something to me even thought I'm not in the target. It can't all be spillover, can it?

J.N.   I think part of it, Tom, is the patients that the products end up touching, you somehow are aware that, okay, they've got an AIDS drug, or they've got a, you know, heavy duty critical care product and some lifesaving product, the stent. And I think that the technology part of it, you see enough in TV and movies and read the *Wall Street Journal,* healthcare articles or whatever the sources may be. And that actually adds to what the company is able to do with its brands.

T.O.   Yeah, because I would say part of your equity . . . a lot of your equity comes from non-clinicians who just believe in the brand. And it may be because these patients are such incredible brand ambassadors and Guidant just being a good corporate citizen. If you keep up on business, Guidant is certainly a company you read about it. Good brand name exposure without much advertising at all.

T.O.   OK. Let me ask you . . . if you had two or three attributes that make for a strong brand, not only your own, but any brand what do you think they are? It's a hard question.

J.N.   It's a hard question. I think the definition of a strong brand is a brand that conveys a very clear image, and it is long lasting . . , and the third, if I were to list a third, the word community comes into it. It's not about isolation. It's the opposite. It's this positive feeling of community I see myself being a part of.

T.O.   I know quite a few physicians and they have certain beliefs about a pharmaceutical company or a device company, there's this sort of belief that, you know, I'm one of them . . . I believe in them, what they do, how they do it, their culture . . . I'm part of this community, this collective effort . . . "These guys get it. I mean, these guys really get it" . . . Belief in the collective, duty to the collective . . . community.

J.N.   And the other part, having done this many years, I think the word trust. You know, the doctors that I know really well, I mean, they personally and professionally trust me. And they will ask a question, is this what's going on? And they're just going to listen to my answer. Should I be doing XYZ? They'll ask me that question. Should I be doing this? Is this ready for prime time? And they trust me. And I'm part of the brand; I'm part of the product, the consumer brand.

T.O.   Is that different in some important ways than for a CPG?

J.N.   You know, if I'm working for Procter & Gamble, not that that's an unimportant job . . . it's a working relationship with the user and the ultimate consumer.

T.O.   That's one reason I was so interested in talking to you: it's an interesting problem it crosses so many boundaries, and it's kind of a . . .

J.N.   It's a hybrid, Tom. It's not traditional anything.

T.O.   So you guys do almost no traditional consumer B2C marketing communication, or do you?

J.N.   Very little. We go to trade shows, which are basically medical meetings. You know big medical meetings. We do journal advertising in very scientific journals, the clinical scientific journals. And, again, if you reach a certain scale, like a Medtronic, gosh, probably six, eight months ago was doing some TV and even print ads . . . about sudden cardiac death . . . and, you know, heart failure and defibrillators, which I totally admire them for doing them. That's pretty rare though in this industry. Johnson and Johnson have this campaign for the last couple years. You've probably seen it, about the importance of being a nurse . . . and I admire them for doing that.

T.O.   It's a great campaign.

J.N.   Yeah, but those are the rare, I would say, the rare examples.

T.O.   What's the biggest obstacle in your field to successful branding? Is it because you're a heavy regulated industry? Is it because you don't have the kind of budgets to do big media, or are there any big obstacles?

J.N.   Yeah, obstacle number one is we're a regulated industry, and so any claim we make, any statement we make has to be approved by our regulatory and legal and ultimately FDA. Because our promotional pieces are labeling of the product. And FDA approves all labeling. And so our advertising is labeling. We route all this stuff, it's signed off, it's, you know, regulatory, legal, the whole deal looks at it. So that's not bad. That's fair. But it's different than probably a lot of others. I think the biggest difference is probably the temptation to just rely on technology.

T.O.   That's interesting.

J.N.   The technology will sell itself, Tom. The doctor will recognize the clinical data and the technology, and you know what? We'll just make it. We'll get out of the way, and we'll just make it.

T.O.   It's the old engineer thinking.

J.N.   Yeah, it's engineering and sales, which is where this industry grew up from. And some of that works, and some of that is how the product gets used, but, you know, it's only part of the puzzle.

T.O.   Do you get pushback from the engineering side?

J.N.   Sure. They spend all this time making sure the technology was going to work, and it should just be flying out past the factory doors, right?

T.O.   Let's talk a little bit about when you're looking for talent. When you go out to hire at entry level or slightly above entry level, what sort of educational backgrounds, what sort of talents, skills, traits, what do you look for in somebody in this industry?

J.N.   Typically, and especially for marketing, an MBA. But they could be finance background. They might have an undergrad in engineering or science or more technical. But if they have a different background, they do have to have a strong customer orientation. And those are the ones that are really the exceptionals that we find, and they rise to the top and do the best job with the marketing.

T.O.   What's the most fun part of your job? I mean, what do you look forward to when you're thinking, I get to do this today rather than, oh, I have to do this today?

J.N.   The fun part of my job is working with the most incredible physicians in the world. That is incredibly challenging and humbling and you know what they do and how they do it amazes me every time I'm with one of them.

T.O.   When you really think about the stakes . . .

J.N.   Well, I've watched, Tom, I probably watch about 100 procedures a year. And so I'm watching them . . . do what they do on 100 people a year.

T.O.   Wow. Well, you're doing something important . . . that's got to feel good, doing something with your life that helps people. I would think you'd have to feel good about this company you work for and what you do.

J.N.   I do. I never have a doubt about that, Tom. You know, it's actually something I never think about because I've done it for so long that it's just . . . you know; my normal is so different from anybody else. I don't think about it. I turn the lights on in the morning, it's there. But I know it's so different. But to me, it's my typical.

T.O.   We've talked about how great these physicians are, but you know, if there's no stent to put in, then it doesn't matter how great they are. And so you have to feel good about the product you sell, and at the end of the day you're helping people. I mean people walk out of hospitals because of what you sell compared to other things we could think of, that's got to make you feel pretty good...

J.N.   Yeah. No, it's a constant jolt of adrenalin. It's around every day.

T.O.   You are also a board member for the Center for Brand and Product Management at the University of Wisconsin, so let's talk about education. Do you think that the idea of specialized brand management training is something that's really important, and do you think the Brand Center at Wisconsin in particular can change the way that idea is projected into real industry practice? Is it a better way to go than the standard and very general MBA?

T.O.   Yes, without a doubt. The concentration, the case studies, the amount of focus that goes into the brand and product management and product line strategy and everything that's related to it . . . is far more intense than what I went through in my MBA. Nearly three decades ago. So I think it's that intensity, that depth. It makes it really different.

T.O.   OK. So you'd recommend it?

J.N.   Yes, I would highly, highly, highly recommend it.

T.O.   OK. Thanks. I appreciate it.

Dick Antoine

Senior Vice President, Global Human Resources Officer Procter & Gamble

Conducted by Tom O'Guinn

T.O.   First I'd like to ask you about your job and how you came to this prestigious and powerful position. How did you end up here?

D.A.   Well, I'm not HR by training necessarily, because I'm a chemical engineer from Wisconsin. I have an MBA from Chicago. And I spent the first roughly 25 years of my career in manufacturing, what we call the Product Supply area, the value chain, if you will. I had run the entire U.S. Supply Operation and then the entire Asian Supply Operation.

But at any rate, in Product Supply, I actually did have two things that I guess people felt, or three, qualified me for this job, and then I'll tell you the circumstances of taking this job. One was at one point in time I was the human resources manager for one of our plants. That was a developmental role to better prepare me to be a plant manager, and it was.

Second, since more than half of our people in this company are in the Supply Chain, it's reasonable to assume that I could be "responsible" for all the human assets of the company.

Third, they felt I was business-oriented, and that's what they wanted in this role.

Then what happened in late 1997 was that I was minding my own business in Asia, had just been told that I would stay there for another three years as the product supplier value chain leader for Asia, when I got called to headquarters and the CEO told me that effective January 1, 1998, I'd be the company's HR leader. And I kind of looked over my shoulder and assumed someone else had to have come into the room. And, of course, there wasn't. They asked me to do it, and when I asked why, those were the three reasons that they gave. And so that's how I got into it. It wasn't asked for, but it was what they felt was the right thing to do.

So, I wasn't so sure about it at the beginning. There is a lot of technology in the HR area, just like there is in any other, whether it's finance or marketing or whatever. Marketing people would say, ah, it's just, you know, you look at commercials and . . .

T.O.   Oh, right, sure.

D.A.   . . . you know very well that's not true.

T.O.   Not at all.

D.A.   So that's what happened. So I got into this in January of 1998.

T.O.   That's a great story. I think that's probably regrettably part of public perceptions of both marketing and HR or certainly advertising, "Oh, gee, anybody could do that." I do know that picking the right people for the right job is one of the hardest things humans do. It really is.

Okay, well, so you've been doing this now for almost ten years. What's been your greatest sense of achievement in this role?

D.A.   Oh, I think a couple of things. I led the implementation of our more formalized talent review system into our company back . . . six or seven years ago.

We've always had great people. I take no credit for that. That's been going on for 100-some years. But we didn't necessarily have a good way of thinking about them, making sure we understood who they were and what their assignments were, what assignments they needed and what skills they needed. We've put all that together now in what we call our talent review process, and I'm probably the most proud of putting that in place. And then the recognition in many, many places that we have one of the premiere groups of talent in the world and one of the best systems for managing that talent. That's why we get these recognitions . . . the best places for leaders, highest quality leaders, most admired for leaders and so on, whether you're talking Fortune, Forbes, and all those kind of things. And when these external organizations call, send us surveys, or sometimes have people come in, we then share what we're doing with them, and usually we kind of blow them away with what we're doing as opposed to . . . "Well, they have good people so I guess there's something going on there that must be okay."

T.O.   So you pretty much led the design of a comprehensive set of metrics to do this?

D.A.   Well, I was the one who said we needed a better system. I borrowed the term, by the way, talent review from Coca-Cola, which I'm more than happy to give them credit for. Still it is our talent review process, the talent review system that we use. And that's what we put in place over the last several years. Obviously I had a bunch of people helping me do that. But that's what I feel good about. The other thing that gives me great pride is, for whatever combination of reasons, the HR organization today has very high credibility with the businesses and business unit leaders for what we bring to the party.

And I know we've made tremendous progress over the past decade. We've gotten a lot of recognition and I feel really good about that. And therefore when I leave, it's going to be somebody from within HR that's going to take my place.

T.O.   Have you built that staff yourself?

D.A.   A lot of them were here. I made changes. It was taking some people out and then promoting some people . . . plus building on the . . . talent here. It just maybe wasn't organized in the right way or given the right credibility or whatever. To be clear Tom, they trained me.

For the first two years, the danger of bringing somebody in from the outside, and the thing that I worry about in most companies, goes back to the first part of the conversation where the feeling, and there's actually three or four disciplines where people feel "anyone can do it."

I mean anyone who's smart; anyone who's capable can do it. And the problem is, you know very well in marketing, that's just not true. And in HR, it's not true. And I'll tell you another, a third one that's like that is external relations or public affairs, public relations or whatever you want to call that, there's a belief that anyone can do it. I don't believe that's true there either.

T.O.   I know that's not true.

D.A.   And yet there are CEOs and senior-level managers in many companies that believe it is true for all of those. And I keep saying, well . . . would you make just anyone your CFO? Of course not. You want to know their accounting training, you want to know their financial acumen, you want to know their financial analysis skills and so on, and you should. Those are the same questions or variations of that that you want to be asking about HR and so on. You'd never think of putting an HR person in to lead finance. Why would you think that a finance person can lead HR?

T.O.   I completely agree. I've worked with a lot of companies where the public relations front was hugely important, and they were companies that learned pretty early that if you don't do a good job on that, particularly in highly regulated industries, you've got a world of hurt, and you push your stock value down.

D.A.   That's absolutely right, Tom. So, I think we were able to add some credibility and, I feel best about that. We've put in place a lot of systems. Another thing that I feel great about is we've, and I mean we inclusively, revitalized our training in the company and done some really, really good things. We now have a suite of four courses and we're working on the fifth for senior managers. These would be like the general manager of France, head of our laundry business in North America.

So these would be, call it the top 300 people just below the very top level that some of us would be at. And we started, six years ago, with something we call general manager college, which is a one-week intensive program where we teach them the principles of a high-performing organization. And, then there is a follow-up course to that. And, then there's the third companion course called Inspirational Leadership. All have had tremendous impacts on the entire organization. And the person who's currently the COO, Bob McDonald, and I were the leaders of that as chartered by our CEO, A.G. Lafley. He said I want you two to create "the best General Manager training program anywhere." And then we had to, of course, go create it.

And it's just fantastic, and it has made a major difference, and then it's got spin-offs into other training, and we've brought in a professional training person. So we've got a lot of the stuff, but without the campus that Crotonville has for GE. But we do a lot of the same kind of things that they do, not surprisingly. I do believe, quite honestly, that GE and P&G are the two best at this . . .

T.O.   Well, you've got to feel really proud of that. That's an amazing in-house training system. Well, it's more than training, isn't it? It's an education in a very complete sense

T.O.   OK, so what do you think are the most important attributes of a successful brand or product manager: The big question?

D.A.   Yeah, it is. Yeah.

Well, first of all, they need to be a great leader. As opposed to: we have people who are brilliant marketers, who can develop great copy or great advertising or great, even, blogs and so on that appeal to people. That's really necessary and those people are very, very valuable. But that's not the same as being a brand manager or product manager.

T.O.   No.

D.A.   OK. A brand or product manager has a broader scope than that. Now many great product managers or brand managers need to have highly tuned advertising skills also. So one part of it is to be a great brand manager, you need to have the technical mastery in marketing, but then you also need to be a leader because you've got to bring people together and you need to have high collaboration skills.

In order to do that, you have to really understand the consumer, so there's a consumer knowledge aspect that you've got to be good at. And our good brand managers get out there and meet with consumers and spend time with consumers in focus groups, as one tool. The more powerful tool is, you know, going on home visits. We even have a program in some countries of staying with consumers in their home. I was just talking to one of our general managers in Latin America. The brand managers that work for him in Argentina spent two days in a home of a lower-class person. And he said, what I learned there was just incredible, but they literally lived with them . . .

T.O.   This is an area that I find so interesting because me along with, I don't know, 20 or 30 other people in my field have been arguing for a long time that this type of approach is so much more meaningful than, you know some experiments, all these things have their purpose, but that actually consumption in the situation of very human existence is far more important an insight than what you're going to get in your standard focus group, standard survey or something.

D.A.   Yeah. I think one of the biggest changes we've had in this company, maybe the biggest one, is when our current CEO took over in 2000 and started this mantra of "the consumer is boss," that the consumer is the person that determines what we do and whether we're successful. And then it goes to, if the consumer is my boss, I guess I better figure out what makes my boss tick and how they live and what they do. And so one thing leads from this consumer is boss all the way into these other activities.

But back to the question that you asked about, what makes a great . . . (brand) manager; it's somebody that's a great leader. It's somebody who has tremendous marketing, advertising skills. It's a person who understands that the consumer is boss, and therefore is trying to please the consumer in any way possible, and part of that kit bag is going and doing these in-home visits and store visits and touching and feeling that consumer. And the good brand manager has to have excellent collaboration skills to work with research and development people on the latest technology to satisfy those needs of the consumer. And so those are probably the main things.

T.O.   Those are great. I think the average company in the U.S. lasts 32 years or something like that, and P&G has been around for 170 years. People talk a lot about "P&G culture." Isn't a lot of that culture driven in a major way by HR? You must, one, understand what the P&G culture is. And two, perpetuate the parts of it that you think are essential and tweak it where you think it needs tweaking. So, am I essentially correct about that?

D.A.   Yes, although, Tom, you know, it's our job in HR to make sure that this culture supports the business. But it's also our job to make sure that our "line" people, the 95% of people who are not HR, believe in that culture and cause that culture to live, right?

T.O.   Right.

D.A.   Which is, as you know, the hardest part, to get the line leaders to own the culture, because in HR we can have brilliant ideas on concepts on culture, but if the line managers don't buy into it, the culture that exists out there is the one that they establish, that they set. Now can an individual person change that? Not for the company, no, but they can change it in their organization. And we have to decide if they're moving that culture in the right direction or if you think they're destroying the culture, and then you have to deal with it.

So the hardest part of our job is to get the line and all the rest of the people in the company to own the culture.

T.O.   Right. What would you say is the smartest thing a new hire at any big CPG company or Procter & Gamble specifically could do to advance their career?

D.A.   I don't mean to oversimplify it. I think there are two things. One is to be voracious learners, and I keep telling people, in the first six months try not to change anything because you might find later that 90% of it you're going to change back . . . make changes when you really understand what you are doing.

T.O.   That's great advice . . . for anyone.

D.A.   So for the first six months, don't do that. But you really need to be a voracious learner. You need to learn. Talk to people who have been in the job before. Talk to your people, the brand manager people that are higher up than you. Go to school on the past. You know one advantage of being 170 years old is there's a lot of history.

In this brand let's just say we're talking about a new marketing person. Learn what's happened over the years because we've had obvious successes. And we've had some times where we almost killed the brand or the brand was struggling or whatever. Well, what was different about those? What can you learn from it? And so the voracious learner is critical.

The other things then they've got to learn is they've got to be clear on what are their deliverables. What's expected of them. And we tell people that there are two areas that you must contribute. The second one isn't as important when you're starting out because typically you don't have people working for you, but the first area is: what are the business metrics that you're going to be evaluated on. Some of them are going to be hard number things, like what happened to the share of the business on the brand that you were responsible for.

Others will be soft measures like collaboration with other people that you need to work with . . .

But there are the business results. And then there's the thing that we do expect once you get beyond your first assignment and you have people working for you that will help develop the talent that works for you. That's a clear expectation of everyone in this company.

And we evaluate them. So voracious learners and then evaluated both on building the business and developing the organization.

T.O.   Wonderful. Now, I would like to ask you about another venture with which you are very involved: the Center for Brand and Product Management at the University of Wisconsin-Madison. Can you tell me why you have chosen to give so much of your time and energy to this educational effort? Why is it so special to you?

D.A.   The Center for Brand and Product Management at Wisconsin is offering a very unusual—and perhaps unique—product. That is MBA graduates who have received training and experiences in Product Management rather than the traditional Marketing focus. In P&G we need people with this broader perspective and people who have experience working collaboratively across functions and organizations. We have already hired several people from this program.

And I enjoy the experience of working with the other Advisory Board members, and making the program relevant to CPG companies has been a lot of fun.

T.O.   Great. Thanks so much.

GLOSSARY

A

above-the-line promotion Traditional measured media advertising: any message broadcast to the public through conventional means such as television, the Internet, radio, and magazines.

account executive The liaison between an advertising agency and its clients; the nature of the account executive's job requires excellent persuasion, negotiation, and judgment skills in order to both successfully alleviate client discomfort and sell highly effective, groundbreaking ideas.

account planner A relatively recent addition to many advertising agencies; it is this person's job to synthesize all relevant consumer research and use it to design a coherent advertising strategy.

account planning A system by which, in contrast to traditional advertising research methods, an agency assigns a coequal account planner to work alongside the account executive and analyze research data. This method requires the account planner to stay with the same projects on a continuous basis.

account services A team of managers that identifies the benefits a brand offers, its target audiences, and the best competitive positioning, and then develops a complete promotion plan.

account team A group of people comprising many different facets of the advertising industry (direct marketing, public relations, graphic design, etc.) who work together under the guidance of a team leader to both interface with other members of the account team and team members of their own respective specialties.

Action for Children's Television (ACT) A group formed during the 1970s to lobby the government to limit the amount and content of advertising directed at children.

adaptors In reference to the *adaptation/innovation theory* generated by a study of creativity in employees, adaptors are the ones who, when faced with creative tasks, tend to work within the existing paradigm.

advertisement A specific message that an organization has placed to persuade an audience.

advertiser Business, not-for-profit, or government organization that uses advertising and other promotional techniques to communicate with target markets and to stimulate awareness and demand for its brands.

advertising A paid, mass-mediated attempt to persuade.

advertising agency An organization of professionals who provide creative and business services to clients related to planning, preparing, and placing advertisements.

advertising campaign A series of coordinated advertisements and other promotional efforts that communicate a single theme or idea.

advertising clutter An obstacle to advertising resulting from the large volume of similar ads for most products and services.

advertising plan A plan that specifies the thinking and tasks needed to conceive and implement an effective advertising effort.

advertising response function A mathematical relationship based on marginal analysis that associates dollars spent on advertising and sales generated; sometimes used to help establish an advertising budget.

advertising specialties A sales promotion having three key elements: a message, placed on a useful item, given to consumers with no obligation.

advertising substantiation program An FTC program initiated in 1971 to ensure that advertisers make available to consumers supporting evidence for claims made in ads.

advertorial A special advertising section designed to look like the print publication in which it appears.

advocacy advertising Advertising that attempts to influence public opinion on important social, political, or environmental issues of concern to the sponsoring organization.

aerial advertising Advertising that involves airplanes (pulling signs or banners), skywriting, or blimps.

affirmative disclosure An FTC action requiring that important material determined to be absent from prior ads must be included in subsequent advertisements.

agency of record The advertising agency chosen by the advertiser to purchase media time and space.

alternative press newspapers Newspapers geared toward a young, entertainment-oriented audience.

animation The use of drawn figures and scenes (like cartoons) to produce a television commercial.

appropriation The use of pictures or images owned by someone else without permission.

ARS Persuasion Method Testing service that offers true pre-post attitude testing through a theater-type test in which commercials are embedded in television shows and audience members indicate brand preference.

aspirational groups Groups made up of people an individual admires or uses as role models but is unlikely to ever interact with in any meaningful way.

association tests A type of projective technique that asks consumers to express their feelings or thoughts after hearing a brand name or seeing a logo.

attitude An overall evaluation of any object, person, or issue that varies along a continuum, such as favorable to unfavorable or positive to negative.

attitude-change study A type of advertising research that uses a before-and-after ad exposure design.

attitude study A method of obtaining customer feedback that measures target markets' feelings and opinions about a company's product, as well as that of the competing brand.

audience A group of individuals who may receive and interpret messages sent from advertisers through mass media.

authenticity The quality of genuineness inherent in something. Advertisers value product placement with a high degree of apparent authenticity, as more blatant approaches are easily detected by consumers, resulting in possible disgust or irritation and achieving the opposite of the advertiser's aim.

average quarter-hour persons The average number of listeners tuned to a radio station during a specified 15-minute segment of a daypart.

average quarter-hour rating The radio audience during a quarter-hour daypart expressed as a percentage of the population of the measurement area.

average quarter-hour share The percentage of the total radio audience that was listening to a radio station during a specified quarter-hour daypart.

axis A line, real or imagined, that runs through an advertisement and from which the elements in the ad flare out.

B

balance An orderliness and compatibility of presentation in an advertisement.

barter syndication A form of television syndication that takes both off-network and first-run syndication shows and offers them free or at a reduced rate to local television stations, with some national advertising presold within the programs.

beliefs The knowledge and feelings a person has accumulated about an object or issue.

below-the-line promotion A promotional effort that includes in-store promotions, coupons, dealer discounts, and product placement.

benefit positioning A positioning option that features a distinctive customer benefit.

benefit segmentation A type of market segmenting in which target segments are delineated by the various benefit packages that different consumers want from the same product category.

between-vehicle duplication Exposure to the same advertisement in different media.

bill-back allowances A monetary incentive provided to retailers for featuring a marketer's brand in either advertising or in-store displays.

blackletter A style patterned after monastic hand-drawn letters characterized by the ornate design of the letters. Also called *gothic*.

bleed page A magazine page on which the background color of an ad runs to the edge of the page, replacing the standard white border.

blog (short for Weblog) A personal journal on a Web site that is frequently updated and intended for public access. Such sites are emerging as new and sophisticated sources of product and brand information.

blogger The author of a blog.

border The space surrounding an advertisement; it keeps the ad elements from spilling over into other ads or into the printed matter next to the ad.

brainstorming An organized approach to idea generation; for effective brainstorming, it is necessary to learn about the material in question beforehand, foster a safe environment free of destructive criticism, and openly discuss disagreements that may arise.

brand A name, term, sign, symbol, or any other feature that identifies one seller's good or service as distinct from those of other sellers.

brand advertising Advertising that communicates the specific features, values, and benefits of a particular brand offered for sale by a particular organization.

brand attitudes Summary evaluations that reflect preferences for various products and brands.

brand communities Groups of consumers who feel a commonality and a shared purpose grounded or attached to a consumer good or service.

branded entertainment Embedding one's brand or brand icons as part of any entertainment property (e.g., a sporting event) in an effort to impress and connect with consumers in a unique and compelling way.

brand equity Developed by a firm that creates and maintains positive associations with the brand in the mind of consumers.

brand extension An adaptation of an existing brand to a new product area.

branding The strategy of developing brand names so that manufacturers can focus consumer attention on a clearly identified item.

brand loyalty A decision-making mode in which consumers repeatedly buy the same brand of a product as their choice to fulfill a specific need.

brand-loyal users A market segment made up of consumers who repeatedly buy the same brand of a product.

brand switching An advertising objective in which a campaign is designed to encourage customers to switch from their established brand.

build-up analysis A method of building up the expenditure levels of various tasks to help establish an advertising budget.

business-market sales promotion Promotion designed to cultivate buyers from large corporations who are making purchase decisions.

business markets The institutional buyers who purchase items to be used in other products and services or to be resold to other businesses or households.

business newspapers Newspapers like the *Financial Times,* which serve a specialized business audience.

buzz marketing The process of creating events or experiences that yield conversations that include the brand or product advertisers are trying to sell.

C

cable television A type of television that transmits a wide range of programming to subscribers through wires rather than over airwaves.

cause-related advertising Advertising that identifies corporate sponsorship of philanthropic activities.

cease-and-desist order An FTC action requiring an advertiser to stop running an ad within 30 days so a hearing can be held to determine whether the advertising in question is deceptive or unfair.

celebrity A unique sociological category that matters a great deal to advertisers.

celebrity endorsements Advertisements that use an expert or celebrity as a spokesperson to endorse the use of a product or service.

channel grazing Using a television remote control to monitor programming on other channels while an advertisement is being broadcast.

Chaos Scenario As predicted by Bob Garfield, the mass exodus of advertising revenue from traditional broadcast media due to audience fragmentation and ad-avoidance hardware, which in turn reduces funding for the affected media and serves to limit their product quality, reducing audience size. This of course accelerates diversion of advertising dollars even further until there is little reliance on these media at all for marketing.

circulation The number of newspapers distributed each day (for daily newspapers) or each week (for weekly publications).

classified advertising Newspaper advertising that appears as all-copy messages under categories such as sporting goods, employment, and automobiles.

click fraud The act of clicking on Internet advertising links solely to generate illegitimate revenue for the Web site carrying the ad; can occur by persons paid to do so or by computer programs designed to imitate people.

click-throughs When Web users click on advertisements that take them to the home pages of those advertisers.

client The company or organization that pays for advertising. Also called the *sponsor.*

closing date The date when production-ready advertising materials must be delivered to a publisher for an ad to make a newspaper or magazine issue.

cognitive consistency The maintenance of a system of beliefs and attitudes over time; consumers' desire for cognitive consistency is an obstacle to advertising.

cognitive dissonance The anxiety or regret that lingers after a difficult decision.

cognitive responses The thoughts that occur to individuals at that exact moment in time when their beliefs and attitudes are being challenged by some form of persuasive communication.

cognitive style The unique preference of each person for thinking about and solving a problem. Cognitive style pioneer Carl Jung proposed three different dimensions in which thinking differs: Sensing versus Intuiting, Thinking versus Feeling, and Extraverted versus Introverted.

column inch A unit of advertising space in a newspaper, equal to one inch deep by one column wide.

commission system A method of agency compensation based on the amount of money the advertiser spends on the media.

communication tests A type of pretest message research that simply seeks to see if a message is communicating something close to what is desired.

community A group of people loosely joined by some common characteristic or interest.

comp A polished version of an ad.

comparison advertisements Advertisements in which an advertiser makes a comparison between the firm's brand and competitors' brands.

competitive field The companies that compete for a segment's business.

competitive positioning A positioning option that uses an explicit reference to an existing competitor to help define precisely what the advertised brand can do.

competitor analysis In an advertising plan, the section that discusses who the competitors are, outlining their strengths, weaknesses, tendencies, and any threats they pose.

concept test A type of developmental research that seeks feedback designed to screen the quality of a new idea, using consumers as the final judge and jury.

consent order An FTC action asking an advertiser accused of running deceptive or unfair advertising to stop running the advertisement in question, without admitting guilt.

consideration set The subset of brands from a particular product category that becomes the focal point of a consumer's evaluation.

consultants Individuals who specialize in areas related to the promotional process.

consumer behavior Those activities directly involved in obtaining, consuming, and disposing of products and services, including the decision processes that precede and follow these actions.

consumer culture A way of life centered around consumption.

consumerism The actions of individual consumers to exert power over the marketplace activities of organizations.

consumer-generated content (CGC) Advertisements for products produced either in part or completely by their end users. The recent explosion of consumer-generated content is largely due to the advent of content-sharing Internet Web sites (like YouTube) that essentially enable anyone to post (and view) video content.

consumer markets The markets for products and services purchased by individuals or households to satisfy their specific needs.

consumer-market sales promotion A type of sales promotion designed to induce household consumers to purchase a firm's brand rather than a competitor's brand.

consumer sales promotion A type of sales promotion aimed at consumers that focuses on price-off deals, coupons, sampling rebates, and premiums.

contest A sales promotion that has consumers compete for prizes based on skill or ability.

context effects How the context of the media through which an ad is presented affects consumers' impressions of the ad.

continuity The pattern of placement of advertisements in a media schedule.

continuous scheduling A pattern of placing ads at a steady rate over a period of time.

controlled circulation The number of copies of a newspaper that are given away free.

cookies Online tracking markers that advertisers place on a Web surfer's hard drive to track that person's online behavior.

coolhunts Researchers actually go to the site where they believe cool resides, stalk it, and bring it back to be used in the product and its advertising.

co-op advertising *See* **cooperative advertising**.

cooperative advertising The sharing of advertising expenses between national advertisers and local merchants. Also called *co-op advertising*.

copywriting The process of expressing the value and benefits a brand has to offer, via written or verbal descriptions.

corporate advertising Advertising intended to establish a favorable attitude toward a company as a whole, not just toward a specific brand.

corporate home page A site on the World Wide Web that focuses on a corporation and its products.

corrective advertising An FTC action requiring an advertiser to run additional advertisements to dispel false beliefs created by deceptive advertising.

cost per inquiry (CPI) The number of inquiries generated by a direct-marketing program divided by that program's cost.

cost per order (CPO) The number of orders generated by a direct-marketing program divided by that program's cost.

cost per rating point (CPRP) The cost of a spot on television divided by the program's rating; the resulting dollar figure can be used to compare the efficiency of advertising on various programs.

cost per thousand (CPM) The dollar cost of reaching 1,000 members of an audience using a particular medium.

cost per thousand–target market (CPM–TM) The cost per thousand for a particular segment of an audience.

coupon A type of sales promotion that entitles a buyer to a designated reduction in price for a product or service.

cover date The date of publication appearing on a magazine.

creative abrasion The clash of ideas, abstracted from the people who propose them, from which new ideas and breakthroughs can evolve. *Compare* **interpersonal abrasion**.

creative boutique An advertising agency that emphasizes copywriting and artistic services to its clients.

creative brief A document that outlines and channels an essential creative idea and objective.

creative concept The unique creative thought behind an advertising campaign.

creative plan A guideline used during the copywriting process to specify the message elements that must be coordinated during the preparation of copy.

creative revolution A revolution in the advertising industry during the 1960s, characterized by the "creatives" (art directors and copywriters) having a bigger say in the management of their agencies.

creative selling The act of assisting and persuading customers regarding purchasing decisions; creative selling typically involves products in which customers require extensive knowledge about the product before buying, such as specialty goods or higher-priced items (for example, sports equipment, cookware, insurance, or real estate).

creative services A group that develops the message that will be delivered through advertising, sales promotion, direct marketing, event sponsorship, or public relations.

creative team The copywriters and art directors responsible for coming up with the creative concept for an advertising campaign.

creativity The ability to consider and hold together seemingly inconsistent elements and forces, making a new connection; creativity is essential in the advertising world because successful marketing demands a constant seamless synthesis of the product and entirely different ideas or concepts.

cross-selling Marketing programs aimed at customers that already purchase other products.

culture What a people do—the way they eat, groom themselves, celebrate, mark their space and social position, and so forth.

cume The cumulative radio audience, which is the total number of different people who listen to a station for at least five minutes in a quarter-hour period within a specified daypart.

customer relationship management (CRM) The continual effort toward cultivating and maintaining long-term relationships with customers; many companies have recognized trust and rapport are key elements to repeated sales and thus train their sales teams to emphasize each particular customer's needs rather than the bottom line.

customer satisfaction Good feelings that come from a favorable postpurchase experience.

D

dailies Newspapers published every weekday; also, in television ad production, the scenes shot during the previous day's production.

database agency Agency that helps customers construct databases of target customers, merge databases, develop promotional materials, and then execute the campaign.

dayparts Segments of time during a television broadcast day.

deal-proneness The ease with which a consumer can get a deal, know what a good deal is, operate with knowledge of what a good price would be, and know a seller's cost.

deception Making false or misleading statements in an advertisement.

defamation When a communication occurs that damages the reputation of an individual because the information was untrue.

delayed response advertising Advertising that relies on imagery and message themes to emphasize the benefits and satisfying characteristics of a brand.

demographic dividend Situation in developing nations such as China, Brazil, and Mexico where falling labor costs, a younger and healthier population, and the entry of millions of women into the work force produce a favorable climate for economic expansion.

demographic segmentation Market segmenting based on basic descriptors like age, gender, race, marital status, income, education, and occupation.

design The structure (and the plan behind the structure) for the aesthetic and stylistic aspects of a print advertisement.

designers Specialists intimately involved with the execution of creative ideas and efforts.

developmental copy research A type of copy research that helps copywriters at the early stages of copy development by providing audience interpretations and reactions to the proposed copy.

dialogue Advertising copy that delivers the selling points of a message to the audience through a character or characters in the ad.

dialogue balloons A type of projective technique that offers consumers the chance to fill in the dialogue of cartoonlike stories, as a way of indirectly gathering brand information.

differentiation The process of creating a perceived difference, in the mind of the consumer, between an organization's brand and the competition's.

digital video (DV) A less expensive and less time-consuming alternative to film, it produces a better quality image than standard videotape.

direct broadcast by satellite (DBS) A program delivery system whereby television (and radio) programs are sent directly from a satellite to homes equipped with small receiving dishes.

direct mail A direct-marketing medium that involves using the postal service to deliver marketing materials.

direct marketing According to the Direct Marketing Association, "An interactive system of marketing which uses one or more advertising media to affect a measurable response and/ or transaction at any location."

direct-marketing agency Agency that maintains large databases of mailing lists; some of these firms can also design direct-marketing campaigns either through the mail or by telemarketing. Also called a **direct response agency**.

direct response Copy research method measuring actual behavior of consumers.

direct response advertising Advertising that asks the receiver of the message to act immediately.

direct response agency Also called direct marketing agency.

direct response copy Advertising copy that highlights the urgency of acting immediately.

display advertising A newspaper ad that includes the standard components of a print ad—headline, body copy, and often an illustration—to set it off from the news content of the paper.

display/banner ads Advertisements placed on World Wide Web sites that contain editorial material.

domain name The unique URL through which a Web location is established.

door-to-door sampling A type of sampling in which samples are brought directly to the homes of a target segment in a well-defined geographic area.

double-page spreads Advertisements that bridge two facing pages.

E

e-business A form of e-advertising and/or promotion in which companies selling to business customers rely on the Internet to send messages and close sales.

e-commerce agency Agency that handles a variety of planning and execution activities related to promotions using electronic commerce.

economies of scale The ability of a firm to lower the cost of each item produced because of high-volume production.

editing In television ad production, piecing together various scenes or shots of scenes to bring about the desired visual effect.

effective frequency The number of times a target audience needs to be exposed to a message before the objectives of the advertiser are met.

effective reach The number or percentage of consumers in the target audience that are exposed to an ad some minimum number of times.

elaboration likelihood model (ELM) A model that pertains to any situation where a persuasive communication is being sent and received.

electronic, laser, and inkjet printing A printing process that uses computers, electronics, electrostatics, and special toners and inks to produce images.

electronic mailing list A collection of e-mail addresses.

embedded Tightly connected to a context.

emergent consumers A market segment made up of the gradual but constant influx of first-time buyers.

emotional benefits Those benefits not typically found in some tangible feature or objective characteristic of a product or service.

ethics Moral standards and principles against which behavior is judged.

ethnic newspapers Newspapers that target a specific ethnic group.

ethnocentrism The tendency to view and value things from the perspective of one's own culture.

evaluative copy research A type of copy research used to judge an advertisement after the fact—the audience expresses its approval or disapproval of the copy used in the ad.

evaluative criteria The product attributes or performance characteristics on which consumers base their product evaluations.

event-planning agencies Experts in finding locations, securing dates, and putting together a "team" of people to pull off a promotional event.

event sponsorship Providing financial support to help fund an event, in return for the right to display a brand name, logo, or advertising message on-site at the event.

extended problem solving A decision-making mode in which consumers are inexperienced in a particular consumption setting but find the setting highly involving.

external facilitator An organization or individual that provides specialized services to advertisers and agencies.

external lists Mailing lists purchased from a list compiler or rented from a list broker and used to help an organization cultivate new business.

external position The competitive niche a brand pursues.

external search A search for product information that involves visiting retail stores to examine alternatives, seeking input from friends and relatives about their experiences with the products in question, or perusing professional product evaluations.

eye-tracking systems A type of physiological measure that monitors eye movements across print ads.

F

fact sheet radio ad A listing of important selling points that a radio announcer can use to ad-lib a radio spot.

Federal Trade Commission (FTC) The government regulatory agency that has the most power and is most directly involved in overseeing the advertising industry.

fee system A method of agency compensation whereby the advertiser and the agency agree on an hourly rate for different services provided.

field work Research conducted outside the agency, usually in the home or site of consumption.

film The most versatile and highest quality medium for television ad production.

first cover page The front cover of a magazine.

first-run syndication Television programs developed specifically for sale to individual stations.

flexography A printing technique similar to offset printing but that uses water-based ink, allowing printing to be done on any surface.

flighting A media-scheduling pattern of heavy advertising for a period of time, usually two weeks, followed by no advertising for a period, followed by another period of heavy advertising.

focus group A brainstorming session with a small group of target consumers and a professional moderator, used to gain new insights about consumer response to a brand.

"forgetting function" Idea that people's forgetting is fairly predictable and seems to obey a mathematical function.

formal balance A symmetrical presentation in an ad—every component on one side of an imaginary vertical line is repeated in approximate size and shape on the other side of the imaginary line.

fourth cover page The back cover of a magazine.

frame-by-frame test Copy research method that works by getting consumers to turn dials (like/dislike) while viewing television commercials in a theater setting.

free premium A sales promotion that provides consumers with an item at no cost; the item is either included in the package of a purchased item or mailed to the consumer after proof of purchase is verified.

free-standing insert (FSI) A newspaper insert ad that contains cents-off coupons for a variety of products and is typically delivered with Sunday newspapers.

frequency The average number of times an individual or household within a target audience is exposed to a media vehicle in a given period of time.

frequency-marketing programs Direct-marketing programs that provide concrete rewards to frequent customers.

frequency programs A type of sales promotion that offers consumers discounts or free product rewards for repeat purchase or patronage of the same brand or company.

fulfillment center Centers that ensure customers receive the product ordered through direct mail.

full position A basis of buying newspaper ad space, in which the ad is placed near the top of a page or in the middle of editorial material.

full-service agency An advertising agency that typically includes an array of advertising professionals to meet all the promotional needs of clients.

functional benefits Those benefits that come from the objective performance characteristics of a product or service.

G

gatefold ads Advertisements that fold out of a magazine to display an extra-wide ad.

gay and lesbian newspapers Newspapers targeting a gay and lesbian readership.

gender The social expression of sexual biology or choice.

general-population newspapers Newspapers that serve local communities and report news of interest to the local population.

geodemographic segmentation A form of market segmentation that identifies neighborhoods around the country that share common demographic characteristics.

geographic scope Scope of the geographic area to be covered by advertising media.

geo-targeting The placement of ads in geographic regions where higher purchase tendencies for a brand are evident.

global advertising Developing and placing advertisements with a common theme and presentation in all markets around the world where the firm's brands are sold.

global agencies Advertising agencies with a worldwide presence.

globalized campaigns Advertising campaigns that use the same message and creative execution across all (or most) international markets.

government officials and employees One of the five types of audiences for advertising; includes employees of government organizations, such as schools and road maintenance operations, at the federal, state, and local levels.

gravure A print production method that uses a plate or mat; it is excellent for reproducing pictures.

Great Depression A period (1929–1941 for the United States) in which the vast majority of people in many countries suffered from a severe economic decline.

green marketing Corporate efforts that embrace a cause or program in support of the environment. Green marketing is currently of particular importance, as the public is becoming increasingly aware and concerned about the urgency of environmental issues.

gross domestic product (GDP) A measure of the total value of goods and services produced within an economic system.

gross impressions The sum of exposures to all the media placement in a media plan.

guaranteed circulation A stated minimum number of copies of a particular issue of a magazine that will be delivered to readers.

guerrilla marketing Edgy, inexpensive promotional initiatives executed in major urban markets.

H

habit A decision-making mode in which consumers buy a single brand repeatedly as a solution to a simple consumption problem.

headline The leading sentence or sentences, usually at the top or bottom of an ad, that attract attention, communicate a key selling point, or achieve brand identification.

heavy users Consumers who purchase a product or service much more frequently than others.

high-definition television (HDTV) Television that displays picture and produces sound from a satellite that sends a digital signal.

highly industrialized countries Countries with both a high GNP and a high standard of living.

hits The number of pages and graphical images requested from a Web site.

household consumers The most conspicuous of the five types of audiences for advertising; most mass media advertising is directed at them.

households using television (HUT) A measure of the number of households tuned to a television program during a particular time period.

I

illustration In the context of advertising, the drawing, painting, photography, or computer-generated art that forms the picture in an advertisement.

illustration format The way the product is displayed in a print advertisement.

implicit memory measures Techniques used to obtain feedback that determines consumers' recognition of products (and thus marketing success), characterized by questions or tasks that do not explicitly make reference to the advertisement in question. The perceived advantage of this type of test is a more subconscious, unadulterated response.

Industrial Revolution A major change in Western society beginning in the mid-eighteenth century and marked by a rapid change from an agricultural to an industrial economy.

industry analysis In an advertising plan, the section that focuses on developments and trends within an industry and on any other factors that may make a difference in how an advertiser proceeds with an advertising plan.

inelasticity of demand Strong loyalty to a product, resulting in consumers being less sensitive to price increases.

influencer marketing A series of personalized marketing techniques directed at individuals or groups who have the credibility and capability to drive positive word of mouth in a broader and salient segment of the population.

infomercial A long advertisement that looks like a talk show or a half-hour product demonstration.

informal balance An asymmetrical presentation in an ad—nonsimilar sizes and shapes are optically weighed.

in-house agency The advertising department of a firm.

inquiry/direct response measures A type of posttest message tracking in which a print or broadcast advertisement offers the audience the opportunity to place an inquiry or respond directly through a reply card or toll-free number.

in-store sampling A type of sampling that occurs at the point of purchase and is popular for food products and cosmetics.

integrated brand promotion (IBP) The use of various promotional tools, including advertising, in a coordinated manner to build and maintain brand awareness, identity, and preference.

integrated marketing communications (IMC) The process of using promotional tools in a unified way so that a synergistic communications effect is created.

interactive agencies Advertising agencies that help advertisers prepare communications for new media like the Internet, interactive kiosks, CD-ROMS, and interactive television.

interactive media Media that allow consumers to call up games, entertainment, shopping opportunities, and educational programs on a subscription or pay-per-view basis.

intergenerational effect When people choose products based on what was used in their childhood household.

internal lists An organization's records of its customers, subscribers, donors, and inquirers, used to develop better relationships with current customers.

internal position The niche a brand achieves with regard to the other similar brands a firm markets.

internal search A search for product information that draws on personal experience and prior knowledge.

international advertising The preparation and placement of advertising in different national and cultural markets.

international affiliates Foreign-market advertising agencies with which a local agency has established a relationship to handle clients' international advertising needs.

Internet A vast global network of scientific, military, and research computers that allows people inexpensive access to the largest storehouse of information in the world.

Internet experiment A method of obtaining consumer feedback that uses a controlled manipulation of some sort of content offered to consumers visiting a Web site.

interpersonal abrasion The clash of people, often resulting from an inability to regard idea feedback as separate from personal feedback, from which communication shuts down and new ideas get slaughtered. *Compare* **creative abrasion**.

involvement The degree of perceived relevance and personal importance accompanying the choice of a certain product or service within a particular context.

IRI Behavior Scan Supplier of single-source data testing.

J, K, L

layout A drawing of a proposed print advertisement, showing where all the elements in the ad are positioned.

less-developed countries Countries whose economies lack almost all the resources necessary for development: capital, infrastructure, political stability, and trained workers.

letterpress The oldest and most versatile method of printing, in which text and images are printed from a plate or mat.

libel Defamation that occurs in print and would relate to magazine, newspaper, direct mail, or Internet reports.

life-stage A circumstantial variable, such as when a family's youngest child moves away from home, which changes the consumption patterns of the family.

lifestyle segmentation A form of market segmenting that focuses on consumers' activities, interests, and opinions.

limited problem solving A decision-making mode in which consumers' experience and involvement are both low.

live production The process of creating a live television commercial, which can result in realism and the capturing of spontaneous reactions and events but comes with a loss of control that can threaten the objectives of the commercial.

live script radio ad A detailed script read by an on-air radio personality.

local advertising Advertising directed at an audience in a single trading area, either a city or state.

local agency An advertising agency in a foreign market hired because of its knowledge of the culture and local market conditions.

localized campaigns Advertising campaigns that involve preparing different messages and creative executions for each foreign market a firm has entered.

local spot radio advertising Radio advertising placed directly with individual stations rather than with a network or syndicate.

local television Television programming other than the network broadcast that independent stations and network affiliates offer local audiences.

logo A graphic mark that identifies a company and other visual representations that promote an identity for a firm.

M

Madison & Vine A reference to continually converging advertising and entertainment, coined from the names of two renowned avenues that represent the two industries, respectively.

mailing list A file of names and addresses that an organization might use for contacting prospective or prior customers.

mail sampling A type of sampling in which samples are delivered through the postal service.

marcom manager A marketing-communications manager who plans an organization's overall communications program and oversees the various functional specialists inside and outside the organization to ensure that they are working together to deliver the desired message to the customer.

marketing The process of conceiving, pricing, promoting, and distributing ideas, goods, and services to create exchanges that benefit consumers and organizations.

marketing database A mailing list that also includes information collected directly from individual customers.

marketing mix The blend of the four responsibilities of marketing—conception, pricing, promotion, and distribution—used for a particular idea, product, or service.

market niche A relatively small group of consumers who have a unique set of needs and who typically are willing to pay a premium price to a firm that specializes in meeting those needs.

market segmentation The breaking down of a large, heterogeneous market into submarkets or segments that are more homogeneous.

markup charge A method of agency compensation based on adding a percentage charge to a variety of services the agency purchases from outside suppliers.

mash-up A combination of one or more Web sites into a single site for purposes of analyzing or comparing information side-by-side.

meaning What an advertisement intends or conveys.

measured media Media that are closely measured to determine advertising costs and effectiveness: television, radio, newspapers, magazines, and outdoor media.

mechanical A carefully prepared paste-up of the exact components of an advertisement, prepared specifically for the printer.

media buying Securing the electronic media time and print media space specified in a given account's schedule.

media-buying service An independent organization that specializes in buying media time and space, particularly on radio and television, as a service to advertising agencies and advertisers.

media class A broad category of media, such as television, radio, or newspapers.

media impressions Instances in which a product or brand is exposed to potential consumers by direct newspaper, television, radio, or magazine coverage (rather than the payment of these media as venues in which to advertise). The effectiveness of sponsorship spending is often judged by the comparison of media impressions to traditional media advertising, such as commercials.

media mix The blend of different media that will be used to effectively reach the target audience.

media plan A plan specifying the media in which advertising messages will be placed to reach the desired target audience.

media planning and buying services Services related to media planning or buying that are provided by advertising agencies or specialized media-buying organizations.

media specialists Organizations that specialize in buying media time and space and offer media strategy consulting to advertising agencies and advertisers.

media vehicle A particular option for placement within a media class (e.g., *Newsweek* is a media vehicle within the magazine media class).

medium The means by which an illustration in a print advertisement is rendered: either drawing, photography, or computer graphics.

members of business organizations One of the five types of audiences for advertising; the focus of advertising for firms that produce business and industrial goods and services.

members of a trade channel One of the five types of audiences for advertising; the retailers, wholesalers, and distributors targeted by producers of both household and business goods and services.

merchandise allowances A type of trade-market sales promotion in which free products are packed with regular shipments as payment to the trade for setting up and maintaining displays.

message strategy A component of an advertising strategy, it defines the goals of the advertiser and how those goals will be achieved.

message weight A sum of the total audience size of all the media specified in a media plan.

missionary salesperson A person who proactively contacts customers after a purchase has been made, in order to ensure customer satisfaction and foster goodwill, by asking if the customer has questions about the product, providing additional information, and checking to see if the customer's current needs have changed (and may present an opportunity for further sales).

miscellaneous In regard to font styles, a category that includes display fonts that are used not for their legibility, but for their ability to attract attention. Fonts like garage and novelty display belong in this category.

Mobile-Fi Wireless Internet technology having multi-mile access and the capability of accessing the Net while the user is moving in a car or train.

mobile sampling A type of sampling carried out by logo-emblazoned vehicles that dispense samples, coupons, and premiums to consumers at malls, shopping centers, fairgrounds, and recreational areas.

monopoly power The ability of a firm to make it impossible for rival firms to compete with it, either through advertising or in some other way.

multi-attribute attitude models (MAAMS) A framework and set of procedures for collecting information from consumers to assess their salient beliefs and attitudes about competitive brands.

N

narrative Advertising copy that simply displays a series of statements about a brand.

narrowcasting The development and delivery of specialized television programming to well-defined audiences.

national advertising Advertising that reaches all geographic areas of one nation.

National Advertising Review Board A body formed by the advertising industry to oversee its practice.

national spot radio advertising Radio advertising placed in nationally syndicated radio programming.

need state A psychological state arising when one's desired state of affairs differs from one's actual state of affairs.

network radio advertising Radio advertising placed within national network programs.

network television A type of television that broadcasts programming over airwaves to affiliate stations across the United States under a contract agreement.

newly industrialized countries Countries where traditional ways of life that have endured for centuries change into modern consumer cultures in a few short years.

newspaper sampling Samples distributed in newspapers to allow very specific geographic and geodemographic targeting.

nonusers A market segment made up of consumers who do not use a particular product or service.

normative test scores Scores that are determined by testing an ad and then comparing the scores to those of previously tested, average commercials of its type.

O

objective-and-task approach A method of advertising budgeting that focuses on the relationship between spending and advertising objectives by identifying the specific tasks necessary to achieve different aspects of the advertising objectives.

off-invoice allowance A program allowing wholesalers and retailers to deduct a set amount from the invoice they receive for merchandise.

off-network syndication Television programs that were previously run in network prime time.

offset lithography A printing process in which a flat, chemically treated surface attracts ink to the areas to be printed and repels ink from other areas; the inked image is then transferred to a rubber blanket on a roller, and from the roller the impression is carried to paper.

online editing The transferring of the finalized rough cut of a television ad onto one-inch videotape, which is of on-air quality suitable for media transmission.

on-package sampling A type of sampling in which a sample item is attached to another product package.

on-sale date The date on which a magazine is issued to subscribers and for newsstand distribution.

opt-in e-mail A list of Web site visitors who have given their permission to receive commercial e-mail about topics and products that interest them.

order taking The practice of accepting and processing needed customer information for pre-arranged merchandise purchase, or scheduling services that a consumer will purchase once rendered. While their role in the transaction process rarely involves communicating large amounts of information, order takers must be able to answer customer questions and be accommodating and considerate.

out-of-home media The combination of transit and billboard advertising.

P

packaging The container or wrapping for a product; packaging serves as an important vessel for product information and user appeal, as it is often viewed by the customer in a potential buying situation.

page views The record of the pages (as indicated by the request for the HTML files that comprise them) that have been sent to a user's computer. Page views provide somewhat inaccurate user documentation because they do not distinguish between repeat and initial visitors, or track whether a user has viewed more than one screen of the page if it takes up several screens.

paid circulation The number of copies of a newspaper sold through subscriptions and newsstand distribution.

paid search Process by which companies pay Web search engines and portals to place ads in or near relevant search results.

parallel layout structure A print ad design that employs art on the right-hand side of the page and repeats the art on the left-hand side.

participation A way of buying television advertising time in which several different advertisers buy commercial time during a specific television program.

pass-along readership An additional number of people, other than the original readers, who may see a magazine.

pay-for-results A compensation plan that results when a client and its agency agree to a set of results criteria on which the agency's fee will be based.

percentage-of-sales approach An advertising budgeting approach that calculates the advertising budget based on a percentage of the prior year's sales or the projected year's sales.

peripheral cues The features of an ad other than the actual arguments about the brand's performance.

permanent long-term displays P-O-P materials intended for presentation for more than six months.

permission marketing Web users agree to receive e-mails from organizations.

personal selling The face-to-face communications and persuasions process, often used with products that are higher-priced, complicated to use, must be tailored to individual user needs, involve a trade-in, or are judged at the point of purchase.

physiological assessment The interpretation of certain biological feedback generated from viewers who are exposed to an ad. Although physiological assessment has advanced with devices such as MRIs and PT scans, its overall value is still questionable.

pica A measure of the width or depth of lines of type.

picturing Creating representations of things.

pilot testing A form of message evaluation consisting of experimentation in the marketplace.

point A measure of the size of type in height.

point-of-entry marketing Advertising strategies designed to win the loyalty of consumers whose brand preferences are still under development in hopes of gaining their loyalty.

point-of-purchase (P-O-P) advertising Advertising that appears at the point of purchase.

pop-up/pop-under ad An Internet advertisement that appears as a Web site page is loading or after a page has loaded.

portal A starting point for Web access and search.

positioning The process of designing a product or service so that it can occupy a distinct and valued place in the target consumer's mind, and then communicating this distinctiveness through advertising.

positioning strategy The key themes or concepts an organization features for communicating the distinctiveness of its product or service to the target segment.

preferred position A basis of buying newspaper ad space, in which the ad is placed in a specific section of the paper.

premiums Items that feature the logo of a sponsor and that are offered free, or at a reduced price, with the purchase of another item.

preprinted insert An advertisement delivered to a newspaper fully printed and ready for insertion into the newspaper.

preproduction The stage in the television production process in which the advertiser and advertising agency (or in-house agency staff) carefully work out the precise details of how the creative planning behind an ad can best be brought to life with the opportunities offered by television.

price/cost transparency Ease with which consumers can find out the price of a product and the seller's cost.

price-off deal A type of sales promotion that offers a consumer cents or even dollars off merchandise at the point of purchase through specially marked packages.

primary demand The demand for an entire product category.

primary demand stimulation Using advertising to create demand for a product category in general.

principle of limited liability An economic principle that allows an investor to risk only his or her shares of a corporation, rather than personal wealth, in business ventures.

principles of design General rules governing the elements within a print advertisement and the arrangement of and relationship between these elements.

proactive public relations strategy A public relations strategy that is dictated by marketing objectives, seeks to publicize a company and its brands, and is offensive in spirit rather than defensive.

production facilitator An organization that offers essential services both during and after the production process.

production services A team that takes creative ideas and turns them into advertisements, direct mail pieces, or events materials.

production stage The point at which the storyboard and script for a television ad come to life and are filmed. Also called the *shoot*.

production timetable A realistic schedule for all the preproduction, production, and postproduction activities involved with making a television commercial.

product placement The sales promotion technique of getting a marketer's product featured in movies and television shows.

professionals One of the five types of audiences for advertising, defined as doctors, lawyers, accountants, teachers, or any other professionals who require special training or certification.

program rating The percentage of television households that are in a market and are tuned to a specific program during a specific time period.

projective techniques A type of developmental research designed to allow consumers to project thoughts and feelings (conscious or unconscious) in an indirect and unobtrusive way onto a theoretically neutral stimulus.

promotion agencies Specialized agencies that handle promotional efforts.

psychographics A form of market research that emphasizes the understanding of consumers' activities, interests, and opinions.

publicity Unpaid-for media exposure about a firm's activities or its products and services.

public relations A marketing and management function that focuses on communications that foster goodwill between a firm and its many constituent groups.

public relations audit An internal study that identifies the characteristics of a firm or the aspects of the firm's activities that are positive and newsworthy.

public relations firms Firms that handle the needs of organizations regarding relationships with the local community, competitors, industry associations, and government organizations.

public relations plan A plan that identifies the objectives and activities related to the public relations communications issued by a firm.

puffery The use of absolute superlatives like "Number One" and "Best in the World" in advertisements.

Pull marketing A method of promotion characterized by voluntary consumer exposure, in which, due to carefully generated interest on the part of the advertiser, the consumer actively seeks out information relating to the product or brand.

pulsing A media-scheduling strategy that combines elements from continuous and flighting techniques; advertisements are scheduled continuously in media over a period of time, but with periods of much heavier scheduling.

purchase intent A measure of whether or not a consumer intends to buy a product or service in the near future.

Pure Food and Drug Act A 1906 act of Congress requiring manufacturers to list the active ingredients of their products on their labels.

Push marketing A method of promotion characterized by involuntary consumer exposure (such as commercials during television and radio programming and advertisements in magazines), in which the advertiser actively seeks to enter consumer consciousness.

push money A form of trade incentive in which retail salespeople are offered monetary reward for featuring a marketer's brand with shoppers.

push strategy A sales promotion strategy in which marketers devise incentives to encourage purchases by members of the trade to help push a product into the distribution channel.

Q, R

radio networks A type of radio that delivers programming via satellite to affiliate stations across the United States.

radio syndication A type of radio that provides complete programs to stations on a contract basis.

rate card A form given to advertisers by a newspaper and containing information on costs, closing times, specifications for submitting an ad, and special pages or features available in the newspaper.

ratings point A measure indicating that 1 percent of all the television households in an area were tuned to the program measured.

reach The number of people or households in a target audience that will be exposed to a media vehicle or schedule at least one time during a given period of time. It is often expressed as a percentage.

reactive public relations strategy A public relations strategy that is dictated by influences outside the control of a company, focuses on problems to be solved rather than opportunities, and requires defensive rather than offensive measures.

readership A measure of a newspaper's circulation multiplied by the number of readers of a copy.

rebate A money-back offer requiring a buyer to mail in a form requesting the money back from the manufacturer.

recall tests Tests of how much the viewer of an ad remembers of the message; they are used to measure the cognitive residue of the ad. These are the most commonly employed tests in advertising.

recognition In a test, when the audience members indicate that they have seen an ad before.

recognition tests Tests in which audience members are asked if they recognize an ad or something in an ad. These are the standard cognitive residue test for print ads and promotion.

regional advertising Advertising carried out by producers, wholesalers, distributors, and retailers that concentrate their efforts in a particular geographic region.

repeat purchase A second purchase of a new product after trying it for the first time.

repositioning Returning to the process of segmenting, targeting, and positioning a product or service to arrive at a revised positioning strategy.

resonance test A type of message assessment in which the goal is to determine to what extent the message resonates or rings true with target audience members.

RFM analysis An analysis of how recently and how frequently a customer is buying from an organization, and of how much that customer is spending per order and over time.

rich media/video and audio The process in which a Web ad uses advanced technology like streaming video or audio that interacts with the user when the user's mouse passes over the ad.

riding the boards Assessing possible locations for billboard advertising.

rituals Repeated behaviors that affirm, express, and maintain cultural values.

roman The most popular category of type because of its legibility.

rough cut An assembly of the best scenes from a television ad shoot edited together using digital technology.

rough layout The second stage of the ad layout process, in which the headline is lettered in and the elements of the ad are further refined.

RSS (Really Simple Syndication) A channel or feed (often commercial in nature) that a computer user is linked to from visited blogs, podcasts, or other content on the Internet.

run-of-paper or **run-of-press (ROP)** A basis of buying newspaper or magazine ad space, in which an ad may appear anywhere, on any page in the paper or magazine.

S

sales promotion The use of incentive techniques that create a perception of greater brand value among consumers or distributors.

salient beliefs A small number of beliefs that are the critical determinants of an attitude.

sampling A sales promotion technique designed to provide a consumer with a trial opportunity.

sans serif A category of type that includes typefaces with no small lines crossing the ends of the main strokes.

satellite and closed-circuit A method of transmitting programming to highly segmented audiences.

scratch track A rough approximation of the musical score of a television ad, using only a piano and vocalists.

script (television) The written version of an ad; it specifies the coordination of the copy elements with the video scenes.

script (typeface) A style of print in which letters connect to one another, resembling handwriting; often used for occasions in which elegance or particularly high quality is appropriate (wedding invitations, etc).

search engine A software tool used to find Web sites on the Internet by searching for keywords typed in by the user.

search engine optimization (SEO) Utilizing a search engine to a company's best advantage.

secondary data Information obtained from existing sources.

second cover page The inside front cover of a magazine.

Second Life The most prominent network of the virtual world phenomenon, in which participants log into a space as an avatar (alternate identity/character), then use their mouse and keyboard to perform a variety of activities that simulate those people perform in the real world. Often the line between the real world and the virtual one can become blurred, and users may indeed do "real" activities (such as conducting business) in a virtual setting.

selective attention The processing of only a few advertisements among the many encountered.

selective demand stimulation Using advertising to stimulate demand for a specific brand within a product category.

self-liquidating premium A sales promotion that requires a consumer to pay most of the cost of the item received as a premium.

self-reference criterion (SRC) The unconscious reference to one's own cultural values, experiences, and knowledge as a basis for decisions.

self-regulation The advertising industry's attempt to police itself.

sentence and picture completion A type of projective technique in which a researcher presents consumers with part of a picture or a sentence with words deleted and then asks that the stimulus be completed; the picture or sentence relates to one or several brands.

serif The small lines that cross the ends of the main strokes in type; also the name for the category of type that has this characteristic.

share of audience A measure of the proportion of households that are using television during a specific time period and are tuned to a particular program.

share of voice A calculation of any advertiser's brand expenditures relative to the overall spending in a category.

short-term promotional displays P-O-P materials that are used for six months or less.

single-source data Information provided from individual households about brand purchases, coupon use, and television advertising exposure by combining grocery store scanner data with TV-viewing data from monitoring devices attached to the households' televisions.

single-source tracking measures A type of posttest message tracking that provides information about brand purchases, coupon use, and television advertising exposure by combining grocery store scanner data and devices that monitor household television-viewing behavior.

situation analysis In an advertising plan, the section in which the advertiser lays out the most important factors that define the situation, and then explains the importance of each factor.

slander Oral defamation that in the context of promotion would occur during television or radio broadcast of an event involving a company and its employees.

slogan A short phrase used in part to help establish an image, identity, or position for a brand or an organization, but mostly used to increase memorability.

slotting fees A type of trade-market sales promotion in which manufacturers make direct cash payments to retailers to ensure shelf space.

social meaning What a product or service means in a societal context.

space contract A contract that establishes a rate for all advertising placed in a magazine by an advertiser over a specified period.

space order A commitment by an advertiser to advertising space in a particular issue of a magazine. Also called an *insertion order*.

spam To post messages to many unrelated newsgroups on Usenet.

split-list experiment A type of pilot testing in which multiple versions of a direct mail piece are prepared and sent to various segments of a mailing list; the version that pulls the best is deemed superior.

split-run distribution A type of pilot testing in which two different versions of an advertisement are placed in every other issue of a magazine; the ads are then compared on the basis of direct response.

split-transmission A type of pilot testing in which two different broadcast signals (which become advertisements when viewed on television) are simultaneously sent to two groups of households for reaction comparison.

sponsorship A way of buying television advertising time in which an advertiser agrees to pay for the production of a television program and for most (and often all) of the advertising that appears in the program.

spot advertising A way of buying television advertising time in which airtime is purchased through local television stations.

square root law The recognition of print ads increases with the square of the illustration.

standard advertising unit (SAU) One of 57 defined sizes of newspaper advertisements.

Starch Readership Services An example of a company that performs recognition tests.

sticky site A site that is able to attract visitors over and over again and keep them for a long time.

still production A technique of television ad production whereby a series of photographs or slides is filmed and edited so that the resulting ad appears to have movement and action.

storyboard A frame-by-frame sketch or photo sequence depicting, in sequence, the visual scenes and copy that will be used in an advertisement.

story construction A type of projective technique that asks consumers to tell a story about people depicted in a scene or picture, as a way of gathering information about a brand.

STP marketing (segmenting, targeting, positioning) A marketing strategy employed when advertisers focus their efforts on one subgroup of a product's total market.

straight-line copy Advertising copy that explains in straightforward terms why a reader will benefit from use of a product or service.

stratification (social class) A person's relative standing in a social system as produced by systematic inequalities in things such as wealth, income, education, power, and status. Also referred to as *social class*.

subhead In an advertisement, a few words or a short sentence that usually appears above or below the headline and includes important brand information not included in the headline.

subliminal advertising Advertising alleged to work on a subconscious level.

support media Media used to reinforce a message being delivered via some other media vehicle.

surfing Gliding from Web site to Web site using a search engine, direct links, or word of mouth.

surveys A method of soliciting customer feedback through questions related to a viewed ad; surveys are administered in various ways, such as over the telephone or on the Internet, as well as at different lengths of time after the viewing takes place.

sweepstakes A sales promotion in which winners are determined purely by chance.

switchers A market segment made up of consumers who often buy what is on sale or choose brands that offer discount coupons or other price incentives. Also called *variety seekers*.

symbolic value What a product or service means to consumers in a nonliteral way.

T

target audience A particular group of consumers singled out for an advertisement or advertising campaign.

target segment The subgroup (of the larger market) chosen as the focal point for the marketing program and advertising campaign.

taste A generalized set or orientation to consumer preferences.

telemarketing A direct-marketing medium that involves using the telephone to deliver a spoken appeal.

television households An estimate of the number of households that are in a market and own a television.

testimonial An advertisement in which an advocacy position is taken by a spokesperson.

third cover page The inside back cover of a magazine.

thought listing A type of pretest message research that tries to identify specific thoughts that may be generated by an advertisement.

three-point layout structure A print ad design that establishes three elements in an ad as dominant forces.

thumbnails, or thumbnail sketches The rough first drafts of an ad layout, about one-quarter the size of the finished ad.

TiVo A service that automatically records a consumer's favorite television shows every time they air and allows consumers to skip commercials.

top-level domain (TLD) The suffix that follows the Web site name.

top-of-the-mind awareness Keen consumer awareness of a certain brand, indicated by listing that brand first when asked to name a number of brands.

tracking studies Studies that document the apparent effect of advertising over time, assessing attitude change, knowledge, behavioral intent, and self-reported behavior. They are one of the most commonly used advertising and promotion research methods.

trade journals Magazines published specifically for members of a trade that carry highly technical articles.

trade-market sales promotion A type of sales promotion designed to motivate distributors, wholesalers, and retailers to stock and feature a firm's brand in their merchandising programs.

trade reseller Organizations in the marketing channel of distribution that buy products to resell to customers.

trade shows Events where several related products from many manufacturers are displayed and demonstrated to members of the trade.

transit advertising Advertising that appears as both interior and exterior displays on mass transit vehicles and at terminal and station platforms.

trial offers A type of sales promotion in which expensive items are offered on a trial basis to induce consumer trial of a brand.

trial usage An advertising objective to get consumers to use a product new to them on a trial basis.

type font A basic set of typeface letters.

U

ultrabroadband Wireless Internet technology allowing people to move extremely large files quickly over short distances.

unfair advertising Defined by Congress as "acts or practices that cause or are likely to cause substantial injury to consumers, which is not reasonably avoidable by consumers themselves and not outweighed by the countervailing benefits to consumers or competition."

unique selling proposition (USP) A promise contained in an advertisement in which the advertised brand offers a specific, unique, and relevant benefit to the consumer.

unique visitors The name used to describe different "people" who visit a Web site (determined from the user's registration with the site). Because unique visitors are also sometimes distinguished by the different IP numbers used by Internet services that connect users, and these services often use changing IP numbers, the record of unique visitors may reflect the same user as many different users.

unit-of-sales approach An approach to advertising budgeting that allocates a specified dollar amount of advertising for each unit of a brand sold (or expected to be sold).

unmeasured media Media less formally measured for advertising costs and effectiveness (as compared to the measured media): direct mail, catalogs, special events, and other ways to reach business and household consumers.

Usenet A collection of more than 13,000 discussion groups on the Internet.

user positioning A positioning option that focuses on a specific profile of the target user.

V

value A perception by consumers that a product or service provides satisfaction beyond the cost incurred to acquire the product or service.

value proposition A statement of the functional, emotional, and self-expressive benefits delivered by the brand, which provide value to customers in the target segment.

values The defining expressions of culture, demonstrating in words and deeds what is important to a culture.

variety seekers *See* **switchers**.

variety seeking A decision-making mode in which consumers switch their selection among various brands in a given category in a random pattern.

V-chip A device that can block television programming based on the recently developed program rating system.

vertical cooperative advertising An advertising technique whereby a manufacturer and dealer (either a wholesaler or retailer) share the expense of advertising.

video on demand (VOD) A cable television service that enables subscribers to select and watch a selection of videos at any time.

videotape An option for television ad production that is less expensive than film but also of lower quality.

viral marketing The process of consumers marketing to consumers over the Internet through word of mouth transmitted through e-mails and electronic mailing lists.

virtual mall A gateway to a group of Internet storefronts that provides access to mall sites by simply clicking on a storefront.

visits The number of occasions on which a user X looked up Y Web site during Z period of time.

voice-response analysis A type of physiological assessment performed by computers to measure the inflections in a test subject's voice for excitement and other physiological states; deemed largely unreliable because it is impossible to tell whether a reaction is due to the ad or any number of other undeterminable factors.

W

Web analytic software Measurement software that not only provides information on hits, pages, visits, and users, but also allows a site to track audience traffic within itself. Web analytic software can detect which pages are more popular, when they are viewed, how long they are viewed, etc.

Web site A collection of Web pages, images, videos, and other digital content that is hosted on a Web server.

white space In a print advertisement, space not filled with a headline, subhead, body copy, or illustration. White space is not just empty space: it is typically used to mark qualities that include luxury, elegance and simplicity.

widget A software module that people can drag and drop on to their personal Web page of their social network (for example, Facebook) or on to a blog. For a fee (per click), advertisers can create widgets that feature their brands or that direct the user to an e-commerce site.

WiFi Wireless technology allowing Internet access connections to reach out about 300 feet.

WiMax A wireless Internet technology similar to WiFi but capable of creating a hot spot with a range of 25-30 miles.

within-vehicle duplication Exposure to the same advertisement in the same media at different times.

World Wide Web (WWW) A universal database of information available to Internet users; its graphical environment makes navigation simple and exciting.

X, Y, Z

Zaltman Metaphor Elicitation Technique (ZMET) A research technique to draw out people's buried thoughts and feelings about products and brands by encouraging participants to think in terms of metaphors.

NAME/BRAND/COMPANY INDEX

Page references in **bold** print indicate ads or photos. Page references in *italics* indicate tables, charts or graphs. Page references followed by "n" indicate footnotes.

SUBJECT INDEX

Page references in **bold** print indicate ads or photos. Page references in *italics* indicate tables, charts or graphs. Page references followed by "n" indicate footnotes.

A

Above-the-line promotion, 455
Abrasion, 331–332
Accommodation, 15
Accountability, 99, 451, 566
Account executives, 272, 322–324, **323**, 328, *429*
Account planners, 63, 277–278
Account planning systems, 228, **256**, 256–257
Account services, 62
Account teams, 328
Action for Children's Television, 95, 124, 129
Activities. *See* Psychographics
Administrative services, 64
Adver-gaming, 610. *See also* Video game advertising
Advertainment. *See* Branded entertainment
Advertisements
  ads on demand, 48
  avoidance of, 454, **600**, 600–601
  definition of, 12
  information in, 23, 112–113, **114**, 155–157
  length and size of, 464–465
  locations of, 436, 501–502
  meaning transmission and, 190–192, **191**
  for media buyers, 477, **477**
  research on (*See* Copy research)
  run-of-paper, 494, 501
  run-of-station, 517
  self-awareness in, **100**, 100–101, **101**
  "smart ads," 7
  values and, 175, 294
Advertisers
  advertising spending by, 49–50, *50*
  categories of, 52–55
  definition of, 52

editorial content influence and, 122, 140
industry trends and, 44–49
role of, in IBP, 55
structure of advertising industry and, 51
top ten, in magazines, *496*
Advertising
  definitions of, 8–11
  ethical aspects of, 123–126
  history of (*See* Evolution, of advertising)
  purpose of, 44
  social aspects of (*See* Social aspects of advertising)
  spending on, 49–50, *50*, **51**
  types of, 29–32
Advertising agencies
  accountability of, 99, 451
  account planning in, 256–257
  advertising plans and, 262–268, 272, 277, 280–281
  agency of record, 480
  auditing firms and, 66
  British, 98
  compensation of, **64**, 64–66, 449–450
  consolidation of, 45, 96
  creativity and, 319–333
  definition of, 55
  founding of, 81
  globalization and, 45, 58
  industry trends and, 44–49
  in-house, 58
  international advertising and, 300–302, **301**
  mass media and, 42–44
  media buying and, 480
  minority employment in, 95
  profitability of, 450–451
  ranking of, *56*
  regulatory activities of, 136
  research departments in, 227–229
  services of, 61–64

specialized, 46, 58
structure of advertising industry and, 51
types of, 55–59, **62**
Advertising and promotions industry
  advertising plans and, 267
  benchmarks in, 276
  scope of, 49–51
  self-regulation of, 130, 133–137, *134*
  structure of, 51–70, **52**
  advertisers, 52–55
  advertising agencies, 55–59
  agency compensation, 64–66
  agency services, 61–64
  external facilitators, 66–68
  media organizations, 51, 68–70
  promotion agencies, 59–61
  target audiences, 70
  trends affecting, 44–49
Advertising associations, 136
Advertising campaigns, 12, 302–305. *See also specific campaigns in Name Index*
Advertising clutter, 167–168, 167n, **168**, 491, 499, 509–510. *See also* Clutter
Advertising plans, 264–281
  advertising agencies and, 262–268, 272, 277, 280–281
  budgeting and, 272–277
  components of, **265**
  evaluation of, 280
  example of, 262–264
  execution of, 278–279
  international (*See* International advertising)
  introduction of, 264
  media plans and, 278–279, 457
  objectives of, 268–272
  situation analysis and, 265–268
  strategy and, 277–278
Advertising research. *See* Research
Advertising research firms, 66–67

Advertising response functions, 274, **274**
Advertising specialties, 571–572, **572**, 580
Advertising substantiation program, 132, 132n
Advertorials, 351
Advocacy, 110, 123, 129–130, 663, 668. *See also* Social issues
Advocacy advertising, 668
Aerial advertising, 11, 588–589
Affective association, 351–358
Affirmative disclosure, 132
Afghanistan, *292*
African Americans, 95, **95**, 183–184, **184**, 186
Age, 201, 205, 294. *See also* Demographics
Agencies. *See* Advertising agencies; Database agencies; Direct response agencies; E-commerce agencies; Event-planning agencies; Interactive agencies; Promotion agencies
Agency of record, 480
Aided recall, 244
Alcohol consumption, **112**, 112–113, 124–125
All-in-one single-source data, 255
Allowances, 146, 577–578
Alternative evaluation, 155–157
Alternative press newspapers, 492
AM (amplitude modulation), 513
American Dreams segment, 206
Animation, 440
Announcements, 392
Anxiety advertisements, **361**, 361–362
Appropriation, 144
Art, advertising as, 84, **85**, 119–121, **121**, 241, 377
Art departments, *429*
Art direction, 424–426, **425**, 426–431

CREDITS

tesy, George Weston Bakeries. **5.16** ©Chris Allen. **5.17** Courtesy, GlaxoSmithKline and Arnold Worldwide. **5.18** Used with permission of Unilever. **5.21** Courtesy, New Orleans Conventions & Visitors Center. **5.22** Courtesy, Singapore Tourist Board and Batey Ads USA **5.23** ©T. O'Guinn. **5.25** ©Ketel One. Used with permission. **5.26** ©T. O'Guinn. **5.27** KRAFT is a registered trademark. Used with permission of Kraft Foods. **5.28** Courtesy of SPLENDA® No Calorie Sweetener. **5.29** ©Procter & Gamble. Used with permission. **5.30** HORMEL & CURE 81 are registered trademarks of Hormel Foods, LLC and are used with permission of Hormel Foods. **5.31**™/®"M&M's," "M," and the "M&M's" Characters are registered trademarks of Mars Incorporated and its affiliates. All are used with permission. Mars Incorporated is not associated with Advertising and Integrated Brand Promotion or O'Guinn, Allen & Semenik, the authors. **5.32** Photo courtesy of Target Stores, Minneapolis. **5.33** Courtesy, G-Unit Clothing Company. **5.34** AP Topic Gallery. **5.35** ©CBS/Landov. **5.36** AP Topic Gallery. **5.37** ©Sesame Workshop. Sesame Street Tickles and their logos are trademarks and or service marks of Sesame Workshop. All rights reserved. **5.38** ©AP Photo/Andy Wong. **5.40** ©Honda. Used with permission. **5.41** Courtesy, Ford Motor Company. **5.42** Courtesy, Wahl's Trimmers. **5.43** ©AP Photo/M. Sajjad. **5.44** Courtesy of Lexus, a division of Toyota USA; ad developed by Team One, El Segundo, CA. **5.45** ©T. O'Guinn. **5.46** ©1997 American Express Financial Division. **5.47** Volvo Cars of North America, LLC. **5.48** Commercial Closet Association. **5.49** Courtesy of Saturn Corporation. **5.50** ©T. O'Guinn. **5.52** Courtesy, Johnston & Murphy, Nashville, TN. **5.53** ©T. O'Guinn.

CHAPTER 6

6.00 ©Unilever USA. **6.01** ©Procter & Gamble. Used by permission. **6.02** ©Procter & Gamble. Used by permission. **6.04** Neither the United States Marine Corp nor any other component of the Department of Defense has approved, endorsed, or authorized this product. USMC advertising creative by J. Walter Thompson. **6.05** Courtesy, Hard Candy. **6.06** www.wellsfargo.com. Used with Permission. Ad no longer valid as an offer of product. **6.07** Simmons Market Research Bureau. **6.08** Courtesy, Pillsbury; Created by Foote, Cone & Belding, San Francisco. **6.09** Courtesy, Pillsbury; Created by Leo Burnett, Chicago. **6.11** Courtesy of TIGI Bed Head. **6.12** Courtesy of TIGI Catwalk. **6.13** Xerox Developing Markets Operations. **6.14** Courtesy, UPS. **6.15** Created in house by Svetlana Electron Devices. Creative Director Jerri Batres; Photographer Jared Cassidy. **6.16** ©Chris Allen. **6.17** Copyright State Farm Mutual Automobile Insurance Company, 1996. Used by permission. **6.18** Courtesy of Pontiac Division, General Motors Corporation. **6.19** Courtesy, Colgate-Palmolive Company. **6.20** Courtesy of UNICEF; Ad Agency: Loyalty Partner GmbH, München. **6.21** ©2004 Hoyu Co., Ltd. **6.22** ©Unilever USA. **6.23** Saatchi & Saatchi, New York. **6.24** Courtesy of Nova Cruz Products and Lunar Design.

CHAPTER 7

7.00 Courtesy, The Coca-Cola Company. **7.01** Courtesy of Volkswagen of America, Inc. **7.02** Oldsmobile Division of General Motors. **7.03** Warner Brothers Entertainment, Inc. **7.05** Leo Burnett Advertising, Sao Paulo Brazil. **7.06** M&M'S® is a registered trademark owned by Mars, Incorporated and its affiliates. This trademark is used with permission. Mars, Incorporated is not associated with Cengage Learning. Advertisement printed with permission of Mars, Incorporated. ©Mars, Inc. 2008. **7.07** AP Topic Gallery. **7.09** U.S. Census Bureau. **7.10** Courtesy, Eurobarometer.ec.europa.eu. **7.11** Courtesy, British Petroleum. **7.12** Claritas Inc. PRIZM NE. **7.14** ©David Young-Wolff/PhotoEdit, Inc. **7.16** Courtesy, The Coca-Cola Company. **7.17** Courtesy, Delta Air Lines. **7.18** Reproduced by permission of Altoids; Ad Agency: Leo Burnett, Chicago. **7.19** Client: Mars. Agency: D'Arcy, London Art Director: Susan Byrne, Michelle Power. Copyrighter: Michelle Power, Susan Byrne. Photographer: Julie Fisher. **7.20** Courtesy, Bruzzone Research Company. **7.21** Courtesy, Bruzzone Research Company. **7.22** Reprinted with permission of General Motors Corporation. **7.23** Courtesy, Ford Motor Company. **7.24** Reprinted with permission of General Motors Corporation. **7.25** The Pepsi Globe Design and MORE HAPPY are trademarks of Pepsico, Inc. Used with permission. **7.26** Courtesy of Diamond Information Center. **7.27** Reproduced courtesy of Lever Bros. Co. **7.28** Screen grabs courtesy of Jaguar Cars North America 2001. **7.29** ©T. O'Guinn. **7.30** ©Photodisc/Getty Images. **7.31** American Association of Advertising Agency Magazine.

CHAPTER 8

8.00 Used with permission from Cincinnati Bell. All rights reserved. **8.01, 8.02, 8.03** Courtesy of ©Apple Computer, Inc. **8.05** ©1996 American Express Travel Related Services Company, Inc. Reprinted with permission. **8.06** ©American Express. All rights Reserved. Reprinted with Permission. **8.07** Courtesy of the Pillsbury Company. **8.08** Courtesy, Uno Restaurant Holding Group Corp. **8.09** Used with permission from Cincinnati Bell. All rights reserved. **8.10** ©2003 Bose Corporation. Reprinted with Permission. **8.11** Courtesy ©Sony Electronics, Inc. **8.15** ©Chris Allen. **8.16** Courtesy, Danskin, Inc. **8.17, 8.18** Courtesy, The Gillette Company.

CHAPTER 9

9.00 ©Procter & Gamble. Used by permission. **9.01** ©Procter & Gamble. Used by Permission. **9.02** Courtesy, Jack Daniels Distillery. **9.03** Courtesy, LG Electronics, Inc. **9.06** ©Heineken Brouwrijen V.V. **9.07** ©Chris Allen. **9.08** Courtesy of Mövenpick-Holding, Switzerland. **9.09** Courtesy, Van Cleef & Arpels. **9.10** Courtesy of FashionMall.com. **9.11** Tourism Authority of Thailand. **9.12** Courtesy, Sears Roebuck Company. **9.13** Courtesy, SkyPort T.V. of Japan. **9.15** Jessica Alba ©2002 America's Dairy Farmers & Milk Processors. **9.16** Courtesy, German Agricultural Co-op. **9.17** Nokia Mobile Phones, Prague, Czech Republic. **9.18** Advertising Agency: IDUE.

CHAPTER 10

10.00 1950-1-1 Picasso, Pablo, Self Portrait with Palette, 1906, Philadelphia Museum of Art: A.E. Gallatin Collection. **10.01** The BURGER KING® trademarks and King character are used with permission from Burger King Brands, Inc. **10.02** FOX TROT ©2004 Bill Amend. Reprinted with permission of UNIVERSAL PRESS SYNDICATE. All rights reserved. **10.03** Courtesy of Target Corporation. **10.04** 1950-1-1 Picasso, Pablo, Self Portrait with Palette, 1906, Philadelphia Museum of Art: A.E. Gallatin Collection. **10.05** AP/Topic Gallery. **10.06** Doing Business: The Art of David Ross, p. 10 Andrews and McMeel. A Universal Press Syndicate Co. 4520 Main St., Kansas City, MO 64111. Library of Congress #96-83993 TCRN:0-8362-2178-8. **10.07** ibidphoto.com. **10.08** Courtesy, Team One Advertising. **10.09** Ingalls Advertising. **10.10** Chairman Emeritus, Borders Perrin and Norrnader, Inc. Advertising Agency, Portland, OR. **10.11** Courtesy, Foote, Cone & Belding. **10.12, 10.13** Courtesy, Project Research, Inc. **10.16** ©Workbook Stock/Jupiter Images.

CHAPTER 11

11.00 Courtesy, Nissan North America, Inc.; Advertising: Team One; Photographer: Scott Downing. **11.01** Courtesy of Apple Computer, Inc.; ad by TBWA\CHAIT\Day; Photo by Hunter Freeman. **11.02** Courtesy, Apple Computer, Inc.; Ad Agency: TBWA Chiat Day, LA; Photographer: Matthew Welch; Model: Emory Livers/LA Models. **11.03** Courtesy, Apple Computer, Inc. **11.05** Photo by Peter S. Sheldon. **11.06** Kibbles 'n Bits is a registered trademark of Del Monte Corporation. ©Del Monte Foods 2004. All Rights Reserved. **11.07** Courtesy, Nissan North America, Inc.; Advertising: Team One; Photographer: Scott Downing. **11.08** KIA Motors America Inc. **11.09** ©Procter & Gamble. Used by permission. **11.10** J.C. Penny Corporation, Inc. **11.11** Courtesy, Castrol NA, Inc. www.castrolusa.com. **11.12** Courtesy, Nissan North America, Inc.; Advertising: Team One; Photographer: Scott Downing. **11.13** Courtesy of D.C. Shoes, Inc. **11.14** Courtesy of Skechers USA, Inc. **11.15** Courtesy of Biersdorf, Inc. **11.16** Courtesy GM Corp., Detroit, MI. **11.17** Courtesy of West-Point Stevens, Inc. and Chillingworth/Redding, Inc. **11.18** Courtesy, The Onion. **11.19** Courtesy of Motorola, Inc. **11.20a** www.azzure-denim.com. **11.20b** Photography: Peter Arnell; Ad, Arnell Group. **11.20c** Courtesy of Skyy Spirits, Importer of Cutty Sark Scots Whisky. **11.20d** Courtesy of Patrick Cox International, London, England. Photography by Sølve Surdsbø. **11.20e** ©The Procter & Gamble Company. Used by permission. **11.20f** Courtesy, Harrah's Las Vegas. **11.21** Reprinted with permission from the April 5, 2004 issue of ADVERTISING AGE. Copyright ©Crain Communications Inc. 2004. **11.21** Courtesy of Omega Research and Development. Douglas, GA. **11.23** Courtesy of Electrolux. **11.24** Ad designed by LVI and Golden Proportions Marketing. **11.25** Courtesy, Wm. Wrigley Jr. Company. **11.26** ©Miller Brewing Company. **11.27** Cheryl Heller Design; Art Direction, copy, Heller Communications. **11.28** ©Courtesy, Verizon Communications, Inc. **11.29** ©Courtesy, NBC/Universal Studios. **11.30** Photo by Susan van Etten. **11.33** Courtesy, Skyy Spirits. **11.34** Courtesy, Prada; photographer, Norbert Schoerner. **11.35a** Courtesy, Messner, Vetere, Berger, McNamee, Scjmettere/Euro RSCG; photographer, Guzzman; model, Jennifer Williams for T Models. **11.35b** Courtesy of Pernod-Ricard USA (Wild Turkey Ad). **11.35c** Courtesy, Sony Computer Entertainment America. **11.35d** Courtesy, DieselStyleLab. **11.35e** Image Courtesy of Kohler Co.

CHAPTER 12

12.00 Courtesy Jamaica Tourism. **12.01** Courtesy, Cengage Learning (formerly Thomson Learning). **12.02** Courtesy, Saatchi &

Saatchi, Singapore. **12.03** Courtesy, TWBA/PARIS. **12.04** Courtesy, AVIS. **12.05** Courtesy, Ogilvy & Mather. **12.06, 12.07, 12.08** ©2001 MasterCard International Incorporated. All rights reserved. **12.09** MatosGrey, Sao Paulo, Brazil. **12.10** ©Manolo Moran. **12.11** Courtesy of Mt. Sinai Hospital; Ad Agency: Devito/Verdi, NY, NY. **12.12** ©2004 General Motors Corporation. Used with permission of HUMMER and General Motors. **12.13** Courtesy of Roxio Inc. **12.14** Women.com was acquired by iVillage in 2001. Used by permission of iVillage.com. **12.15** Courtesy, BMW. **12.16** Courtesy Jamaica Tourism. **12.17** Courtesy of Oregon Food Bank. **12.18** Courtesy, Cattlemen's Beef Board. **12.19** ©Harley-Davidson Motor Company. Used with permission. **12.20** Courtesy of The Clorox Company. **12.21** Courtesy of Nicorette & The American Cancer Society. **12.22** Registered trademark ®GarageBand.com. **12.23** ©2004 Johnsonville Sausage, LLC. **12.24** ©The Procter & Gamble Company. All rights reserved. **12.25** John Michael Linck, Wooden Toymaker www.woodentoy. com. **12.26** Courtesy, Saatchi & Saatchi Australia. **12.27** Cliff Freeman & Partners. **12.28** ©Stephen Frisch/Stock Boston. **12.29** Courtesy of Honda. **12.30** Courtesy of John Hancock Insurance Company. **12.33** © DILBERT@UFS. Reprinted by permission.

CHAPTER 13

13.00 Courtesy, First Base Imaging, London. **13.01** Courtesy, homestore.com. **13.02** Courtesy, XM. **13.03** Ubachs Wisbrun. **13.04** ©Procter & Gamble. Used with permission. **13.05** Kai Zastrow, Amsterdam. **13.06** Courtesy, Beck & Co. **13.07, 13.08** ©2004 Motorola, Inc. **13.09** OraLabs, Inc. **13.10** Courtesy, Boeri; Art Director, Mary Ric; Copy, Steven Meitelski; Photo: Craig Orsini. **13.11** ©MINI, a division of BMW NA, LLC. **13.12** Courtesy, First Base Imaging, London. **13.13** Courtesy of Parmalat. **13.14** Courtesy, Land Rover North America. **13.15, 13.16** Courtesy of Volkswagen of America, Inc. **13.17** Courtesy, Lowe's. **13.18** Reprinted with permission from Hidesign. **13.19** Client: The Epiphone Company, a division of Gibson Guitar Corp.; Agency: CORE, St. Louis; Creative Director: Eric Tilford; Art Director: Eric Tilford; Copy Writer: Wade Paschall; Strategy: Jeff Graham; Photographer: James Schwartz. **13.20–13.23** Courtesy Arnold, Finnegan & Martin. **13.25** ©Style West. Used with permission. **13.26** Courtesy of Kohler, Inc. **13.27** Courtesy, Elvis Presley Enterprises, Inc. **13.28** Reprinted by permission of Krispy Kreme Doughnut Corporation. **13.29** Courtesy, Frito-Lay, a division of PepsiCo. **13.30** ©The Kobal Collection. **13.31** ©Paramount, Courtesy, The Kobal Collection. **13.33** ®/™Cheddar Cheese Combos is a registered trademark of Mars, Incorporated and its affiliates. It is used with permission. Mars, Incorporated is not associated with Cengage Learning. Advertisement printed with permission of Mars, Incorporated. ©Mars, Inc. 2005. **13.34** COMBOS® and SKITTLES® are registered trademarks owned by Mars, Incorporated and its affiliates. These trademarks are used with permission. Mars, Incorporated is not associated with Cengage Learning. Advertisements printed with permission of Mars, Incorporated. ©Mars, Inc. 2008. **13.35** Courtesy, Democratic National Committee. **13.36** Courtesy, Miller Brewing Company. **13.37** Courtesy of Hewlett Packard. **13.39, 13.40** Courtesy, Miller Brewing Company. **13.41** ©The Kobal Collection. **13.42** ©Universal, Courtesy, The Kobal Collection.

CHAPTER 14

14.00 Courtesy of The Paley Center for Media. Used with permission. **14.01a** ©Bettmann/CORBIS. **14.01b** ©EPA/Rhona Wise/Landov. **14.03** Reprinted with permission from the November 10, 2004 issue of ADVERTISING AGE. Copyright ©Crain Communications Inc. 2004. **14.04** The Wall Street Journal. **14.05** Shopping.com Ltd. www .shopping.com. **14.06** ©State Farm Mutual Automobile Insurance Company 2007. Used by permission. **14.11** Courtesy of The Paley Center for Media. Used with permission. **14.13** Ad courtesy of Telemundo Network, the NBC Agency and Red Tettemer. Photo courtesy of Juan Manuel Garcia. **14.15** Courtesy, Saatchi & Saatchi: Michael Rausche, David Lebon, John Early. **14.16** ConAgra Foods, Inc. **14.22** Courtesy, Christie's. **14.23** Courtesy of Sunglass Hut & Universal Studios. **14.25** ©Chad Buchanan/Getty News Entertainment. **14.30** Courtesy, Men's Health, Rodale, Inc. Photographer: Deborah Jaffe. **14.31** Courtesy, Everland Entertainment. **14.32** Courtesy of Gospel Music Channel. **14.33** Courtesy, Donner Advertising. Photos: ©Rausser/Getty Images. ©Photodisc/Getty Images. **14.36** Courtesy of the Newspaper Network.

CHAPTER 15

15.00 ©Keokee Co. Publishing, Inc. **15.01** Courtesy, Delta Air Lines; Created by SS+K, a creatively-driven, strategic communications firm. **15.03** Courtesy, Tire America. **15.04** ©Reuters/Robin Jerstad/

Landov. **15.05** Cengage Learning. **15.06** Courtesy, Zale Corporation. **15.07** Photo courtesy of Pizza Hut. **15.08** Reprinted by permission of Newspaper National Network. **15.09** ©Keokee Co. Publishing, Inc. **15.12** Cover Photo by James McLaughlin/FPG From Men's Journal. March 1998. From Men's Journal LLC 1998. All rights reserved. Reprinted by permission. **15.13** Courtesy of Escort, Inc. Used by permission. **15.14** Clarins S.A. **15.15** AP/Topic Gallery. **15.18** Company: Lenox Brands 1998; Agency: Grey Advertising, NY. **15.19** Courtesy, Fujitsu Computer Systems Corporation. **15.22** ©2003 Speed Channel Inc. **15.24** Sirius Satellite Radio. Creative by Crispin, Porter & Bogusky, Miami. **15.26** Courtesy, Clear Channel Worldwide.

CHAPTER 16

16.00 Copyright ©2007, Linden Research, Inc. All rights reserved. **16.01** Courtesy, Unilever USA, Inc. **16.02** Copyright ©2007 ASK, Inc. All rights reserved. ASK.com is a registered trademark of ASK, Inc. **16.05** Courtesy of Advertising.com. **16.06** L-Soft International, developers of LISTSERV®. **16.07** Reproduced with permission of Yahoo! Inc. YAHOO! and the YAHOO! Logo are trademarks of Yahoo! Inc. **16.08** Used with permission of CNET Networks, Inc. Copyright ©1995–2004 CNET Networks, Inc. All rights reserved. **16.09** Latina. com 2002. **16.12** ©Health Grades, Inc. **16.13** Courtesy Forrester.com. **16.14** Courtesy InetGiant, Inc. **16.15** ©Saturn Corporation. Used with permission. **16.16** Permission granted by Binney & Smith. **16.17** Copyright ©2007, Linden Research, Inc. All rights reserved. **16.18** Copyrights ©1998–2004 PrintingForLess.com. **16.19** Copyright ©1999–2004 iWon.com. All rights reserved. iWon is a registered trademark of The Excite Network, Inc. **16.20** Courtesy, VeriSign, Inc. **16.22** Nielsen Media Research. **16.23** Courtesy of Collabrio.com. **16.24** AP/Topic Gallery.

CHAPTER 17

17.00 ©Crayons, Inc. **17.01** GLAD® and ODOR SHIELD® are Registered Trademarks of The Glad Products Company. Used with permission. **17.02** Courtesy, Oreck Corporation. **17.05** Photo by Jeff Greenberg/Thomson Learning (now Cengage Learning). **17.06** ©Vitro Robertson. **17.07** Courtesy of Campbell Soup Company. **17.09, 17.10** ©Susan Van Etten. **17.11** Reproduced by permission of Marriott International, Inc. **17.12** Photo courtesy of Omega Ltd. **17.13** ©Rachel Epstein/PhotoEdit, Inc. **17.14** ©Bonnie Kamin/PhotoEdit Inc. **17.15** ©Novastock/Index Stock Imagery. **17.16** Photo by Susan Van Etten. **17.17** ©Chris Allen. **17.18** ©Bettmann/CORBIS. **17.19** Courtesy of Horst Salons. **17.20** Courtesy of David Auerbach Opticians. **17.21, 17.22, 17.23** ©Chris T. Allen. **17.24** ©Crayons, Inc.

CHAPTER 18

18.00, 18.01, 18.02 ©Procter & Gamble. Used by permission. **18.03** Courtesy of TiVo, Inc. **18.04** Cincinnati Flying Pig Marathon; Photographer: Mark Bowen. **18.05** Courtesy, PUMA; Photographer, Warwick Saint @ Michele Filomeno Agency USA. **18.06, 18.07** ©Procter & Gamble. Used by permission. **18.08** Courtesy, JBL Harman International. **18.10** BMW of North America LLC. **18.11, 18.12** ©Roger Padgett/Reuters/Landov. **18.13, 18.14, 18.15** Courtesy of the Procter & Gamble Company. Used with permission.

CHAPTER 19

19.00 Courtesy, Wyoming Travel &Tourism. **19.01** Courtesy of Best Buy Co., Inc., Minneapolis, MN. **19.02** Adirondack Country Store; www.adirondackcountrystore.com. **19.04** Courtesy of Stairmaster Co., Kirkland, WA. **19.05** Courtesy, Wyoming Travel & Tourism. **19.06, 19.07** ©Cabela's. Used with permission. **19.08** Courtesy, Sunglass Hut International. **19.09** Courtesy, Zeroknowledge Systems, Inc. **19.10** Courtesy, United States Postal Service. **19.11** Courtesy of Colette Stewart, Owner of Montana Fleece & Flannel, Livingston, MT. **19.12** Courtesy, YesMail.com. Used with permission. **19.13** Courtesy, Oreck Corporation. **19.14, 19.15** ©Jeff Greenberg/PhotoEdit, Inc. **19.16** ©Chris Allen. **19.17** ©Susan Van Etten.

CHAPTER 20

20.00, 20.01, 20.02, 20.03, 20.04 ©The Procter & Gamble Company. Used by permission. **20.05** ©DILBERT reprinted by permission of United Features Syndicate, Inc. **20.06** ©2000 JABRA Corporation. **20.07** Myriad Genetics, Inc. **20.08** ©Jim Borgman, 09/06/2002. Reprinted by special permission, Universal Press Syndicate. **20.09** Courtesy of Korey Kay & Partners www.koreykay.com. **20.10** Council for Biotechnology Information. **20.11** ©Susan Van Etten. **20.12** ©Elkay Manufacturing. **20.13** ©Michael Newman/PhotoEdit, Inc. **20.14** Permission granted by HP, through Creative i Advertising. **20.15** Bristol-Myers Squibb. **20.16** Courtesy, Anheuser Busch Companies, Inc.